UGANDA

PHILIP BRIGGS

WITH ANDREW ROBERTS

www.bradtguides.com

Bradt Guides Ltd, UK
The Globe Pequot Press Inc, USA

Bradt GUIDES
TRAVEL TAKEN SERIOUSLY

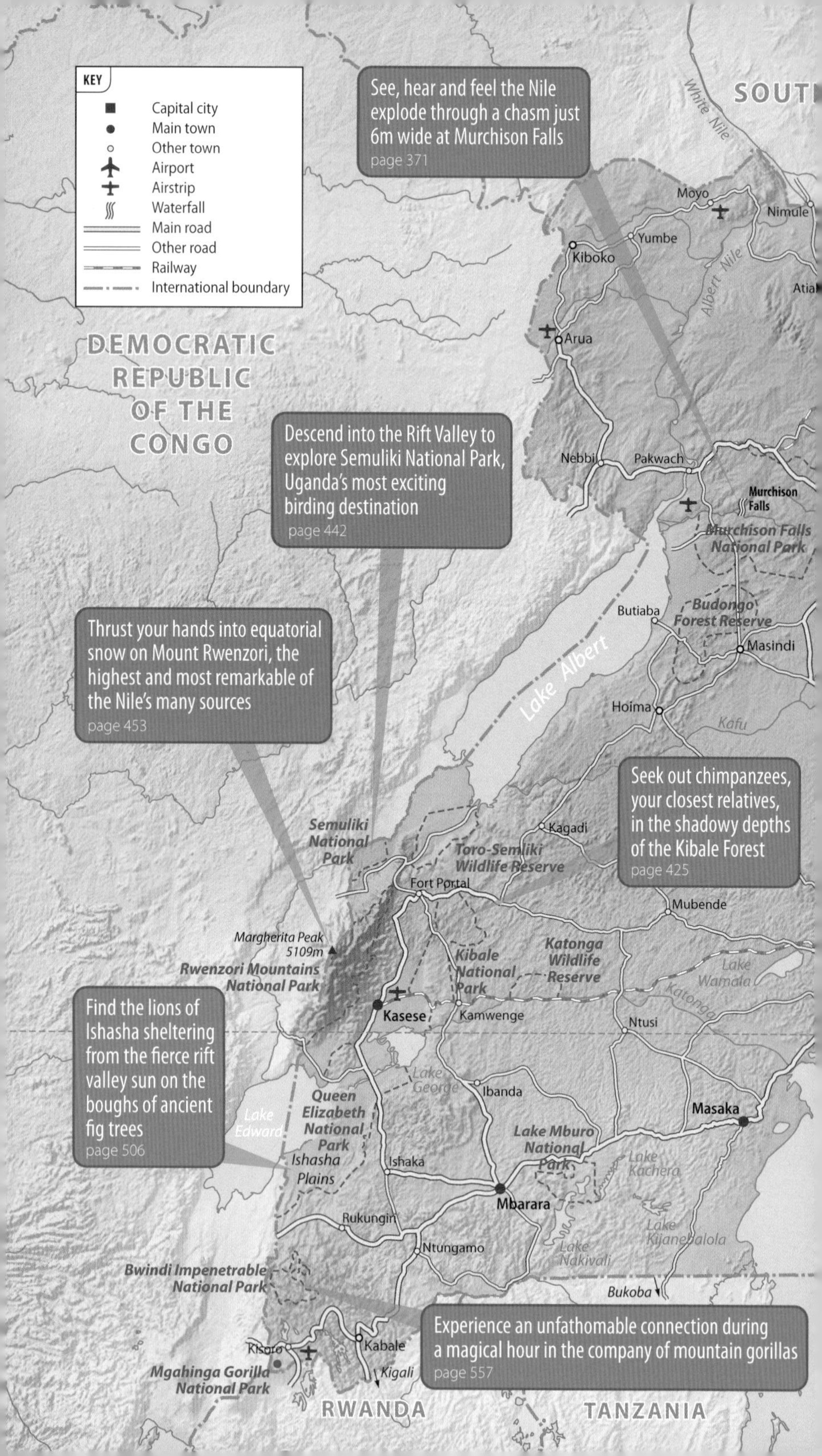

KEY
Capital city
Main town
Other town
Airport
Airstrip
Waterfall
Main road
Other road
Railway
International boundary
See, hear and feel the Nile explode through a chasm just 6m wide at Murchison Falls
page 371
Descend into the Rift Valley to explore Semuliki National Park, Uganda's most exciting birding destination
page 442
Thrust your hands into equatorial snow on Mount Rwenzori, the highest and most remarkable of the Nile's many sources
page 453
Seek out chimpanzees, your closest relatives, in the shadowy depths of the Kibale Forest
page 425
Find the lions of Ishasha sheltering from the fierce rift valley sun on the boughs of ancient fig trees
page 506
Experience an unfathomable connection during a magical hour in the company of mountain gorillas
page 557
DEMOCRATIC REPUBLIC OF THE CONGO
SOUTH
RWANDA
TANZANIA
White Nile
Albert Nile
Moyo
Nimule
Yumbe
Kiboko
Atiak
Arua
Nebbi
Pakwach
Murchison Falls
Murchison Falls National Park
Butiaba
Budongo Forest Reserve
Masindi
Lake Albert
Hoima
Kafu
Kagadi
Semuliki National Park
Toro-Semliki Wildlife Reserve
Fort Portal
Mubende
Margherita Peak 5109m
Rwenzori Mountains National Park
Kibale National Park
Katonga Wildlife Reserve
Lake Wamala
Katonga
Kasese
Kamwenge
Ntusi
Lake George
Ibanda
Queen Elizabeth National Park
Lake Edward
Ishasha Plains
Masaka
Lake Mburo National Park
Lake Kachera
Ishaka
Mbarara
Rukungiri
Ntungamo
Lake Kijanebalola
Lake Nakivali
Bwindi Impenetrable National Park
Bukoba
Kisoro
Kabale
Kigali
Mgahinga Gorilla National Park

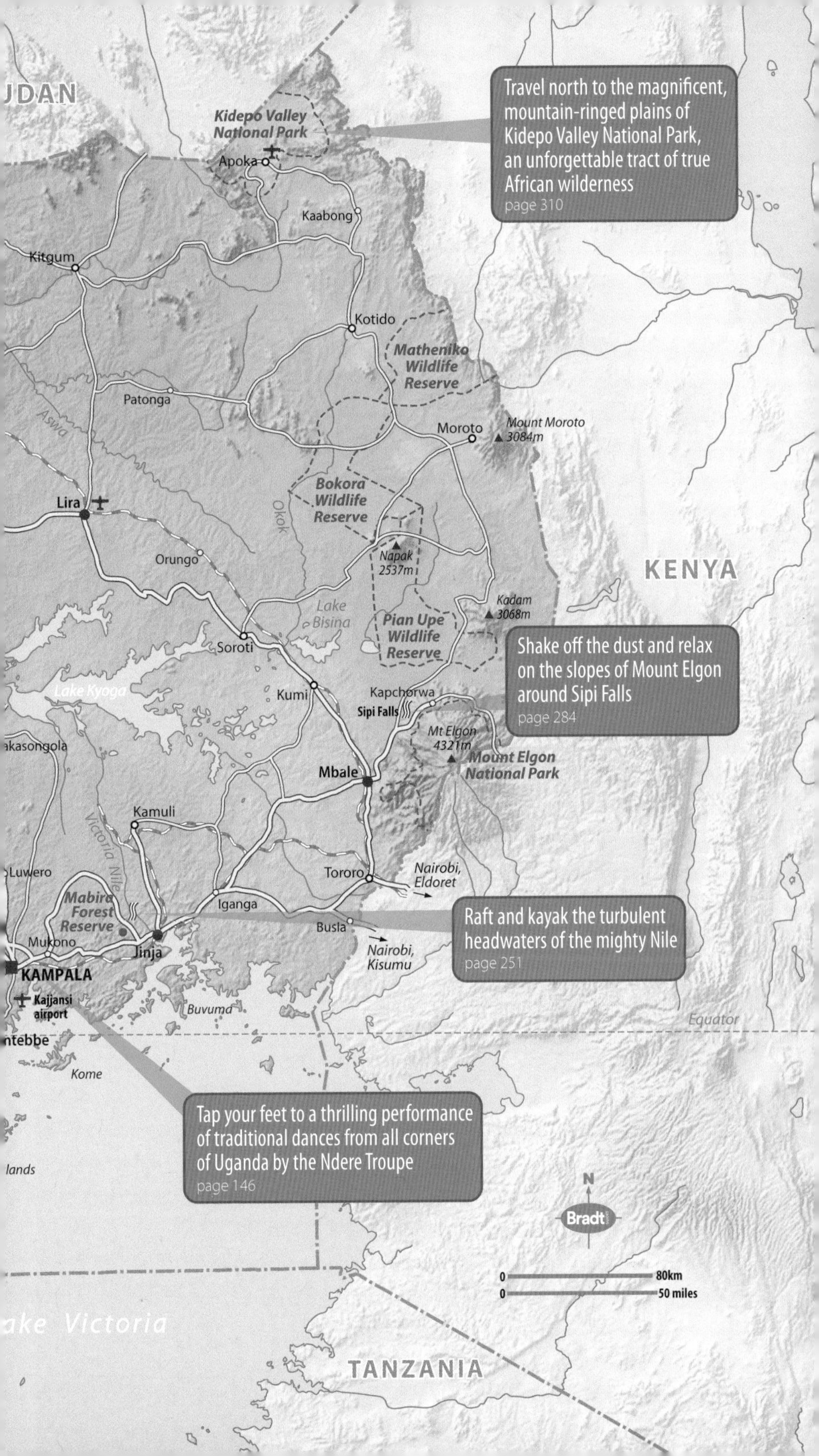

Travel north to the magnificent, mountain-ringed plains of Kidepo Valley National Park, an unforgettable tract of true African wilderness
page 310
Shake off the dust and relax on the slopes of Mount Elgon around Sipi Falls
page 284
Raft and kayak the turbulent headwaters of the mighty Nile
page 251
Tap your feet to a thrilling performance of traditional dances from all corners of Uganda by the Ndere Troupe
page 146
UDAN
Kidepo Valley National Park
Apoka
Kaabong
Kitgum
Kotido
Matheniko Wildlife Reserve
Patonga
Aswa
Moroto
Mount Moroto 3084m
Lira
Bokora Wildlife Reserve
Okok
Napak 2537m
Orungo
KENYA
Kadam 3068m
Lake Bisina
Pian Upe Wildlife Reserve
Soroti
Lake Kyoga
Kumi
Kapchorwa
Sipi Falls
Mt Elgon 4321m
Mount Elgon National Park
akasongola
Mbale
Kamuli
Victoria Nile
Luwero
Tororo
Nairobi, Eldoret
Mabira Forest Reserve
Iganga
Busia
Mukono
Jinja
Nairobi, Kisumu
KAMPALA
Kajjansi airport
Buvuma
Equator
ntebbe
Kome
lands
N
Bradt
0 80km
0 50 miles
ake Victoria
TANZANIA

UGANDA DON'T MISS...

TREE-CLIMBING LIONS
The unusual tree-climbing behaviour of Ishasha's lion prides makes these felines unusually easy to spot PAGE 506
(AVZ)

FORT PORTAL REGION
Between the Rwenzori and the forest of Kibale National Park, the landscape is one of lush vegetation PAGE 401
(AVZ)

WHITE-WATER RAFTING
Every year, thousands of adventure seekers enjoy thrills and spills on the turbulent headwaters of the Nile near Bujagali PAGE 251
(SS)

MOUNTAIN GORILLA TRACKING
Few visitors are unmoved by the magical hour spent in the presence of a group of mountain gorillas PAGE 537
(AVZ)

MURCHISON FALLS
At Murchison Falls, the Nile explodes through a 6m-wide gorge to form the most dramatic feature along its 6,650km course PAGE 371
(AVZ)

UGANDA
IN COLOUR

above (AVZ) Towering above the plains of eastern Uganda, Mount Kadam marks the gateway into the vast and undeveloped region of Karamoja PAGE 302

below (AVZ) A traditional Tepith homestead on Mount Moroto in the heart of Karamoja PAGE 303

Circumcision ceremonies are still carried out by the Bagisu, a Bantu-speaking people from the western slopes of Mount Elgon PAGE 278 above (AVZ)

The Batwa are one of Africa's oldest hunter-gatherer groups, and still inhabit villages around Lake Bunyonyi PAGE 540 right (AVZ)

Visits to Karamojong communities often include traditional dance performances PAGE 307 below (AVZ)

above (AVZ) Every Monday, Moroto comes alive as the Karamojong hawk livestock and other rural produce at Naitakwai Cattle Market PAGE 306

left (AVZ) The small village of Mpambire is the traditional home of the Buganda royal drum-makers PAGE 187

below (AVZ) Brightly coloured stools for sale at a stall along the Mbarara Road

The Igongo Cultural Centre in Masaka preserves and promotes the history and traditional culture of the former Ankole Kingdom PAGE 224 above (AVZ)

In much of rural Uganda, far from mains electricity, flour is still made with a grinding stone right (AVZ)

Fishermen cast their lines from a traditional Ssese canoe at the Source of the Nile PAGE 247 below (AVZ)

JOIN
THE TRAVEL CLUB
THE MEMBERSHIP CLUB FOR SERIOUS TRAVELLERS
FROM BRADT GUIDES
Be inspired
Free books and exclusive insider travel tips and inspiration
Save money
Special offers and discounts from our favourite travel brands
Plan the trip of a lifetime
Access our exclusive concierge service and have a bespoke itinerary created for you by a Bradt author
Join here:
bradtguides.com/travelclub
Membership levels to suit all budgets
Bradt GUIDES
TRAVEL TAKEN SERIOUSLY

AUTHOR

Philip Briggs (e philip.briggs@bradtguides.com) has been exploring the highways, byways and backwaters of Africa since 1986, when he spent several months backpacking on a shoestring from Nairobi to Cape Town. In 1991, he wrote the Bradt guide to South Africa, the first such guidebook to be published internationally after the release of Nelson Mandela. Over the rest of the 1990s, Philip wrote a series of pioneering Bradt travel guides to destinations that were then – and in some cases still are – otherwise practically uncharted by the travel publishing industry. These included the first dedicated guidebooks to Tanzania, Uganda, Ethiopia, Malawi, Mozambique, Ghana and Rwanda, new editions of which have been published regularly ever since. More recently, he has authored guides to Somaliland, Suriname, Sri Lanka and The Gambia, all published by Bradt. He spends at least four months on the road every year, usually accompanied by his wife, travel photographer Ariadne Van Zandbergen, and spends the rest of his time battering away at a keyboard in the sleepy coastal village of Wilderness in South Africa's Western Cape.

UPDATER

Andrew Roberts has lived in Uganda since 1993. Born in Britain, he first visited the country with a backpack in 1990 and returned three years later to help the Ugandan Forest Department set up ecotourism projects. He's still there and has now been married to Sarah for long enough for their two daughters to grow up and buzz off to the UK. They have no intention of following them. Andrew considers himself lucky to have worked in every national park in Uganda, settings which he greatly prefers to his office in Kampala. He has updated several previous editions of Bradt's *Uganda* and also produces tourist maps of Uganda and East Africa. His 2022 magnum opus, *Uganda Safari*, is the only other book you could possibly want to read about this splendid country.

MAJOR CONTRIBUTOR

Ariadne Van Zandbergen, who took most of the photographs for this book, is a freelance photographer and content creator. Born and raised in Belgium, she travelled through Africa from Morocco to South Africa in 1994/95 and is now resident in Wilderness, South Africa. She has visited 25 African countries and her photographs have appeared in numerous books, magazines, newspapers, maps, periodicals and pamphlets. She has her own online photo library (w africaimagelibrary.com).

Tenth edition published January 2025
First published 1994
Bradt Travel Guides Ltd
31a High Street, Chesham, Buckinghamshire, HP5 1BW, England
www.bradtguides.com
Print edition published in the USA by The Globe Pequot Press Inc,
PO Box 480, Guilford, Connecticut 06437-0480

Project Manager: Susannah Lord
Cover research: Pepi Bluck, Perfect Picture

ISBN: 9781804692158

British Library Cataloguing in Publication Data
A catalogue record for this book is available from the British Library

Photographs Ariadne Van Zandbergen (www.africaimagelibrary.com) (AVZ); Adrift UG (AU); Dreamstime.com: Altaoosthuizen (A/D), Andrey Gudkov (AG/D), Dmitrii Pichugin (DP/D), Dvrcan (D/D), Nmcavaney (N/D), Turfantastik (T/D); Shutterstock.com: A.F.Smith (AFS/S); SuperStock (SS)

Front cover Chimpanzee (*Pan troglodytes*), Kibale Forest National Park (AVZ)
Back cover, clockwise from left Tree-climbing lion (*Panthera leo*) (AVZ); a dugout canoe on Lake Bunyonyi (DP/D); grey crowned crane (*Balearica regulorum*) (AVZ)
Title page, clockwise from left A Karamojong boy drinking milk from a calabash, in a village near Mount Kadam; mountain gorilla (*Gorilla beringei beringei*) in Bwindi Impenetrable National Park; colourful stools for sale at a roadside store (all AVZ)
Part openers page 97: View over Kampala from Kibuli Mosque (D/D); page 227: Bujagali Falls (DP/D); page 329: Giraffes, Murchison Falls National Park (N/D); page 397: Queen Elizabeth National Park (DP/D); page 509: Mountain gorillas, Bwindi Impenetrable National Park (AG/D)

Maps David McCutcheon FBCart.S. FRGS, assisted by Daniella Levin

Typeset by Ian Spick, Bradt Travel Guides Ltd
Production managed by Gutenberg Press Ltd; printed in Malta
Digital conversion by www.dataworks.co.in

Paper used for this product comes from sustainably managed forests, and recycled and controlled sources.

Acknowledgements

PHILIP BRIGGS So many people contributed towards putting together the tenth edition of this guidebook – not to mention earlier versions – that it is difficult to know where to start!

First up, immense thanks to Andrew Roberts for his efforts updating three previous editions, in addition to this tenth one. On the home front, I'm grateful as ever to my wife, Ariadne Van Zandbergen, to the Bradt production team, and to Vince Hart for joining me on part of an update trip in 2023. Also, thanks to Sam Mwandha, Executive Director of the Uganda Wildlife Authority for his organisation's invaluable support, to Charlotte Beauvoisin and Alfie Pearce-Higgins for taking the time to provide valuable text boxes, and to the many readers whose contributions have helped improve the book.

I am also grateful to the many readers and people in the tourist industry who helped support this project in various ways. Listed alphabetically by first name, these include Adele Cutler, Amos Wekesa, Anna Santa Drale DeBoer, Asha and Steve Williams, Crystal Mbabazi, Debbie Willis, Ivan Mbabazi Batuma, Jane and Paul Goldring, Johnny Wright, Julia Lloyd, Laura van Dijk, Lizzie Wright, Merryde Loosemore, Miha Logar, Phillip Kiboneka, Ralph Shenk, Robert Akuguzibwe, Sylvia Tumusiime and Wim Kok.

ANDREW ROBERTS First of all, thanks to Philip Briggs for handing over his book for me to give it another going over. In Uganda, I'm as grateful as ever to my wife Sarah for her support, and, in the UK, to the Bradt production team – in particular Susannah Lord and cartographer David McCutcheon – for pulling it all together. Also, thanks to Sam Mwandha of the Uganda Wildlife Authority together with Paul Ninsiima, Leslie Muhindo, Justine Namara, Mabel Nabitosi, Dorcus Rukundo and Grace Mbeezi at Kampala HQ and Jesca Kabagenyi, Nakami Lydia in Kibale National Park and Aggie Nakidde in Bwindi for their assistance. Also to Charlotte Beauvoisin and the many readers whose contributions have been reproduced on the Bradt Uganda update website.

I am also grateful in various ways to many people, most of them in the tourist industry, who helped support this project. Listed in no particular order, these include Saleh Naminya at Casa in Mbale, Noah Wafula at Buhoma Lodge, Grisson Muhindo and Masereka Hannington at Kibale Primate Lodge, Nick and Elaine Roberts at Nkima Lodge, Ruben Vandenhoeke of Nature Lodges, Steve and Asha Williams, Neil Blazevic of Bushbaby Lodge, Isiah Weboya at Mount Elgon Hotel, Mike Rourke at Anyadwe House, Fred at Entebbe Forest Lodge, Chris Wilson, Atwurun Isaac of Timisha Hotel in Soroti and Gipir & Labongo in Pakwach, Kikonko Lodge, Lydia Nandudu of Nkuringo Safari Lodge, Wildwaters Lodge, Grace Kooja at Kon Tiki in Hoima, Jane and Paul Goldring, Phillip Kiboneka and Judith at Kasenyi

Safari Lodge, 2 Friends in Jinja, Bingo Small at Bujagali, the Riverside Inn, Kabale, Murchison River Lodge, Arra Fishing Lodge, Theo Vos of Kara Tunga, Bart Munting and Wellington Insgusya at Kiho Lodge.

AUTHOR'S STORY *Philip Briggs*

My first visit to Uganda, in late 1988, was decidedly lacking in premeditation. I'd flown from London to Nairobi with broad thoughts of travelling through Tanzania to South Africa over a few months. But on my first night in town, I had a couple of beers with an enthused Canadian who'd just bussed back from Uganda, and was persuaded to revise my plans.

My memories of that first trip to Uganda reflect the decades of war and deprivation that had culminated in the coup of 1986. Bananas, bananas everywhere and nothing else to eat. Buses that took a day to cover 100km of violently pot-holed road. Heaped toilet bowls whose flush mechanism was habitually disused after years without running water. Buildings scarred with bullet holes. The pitiful war orphans who accosted me at every turn.

But there was also much to enjoy. I was enchanted by the verdant landscapes of the west, thrilled by a semi-successful gorilla track in what was then the Impenetrable Forest Reserve (heard them, could see where they were, never actually saw them – all in all, a reasonable return for an investment of US$1), and felt a growing empathy with the guarded optimism, expressed by most of the Ugandans to whom I spoke, that the dark days just might be in the past.

And, with the notable exception of the civil war in the far north, so they were. By 1992, Uganda, once a byword for the worst malaises associated with post-independence Africa, was sufficiently stable for Bradt to commission me to research and write a guidebook to the country. Since then, it's been my privilege to watch and document Uganda as it embarked on one of the most staggering economic and political transformations of our time, to become, in the words of a recent Oxfam report, 'an inspirational economic success story, and a symbol of a more vibrant, successful Africa'.

Contents

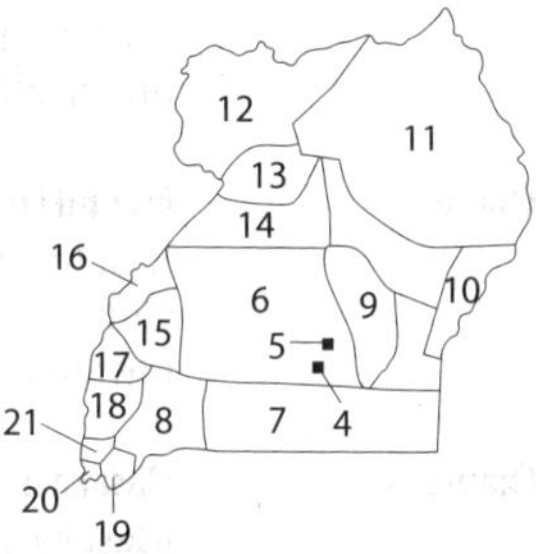

LIST OF MAPS

Introduction

Exactly thirty years ago, in the introduction to the first edition of this guide, I wrote that Uganda's attractions 'tend towards the low-key'. Many years later, when I re-read this assertion for the first time in years, my initial reaction was – well – bemusement, unease, even embarrassment.

Meeting the eyes of a mountain gorilla on the bamboo-clumped slopes of the Virungas? Rafting Grade 5 rapids on the Nile? Following a narrow rainforest trail awhirl with the heart-stopping pant-hoot chorusing of chimpanzees? Cruising the Kazinga Channel in the shadow of the Rwenzori while elephants drink from the nearby shore? Watching a prehistoric shoebill swoop down on a lungfish in the brooding reed beds of Mabamba Swamp? The roaring, spraying sensory overload that is standing on the tall rocks above Murchison Falls... Low-key? Goodness me – short of landing on the moon, what exactly would I have classified as a must-do or must-see attraction when I wrote that line?

But as I flicked through that yellowing first edition, all 150 pages of it, my unease slowly dissipated. It had not, I realised, been a reflection of any significant change in my own perceptions during the intervening decades, but rather of the remarkable strides made by Uganda in general, and its tourist industry specifically.

Uganda has changed. And how! When I first visited in 1988, Uganda's economy, infrastructure and human spirit – every aspect of the country, really – were still tangibly shattered in the aftermath of a 15-year cycle of dictatorship and civil conflict that had claimed an estimated 1 million human lives. Come 1992, when I researched the first edition of this guide, Uganda was visibly on the mend, but, a steady trickle of backpackers aside, its tourist industry remained in the doldrums. Incredible as it seems today, there was no facility to track gorillas within Uganda in 1992, no white-water rafting, no realistic opportunity to get close to chimpanzees, and the likes of Queen Elizabeth and Murchison Falls national parks were practically void of game. Many other tourist sites that today seem well established either didn't exist in their present form, were off-limits or unknown to travellers, or were far less accessible than they are now.

Uganda today does not lack for accessible travel highlights. There is the opportunity to trek within metres of one of the world's last few hundred mountain gorillas, arguably the most exciting wildlife encounter Africa has to offer – though observing chimps in the Kibale or Budongo runs it a damn close second. There is the staggering recovery made by Uganda's premier savannah reserves, where these days one can be almost certain of encountering lions, elephants and buffaloes, etc. There are the Rwenzori and Mount Elgon, where one can explore East Africa's bizarre montane vegetation without the goal-oriented approach associated with ascents of mounts Kilimanjaro or Kenya. And there is the Jinja Nile corridor which – with white-water rafting, kayaking, quad biking and bungee-jumping – is East Africa's answer to that more southerly 'adrenalin capital', Victoria Falls.

Nor does Uganda lack for tourist facilities. Thirty years ago, international-class hotels and restaurants were all but non-existent outside the capital. Today, by contrast, practically every major attraction along the main tourist circuits is serviced by at least one luxury lodge and/or tented camp. Trunk roads have improved beyond recognition, as has the overall standard of local tour operators, public transport, budget accommodation, restaurants and service in general.

It should be noted, too, that the country's natural attractions far exceed the opportunity to see gorillas and lions and so on. Somebody once said that if you planted a walking stick overnight in the soil of Uganda, it would take root before the morning dawned. And it is certainly true that of all Africa's reasonably established safari destinations, Uganda is the most green, the most fertile – the most overwhelmingly tropical!

Uganda, in an ecological nutshell, is where the eastern savannah meets the West African jungle – and it really does offer visitors the best of both these fantastic worlds. In no other African destination can one see a comparable variety of primates with so little effort – not just the great apes, but also more than ten monkey species, as well as the tiny wide-eyed bushbaby and peculiar potto. And if Uganda will have primate enthusiasts wandering around with imbecile grins, it will have birdwatchers doing cartwheels. Uganda is by far the smallest of the four African countries in which more than 1,000 bird species have been recorded, and it is particularly rich in western rainforest specialists – in practical terms, undoubtedly the finest birdwatching destination in Africa.

And yet for all that, Uganda does feel like a more intimate, unspoilt and – dare I say it? – low-key destination than its obvious peers. For starters, it has no semblance of a package tourist industry: group tours seldom exceed eight in number, and even the most popular game-viewing circuits retain a relatively untrammelled atmosphere. The country's plethora of forested national parks and reserves remain highly accessible to independent travellers and relatively affordable to those on a limited budget, as do such off-the-beaten-track gems as the Ssese Islands, Katonga Wildlife Reserve, Sipi Falls and the Toro Crater Lakes.

Uganda has changed. A full 45 years after Idi Amin was booted into exile, and close to four decades since President Museveni took power, the country bears few obvious scars of what came before. Today, Uganda enjoys one of the healthiest reputations of any African country when it comes to crime directed at tourists. The level of day-to-day hassle faced by independent travellers is negligible. And Ugandans as a whole – both those working within the tourist industry and the ordinary man or woman on the street – genuinely do come across as the warmest, friendliest and most relaxed hosts imaginable.

It's been with growing pleasure that I've documented Uganda's progress, as a country and as a tourist destination, over the course of ten editions of this guidebook. And this progress is, I hope, reflected in the evolution of the book – from its backpacker-oriented earliest incarnation into this expanded tenth edition, which provides thorough coverage of all aspects of the country for all tastes and budgets. But progress begets progress, and doubtless the next few years will see a host of new and exciting tourist developments in Uganda.

KEY TO SYMBOLS

Symbol	Meaning
	International boundary
	Surfaced road
	Main unsurfaced road
	Minor unsurfaced road
	Railway
	Airport/airstrip
	Vehicle/passenger ferry
	Petrol station/garage
	Bus station
	Taxis
	Tourist information
	Museum/art gallery
	Theatre/cinema
	Historic building/palace
	Historic castle/fortification
	Statue/monument
$	Bank
	Post office
	Hospital/clinic etc
	Hotel/inn
	Camping
	Lodge/camp
	Restaurant
	Café
	Bar
☆	Nightclub/casino
	Church/cathedral
	Mosque
	Hindu temple
	Sikh temple
	Archaeological/historic site
	Rafting/watersports
	Golf course
	Garden
	Cave/rock shelter
	Waterfall
	Scenic viewpoint
▲	Summit (height in metres)
	Stadium/sports facility
	National park
	Marsh
	Urban park
	Market

UPDATES WEBSITE

At Bradt Guides we're aware that guidebooks start to go out of date on the day they're published – and that you, our readers, are out there in the field doing research of your own. You'll find out before us when a fine new family-run hotel opens or a favourite restaurant changes hands and goes downhill. So why not write and tell us about your experiences? Key updates will be posted to Bradt's Uganda travel news website (w bradtugandaupdate.wordpress.com), a free online forum, administered by author Philip Briggs, where travellers (and people in the tourist industry) can catch up with the latest travel news, trip reports and factual updates. Feedback can be posted to the forum directly, or emailed to Philip (e philip.briggs@bradtguides.com).

It's easy to keep up to date with the latest posts by following Philip on Twitter (𝕏 philipbriggs). You can also add a review of the book to w bradtguides.com or Amazon.

HOW TO USE THIS GUIDE

AUTHOR'S FAVOURITES Finding genuinely characterful accommodation or that unmissable off-the-beaten-track café can be difficult, so the author has chosen a few of his favourite places throughout the country to point you in the right direction. These 'author's favourites' are marked with a ✷.

ACCOMMODATION PRICE CODES Throughout this guide we have used price codes to indicate the cost of those places to stay listed in the guide. These codes are based on the price of a standard room with double occupancy, as follows:

$	under US$20
$$	US$20–75
$$$	US$75–200
$$$$	US$200–400
$$$$$	US$400–800
$$$$$$	over US$800

Please note that codes are reflective of price only and are not an indication of quality or star rating.

PRICES To pre-empt an ever-sliding exchange rate, and to help readers at the planning stage of the trip, all prices in this book are quoted in US dollars, using a rate of US$1 = Ush3,750, often rounded to the nearest dollar. However, as always, be assured that the prices given will most likely change during the lifetime of this edition.

MAPS

Keys and symbols Maps include alphabetical keys covering the locations of those places to stay, eat or drink that are featured in the book. Note that regional maps may not show all hotels and restaurants in the area: other establishments may be located in towns shown on the map.

Grids and grid references Several maps use gridlines to allow easy location of sites. Map grid references are listed in square brackets after the name of the place or site of interest in the text, with page number followed by grid number, eg: [107 C3].

Part One

GENERAL INFORMATION

UGANDA AT A GLANCE

Area 235,796km² (91,041 square miles), similar to Great Britain or the state of Oregon
Location Equatorial Africa between latitudes 4°12′ N and 1°29′ S and longitudes 29°35′ W and 25°E. Bordered by Rwanda (169km) and Tanzania (396km) to the south, Kenya (933km) to the east, South Sudan (435km) to the north and the Democratic Republic of Congo (DRC) for 765km to the west.
Altitude 85% of the country lies between 900m and 1,500m above sea level. The lowest region is the Lake Albert basin (620m) and the Albert Nile. The highest point is Mount Stanley (Rwenzori) at 5,109m.
Population 45.9 million (2024 census), 35 million (2014 census), 28 million (2002), 16.7 million (1991), 12.6 million (1980), 9.5 million (1969), 6.5 million (1959), 5 million (1940), 3.5 million (1931), 2.9 million (1921) and 2.5 million (1911)
Capital Kampala (population 1,875,834; 2024 census)
Other major towns Towns with populations of more than 100,000 include Kira, Mbarara, Mukono, Gulu, Hoima, Masaka, Kasese, Lira and Mbale
Language English, the official language, is spoken by most reasonably educated Ugandans. Among the country's 33 indigenous languages, Luganda is the closest to being a lingua franca.
Religion Christian (85%), Islam (12%), also some Hindu and Jewish, while tribes such as the Karamojong adhere to a traditional animist faith
Currency Uganda shilling; exchange rates in November 2024 were US$1= Ush3,668, £1 = Ush4,766, €1 = Ush3,972
Head of State President Yoweri Museveni (since 1986)
Time zone GMT+3
International dial code +256 (Kampala: 414)
Electricity 240 volts at 50Hz
Mineral resources Copper, cobalt, limestone, salt, alluvial gold, oil
Major exports Coffee, fish, tea, tobacco
Other crops Bananas, maize, millet, sorghum, cotton, rice, cassava, groundnuts, potatoes
GDP US$45.5 billion in 2022 with a recent annual growth rate of around 3%
Human development Average life expectancy 64.5 years; under-five mortality rate 4.9%; adult (age 15–49) HIV/AIDS prevalence 7.3% (estimate); primary school completion 51%; secondary school enrolment 25%; adult literacy 78%; access to safe water 66%; access to electricity 18%
Land use Arable land 25%; agriculture 9%; pasture 9%; forest and woodland 28%; open water 18%; marsh 4%; other 7%
National flag Two sets of black, yellow and red horizontal stripes, with a white central circle around the national bird, the grey crowned crane
National anthem
'Oh! Uganda, May God uphold thee, We lay our future in thy hand,
United, free, for liberty, Together, We always stand.
Oh! Uganda the land of freedom, Our love and labour we give,
And with neighbours all at our country's call, In peace and friendship we'll live.
Oh! Uganda the land that feeds us, By sun and fertile soil grown,
For our own dear land we'll always stand, The Pearl of Africa's crown'

1

Background Information

GEOGRAPHY

Uganda lies in the east-central African interior more than 500km inland of the Indian Ocean, and is one of only 13 countries worldwide run through by the equator. It stands on an elevated basin that separates the eastern branch of the Great Rift Valley, running through Kenya and Tanzania, from the western branch, which is also known as the Albertine Rift (after Lake Albert) and forms the border between Uganda and the Democratic Republic of Congo (DRC). Most of Uganda is set at altitudes of greater than 1,000m, the main exception being parts of the Albertine Rift floor, where Lake Albert, at an elevation of 620m above sea level, is the lowest point in the country.

Topographically, much of Uganda is gently undulating or flat. The most mountainous area is the far southwest, where the steep slopes of Kigezi subregion are mostly covered in terraced cultivation, though patches of natural cover remain, most famously the rainforest protected within Bwindi Impenetrable National Park. The Congolese border immediately north of Kigezi is demarcated by Africa's third-highest massif, the 70km-long and 30km-wide Rwenzori, whose 5,109m Margherita Peak is topped only by mounts Kilimanjaro and Kenya. Several other large mountains are associated with Uganda's border regions. The Virungas, on the border with Rwanda and the DRC, is a string of freestanding volcanic peaks whose tallest Ugandan summit rises to 4,127m, while the 4,321m Mount Elgon on the Kenyan border has the largest base of any of the world's volcanically formed massifs. Other major mountains include Moroto (3,084m), Kadam (3,068m) and Morungole (2,750m) on the Kenyan border north of Elgon. Several other smaller volcanic mountains can be found in the north and east, while a field of more than 100 crater lakes (and many more dry craters) set below the Rwenzori foothills from Fort Portal south to Kichwamba provides further evidence of the country's geologically volatile past.

With the exception of the semi-arid northeast, Uganda is characterised by high precipitation and fertile soils. Indeed, close on 25% of the country's surface comprises water. In the southeast, Lake Victoria, the largest lake in Africa and second-largest freshwater body in the world, is shared between Uganda, Tanzania and Kenya. In the west, lakes Albert, Edward and George lie on the Albertine Rift floor straddling or close to the Congolese border. Smaller lakes include Wamala near Mityana, Bunyonyi and Mutanda in the southwest, and Bisina and Opeta in the east. In addition, more than 100 crater lakes are dotted around the Rwenzori foothills. At Jinja, on the Lake Victoria shore, Owen Falls (now submerged by the Owen Falls Dam) is the primary source of the White Nile, the world's longest river, which passes through the marshy and ill-defined Lake Kyoga in central Uganda, then through the northeast corner of Lake Albert, before crossing into Sudan and on to the Mediterranean.

CLIMATE

Uganda's equatorial climate is significantly tempered by its elevated altitude. In most parts of the country, the daily maximum is between 20°C and 27°C and the minimum is between 12°C and 18°C. The highest temperatures in Uganda occur on the plains immediately east of Lake Albert, while the lowest have been recorded on the glacial peaks of the Rwenzori. Except in the dry north, where in some areas the average annual rainfall is as low as 100mm, most parts of Uganda receive an

CLIMATE CHART

KAMPALA (1,155m)	Jan	Feb	Mar	Apr	May	Jun	Jul	Aug	Sep	Oct	Nov	Dec
Ave max (°C)	28	28	27	26	26	25	25	26	27	27	27	27
Ave min (°C)	18	18	18	18	17	17	17	16	17	17	17	17
Rainfall (mm)	45	60	125	170	135	75	50	85	90	100	125	105

ENTEBBE (1,145m)	Jan	Feb	Mar	Apr	May	Jun	Jul	Aug	Sep	Oct	Nov	Dec
Ave max (°C)	27	26	26	25	25	25	25	25	26	26	26	26
Ave min (°C)	17	18	18	18	17	16	16	16	16	17	17	17
Rainfall (mm)	75	95	155	250	240	115	75	75	75	80	130	115

FORT PORTAL (1,540m)	Jan	Feb	Mar	Apr	May	Jun	Jul	Aug	Sep	Oct	Nov	Dec
Ave max (°C)	27	27	26	26	25	25	25	25	25	25	25	26
Ave min (°C)	12	13	14	14	14	13	13	13	13	14	14	12
Rainfall (mm)	20	75	125	190	130	85	60	110	195	210	165	75

KABALE (1,950m)	Jan	Feb	Mar	Apr	May	Jun	Jul	Aug	Sep	Oct	Nov	Dec
Ave max (°C)	24	24	23	22	22	23	23	24	24	24	23	23
Ave min (°C)	10	10	11	12	11	10	9	10	11	11	11	10
Rainfall (mm)	50	100	125	120	95	25	20	45	95	100	115	90

GULU (1,110m)	Jan	Feb	Mar	Apr	May	Jun	Jul	Aug	Sep	Oct	Nov	Dec
Ave max (°C)	32	32	31	29	28	28	26	27	28	29	29	31
Ave min (°C)	17	18	18	18	18	17	17	17	17	17	17	16
Rainfall (mm)	10	35	85	160	200	140	155	215	165	140	95	30

MASINDI (1,145m)	Jan	Feb	Mar	Apr	May	Jun	Jul	Aug	Sep	Oct	Nov	Dec
Ave max (°C)	31	31	30	29	29	28	27	27	28	29	30	30
Ave min (°C)	12	12	13	13	13	12	12	12	12	12	13	12
Rainfall (mm)	20	50	10	140	135	95	100	45	120	125	110	45

MBALE (1,150m)	Jan	Feb	Mar	Apr	May	Jun	Jul	Aug	Sep	Oct	Nov	Dec
Ave max (°C)	32	32	31	29	28	28	27	28	28	29	30	32
Ave min (°C)	16	17	17	17	17	16	16	15	15	16	16	16
Rainfall (mm)	25	60	90	160	175	130	110	135	105	80	65	27

JINJA (1,145m)	Jan	Feb	Mar	Apr	May	Jun	Jul	Aug	Sep	Oct	Nov	Dec
Ave max (°C)	29	30	29	28	27	27	27	28	28	29	30	29
Ave min (°C)	15	15	15	15	15	14	14	15	15	15	15	14
Rainfall (mm)	50	70	120	170	130	65	50	105	80	95	100	85

NATIONAL PARKS

	Area	Habitat	Special attractions
Bwindi Impenetrable	310km^2	forest	mountain gorillas, forest birds
Kibale	766km^2	forest	chimpanzees, monkeys, forest birds
Kidepo Valley	1,344km^2	savannah	dry-country antelopes, predators & birds
Lake Mburo	256km^2	savannah	wide variety of antelope & waterbirds
Mgahinga Gorilla	33km^2	montane	mountain gorillas, hiking, volcanic peaks
Mount Elgon	1,145km^2	montane	hiking, forest birds
Murchison Falls	3,900km^2	savannah	Murchison Falls, big game, waterbirds
Queen Elizabeth	1,978km^2	savannah	big game, chimps, 612 bird species
Rwenzori	996km^2	montane	hiking, forest birds, Afro-montane plants
Semliki	220km^2	forest	hot springs, rift valley setting, 45 birds found nowhere else in Uganda

annual rainfall of between 1,000mm and 2,000mm. There is wide regional variation in rainfall patterns. In western Uganda and the Lake Victoria region it can rain at almost any time of year. Historically, the wet seasons were expected between mid-September and November, and March and May (see opposite). These patterns are increasingly flexible, however, and it is not uncommon for the November rains to extend over Christmas into the New Year.

CONSERVATION AREAS

Uganda's list of gazetted conservation areas embraces ten national parks and several other wildlife and forest reserves. National parks have a higher status and conservation priority than other reserves, and from the visitor's point of view they are generally better developed for tourism. Although several other wildlife reserves exist, most are merely adjuncts to one of the savannah national parks. The only ones that have tourist facilities are Toro-Semliki, Katonga, Bugungu, Pian Upe, Kabwoya and Kyambura wildlife reserves. Of these, Toro-Semliki, Katonga and Pian Upe are earmarked for eventual upgrade to full national park status. Also of interest to tourists are forest reserves such as Budongo, Kalinzu, Mpanga and Mabira. Chimp tracking in Budongo and Kalinzu is cheaper than in the national parks.

Several other sites are also of interest for their natural history. These include Lake Nkuruba and Bigodi Wetland near Fort Portal, Lake Bunyonyi and the Echuya Forest in Kigezi, and the Sipi Falls near Mbale. For birders in particular, it is easy to view Uganda, with its lush natural vegetation and dense tropical cultivation, as nothing less than one giant nature sanctuary. Even around the capital, the small relict forest protected in the Entebbe Botanical Garden offers an excellent introduction to Uganda's forest birds, while gardens in suburban Kampala offer the opportunity to see such colourful species as Ross's turaco, woodland kingfisher, white-throated bee-eater and a variety of robin-chats and weavers.

HISTORY

A lack of coherent written records exist pertaining to the East African interior prior to the mid 19th century, making it difficult for scholars to accurately determine the region's early history. Despite this, however, academics have two main resources

BANANA REPUBLIC

With its distinctive tall green stem topped by a luxuriant clump of thick, wide leaves, the banana (or plantain) is such an integral feature of the Ugandan landscape that it may come as a surprise to learn that it is not indigenous to the country. Kiganda folklore claims that the first banana plant was brought to the kingdom by Kintu, whose shrine lies on a hill called Magonga (almost certainly a derivative of a local name for the banana) alongside a tree said to have grown from the root of the plant he originally imported. If this legend is true, it would place the banana's arrival in Uganda in perhaps the 13th–15th century, probably from the Ethiopian Highlands. Most botanists argue, however, that the immense number of distinct varieties grown in modern Uganda could not have been cultivated within so short a period – a time span of at least 1,000 years would be required.

Only one species of banana (*Musa ensete*) is indigenous to Africa, and it doesn't bear edible fruit. The more familiar cultivated varieties have all been propagated from two wild Asian species (*M. acuminata* and *M. balbisiana*), and hybrids thereof. Wild bananas are almost inedible and riddled with hard pits, and it is thought that the first edible variety was cultivated from a rare mutant of one of the above species about 10,000 years ago – making the banana one of the oldest cultivated plants in existence. Edible bananas were most likely cultivated in Egypt before the time of Christ, presumably having arrived there via Arabia or the Indian Ocean. The Greek sailor and explorer Cosmas Indicopleustes recorded that edible bananas grew around the port of Adulis, in present-day Eritrea, CAD525 – describing them as 'moza, the wild-date of India'.

The route via which the banana reached modern-day Uganda is open to conjecture. The most obvious point of origin is Ethiopia, the source of several southward migrations in the past two millennia. But it is intriguing that while the banana is known by a name approximating to the generic Latin *musa* throughout Asia, Arabia and northeast Africa – *moz* in Arabic and Persian, for instance, or *mus* or *musa* in various Ethiopian languages and Somali – no such linguistic resemblance occurs in East Africa, where it is known variously as *ndizi*, *gonja*, *matoke*, etc. This peculiarity has been cited to support a hypothesis that the banana first travelled between Asia and the East African coast either as a result of direct trade or else via Madagascar, and that it was entrenched there before regular trade was established with Arabia. A third possibility is that the banana reached Uganda via the Congolese Basin, possibly in association with the arrival of Bantu speakers from West Africa.

However it arrived in Uganda, the banana has certainly flourished there, forming the main subsistence crop for an estimated 40% of the population. Some 50 varieties are grown in the country, divided into four broad categories based on their primary use – *matoke* for boiling, *gonja* for roasting, *mbide* for distillation into banana beer (*mwenge*) or wine (*mubisi*), and the more familiar sweet *menvu* eaten raw for a snack or dessert. Within these broad categories, many subtleties of nomenclature and cultivation are applied to different varieties. And first-time visitors to Uganda might take note of the above names when they shop for bananas in the market – or sooner or later you'll bite into what looks to be a large, juicy sweet banana, but is in fact a foul and floury uncooked *matoke* or *gonja*!

The banana's uses are not restricted to feeding bellies. The juice from the stem is traditionally regarded to have several medicinal applications, for instance as a cure for snakebite and for childish behaviour. Pulped or scraped sections from the stem also form very effective cloths for cleaning. The outer stem can be plaited to make a strong rope known as *byai* in Luganda, while the cleaned central rib of the leaf is used to weave fish traps and other items of basketry. The leaf itself forms a useful makeshift umbrella, and was traditionally worn by young Buganda girls as an apron. The dried leaf is a popular bedding and roofing material, and also used to manufacture the head pads on which Ugandan women generally carry their loads.

The banana as we know it is a cultigen – modified by humans to their own ends and totally dependent on them for its propagation. The domestic fruit is the result of a freak mutation that gives the cells an extra copy of each chromosome, preventing the normal development of seeds, thereby rendering the plant edible, but also sterile. Every cultivated banana tree on the planet is effectively a clone, propagated by the planting of suckers or corms cut from 'parent' plants. This means that, unlike sexually reproductive crops, which experience new genetic configurations in every generation, the banana is unable to evolve mechanisms to fight off new diseases.

In early 2003, a report in the *New Scientist* warned that cultivated bananas could become extinct, because of their lack of defence against a pair of fungal diseases rampant in most of the world's banana-producing countries. These are black sigatoka, an airborne disease first identified in Fiji in 1963, and the soil-borne Panama disease, also known as fusarium wilt. Black sigatoka can be kept at bay by regular spraying – every ten days or so – but it is swiftly developing resistance to all known fungicides, which in any case are not affordable to the average subsistence farmers. There is no known cure for Panama disease.

So far as can be ascertained, Panama disease does not affect any banana variety indigenous to Uganda, but it has resulted in the disappearance of several introduced varieties. Black sigatoka, by contrast, poses a threat to every banana variety in the world, and it became widespread in Uganda during the mid-2000s. Buganda was especially hard hit – a progressive reduction exceeding 50% was experienced in the annual yield of the most seriously affected areas. In addition to reducing the yield of a single plant by up to 75%, black sigatoka can also cut its fruit-bearing life from more than 30 years to less than five. As a result, banana production in Uganda dropped from 10.5 million tonnes in 2002 to a low of 4.3 million tonnes in 2016.

A potential solution to this is genetic modification (GMO), which might for instance entail introducing a gene from a wild species to create a disease-resistant edible banana. The first trials of GMO bananas took place in Uganda in 2007 and met with some success: four of the six new strains tested proved to be 100% resistant to black sigatoka. These strains have yet to be planted on a large scale commercially, since the farming of GMO crops was illegal in Uganda prior to 2017, and it still remains an emotive and controversial subject. A less controversial development, funded by a US$13 million grant from the Bill and Melinda Gates Foundation in 2014, has been the creation of high-yield disease-resistant banana hybrid varieties by the International Institute of Tropical Agriculture. The introduction of these hybrid varieties to East Africa over recent years has done much to turn around the situation, and recent banana yields have been excellent. Indeed, in 2023, Uganda's yielded a record crop of 11 million tonnes, making it the world's second-largest banana producer after India (it is also the world's largest per capita consumer; the average Ugandan eats around 700g of bananas daily).

NATIONAL PARK AND RESERVE FEES

The Uganda Wildlife Authority or UWA (pronounced *ooh-er!*) is the body responsible for Uganda's national parks and wildlife reserves. See page 5.

Visiting fees for UWA's protected areas fall into three categories. Murchison Falls is Category A+ while Queen Elizabeth, Bwindi Impenetrable, Mgahinga Gorilla, Lake Mburo, Kibale and Kidepo Valley national parks are Category A. Semuliki, Mount Elgon and Rwenzori Mountains national parks and Toro-Semuliki, Katonga and Pian Upe wildlife reserves are classed as Category B. All other wildlife reserves are Category C. A new category, D, applies only to the Kapkwai sector of Mount Elgon National Park, where activity fees but no entrance fees are charged.

The UWA tariff charges separate fees for park entrance and activities to the four categories of tourist described below.

East African Citizens (EAC) Citizens of the East African Community, ie: Uganda, Kenya, Tanzania, Rwanda, Burundi, South Sudan and Somalia.
Foreign Residents (FR) Foreigners living within the EAC and who can show proof of residency or a work permit.
Foreign Non Residents (FNR) Tourists resident in countries outside Africa.
Rest of Africa (ROA) Citizens of all countries in Africa beyond the EAC. This new category offers discounts for park entrance and gorilla tracking, while all other activities are charged at the FNR rate.

The prices given below will apply until a new two-year tariff comes into operation in July 2026. For prevailing rates visit UWA's website (w ugandawildlife.org) and click on the orange 'UWA Rates' tab (top right).

Entrance to Murchison Falls (**Category A+**) currently costs US$45/35/30 FNR/FR/ROA. Entrance to **Category A** protected areas is US$40/30/25 FNR/

from which to work in the form of archaeological evidence and oral tradition – although both of these tend to be patchy and riddled with contradictions, making them open to a diversity of interpretations. All the same, the ancient legends associated with the various Ugandan kingdoms and the more objective evidence unearthed by modern archaeologists display a high level of mutual corroboration when it comes to certain key events in Uganda between AD1100 and the present, suggesting that many local oral traditions, when stripped of overt mythologising, amount to a reasonably accurate account of actual events.

EARLY PREHISTORY It is widely agreed that the entire drama of human evolution was enacted in the Rift Valley and plains of East Africa. Although the fossil record is patchy, the combination of DNA evidence and various hominid bones unearthed in the region suggest that the ancestors of modern humans and modern chimpanzees diverged in the Ethiopian and Kenyan Rift Valley roughly 5 million to 6 million years ago. Uganda has presumably supported hominid life for as long as any other part of East Africa, an assertion supported by the recent discovery of several fossils belonging to the semi-bipedal proto-hominid *Ugandapithecus major* in the vicinity of Moroto. These include a complete 20-million-year-old fossil skull unearthed on the slopes of Mount Napak in 2011, and now on display in the Uganda Museum in Kampala.

FR/ROA and US$35/25/20 FNR/FR/ROA for **Category B**. **Category C** reserves cost US$10/5/5 FNR/FR/ROA. Children (5–15 years) pay US$25/15/10 FNR/FR/ROA for the Category A+ park, US$20/10/5 for **Category A** and US$5 for others. Permits are valid for 24 hours from time of entrance. In addition, 4x4 vehicles registered in Uganda pay an entrance fee of Ush30,000 (around US$8) while a stiffer US$150 applies to foreign vehicles. Ugandan saloon cars pay Ush20,000 (US$6), and foreign ones US$40. An additional US$3/10 is levied on Ugandan/foreign vehicles entering Murchison to discourage use of the park's new tarmac road as a short cut to West Nile. In addition to these vehicle fees, self-driving visitors (tour groups are exempt) now pay an additional US$10 per car per day for a self-guided game drive. You might think that this is like buying a ticket for a seat in a cinema and then being charged extra to watch the film, and you'd be right. Motorcycles (including bodas) are prohibited in the parks except by special arrangement. Vehicle fees do not apply to forested parks such as Kibale and Mgahinga. Fees are payable in shillings or dollars. The Reservations Office at UWA HQ in Kampala will accept payments in cash, by bank transfer or credit/debit card or by Mobile Money (page 80). Cash payments are not accepted in the parks, however, so you'll need to be prepared to pay by card or Mobile Money.

Additional rates apply for park activities including gorilla and chimpanzee tracking. These are listed under the relevant sections in the regional parts of the guide.

Independent travellers should note that fees paid for activities booked in advance can no longer be refunded or the activity rescheduled. In other words, if you don't turn up for a boat trip booked for Thursday, then it's hard cheese. Fortunately, with the exceptions of gorilla and chimp tracking, there are few activities that can't just as easily be booked and paid for on the spot.

Stone Age implements dating to more than a million years ago have been discovered throughout East Africa, and it is highly probable that this earliest of human technologies arose in the region. For a quarter of a million years prior to around 8000BC, Stone Age technology was spread throughout Africa, Europe and Asia, and the design of common implements such as the stone axe was identical throughout this area. The oldest Stone Age sites in Uganda, Nsongezi on the Kigezi River and Sango Bay on Lake Victoria, were occupied between 150,000 and 50,000 years ago.

The absence of written records means that the origin and classification of the modern peoples of East and southern Africa are a subject of some academic debate. Broadly speaking, it is probable that East Africa has incurred two major human influxes since 1000BC, on both occasions, by people from West Africa.

The first of these influxes probably originated somewhere in modern-day DRC about 3,000 years ago. The descendants of these invaders, known locally as the Bambuti or Batwa, were slightly built hunter-gatherers similar in culture and physique to the Khoisan-speaking peoples of southern Africa and the Pygmoid people who still live in certain rainforests near the Congolese border. The rock paintings on several shelters near Mbale in eastern Uganda show strong affinities with rock art associated with Khoisan-speaking hunter-gatherers elsewhere in the continent, suggesting that at one time these people occupied most of Uganda, as did they most of East and southern Africa at the beginning of the 1st millennium AD.

The second human influx, which reached the Lake Victoria hinterland in roughly 200BC, apparently coincided with the spread of Iron Age technology in the region. There is good reason to suppose that the people who brought iron-working techniques into the region were the ancestors of the Bantu speakers who probably occupied most of sub-equatorial Africa by AD500. Few conclusive facts are known about the political and social structures of the early Bantu-speaking peoples who inhabited Uganda, but it is reasonable to assume that they lived in loosely assembled chiefdoms similar to the pre-colonial *ntemi* structures which existed in the Tanzanian interior until colonial times.

It has been established beyond doubt that relatively centralised political systems made an early appearance in Uganda. The origin of the first of these kingdoms, Bunyoro-Kitara, is shrouded in legend, and the rough date of its foundation has yet to be determined by scholars. Nevertheless, a number of archaeological sites in the Mubende and Ntusi districts of central Uganda suggest that Bunyoro-Kitara was established long before AD1500.

THE BATEMBUZI AND BACHWEZI (AD1100–1500) A creation myth common to Kiganda, Kinyoro and several other Ugandan oral traditions asserts that the first man on earth was Kintu, a divinely created being who lived in the vicinity of Wanseko and went on to marry Nambi, the daughter of his creator Ggulu (page 166). Traditions are vague on how long ago this event occurred, but they do assert that the first dynasty to rule over Bunyoro-Kitara, the Batembuzi, lived between AD1100 and AD1350, and ample physical evidence at Ntusi would seem to confirm that a highly centralised society existed in this area as early as the 11th century.

The origin of the Batembuzi is obscured by legend and myth, but they must have ruled for several generations, as various local traditions list between ten and 22 dynastic kings. Oral traditions name Ruhanga, the King of the Underworld, as the founder of the dynasty (the Kinyoro Underworld is evidently closer to the Christian notion of heaven than to that of hell) and they consider the Batembuzi to have been deities with supernatural powers. Descriptions of the Batembuzi's physical appearance suggest that they may have migrated to the area from modern-day Sudan or Ethiopia. Whatever their origins, they evidently became culturally and linguistically integrated into the established Bantu-speaking culture of Bunyoro-Kitara.

Most traditions identify Isuza as the last Batembuzi ruler. Isuza is said to have fallen in love with a princess of the Underworld, and to have followed her into her homeland, from where he couldn't find his way back to Bunyoro-Kitara. Years later, Isuza's son Isimbwa visited Bunyoro-Kitara, and he impregnated the only daughter of the unpopular stand-in king, Bukuku. Their child, Ndahura, was thrown into a river shortly after his birth at the order of Bukuku, who had been told by diviners that he should fear any child born by his daughter; but his umbilical cord stuck in a tree, keeping him afloat, and he was rescued by a royal porter. Ndahura was raised by the porter and, after he reached adulthood, he drove Bukuku's cattle from his home, stabbed the king in the back, and claimed the throne as his own. His claim was supported by the people of Bunyoro-Kitara, who accepted that the true royal lineage was being restored because of Ndahura's striking physical resemblance to his grandfather Isuza.

Ndahura – 'the uprooter' – is remembered as the founder of the Bachwezi dynasty. The Bachwezi were most probably migrants from Ethiopia or Sudan (hence the physical resemblance between Ndahura and Isuza?), who, like the Batembuzi before them, adopted the language and culture of the local Bantu speakers over whom they assumed rule. Ndahura was almost certainly a genuine historical figure,

A NOTE ON TERMINOLOGY

Most Bantu languages use a variety of prefixes to form words so that several similar words are made from a common root. When discussing the various peoples and kingdoms of Uganda, this can be somewhat confusing.

The most common prefixes are *mu-*, *ba-* and *bu-*, the first referring to an individual, the second to the people collectively, and the third to the land they occupy. In other words, a Muganda is a member of the Baganda, the people who live in Buganda. The language of the Baganda is Luganda and their religion and customs are Kiganda. To use another example, the Banyoro live in Bunyoro, where they speak Runyoro and follow Kinyoro customs.

There is not a great deal of consistency in the use of these terms in the English-language books. Some use the adjective *Ganda* to describe, for instance, the *Ganda kabaka* (King of Buganda). Others will call him the Muganda or Baganda kabaka. Standards are more flexible when dealing with ethnic groups other than the Baganda: the Ankole people are usually referred to as the Banyankole but I've never seen the kingdom referred to as Bunyankole; the people of Toro are often referred to as the Batoro but I've not come across the term Butoro. In this following historical account, I've generally stuck with what seems to be the most common usage: prefixes for -ganda, -nyoro and -soga; no prefixes for Ankole and Toro.

The name 'Uganda' of course derives from the word *Buganda*. The reason why the British protectorate came to be known by this abbreviated name is probably that most Europeans had their initial contact with Buganda through KiSwahili-speaking guides and translators. In KiSwahili, the prefix *u-* is the equivalent of the Luganda *bu-*, so that the Swahili speakers would almost certainly have referred to the Ganda kingdom as Uganda. Although many Baganda writers evidently find it annoying that their country has been misnamed in this way, it does simplify my task that there is a clear distinction between the name of Uganda the country and that of Buganda the kingdom.

When referring to the leaders of the various Ugandan groups, the title *kabaka* is bestowed on the Baganda king, the title *omukama* on the Banyoro and Batoro kings, and *omugabe* on the Ankole king.

and he probably came to power in the second half of the 14th century. In addition to having supernatural powers, Ndahura is traditionally credited with introducing Ankole cattle and coffee cultivation to Uganda.

The Mubende and Ntusi areas are identified by all traditional accounts as lying at the heart of Bunyoro-Kitara during the Bachwezi era, an assertion which is supported by a mass of archaeological evidence, notably the extensive earthworks at Bigo bya Mugyenyi and Munsa. This suggests that the Bachwezi Empire covered most of Uganda south and west of the Nile River. Traditional accounts claim that it covered a much larger area, and that Ndahura was a militant expansionist who led successful raids into parts of western Kenya, northern Tanzania and Rwanda.

Ndahura was captured during a raid into what is now northern Tanzania. He eventually escaped, but he refused to reclaim the throne, instead abdicating in favour of his son Wamala. Ndahura then disappeared, some claim to the Fort Portal region. He abandoned his capital at Mubende Hill to his senior wife, Nakayima, who founded a hereditary matriarchy that survived into the colonial era. Wamala moved his capital to an unidentified site before eventually relocating it to Bigo bya Mugyenyi.

Considering the immense Bachwezi influence over modern Uganda – almost all the royal dynasties in the region claim to be of direct or indirect Bachwezi descent – it is remarkable that they ruled for only two generations. Tradition has it that Wamala simply disappeared, just like his father before him, thereby reinforcing the claim that the Bachwezi were immortal. It is more likely that the collapse of the dynasty was linked to the arrival of the Luo in Bunyoro-Kitara towards the end of the 15th century. Whatever their fate, the Bachwezi remain the focus of several religious cults, and places like the Nakayima Tree on Mubende Hill and the vast earthworks at Bigo bya Mugyenyi near Ntusi are active sites of Bachwezi worship to this day.

BUNYORO, BUGANDA AND ANKOLE (1500–1650) In the second half of the 15th century, the Nilotic-speaking Luo left their homeland on the plains of southeastern Sudan, and migrated southwards along the course of the Nile River into what is now Uganda. After settling for a period on the northern verge of Bunyoro-Kitara at a place remembered as Pubungu (probably near modern-day Pakwach), they evidently splintered into three groups. The first of these groups remained at Pubungu, the second colonised the part of Uganda west of the Nile, and the third continued southwards into the heart of Bunyoro-Kitara.

It was probably the Luo invasion which ended Bachwezi rule over Bunyoro-Kitara. The Bachwezi were succeeded by the Babiito dynasty, whose founder Rukidi came to Bunyoro from Bukidi (a Runyoro name for anywhere north of Bunyoro). The tradition is that Rukidi was the son of Ndahura and a Mukidi woman, and that he was invited to rule Bunyoro by the Bachwezi nobles before they disappeared. Many modern scholars feel that the Luo captured Bunyoro by force, and that they integrated themselves into the local culture by claiming a genetic link with the Bachwezi, adopting several Bachwezi customs and rapidly learning the local Runyoro tongue.

The arrival of the Luo coincided with the emergence of several other kingdoms to the south and east of Bunyoro, notably Buganda and Ankole in modern-day Uganda, as well as Rwanda, Burundi and the Karagwe kingdom in what is now northwest Tanzania. All these kingdoms share a common Bachwezi heritage. Kinyoro and Kiganda traditions agree that Buganda was founded by an offshoot of the Babiito dynasty, while Ankole traditions claim that Ruhinda, the founder of their kingdom, was yet another son of Ndahura. Ankole retained the strongest Bachwezi traditions, and its most important symbol of national unity was a royal drum or Bagyendwaza said to have been owned by Wamala.

Bunyoro was the largest and most influential of these kingdoms until the end of the 17th century. It had a mixed economy, a loose political structure, and a central trade position on account of its exclusive control of the region's salt mines. Bunyoro was presided over by an *omukama*, who was advised by a group of special counsellors. The omukama was supported at a local level by several grades of semi-autonomous chiefs, most of whom were royally appointed loyalists of aristocratic descent.

Prior to 1650, Buganda was a small kingdom ruled over by a *kabaka*. Unlike those in Bunyoro, the local chiefs in Buganda were hereditary clan leaders and not normally of aristocratic descent. Buganda was the most fertile of the Ugandan kingdoms, for which reason its economy was primarily agricultural. Ankole, by contrast, placed great importance on cattle, and its citizens were stratified into two classes: the cattle-owning Bahima, who claimed to be descendants of Ruhinda, and the agriculturist Bairu. Ankole was ruled by an *omugabe*. As with the Omukama of

Bunyoro and the Kabaka of Buganda, this was a hereditary title normally reserved for the eldest son of the previous ruler. Positions of local importance were generally reserved for Bahima aristocrats.

Another identifiable polity to take shape at around this time was the Busoga, which lies to the east of Buganda and is bordered by Lake Kyoga to the north and Lake Victoria to the south. The Basoga show strong linguistic and cultural affiliations to the Baganda, but their oral traditions suggest that their founder, remembered by the name of Mukama, came from the Mount Elgon region and had no Bachwezi or Babiito links. Busoga has apparently assimilated a large number of cultural influences over the centuries, and it seems to have remained curiously detached from the mainstream of Ugandan history, probably by allying itself to the dominant power of the time.

An indication of Bunyoro's regional dominance in the 16th century comes from the traditional accounts of the wars fought by Olimi I, the fifth omukama. Olimi is said to have attacked Buganda and killed the kabaka in battle, but he declined to occupy the conquered territory, opting instead to attack Ankole (of the several explanations put forward for this superficially peculiar course of action, the only one that rings true is that Olimi was after cattle, which were scarce in Buganda but plentiful in Ankole). Olimi occupied Ankole for some years, and according to Kinyoro traditions he withdrew only because of a full solar eclipse, an event which Banyoro traditionalists still consider to be portentous. If this tradition is true (and there is no reason to doubt it), Olimi must have been ruling Bunyoro at the time of the solar eclipse of 1520. Assuming that the four Babiito rulers who preceded Olimi would together have ruled for at least 30 or 40 years, this suggests that the Babiito dynasty and the Buganda and Ankole kingdoms were founded between 1450 and 1500.

BUNYORO, BUGANDA AND ANKOLE (1650–1850) At its peak in the 17th century, Bunyoro covered an area of roughly 80,000km^2 south and west of the Nile and Lake Victoria. Buganda was at this time no more than 15,000km^2 in area, and Ankole covered a mere 2,500km^2 north of the Kagera River. Similar in size to Buganda, the relatively short-lived Kingdom of Mpororo, founded in about 1650, covered much of the Kigezi region of Uganda, as well as parts of what is now northern Rwanda, until its dissolution in the mid 17th century.

The period between 1650 and 1850 saw Bunyoro shrink to a fraction of its former area and relinquish its regional dominance to Buganda. The start of this decline can be traced to the rule of Omukama Cwa I (or Cwamali) in the late 17th or early 18th century. During Cwa's reign, Bunyoro suffered an epidemic of cattle disease. Cwa ordered all the cattle in the kingdom to be killed, and he then raided Ankole to seize replacements. Cwa occupied Ankole for three years, after which he attempted to extend his kingdom into Rwanda. He was killed in Rwanda and his returning troops were evicted from Ankole by Omugabe Ntare IV, who thereby earned himself the nickname Kitabunyoro – 'the scourge of Bunyoro'. After chasing out the Banyoro, Ntare IV extended Ankole's territory north to the Katonga River.

Bunyoro descended into temporary disarray as the aristocracy tried to cover up the omukama's death, and the empty throne was seized by one of his sisters, stimulating a succession war that lasted for several years. Buganda took advantage of Bunyoro's weakness by taking control of several of its allied territories, so that in the years following Cwa's death it doubled in area. It is unclear whether Buganda acquired these territories by conquest or merely by exploiting the faltering loyalty of chiefs who were traditionally allied with Bunyoro.

Also linked to the upheavals following Cwa's death was the migration of the Palwo, the name given to the Luo speakers who had settled in the north of Bunyoro two centuries earlier. Some of the Palwo settled in Acholi, the part of northern Uganda east of the Albert Nile, where they founded several small Luo-speaking kingdoms modelled along the traditions of Bunyoro. Others migrated through Busoga in eastern Uganda to the Kisumu region of what is now western Kenya, where they are still the dominant group. A few groups settled in Busoga, south of modern-day Tororo, to found a group of small kingdoms known collectively as Jopadhola.

In 1731, Omukama Duhaga took the Banyoro throne. Kinyoro traditions remember him as being small, light-skinned, hairy and difficult, and as having had the second-greatest number of children of any omukama (the third omukama, Oyo I, reputedly had 2,000 children, a record which will take some beating). During Duhaga's 50-year reign, Buganda annexed the area around Lake Wamala, as well as the land immediately west of the Victoria Nile, from where it plundered large parts of Busoga. Duhaga died in battle along with 70 of his sons, attempting to protect Bunyoro from Baganda expansionists.

By the reign of Omukama Kyebambe III (1786–1835), Buganda was firmly entrenched as the major regional power. During the late 17th century, Kabaka Mutebi consolidated his power by dismissing some traditional clan leaders and replacing them with confirmed loyalists; by the end of the 18th century, practically every local chief in Buganda was one of the so-called 'king's men'. Buganda forged loose allegiances with Busoga and Karagwe (in northern Tanzania), and they maintained a peaceful equilibrium with Ankole, which had in the meantime further expanded its territory by absorbing several parts of the former Mpororo kingdom. Towards the end of Kyebambe III's rule, Bunyoro was dealt a further blow as several local princes decided to rebel against the ageing omukama. The most significant rebellion was in Toro, where a prince called Kaboyo declared autonomous rule in 1830, depriving Bunyoro of its important salt resources at Katwe.

By the mid 19th century, Buganda stretched west from the Victoria Nile almost as far as Mubende and over the entire Lake Victoria hinterland as far south as the Kagera River. Ankole covered an area of roughly 10,000km^2 between the Katonga and Kagera rivers, and the newly founded Toro kingdom occupied a similar area north of the Katonga. Bunyoro had been reduced to a quarter of its former size; although it had retained the Nile as its northern boundary, there was now no point at which it stretched further than 50km south of the Kafu River.

BUNYORO AND EGYPT (1850–89) The death of Omukama Kyebambe III was followed by a period of internal instability in Bunyoro, during which two weak omukamas ruled in succession. In 1852, the throne was seized by Kamurasi, who did much to stop the rot, notably by killing a number of rebellious princes at the Battle of Kokoitwa. Kamurasi's rule coincided with the arrival of Arab traders from the north, who were admitted into Bunyoro in the recognition that their support could only strengthen the ailing kingdom. The Arabs based themselves at Gondoroko, from where they led many brutal raids into the small and relatively defenceless Luo kingdoms of Acholi.

In 1862, Kamurasi's court welcomed John Speke and James Grant, the first Europeans to reach Bunyoro. Two years later, Bunyoro was entered from the north by Samuel Baker, a wealthy big-game hunter and incidental explorer who travelled everywhere with his wife. The Bakers spent a year in Bunyoro, during which time they became the first Europeans to see Lake Mwatanzige, which they renamed Lake Albert. Baker also developed an apparently irrational antipathy towards his royal host, which almost certainly clouded his judgement when he returned to the region eight years later.

The years following the Bakers' departure from Bunyoro saw radical changes in the kingdom. Omukama Kamurasi died in 1869, prompting a six-month succession battle that resulted in the populist Kabalega ascending to the throne. Omukama Kabalega is regarded by many as the greatest of all Banyoro rulers who, were it not for British intervention, would surely have achieved his goal of restoring the kingdom to its full former glory. Kabalega introduced a set of military and political reforms which have been compared to those of Shaka in Zululand: he divided the army into battalions of 1,500 men, each of which was led by a trained soldier chosen on merit as opposed to birth, and he minimised the influence of the eternally squabbling Banyoro aristocracy by deposing them as local chiefs in favour of capable commoners with a sound military background.

In 1871, the imperialist Khedive Ismail of Egypt appointed the recently knighted Sir Samuel Baker to the newly created post of Governor General of Equatoria, a loosely defined province in the south of Egyptian-ruled Sudan. When Baker assumed his post in 1872, he almost immediately overstepped his instructions by declaring Bunyoro to be an annexe of Equatoria. Kabalega responded to Baker's pettiness by attacking the Egyptian garrison at Masindi. Baker was forced to retreat to Patiko in Acholi, and he defended his humiliating defeat by characterising Kabalega as a treacherous coward, thereby poisoning the omukama's name in Europe in a way that was to have deep repercussions on future events in Uganda.

The second Governor General of Equatoria, General Gordon, knew of Kabalega only what his biased predecessor had told him. Gordon further antagonised the omukama by erecting several forts in northern Bunyoro without first asking permission. Kabalega refrained from attacking the forts, but relations between Bunyoro and the Egyptian representative became increasingly uneasy. Outright war was probably averted only by the appointment of Emin Pasha as governor general in 1878. Sensibly, Emin Pasha withdrew from Bunyoro; and, instead of using his position to enact a petty vendetta against Kabalega, he focused his energy on the altogether more significant task of wresting control of the West Nile and Acholi regions from Arab slave traders. In 1883, following the Mahdist rebellion in Sudan, Emin Pasha and his troops were stranded in Wadelai. In 1889, they withdrew to the East African coast, effectively ending foreign attempts to control Uganda from the north.

The combined efforts of Baker and Gordon did little to curb Kabalega's empire-building efforts. In 1875, the Banyoro army overthrew Nyaika, the King of Toro, and the breakaway kingdom was reunited with Bunyoro. Kabalega also reclaimed several former parts of Bunyoro which had been annexed to Buganda, so that Bunyoro doubled in area under the first 20 years of his rule. Even more remarkably, Kabalega's was the first lengthy reign in centuries during which Bunyoro was free of internal rebellions. Following Emin Pasha's withdrawal from Equatoria in 1889, the continued expansion, stability and sovereignty of Bunyoro under Kabalega must have seemed assured.

EUROPEANS IN BUGANDA (1884–92) In the mid 19th century, when the first Swahili slave traders arrived in central Africa from the east coast, the dominant regional power was Buganda, ruled over by Kabaka Mutesa from his capital at Kampala. Mutesa allowed the slave traders to operate from his capital, and he collaborated in slave-raiding parties into neighbouring territories. The Swahili converted several Baganda clan chiefs to their Islamic faith, and later, when Kampala was descended upon by the rival French Catholics and British Protestants, even more chiefs were attracted away from traditional Kiganda beliefs. Mutesa's court rapidly descended into a hotbed of religious rivalry.

Mutesa died in 1884. His son and successor, Mwanga, was a volatile and headstrong teenager who took the throne as religious rivalries in Buganda were

IN THE COURT OF MUTESA

In 1862, John Speke spent weeks kicking his heels in the royal capital of Buganda, awaiting permission to travel to the river he suspected might be the source of the Nile. His sojourn is described in four long and fascinating chapters in *Journal of the Discovery of the Source of the Nile*, the earliest and most copious document of courtly life in the kingdom.

The following extracts provide some idea of the everyday life of the subjects of Kabaka Mutesa – who is remembered as a more benevolent ruler than his predecessor Suuna or successor Mwanga. The quotes are edited to modernise spellings and cut extraneous detail.

> A more theatrical sight I never saw. The king, a good-looking, well-figured, tall young man of 25, was sitting on a red blanket spread upon a platform of royal grass, scrupulously well dressed in a new *mbugu*. His hair was cut short, excepting on the top, where it was combed up into a high ridge, running from stem to stern like a cockscomb. On his neck was a large ring of beautifully worked small beads, forming elegant patterns by their various colours. On one arm was another bead ornament, prettily devised; and on the other a wooden charm, tied by a string covered with snakeskin. On every finger and every toe, he had alternate brass and copper rings; and above the ankles, halfway up to the calf, a stocking of very pretty beads. Everything was light, neat, and elegant in its way; not a fault could be found with the taste of his 'getting up'.

> Both men, as is the custom in Uganda, thanked Mutesa in a very enthusiastic manner, kneeling on the ground – for no-one can stand in the presence of his majesty – in an attitude of prayer, and throwing out their hands as they repeated the words *N'yanzig, N'yanzig, ai N'yanzig Mkahma wangi*, etc, etc, for a considerable time; when, thinking they had done enough of this, and heated with the exertion, they threw themselves flat upon their stomachs, and, floundering about like fish on land, repeated the same words over again and again, and rose doing the same, with their faces covered with earth; for majesty in Uganda is never satisfied till subjects have grovelled before it like the most abject worms …

> The king loaded one of the carbines I had given him with his own hands, and giving it full-cock to a page, told him to go out and shoot a man in the outer court; which was no sooner accomplished than the little urchin returned to announce his success, with a look of glee such as one would see in the face of a boy who had robbed a bird's nest, caught a trout, or done any other boyish trick. I never heard, and there appeared no curiosity to know, what individual human being the urchin had deprived of life …

> The Namasole entered on a long explanation, to the following effect. There are no such things as marriages in Uganda; there are no ceremonies attached to it. If any man possessed of a pretty daughter committed an offence, he might give her to the king as a peace offering; if any neighbouring king had a pretty daughter, and the King of Uganda wanted her, she might be demanded as a fitting tribute. The men in Uganda are supplied with women by the king, according to their merits, from seizures in battle abroad, or seizures from refractory officers at home. The women are not regarded as property, though many exchange their daughters;

building to a climax. Mwanga attempted to play off the various factions; he succeeded in alienating them all. In 1885, under the influence of a Muslim adviser, Mwanga ordered the execution of Bishop Hannington and 50 Christian converts (many of whom were roasted to death on a spit). In 1887, Mwanga switched allegiance to the

and some women, for misdemeanours, are sold into slavery; while others are flogged, or are degraded to do all the menial services of the house …

Congow was much delighted with my coming, produced *pombe*, and asked me what I thought of his women, stripping them to the waist. I asked him what use he had for so many women? To which he replied, 'None whatever; the king gives them to us to keep up our rank, sometimes as many as one hundred together, and we either turn them into wives, or make servants of them, as we please …'

The king was giving appointments, plantations, and women, according to merit, to his officers. As one officer, to whom only one woman was given, asked for more, the king called him an ingrate, and ordered him to be cut to pieces on the spot; and the sentence was carried into effect – not with knives, for they are prohibited, but with strips of sharp-edged grass, after the executioners had first dislocated his neck by a blow delivered behind the head …

Nearly every day, I have seen one, two, or three of the wretched palace women led away to execution, tied by the hand, and dragged along by one of the body-guard, crying out, as she went to premature death, at the top of her voice, in the utmost despair and lamentation; and yet there was not a soul who dared lift hand to save any of them, though many might be heard privately commenting on their beauty…One day, one of the king's favourite women overtook us, walking, with her hands clasped at the back of her head, to execution, crying in the most pitiful manner. A man was preceding her, but did not touch her; for she loved to obey the orders of her king voluntarily, and in consequence of previous attachment, was permitted, as a mark of distinction, to walk free. Wondrous world!…

A large body of officers came in with an old man, with his two ears shorn off for having been too handsome in his youth, and a young woman who had been discovered in his house. Nothing was listened to but the plaintiff's statement, who said he had lost the woman for four days, and, after considerable search, had found her concealed by the old man. Voices in defence were never heard. The king instantly sentenced both to death; and, to make the example more severe, decreed that, being fed to preserve life as long as possible, they were to be dismembered bit by bit, as rations for the vultures, every day, until life was extinct. The dismayed criminals, struggling to be heard, in utter despair, were dragged away boisterously in the most barbarous manner, to the drowning music of drums…

A boy, finding the king alone, threatened to kill him, because he took the lives of men unjustly. The king showed us, holding the pistol to his cheek, how he had presented the muzzle to the boy, which so frightened him that he ran away…The culprit, a good-looking young fellow of 16 or 17, brought in a goat, made his *n'yanzigs*, stroked the goat and his own face with his hands, *n'yanzigged* again with prostrations, and retired…There must have been some special reason why, in a court where trifling breaches of etiquette were punished with a cruel death, so grave a crime should have been so leniently dealt with; but I could not get at the bottom of the affair.

traditionalist Kiganda chiefs, who in return offered to help him expel converts of all persuasions from Buganda. Threatened with expulsion, Muslims and Christians combined forces to launch an attack on the throne. Mwanga was overthrown in 1888. His Muslim-backed replacement, Kiwewa, persecuted Christians with even greater fervour than Mwanga had in 1885–86, but when Kiwewa's Kiganda leanings became apparent the Muslims rebelled and installed yet another leader. Events came to a head in 1889, when a civil war erupted between the Christian and Muslim factions, the result of which was that all Muslims were driven from the capital, later to join forces with Kabalega in Bunyoro. Mwanga was reinstalled as kabaka.

The rival European powers were all eager to get their hands on the well-watered and fertile Kingdom of Buganda, where, with the Muslims safely out of the way, rivalry between Francophile Catholics and Anglophile Protestants was increasingly open. In February 1890, Carl Peters arrived at Mengo clutching a treaty with the German East Africa Company. Mwanga signed it readily, possibly in the hope that German involvement would put an end to the Anglo-French religious intrigues which had persistently undermined his throne. Unfortunately for Mwanga, German deliverance was not to be: a few months after Peters' arrival, Germany handed Buganda and several other African territories to Britain in exchange for Heligoland, a tiny but strategic North Sea island.

In December 1890, Captain Frederick Lugard, the representative of the British East Africa Company, arrived at Kampala hoping to sign a treaty with an unimpressed Mwanga. The ensuing religious and political tensions sparked a crisis in January 1892, when a Catholic accused of killing a Protestant was acquitted by Mwanga on a plea of self-defence. Lugard demanded that the freed man be handed to him for a retrial and possible execution. Mwanga refused, on the rightful grounds that he was still the kabaka. Lugard decided it was time for a show of strength, and with the support of the Protestants he drove Mwanga and his Catholic supporters to an island on Lake Victoria. He then sent troops to rout Mwanga from the island; the kabaka fled to Bukoba in Karagwe (northern Tanzania) before returning in March to his kingdom, which was by then on the verge of civil war. Mwanga was left with no real option but to sign a treaty recognising the Company's authority in Buganda.

Lugard returned to Britain in October 1892, where he rallied public support for the colonisation of Buganda, and was instrumental in swaying a Liberal government which under Gladstone was opposed to the acquisition of further territories. In November, the British government appointed Sir Gerald Portal as the commissioner to advise on future policy towards Buganda. Portal arrived in Kampala in March 1893, to be greeted by a flood of petitions from all quarters. Swayed by the fact that missionaries of both persuasions felt colonisation would further their goals in the kingdom, Portal raised the Union Jack over Kampala in April; a month later he signed a formal treaty with the unwilling but resigned Mwanga, offering British protectorateship over Buganda in exchange for the right to collect and spend taxes.

THE CREATION OF UGANDA (1892–99) The protectorate of Uganda initially had rather vague boundaries, mimicking those of the indigenous kingdom to which it nominally offered protection. It is not at all clear to what extent the early British administrators conceived of their protectorate extending beyond the boundaries of the kingdom, but all accounts suggest that Uganda was as chaotic an assemblage as can be imagined.

Captain Lugard had done a fair bit of tentative territorial expansion even before he signed a treaty with Buganda. It was evidently his intention to quell Bunyoro's rampant Omukama Kabalega, against whom he had been prejudiced by the combination of Baker's poisonous reports, and the not entirely unpredictable antipathy held for the Banyoro in Buganda. In August 1891, Lugard signed a treaty with the Omugabe of Ankole in a vain attempt to block arms reaching Bunyoro from the south. Lugard drove the Banyoro army out of Toro and installed Kasagama, an exiled prince of Toro, to the throne. He then built a line of forts along the southern boundary of Bunyoro, effectively preventing Kabalega from invading Toro. The grateful Kasagama was happy enough to reward Lugard's efforts by signing a treaty of friendship between Britain and Toro.

Britain's predisposition to regard Kabalega as a villain became something close to a legal obligation following the treaty of protectorateship over Buganda, and it was certainly parallelled by the residual suspicion of foreigners held by Kabalega after the Equatoria debacle. Elements opposing British rule over Buganda fled to Kabalega's court at Mparo (near Hoima), notably a group of Muslim Baganda and Sudanese soldiers whose leader Selim Bey was deported in 1893 following a skirmish with the imperial authorities in Entebbe. With the assistance of the Baganda exiles, Kabalega reinvaded Toro in late 1893, driving Kasagama into the Rwenzori Mountains and the only British officer present back to Buganda.

In December 1893, Colonel Colville led a party of eight British officers, 450 Sudanese troops and at least 20,000 Baganda infantrymen on to Mparo. Kabalega was too crafty to risk confrontation with this impressive force: he burnt his capital and fled with his troops to the Budongo Forest. During 1894, Kabalega led several successful attacks on British forts, but as he lost more men and his supplies ran low, his guerrilla tactics became increasingly ineffective. In August 1894, on the very same day that the formal protectorateship of Uganda was announced by Colville, Kabalega launched his biggest assault yet on the fort at Hoima. The fort was razed, but Kabalega lost thousands of men. He was forced to leave Bunyoro to go into hiding in Acholi and Lango, from where he continued a sporadic and increasingly unsuccessful series of attacks on British targets. Kabalega's kingdom was unilaterally appended to the British protectorate on 30 June 1896; the first formal agreement between Britain and Bunyoro was signed only in 1933.

Meanwhile, back in Kampala, Kabaka Mwanga and his traditionalist chiefs were becoming frustrated at the power which the British had invested in Christian converts in general and Protestants in particular. In July 1897, Mwanga left Kampala and raised a few loyalist troops to launch a feeble attack on the British forces. Swiftly defeated, Mwanga fled to Bukoba where he was captured by the German authorities. The British administration officially deposed Mwanga and they installed his one-year-old son Chwa as kabaka under the regency of three Protestant chiefs led by Apollo Kaggwa. The administration adopted the same tactic in Bunyoro, where a blameless 12-year-old son of Kabalega was installed as omukama in 1898 – only to be removed four years later for what the administration termed incompetence!

Mwanga escaped from his German captors in late 1897, after which he joined forces with his former rival Kabalega. After two years on the run, Mwanga and Kabalega were cornered in a swamp in Lango. Following a long battle, Kabalega was shot (a wound which later necessitated the amputation of his arm) and the two former kings were captured and exiled to the Seychelles, where Mwanga died in 1903 and Kabalega died 20 years later. Kabalega remained the spiritual leader of Bunyoro until his death: it is widely held that the unpopular Omukama Duhaga II, installed by Britain in place of his 'incompetent' teenage brother, was tolerated by the Banyoro only because he was Kabalega's son.

Ankole succumbed more easily to British rule. Weakened by smallpox and rinderpest epidemics in the 1870s, the kingdom then suffered epidemics of tetanus and jiggers in the early 1890s, and it only just managed to repel a Rwandan invasion in 1895. Omugabe Ntare died later in the same year, by which time all the natural heirs to the throne had died in one or other epidemic. Following a brief succession war, a youthful nephew of the Ntare was installed on the throne. In 1898, Britain occupied the Ankole capital at Mbarara; the battered kingdom offered no resistance.

The southeast also fell under British rule without great fuss, because of the lack of cohesive political systems in the region. Much of the area was brought into the protectorate through the efforts of a Muganda collaborator called Semei Kakungulu who, incidentally, had assisted in the capture of Kabalega and Mwanga in Lango. Kakungulu set up a fiefdom in the Lake Kyoga region, where he installed a rudimentary administrative system over much of the area west of what is now the Kenyan border and south of Mount Elgon. Characteristically, the British administration eventually demoted Kakungulu to a subordinate role in the very system which he had implemented for them. Kakungulu's life story, as recounted in Michael Twaddle's excellent biography (page 583), is as illuminating an account as any of the formative days of the protectorate.

By the end of the 19th century, the Uganda Protectorate formally included the Kingdoms of Buganda, Bunyoro, Ankole and Toro. Three of them were ruled by juveniles, while Toro was under the rule of the British-installed Kasagama. Whether through incompetence or malicious intent, the British administration was in the process of creating a nation divided against itself: firstly by favouring Protestants over Baganda of Catholic, Muslim or traditionalist persuasion, and secondly by replacing traditional clan leaders in other kingdoms with Baganda officials. In this respect, the arrogant, myopic and partial British administrators who were imposed on Uganda in the late 19th century unwittingly but surely sowed the seeds of future tragedy.

BRITISH RULE (1900–52) The first governor of Uganda was Sir Harry Johnston, who arrived fresh from having led a vigorous anti-slaving campaign in Malawi in the 1890s. Johnston's instructions were to place the administration of the haphazardly assembled Uganda Protectorate under what the Marquis of Salisbury termed 'a permanently satisfactory footing'. In March 1900, the newly appointed governor of Uganda signed the so-called Buganda Agreement with the four-year-old kabaka. This document formally made Buganda a federal province of the protectorate, and it recognised the kabaka and his federal government conditional upon their loyalty to Britain. It divided Buganda into 20 counties, each of which had to pass the hut and gun taxes collected in their region to the central administration, and it forbade further attempts to extend the kingdom, a clause inserted mostly to protect neighbouring Busoga.

The Buganda Agreement also formalised a deal which had been made in 1898, in recognition of Buganda's aid in quelling Kabalega. Six former counties of Bunyoro were transferred to Buganda and placed under the federal rule of the kabaka, a decision described by a later district commissioner of Bunyoro as 'one of the greatest blunders' ever made by the administration of the protectorate. For lying within the Lost Counties (as the six annexed territories came to be called) were the burial sites of several former omukamas, as well as Mubende, a town which is steeped in Kinyoro traditions and the normal coronation site of an incoming omukama. In 1921, the Banyoro who lived in the Lost Counties formed the Mubende Bunyoro Committee to petition for their return to Bunyoro. This, and at least three subsequent petitions, as well as five petitions made by the omukama between 1943 and 1955, were all refused by the British administration on the basis that 'the boundaries laid down in 1900 could not be changed in favour of Bunyoro'. The issue of the Lost Counties caused Banyoro resentment throughout the colonial era, and it is arguably the trigger which set in motion the tragic events that followed Uganda's independence.

When Johnston arrived in Kampala in 1900, Uganda's borders were ill-defined. The first 15 years of the 20th century saw the protectorate expand further to incorporate yet more disparate cultural and linguistic groups, a growth which was motivated as much as anything by the desire to prevent previously unclaimed territories from falling into the hands of other European powers. The Kigezi region, a mishmash of small kingdoms which bordered German and Belgian territories to the south and west, was formally appended to Uganda in 1911. Baganda chiefs were installed throughout Kigezi, causing several uprisings and riots until the traditional chiefs were restored in 1929.

In the first decade of protectorateship, Britain had an inconsistent and ambiguous policy towards the territories north of the Nile. In 1906, it was decided not to incorporate them into Uganda, since they were not considered to be appropriate for the Kiganda system of government which was being imposed on other appended territories. More probably the administration was daunted by the cost and effort that would be required to subdue the dispersed and decentralised northern societies on an individual basis. In any event, the policy on the north was reversed in 1911, when the acting governor extended the protectorate to include Lango, and again in 1913, when Acholi and Karamoja were placed under British administration. The final piece in the Ugandan jigsaw was West Nile Province: leased to the Belgian Congo until 1910, after which it was placed under the administration of Sudan, West Nile was found a permanent home as part of Uganda in 1914.

Obsessed with the idea of running the protectorate along what it termed a Kiganda system of indirect rule, the British administration insisted not only on exporting its bastardised Kiganda system throughout the country, but also on placing its implementation in the hands of Baganda officials. In effect, Britain ruled Uganda by deploying the Baganda in a sub-imperialistic role; as a reward for their doing the administration's dirty work, Buganda was run as a privileged state within a state, a status it enjoyed right through to independence, when it was the only former kingdom to be granted full federality.

This divisive arrangement worked only because the administration had the legal and military clout to enforce it – even then, following regular uprisings in Bunyoro and Kigezi, traditional chiefs were gradually reinstated in most parts of the country. The 1919 Native Authority Ordinance delineated the powers of local chiefs, which were wide-ranging but subject always to the intervention of British officials. The Kiganda system was inappropriate to anywhere but Buganda, and it was absolutely absurd in somewhere like Karamoja, where there were no traditional chiefs, and decisions were made on a consensual basis by committees of recognised elders.

For all its flaws, the administrative system which was imposed on Uganda probably gave indigenous Ugandans far greater autonomy than was found elsewhere in British-ruled Africa. The administration discouraged alien settlement and, with the introduction of cotton, it helped many regions attain a high degree of economic self-sufficiency. Remarkably, cotton growing was left almost entirely to indigenous farmers – in 1920, a mere 500km^2 of Uganda was covered in European-run plantations, most of which collapsed following the global economic slump of the 1920s and the resultant drop in cotton prices. Political decentralisation was increased by the Local Government Ordinance of 1949, which divided Uganda along largely ethnic lines into 18 districts, each of which had a district council with a high degree of federal autonomy. This ordinance gave even greater power to African administrators, but it also contributed to the climate of regional unity and national disunity which characterised the decades immediately preceding and following Uganda's independence.

The area that suffered most from this federalist policy was the 'backward' north. Neglected in terms of education, and never provided with reliable transport links whereby farmers could export their product to other parts of the country, the people of the north were forced to send their youngsters south to find work. There is some reason to suppose it was deliberate British policy to underdevelop an area which had become a reliable source of cheap labour and of recruits to the police and army. This impression is reinforced by the fact that when Africans were first admitted to the Central Legislative Council, only Buganda, the east and the west were allowed representation – the administrative systems which had been imposed on the north were 'not yet in all districts advanced to the stage requiring the creation of centralised native executives'. In other words, instead of trying to develop the north and bring it in line with other regions in Uganda, the British administration chose to neglect it.

Writing before Idi Amin ascended to power, the Ugandan historian Samwiri Karugire commented that 'the full cost of this neglect has yet to be paid, not by the colonial officials, but by Ugandans themselves'. More recent writers have suggested that it is no coincidence that Milton Obote and Idi Amin both hailed from north of the Nile.

THE BUILD-UP TO INDEPENDENCE (1952–62) The cries for independence which prevailed in most African colonies following World War II were somewhat muted in Uganda. This can be attributed to several factors: the lack of widespread alien settlement, the high degree of African involvement in public affairs prior to independence, the strongly regional character of the protectorate's politics, and the strong probability that the status quo rather suited Uganda's Protestant Baganda elite. Remarkably, Uganda's first anti-colonial party, the Uganda National Congress (UNC), was founded as late as 1952, and it was some years before it gained any marked support, except, significantly, in parts of the underdeveloped north.

The first serious call for independence came from the most unlikely of sources. In 1953, the unpopular Kabaka Mutesa II defied the British administration by vociferously opposing the mooted federation of Uganda with Kenya and Tanzania. When the Governor of Uganda refused to give Mutesa any guarantees regarding federation, Mutesa demanded that Buganda – alone – be granted independence. The governor declared Mutesa to be disloyal to Britain, deposed him from the throne, and exiled him to Britain. This won Mutesa immense support, and not only in Buganda, so that when he was returned to his palace in 1955, it was as something of a national hero. Sadly, Mutesa chose not to use his popularity to help unify Uganda, but concentrated instead on parochial Kiganda affairs. A new Buganda Agreement was signed on 18 October 1955, giving the kabaka and his government even greater federal powers – and generating mild alarm among the non-Baganda.

Uganda's first indigenous party of consequence, the Democratic Party (DP), was founded in 1956 by Matayo Mugwanya after Mutesa had rejected him as a candidate for the Prime Minister of Buganda on the grounds of his Catholicism. The party formed a platform for the legitimate grievances of Catholics, who had always been treated as second-class citizens in Uganda, and it rose to some prominence after party leadership was handed to the lawyer Benedicto Kiwanuka in 1958. However, the DP was rightly or wrongly perceived by most Ugandans as an essentially Catholic party, which meant it was unlikely ever to win mass support.

The formation of the Uganda People's Union (UPU) came in the wake of the 1958 election, when for the first time a quota of Africans was elected to national government. The UPU was the first public alliance of non-Buganda leaders, and as such it represented an important step in the polarisation of Ugandan politics: in essence, the Baganda versus everybody else. In 1959, the UNC split along ethnic lines, with the non-Baganda faction combining with the UPU to form the Uganda People's Congress (UPC), led by Milton Obote. In 1961, the Baganda element of the UNC combined with members of the federal government of Buganda to form the overtly pro-Protestant and pro-Baganda Kabaka Yekka (KY) – which literally means 'The Kabaka Forever' (and was nicknamed 'Kill Yourselves' by opponents).

As the election of October 1961 approached, the DP, UPC and KY were clearly the main contenders. The DP won, largely through a Baganda boycott which gave them 19 of the seats within the kingdom – in East Kyaggwe, for instance, only 188 voters registered out of an estimated constituency of 90,000. The DP's Benedicto Kiwanuka thus became the first Prime Minister of Uganda when self-government was granted on 1 March 1962 – the first time ever that Catholics had any real say in public matters. Another general election was held in April of that year, in the build-up to the granting of full independence. As a result of the DP's success the year before, the UPC and KY formed an unlikely coalition, based on nothing but their mutual non-Catholicism. The UPC won 43 seats, the DP 24 seats, and the KY 24 (of which all but three were in Buganda), giving the UPC–KY alliance a clear majority and allowing Milton Obote to lead Uganda to independence on 9 October 1962.

THE FIRST OBOTE GOVERNMENT (1962–71) Obote, perhaps more than any other Commonwealth leader, inherited a nation fragmented along religious and ethnic lines to the point of ungovernability. He was also handed an Independence Constitution of singular peculiarity: Buganda was recognised as having full federal status, the other kingdoms were granted semi-federal status, and the remainder of the country was linked directly to central government. His parliamentary majority was dependent on a marriage of convenience based solely on religious grounds, and he was compelled to recognise Kabaka Mutesa II as head of state. Something, inevitably, was going to have to give.

The Lost Counties of Bunyoro became the pivotal issue almost immediately after independence. In April 1964, Obote decided to settle the question by holding a referendum in the relevant counties, thereby allowing their inhabitants to decide whether they wanted to remain part of Buganda or be reincorporated into Bunyoro. The result of the referendum, almost 80% in favour of the counties being reincorporated into Bunyoro, caused a serious rift between Obote and Mutesa. It also caused the fragile UPC–KY alliance to split; no great loss to Obote since enough DP and KY parliamentarians had already defected to the UPC for him to retain a clear majority.

Tensions between Obote and Mutesa culminated in the so-called Constitutional Crisis of 1966. On 22 February, Obote scrapped the Independence Constitution, thereby stripping Mutesa of his presidency. Mutesa appealed to the UN to intervene. Obote sent the army to the royal palace. Mutesa was forced to jump over the palace walls and into exile in London, where he died, impecunious, three years later. Ominously, an estimated 2,000 of the Baganda who had rallied around their king's palace were loaded on to trucks and driven away. Some were thrown over

Murchison Falls. Others were buried in mass graves. Most of them had been alive when they were taken from the palace.

In April 1966, Obote unveiled a new constitution in which he abolished the role of prime minister and made himself 'Life President of Uganda'. In September 1967, he introduced another new constitution wherein he made Uganda a republic, abolished the kingdoms, divided Buganda into four new districts, and gave the army unlimited powers of detention without trial. In sole control of the country, but faced with smouldering Baganda resentment, Obote became increasingly reliant on force to maintain a semblance of stability. In September 1969, he banned the DP and other political parties. A spate of detentions followed: the DP leader Benedicto Kiwanuka, perceived dissidents within the UPC, the Baganda royal family, Muslim leaders, and any number of lawyers, students, journalists and doctors.

On 11 January 1971, Obote flew out of Entebbe for the Commonwealth Conference in Singapore. He left behind a memorandum to the commander of the Ugandan army, demanding an explanation not only for the disappearance of US$4 million from the military coffers, but also for the commander's alleged role in the murder of a brigadier and his wife in Gulu a year earlier, a dual murder for which he was due to be brought to trial. The commander decided his only option was to strike in Obote's absence. On 25 January 1971, Kampala was rocked by the news of a military coup, and Uganda had a new president – a killer with the demeanour of a buffoon, and charisma enough to ensure that he would become one of the handful of African presidents who have achieved household-name status in the West.

THE AMIN YEARS (1971–79) Idi Amin was born in January 1928 of a Muslim father and Christian mother at Koboko near the border with the DRC and Sudan. As a child, he moved with his mother to Lugazi in Buganda. Poorly educated and barely literate, Amin joined the King's African Rifles in 1946. He fought for Britain against the Mau-Mau in Kenya, after which he attended a training school in Nakuru. In 1958, he became one of the first two Africans in Uganda to be promoted to the rank of lieutenant. In 1962, he showed something of his true colours when he destroyed a village near Lake Turkana in Kenya, killing three people without provocation; a misdeed for which he only narrowly escaped trial, largely through the intervention of Obote.

By 1966, Amin was second in command of the Ugandan army, and, following the 1966 Constitution Crisis, Obote promoted him to the top spot. It was Amin who led the raid that forced Mutesa into exile, Amin who gave the orders when 2,000 of the kabaka's Baganda supporters were loaded into trucks and killed, and Amin who co-ordinated the mass detentions that followed the banning of the DP in 1969. For years, Amin was the instrument with which Obote kept a grip on power, yet, for reasons that are unclear, by 1970 the two most powerful men in Uganda were barely talking to each other. It is a measure of Obote's arrogance that when he wrote that fateful memorandum before flying to Singapore, he failed to grasp not only that its recipient would be better equipped than anybody else to see the real message, but also that Amin was one of the few men in Uganda with the power to react.

Given the role that Amin had played under Obote, it is a little surprising that the reaction to his military takeover was incautious jubilation. Amin's praises were sung by everybody from the man in the street to the foreign press and the Baganda royals whose leader Amin had helped drive into exile. This, quite simply, was a reflection less of Amin's popularity than of Obote's singular unpopularity. Nevertheless, Amin certainly played out the role of a 'man of peace', promising a rapid return to civilian rule, and he sealed his popularity in Buganda by allowing the preserved body of Mutesa to be returned for burial.

On the face of it, the first 18 months of Amin's rule were innocuous enough. Arguably the first public omen of things to come occurred in mid 1972, when Amin expelled all Asians from the country, 'Africanised' their businesses, and commandeered their money and possessions for 'state' use. In the long term, this action proved to be an economic disaster, but the sad truth is that it won Amin further support from the majority of Ugandans, who had long resented Asian dominance in business circles. Even as Amin consolidated his public popularity, behind the scenes he was reverting to type; this was, after all, a man who had escaped being tried for murder not once but twice. Amin quietly purged the army of its Acholi and Lango majority: by the end of 1973, 13 of the 23 officers who had held a rank of lieutenant colonel or higher at the time of Amin's coup had been murdered. By the end of 1972, eight of the 20 members of Obote's 1971 cabinet were dead, and four more were in exile. Public attention was drawn to Amin's actions in 1973, when the former prime minister, Benedicto Kiwanuka, was detained and murdered by Amin, as was the Vice Chancellor of Makerere University.

By 1974, Amin was fully engaged in a reign of terror. During the eight years he was in power, an estimated 300,000 Ugandans were killed by him or his agents (under the guise of the State Research Bureau), many of them tortured to death in horrific ways. His main targets were the northern tribes, intellectuals and rival politicians, but any person or group that he perceived as a threat was dealt with mercilessly. Despite this, African leaders united behind Uganda's despotic ruler: incredibly, Amin was made President of the Organisation of African Unity (OAU) in 1975. Practically the sole voice of dissent within Africa came from Tanzania's Julius Nyerere, who asserted that it was hypocritical for African leaders to criticise the white racist regimes of southern Africa while ignoring similarly cruel regimes in 'black' Africa. Nyerere granted exile to several of Amin's opponents, notably Milton Obote and Yoweri Museveni, and he refused to attend the 1975 OAU summit in Kampala.

As Amin's unpopularity with his own countrymen grew, he attempted to forge national unity by declaring war on Tanzania in 1978. Amin had finally overreached himself; after his troops entered northwest Tanzania, where they bombed the towns of Bukoba and Musoma, Tanzania and a number of Ugandan exiles retaliated by invading Uganda. In April 1979, Amin was driven out of Kampala into an exile from which he would never return prior to his death of multiple organ failure in a Saudi Arabian hospital in August 2003.

UGANDA AFTER AMIN (1979–86) When Amin departed from Ugandan politics in 1979, it was seen as a fresh start by a brutalised nation. As it transpired, it was Uganda's third false dawn in 17 years – most Ugandans now regard the seven years which followed Amin's exile to have been worse even than the years which preceded it.

In the climate of high political intrigue which followed Amin's exile, Uganda's affairs were stage managed by exiled UPC leaders in Arusha (Tanzania), most probably because the UPC's leader Milton Obote was understandably cautious about announcing his return to Ugandan politics. The semi-exiled UPC installed Professor Lule as a stand-in president, a position which he retained for 68 days. His successor, Godfrey Binaisa, fared little better, lasting eight months before he was bundled out of office in May 1980. The stand-in presidency was then assumed by two UPC loyalists, Paulo Muwanga and David Oyite-Ojik, who set an election date in December 1980.

The main rivals for the election were the DP, led by Paul Ssemogerere, and the UPC, still led by Milton Obote. A new party, the Uganda Patriotic Movement (UPM), led by Yoweri Museveni, was formed a few months prior to the election. Uganda's first election since 1962 took place in an atmosphere of corruption and intimidation. Muwanga and Oyite-Ojik used trumped-up charges to prevent several DP candidates from standing, so that the UPC went into the polling with 17 uncontested seats. On the morning of 11 December, it was announced that the DP were on the brink of victory with 63 seats certain, a surprising result that probably reflected a strong anti-Obote vote from the Baganda. In response, Muwanga and Oyite-Ojik quickly drafted a decree ensuring that all results had to be passed to them before they could be announced. The edited result of the election saw the DP take 51 seats, the UPM one seat, and the UPC a triumphant 74. After some debate, the DP decided to claim their seats, despite the overwhelming evidence that the election had been rigged.

Yoweri Museveni felt that people had been cheated by the election, and that under Obote's UPC the past was doomed to repeat itself. In 1982, Museveni formed the National Resistance Movement (NRM), an army largely made up of orphans left behind by the excesses of Amin and Obote. The NRM operated from the Luwero Triangle in Buganda north of Kampala, where they waged a guerrilla war against Obote's government. Obote's response was characteristically brutal: his troops waded into the Luwero Triangle killing civilians by their thousands, an ongoing massacre which exceeded even Amin's. The world turned a blind eye to the atrocities in Luwero, and so it was left to 'dissident' members of the UPC and the commander of the army, Tito Okello, to suggest that Obote might negotiate with the NRM in order to stop the slaughter. Obote refused. On 27 July 1985, he was deposed in a bloodless military coup led by Tito Okello. For the second time in his career, Obote was forced into exile by the commander of his own army.

Okello assumed the role of head of state and he appointed as his prime minister Paulo Muwanga, whose role in the 1980 election gave him little credibility. With some misgivings, the DP allied itself with Okello, largely because Ssemogerere hoped he might use his influence to stop the killing in Luwero. In a statement made in Nairobi in August 1985, Museveni announced that the NRM was prepared to co-operate with Okello, provided that the army and the other instruments of oppression used by previous regimes were brought under check. The NRM entered into negotiations with Okello, but after these broke down in December 1985, Museveni returned to the bush. On 26 January 1986, the NRM entered Kampala, Okello surrendered tamely, and Museveni was sworn in as president – Uganda's seventh head of state in as many years.

THE NRM GOVERNMENT (1986–PRESENT) In 1986, Museveni took charge of a country that had been beaten and brutalised as have few others. There must have been many Ugandans who felt this was yet another false dawn, as they waited for the cycle of killings and detentions to start all over again. Certainly, to the outside world, Uganda's politics had become so confusing in all but their consistent brutality that the NRM takeover appeared to be merely another instalment in an apparently endless succession of coups and civil wars.

But Museveni was far from being another Amin or Obote. He shied away from the retributive actions which had destroyed the credibility of previous takeovers; he appointed a broad-based government which swept across party and ethnic lines, re-established the rule of law, appointed a much-needed Human Rights Commission, increased the freedom of the press, and encouraged the return of Asians and other exiles. On the economic front, he adopted pragmatic policies and encouraged foreign investment and tourism, the result of which was an average growth rate of 10% in his first decade of rule. Museveni has also tried to tackle corruption, albeit with limited success, by gradually cutting the civil service. Most significantly, Uganda under Museveni has visibly moved away from being a society obsessed with its ethnic and religious divisions. From the most unpromising material, Museveni has, miraculously, forged a real nation.

In 1993, Museveni greatly boosted his popularity (especially with the influential Baganda) by his decision to grant legal recognition to the old kingdoms of Uganda. In July 1993, the Cambridge-educated son of Mutesa II, Ronald Mutebi, returned to Uganda after having spent over 20 years in Britain; in a much-publicised coronation near Kampala, he was made the 36th Kabaka of Buganda. The traditional monarchies of Bunyoro and Toro have also been restored, but not that of Ankole.

In the 1990s, the most widespread criticism of Museveni and the NRM was their tardiness in moving towards a genuine multi-party democracy. At the time, Museveni argued, convincingly enough, that Uganda needed stability offered by a 'no party' system rather than a multi-party system that risked igniting the ethnic passions that had caused so much misery in its first two decades of independence. As a result, the NRM remained the only legal political party until 2005, though the country's first open presidential elections were held in 1996, slightly more than ten years after Museveni had first assumed power. Museveni won this formality with an overwhelming 74% of the vote, as compared with the 23% polled by his main rival, Paul Ssemogerere, a former DP leader who once served as prime minister under Museveni. A similar pattern was registered in the 2001 presidential elections, which returned Museveni to power with 70% of the vote, as compared with the 20% registered by his main rival Kizza Besigye. At the time, and for several years afterwards, Museveni reiterated his commitment to stand down from the presidency in 2006, in accordance with the maximum of two presidential terms specified by a national constitution drawn up years earlier by the NRM constitution.

Museveni then made two crucial about-turns. Firstly, he advocated a return to multi-party politics and held a national referendum that demonstrated the move was supported by 92.5% of voters. Only weeks later, he pushed a constitutional amendment through parliament to scrap presidential term limits, clearing the way for him to seek a third term in the looming elections. In November, barely three months before the election was due, the main opposition leader Kizza Besigye, recently returned from exile, was arrested and charged with terrorism, only to be released on bail in January 2006. A month later, Uganda's first multi-party election in 25 years was largely held to be free and fair by international observers, though this verdict was loudly disputed by Besigye, who polled 37% of the vote as compared with Museveni's 59%. Once again, this result can be viewed as ambiguous – the gap between the two primary candidates, though by no means insubstantial, had halved since the 2001 presidential election, and it is difficult to say to what extent the vote for Museveni represented overt support for his presidency and to what extent it simply reflected a fear of change.

There is no doubt that Uganda has made fantastic progress under Museveni's rule. Kampala today is unrecognisable from the shattered capital that the NRM inherited in 1986, while most smaller towns have been visibly bolstered by the consistent economic growth of the past three decades. Tragically, however, while most of the country thrived during the first 20 years of the Museveni era, the north suffered terribly at the hands of the Lord's Resistance Army (LRA; page 322), a rebel organisation whose primary manifesto appeared to be the slaughter

UGANDA'S INTERNATIONAL ART RENAISSANCE

Alexander Calder and Dr Joseph Kivubiro

Since its foundation in 1937, the School of Fine Art at Kampala's Makerere University has been the nucleus for East Africa's most influential and widespread contemporary art movement. While indigenous arts have flourished and evolved for centuries throughout East Africa, Makerere provided the region's first formal instruction in modern fine-art techniques, including drawing, painting and modern sculpture. Over the years, many students and graduates of this school became recognised innovators of striking new techniques and original styles.

During the particularly active 1950s and 60s, artists held solo and group exhibitions at numerous locations. Growing interest in exhibitions by local artists led to the establishment of sizeable art collections by public museums, corporations and government institutions throughout the country.

Until 1961, Makerere generally emphasised representative art, using drawing, perspective and shading in compositions inspired by local imagery. Following independence, however, a cadre of leading artists embraced a new role as visual cultural historians, producing interpretative works that document the early post-independence era – often using representative forms and figures to symbolise uncertainties and ideals within a rapidly changing society.

In 1966, artist Norbert Kaggwa underscored the importance of representational art in Uganda's rapidly evolving culture:

> Wedged into a single generation, my own, is a double vision; we are the beginning of an industrialised, urban society and we are probably – to be realistic – the end of the nomadic and village ways of life. The two eras are usually separated by hundreds of years. Here they are separated by a few dozen miles. I am personally very moved by this phenomenon and feel some special responsibility towards it. This is at least one of the reasons why I am a realistic and not an abstract painter. In one way, I suppose, I consider myself as much a cultural historian as an artist…or rather, in my case, they are one and the same thing.

Artists debated their perceived role and the purpose of their works against the backdrop of independence. Art of this period consequently benefited from rich cross-fertilisation: several artists embraced both idioms to find unique and expressive visual forms that drew from abstract as well as representational influences. The late Henry Lumu, Augustine Mugalula Mukiibi, Teresa Musoke and Elly Kyeyune were early leaders of Uganda's emerging Modernist school, spawning the distinctive semi-abstract styles that characterised much art of this era.

In 1968, Makerere graduate Henry Lumu was hired as art director by Uganda National Television, initiating regular broadcasts of televised art-instruction classes. Exposure through this new medium further stimulated Kampala's burgeoning art community, which by that time extended well beyond the campus. The Uganda Art Club organised exhibitions throughout Kampala in the early to mid 1970s, prompting prominent hotels, banks and commercial buildings to amass and display collections of outstanding original works. During this period, artists attained unprecedented standing within Kampala's thriving cosmopolitan circles and among the country's elite.

By the late 1970s, political unrest had taken a dreadful toll among Uganda's artistic community. Professionals and intellectuals were targeted by the Obote and Amin regimes, and museums and galleries were looted or reoccupied – destroying numerous significant art collections. Forced to choose between seclusion, alternative occupations or self-imposed exile, many Ugandan artists emigrated to Kenya, South Africa, Europe or North America. The expatriate artists incorporated visual elements from their new surroundings into mediums, styles and colour palettes that still remained faithful to their Ugandan experience.

A large number of artists, including Henry Lumu, Joseph Mungaya, Dan Sekanwagi, Emmy Lubega, David Kibuuka, Jak Kitarikawe, David Wasswa Katongole and James Kitamirike, left for neighbouring Kenya. The colourful, innovative and uniquely stylised works of the Ugandan painters transformed Nairobi's art scene. Kenyan artist Nuwa Nnyanzi reflected recently: 'The impact of Ugandan artists in Kenya in the seventies and eighties was so great that it is still felt and highly visible today.'

Restored political stability in the late 1980s encouraged the homecoming or resurfacing of many Ugandan artists. Expressing rediscovered peacetime ideals through their art, many artists also reminded their audience of struggles and horrors endured during the troubled years. Exhibitions by Ugandan artists were held regularly at London's Commonwealth Institute, while other shows opened in Paris and Vienna. In 1992, President Museveni marked the opening of a Vienna show featuring Geoffrey Mukasa and Fabian Mpagi with these remarks:

> As those destructive years have regrettably shown, art cannot flourish in a situation plagued with terror and human indifference. Peace and security have returned to our country. We have gone a long way to encourage the revival of arts. The fine works exhibited are a vivid testimony that art has come to life again in Uganda. Certainly, both the public and the critics will recognise that Uganda has taken up her place in the world of modern art. It is an opportune moment for us to portray through these paintings a promising new picture of the 'New Uganda'.

Exhibitions by and for Ugandan artists have also been held in Stockholm, Amsterdam, Berlin, Frankfurt, Rome, Johannesburg and seven cities in the USA. In North America, expatriate artists such as James Kitamirike, David Kibuuka, Dan Sekanwagi and Fred Makubuya have united to spearhead renewed interest in their art through the Fine Arts Center for East Africa, which opened in San Francisco in 1998. Organising group exhibitions in the USA and Canada, this active contingent of artists continues to garner recognition for their innovative styles, mediums and potent individual voices within Uganda's art movement.

In Kampala today, Uganda's renewed art scene embodies a vibrant and vital country redefining its past yet also reaching for a hopeful future. Sharing their unique visual arts legacy, Uganda's fine-art pioneers have become the country's cultural ambassadors, creating global awareness of their homeland's unique colours, cultures, peoples and art.

Locations to view art in Kampala are listed on page 146.

Reprinted with minor edits from the website of the Fine Arts Center for East Africa in San Francisco, with permission from Alexander Calder (+1 415 333 9363; e gadart@aol.com)

of unarmed civilians. Although protracted negotiations between the LRA and the government failed to result in a formal peace agreement, the former withdrew from Uganda into the Congo in 2005, and the north has been at peace – and enjoying a considerable economic revival of its own – ever since. The progress of Uganda post-1986 was showcased to the world in November 2007 when Uganda hosted Queen Elizabeth II and 57 heads of state for the Commonwealth Heads of Government Meeting (CHOGM).

Since CHOGM, it has been more of the same. Museveni winning elections in 2011, 2016 and 2021. Though in each case his opponents have cried foul and petitioned to have the result overturned, it is probable that NRM victories were genuine. That said, cracks are appearing in Museveni's once solid bedrock of support, even within the NRM, with a significant number of MPs opining that it might be time for the ageing president to retire to his farm at Rwakitura and make way for fresh blood. Dwindling margins of victory since 2011 also indicate that support among the electorate is also wavering, particularly among more educated and urbanised Ugandans. Unquestioned allegiance to the NRM is not helped by regular corruption scandals and accusations of skulduggery which suggest that senior government officials consider themselves above the law and accountable to themselves rather than their voters. In 2011, the Ministry of Health was embroiled in a scandal concerning the loss of at least US$10 million from a Global Fund dedicated to fight AIDS, tuberculosis and malaria. Vulnerable voters also lost out in 2013 when senior officials in the Office of the Prime Minister were unable to account for billions of shillings of donor money meant to rebuild northern Uganda, a blip that led to the withholding of aid by several donor countries. More recently, questions have been asked about the use of millions of dollars secured from international agencies to manage the Covid-19 crisis.

Ironically, Uganda's most successful attempt to shoot itself in the foot was portrayed as a move to reflect the views of the electorate when a draconian Anti-Homosexuality Act (AHA) was passed in 2013. Hitherto, intolerance of homosexuality in Uganda had been largely a latent affair until the subject was elevated by evangelical preachers, often from or funded from the USA. Though this was overturned by the Supreme Court the same year, it would only be a temporary respite for Uganda's LGBTQIA+ community, the AHA being revived in 2022.

In December 2017, the Ugandan parliament voted overwhelmingly in favour of a constitutional amendment, proposed by the NRM, to lift the existing age limit of 75 for presidential candidates. In due course, Museveni stood for and was returned for a sixth term in January 2021. This formality was notable for the absence of Museveni's long-term opponent, Kizza Besigye, from the fray and the emergence of one Robert Kyagulani, MP and leader of the National Unity Party. From humble beginnings, Kyagulani had risen to prominence as pop star Bobi Wine before being elected to parliament, where he styled himself the people's president. Though his angry charisma and energy struck a chord with many, particularly among the youth, the electorate remained unconvinced; though it might be argued that the NRM held all the aces, using restrictions attached to the Covid-19 crisis to stifle Kyagulani's campaign.

Indeed, for many, the election took second place to privations caused by the pandemic, during which Ugandans endured two nationwide lockdowns, as well as prolonged closures of schools (the world's longest), churches, mosques, gyms, bars and restaurants. Traffic across international borders was limited to commercial trucks while Entebbe International Airport was closed to commercial airlines for six months. The first lockdown, promptly imposed in the first weeks of the global pandemic in March 2020, is credited with buying time while vaccines were developed. Though these were rolled out with commendable efficiency in early 2021, initial uptake was low and it was during a second lockdown in July/August that year that mortality rates spiked. Even this surge was, however, low compared with fatalities elsewhere and to date just 3,600 deaths have been attributed to the virus. That said, economic hardship caused by Covid-related restrictions was keenly felt, especially within the low-income, hand-to-mouth urban sector with many arguing that they would prefer the possibility of dying from Covid than the certainty of starvation.

In 2022, the notorious Anti-Homosexuality Act was revived and, having been passed by Parliament was signed into law by the president in 2023 (see also page 77). International condemnation was immediate with the World Bank and several other funding agencies halting support to Uganda while the US has imposed economic restrictions and denied visas to senior officials. The saga is not yet over, however, for at the time of writing, legal challenges are being mounted to fight the AHA. For Museveni, its repeal would not be a disaster. In signing the act, he had boosted his star by listening to the will of (most of) his people, and if he was to be ultimately thwarted by the courts, that in itself would be pronounced a sign of a healthy and independent judiciary. Meanwhile foreign funding would resume, the stain on Uganda's reputation would fade with time and the world would move on.

What of the future? Museveni has already indicated that he will be standing for – and could reasonably be expected to win – a seventh term, an event that will mark 40 years in power. Additional intrigue has, however, been added by the announcement that his son, 49-year-old General Muhoozi Kainerugaba, who many expect to step in as the NRM's main man, will also be running for office in 2026.

GOVERNMENT

Uganda is a republic presided over by a president who serves as the head of state and head of government. The ruling party is the National Resistance Movement (NRM), which seized power in 1986 to end the 15-year era of despotic rule and civil war initiated by a coup led by Idi Amin in 1971. President Yoweri Museveni of the NRM has served as president since 1986, having won his sixth presidential election in 2021. The post of prime minister, abolished under Milton Obote in 1966 but reinstated in 1980, has been held by six different NRM members since 1986. The incumbent since September 2021 is Robinah Nabbanja. The cabinet currently comprises another 30 cabinet ministers and 49 Ministers of State, and is dominated by NRM members. The parliament comprises 426 elected members of whom 337 belong to the NRM, and 57 to the National Unity Platform (NUP), currently the largest opposition party.

Uganda is a democracy, and it has held elections every five years since 1996, However, the 'no party' system once espoused by the NRM, ostensibly to reduce sectarian violence, put a curb on multi-party activity until 2005, when the ban was cancelled by a constitutional referendum.

Uganda has undergone several internal administrative reforms since the early 20th century. In the colonial era, the protectorate was divided into 14 administrative regions, including the Kingdoms of Buganda, Ankole, Bunyoro and Toro. Today, the country is divided into Central, Eastern, Northern and Western administrative regions, and these are further subdivided into 121 districts (most named after their main town) as well as the city of Kampala. The districts are clustered into 14 subregions: Acholi, Ankole, Buganda, Bugisu, Bukedi, Bunyoro, Busoga, Karamoja, Kigezi, Lango, Sebei, Teso, Toro and West Nile. Although these subregions seem to possess a limited significance as administrative entities, they closely resemble the original kingdoms and other ethnically defined divisions delineated by the British government in the early 20th century, and their names are still in wide vernacular use a century later.

ECONOMY

Uganda's free-market economy has experienced a steady per-annum growth of around 5% over the last 30-odd years, largely due to the atmosphere of political stability fostered by the NRM and economic reforms implemented by President Museveni in the early years of his rule. As a result, the national GDP (based on purchasing-power-parity) has soared from around US$7 billion in 1986 to US$45 billion today, and it is likely to remain one of the world's fastest-growing economies in the coming decade. An important impetus for this growth has been the expansion of the service and industrial sectors since Museveni took power in 1986. Back then, the agricultural sector – despite having been undermined by the long years of civil strife under his predecessor – accounted for about 60% of the national GDP, and more than 90% of Ugandans were subsistence farmers or employed in agriculture-related fields. Today, by contrast, the industrial and service sectors contribute 25% and 50% of the GDP, respectively, while the agricultural sector's input has dropped to 24% (though it still employs 70% of the workforce of 18.8 million). Fertile soils and high rainfall have ensured that Uganda has been self-sufficient in food ever since independence. The major export crop is coffee, followed by tea, cut flowers and tobacco. Notable industries include sugar refinement, textiles, and cement and steel production. Historically, mining has not played a large role in the Ugandan economy, not unless you count salt extraction in the west, at sites such as Lake Katwe, but this is set to change with the reopening of the Kilembe copper mine near Kasese and discovery of oil in the vicinity of Lake Albert in the Rift Valley. As might be expected, most economic and social indicators have improved greatly in recent years, though 40% of the population still lives below the international poverty line of US$2.15 per day.

PEOPLE

The 2024 census shows Uganda to have a population of 45.9 million, an increase of 11.3 million (32%) since the last census recorded 35 million in 2014, and a near sixfold increase (555%) since independence when the population stood at about 7 million. The annual growth rate, however, is slowly shrinking from 3.2% to 2.9% in 2024. The majority of Uganda's people are concentrated in the south and west. The most populous ethnic group is the Bantu-speaking Baganda, which accounts for about 18% of the population and is centred on Kampala. Other numerically significant Bantu-speaking groups are the Busoga (10%), Banyankole (8%) and Bakiga (8%). The east and north of the country are populated by several Nilotic- or Cushitic-speaking groups, including the Teso, Karamojong, Acholi and Lango.

The table opposite compares population data for Uganda's ten largest cities as ranked in the 2024 census with those in previous censuses. Note that the comparison is somewhat skewed since only cities are shown. At the time of writing, data for Kampala's satellite towns (Mukono, Nansana and Kira all feature prominently in the 2014 count) were yet to be released. Still, it provides a good indicator of the

POPULATION TRENDS

	1959		1991		2002		2014		2024	
1	Kampala	46,000	Kampala	775,000	Kampala	1,200,000	Kampala	1,568,900	Kampala	1,875,000
2	Gulu	30,000	Jinja	65,000	Gulu	113,000	Kira	353,400	Arua	380,824
3	Lira	14,000	Mbale	54,000	Lira	89,500	Mbarara	202,800	Jinja	292,368
4	Jinja	11,500	Masaka	49,500	Jinja	86,500	Mukono	170,200	Mbale	289,941
5	Mbale	11,000	Entebbe	42,700	Mbale	70,000	Nansana	162,700	Masaka	285,509
6	Mbarara	8,500	Mbarara	41,000	Mbarara	69,000	Gulu	161,200	Mbarara	261,656
7	Masaka	8,000	Soroti	40,900	Masaka	61,000	Hoima	108,700	Lira	246,437
8	Entebbe	7,000	Gulu	38,300	Entebbe	57,000	Masaka	107,700	Gulu	232,723
9	Kasese	6,000	Njeru	37,000	Kasese	53,000	Kasese	106,300	Hoima	141,442
10	Njeru	5,000	Fort Portal	32,800	Mukono	47,000	Lira	104,200	Fort Portal	135,775

dramatic post-independence shifts in urban growth around the country. Kampala remains, obviously, the most populous city by far with a population approaching 1.9 million. This, however, is only half of the story, the city merely being the nucleus of a conurbation with a predicted population of over 4 million.

LANGUAGE

The official language, English, is spoken as a second language by most educated Ugandans. More than 33 local languages are spoken in different parts of the country. Most of these belong to the Bantu language group: for instance, Luganda, Lusoga and Lutoro. Several Nilotic and Cushitic languages are spoken in the north and east, some of them by only a few thousand people. Many Ugandans speak a limited amount of Swahili, a coastal language which spread into the East African interior via the 19th-century Arab slave traders.

RELIGION

Religion plays a far larger role in day-to-day life in Uganda than it does in most Western countries, with fewer than 1% of the population claiming to be atheist or agnostic. Freedom of religion is a constitutional right, though the activities of certain groups classified as cults is restricted. Christianity dominates. The Roman Catholic Church can claim around 42% of the total population, while the Church of Uganda (an offshoot of the Church of England) accounts for another 36%, and 7% are Jehovah's Witnesses or belong to a Pentecostal church. Partially as a legacy of the Arab trade with Buganda in the late 19th century, roughly 12% of Ugandans are Muslim (mostly Sunni), with the majority living in the eastern half of the country. Today, there is little or no friction between Christian and Muslim, though post-independence political conflict did follow Catholic-Protestant lines. In most rural areas, these non-indigenous faiths have not entirely displaced traditional beliefs, so that an estimated 25% of the Christian and Islam population might still partake in traditional religious practices such as making sacrifices to clan ancestors or other spirits. Other minority religions are Hindu, Bahá'í and a unique variant on Judaism practised by the Abayudaya of Mbale. The main centre of animism is the northeast, where the Karamoja – like the affiliated Maasai and other Rift Valley pastoralists – largely shun any outside faith in favour of their own traditional beliefs.

EDUCATION

Uganda has a high standard of education by African standards, but is rather less impressive by global ones. Since independence, the schooling system has comprised seven years of primary education followed by six years of secondary education. Attendance rates were very low in the 1970s and 1980s, as reflected in a low adult literacy rate (just under 75%) but have soared since the introduction of a Universal Primary Education (UPE) system in 1997. UPE allows for free primary education in

RUNNING IN UGANDA *Alfie Pearce-Higgins*

Uganda may lack the running reputation of neighbouring Kenya or Ethiopia, but it is still capable of producing great athletes. In 2012 Stephen Kiprotich became a national sensation when he took gold in the marathon at the London Olympics (one of only two such medals in Uganda's history), which helped to boost the popularity of running among the growing urban middle class. Four years later, David Emong became Uganda's first ever Paralympic medal winner, taking silver in the 1,500m in Rio de Janeiro.

For energetic visitors wanting to enjoy their own Kiprotich moment, there is no shortage of opportunities. Whether you are after a gentle jog or a 50km race, Uganda offers some excellent runs. Some might require dodging bodas, wildlife or pot-holes and many will involve being laughed at by confused locals, but few will be boring. Here is a selection of our favourite races and routes.

RUNNING THE RIFT Each November, Kyaninga Lodge (page 417) hosts 42km, 21km and 10km races that snake along the edge of the Western Rift Valley. Participants are treated to spectacular views of the valley floor with the Rwenzori Mountains towering in the distance and have the opportunity to cool off afterwards in the refreshing (and bilharzia-free) crater lake. All proceeds go to the Kyaninga Child Development Centre. In 2018, the organisers added a bike race (Ride the Rift), a 100km uphill slog from Lake Albert to Kyaninga. The lodge also hosts a popular triathlon each May.

UGANDA MARATHON First held in 2015, the Uganda Marathon (42km, 21km, 10km; w ugandamarathon.com) is held in Masaka and raises money for local community projects. Each year several hundred runners travel to Uganda, many of whom combine the race with an organised seven-day tour of the country.

LAKE MBURO NATIONAL PARK The area bordering the park offers one of the best opportunities to run alongside wildlife in Uganda. It abounds with zebra, impala and other antelope, and there's the occasional leopard and hippo to watch out for (if in doubt ask for guidance on routes and wildlife risk). Mihingo Lodge (page 213) offers guided runs just outside the park (or you can just run alone) and together with Activate Uganda (see opposite).

LAKE MUTANDA Most lodges and hotels in Uganda will point guests in the right direction for an enjoyable run, but Mutanda Lake Resort (page 544) deserves special mention for its running opportunities. Dirt roads and tracks circle the entire

government schools for up to four children per family, and it resulted in a threefold increase in primary school attendance from 2 million in 1986 to more than 6 million at the turn of the millennium. By 2012, primary school attendance stood at almost 95% (compared with 68% in 1995), and the literacy rate of young adults (aged 15–24) had improved to 87.5%. More recent figures are unavailable, but these are likely to have increased slightly since then. That said, only 25% of Ugandans continue on to secondary school, which follows the old British system of four years of O-levels followed by two years of A-levels. Fewer than 4% of Ugandans complete tertiary education.

lake, making life easier for the navigationally challenged. A full lap of the lake is almost exactly a marathon but there are also a range of shorter options on offer.

ELGON AND THE RWENZORI Uganda's two largest mountains are both open to hikers. For those who find walking a bit pedestrian, running is an option, although both areas involve significant challenges including the risk of altitude sickness. The Elgon region requires visitors to be accompanied by a UWA ranger so any would-be runners will face the challenge of finding a guide fit enough and willing to accompany them (at the time of writing, Rodgers is the best option). Meanwhile in the Rwenzori, the trails are often so boggy or steep that only the most technical of runners will succeed in breaking out of a walk, but Sam of Rwenzori Trekking Services (page 459) has occasionally been persuaded to accompany runners.

JINJA For those staying in or near Jinja running can be an excellent way to explore the surrounding areas. On both sides of the river a network of trails covers the fertile land and runners can look forward to passing through fields, over streams and into settlements and villages, where one can rely on a welcoming reception.

ACTIVATE UGANDA This enthusiastic Kampala-based operator (w activateuganda.com) organises a series of popular running and mountain-biking trail races throughout the year. The Source of the Nile Race (September) includes a 50km option making it Uganda's only ultra-marathon (although depending on the quality of the course markings many races in Uganda can easily turn into impromptu ultra-marathons). Other highlights of Activate Uganda's calendar include the Mpanga Forest Trail Race (November) and the Iron Hammer Run (July), both conveniently located within an hour of Kampala and including 21km, 12km and 5km options.

KAMPALA The busy, polluted streets of Kampala are far from a runner's paradise. However, each morning and evening one will find a committed bunch of Ugandans and expatriates sweating their way up some of the city's hills, where the air is (slightly) cleaner and the streets (marginally) quieter. Popular Strava segments are keenly fought over. Uganda's most serious road race is the MTN Kampala Marathon (w mtn.co.ug), which takes place each November. Big prize money means the event attracts a selection of elite runners from across East Africa, while thousands of locals run (or walk) the 10km option.

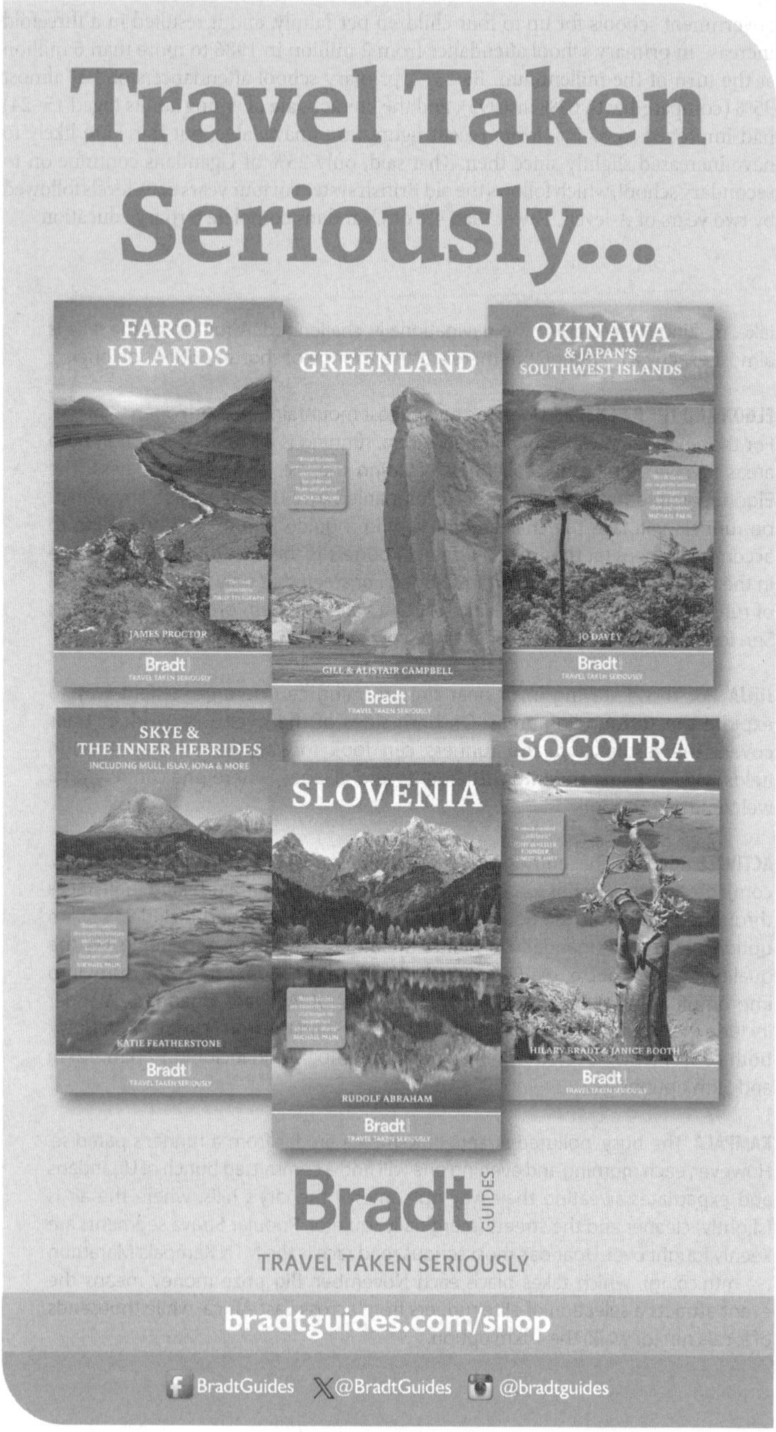
Travel Taken Seriously...
FAROE ISLANDS
JAMES PROCTOR
Bradt
TRAVEL TAKEN SERIOUSLY
GREENLAND
GILL & ALISTAIR CAMPBELL
Bradt
TRAVEL TAKEN SERIOUSLY
OKINAWA & JAPAN'S SOUTHWEST ISLANDS
JO DAVEY
Bradt
TRAVEL TAKEN SERIOUSLY
SKYE & THE INNER HEBRIDES
INCLUDING MULL, ISLAY, IONA & MORE
KATIE FEATHERSTONE
Bradt
TRAVEL TAKEN SERIOUSLY
SLOVENIA
RUDOLF ABRAHAM
Bradt
TRAVEL TAKEN SERIOUSLY
SOCOTRA
HILARY BRADT & JANICE BOOTH
Bradt
TRAVEL TAKEN SERIOUSLY
Bradt GUIDES
TRAVEL TAKEN SERIOUSLY
bradtguides.com/shop
BradtGuides
@BradtGuides
@bradtguides

ꞏn adult male
nountain gorilla,
nown as a
ilverback, can be
p to three times as
ulky as its average
uman counterpart
AGE 39
VZ)

The world's largest living primate, the iconic mountain gorilla has a range confined to the Virunga volcanoes (which are split between Uganda, Rwanda and the DRC) and Bwindi Impenetrable National Park. Roughly 1,000 individuals survive, living in tight-knit family groups that consist of at least one silverback male (below), a few females (left), and several youngsters (above) (AVZ) PAGE 39

Chimpanzees are more closely related to humans than any other living primate, and their distinctive 'pant-hoot' call (pictured below) means you're likely to hear them before you see them. They live in extended communities of up to 100 individuals. Habituated chimps can be tracked in several Ugandan forests, most notably Kibale, Budongo and Kalinzu (AVZ) PAGE 40

above left (AVZ) An agile adult black-and-white-colobus is capable of jumping up to 30m PAGE 40

above right (AVZ) The Angola colobus is superficially similar in appearance to its black-and-white relation, but can be distinguished from it by its much darker and less shaggy tail PAGE 40

below left (AVZ) Kibale National Park is an excellent place to spot the endangered Ugandan red colobus PAGE 40

below right (AVZ) Omnivorous and highly adaptable, the Anubis baboon is frequently seen on the fringes of forest reserves PAGE 40

The blue monkey is a common resident of many Ugandan forests PAGE 41 above left (AVZ)

The vervet monkey, a widespread woodland and savannah species, occurs throughout the country, both in and out of national parks PAGE 41 above right (AVZ)

While most other Ugandan primates are arboreal forest dwellers, the patas monkey is a predominantly terrestrial creature of open savannah PAGE 40 below (AVZ)

above left (AVZ) Tracking golden monkeys in the bamboo zone of the Virungas is a highlight of visiting Mgahinga Gorilla National Park PAGE 41

above right (AVZ) The distinctive red-tailed monkey can be identified by its conspicuous white nose spot and long, russet tail PAGE 41

below (AVZ) L'Hoest's monkeys prefer dense secondary forest, making them very difficult to see PAGE 41

The bearded De Brazza's monkey is an uncommon resident of Mount Elgon and Semuliki national parks PAGE 41 above left (AVZ)

The greyish-black Uganda mangabey, first recognised as a full species in 2007, is endemic to the country PAGE 42 above right (AVZ)

Six galago species are found in Uganda, including the cat-like greater galago PAGE 42 below (AVZ)

above left & right (AVZ) Africa's largest carnivore, the lion is a primarily nocturnal hunter, and prides spend their days lying in the shade PAGE 42

below (AVZ) Owing to its highly secretive, solitary nature, the leopard is difficult to see, even in parks where it is common PAGE 43

The cheetah's lithe form helps it to hunt using speed rather than stealth PAGE 43

above (AVZ)

The African wild cat is ancestral to the domestic tabby, which explains its familiar appearance PAGE 43

right (AVZ)

The serval is a medium-sized cat often confused with the larger cheetah thanks to its sleek build and pale, spotted coat PAGE 43

below (AVZ)

above (AVZ) The black-backed jackal is an omnivore that will hunt small mammals but also eats carrion, fruit and bulbs PAGE 44

left (AVZ) The distinctive bat-eared fox is commonly sighted in Kidepo and Pian Upe PAGE 44

below (AVZ) The side-striped jackal is the most widespread canid in Uganda PAGE 43

Within Uganda, the striped hyena – a scarcer and more strictly nocturnal creature than the related spotted hyena – is restricted to the Kidepo Valley PAGE 44

above (AVZ)

Despite its reputation as a scavenger, the spotted hyena is adept at hunting animals as large as wildebeest PAGE 44

right (AVZ)

The African wild dog was extinct in Uganda, but following recent sightings in Kidepo Valley, hope remains that this wandering canid will recolonise its former habitats PAGE 44

below (AVZ)

above (AVZ) The large-spotted genet is sometimes observed slinking around campsites and lodges after dark PAGE 45

left (AVZ) The spotted-necked otter is common in and around Lake Bunyonyi PAGE 45

below (AVZ) A highly adaptable hunter, the honey badger (or ratel) is widespread in Uganda but rarely seen PAGE 45

As its name implies, the dwarf mongoose is the smallest of the African mongoose species PAGE 45 — above (AVZ)

The long tail of the slender mongoose is distinctively black tipped PAGE 45 — right (A/D)

A habituated banded mongoose troop can be tracked on the Mweya Peninsula in Queen Elizabeth National Park PAGE 45 — below (AVZ)

above (AVZ) The handsome roan antelope is present only in small numbers in Pian Upe PAGE 46

below left (AVZ) Jackson's hartebeest is found in most of Uganda's savannah reserves PAGE 46

below right (AVZ) The Defassa waterbuck is distinguished by its shaggy grey-brown coat, white rump and large curved horns PAGE 46

Distinctive white side-stripes mark the coat of greater kudu PAGE 46

above (AVZ)

A male common eland can stand up to 1.8m tall, making it Africa's largest antelope PAGE 46

right (AVZ)

The topi is similar in size and build to a hartebeest, but has a much darker coat PAGE 46

below (AVZ)

above left (AVZ) Unlike other duikers, the grey duiker occurs not in forest but in woodland and savannah habitats PAGE 47

above right (AVZ) The forest-dwelling red duiker forages on leaves, fruits and flowers fallen from the canopy PAGE 48

left (AVZ) True to its name, the klipspringer ('rock-jumper' in Afrikaans) is often found in the vicinity of kopjes or cliffs PAGE 48

below (AVZ) The gazelle-like oribi is usually seen in pairs or small groups in tall grassland PAGE 48

bottom (AVZ) The bohor reedbuck is present in all four of Uganda's savannah national parks PAGE 47

The impala has decidedly springy legs that enable it to broad-jump over 10m PAGE 47 above left (AVZ)

Once-numerous Ugandan populations of Grant's gazelle have been reduced to a mere 100 animals roaming the reserves of Karamoja PAGE 47 above right (AVZ)

The bushbuck is probably the most widespread antelope in Uganda PAGE 47 below left (AVZ)

The semi-aquatic sitatunga is uniquely adapted to its favoured habitat of papyrus swamps PAGE 47 below right (AVZ)

The graceful Ugandan kob is the national animal of Uganda and appears on its coat of arms PAGE 46 bottom (AVZ)

above (AVZ) Female elephants form closely knit clans, with the eldest female taking the matriarchal role PAGE 48

left (AVZ) Large and lumbering as it might look, the largely aquatic hippo can move surprisingly quickly when threatened PAGE 49

below (AVZ) Although they are often seen in large herds, zebras actually form relatively small stable social groups PAGE 50

Africa's only wild ox, the African buffalo lives in large herds on Uganda's savannah plains PAGE 49 above left (AVZ)

Africa's second-largest land animal, the southern white rhino has been introduced to Ziwa Rhino and Wildlife Ranch in place of the extinct northern white rhino, and can be tracked on foot there PAGE 49 above right (AVZ)

Rothschild's giraffe is most common in Murchison Falls National Park, where herds of up to 50 are frequently encountered on the plains to the north of the Nile PAGE 49 below (AVZ)

above (AVZ) Hidden deep in the forest interior and emerging only at night, the giant forest hog is a rare sight in Uganda PAGE 50

left (AVZ) Bushpigs are similar in appearance to warthogs, but distinctly hairier and bulkier PAGE 50

below (AVZ) Warthogs are the most common wild pigs in Uganda, and likely to be seen in any savannah habitat, occasionally with a few crow-like piapiacs hitching a ride PAGE 50

Uganda is home to five hyrax species, including the tree hyrax (left) and rock hyrax (right) PAGE 50

above left & above right (AVZ)

The rather bizarre-looking aardvark is widespread in Uganda, but rarely seen due to its nocturnal habits PAGE 50

right (AVZ)

The pangolin is the only mammal wholly covered in scales PAGE 50

below (AVZ)

above left (AVZ) The puff adder is the most commonly encountered venomous snake in Uganda PAGE 58

above right (AVZ) Several cobra species are found in Uganda, including the venomous forest cobra PAGE 59

left (AVZ) Bright green and slender, bush snakes have distinctive flat heads and long tails

below (AVZ) Nile crocodiles can grow up to 6m in length, and are mainly seen on the Nile in Murchison Falls National Park PAGE 55

Agama lizards are often found basking in the grounds of rural lodges PAGE 60 — above left (AVZ)

Named after its gold-and-black mottled shell, the leopard tortoise is the most common terrestrial tortoise in the region PAGE 60 — above right (AVZ)

Often spotted in the forests of Bwindi, the Rwenzori three-horned chameleon can grow up to 30cm long PAGE 59 — above (AVZ)

A massive lizard often seen on riverbanks, the Nile monitor could be mistaken for a small crocodile PAGE 60 — below (AVZ)

Uganda's wealth of wetland habitats, from the Nile River to the great lakes of the Albertine Rift, make it a magnet for water-associated birds

above left (AVZ) Saddle-billed stork (*Ephippiorhynchus senegalensis*)

above centre (AVZ) Marabou stork (*Leptoptilos crumeniferus*)

above right (AVZ) Flamingo (*Phoenicopterus roseus*)

left (AVZ) Hamerkop (*Scopus umbretta*)

below left (AVZ) Grey crowned crane (*Balearica regulorum*)

below right (AVZ) Shoebill (*Balaeniceps rex*)

Goliath heron (*Ardea goliath*) above left (AVZ)

Malachite kingfisher (*Alcedo cristata*) top right (AVZ)

Pink-backed pelican (*Pelecanus rufescens*) above right (AVZ)

African jacana (*Actophilornis africanus*) below left (AVZ)

White-faced whistling duck (*Dendrocygna viduata*) below right (AVZ)

Uganda supports a wide diversity of raptorial birds, from hefty eagles and vultures to nocturnal owls and acrobatic kestrels and falcons.

above left (AVZ) Dark chanting goshawk (*Melierax metabates*)

above right (AVZ) Spotted eagle owl (*Bubo africanus*)

left (AVZ) Greater kestrel (*Falco rupicoloides*)

below left (AVZ) Palmnut vulture (*Gypohierax angolensis*)

below right (AVZ) Lappet-faced vulture (*Torgos tracheliotos*)

Grey kestrel (*Falco ardosiaceus*) above left (AVZ)

Verraux's eagle owl (*Bubo lacteus*) above right (AVZ)

Rüppell's vulture (*Gyps rueppellii*) below left (AVZ)

African fish eagle (*Haliaeetus vocifer*) below right (AVZ)

More than half of Uganda's bird species are passerines, an order of (mostly smallish) perching birds distinguished by a trademark toe arrangement of three pointing forward and one to the back.

above left (AVZ) Rüppell's starling (*Lamprotornis purpuroptera*)

above right (AVZ) Red-chested sunbird (*Cinnyris erythrocerca*)

left (AVZ) White-necked raven (*Corvus albicollis*)

below left (AVZ) Olive thrush (*Turdus olivaceus*)

below right (AVZ) Silverbird (*Empidornis semipartitus*)

Yellow-backed weaver (*Ploceus melanocephalus*) above left (AVZ)

Baglafecht weaver (*Ploceus baglafecht*) above right (AVZ)

Yellow-throated longclaw (*Macronyx croceus*) right (AVZ)

Red-throated alethe (*Alethe poliophrys*) below left (AVZ)

Black-crowned waxbill (*Estrilda nonnula*) below right (AVZ)

Birds of the various non- and near-passerine orders tend to be larger than passerines and include such colourful charmers as turacos, hornbills and bee-eaters.

above left (AVZ) Abyssinian ground hornbill (*Bucorvus abyssinicus*)

above right (AVZ) Northern red-billed hornbill (*Tockus erythrorhynchus*)

left (AVZ) Black-headed lapwing (*Vanellus tectus*)

below left (AVZ) Black-bellied bustard (*Eupodotis melanogaster*)

below right (AVZ) Red-necked spurfowl (*Pternistis afer*)

Bare-faced go-away bird (*Corythaixoides personatus*) above left (AVZ)

Great blue turaco (*Corythaeola cristata*) above right (AVZ)

Abyssinian roller (*Coracias abyssinica*) right (AVZ)

Red-throated bee-eater (*Merops bullocki*) below left (AVZ)

Woodland kingfisher (*Halcyon senegalensis*) below right (AVZ)

A red-chested sunbi
(*Cinnyris erythrocerc*
feeding chicks in
a nest, in Queen
Elizabeth National P
(AVZ)

2

Wildlife Guide

Uganda differs from any other recognised African safari destination in that it has a relatively high proportion of closed canopy forest. This embraces a wide variety of forest types, with different ecological affinities. The Afro-montane forest of Mount Elgon, for instance, is similar in composition to more easterly habitats on Kilimanjaro and Mount Kenya, whereas the lowland forest of Semuliki National Park is effectively an extension of the more westerly lowland rainforest that blankets the Congo Basin. Uganda thus harbours a wide variety of vertebrate and other species absent elsewhere in East and southern Africa, and the accessibility of its major forests by comparison to those in West Africa makes it an unbeatable destination for viewing African forest creatures – from gorillas and chimps to a colourful array of butterflies and birds – in their natural habitat.

When it comes to more conventional plains wildlife, Uganda doesn't quite bear comparison to top-ranking safari destinations such as Tanzania or Kenya. Nevertheless, Queen Elizabeth, Murchison Falls and Kidepo Valley national parks are now largely recovered from the heavy poaching that took place over 1970–86, and perennial safari favourites such as lion, elephant, buffalo, giraffe and even leopard are now quite easily seen there.

A striking feature of Uganda, with the exception of the semi-desert and dry acacia woodland of the northeast, is its relatively moist climate. The countryside is generally far greener and more fertile than elsewhere in East Africa, and lakes, rivers and other wetland habitats account for almost 25% of the country's surface area. Aquatic wildlife abounds, from hippos and otters to herons and the papyrus-associated shoebill, the last more easily seen in Uganda than anywhere else.

Although most of Uganda is topographically relatively undramatic – essentially an undulating plateau perched at altitudes of 1,000–1,200m between the eastern and western arms of the Rift Valley – it is bordered by some of the continent's most impressive mountains, including the Rwenzori and Virunga ranges, and standalone Mount Elgon. The upper reaches of these mountains support a cover of Afro-alpine moorland, a fascinating and somewhat other-worldly habitat noted for gigantism among plants such as lobelias, heather and groundsel, as well as habitat-specific creatures such as the dazzling scarlet-tufted malachite sunbird.

MAMMALS

The official Ugandan mammal checklist of 343 species comprises 133 larger mammals, 94 bats, 70 rats and mice, 33 shrews and otter shrews, eight gerbils, four elephant shrews and a solitary golden mole. Several useful field guides to African mammals are available for the purpose of identification (page 583), but since they tend to lack specific distribution details for individual countries, the

ANIMAL TAXONOMY

In this chapter, I've made widespread use of taxonomic terms such as genus, species and race. Some readers may not be familiar with these terms, so a brief explanation follows.

Taxonomy is the branch of biology concerned with classifying living organisms. It uses a hierarchical system to represent the relationships between different animals. At the top of the hierarchy are kingdoms, phyla, subphyla and classes. All vertebrates belong to the animal kingdom, phylum Chordata, subphylum Vertebrata. There are five vertebrate classes: Mammalia (mammals), Aves (birds), Reptilia (reptiles), Amphibia (amphibians) and Pisces (fish). Within any class, several orders might be divided in turn into families and, depending on the complexity of the order and family, various suborders, subfamilies and other subdivisions. All baboons, for instance, belong to the Primate order, suborder Haplorhini (monkeys and apes), family Cercopithecidae (Old World Monkeys) and subfamily Cercopithecinae (cheek-pouch monkeys, ie: guenons, baboons and mangabeys) and tribe Papionini (baboon-like monkeys).

The Linnaean scheme of nomenclature, devised in the 18th century by the Swedish botanist Carolus Linnaeus, assigns every living organism a scientific binomial, which is a two-part name that indicates both its genus and species. Thus *Papio cynocephalus* is the yellow baboon and *Papio anubis* the olive baboon. These names are derived from Greek, Latin or a combination of the two, and it is conventional to italicise them.

Taxonomic constructs are designed to approximate the real genetic and evolutionary relationships between various living creatures, and on the whole they succeed. But equally the science exists to help humans understand a reality that is likely to be more complex and less absolute than any conceptual structure used to contain it. This is particularly the case with speciation – the evolution of two or more distinct species from a common ancestor – which might occur over many thousands of generations, and like many gradual processes may lack for any absolute landmarks.

Simplistically, the process of speciation begins when a single population splits into two mutually exclusive breeding units. This can happen as a result of geographic isolation (for instance mountain and lowland gorillas), habitat differences (forest and savannah elephants) or varied migratory patterns (the six races of yellow wagtail intermingle as non-breeding migrants to Africa during the northern winter, but they all have a discrete Palaearctic breeding ground). Whatever the reason, the two breeding communities will share an identical gene pool when first they split, but as generations pass they will accumulate a number of small genetic differences and eventually marked racial characteristics. Given

following notes emphasise local distribution and habitat, and are intended to serve as a Uganda-specific supplement to such a proper field guide.

PRIMATES Primates are exceptionally well represented, with 15 diurnal and seven nocturnal species listed, though the taxonomic status of many is controversial, and some go by several different common names.

Apes The great apes of the family Pongidae are so closely related to humans that a less partial observer might well place them in the same family as us (it is thought

long enough, the two populations might even deviate to the point where they wouldn't or couldn't interbreed, even if the barrier that originally divided them was removed.

The taxonomic distinction between a full species and a subspecies or race of that species rests not on how similar the two taxa are in appearance or habit, but on the final point above. Should it be known that two distinct taxa freely interbreed and produce fertile hybrids where their ranges overlap, or it is believed that they would in the event that their ranges did overlap, then they are classified as races of the same species. If not, they are regarded as full species. The six races of yellow wagtail referred to previously are all very different in appearance, far more so, for instance, than the several dozen warbler species of the genus *Cisticola*, but clearly they are able to interbreed, and they must thus be regarded as belonging to the same species. And while this may seem a strange distinction on the face of things, it does make sense when you recall that humans rely mostly on visual recognition, whereas many other creatures are more dependent on other senses. Those pesky cisticolas all look much the same to human observers, but each species has a highly distinctive call and in some cases a display flight that would preclude crossbreeding whether or not it is genetically possible.

The gradual nature of speciation creates grey areas that no arbitrary distinction can cover – at any given moment in time there might exist separate breeding populations of a certain species that have not yet evolved distinct racial characters, or distinct races that are on their way to becoming full species. Furthermore, where no conclusive evidence exists, some taxonomists tend to be habitual 'lumpers' and others eager 'splitters' – respectively inclined to designate any controversial taxa racial or full specific status. For this reason, various field guides often differ in their designation of controversial taxa.

Among African mammals, this is particularly the case with primates, where in some cases up to 20 described taxa are sometimes lumped together as one species and sometimes split into several specific clusters of similar races. Our earlier baboon example is a case in point: some taxonomists regard olive and yellow baboon to represent a single species (conspecific) on the basis that they often interbreed where their ranges overlap. These taxonomists thus assign them trinomials, in this case *P. c. cynocephalus* and *P. c. anubis*, whose third part indicates the race. Such ambiguities can be a source of genuine frustration, particularly for birdwatchers obsessed with ticking 'new' species, but they also serve as a valid reminder that the natural world is and will always be a more complex, mysterious and dynamic entity than any taxonomic construct designed to label it.

that the chimpanzee is more closely related to humans than it is to any other ape). There are four ape species, of which two are found in Uganda (for further details, see below).

Mountain gorilla (*Gorilla b. beringei*) This high-altitude subspecies of the eastern gorilla is the bulkiest member of the primate family, standing up to 1.8m high and weighing up to 210kg. An Albertine Rift Endemic, it is found in only two localities, namely the Virunga Mountains (shared between Uganda, DRC and Rwanda) and Uganda's Bwindi Impenetrable National Park, and the global population stands at slightly more than 1,000. In October 2018, the status of the mountain gorilla on the IUCN Red List was changed from 'Critically Endangered' to 'Endangered'. More detailed information on gorilla behaviour can be found on page 552.

Common chimpanzee (*Pan troglodytes*) This distinctive black-coated ape, more closely related to man than to any other living creature, lives in large, loosely bonded communities based around a core of related males with an internal hierarchy topped by a benevolent alpha male. Chimpanzees are typical animals of the rainforest and woodlands from Guinea to western Uganda, which supports a population estimated at around 5,000 across a dozen sites. Chimps have been habituated to tourists in Kibale National Park, Kyambura Gorge (Queen Elizabeth National Park), Kaniyo Pabidi (Murchison Falls Conservation Area) and Kalinzu Forest Reserve. For more details about chimp behaviour and ecology, see page 430.

Monkeys All the monkeys found in Uganda are members of the family Cercopithecidae (Old World Monkeys), and they break up into two subfamilies, the leaf-eating colobus monkeys of the Colobinae and more generalised cheek-pouched monkeys of the Cercopithecinae.

Black-and-white colobus (*Colobus guereza*) Also known as the guereza, this beautifully marked and distinctive monkey has a black body, white facial markings, long white tail and, in some races, a white side-stripe. It lives in small groups and is almost exclusively arboreal. An adult is capable of jumping up to 30m, a spectacular sight with its white tail streaming behind. It is probably the most common and widespread forest monkey in Uganda, occurring in most sizeable forest patches and even in well-developed riparian woodland.

Angola colobus (*Colobus angolensis*) Closely related and similar in appearance to the black-and-white colobus, the Angola colobus is represented in Uganda by the race *C. a. ruwenzorii*, which inhabits montane forests along the Albertine Rift.

Ugandan red colobus (*Procolobus tephrosceles*) Split from the western red colobus (*P. badius*) in 2001, this relatively large red-grey monkey has few distinguishing features other than its slightly tufted crown. It is highly sociable and normally lives in scattered troops of 50 or more animals. Confined to a few localities along the Albertine Rift in Uganda and Tanzania, it is IUCN Red-Listed as 'Endangered', but is quite common in Kibale National Park, and is often seen on the swamp walk through the neighbouring Bigodi Wetland Sanctuary.

Anubis baboon (*Papio anubis*) Also known as the olive baboon, this heavily built and mainly terrestrial baboon can be distinguished from any other Ugandan monkey by its larger size and distinctive dog-like head. It lives in large troops with a complex and rigid social structure held together by matriarchal lineages. Males frequently move between troops in their search for social dominance. Omnivorous and highly adaptable, the Anubis is widespread and common in Uganda, where it is frequently seen on the fringes of forest reserves and even along the roadside.

Patas monkey (*Erythrocebus patas*) Another terrestrial primate, restricted to the dry savannah of north-central Africa, the patas (also known as the hussar monkey) could be confused with the vervet monkey, but it has a lankier build, a light reddish-brown coat, and a black stripe above the eyes (the vervet is greyer and has a black face mask). In Uganda, the patas monkey is restricted to the extreme north, where it can be seen in Kidepo Valley and Murchison Falls national parks, as well as the Pian Upe Wildlife Reserve. The race found in Uganda is the Nile patas or nisras (*E. p. pyrrhonotus*).

Vervet monkey (*Chlorocebus pygerythrus*) This light-grey monkey is readily identified by its black face and the male's distinctive blue genitals. Associated with a wide variety of habitats, it's the only guenon you're likely to see outside of forests and it is thought to be the most numerous monkey species in the world. It is sometimes listed a subspecies of the grivet monkey (*C. aethiops*). Vervet monkeys are widespread and common in Uganda, even outside of national parks, but they are absent from forest interiors and Afro-alpine habitats.

Blue monkey (*Cercopithecus mitis*) The blue monkey is the most widespread forest guenon in East Africa – uniform dark blue-grey in colour except for its white throat and chest patch, with thick fur and backward-projecting hair on its forehead. The blue monkey is common in most Ugandan forests, where it lives in troops of between four and 12 animals and frequently associates with other primates. It is also known as the diademed guenon, samango monkey, Sykes' monkey and gentle monkey, and several races are recognised.

Golden monkey (*Cercopithecus kandti*) Formerly treated as a subspecies of blue monkey, this bamboo-associated species is an endangered Albertine Rift Endemic named for the orange-gold patch on its upper flanks and back. Formerly more widespread, it is now near-endemic to the Virunga volcanoes, where it is the most common primate. A habituated troop can be visited in Mgahinga Gorilla National Park.

Silver monkey (*Cercopithecus doggetti*) Also recently split from the blue monkey, this forest-dwelling species has a rather uniform silver-grey coat. It is unclear which Ugandan populations still listed as blue monkey actually belong to this species.

Red-tailed monkey (*Cercopithecus ascanius*) A widespread forest guenon, the red-tailed monkey is brownish in appearance with white cheek whiskers, a coppery tail and a distinctive heart-shaped white patch on its nose, giving rise to the more descriptive alternative name white-nosed monkey. It is normally seen singly, in pairs or in small family groups, but it also associates with other monkeys and has been known to accumulate in groups of up to 200. It regularly interbreeds with blue monkeys in Kibale Forest. It also occurs in Semuliki and Queen Elizabeth national parks, as well as in Budongo, Mpanga and several other forest reserves.

De Brazza's monkey (*Cercopithecus neglectus*) This spectacular thickset guenon has a relatively short tail, a hairy face with a reddish-brown patch around its eyes, a white band across its brow and a distinctive white moustache and beard. Primarily a West African species, De Brazza's monkey is very localised in East Africa, most likely to be seen in the vicinity of Mount Elgon and Semuliki national parks.

L'Hoest's monkey (*Cercopithecus lhoesti*) This handsome Albertine Rift Endemic is often more difficult to see than most of its relatives, largely because of its terrestrial habits and a preference for dense secondary forest. It has a black face and backward-projecting white whiskers that partially cover its ears, and is the only guenon which habitually carries its tail in an upright position. L'Hoest's monkey is very common in Bwindi Impenetrable National Park, but it also occurs in Kibale Forest and Queen Elizabeth national parks.

Uganda mangabey (*Lophocebus ugandae*) Endemic to Uganda, this heavy greyish-black monkey was split from the grey-cheeked mangabey (*L. albigena*) in 2007. It has few distinguishing features, but can be determined from other forest monkeys by its baboon-like mannerisms, shaggier appearance, light-grey cheeks and slight mane. A resident of lowland and mid-altitude forests, it is most likely to be seen in Mabira Forest, Bugoma Forest or Kibale National Park.

Nocturnal primates Seldom observed on account of their nocturnal habits, the prosimians are a relict group of primitive primates more closely related to the lemurs of Madagascar than to the diurnal monkeys and apes of the African mainland.

Galagos Also called bushbabies, these small nocturnal primates are widespread in wooded habitats in sub-Saharan Africa and their piercing cry is one of the region's most distinctive night sounds. If you want to see a bushbaby, trace the cry to a tree, then shine a torch into it and you should easily pick out the bushbaby's large round eyes. Six galago species are found in Uganda, of which the lesser galago (*Galago senegalensis*) is the most common. An insectivorous creature, only 17cm long excluding its tail, the lesser bushbaby is a creature of woodland as opposed to true forest, and it has been recorded in all of Uganda's savannah reserves. The much larger and rather catlike silvery greater galago (*Otolemur monteiri argentatus*), though restricted to woodland habitats in the Lake Victoria basin, commonly visits Mihingo Lodge in Lake Mburo National Park shortly after dark.

Potto (*Perodicticus potto*) This medium-sized sloth-like creature inhabits forest interiors, where it spends the nights foraging upside down from tree branches. It can sometimes be located at night by shining a spotlight into the canopy. The potto occurs in Kibale, Bwindi and Queen Elizabeth national parks, as well as most other major rainforests, and it is most likely to be seen on guided night walks in Kibale Forest.

CARNIVORES A total of 38 carnivores have been recorded in Uganda: five canid species; seven felines; three hyenas; ten mongooses; six mustelids (otters, badgers and weasels); and seven viverrids (civets and genets).

Felines

Lion (*Panthera leo*) The largest African carnivore, and the one animal that everybody wants to see on safari, the lion is the most sociable of the large cats, living in loosely structured prides of typically five to 15 animals. Primarily a nocturnal hunter, its favoured prey are buffalo and medium-to-large antelope such as Ugandan kob. Females, working in teams of up to eight animals, are responsible for most hunts. Rivalry between male lions is intense: prides may have more than one dominant male working in collaboration to prevent a takeover and young males are forced out of their home pride at about three years of age. Pride takeovers are often fought to the death; after a successful one, it is not unusual for all the male cubs to be killed. Lions are not very active by day: they are most often seen lying in the shade looking the picture of regal indolence. They occur naturally in most woodland and grassland habitats, and are now fairly common in the Murchison Falls, Queen Elizabeth and Kidepo Valley national parks, but are scarce or absent elsewhere.

Leopard (*Panthera pardus*) The most common of Africa's large felines, the leopard often lives in close proximity to humans, but it is rarely seen because of its secretive, solitary nature. Leopards hunt using stealth and power, often getting to within 5m of their intended prey before pouncing, and they habitually store their kill in a tree to keep it from being poached by other large predators. They can be distinguished from cheetahs by their rosette-shaped spots and more powerful build, as well as by their preference for wooded or rocky habitats. Leopards are found in virtually all habitats which offer adequate cover, and are present in most Ugandan national parks and forest reserves. The only places in Uganda where they are seen with regularity is along the Channel Drive in Queen Elizabeth National Park, around Pakuba Lodge in Murchison Falls National Park, and on night drives in Lake Mburo National Park.

Cheetah (*Acinonyx jubatus*) Superficially similar to the leopard, the cheetah is the most diurnal of Africa's cat species, and it hunts using speed as opposed to stealth. Cheetahs are the fastest land mammals, capable of running at up to 70km/h in short bursts. Male cheetahs are strongly territorial and in some areas they commonly defend their territory in pairs or trios. Cheetahs are the least powerful of the large predators: they are chased from a high percentage of their kills and 50% of cheetah cubs are killed by other predators before they reach three months of age. Like leopards, cheetahs are heavily spotted and solitary in their habits, but their greyhound-like build, distinctive black tear-marks and preference for grassland and savannah habitats preclude confusion. In Uganda, cheetahs are most common in the little-visited Pian Upe Wildlife Reserve, but they are also present in Kidepo Valley National Park, and have very occasionally been reported from the north of Murchison Falls National Park.

Smaller cats The lynx-like **caracal** (*Caracal caracal*) is a medium-sized cat found in open habitats, and easily identified by its uniform reddish-brown coat and tufted ears. In Uganda, it occurs only in Kidepo Valley National Park. The **African golden cat** (*Caracal aurata*) is a rarely seen creature of the West African forest: it is widespread in western Uganda, where it has been recorded in every forested national park except Semuliki. The slightly larger **serval** (*Leptailurus serval*) has a pale spotted coat, making it possible to confuse it with some genet species. It favours moister habitats than the caracal, ranging from woodland to forest, and it is widespread in Uganda. The **African wild cat** (*Felis silvestris*), reminiscent of the domestic tabby, to which it is thought to be ancestral, is found in most savannah habitats in Uganda.

Canids The Canidae is a family of medium-sized carnivores of which the most familiar is the domestic dog. Five species – all recognisably dog-like in appearance and habits – are present in Uganda, though none is very common.

Jackals and wolves Jackals are small to medium-sized dogs associated with most savannah habitats. Although often portrayed as carrion-eaters, they are in fact opportunistic omnivores, hunting a variety of small mammals and birds with some regularity and also eating a substantial amount of fruit and bulbs. The most widespread canid in Uganda is the **side-striped jackal** (*Lupulella adustus*), which occurs in all four savannah national parks as well as in Bwindi and Mgahinga, and is most likely to be seen in the north of Murchison Falls. Within Uganda, the similar **black-backed jackal** (*L. mesomelas*) is restricted to Kidepo Valley National Park, Pian Upe and environs. Formerly thought to be an African form of the Eurasian golden jackal, the **African wolf** (*Canis lupaster*), though it appears on the national checklist, has been recorded in no national park and is presumably a vagrant. All three species are very similar in appearance, but recent DNA testing revealed that the African wolf is a distinct species, one more closely related to the coyote, grey wolf and Ethiopian wolf than it is to other African jackals. As a result, the black-backed and side-striped jackal are now placed in an endemic African genus Lupulella.

Bat-eared fox (*Otocyon megalotis*) This small but striking silver-grey insectivore, rendered unmistakable by its huge ears and black eye-mask, is most often seen in pairs or small family groups during the cooler hours of the day. Associated with dry open country, the bat-eared fox is quite common in the Kidepo and Pian Upe, but absent elsewhere in Uganda.

African wild dog (*Lycaon pictus*) The largest African canid, and the most endangered after the rare Ethiopian wolf, the African wild dog (also known as the hunting or painted dog) is distinguished by its cryptic black, brown and cream coat. It is officially extinct in roughly half the countries it once inhabited, Uganda included, but recolonisation is not out of the question, since it is a great wanderer and small populations persist in parts of Kenya and northern Tanzania. Indeed, two individual African wild dogs were seen and photographed by a ranger in Kidepo Valley National Park in 2023, the first such record in Uganda since the 1980s.

Other carnivores

Spotted hyena (*Crocuta crocuta*) In Uganda, as elsewhere in Africa, the spotted hyena is by far the most common member of a family of large, hunchbacked carnivores whose somewhat canid appearance belies a closer evolutionary relationship to mongooses and cats. Often portrayed as an exclusive scavenger, the spotted hyena is an adept hunter capable of killing an animal as large as a wildebeest. In ancient times, the spotted hyena was thought to be hermaphroditic: the female's vagina is blocked by a false but remarkably realistic-looking scrotum and penis. Most hyena species live in loosely structured clans of around ten animals, and their social interaction is fascinating to observe. Clans are led by females, which are stronger and larger than males. The spotted hyena is bulky with a sloping back, a light-brown coat marked with dark-brown spots and an exceptionally powerful jaw which enables it to crack open bones and slice through the thickest hide. The spotted hyena is found in all of Uganda's savannah national parks, as well as in Mgahinga, but is only seen with great regularity in Queen Elizabeth. Note that the secretive **striped hyena** (*Hyaena hyaena*) and the insectivorous **aardwolf** (*Proteles cristatus*) are present but uncommon in Kidepo Valley National Park and environs.

African civet (*Civettictis civetta*) This bulky, long-haired, cat-like viverrid has been kept in captivity for thousands of years (its anal secretions were used in making perfumes until a synthetic replacement was found). Surprisingly, little is known about their habits in the wild. Civets are widespread and common in most wooded habitats, and they have been recorded in most of Uganda's national parks, but they are seen very rarely on account of their secretive, nocturnal habits.

Genets (*Genetta* spp) Closely related to civets, but often referred to mistakenly as cats because of various superficial similarities in appearance, genets are slender, low-slung viverrids characterised by beautiful spotted coats and extraordinarily long tails. Secretive except when habituated, and subject to some taxonomic debate, genets are attracted to human waste and are occasionally seen slinking around campsites and lodges after dark. The **servaline genet** (*G. servalina*), **large-spotted genet** (*G. tigrina*) and **small-spotted genet** (*G. genetta*) are all widespread in Uganda, with the latter two generally occurring in more lightly wooded areas than the former, and sometimes observed on night drives in the Toro-Semliki Wildlife Reserve. A West African species, the **giant forest genet** (*G. victiriae*), has been recorded in Maramagambo Forest in Queen Elizabeth National Park.

Otters Three species of these familiar aquatic predators occur in sub-Saharan Africa, and their ranges overlap in western Uganda, where all three have been recorded in certain areas such as Lake Mburo National Park. The **Cape clawless otter** (*Aonyx capensis*) and **Western clawless otter** (*A. congica*), regarded to be conspecific by some authorities, are the largest African otters, growing up to 1.6m long, with a rich brown coat and pale chin and belly. Associated with most wetland habitats, the clawless otters are most active between dusk and dawn, and are hence less likely to be observed than the smaller and darker **spotted-necked otter** (*Lutra maculicollisi*), a diurnal species that is unusually common and visible on Lake Bunyonyi in Kigezi.

Honey badger (ratel) (*Mellivora capensis*) The ratel is a medium-sized mustelid with a puppy-like head, black sides and underparts and a grey-white back. It is an adaptable creature, eating whatever comes its way – it's said that they've been known to kill buffaloes by running underneath them and biting off their testicles which, if true, is certainly taking opportunism to a wasteful extreme. When not bobbitting bovines, the ratel occasionally indulges in a symbiotic relationship with a bird called the greater honeyguide: the honeyguide takes the ratel to a beehive, which the ratel then tears open, allowing the honeyguide to feed on the scraps. Ratels are widespread in Uganda, but uncommon and rarely seen. Other mustelids found in Uganda include the **zorilla** (or striped polecat; *Ictonyx striatus*) and the **striped weasel** (*Poecilogale albinucha*).

Mongooses Ten mongoose species have been recorded in Uganda, none of which – as is commonly assumed – feeds predominantly on snakes. Five species are widespread and common enough to have been recorded in at least half the national parks. They are the **marsh mongoose** (*Atilax paludinosus*), **Egyptian mongoose** (*Herpestes ichneumon*), **slender mongoose** (*Herpestes sanguineus*), **white-tailed mongoose** (*Ichneumia albicauda*) and **banded mongoose** (*Mungos mungo*). Of these the banded mongoose is the most regularly observed, particularly on the Mweya Peninsula in Queen Elizabeth National Park.

ANTELOPE Thirty antelope species – about one-third of the African total – are listed on the checklist for Uganda, a figure that fails to acknowledge a recent rash of near or complete local extinctions. There are probably no more than ten roan antelope remaining in Uganda, for example, while no oryx are left at all. Of the species that do still occur, six fall into the category of large antelope, having a shoulder height of above 120cm (roughly the height of a zebra); nine are in the category of medium-sized antelope, having a shoulder height of between 75cm and 90cm; and the remainder are small antelope, with a shoulder height of between 30cm and 60cm.

Large antelope

Common eland (*Taurotragus oryx*) The world's largest antelope is the common or Cape eland which measures over 1.8m in height, and which can be bulkier than a buffalo. The eland has a rather bovine appearance: fawn-brown in colour, with a large dewlap and short, spiralled horns, and in some cases light-white stripes on its sides. The common eland occurs in open habitats throughout eastern and southern Africa. In Uganda, it is most likely to be seen in Lake Mburo National Park, but also occurs in Kidepo Valley and Pian Upe Wildlife Reserve.

Greater kudu (*Tragelaphus strepsiceros*) This is another very large antelope, measuring up to 1.5m high, and it is also strikingly handsome, with a grey-brown coat marked by thin white side-stripes. The male has a small dewlap and large spiralling horns. The greater kudu lives in small groups in woodland habitats. In Uganda, it occurs only in small numbers in Kidepo.

Hartebeest (*Alcelaphus buselaphus*) This large and ungainly looking, tan-coloured antelope – a relative of the wildebeest, which is absent from Uganda – has large shoulders, a sloping back and relatively small horns. It lives in small herds in lightly wooded and open savannah habitats. The typical hartebeest of Uganda is **Jackson's hartebeest** (*A. b. jacksoni*), though it is replaced by the **Lelwel hartebeest** (*A. b. lelweli*) west of the Nile. The closely related and similarly built **topi** (*Damaliscus lunatus jimela*) has a much darker coat than the hartebeest, and distinctive blue-black markings above its knees. Jackson's hartebeest is most frequently seen in Murchison Falls, though it also occurs in Kidepo Valley.

Defassa waterbuck (*Kobus ellipsiprymnus defassa*) Shaggy-looking, with a grey-brown coat, white rump and large curved horns, the Defassa waterbuck is considered by some authorities to be a distinct species, *K. defassa* (the common waterbuck found east of the Rift Valley has a white ring on its rump), but the two races interbreed where they overlap. Defassa waterbuck live in small herds and are most often seen grazing near water. They are found in suitable habitats in all four of Uganda's savannah national parks.

Roan antelope (*Hippotragus equinus*) This handsome animal has a light red-brown coat, short backward-curving horns and a small mane on the back of the neck. It is present only in small numbers in Pian Upe having become locally extinct in Kidepo Valley and Lake Mburo national parks.

Lowland bongo (*Tragelaphus eurycerus eurycerus*) The presence of the bongo in the forested Semuliki National Park was established by a camera trap in 2017. The largest of the forest antelopes – a male may stand 1.3m at the shoulder – the bongo has a reddish-brown coat and a striking pattern of vertical white stripes on its flanks.

Medium-sized antelope

Ugandan kob (*Kobus kob thomasi*) Uganda's national antelope is a race of the West African kob confined to grassy floodplains and open vegetation near water in Uganda and South Sudan. Although closely related to waterbuck and reedbuck, the kob is reddish-brown in colour and similar to the impala, but bulkier in appearance and lacking the impala's black side-stripe. Ugandan kob live in herds of up to 100 animals in Queen Elizabeth and Murchison Falls and neighbouring conservation areas, as well as in Toro-Semliki and Katonga wildlife reserves.

Bushbuck (*Tragelaphus scriptus*) Probably the most widespread antelope in Uganda is the bushbuck, which lives in forest, riverine woodland and other thicketed habitats. The male bushbuck has a dark chestnut coat marked with white spots and stripes. The female is lighter in colour and vaguely resembles a large duiker. Although secretive and elusive, the bushbuck is very common in suitable habitats in most forests and national parks in Uganda.

Sitatunga (*Tragelaphus spekei*) This semi-aquatic antelope is similar in appearance to the closely related bushbuck, but the male is larger with a shaggier coat, both sexes are striped, and it has uniquely splayed hooves adapted to its favoured habitat of papyrus and other swamps. It is found in suitable habitats throughout Uganda, including six national parks, but is likely to be seen only in the Katonga Wildlife Reserve.

Lesser kudu (*Tragelaphus imberbis*) This pretty, dry-country antelope is similar in appearance to the greater kudu, but much smaller and more heavily striped (greater kudu have between six and ten stripes; lesser kudu have 11 or more). Lesser kudu are present in Pian Upe and environs.

Grant's gazelle (*Gazella granti*) Yet another dry-country antelope which in Uganda has been reduced to 100 animals roaming the contiguous Pian Upe, Matheniko and Bokora wildlife reserves in Karamoja, this typical gazelle is lightly built, tan in colour, and lives in herds.

Reedbuck (*Redunca* spp) Also restricted to Kidepo is the **mountain reedbuck** (*R. fulvorufula*), a grey-brown antelope with small crescent-shaped horns. The very similar **Bohor reedbuck** (*R. redunca*) is more widespread, occurring in all four savannah national parks. Both reedbuck species are usually seen in pairs in open country near water, with the mountain reedbuck occurring at higher altitudes.

Impala (*Aepyceros melampus*) This slender, handsome antelope, though superficially similar to the gazelles, belongs to a separate subfamily that is more closely related to hartebeest and oryx. The impala can be distinguished from any gazelle by its chestnut colouring, sleek appearance and the male's distinctive lyre-shaped horns. An adult impala can jump up to 3m high and has been known to broad-jump for over 10m. Impala live in herds of between 20 and a few hundred animals. They favour well-wooded savannah and woodland fringes, and are often abundant in such habitats. In Uganda, impalas are found only in Lake Mburo National Park and Katonga Wildlife Reserve.

Small antelope Nine of the small antelope species present in Uganda are duikers, a family of closely related antelopes which are generally characterised by their small size, sloping back, and preference for thickly forested habitats. Between 16 and 19 duiker species are recognised, many of them extremely localised in their distribution.

Grey duiker (*Sylvicapra grimmia*) Also known as the common or bush duiker, this is an atypical member of its family in that it generally occurs in woodland and savannah habitats. It has a grey-brown coat with a vaguely speckled appearance. The grey duiker is widespread in East and southern Africa, and it occurs in all four of Uganda's savannah national parks as well as in Mount Elgon.

Forest duikers (*Cephalophus* spp) The striking **yellow-backed duiker** (*C. sylviculter*) is also atypical of the family, owing to its relatively large size – heavier than a bushbuck – rather than any habitat preference. It is a West African species, but has been recorded in several forests in western Uganda, including those in Bwindi, Mgahinga, Rwenzori and Queen Elizabeth national parks; it's sometimes encountered fleetingly along the forest track leading uphill from the Buhoma headquarters at Bwindi. Of the more typical duiker species, **Harvey's red duiker** (*C. harveyi*) is a tiny chestnut-brown antelope found in forested parts of Queen Elizabeth National Park and in the Kibale Forest. The **blue duiker** (*C. monticola*), even smaller and with a grey-blue coat, is known to occur in Queen Elizabeth, Murchison Falls, Kibale and Bwindi national parks. **Peter's duiker** (*C. callipygus*) has been recorded in Bwindi, Kibale and Queen Elizabeth; the **black-fronted duiker** (*C. nigrifrons*) in Mgahinga and Bwindi; and there have been unconfirmed sightings of the **white-bellied duiker** (*C. leucogaster*) for Bwindi and Semuliki. The **red-flanked duiker** (*C. rufilatus*) and **Weyn's duiker** (*C. weynsi*) have not been recorded in any national park, but they most probably occur in the Budongo Forest.

Bates's pygmy antelope (*Neotragus batesi*) Not a duiker, but similar both in size and its favoured habitat, this diminutive antelope – the second-smallest African ungulate – is a Congolese rainforest species that has been recorded in Semuliki National Park and in forests within and bordering the southern half of Queen Elizabeth National Park.

Klipspringer (*Oreotragus oreotragus*) This distinctive antelope has a dark-grey bristly coat and an almost speckled appearance. It has goat-like habits and is invariably found in the vicinity of kopjes or cliffs (the name 'klipspringer' means 'rock-jumper' in Afrikaans). It lives in pairs in suitable habitats in Kidepo Valley and Lake Mburo national parks.

Oribi (*Ourebia ourebi*) This endearing gazelle-like antelope has a light red-brown back, white underparts, and a diagnostic black scent gland under its ears. It is one of the largest 'small' antelopes in Africa, not much smaller than a Thomson's gazelle. When disturbed, the oribi emits a high-pitched sneezing sound, then bounds off in a manner mildly reminiscent of a pronking springbok. The oribi favours tall grassland, and it occurs in all of the savannah national parks except for Queen Elizabeth. It is remarkably common in the Borassus grassland in the northern part of Murchison Falls National Park, most often seen in pairs or groups of up to five animals, consisting of one male and his 'harem', but also sometimes in larger groups.

Guenther's dik-dik (*Madoqua guentheri*) This pretty, small antelope has a dark red-brown coat and distinctive white eye markings. It is found in the dry savannah in and around Kidepo Valley.

OTHER HERBIVORES

Elephants (*Loxodonta spp*) The world's largest land animal is also one of the most intelligent and entertaining to watch. A fully grown elephant is about 3.5m high and weighs around 6,000kg. Female elephants live in closely knit clans in which the eldest female takes a matriarchal role over her sisters, daughters and granddaughters. Mother–daughter bonds are strong and may exist for up to 50 years. Males generally leave the family group at around 12 years, after which they either roam around on their own or form bachelor herds. Under normal circumstances, elephants range widely in search of food and water but, when concentrated populations are forced to live in conservation areas, their habit of uprooting trees can cause serious environmental damage.

Recent DNA testing has revealed that two distinct African elephant species should be recognised. These are the familiar **African bush elephant** (*L. africana*) of East and southern Africa and the smaller, straighter-tusked and slightly hairier **African forest elephant** (*L. cyclotis*) of the West African rainforest. Despite severe poaching in the past, the African bush elephant occurs in all Ugandan national parks except for Lake Mburo, and is most likely to be seen in Murchison Falls, Queen Elizabeth and Kidepo. The two species co-exist in parts of western Uganda, most notably Tori-Semliki Wildlife Reserve and Bwindi Impenetrable National Park, where they generally maintain separate herds, though they have been known to interbreed. The African bush elephant is listed as Endangered by the IUCN and the African forest elephant was reassessed as Critically Endangered in 2021.

Rhinoceros The **black rhinoceros** (*Diceros bicornis*) and **northern white rhinoceros** (*Ceratotherium simum cottoni*) both occur naturally in Uganda, but they have been poached to local extinction. A population of southern white rhino, originating from South Africa but relocated from introduced populations in Kenya and the USA, can be tracked on foot in Ziwa Rhino and Wildlife Ranch north of Kampala.

Hippopotamus (*Hippopotamus amphibius*) This large, lumbering aquatic animal occurs naturally on most African lakes and waterways, where it spends most of the day submerged, before emerging from the water to graze at night. Hippos are strongly territorial, with herds of ten or more animals being presided over by a dominant male. The best places to see them are in Murchison Falls, Queen Elizabeth and Lake Mburo national parks, where they are abundant in suitable habitats. Hippos are still quite common outside of reserves, and they are responsible for killing more people than any other African mammal.

African buffalo (*Syncerus caffer*) Africa's only wild ox species is an adaptable and widespread creature that lives in large herds on the savannah and smaller herds in forested areas. Herds are mixed-sex and normally comprise several loosely related family clans and bachelor groups. Buffaloes can be seen in just about all of Uganda's national parks and large forests. In Queen Elizabeth and Murchison Falls national parks, you may see hybrids of the **savannah buffalo** (*S. c. caffer*) of East Africa and the **red buffalo** (*S. c. nanus*) of the West African forest.

Giraffe (*Giraffa camelopardalis*) The world's tallest animal (up to 5.5m) lives in loosely structured mixed-sex herds, typically numbering between five and 15 animals. As herd members may be dispersed over an area of up to 1km, they are frequently seen singly or in smaller groups, though unusually large aggregations are often seen in Uganda. The long neck of the giraffe gives it a slightly ungainly appearance when it ambles; giraffes look decidedly absurd when they adopt a semi-crouching position in order to drink.

The subspecies found in Uganda is traditionally referred to as **Rothschild's giraffe** (*G. c. rothschildi*), which is listed as Near-Threatened by the IUCN. This is the only type of giraffe to be born with five ossicones (horn-like skin-covered bones) as opposed to two or three, and it is sometimes regarded to be a full species. Uganda is the main global stronghold for Rothschild's giraffe, supporting around 2,000 adults, a tally that has more than doubled since the turn of the millennium, and which probably represents 90% of the global wild population. The vast majority of these giraffes occur in the northern part of Murchison Falls National Park. A small herd is also present in Kidepo Valley, while giraffes from northern Murchison Falls have been relocated to Lake Mburo National Park, the southern half of Murchison Falls and Pian Upe Wildlife Reserve.

DNA tests undertaken in 2016 suggest that Rothschild's giraffe is a regional ecotype of the genetically identical **Nubian giraffe** (*G. c. camelopardalis*) and should probably be referred to by this name in future, but this change has yet to be widely adopted. As a result, the Nubian giraffe is currently listed as Critically Endangered, on the basis that fewer than 500 individuals survive in the wild, split between South Sudan and western Ethiopia. Should the IUCN opt to lump Rothschild's giraffe with Nubian giraffe, that status might well be changed to Near Threatened.

Plains zebra (*Equus quagga*) This unmistakable striped horse, also known as the common zebra, is common and widespread throughout East and southern Africa. Zebras are often seen in large herds but their basic social unit is the small, relatively stable family group, which typically consists of a stallion, up to five mares, and their collective offspring. In Uganda, zebras are present only in Lake Mburo and Kidepo Valley national parks.

Swine The most visible pig species in Uganda is the **warthog** (*Phacochoerus africanus*), a common resident of the savannah national parks. Warthogs are uniform grey in colour and both sexes have impressive tusks. They are normally seen in family groups, trotting away briskly in the opposite direction with their tails raised stiffly and a determinedly nonchalant air. The bulkier and hairier **bushpig** (*Potamochoerus porcus*) is found mainly in thickets and dense woodland. Although bushpigs occur in all national parks except for Rwenzori, they are not often seen because of their nocturnal habits and the cover afforded by their favoured habitat. The **giant forest hog** (*Hylochoerus meinertzhageni*) is the largest African pig species. It is a nocturnal creature of the forest interior, and so very rarely seen, but it probably occurs in all national parks in western Uganda, and is often seen by day along Channel Drive in Queen Elizabeth National Park.

Hyraxes and other oddities Uganda's five hyrax species are guinea pig-like animals, often associated with rocky habitats, and related more closely to elephants than to any other living creatures – difficult to credit until you've heard a tree hyrax shrieking with pachydermal abandon through the night. Four types of **pangolin** (similar in appearance to the South American scaly anteaters) occur in Uganda, as does the **aardvark**, a bizarre, long-snouted insectivore which is widespread in savannah habitats but very seldom seen because of its nocturnal habits. Also regarded as large mammals by the official checklist are 12 squirrel species, three flying squirrels (anomalures), three porcupines, three hares, two cane-rats, a hedgehog and the peculiar chevrotain.

BIRDS

Uganda is arguably the most attractive country in Africa to birdwatchers, not only because of the unusually high number of species recorded within its borders, but also because it offers easy access to several bird-rich habitats that are difficult to reach elsewhere. Uganda's remarkable avian diversity – 1,075 species recorded in an area similar to that of Great Britain – can be attributed to its location at a transitional point between the East African savannah, the West African rainforest and the semi-desert of the north.

Indicative of Uganda's transitional location is the fact that only one or two bird species are endemic to the country: Fox's weaver (associated with waterside vegetation in the southeast) and possibly Stuhlmann's double-collared sunbird (an Albertine Rift Endemic whose range might now be limited to the Ugandan slopes of the Rwenzori as a result of habitat loss). However, if you take only East Africa into consideration, then approximately 150 bird species (more than 10% of the regional checklist) are found only in Uganda. This list includes seven of the 20 hornbill species recorded in the region, five out of 14 honeyguides, seven out of 21 woodpeckers, 11 out of 36 bulbuls and greenbuls, and five out of 20 bush-shrikes, as well as 13 members of the thrush family, 11 warblers, ten flycatchers, eight sunbirds, eight weavers, eight finches, four tinkerbirds, four pigeons or doves, three kingfishers, three sparrowhawks, three cuckoos and three nightjars.

Most of these 'Uganda specials' are West African and Congolese forest birds that would be very difficult to see elsewhere, for the simple reason that the other countries in which they occur are poorly developed for tourism. The rainforests of western Uganda must be seen as the country's most important bird habitat, and the one that is of greatest interest to birdwatchers, particularly if they are already reasonably familiar with typical East African birds. The most alluring forest in terms of localised species is probably Semliki, closely rivalled by Budongo, Kibale and Bwindi. However, in practical terms, Kibale Forest is probably Uganda's best single stop for forest birds, because of the proficiency of the guides who take tourists into the forest and the nearby Bigodi Swamp Walk. That said, just about any forest in Uganda will be rewarding; even the relatively tame botanical garden in Entebbe will throw up several interesting species.

Unfortunately, most forest birds are very secretive, and it can be difficult to get even a glimpse of them in the dense undergrowth, let alone a clear enough look to make a positive identification. You would probably identify more bird species in 10 minutes at the Entebbe Botanical Gardens than you would in an afternoon walking through the Semliki Forest. For this reason, first-time visitors to Africa might do better concentrating on locations other than forests – if you want to see a wide range of Ugandan birds, try to visit Entebbe (water and forest birds), Lake Mburo (water- and acacia-associated birds), Queen Elizabeth (a wide variety of habitats; over 600 species recorded), Murchison Falls (a wide variety of habitats; the best place in East Africa to see the papyrus-associated shoebill) and Kidepo (northern semi-desert specials; over 50 raptors recorded).

Few visitors to Uganda will depart totally unmoved by its avian wealth, but different people arrive in the country with a wide variety of expectations. Those European visitors for whom birdwatching ranks as a pursuit on a perversity level with stamp collecting might well revise that opinion when first confronted by a majestic fish eagle calling high from a riverine perch, or a flock of Abyssinian ground hornbills marching with comic intent through the savannah. First-time African visitors with a stated interest in birds are more likely to be blown away by their first sighting of a lilac-breasted roller or Goliath heron than by most of the country's long list of western forest specials. Birdwatchers based in Africa's savannah belt will generally want to focus more on forest birds, but mostly on such common and iconic species as great blue turaco or black-and-white casqued hornbill rather than on glimpsing a selection of more localised but duller forest greenbuls. The more experienced the individual birdwatcher in African conditions, the greater the priority they will place on the pursuit of Albertine Rift Endemics

ALBERTINE RIFT ENDEMICS

Most of Uganda's forest inhabitants have a wide distribution in the Democratic Republic of Congo (DRC) and/or West Africa, while a smaller proportion comprises eastern species that might as easily be observed in forested habitats in Kenya, Tanzania and in some instances Ethiopia. A significant number, however, are endemic to the Albertine Rift: in other words, their range is more-or-less confined to montane habitats associated with the Rift Valley Escarpment running between Lake Albert and the north of Lake Tanganyika. The most celebrated of these regional endemics is of course the mountain gorilla, confined to the Virungas and Bwindi Mountains near the eastern Rift Valley Escarpment. Other primate species endemic to the Albertine Rift include golden monkey and Rwenzori colobus. Eight endemic butterflies have been described, and are regarded as flagship species for the many hundreds of invertebrate taxa that occur nowhere else in the world.

Of the remarkable tally of 38 range-restricted bird species listed as Albertine Rift Endemics, roughly half are regarded to be of global conservation concern. All 38 of these species have been recorded in the DRC, and nine are endemic to that country, since their range is confined to the western escarpment forests. More than 20 Albertine Rift Endemics are resident in each of Uganda, Rwanda and Burundi, while two extend their range southward into western Tanzania. All 25 of the Albertine Rift Endemics recorded in Uganda occur in Bwindi National Park, including the highly sought African green broadbill, which is elsewhere known only from the Itombwe Mountains and Kahuzi-Biega National Park in the DRC. Other important sites in Uganda are the Rwenzori Mountains with 17 Albertine Rift Endemics, the Virungas with 14 and the Echuya Forest with 12.

Outside Uganda, all but one of the 29 endemics that occur on the eastern escarpment have been recorded in Rwanda's Nyungwe Forest, a readily accessible site that is highly recommended for the opportunity to observe several species absent from, or not as easily located in, Uganda. Inaccessible to tourists at the time of writing, the Itombwe Mountains, which rise from the Congolese shore of northern Lake Tanganyika, support the largest contiguous block of montane forest in East Africa. This range is also regarded to be the most important site for montane forest birds in the region, with a checklist of 565 species including 31 Albertine Rift Endemics, three of which are known from nowhere else in the world. The most elusive of these birds is the enigmatic Congo bay owl, first collected in 1952, and yet to be seen again, though its presence is suspected in Rwanda's Nyungwe Forest.

Several Albertine Rift forest endemics share stronger affinities with extant or extinct Asian genera than they do with any other living African species, affirming the great age of these forests, which are thought to have flourished during prehistoric climatic changes that caused temporary deforestation in lower-lying areas such as the Congo Basin. The Congo bay owl, African green broadbill and Grauer's cuckoo-shrike, for instance, might all be classed as living fossils – isolated

and Semliki 'specials'. At the extreme end of the scale, there are those whose life's mission is to tick every bird species in the world, in which case dedicating several days to seeking out the endemic Fox's weaver might rank above all other considerations in planning a Ugandan itinerary.

Uganda's appeal as a birding destination has been enhanced in recent years by improving avian knowledge, and general guiding practices, on the part of

relics of a migrant Asian stock that has been superseded elsewhere on the continent by indigenous genera evolved from a common ancestor.

Among the other mammal species endemic to the Albertine Rift, the Rwenzori dwarf otter-shrew is one of three highly localised African mainland species belonging to a family of aquatic insectivores that flourished some 50 million years ago and is elsewhere survived only by the related tenrecs of Madagascar. A relict horseshoe bat species restricted to the Rwenzori and Lake Kivu is anatomically closer to extant Asian forms of horseshoe bat and to ancient migrant stock than it is to any of the 20-odd more modern and widespread African horseshoe bat species, while a shrew specimen collected only once in the Itombwe Mountains is probably the most primitive and ancient of all 150 described African species.

A full list of the Albertine Rift Endemic birds that occur in Uganda follows, with species regarded to be of global conservation concern marked with an asterisk. All are present in Bwindi National Park; those present elsewhere are indicated as M (Mgahinga), E (Echuya), R (Rwenzori) and/or K (Kibale Forest).

Handsome francolin	*Francolinus nobilis*	M E R
Rwenzori turaco	*Tauraco johnstoni*	M E R
Rwenzori nightjar	*Caprimulgus rwenzori*	E R
Dwarf honeyguide	*Indicator pumilio* *	
African green broadbill	*Pseudocalyptomena grauri* *	
Kivu ground thrush	*Zoothera tanganjicae* *	M E
Red-throated alethe	*Alethe poliophrys*	E R
Archer's robin-chat	*Cossypha archeri*	M E R
Rwenzori apalis	*Apalis rwenzori*	M E R K
Mountain masked apalis	*Apalis personata*	M E R
Grauer's swamp-warbler	*Bradypterus grauri* *	M E R
Grauer's warbler	*Graueria vittata*	
Neumann's warbler	*Hemetisia neumanni*	
Red-faced woodland warbler	*Phylloscopus laetus*	M E R K
Yellow-eyed black flycatcher	*Melaeornis ardesiascus*	E
Chapin's flycatcher	*Musicapa lendu* *	
Rwenzori batis	*Batis diops*	M E R
Stripe-breasted tit	*Parus fasciiventer*	M E R
Blue-headed sunbird	*Nectarinia alinae*	E R K
Regal sunbird	*Nectarinia regia*	M E R
Rwenzori double-collared sunbird	*Cinnyris stuhlmanni*	R
Purple-breasted sunbird	*Nectarinia purpureiventris*	E R K
Dusky crimsonwing	*Cryptospiza jacksoni*	M E R K
Shelley's crimsonwing	*Cryptospiza shelleyi* *	M R
Strange weaver	*Ploceus alienus*	M E R

local guides. The best of these are capable of identifying most species by call, and even calling up the more responsive species. In the parks and reserves you'll meet some ranger guides whose knowledge compares favourably with their counterparts in any part of Africa. Birding capabilities do vary from one guide to the next, however, so specify your interest when you ask for a guide. Better still, to secure the services of a guide for a nationwide tour of birding

WEAVERS

Placed by some authorities in the same family as the closely related sparrows, the weavers of the family Ploceidae are a quintessential part of Africa's natural landscape, common and highly visible in virtually every habitat from rainforest to desert. The name of the family derives from the intricate and elaborate nests – typically but not always a roughly oval ball of dried grass, reeds and twigs – that are built by the dextrous males of most species.

It can be fascinating to watch a male weaver at work. First, a nest site is chosen, usually at the end of a thin hanging branch or frond, which is immediately stripped of leaves to protect against snakes. The weaver then flies back and forth to the site, carrying the building material blade by blade in its heavy beak, first using a few thick strands to hang a skeletal nest from the end of a branch, then gradually completing the structure by interweaving numerous thinner blades of grass into the main frame. Once completed, the nest is subjected to the attention of his chosen partner, who will tear it apart if the result is less than satisfactory, and so the process starts all over again.

All but 12 of the 113 described weaver species are resident on the African mainland or associated islands, with some 40 represented within Uganda alone. A full 25 of the Ugandan species are placed in the genus *Ploceus* (true weavers), which is surely the most characteristic of all African bird genera. Most of the *Ploceus* weavers are slightly larger than a sparrow, and display a strong sexual dimorphism. Females are with few exceptions drab buff or olive-brown birds, with some streaking on the back, and perhaps a hint of yellow on the belly.

Most male *Ploceus* weavers conform to the basic colour pattern of the 'masked weaver' – predominantly yellow, with streaky back and wings, and a distinct black facial mask, often bordered orange. Eight Ugandan weaver species fit this masked weaver prototype more-or-less absolutely, and a similar number approximate it rather less exactly, for instance by having a chestnut-brown mask, or a full black head, or a black back, or being more chestnut than yellow on the belly. Identification of the masked weavers can be tricky without experience – useful clues are the exact shape of the mask, the presence and extent of the fringing orange, and the colour of the eye and the back.

The golden weavers, of which only two species are present in Uganda, are also brilliant yellow and/or light orange with some light streaking on the back, but they lack a mask or any other strong distinguishing features. The handful of forest-associated *Ploceus* weavers, by contrast, tend to have quite different and very striking colour patterns, and although sexually dimorphic, the female is often as boldly marked as the male. The most aberrant among these are Vieillot's and Maxwell's black weavers, the males of which are totally black except for their eyes,

hotspots, contact the Uganda Bird Guides Club (f UgBirdGuidesClub), an organisation whose membership includes most of the country's best privately operating bird guides. Their website also contains plenty of useful information including a national checklist and lists for different regions and Important Bird Areas. An essential purchase is Stevenson and Fanshawe's *Birds of East Africa*, which includes accurate depictions, descriptions and distribution details for every species recorded in the country. Harder to obtain, but worth locating for its detailed site descriptions, is the out-of-print *Where to Watch Birds in Uganda* by Russouw and Sacchi.

while the black-billed weaver reverses the prototype by being all black with a yellow facemask.

Among the more conspicuous *Ploceus* species in Uganda are the black-headed, yellow-backed, slender-billed, northern brown-throated, orange and Vieillot's black weavers – for the most part gregarious breeders forming single or mixed species colonies of hundreds, sometimes thousands, of pairs. The most extensive weaver colonies are often found in reed beds and waterside vegetation – the mixed species colonies in Entebbe Botanical Garden or Ngamba Island are as impressive as any in Uganda. Most weavers don't have a distinctive song, but they compensate with a rowdy jumble of harsh swizzles, rattles and nasal notes that can reach deafening proportions near large colonies. One of the more cohesive songs you will often hear seasonally around weaver colonies is a cyclic 'dee-dee-dee-Diederik', often accelerating to a hysterical crescendo when several birds call at once. This is the call of the Diederik cuckoo, a handsome green-and-white cuckoo that lays its eggs in weaver nests.

Oddly, while most East African *Ploceus* weavers are common, even abundant, in suitable habitats, seven highly localised species are listed as range-restricted, and three of these – one Kenyan endemic and two Tanzanian endemics – are regarded to be of global conservation concern. Of the other four, Fox's weaver (*Ploceus spekeoides*) is the only bird species endemic to Uganda: a larger-than-average yellow-masked weaver with an olive back, yellow eyes and orange-fringed black facemask, confined to acacia woodland near swamps and lakes east of Lake Kyoga. The strange weaver (*Ploceus alienus*) – black head, plain olive back, yellow belly with chestnut bib – is an Albertine Rift Endemic restricted to four sites in Uganda.

Most of the colonial weavers, perhaps relying on safety in numbers, build relatively plain nests with a roughly oval shape and an unadorned entrance hole. The nests of certain more solitary weavers, by contrast, are far more elaborate. Several weavers, for instance, protect their nests from egg-eating invaders by attaching tubular entrance tunnels to the base – in the case of the spectacled weaver, sometimes twice as long as the nest itself. The thick-billed weaver (a peculiar, larger-than-average brown-and-white weaver of reed beds, distinguished by its outsized bill and placed in the monospecific genus *Amblyospiza*) constructs a large and distinctive domed nest, which is supported by a pair of reeds, and woven as precisely as the finest basketwork, with a neat raised entrance hole at the front. By contrast, the scruffiest nests are built by the various species of sparrow- and buffalo-weaver, relatively drab but highly gregarious dry-country birds, poorly represented in Uganda except for in the vicinity of Kidepo.

REPTILES

NILE CROCODILE The order Crocodilia dates back at least 150 million years, and fossil forms that lived contemporaneously with dinosaurs are remarkably unchanged from their modern ancestors. The largest species are the Australian saltwater and the African Nile crocodiles which regularly attain lengths of up to 6m. Widespread throughout Africa, the Nile crocodile (*Crocodylus niloticus*) was once common in most large rivers and lakes, but it has been exterminated in many areas in the past century – hunted professionally for its skin as well as by vengeful local villagers. Contrary to popular legend, Nile crocodiles generally feed mostly on fish, at least where densities are sufficient. They will also prey on drinking or swimming mammals where the opportunity presents itself, dragging their victim underwater until it drowns, then storing it under a submerged log or tree until it has decomposed sufficiently for them to eat. A large crocodile is capable of killing

BUTTERFLIES

Uganda's wealth of invertebrate life – more than 100,000 species have been identified countrywide – is largely overlooked by visitors, but is perhaps most easily appreciated in the form of butterflies and moths of the order **Lepidoptera**. An astonishing 1,200 butterfly species, including almost 50 endemics, have been recorded in Uganda, as compared with fewer than 1,000 in Kenya, roughly 650 in the whole of North America, and a mere 56 in the British Isles. Several forests in Uganda harbour 300 or more butterfly species, and one might easily see a greater selection in the course of a day than one could in a lifetime of exploring the English countryside. Indeed, I've often sat at one roadside pool in the like of Kibale or Budongo forests and watched ten to 20 clearly different species converge there over the space of 20 minutes.

The Lepidoptera are placed in the class Insecta, which includes ants, beetles and locusts among others. All insects are distinguished from other invertebrates, such as arachnids (spiders) and crustaceans, by their combination of six legs, a pair of frontal antennae, and a body divided into a distinct head, thorax and abdomen. Insects are the only winged invertebrates, though some primitive orders have never evolved them, and other more recently evolved orders have discarded them. Most flying insects have two pairs of wings, one of which, as in the case of flies, might have been modified beyond immediate recognition. The butterflies and moths of the order Lepidoptera have two sets of wings and are distinguished from all other insect orders by the tiny ridged wing scales that create their characteristic bright colours.

The most spectacular of all butterflies are the swallowtails of the family **Papilionidae**, of which roughly 100 species have been identified in Africa, and 32 in Uganda. Named for the streamers that trail from the base of their wings, swallowtails are typically large and colourful, and relatively easy to observe when they feed on mammal dung deposited on forest trails and roads. Sadly, this last generalisation doesn't apply to the African giant swallowtail (*Papilio antimachus*), a powerful flier that tends to stick at canopy levels and seldom alights on the ground, but the first two generalisations certainly do. With a wingspan known to exceed 20cm, this black, orange and green gem, an endangered West African species whose range extends into Bwindi, Kibale, Semliki, Budongo and Kalinzu forests, is certainly the largest butterfly on the continent, and possibly the largest in the world. One of the most common large swallowtails in Uganda is *Papilio nobilis*, which has golden or orange wings, and occurs in suburban gardens in Kampala, Entebbe, Jinja and elsewhere.

The **Pieridae** is a family of medium-sized butterflies, generally smaller than the swallowtails and with wider wings, of which almost 100 species are present in Uganda, several as seasonal intra-African migrants. Most species are predominantly white in colour, with some yellow, orange, black or even red and blue markings on the wings. One widespread member of this family is the oddly named angled grass yellow (*Eurema desjardini*), which has yellow wings marked by a broad black

a lion or wildebeest, or an adult human for that matter, and in certain areas such as the Mara or Grumeti rivers in the Serengeti, large mammals do form their main prey. Today, large crocodiles are mostly confined to protected areas. The gargantuan specimens that lurk on the sandbanks along the Nile below Murchison Falls National Park are a truly primeval sight, silent and sinister, vanishing under the water when

band, and is likely to be seen in any savannah or forest-fringe habitat in southern Uganda. The orange-and-lemon *Eronia leda* also has yellow wings, but with an orange upper tip, and it occurs in open grassland and savannah countrywide.

The most diverse family of butterflies within Uganda is the **Lycaenidae**, with almost 500 of the 1,500 African species recorded. Known also as gossamer wings, this varied family consists mostly of small to medium-sized butterflies, with a wingspan of 1–5cm, dull underwings, and brilliant violet blue, copper or rufous-orange upper wings. The larvae of many Lycaenidae species have a symbiotic relationship with ants – they secrete a fluid that is milked by the ants and are thus permitted to shelter in their nests. A striking member of this family is *Hypolycaena hatita*, a small bluish butterfly with long tail streamers, often seen on forest paths throughout Uganda.

Another well-represented family in Uganda, with 370 species present, is the **Nymphalidae**, a diversely coloured group of small to large butterflies, generally associated with forest edges or interiors. The Nymphalidae are also known as brush-footed butterflies, because their forelegs have evolved into non-functional brush-like structures. One of the more common and distinctive species is the African blue tiger (*Tirumala petiverana*), a large black butterfly with about two-dozen blue-white wing spots, often observed in forest paths near puddles or feeding from animal droppings. Another large member of this family is the African queen (*Danaus chrysippus*), which has a slow, deliberate flight pattern, orange or brown wings, and is as common in forest-edge habitats as it is in cultivated fields or suburbia. Also often recorded in Kampala gardens is the African mother of pearl (*Salamis parhassus*), a lovely light-green butterfly with black wing dots and tips.

The family **Charaxidae**, regarded by some authorities to be a subfamily of the Nymphalidae, is represented in Uganda by 70 of the roughly 200 African species. Typically large, robust, strong fliers with one or two short tails on each wing, the butterflies in this family vary greatly in coloration, and several species appear to be scarce and localised since they inhabit forest canopies and are seldom observed. Bwindi is a particularly good site for this family, with almost 40 species recorded, ranging from the regal dark-blue charaxes (*Charaxes tiridates*; black wings with deep-blue spots) to the rather leaf-like green-veined charaxes (*Charaxes candiope*).

Rather less spectacular are the 200 grass-skipper species of the family **Hersperiidae** recorded in Uganda, most of which are small and rather drably coloured, though some are more attractively marked in black, white and/or yellow. The grass-skippers are regarded as the evolutionary link between butterflies and the generally more nocturnal moths, represented in Uganda by several families of which the most impressive are the boldly patterned giant silk-moths of the family **Saturniidae**.

For those with more than a passing interest in Uganda's butterflies, Nanny Carter and Laura Tindimubona's *Butterflies of Uganda* (Uganda Society, 2002) illustrates and describes roughly 200 of the more common and striking species, with basic information about distribution and habitat.

CHAMELEONS

Common and widespread in Uganda, but not easily seen unless they are actively searched for, chameleons are arguably the most intriguing of African reptiles. True chameleons of the family Chamaeleontidae are confined to the Old World, with the most important centre of speciation being the island of Madagascar, to which about half of the world's 120 recognised species are endemic. Aside from two species of chameleon apiece in Asia and Europe, the remainder are distributed across mainland Africa.

Chameleons are best known for their capacity to change colour, a trait that has often been exaggerated in popular literature, and which is generally influenced by mood more than the colour of the background. Some chameleons are more adept at changing colour than others, with the most variable being the **common chameleon** (*Chamaeleo chamaeleon*) of the Mediterranean region, with more than 100 colour and pattern variations recorded. Many African chameleons are typically green in colour but will gradually take on a browner hue when they descend from the foliage in more exposed terrain, for instance while crossing a road. Several change colour and pattern far more dramatically when they feel threatened or are confronted by a rival of the same species. Different chameleon species also vary greatly in size, with the largest being **Oustalet's chameleon** (*Furcifer oustaleti*) of Madagascar, known to reach a length of almost 80cm.

A remarkable physiological feature common to all true chameleons is their protuberant round eyes, which offer a potential 180° vision on both sides and are able to swivel around independently of each other. Only when one of them isolates a suitably juicy-looking insect will the two eyes focus in the same direction as the chameleon stalks slowly forward until it is close enough to use the other unique weapon in its armoury. This is its sticky-tipped tongue, which is typically about the same length as its body and remains coiled up within its

the launch approaches too closely. Other reliable sites for crocs are Lake Mburo and increasingly the Kazinga Channel in Queen Elizabeth National Park.

SNAKES A wide variety of snakes is found in Uganda, though – fortunately, most would agree – they are typically very shy and unlikely to be seen unless actively sought. One of the snakes most likely to be seen on safari is Africa's largest, the **rock python** (*Python sebae*), which has a gold-on-black mottled skin and regularly grows to lengths exceeding 5m. Non-venomous, pythons kill their prey by strangulation, wrapping their muscular bodies around it until it cannot breathe, then swallowing it whole and dozing off for a couple of months while it is digested. Pythons feed mainly on small antelopes, large rodents and similar. They are harmless to adult humans, but could conceivably kill a small child. A slumbering python might be encountered almost anywhere in East Africa, and one reasonably relaxed individual is often present at the bat cave near the visitors' centre in Maramagambo Forest, Queen Elizabeth National Park.

Of the venomous snakes, one of the most commonly encountered is the **puff adder** (*Bitis arietans*), a large, thick resident of savannah and rocky habitats. Although it feeds mainly on rodents, the puff adder will strike when threatened, and it is rightly considered the most dangerous of African snakes, not because it is especially venomous or aggressive, but because its notoriously sluggish disposition

mouth most of the time, to be unleashed in a sudden, blink-and-you'll-miss-it lunge to zap a selected item of prey. In addition to their unique eyes and tongues, many chameleons are adorned with an array of facial casques, flaps, horns and crests that enhance their already somewhat fearsome prehistoric appearance.

In Uganda, you're most likely to come across a chameleon by chance when it is crossing a road, in which case it should be easy to take a closer look at it, since most chameleons move painfully slowly and deliberately. Chameleons are also often seen on night game drives, when their ghostly nocturnal colouring shows up clearly under a spotlight – as well as making it pretty clear why these strange creatures are regarded with both fear and awe in many local African cultures. More actively, you could ask your guide if they know where to find a chameleon – a few individuals will be resident in most lodge grounds.

The **flap-necked chameleon** (*Chamaeleo dilepis*) is probably the most regularly observed species of savannah and woodland habitats in East Africa. Often observed crossing roads, the flap-necked chameleon is generally around 15cm long and bright green in colour with few distinctive markings, but individuals might be up to 30cm in length and will turn tan or brown under the right conditions. Another closely related and widespread savannah and woodland species is the similarly sized **graceful chameleon** (*Chamaeleo gracilis*), which is generally yellow-green in colour and often has a white horizontal stripe along its flanks.

Characteristic of East African montane forests, **three-horned chameleons** form a closely allied species cluster of some taxonomic uncertainty. Darker and much larger than the savannah chameleons, the males of all taxa within this cluster are distinguished by a trio of long nasal horns that project forward from their face. Within Uganda, the spectacular Rwenzori three-horned chameleon (*Trioceros johnstoni*), which grows up to 30cm long, is often seen in and around Bwindi National Park.

means it is more often disturbed than other snakes. The related **Gabon viper** is possibly the largest African viper, growing up to 2m long, very heavily built, and with a beautiful cryptic geometric gold, black-and-brown skin pattern that blends perfectly into the rainforest litter it inhabits. Although highly venomous, it is more placid and less likely to be encountered than the puff adder.

Several **cobra** species (*Naja* spp.), including the spitting cobra, are present in Uganda, most with characteristic hoods that they raise when about to strike, though they are all very seldom seen. Another widespread family is the **mambas** (*Dendroaspis spp.*), of which the black mamba (*D. polylepis*) – which will only attack when cornered, despite an unfounded reputation for unprovoked aggression – is the largest venomous snake in Africa, measuring up to 3.5m long. While the dangers from these snakes are well documented, those of two of Africa's most toxic species – the variably coloured, arboreal **boomslang** (*Dispholidus typus*) and its relative, the twig-coloured **twig snake** (*Thelotornis* spp.) – were long underrated. In fact both were long considered harmless to humans, being back-fanged (meaning that they have to work at biting humans) and characteristically inoffensive. Nevertheless, their venom, if injected effectively, is deadly. Even so, African records contain just one confirmed fatality for each snake, both involving herpetologists subscribing to the 'harmless' theory.

Most snakes are in fact non-venomous and not even potentially harmful to any other living creature much bigger than a rat. One of the more common non-venomous snakes in the region is the **emerald snake** (*Hapsidophrys smaragdinus*; sometimes mistaken for a boomslang, though the latter is never as green and more often than not brown), which feeds mostly on amphibians. The **mole snake** (*Pseudaspis cana*) is a common and widespread grey-brown savannah resident that grows up to 2m long, and feeds on moles and other rodents. Unusually, its fangs protrude as frontal spikes in order to spear prey in tunnels. The remarkable **egg-eating snakes** (*Dasypeltis* spp.) live exclusively on birds' eggs, dislocating their jaws to swallow the egg whole, then eventually regurgitating the crushed shell in a neat little package. Many snakes will take eggs opportunistically, for which reason large-scale agitation among birds in a tree is often a good indication that a snake (or small bird of prey) is around.

LIZARDS All African lizards are harmless to humans, with the arguable exception of the **Nile monitor** (*Varanus niloticus*), which could in theory inflict a nasty bite if cornered. Two species of monitor occur in East Africa, the **water** and the **savannah**, the latter growing up to 2.2m long and occasionally seen in the vicinity of termite mounds, the former slightly smaller but far more regularly observed by tourists, particularly along the Kazinga Channel in Queen Elizabeth National Park. Their size alone might make it possible to fleetingly mistake a monitor for a small crocodile, but their more colourful yellow-dappled skin precludes sustained confusion. Both species are predatorial, feeding on anything from birds' eggs to smaller reptiles and mammals, but will also eat carrion opportunistically.

Visitors to East Africa will soon become familiar with the **tropical house gecko** (*Hemidactylus mabouia*), an endearing bug-eyed, translucent white lizard, which as its name suggests reliably inhabits most houses as well as lodge rooms, scampering up walls and upside down on the ceiling in pursuit of pesky insects attracted to the lights. Also very common in some lodge grounds are various **agama** species, (*Agama* spp.) distinguished from other common lizards by their relatively large size of around 20–25cm, basking habits, and almost plastic-looking scaling – depending on the species, a combination of blue, purple, orange or red, with the flattened head generally a different colour from the torso. Another common family are the **skinks** (family Scincidae): small, long-tailed lizards, most of which are quite dark and have a few thin black stripes running from head to tail.

TORTOISES AND TERRAPINS These peculiar reptiles are unique in being protected by a prototypal suit of armour formed by their heavy exoskeleton. The most common of the terrestrial tortoises in the region is the **leopard tortoise** (*Stigmochelys pardalis*), which is named after its gold-and-black mottled shell, can weigh up to 30kg, and has been known to live for more than 50 years in captivity. It is often seen motoring along in the slow lane of game reserve roads in Uganda. Four species of terrapin – essentially the freshwater equivalent of turtles – are resident in East Africa, all somewhat flatter in shape than the tortoises, and generally with a plainer brown shell. They might be seen sunning on rocks close to water or peering out from roadside puddles. The largest is the **Nile soft-shelled terrapin** (*Trionyx triunguis*), which has a wide, flat shell and in rare instances might reach a length of almost 1m.

3

Practical Information

WHEN AND WHERE TO VISIT

Equator-straddling Uganda has a warm to hot climate all year through with limited temperature variations but a strongly seasonal rainfall pattern. The wettest months in most parts of the country are April, May, October and November, when camping can be unpleasant and hiking on the Rwenzori is particularly miserable. Abundant rainfall also means that large wildlife tends not to congregate conveniently around water sources in the national parks. On the other hand, landscape photographers will revel in the haze-free skies of the rainy season. That said, the seasons are becoming less defined.

The highlight and focal point of many a visit to Uganda is tracking mountain gorillas in Bwindi Impenetrable National Park in the extreme southwest. Consequently, most formal itineraries follow an established circuit between Kampala and the southwest, an area blessed with a high density of natural attractions and a good tourist infrastructure. A typical tour heads west from Kampala (or the international airport at nearby Entebbe) to the scenic Fort Portal area, where the main attraction is chimpanzee tracking in forested Kibale National Park, followed by a two- to three-night visit to Queen Elizabeth National Park (QENP) at the foot of the Rwenzori Mountains. South of QENP, Bwindi now offers no fewer than four separate gorilla tracking locations. It's a long haul from Bwindi back to Kampala/Entebbe and many tour operators now offer their clients an overnight break at Lake Mburo National Park. It is possible to cover this itinerary in seven days (ten would be better) and many people do. However, those with time and flexibility to delay and detour will discover much more. Days can be spent exploring the Fort Portal and Rwenzori area, while Lake Bunyonyi and the Virunga volcanoes are worthwhile diversions near Bwindi. Visitors intent on reaching true East African wilderness (a rare commodity in the densely populated south of Uganda) will want to head north to the Murchison Falls and Kidepo Valley national parks. These experiences do, however, incur a cost of increased travel time and expenditure. Visitors with time for a day trip at the end of their visit invariably head east from Kampala to visit the famed source of the Nile at Jinja. If this event represents a tick on a list rather than a life-affirming experience, the same cannot be said for Jinja's other main attraction: the menu of adventure sports offered along the Nile corridor north of the town. Activities such as white-water rafting, kayaking, bungee-jumping and quad-biking attract a steady flow of the young and young at heart.

TOURIST INFORMATION

Useful websites include those operated by the **Uganda Tourism Board** (UTB; w exploreuganda.com) and **Uganda Wildlife Authority** (w ugandawildlife.org) along with the privately run w traveluganda.co.ug. The website for the car-hire company **Roadtrip Uganda** (w roadtripuganda.com) has a selection of practical itineraries with an emphasis on camping, while comprehensive coverage of the southwest, including a fun new video map, can be found on w gorillahighlands.com. For updates to this book, visit w bradtguides.com/updates. An excellent database of rock climbs compiled by Matt Battani can be found at w thecrag.com/climbing/uganda/guide. Another, more fun resource is the award-winning blog *Diary of a Muzungu* (w diaryofamuzungu.com). A superb free resource for birders is Derek Kverno's w birdinguganda.blogspot.com.

TOUR OPERATORS

An ever-growing number of local and international tour operators offer a range of standard and customised private safaris to Uganda. Two-week itineraries typically cover the full western circuit from Murchison Falls to Lake Mburo via Kibale Forest, Queen Elizabeth and Bwindi or Mgahinga national parks, sometimes nipping across the border to Rwanda to go gorilla tracking when no permits are available within Uganda. Shorter itineraries generally omit the long drive to and from Murchison Falls, and one-stop gorilla tours of three days' duration are also available out of Kampala. Several other variations are available, depending on the individual's interests and how much time they have available. The high cost of vehicle maintenance, fuel and upmarket accommodation in Uganda is reflected in the price of private safaris, but this can be reduced by using cheaper accommodation, such as the Red Chilli Rest Camp at Paraa at Murchison Falls or Mweya Hostel in QENP, or by camping.

Uganda, mercifully, shows no signs of trying to establish itself as a package destination, nor is it likely to for as long as its premier attraction remains the relatively exclusive experience of tracking mountain gorillas in Bwindi or the Virungas. The country is, however, well suited to small group tours that offer the same standard of accommodation and service as private safaris, but generally at a reduced individual price because transport and related costs are divided between several passengers. In addition to general group tours, packages are also available for special-interest groups such as birdwatchers, primate enthusiasts and photographers.

The following locally based and international operators can all be recommended as experienced and reliable. Note that contacts for companies that operate offices in Uganda and abroad are combined in the *Uganda* section below. Alternatively, w travellocal.com is a reputable UK-based agent whose website allows customers to communicate directly with selected local operators, as well as book their trips.

OPERATORS IN UGANDA

Large operators When selecting a tour operator, be sure to choose one with some form of accreditation. Two main systems of registration operate in Uganda, operated by AUTO (Association of Ugandan Tour Operators), a long-serving private sector body, and the government-operated UTB. Historically, AUTO membership has been taken as the industry standard, implying an acceptable standard of operation, experience and integrity. However, with the government taking a growing interest in regulation, UTB listing is becoming equally important. If you're an independent traveller selecting a safari outfit to book your gorilla- or chimp-tracking permit (page 560), make sure they are on the UTB list; you'll have more come-back in the event of problems.

The companies listed opposite all have solid reputations and are all members of AUTO, and will all be registered with UTB too. The AUTO website (w auto.or.ug) lists plenty more companies which you might consider, supplemented ideally by some online research for feedback from previous customers.

As regards payment, we suggest that transfers should only be made electronically to a company-named bank account. Be wary if your chosen tour company suddenly asks for payment details to be sent to an alternative account or a transfer agency such as Western Union, or if the email address used changes.

Looking online, you'll come across a growing choice of smaller operators, often Ugandan safari guides setting up on their own with a vehicle. These are more likely to be registered with UTB than AUTO. If booking a freelance tour guide or birding guide, check their status with the Uganda Safari Guides Association (USAGA; w ugasaf.org) or the Uganda Bird Guides Club (w ugandabirdguidesclub.org). Note that local operators that specialise in certain regions, for instance, Kara Tunga in Karamoja and Yebo Tours in Masindi are listed in the relevant regional chapter.

Across Africa m 0701 630684; e manager@across-africa.de; w acrossafrica.travel
The Adventure Committee m 0788 158187; e safari@theadventurecommittee.com; w theadventurecommittee.com
Africa Beyond Borders m 0773 599507; e reservations@aroundafricasafari.com; w aroundafricasafari.com
Africa Nziza Odysseys m 0782 774005; e reservations@africanzizaodysseys.com; w africanzizaodysseys.com
Africa's Great Exploration Safaris ☎ 041 4662300; m 0776 723274; e info@agesafaris.com; w agesafaris.com
Around Africa Safaris m 0773 599507; e reservations@aroundafricasafari.com; w aroundafricasafari.com
BIC Tours m 0776 527333; e info@bic-tours.com; w bic-tours.com. English & Japanese spoken.
Buffalo Safaris m 0758 098428; e info@buffalosafaricamps.com; w buffalosafaricamps.com
Destination Jungle m 0712 385446; e d.jungle@safaritoeastafrica.com; w safaritoeastafrica.com
Exclusive Safaris m 0782 250610; e enquiries@exclusiveugandasafaris.com; w exclusiveugandasafaris.com
Gorilla Tours m 0777 820071; e postmaster@gorillatours.com; w gorillatours.com
Great Lakes Safaris m 0770 486002; e info@greatlakessafaris.com; w greatlakessafaris.com
Kagera Safaris ☎ 039 2176513; m 0782 477992; e info@kagerasafaris.com; w kagerasafaris.com
Kazinga Tours m 0772 552819; e mail@kazingatours.com; w kazingatours.com
Matoke Tours ☎ 039 3202907; e contact@matoketours.com; w matoketours.com
Nkuringo Safaris m 0785 999900; e info@nkuringosafaris.com; w nkuringosafaris.com
Primate Watch Safaris Ltd ☎ 041 4266824; e info@primatewatchsafaris.com; w primatewatchsafaris.com
Ranger Africa Safaris m 0772 853372; e enquiries@rangerafricasafaris.com; w rangerafricasafaris.com
Speke Uganda Holidays m 0701 207009; e info@spekeugandaholidays.com; w spekeugandaholidays.com
Sun Africa Expeditions m 0782 172312/0781 486219; e info@sunafricaexpeditions.com; w sunafricaexpeditions.com

High-end operators In addition to those listed above, which are solid mid-range outfits, the following are experienced and genuinely high-end operators with the vehicles and, in most cases, the lodges to ensure a top-notch safari.

Classic Africa Safaris m 0772 642527; e gm@classicafricasafaris.travel; w classicugandasafaris.travel. Uniquely in this category, this first-rate outfit doesn't have its own luxury lodges but its vehicles are in a class of their own.

The Uganda Safari Company (TUSC) ☎ 041 4251182; **m** 0787 433710; **e** info@safariuganda.com; **w** safariuganda.com. Long-serving TUSC is affiliated to Wildplaces Africa (**w** wildplacesafrica.com), which operates superb lodges in Murchison Falls, Queen Elizabeth & Bwindi national parks & the Semliki Valley.

Volcanoes Safaris ☎ 041 4346464; **m** 0772 741720; **e** enquiries@volcanoessafaris.com; **w** volcanoessafaris.com. High-end company with 25 years' experience, with posh lodges servicing Mgahinga, Kibale, Bwindi & Kyambura Gorge.

Wild Frontiers **m** 0772 721479; **w** wildfrontiersuganda.com. One of Uganda's oldest & best tour operators, Wild Frontiers operates luxury camping safaris plus superb lodges in Bwindi & Queen Elizabeth national parks.

Specialist operators

Birding

Avian Safaris **m** 0782 475961; **e** info@aviansafaris.com; **w** aviansafaris.com. Talented team of young & capable bird guides.

Eco-Specialists Tours **m** 0751 955671, 0714 871145; **e** info@ecotoursuganda.com; **w** ecotoursuganda.com. With 30 years' birding experience behind them, the Mabira Forest guides have formed their own company.

Emmy Gongo **m** 0772 853372; **e** emmygongo@yahoo.com. Born on the edge of Bwindi Forest, Emmy is one of Uganda's best-known birding guides.

Cycling

These operators both offer day trips from Kampala's Ggaba port to Bule landing & beyond (page 161), as well as extended upcountry bike trips tailored to requirements.

Go Free Uganda **m** 0779 767372; **e** gofreeuganda@gmail.com; **w** gofreeuganda.com

Red Dirt Biking **m** 0762 133784; **e** thies@reddirtuganda.com; **w** reddirtuganda.com

Other

Herping Tours **m** 0756 264190, 0705 374767; **e** herpingtoursug@gmail.com; **w** herpingtoursafaris-smc.com. In addition to locating the usual quadrupeds, this outfit based in Kampala also specialises in finding snakes.

Women Tour Uganda **m** 0779 767372; **e** gofreeuganda@gmail.com; **w** gofreeuganda.com. This operator caters for strictly female-only safari groups with a female guide & male driver.

INTERNATIONAL OPERATORS

UK

Aardvark Safaris ☎ 01980 849160; **e** mail@aardvarksafaris.com; **w** aardvarksafaris.co.uk. Private & small-group tailored itineraries.

Cox & Kings Travel ☎ 020 3813 9460; **e** info@coxandkings.co.uk; **w** coxandkings.co.uk

Explore Worldwide ☎ 01252 888781; **e** hello@explore.co.uk; **w** explore.co.uk

Gane & Marshall ☎ 01822 600600; **e** info@ganeandmarshall.com; **w** ganeandmarshall.com

Imagine Africa ☎ 020 3468 0785; **e** info@imagineafrica.co.uk; **w** imagineafrica.co.uk

Journeys by Design ☎ 01273 623790; **e** info@journeysbydesign.com; **w** journeysbydesign.com

Natural World Safaris ☎ 01273 691642; **e** sales@naturalworldsafaris.com; **w** naturalworldsafaris.com

Rainbow Tours ☎ 020 7666 1276; **e** info@rainbowtours.co.uk; **w** rainbowtours.co.uk

Royle Safaris ☎ 0845 226 8259; **e** info@royle-safaris.co.uk; **w** royle-safaris.co.uk

Safari Consultants ☎ 01787 888590; **e** info@safariconsultantuk.com; **w** safari-consultants.co.uk

World Odyssey ☎ 01905 731373; **e** info@world-odyssey.com; **e** info@world-odyssey.com; **w** world-odyssey.com

Yellow Zebra ☎ 0203 9449387; **e** reservations@yellowzebratravel.com; **w** yellowzebrasafaris.com

USA

Aardvark Safaris ☎ +1 858 523 9000; **w** aardvarksafaris.com

The African Adventure Company ☎ +1 800 882 9453; **e** safari@africanadventure.com; **w** africanadventure.com

Germany

Hauser Exkursionen International ☎ +49 89 235 0060; e info@hauser-exkursionen.de; w hauser-exkursionen.de
Safari Uganda ☎ +49 06 207 7378; e kontakt@safariuganda.de; w safariuganda.de
Wigwam ☎ +49 83 799 2060; e info@wigwam-tours.de; w wigwam-tours.de

South Africa

Pulse Africa ☎ +27 11 325 2290; e info@pulseafrica.com; w pulseafrica.com
Wild Frontiers ☎ +27 11 702 2035; e reservations@wildfrontiers.com; w wildfrontiers.com

RED TAPE

VISAS A valid passport is required to enter Uganda. Entry may be refused if it is set to expire within six months of your intended departure date. Should your passport be lost or stolen while you are on the road, it will be easier to get a replacement if you have a photocopy or photograph of the important pages.

Nationals of most countries require a **visa** in order to enter Uganda. Though available on arrival at overland entry points, they are no longer available at the airport and you should apply for an e-visa online at w visas.immigration.go.ug at least five working days before the intended date of travel. This will usually be approved by email within three working days of application; you'll need to download, print and carry the approval letter with you. A standard single-entry visa, valid for 90 days, costs US$50. Multiple-entry visas cost US$100/150/200 for a period of 12/24/36 months. To confirm these rates, see w immigration.go.ug/content/visas-and-passes. It is also possible to apply for a 90-day East African Tourist Visa, valid for Uganda, Rwanda and Kenya for US$100. Be aware that there have been incidents of Ugandan immigration officials rejecting these as fakes (the official line is that these are issued in Kenya where the process is subject to periodic scams) and making arrivals pay for a visa.

Don't overstay your visa or the date of the immigration stamp in your passport, or you'll be liable for a fine. And note that, even though you hold a three-month visa, immigration authorities may only stamp your passport for a period of one month or less. This can be extended to three months at any immigration office in Kampala or upcountry. Irrespective of what they might tell you, there is no charge for this. In Kampala, you may be asked to provide an official letter from a sponsor or the hotel where you are staying.

For **security** reasons, it's advisable to detail all your important information in one document, which you can then print out and distribute in your luggage, and/or store on a smartphone, and/or email to your webmail address and a reliable contact at home. The sort of things you want to include on this are travel insurance policy details and 24-hour emergency contact number, passport number, details of relatives or friends to be contacted in an emergency, bank and credit card details, camera and lens serial numbers, etc.

DRIVING If there is any possibility you'll drive in Uganda, bring a valid driving licence; you'll need to show it at regular police checkpoints. Your domestic driving licence is OK for up to three months. Alternatively, if you're reluctant to take the original, you could carry an international driving licence (which can be bought from any AA office in most countries). If you spend longer than three months in Uganda, you must either obtain a local licence or carry an international driving licence. Instead of an original, first show a photocopy or a photo on your phone just in case the officer wants to keep it for some reason.

IMMUNISATIONS The situation with yellow fever vaccination changes periodically, but as things stand, all travellers aged one year or over must have an international health certificate showing they have had a vaccination when they enter Uganda and upload it when applying for an e-visa. Note that in 2016, the WHO extended the period of validity for an international certificate of vaccination against yellow fever from ten years to life.

CUSTOMS The following items may be imported into Uganda without incurring customs duty: 400 cigarettes or 500g of tobacco; one bottle of spirits and wine and 2.5 litres of beer; 1oz bottle of perfume. Souvenirs may be exported without restriction but game trophies such as tooth, bone, horn, shell, claw, skin, hair, feather or other durable items are subject to export permits.

EMBASSIES More than 50 embassies, high commissions and other diplomatic missions can be found in the capital. A comprehensive list of foreign high commissions and embassies in Kampala, is available at w embassypages.com/uganda.

GETTING THERE AND AWAY

BY AIR For obvious reasons, the most convenient means of reaching Uganda from Europe and North America is by air. An established specialist UK operator is **Africa Travel** (020 7387 1211; w africatravel.co.uk), and reputable agents specialising in round-the-world tickets rather than Africa specifically are **Trailfinders** (020 7084 6500; w trailfinders.com) and **STA** (0333 321 0099; w statravel.co.uk). Recently revived, the national carrier, **Uganda Airlines** (w ugandaairlines.com), hopes to initiate a direct connection with London by the end of 2024. This will be a welcome development for travellers from the UK since all current flights to Uganda involve a change along the way. The following international airlines fly to Entebbe.

Brussels Airlines w brusselsairlines.com
EgyptAir w egyptair.com
Emirates w emirates.com
Ethiopian Airways w flyethiopian.com
Etihad Airways w etihad.com
Kenya Airways w kenya-airways.com
KLM Royal Dutch Airlines w klm.com
Qatar w qatarairways.com
RwandAir w rwandair.com
South Africa Airways w saa.co.za
Turkish Airlines w turkishairlines.com

Arrival and departure Practically all fly-in visitors land at Entebbe International Airport (w entebbe-airport.com), which lies on the Lake Victoria shore about 3km from Entebbe town and 40km from Kampala. Immigration formalities are straightforward enough (though you may wonder on what grounds Uganda claims to be Africa's friendliest country) so unless two major airlines have arrived around the same time, the queue shouldn't take too long to clear. If you arrive outside banking hours, there are ATMs and 24-hour foreign-exchange facilities at the airport.

Airport transfers can be arranged in advance through any hotel in Entebbe (indeed, many include it in the room rate) and most tour operators and upmarket hotels in Kampala. Failing that, special hire taxis licensed to operate within the airport are marked 'Airport Taxi' and identified by their yellow stripe. Expect to pay US$8–10 to Entebbe and US$30–35 to Kampala, depending on your bargaining skills.

An increasingly popular option for people whose main interest in Uganda is gorilla tracking in the southwest is to fly into Kigali, the capital of Rwanda, and transfer by road from there. It's quite a distance – 145km/3–4 hours to get from

Kigali to Mgahinga, or 170–220km/4–6 hours to Bwindi, depending on where exactly – and you need to allow time for the border crossing, but it is still a lot quicker than driving from Entebbe.

By prior arrangement with immigration, international charter flights can sometimes land at other airstrips around the country such as Kihihi (for Bwindi NP), Pakuba (Murchison Falls NP), Kakira (Jinja) and Apoka (Kidepo Valley NP).

OVERLAND Uganda borders five countries. Of these, many visitors cross in or out of Uganda overland from Kenya, Tanzania and Rwanda, but the DRC and South Sudan are effectively off-limits to casual travel. Uganda's land borders are generally very relaxed, provided that your papers are in order.

To/from Kenya Crossing between Kenya and Uganda couldn't be more straightforward. The current pick of the direct coach services between Kampala and Nairobi is **Mash** (m 0774 082853; f Mash Poa Bus Company; w mashpoa.co; US$25), which departs twice daily from their Rubaga Road office, via a sub office on De Winton Road (opposite the National Theatre) and docks at the rough (River Rd) end of Nairobi city centre from which, rather than walk, it's safer to take a taxi to your next destination. You can also do the trip in hops, stopping at the likes of Jinja and Busia in Uganda, and Kisumu and Nakuru in Kenya. The direct rail service between Nairobi and Kampala foundered years ago, but it is possible to take a **train** from Nairobi as far as Kisumu. Plenty of **public transport** runs on from Kisumu to the Ugandan border at Busia, where buses to Kampala tend to pass through in the early morning, but matatus run throughout the day.

To/from Tanzania The best route depends on which part of Tanzania you want to visit. The only direct road between the two countries connects Masaka to the port of Bukoba, crossing at the Mutukula border post. It is possible to travel between Kampala and Bukoba in hops, but far easier to take the direct **Friends Safaris** bus (m 0759 176330) from their office in Old Kampala. These leave at 05.00 and 14.00 and tickets cost US$10. Friends Bus also runs to Mwanza (US$18; though it is more interesting to leave the bus in Bukoba and take the thrice-weekly ferry across Lake Victoria). If heading from Kampala to Arusha and Moshi it's quicker and more comfortable to travel via Nairobi. Regular shuttle buses run between Nairobi and Arusha and take around 5 hours.

To/from Rwanda Two main border crossings connect Uganda and Rwanda. Cyanika lies 15km south of Kisoro while Katuna is 21km south of Kabale. There's also an additional crossing at Mirama Hills, 30km from Ntungamo. It's perfectly straightforward to drive yourself so long as you remember that the Rwandan authorities consistently expect vehicles to drive on the right, have appropriate insurance and carry breakdown warning triangles. **Jaguar Executive Coaches** (m 0774 537799 or +250 (0)772 827022; f) run four buses daily from Kampala to Kigali from their stage on Namirembe Road, 500m uphill from the main cluster of bus and taxi parks around Nakivubo Stadium (US$18). Visas, if required, can be obtained at the border. If you care to chance it (page 65), both countries are also covered in the East Africa e-visa.

To/from South Sudan The 'Nile Route' via Juba was very popular with travellers before it was closed for years by the long-running civil war in Sudan and northern Uganda. When the independent Republic of South Sudan was excised from the

Republic of the Sudan in 2011, there were hopes that this might once again be possible but these quickly evaporated after South Sudan became embroiled in its own civil war in 2014. Though this has finally calmed down, and you can fly to Juba from Entebbe or travel by bus from Kampala to Juba, we still wouldn't recommend doing so without a good reason.

LOL buses depart the Namayiba Bus Terminal in Old Kampala at 03.00 and take anything from 12 hours upwards to get to Juba, depending on road conditions and breakdowns. Don't think about travelling without seeking current information regarding availability of visas on arrival at Nimule border crossing or Juba Airport.

To/from DRC There are several routes between Uganda and the Democratic Republic of Congo. From north to south, the main ones are Arua–Aru, Ntoroko–Kasenyi (a boat crossing on Lake Albert), Bwera–Kasindi, Ishasha, and Bunagana. Of these, only the last sees much in the way of tourist traffic, this being the most convenient crossing for tracking mountain gorillas in the Virunga National Park, and visiting other locations such as Nyiragongo Volcano. Bunagana is 8km from Kisoro and served by daily buses from Kampala. Note, however, that Virunga National Park is currently closed due to security concerns and travel to eastern Congo is frequently complicated by some form of instability. Be sure to seek reliable and up-to-date information before considering crossing into the DRC. See also the dedicated chapter about eastern Congo in the Bradt Guide to Rwanda.

HEALTH *With Dr Daniel Campion*

Uganda, like most parts of Africa, is home to several tropical diseases unfamiliar to people living in more temperate climates. However, with adequate preparation and a sensible attitude to malaria prevention, the chances of serious mishap are small. In fact, as in much of Africa, it is road travel that presents the greatest risk to life and limb.

Private clinics, hospitals and pharmacies can be found in most large towns, and doctors generally speak good English (see page 148 for suggestions in Kampala).

Consultation fees and laboratory tests are inexpensive when compared with most Western countries, so if you do fall sick, don't allow financial considerations to dissuade you from seeking medical help. Commonly required medicines such as broad-spectrum antibiotics, painkillers, asthma inhalers and various antimalarial treatments are widely available over the counter. If you are on any short-term medication prior to departure, or you have specific needs relating to a less common medical condition (for instance if you are allergic to bee stings or nuts), then bring necessary treatment with you.

PREPARATIONS Sensible preparation will go a long way to ensuring your trip goes smoothly. The following summary points are worth emphasising:

- Don't travel without comprehensive medical **travel insurance** that will fly you home in an emergency.
- Make sure all your **immunisations** are up to date. A yellow-fever certificate is required from all travellers aged one and over. Requirements may vary periodically in response to outbreaks. If the vaccine is not suitable for you then you should discuss your travel plans with a travel health expert, as the risk from travelling unvaccinated is significant. If your onward travel from Uganda is to a country that requires a yellow-fever certificate for entry (eg: South Africa), then

ensure that you are carrying your certificate or yellow fever exemption where appropriate. It's also unwise to travel in the tropics without being up to date on tetanus, polio and diphtheria (given as an all-in-one vaccine) and hepatitis A. Immunisation against meningitis, typhoid, hepatitis B, rabies, or (rarely) tuberculosis may also be recommended.

- The biggest health threat is malaria. Although two new malaria vaccines have been introduced as part of childhood immunisation programmes in Africa, they are neither recommended nor available for travellers. A variety of prescription medications is used to prevent this mosquito-borne disease, including mefloquine, atovaquone/proguanil (Malarone) and the antibiotic doxycycline. The most suitable choice of drug varies depending on the individual and the country they are visiting, so visit your GP or a travel clinic for medical advice. If you will be spending a long time in Africa and visiting remote areas, consider taking an emergency treatment kit in addition to prophylaxis. Artemether and lumefantrine combination therapy (Coartem) is often used. It is also worth noting that no homeopathic prophylactic for malaria exists, nor can any traveller acquire effective 'natural' immunity to malaria after infection. Those who don't make use of preventative drugs risk their life in a manner that is both foolish and unnecessary.
- Though an advisable precaution for everyone, **pre-exposure rabies vaccination**, involving three doses taken over 21–28 days, is particularly important if you intend to have contact with animals, or are likely to be 24 hours away from medical help. More rapid courses are available if time is short, but require an additional booster after a year.
- Anybody travelling away from major centres should carry a **personal first-aid kit**. Contents might include an antiseptic, Band-Aids, suncream, insect repellent, aspirin or paracetamol, antifungal cream (eg: clotrimazole), loperamide for diarrhoea (and possibly prescribed antibiotics for severe diarrhoea if you are at high medical risk), antibiotic eye drops, tweezers, condoms or femidoms, a digital thermometer and a needle-and-syringe kit with an accompanying letter from a health-care professional.
- Bring any **drugs or devices relating to known medical conditions** with you. That applies both to those who are on medication prior to departure, and those who are, for instance, allergic to bee stings, or are prone to attacks of asthma.
- Prolonged immobility on long-haul flights can result in **deep vein thrombosis** (DVT), which can be dangerous if the clot travels to the lungs to cause pulmonary embolus. The risk increases with age, and is higher in obese or pregnant travellers, heavy smokers, those taller than 6ft/1.8m, and anybody with a history of clots, recent major operation or varicose veins surgery, cancer, a stroke or heart disease. If any of these criteria apply, consult a doctor before you travel.

Travel clinics and health information A full list of current travel clinic websites worldwide is available on w istm.org. For other journey preparation information, consult w travelhealthpro.org.uk (UK) or w wwwnc.cdc.gov/travel (USA). All advice found online should be used in conjunction with expert advice received prior to or during travel.

ON THE ROAD

Malaria This potentially fatal disease is widespread in tropical Africa. Within Uganda, it is possible to catch malaria almost anywhere below the 2,000m contour (everywhere, that is, except the upper slopes of high mountains such as the Rwenzori, Virunga and Elgon). In mid-altitude locations, malaria is largely but not entirely seasonal, with the highest risk occurring during the rainy seasons (March to May and October to December). Moist and low-lying areas such as the Nile at Murchison Falls are high risk throughout the year, but the risk is greatest during the rainy season. This localised breakdown might influence what long-term foreign residents in Uganda do about malaria prevention, but all travellers to Uganda must assume that they will be exposed to malaria throughout their trip and should take suitable preventative drugs and other precautions.

Since no malaria prophylactic is 100% effective, it makes sense to take all reasonable precautions against being bitten by the nocturnal *Anopheles* mosquitoes that transmit the disease (page 72). Malaria usually manifests within two weeks of transmission (though it can be as short as seven days), but it can take months, which means that short-stay visitors are most likely to experience symptoms after they return home. These typically include a rapid rise in temperature (over 38°C), and any combination of a headache, flu-like aches and pains, a general sense of disorientation, and possibly even nausea and diarrhoea. The earlier malaria is detected, the better it usually responds to treatment. So if you display possible symptoms, get to a doctor or clinic immediately. A simple test, available at even the most rural clinic in Africa, is usually adequate to determine whether you have malaria. And while experts differ on the question of self-diagnosis and self-treatment, the reality is that if you think you have malaria and are not within easy reach of a doctor, it would be wisest to start treatment. If you use a self-treatment kit, you should still seek medical assistance as soon as possible, for definitive diagnosis and treatment.

Travellers' diarrhoea Many visitors to unfamiliar destinations suffer a dose of travellers' diarrhoea, usually as a result of consuming contaminated food or water, and Uganda seems to be particularly bad in this respect. Rule one in avoiding diarrhoea and other sanitation-related diseases is arguably to wash your hands regularly, especially before snacks and meals, and after handling money (the low denomination Ush1,000 notes in particular are often engrained with filth). As for what food you can safely eat, a useful maxim is 'peel it, boil it, cook it or forget it'. This means that fruit you have washed and peeled yourself should be safe, as should hot cooked foods. However, raw foods, cold cooked foods, salads, fruit salads prepared by others, ice cream and ice are all risky. It is rarer to get sick from drinking contaminated water but it can happen: use drinking water to brush your teeth. Bottled water is safe and widely available, although if you want to limit plastic waste, buying your own filter bottle such as Aquapure is an eco-friendly alternative.

If you suffer a bout of diarrhoea, it is dehydration that makes you feel awful, so drink lots of water and other clear fluids. These can be infused with sachets of oral rehydration salts, though any dilute mixture of sugar and salt in water will do you good, for instance a bottled soda with a pinch of salt. If diarrhoea persists beyond a couple of days, it is possible it is a symptom of a more serious sanitation-related illness (typhoid, cholera, hepatitis, dysentery, worms, etc), so see a doctor. If the diarrhoea is greasy and bulky, and is accompanied by sulphurous (eggy) burps, one likely cause is the parasite *Giardia*, which can cause persistent symptoms but is treatable. Again, seek medical advice if you suspect this.

Schistosomiasis Also known as bilharzia, schistosomiasis is an unpleasant parasitic disease transmitted by freshwater snails most often associated with reedy shores. It cannot be caught in hotel swimming pools, but should be assumed to be present in any freshwater river, pond, lake or similar habitat, probably even those advertised as 'bilharzia free'. The riskiest shores will be within 200m of villages or other places where infected people use water and wash clothes. Ideally, however, you should avoid swimming in any fresh water other than an artificial pool. Applying DEET insect repellent and drying off vigorously with a towel may reduce your risk after exposure, but should not be relied upon. Schistosomiasis is often asymptomatic in its early stages, but some people experience an intense immune reaction, including fever, cough, abdominal pain and an itching rash, around four to six weeks after infection. Later symptoms vary but often include a general feeling of tiredness and lethargy. Schistosomiasis can be tested for at specialist travel or tropical medicine clinics, ideally at least six weeks after likely exposure. Fortunately, it is easy to treat at present.

Meningococcal disease The most common forms of meningococcal disease are meningitis (infection of the protective lining around the brain) and septicaemia (blood poisoning). Transmitted by close contact and respiratory droplets, this bacterial infection can kill within hours of the appearance of initial symptoms, typically a combination of a blinding headache, light sensitivity, blotchy rash and high fever. Admission to hospital and prompt antibiotic treatment are required. Outbreaks tend to be localised and are usually reported in newspapers. Fortunately, immunisation protects against the most serious bacterial form of meningitis. Nevertheless, other less serious forms exist, and a severe headache and fever – possibly also symptomatic of typhoid or malaria – should be sufficient cause to visit a doctor immediately.

Rabies This deadly disease can be carried by any mammal and is usually transmitted to humans via a bite or deep scratch. Beware village dogs, bats and habituated monkeys, but assume that *any* mammal that bites or scratches you might be rabid. Even a lick over broken skin or on a mucous membrane such as the mouth or eyes could transmit the virus. First, scrub the wound with soap under a running tap, or while pouring water from a jug, then pour on a strong iodine or alcohol solution, which will guard against other infections and might reduce the risk of the rabies virus entering the body. Whether or not you underwent pre-exposure vaccination, it is vital to obtain post-exposure prophylaxis as soon as possible after the incident. However, if you have had the vaccine before exposure, treatment is very much easier. It removes the need for a human blood product (rabies immunoglobulin or RIG) which is expensive and often not available in Uganda. Death from rabies is probably one of the worst ways to go, and once you show symptoms it is too late to do anything – the mortality rate is 100%.

Ebola Outbreaks of this viral haemorrhagic fever have occurred regularly in Uganda, most recently in 2023. These outbreaks are usually contained quickly and the risk to travellers continues to be extremely low, unless there has been contact with blood or other body fluids from infected people. It is still wise, however, to avoid eating bush meat and handling animals.

Tetanus Tetanus is caught through deep dirty wounds, including animal bites, so ensure that such wounds are thoroughly cleaned. Immunisation protects for ten years, provided you don't have an overwhelming number of tetanus bacteria on board. If you haven't had a tetanus shot in ten years, or you are unsure, get a booster immediately.

HIV HIV prevalence is gradually decreasing in Uganda, but it remains a concern and other sexually transmitted infections are common. Barrier contraceptives such as condoms greatly reduce the risk of transmission.

Tick bites Ticks may spread African tick bite fever (ATBF) along with a few dangerous rarities. They should ideally be removed whole, and as soon as possible, to reduce the chance of infection. You can use special tick tweezers, which can be bought in good travel shops; or failing this, with your fingernails, grasp the tick as close to your body as possible, and pull it away steadily and firmly at right angles to your skin without jerking or twisting. Applying irritants (eg: Olbas oil) or lit cigarettes is to be discouraged as a means of removal since they can cause the ticks to regurgitate and therefore increase the risk of disease. Once the tick is removed, if possible douse the wound with alcohol (any spirit will do), soap and water, or iodine. If travelling with small children, remember to check their heads, and particularly behind the ears, for ticks. Spreading redness around the bite and/or fever and/or aching joints after a tick bite imply that you have an infection that requires antibiotic treatment. In this case seek medical advice.

Skin infections Any mosquito bite or small nick is an opportunity for a skin infection in warm humid climates, so clean and cover the slightest wound in a good drying antiseptic such as dilute iodine, gentian violet or potassium permanganate. Prickly heat is a fine pimply rash that can be alleviated by cool showers, dabbing (not rubbing) dry and talc, and sleeping naked under a fan or in an air-conditioned

AVOIDING MOSQUITO AND INSECT BITES

The *Anopheles* mosquitoes that spread malaria are active at dusk and after dark. Most bites can thus be avoided by covering up at night. This means donning a long-sleeved shirt, trousers and socks from around 30 minutes before dusk until you retire to bed, and applying a DEET-based insect repellent (around 50% DEET) to any exposed flesh. Icaridin is an effective alternative. It is best to sleep under a net, or in an air-conditioned room, though burning a mosquito coil and/or sleeping under a fan will also reduce (though not entirely eliminate) bites. Travel clinics usually sell a good range of nets and repellents, as well as permethrin treatment kits, which will render even the tattiest net a lot more protective, and helps prevent mosquitoes from biting through a net when you roll against it. These measures will also do much to reduce exposure to other nocturnal biters. Bear in mind, too, that most flying insects are attracted to light: leaving a lamp standing near a tent opening or a light on in a poorly screened hotel room will greatly increase the insect presence in your sleeping quarters.

It is also advisable to think about avoiding bites when walking in the countryside by day, especially in wetland habitats, which often teem with diurnal mosquitoes. Wear a long loose shirt and trousers, preferably 100% cotton, as well as proper walking or hiking shoes with heavy socks (the ankle is particularly vulnerable to bites), and apply an insect repellent to any exposed skin. If you are very prone to being bitten, consider using a permethrin-based clothing spray (eg: EX4 clothing spray). This can be done in advance of travel and the permethrin will survive around six washes. Mosquitoes landing on the clothes then die, rather than biting through the fabric.

room. Fungal infections also get a hold easily in hot moist climates, so wear 100% cotton socks and underwear and shower frequently.

Eye problems Bacterial conjunctivitis (pink eye) is a common infection in Africa, particularly for contact-lens wearers. Symptoms are sore, gritty eyelids that often stick closed in the morning. They will need treatment with antibiotic drops or ointment. Lesser eye irritation should settle with bathing in salt water and keeping the eyes shaded. If an insect flies into your eye, extract it with great care, ensuring you do not crush or damage it, otherwise you may get a nastily inflamed eye from secreted toxins.

Sunstroke and dehydration Overexposure to the sun can lead to short-term sunburn or sunstroke and increases the long-term risk of skin cancer. Wear a T-shirt and waterproof sunscreen when swimming. When visiting outdoor historical sites or walking in the direct sun, cover up with long, loose clothes, wear a hat, and use sunscreen. The glare and the dust can be hard on the eyes, so bring UV-protecting sunglasses. A less direct effect of the tropical heat is dehydration, so drink more fluids than you would at home.

Snakes, spiders and scorpions Venomous snakes, spiders and scorpions are present but unobtrusive, though you should be wary when picking up the wood or stones under which they often hide. Snakes generally slither away when they sense the seismic vibrations made by footfall, but be aware that rocky slopes and cliffs are a favoured habitat of the slothful puff adder, which may not move off in such circumstances. Good walking boots protect against the 50% of snakebites that occur below the ankle, and long trousers help deflect bites higher on the leg. But lethal bites are a rarity – in South Africa, which boasts its fair share of venomous snakes, more people are killed annually by lightning! Only a small fraction of snakebites deliver enough venom to be life-threatening, but it is important to keep the victim calm, immobilise the affected area, and seek urgent medical attention.

Other insect-borne diseases (including dengue and Zika virus) Although malaria is the insect-borne disease that attracts the most attention in Africa, and rightly so, there are others, most too uncommon to be a significant concern to short-stay travellers. These include dengue fever, zika virus and other arboviruses (spread by diurnal mosquitoes), sleeping sickness (tsetse flies), and river blindness (blackflies). Bearing this in mind, however, it is clearly sensible, and makes for a more pleasant trip, to avoid insect bites as far as possible (see opposite). Two nasty (though ultimately relatively harmless) flesh-eating insects associated with tropical Africa are *tumbu* or *putsi* flies, which lay eggs, often on drying laundry, that hatch and bury themselves under the skin when they come into contact with humans, and jiggers, which latch on to bare feet and set up home, usually at the side of a toenail, where they cause a painful boil-like swelling. Drying laundry indoors and wearing shoes are the best way to deter this pair of flesh-eaters.

Anyone who is planning a pregnancy and is travelling to an area where there is Zika virus (including Uganda, where it was first discovered) should be mindful of the guidance to wait before conceiving. Women travelling without their partners are advised to use barrier precautions for two months after leaving a Zika area; women travelling with their male partners should use barrier precautions during the trip and for three months afterwards.

SAFETY AND SECURITY

Uganda has been an acceptably safe travel destination since Museveni took power in 1986. The only region that subsequently experienced long-term instability is the north, but even that has settled down since 2006. Kampala, like most cities around the world, is vulnerable to terrorist attacks, as demonstrated in 2010 when 74 people were killed in twin blasts at two venues showing World Cup matches on television. More recently, in 2019, an American tourist and local driver were kidnapped at gunpoint during a game drive in the Ishasha Sector of Queen Elizabeth National Park; both were rescued unharmed a few days later after the Ugandan government reputedly paid a portion of the demanded ransom. More seriously, two British tourists and their driver were killed in the northern part of the same park by Congo-based rebels allied to Islamic State in late 2023. Despite these incidents, it might be noted that the most significant threat to life and limb in Uganda comes not from banditry or terrorism, but rather from the malaria parasite and car, boda or boat accidents.

In case of emergency or difficulty in contacting local police anywhere in Uganda, call the Police HQ Operations Room at 0800 199699 (toll free), 041 4256367 or m 0714 667743. If you have problems with these numbers, call the Police HQ Command Centre at 0800 199399.

THEFT Uganda is widely and rightly regarded as one of the most crime-free countries in Africa, certainly as far as visitors need be concerned. Muggings are comparatively rare, even in Kampala, and it is largely free of the sort of con tricks that abound in places like Nairobi. Even petty theft such as pickpocketing and bag snatching is relatively unusual, though it does happen from time to time. Walking around large towns at night is reputedly safe, though it would be tempting fate to wander alone along unlit streets. On the basis that it is preferable to err on the side of caution, here are a few tips that apply to travelling anywhere in East and southern Africa:

- Most casual thieves operate in busy markets and bus stations. Keep a close watch on your possessions in such places, and avoid having valuables or large amounts of money loose in your daypack or pocket.
- Keep all your valuables and the bulk of your money in a moneybelt that can be hidden beneath your clothing. A belt made of cotton or another natural fabric is most pleasant on the skin, but such fabrics tend to soak up sweat, so wrap everything inside in plastic. Never show this moneybelt in public, and keep any spare cash you need elsewhere on your person.
- Where the choice exists between carrying valuables on your person or leaving them in a locked room, we would generally favour the latter option, though you need to use your judgement and be sure the room is absolutely secure.
- Leave any jewellery of financial or sentimental value at home.
- Bash and grab incidents involving boda bodas are on the increase, so be alert when walking in urban areas, particularly in Kampala, and keep car doors locked in traffic.

BRIBERY AND BUREAUCRACY For all you read about the subject, bribery is not a major issue for travellers in Africa, especially if you are travelling on public transport or as part of a tour. Travellers driving themselves are vulnerable to being asked for a bribe by traffic police, but less so in Uganda than in the likes of Mozambique and Kenya.

When dealing with African bureaucrats, a big factor in determining how you are treated will be your own attitude. If you come across as friendly and patient, and accept that the person to whom you are talking does not speak English as a first language and may have difficulty following everything you say, it should all go smoothly. Treat people with respect rather than disdain, in Uganda as elsewhere, and they'll tend to treat you in the same way.

LARGE WILDLIFE Don't confuse habituation with domestication. Most wildlife in Africa is genuinely wild, and might attack a person given the right set of circumstances. Fortunately, however, most wild animals fear people far more than we fear them, and their normal response to any human encounter is to leg it as quickly as possible, which means such attacks are rare, and they almost always stem from a combination of poor judgement and poorer luck.

The need for caution is greatest near water, particularly around dusk and dawn, when hippos are out grazing. Responsible for more human fatalities than any other large mammal, hippos are not actively aggressive to humans, but they do panic easily and tend to mow down any person that comes between them and the safety of the water, usually with fatal consequences. Never cross deliberately between a hippo and water, and avoid well-vegetated riverbanks and lakeshores in overcast weather or low light unless you are certain no hippos are present. Be aware, too, that any path leading through thick vegetation to an aquatic hippo habitat was most probably created by grazing hippos, so there's a real risk of a heads-on confrontation in a confined channel at times of day when hippos might be on land.

Crocodiles are more dangerous to locals but represent less of a threat to travellers, since they are unlikely to attack outside of their aquatic hunting environment. So don't bathe in any potential crocodile habitat unless you have reliable local information that it is safe. It's also wise to keep a berth of a metre or so from the shore, since a large and hungry individual might occasionally drag in an animal or person from the water's edge.

There are parts of Uganda where hikers might stumble across an elephant or a buffalo, the most dangerous of Africa's terrestrial herbivores. Elephants almost invariably mock charge and indulge in some hair-raising trumpeting before they attack in earnest. Provided that you back off at the first sign of unease, they seldom take further notice of you. If you see them before they see you, give them a wide berth, bearing in mind they are most likely to attack if surprised at close proximity. If an animal charges you, the safest course of action is to head for the nearest tree

TRAVELLING WITH CHILDREN *From a letter by Steve Lenartowicz*

Ugandans are very interested in children and make them most welcome. On buses and matatus, the rule seems to be that you pay full fare for the seats you occupy, and so children sitting on a lap go free. Similarly, hotels are usually happy for children (and adults!) to share beds, and we usually negotiated to pay per bed rather than per person. Often, hotels were able to provide an extra bed or mattress on the floor. We travelled light, taking no camping gear or bedding, but we carried mosquito nets and often used them (although mosquitoes were never bad). Don't take white clothing, as the ubiquitous red dust and mud get everywhere. It was easier to order adult portions of meals and to share them rather than to try to negotiate children's portions. National park fees are significantly reduced for children.

and climb it. And should an elephant or buffalo stray close to your campsite or lodge, do suppress any urge to wander closer on foot – it may well react aggressively if surprised!

An elephant is large enough to hurt the occupants of a vehicle, so if it doesn't want your vehicle to pass, back off and wait until it has crossed the road or moved off. Never switch off the engine around elephants until you're certain they are relaxed, and avoid allowing your car to be boxed in between an elephant and another vehicle (or boxing in another vehicle yourself). If an elephant does threaten a vehicle in earnest and backing off isn't an option, then revving the engine hard will generally dissuade it from pursuing the contest.

Monkeys, especially vervets and baboons, can become aggressive where they associate people with food. For this reason, feeding monkeys is highly irresponsible, especially as it may ultimately lead to their being shot as vermin. If you join a guided tour where the driver or guide feeds any primate, tell them not to. Although most monkeys are too small to be more than a nuisance, baboons have killed children and maimed adults with their vicious teeth. Unless trapped, however, their interest will be food, not people, so in the event of a genuine confrontation, throw down the food before the baboon gets too close. If you leave food (especially fruit) in your tent, monkeys might well tear it down. Chimps and gorillas are potentially dangerous, but they are only likely to be encountered on a guided forest walk, where you should obey your guide's instructions at all times.

Despite their fierce reputation, large predators generally avoid humans and are only likely to kill accidentally or in self-defence. Lions are arguably the exception, though they seldom attack unprovoked. Should you encounter any large predator on foot, be aware that running away might well trigger its 'chase' instinct, and that it will win the race. Better to stand still and/or back off very slowly, preferably without making eye contact. If (and only if) the animal looks really menacing, then noisy confrontation is probably a better tactic than fleeing. Sleeping in a sealed tent practically guarantees your safety – but don't sleep with your head sticking out or you risk being decapitated through predatorial curiosity. Never store meat in the tent.

When all's said and done, Africa's most dangerous creature, exponentially so, is the malaria-carrying mosquito (page 70). Humans, particularly when behind a steering wheel, come in a close second!

CAR ACCIDENTS Dangerous driving is probably the biggest threat to life and limb in most parts of Africa. On a self-drive visit, drive defensively, being especially wary of stray livestock, gaping pot-holes, and imbecilic or bullying overtaking manoeuvres. Many vehicles lack headlights and most local drivers are reluctant headlight-users, so avoid driving at night and pull over in heavy storms. On a chauffeured tour, don't be afraid to tell the driver to slow or calm down if you think he is driving too fast or being reckless.

WOMEN TRAVELLERS Women generally regard sub-equatorial Africa as one of the safest places in the world to travel alone. Uganda in particular poses few if any risks specific to female travellers. It is reasonable to expect a fair bit of flirting and the odd direct proposition, especially if you mingle with Ugandans in bars, but a firm 'no' should be enough to defuse any potential situation. And, to be fair to Ugandan men, you can expect the same sort of thing in any country, and for that matter from many male travellers. Ugandan women tend to dress conservatively. It will not increase the amount of hassle you receive if you avoid wearing clothes that, however unfairly, may be perceived to be provocative, and it may even go some way to decreasing it.

More mundanely, tampons are not readily available in smaller towns, though you can easily locate them in Kampala, Entebbe and Jinja, and in game lodge and hotel gift shops. When travelling in out-of-the-way places, carry enough tampons to see you through to the next time you'll be in a large city, bearing in mind that travelling in the tropics can sometimes cause heavier or more irregular periods than normal. Sanitary pads are available in most towns of any size.

LGBTQIA+ TRAVELLERS Homosexual activity is illegal in Uganda, and has been since colonial times. In 2009, existing anti-homosexuality laws were amplified by the submission to parliament of a draconian, so-called 'Kill the Gays' bill that caused a furore in the international community, and led to threats of withdrawal of aid and the like. The Anti-Homosexuality Act (AHA) was eventually passed in February 2014, albeit in a watered-down form. In reality, it contained little that was not already tackled under Ugandan law; its content being little more than a populist repackaging of colonial-era legislation enacted during an era when British attitudes were less liberal than today. The AHA was overturned by the Supreme Court on 8 August 2014 and a pioneering Gay Pride rally was held outside Kampala in 2015 on the first anniversary of this ruling. Any thoughts that this represented a more enlightened stance on homosexuality were, however, crushed in August 2016, when police officers set upon the second Gay Pride rally, beating and arresting several participants. Subsequent Gay Pride marches were cancelled due to threats of similar police intervention. From that point, it went from bad to worse for the LGBTQIA+ community, with the AHA being revived and signed into law in 2023 (page 31). In its present form it includes the death penalty for anyone convicted of aggravated homosexuality or the transmission of a life-changing disease such as AIDS and lengthy prison sentences for people convicted of the disturbingly vague-sounding offence of 'promoting homosexuality'.

There is no denying that the AHA saga reflects a deep-held anti-LGBTQIA+ sentiment among the general populace of Uganda (93% of which believes that homosexual lifestyles are immoral and should not be socially acceptable, according to the Pew Global Attitudes Project of 2014). That said, this was a largely latent prejudice before right-wing American evangelists elevated low-level disapproval into a full-blown crusade. These groups had done their homework well, establishing that this was fertile ground in which their vitriolic outpourings might bear fruit. Specifically, they saw that they might exploit a perception – widespread throughout Africa – that homosexuality (unlike American evangelism, or more conventional Christianity for that matter) is an un-African activity introduced by foreigners to fulfil a Western agenda.

Museveni remains obstinate in the defence of the AHA and in stating that he will not be dictated to by Western leaders; he has a point given the conflicting nature of the demands being made on him. Should he listen to the US government, which insists that the ill-treatment of LGBTQIA+ people is unacceptable and has imposed penalties on Uganda by way of punishment? Or ought he to side with the American Christians that have persuaded his people that homosexuals are an abomination? By the same token, Britain has changed its tune since its own legislators laid down the core of the AHA during the protectorate era (page 18). Though the true victims of the AHA are obviously members of Uganda's beleaguered LGBTQIA+ community, one has to ask whether Ugandans as a whole are the dupes of conflicting views and changing tolerances in the world beyond.

INFORMATION ON TRAVELLING WITH A DISABILITY

The UK's **gov.uk** website (w gov.uk/guidance/foreign-travel-for-disabled-people) provides general advice and practical information for travellers with disabilities preparing for overseas travel. **Accessible Journeys** (w disabilitytravel.com) is a comprehensive US site written by wheelchair users who have been researching wheelchair-accessible travel full-time since 1985. There are many tips and useful contacts (including lists of travel agents on request) for slow walkers, wheelchair travellers and their families, plus informative articles, including pieces on disabled travelling worldwide. The company also organises group tours. **Global Access News** (w globalaccessnews.com/index.htm) provides general travel information, reviews and tips for travelling with a disability. The **Society for Accessible Travel and Hospitality** (w sath.org) also provides some general information.

Whether or not the AHA survives its second incarnation, it should not be seen as a practical obstacle to LGBTQIA+ travellers visiting Uganda, provided they are willing to be discreet about their sexuality. Some, however, might well regard it to be an ethical stumbling block.

WHAT TO TAKE

The key to packing for a country like Uganda is finding the right balance between bringing everything you might possibly need and carrying as little luggage as possible, something that depends on your own priorities and experience as much as anything. Worth stressing is that most genuine necessities are surprisingly easy to get hold of in main centres, and that most of the ingenious gadgets you can buy in camping shops are unlikely to amount to much more than dead weight on the road. If it came to it, a hardy backpacker could easily travel in Uganda with little more than a change of clothes, a few basic toiletries and a medical kit.

CARRYING YOUR LUGGAGE A normal suitcase is ideal for organised tours, or for those who are travelling mostly by air or private transport. Ideally, buy a suitcase that easily slings across your back, or that rolls, or both. Travellers using public transport should either use a backpack or a suitcase that converts into one. Make sure your luggage is designed in such a manner that it can easily be padlocked. This won't prevent a determined thief from slashing it open, but it is a real deterrent to casual theft.

CAMPING EQUIPMENT Travellers on a tight budget might want to bring a lightweight but mosquito-proof tent to Uganda, along with a sleeping bag and roll-mat. There is no real need to carry a stove, as firewood is available at most campsites where meals cannot be bought. Cheap cutlery, plastic cups and plates, and lightweight metal pans (*suferias*) are the norm for most Ugandans and are available everywhere.

CLOTHES Uganda has a warm climate so bring plenty of light clothing, ideally made from natural fabrics, such as cotton, though many people prefer quick-dry synthetic trousers designed specifically for tropical travel. Western Uganda has a wet climate, and showers are normal even during the supposed dry seasons, so a light waterproof jacket is close to essential. At higher altitudes (for instance in Fort Portal) it can cool down in the evening, so bring at least one warm sweater, fleece jacket or sweatshirt.

If you intend to hike on Mount Elgon or the Rwenzori, you will need seriously warm clothing. As for footwear, those tracking gorillas in Bwindi or undertaking montane hikes elsewhere ideally require waterproof hiking boots that won't slip easily in mud or on wet leaves and rocks. Elsewhere, a good pair of walking shoes with solid ankle support should be sufficient. It's also useful to carry sandals, flip-flops or other light semi-open shoes – just watch out for irregular pavements! Rather than spending a fortune outfitting yourself for Africa before leaving home, you might follow the lead of informed travellers and volunteers who pack a minimum of clothes and buy the remainder in Kampala's superb Owino Market (or at similar locations in major towns), where secondhand clothes bought in bulk from charity shops for export to Uganda sell for a fraction of what they would in Europe or North America.

OTHER USEFUL ITEMS Bring a universal electric socket adaptor for charging your batteries in hotel rooms. A torch will be useful during power cuts. Some people wouldn't travel without a good pair of earplugs to help them sleep through traffic noise or mosque calls, while a travel pillow might make long bus journeys that bit easier to endure. Carry a small first-aid kit, the contents of which are discussed on page 69. A pack of wet or facial cleansing wipes can help maintain a semblance of cleanliness on long, dusty journeys, and anti-bacterial gel is a good way of making sure you don't make yourself sick with your own grime if you're eating on the move.

All the toilet bag basics (soap, shampoo, conditioner, toothpaste, toothbrush, deodorant, basic razors) are very easy to replace as you go along, so there's no need to bring family-sized packs. If you wear contact lenses, be aware that the various cleansing and storing fluids are not readily available, and, since many people find the intense sun irritates their eyes, you might consider reverting to glasses. Disposable contact lenses are another option. Most budget hotels provide toilet paper and many also provide towels, but if you are travelling on the cheap, it is worth taking your own.

If you're interested in wildlife, nothing will give you such value-for-weight entertainment as a pair of light binoculars, which allow you to get a good look at the colourful local birds, and to watch distant mammals in game reserves. For most purposes, 7x21 compact binoculars will be fine, though some might prefer 7x35 traditional binoculars for their larger field of vision. Serious birdwatchers will find a 10x magnification more useful.

Novels are difficult to get hold of outside Kampala and your best bet is to carry an e-book tablet loaded with reading material. If you prefer the real thing, bring a supply of books with you or visit Kampala's excellent Aristoc bookshop in Garden City Mall (page 147).

These days it seems to be standard practice to move around with either a tablet or notebook computer. If entertainment and internet access are your priorities, and your typing requirements are limited to the odd email, a tablet (fitted with a full-body protective casing) is ideal. If your surfing requirements can await the increasingly frequent occasions when you reach a Wi-Fi hotspot, then all well and good. If not, bring a model with 3G capability, fit it with a local SIM card loaded with data credit (page 91), and you can access the internet anywhere your chosen network provides a signal.

MONEY AND BUDGETING

The local currency is the Uganda shilling, which traded at around Ush3,000 to the US dollar in late 2024. Notes are printed in denominations of Ush50,000, 20,000,

10,000, 5,000 and 1,000. Ush500, 200, 100 and 50 notes have been replaced by coins and are no longer legal tender. Ush1,000 notes are in the process of being phased out in favour of an equivalent coin, but this isn't happening in any rush. Most visitors rely primarily on a credit or debit card, which can be used to draw local currency at ATMs countrywide, and supplement it with some hard currency cash as a fall-back (travellers' cheques are no longer accepted).

CASH US dollar, pound sterling and euro banknotes can be changed for local currency in a matter of minutes at any bank or foreign exchange (forex) bureau. With US dollars specifically, bills issued before 2009 are not accepted. Nor are torn or blemished notes of any currency, no matter how insignificant the damage. Large-denomination hard currency bills attract a better exchange rate than denominations of 20 or less, though the latter can be useful in some situations. In Kampala, ubiquitous forex bureaux tend to offer better exchange rates than banks, and are less bureaucratic (no ID required and the receipt serves only as a souvenir). Outside Kampala, there are fewer forex bureaux, so you'll mostly depend on banks. Banks are open from 09.00 to 15.00 on weekdays (though some banks in Kampala stay open later) and from 09.00 to noon on Saturdays. Forex offices may open earlier and typically close at 17.00 Monday to Saturday. You'll struggle to find anywhere to change money on a Sunday. If you have shillings left over at the end of the trip, it's perfectly straightforward to convert them back to foreign currency in a matter of minutes at any forex bureau, albeit at a slight loss.

CREDIT AND DEBIT CARDS All large towns and many smaller ones have at least one 24-hour ATM where local currency can be drawn against any international PIN-protected credit/debit card with a Visa or Mastercard logo. Stanbic ATMs are both reliable and widespread, and allow for daily withdrawals of up to Ush1,000,000 (around US$270). Larger towns also usually have branches of Standard Chartered, DFCU, Kenya Commercial Bank, Centenary and Absa. Charges are levied for withdrawals, but it tends to more-or-less balance out against the charges on cash forex transactions with the exception of Absa, which charges US$8 commission, irrespective of the sum requested. Charges for Centenary ATMs are reportedly the lowest, though its grassroots client base can mean long queues. If you'll be dependent on a card, alert your bank in advance to the dates you will be travelling so they won't be concerned about unusual foreign transactions. It might also be prudent to contact them to check your card's compatibility with East African systems and find out what they will charge in addition to locally levied fees. Other than cash withdrawals, use of debit/credit cards in Uganda is far less widespread than you will be used to, though they are becoming accepted in a growing number of supermarkets, hotels and restaurants in Kampala and Entebbe, as well as some brand-name fuel stations further afield. For small purchases and upcountry, you should expect to pay with cash or Mobile Money (see below).

MOBILE MONEY If you're going to be in Uganda for a while, and if you're going to visit the national parks, you'll probably want to obtain a phone line with a local mobile operator (page 91) and take advantage of their 'electronic wallet' service. There are several options but MTN's Mobile Money is the most widespread. Having used cash to load money on to your account, you can then withdraw funds (at a small fee) from any of the 50,000-plus Mobile Money agents nationwide (assuming that they have sufficient cash to oblige). You can also use Mobile Money to pay for services. The most common scenario is to send money to another registered number; you'll be asked to add a little extra to cover the vendor's withdrawal charge. Some larger businesses, such as supermarkets and fuel stations, use the 'MoMo' variation whereby you enter their merchant code (there are no additional fees). MoMo is also used for payments at Uganda Wildlife Authority (UWA) entrance gates, each of which has its own code. See w mtn.co.ug for further details.

MONEY TRANSFERS Transferring funds between banks in Europe/North America and Uganda remains surprisingly slow, taking several days. Fortunately, there are quicker options, the simplest being for your benefactor to send money to your home bank account and leave you to do the rest with your trusty ATM card. Alternatively, they could send funds, via a choice of online intermediaries, to your Ugandan Mobile Money account (see opposite). Both options are cheaper than the once-standard course of action, which was to have money sent via Western Union or MoneyGram to be collected in Ugandan shillings from a local agent.

PRICES QUOTED IN THIS BOOK Practically everything in Uganda can be paid for using the Uganda shilling, irrespective of the currency in which a price is quoted. For example, UWA tariffs for entrance fees and activities are quoted in US dollars, but can be paid either in US dollars or in Uganda shillings. However, in order to pre-empt an ever-sliding exchange rate, and to help readers at the planning stage of the trip, all prices in this book are quoted in US dollars, using a rate of US$1 = Ush3,750, often rounded to the nearest dollar. As always, be assured that the prices given in this book will most likely change during the lifetime of this edition. These may be minor or they may be quite spectacular due to local or global factors, such as worldwide economic squeezes, fluctuating fuel prices, highs and lows in the US dollar exchange rate and the considerable expense of bankrolling local general elections.

BUDGETING Independent travel in Uganda is no longer inexpensive – a trend that actually has much to do with rising expectations on the part of travellers – and your budget will depend greatly on how and where you travel. The following guidelines may be useful to people trying to keep costs to a minimum.

In most parts of the country, it will be difficult to keep your basic travel expenses (food, transport and accommodation) to much below US$50 per day, though you could do so by camping or staying in shoestring lodges. Typically, a double room in a basic (but acceptable) local hotel will cost US$15–25, camping around US$5 per person, and a simple meal US$2–7 depending on whether you are content to stick to the predictable local fare or want to eat a more varied menu. Bus fares are mostly in the Ush10,000–40,000 range, so transport costs will probably work out at around US$6–12 daily, assuming that you're on the move every other day or thereabouts. If you don't want *always* to stay in the most affordable room and *always* to go for the cheapest item on the menu, I would bank on spending around US$50–60 per day on basic travel costs. You could travel a lot more comfortably on US$75–100 per day.

Unless you go on an organised safari, the only expenses over and above your basic travel costs will be incurred in national parks where you can expect to spend around US$80 per day for every 24-hour period in entrance and activity fees, as well as inflated meal prices.

If funds are tight, it is often a useful idea to separate your daily budget from one-off expenses. At current prices, a daily budget of around US$50 with US$800 set aside for expensive one-off activities (and another US$800 if gorilla tracking) would be comfortable for most travellers.

GETTING AROUND

BY AIR Since few major urban centres lie more than 5–6 hours' drive from the capital, flying has never been an option for most people, though some more upmarket safaris now use flights to cut the driving time between Murchison Falls National Park and Queen Elizabeth or Bwindi Impenetrable national parks. The only destination in Uganda that is reached by air almost as often as it is by road is Kidepo Valley National Park, since the drive up from Kampala cannot be accomplished comfortably in one day.

The most useful airline for travellers is **Aerolink** (w aerolinkuganda.com), which (subject to demand) runs a daily return flight from Entebbe west to Semliki, Kasese, Mweya (Queen Elizabeth), Kihihi (for Ishasha and Buhoma), Kisoro, and north to Bugungu, Chobe, Pakuba and Kidepo. **Eagle Air** (w eagleair-ug.com) will get you up to Arua. Note that the above flights are subject to a minimum number of passengers and there are often diversions to other destinations.

SELF-DRIVE By African standards, Uganda's major roads are generally in good condition. Decent surfaced roads radiate out from Kampala, running east to Jinja, Busia, Malaba, Tororo, Mbale and Soroti, south to Entebbe, southwest to Masaka, Mbarara and Kabale, west to Fort Portal, northwest to Hoima, north to Gulu, and northeast to Gayaza and Kayunga (and on to Jinja). Other surfaced roads connect Karuma Falls to Arua, Mbale to Sipi Falls, Masaka to the Tanzanian border, Mbarara to Ibanda, and Ntungamo to Rukungiri. Most other roads are unsurfaced and tend to be variable in condition from one season to the next, with surfaces being trickiest during the rains. Road conditions described in this guide are of necessity a snapshot of conditions at the time of research and should not be taken as gospel. When in doubt, ask local advice – if matatus are getting through, then so should any 4x4, so the taxi park is always a good place to seek current information.

The main hazard on Ugandan roads is the road hog mentality of, and risks taken by, other drivers. Matatus in particular are given to overtaking on blind corners, while coaches routinely bully their way along trunk routes at up to 120km/h, forcing drivers of smaller vehicles to keep an eye on their rear-view mirror and pull off the road to let them pass. Bearing the above in mind, a coasting speed of 80km/h in the open road is comfortable without being over cautious, and it's not a bad idea to slow down and cover the brake in the face of oncoming traffic. In urban situations, particularly downtown Kampala, right of way essentially belongs to whoever is prepared to force the issue – a considered blend of defensive driving tempered by outright assertiveness is required to get through safely without becoming too bogged down in the traffic.

A peculiarly African road hazard – one frequently taken to extremes in Uganda – is the giant speed bump. A lethal bump might be signposted in advance, it might be painted in black-and-white stripes, or it might simply rear up without warning above the road like a macadamised wave. Other regular obstacles include weaving bicycles laden with banana clusters, as well as livestock and pedestrians blithely wandering around in the middle of the road. Piles of foliage placed in the road at a few metres' interval warn of a broken-down vehicle ahead. Note too that indicator lights are not used to signal an intent to turn, but are switched on when approaching oncoming traffic to suggest that following drivers should not overtake. Ugandans also display a strong aversion to switching on their headlights except in genuine darkness. In rainy, misty or twilight conditions, don't expect to be alerted to oncoming traffic by headlights, or for that matter expect drivers to avoid overtaking or speeding simply because they cannot see more than 10m ahead. It's strongly recommended that you avoid driving at night on main highways altogether, but if you do, be warned that a significant proportion of vehicles lack a full complement of functional headlights, so never assume a single glow indicates a motorcycle! Another very real danger is unlit trucks that have broken down in the middle of the road.

If you decide to rent a self-drive vehicle, check it over carefully and ask to take it for a test drive. Even if you're not knowledgeable about the working of engines, a few minutes on the road should be sufficient to establish whether it has any seriously disturbing creaks, rattles or other noises. Check the condition of the tyres (bald is beautiful might be the national motto in this regard) and that there is at least one spare, better two, both in a condition to be used should the need present itself. If the tyres are tubeless, an inner tube of the correct size can be useful in the event of a repair being required upcountry. Ask to be shown the wheel spanner, jack, the thing for raising the jack and (a legal requirement) a pair of red warning triangles. If the vehicle is a high-clearance 4x4 make sure that the jack is capable of raising the wheel high enough to change it. Ask also to be shown filling points for oil, water and petrol and check that all the keys do what they are supposed to do – we've left Kampala before with a car we later discovered could not be locked! Once on the road, check oil and water regularly in the early stages of the trip to ensure that there are no existing leaks.

Ugandans follow the British custom of driving on the left side of the road, albeit somewhat loosely on occasions. The following documentation is required at all times: vehicle registration book (a photocopy is acceptable); a window sticker indicating valid insurance (check this on a hire car too), and driving licence. Your own domestic licence is acceptable for up to three months, but in practice it's preferable to have an international licence. If you're nicked for speeding (the limit is 100km/h on the open, tarmac road, 80km/h on murram and 50km/h in built-up areas, unless otherwise indicated), not having valid insurance, or any other transgression, the worst case scenario is that you'll be presented with a charge sheet to clear at a bank within 28 days. As often as not, however, after a few minutes or so of friendly back and forth (remain polite, admit guilt, plead stupidity), you'll be let on your way. Still, it's safest to show the officer a photocopy of your licence or an expendable international licence, just in case they decide to retain it until you pay the fine.

Filling stations charge around US$1.50 per litre for petrol and slightly less for diesel. Fuel from Shell and Total stations is considered most reliable and both brands have at least one outlet in larger towns. Otherwise, every town has a selection of filling stations of more parochial affiliation, and while many of these are fine to use, others might stock diluted or dirty fuel, and it is difficult to know which can be relied upon (though any station selling fuel more cheaply than its branded peers might be assumed to be suspect). Uganda being quite a small country by African standards, you're unlikely to drive too long without an opportunity to refuel, but there are a few stretches – notably the Arua road beyond Karuma, or the drive from Kasese to Kisoro via Bwindi, and Karamoja in general – where branded filling stations are few and far between, so plan ahead. It is also always worth filling up before you enter any national park where you expect to do a few game drives (ie: Murchison Falls, Queen Elizabeth, Lake Mburo or Kidepo Valley). In more remote areas, filling stations may be absent altogether and self-drivers who forgot to fill up in advance will be reliant on buying fuel in jerry cans. This tends to be both pricey and highly suspect (even if the fuel is pure, the container may be dirty) so it would be prudent to use a piece of material to filter the fuel as you empty it into the tank.

Car hire Poor roads make vehicle hire relatively costly in Uganda. Most expat-/tourist-oriented safari companies charge well in excess of US$100 per day for a 4x4 with driver (but excluding fuel), but it's still possible to get some good deals.

Alpha Rent A Car m 0772 436346; e alphabetarentals@gmail.com; w alpharentals.co.ug. This reliable & highly recommended Kampala-based company offers excellent rates. A 4x4 for upcountry use with a driver excluding fuel costs US$100/day. A saloon used around Kampala costs US$50 with a driver & fuel, or US$40 without fuel.

Buffalo Safari Camps m 0782 805639; e info@buffalosafaricamps.com; w buffalosafaricamps.com. Open top 4x4 vehicle hire from US$70/day excluding fuel. Camping equipment also available.

Roadtrip Uganda m 0773 363012; e info@roadtripafrica.com; w roadtripafrica.com. Rav4 & Landcruiser vehicles with everything you need for a self-drive safari in Uganda. Check the website for prices; it's also an excellent general reference for travelling in Uganda.

MOUNTAIN BIKING Uganda is relatively compact and flat, making it ideal for travel by mountain bike. New-quality bikes are not available in Uganda so you should try to bring one with you (some airlines are more flexible than others about carrying bicycles; you should discuss this with your airline in advance). However, if you are prepared to look around Kampala, secondhand bikes can be bought from a few private importers; though you'll get plenty of options for less, US$200 should get you a pretty decent machine. There's a huge choice in the basement of the Energy Centre building on Market Street near Nakasero Market. Main roads in Uganda are generally in good condition and buses will allow you to take your bike on the roof, though expect to be charged extra for this. Minor roads are variable in condition, but in the dry season you're unlikely to encounter any problems. Several of the more far-flung destinations mentioned in this book would be within easy reach of cyclists.

Before you pack that bicycle, do consider that cyclists – far more than motorists – are exposed to an estimable set of hazards on African roads. A 'might-is-right' driving mentality is doubly concerning to cyclists, who must expect to be treated as second-class road users, and need to display constant vigilance against speeding buses, etc. It is routine for motorised vehicles to bear down on a bicycle as if it simply didn't exist, hooting at the very last minute, and enforcing the panicked cyclist to veer off the road abruptly, sometimes resulting in a nasty fall. Should this not put you off, do at least ensure that your bicycle is fitted with good rear-view mirrors, a loud horn and luminous strips, and that you bring a helmet and whatever protective gear might lessen the risks. Cycling at night is emphatically not recommended.

The **International Bicycle Fund** (w ibike.org/publications.htm) produces a useful publication called *Bicycling in Africa*, as well as several regional supplements including one about Malawi, Tanzania and Uganda.

PUBLIC TRANSPORT Following the permanent suspension of most passenger train services, public transport in Uganda essentially boils down to buses and other forms of motorised road transport supplemented by ferry and small boat services on various rivers and lakes.

Buses Coach and bus services cover all major routes, and are probably the safest form of public transport in Uganda. On all trunk routes, the battered old buses of a few years back have been replaced or supplemented by large modern coaches that typically maintain a speed of 100km/h or faster, allowing them to travel between the capital and any of the main urban centres in western Uganda in less than 5 hours, generally at a cost of less than US$10. While Link Bus (w link.co.ug) is the most popular operator on tarmac routes in the southern half of Uganda, other operators are listed in the Kampala and relevant regional chapters.

A **word of warning**: there have been a few incidents in East Africa in recent years whereby travellers accept drugged food from fellow passengers and awake much later to find themselves relieved of their belongings. Though 99% of offers of refreshment will be made from genuine courtesy, a polite refusal may be the safest option.

Matatus In addition to buses, most major routes are covered by a regular stream of white minibuses referred to locally as matatus or (rather confusingly) taxis. Generally, these have no set departure times, but simply leave when they are full. Matatus tend to charge slightly higher fares than buses, and the drivers tend to be more reckless, but they allow more flexibility, especially for short hops. It's customary on most routes to pay shortly before arriving rather than on departure, so there is little risk of being overcharged provided that you look and see what other passengers are paying. A law enforcing a maximum of three passengers per row is stringently adhered to in most parts of Uganda, and seat belts are now mandatory. All minibus-taxis by law now have to have a distinctive blue-and-white band round the middle, and special hire cars have to have a black-and-white band. Throughout this book, we use the term matatu (as opposed to taxi) to describe this form of transport, but we follow the local custom of referring to the terminal from where they depart as the 'taxi park'.

Shared taxis Shared taxis, generally light saloon cars that carry four to six passengers, come into their own on routes that attract insufficient human traffic for a matatu. They tend to be crowded and slow in comparison with minibuses, and on routes where no other public transport exists, fares are often highly inflated. Drivers habitually overcharge tourists, so establish the price in advance.

Boda One of the most popular ways of getting around in Uganda is the bicycle-taxi or boda (or *boda-boda* in full, since they originated as a means of smuggling goods from border to border along rural footpaths). Now fitted with pillions instead of panniers, and powered by foot or by 100cc engines, they are a convenient form of suburban transport and also great for short side trips where no public transport exists. Fares are negotiable and affordable, starting at Ush1,000 – about US$0.25. If you're reliant on public transport it's inevitable that you'll use a boda at some stage, but before hopping aboard you should be aware of their poor safety record. Boda riders are invariably lacking in formal training and road safety awareness, and many also seem to be in short supply when it comes to common sense. As a result, accidents – often fatal – are frequent.

By all means use bodas, but do try to identify a relatively sensible-looking operator, ideally of mature years. Older riders are generally better than 16-year-old village kids with no comprehension of traffic. Tell your driver to go slowly and carefully and don't be afraid to tell them to slow down (or even stop for you to get off) if you don't feel safe. Officially, helmets for boda passengers are mandatory, but the law is rarely enforced.

Though boda muggings are largely confined to Kampala (see warning on page 74), we have heard reports of similar incidents at night in Fort Portal. Presumably it could happen elsewhere, too, so keep your wits about you.

Special hire You won't spend long in Uganda before you come across the term 'special hire', which means hiring a vehicle privately to take you somewhere, ie: what you'll probably know as a taxi. Their use is most widespread in urban areas, but you may encounter situations elsewhere where a boda ride is a little too long, muddy and/or wet for comfort, or in a national park where bodas are prohibited. If you opt for a special-hire vehicle, bargain hard.

Ferry services A variety of craft shuttle across rivers and lakes throughout the country. Of these, the most organised are the ferry services operated by the Uganda National Road Authority (UNRA). These generally start operations around first light and run according to a timetable throughout the day until dusk (w unra.go.ug/services/ferry-services). Though intervals obviously vary with the tract of water to be negotiated, the one constant is that one or two crossings are skipped in the middle of the day to provide a staff lunchbreak. This can cause a rush for the ferry just before lunch and a backlog of vehicles awaiting the post-lunch crossing. Time your arrival accordingly, bearing in mind that entertainment value at rural ferry landings is often limited. Flatbed ferries carry 10–12 standard vehicles and up to 300 passengers while large craft making daily trips to islands out on Lake Victoria carry more. Though there is no charge for the smaller ferries, fees are levied on vehicles and travellers bound to/from the islands. Drivers must register themselves, passengers and their vehicles prior to crossing; foot travellers must also register with ID. Do this immediately to ensure nobody way back in the queue snaffles your place; that said, officials at some landings helpfully list registration numbers of queued vehicles to ensure fair play.

If you're not tied to a vehicle, and the ferry is over on the other side of the river or bay, you can simply hire a motorised canoe to zip across the water. Elsewhere, wooden canoes of varying size (the standard length is 10m) are used to shuttle around the larger lakes. Think carefully before using these, however. Overloading small passenger boats is customary in Uganda, and fatal accidents are commonplace, often linked to the violent storms that can sweep in from nowhere throughout the year.

ACCOMMODATION

The number of hotels in Uganda has grown enormously in recent years. Indeed, wherever you travel, and whatever your budget, you'll seldom have a problem finding suitable accommodation. Most towns have a good variety of moderately priced and budget hotels, and even the smallest villages will usually have somewhere you can stay for a couple of dollars. Upmarket accommodation, on the other hand, is centred on major towns and tourist centres such as national parks. All accommodation entries in this travel guide are placed in one of six categories: luxury/exclusive, upmarket, moderate, budget, shoestring and camping. The purpose of this categorisation is twofold: to break up long hotel listings that span a wide price range, and to help readers isolate the range of hotels that will best suit their budget and taste. Any given hotel is categorised on its overall feel as much as its actual prices and in the context of general accommodation standards in the town or reserve where it is situated. Comments relating to the value for money represented by any given hotel should also be read in the context of the individual town and of the stated category. In other words, a hotel that seems to be good value in one town might not be such a bargain were it situated in a place where rates are generally cheaper. Likewise, a hotel that we describe as good value in the upmarket category will almost certainly feel madly expensive to a traveller using budget hotels.

Broadly speaking, hotels placed in the luxury bracket are truly world-class institutions, whereas lodges and tented camps listed as exclusive meet the highest standards that could reasonably be expected in a bush setting while also possessing a strong individual flair. Upmarket hotels often have all the facilities you'd expect of a three- to four-star hotel, making them top-drawer for Uganda, but not quite so outstanding by global standards. Moderate hotels are more middling in quality but would still come across as very comfortable to tourists used to developing world standards. Budget accommodation mostly consists of ungraded accommodation that is aimed primarily at the local market but would still be considered reasonably comfortable by hardened backpackers, often with facilities such as en-suite hot showers, satellite TV and good netting. Shoestring accommodation consists of the cheapest rooms around, usually unpretentious local guesthouses, often with shared bathrooms. Camping generally refers to sites where you would pitch your own tent (as opposed to camps with standing tents).

Note that most East African hotels refer to a room that has en-suite shower and toilet facilities as 'self-contained'. Several hotels offer accommodation in *bandas*, a term used widely to designate detached rooms or cottages. Be aware that Ugandan usage of the terms single, double and twin is inconsistent with Western conventions. A room with one double bed is often referred to as a single room, while one with two beds may be termed a double rather than a twin. For this reason, couples should make a habit of looking at a 'single' room before assuming they need to pay extra for a double or twin.

Hotels assigned as author's favourites (indicated by a ✱ before the listing) stand out as being unusually characterful, service-oriented, or good value – often, all three! As an easy visual reference, all hotels are assigned a price band, based on the price of a standard room with double occupancy, as follows:

$	under US$20
$$	US$20–75
$$$	US$75–200
$$$$	US$200–400
$$$$$	US$400–800
$$$$$$	over US$800

Note that prices are not included in listings for the last two categories. One reason is that while the minutiae of accommodation costs is useful to budget travellers, it is of less concern to those accustomed to frequenting these upper bandings. It also pre-empts unhelpful calculations against the overall cost of an upmarket safari. Readers should not necessarily be deterred by the rates and daunting numbers of **$** signs shown. These present a worst-case scenario, being high season rack rates, and discounts during low season months and for local/East African residents are often available.

EATING AND DRINKING

EATING OUT If you are not too fussy and don't mind a lack of variety, you can eat cheaply almost anywhere in Uganda. In most towns numerous local restaurants (often called *hotelis*) serve unimaginative but filling meals for under US$2. Typically, local food is based around a meat or chicken stew eaten with one of four staples: rice, chapati, *ugali* or *matoke*. *Ugali* is a stiff maize porridge eaten throughout sub-Saharan Africa. *Matoke* is a cooked plantain dish, served boiled or in a mushy

THE HUMBLE ROLEX

A welcome, if humble, addition to Kampala's edible offerings is the 'rolex'. This is nothing more (or less) than a freshly cooked chapati enhanced by a fresh omelette, chopped onions, tomatoes, green peppers and finely sliced cabbage. The latter items are rolled up inside the former, hence the name, and popped into a polythene bag. You'll find rolex street vendors armed with metal hot plates, a charcoal stove and a chopping board in all popular nightspots of 'local' flavour. It's exactly the sort of street food your mother warned you against eating in Africa, so rolexes are obviously a firm favourite with backpackers, gap-year students and volunteers. Expect to pay around US$0.50.

heap, and is the staple diet in many parts of Uganda. Another Ugandan special is groundnut sauce. *Mandazi*, the local equivalent of doughnuts, are tasty when they are freshly cooked, but rather less appetising when they are a day old. Mandazi are served at hotelis and sold at markets. You can often eat very cheaply at stalls around markets and bus stations.

Cheap it may be, but for most travellers the appeal of this sort of fare soon palls. In larger towns, you'll usually find a couple of better restaurants (sometimes attached to upmarket or moderate hotels) serving Western or Indian food for around US$5–8. There is considerably more variety in Kampala, where for US$10–15 per head you can eat very well indeed. Upmarket lodges and hotels generally serve high-quality food. Vegetarians are often poorly catered for in Uganda (the exception being Indian restaurants), and people on organised tours should ensure that the operator is informed in advance about this or any other dietary preference.

COOKING FOR YOURSELF The alternative to eating at restaurants is to put together your own meals at markets and supermarkets. The variety of foodstuffs you can buy varies from season to season and from town to town, but in most major centres you can rely on finding a supermarket that stocks frozen meat, a few tinned goods, biscuits, pasta, rice and chocolate bars. Fruit and vegetables are best bought at markets, where they are very cheap. Potatoes, sweet potatoes, onions, tomatoes, bananas, sugarcane, avocados, paw-paws, mangoes, coconuts, oranges and pineapples are available in most towns. For hikers, packet soups and noodles are about the only dehydrated meals that are available throughout Uganda. If you have specialised requirements, you're best off doing your shopping in Kampala, where a wider selection of goods is available in the supermarkets.

DRINKS The usual brand-name soft drinks are widely available in Uganda and cheap by international standards. You can buy imported South African fruit juices at supermarkets in Kampala and other large towns. Don't assume that tap water is safe to drink; boiled or self-treated water or bottled mineral water is a more sensible option.

Locally, the most widely drunk hot beverage is *chai*, a sweet tea where all ingredients are boiled together in a pot. In some parts of the country *chai* is often flavoured with spices such as ginger (an acquired taste, in the author's opinion). Coffee is one of Uganda's major cash crops, but brewed locally it almost invariably tastes insipid and watery, except at upmarket hotels and restaurants, and specialist coffee shops.

The main alcoholic drink is lager beer, and several brands are available. Most come in 500ml bottles, which cost around US$1.20 in local bars and up to US$4 in some upmarket hotels. Nile Special is probably the most popular tipple with travellers, at least initially; after a few experiments, many opt for the milder Club and Bell. If you've never been to Africa before, you might want to try the local millet beer, which outsells any other brand tenfold, though for most visitors once is enough.

A selection of superior plonk-quality South African wines is available in most tourist-class hotels and bars, as well as in some supermarkets, starting at around US$10–20 per bottle. Local gins can be bought very cheaply in a variety of bottle sizes as small as a pocket-sized 250ml.

PUBLIC HOLIDAYS

In addition to the following fixed public holidays, Uganda recognises as holidays the Christian Good Friday and Easter Monday and the Muslim Eid-el-Fitr and Eid-el-Adha. Expect any institutions that would be closed on a Sunday – banks and forex bureaux, for instance, or government and other offices – to also be closed on any public holiday, but most shops and other local services will function as normal. Public transport is typically more intermittent than normal on public holidays, but it still operates.

1 January	New Year's Day
26 January	NRM Liberation Day
16 February	Archbishop Janani Luwum Day
8 March	International Women's Day
1 May	Labour Day
3 June	Martyrs' Day
9 June	National Heroes' Day
9 October	Independence Day
25 December	Christmas Day
26 December	Boxing Day

SHOPPING

A good range of imported goods is available in Kampala, though prices are often inflated. Most upcountry towns, especially those with significant expatriate communities or tourist flow, have at least one well-stocked supermarket, along with any number of smaller shops selling toilet rolls, soap, toothpaste, pens, batteries and locally produced foodstuffs. Normal shopping hours are between 08.30 and 18.00.

Typical **crafts and curios** include carvings, batiks, musical instruments, wooden spoons, various soapstone and malachite knick-knacks and masks. As yet, however, relatively few items are produced in country, the majority coming from Kenya or Congo. In Kampala, craft markets are found next to the National Theatre and on Buganda Road, while most upcountry tourist destinations have at least one shop or cluster of stalls as listed in the relevant chapters.

MEDIA AND COMMUNICATIONS

NEWSPAPERS Uganda has a good English-language press. The daily ***New Vision*** (w newvision.co.ug) and ***Daily Monitor*** (w monitor.co.ug) offer the best

FESTIVALS IN UGANDA

Charlotte Beauvoisin (w diaryofamuzungu.com)

Ugandans love to party. Not only do locals enjoy 'making noise', but the equatorial weather makes the Pearl of Africa perfect for festivals virtually all year round. Consequently, over the past decade Uganda has seen the mushrooming of a variety of arts and music festivals.

Kampala has an eclectic range of cultural activities, but you need to be in the city or active on social media to track events down. Social media pages are more up to date than official websites, but that's no guarantee you won't miss anything. An annual event may suddenly stop – or resume – at a few weeks' notice.

That said, one reliable platform is the German Goethe-Zentrum Kampala (w goethezentrumkampala.org) which collaborates with local and international artists to put on photo exhibitions, performance poetry, the Ngalabi Short Film Festival and the International Hip-Hop Week every November.

Every June, L'Alliance Française (f afkampala) organises the Fête de la Musique (World Music Day). This and other events promoting La Francophonie – loosely translated as art and culture of the French-speaking world – are open to all-comers (meaning a knowledge of French is not compulsory!)

While traditionally Uganda is known as a safari destination, there is life beyond wildlife and, boy, does Kampala sock it to you. Famed across the region for its legendary nightlife, the capital's festival scene is one to watch, although it's interesting to note that the two biggest festivals are now outside Kampala: one on an island in Lake Victoria and the other in Jinja, to the east.

More sedate events include the **Kampala International Theatre Festival** (w kampalainternationaltheatrefestival.com) every November. The **Kampala Music School** (f) has a regular programme of (mostly) classical music concerts throughout the year. The **Kampala Singers** lead celebrations every Easter and Christmas at Namirembe Cathedral.

NYEGE NYEGE INTERNATIONAL MUSIC AND ARTS FESTIVAL (w nyegenyege.com) Celebrating its ninth edition in November 2024, 'Africa's Best Underground Music Festival' and certainly Uganda's most talked-about annual event, takes place on the banks of the River Nile in Jinja, 2 hours' drive from Kampala. Half of Kampala decamps to the Source of the Nile for the weekend. Officially, *nyege*

local and international coverage. The weekly ***East African*** (w theeastafrican.co.ke) has excellent regional coverage and comment. The bi-weekly ***Independent*** (w independent.co.ug), produced by independent journalist Andrew Mwenda, provides insightful coverage of current controversies.

RADIO AND TELEVISION A varied selection of local and national radio stations service Uganda, most of them privately run, offering listeners a lively mix of talk, hard and soft news, local and other current music – not to mention a litany of country and disco staples you'd probably forgotten about! For entertainment from the outside world, BBC World Service relays through a number of regional stations (in Kampala, Capital Radio on 91.3 FM) while Touch FM (95.9 FM) gives regular airtime to classic rock staples. The national television channels aren't up to much, but most international hotels and many smaller ones subscribe to DSTV, a multi-channel satellite service featuring the likes of CNN or Sky News as well as movie and sports channels. Bars and restaurants with DSTV tend to be packed on

nyege stands for 'peace, respect and abundant joy; it stands for Africa and Africans, for underground music and musicians'. Unofficially, though, *nyege nyege* can be translated as 'the urge to dance' (or 'feeling horny' in Kenya's Sheng dialect). The festival has not been without controversy. According to UK-based club promoter Boiler Room, 'There are festivals and there is Nyege Nyege.'

BAYIMBA INTERNATIONAL FESTIVAL OF THE ARTS (w bayimba.org/events) Established in 2008, this multi-day festival of music and dance, poetry, comedy, film, fashion and the visual arts takes place on its very own island – Lunkulu – on Lake Victoria. Unlike the sometimes frenetic Nyege Nyege, the more intimate Bayimba has a more grown-up following. Bayimba's intentions are laudable: the festival is not just about having a good time but also about showcasing homegrown talents. The 2024 event takes place in September. Other Bayimba events include the Amakula Film Festival and the Reggae Fest and Comedy Weekends.

ROLEX FESTIVAL (w rolexinitiative.com; f) *'In Uganda, we don't wear rolex, we eat them'* reads a popular T-shirt slogan, and Ugandan beauty queen Mirembe pushed this up a notch by taking Uganda's most popular street food to a new level. A feature on CNN made the rolex 'rolled eggs' in a chapati go viral. Now it's the theme of an annual day-long festival, where revellers dance to live music while snacking on various variations of the rolex. Cleverly, the Rolex Initiative has birthed job creation and skilling of thousands of fast-food street vendors across the country.

BLANKETS AND WINE (f BlanketsNWineUG) For those who don't have a whole weekend to lose, these boozy Sunday picnics could be the answer. Hugely popular with Kampala's fashionista crowd, expect to pay an arm and a leg for the entrance tickets and cocktails – and the new frock, of course.

KLA ART (w klaart.org) Organised every two years by 32° East and the Ugandan Arts Trust, KLA ART celebrates public art, with each edition revolving around a unique theme. Artists craft their pieces, which are showcased primarily in outdoor spaces across various locations in Kampala during the month of August.

Saturday and Sunday afternoons and evenings during the English football season, and for all other major football events.

TELEPHONE Uganda's land telephone system is reasonably efficient, but mobile phones rule. If you bring your mobile from home, you'll enjoy international roaming – albeit at a significant cost – through a local network. Far cheaper, however, especially if you also want to make use of data and Mobile Money services, is to bring a compatible phone with you and insert a local SIM card, which costs next to nothing. MTN (w mtn.co.ug) is the provider best suited to travellers due to its excellent countrywide network. Airtime cards are available everywhere, and local and international calls and data bundles are cheap.

Both land and mobile numbers are included in this guidebook. All numbers are ten digits. Landline numbers start with 03 or 04 and are listed in the format nnn nnnnnnn. Mobile numbers start with 07 and are listed in the format nnnn nnnnnn. Generally, you're likely to get through to mobile phones more quickly than to landlines. Note, however, that many of the mobile numbers listed in this book belong to somebody's personal device, so they are more likely to become obsolete than landlines. Calling from overseas, the international code is +256, and you need to drop the leading zero from the local number.

INTERNET AND EMAIL Practically all hotels that cater to tourist or business travellers on a regular basis offer free Wi-Fi to their guests, though reception can be very spotty and slow, especially in smaller towns and rural areas. Smarter restaurants and cafés often also offer free Wi-Fi to patrons. Despite this, it is worth buying a local MTN SIM card for your smartphone and loading it up with a data bundle, which will give you more-or-less permanent access to the internet, email and various apps for next to no cost. Even so, access may be slow or erratic outside the cities so best to warn anxious loved ones at home or business associates that contact may be intermittent.

Email and internet are not really a standard medium of communication in Uganda. Except at the very top end of the price scale, few hotels and other institutions have websites or email addresses, and even if they do in theory, the URLs and email addresses printed boldly on business cards or signposts are often misspelt, non-existent or lapsed. We have done our best to validate all URLs and any improbable-looking email addresses before including them in this book, but even this can be problematic, as domains we discover to be expired or suspended might yet be reactivated, and email addresses whose inbox is so full that new emails sent to them bounce back might one day be emptied. Furthermore, even where addresses are valid, a great many Ugandans are not in the habit of replying to emails, so you are far more likely to get somewhere by phoning or using WhatsApp instead. We also occasionally list Facebook pages, although, as another minor complication, Facebook was banned by the regulatory authority in Uganda; a retaliatory action after the disconnection of accounts linked to supposed electoral malpractice in 2021. Facebook can still be accessed through VPNs, which, though also illegal, are used by everyone including the police.

POST AND COURIER SERVICES If you need to send anything weightier than a few megabytes upcountry in Uganda, it can be sent fastest (and reliably and cheaply) by bus, assuming your dispatch and collection points both lie on an established route. Take it to the company office in Town A to be collected from the same in Town B later that day or, latest, the following morning. Useful, for example, if you need a new tyre sent upcountry. You'll find the Link Bus to be most efficient in this regard.

For international deliveries, the postal service – once extremely efficient – is now slow and erratic and it is safer to use a courier service such as **DHL** (☎ 031 2210006; w dhl.com).

CULTURAL ETIQUETTE

Ugandans are generally relaxed, friendly and tolerant in their dealings with tourists, and you would have to do something pretty outrageous to commit a serious faux pas there. But, like any country, it does have its rules of etiquette, and while allowances will always be made for tourists, there is some value in ensuring that they are not made too frequently!

GENERAL CONDUCT Perhaps the single most important point of etiquette to be grasped by visitors to Africa is the social importance of formal greetings. Rural Africans tend to greet each other elaborately, and if you want to make a good impression on somebody who speaks English, whether they be a waiter or a shop assistant (and especially if they work in a government department), you would do well to follow suit. When you need to ask directions, it is rude to blunder straight into interrogative mode without first exchanging greetings. Most Ugandans speak some English, but for those who don't the Swahili greeting '***jambo***' delivered with a smile and a nod of the head will be adequate.

Among Ugandans, it is considered to be in poor taste to display certain emotions publicly. Affection is one such emotion: it is frowned upon for members of the opposite sex to hold hands publicly, and kissing or embracing would be seriously offensive. Oddly, it is quite normal for friends of the same sex to walk around hand in hand. Male travellers who get into a long discussion with a male Ugandan shouldn't be surprised if that person clasps them by the hand and retains a firm grip on their hand for several minutes. This is a warm gesture, one particularly appropriate when the person wants to make a point with which you might disagree.

Recent events, however, mean that this practice and handshakes in general are being relegated to history. Thanks to Covid-19 and occasional outbreaks of Ebola, a fist bump is now usually as far as it goes. If you're inclined to lament this erosion of an age-old cultural practice, google the stats concerning post-lavatory hand-washing in Uganda and you'll see things rather differently.

TIPPING AND GUIDES The question of where and when to tip can be difficult in a foreign country. In Uganda, it is customary to tip your driver/guide at the end of a safari or hike, as well as any cook or porter who accompanies you. A figure in the region of US$10 per day would be a fair benchmark, though do check this with your safari company in advance. It is not essential to tip the guides who take you around in national parks and other reserves, but it is recommended. A similar sum in shillings would be appreciated, especially if the guide has found you that lion, leopard or shoebill. In both cases, feel free to give a bigger or smaller tip based on the quality of service.

In some African countries, it is difficult to travel anywhere without being latched on to by a self-appointed guide, who will often expect a tip over and above any agreed fee. This sort of thing is unusual in Uganda, but if you do take on a freelance guide, then it is advisable to clarify in advance that whatever price you agree is final and inclusive of a tip.

It is not customary to tip for service in local bars and eateries, but if you feel like doing so, it will be appreciated. A 5% tip would be acceptable and 10% generous. Generally, any restaurant that caters primarily to tourists and to wealthy Ugandan residents will automatically add a service charge to the bill, but since there's no telling where that service charge ends up, it would still be reasonable to reward good service with a 10% tip.

BARGAINING AND OVERCHARGING Prices in hotels, restaurants and shops are generally fixed, and overcharging in such places is very unusual. For this reason, the need to bargain generally exists only in reasonably predictable circumstances, for instance when chartering a private taxi, organising a guide, or buying curios and to a lesser extent other market produce.

The main instance where bargaining is essential is when buying curios. However, the fact a curio seller is open to negotiation does not mean that you were initially being overcharged or ripped off. Curio sellers will generally quote a price knowing full well that you are going to bargain it down (they'd probably be startled if you didn't) and it is not necessary to respond aggressively or in an accusatory manner. To get a feel for prices, check a few similar items at different stalls before you actually buy anything.

At markets and stalls, bargaining is the norm, even between locals, and the healthiest approach is to view it as an enjoyable part of the African experience. There will normally be an accepted price band for any particular commodity. To find out what it is, listen to what other people pay and try a few stalls. A ludicrously inflated price will always drop the moment you walk away. It's simpler when buying fruit and vegetables, which are generally piled in heaps for a set price. You'll elicit a smile and a few extra items thrown in if you ask '*Yongela ko*' meaning 'addition'. Above all, bear in mind that when somebody is reluctant to bargain, it may be because they asked a fair price in the first place.

Matatu conductors often try to overcharge tourists, so check the correct ticket price in advance, and try to book your ticket the day before you travel. Failing that, you will have to judge for yourself whether the price is right, and if you have reason to think it isn't, then question the conductor. In such circumstances, it can be difficult to find the right balance between standing up for your rights and becoming overtly obnoxious.

A final point to consider on the subject of overcharging and bargaining is that it is the fact of being overcharged that annoys; the amount itself is generally of little consequence in the wider context of a trip to Uganda. So while travellers shouldn't allow themselves to be routinely overcharged, there are occasions when it helps to retain some perspective with respect to relative incomes. If you find yourself quibbling over a pittance with an old lady selling a few piles of fruit by the roadside, you might bear in mind that the notion of a fixed price is a very Western one. When somebody is desperate enough for money, or afraid that their perishable goods might not last another day, it may well be possible to push them down to a price lower than they would normally accept. In such circumstances, it might be kinder to err on the side of generosity.

GETTING INVOLVED

It goes without saying, or it ought to, that you'll observe a vast difference in Uganda between your standard of living and that of many local people, and many visitors are moved to help. To do so effectively and appropriately can, however, be difficult; there are plenty of tricksters looking to fleece well-meaning donors with school-fee scams, as well as the odd dodgy pastor using bogus community campsites/volunteer schemes to line their own pockets. Rather than handing out cash, a good way to be certain of making a difference is to stuff empty spaces in your rucksack with items that are hugely useful but which are costly or unavailable in Uganda. Check out the website of **Sanyu Babies Home** (☎ 041 4274032; m 0712 370950; e barbara@sanyubabies.com; w sanyubabies.com) before you travel, a charitable foundation that cares for orphaned, destitute and abandoned babies until they are adopted or graduate to orphanages. Sanyu Babies Home also welcomes volunteers and paying guests; accommodation on site is provided in a pleasantly homely guesthouse (US$25 shared facilities). The home is found on the side of Namirembe Hill on Natete Road just before Mengo Hospital.

Volunteers for Sustainable Development (VFSD; m 0782 808257, 0753 301879; e volunteers.vfsd@gmail.com), a small organisation established by local residents, is doing its best to provide a life for a handful of orphans in Bwaise, Kampala's largest slum. It's a truly humbling initiative, tackling overwhelming odds, and every little helps. Assistance can take the form of volunteering, simply spending time with the kids to help them practise their English, donating funds (supporters in the US have set up a 501C facility) or taking the VFSD slum tour (page 137) to better understand the reality of life in Bwaise.

If you're moved to support the Uganda Wildlife Authority's struggle to protect Uganda's wildlife, visit w ugandacf.org to learn about the work of the **Uganda Conservation Foundation**. UCF helps UWA with much-needed infrastructure, equipment, training and support for research. Recent activities include the construction of ranger posts in Queen Elizabeth and Murchison Falls national parks, donation of bicycles and patrol boats, training of boat coxwains, a hippo survey in Queen Elizabeth and the refurbishment of a veterinary vehicle for Murchison Falls. Administration costs are kept to a minimum and 90% of funding is channelled directly into conservation action. If you would like to support UCF from the US, a 501C facility can be accessed on the website.

Part Two

ENTEBBE, KAMPALA AND SOUTH-CENTRAL UGANDA

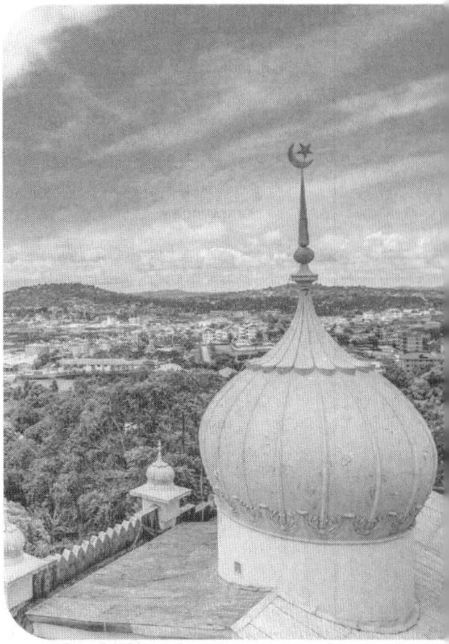

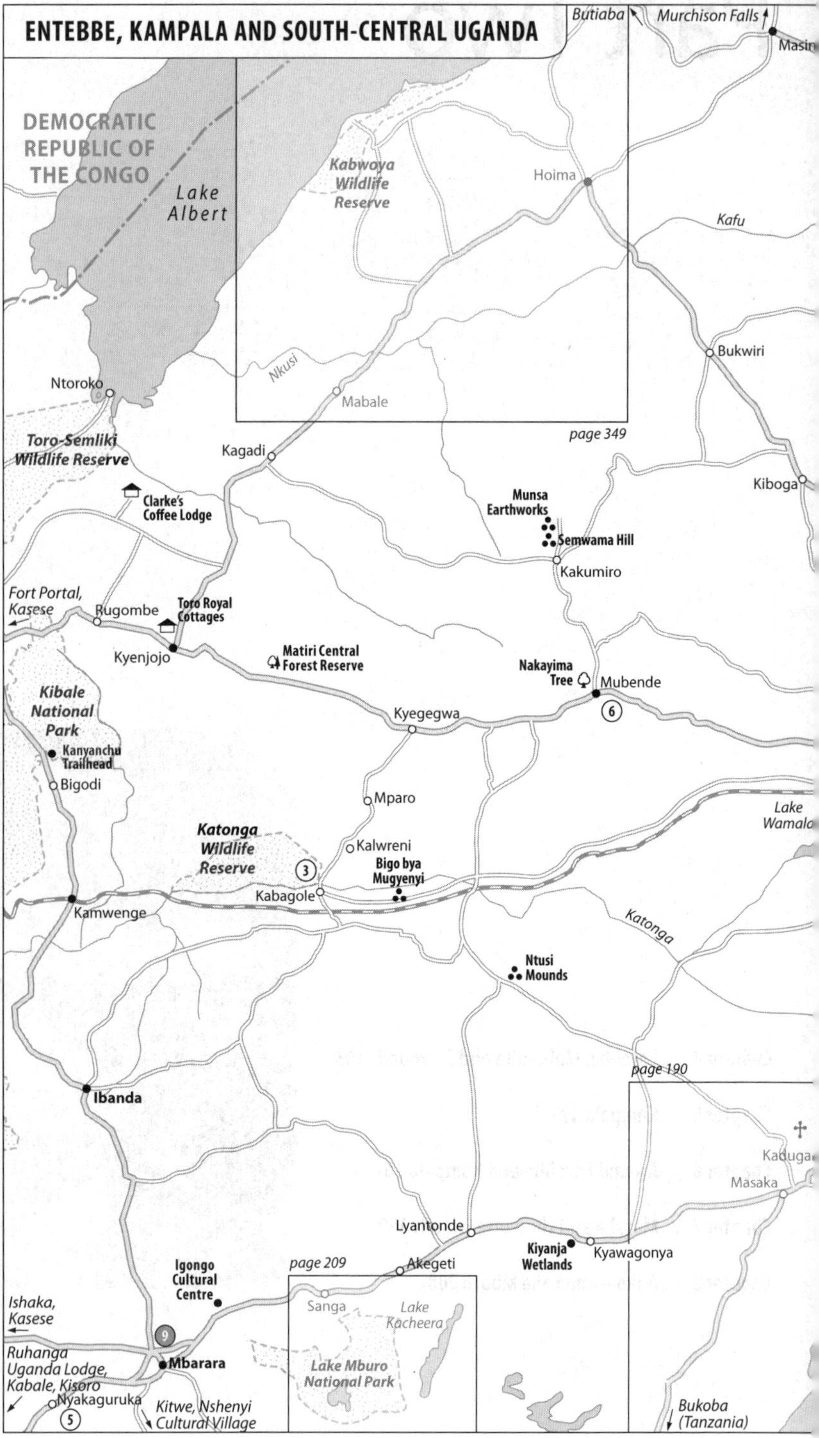
ENTEBBE, KAMPALA AND SOUTH-CENTRAL UGANDA
Butiaba
Murchison Falls
Masin
DEMOCRATIC REPUBLIC OF THE CONGO
Lake Albert
Kabwoya Wildlife Reserve
Hoima
Kafu
Nkusi
Mabale
Bukwiri
Ntoroko
page 349
Toro-Semliki Wildlife Reserve
Kagadi
Kiboga
Clarke's Coffee Lodge
Munsa Earthworks
Semwama Hill
Kakumiro
Fort Portal, Kasese
Rugombe
Toro Royal Cottages
Kyenjojo
Matiri Central Forest Reserve
Nakayima Tree
Mubende
Kibale National Park
Kyegegwa
Kanyanchu Trailhead
Bigodi
Mparo
Lake Wamala
Katonga Wildlife Reserve
Kalwreni
Bigo bya Mugyenyi
Kabagole
Kamwenge
Katonga
Ntusi Mounds
page 190
Ibanda
Kaduga
Masaka
Lyantonde
Kiyanja Wetlands
Kyawagonya
Igongo Cultural Centre
page 209
Akegeti
Sanga
Lake Kacheera
Ishaka, Kasese
Ruhanga Uganda Lodge, Kabale, Kisoro
Mbarara
Lake Mburo National Park
Nyakaguruka
Kitwe, Nshenyi Cultural Village
Bukoba (Tanzania)

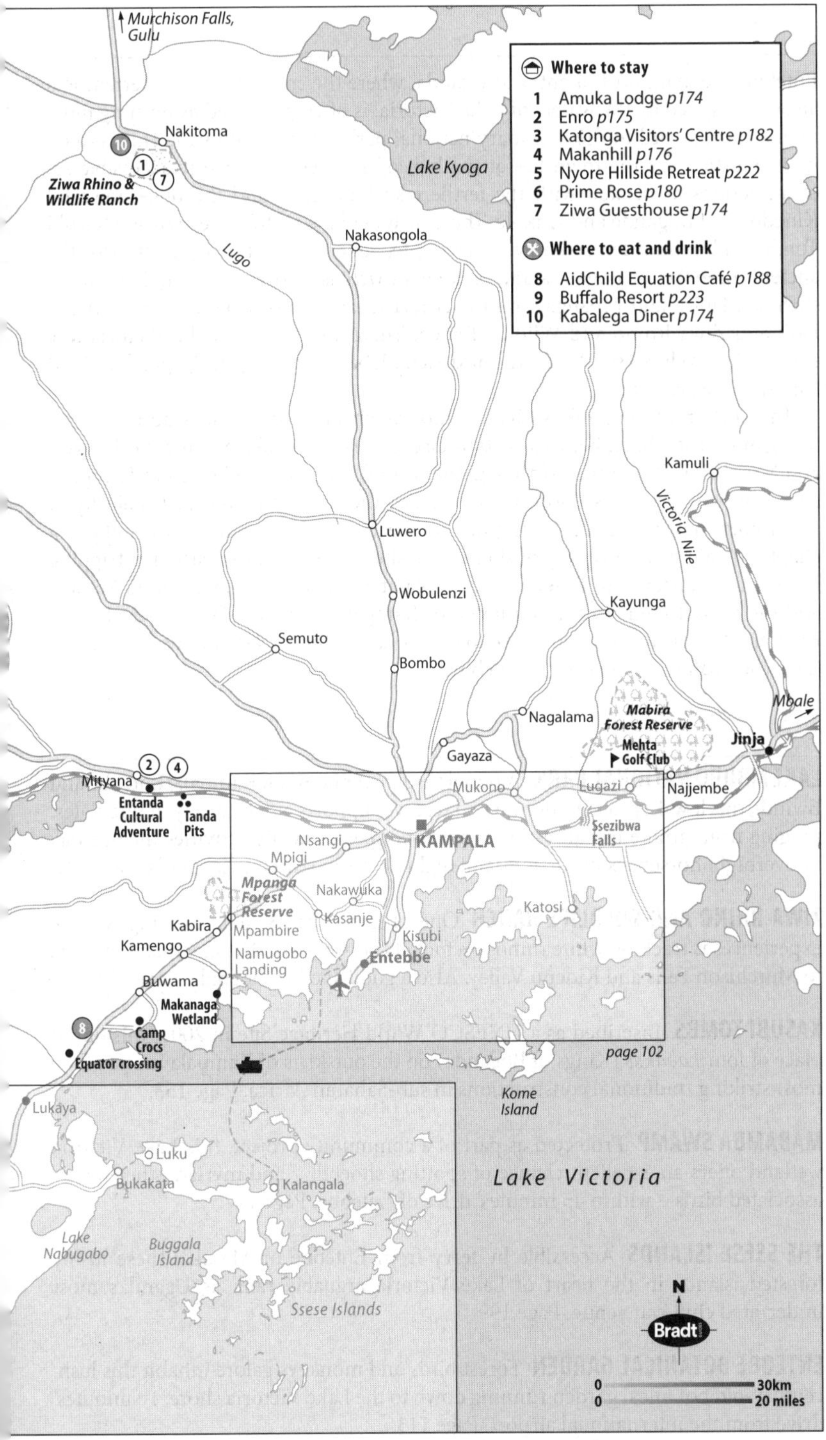

Murchison Falls, Gulu
Where to stay
1 Amuka Lodge p174
2 Enro p175
3 Katonga Visitors' Centre p182
4 Makanhill p176
5 Nyore Hillside Retreat p222
6 Prime Rose p180
7 Ziwa Guesthouse p174
Where to eat and drink
8 AidChild Equation Café p188
9 Buffalo Resort p223
10 Kabalega Diner p174
Nakitoma
Ziwa Rhino & Wildlife Ranch
Lake Kyoga
Lugo
Nakasongola
Kamuli
Victoria Nile
Luwero
Wobulenzi
Kayunga
Semuto
Bombo
Mbale
Nagalama
Mabira Forest Reserve
Jinja
Mehta Golf Club
Gayaza
Mityana
Entanda Cultural Adventure
Tanda Pits
Mukono
Lugazi
Najjembe
Ssezibwa Falls
Nsangi
KAMPALA
Mpigi
Mpanga Forest Reserve
Nakawuka
Kasanje
Katosi
Kabira
Mpambire
Kisubi
Kamengo
Namugobo Landing
Entebbe
Buwama
Makanaga Wetland
Camp Crocs
Equator crossing
page 102
Kome Island
Lukaya
Luku
Bukakata
Kalangala
Lake Victoria
Lake Nabugabo
Buggala Island
Ssese Islands
N
Bradt
0 30km
0 20 miles

OVERVIEW

Entebbe, the main port of entry to Uganda, where the country's only international airport is lapped by the waters of Lake Victoria, is often perceived as nothing more than a springboard to the legendary national parks of the southwest. This is to do it an injustice, for the town lies at the hub of a varied and readily accessible set of attractions associated with the fertile lake hinterland and the once-powerful Kingdoms of Buganda and Ankole. These include the UNESCO-recognised Kasubi Tombs and several lesser-known sacred sites associated with the Bachwezi, the ancient forebears of Buganda and Ankole, as well as bird-rich, jungle-like forests such as Mabira and Mpanga, and the acacia savannahs of Lake Mburo National Park and Ziwa Rhino and Wildlife Ranch. There are gems on Lake Victoria too, such as the lovely Ssese Islands, the bird-rich Mabamba Swamp and Ngamba Island Chimpanzee Sanctuary.

This section of the book is divided into five chapters. It starts, as do most trips to Uganda, with Entebbe; this section also covers Mabamba Swamp to the west and Murchison Bay to the northeast. The second chapter is dedicated to Kampala, a substantially pruned section that recognises the reality that the vast majority of safari-goers now bypass the metropolis and head directly upcountry. The following chapter details a wide variety of standalone sites situated within easy day-tripping or overnight distance of Entebbe and the capital. The next chapter covers Masaka and the Ssese Islands to the southwest of Kampala, while the last one deals with Mbarara, the principal town of Ankole, and Lake Mburo National Park, which is the closest safari destination to Entebbe.

HIGHLIGHTS

LAKE MBURO NATIONAL PARK A popular stopover between Kampala/Entebbe and Bwindi, this low-key, acacia-dominated reserve supports a rich variety of ungulates, ranging from giraffe to half-a-dozen antelope species, while activities include day or overnight horseback excursions and night drives in search of leopards. Page 209.

ZIWA RHINO AND WILDLIFE RANCH One of East Africa's most exciting wildlife experiences is tracking white rhinos on foot at this well-wooded sanctuary en route to Murchison Falls and Kidepo Valley. Also a good site for shoebills. Page 172.

KASUBI TOMBS Inscribed as a UNESCO World Heritage Site in 2001, this burial place of four *kabakas* (Kings of Buganda) on the outskirts of Kampala is one of the most striking traditional constructions in sub-Saharan Africa. Page 153.

MABAMBA SWAMP Protected as part of a community project, this Lake Victoria wetland offers an excellent chance of spotting shoebill – and myriad other water-associated birds – within 45 minutes' drive of Entebbe. Page 117.

THE SSESE ISLANDS Accessible by ferry from Entebbe or Masaka, these lushly forested islands in the heart of Lake Victoria arguably rank as Uganda's most underrated chill-out venue. Page 199.

ENTEBBE BOTANICAL GARDEN Forest birds and monkeys galore inhabit this lush, century-old botanical garden running down to the Lake Victoria shore, 10 minutes' drive from the international airport. Page 113.

KAMPALA It may not be one of the world's most compelling capitals, but perennially gridlocked Kampala – Uganda's only genuine city – has the country's liveliest nightlife and restaurants, as well as housing the national museum. Page 121.

TANDA PITS This revered sacrificial site an hour's drive west of Kampala ranks as probably the most important traditional shrine in Buganda, with strong links to the creation legend associated with the medieval Bachwezi cult. Page 176.

MABIRA FOREST RESERVE The most important biodiversity hotspot within day-tripping distance of Kampala is home to 300 bird species, the endemic Uganda mangabey, and a thrilling new canopy zip line connecting six platforms. Page 168.

NAKAYIMA TREE The best-known Bachwezi-associated sacrificial site in Buganda, the magnificently buttressed, centuries-old Nakayima Tree is associated with the eponymous fertility spirit and attended by a powerful matriarchal priestess. Page 180.

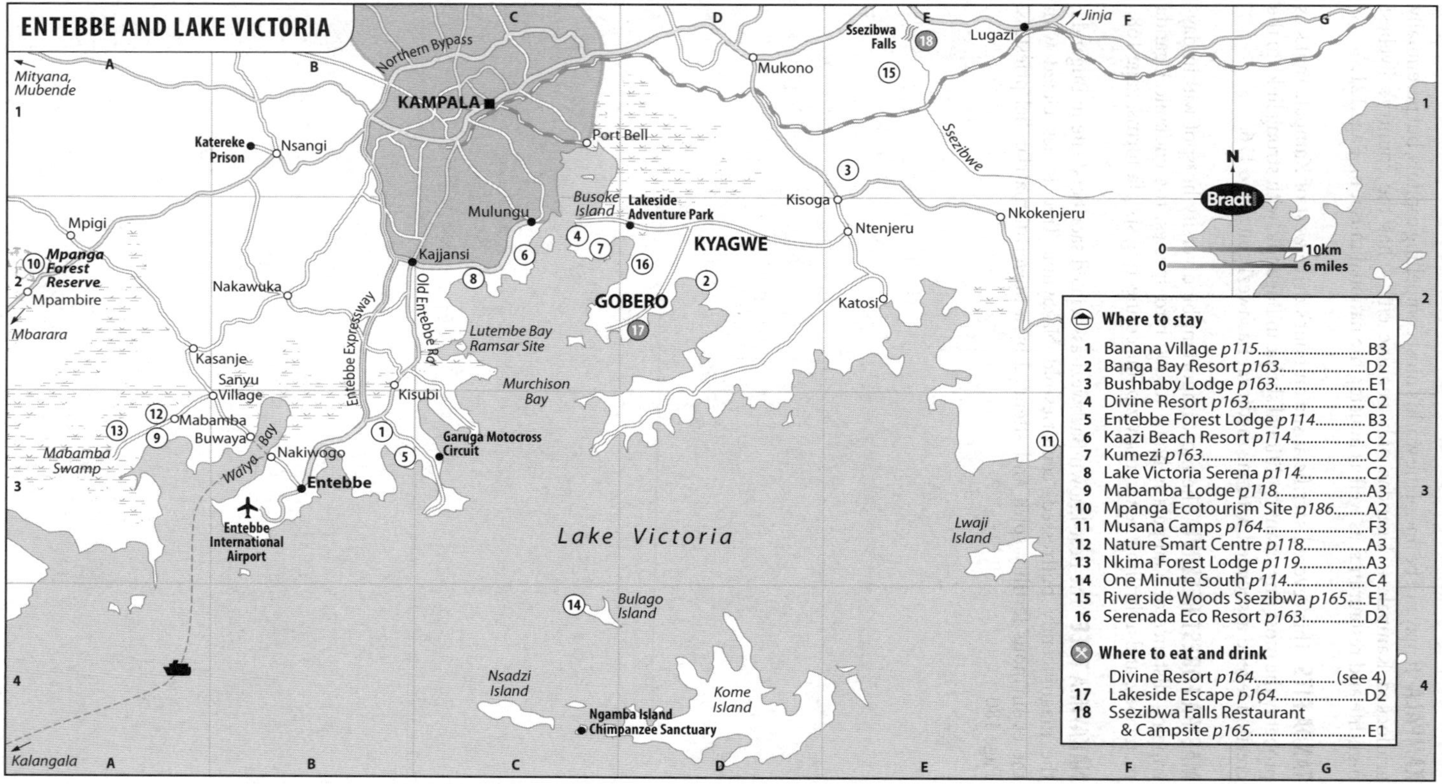
ENTEBBE AND LAKE VICTORIA
Mityana, Mubende
Katereke Prison
Nsangi
Mpigi
Mpanga Forest Reserve
Mpambire
Mbarara
Nakawuka
Kasanje
Sanyu Village
Mabamba
Buwaya
Mabamba Swamp
Waiya Bay
Nakiwogo
Entebbe
Entebbe International Airport
Kalangala
Northern Bypass
KAMPALA
Port Bell
Mulungu
Kajjansi
Entebbe Expressway
Old Entebbe Rd
Kisubi
Garuga Motocross Circuit
Lutembe Bay Ramsar Site
Murchison Bay
Busoke Island
Lakeside Adventure Park
GOBERO
KYAGWE
Mukono
Kisoga
Ntenjeru
Katosi
Ssezibwa Falls
Lugazi
Jinja
Ssezibwe
Nkokenjeru
Lake Victoria
Bulago Island
Nsadzi Island
Ngamba Island Chimpanzee Sanctuary
Kome Island
Lwaji Island
Bradt
N
0 10km
0 6 miles
Where to stay
1 Banana Village p115 ... B3
2 Banga Bay Resort p163 ... D2
3 Bushbaby Lodge p163 ... E1
4 Divine Resort p163 ... C2
5 Entebbe Forest Lodge p114 ... B3
6 Kaazi Beach Resort p114 ... C2
7 Kumezi p163 ... C2
8 Lake Victoria Serena p114 ... C2
9 Mabamba Lodge p118 ... A3
10 Mpanga Ecotourism Site p186 ... A2
11 Musana Camps p164 ... F3
12 Nature Smart Centre p118 ... A3
13 Nkima Forest Lodge p119 ... A3
14 One Minute South p114 ... C4
15 Riverside Woods Ssezibwa p165 ... E1
16 Serenada Eco Resort p163 ... D2
Where to eat and drink
Divine Resort p164 ... (see 4)
17 Lakeside Escape p164 ... D2
18 Ssezibwa Falls Restaurant & Campsite p165 ... E1

4

Entebbe, Mabamba and Surrounds

Tropical and verdant Entebbe, capital of Uganda during the colonial era, stands on the Lake Victoria shore a few hundred metres north of the equator and only 40km south of the modern capital Kampala. Though modestly proportioned by comparison with Kampala, Entebbe has long been the main port of entry to Uganda, thanks to the presence of the country's only international airport on the adjacent lakeshore. Yet for all its logistical significance, Entebbe is a remarkably unfocused and green town, carved haphazardly into the lakeshore jungle in such a manner that one might reasonably wonder whether most of its 70,000-plus residents haven't packed up their tents and gone on holiday.

Back in 1913, Sir Frederick Treves arrived at Entebbe fresh from the ports of Mwanza and Kisumu, and described it as: 'the prettiest and most charming town of the lake…a summer lake resort where no more business is undertaken than is absolutely necessary. The town spreads in a languid careless way to the lake…the golf links are more conspicuous than the capital.' Almost a century later, as Entebbe entered the new millennium, it remained much as Treves had described it: surely the only former or extant African capital whose tallest buildings were dwarfed by the antiquated trees of the botanical garden, and whose golf course was more expansive than the nominal town centre.

Even today, Entebbe retains an unusually green feel, not least because its main roads divert around the market suburb of Kitoro (which shelters a sizeable proportion of those seemingly absent residents). But, make no mistake, business is booming, much of it on the back of a service industry catering to a steady influx of UN personnel, tourists and other newly arrived air passengers. Indeed, unlike its soporific turn-of-the-millennium incarnation, Entebbe today is home to more than 100 hotels and guesthouses, not to mention an excellent selection of eateries, banks, bars, shops, and a pair of modern malls.

Entebbe's hotels vary widely in standard and character, but tend to be pricey in comparison with other towns in Uganda. This would appear to present a dilemma: pay over the odds to stay in Entebbe, or head to Kampala for better value for money. The answer, assuming you're just there for a night or two, and that natural history is your priority, is a no-brainer: stay in Entebbe. Any financial saving made in Kampala will be offset by the tedium of sitting in the capital's appalling traffic. Far better to use that time ticking off birds in Entebbe Botanical Garden, exploring the neighbouring Uganda Wildlife Education Centre, or relaxing on the beach before heading directly upcountry the following day. If you plan on dallying longer, Entebbe is also a better base than Kampala for visits to two of the most compelling wildlife destinations in the vicinity of the two cities: the Jane Goodall-sanctioned chimpanzee orphanage on Ngamba Island, and the bird-rich Mabamba Swamp with its easily spotted shoebills. Furthermore, a night in Entebbe prior to departure will eliminate the possibility of missing your flight due to congestion in or en route from Kampala.

HISTORY

Entebbe has been the main port of arrival for international visitors to Uganda for about as long as the country has been receiving them. The first such newbies consisted of a boatload of French missionaries who landed there in 1879 following a 300km lake crossing from Mwanza in present-day Tanzania. Theirs was a stormy and dangerous journey (legend has it that the boat disintegrated as soon as they made landfall) but the journey to Uganda soon became more comfortable with the completion of the Uganda Railway in 1901. A two-day train ride brought travellers from Mombasa to the Lake Victoria port of Kisumu for an overnight steamer voyage to Entebbe pier. Conveniently for arriving civil servants, Entebbe was the capital of the Uganda Protectorate with the offices of the British administration 5 minutes' walk uphill from the pier.

During the 1930s, Entebbe surrendered its mantle as Uganda's *entrepôt* to Kampala, firstly when the railway was extended there, leaving the lake steamers high and dry, and secondly with the introduction of the Empire flying boat service from the UK, which landed in the relatively sheltered bay off Kampala's Port Bell rather than on Entebbe's choppy waters. Entebbe regained its status after technological advances made during World War II enabled non-stop flights from Europe to land there. Entebbe's bumpy airstrip was upgraded to create Uganda's first international airport in 1951. This first terminal (which was the site of the 1976 Entebbe Raid described below) is now the UN Regional Service Centre (which co-ordinates UN activities in Uganda's more temperamental neighbours), while passenger traffic passes through a second terminal. Entebbe served as the

THE ENTEBBE INCIDENT

Entebbe achieved instant immortality on 27 June 1976 when an Air France airbus flying from Israel was hijacked by Palestinian terrorists and forced to land there. Non-Jewish passengers were released and the remainder held hostage against the demand that certain terrorists be freed from Israeli jails. In response, on 4 July 1976, a group of Israeli paratroopers stormed the airport in a daring surprise raid that resulted in all the hostages being freed. During the hijack, Amin pretended to play a mediating role between the Israeli government and the hijackers, but his complicity soon became apparent. A 75-year-old Israeli woman called Dora Bloch, who had been rushed into a Ugandan hospital after choking on her food, was killed by Amin's agents. Afterwards, incensed that the Israelis had been allowed to refuel in Nairobi before flying to Entebbe, Amin killed some hundreds of Kenyans resident in Uganda and broke off relations with his eastern neighbour, effectively ending the already tenuous East African community.

The dramatic events of 1976 have been re-enacted in numerous movies. Quickest off the mark was *Victory at Entebbe*, an all-star, made-for-TV affair that featured the likes of Anthony Hopkins, Elizabeth Taylor, Richard Dreyfuss and Kirk Douglas, and was first broadcast in December 1976. Newer but somewhat less stellar is the 2018 release simply called *Entebbe* in the UK and *7 days in Entebbe* in the USA.

EARLY DAYS IN ENTEBBE

The name 'Entebbe' derives from the Luganda phrase 'Entebe za Mugala' ('Headquarters of Mugala', head of the lungfish clan) and thus literally means 'Headquarters' – somewhat prescient, given that it would later serve as the British administrative capital of Uganda. Entebbe's prominence as a harbour is essentially a modern phenomenon: even into the 1890s, it was too remote from the centre of Baganda political activity to be of comparable significance to Munyonyo and Kaazi on Murchison Bay. But Entebbe's potential was hinted at as early as 1879 by the French missionaries Lourdel and Amans, who noted that 'the port...is large and very well sheltered; on the shore there are no more than three or four houses for travellers'.

Entebbe's potential was first realised in 1896, with the arrival of a European steamship on Lake Victoria – shipped from Scotland to Mombasa, from where it was transported to Port Florence (Kisumu) in pieces by a caravan of porters! And it was sealed in 1901, when the railway line from Mombasa finally reached Port Florence, allowing travellers to and from the coast to reach Entebbe directly by the combination of train and ferry. Within two years, Entebbe had replaced Kampala as the colonial administrative capital – though Kampala would remain capital of the Buganda kingdom throughout the colonial era.

W E Hoyle, who arrived in Uganda in 1903, would later recall that Entebbe, not Kampala, 'was then regarded as the "metropolis" of Uganda'. This switch evidently occurred in 1901, judging by a lamentation published in the *Mengo Notes* late that year: 'The traders in Uganda are not very numerous...we know of...only two Germans [who] have both left Kampala and now appear to be doing chiefly wholesale business in Entebbe.' By 1903, certainly, Entebbe had a greater population of European residents than Kampala, most prominently the commissioner of Uganda and his administrative officers, who were 'mostly living in houses with thatched roofs'. By 1904, Entebbe even boasted a hotel, the Equatorial, evidently the precursor of the present-day Lake Victoria Hotel, owned by an Italian couple whose 'charming daughter', according to Hoyle, 'became engaged to the first English postmaster...' Neither spoke the other's language, but both knew Swahili, so that little problem was solved.

Entebbe served as administrative capital of Uganda into the 1960s, and still houses a few government departments to this day, but its claims to outrank Kampala in the metropolitan stakes were rather more short-lived. Sir Frederick Treves wrote in 1913 that Entebbe 'is as unlike a capital as any place can well be, while as for administration it must be of that kind which is associated with a deck-chair, a shady veranda, the chink of ice on glass, and the curling smoke of a cigar'. Norma Lorimer, who visited 'gay little' Entebbe in the same year, paints a more pastoral picture: 'very tidy and clean and civilised...its gardens by the lake, full of gorgeous flowering trees and ferns, its red roads with no dust, and its enchanting views of the islands...Baganda moving about in their white *kanzus* on the red roads, silhouetted against a background of deep blue sky and tropical vegetation.'

seat of government for much of the colonial era, but relinquished this status to Kampala – traditionally, the head of the Buganda kingdom – following independence in 1962.

GETTING THERE AND AWAY

BY AIR Uganda's main port of entry is Entebbe International Airport, 3km from Entebbe town. For arrival procedures at Entebbe, and a full list of international airlines that fly there, see page 66.

BY PUBLIC TRANSPORT The road to Kampala is well served by matatus, which leave the capital every few minutes from the Old Taxi Park. Additional parks for Entebbe can be found 15 minutes' walk away behind the Nakivubo Stadium and in shabby Katwe suburb, but neither are in areas you'd want to aim for after dark. Some taxis head straight down the old Entebbe Road while others follow the new Expressway. If travelling in the opposite direction, you'll find Entebbe's taxi park [110 B4] tucked away in the warts-and-all suburb of Kitoro, 1km south out of the town centre, off the Airport Road. You can also board matatus to Kampala opposite the Municipal Council office next to the golf club. If you're using public transport to travel from Entebbe to southwestern Uganda (or vice versa), you can dodge Kampala's central taxi/bus parks. Take a matatu to Natete taxi park on the southern edge of the city and transfer to a vehicle headed to your destination.

BY CAR Self-driving between Kampala and Entebbe used to be a bumper-to-bumper procession, especially during peak hours, when queues to enter or leave the capital extended out for some kilometres. But while the interminable crawl still exists on the old Entebbe Road, self-drivers can now bypass it by taking the splendid new dual-carriage Entebbe Expressway, a toll road (US$1.50) that diverges from the old road about 8km out of Entebbe to join Kampala's Northern Bypass at Busega and connect to routes to western and northern Uganda. If driving out from Kampala, try to avoid joining the Expressway at the congested Busega intersection. If in northern Kampala, approach using the Northern Bypass; if in the south or southeast, utilise another dual carriageway that runs west from the southeastern lake suburb of Munyonyo to join the Expressway (and old Entebbe Road) at Kajanssi.

The Expressway remains surprisingly lightly trafficked, from which we might infer that the ongoing congestion on the Old Entebbe Road is because most drivers are involved in short, local hops rather than a full Kampala–Entebbe commute. This is a bonus during the day but less so at night, when the Expressway can feel lonely and potentially vulnerable; indeed the road gained a reputation for banditry soon after opening. Recent consultations with the authorities suggest that police patrols on the road are considered adequate to discourage wrongdoers. That said, many drivers still prefer to take the old Entebbe Road after hours and it would be prudent to ask for an update.

If driving yourself to Masaka and beyond, you can avoid the chaos of Kampala entirely (and save yourself a useful US$1.50) by heading north along the old Entebbe Road for 12km to Kisubi, then turning left as if heading to Mabamba Swamp, and zigzagging cross-country on dirt roads via Nakawuka and Kasanje to reach the Masaka Road near Mpigi. See page 189 for further details.

BY FERRY Entebbe's Nakiwogo port [107 A1] offers a free vehicle ferry across Waiya Bay to Buwaya, 20km from Mpigi, which shuttles across the bay throughout the day from around 07.30. This is not necessarily a time saver since a backlog of waiting vehicles may mean you have to wait for a second or even third crossing. Nor is it particularly convenient for pedestrians headed upcountry since you'll probably

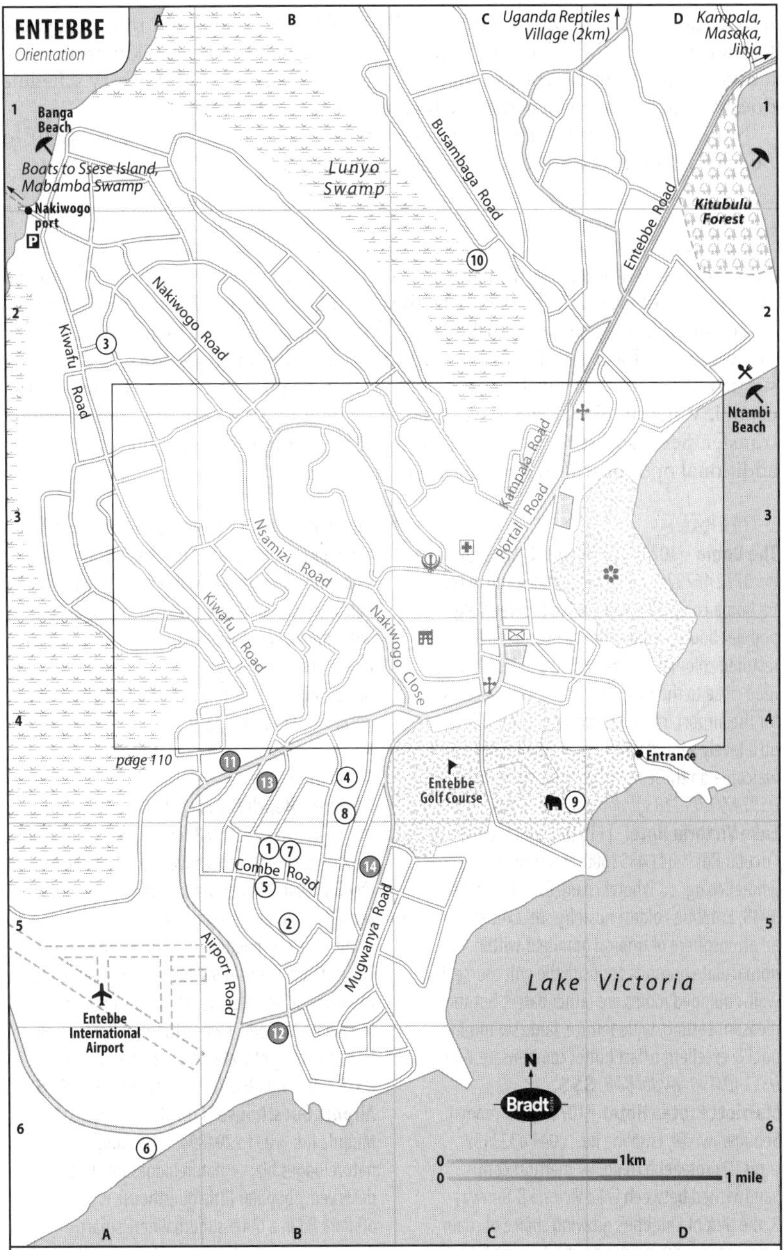

For listings, see from page 108

Where to stay

1	Airport Guesthouse	B5
2	Askay Hotel Suites	B5
3	Blue Monkey Guesthouse	A2
4	The Boma	B4
5	The Guineafowl	B5
6	Marriott Protea	A6
7	No 5 Boutique	B5
8	Sunset Entebbe	B4
9	Uganda Wildlife Education Centre	C4
10	ViaVia	C2

Where to eat and drink

11	4 Point	B4
12	Faze 3	B6
13	Muti	B4
14	Thai	B5

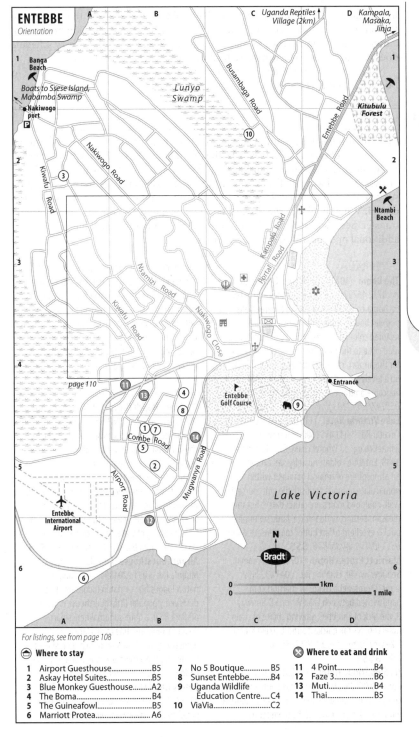

have to take a boda to Mpigi, where you'll be unlikely to find public transport going further west than Masaka. It is, however (if you're happy with a 16km boda ride), a useful route from Entebbe to Mabamba Swamp (page 117). If the ferry schedule doesn't match yours, you can hire a boat to cross the bay for about US$3.

Nakiwogo is also the site of the daily passenger/vehicle ferry (dep 14.00) to Buggala Island in the Ssese Archipelago (page 199).

WHERE TO STAY

More than 100 hotels, guesthouses and other accommodation options are scattered around Entebbe, and the following listings are highly selective. Room prices tend to be considerably higher than in Kampala, a generalisation that includes the cluster of overpriced local guesthouses around the taxi park in the scruffy but bustling suburb of Kitoro, so travellers on a tight budget might prefer to head north to the capital. When booking, check whether your hotel offers a complimentary airport transfer. See also listings for Kampala Road and Murchison Bay on page 114 for additional options within reach of the airport.

UPMARKET

The Boma [107 B4] (16 rooms) Gowers Rd; m 0772 467929; e bomareception@gmail.com; w boma.co.ug. This welcoming & perennially popular boutique guesthouse occupies a tastefully restored colonial homestead on a quiet suburban road close to the town centre. It's well placed for the airport, rates include a full English b/fast on a lovely veranda, & the swimming pool is welcome on those hot equatorial afternoons. *US$147/170/218 sgl/dbl/trpl B&B.* **$$$**

Lake Victoria Hotel [110 D4] (144 rooms) Circular Rd; 041 4351600; e reservations@lvhotel.co.ug; w lvhotel.co.ug. Established in 1948, Entebbe's oldest hostelry still exudes an atmosphere of tropical grandeur within immaculate grounds opposite the golf course. The well-equipped rooms are rather dated, but the pleasant setting, wide terrace, large swimming pool & excellent b/fast buffet compensate. *From US$140/190 sgl/dbl B&B.* **$$$**

Marriott Protea Hotel [107 A6] (73 rooms) Sebugwawo Dr, Entebbe Rd; 041 4323132; e res1@proteaebb.co.ug; w marriott.com. Sandwiched between Lake Victoria & Runway 2, the pick of Entebbe's growing choice of chain hotels enjoys the quickest airport access & best lake view in town. *From US$215/250 sgl/dbl B&B.* **$$$$**

No 5 Boutique Hotel [107 B5] (15 rooms) Edna Rd; m 0797 282908; e bookings@hotelnumber5.com; w hotelnumber5.com. Set in quiet suburbia within walking distance of the town centre, this modern, top-of-the-range boutique hotel overlooks a palm-shaded garden with a lovely swimming pool area & well-equipped gym. The balcony restaurant offers fine dining complete with international wine list, while a ground floor diner serves oven-baked pizzas & fresh pasta dishes. Airport transfers US$10. *US$415/450 sgl/dbl or twin B&B.* **$$$$$**

MODERATE

2 Friends Beach Hotel [110 G1] (16 rooms) Nambi Rd; m 0755 148873; e stay@2friends.info; w 2friendshotel.com. Conveniently located for Victoria Mall (10mins' walk) & the lakeshore (30 seconds), this owner-managed lodge centres on a small, cosy compound with swimming pool & bar. The outlook is considerably more expansive from the lake-facing balconies of the 1st-floor rooms & the adjacent, hotel-owned Hinriksh Restaurant, one of a string of waterfront eateries (mains cost US$8–20). *From US$100/120 sgl/dbl B&B.* **$$$**

Airport Guesthouse [107 B5] (10 rooms) Mugula Rd; 031 2294894; e booking@naturelodges.biz; w naturelodges.biz. This deservedly popular little guesthouse is found off Park Rd in a quiet suburb where smart & comfortable en-suite rooms face a pretty garden with much to offer birders. Conveniently located for the airport & very reasonably priced. *US$60/70/90 sgl/dbl/trpl B&B.* **$$$**

Gately Inn [110 E3] (11 rooms) Portal Rd; 041 4321313; m 0777 555966; e gatelyinnoffice@gmail.com; w gatelyinn.com. The en-suite rooms & cottages at this attentively managed guesthouse use natural materials such as stone, reed, wood, rough plaster & traditional fabrics. The comfortable terrace restaurant serves good food & is a delightful spot to spend time. Light sleepers might be put off by the traffic noise. Good value following a plunge in rates. *From US$60/90 sgl/dbl B&B.* **$$$**

The Guineafowl [107 B5] (7 rooms) Mugula Rd; m 0771 980390; e info@theguineafowlentebbe.com; w theguineafowlentebbe.com. Top value in its range is this outstanding owner-managed boutique guesthouse notable for its vibrant but uncluttered décor, cheerful & engaged staff, pan-African music selection & lovely setting in a sprawling, tree-shaded garden alive with birds & scattered with tables & chairs. Airy en-suite rooms have walk-in nets & modern bathroom with quality fittings. The cosmopolitan & imaginative all-day menu is strong on salads, wraps & pitas, pasta & grills, mostly in the US$6–8 range, & has a good dessert & smoothie & juice selection. Excellent value. *From US$70–85/85–95 sgl/dbl B&B; US$20 pp camping.* **$$$**

Karibu Entebbe [110 B1] (9 rooms) 84 Nsamizi Rd; m 0777 044984; e night@karibuguesthouse.com; w karibuguesthouse.com. A favourite with travellers flying in or out of the nearby airport, this boutique guesthouse has stylish rooms finished with meticulous attention to detail. A swimming pool is tucked away in the pretty garden while the well-appointed terrace restaurant serves beautifully presented Mediterranean-influenced dishes. *US$180/216 sgl/dbl B&B.* **$$$$**

Papyrus Guesthouse [110 B1] (15 rooms) Uringi Cres; m 0787 778424; e papyrusguesthouse@nkuringolodges.com; w papyrusguesthouse.com. Centred on a 1940s residence, this reputable guesthouse is located 15mins' drive from the airport & 1km north of the town centre. While rooms in the old house are decent value, treat yourself to a modern room in the garden to best appreciate the compact but lush compound. *US$55/110 sgl/dbl; garden rooms US$68/130 sgl/dbl B&B.* **$$$**

BUDGET

Anderita Beach Hotel [110 G1] (40 rooms) Nambi Rd; m 0772 665616; e reservations@anderitabeachhotel.com; w anderitabeachhotel.com. This unremarkable but attractively priced hotel is notable for its splendid location on Nambi Rd opposite a line of waterfront bars & restaurants, which include one owned by the Anderita. *From US$45/60/70 sgl/dbl/twin en-suite rooms.* **$$**

Askay Hotel Suites [107 B5] (19 rooms) Mugula Rd; m 0789 300000; e info@askayhotelsuites.com; w askayhotelsuites.com. Set in a green garden & with comfortable rooms provided with AC & DSTV, this smart 3-storey hotel is the best-value central option in this category. *US$45/55/80 sgl/dbl/suite.* **$$$**

Blue Monkey Guesthouse [107 A2] (6 rooms) Buwaya Rise; m 0782 942237; e guesthouse@bluemonkey.ug; w bluemonkey.ug. This German-owned & -managed guesthouse stands in a pretty suburban garden 3km north of the town centre. Small but cheerful en-suite rooms are decorated with ethnic fabrics & come with 2m-long bed, fitted nets, locally crafted toiletries & filtered drinking water. No restaurant but can arrange take-aways. *US$48/53 sgl/dbl using shared bathroom; US$48 dbl tent; US$75 en-suite dbl. All rates B&B.* **$$–$$$**

Sunset Entebbe [107 B4] (18 rooms) Church Rd; m 0776 323501; e enquiries@sunsetentebbe.com; w sunsetentebbe.com. Housed in a colonial bungalow in a pretty garden, this guesthouse offers comfortable, tiled en-suite rooms with nets, fan & DSTV. *From US$50/70 sgl/dbl B&B.* **$$**

Uganda Wildlife Education Centre (UWEC) [107 C4] (8 cottages) t 041 4320520; e reservation@uwec.ug; w uwec.ug. Ever wondered what happens in a zoo when the visitors go home? Try the basic but roomy en-suite bandas at UWEC. Twin beds are provided downstairs & on a mezzanine platform. Meals are available in the UWEC café. The cottages are several hundred metres inside the zoo; hire a boda if you've got luggage & no vehicle. *US$40/50/120 sgl/dbl/family cottage. Rates inc UWEC entrance fee but exc meals which are available in the café. US$20 pp camping; advance booking required.* **$$**

✷ **ViaVia** [107 C2] (16 rooms & 1 dorm) Kisalu Rd; ⊕ 0.0783575, 32.4720319; m 0781 524991, 0792 333066; e traveluganda@viavia.world; w entebbe.viavia.world. This eco-friendly Belgian-owned & -managed travellers' lodge stands in a large garden whose ponds & fruiting trees attract daily visits by the gorgeous Ross's & great blue turaco as well as more sporadic showings by bushbuck, sitatunga & vervet monkey. A sociable

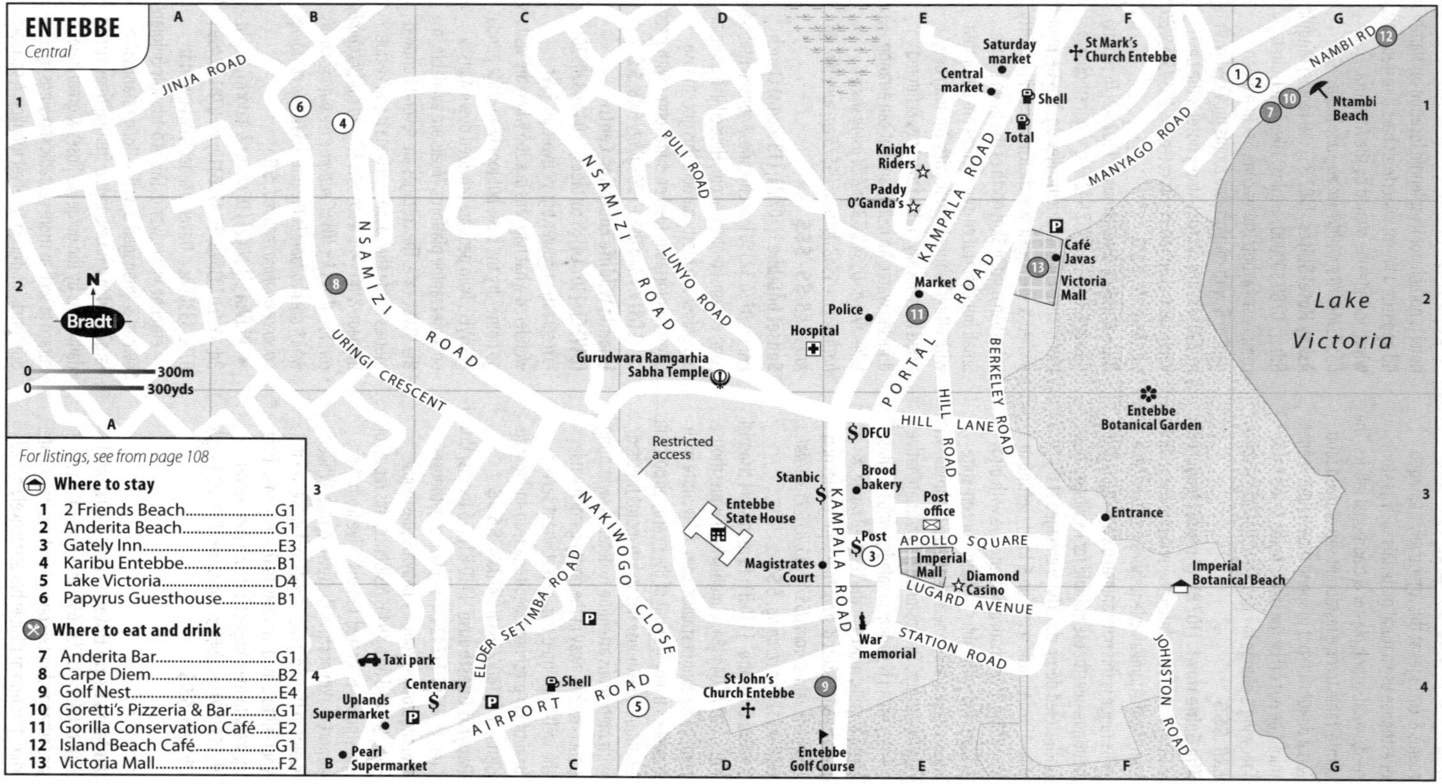
ENTEBBE
Central
JINJA ROAD
NSAMIZI ROAD
URINGI CRESCENT
PULI ROAD
LUNYO ROAD
NAKIWOGO CLOSE
ELDER SETIMBA ROAD
AIRPORT ROAD
KAMPALA ROAD
PORTAL ROAD
HILL LANE
HILL ROAD
BERKELEY ROAD
MANYAGO ROAD
NAMBI RD
APOLLO SQUARE
LUGARD AVENUE
STATION ROAD
JOHNSTON ROAD
Saturday market
Central market
St Mark's Church Entebbe
Shell
Total
Knight Riders
Paddy O'Ganda's
Café Javas
Victoria Mall
Market
Police
Hospital
Gurudwara Ramgarhia Sabha Temple
DFCU
Restricted access
Stanbic
Brood bakery
Post office
Post
Entebbe State House
Magistrates Court
Imperial Mall
Diamond Casino
War memorial
St John's Church Entebbe
Entebbe Golf Course
Taxi park
Centenary
Uplands Supermarket
Pearl Supermarket
Ntambi Beach
Lake Victoria
Entebbe Botanical Garden
Entrance
Imperial Botanical Beach
Bradt
N
0 300m
0 300yds
For listings, see from page 108
Where to stay
1 2 Friends Beach........G1
2 Anderita Beach........G1
3 Gately Inn........E3
4 Karibu Entebbe........B1
5 Lake Victoria........D4
6 Papyrus Guesthouse........B1
Where to eat and drink
7 Anderita Bar........G1
8 Carpe Diem........B2
9 Golf Nest........E4
10 Goretti's Pizzeria & Bar........G1
11 Gorilla Conservation Café........E2
12 Island Beach Café........G1
13 Victoria Mall........F2

& shady terrace restaurant/bar serves full meals (US$7–8), snacks (US$3–4) & draught beer, supported by live music on Fri nights. Brightly decorated en-suite rooms have fitted nets & private balcony, & there is also a 6-bed dorm & glamping yurts (shared facilities) on platforms overlooking the wetland. Other attractions include a spa & massage centre, book swap & table tennis. Reception can arrange day excursions to Mabamba Swamp, sunset cruises & various boda, bicycle & walking tours. *US$40/50/60 sgl/dbl/twin garden room; US$60/80 sgl/dbl pond-view room; US$60/70 glamping sgl/dbl; US$15 pp dorm bed; US$12 pp camping. All rates B&B.* **$$–$$$**

WHERE TO EAT AND DRINK

Entebbe offers a broad choice of international cuisine and most restaurants are easy to reach on foot or by boda (unlike in Kampala where the appeal of going out for a meal is diminished by the bother of getting there). The only location to vaguely resemble an entertainment hub is the lakeside Nambi Road, whose selection of eateries includes Goretti's Pizzeria, a few restaurants owned by nearby hotels, plus a few basic beer 'n' barbecue snack joints.

MODERATE TO EXPENSIVE

Carpe Diem [110 B2] Uringi Cres; m 0785 711332. This terraced diner on the hillside above Kitoro offers a great view over Waiya Bay, making it a perfect place to end the day with a sundowner drink while choosing from an attractively varied menu that includes seafood options. *Mains US$7–12; seafood US$15–20.*

Faze 3 [107 B6] Circular Rd; 039 3671345. Excellent steaks & whole tilapia. The lake-facing deck attracts a welcome breeze, but you may prefer to eat indoors if the lake flies are out. *Mains US$8–12.*

Goretti's Pizzeria & Bar [110 G1] Nambi Rd; m 0772 308887. This popular Italian-themed eatery has a wood-fired pizza oven & a smashing location right beside the lake. Service can be slow, so it's not the place to eat before a flight. *Meals US$8–13.*

Thai Restaurant [107 B5] Circular Rd; m 0782 030284. A tempting Thai menu has popped up at a few locations around Entebbe in recent years, its current home being the green garden setting of the Entebbe Palm Hotel. *US$10–14 main & rice.*

CHEAP TO MODERATE

4 Point [107 B4] Airport Rd; 039 2001517. Popular with the local UN crowd, this open-plan diner boasts Entebbe's most ambitious menu with hit & occasional miss interpretations on Indian, Chinese, Thai & Mexican themes. *Mains US$8–12.*

Anderita Bar [110 G1] Nambi Rd. This basic waterfront bar, situated directly opposite the eponymous hotel, is a pleasant spot to enjoy a cheap drink & snack.

Golf Nest [110 E4] Airport Rd; m 0772 555360; 08.30–21.30 daily. A leafy colonial relict with an appealingly rundown demeanour that evokes what passed for an upmarket eating experience in Uganda in the early 1990s, the unpretentious veranda restaurant at the golf club offers grills, stews & burgers. Whole grilled tilapia is a speciality. *Mains in the US$4–5 range.*

Gorilla Conservation Café [110 E2] Portal Rd. Set in a restored bungalow on the main road through town, this relaxed coffee shop offers a pleasant alternative to the brand-name eateries in nearby Victoria Mall, serving burgers, sandwiches, wraps, etc. Profits go to the NGO Conservation Through Public Health. *US$6–9.*

Island Beach Café [110 G1] Nambi Rd; m 0755 200234; 08.30–21.30 daily. Ethiopian-owned beach house serving spicy Ethiopian dishes as well as steaks, fish & other grills. *Mains US$6–8.*

Muti [107 B4] Queen's Rd; m 0789 593196. Delightful suburban garden café set in appealingly dense tropical vegetation. A large pizza & burger selection is supplemented by salads, pasta dishes, sandwiches & a good b/fast selection. *Most dishes in the US$5–10 range.*

Victoria Mall [110 F2] Entebbe's smartest shopping mall offers branches of Café Javas & KFC within & a smart, covered shawarma den without. Though the choice in the 1st-floor food hall remains limited after the Covid-19 pandemic, a wall of foliage provided by the forest trees in the adjacent Botanical Garden creates a marvellous backdrop.

ENTERTAINMENT AND NIGHTLIFE

NIGHTCLUBS A few late-night venues are located on Kampala Road, 500m downhill from the town centre behind the Shell and Total fuel stations. The pick of these are currently **Paddy O' Gandas** [110 E1] and **Knight Riders** [110 E1]. The **Diamond Casino** [110 E3] is on Lugard Avenue next to Imperial Mall.

CINEMA The two-screen Nu Max cinema (m 0707 000488) in the Victoria Mall [110 F2] shows recent international releases. Afternoon and evening screenings.

SHOPPING

Victoria Mall [110 F2], just south of the main road on the way to Kampala, is your go-to destination for pre-safari requirements. The **MTN** service centre will register you for a local SIM and phone/internet package while **Carrefour supermarket** ⌚ 08.00–21.00 Mon–Sat, 08.30–19.00 Sun) is the town's best one-stop source of meats, bread, vegetables, packaged goods and beer, wine and other beverages (if, however, quality rather than convenience is paramount, for bakery products you'll need the Dutch-owned **Brood bakery** [110 E3] and for meats and cheeses, the **Quality Cuts delicatessen** (m 0707 571600) in Imperial Mall [110 E3]). Also in Victoria Mall, **Lifestyle Tactical Training** [110 E3] (m 0754 244838; f lifestyletacticaluganda) sells imported rucksacks, hiking boots, multitools and torches, though with hefty price tags. There are also plenty of options for a lunch stop (page 111).

Elsewhere, you'll find **Pearl Supermarket** [110 B4] at the turning off Airport Road into Kitoro, and the perennial **Uplands Supermarket** [110 B4], aka 'John's shop', 100m further down the same road. The main market for fresh produce is also in Kitoro. Decent **gift shops** are found at the Uganda Wildlife Education Centre, Gately Inn, and on Lugard Avenue opposite the Imperial Mall.

OTHER PRACTICALITIES

HAIRDRESSING Aisha Salon in Victoria Mall [110 F2] keeps the UN crowd looking neat and tidy.

MEDICAL The best clinic is the branch of Kenya's **AAR Health Centre** [110 F2] (m 0781 039614/0715 159573; ⌚ 09.00–21.00 Mon–Sat, 10.00–16.00 Sun) in Victoria Mall. Pharmacies are prevalent throughout the town.

LUGGAGE STORAGE The Lake Victoria Hotel (page 108) is usually happy to store luggage for day visitors using the swimming pool or taking lunch.

SWIMMING The pool at the Lake Victoria Hotel (page 108) is open to non-residents for US$6.50.

WHAT TO SEE AND DO

If you're exploring the town independently, look for the Entebbe title (No 13) in the Uganda Maps series. Otherwise, a free app and downloadable map of historical buildings in Entebbe, supported by the European Union, was published by the Cross-Cultural Foundation of Uganda in 2019 and is available at w crossculturalfoundation.or.ug/historical-sites-more-resources.

ENTEBBE BOTANICAL GARDEN [110 F2–3] (entrance US$3/6 FR/FNR) Established in 1902, Entebbe's botanical garden is an attractively laid-out mix of indigenous forest, cultivation and horticulture, and a highly attractive destination to birdwatchers. The botanical garden offers an excellent introduction to Uganda's birds, ranging from Lake Victoria specials such as grey kestrel, yellow-throated leaflove, slender-billed weaver, orange weaver and Jackson's golden-backed weaver to the more widespread but nonetheless striking black-headed gonolek, red-chested sunbird, grey-capped warbler and brown-throated wattle-eye. The impressive palmnut vulture and African fish eagle are both common, while forest birds include the splendid Ross's and great blue turaco, African grey parrot, and noisy black-and-white casqued hornbill. As for mammals, the sitatunga and hippos that once frequented the lakeshore are long gone, but you can be confident of seeing vervet and black-and-white colobus monkeys, as well as tree squirrels.

At bizarre variance to the idea of the gardens as a peaceful retreat, the pretty lakeside at the southern end of the gardens is now occupied by the lively Forest Beach, a low-key resort. Here, should you so wish, you can put away your binoculars and join a host of young Ugandans as they enjoy boat rides, frolic in the shallows (beware of bilharzia; page 70) and oscillate to music played at memorable volume (but which, thanks to surrounding vegetation, is inaudible from the rest of the gardens).

UGANDA WILDLIFE EDUCATION CENTRE [107 C4] (041 4320520; m 0788 788456, 0707 750108; e info@uwec.ug; w uwec.ug; 08.30–18.30 daily; entrance US$10/15 FR/FNR) Established as a sanctuary for animals unable to fend for themselves in the wild, this orphanage has played an important role in the protection of rare and threatened animals. Residents include a few lions (whose nocturnal vocalisations add a distinct sense of place to a night in any nearby hotel), a pair of reintroduced black rhinos, and a variety of smaller predators that are seldom seen in the wild. The aviary provides the most reliable opportunity in Uganda to get a close-up shot of the renowned shoebill. Other, costlier options include a 2–3-hour 'Behind the Scenes' tour (US$50/70 pp FR/FNR; children half price; starts 09.00 & 14.30), 'Chimpanzee Close Up' (US$290 pp; starts 07.30) and 'Keeper for a Day' (US$75/150 pp FR/FNR).

GOLF [110 D4] (041 4322067; w entebbeclub.org; non-members US$20, club hire & caddies available) The open expanse of the 18-hole golf course sloping towards Lake Victoria is Entebbe's most distinctive feature on the drive towards the airport. It's one of few clubs worldwide where a hooked drive on the third might hit a rhino (in the neighbouring Wildlife Education Centre). Golfers should try for early-morning or late-afternoon starts to avoid the heat of the day.

UGANDA REPTILES VILLAGE [107 D1] (m 0782 349583; w ugandareptiles.com; entrance US$4) Established to encourage Ugandans to respect reptiles and in particular snakes, rather than automatically battering them to death, this worthwhile destination lies on the northwestern edge of Entebbe, 3km off the main road. You'll find a variety of snakes, chameleons, monitor lizards and a couple of crocodiles. It's a pretty site on the edge of the extensive Waiya Swamp; boat and birding voyages are available on a channel cut through to the open lake. Bottled refreshments are available but no food. A boda from Entebbe costs about US$2.

THE KAMPALA ROAD AND MURCHISON BAY

As far as most visitors to Uganda are concerned, the 40km Entebbe–Kampala peninsula is nothing more than a transit route between the capital and the airport. It does, however, provide access to a few low-key attractions, some decent scenery and some worthwhile accommodation. While the road corridor itself is now a ribbon of development, it runs parallel to the scenic Murchison Bay, which extends north from Entebbe for 40km before terminating at Kampala's Port Bell. A number of side roads, indicated on the 'Uganda Maps' Sheet No 3, *Beyond Kampala*, run east to the shores of Murchison Bay leaving the suburban sprawl behind to explore some still-unspoiled countryside.

WHERE TO STAY AND EAT These listings include accommodation in Murchison Bay (extending south to Bulago Island) and along its western margin. For accommodation on the eastern side (accessed from Kampala's Ggaba port), see page 163.

Exclusive

Entebbe Forest Lodge [102 B3] (8 rooms) Garuga Peninsula; ⊕ 0.0755224, 32.5417631; t 0703 927726; e manager@ebbforestlodge.com; w ebbforestlodge.com. This splendid & potentially game-changing lodge offers upmarket arrivals the opportunity of starting their safari cocooned by 15 acres of tropical forest on the shores of Lake Victoria. There are of course more convenient options in Entebbe town, but the 35min/15km drive to the lodge is not excessive & the prospect of planned boat transfers from a marina by the airport sounds particularly exciting. Accommodation is in luxurious & meticulously finished stone & wood cottages, some with balconies facing the forest, others looking toward the lake; ideal locations to get your birding checklists off to a good start. If you're safari-bound, take the opportunity to relax by the pool, enjoy a massage in a forest glade, amble around the manicured lawns & enjoy your sundowner on the wave-cut platform beside the lake; upcountry Uganda will be an altogether dustier & more bumpy affair. **$$$$$**

One Minute South [102 C4] (5 rooms) Bulago Island; m 0776 709970; e ali@oneminutesouth.com; w oneminutesouth.com. This gorgeous & characterful private house occupies a terrific clifftop site overlooking the lake on a 500-acre private island. In addition to a pool with a view, a network of trails explores a fabulous mosaic of forest, grassland, panoramic hilltops & lovely lakeshores. 20mins' walk away, the upmarket Pineapple Bay Resort is a marvellously scenic destination for a drink. A flat fee gets you the run of the property, perhaps as the ultimate house party destination, or a delightfully self-indulgent getaway for a couple, or a once-in-a-lifetime trip for a group of fishing enthusiasts – following the creation of a Lake Protection Area around the island (marine park status is mooted), some impressively large Nile Perch have been hauled out in the vicinity. *US$700/night, sleeps up to 13 in 5 bedrooms. Add US$40 pp/day for FB meals. Rate exc US$500 for the return boat transfer on the beautiful* Silver Fulu *dhow (smaller & cheaper craft are available).* **$$$$$**

Upmarket

Kaazi Beach Resort [102 C2] (18 rooms) ⊕ 0.21989, 32.61913; m 0787 475009; e info@kaazibeachresort.com; w kaazibeachresort.com. Located beside Lake Victoria, just off the Munyonyo–Kajjansi highway & 2km west of Munyonyo, this new resort combines easy access to Kampala & the Entebbe Expressway. The lake views – fringed variously by swamp, suburbs & forest – can be enjoyed from the restaurant terrace (mains on the wide-ranging menu cost US$7–10); from the bedrooms (all have a veranda or balcony); from the large swimming pool (Ush15,000 to non-residents); or by chartering a boat & getting out on the water. In the opposite direction, the 1km approach to the resort is through several hectares of forest & bush owned by the Scouts Association, which should provide some worthwhile birding. *US$100/120 sgl/dbl B&B.* **$$$**

Lake Victoria Serena [102 C2] (120 rooms) 5km off Entebbe Rd; t 041 7121000; e lakevictoria@serena.co.ug;

w serenahotels.com. This 100ha lakeshore development has a striking main building with a high, airy atrium inspired by Zanzibari architecture, while accommodation blocks are modelled on Roman insulae complete with classical arches, pastel-toned walls & terracotta roofs. There's a beautiful swimming pool, a gym/sauna & a daunting 9-hole lakeside golf course rippling with water hazards (US$25/35 guests/visitors). For sheer style, the veranda of the golf clubhouse, which faces a tiny island containing the 9th green beyond a small but extremely exclusive marina, is difficult to beat in Uganda. A smashing location for a meal (US$10–15) or drink while easy airport access makes it an ideal location to spend a relaxing afternoon before a flight. *From US$303/350 sgl/dbl B&B; check website for specials.* **$$$$**

Budget

Banana Village [102 B3] (10 cottages) Off Garuga Rd; m 0706 115356, 0755 522552; e bananavillage@hotmail.com; w bananavillageuganda.com. This appealingly rustic lodge 10km north of Entebbe offers a selection of en-suite cottages in a garden site adjoining remnant forest. Birders will enjoy looking for the 100+ resident species while others relax around the swimming pool & garden bar. *From US$22/40/48 sgl/dbl/trpl B&B.* **$$**

WHAT TO SEE AND DO

Lutembe Bay Ramsar Site [102 C2] This small (just 98ha) wetland on the eastern side of the Kampala–Entebbe Road is notable for seasonal Palaearctic (26 species) and Afro-tropical (15) migrants. Regular surveys by Nature Uganda have recorded an average of 1,429,829 wetland birds. These include an average of 1,048,602 white-winged black terns, a figure representing more than half of the global population. The 108 species of waterbird recorded at the site include the globally vulnerable shoebill, Madagascar squacco heron, and the papyrus yellow warbler, the near-threatened papyrus gonolek, great snipe, African skimmer and pallid harrier, and 24 regionally threatened species such as the northern brown-throated weaver, great cormorant, slender-billed gull and (as previously mentioned) quite a lot of white-winged black terns. As far as getting there is concerned, contact one of the specialist bird guides (page 64) and arrange an excursion to get the best out of your visit.

Garuga Motocross Circuit (m 0703 122169; f UgandaMotorcrossTrackGaruga) [102 C3] Uganda MotoX Club puts on regular weekend events at its lakeside circuit, 10km off the Entebbe–Kampala Road on Garuga Peninsula. Competitions, which include club, national and regional-level events, make for a fun afternoon out.

NGAMBA ISLAND CHIMPANZEE SANCTUARY

[102 C4] (041 4320662; m 0758 221880; e reservations@ngambaisland.org; w ngambaisland.org) Situated 23km southeast of Entebbe, Ngamba is a formerly uninhabited 50ha island in the Kome Archipelago, which is separated from the northern shore of Lake Victoria by the 10km-wide Damba Channel. Supporting a rainforest environment that includes 50-plus plant species utilised by free-ranging chimps, Ngamba was established as a sanctuary in 1998, when 19 orphaned chimps, all of which had been saved from a life in captivity or a laboratory, were relocated there. Today, 53 chimpanzees, many captured illegally in the forests of the DRC and smuggled across to Uganda for trade, are resident on Ngamba.

The island is divided into two unequal parts, separated by an electric fence. On one side of the fence, a tented camp, visitors' centre and staff quarters extend over an area of about 1ha on a partially cleared stretch of northwestern shore notable for its immense weaver colonies. The rest of the island is reserved more-or-less exclusively for the chimps and their attendants.

The fenced-off part of the island offers plenty of room for the chimps to roam, but it isn't large enough to sustain the entire community – indeed, its area corresponds roughly to the natural range of one chimpanzee – so the chimps are fed a porridge-like mixture for breakfast, and then fruits and vegetables twice during the day. The fruits are given to the chimps from a viewing platform, which provides an opportunity for visitors to observe and photograph them through a fence.

The sanctuary aims to provide the best facilities and care to the captive chimpanzees, who are given the choice of staying in the forest overnight or returning to a holding facility built to enhance social integration and veterinary management. The management has elected not to allow the chimps to breed, so sexually mature females are given a contraceptive implant, which doesn't disrupt the community's normal sexual behaviour, but does prevent pregnancy. Accidents happen here as elsewhere, however, so the island's chimp community does include a few unplanned youngsters that were born there.

Ngamba Island is the flagship project of the Chimpanzee Sanctuary and Wildlife Conservation Trust, an affiliate of the Jane Goodall Institute. Proceeds from tourist visits contribute directly to the maintenance of the sanctuary and related projects, including an ongoing census of Uganda's wild chimpanzees, snare-removal programmes, and education and outreach initiatives in local communities.

Chimps aside, the public area of Ngamba hosts plenty of other wildlife. This includes some of the most monstrously large monitor lizards you're likely to see anywhere in Africa, and a good variety of aquatic birds including water thick-knee, spur-winged lapwing, hamerkop and various egrets and herons. It's a very pleasant, tranquil spot to hang out for a couple of hours, or even overnight.

GETTING THERE AND AWAY Motorboat crossings from Entebbe leave at 09.00 and 12.45 daily, take 45 minutes, and are operated by Ngamba itself, as well as by Wild Frontiers (page 64). The round trip costs US$365/188/132/110 per person for one/two/three/four-plus people, inclusive of entrance and chimpanzee-viewing fees. The only alternative to the boats is a helicopter charter. Transport can be arranged directly with Wild Frontiers or by using the sanctuary's contact details, or through any other operator in Kampala or Entebbe.

WHERE TO STAY AND EAT

Ngamba Eco-Lodge (4 cottages) ⊕ -0.10013, 32.65224; \ 041 4320662; m 0758 221880; e reservations@ngambaisland.org; w ngambaisland.org. This small camp next to the landing jetty offers accommodation in cosy stilted stone cottages with private verandas, solar lighting & en-suite hot shower. A good restaurant specialises in fish-based meals, & there's wonderful birdwatching. It's particularly beautiful in the evening, since it faces west to catch the sunset, & you'll see thousands of fruit bats streaming out of the forest. Rates are included in a variety of 2-plus night packages; details are found on the website. **$$$$$$**

WHAT TO SEE AND DO Day trips are timed to coincide with supplementary feeding times (11.00 and 14.30), when the chimpanzees come to within metres of a raised viewing platform, offering an excellent opportunity to observe and photograph one of our closest animal relatives. For overnight visitors, kayaks are available to explore the island bays and go searching for monitor lizards, otters and some of the 154 recorded bird species. Other optional activities include a visit to a local fishing village, a sunset cruise, and fishing, all of which can be arranged through the camp.

MABAMBA SWAMP

[102 A3] (m 0780 351047, 0784 751923; e mabambaswampshoebill@gmail.com) Only 12km west of Entebbe as the crow flies, the 100km^2 Mabamba Swamp is a Ramsar site and Important Bird Area that extends across a shallow marshy bay on the northern shore of Lake Victoria. Some 300 bird species have been recorded in the swamp, including an alluring selection of water-associated species, and it is also home to a relict population of sitatunga antelope and more than 200 varieties of butterfly. The prime attraction of Mabamba, however, is that it is the most reliable place in the vicinity of Entebbe – indeed, perhaps anywhere in the country – to look for the charismatic shoebill in the wild.

Dugout canoe trips into the swamp run out of the tiny village of Mabamba, where the local boaters have organised themselves into a community-based ecotourism project – the Mabamba Wetland Tourism Association (MWTA) – that has also played an important role in conserving the few shoebills left in the area. It's no longer quite the budget excursion it once was: a canoe capable of carrying up to three passengers now costs US$60, while the local authority levies a US$8 head tax for local development, a worthy aim but one that clearly excludes any remedial works on the roads between Buwaya and Kasanje to Mabamba. There is, however, a lot to be said for having a single organisation to deal with and fixed prices. It's also an undisputedly great day out, especially if combined with a boat ride from Entebbe (page 100), and the enthusiastic guides are usually able to locate a shoebill fairly quickly.

Trips starting at around 08.00 (earlier if you're hoping to find a papyrus gonolek) and after 15.00 are recommended though the truth is that you can expect to find a shoebill any time of day. The real reason for these timings is to avoid the heat of the day in a small, uncovered boat. Even if you're out of luck on the shoebill front, the general birdlife is fantastic, with a good chance of spotting localised species such as African pygmy goose, lesser jacana, gull-billed tern, purple swamphen, African fish eagle, African marsh harrier, osprey, African grey parrot, blue-headed coucal, blue-breasted bee-eater and the papyrus-specific Carruthers's cisticola, papyrus gonolek and white-winged warbler. And if you are very lucky, you might even catch a glimpse of a sitatunga.

GETTING THERE AND AWAY Mabamba is easily visited as a day trip from Kampala or Entebbe, though serious birders and wildlife enthusiasts might prefer to base themselves at Mabamba Lodge or Nkima Forest Lodge, which are closer to the swamp. Mabamba also makes for a straightforward and popular diversion for those travelling to or from destinations further southwest, such as Lake Mburo or Bwindi Impenetrable national parks.

Organised tours The easiest way to visit Mabamba is on a day tour, which can be organised through any operator in Kampala or Entebbe. Expect to pay around US$150 per party for up to three people, plus US$30 for every additional person, for a half-day trip inclusive of hotel pickup within Entebbe, road transport to the swamp and guided dugout trip. Trips can also be organised by boat, as described above.

Self-drive Despite their close geographical proximity, Entebbe and Mabamba lie at least 40km apart by (mostly unsurfaced) roads, and the drive takes at least 1 hour. The most direct road-only route out of Entebbe involves following the surfaced

Kampala Road north for about 12km to Kisubi [102 B2] (⊕ 0.13031, 32.53293), then following a good dirt road northwest for about 15km to Nakawuka [102 B2] (⊕ 0.18858, 32.46215), where another left turn leads after 6km to the small town of Kasanje [102 A2] (⊕ 0.15295, 32.39934). Turn left again at an outsized roundabout and after 3.5km, you'll reach a minor road on the right in a small trading centre known as Sanyu Village, after a conspicuous sign for a local Born Again church (⊕ 0.12569, 32.41031). Follow this for 9km to reach Mabamba [102 A3] (⊕ 0.07591, 32.35071). Coming from Kampala or Masaka, follow the main road to Mpigi, then turn south at a junction a short way further east (⊕ 0.21926, 32.33349) and follow it for 12km to Kasanje, where you need to go straight across the roundabout mentioned above, then continue as if coming from Entebbe. A shorter route from Kampala leaves south from the Masaka Road at Natete traffic lights and runs through Kasenge, Nasagi and Nakawuka to Kasanje. It's a slow and bumpy drive though, taking about 90 minutes to Mabamba.

An alternative route from Entebbe entails catching the car ferry that shuttles across Waiya Bay every half an hour between Nakiwogo and Buwaya. From the latter, its only 17km to Mabamba via Sanyu Village (reached from the opposite direction) so the route is far shorter in terms of distance, but there are often long waits for the ferry from the Entebbe side, especially after the lunchtime break (see page 106 regarding ferry transport).

By boat All things considered, driving yourself to Mabamba is a sufficiently bothersome business that unless you're driving from or headed to western Uganda, you're best leaving your car in Entebbe and taking to the water. After you've crossed on the Nakiwogo ferry as a foot passenger, the MWTA will collect and return you to Buwaya for US$26. Transfers can also be arranged by Nkima Lodge (US$16 one-way). Even better, you can hire a motorised canoe from Nakiwogo for a 45-minute chug to the edge of Mabamba Swamp, where you'll transfer to a paddle canoe to seek out your shoebill – just be sure to prearrange this with the MWTA! Your boatman will wait for you and take you back to Nakiwogo (the return trip costs US$40). Alternatively, you might let Wild Frontiers (page 64) handle all arrangements and in rather more style. Expect to pay US$450, including fees for Mabamba Swamp, to be whizzed across the Waiya Bay with up to five companions in a speedboat.

Public transport Mabamba is quite easily reached by public transport. Coming from Entebbe, take a boat or ferry from Nakiwogo to Buwaya, then hire a boda from there. If you're in Kampala, around ten matatus daily ply back and forth to Mabamba village from the New Taxi Park. Alternatively, catch a matatu to Mpigi, then another on to Kasanje, from where you can hire a boda to Mabamba.

WHERE TO STAY AND EAT

✱ **Mabamba Lodge** [102 A3] (5 cottages) ⊕ 0.09354, 32.37392; m 0783 915678, 0753 628839; e info@mabambalodge.com; w mabambalodge.com. This attractive lodge runs down to the open waters of Lake Victoria a short distance east of Mabamba Swamp. Accommodation is in charming stone & thatch cottages with imaginative contemporary African décor. It's a very friendly place, the fusion cuisine – cooked by the owners – is superb, & the gardens are bursting with birdlife including the likes of great blue turaco, black-&-white casqued hornbill & broad-billed roller. The management can arrange boat trips into the swamp, leaving right from their own jetty. *From US$200 dbl FB.* **$$$$**

Nature Smart Centre [102 A3] (4 rooms) ⊕ 0.09007, 32.36323; m 0752 449729. Situated in a neat village garden about 1km from Mabamba

Swamp, this place accommodates budget travellers in simple A-frame rooms that look like they could be rather sweaty in the midday heat. There's an on-site restaurant & small museum. *US$20/30 pp with shared/en-suite amenities.* **$**

✱ **Nkima Forest Lodge** [102 A3] (6 cottages) ⊕ 0.08797, 32.35467; m 0793 327469, 0701 865056; e info@nkimaforestlodge.com; w nkimaforestlodge.com. Set in the midst of a 27ha indigenous hilltop forest overlooking Mabamba Swamp, & only 3.5km away from it by road, this terrific owner-managed lodge is an ideal first stop in Uganda for dedicated birders & wildlife lovers arriving at Entebbe Airport; alternatively, it's also a great coda to a safari, especially if a shoebill eluded you upcountry. Family & dbl bandas are artfully placed on the forested hillside so that the elevated private balconies are, if not exactly in the canopy, definitely up in that direction. There's also a stone swimming pool & a brightly decorated lounge/dining area, while 5mins' walk away a lovely sundowner spot provides a panoramic view of the lake & surrounding wetlands. Local wildlife includes red-tailed & vervet monkey, bushbuck & a wide range of forest birds including great blue & Ross's turaco, African grey parrot, snowy-headed robin-chat & the elusive white-spotted flufftail. Day visitors to the swamp are welcome to drop in for a 3-course lunch (US$12 pp) but should ideally call a couple of hours ahead. Very good value. Nkima can collect you from Buwaya ferry landing (US$16) or all the way from the airport (US$45), see options for reaching Mabamba on page 117. *US$155/240/320 sgl/dbl/trpl FB, discounts available for Ugandan residents &/or longer stays; US$12 pp camping.* **$$$$**

5

Kampala

Extending over a series of rolling hills and swampy valleys at the head of Lake Victoria's Murchison Bay, Kampala, the economic and social hub of Uganda, is the archetypal African capital. More verdant than many of its counterparts and not quite so populous or chaotic as some (though great efforts are being made to remedy these latter deficiencies), it follows a pattern duplicated across sub-Saharan Africa. At its core is a compact and bustling high-rise city centre surrounded by green and carefully laid out suburbs of many years standing. In Kampala's case, these were invariably built on distinctive hills divided by valleys of swamp. Some 30 years ago, when Kampala was home to a modest community of 874,000 people occupying just 200km^2, these suburbs merged gently into a rustic hinterland. Now, however, they are isolated islands of greenery rising out of a mishmash of more recent development, the swamps have been settled and an outer ring of habitation extends ever deeper into what was, until recently, farmland. This sprawl accommodates, in drastically differing degrees of comfort, an additional 3 million people and, with the population of Greater Kampala growing at 5% a year, the city is set to pass the 4 million mark in 2025. Brown now outstrips green as the dominant colour. Clay-tiled roofs scattered across hillsides indicate a burgeoning middle class, while on swampy valley floors acres of rusting tin roofs shelter tens of thousands of less privileged city dwellers. In between these extremes, miles of houses and small businesses line arterial roads that push outwards through a conurbation that now covers over 1,000km^2. The consequence for the aspiring safari-goer is that with fresh air and open countryside more distant by the year, an hour or so must be set aside just to get out of town. On the bright side, bearing in mind that Kampala is at least ten times larger than anywhere else in Uganda, the settlements that lie ahead along your route – the likes of Mbale, Fort Portal, Jinja, Kabale – all retain pleasant, small-town atmospheres in which congestion and pollution are unlikely to feature.

All of the above raises the question, how relevant is Kampala to a visit to Uganda? If you're looking for a smart, international-standard hotel (or a good-value budget hotel), a wide choice of cuisine, shopping opportunities, live music, clubbing and the latest movie – or just a taste of urban African life – you'll probably love the city; and compared with the likes of Nairobi or Dar es Salaam, it's still remarkably safe to explore. If, however, your main interest is Uganda's natural history, then you're much better off giving the city a wide berth, staying a night in Entebbe and heading upcountry. As a further disincentive, compared with, say, Nairobi, genuine sightseeing opportunities within the conurbation are limited and, at best, low key. Should you attempt a tour of the city, your overriding memory will likely be of the horrendous traffic as the population, swollen by daily commuters from surrounding districts, attempts to move around in an assortment of private vehicles, buses, matatus and bodas. If you *do* decide to stay in Kampala, establish

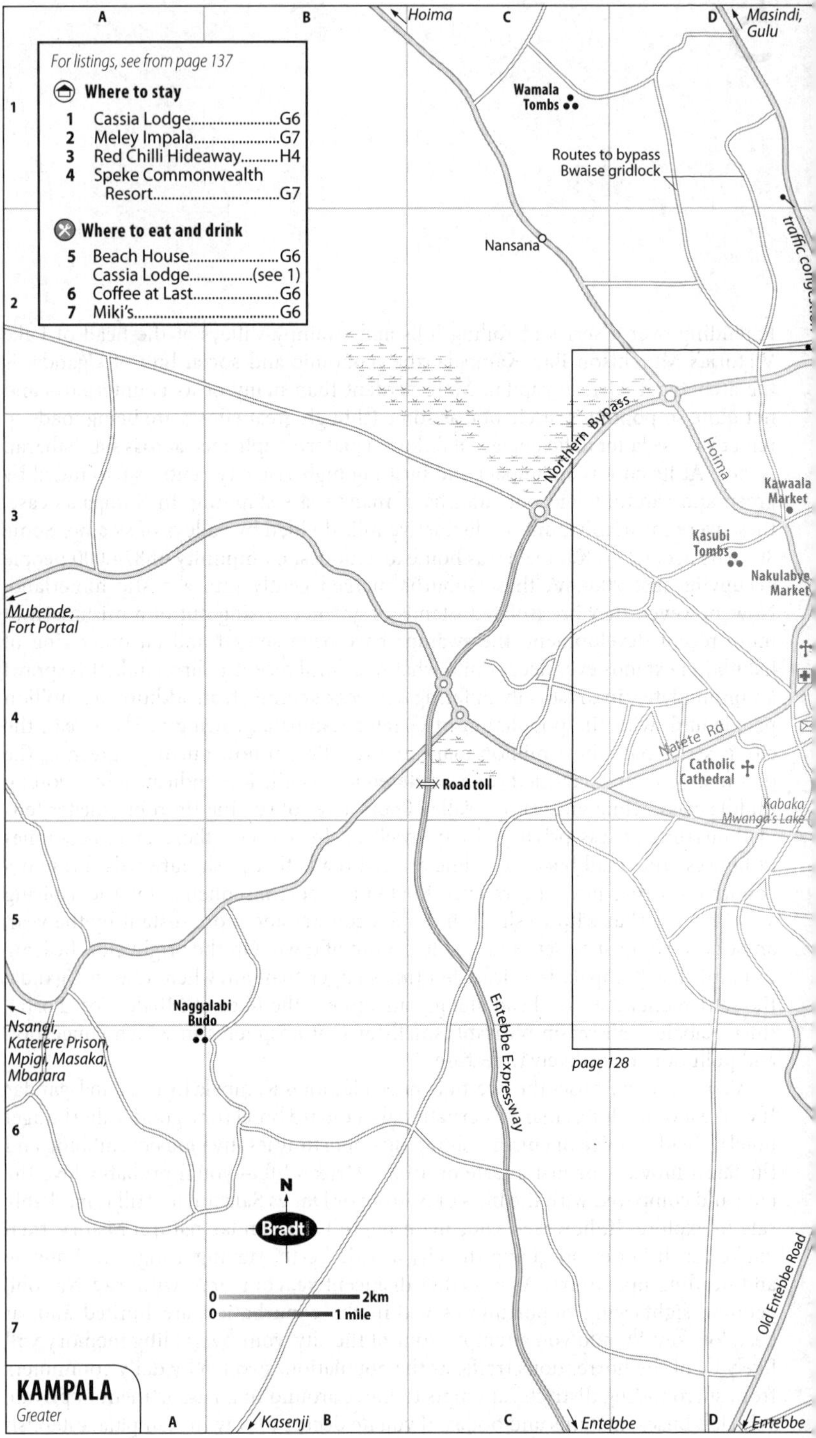
For listings, see from page 137
Where to stay
1 Cassia Lodge....G6
2 Meley Impala....G7
3 Red Chilli Hideaway....H4
4 Speke Commonwealth Resort....G7
Where to eat and drink
5 Beach House....G6
Cassia Lodge....(see 1)
6 Coffee at Last....G6
7 Miki's....G6
Hoima
Masindi, Gulu
Wamala Tombs
Routes to bypass Bwaise gridlock
Nansana
traffic congestion
Northern Bypass
Hoima
Kawaala Market
Kasubi Tombs
Nakulabye Market
Mubende, Fort Portal
Natete Rd
Catholic Cathedral
Road toll
Kabaka Mwanga's Lake
Entebbe Expressway
Naggalabi Budo
Nsangi, Katerere Prison, Mpigi, Masaka, Mbarara
page 128
Bradt
N
0 2km
0 1 mile
Old Entebbe Road
KAMPALA
Greater
Kasenji
Entebbe
Entebbe
A
B
C
D
1
2
3
4
5
6
7

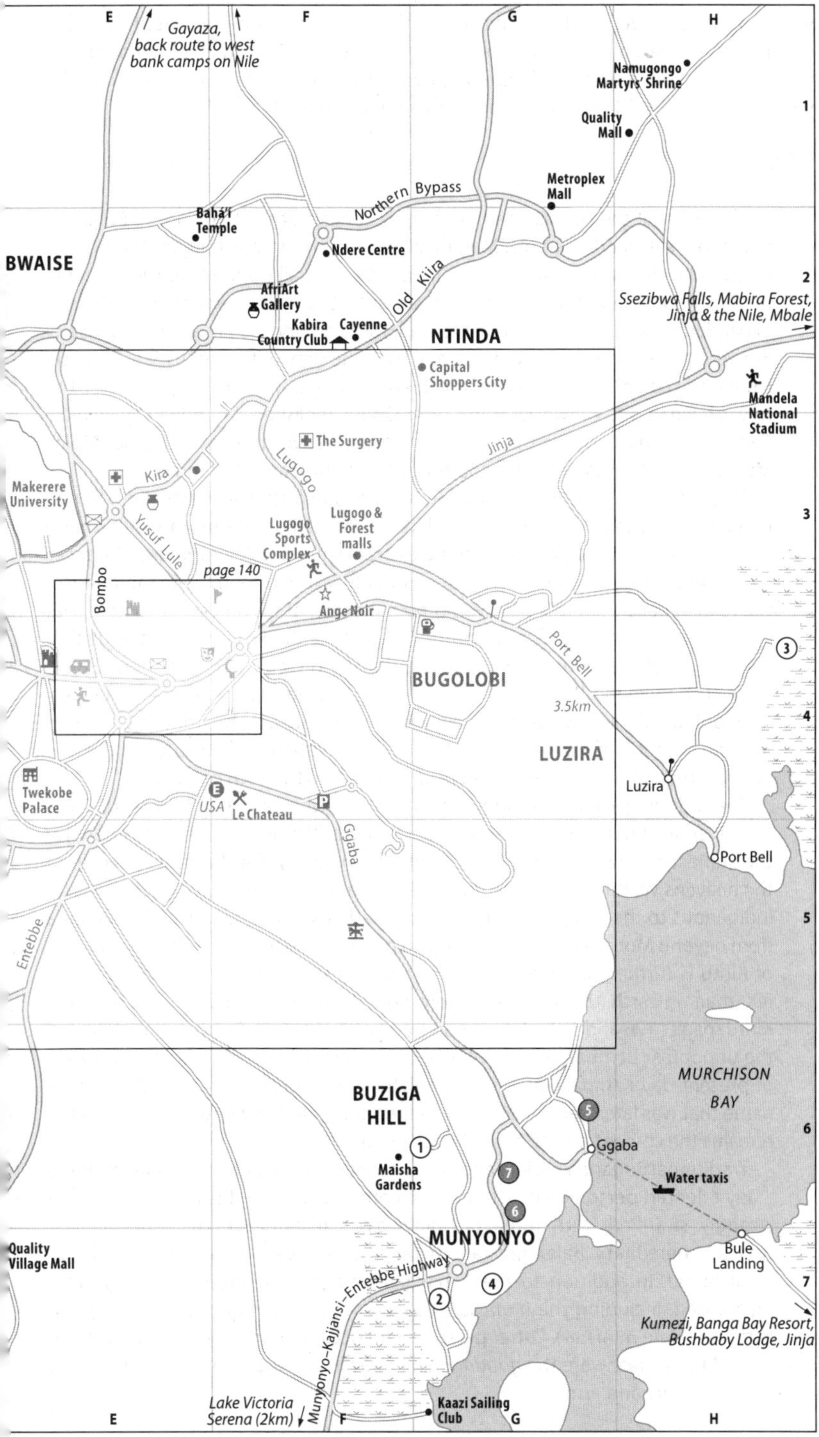
E
F
G
H
Gayaza, back route to west bank camps on Nile
Namugongo Martyrs' Shrine
Quality Mall
Metroplex Mall
Northern Bypass
Bahá'í Temple
Ndere Centre
BWAISE
AfriArt Gallery
Old Kiira
Ssezibwa Falls, Mabira Forest, Jinja & the Nile, Mbale
Kabira Country Club
Cayenne
NTINDA
Capital Shoppers City
Mandela National Stadium
The Surgery
Jinja
Lugogo
Makerere University
Kira
Yusuf Lule
Lugogo Sports Complex
Lugogo & Forest malls
page 140
Bombo
Ange Noir
Port Bell
BUGOLOBI
3.5km
LUZIRA
Luzira
Twekobe Palace
USA
Le Chateau
Ggaba
Port Bell
Entebbe
MURCHISON BAY
BUZIGA HILL
Ggaba
Maisha Gardens
Water taxis
MUNYONYO
Bule Landing
Quality Village Mall
Munyonyo–Kajjansi–Entebbe Highway
Kumezi, Banga Bay Resort, Bushbaby Lodge, Jinja
Lake Victoria Serena (2km)
Kaazi Sailing Club
1
2
3
4
5
6
7

what you want to do and find lodgings in that area. Spending the evening sitting in 'the jam' instead of a selected restaurant or cinema is no fun at all. Of course, if you're at home on a boda boda and happy for the lunatic of your choice to whizz you through the gridlock, then ignore this advice and have fun!

BUGANDA: AN INTRODUCTION

Kampala lies at the political and geographical heart of the Kingdom of Buganda, home to the Baganda (singular Muganda), who form the largest single ethnic group in Uganda, comprising more than 20% of the national population. The kingdom originally consisted of four counties: Kyadondo, Busiro, Busujju and Mawokota. It expanded greatly during the early to mid 18th century, mainly at the expense of Bunyoro, to extend over 20 counties, as well as the semi-autonomous Ssese Islands. During the colonial era, Buganda remained a kingdom with unique privileges, but it was relegated to provincial status after Obote abolished the monarchy in 1966. Today, Buganda is divided across nine administrative districts: Kampala, Mpigi, Mukono, Masaka, Kalangala, Kiboga, Rakai, Sembabule and Mubende.

Buganda is ruled by a kabaka, an autocratic monarch whose position, though hereditary, is confined to no single clan. Traditionally, the kabaka would marry into as many clans as possible – the explorer Henry Stanley estimated Mutesa's female entourage to number 500, of whom at least one-tenth were members of the royal harem – and his heir would take the clan of his mother, a custom that encouraged loyalty to the throne insofar as each of the 52 clans could hope that it would one day produce a king. Mutesa, who held the throne when John Speke (page 16) arrived in Buganda in 1862, is listed by tradition as the 30th kabaka. Although the dates of Mutesa's predecessors' reigns are a matter for conjecture, an average duration of a decade would place the foundation of Buganda in the mid 16th century, while 20 years would push it back into the 13th century.

The founding Kabaka of Buganda was Kintu, who, it is widely agreed, came to power after defeating a despotic local ruler called Bemba. Kintu is otherwise the subject of several conflicting traditions. Some say that he descended from the heavens via Bunyoro, others that he originated from the Ssese Islands, or was indigenous to the area, or – most credible perhaps – that he arrived in Buganda from beyond Mount Elgon, suggesting an origin in Sudan or Ethiopia. The identity of Kintu is further confused by the Kiganda creation legend asserting that the first man on earth, though presumably a totally different person, was also called Kintu (pages 126 and 176). A common tradition holds that Kintu, having defeated the unpopular Bemba, took over his house at Nagalabi Buddo, about 20km west of present-day Kampala, as a spoil of victory. The house was called Buganda, a name that was later transferred to all the territory ruled by Kintu. Nagalabi Buddo remains the coronation site of the kabaka to this day.

Traditional Buganda society allowed for some upward and downward mobility – any talented person could rise to social prominence – but it was nevertheless strongly stratified, with three distinct classes recognised. The highest class was the hereditary Balangira (aristocracy), which based its right to rule on royal blood. In addition to the kabaka, several aristocratic figureheads were recognised, including the *namasole* (queen mother), *lubuga* (king's sister) and *katikiro* (prime minister). Other persons who occupied positions of political and social importance were the *gabunga* and *mujasi*, the respective commanders of the royal navy and army.

HISTORY

Back in the day – 18 December 1890, to be precise – Kampala's first foreign visitor found the site of Uganda's future capital an altogether wilder setting. Indeed, the low

The middle class in Baganda society consisted of chiefs or *baami*. Initially, the status of the baami was hereditary, enjoyed solely by the *bataka* (clan heads). After 1750, however, *bakopi* men could be promoted by royal appointment to baami status, on the basis of distinguished service and/or ability. A hierarchic system of chieftaincy existed, corresponding with the importance of the political unit over which any given chief held sway. The most important administrative division was the Saza (county), each of which was ruled by a Saza chief. These were further subdivided into Gombolola (sub-counties), then into parishes and sub-parishes, and finally Bukungu, which were more-or-less village units. The kabaka had the power to appoint or dismiss any chief at will, and all levels of baami were directly responsible to him.

At the bottom of the social strata was the serf class known as the *bakopi*: literally, the people who don't matter. The bakopi were subsistence farmers, whose labour (as tends to be the case with those who matter not to their more socially elevated masters) formed the base of Buganda's agricultural economy. Many bakopi kept chickens and larger livestock, but they were primarily occupied with agriculture – the local staple of bananas, supplemented by sweet potatoes, cassava, beans and green vegetables. The bakopi were dependent on land to farm, but they had no right to it. All land in Buganda was the property of the kabaka, who could allocate (or rescind) the right of usage to any subsidiary chief at whim. The chiefs, in turn, allocated their designated quota of land as they deemed fit – a scenario that encouraged the bakopi to obedience. Peasant men and women were regularly sacrificed by the aristocracy – Kabaka Suuna, during one bout of illness, is said to have ordered 100 bakopi to be slaughtered daily until he was fully recovered.

Kiganda, the traditional religion of Buganda (discussed more fully on page 166), is essentially animist, in thrall not to a supreme being but rather a variety of ancestral and other spirits. Temples dedicated to the most powerful spirits were each served by a medium and a hereditary priest, who would liaise between the spirit and the people. The priests occupied a place of high religious and political importance – even the most powerful kabaka would consult with appropriate spirit mediums before making an important decision or going into battle. The kabaka appointed at least one female slave or relative to tend each shrine and provide food and drink to its priest and medium.

The traditions of Buganda are enormously complex, and the kingdom's history is packed with incident and anecdote. The above is intended as a basic overview, to be supplemented by more specific information on various places, events, characters and crafts elsewhere in this book. Readers whose interest is whetted rather than sated by this coverage are pointed to the tours offered by the recently formed Buganda Tourist Board (w bhtb.or.ug). These might be supplemented by Richard Reid's excellent *Political Power in Pre-Colonial Buganda* (James Currey, 2002) which offers comprehensive information on most aspects of traditional Baganda society. Many old and out-of-print editions of the *Uganda Journal* also contain useful essays on pre-colonial Buganda. These can be viewed at the Uganda Society Library in the Uganda Museum in Kampala (page 148) or online (w ufdc.ufl.edu).

THE TWO KINTUS

Intriguingly, Kiganda tradition holds that Kintu, the founding Kabaka of Buganda, shares his name with Kintu, the first man on earth (page 176). As a result, outsiders tend to assume that these two seminal personages are one and the same figure, a more-or-less mythical embodiment of the creation both of mankind and of Buganda. Muganda traditionalists, however, tend to assert otherwise. Yes, many would concede that Kintu and his wife Nambi, the first people on earth, are allegorical 'Adam and Eve'-like figures whose story has little basis in historical fact. But not so Kintu, the founder of Baganda, who is both a wholly separate person, and a genuine historical figure.

The 'two Kintus' claim is legitimised by the contrast between the unambiguous absence of other humans in the creation myth, and the presence of humanity explicit in any foundation legend in which one king defeats another king and rules over his former subjects. There is a popular Kiganda saying, derived from the mythical Kintu's last words, that translates as 'Kintu's children will never be removed from the face of the earth'. And if this saying does pre-date the foundation of Buganda, then it is plausible – even likely – that the founder of Buganda would have adopted Kintu as his throne name, with the deliberate intention of legitimising his rule by association with the mythical father of mankind.

hill allocated by Kabaka Mwanga of Buganda to Frederick Lugard of the Imperial British East Africa Company for his camp was known locally as *'kasozi ka impala'* after the antelopes that grazed there. Not that the area was lacking in significance: Lugard's occupation of the stumpy *kasozi ka impala* was due to the fact that most of the hills in the vicinity were considered royal ground, having at one time (or indeed several times) been used by the *kabakas* for their *kibugas* (citadels). Since a kabaka might occupy a series of hills during the course of his reign, and since Mwanga was the 31st of the line, non-royal summits were in short supply. Mutesa I, for example, was occupying a palace on Banda Hill when the explorers Speke and Grant reached Buganda in 1864, but by the time Henry Stanley arrived in 1875, he had relocated to Rubaga Hill and would later move again, to Kasubi, a site that his father, Kabaka Suuna II, had occupied in the 1850s. With the subsequent proclamation of the Uganda Protectorate in 1896, and the transfer of power from the kabaka's hill to the *kasozi ka impala*, the latter gave its name, albeit somewhat mangled, to the settlement that grew up around it.

By independence, Kampala had grown into a city of 167,000 and in the subsequent decade was widely regarded as the showpiece of the East African community: a spacious and well-planned garden city with a cosmopolitan atmosphere and bustling trade. It was also a cultural and educational centre of note, with Makerere University regarded as the academic heart of East Africa. Under Idi Amin, however, Kampala's status started to deteriorate, especially after the Asian community was forced to leave Uganda. By 1986, when the civil war ended, Kampala was in complete chaos: skeletal buildings scarred with bullet holes dotted the city centre, shops and hotels were boarded up after widespread looting, and public services had ground to a halt, swamped by the huge influx of migrants from war-torn parts of the country.

Nearly 40 years on, Kampala is unrecognisable from the dire incarnation of the mid 1980s. The main shopping area along Kampala Road might be that of any

African capital, while the edge of the city centre has seen the development of a clutch of bright, modern supermarkets and shopping malls. The area immediately north of Kampala Road, where foreign embassies and government departments rub shoulders with renovated tourist hotels, is as smart as any part of Nairobi or Dar es Salaam. Admittedly, it's a different story downhill of Kampala Road where overcrowded backstreets, congested with hooting matatus and swerving boda drivers, reveal a more representative face of Kampala – the city as most of its residents see it.

GETTING THERE AND AWAY

BY ROAD Kampala lies 40km north of Entebbe International Airport and can be reached either along the old Entebbe Road, through 40km of corridor development or using the nippy new Entebbe Expressway as already described on page 106.

BY RAIL No regional railway services currently operate in Uganda; the best that train buffs can currently hope for is a twice-daily shuttle between Kampala Railway Station and Namanve Industrial Estate, 10km east. This is set to change, however. In 2023, a Spanish company, Imathia Construction, was contracted to renovate the line between Kampala and Mukono, 20km east. After achieving this modest goal they will aim for Lugazi (near Mabira Forest) and Jinja before setting their sights on Tororo and the Kenyan border.

BY BOAT Despite the potential that the world's second-largest freshwater body presents for regional navigation, no passenger services connect Uganda to Tanzania or Kenya.

ROAD TRANSPORT

Buses Bus services from Kampala to upcountry destinations operate from various terminals in the central Nakivubo Valley. These lie near the two taxi parks, enhancing the general aura of chaos in this astonishingly congested part of town – even bodas take roundabout routes to avoid the 300m section of Namirembe Road which runs through the middle of the fun.

The two main terminals are Kasenyi and Namayiba (pronounced Namaiba). **Kasenyi** [140 B4] lies in the most congested part of the valley, 100m behind Namirembe Road next to the Nakivubo Stadium, while **Namayiba** [140 A2] sits a short distance north in quieter Old Kampala and is accessible by vehicle. Some companies have their own private parks, also in or close to the Nakivubo Valley, which are specified in the bus company listings on page 132.

Timetables are rare. Instead, buses depart regularly – every 1–2 hours from around 07.00 until early afternoon – to most regional centres. The exceptions are distant destinations such as Bwindi, Kitgum, Soroti and Kisoro, which are usually limited to a reasonably punctual early morning and evening departure. Note that public transport fares increase immediately before holiday periods such as Easter and Christmas when Kampala's multi-tribal society moves out en masse to their home areas. These increases are only partially due to opportunistic profiteering; they also compensate for vehicles returning almost empty to Kampala at these times.

Details of buses plying the route between Kampala and upcountry destinations are given on page 132 and in relevant chapters. The fastest means of travel is with private bus companies who have an obvious interest in getting from A to B as

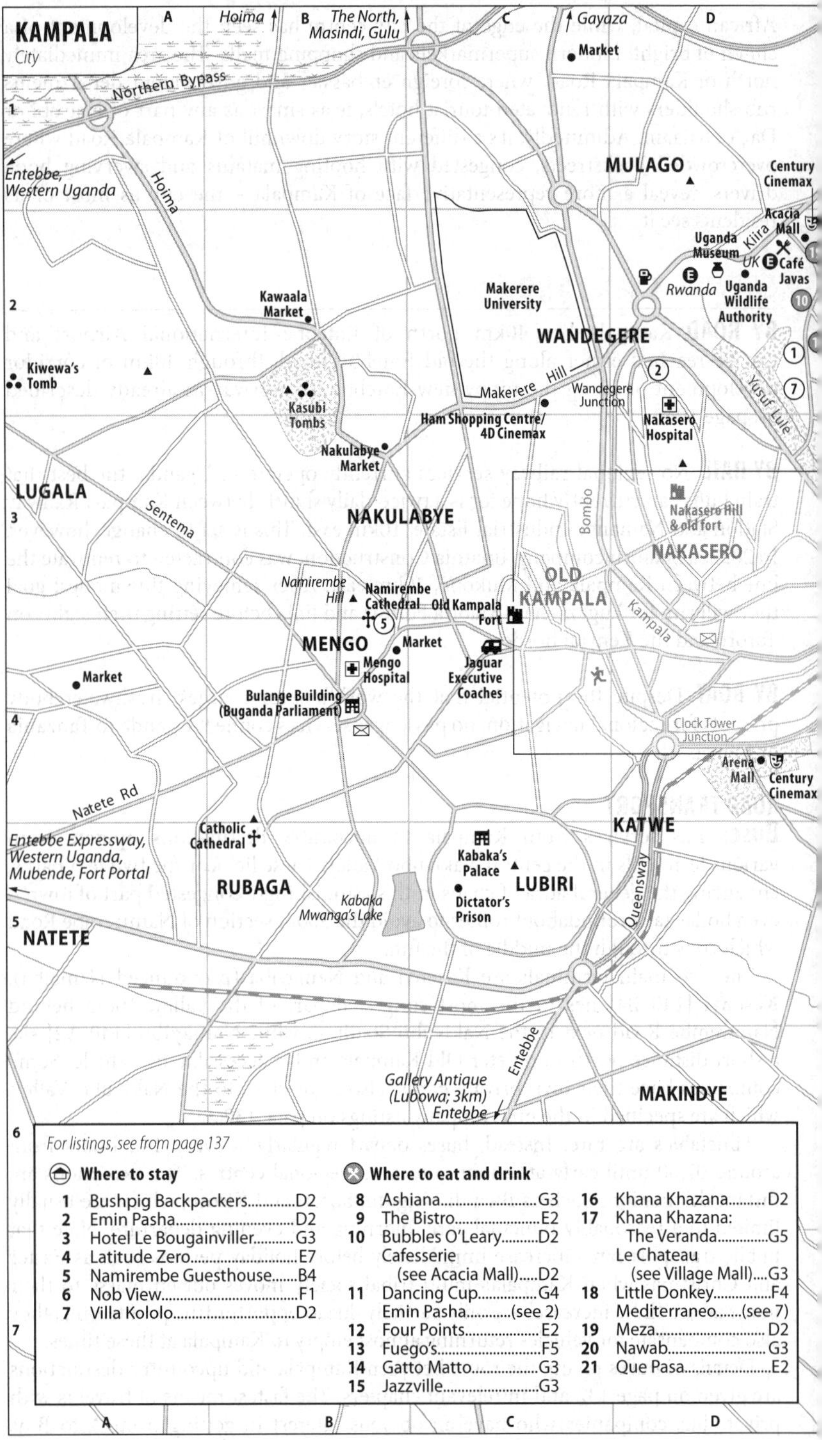

For listings, see from page 137

Where to stay

1 Bushpig Backpackers............D2
2 Emin Pasha............................D2
3 Hotel Le Bougainviller...........G3
4 Latitude Zero.........................E7
5 Namirembe Guesthouse.......B4
6 Nob View................................F1
7 Villa Kololo...........................D2

Where to eat and drink

8 Ashiana.........................G3
9 The Bistro.....................E2
10 Bubbles O'Leary..........D2
Cafesserie (see Acacia Mall).....D2
11 Dancing Cup...............G4
Emin Pasha...........(see 2)
12 Four Points...................E2
13 Fuego's.........................F5
14 Gatto Matto.................G3
15 Jazzville........................G3
16 Khana Khazana..........D2
17 Khana Khazana: The Veranda..............G5
Le Chateau (see Village Mall)....G3
18 Little Donkey...............F4
Mediterraneo.......(see 7)
19 Meza............................D2
20 Nawab..........................G3
21 Que Pasa......................E2

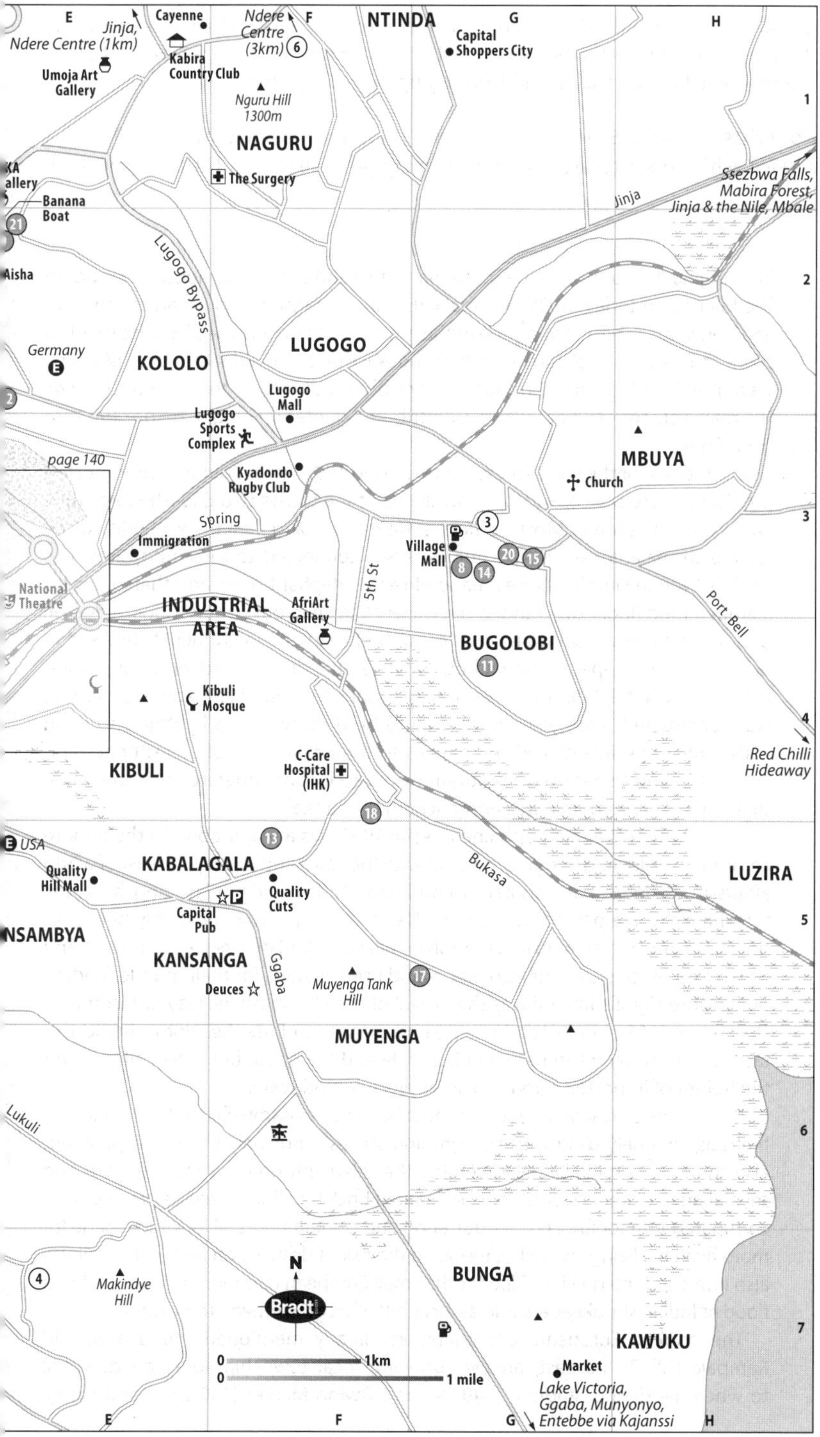
E
F
G
H
1
2
3
4
5
6
7
Jinja, Ndere Centre (1km)
Cayenne
Ndere Centre (3km)
6
NTINDA
Capital Shoppers City
Umoja Art Gallery
Kabira Country Club
Nguru Hill 1300m
NAGURU
The Surgery
Banana Boat
21
Aisha
Lugogo Bypass
Jinja
Ssezbwa Falls, Mabira Forest, Jinja & the Nile, Mbale
LUGOGO
Germany
KOLOLO
2
Lugogo Mall
Lugogo Sports Complex
page 140
Kyadondo Rugby Club
MBUYA
Church
Spring
Immigration
3
Village Mall
8
14
20
15
National Theatre
INDUSTRIAL AREA
AfriArt Gallery
5th St
Port Bell
BUGOLOBI
11
Kibuli Mosque
KIBULI
C-Care Hospital (IHK)
Red Chilli Hideaway
18
13
USA
Quality Hill Mall
KABALAGALA
Bukasa
LUZIRA
Quality Cuts
Capital Pub
NSAMBYA
KANSANGA
Ggaba
17
Deuces
Muyenga Tank Hill
MUYENGA
Lukuli
4
Makindye Hill
N
Bradt
BUNGA
KAWUKU
0
1km
0
1 mile
Market
Lake Victoria, Ggaba, Munyonyo, Entebbe via Kajanssi

quickly as possible. If safety is your priority, however, it's generally accepted that the slower Post Bus is the best option, should it resume (see below). For details of international bus services to and from Kampala, see page 67.

Post Bus (☎ 041 4255511/5; m 0775 185112) At the time of writing, the Post Bus service, which operates from Kampala's main post office [140 D4], is suspended.

EARLY DAYS IN KAMPALA

The original city centre – little more than a fort and a few mud houses – stood on the hill known today as Old Kampala. Its early expansion and urbanisation from 1897 onwards is best catalogued in the memoirs of two early settlers, the medical pioneer Sir Albert Cook (arrived 1897) and W E Hoyle (arrived 1903), both of which were published in early (and long out of print) editions of the *Uganda Journal*, the main sources of what follows. Unattributed quotes relating to before 1903 are from Cook.

Conditions for the few settlers in Kampala in 1897 were rudimentary. Imported provisions were scarce, and when available at the town's two English stores they were very expensive. Most settlers suffered ongoing health problems, often related to malaria, which had not yet been connected to mosquito bites. The settlers lived in simple abodes made of reeds, elephant grass and thatch, with a stamped mud floor 'cow-dunged once a week to keep out jiggers'. Cook, a doctor, performed his first operations 'on a camp bedstead, the instruments sterilised in our cooking saucepans, and laid out in vegetable dishes filled with antiseptics'. A 12-bed hospital, built in the local style, opened in May 1897, and a larger one was constructed three years later, only to be destroyed in a lightning strike in 1902. Still, Cook 'introduced the natives to the advantages of anaesthetics and antiseptics' and also started a programme of vaccinations after a chief warned him that a smallpox epidemic was approaching the capital.

The arrival of the telegraph line in April 1900 was a major boon to the remote community, allowing it regular contact with the coast and to keep abreast of world affairs. Cook notes that: 'this happy condition of affairs did not last long, however, for where the line passed through the Nandi country it was constantly being cut down. On one occasion no less than sixty miles [100km] of wire were removed and coiled into bracelets or cut into pieces and used as slugs for their muzzle-loading guns.' More significant still was the arrival of the Mombasa Railway at Kisumu, in December 1901, connected by a steamer service to Entebbe. Not only did this facilitate personal travel between Kampala and the coast, but it also allowed for the freight of imported goods on an unprecedented scale.

Prior to the arrival of the railway, most buildings in Kampala had been thatched firetraps, routinely destroyed by lightning strikes – not only Cook's hospital, but also the first cathedral at Namirembe, the telegraph office, a trading store and several private homesteads. Now, permanent brick buildings could be erected, with corrugated-iron roofing, proper guttering and cement floors, all of which made for more hygienic living, as well as reducing the risk of destruction by fire. The railway also improved the quality of life for the small European community by attracting 'a flood of Indian shopkeepers' and associated 'influx of European trade goods'.

The original European settlement, as already mentioned, stood atop Old Kampala Hill. To its east, an ever-growing local township sprawled downhill to where Nakivubo Stadium [140 B4] and Owino Market [140 B5] stand today.

Assuming it is revived, and we are assured it soon will be, you can expect buses to depart each morning at 07.00 for Kisoro, Lira and Kitgum and at 08.00 for Gulu and Kabale. Along the way, they stop in numerous towns (22 in the case of the Gulu bus) to drop off and collect mail and passengers. Tickets to these final destinations should cost around US$10; fares to towns along the way are accordingly cheaper.

The present-day city centre took shape as an indirect result of the improved transportation to the coast via Kisumu. It was, Hoyle writes: 'realised by the government that the space below Kampala Fort was inadequate to meet growing trade, and they decided to start a new township on the more expansive hill named Nakasero, half a mile [0.8km] to the east. Already by 1903 a new fort had been built there [and] by 1905 practically all government offices and staff and traders' shops had been moved to Nakasero.' Over the next few years, writes Cook, the government had 'good roads cut and well laid out in the new town…bordered with trees' – essentially the nascent modern city centre, which slopes across the valley dividing Old Kampala from Nakasero Hill.

The Mombasa Railway also facilitated the export trade out of Uganda, which until 1906 consisted primarily of wild animal produce such as hide, skins and ivory, controlled by an Italian and an American firm, as well as the Indian storekeeper Allidina Visram. Hoyle writes: 'It was a memorable sight to see frequent safaris laden with ivory tusks filing towards Kampala from the strip of country between the Congo Free State and Uganda Protectorate, which at that point was in dispute, a kind of no-man's-land and therefore the elephant-hunters' paradise.' Hoyle writes elsewhere of Allidina Visram's store that in 1903 it was 'to Europeans, the most important…existence almost entirely depended on [it], for his firm not only supplied the necessities of life, but in the absence of any bank it provided ready money in exchange for a cheque'.

Oddly, perhaps, English money held no currency in Kampala's early days. The Indian rupee was effectively the official currency, equivalent to one English shilling and four pence. But Hoyle writes that: 'the most generally used currency among the Baganda was cowrie shells…one thousand to the rupee…through which a hole had been made for threading…using banana fibre. The Baganda were very adept at counting shells, usually strung in hundreds…It was amusing, having paid a porter…five thousand shells, to see him sit down and count them… report that he was one, two, or maybe up to five short, and it was easier to throw these to him from a quantity of loose shells kept in a bag for that purpose.' Cowries continued in general use until about 1905, and were still employed in petty trade until 1922, when the shilling was introduced.

Last word to Hoyle, and an improbable anecdote relating to Sir Hesketh Bell, Governor of Uganda from 1905–09: 'Bell conceived the idea that elephants might be trained to do the many useful jobs they do in India. The experiment was made of bringing a trained elephant from India. It was a great business getting the elephant aboard the [ferry] at Kisumu and landing it in Entebbe. [Bell] came to Kampala to make a triumphant entry riding the elephant, mounting it two miles outside the township. He was greeted by a large crowd of Europeans and Baganda. Some young elephants were caught, but the experiment of training them was not successful, and eventually the Indian elephant was sold to a menagerie in Europe.'

BUGANDA'S FIRST FEMINIST?

The life of a *mumbeja* – a Muganda princess – wasn't quite as romantic as it might sound. The sisters of the kabaka generally lived as ladies-in-waiting to the king, at risk of being put to death for any perceived breach of conduct. Marriage was forbidden to the king's sisters and daughters, as was casual sex or becoming pregnant – and the punishment for transgressing any of these taboos was death by cremation.

The first princess to break the mould was Clara Nalumansi, a daughter of Mutesa I. Nalumansi angered Mwanga by converting to Islam during the first year of his reign, and further aggravated him by publicly reconverting to Catholicism in May 1886. Then, in early 1887, Princess Clara capitalised on her rights as a Christian – in the process scandalising the whole of Buganda – by tying the marital knot with another convert, a former page of Mwanga named Yosef Kadu.

The admirable princess didn't stop there. Shortly after her marriage, Clara was appointed to succeed the recently deceased *namasole* of Kabaka Junju, a charge that, traditionally, would have entailed her moving permanently to a house alongside Junju's tomb and tending the royal shrine in solitude for the rest of her days. Instead, Clara and Yosef arrived at the tomb, chased away the attendant spirit medium, then cleared the previous namasole's house of every last fetish and charm, and dumped the lot on a bonfire.

Clara's next move? Well, it's customary for the umbilical cord of a Muganda princess – and all other royals for that matter – to be removed with care and preserved until they die, when it is buried with the rest of the body. So Clara dug out her umbilical cord from wherever it was stored, cut it into little pieces, and chucked it out – leading to further public outcry and a call for both her and her husband to be executed.

The general mood of unrest in Buganda in late 1887 diverted attention from the Christian couple and gave them temporary respite. But not for long. In December, Clara placed herself back in the spotlight when she arranged for an immense elephant tusk, placed by her grandfather Kabaka Suuna at a shrine dedicated to the water god Mukasa, to be removed from its sacred resting place.

The errant princess's luck ran out in August 1888, a month before Mwanga was forced into exile, when she was killed by a gunshot fired by a person or persons unknown. Not entirely incredibly, her relatives claimed that the assassination was arranged by Mwanga, who – characteristically paranoid – feared that the English Christians might follow the British example and name the princess as the new ruler of Buganda.

More than a century after her death, it's impossible to know what to make of Princess Clara Nalumansi's singular story. Quite possibly she was just religiously motivated, recently converted to Christianity and set on a self-destructive collision course with martyrdom. But it's more tempting, and I think credible, to remember her as a true rebel: a proto-feminist whose adoption of Christianity was not a matter of blind faith, but rather a deliberately chosen escape route from the frigid birthright of a *mumbeja*.

Private bus companies The better private bus services all have, if not fixed, at least regular departure times, with one or another coach leaving in either direction between Kampala and the likes of Mbale, Mbarara, Kabale and Kasese. Note that reliable company phone numbers are rare; contacts tend to be personal mobile numbers for employees, which regularly become obsolete. As such, they have generally not been included in the listings below. Moreover, few companies in Namayiba or Kasenyi have offices; just find your bus, buy a ticket and hop aboard.

Services from Kasenyi Bus Terminal

Bismarken Bus Reliable service to Kabale (5–6hrs; US$10) & Kisoro (8–9hrs; US$10). Departs at 05.30, 07.00 & 10.00. Also travels to Butogota (20km from Buhoma; 19.30; 8hrs; US$11).

Courier Bus Daily to Lira (8–9hrs; US$10) via Soroti (6–7hrs; US$7).

Gateway Bus Though usually best avoided, this is the only option for travelling to Kaabong (for Kidepo National Park) via Soroti & Kotido (dep 03.00; 12hrs; US$12).

Highway Bus Buses running directly to the Buhoma Gate of Bwindi Impenetrable National Park (dep 07.30; 10–12hrs; US$13).

Kalita Coaches m 0756 897930. Long-serving operator running west to Mubende (2hrs; US$5), Fort Portal (4hrs; US$8) & Kasese (5–6hrs; US$10).

Link Bus ☎ 041 4255426; e info@link.co.ug; w link.co.ug. The pick of Uganda's bus companies, this large & reliable operator runs daily – sometimes several times – to the following destinations: Hoima (3hrs; US$4) & onwards to Wanseko (5hrs; US$6) or Kaiso-Tonya (4hrs; US$5); Masindi (3hrs; US$4); Kasese (5–6hrs; US$10); Fort Portal (4hrs; US$10) & onwards to Bundibugyo (5–6hrs; US$10) or Kasese (5–6hrs; $12) & Mutukula (Tanzanian border; 4hrs; US$5) via Masaka. In most cases, upcountry destinations operate from their own terminal. Link's useful website lists current destinations with up-to-date contacts for each.

Savanna & Starlink Buses to Kihihi (between Bwindi & Ishasha) via Ntungamo (05.30; 7hrs; US$8).

Services from Namayiba Bus Terminal

Robelyn, Friendship & Makome These buses are the preferred choices to travel to Kitgum. Early morning & evening departures (6–7hrs; US$13).

YY Coaches f yycoaches. Daily coaches to Mbale (5hrs; US$8).

Other services

Gaagaa Coaches [140 C3] Arua Stage on Johnstone St. The best operator to West Nile runs 3 buses daily (8–10hrs; US$12), starting at 07.00, to Arua via Pakwach.

Jaguar Executive Coaches [128 C4] Namirembe Rd; m 0782 811128. The top operator for Kabale or Kisoro (& to the Rwandan capital Kigali) runs several executive buses daily to Kisoro or Kigali via Kabale. Buses to Kigali via Kabale with Trinity Coaches leave from across the road.

Zawadi Buses [140 B1] William St. Daily buses to Gulu (8hrs; US$8). The service continues north from Gulu to Adjumani (7hrs; US$12) & Moyo (9hrs; US$13), the latter stage including a memorable ferry crossing over the Nile at Laropi.

Matatus These days, buses rather than matatus are the preferred option for long-distance travel to/from Kampala. Understandably, few people want to spend hours crammed into a hot, cramped metal box being driven at frightening speed by a person lacking the most basic of precautionary instincts and (very possibly) a driving licence. However, matatus do still play a role for destinations within an hour or so of Kampala and if you are in a hurry to travel further afield. Though matatus are more expensive than buses, departures are more regular – before noon, you're unlikely to wait for more than 30 minutes for a matatu to leave for Jinja, Tororo, Mbale, Kabale, Kasese, Mityana, Mubende, Fort Portal, Masindi, Gulu or Hoima. Matatus to destinations west of the city leave from the **New Taxi Park** [140 B4], while matatus to destinations east of Kampala leave from the **Old Taxi Park** [140 C4]. Local matatus leave for Entebbe from both taxi parks every few minutes.

GETTING AROUND

Getting around Kampala is hard work. Mobility during weekdays is reduced during prolonged morning and evening rush hours, and Saturdays are often little better.

Poor road conditions don't help and nor do apparently spontaneous decisions to close them in attempts to fix them. Floods caused by heavy rain compounds the misery. Though there are few reasons to visit the city centre, heavy traffic and minimal off-street parking opportunities reinforce the decision to limit your activities to the suburbs. Establish what you want to do and stay in the relevant part of town. It is no longer practical, for example, to check into the Speke Commonwealth Resort in Munyonyo and expect a fun evening out at the Ndere Centre (page 146) – unless you're prepared for a 40km trip using the city's outer ring roads. If you're

KAMPALA – GETTING ORIENTED

Kampala might have long outgrown its initial seven hills but it's still a simple matter to stay oriented within the urban sprawl. Uganda's capital covers a landscape of distinct hills separated by swampy valleys draining into Lake Victoria. Many of these hills, both the historic seven (those included here are marked *) and others settled more recently, bear landmarks that mean that you need never get completely lost in Greater Kampala. This happy situation contrasts with, say, Nairobi and Dar es Salaam, where geography is less helpful.

The city's most obvious reference point is the modern multi-storeyed city centre on Nakasero Hill. This is ringed by more discreet, but no less identifiable, landmarks on neighbouring summits. These are described here moving clockwise around Nakasero, starting with **Old Kampala Hill*** (page 150), just a few hundred metres southwest of the city centre. This stumpy knoll attained initial significance as the site of Lugard's 1899 encampment, but since the 1970s has provided central Kampala with its most dramatic reference point. Initially, this was the shell of an unfeasibly tall tower, noted for a distinct list halfway up, rising above an incomplete mosque initiated by Idi Amin. This well-loved folly was demolished around 2001 to make way for the magnificent National Mosque (page 150) with its more practically proportioned tower. Due south of Old Kampala, the kabaka's palace stands on the broad, low hill of **Lubiri*** (page 153). This circular area, a full kilometre in diameter, remains mostly undeveloped and is conspicuous as a green expanse, enclosed within a crumbling brick wall in an area of low-rent housing and workshops. Lubiri is neighboured by **Namirembe*** and **Rubaga*** hills, topped by the Anglican and Catholic cathedrals respectively. St Paul's on Namirembe is identified by its dome (more modest than that of its London namesake but still striking) and Rubaga Cathedral by two bell towers. Moving northeast from Namirembe, the white bell tower of Uganda's oldest university is visible on the leafy ridge of Makerere. Looking north from Kisementi and Kiira Road, the striking Bahá'í temple is conspicuous on a grassy hill off the Gayaza Road. Immediately behind Kisementi is leafy Kololo, the city's highest hill and the site of many embassies and diplomatic residences. South of Jinja Road, a cluster of white minarets and palm trees mark **Kibuli* Mosque** [129 E4], where Uganda's first Islamic visitors settled in the mid 19th century. Just south of Kibuli is the upmarket Muyenga Hill, on which posh homes mushroomed during Kampala's 1990s renaissance. Popularly known as 'Tank Hill' after the conspicuous municipal water reservoirs on its summit, Muyenga is an effective beacon for the nightspots of Kabalagala and Ggaba Road at its base.

flexible, and plan on spending some time in the capital, it's worth timing your visit to coincide with school holidays when traffic is considerably lighter. The long break, dividing school years, is usually December to mid-February and there are shorter breaks around Easter and in August.

MATATUS A steady stream of matatus plies most trunk roads through Kampala, picking up and dropping off passengers more-or-less at whim, and charging around US$0.40–2 per person depending on the routing.

Matatu routes are not numbered, which can be confusing. Heading from the suburbs into central Kampala is pretty straightforward, however, since you can safely assume that any minibus pointed towards the city centre along a trunk route is going your way.

Heading out of town can be more daunting. If you're going anywhere along the Natete and Hoima roads (for instance Namirembe Guesthouse or Kasubi Tombs) you need to head to the New Taxi Park. Matatus to most other parts of the city leave from the nearby Old Taxi Park.

Sitting in a matatu crawling out of a central taxi park is hot, slow and uncomfortable, and you may prefer to walk or boda to an alternative taxi stage. On Kampala Road, matatus parked around the Total fuel station [141 E4] at the end of Parliament Avenue run to Red Chilli Hideaway (page 142) and other places along Port Bell Road, while those at the junctions with Burton Street will take you to Bombo Road, Makerere University, the National Museum and Kisementi. Following a couple of incidents involving commuters, Red Chilli Hideaway advise you to board a matatu at a recognised stage rather than one slowing to a speculative crawl beside you. If you must do the latter, do check that the vehicle contains an acceptable mixture of male/female/old/young passengers. If the demographics are limited to a clutch of feral-looking young men, decline the invitation.

TAXIS (SPECIAL HIRE) Conventional taxis – generally referred to as special hires – are usually easy to locate within the city centre and normally charge a negotiable US$4–6 or so for short trips and up to US$20 for longer rides or travel during congested hours. Taxi stands can be found outside most of the upmarket hotels, on Dastur Street close to the intersection with Kampala Road, on Ben Kiwanuka Street opposite the Old Taxi Park, near the junction of Navibuko and Kyagwe streets behind the New Taxi Park, and at the roundabout at the junction of Bombo and Makerere Hill roads. Any hotel or decent restaurant will be able to call a special- hire taxi for you.

UBER For a while, rather than finding a taxi and haggling a price, it was cheaper and more convenient to have an Uber come to collect you, assuming you got a driver who could read the map on the app. Ultimately though, the system proved more popular with passengers than operators, as drivers became disillusioned with the discrepancies between calculated fares and journey times during peak hours. Uber still persists, though be aware of dodges, once your driver has collected you, to bypass the app and revert to a negotiated rate. Depending on your destination and time of day, you may struggle to find an Uber driver prepared to take you.

BODA The easiest way to negotiate Kampala traffic is by boda boda (motorbike taxi). However, you shouldn't hop aboard without first reading about their poor road safety record on page 85. Fares start at US$0.25.

Vehicle congestion means that bodas have an essential role to play and there are initiatives to help commuters get around in greater safety. One such venture is Safe

Boda, whose drivers are distinguished by orange helmets (including one for the passenger) and a reflective vest bearing the owner's name. They can be hailed on the street, called on ☎ 0800 300200 (toll free) or summoned using an Uber-style app (available on Google Play or the App Store) which also calculates the fare for the journey. The city's 8,000 Safe Boda riders are trained in safe driving techniques, though in the rough and sometimes tumble of the streets, their application is inconsistent.

Given that bodas represent the main source of employment for young men in Kampala, it is inevitable that they now provide ample opportunities for crime. If possible, when riding a boda, keep hold of your bags on your lap rather than on your back. Pedestrians should also beware, especially after dark, of bag snatchers. Disturbingly, these incidents are no longer perpetrated by a single boda rider with a passenger-accomplice but now involve gangs working together. Finally, before you leave a bar late at night and hop on a motorcycle with an unknown male, ask yourself, 'Would I do this at home?' Most establishments can recommend a known boda rider or (preferably) a special-hire driver (page 86).

TOURIST INFORMATION AND TOUR OPERATORS

TOURIST INFORMATION At the time of writing, Kampala has no tourist information office, the closest thing being the Booking Office at UWA Headquarters on Kira Road where staff are at least well informed about the parks and reserves. A tourist information centre has opened in the grounds of the Sheraton Hotel [141 E3]. A joint venture between UWA and the Kampala city council, this promotes Uganda's remarkable natural heritage (not too difficult) and the so-called attractions of the capital (tricky one, that). Elsewhere, the city's backpacker haunts such as Bushpig Backpackers, Red Chilli Hideaway and City Annex Hotel are good sources of current information for budget travellers.

Look out for the locally produced ad-mags *The Eye* and *Expats in Uganda* at upmarket hotels, bookshops and tour agents. These contain useful nationwide listings for hotels, national park fees, buses, airlines, rafting companies, safari companies, etc, plus a few general articles including lodge and restaurant reviews and plenty of ads.

TOUR OPERATORS Heavy traffic means that conventional four-wheeled transport can be a slow and bothersome way to see the city. You'll see (and smell) much more on foot or on a boda, and although you could find the sights of central Kampala perfectly well with the aid of this book, your day will be infinitely more enjoyable with a good guide.

Full details of international and local tour operators servicing Uganda are listed on page 6.

Kampala Sightseeing Bus m 0778 285666; w promoteugandasafaris.co.ug. If you'd prefer to tour the city in a little more comfort, hop aboard the Sightseeing Bus. Tickets for a circuit around the standard landmarks on this smart new double-decker (open top & AC below) cost US$40 excluding entrance fees. Tours leave from the Hotel Africana at 09.00 & 14.00 & take 3–4hrs.

✱ **Kampala Walking Tours** m 0774 596222; w kampalawalkingtours.com. You'll have a great time exploring the city with the personable & informed Zulaika Birungi of Kampala Walking Tours. From the main post office [140 D4], Zulaika will take you downhill into the chaotic taxi parks & labyrinthine markets on the floor of the Nakivubo Valley. Then, if you're up for more, she'll lead you up the opposite hillside to the vantage points provided by the National Mosque [140 B4] & Namirembe Cathedral [128 B3] before concluding with the tour of the Kabaka's Palace in Mengo [128 C5]. A 3hr tour of Nakivubo costs US$25 pp; a 6hr tour, continuing to Mengo, is US$30 pp. Cost

'SLUM TOURS'

Every large African city has its slums and Kampala is no exception. The largest of these is Bwaise on the Gulu Road just outside the Northern Bypass. Most people's experience of this area is limited to its notorious traffic jam on the way to/from Murchison Falls. What goes unseen are the difficulties faced by Bwaise's 50,000 residents to secure basic needs such as water, nutrition, sanitation, education, housing and some sort of income. Elsewhere, similar difficulties beset the occupants of Namuwongo Slum, a linear shanty that has sprung up along a disused, swamp-edge railway corridor running down to the lake at Port Bell. The location represents a poignant juxtaposition of the haves and have-nots, being just 5 minutes' drive from the splendours of the city centre and directly between Muyenga and Bugolobi, two of the city's more affluent suburbs.

Two worthy initiatives have been set up to help visitors gain an understanding of the problems faced by people living in these slums and, in some small way, raise funds to tackle some of them. In Bwaise, life-long resident Salim Semambo has set up a small organisation, **Volunteers for Sustainable Development** ✷ (VFSD; m 0782 808257, 0753 301879; e volunteers.vfsd@gmail.com; f @slumtourkampala), to provide a very basic home for 26 orphaned or abandoned kids, many of them HIV positive. Their main source of income is a guided walk through this little-known side of Kampala. It is an extraordinary and humbling experience in which you'll find harsh realities countered by the optimism, friendliness and resilience of local residents, and by the determination of VFSD to make a tiny difference in the face of monumental odds. The tour costs US$25 and the proceeds, as you'll see, really do make a difference.

In Namuwongo, **Hands for Hope** (m 0772 913001; e info@onlinehope.org; w ugandahandsforhope.org), a UK-registered charity, started a protection centre for vulnerable children, an initiative that subsequently expanded into a nursery, primary and secondary school. A Hands for Hope tour offers visitors the chance to walk through the slum, meet community members, see the good works done by the schools and have lunch. There is actually no charge for the experience but obviously you'll do the decent thing and make a generous donation to the cause.

excludes nominal entrance fees at the mosque & palace. Highly recommended.

Walter's boda-boda tours m 0787 492781; w walterstoursinuganda.com. Rather than crawling through traffic in a safari car, Walter Wandera & his mates can take you around the city sights by boda. He & his team are exceedingly safety conscious & helmets are provided. Excursions cost US$35–45 pp, depending on group size.

WHERE TO STAY

The choice of accommodation in Kampala has come a long way since the early 90s when there were two established options: backpackers slept on the floor of the YMCA, while NGO and business travellers stayed in the Sheraton. Today, there's an abundance of hotels in every budget category and the listings on page 138 are highly selective. They are also very brief for the simple reason that they are likely to be of little interest to readers.

As far as budget/backpacker/volunteer accommodation goes, there are three main options. The centrally located City Annex is popular with folk who want to be, well, centrally located. Party people will be in heaven 2km north where the Bushpig Backpackers is perfectly placed to plunder the Kisementi/Acacia Avenue cluster of bars, restaurants and cinema. Some 15km out of town, the purpose-built Red Chilli Hideaway is anything but central but its excellent facilities and quiet location make it popular with volunteer groups and older visitors. Note that the city's oldest backpacker haunt, Kampala Backpackers, closed in 2022.

CITY CENTRE

Exclusive

✷ **Emin Pasha Hotel** [128 D2] (46 rooms) 27 Akii Bua Rd, Nakasero; ☎031 2264712; e info@eminpasha.com; w eminpasha.com. Centred on a carefully restored 1930s town house on leafy Nakasero Hill, 1km north of the city centre, the Emin Pasha is far & away the most characterful of central Kampala's hotels, with terraces, balconies & courtyards abounding above a landscaped garden & swimming pool. The recent addition of 2 extension blocks (doubling the hotel's capacity) have greatly enhanced the development, blocking out the multi-storeyed towers mushrooming beyond to create a secluded & quite delightful haven within. The rates are remarkably good value. *From US$180/210 B&B*. **$$$$**

Upmarket

Kampala Serena [141 F2] (150 rooms) Nile Av; ☎031 2309000; e kampala@serenahotels.com; w serenahotels.com. The former Nile Hotel, a facility remembered for its gruesome associations with Idi Amin's secret service, was reborn as the Kampala Serena in 2006, marking a major quantum leap in Ugandan hotel standards. Outside are beautifully landscaped grounds, a 6ha site replete with cliffs, lakes & waterfalls. The interior is equally grand, having been infused with a Moroccan flavour & seasoned by a dash of explorers-era nostalgia. From *US$303/322 sgl/dbl B&B*. **$$$$**

Moderate

Fairway Hotel [141 F1] (72 rooms) 1 Kafu Rd; ☎041 4259571; m 0789 493088; e booking@fairwayhotel.co.ug; w fairwayhotel.co.ug. If you last visited Kampala in 1969, you might well have stayed in the brand-new Fairway Hotel, Kampala's first international-standard hotel, & 50+ years on, its doors are still open. While new & more polished pretenders now tussle for the 'international' mantle, the Fairway still delivers the goods. Facilities include a gym, swimming pool & conference centres. The 2 popular outside restaurants & bar are preferable to the dining rooms inside. The refurbished rooms have AC & DSTV. *US$155/190 std sgl/dbl; US$235/270 exec sgl/dbl. B&B*. **$$$–$$$$**

Speke Hotel [141 E3] (50 rooms) Nile Av; ☎041 4259221; e reservations@spekehotel.com; w spekehotel.com. The last of the central hotels to retain any period character, the Speke enjoys a prime location & has a selection of restaurants on the premises. The long veranda facing Speke Av, a popular rendezvous spot, is Kampala's answer to the frontages of Nairobi's historic Norfolk & New Stanley hotels. The peaceful atmosphere is dispelled at night by the adjacent Rock Bar, a nightspot famous for its particularly persistent sex workers, so ask for a room at the rear. *US$70/80 sgl/dbl B&B*. **$$$**

Budget

Hotel City Square [140 D4] (22 rooms) Kampala Rd; m 0759 983814. Overlooking City Sq, this outdated, lino-tiled budget option is only 200m from the post office & will be ideal if the currently suspended Post Bus resumes its 08.00 departures to upcountry destinations. Otherwise, it's poor value compared with the Nakivubo listings opposite. *US$16/21 sgl/dbl B&B*. **$$**

Shoestring

✷ **City Annex** [141 G3] (31 rooms) De Winton Rd; m 0775 958867; e ncahotel@gmail.com. This rambling city-centre hotel was long a favourite of backpackers & volunteers, being conveniently placed for bars, restaurants, the Garden City & Oasis malls, & several Nairobi-bound buses. However, with only Mash Bus remaining on De Winton Rd, & the entertainment focus shifting to Acacia Mall & Kisementi, 2km north, the location no longer exerts the same pull. Though a variety of rooms are available, major improvements are needed to compete with newer offerings in the Nakivubo listings below. *US$11–22 sgl/twin with shared bathrooms, US$24 en-suite dbl. B&B.* **$$**

NAKIVUBO (BUS AND TAXI PARKS)

The hotels listed here are centrally located but presented separately due to their proximity to the main bus & taxi parks around Nakivubo Stadium. These options are strictly for those using public transport; permanent traffic congestion means that this is not an area to bring a vehicle. Most of Nakivubo's 'classic' shoestring hotels have been replaced by shop premises, so the listings below present the best acceptable options. If you really are strapped for cash, you'll find the dreadful Samalien, Mukwano & ABC guesthouses on the back road behind Nakivubo Place [140 C5].

Budget

Namayiba Park Hotel [140 A2] (45 rooms) Rhashid Khamis Rd; m 0707 303008, 0780 392461. If this new & seriously smart 6-floor hotel was in a more auspicious location, you'd happily pay 5 times the asking price. As it is, the park in question is Old Kampala's crowded & chlorophyll-free Namayiba Bus Terminal. Ideal for bus travellers arriving late or departing early from Namayiba but not Kasenyi. It would also be a feasible base for exploring the historic sites of Western Kampala. *US$16/18/26/32 sgl/deluxe sgl/dbl/twin B&B.* **$$**

Victoria Mews [140 C5] (90 rooms) Nakivubo Pl; m 0776 891622. Rising 6 floors above the floor of the Nakivubo Valley between Owino Market & the Old Taxi Park, this smart new landmark is another convenient & unexpectedly comfortable place to aim for when you arrive at one of the central bus parks. *US$26/40 sgl/dbl B&B.* **$$**

WESTERN KAMPALA

For 20 years, budget travellers were a familiar sight in taxis headed to & from the Kampala Backpackers in the western suburb of Mengo & local markets, bars & diners all profited from their presence. Since this closed in 2022, travellers have had little reason to stay this side of town, though the area's historical sites remain of interest (page 151).

Budget

Namirembe Guesthouse [128 B4] (40 rooms) 039 3109937; e info@namirembe-guesthouse.com; w namirembe-guesthouse.com. The Church of Uganda's sprawling guesthouse just below Namirembe Cathedral has long provided a secure & convenient choice for a respectable & invariably Church-oriented clientele of mature age. The 2nd-floor rooms in the new block enjoy a fabulous view of the metropolis, as does the thatched Coffee & Juice Bar. *New block US$40/50/60 sgl/dbl/twin en suite; old block US$20/30/40/45 sgl/dbl/twin/trpl en suite. All rates B&B.* **$$**

NORTHEAST KAMPALA

Kololo, Kampala's most affluent residential district, covers the hill immediately east of the city centre beyond the golf course. Historically associated with embassies & the diplomatic residences, this part of the city has always been thin on the ground when it comes to options for affordable accommodation. Though the higher slopes of the hill remain as exclusive as ever, budget options now exist on the periphery, temptingly close to the entertainment hotspots of Kisementi & Acacia Av (page 144). Further east, the more affordable suburbs of Ntinda & Naguru are the stronghold of Uganda's emergent middle class. Proximity to the Northern Bypass & the Ndere Centre (page 146) are the main reasons for seeking a hotel in this latter part of town.

Kololo

Exclusive

✷ **Villa Kololo** [128 D2] (8 rooms) 31 Acacia Av; 041 4500533; m 0701 098732; e villakololo@gmail.com; w villakololo.com. Part of the atmospheric Mediterraneo restaurant (page 144), the intimate Villa Kololo stands apart from Kampala's blander international offerings. The charm lies in the array of contrasting spaces & eclectic array of antique furniture. A private 1st-floor balcony enjoys a terrific view towards Nakasero Hill. *US$110/130 sgl/dbl B&B.* **$$$**

Budget

✷ **Bushpig Backpackers** [128 D2] (24 rooms) Acacia Av; m 0772 285234; e bookings@bushpigkampala.com; w bushpigkampala.com. Kampala's first boutique backpacker hostel occupies a converted 3-storey apartment block at the bottom half of leafy Acacia Av, close to a cluster of smart bars & restaurants. Facilities include a bar & restaurant/pizzeria (meals US$7–10). Bushpig also scores over its rivals with a broader, smarter choice of rooms, which represent extraordinary

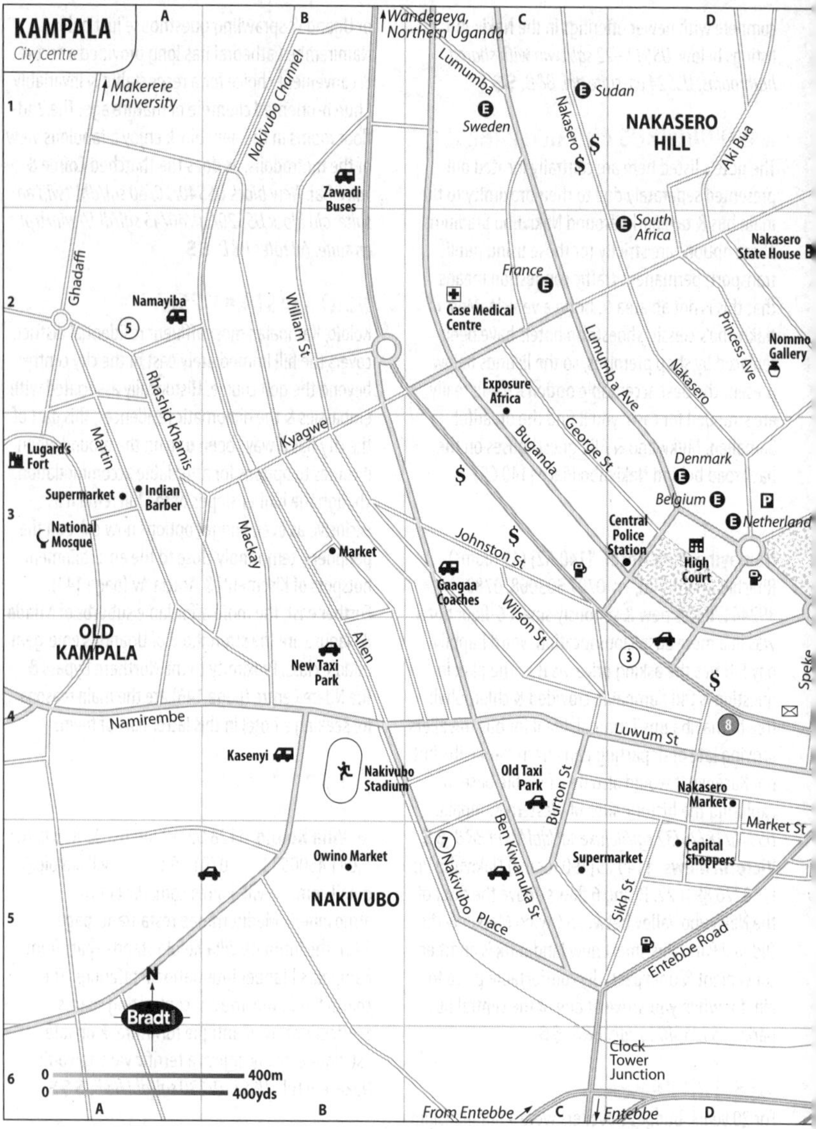

value for the location. *US$15/25/44/54 dorm/small sgl/twin/trpl (all shared bathrooms); US$50/60 sgl/dbl en suite. B&B. Long-stay discounts.* **$$**

Ntinda and Bukoto

Nob View [129 F1] (80 rooms) Commercial Rd, off Kira Rd; **m** 0774 225584; **w** nobviewhotel.com. Should you need a decent budget hotel with a swimming pool in northeast Kampala, look no further. Upper rooms on the south side have a balcony with a view. Turn off Kira Rd between the Shell & Total fuel stations in Ntinda. *US$28/34/34 sgl/dbl/twin.* **$$**

BUGOLOBI AND LUZIRA

For a few years in the 1930s, this southeastern corner of the city was an international gateway to Uganda, when flying boats from Europe landed on Lake Victoria at nearby Luzira. Transit passengers spent the night in a Bugolobi hotel

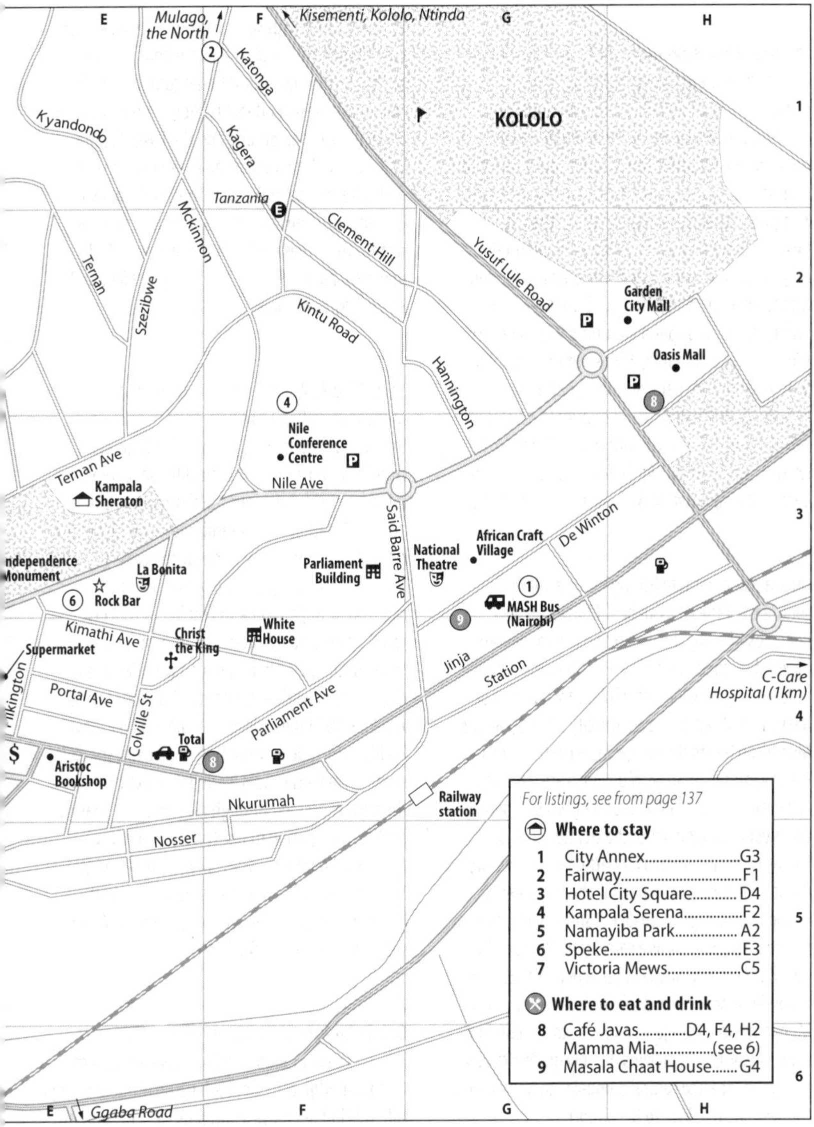

before continuing south. World War II & associated advances in long-distance air travel ended the flying boat service, relegating Luzira to a relative backwater. Today, its relevance to international visitors is as the home of the popular, budget-oriented Red Chilli Hideaway.

Moderate

Hotel Le Bougainviller [129 G3] (34 rooms) Katazamiti Rd, Bugolobi; 039 3220966; e hotelbougainviller@gmail.com; w bougainviller.co.ug. Inspired by classic Mediterranean villa architecture, this French-owned hotel surrounds a terraced & landscaped courtyard with a small swimming pool. The airy, spacious rooms have stone-tiled floors & glass doors lead out to the patio & central garden. If eating in doesn't appeal, there are plenty of options across the road in & around Village Mall. *US$116/131 sgl/dbl std, US$126/141 suites, US$136/151 duplex rooms. All rates B&B.* **$$$**

Budget

✷ Red Chilli Hideaway [123 H4] (30 rooms) Butabika Rd, near Luzira; ☎ 039 3202903 (office); m 0772 709151; e reservations@redchillihideaway.com; w redchillihideaway.com. This excellent hostel occupies purpose-built premises on a 2ha site in Butabika in southeast Kampala. It really is a hideaway, on the city's farthest extremity overlooking wetland on the edge of Lake Victoria. Check the website for details & for directions if self-driving. Once there, there are plenty of ways to spend your time with a library, table tennis, pool table, 16m swimming pool & indoor & outdoor bars. Accommodation options are varied. *US$8 camping; US$12 dorm; US$30/35/40 sgl/dbl/trpl with shared bathroom; US$50/55/60 en-suite sgl/dbl/trpl. Flat (self-contained dbl with kitchen, living room) US$75. Rates exc b/fast.* **$$**

GGABA AND MUNYONYO

Once a pair of remote fishing villages 14km southeast of the city, Ggaba & Munyonyo have been absorbed by the expanding metropolis, an inexorable spread curtailed – for the time being at least – by Lake Victoria. If plans for a bridge or ferry are realised, however, the city will leap across Murchison Bay to Busoke on the eastern shore. In the meantime, Ggaba & Munyonyo are, after the entertainment hub in & around Kisementi, perhaps the most relevant parts of the city for tourists. Firstly, there are options for getting out of the city & out on to Lake Victoria, while the still green & unspoilt landscape of Busoke, 15mins across the bay, is gaining popularity as a safe, scenic & accessible destination for cycling & other activities (page 162). Secondly, a new 10km dual carriageway now links Munyonyo to the Kajjansi entrance to the Entebbe Expressway, making it considerably quicker to drive to Entebbe than to central Kampala, guaranteeing a congestion-free drive to the airport.

Also included in this section are a couple of hotels on the distinctive Buziga-Konge-Makindye ridge which runs north from Munyonyo, parallel to Ggaba Rd. With panoramic views of the city in one direction & the lake in the other, the higher contours are exclusive enclaves for monied Ugandans & a few expats.

Exclusive

Speke Commonwealth Resort [123 G7] (449 rooms) Munyonyo; ☎ 041 4227111; e reservations@spekeresort.com; w spekeresort.com. Regularly hogging the limelight for this or that high-level international conference, this top-quality resort offers luxurious rooms & suites set in landscaped grounds on the Lake Victoria waterfront. With an Olympic-sized pool, marina & stables on site, swimming, horseriding, fishing & boat excursions are all possible diversions. A restaurant serves continental meals for US$12 upwards. *From US$182/201/225 sgl/dbl/suite B&B. W/end discounts apply.* **$$$$**

Upmarket

✷ Latitude Zero [129 E7] (47 rooms) Munyonyo; ☎ 0312 418300; e 0@thelatitudehotels.com; w thelatitudehotels.com. Melding a mix of Arabic, African & colonial influences, this luxurious hotel offers sumptuous accommodation & panoramic views on Makindye ridge. It's a strategic location, with access to the city centre as good as it gets while the Munyonyo-Kajjansi link to Entebbe Airport is just 15mins away. 2 ground-floor restaurants offer continental/Ugandan food & Italian menus respectively, while a 3rd on the 2nd floor serves Japanese & Chinese dishes & enjoys a lake view. Facilities include a swimming pool, gym, spa & short-term workspaces. Varied & eclectic design themes (expressed through carved doors, masks, basketwork, period maps, tribal jewellery & portraits, knobkerrie assemblages, tribal prints & so on) extend to the rooms, which are both luxurious & reasonably priced. *US$140/170 exec/superior rooms B&B.* **$$$**

Moderate

Cassia Lodge [123 G6] (30 rooms) Buziga Hill; m 0786 115085; e info@cassialodge.com; w cassialodge.com. Set high up on affluent Buziga Hill, this lodge enjoys a fabulous view of southern Kampala, the lake, & its adjoining wetlands. Though a swimming pool & an excellent 1st-floor restaurant (page 145) are provided, Latitude Zero (see above) is altogether classier & better value. *US$140/160 sgl/dbl B&B.* **$$$$**

Budget

Meley Impala Hotel [123 G7] (31 rooms) Munyonyo; m 0708 382984; e meleyimpalahotel@gmail.com.This hotel is conveniently placed off Salaama Rd just metres from the Munyonyo–Kajjansi highway. A restaurant & 3-storey extension is eating into the garden but it remains a pleasant spot. The tiled rooms are reasonable value for money – though some are smarter & more spacious than others. Outside the hotel is a shrine to St Andrew Kaggwa, a Baganda Christian who fell victim to the murderous 19th-century Kabaka Mwanga. *US$50/57/66 sgl/dbl/exec dbl B&B.* **$$**

WHERE TO EAT AND DRINK

Over the past 15 years, Kampala has become a diner's paradise, with hundreds of restaurants springing up all over the city to cater for all tastes and budgets. There are also, of course, numerous small take-aways, pork joints, roadside chicken grills and market stalls, which offer cheap and reasonable local food.

While plenty of low-key centres exist, there are three main clusters that are, not coincidentally, found in the most popular suburbs for diplomats, NGO workers and other expatriates. The greatest choice is found in and around **Kisementi and Acacia Avenue**, 1.5km north of the city centre, while additional hubs are found on **Muyenga Hill**, 3km to the south, and **Bugolobi**, 3km to the east.

In addition to the restaurants listed here, **Red Chilli Hideaway** (see opposite) and most other hotels in the upmarket and moderate ranges in Kisementi and Acacia Avenue have restaurants serving cuisine to guests and outsiders. The list below is only a small selection of what's on offer. For a fuller picture (at least of Kampala's smarter eateries), get hold of the free monthly ad-mags *The Eye* and *Expats in Uganda* for updated listings and restaurant reviews.

CITY CENTRE

Opportunities for fine dining outside the main hotels are limited indeed in the city centre these days. With virtually all quality restaurants having moved out to the suburbs, eateries outside the main hotels cater primarily for office workers & the 2 central branches of Café Javas are as good as it gets.

Café Javas [140 D4] Kampala Rd, opposite the post office; [141 F4] cnr Parliament Av; [141 H2] Oasis Mall. This popular Kenyan restaurant chain has 2 branches in the city centre & others in Kisementi, Namirembe, Acacia Mall, Lugogo Mall and on Acacia Av, Bombo Rd & Jinja Rd. The menu includes pies, burgers, steaks, wraps, quesadillas, salads & a range of cakes for afters. The prices aren't cheap but the main courses will often feed 2. *Mains US$5–11.*

Emin Pasha Hotel [128 D2] Akii Bua Rd; 031 2264712. The terraced Brasserie restaurant at Kampala's first boutique hotel (page 138) is a delightful setting for a special occasion, especially if someone else is paying! *Starters US$8–10, main courses US$10–30, desserts US$10.*

Mamma Mia [141 E3] Speke Hotel; 041 4346340; m 0772 630211. The corner plot of Nile/Kimathi Avs has served Italian food since the mid 1960s (with a few excusable interruptions in service). Located within the Speke Hotel complex, this restaurant is popular for lunch & dinner alike. *Meals US$8.*

Masala Chaat House [141 G4] De Winton Rd; 0772 510145. The thalis at this informal & affordable Indian restaurant opposite the National Theatre have long been a travellers' favourite. *Main course US$6–9.*

BUGOLOBI AND LUGOGO

With heavy traffic complicating excursions to Kabalagala & the city centre, the residents of Bugolobi & Mbuya were once all dressed up, with no place to go. Local entrepreneurs have responded by providing a range of opportunities to dine & party.

Ashiana [129 G3] Bandali Rise; f ashianabugolobi. Top-quality curries. *Main course exc rice/naan US$9.*

Dancing Cup [129 G4] Luthuli Av; f dancingcupbugolobi. The D-Cup provides a relaxed setting for a drink &/or a meal chosen from a diverse menu supplemented by daily specials. As an added bonus, the prices are carefully pitched to keep the riffraff out. *Mains US$8–10.*

Gatto Matto [129 G3] Bandali Rise, behind Village Mall; f GattoMatto.Kampala. With cosy seating & warm night-time illuminations, this garden bar-restaurant is a deservedly popular spot for an evening drink. Live music on Tue. *Meals in the US$7–10 range.*

Jazzville [129 G3] Bandali Rise. Popular & classy bar offering *muchomo* (roast meat) & with live music every evening until 23.00. *US$3–4.*

Nawab [129 G3] Bandali Rise; m 0709 743524. Affordable curry house with standard & combo menus plus delivery service. *Main course exc rice/naan US$7.*

KOLOLO

The western side of the upmarket Kololo Hill has become Kampala's main destination for eating out. You'll find an abundance of restaurants in & around Kisementi & the monolithic Acacia Mall, & along nearby Bukoto St & Acacia Av. The handful listed here really is the tip of the iceberg.

Kisementi

The Bistro [129 E2] f thebistrokampala. Hidden from the touts, peddlers & hawkers of the Kisementi car park (& other members of the budget dining classes) by a screen of foliage, this posh eatery offers diners a choice between a shady, stone-flagged terrace & a cool, AC interior. A wide-ranging selection of burgers, pastas, salads, grills & curries keeps everyone happy. *Main courses US$8–14.*

✷ **Cafesserie** [128 D2] Acacia Mall; w cafesserie.com. The terrace at the entrance to Kampala's most fashionable mall is the place to be seen at brunch, lunch &/or dinnertime. Splash out on a grill/salad/pasta before a little treat from Kampala's best selection of freshly made ice cream. *Mains US$10–12.*

Meza [128 D2] This storeyed, open-fronted restaurant stands directly opposite the entrance to Acacia Mall. Whether you content yourself with a shawarma wrap or upgrade to a shawarma-plate, grill or burger, Meza is a convenient & affordable option. *Wraps US$4.*

Que Pasa [129 E2] m 0783 874469; f quepasakampala. Further evidence in support of Kisementi's claim as home to Uganda's most varied selection of international menus is provided by this corner-plot *cantina*. The popularity of the Tex Mex menu is boosted by a daily happy hour for beers & cocktails. *Snack items US$4, meals US$9.*

Acacia Avenue

Bubbles O' Leary [128 D2] Acacia Av; f BubblesOLearys. Authentic Irish pub (fittings imported from a bankrupt bar in Eire) but without the authentic Guinness. Popular with young expats & Ugandans.

✷ **Four Points** [128 E2] Acacia Av; 020 0730000; e info@fourpointskampala.com; w fourpoints.com/kampala. Overlooking Kololo & the golf course, the open-sided 8th-floor bar-restaurant of this posh new business hotel provides the best high-rise view of the city available to the general public. *Beers US$2.50, main courses US$15–25.*

✷ **Khana Khazana** [128 D2] Acacia Av; 041 4233049; ⏲ closed Mon. One of Kampala's most atmospheric restaurants, KK serves rich & creamy dishes from across India. Splash out. *Main exc rice & naan US$9.*

✷ **Mediterraneo** [128 D2] Villa Kololo; 041 4500533; m 0701 098732. Kampala's most distinctive Italian restaurant comprises a mélange of decks, shades & shelters decorated with antique fittings & furniture. *Main course US$10–30.*

MUYENGA AND KABALAGALA

For years, Kabalagala ('Kabs' to those in the know) was notorious for Kampala's densest concentration of bars, restaurants, roadside grills & unattached ladies. Though its star is waning, there are still plenty of options for a fun evening out.

Fuego's [129 F5] Zimwe Rd; f Fuego.Cocktails. Restaurant. Turn left off Tank Hill Rd at Reste Corner junction at the very top of Kabalagala. Popular garden bar/restaurant attached to a converted residential house. *Meals US$8–10.*

Khana Khazana: The Veranda [129 G5] Tank Hill Rd; m 0752 224003. Sister to the legendary Khana Khazana restaurant in Kololo (see above), the Veranda provides Ggaba Rd residents with terrific Indian food without having to battle across town. *Main exc rice & naan US$9.*

Le Chateau [129 G3] Ggaba Rd; m 0761 840795; w lechateaukla.com. Perennially popular, Le Shat has been a venue for a special occasion for nigh on 30 years now. Located within the small & exclusive Quality Hill Mall, its airy, thatched premises offer a peaceful haven just off the busy Ggaba Rd, while the Belgian menu (US$12–20) is a definitive notch above anything else in the vicinity; our favourites are the lamb shanks & cowboy steaks. Mains US$8–18. The adjacent **La Patisserie** (m 0761 047320) is an equally popular & more affordable spot for pastries, coffees, baguettes, steaks, wraps, etc, while your view of the humble burger (US$8) will be elevated by a visit to the grill in the exclusive & appropriately priced **Le Gourmet supermarket**.

Little Donkey [129 F4] Kisugu Rd, near International Hospital; f littledonkeykampala. This great little restaurant has a cool atmosphere & good Mexican food. Proceeds support an organisation called S7 (ie: the year after S6, the final year in a Ugandan school) to increase options for school leavers. *US$4–8.*

GGABA AND MUNYONYO

While options in & around Ggaba fishing village are predictably basic, the affluent Munyonyo suburb is seeing a sudden growth in dining opportunities. The listings here cater for moderate budgets but, if a splurge is in order, head for the Speke Commonwealth Resort (page 142) or the plush Lake Victoria Serena (10mins away down the new Kajjansi highway).

Beach House [123 G6] Ggaba. The starting point for trips across the bay to Busoke, this downsized & downmarket version of the sprawling Speke Resort is a decent enough spot for a communal platter of whole tilapia & chips. *US$10.*

Cassia Lodge [123 G6] Munyonyo; m 0786 115085; e info@cassialodge.com; w cassialodge.com. Kampala's most spectacularly placed dining terrace overlooks Murchison Bay from the upper slopes of Buziga Hill. Better known for its accommodation, but the rates compare poorly with newer ventures. *Continental meals US$12.*

Coffee at Last [123 G6] Munyonyo Rd, off Ggaba Rd. In addition to a tempting array of grills, wraps, salads, juices & coffees, this popular coffee house is notable for elevating the humble rolex (page 88) from a snack to a feast. *Mains from US$5.*

Miki's [123 G6] Munyonyo Rd, off Ggaba Rd. This roadside bar & pizzeria is popular with locals & expats. *From US$6.*

ENTERTAINMENT AND NIGHTLIFE

BARS AND NIGHTCLUBS It's perfectly possible to visit any of the places mentioned in the previous section for a meal and a couple of drinks and retire happily before midnight. However, if that doesn't appeal, the locations listed below will keep you entertained until very late.

A word of warning. If you're out late on a Friday night (or theoretically at any time) carry a copy of your passport and visa page. We've heard of police asking tourists for copies of ID and charging those unable to oblige with immigration offences. On a Friday, this either means a weekend in the cells or an off-the-record contribution to the police welfare fund.

City centre

Rock Bar [141 E3] f rockbarkampala. Next to the Speke Hotel (page 138). The city centre's liveliest hangout is notable for its clientele of unattached & commercially minded women.

Kabalagala/Kansanga

Capital Pub [129 F5] Kabalagala. This noisy, sprawling & crowded bar in the heart of the Kabalagala cluster still rocks after all these years. First-time male visitors will be surprised at how the ladies are drawn to your wit & good looks like moths to a flame. Nothing to do with your wallet. Definitely not.

Deuces [129 F5] Ggaba Rd. Deuces occupies the premises of the famous Al's Bar, an institution that rocked Ggaba Rd into the small hours for over 20 years. The choice of music has fast forwarded a couple of decades & it's less intense than back in the day, but still popular with the late night/early morning crowd.

Industrial area off Jinja Road

Off Jinja Rd [129 E3], between 1st & 3rd streets. If your idea of a good time is music recorded since the millennium played at a volume that limits communication to sign language, then several nightclubs in this area will appeal.

ENTERTAINMENT

Cinema Century Cinemax's three-screen cinema in **Acacia Mall** [128 D2] shows brand-new international releases opening within a day or so of their premieres in London and New York (and at a fraction of the cost). Century Cinemax also operates in Arena Mall [128 D4] and Metroplex Mall [123 G1] on the Northern Bypass beyond Ntinda. Find current showings at w centurycinemax.co.ug or phone m 0700 660415. Less plush (and less current too) is the **4D Cinemax** [128 C2] (☎ 039 2080424) in Ham Shopping Centre opposite the main entrance to Makerere University.

Theatres and live performances Kampala has an active English-language theatre community, which mainly stages locally written plays in English. The **National Theatre** [141 G3] (☎ 041 4254567), which opened in 1959 on the corner of Said Barré Avenue and De Winton Road, puts on productions most weekends. Tickets cost around US$5–6.50. Rather smarter is the **La Bonita** [141 E3] theatre (f theatre.labonita) on Colville Street, home to The Ebonies, Kampala's most popular performing group, and a plush restaurant.

The **Ndere Centre** [123 F2] (☎ 041 4288123; m 0772 700117; w ndere.com), a purpose-built venue, set in large lawns to the northeast of the metropolis at Ntinda, is home to the well-known Ndere Troupe, which performs traditional dance and music from all corners of Uganda. The thrice-weekly shows (Wed, Fri & Sun between 18.00 & 21.00) are quite fantastic, though at US$24 for tourists and foreign residents alike, it's a rare family destination for the latter. The Ndere Centre lies between Ntinda crossroads and Kisaasi-Ntinda roundabout on the Northern Bypass.

Art scene Kampala has a vibrant art scene with several good art galleries and other venues scattered around the city. The Faculty of Fine Arts in **Makerere University** [128 C2] has some impressive resources and displays works by several of the country's leading or most promising talents. Artists often being free-spirited types, it's best to phone before visiting.

AfriArt Gallery [129 F4] Plot 110, 7th St Industrial Area; w afriartgallery.org

AKA Gallery [129 E1] Bukoto St, Kamwokya; w akagalleryuganda.com

Gallery Antique [128 C6] Lubowa, off Entebbe Rd; m 0772 430338; w africagalleryantique.com. Contemporary art plus a wide selection of genuine tribal & antique artefacts from across east & central Africa.

Nommo Gallery [140 D2] Princess Av, on the edge of the city centre in Nakasero

Umoja Art Gallery [129 E1] Off Kyebando-Kabira Rd, near Kampala International School Uganda (KISU); ⊕ 0.35410569, 32.5953868; w umojartgallery.org

SHOPPING

SHOPPING MALLS Kampala is served by a growing number of shopping malls, mostly in suburban locations. However, the choice and appeal of the goods available varies greatly and the outlet of most interest to tourists is likely to be the supermarket.

Acacia Mall [128 D2] w theacaciamall.com. Though the closure of its bookshop has dented the appeal of Kampala's smartest mall to all right-minded shoppers, you can still take in a film at the Metroplex cinema, buy socks at Woolworths & get your groceries at a Carrefour supermarket.

There are also plenty of opportunities for eating out, including KFC, the fashionable Cafesserie restaurant (page 144) & Nawab, an excellent Indian restaurant. The food hall offers a good choice of menus, as well as a great view towards leafy Nakasero Hill.
Arena Mall [128 D4] Kampala's newest mall enjoyed a slow start, its fortunes stalled by Covid-19 & interminable roadworks relating to Kampala's first flyover project. It is, however, conveniently located at the city end of the Ggaba Rd corridor & contains a Metroplex cinema, Carrefour supermarket & a Cafesserie restaurant.
Village Mall [129 G3] f villagemallug. Out in Bugolobi suburb, this smart mall has a Carrefour supermarket, a bookshop (which includes a good selection of local-interest publications) & branches of Brood bakery, KFC & Cafesserie.

SUPERMARKETS You'll find most of your day-to-day requirements in small suburban supermarkets, though the choice and quality has condensed in recent years to accommodate local tastes and budgets. Larger and more varied supermarkets include branches of the **Quality** chain in Old Kampala [140 A3], Lubowa [123 E7], and Naalya [123 H1]; while the French-owned **Carrefour** is represented at Lugogo Mall [129 F3], Acacia Mall [128 D2], Village Mall [129 G3] and Metroplex Mall [123 G1]. **Capital Shoppers** has branches in Garden City [141 H2], Ntinda's Capital Shoppers City [129 G1], and in the city centre on Dastur Street [140 D5].

If you're stocking up for a safari and want to avoid the usual packaged or frozen foodstuffs, **Quality Cuts** (outlets in the tiny Quality Hill Mall on Ggaba Road in Kabalagala [129 F5] and at Lugogo Mall [129 F3]) offer a decent selection of meats and cheeses.

BAKERIES Salt bread, as well as the locally preferred sweet variety, is widely available these days. For buns, baguettes, croissants, etc, visit **La Patisserie** also in Quality Hill Mall or the Dutch-owned **Brood Bakery** [129 G3] (Village Mall, Bugolobi; also Reste Corner, Muyenga).

BOOKSHOPS The excellent **Aristoc Bookshop** has a branch on Kampala Road [141 E4] and another which represents the last surviving highlight of Garden City Mall [141 H2]. You'll find an impressive selection of current novels, travel guides, field guides, tourist maps and publications about Ugandan history. The closest competition is **Bookpoint** [129 G3] in the Village Mall in Bugolobi.

HANDICRAFTS AND CURIOS Though home-produced crafts are increasing and improving, most local craft shops are still dominated by ubiquitous Kenyan carvings of animals and Maasai warriors. For the greatest choice of vendors (rather than choice of items), visit the **African Craft Village** [141 G3] behind the National Theatre and the **Exposure Africa** [140 C2] collective on Buganda Road.

By far the best selection of quality crafts is found in the **Banana Boat** (m 0705 665423; e crafts@bananaboat.co.ug; w bananaboat-ug.com) shops located at Kisementi [129 E2] and Lugogo Mall [129 F3]. These contain an excellent variety of items produced by over 90 small Ugandan artisans and workshops, many of them exclusively for Banana Boat. Bespoke items include jewellery, prints and handmade paper products as well as tribal art, guidebooks and maps.

OTHER PRACTICALITIES

CLUBS AND SOCIETIES Travellers with special interests may want to contact the following clubs and societies. A fuller list is contained in Kampala's free monthly ad-mag, *The Eye*.

Kampala Group of Bikers
f kampalagroupbikers. Kampala-based group of keen mountain bikers. Meets on Sun at Kabira Country Club [123 F2] car park at 08.00 for circuits of varying length & difficulty (up to 60km). KGB members also organise regular excursions to challenging destinations & events upcountry.

Mountain Club of Uganda e info@mcu.ug; w mcu.ug; f. Regular meetings, usually on the 1st Thu of each month (check the website for locations) & a programme of events in Kampala & beyond.

Nature Uganda ☎ 041 4540719; w natureuganda.org. Ring for details of free monthly nature walks around Kampala.

Uganda Bird Guides Club m 0777 912938; e info@ugandabirdguides.org; w ugandabirdguides.org. Most of the country's top bird guides belong to this club, which is well worth contacting if you're looking for a reliable freelance guide with local knowledge.

COMMUNICATIONS

Post office

The main **post office** [140 D4] is on the corner of Kampala and Speke roads with sub-post offices in Mengo, Ntinda, Wandegeyre and Nakawa (see also page 92).

Internet and email

The advent of smartphones has all but eliminated internet cafés in Kampala. However, most suburbs still contain a couple of basic setups while most hotels offer free Wi-Fi for guests, as do the Café Javas restaurants.

HAIR AND BEAUTY SALONS Recommended salons include 5enses [sic] at **Cayenne** in Ntinda [123 F2] (m 0772 587603), **Aisha** at Kisementi [128 D2] (☎ 041 4344366) and **Sparkles** in the Lugogo, Garden City and Oasis malls (m 0783 926871). Several of the upmarket hotels in the city centre also have in-house salons.

For gents' haircuts, the most reliable place is **Aisha** [128 D2] (US$8.50) in Kisementi Plaza, while at other locations, such as **Sparkles** and the **Indian barber** [140 A3] (US$3) near Quality Supermarket in Old Kampala, the outcome really is a matter of luck.

LIBRARIES The **Uganda Society** [128 D2] (m 0782 353775, 0787 818132; e ugandasocietysince1923@gmail.com; f; ⏲ 08.00–17.30 Mon–Sat, closed pub hols; a nominal daily membership fee is charged to casual visitors), in the Uganda Museum building on Kira Road, houses what is probably the most comprehensive public collection of current and out-of-print books about Uganda.

MEDICAL SERVICES The standard of health care in Kampala is constantly improving, and while not up to Western standards for serious medical attention, you'll find the city's better hospitals and clinics far superior in terms of speed of medical consultations, laboratory services, referrals and cost, though the associated bureaucracy can be a chore. Those listed below are generally considered competent by expats and travellers, but your hotel may be able to suggest other options in your vicinity.

C-Care Hospital [129 F4] St Barnabas Rd, Namuwongo; ☎ 031 2200400; e ihk@img.co.ug; w ihk.img.co.ug. This efficient & modern hospital was previously, & is still usually known as, International Hospital Kampala (IHK). If admitted for treatment, it's a good idea to start the final paperwork a couple of days before you expect to be discharged.

Case Medical Centre [140 C2] 69–71 Buganda Rd; ☎ 041 4250362, 24hr emergency line: ☎ 031 2250362. Modern, well-equipped clinic close to the city centre.

Nakasero Hospital [128 D2] Akii Bua Rd near Emin Pasha Hotel; ☎ 0800 200035, 24hr emergency line: ☎ 039 3224681; w nakaserohospital.com. Excellent general & specialist medical care.

Set against a backdrop of seven hills, Kampala is your archetypal African capital – a mixture of high-rise developments and suburban sprawl PAGE 121

above (T/D)

The striking Bahá'i Temple on Kikaya Hill is the only place of worship of its kind in the whole of Africa PAGE 160

right (D/D)

Today, Old Kampala is the focal point of the city's Islamic community and the site of an imposing mosque PAGE 150

below (D/D)

above (AVZ) Horseback safaris are a great opportunity to get close to animals in Lake Mburo National Park, as they are far more relaxed around horses than cars PAGE 217

left (AVZ) Budongo Forest Reserve is one of Uganda's key birdwatching destinations, with over 360 species recorded PAGE 355

below (AVZ) Head for any high spot in Queen Elizabeth National Park for stunning vistas over its sweeping plains PAGE 469

A boat trip along the Victoria Nile is one of the highlights of a visit to Murchison Falls National Park PAGE 386 above (AVZ)

A popular activity in Mgahinga Gorilla National Park is the vertiginous scramble up the 3,669m-high volcanic peak of Sabyinyo PAGE 538 right (AVZ)

Navigating the frothing white waters of the Upper Nile at Jinja is a trip highlight for any adrenaline junkie PAGE 251 below (AU)

above (SS) The trails to the snow peaks of the Rwenzori Mountains follow the floors of glacier-carved chasms inhabited by surreal groves of giant groundsel PAGE 453

below (AVZ) On its way downhill from Mount Elgon's central caldera, the Sipi River plunges over ochre basalt cliffs to create the massif's emblematic waterfall PAGE 284

below right (AVZ) Bwindi Impenetrable National Park was not named lightly – as you'll appreciate as you traverse its steep, soggy and densely vegetated slopes in search of gorillas PAGE 546

Ringed by distant mountains in Uganda, Kenya and South Sudan, the plains of Kidepo Valley National Park are one of Africa's great wildernesses PAGE 310

above (AVZ)

Jewel-like Lake Kifuruka is just one of the 30-plus crater lakes that stud the Rwenzori footslopes near Fort Portal PAGE 424

right (AVZ)

In the shadow of the Kijura Escarpment, Ugandan kob graze the Rift Valley plains in Toro-Semliki Wildlife Reserve PAGE 437

below (AVZ)

above (SS) Bordering the park's eastern rim, the densely forested Kyambura Gorge hosts Queen Elizabeth National Park's only habituated chimpanzee community PAGE 496

below (AVZ) The zig-zag outline of the Virunga volcanoes provides a dramatic backdrop to the placid waters of Lake Mutanda PAGE 542

The northern plains of Queen Elizabeth National Park are potted with a series of magnificent explosion craters, each with its own microhabitat PAGE 478 above (AVZ)

Lovely Lake Bunyonyi is an excellent spot to chill out for a few days before or after gorilla tracking PAGE 517 below (AFS/S)

GT
Ganders Travel
Exceptional holidays thoughtfully planned
Africa and Indian Ocean Travel Specialists
E—Lucinda@ganderstravel.com
www.ganderstravel.com
T—07552 198394

The Surgery [129 F1] Naggulu Dr; ⊕ 0.341490, 32.6020; ☎ 031 2256001/2/3; 24hr emergency & ambulance service: m 0752 756003; w thesurgeryuganda.org. Originally the clinic in the British High Commission, this is the choice of many expats. Many travellers have also found the website a useful resource.

DENTAL SERVICES Kampala has a small clique of competent dentists including **Jubilee Dental Practice** (☎ 041 4344647) and **Doctors A & G Madan** (m 0772 433058/9). The well-equipped dental clinic at **Mengo Hospital** [128 B4] (☎ 041 4272861) is equally efficient and more reasonably priced than most.

NATIONAL PARKS AND RESERVES The **Uganda Wildlife Authority** [128 D2] is in charge of all of Uganda's national parks and game reserves. The booking office (☎ 041 4355000; e info@ugandawildlife.org; w ugandawildlife.org; ⊙ 08.00–13.00 & 14.00–17.00 Mon–Fri, 09.00–13.00 Sat) is located in the UWA headquarters on Kira Road between the Uganda Museum and the British High Commission. Gorilla-viewing permits for Bwindi and Mgahinga can be booked and paid for here, as can banda accommodation in the various national parks and game reserves, and you can also pick up some informative brochures.

WHAT TO SEE AND DO

The Uganda Museum, Kasubi Tombs and other sites of interest situated more-or-less within the city limits of Kampala are covered on the following pages. As with any city, however, just strolling around can be illuminating; the contrast between the leafy avenues above Kampala Road and the bustling commercial streets running downhill towards the bus and taxi parks is striking. It is also possible to take a boda tour (page 137), while an app and downloadable map of historical buildings in Kampala, supported by the European Union, was published by the Cross-Cultural Foundation of Uganda in 2019 and is available at w crossculturalfoundation.or.ug/historical-sites-more-resources. Sites of interest in Entebbe are covered in the previous chapter, while those further afield from Kampala are covered in *Chapter 6*.

CITY CENTRE Kampala's modern city centre – which sprawls across a valley about 2.5km east of Kabaka Mwanga's former capital on Kasubi Hill, immediately east of Lugard's original fort on Old Kampala Hill – boasts little in the way of compelling sightseeing. The most important cluster of architecturally noteworthy buildings is centred on the acacia-lined **Parliament Avenue** [141 F4] on the east side of the city centre. On Parliament Avenue itself, the imposing though not exactly inspiring **Parliament Building** [141 F3], built during the colonial era and still the seat of national government today, is a vast white monolith entered via an angular concrete arch, built to commemorate independence in 1962. On the same block lies the so-called **White House** [141 F4], occupied by the Kampala City Council, while immediately to its east, on De Winton Road, stand the **National Theatre** [141 G3] and attached **African Craft Village**. Also of minor interest is the **railway station** [141 G4], which lies on Jinja Road about 200m further south. Built in the 1920s, it has fallen into virtual disuse since passenger services out of Kampala were suspended in 1995.

On Nile Avenue, the **Independence Monument** [141 E3], just outside the fenced gardens, is worth a minor diversion – a tall, attractively proportioned neo-traditional statue of a mother and child emerging from mummy-like bandages of colonial bondage. The attractive gardens behind the statue were originally created to commemorate the jubilee of King George VI and now form the grounds of the Kampala Sheraton. Once a popular lunchtime space, they are today closed to the general public, security reasons being the rather lame excuse.

You'll find an altogether more vibrant taste of city life in the busy commercial streets between Kampala Road and the taxi parks on the floor of the Nakivubo Valley. If these roadways are not adventure enough, try to find an indoor route through a series of shop-filled complexes around William and Wilson streets, a block below Kampala Road. Other than advising that a downhill trend will lead to the taxi parks, I can give no further clues as to how to navigate their incredibly crowded passages; indeed, I'm not sure I've ever taken the same route twice.

OLD KAMPALA Old Kampala Hill [140 A3], which rises gently to the immediate west of the city centre, 10 minutes' walk from the New Taxi Park, was the site of the original fort and capital founded by Captain Frederick Lugard in 1890. Enclosed within the oval Old Kampala Road, the hill is dotted with a few fine colonial-era buildings of Asian design, now generally rather rundown though some have been renovated.

Old Kampala is most notable today as the focal point for Kampala's Islamic community and the site of the imposing **National Mosque** [140 A3] (🕘 09.00–18.00 Mon–Thu, Sat & Sun, 09.00–11.00 & 14.30–18.00 Fri; tour US$4). It was initiated by Idi Amin in the 1970s, but the project stalled after the dictator's overthrow and was only completed in 2006 with funds provided by the late Libyan leader, Colonel Gaddafi. When work on the mosque restarted after a 25-year delay, Amin's concrete monolith was demolished to make way for today's magnificent copper-domed structure.

Given the dearth of sightseeing highlights in Kampala, a visit to the mosque is a popular – and genuinely worthwhile – diversion. Visitors are welcomed and you'll find a tourism office (m 0772 502037) just inside the main gate. There is no need to book a daytime tour (US$6.60 pp) but a sunrise visit must be arranged in advance: starting at 06.30, this enables you to climb the tower and watch dawn break over the city. Women will be provided with shawls to wear. Men may wear shorts that extend below the knee, but if they are deemed too short, a kanzu will be provided.

The highlights are the main hall and the ascent of the minaret. The former is an imposing space which, carpeted but otherwise unfurnished, is dominated by a forest of massive columns that support the roof and copper dome. European, Arab and African influences meld with Italian stained-glass windows, Ugandan timber and an Arabian mosaic on the underside of the dome above a massive and magnificent metal chandelier. Inside the minaret, 306 steps spiral upwards to provide a superbly giddy 360° view over the city.

Part of the complex, but accessed from Old Kampala Road, is a period building with a vaguely Arcadian frontage. This is an approximation of a historic building that was demolished to make way for the mosque car park. Though known as the Old Fort, it was built some years after Lugard's occupation in 1908 and was actually Kampala's first museum. Entrance costs US$5 though there's little to see inside the building and the compound is of greater interest as the site of a bustling craft market on Fridays.

MAKERERE UNIVERSITY [128 C2] The main campus of Uganda's respected Makerere University, which was founded in 1922, lies about 1km north of the city centre and can be entered via the main gate on Makerere Hill Road, some 200m west of Wandegeyre traffic lights on Bombo Road. The **university library** has an extensive Africana section, the **campus bookshop** stocks a selection of local-interest academic works, and the gallery in the **Faculty of Fine Arts** has regular exhibitions. The spacious green grounds possess an aura of academic gentility at odds with the hustle and bustle of downtown Kampala, while the older buildings – in particular the whitewashed **Main Hall** with its handsome bell tower – will be of interest to students of colonial architecture. Those interested in contemporary buildings can also learn a thing or two (mainly about the things that architects expect to get away with these days) from recent additions to the campus.

UGANDA MUSEUM [128 D2] (Kira Rd, about 2km from the city centre; ⌚ 08.00–17.00 daily; a small entrance fee is charged) The Uganda Museum is the oldest in East Africa, and perhaps the best, rooted in an ethnographic collection first exhibited in 1905 in a small Greek temple near Lugard's Fort on Old Kampala Hill. Formally established in 1908, the museum was initially known locally as Enyumba ya Mayembe (House of Fetishes) and its exhibits were believed to bestow supernatural powers on the colonial administration. In 1954, the museum relocated to its present site on Kira Road. For those with an interest in pre-colonial African history, there are stimulating displays on the Nakayima Tree, Ntusi and Bigo bya Mugyenyi, as well as other aspects of Ugandan history. Of more general interest is a fantastic collection of traditional musical instruments from all over the continent, and the ethnographic gallery, which houses a variety of exhibits relating to traditional Ugandan lifestyles. To get there on foot or in a private vehicle, follow Kampala/Bombo Road north out of the city centre, turning right at the traffic lights at Wandegeyre into Haji Kasule Road, crossing straight across another roundabout after 400m into Kira Road. The museum is clearly signposted to the right, 600m past this roundabout. Matatus between the New Taxi Park and Kamwokya will drop passengers roughly opposite the museum entrance, and can be picked up at taxi ranks along Kampala/Bombo Road north of the junction with Burton Road. The **Uganda Society Library** in the main museum building (⌚ 08.00–19.30 Mon–Sat) has a comprehensive collection of antique books and recently published works relating to Uganda.

NATETE ROAD A number of minor historical sites lie within 1km of the Natete Road, which runs west out of central Kampala in the direction of Masaka.

Namirembe Cathedral [128 B3] The Anglican (now Church of Uganda) cathedral perched atop Namirembe Hill, roughly 1.5km west of the city centre off Natete Road, is one of the most impressive colonial-era constructions in Kampala, and it also offers superb views over the city centre and suburbs. The original cathedral, completed in 1903 and consecrated a year later (page 152), was built entirely by Baganda artisans, albeit under the supervision of a British missionary, and could hold a congregation of 3,000 people. It was described contemporaneously by W E Hoyle as 'a remarkable building with walls of sun-dried bricks, and brick columns supporting the thatch roof, containing 120 tonnes of thatch [and a] ceiling covered with washed reeds of elephant grass'. This building was destroyed by lightning in 1910 and the present cathedral, a more conventional red-brick structure, built to vast dimensions and graced by some attractive stained-glass windows, was completed in 1919. The cemetery contains the grave of Bishop Hannington, murdered near Jinja in 1885, as well as that of Sir Albert Cook, a pioneering medical doctor who arrived in Kampala in 1896 and whose extensive writings about the early colonial era are quoted elsewhere in this guide. Brass memorial plaques on the wall testify to the often short lives of Europeans in those early days.

THE CONSECRATION OF NAMIREMBE CATHEDRAL

The consecration of Namirembe Cathedral on 21 July 1904 was described vividly in the Mengo Notes *a month after the event:*

A great crowd began to assemble at 06.00, and…the crush at the doors [was] so great that they had to be opened to prevent people being crushed to death. There was a considerable amount of struggling and good-natured fighting among the Baganda desirous of gaining entrance, for not more than 3,000 could get in, and the crowd must have numbered nearly 10,000…Numbers climbed through the windows and jumped down on to those seated inside… Mr Savile had a bone in the hand broken in trying to repress a rush. To while away the time of waiting Mr Hattersley gave half an hour's organ recital… The European and native clergy, over 40 in number, assembled at the west door, and all in procession marched up to the church, repeating the opening sentences of the Consecration Service…in English and Luganda…Then came morning prayer…and the wonderful way in which the congregation responded, and joined in the hymns and chants, will long be remembered.

Instead of dispersing, the vast crowd unable to gain entrance to the service had filled all the school rooms around the church, and still enough remained to nearly fill the yard. [They] contributed to the collection just as though they had taken part in the service. This considerably delayed matters, and it seemed as though the bringing in of offerings would never cease… The collection consisted of rupees, rice, and cowrie shells…in bundles more than enough to fill a whole collecting bag. Then came goats led up by ropes to the communion rails…fowls in a coop and singly; one, trussed feet and wings, was solemnly handed by the sideman to the Bishop along with his bag of shells…More than 30 head of cattle had been sent in by chiefs, but it was wisely decided that it would not be well to admit these to the church. The proceeds of the collection thus totalled up to over £80, the exact amount we cannot give, as the cattle have not all been sold at the time of writing.

Bulange Building [128 B4] Less than 500m past the turn-off to Namirembe, the impressive Bulange Building – the traditional seat of the Buganda Parliament – stands on the south side of Natete Road, directly opposite the junction with Sentema Road. Though the Bulange's high roof, capped with a trio of spires, is visible from the main road, to see the building properly you'll have to leave Natete Road to find the main entrance at the head of a straight, tree-lined avenue known as Kabaka Njagala ('the king is coming') which runs for a mile to the Kabaka's Palace (see opposite) on the facing hill. Visits to the Bulange (US$10) should be arranged (unless the building is in official use) at a tourism office just outside the main gate.

Kabaka Mwanga's Lake, Rubaga Cathedral and the Kabaka's Palace In 1885, Mwanga initiated an ultimately overambitious scheme of digging a 15km canal from his palace to Lake Victoria. Work was abandoned when Buganda's quarrelling Christian and Muslim factions united long enough to drive the kabaka from his capital. Today, a 400m-long lake in the valley between Mengo and Rubaga Hills [128 B5] is all that remains of the project.

The lake was at one time more of a health hazard than a tourist attraction, though the shores have been tidied up a bit and there are some interesting birds to be seen –

notably large colonies of cattle egrets and weavers and possibly crowned cranes and maribou storks. Follow the Natete Road out of the city centre for about 2km then turn left just beyond the spired Bulange Building. As you descend the hill, you'll see the lake. The shore can be reached about 1km further on, by taking a steep dirt road on your left.

The lake can easily be visited in conjunction with the **Catholic cathedral** [128 B5] on Rubaga Hill, which lies about 500m south of Natete Road along Mutesa Road. Though neither as old nor as impressive as its Church of Uganda equivalent at Namirembe, it is notable for stained-glass windows depicting the story of the Uganda Martyrs. Also close to the lake is the **Kabaka's Palace** [128 C5] on the low Lubiri Hill, the site chosen by Mwanga after his coronation in 1884. The ill-fated Kabaka Edward Mutesa was driven from this palace in 1966 by Idi Amin on Obote's orders. The army subsequently occupied the site until 1993, gaining a reputation for terror. Hundreds were taken through its gates by the agents of Amin and Obote, never to be seen again, while ill-paid and ill-disciplined troops terrorised the leafy suburbs of Rubaga and Mengo. The Buganda kingdom is once more in possession of Lubiri Hill and you'll find an informed guide to show you round at the tourism office just inside the main gate (US$10 pp). The restored Kabaka's Palace is closed to the public and the 'attractions' mostly relate to the Amin and Obote regimes. The centrepiece – the so-called Dictators' Prison – is a complex of underground cells and execution chambers decorated by some movingly defiant graffiti scrawled in charcoal by the doomed inmates (you'll need a translator). It's a grim hark back to a darker time and it's a relief to emerge into Mengo's picturesque environs and be thankful that those days are past.

HOIMA ROAD Two important sets of royal tombs, collectively housing the bodies of the four kabakas of Buganda to have died since the 1850s, lie within easy reach of the road running northwest from central Kampala towards Hoima. Though Kasubi Tombs are better known, a visit to the Wamala Tomb is no less worthwhile (its caretakers are less accustomed to tourist visits) and now also certainly cheaper.

Kasubi Tombs (m 0777 253155; ⌚ 08.00–07.00 daily; US$20, foreign residents US$15, inc guide) In 1882, Kabaka Mutesa relocated his kibuga (palace) to Nabulagala Hill, briefly the capital of his father, Suuna II, some 30 years earlier, and renamed it Kasubi Hill after his birthplace some 50km further east. Mutesa constructed a large hilltop palace called Muziba Azala Mpanga (roughly translating as 'a king is born of a king'), where he died in 1884 following a prolonged illness. As was the custom, Kasubi Hill was abandoned after the king's death – his successor Mwanga established a new capital at Mengo Hill – but, rather less conventionally, Mutesa was the first kabaka to be buried with his jawbone intact, in a casket built by the Anglican missionary Alexander Mackay. In a further break with tradition, Kasubi rather than Mengo was chosen as the burial place of Kabaka Mwanga in 1910, seven years after his death in exile (page 154). It also houses the tombs of his successor, Daudi Chwa II, who ruled from 1897 to 1939, and of Edward Mutesa II, whose body was returned to Uganda in 1971, two years after his death in exile.

Until 2010, the tombs comprised a huge domed structure of poles, reeds and thatch, which – aside from the addition of a concrete base – seemed to have changed little in appearance over the intervening 130 years. Unfortunately, on the night of 16 March 2010, the building, due to causes still unknown, burned down. The structure, reduced to an arching framework of hitherto unsuspected (or at least unmentioned) metal beams, remained under a patchwork of gaudy orange tarpaulins for almost three years before a Ush10 billion reconstruction programme started in January

THE FUNERAL OF KABAKA MWANGA

Edited from the Uganda Notes *of September 1910*

Mwanga was deported in the year 1899 [and] moved to the Seychelles, where he died in May 1903...Nothing can be more distressing to the Baganda mind than that a near relative should not be buried in his own Butaka [home]...So the leading chiefs and the descendants of Mwanga have been agitating to exhume the body and have it transferred to Uganda, and at last permission was obtained.

2 August [1910] was a day of great excitement, and business, as far as natives was [sic] concerned, was suspended. A large crowd proceeded to meet the steamer at Kampala Port to bring up the large packing case in which was enclosed the leaden coffin containing the body of the deceased king [Mwanga], and at 15.00 an enormous concourse followed the body to Namirembe Cathedral...The funeral cortège entered the church, filling it from end to end, and part of the Burial Service was read...The body was then removed to Kasubi, the burial place of King Mutesa...[where] a vault had been carefully prepared of brick and cement, and a double coffin was in readiness.

On the morning of Wednesday [3 August], everyone of any importance in or near Mengo was present at the tomb and the gruesome process of opening the leaden shell in order to examine the remains was gone through. Repugnant though it seems to open a coffin so many years after a death has taken place, it was insisted that as King Daudi had never seen his father in the flesh he must on no account miss seeing his corpse, and to the surprise of everyone concerned the features were quite recognisable...Daudi took hold of a barkcloth together with Mugemo and Kago and covered up the corpse, this being the custom of a son whose father is dead, and then the body was buried...In the afternoon the concluding part of the Burial Service was read; Bishop Tucker and a very large number of Europeans were present, together with a crowd of natives, to perform the last rites.

To follow old custom, Mwanga should really have been buried inside his own court [on Mengo Hill], and many of the natives were inclined to follow precedent; but it was finally decided that if he were to be buried in Mengo, the Kabaka Daudi would have to turn out [of his] comfortable and permanent residence, [which] seemed inadvisable, especially when there is the difficulty of securing a suitable

2013. This was finally completed in 2024, since when it has been business as usual. A total of 52 giant reed rings in the roof of the new hut once again represent each of the clans of Buganda, while a giant veil – created from countless pieces of barkcloth – screen the four tombs from the vulgar gaze of the public. Unfortunately, a fascinating collection of irreplaceable artefacts which stood in front of the curtain – including portraits of the four monarchs, traditional musical instruments, weapons, shields, fetishes, gifts from Queen Victoria and a stuffed leopard kept as a pet by Mutesa I – were destroyed in the fire and what you'll see now are replicas.

Interestingly, the restoration provided the Baganda with the opportunity to reconstruct the tombs using their original design. Historically, it transpired, the tomb of a kabaka was an even structure resembling a huge, thatched wigwam, some 16m tall. The significantly lower, dome-like structure destroyed in 2010 was a British imposition dating back to 1938 when the introduction of load-bearing concrete beams enabled the height of the structure to be reduced by 6m. Whether this was (as some academics claim) a deliberate attempt to hijack Baganda tradition and

site for the new court in the Capital. On the morning of Thursday 4 August, a very interesting ceremony took place, which had been deemed impossible until such time as Mwanga should be buried in his own country.

The following is a translation of an account of the ceremony, written by the Rev Henry Wright Duta:

> [King Daudi] came and stood outside his court [on] the coronation chair...Mugema opened proceedings by bringing a barkcloth and hanging it about the king from his shoulders...He then put on a calfskin to remind [Daudi] that his first forefather was thus dressed...Then came Kasuju, who brought a second barkcloth and also a leopard skin, with which he also proceeded to dress the king...the meaning of the leopard skin is that it separates him from all other princes and makes him into the king...The reason why he is dressed in two barkcloths is because he is called the 'father of twins', that is to say he gives birth to many people and he rules over many people.
>
> [Kasuju] brought the king a sword...saying 'take this sword and with it cut judgement in truth (distribute justice equally and fairly), anyone who rebels against you, you shall kill with this sword'. Then they brought before him the drum which is called Mujagazo which is very old indeed and which has carved on it a python (once sacred to the Baganda)...this is supposed to be the drum which Kimera had with him when he came from Bunyoro...A shield was then presented to the king and...two spears...[and] a bow and arrows...the weapons with which Kimera first came to Uganda...Then came a long string of people bringing offerings too numerous to mention.
>
> After that the king was placed on the shoulders of Namutwe so that the crowd might all have a good look at him, saying 'This is your king' and the crowd set up a loud yell beating their hands with their mouths to produce a tremulant effect. Then the king together with the Lubuga (queen sister) and an old woman to represent the head of the king's wives were all carried on the shoulders of their attendants back into the [royal] Court...Then came the whole of the visitors to the king to congratulate him on his accession, he sitting down on the seat called Mubanga, which resembles a drum, and old Prince Mbogo, the brother of [the late king] Mutesa, came and wrapped some cents around his wrist in place of the cowrie shells which used to obtain here. Every member of the king's tribe – princes, princesses and everyone else who could be present – brought him presents of money...and for days afterwards all his relatives came in batches and went through the same ceremony.

anchor it in the shadow of British authority, or an attempt to reduce the building's vulnerability to lightning, is not clear. Whatever the truth, it was in their original – and more imposing – form that the tombs were revealed in 2024.

The tombs are maintained by the wives of the various kings – or more accurately by female descendants of their long-deceased wives – some of whom live on the property. Many of the kings' wives, sisters and other female relations are also buried at Kasubi in several smaller buildings that flank the driveway. The complex is entered via a large traditional reception hut known as a bujjabukula. This is tended by the chief gateman, known as Mulamba (a hereditary title), who customarily dresses in a brilliant yellow barkcloth robe, as do his assistants. The history, as delivered by your guide, is of undeniable interest but for US$20, one can't help feeling that as the centrepiece of Ganda culture (and a UNESCO World Heritage Site to boot), Kampala's only boda fide tourist attraction might offer more than a large grass hut, perhaps a properly equipped visitor centre, coffee shop, dancing, craft displays and so on.

JAWBONE SHRINES

The Baganda traditionally believe that the spirit of a dead man resides in his jawbone, for which reason it is customary for the jawbone of a deceased king to be removed and preserved in a separate shrine before the rest of the body is buried. The jawbone shrine is normally located at the last capital site used by the dead ruler and is housed within a miniature reproduction of his palace. Jawbone shrines associated with almost all of the kabakas who preceded Mutesa I lie scattered across an area of less than 500km^2 northwest of present-day Kampala. Most are now untended and have suffered from serious neglect over the past century, but their location remains well known to locals.

According to the historian Roland Oliver: 'after the dislocation of the jawbone, the body of the king was handed over to the chief executioner, Senkaba, who took it away…to the royal cemetery. There, the body was placed on a bed and certain friends and officials of the dead kabaka were killed and their bodies were thrown upon the heap. These sites did not, like the jawbone shrines, become places of pilgrimage. Nevertheless they were guarded by Senkaba and his representatives.' While jawbone shrines are associated with one specific king, the royal burial grounds are more centralised entities. At least ten tombs of the earlier kings are situated within a 1km^2 area at Gombe, 20km north of Kampala, while a similar number of more recent kings are buried at Merera along the Hoima Road.

The last ruler of Buganda to receive a traditional royal burial was Kabaka Suuna II, whose jawbone shrine is preserved in a large traditional structure at the site of his last *kibuga* (capital) at Wamala. Suuna's successors – influenced by Islam and Christianity – were buried at Kasubi with their jawbones intact. There is some ambiguity about where the rest of Suuna's remains are located: one tradition asserts that he was the last king to be buried at Merera, while others claim that he was buried at Wamala. The most likely explanation is that Suuna was originally buried at Merera, but his body was later exhumed by his son Mutesa I to be buried alongside the jawbone at Wamala.

To get there from the city centre, follow Makerere Hill Road west from Wandegere crossroads for almost 2km to Nakulabye roundabout. Turn right and 2km further on you'll reach Kawaala Market traffic lights at a five-way junction. The tombs, signposted to the left, are about 500m uphill along Masiro Road. Plenty of matatus run from the city centre to Kasubi Market.

Wamala Tomb [122 C1] Situated on the crest of a low hill some 12km northwest of central Kampala, Wamala Tomb is housed in an attractive, traditional, thatched domed building, slightly smaller and older than its counterpart at Kasubi. The hill is the former palace and sacred resting place of Kabaka Mutesa I's father and predecessor Kabaka Suuna, who ascended the throne c1830 and died in 1856. Suuna is remembered as a despotic ruler and keen hunter. The menagerie he maintained at Wamala – said to have included lions, leopards, elephants and various smaller creatures – sufficiently impressed the first Arab traders to reach Buganda that word of it reached Sir Richard Burton at the Swahili Coast.

Wamala is neither as well known as Kasubi, nor as carefully tended, but it is just as interesting in its comparatively low-key way. A diverse array of royal artefacts – spears, shields, drums and other musical instruments – is displayed in front of the barkcloth drape that veils the tomb itself. Opposite the main building stands the former palace and tomb of Suuna's mother, Namasole Kanyange, who according to tradition was a very beautiful woman and also highly influential – it's said that Suuna insisted the namasole live alongside him so that he could keep an eye on her doings. In keeping with Kiganda royal custom, Kanyange appointed a successor as namasole before her death. The lineage survives to this day: the fourth namasole to Suuna is resident at Wamala and still performs traditional duties such as tending the royal tomb.

To reach Wamala, follow the Hoima Road out of Kampala past the junction for Kisubi to cross the Northern Bypass into the elongated and congested corridor of Nansana. After 4km, just before the road crosses the remnants of a swamp, you'll need to turn right (⊕ 0.3856022, 32.5152264). On reaching a T-junction after 1.5km, turn right to find the tombs occupying a rare island of greenery on the summit of the now developed Wamala Hill.

GGABA AND MUNYONYO The twin ports of Ggaba [123 G6] and Munyonyo [123 G7] lie about 2km apart near the southwest of Murchison Bay on Lake Victoria, some 10km southeast of central Kampala. Both are worthwhile goals for a day's outing as well as acting as embarkation points for excursions across the bay to Busoke Island (page 162). Ggaba is a compact, bustling settlement with a busy market that spills down to a waterfront that used to consist of a grim and muddy littoral. This has been tidied up with the construction of a number of stone quays. While the vegetable market, fish auction and fish-smoking activities remain as sensory as ever, the quays have become a popular spot for residents and visitors to take the lake air and perhaps a drink at a makeshift bar. Folk do much the same in more spacious surroundings at the historically more significant port of Munyonyo, 2km south and 500m off the roundabout that marks the start of the new Kajjansi dual carriageway. A recent rise in lake level, however, means that much of the action has shifted outside the gates of the original landing, where you'll find a cluster of hugely popular outlets renowned for their Ugandan-style fish (whole fried tilapia) and chips. If asking directions, note that locals now know the landing as Mulungu while 'Munyonyo' refers to the upmarket suburb in the immediate hinterland.

Munyonyo (or Mulungu) was – and technically still is – the royal port to which the Bagandan kabakas led their entourages in periodical exoduses from their Kampala palaces. During the 19th century it was home to a large canoe fleet reserved for the kabaka – mainly for pleasure cruises and hunting expeditions, but also on standby to evacuate the king in times of emergency.

Speke and Stanley both accompanied Kabaka Mutesa to the lakeshore, where the former considered 'the royal yachting establishment' at Munyonyo to be 'the Cowes of Uganda'. Today, however, the title would go to the plush marina stocked with modern speedboats and cabin cruisers at the neighbouring **Speke Commonwealth Resort** (page 142). This sprawling development is set in beautifully landscaped gardens with a magnificent tropical lakeshore setting opposite the forested Buliguwe Island. A US$12 day entrance fee allows access to an Olympic-sized swimming pool, gym and restaurant (meals US$10). This is a great place to chill out should you have a spare day in the capital, or if you have a few hours to spare before whizzing down the new Kajjansi highway to the airport. For those using public transport, a steady stream of matatus connects the Old Taxi Park in Kampala to both Ggaba and Munyonyo.

Boat trips on the lake A variety of craft with pilots are available to get you on to the lake for voyages of varying duration. For a budget cruise, there are plenty of 9m-long wooden Ssese canoes, with sunshade and lifejackets, to take a group out from Ggaba or Mulungu landings for around US$3 pp. Rather more comfortable is *Catch 22* (m 0783 129738), a slow and steady covered craft which can carry 12 for birding and fishing trips and day/sundowner/moonlight cruises (2–3hrs; US$30 pp or min US$100). The marina at Speke Commonwealth Resort (m 0752 711008) also operates a variety of craft, the most practical being the motorised canoes which will take seven passengers out for US$26/hour while speedboats with the same capacity cost US$80/hour. Slower but considerably grander are the *Silver Fulu* (m 0776 709970) and *Mvule Boat* (m 0705 413581), both being magnificent, 15m-long dhow-like creations. The *Fulu* operates as far out as Bulago Island (US$500 return) while the *Mvule Boat* (US$400 for 4hrs) is ideal for a family or group looking to chillax with wine and nibbles (board games, paddleboards and kayaks are also included) in Murchison Bay.

Maisha Gardens [123 F6] (m 0701 712712; e fibby@maishafilmlab.org; w maishafilmlab.org) Close to Munyonyo, high on the increasingly suburban Buziga Hill, Maisha Gardens provides a green sanctuary for humans as well as birds, including a flock of Ross's turaco. Billed as a multi-disciplinary art space, it offers a regular programme of events including performances of music and dance (entrance is typically US$5) and gatherings of the artistically inclined (musicians, painters, gardeners, musicians, etc). More superficially, Maisha is a lovely place to relax and it is open to the non-creative masses on Sundays and Mondays (US$1.50), on condition that they leave their alcohol, plastics and Bluetooth speakers at home.

NAMUGONGO MARTYRS' SHRINE [123 H1] Situated about 12km northeast of the city centre, Namugongo, an established place of execution in pre-colonial Buganda, is remembered today for the massacre that took place there on 3 June 1886 at the order of Kabaka Mwanga (page 185). In the last week of May, an unknown number of Baganda men and women, suspected or known to have been baptised, were detained near Mengo and forced to march, by some accounts naked, to Namugongo, where they were imprisoned for several days while a large pyre was prepared. On the morning of 3 June, those prisoners who had not already done so were given one final opportunity to renounce their recently adopted faith. Whether any of the neophyte Christians accepted this offer goes unrecorded, but 26 known individuals, divided evenly between Catholic and Protestant, declined. Charles Lwanga, the leader of the Catholic contingent, was hacked apart and burnt alive on the spot. Later in the day, the remaining individuals were bound in reed mats, thrown on to the pyre, and roasted alive. The 26 remembered victims of the massacre were all baptised, and thus known to one or other mission by name, but contemporary reports indicate that more than 30 people were thrown on to the fire.

In 1920, Pope Benedict XV paved the way for future canonisation by declaring blessed the 13 known Catholic martyrs at Namugongo, together with another nine Catholic victims of separate killings in May 1886. The 22 Catholic martyrs were finally canonised by Pope Paul VI on 18 October 1964 during the Vatican II Conference. In July 1969, Pope Paul VI visited Uganda – the first reigning pope to set foot in sub-Saharan Africa – to make a pilgrimage to Namugongo, where he instructed that a shrine and church be built on the spot where Lwanga had been killed. The **Church of the Namugongo Martyrs**, dedicated in 1975 and subsequently named a basilica, is an unusual and imposing structure, modernistic and metallic

THE KIBUGA OF BUGANDA

The centre of political power in Buganda for several centuries prior to the colonial era was the kibuga (capital) of the kabaka (king), generally situated on a hilltop for ease of defence. Based on the knowledge that at least ten different kibuga sites were used by three kabakas between 1854 and 1894, it would appear that the capital was regularly relocated, possibly for security reasons. It was also customary for a kibuga to be abandoned upon the death of its founder, at least until 1894, when Kabaka Mwanga founded a new capital on Mengo Hill, one that remained in use until the Baganda monarchy was abolished in 1966. Mengo Palace, damaged by the military during the Amin era, remains in poor shape, but following the reinstitution of the monarchy in 1993, a new kibuga was established 10km east of Kampala at Banda.

Banda was also the site of the first capital of Kabaka Mutesa, visited in 1862 by Speke, who wrote: 'the palace or entrance quite surprised me by its extraordinary dimensions, and the neatness with which it was kept. The whole brow and sides of the hill on which we stood were covered with gigantic grass huts, thatched as neatly as so many heads dressed by a London barber, and fenced all round with the tall yellow reeds of the common Uganda tiger-grass; while within the enclosure, the lines of huts were joined together, or partitioned off into courts, with walls of the same grass.' The next European visitor to Mutesa's capital – by then relocated to Rubaga – was Stanley, in 1875, who was equally impressed: 'Broad avenues [of] reddish clay, strongly mixed with the detritus of hematite…led by a gradual ascent to the circular road which made the circuit of the hill outside the palace enclosure…his house is an African palace, spacious and lofty.' Visitors to Kabaka Mwanga's kibuga some ten years later were less complimentary – Gedge, for instance, described it as a 'miserable collection of huts [where] dirt and filth reign supreme' – but this was probably a temporary decline linked to the instability that characterised Mwanga's early rule.

The most detailed description of a kibuga was published by the Rev John Roscoe in 1911:

> The king lived upon a hill situated in the neighbourhood of the lake. The summit of the hill was levelled, and the most commanding site overlooking the country was chosen for the king's dwelling houses, court houses, and shrine for fetishes, and for the special reception room…The whole of the royal enclosure was divided up into small courtyards with groups of huts in them; each group was enclosed by a high fence and was under the supervision of a responsible wife. Wide paths between high fences connected each group of houses with the king's royal enclosure. In the reign of the famous King Mutesa, there were several thousand residents in the royal enclosure; he had five hundred wives, each of whom had her maids and female slaves; and in addition to the wives there were fully two hundred pages and hundreds of retainers and slaves. A high fence of elephant grass surrounded the royal residence, so that it was impossible for an enemy with the ordinary primitive weapons to enter…There was one plan followed, which has been used by the kings for years without variation. The [royal] enclosure was oval shaped, a mile in length and half a mile wide, and the capital extended five or six miles in front and two miles on either side.

in appearance, but based on the traditional Kasiisira style (epitomised, ironically, by the tombs of Mwanga and three other kabakas at Kasubi).

The 3 June massacre remains a public holiday in Uganda and is marked worldwide on the Church calendar in honour of the Uganda Martyrs. Namugongo was visited by Archbishop Robert Runcie of Canterbury in 1984, by Pope John Paul II in 1993 and Pope Francis in November 2015.

The actual site of the martyrdom is occupied by a Protestant shrine, 500m east of the Catholic basilica. Until recently, this was a comparatively low-key affair but the complex now contains a substantial memorial building. The centrepiece is a life-size sculpture that illustrates the terrible – and varied – events of 3 June 1886 in graphic detail.

BAHÁ'Í TEMPLE [123 E2] Opened on 15 January 1962, the Bahá'í Temple on Kikaya Hill, 6km from Kampala on the Gayaza Road, is the only place of worship of its kind in Africa. It is the spiritual home to the continent's Bahá'í, adherents to a rather obscure faith founded by the Persian mystic Bahá'u'lláh in the 1850s. Born in Tehran in 1812, Bahá'u'lláh was the privileged son of a wealthy government minister, but he declined to follow his father into the ministerial service, instead devoting his life to philanthropy.

In 1844, Bahá'u'lláh abandoned his Islamic roots to join the Bábí cult, whose short-lived popularity led to the execution of its founder and several other leading figures by the religious establishment – a fate escaped by Bahá'u'lláh only because of the high social status of his family. Bahá'u'lláh was nevertheless imprisoned, with his feet in stocks and a 50kg metal chain around his neck in Tehran's notoriously unsanitary and gloomy Black Pit. It was while imprisoned that Bahá'u'lláh received the Godly vision that led to the foundation of Bahá'í. Upon his release, Bahá'u'lláh dedicated the remaining 40 years of his life to writing the books, tracts and letters that collectively outlined the Bahá'í framework for the spiritual, moral, economic, political and philosophical reconstruction of human society.

Bahá'í teaches that heaven and hell are not places, but states of being defined by the presence or absence of spirituality. It is an inclusive faith, informed by all other religions – Hindu, Christian, Jewish, Zoroastrian, Buddhist and Islamic holy texts are displayed in the temple – which it regards to be stepping stones to a broader, less doctrinal spiritual and meditative awareness. It is also admirably egalitarian: it regards all humankind to be of equal worth, and any member of the congregation is free to lead prayers and meditations. Although not a didactic religion, Bahá'í does evidently equate spiritual well-being with asceticism: the consumption of alcohol and intoxicating drugs is discouraged in Bahá'í writings, and forbidden in the temple grounds, along with loud music, picking flowers and 'immoral behaviour'.

The Bahá'í Temple in Kampala, visible for miles around and open to all, is set in neatly manicured gardens extending over some 30ha atop Kikaya Hill. The lower part of the building consists of a white nonagon roughly 15m in diameter, with one door on each of its nine shaded faces. This is topped by an immense green dome, covered with glazed mosaic Italian tiles, and a turret that towers 40m above the ground. The interior, which can seat up to 800 people, is illuminated by ambient light filtered through coloured glass windows, and decorated with lush Persian carpets. Otherwise, it is plainly decorated, in keeping with the Bahá'í belief that it would belittle the glory of God to place pictures or statues inside His temple. A solitary line of Arabic text repeated on the wall at regular intervals approximately translates to the familiar Christian text Glory of Glories.

6

Around Entebbe and Kampala

This chapter covers a mixed bag of natural and cultural attractions that lie close enough to the capital to appeal to residents of Entebbe or Kampala, or visitors with a spare day or two at the start or end of a business trip or longer safari. Note that worsening traffic within Kampala and associated arterial roads mean that many destinations once feasible as round day trips are now more enjoyable if planned as overnight or weekend excursions.

For wildlife enthusiasts, these destinations include a few genuine highlights, most notably tracking rhinos on foot at Ziwa, but also more low-key forest reserves such as Mabira and Mpanga. The area around Kampala and Entebbe also houses several important traditional Kiganda shrines, most accessibly the Tanda Pits, Nakayima Tree and Ssezibwa Falls, while the Canopy Skyway Zipline at Griffin Falls provides an adrenalin-charged taster for the type of activities on offer at nearby Bujagali and Kalagala Falls (page 249).

Although the destinations included in this chapter can all be visited as round trips out of the capital, most lie en route to other popular attractions further afield – Ziwa, for instance, could easily be visited on the way to the far north, while Mpanga Forest makes for an enjoyable diversion coming to or from the southwest – so they have been structured to follow the main roads out of the capital: east towards Jinja; north towards Masindi and Gulu; west towards Fort Portal; and southwest towards Masaka.

EAST TOWARDS JINJA

Two transport corridors run east–west between Kampala and Jinja: the busy, 85km Jinja Road and a quieter, parallel route, 15km to the south. A few low-key attractions are found along the main road, the primary diversion, easily visited as a day trip from Kampala or Jinja, being the Mabira Forest Reserve. This offers excellent birding and monkey viewing as well as a selection of overnight accommodation and the country's first canopy zipline. Lesser or more esoteric attractions are the legend-steeped Ssezibwa Falls only 40km east of Kampala, and the superb Mehta Golf Course outside Lugazi.

Visiting any of these is, however, currently a slow and bothersome process due to long, slow-moving queues of traffic following trucks crawling to and from Kenya. The southerly route also has its issues, notably because the first stage, from Kampala's Ggaba port to Bule landing, involves a 15-minute boat ride, which rules out the use of a car but not a mountain bike or motorbike. From Bule, a second stage runs on rough murram for 17km to Ntenjeru, where quiet tarmac roads connect to both Jinja and Mukono – useful if you do want to bring a vehicle round from Kampala. The primary appeal of the Bule–Jinja corridor, which runs through Lake Victoria's rural hinterland, is the opportunity to discover lovely and unspoiled countryside just a couple of kilometres outside the capital. Inevitably perhaps, scenic highlights are lake-oriented and vary from tantalising glimpses to full-frontal prospects of watery horizons. Some are seen from tarmac, others from dirt roads on remote hilltops, while still more can be appreciated at leisure from a variety of shoreline resorts.

BUSOKE AND BEYOND For the benefit of those desperate for some proper countryside, we'll kick off with the fastest route out of town. As will quickly become apparent, towards most points of the compass, the distinction between Kampala and the surrounding countryside is blurred by kilometres of relentless suburban tat. To the southeast, however, the expansion is abruptly curtailed by the waters of Lake Victoria's Murchison Bay. Directly opposite lies Busoke Island. Though so called since it is entirely surrounded by water and swamp, it is connected to the 'mainland' by a short causeway, thus enabling wider exploration. In dramatic contrast to the sprawling urb, Busoke and beyond remains as green and rustic as anywhere in central Uganda. With an abundance of lake viewpoints, wetlands and forests and a few choice lodgings, it is fast becoming appreciated as a great place to explore, particularly by cyclists and motorbikers. This idyll won't last forever, however, for there are plans for a bridge or ferry that would enable the metropolis to leap across the bay.

Getting there and away The springboard for visits to Busoke and beyond is the Kampala suburb of Ggaba, where boats from the scruffy landing site designated as Ggaba port (page 157) shuttle across to Bule and Kisinsi landings. Public boats from Ggaba leave when full and cost around US$1.50 per person. Alternatively, 'special hire' boats will take you across the bay for US$5 or US$2–3 per person, whichever sum best favours the boatman. If secure parking is required, you can leave your vehicle at the nearby Beach House resort (US$1.50), where staff will be happy to call a boat for you. Note that these are passenger boats only, so on arrival at Bule, you'll either need your own bicycle or motorbike, or to hire a boda boda or have a prearranged vehicle pickup. If you want to explore the area with your own vehicle, you'll need to follow the main Jinja Road to the eastern edge of Mukono town and follow the surfaced Katosi road south. Turn left at Kisoga, after 15km, to explore the 60km of lake hinterland between Katosi and Jinja. Otherwise keep straight for another 4km, where a right turn on to a variable dirt road at Ntenjeru passes turnings for various lake resorts before terminating at Bule after 17km. There you can gaze across the bay to Ggaba, just 15 minutes away by boat, in the knowledge that the drive there will take at least 3 hours.

Getting around Busoke Island and the wider Kyagwe County are best explored with a mountain bike and parties of puffing expats trailing behind a sinewy Ugandan guide are a common sight at weekends. If you don't have your own bike, contact the two cycling operators listed in the specialist tour operator section on page 64, who will provide everything you need for a great day out. Both charge around US$50 for an excursion with boat transfers to/from Bule, bike hire and lunch or snacks.

If you're not ready to cross back to the capital (always a depressing event), a variety of lodgings are listed opposite. If you're up for greater distances, you could spend a delightful couple of days exploring the area between Murchison Bay and Jinja. See 'Uganda Maps' Sheet 3: *Beyond Kampala* for inspiration.

Where to stay

Upmarket

Divine Resort [102 C2] (6 cottages) m 0770 674066, 0200 959850; e reservations@divineresort.co.ug; w divineresort.co.ug. Currently the place for the monied classes to hang out, this exclusive offshore resort is by far the closest to Kampala, being just 5mins from Ggaba by speedboat. *Spacious cottages cost US$200 sgl/dbl B&B inc boat transfers.* **$$$**

Moderate

Banga Bay Resort [102 D2] (24 cottages) m 0772 462646. While the drive out from Kampala via Mukono would be a bit of a chore, this new lodge at the head of Gobero Bay is easily accessible by bike, boda or special hire from Bule landing. Lakefront lawns are backed by a row of forgettable bandas redeemed by a modern-looking & open-sided lodge building. The centrepiece of the latter is a state-of-the-art island kitchen where you can sit at the counter & enjoy the lake outlook while chatting to the chef as he prepares your order; you'll find his labours worthwhile & reasonably priced for the location (mains US$4–8). Now look carefully into the shady pine grove at the back & you'll see, perfectly camouflaged, a group of delightful thatched chalets built, all eaves & no walls, in Viking style. *US$45 sgl/dbl bandas; US$80 sgl/dbl chalet. B&B.* **$$**

✱ **Kumezi** [102 C2] (3 cottages) m 0772 462646; e ugandamaps@gmail.com. Located at the end of a peninsula on Wavimenya Bay, this self-catering setup is perfectly placed for a getaway from Kampala. A thatched clifftop house (1 bedroom with lounge & fully equipped kitchen) is supplemented by 2 adjacent en-suite dbl cottages. If a daybed alcove in the lounge is used, Kumezi can sleep 8. Other residents include red-tailed monkeys, otters & monitor lizards, while a wealth of birdlife includes turacos, hornbills, fish eagles & various storks & herons. A croquet lawn & swimming pool provide diversions on site, & there is plenty of scope for exploration on local roads & paths. Boats to Kumezi can be hired from Beach House in Ggaba (40mins) or vehicle pickup can be arranged from Bule landing (15mins away). Advance booking is essential. *US$100 for the main house; US$50 for each additional cottage.* **$$$**

Budget

Serenada Eco Resort [102 D2] (14 rooms/tents) m 0772 428456/493033; e serenadakyaggwe@gmail.com, info@serenadaecoresort.com; w serenadaecoresort.com. This pretty resort occupies a series of clearings around an attractive, forest-shaded beach beside Wavimenya Bay, 40mins' boat ride from Ggaba. Chill by the lake or go kayaking, walk in the forest, tick off birds (the list stands at 200 species) & climb nearby Kyasa Hill. A variety of basic accommodation includes Dream Cottage, a cosy & privately positioned en-suite timber cabin (US$125/185 HB) & a row of standing tents (shared facilities; US$25 pp B&B). **$$–$$$**

Further afield

Other than the 2 listings below, lodgings of the standard you deserve are non-existent along the Katosi–Jinja road corridor, so, if cycling, plan accordingly. The ride down to the busy fishing village of Senyi is a delightful one, but there is no accommodation. If you can't make it down to Musana Camps or back up to a couple of acceptable lodges at Nkokenjeru on the main road, you'll need to make do with the grim New Lion Inn behind a noisy bar in Ssi trading centre, 15km away (US$8 sgl/dbl exc b/fast).

✱ **Bushbaby Lodge** [102 E1] (14 rooms) m 0782 960742, 0788 104752; e booking@staybushbaby.com; w staybushbaby.com. This delightful Ugandan-Canadian venture lies at the heart of a 100-acre family farm near Kisoga on the tarmac Mukono–Katosi road. Popular with expat & Ugandan families, it's a place where you can do as much or as little as you like. If the passive appeal of the rural setting wanes, more active diversions include a dip in the pool, horseriding, cycling (Ssezibwa Falls – page 164 – is 15km away along rural back routes), a farm tour, forest walk & birding. The dining experience is both delicious & diverse, with home-produced meat & vegetables served, variously, in the restaurant, by the campfire or in a forest glade. Further variation for longer stays is ensured by a meat smoker, barbecue, & a pizza oven. Bushbaby is a worthwhile day destination for the 3-course lunch (US$20 pp), but then you'd miss b/fast, arguably the best time of day with mist in the valley & the morning sun glinting on gates, fences & other pastoral paraphernalia. Coming from Mukono, Bushbaby is signposted to the left, immediately after a Stabex fuel station & just before Kisoga town. Another signpost, 1.3km further on, indicates the turning into the estate. Alternatively, cross from Ggaba to Bule landing where a special hire (US$30 1-way) can be prearranged to collect you. *US$100/120 sgl/dbl B&B or US$140/200 FB.* **$$$**

✷ **Musana Camps** [102 F3] (3 guesthouses, dorms) ⊕ 0.09298720, 32.9496967; m 0759 220943; e bookings@musanacamps.com. Golly, this place was a find! A good 25km off of the Kisoga–Jinja tarmac, at the end of some particularly steep & rough dirt roads, this Christian setup is scattered across 600 acres of natural habitat – bush, grassland & forest – on a dramatic escarpment facing Lake Victoria & a scattering of islands. There's a choice of self-catering guesthouses, including a commodious 4-bedroom house (2 en suite, 2 sharing a bathroom) with a huge open-plan sitting room/kitchen & a similarly oversized lake-facing veranda. Visit the waterfall, work on the bird list (currently 142 species), take a boat on the lake or simply sit on your veranda to enjoy the phenomenal view & appreciate Speke's conviction that his Victoria Nyanza must – *surely* – be the Source of the Nile. A campsite & dorms cater mainly to groups coming for a variety of activities, including a rope course, hikes, swimming, orienteering, etc. Alcohol is neither sold nor approved of at Musana, so be discreet & remember to observe the high standards of behaviour we expect from our readers. Though the shortest road to Musana leaves the Kisoga–Jinja road at Nkokenjuru, the best route turns off 8km further east & passes via Ssi trading centre. *Dbl guesthouse US$40; 4-room guesthouses cost US$105 & 120. Rates exc meals. Camping US$8; dorm bed US$40 FB.* **$$$**

✗ Where to eat and drink

✷ **Divine Resort** [102 C2] See page 163. Just 5mins from Kampala by fast boat, this exclusive resort offers a range of delicious grills, stir fries & salads for around US$12. The lakeside deck looks towards Kampala in one direction, with the forested hills of Busoke in the other. The latter backdrop is blotted out each time a speedboat docks for high-heeled & bottom-heavy divas to teeter ashore & pout & pose for selfies on the jetty. Live music at w/ends. Advance booking recommended.

Lakeside Escape [102 D2] m 0772 367972. The appeal of this sprawling Gobero Bay resort lies in its location, 20km from Bule & perfectly placed as a halfway lunch spot for cyclists. Though the welcome & fare are nothing to write home about, the alternative is a roadside rolex in Kabanga trading centre, 6km away. *Main courses US$8–9.*

SSEZIBWA FALLS RESORT [102 E1] (⊕ 0.35867, 32.8659; ⌚ 08.30–18.00 daily; entry US$5.50) A notable beauty spot and focal point of Kiganda legends, the Ssezibwa Falls Resort is a private ecotourism venture offering a variety of guided nature and cultural walks, as well as an attractive terrace restaurant and campsite. In the 19th century, the waterfall, which lies on the Ssezibwa River, was a favourite spot of Kabaka Mwanga and Kabaka Mutesa II, both of whom planted trees there that still flourish today (an act emulated by Kabaka Ronald Mutebi II in 2002).

According to legend, the Ssezibwa River is not a natural phenomenon, but the progeny of a pregnant woman called Nakangu, who lived many hundreds of years ago and belonged to the Achibe (ox) clan. She was expected to give birth to twin children, but instead what poured from her womb was a twin river, one that split into two distinct streams around an island immediately below the waterfall. The spirits of Nakangu's unborn children – Ssezibwa and Mobeya – each inhabit one of these streams, for which reason it used to be customary for any Muganda passing the river's source at Namukono, some 20km further east, to throw a handful of grass or stones into it for good luck. Even today, a thanksgiving sacrifice of barkcloth, beer and a cockerel is made at the river's source every year, usually led by a Ssalongo (father of twins).

Given the supernatural significance that many Ugandan societies attach to twins, it is unsurprising that a number of shrines are maintained among the colourful quartzite rocks over which the river tumbles for perhaps 15m before it divides into two. Various gaps in the rock are dedicated to specific lubaale, among them the river spirit Mukasa, the hunting spirit Ddunga and the rainbow spirit Musoke. A fertility shrine in the rocks adjacent to the falls is associated with the thunder spirit Kiwanuka, and generally used for individual rather than communal sacrifices. Women who have been blessed with twins (one child being indisputably human while the other is associated with a benevolent spirit manifested in a python or leopard), often visit this shrine to leave eggs for the python spirit or a cock for its feline counterpart. Communal ceremonies, in which nine pieces of meat are sacrificed at the appropriate spirit's shrine, are also still held at the waterfall. Tourists are welcome to visit on such occasions, but unfortunately their timing is difficult to predict – ceremonies are not held every year, and the date is usually announced at short notice when a medium is consulted by a hungry spirit. Certain spirits, after having accepted a sacrifice and taken the requested action, appreciate having a live sheep or cock – white for Mukasa, brown for Kiwanuka – thrown over the waterfall itself, and they always ensure that the animal survives.

Getting there and away Ssezibwa Falls Resort lies 40km east of Kampala. It can be reached by following the Jinja Road as far as Kayanja trading centre, where a green, tea-covered hill comes into view. At the signposted junction (⊕ 0.37256, 32.87338), turn right and continue south for almost 2km, then turn right again on to a signposted track that brings you to the entrance gate after 350m. Using public transport, any eastbound matatu out of Kampala's Old Taxi Park can drop you at Kayanja, from where it is a 30-minute walk to the resort.

Where to stay and eat

Riverside Woods Ssezibwa [102 E1] ⊕ 0.3385857, 32.8647312; m 0783 920588; e riversidewoods.ssezibwa@gmail.com. This hillside lodge overlooks the papyrus-filled Ssezibwa Valley, 2.5km beyond the Falls & 4km from the Jinja highway. The attraction of the cottage accommodation will depend on circumstances. Those who have pedalled from afar will be quite appreciative; others with 4 wheels may be inclined to push on elsewhere. While the southerly approach from Kisoga & Bushbaby Lodge is doable by mountain bike, it is less fun in a car. *Thatch cottages US$40/52 sgl/dbl; iron-roofed cottages US$52 twin B&B.* **$$**

Ssezibwa Falls Restaurant & Campsite [102 E1] m 0704 022096, 0756 677768; e ssezibwafallsresort@yahoo.com; ⌚ 08.30–18.00 daily, but the restaurant will close later if the campsite is in use. Offering a pretty view over the Ssezibwa River from its shady terrace, this thatched restaurant serves a selection of grills, curries, sandwiches & salads in the US$4–7 range. Camping is permitted for US$5.50 pp.

What to see and do Ssezibwa Falls is a very pretty spot and there are worse ways to spend an afternoon than chilling on the restaurant terrace enjoying the scenery, passing birdlife and a cold drink. For more energetic visitors, a variety of guided walks is offered for US$7–10 per person, the most interesting of which is a cultural walk that provides extensive background to the waterfall's history and associated legends. Bird walks don't really compare with what's on offer at nearby Mabira Forest, but they do offer Uganda newbies a good opportunity to seek out such charismatic species as great blue turaco and black-and-white casqued hornbill. Also available are longer (up to 3-hour) forest walks and hikes outside the resort.

KIGANDA RELIGION

The traditional religion of Buganda is called Kiganda, and as is the case in many traditional African cultures, it revolves largely around the appeasing and petitioning of various ancestral and animist spirits, some malevolent and others benign, in order, for instance, to prevent the former from wreaking destruction on the kingdom, or to ensure the latter grant it a bountiful harvest. But Kiganda is unusual in that it has a core of monotheism. The supreme being of the Baganda is Katonda – literally, Creator – who is not of human form, and has neither parents nor children, but who brought into being the heavens, the earth, and all they contain. Katonda is the most powerful denizen of the spiritual world, but somewhat detached from human affairs, which means he requires little attention by comparison to various subordinate spirits with a more hands-on approach.

Ranking below Katonda, the *balubaale* (singular *lubaale*) are semi-deities who play a central role in day-to-day affairs affecting Buganda. At least 30 balubaale are recognised (some sources claim a total of 70), and many are strongly associated with specific aspects or attributes of life. The balubaale have no equivalent in the Judaic branch of religions. Certainly not gods, they are more akin perhaps to a cross between a saint and a guardian angel – the spirits of real men (or more occasionally women) whose exceptional attributes in life have been carried over into death. Traditionally, the balubaale form the pivot of organised religion in Buganda: prior to the introduction of outside religions they were universally venerated, even above the kabaka (king), who in all other respects was an absolute ruler.

The most popular lubaale is Mukasa, a spirit of lakes and rivers honoured at many temples around Buganda. Mukasa is strongly associated with Lake Victoria, so it's no surprise that the most important shrine to his spirit is located in the Ssese Archipelago, on Bubembe Island, to where the kabaka would send an annual offering of cows and a request for prosperity and good harvests. Mukasa is also associated with fertility: childless women would regularly visit an adjacent shrine on Bubembe, dedicated to his wife Nalwanga, to ask her to seek her husband's blessing. Another important lubaale is Wanga, the guardian of the sun and moon, who as such has no earthly shrine. Wanga is the father of Muwanga, literally 'the most powerful'. Other prominent male balubaale with specific areas of interest include Musoke (rainbows), Kawumpuli (plagues), Ndahura (smallpox), Kitinda (prosperity), Musisi (earthquakes), Wamala (Lake Wamala) and Ddunga (hunting).

Female balubaale are fewer, and in most cases their elevated status is linked to kinship with a male lubaale, but they include Kiwanuka's wife Nakayage (fertility) and Kibuuka's mother Nagaddya (harvests). Nabuzaana, the female lubaale of obstetrics, is possibly unique in having no kin among the other balubaale, and also in that she is tended by priestesses of Banyoro rather than Baganda origin. The male lubaale Ggulu, guardian of the sky, is a confusing figure. Listed in some traditions as the creator, his existence, in common with that of Katonda, pre-dated that of humanity, and he has no earthly shrine, furthering the suggestion that unlike other balubaale he is not the spirit of a dead person. Ggulu's children include the lightning spirit Kiwanuka as well as Walumbe, the spirit of sickness and death.

The balubaale are expected to intercede favourably in national affairs related to their speciality when petitioned with sacrifices and praise. Sacrifices to the water spirit Mukasa might be made during periods of drought, in case he has forgotten that the people need rain. The rainbow spirit Musoke, by contrast, might be placated with sacrifices after extended rains that prevent harvesting or ploughing, and he will signal his assent to stop the rain with a rainbow. In past times, all the major temples would be consulted and offerings made before any major national undertaking – a coronation, for instance, or a war – and any kabaka who ignored this custom was inviting disaster. One main shrine or *ekiggwa* is dedicated to each lubaale, though many are also venerated at a number of lesser shrines scattered around Buganda. Every shrine is tended by a *mandwa*: a priest or medium who is on occasion possessed by the shrine's spirit and acts as its oracle. The mandwa for any given temple might be male or female, but will usually come from a specific clan associated with that temple. The three main shrines dedicated to Katonda – all situated in Kyagwe, near the Mabira Forest – are, for instance, tended by priests of the Njovu (elephant) clan. Sacred drums, ceremonial objects and sometimes body parts of the deceased are stored in the temple, the upkeep of which is governed by elaborate customs.

While a relatively small cast of balubaale is concerned with national affairs, the day-to-day affairs of local communities and of individual Muganda are governed by innumerable lesser spirits. These are divided into two main categories: *mizimu* (singular *omuzimu*) are the spirits of departed ancestors, while *misambwa* (singular *omusambwa*) are spirits associated with specific physical objects such as mountains, rivers, forests or caves. Dealings with the ancestral spirits are a family matter, undertaken at a household shrine where small items, such as cowries or beans, are offered on a regular basis, while a living sacrifice of a chicken or goat might be offered before an important event or ceremony. Appeasing the misambwa, by contrast, is a community affair, with communal offerings made on a regular basis.

The place of Kiganda in modern Buganda is difficult to isolate. In the latter half of the 19th century, when the kingdom was first infiltrated by evangelical foreigners – initially just Arabs, later also Europeans – a significant number of Muganda, especially the elite, converted to an outside religion. Thereafter, the converts tended to regard their indigenous spiritual traditions as backward and superstitious, a stance that caused considerable friction within the kingdom during the 1880s. The trend against traditionalism continued throughout the 20th century. Today, most if not all Baganda profess to be either Christian or Muslim, and certainly very few educated and urbanised Baganda take Kiganda traditions very seriously, if they consider them at all.

In rural Buganda, by contrast, many people still adhere partially or concurrently to two apparently contradictory religious doctrines. In other words, they might be dedicated Christians or Muslims, but in times of trouble they will as likely consult a traditional oracle or healer as they will a priest or imam or a Western doctor. This dualism in Buganda is perhaps less conspicuous to outsiders than it would be in many other parts of Africa. But its existence is confirmed by the fact that sacrificial shrines such as Ssezibwa Falls, Tanda Pits and the Nakayima Tree remain active focal points for traditionalist cults – far more so perhaps today than they did ten or 20 years before that. Outside of Buganda, post-1986 Christian cults centred on the Acholi and Bakiga mediums Alice Lakwena and Credonia Mwerinde; though very different, both possessed undeniable traditionalist undertones. And so, it is out of respect for Kiganda traditions, rather than any wish to offend the many Baganda who reject them, that this box has been written not in the past tense but in the present.

MEHTA GOLF CLUB A contender for the most scenic golf course in Uganda, this compact nine-holer on the northeastern outskirts of Lugazi town, midway between Kampala and Jinja, has to be seen to be believed. The creation of the Asian owners of the town's sugar factory, it is a surreal golfing paradise set in a lush valley hidden from the gaze of the masses toiling in the factory and in the surrounding cane plantations. Good curry lunches can be arranged, and there are a few simple hotels in town. To get there coming from Kampala, turn left at the main traffic circle in Lugazi (⊕ 0.36938, 32.94089) and continue north for about 1.8km to the clubhouse. For further details, contact the factory management at ☏ 041 4448279; m 0703 666308.

MABIRA FOREST RESERVE The 306km^2 Mabira Forest Reserve, whose southern extremities are skirted by the main Kampala–Jinja Road as it runs between Lugazi and Njeru, ranks as the largest remaining block of moist semi-deciduous forest in central or eastern Uganda. Although it suffered from heavy logging in the colonial era and substantial encroachment in the 1980s, Mabira remains the most important biodiversity hotspot within easy day-tripping distance of Kampala, with a bird checklist of more than 300 species and a varied mammalian fauna that includes the endemic Uganda mangabey. Highly accessible, whether as a round trip from Kampala or en route to Jinja, Mabira is now serviced by a decent selection of accommodation, while the lovely forest interior can be explored along a network of walking trails, making it a highly attractive goal for jaded city dwellers and freshly arrived travellers alike. And if tranquil isn't your thing, then the Mabira Canopy Super Skyway surely will be: this under-publicised zipline system, connecting six lofty canopy platforms, offers an adrenalin surge to match the white-water rafting on the nearby Upper Nile.

History The first attempt to exploit Mabira was initiated in 1900, when the colonial administration leased the forest to the Mabira Forest Rubber Company, which intended to reap an annual harvest of around 250,000kg from the estimated half-a-million African silk rubber (*Funtumia elastica*) trees that grow wild there. This plan was quickly scrapped as uneconomic, due to the high cost of clearing around these low yield trees, but the forest was heavily exploited for timber, even after it was gazetted as the Mabira Forest Reserve in 1932. After independence, Mabira's proximity to Kampala and Jinja led to an estimated 1,500 tonnes of charcoal being extracted from it annually throughout the 1960s. Less reversible was the damage done during the civil war of the early 1980s, when roughly 25% of the forest was cleared or otherwise degraded by subsistence farmers, who were eventually evicted in 1988. Since then, much of the degraded forest has recovered through the replanting of indigenous trees, and illegal felling has practically ceased.

A more recent, and more serious, threat to the integrity of Mabira was a 2007 government proposal to de-gazette one-third of the forest reserve and transfer ownership to the Lugazi-based Sugar Corporation of Uganda for conversion to sugarcane plantations. This proposal sparked widespread and unexpectedly passionate public protest, ranging from reasoned letters to the press and the vociferous intervention of Kabaka Ronald Mutebi II of Buganda to a riot in the middle of Kampala that led to three fatalities. Possibly because the furore exploded during the build-up to the prestigious Commonwealth Heads of Government Meeting (CHOGM) held in Kampala in November 2007, the proposal was quickly scrapped. It was briefly resurrected and then shelved again in 2011, since when the government has been silent on the issue. The short-term future of the forest

THE NAKALANGA OF MABIRA

The first European survey of Mabira Forest referred to it as Mabira Nakalanga, which translates as Nakalanga Forest, since Mabira is simply a generic Luganda term used to denote any large forest. In reality, then, the local Baganda would have known the forest as Nakalanga, which is also the name of a mischievous spirit said to inhabit it. According to folklore, Nakalanga is associated with one specific stream that runs through Mabira Forest, the source of which was until recent times the site of an important sacrificial shrine consisting of several huts.

Several early colonial writers reported that Mabira harboured a Pygmy tribe called the Banakalanga (people of Nakalanga) and assumed that these people were related to the Batwa Pygmies of the Congolese border area. Local Luganda legend, however, doesn't regard the Banakalanga as a tribe, but rather as spirits of nature. The belief is that the forest spirit punishes families that have fallen out of favour by cursing one of its children to be a puny and often mildly deformed dwarf.

In the 1950s, Rapper and Ladkin of the Uganda Medical Service investigated the Nakalanga phenomenon and determined that the dwarfism sufferers did indeed appear to be born randomly to physiologically normal parents with other healthy offspring. They concluded that the Banakalanga were affected by a form of infantilism linked to a pituitary defect, one that generally first showed itself when the afflicted person was about three years of age. The disease, Rapper and Ladkin believed, was pathological rather than genetic in origin, but its precise cause was indeterminate, as was its apparent restriction to one small area around Mabira Forest. Subsequent studies confirmed that Nakalanga dwarfism is a complication of a pituitary malfunction caused by onchocerciasis (a disease spread by the *Simulium* blackfly) and note that the condition also occurs in the Kabarole District of western Uganda.

Interestingly, the first written references to the Banakalanga interchangeably calls them the Bateemba (people of the nets), evidently in reference to a hunting method used by Pygmoid peoples elsewhere in Africa. Furthermore, according to Rapper and Ladkin, a local Saza chief interviewed back in the early 20th century told his interrogators that a tribe of true Pygmies did once live in the forest, but it vanished sometime before Europeans arrived in the area. It seems probable, then, that both Nakalanga and the medical condition attributed to the spirit's mischief-making derive their name from that of a Pygmoid tribe which once inhabited Mabira Forest.

reserve thus looks reasonably secure, but many environmentalists fear that it is only a matter of time before the proposal is revived.

Flora and fauna The reserve is primarily composed of moist semi-deciduous forest, with some 202 tree species identified to date, including the only known Ugandan specimens of *Diphasia angolensis*. The forest is interspersed with patches of open grassland, while several of the valleys support extensive papyrus swamps. Large mammals are relatively scarce in Mabira today, though a small population of elephant was present as recently as the 1950s. Primates include red-tailed monkey and black-and-white colobus, but Mabira is particularly important as a stronghold for the Uganda mangabey, a national endemic first recognised in 2007. More than 300 species of moth and butterfly have been identified in the forest.

Mabira ranks as one of the most important ornithological sites in Uganda, with a checklist of 315 (mostly forest-associated) species, including several rarities. Conspicuous larger birds include the stunning great blue turaco and more familiar African grey parrot, while three forest hornbill species and a variety of colourful sunbirds are often seen around the camp. Mabira is one of only two places in East Africa where the pretty tit hylia has been recorded, and this rare bird is seen here with surprising regularity. It is also one of the few places in Uganda where the localised forest wood-hoopoe, African pitta, purple-throated cuckoo-shrike, red-tailed leaflove, Weyn's weaver and Nahan's francolin are regular. Note, however, that the forest's reputation as a good place to see the rare blue swallow is based on one vagrant sighting many years ago.

Fees Entrance to the reserve costs US$5.50 per person. An additional US$9 per person is charged for a guided walk, while US$23/35 per group of up to six is levied for a half-/full-day birding excursion.

Getting there and away Mabira Forest Reserve is easily accessible by private vehicle or public transport since the surfaced Kampala–Jinja Road runs right through it. There are two main access points: the small town of Lugazi, 50km east of Kampala and 35km west of Jinja, is the springboard for Griffin Falls Camp and the Canopy Skyline, which both lie a few kilometres north of the main road, while Najjembe, 10km closer to Jinja, is the junction village for the Mabira Forest Eco-Tourism Project and Rainforest Lodge.

To get to Griffin Falls Camp, first head to Lugazi, then branch to the north at a large junction (⊕ 0.3687, 32.93636) immediately west of the taxi park. Follow this road for 800m, passing a small market to your left, until you reach a T-junction (⊕ 0.37558, 32.93623) in front of a sugarcane plantation where you need to turn left. From here, it's a fairly straightforward 9km drive, with all junctions signposted, to the village of Wuswa (⊕ 0.42936, 32.95182), then another 1km to the camp. Using public transport, plenty of matatus run to Lugazi from Kampala or Jinja throughout the day, and a boda onwards to Griffin Falls Camp should cost around US$3.

At Najjembe (⊕ 0.39558, 33.00888), a clearly signposted track leads south from the main crossroads to reach the Rainforest Lodge after 2km. Across the road, the road through the village passes the Mabira Forest Eco-Tourism Project after 500m. Unfortunately, since it is perfectly placed for travellers using public transport between Kampala and Jinja, this site is currently all but closed down.

Where to stay and eat Although the lodges listed here are found on the *Bujagali, Kalagala, Upper Nile and Mabira Forest* map in *Chapter 9*, they are included in this section as they are best visited on a return trip from Kampala.

Upmarket

Rainforest Lodge [250 A6] (12 cottages) ⊕ 0.38191, 33.01703; m 0782 574271, 0701 563437; e reservations@geolodgesafrica.com; w geolodgesafrica.com. This attractive & – given the unforgiving rainforest setting – remarkably well-maintained lodge stands on the forested Gangu Hill 2km south of Najjembe, where it provides accommodation in beautifully furnished stilted timber cottages. Private balconies look into the canopy where hornbills, turacos & red-tailed monkeys abound, & an elevated restaurant building & swimming pool-sauna area enjoy similar views. Fantastic value for B&B, though less so if you intend to eat more than once a day. *US$100/180 sgl/dbl B&B; US$180/300 sgl/dbl FB.* **$$$$**

Budget

✷ **Griffin Falls Camp** [250 A6] (6 rooms & dorms) ⊕ 0.43685, 32.95416; m 0751 955671, 0754 031769; e info@mabiraforestcamp.com, griffinfalls@yahoo.com; w mabiraforestcamp.com. This basic ecotourism camp is set in a forest clearing near the village of Wuswa, 10km from Lugazi. Accommodation – twin bandas & 4-bed dorms – is simple but adequate with camping an additional option. A restaurant serves a reasonably varied menu, with most mains priced at around US$8, & beers & sodas are sold. Activities include guided forest walks, birding, mangabey tracking & the canopy skyway zipline. Best to phone in advance to book accommodation & meals. *US$26/40 sgl/twin en-suites; US$12 pp per dorm bed; US$3 pp camping.* **$$**

What to see and do

Griffin Falls

Forest walks It is possible to explore motorable tracks through the forest unaccompanied, but you'll benefit greatly from taking a guide to discover the excellent network of forest trails that emanates from Griffin Falls Camp. Non-specialised walks are cheaper than dedicated birding walks, but the latter increase your chance of seeing rare birds as you'll be allocated a guide with a good knowledge of bird calls, which can be invaluable when it comes to locating more elusive species in the dense forest. The main attraction at Griffin Falls Camp is the 30-minute forest walk to the pretty Griffin Falls, where all three types of monkey might be seen – though be prepared for the water to have a slight whiff of molasses, thanks to effluent dumped into the Musamya River from the Sugar Corporation of Uganda's factory at Lugazi.

Canopy Super Skyway (3hrs; US$50/17 for foreigners/Ugandans irrespective of group size – it will run even if only one person wants to go) Opened in 2014, this thrilling 250m canopy zipline, the first of its kind in Uganda, connects six canopy platforms, the tallest being 40m above the ground, alongside the Musamya River 15 minutes' walk from Griffin Falls Camp. The excursion leaves from Griffin Falls Camp at 08.00 and 14.00 daily, and can also be booked as a day trip out of Jinja/Kampala, inclusive of transport, lunch and nature walk, for US$80/100 per person, with a minimum group size of three – contact Griffin Falls Camp for details.

Mangabey tracking (US$14 pp) The Uganda mangabey (*Lophocebus ugandae*) is a recently described endemic monkey that was split from the more widespread grey-cheeked mangabey in 2007. The only primate species endemic to Uganda, it is significantly smaller than other mangabeys – a group of monkeys closely related to baboons – and easily distinguished from other monkeys in Mabira by its overall dark coloration with a pale ruff. Several troops living in the vicinity of Griffin Falls Camp have been habituated, and can be tracked, ideally leaving first thing in the morning, when sightings are almost certain, though nothing is guaranteed. The excursion normally takes 3–4 hours, but might take longer if the monkeys prove difficult to locate.

Mountain biking Mountain-bike trails have been cut in the vicinity of Griffin Falls Camp, but no bicycles are available to hire, so you'll need your own.

Najjembe Sadly, the once-active Mabira Forest Eco-Tourism Site at Najjembe is practically defunct, though forest walks are still an option. The US$14 fee includes a guide who knows the trails, but if you're expecting any sort of birding expertise, you should arrange for a guide to travel over from the Griffin Falls site. In theory, you can still pitch a tent and eat out on barbecue chicken from the roadside market; however, if the 24/7 traffic noise from the main road isn't sufficient deterrent, the run-down communal facilities probably will be. Note, too, that if a new tariff (see rates for Mpanga Forest on page 186) is implemented, Mabira will be poor value indeed unless significant improvements are made.

NORTH TOWARDS MASINDI AND GULU

The 170km trunk road running from Kampala to Kafu Bridge via Bombo and Luwero is traversed by practically all tourists heading further north, whether they intend to branch left for Masindi or Murchison Falls National Park immediately after crossing the Kafu River, or to continue straight ahead for Pakwach, Gulu, Lira or Kidepo Valley National Park. Despite the strategic importance of this road, it carries a relatively low volume of traffic, at least once you've cleared Luwero, and is rather short on tourist attractions. The one rather thrilling exception, signposted to the left 8km before Kafu Bridge, is Ziwa Rhino and Wildlife Ranch, which offers northbound travellers the opportunity to track an introduced population of white rhinos on foot, and also makes for a great day or overnight bush break from the capital. Another important landmark only 2km past the junction for Ziwa is the excellent Kabalega Diner, now entrenched as *the* place to break for a bite, drink or leg stretch before crossing the Kafu River, which effectively marks the boundary between southern Uganda and the north.

ZIWA RHINO AND WILDLIFE RANCH (formerly Ziwa Rhino Sanctuary; m 0785 552801; e info@ziwarhinoandwildliferanch.com; w ziwarhinoandwildliferanch.com; ⌚ main gate 07.00–17.00 daily; entrance US$50/45 FNR/FR) A 70km^2 tract of tangled woodland situated a short way south of the Kafu River, Ziwa Rhino and

RHINOS IN UGANDA

Historically, Uganda's main white rhino stronghold is West Nile, which supported a population estimated at 350 individuals in 1955. Back then, Murchison Falls and Kidepo Valley National Park were home to a similar number of black rhino. By the mid 1960s, however, the country's white rhino population had plummeted to 80, split between West Nile's Ajai Wildlife Reserve and a herd of 15 introduced to Murchison Falls. No figures for black rhino are available, but they had also become scarce by the late 1960s. Today, both species are naturally extinct in Uganda, with the last documented sightings of white and black rhino being in 1982 and 1983 respectively. The main cause of this rapid decline was commercial poaching – rhino horns, used as dagger handles in the Middle East and as an aphrodisiac in parts of Asia, fetch up to US$1 million on the black market – exacerbated by the lawlessness that prevailed during and after the rule of Idi Amin.

In 2001, the NGO Rhino Fund Uganda bought a pair of 2½-year-old white rhinos from Kenya's Solio Ranch, flew them to Entebbe to a festive reception, then interred them in the Uganda Wildlife Education Centre, a respected zoo-like facility where they remain to this day. This led to the initiation of a longer-term reintroduction programme centred on Ziwa Rhino and Wildlife Ranch, a former cattle ranch, now sealed off within a 2m-high electric fence, in Nakasongola District. In 2005, four southern white rhinos from Kenya were introduced to Ziwa, supplemented a year later by two more individuals from Disney Animal Kingdom

Wildlife Ranch is the only place in Uganda where rhinos can be seen in a more-or-less wild state, thanks to an ongoing introduction programme (see below) now jointly managed with the Uganda Wildlife Authority. The sanctuary's main attraction is a white rhino population of more than 40 (and growing), which can be tracked on foot by day or overnight visitors in the company of an experienced ranger. It is also home to around 20 other large mammal species, most conspicuously warthog, vervet monkey, black-and-white colobus, bushbuck, impala and waterbuck, while plans to introduce giraffe, hartebeest and zebra will increase the appeal further. Ziwa also boasts an impressive checklist of 300-plus bird species include shoebill, which can be tracked by canoe or on foot in Lugogo Swamp. With accommodation to suit all budgets, the sanctuary makes for a great overnight bush break out of Kampala, as well as being conveniently located for a day visit or overnight stop en route from the capital to Murchison Falls, Gulu or elsewhere in the north.

Getting there and away The junction (⊕ 1.5076, 32.09613) for Ziwa Rhino and Wildlife Ranch is clearly signposted on the west side of the Gulu Road as it passes through the small trading centre of Nakitoma (pronounced 'Nachitoma') about 170km north of Kampala and 8km before Kafu Bridge. From the junction, it's about 2.5km to the entrance gate (⊕ 1.48583, 32.09564), then another 5km to the sanctuary headquarters (⊕ 1.44783, 32.07738), which is also the site of Ziwa Guesthouse (page 174) and the departure point for all activities. For Amuka Lodge, which lies 6km from the entrance, follow the road towards the headquarters for 2.5km, then turn right at the signposted junction (⊕ 1.46671, 32.08745).

Where to stay and eat *Map, page 98*

In addition to places to eat and sleep within the sanctuary, there are further options close by on the main Kampala–Gulu road.

USA. In 2009, a rhino was born on Ugandan soil for the first time in almost three decades, and named Obama, on account of its half-Kenyan, half-American ancestry. Today, thanks to a successful breeding program, the ranch supports more than 40 white rhinos, including four survivors from the original founding population of six. Once numbers have grown sufficiently, the long-term intention is to release a few individuals into Ajai Wildlife Reserve, Murchison Falls and possibly a few other national parks.

Admirable as the programme at Ziwa may be, it is arguably of greater symbolic and touristic value than ecological worth. This is because the imported white rhinos all belong to the southern subspecies *Ceratotherium s. simum,* whose natural range extends little further north than the Zambezi River (though it has since been introduced to Kenya). Unfortunately, the northern subspecies (*C. s. cottoni*) – which once ranged across northwest Uganda, northeast DRC, southeast CAR and southwest South Sudan – is now practically extinct. The world's last wild population of northern white rhinos, a herd of six living in DRC's Garamba National Park, were shot dead by poachers in 2006. True, two female northern white rhinos still survive in captivity, housed in a large pen in Kenya's Ol Pejeta Conservancy, but since both are incapable of natural reproduction, and the last living male died in captivity aged 45 in 2018, the last slim hope for this subspecies is the use of in vitro fertilisation (IVF) techniques.

Amuka Lodge (9 rooms) ⊕ 1.46991, 32.06558; m 0771 600812; e info@amukalodgeuganda.com; w amukalodgeuganda.com. This wonderfully isolated family-run lodge is carved into the bush about 6km by road from the sanctuary headquarters. The widely spaced-out rooms all have a tiled floor, earthy décor, dbl bed with nets, en-suite hot shower & private balcony, & there are also 3 family rooms with 2 additional sgl beds. Amenities include a small swimming pool on the deck & campfires at night. The 3-course meals come highly praised. *US$201/378 sgl/dbl B&B.* **$$$$**

Kabalega Diner ⊕ 1.51305, 32.07661; ☎ 041 4691910; m 0774 582296; e kabalegadinerug@gmail.com; ⏲ 07.00–19.00 daily. Perhaps the best out-of-town roadside eatery in Uganda, Kabalega Diner now also offers accommodation. Located on the left side of the Gulu Rd 2km north of the junction for Ziwa & 5km before the turn-off for Masindi, it is a more-or-less mandatory stop for safari-goers bound for Murchison or Kidepo; as well as an excellent menu, clean, flushing toilets are a far from insignificant consideration. It is also ideally placed to accommodate &/or feed visitors to Ziwa. B/fasts, soups, salads & sandwiches are in the US$5–6 range, while pizzas, curries, stir-fries, burgers & grills (including several vegetarian options) mostly cost US$7–9. As regards accommodation, a pair of dbl rooms are priced at US$50, a twin at US$63 while some tents sharing an outside bathroom cost US$30. All rates B&B.

Ziwa Guesthouse ⊕ 1.44783, 32.07738; m 0785 552801; e info@ziwarhinoandwildliferanch.com; w ziwarhinoandwildliferanch.com. Situated alongside the sanctuary headquarters, this unpretentious lodge sprawls across shady park-like gardens frequented by warthog, waterbuck, bushbuck & plentiful birds (not to mention the rhinos that frequently pass through in the evening). For accommodation, 2 guesthouses have a selection of dbl, twin & trpl rooms with nets, en-suite hot shower & shared balcony, & there is also a dorm using common showers. A thatched restaurant, also open to day visitors, offers terrace or indoor seating, an adequately stocked bar & a limited selection of mains in the US$8–10 range. *From US$80/90 sgl/dbl; US$35 pp per dorm bed.* **$$–$$$**

What to see and do Those who arrive with their own transport can use it as required for any of the activities described here. Those without can rent a 4x4 from the sanctuary headquarters at US$25 per group per activity. Note also that those who want to track rhinos and shoebills get a US$10 discount on the package deal. Closed shoes and long trousers are mandatory for all excursions, and insect repellent is recommended in the swamp.

Rhino tracking (2hrs; US$20/30/10 FR/FNR/Ugandan citizen plus US$20 entrance; discounts for children) One of the most exciting wildlife activities on offer anywhere in Uganda, tracking the white rhinos of Ziwa usually takes place on foot, though you may need to drive a short way from the headquarters first, depending on the location of the nearest individuals. Because they are solitary animals, the rhinos are usually seen singly, though youngsters tend to stick close to their mother until they are almost fully grown. The rhinos are very habituated, since they are protected by armed rangers 24/7, so it is often possible to approach them to within 30m. White rhinos are not generally aggressive towards people (certainly not by comparison to their notoriously grouchy black counterparts), but like any wild animal, they can be unpredictable, so it is vital you stick close to the ranger, listen to their instructions, and avoid sudden movements. There are no fixed departure times, but early morning and late afternoon tend to be cooler for walking, and better for photography.

Shoebill canoe safari (4hrs; US$20/25/10 FR/FNR/Ugandan citizen) Best undertaken in the early morning (departing from your lodge at 06.00), the shoebill-tracking excursion involves driving to the edge of Lugogo Swamp, then canoeing or walking – or both – in search of one of the resident shoebills. The activity enjoys a high success rate, but you will seldom get as close to the shoebills as you might in Murchison Falls. Even if you dip on shoebills, plenty of other water-associated birds can be seen in the swamp, as can the localised sitatunga antelope. The activity starts at 06.00, so it is only available to overnight visitors.

Bird and nature walks (2hrs; US$20/20/10 FR/FNR/Ugandan citizen) Shoebills aside, the best way to see a selection of the 330 bird species recorded in Ziwa (along with other larger mammals) is a guided bird or general nature walk using one of four trails that emanate from the headquarters. These are best undertaken from 08.00 to 10.00 or 16.00 to 18.00, when wildlife tends to be most active.

Night walks (2hrs; US$20/10 adult/child) Guided night walks at Ziwa offer a great opportunity to look for nocturnal creatures such as white-tailed mongoose, genets, bushbabies and a variety of owls and night jars. Leopards and even aardvarks are also very occasionally seen. The walks leave at 20.00, so are only available to overnight visitors.

WEST TOWARDS FORT PORTAL

The 300km surfaced road from Kampala to Fort Portal can be covered in a longish half-day, if – as is the case with most tourists – you're concerned solely with getting from A to B. It passes through a lush and densely populated part of Buganda and Bunyoro punctuated by a trio of bustling medium-sized towns, namely Mityana, Mubende and Kyenjojo. Recognised tourist attractions are practically non-existent, but this is arguably compensated for by a number of little-known archaeological sites and sacrificial shrines associated with the medieval Bachwezi kingdom. These include the Tanda Pits and Lake Wamala near Mityana, set within easy day-tripping distance of the capital, as well as the Nakayima Tree and Munsa Earthworks near Mubende, which lies in the far west of Buganda almost exactly halfway to Fort Portal.

MITYANA AND SURROUNDS Sprawling along the Fort Portal Road about 60km west of Kampala, Mityana is a substantial and fast-growing town of 50,000 set in an area steeped in Bachwezi and Kiganda legend. Though inherently unremarkable and arguably too close to Kampala for a rest or an overnight stay, there's some interesting sightseeing in the area, most notably the ancient shrine at the Tanda Pits, but also to a lesser extent the little-visited Lake Wamala.

Getting there and away In theory, Mityana should be only an hour's drive from Kampala, but the congested city traffic means the drive can take twice as long. If you plan on stopping at Tanda, note that the junction is 9km before Mityana coming from Kampala. Inexpensive matatus connect Mityana to Kampala's New Taxi Park and Mubende throughout the day.

Where to stay *Map, page 98*

Enro Hotel (62 rooms) ⊕ 0.39808, 32.05926; m 0772 442007; e enrohotellimited@yahoo.com. This long-serving hotel is located off the Kampala Rd, 500m beyond the Makanhill turning. Acceptable rooms are offered in an older wing & smarter (& correspondingly pricier) ones in a new block. A restaurant, bar & pool are provided. *US$13/32 sgl/dbl in old wing, US$20–3/40/53 exec sgls/dbl/trpls in new wing. All rates B&B.* **$$**

IN THE BEGINNING...

Once upon a time, Ggulu, the creator, sent his daughter Nambi and her siblings on a day trip to earth, where they chanced upon its only human inhabitant: poor lonely Kintu, who lived in the vicinity of Lake Wamala, near present-day Mityana, his sole companion a beloved cow. Nambi was at once attracted to Kintu and upset at his enforced solitude, and she determined there and then to marry and keep him company on earth. Nambi's brothers were appalled at her reckless decision and attempted to dissuade her, eventually reaching the compromise that she and Kintu would return to heaven to ask Ggulu's permission to marry. Ggulu reluctantly blessed the union, but he did advise the couple to descend to earth lightly packed and in secret, to avoid being noticed and followed by Nambi's brother Walumbe, the spirit of disease and death.

The next morning, before dawn, the delighted newlyweds set off for earth, carrying little other than Nambi's favourite chicken. When they arrived, however, Nambi realised that she had forgotten to bring millet to feed the chicken and decided to return to heaven to fetch it. Kintu implored Nambi to stay, fearing that she might encounter Walumbe and suggesting that a substitute chicken feed would surely be available on earth. But Nambi ignored Kintu's pleadings and returned to heaven, where sure enough she bumped into Walumbe, who – curious as to where his sister might be headed so early in the morning – followed her all the way back to join Kintu.

A few years later, Kintu, by then the head of a happy family, received a visit from Walumbe, who insisted that he be given one of their children to help with his household chores. Heedful of his father-in-law's warning, Kintu refused Walumbe,

Makanhill Hotel (25 rooms) 0393 224000. Located in a quiet suburb, this smart new addition to Mityana's listings is prominently signed on the right as you enter the town from Kampala. *US$21/40 sgl/dbl B&B*. **$$**

What to see and do

Tanda Pits (m 0751 777370, 0772 870689; 24hrs daily; entry US$5) An intriguing goal for a day trip out of Kampala or diversion en route to Fort Portal, Tanda comprises a field of around 240 pits scattered in a 10ha rectangle of ancient forest whose undergrowth has been cleared, though its canopy remains intact. Some of the pits are quite shallow, but others are narrow, deep and, according to Kiganda tradition, bottomless. Legend holds that this shady enclave served as the stage for much of the formative earthly action described above. Indeed, a rock shelter only 500m from Tanda is supposedly where Kintu, the first man on earth, settled down with his wife Nambi. As for the pits, they were excavated by Nambi's brother Kayikuzi (literally, 'Digger of Holes') in an unsuccessful attempt to capture their third sibling Walumbe, the spirit of death and disease, and rid the world of his malevolent presence.

Today, Tanda ranks as probably the most important Bachwezi shrine in Buganda. Eighteen of the pits at Tanda are revered as sacrificial sites, each one dedicated to a different Bachwezi spirit. The largest pit and most important shrine, covered in several layers of barkcloth and surrounded by massive clusters of five-fingered spears and gourds, is the one associated with Walumbe, who is said to return there from time to time. Elsewhere, sacrifices are tailored to appease the particular spirit for which they were left. Carved wooden boats and fish skins are littered around the

who was deeply angered and avenged himself by killing Kintu's eldest son. When Kintu returned to heaven to ask for assistance, Ggulu chastised him for ignoring the warning, but he agreed nevertheless to send another son, Kayikuzi, to bring Walumbe back to heaven. Walumbe refused to leave earth, however, so Kayikuzi was forced to try and evict him against his will. The brothers fought violently, but the moment Kayikuzi gained an upper hand, Walumbe vanished underground. Kayikuzi dug several large holes, found Walumbe's hiding place, and the two resumed their fight, but soon Walumbe fled into the ground once again, and so the pattern repeated itself.

After several days, Kayikuzi, now nearing exhaustion, told Kintu and Nambi he would try one last time to catch Walumbe, at the same time instructing them to ensure that their children stayed indoors and remained silent until his task was done. Kayikuzi chased Walumbe out of hiding, but some of Kintu's children, who had disobeyed the instruction, saw the sparring brothers emerge from underground and they started screaming, giving Walumbe the opportunity to duck back into his subterranean refuge. Kayikuzi, angry that his earthly charges had ignored his instructions, told them he was giving up the chase, and the embarrassed Kintu did not argue. He told Kayikuzi to return to heaven and said: 'If Walumbe wishes to kill my children, so be it. I will keep having more, and the more he kills, the more I will have. He will not be able to remove them all from the face of the earth.'

…and so ends the Kiganda creation myth, one whose association between human disobedience and the arrival of death and disease on earth has an oddly Old Testament ring.

shrine for Mukasa, the spirit of lakes and rivers; bottled alcohol and other addictive substances have been sacrificed to Bamweyana, the spirit of madness; while electric sockets, light bulbs and other such appliances are draped from a tree overhanging the shrine to Kiwanuka, the spirit of thunder and lightning.

A truly fascinating repository of Bachwezi tradition, Tanda is far more active than might be expected of an ancient animist shrine in 21st-century Uganda. Tourists are welcome, provided they stick to photographing the actual shrines rather than the (often distraught, bereaved or suffering) locals who come to place sacrifices at them. Unpaid English-speaking guides are available, and highly recommended both for the insight they'll provide into the Kiganda traditions associated with Tanda, and to ensure that you avoid any cultural faux pas, but a fair tip will be expected.

Getting to Tanda could hardly be more straightforward. The junction (⊕ 0.39488, 32.13146), signposted 'Itanda Archaeological Archives and Walumbe Tombs', lies on the south side of the Fort Portal Road about 48km west of Kampala's Busega Roundabout and 9km east of the Enro Hotel in Mityana. It's almost 2km from the junction to the entrance gate (⊕ 0.3852, 32.12795). Those without private transport could either catch a matatu between Kampala and Mityana and walk from the junction, or else charter a boda in Mityana.

Lake Wamala Extending over 180km^2 southwest of Mityana, Lake Wamala was submerged by Lake Victoria until about 4,000 years ago, and it still drains into the larger lake via the rivers Kibimba and Katonga. The lake is named after the last Bachwezi leader, Wamala, and as with so many other sites in this part of Uganda, it has strong associations with traditional religions. One legend has it that the lake was formed by water leaked from a skin-carrier that belonged to King Wamala, while another states that its Bachwezi namesake disappeared into it at a site called Nakyegalika and that his spirit still resides there today. Despite its size and historical associations, Lake Wamala is virtually unknown as a tourist destination. If you want to explore, the best point of access is the village of Naama about 6km west of Mityana. To reach the lake, turn left off the Fort Portal road opposite the Mityana Shell station and drive straight though the town. After about 4km on a brand new tarmac road, turn left (⊕ 0.4081889, 31.9956325) after a swamp crossing on to a variable, 5km dirt road, which will lead you to a boat landing beside the lake. You should be able to organise a dugout canoe to take you across to one of the lake's larger islands or to look for the waterbirds (and reputedly hippos) that frequent the shallows and well-vegetated shore.

Entanda Cultural Adventure (m 0772 340576; e ask@entandatours.com; w entandatours.com) Situated on the eastern outskirts of Mityana, award-winning Entanda runs full- and half-day cultural programmes offering the opportunity to experience a few aspects of traditional Ugandan life. Expect a joyous welcome of dancing and drumming, bountiful organic fruits, a local lunch, information about and demonstrations of traditional games, hunting techniques, barkcloth making, medicine, taboos and totems, and a chance to listen to the traditional wisdom (and bedroom secrets!) of the 'senga'. Tours must be prebooked (this can be done online) and include transport from Kampala.

MUBENDE AND SURROUNDS Roughly midway along the main road between Kampala and Fort Portal, Mubende (population 50,000) ranks among Uganda's prettier small towns, set below and named after a 1,573m-high hill that reputedly served as the 15th-century capital of King Ndahura. More recently, the breezy climate, fertile soil and clear springs of Mubende Hill so impressed the early colonials that it was chosen as the site of a sanatorium where weary Entebbe-based administrators could, according to a contemporary issue of the *Mengo Notes*, 'repair thither for a period of change and invigoration'. These days, Mubende – or rather the bustling stretch of main road 1km south of the more sedate town centre – visibly revels in its status as a halfway snack house where Kampala- or Fort Portal-bound travellers can pause to enjoy a chilled drink and a barbecued chicken-on-a-stick, or whatever other basic refreshments take their fancy. And while most passers-by decline to explore any further, the Mubende area is of some interest for its wealth of important Bachwezi-related sites. The most accessible of these, set atop Mubende Hill, 15 minutes' drive from the town centre, is the splendid Nakayima Tree, an active centuries-old sacrificial shrine whose immense buttresses house the spirit of Ndahura and several other traditional spirits.

History The hill known as Mubende, literally 'Place of Disaster', earned that name in the 16th century, when its summit served as the capital of a notorious king whose reign was characterised by several massacres. But both oral tradition and archaeological evidence suggest the sacred hilltop plateau formerly called Kisozi supported a substantial and important settlement for some centuries before that. In pre-Bachwezi times, Kisozi is said to have been settled by Kamwenge, a sorceress from present-day Ankole. Kamwenge's two sons established themselves as important local rulers, and their hilltop capital became one of the region's largest settlements. Kisozi was later usurped by the Bachwezi ruler Ndahura, who resided there for several years before he abdicated in favour of his son Wamala, and retired to his birthplace near Fort Portal.

Perhaps a century after Ndahura's vanishing act, Kisozi became the capital of the murderous king whose reign is alluded to in the name 'Mubende'. According to tradition, the only person able to persuade this despot to mend his ways was a powerful sorceress of the cow clan whose heroism earned her the soubriquet Nakayima – literally, 'Advocator'. Eventually, however, the king lost patience with all the advocacy, and he attempted to capture Nakayima, who spirited herself away inside a large tree planted many decades earlier in memory of Ndahura. This was the Nakayima Tree: believed ever since to harbour the spirit of Ndahura, who is deified by both the Banyoro and Baganda as the god of smallpox, as well as the spirit of Nakayima, as manifested in an oddly shaped branch that resembles her clan animal, the cow.

Ever since the spirit took refuge in the Nakayima Tree, a hereditary line of priestesses, also known by the title Nakayima, and said by some to descend from the eponymous wife of Ndahura, have maintained it as a sacrificial shrine. The Nakayima priestess is also regularly possessed by the spirit of Ndahura, and her alleged powers include the ability to cure infertility and smallpox. She was probably the most important single spiritual leader in pre-colonial Buganda and Bunyoro, and received regular tributes from the kings of both polities, as well as overseeing various ritual ceremonies that involved the sacrifice of livestock and more occasionally teenage boys and girls.

The decline of the Nakayima lineage started in 1888, when the religious conflict that rocked Buganda forced the incumbent priestess, named Nyanjara, to flee Mubende. Nyanjara returned to Mubende a year later, only to find six of the seven huts traditionally inhabited by the Nakayima had been razed, the sacred drums they held had vanished, and the graves of her predecessors had been defaced. This attack had no immediate impact on the Nyanjara's influence in Bunyoro, which was then relatively unexposed to outside religions – indeed, King Kabalega visited Mubende Hill to pay her tribute in 1899. But as foreign missionaries persuaded the Baganda elite to turn away from traditional beliefs, so the Nakayima's spiritual importance in Buganda diminished.

The last blow came in 1902, when the British administration placed Mubende Hill under the indirect colonial rule of a Muganda chief. Nyanjara retired to Bugogo, where she died five years later, and became the first Nakayima not to be interred in a traditional cemetery near the sacred tree (though eventually she was buried in isolation at the base of Mubende Hill). Her fantastic regalia, confiscated by the colonial authorities, now forms one of the most impressive displays in Kampala's National Museum – together with two large and ancient pots, probably used in Bachwezi-related religious rituals, unearthed during excavations on Mubende Hill.

The present-day status of the Nakayima is unclear. After the death of Nyanjara, no successor to the title emerged until 1926, when a Muhima sorceress took up brief residence on Mubende Hill only to vanish a short while later. Ten years later, another short-lived candidate showed up in the form of a young Ankole girl, dressed in full priestly regalia, who spent several nights screeching at the base of the Nakayima Tree before she too disappeared. All written sources agree that the spirit of Nakayima has been unclaimed ever since. On site, by contrast, an elderly woman living below the tree claims to have served as the Nakayima priestess since the 1960s, and seems to be accepted as such by the many Baganda and Banyoro traditionalists who still come to make sacrifices below there.

Getting there and away Mubende lies about 150km west of Kampala and a similar distance east of Fort Portal. Heavy traffic on the outskirts of Kampala and deteriorating tarmac west of Mityana mean that the drive from the capital now takes about 3½ hours, a good hour longer than the drive from Fort Portal. All buses between Kampala and Fort Portal stop at Mubende, connecting the town to Mityana, Kyenjojo and Fort Portal throughout the day. Regular matatus also run to Mubende to Kampala's New Taxi Park.

Where to stay and eat

These days, Mubende is best known for the roadside market on the Kampala–Fort Portal road which skirts the town centre. Travellers, NGO vehicles and buses all stop here to grab a stick of barbecue chicken or goat with a chapati or bag of soggy chips. Rather than buying skewered meat from the roadside hawkers, seasoned travellers head into the market-sized barbecue shelter to pick a fresh piece straight from the grill.

Prime Rose Hotel [map, page 98] (38 rooms) ⊕ 0.54712, 31.39713; **m** 0776 884321, 0756 884321; **e** info@primerosehotel.com; **w** primerosehotel.com. Situated 200m south of the Kampala Rd & clearly signposted as you enter town from that side, this blandly modern high-rise is easily the best choice in Mubende, & great value too. Comfortable en-suite rooms have nets, DSTV & hot shower, & there's a well-stocked restaurant/bar with garden seating. *US$12/16 sgl/dbl B&B.* **$**

What to see and do

Nakayima Tree (⊕ 0.57355, 31.37761; f nakayima.tree; ⏲ 24hrs daily; entry US$1.50) The best-known Bachwezi-associated sacrificial site in Buganda is the Nakayima Tree, which stands on the plateau-like summit of Mubende Hill close to a sanatorium built by the British in 1908. It isn't difficult to see why this particular tree – estimated by various scientific teams to be between 500 and 1,000 years old – has acquired such a revered status. It is a compelling piece of natural engineering, towering almost 40m above its park-like surrounds like an oversized surrealist sculpture whose fin-shaped buttresses fan out from the base to create around a dozen cavernous hollows, each of which is dedicated to one particular spirit. The most popular spirits associated with the tree are of course Nakayima (fertility and various illnesses) and Ndahura (smallpox), but others with their buttressed 'rooms' include Nabuzana (marriage), Walumbe (death and disease), Mukasa (lakes and rivers) and Bamweyana (madness). As with nearby Tanda, the Nakayima Tree remains an active shrine, visited by Bachwezi cultists from all around Buganda and Bunyoro to pay homage or leave sacrifices (coins, cowrie shells, gourds, food, et al) to the relevant spirit. Every so often, a group of cultists will spend a night by the tree, where they might roast a goat or pig in honour of the incumbent priestess, who claims to have lived below the tree and served in that role since the 1960s (though sceptics might note that she wasn't present on any of our several visits prior to 2015). Other points of interest include some old grinding stones said to date to Bachwezi times.

From central Mubende, the Nakayima Tree can be reached along a steep surfaced road clearly signposted uphill from the roundabout, 100m west of the taxi park. If you're walking, you should make it up in an hour, depending on how often you stop to enjoy the prolific birdlife and views over the town and south to Masaka Hill. Once there, optional guides are available for a nominal flat fee; if the articulate and friendly lady who showed us around is anything to go by, it's well worth the minor investment.

Munsa Earthworks (⊕ 0.8228, 31.31308) Situated 38km north of Mubende, Munsa comprises a maze of deep but silted-up trenches enclosing Bikekete Hill, a prominent granite outcrop riddled with tunnels and caves. Oral tradition links Bikekete and Munsa – derived from the Runyoro 'Mu-ensa', or 'place of ditches' – with the Bachwezi prince Kateboha, who reputedly lived in a cave large enough to seat 50 people. This tradition is supported by archaeological evidence that indicates Bikekete was inhabited in the 14th century, and that the 7m-wide, 3m-deep V-shaped earthworks were excavated to protect his rocky stronghold. Significant discoveries at Bikekete include a clay iron-smelting furnace, innumerable pot shards, glass trade beads from the Swahili Coast, and a small cemetery where one skeleton lay beneath a second inverted one, suggestive of the grisly royal custom that a servant should be buried alive above the king, in order to attend his dead master.

Long-standing talk of developing Munsa as a formal tourist attraction has yet to translate into action. All the same, the earthworks are easy enough to visit. With a torch and a local guide, you can crawl through a tight tunnel into the cave once inhabited by Kateboha, while the outline of the silted-up earthworks is clearly visible from the top of the hill. Look out, too, for a pair of deep, narrow artificial holes in a slab of flat granite 150m south of the hill's base – according to local tradition, these were receptacles from which Kateboha drank beer offerings from his subjects at the start of the harvest season. On the way to or from Munsa, you might also want to investigate Semwama Hill, a massive granite whaleback renowned as the site of a venerable Bachwezi sacrificial shrine set in the twin-chambered cave where Kateboha of Munsa reputedly used to hold council with his elders and advisors.

Munsa Earthworks makes for a feasible day trip out of Mubende, even for those dependent on public transport. It is reached via Kakumiro, a junction village 32km north of Mubende, and no more than an hour's drive, whether in a private vehicle or a matatu. From Kakumiro, follow the Hoima Road 1km north then turn left at the junction (⊕ 0.79047, 31.32474) signposted for Munsa Primary School. The primary school lies about 3.5km along this road, and the inconspicuous track to the earthworks (⊕ 0.81742, 31.32004) runs left from practically opposite it. Roughly 700m down this track, and only 100m before the earthworks, lies the home of the local priest, who is also the official caretaker. If you also want to visit Semwama Hill (⊕ 0.79949, 31.32179), an overgrown 200m track (⊕ 0.79725, 31.32045) to the base of this conspicuous outcrop leads right from the road to Munsa Primary School about 1km past the junction with the Hoima Road. There is no public transport beyond Kakumiro, but you could walk from there to either site in an hour, or charter a boda.

Bigo bya Mugyenyi and the Ntusi Mounds These two archaeologically important but relatively inaccessible sites, neither of which is likely to convey much to a day visitor, lie in the vicinity of Ntusi, a small town situated 75km south of Mubende along a little-used back route to Masaka and Lyantonde. The 15th-century Bigo bya Mugyenyi (literally 'Fort of the Stranger'), situated at the confluence of the Katonga and Kakinga rivers, is the largest of several earthworks excavated by the Bachwezi, but the site has never been cleared and it lacks the impact of Munsa. Older still are the Ntusi Mounds, a pair of immense trash heaps containing bones, pottery shards and other waste material deposited over a 300-year period by the inhabitants of what was probably the largest medieval settlement in the East African interior. The Ntusi Mounds lie within 1km of Ntusi District Headquarters, and can be visited on foot over a couple of hours, but Bigo bya Mugyenyi is a long hour's drive from Ntusi along poor unmarked roads that shouldn't be attempted without a local guide.

KATONGA WILDLIFE RESERVE (entry US$25/35 FR/FNR) The closest wildlife reserve to Kampala as the crow flies, little-known Katonga comprises 207km² of mixed savannah, papyrus swamp and rainforest along the northern edge of the river for which it is named. Geologically, it lies within one of Africa's oldest river valleys – one that once flowed all the way from western Kenya to the Atlantic, and that pre-dates the formation of the Rift Valley, Lake Victoria and even the Nile by many millions of years. Gazetted in 1964, the reserve originally supported large resident herds of zebra, elephant and buffalo, while doubling as part of a game migration corridor between western Uganda, Tanzania and South Sudan. An upgrade to national park status is likely in the near future.

Poaching and cattle encroachment took a heavy toll on the environment and wildlife in the 1970s and 1980s, but improved protection in recent years has ensured that populations are now on the increase. The mammal checklist of 40 species includes black-and-white colobus, olive baboon, Ugandan kob and small numbers of elephant and buffalo, while waterbuck, reedbuck and bushbuck are common and sufficiently habituated to approach on foot. Katonga is one of perhaps three places in East Africa where the secretive sitatunga antelope is reasonably likely to be seen by a casual visitor. Recent reintroductions include a herd of zebra and impala from Lake Mburo National Park. Katonga is also of great interest for its varied birdlife – over 338 species have been recorded – and among the more interesting likely to be seen are blue-headed coucal, Ross's and great blue turaco, crested malimbe and papyrus gonolek.

The main activity is guided half-day walking trails, which cost US$30 per person. Canoe trips through the wetland have been discontinued for safety reasons following the colonisation of the channel by hippos.

Getting there and away The signposted junction for Katonga is Kyegegwa, which lies on the Fort Portal Road, 42km west of Mubende. From here, a 40km dirt road heads south to the entrance gate via Mparo and Kalwreni. It's easy enough to find public transport to Kyegegwa and on to Kalwreni, possibly changing vehicles at Mparo. Kalwreni lies 7km from the entrance gate, so if you can't find transport, you could walk or hire a boda.

It is also possible to approach Katonga from Kibale National Park via Kamwenge, Ibanda and Kabagole. Public transport is plentiful on all legs of this route.

Where to stay and eat The Katonga Visitors' Centre [map, page 98], which overlooks the valley 1km from the entrance gate, is basically a campsite with a covered dining area and ablutions. Water and firewood are provided, but you should bring everything else you require with you. Camping costs US$5 per person. Basic lodgings are also available in the village of Kabagole, which lies on the southern edge of the valley, about 1km from the reserve entrance gate.

SOUTHWEST TOWARDS MASAKA

The main surfaced road running southwest from Kampala is dotted with low-key attractions. The most alluring of these, often visited as a destination in its own right, is the under-publicised Mpanga Forest, which abuts the main road 35km from the capital. Other attractions in the region – most notably perhaps the equator crossing at Nabusanke – are more often visited en route between Kampala and points further southwest, such as Masaka, Lake Mburo National Park or Bwindi Impenetrable National Park.

KATEREKE PRISON [102 B1] (☎ 041 4501866; ⌚ 08.00–17.00 daily; entry US$2) The extensive prison ditch at Katereke is a relic of the instability that characterised Buganda in the late 1880s (page 184). It was constructed by Kabaka Kalema, an Islamic sympathiser who was controversially placed on the throne in October 1888, less than two months after Kabaka Mwanga had been forced into exile. Kalema ordered that every potential or imagined rival to his throne be rounded up and sent to Katereke – which, given the fragility of his position in the divided kingdom, added up to an estimated 40 personages.

One of the first to be imprisoned at Katereke was Kiwewa, who had ruled Buganda for the brief period between Mwanga's exile and Kalema's ascent to the throne. Kiwewa was soon joined by a bevy of his wives, as well as the two infant sons of the exiled Mwanga, and the last two surviving sons of the late Kabaka Suuna. Kalema also feared a secession bid from his own brothers, and even his sisters – like Mwanga before him, Kalema was unsettled by the fact that a woman sat on the English throne – and most of them were imprisoned, too.

Six months into his reign, sensing a growing threat from the budding alliance between the Christian faction in Buganda and its former persecutor Mwanga – the latter by this time openly resident on an island in Murchison Bay, only 10km from the capital – Kalema decided to wipe out the potential opposition once and for all. Most of the occupants of the prison were slaughtered without mercy. Other less significant figures, for instance some of the princesses and one elderly son of Kabaka Suuna, were spared when they agreed to embrace Islam. The massacre wasn't confined to the prison's occupants either: Mukasa, the traditionalist Katikiro who had served under Mwanga, was shot outside his house, which was then set on fire with the body inside. The wives of the former Kabaka Kiwewa, according to Sir John Milner Gray, were 'put to death in circumstances of disgusting brutality'.

Ultimately, this massacre probably hastened Kalema's downfall by strengthening the alliance between Buganda's Christians, who suffered several casualties, and the island-bound Mwanga, left mourning several brothers and sisters as well as his two sons. And the lingering death that Kalema had reserved for his predecessor set many formerly neutral chiefs and other dignitaries against him. Kiwewa was starved of food and water for seven days, then a bullet was put through his weakened body, and finally his remains were burnt unceremoniously in his prison cell – not, in the words of Sir Apollo Kaggwa, 'a fit manner in which to kill a king'.

Katereke Prison lies to the west of Kampala, and can be reached by following the Masaka Road out of town for about 15km, passing through Nsangi trading centre, then about 2km later turning right at a left-hand bend in the road marked by a series of speed bumps. The 2km track to Katereke is marked by a fading mauve signpost (ignore a similar but premature sign 1km back down the road towards Nsangi). It's a surprisingly peaceful and leafy spot, considering its bloody historical associations, and guides are available to show you around what remains of the prison trench.

A visit to Katereke could be combined with a side trip to **Nagalabi Buddo**, which lies about 5km south of Nsangi trading centre and has reputedly served as the coronation site for the kabaka since Buganda was founded.

MPANGA FOREST RESERVE [102 A2] Gazetted in the 1950s, the 45km^2 Mpanga Forest Reserve, situated 36km from Kampala near the small town of Mpigi, makes for a short and agreeably rustic trip out of the capital, or first stop en route to further-flung destinations. It protects an extensive patch of medium-altitude rainforest characteristic of the vegetation that extended over much of the northern

CHAOS IN BUGANDA: 1884–89

The succession of Kabaka Mwanga in October 1884 was an unusually smooth affair, accepted by his brothers and kin without serious infighting, and supported by the majority of Saza chiefs as well as the foreign factions that had by then settled around the royal capital. The five years that followed Mwanga's coronation were, by contrast, the most tumultuous in Buganda's 400-plus years of existence, culminating in three changes of kabaka within 12 months, and paving the way for the kingdom to relinquish its autonomy to a colonial power in 1890.

Mwanga's career comes across as the antithesis of the epithet 'come the moment, come the man'. In 1884, the missionary Alexander Mackay, who had witnessed Mwanga develop from 'a little boy…into manhood' described Mwanga as an 'amiable…young fellow' but 'fitful and fickle, and, I fear, revengeful', noting that 'under the influence of [marijuana] he is capable of the wildest unpremeditated actions'. These misgivings were echoed by other contemporary commentators: Robert Walker, for instance, dismissed Mwanga as 'frivolous…weak and easily led; passionate and if provoked petulant…possessed of very little courage or self-control'.

Whatever his personal failings, Mwanga was also forced to contend with a daunting miscellany of natural disasters, religious tensions and real or imagined political threats. Three months into his reign, he lost several wives and trusted chiefs to an epidemic that swept through his first capital at Nubulagala, while his second capital on Mengo Hill was destroyed by fire in February 1886 and again in 1887. Politically, Mwanga was threatened to the west by a resurgent Bunyoro, whose charismatic leader Kabalega inflicted several defeats on the Kiganda army in the 1880s. From the east, meanwhile, Buganda faced a more nebulous and less quantifiable threat, as news filtered through of the growing number and influence of European colonial agents on the coast.

Buganda (c1884) was riddled with religious factionalism. Kiganda traditionalists had for some time co-existed uneasily with a growing volume of Islamic converts influenced by Arab traders. And both of these relatively established factions faced further rivalry from the late 1870s onwards, following the establishment of Catholic and Anglican missions near the capital. The divisions between these religious factions were not limited to matters purely ecclesiastical. Many established Kiganda and Islamic customs, notably polygamy, were anathema to the Christian missionaries, who also spoke out against participation in the slave trade – the lifeblood of the Arab settlers, and profitable to several prominent Kiganda traditionalists.

Mwanga's personal religious persuasions were evidently dictated by pragmatic concerns. During the early years of his rule, his views were strongly shaped by his *katikiro*, an influential Kiganda traditionalist who distrusted all outside religions, but was relatively sympathetic to Islam as the lesser – or more tolerant towards Kiganda customs – of the two evils. It also seems likely that the traditionalist faction, not unreasonably, perceived a connection between the European missionaries and threat of European imperialism, and thus reckoned it had less to fear from the Arabs.

Three months after he took the throne, Mwanga signalled his hostility to Christianity by executing three young Anglican converts. Then, in October 1885, the king received news of Bishop Hannington's attempt to become the first European through the 'back door' of Busoga. In Kiganda tradition, the back door is used only by close friends or plotting enemies, and Hannington – a stranger to Mwanga – was clearly not the former. Motivated by fear more perhaps than any religious factor, Mwanga ordered the execution of Hannington (page 259).

Weeks after the bishop's death, Joseph Mukasa, a Catholic advisor to the king, criticised Mwanga for having Hannington killed without first giving him an opportunity to defend himself, and was also executed for his efforts. These two deaths led to an increasing estrangement between the kabaka and the missionaries – Mackay included – who resided around his court, fuelled partially by Mwanga's fear of a European reprisal for the attack on Hannington.

Mwanga's distrust of Christianity exploded into blind rage on 25 May 1886. The catalyst for this was probably the subversive actions of his sister Princess Clara Nalumansi (page 132), though it has been suggested by some writers that Mwanga was a homosexual paedophile whose temporary hatred of Christians stemmed from his rejection by a favoured page, recently baptised. Exactly how many Baganda Christians were speared, beheaded, cremated, castrated and/or bludgeoned to death over the next ten days is an open question – 45 deaths are recorded by name, but the actual tally was probably several hundred. The persecution culminated at Namugongo on 3 June 1886, when at least 26 Catholic and Anglican converts, having rejected the opportunity to renounce their new faith, were roasted alive (page 158).

His rage evidently spent, Mwanga set about repairing his relationship with the European missionaries, who had not been directly victimised by the persecution, and who depended on the kabaka's tolerance to continue their work in the kingdom. Tensions resurfaced in June 1887 when, according to Mackay, Stanley's non-military expedition to Equatoria was described to Mwanga by an Arab trader as 'a Mazungu coming here with a thousand guns' – a ploy designed to reawaken the king's concern that Hannington's death would be avenged by his countrymen. In December 1887, Hannington's successor wrote Mwanga a letter, delivered by Rev E C Gordon, stating that: 'we do not desire to take vengeance for this action of yours, we are teachers of the religion of Christ, not soldiers...We believe that you must see now that you were deceived as to the object for which [Hannington] had come.' The increasingly paranoid Mwanga interpreted this as a declaration of war, and Gordon was imprisoned for two months.

During 1888, Mwanga's concerns about a foreign invasion were diverted by the domestic chaos induced by years of vacillation between the religious factions. On 10 September, Mwanga was forced to flee into exile. His successor, a Muslim convert called Kiwewa, enjoyed a six-week reign, marked by violence between the opposing religious factions, before he was ousted by another Muslim convert called Kalema. Under Kalema, Buganda descended into full civil war, with an unexpected reversal of alliances in which the Christian and traditionalist Baganda lent their support to Mwanga, who was restored to power in February 1890. Three months later, Captain Lugard arrived in Kampala waving a treaty of protectorateship with England.

E B Fletcher, who knew Mwanga in his later years, regarded him to be 'nervous, suspicious, fickle, passionate...with no idea whatever of self-discipline, without regard for life or property, as long as he achieved his own end'. Yet in 1936 Fletcher also wrote an essay exonerating many of the king's excesses and flaws as symptomatic of the troubled times through which he'd lived. 'To steer a straight course through a time when such radical changes were taking place', Fletcher concluded, 'needed a man of a strong character, a firm will and wide vision. Those characteristics Mwanga did not possess.'

Lake Victoria hinterland prior to the early 20th century. Although Mpanga harbours a less diverse fauna than the larger forests in the far west of Uganda, its accessibility and proximity to Kampala more than justify a visit. The most readily observed mammal is the red-tailed monkey, though bushpig, bushbuck and flying squirrels are also present. Blue-breasted kingfisher, black-and-white casqued hornbill, African pied hornbill, African grey parrot and great blue turaco are among the more striking and conspicuous of the 180-plus bird species recorded. Resident birds with a rather localised distribution elsewhere in Uganda include shining blue kingfisher, spotted greenbul, Uganda woodland warbler, green crombec, (Frazer's) rufous flycatcher-thrush, Bocage's bush-shrike, pink-footed puff-back and Weyn's weaver. Mpanga Forest is also noted for its butterflies, which are abundant wherever you walk. The site has recently been allocated to a concessionaire, so expect some improvements to infrastructure and facilities. No contacts are available yet but you could call the NFA in Kampala for updates: 031 2264036.

Fees According to the National Forest Authority, the new operator will charge US$5 for foreign tourists to enter the site and an additional US$32 (payable in Uganda shillings) for a forest/birding walk. In this new tariff, which also applies to Mabira Forest, no distinction is made between Foreign Residents and Foreign Non Residents. Lower rates apply to East Africans and Ugandans.

Getting there and away Coming from Kampala, about 3km past the turn-off to Mpigi, the road passes through a dip flanked by the southernmost tip of the forest. Immediately after, a signposted turn-off to the right (⊕ 0.20265, 32.30618) leads to the ecotourism centre after about 500m. It's a nasty corner on a fast road so you might prefer to continue into Mpambire village and turn around to make your approach. Matatus to Mpigi leave Kampala from the New Taxi Park. From Mpigi, a boda to the forest will cost less than US$1. Alternatively, any minibus or bus heading between Kampala and Masaka can drop you at the turn-off 500m from the ecotourism centre.

Where to stay and eat

Mpanga Ecotourism Site [102 A2] ⊕ 0.2061, 32.30189. This pretty camp centres on a grassy picnic area overlooked by the southern edge of the forest & resounding with the calls of hornbills & other forest birds. No details are available yet, but expect some much-needed improvements to the banda accommodation & campsite facilities.

What to see and do A network of wide footpaths initially cut by researchers is now the basis of a selection of forest walks emanating from the Mpanga Ecotourism Centre. You can wander along the footpaths alone if you wish, or take a guide. The undemanding 3km **Base Line Trail** is the main route through the forest, crossing two streams before it emerges on the western margin at Nakyetema Swamp, where sitatunga and shoebill are resident, though seldom seen. The 5km **Hornbill Loop** covers more undulating terrain, and involves fording several streams along minor footpaths, passing a striking tree-root arch along the way. For those with limited time, the 1km **Butterfly Loop** offers a good chance of seeing monkeys and common forest birds, as well as myriad colourful butterflies, and can be completed in less than an hour.

In addition to forest walks, guided visits can also be arranged to two important Kiganda shrines which lie within walking distance of the forest. Less than 1km from the ecotourism centre, **Nakibinge Shrine**, dedicated to the eponymous

16th-century king, is housed in a small thatched building in the style of the Kasubi Tombs. The **Kibuuka Shrine** near Mpigi, 3–4km back along the Kampala Road, is dedicated to a god of war who hailed from the Ssese Islands. Beyond the forest, the **flat-topped hill** south of the main road is worth climbing for the attractive grassland environment and views over the forest and surrounding swamp valleys.

FROM MPANGA TO MASAKA

Mpambire and Kabira About 1km beyond Mpanga Forest, the small village of **Mpambire**, traditional home of the Buganda royal drum-makers, is lined with stalls selling drums (US$15 upwards, depending on size) and other musical instruments. Even if you're not interested in buying drums, it's fascinating to watch the craftsmen at work, and there's no hassle attached to wandering around. At **Kabira**, another 5km further towards Masaka, a row of stalls sells distinctive and colourful baskets and stools. Between these two locations, the road fords an extensive papyrus swamp – stretching all the way to Lake Victoria – in which the shoebill is resident and reportedly sometimes observed from the road.

Makanaga Wetland Effectively a western extension of the better-known Mabamba Swamp [102 A3], Makanaga is a mosaic of shallow open water and papyrus swamps extending across a vast bay on the northern shore of Lake Victoria. As with Mabamba, the wetland's principal attraction is the shoebill, which is regularly seen on dugout trips into the swamps. But a profusion of other water-associated birds is present, particularly on the open shallows, which often host seething flocks of white-winged black tern and various ducks and waders. The rare blue swallow is often observed over fringing grassland between November and January, while the forested verges of the Namugobo boat landing host the likes of great blue turaco, Ross's turaco, African pied hornbill and Weyn's weaver. Namugobo Landing, the best place to arrange a boat into the wetland, lies only 6km from the Masaka Road along a fair dirt road branching south at Kamengo (⊕ 0.14675, 32.22413), about 13km west of Mpanga Forest.

Camp Crocs (m 0754 844944, 0772 832013; e info@ugandacrocs.com; ⏲ 08.00–18.00 daily; entry US$3) Established on the Lake Victoria shore south of Buwawa in 1991, Camp Crocs is a long-serving Nile crocodile farm whose main products are crocodile meat (most of which is consumed locally) and crocodile skin for the lucrative export market. Activities include guided tours of the farm, where you'll see a vast array of farmed Nile crocodiles, from hatchlings to some that are five years old, along with a few venerable man-eaters who were relocated here by UWA from other parts of Uganda where they were harassing the surrounding population. Visitors can hold a half-metre croc (US$5) and, should they wish, feed them a live chicken (US$12 per group). If you still have an appetite after that, an open-air restaurant facing the lake specialises in crocodile steaks and whole tilapia (US$11). Accommodation is available in four spacious clean hillside cabins costing US$40 single/double B&B. Coming from Kampala, Camp Crocs lies 10km south of the Masaka Road along a dirt turn-off signposted at Buwama (⊕ 0.06231, 32.10593). If you miss that turn-off, or are coming in the opposite direction, a second (slightly shorter) road branches south to the camp, close to an isolated Shell fuel station and diner about 4km to the southwest (⊕ 0.0387, 32.07963).

Nabusanke The most popular stop on the Masaka Road, 75km from Kampala, Nabusanke (literally 'Small Parts') is an otherwise unremarkable location shunted into the limelight by the fact that the equator happens to cross the road here. A pair of much-photographed white concrete hoops attest to the fact, while a local entrepreneur has set up buckets and jugs between these unprepossessing landmarks. For a small fee he will demonstrate (or at least intimate) that water swirls in opposite directions in the northern and southern hemispheres.

A long line of roadside craft stalls with the usual mundane offerings lines the equator, as do half-a-dozen small cafés. The most professional of these places is the **AidChild Equation Café** (⊕ -0.00093, 32.03901; m 0779 699922; w aidchild.org/aidchild-businesses; ⏲ 05.00–19.00 daily), which sells a variety of high-quality local crafts and artwork, and serves tasty coffee and muffins, as well as wraps and light meals in the US$3–7 range. There are flushing toilets, too. It's not the cheapest option, but it's good value, and all money raised by AidChild goes to a self-explanatory good cause.

Lukaya If you're travelling by bus, expect to have a potential buffet of barbecue snacks and bottled drinks thrust up to your window at Lukaya, which lies about 30km before Masaka, on the western edge of a 14km-wide swamp close to the shore of Lake Victoria. Look out for colonies of pelicans, and occasionally herons or storks, roosting on roadside trees.

7

Masaka and the Ssese Islands

The Lake Victoria hinterland southwest of Kampala and Entebbe is traversed by almost all tours headed to or (more usually) coming from Bwindi or Queen Elizabeth national parks, but not many bother to explore on their way through. It is a region of few highlights, with its main focal point being the large and well-equipped but unexciting town of Masaka, which is bypassed by the Mbarara Road 2 hours southwest of the capital. Altogether more compelling is pretty Lake Nabugabo, a Ramsar wetland whose reputedly bilharzia-free waters and plentiful birdlife can be enjoyed from a quartet of inexpensive resorts. The region's main attraction, however, is the lovely Ssese Archipelago, whose largest and most developed island, Buggala, is readily accessible by ferry from Entebbe or Masaka.

MASAKA

Uganda's fourth-largest city (population around 285,000), Masaka has an attractive location amid the fertile green hills of the northwestern Lake Victoria hinterland. It was founded as an Indian trading post in the first decade of the 20th century, and its name is said variously to have derived from that of a tree which once grew profusely in the area, or to be a Luganda mispronunciation of an Ankole word for millet. With an economy based largely on agriculture and fishing in the nearby lake, it had grown to become the country's third-largest town prior to 1979, when it was invaded by the Tanzanian forces that ousted Idi Amin (page 191). Masaka experienced further destruction during the civil war of 1981–86, and the town centre retained an aura of economic stagnation for many years after that. Things have perked up in recent years as a result of extensive post-millennial construction and the agricultural wealth of the surrounding countryside, though the southern end of the town centre retains a rather down-at-heel appearance.

Masaka offers little to excite travellers, but it is a popular base with NGOs and volunteers, and some good hostelries and restaurants cater to that market. It also forms a minor route focus, sitting at the junction of the main road between Kampala and Mbarara, the main overland route south to the border with Tanzania, and a side road running east to Lake Nabugabo and the Ssese Islands.

GETTING THERE AND AWAY Masaka lies roughly 140km from Kampala along the surfaced Mbarara Road, which bypasses it at Nyendo some 3km north of the town centre. In a **private vehicle**, the drive takes about 2 hours depending on how quickly you clear Kampala. Coming from Entebbe, the new Entebbe Expressway spares you the worst of the congestion around Kampala. It is also possible to avoid the traffic almost entirely by branching left from the Old Entebbe–Kampala Road at Kisubi, then following a good dirt road northwest for about 15km to Nakawuka (crossing

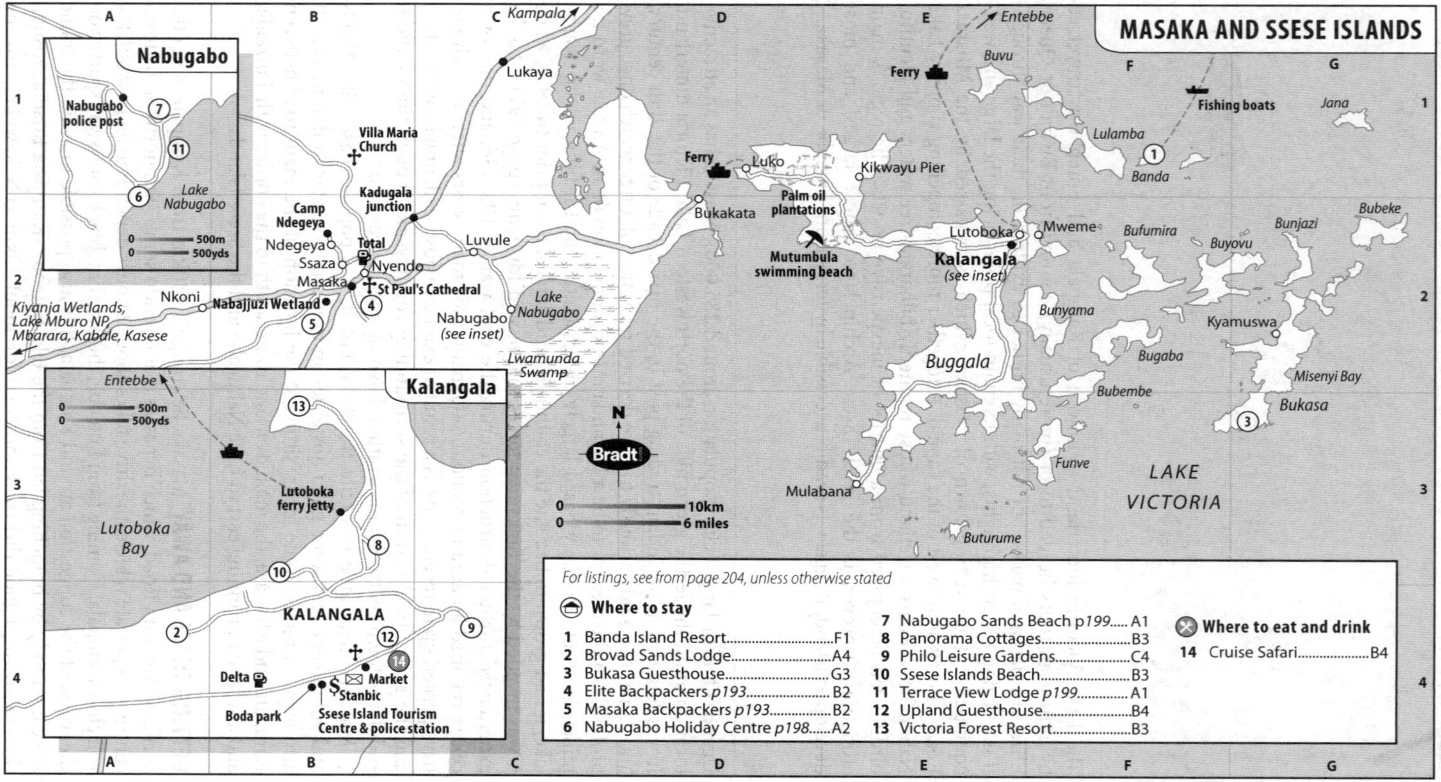
MASAKA AND SSESE ISLANDS
Nabugabo
Nabugabo police post
Lake Nabugabo
0 500m
0 500yds
Kalangala
Entebbe
Lutoboka Bay
Lutoboka ferry jetty
KALANGALA
Delta
Boda park
Stanbic
Market
Ssese Island Tourism Centre & police station
Kampala
Lukaya
Villa Maria Church
Kadugala junction
Camp Ndegeya
Ndegeya
Total
Ssaza
Nyendo
Masaka
St Paul's Cathedral
Luvule
Nkoni
Nabajjuzi Wetland
Kiyanja Wetlands, Lake Mburo NP, Mbarara, Kabale, Kasese
Nabugabo (see inset)
Lake Nabugabo
Lwamunda Swamp
Ferry
Bukakata
Luko
Palm oil plantations
Mutumbula swimming beach
Kikwayu Pier
Entebbe
Ferry
Buvu
Lutoboka
Kalangala (see inset)
Mweme
Lulamba
Banda
Fishing boats
Jana
Bubeke
Bunjazi
Buyovu
Bufumira
Bunyama
Kyamuswa
Buggala
Bugaba
Misenyi Bay
Bubembe
Bukasa
Funve
Mulabana
Buturume
LAKE VICTORIA
Bradt
N
0 10km
0 6 miles
For listings, see from page 204, unless otherwise stated
Where to stay
1 Banda Island Resort F1
2 Brovad Sands Lodge A4
3 Bukasa Guesthouse G3
4 Elite Backpackers p193 B2
5 Masaka Backpackers p193 B2
6 Nabugabo Holiday Centre p198 A2
7 Nabugabo Sands Beach p199 A1
8 Panorama Cottages B3
9 Philo Leisure Gardens C4
10 Ssese Islands Beach B3
11 Terrace View Lodge p199 A1
12 Upland Guesthouse B4
13 Victoria Forest Resort B3
Where to eat and drink
14 Cruise Safari B4

THE SACKING OF MASAKA

In October 1978, Idi Amin ordered his Masaka-based Suicide Battalion and Mbarara-based Simba Battalion to invade Tanzania, under the pretext of pursuing 200 mutineers from his army. In the event, the Ugandan battalions occupied Tanzania's northwestern province of Kagera, and ravaged the countryside in an orgy of rape, theft and destruction that forced about 40,000 people to flee from the area.

In retaliation, Tanzania's Julius Nyerere ordered 45,000 Tanzanian troops, supported by the UNLA (a 1,000-strong army of exiled Ugandans), to drive Amin's army out of Kagera, then to create a military buffer zone by capturing the largest Ugandan towns close to the Tanzanian border, Masaka and Mbarara. Masaka was taken with little resistance on 24 February 1979. The outnumbered Suicide Battalion fled to a nearby hilltop, from where they watched helplessly as first the governor's mansion and several other government buildings collapsed under missile fire, and then shops and houses were ransacked as the Tanzanian soldiers poured into the town centre.

Two days later, Nyerere achieved his stated aims for the campaign with the capture of Mbarara. But in early March it was announced that Amin would be enlisting the help of 2,500 Libyan and PLO soldiers to recapture Masaka and Mbarara, and possibly launch a counterattack on Tanzanian territory. Nyerere decided to retain the offensive, ordering his troops to prepare to march northeast towards the capital. Meanwhile, Radio Tanzania broadcast details of the fall of Masaka and Mbarara across Uganda, demoralising the troops, and prompting several garrisons to mutiny or desert as it became clear their leader's rule was highly tenuous. On 10 April 1979, the combined Tanzanian and UNLA army marched into Kampala, meeting little resistance along the way. Amin, together with at least 8,000 of his soldiers, was forced into exile.

below the expressway after about 5km), from where you can either drive straight along the 15km road to Katende, which straddles the main Kampala–Masaka Road 6km east of Mpigi, or divert left to Kasanje (as for Mabamba Swamp on page 116) where a right turn will reach the main road at Mpigi itself.

Using **public transport**, Global and Link buses both make regular departures from Kampala's Kasenyi Terminal between 05.30 and 20.30. These and most other coaches drop off and pick up passengers at the Masaka Bypass, 3km north of the town centre. In addition, regular matatus run between Masaka's central bus station/taxi park [192 C6] and Kampala's New Taxi Park, Mbarara and the Mutukula border post. Those heading further west, for instance to Kasese or Kabale, will most likely need to change vehicles at Mbarara.

The neighbouring and fast-growing town of Nyendo, which is separated from Masaka by a rapidly contracting swamp, adjoins the eastern end of the Kampala–Mbarara Bypass. As such, it is an important road junction and its taxi park is the best place to pick up matatus heading towards Ntusi, Lake Nabugabo and the Ssese Islands.

WHERE TO STAY Masaka is lacking when it comes to genuinely upmarket accommodation, but it boasts several pleasant and well-priced options in the moderate to shoestring ranges.

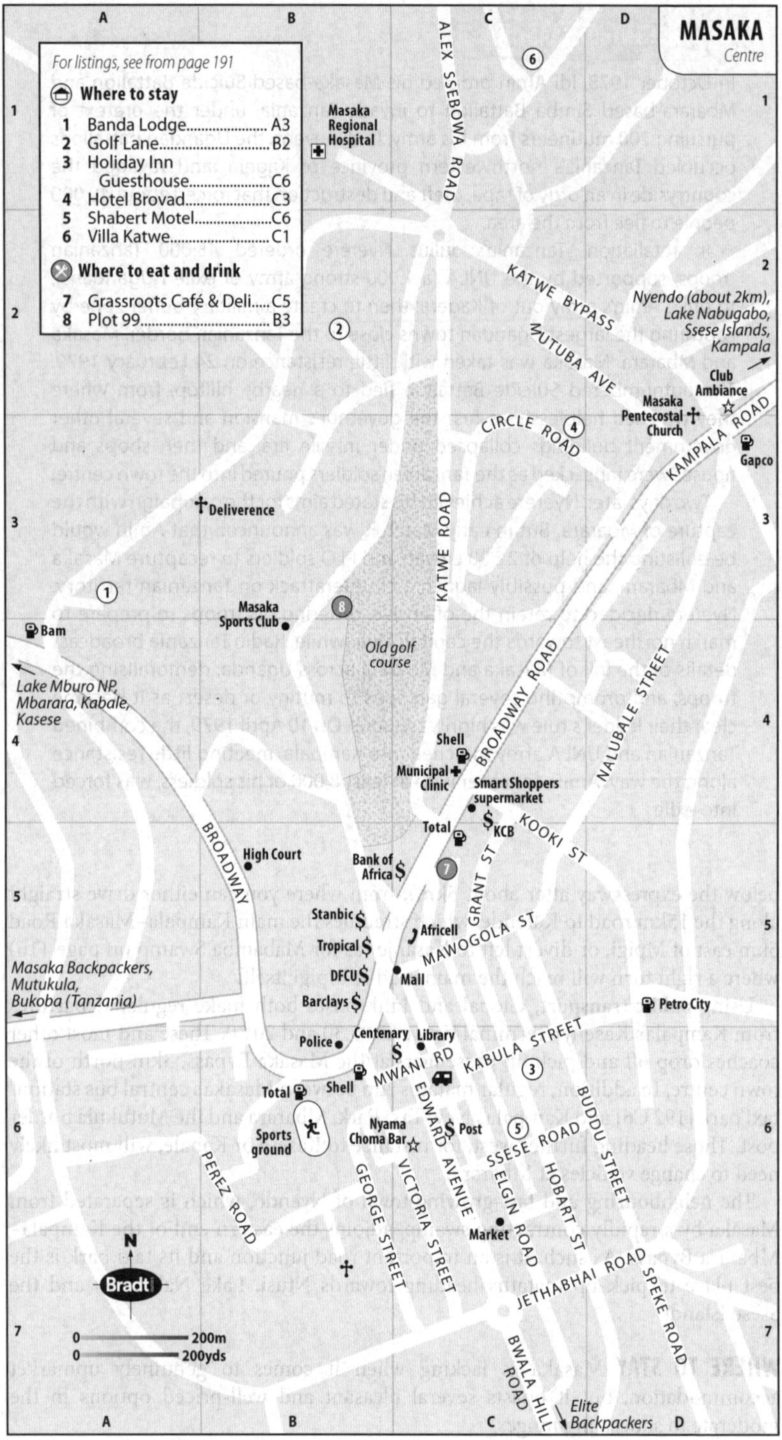
MASAKA
Centre
For listings, see from page 191
Where to stay
1 Banda Lodge.....A3
2 Golf Lane.....B2
3 Holiday Inn Guesthouse.....C6
4 Hotel Brovad.....C3
5 Shabert Motel.....C6
6 Villa Katwe.....C1
Where to eat and drink
7 Grassroots Café & Deli.....C5
8 Plot 99.....B3
Masaka Regional Hospital
ALEX SSEBOWA ROAD
KATWE BYPASS
MUTUBA AVE
Nyendo (about 2km), Lake Nabugabo, Ssese Islands, Kampala
Club Ambiance
Masaka Pentecostal Church
CIRCLE ROAD
KAMPALA ROAD
Gapco
Deliverence
KATWE ROAD
Masaka Sports Club
Bam
Old golf course
Lake Mburo NP, Mbarara, Kabale, Kasese
BROADWAY ROAD
NALUBALE STREET
Shell
Municipal Clinic
Smart Shoppers supermarket
Total
KCB
KOOKI ST
BROADWAY
High Court
Bank of Africa
GRANT ST
Stanbic
Africell
Tropical
MAWOGOLA ST
DFCU
Mall
Masaka Backpackers, Mutukula, Bukoba (Tanzania)
Barclays
Petro City
Police
Centenary
Library
KABULA STREET
MWANI RD
Total
Shell
Sports ground
Nyama Choma Bar
EDWARD AVENUE
Post
SSESE ROAD
BUDDU STREET
PEREZ ROAD
GEORGE STREET
VICTORIA STREET
ELGIN ROAD
HOBART ST
Market
JETHABHAI ROAD
SPEKE ROAD
Bradt
0 200m
0 200yds
BWALA HILL ROAD
Elite Backpackers

Moderate

✷ **Banda Lodge** [192 A3] (7 rooms & 2 dorms) Off Birch Close; m 0708 991826; e bandalodge@gmail.com; w banda.dk. This delightful Danish-managed lodge is set in terraced gardens off the Mbarara Rd, 1km northwest of the town centre. Occupants of the thatched en-suite bandas, rooms (shared facilities) & dorms enjoy the use of a residents-only swimming pool & a pretty garden restaurant. *US$50/75 en-suite bandas sgl/dbl; US$30/40 shared facilities sgl/dbl; US$20 pp dorm. All rates B&B.* **$$$**

Golf Lane Hotel [192 B2] (86 rooms) Kinanina Rd (off Katwe Rd); m 0700 868956. This multi-storey hotel doesn't quite do justice to its hilltop site's potential 360° panorama with its solitary ground-floor terrace. Otherwise, it seems like good value, & the spacious rooms all have wooden furniture, dbl bed with nets, DSTV, plenty of cupboard space, en-suite hot shower & large private balcony. *US$26/40/43 sgl/dbl/twin B&B.* **$$**

Hotel Brovad [192 C3] (250 rooms) Circle Rd; m 0774 195050, 0752 425666; e hotelbrovad2022@gmail.com; w hotelbrovad.com. First & foremost a conference venue, Masaka's smartest city hotel sprawls across pleasant green suburban gardens centred on a large swimming pool that give it an edge over its similarly bland competitors. The carpeted rooms wouldn't win any décor awards, but they are OK value. A restaurant & gym are attached. *US$50/80/120 sgl/dbl/deluxe B&B.* **$$$**

✷ **Villa Katwe** [192 C1] (5 units) Somero Rd; ⊕ 0.327519, 31.73966; m 0708 238093; e info@villakatwe.com; w villakatwe.com. Set in palm-shaded hilltop gardens about 1.5km north of the town centre, this popular lodge has the relaxed & sociable feel of a backpackers but the en-suite accommodation is far superior. Amenities include nightly campfires, book-swap service & cosy lounge. A boda from the town centre costs less than US$1. *US$35 pp en-suite sgl/dbl/trpl; US$60/75/90/105 for 1/2/3/4 people in a 2-bedroom apartment; US$25 pp dorm tent; US$12 pp camping. All rates B&B.* **$$**

Budget

Elite Backpackers [190 B2] (13 rooms & 1 dorm) Bwala Hill Rd; m 0701 351736; e elitebackpackers@gmail.com; w elitebackpackers.com. Situated about 1.5km south of the town centre, this attractive, owner-managed backpackers' has small but smart & colourfully decorated en-suite thatched bandas as well as a 6-bed dorm using common showers. A thatched restaurant offers mains in the US$4–8 range, but self-catering is also permitted. Clearly an active part of the community, Elite facilitates a variety of volunteer opportunities, offers a range of activities though its EBS Safaris subsidiary & hosts cultural performances at w/ends. *US$20/35/35 sgl/dbl/twin B&B; US$10 dorm bed. All B&B. Discounts for volunteers.* **$$**

Shabert Motel [192 C6] (28 rooms) Hobart St; m 0752 646797. Outstanding value in a town that's well endowed with good cheapies, this multi-storey hotel has clean, en-suite tiled rooms with fitted nets, DSTV & hot shower. *US$12 twin.* **$**

Shoestring and camping

Holiday Inn Guesthouse [192 C6] (22 rooms) Hobart St; m 0755 241947, 0756 861864. The best of several decent shoestring options clustered in & around Hobart St, this has large tiled rooms with nets, writing desk & en-suite hot shower. *US$5 sgl using common shower; US$7 sgl/twin with DSTV.* **$**

✷ **Masaka Backpackers** [190 B2] (10 rooms & 2 dorms) ⊕ -0.3634, 31.71463; m 0752 619389; e masakabackpackers@gmail.com; w masakahostels.com. Situated on a rural hilltop 4km out of town off the Mutukula Rd, this long-serving owner-managed retreat offers the option of en-suite rooms, a dorm bed, or pitching your own tent. It also serves tasty meals in the US$4–8 range & has a well-stocked drinks fridge. *US$13/26 sgl/dbl; US$7 pp dorm B&B; US$3 pp camping.* **$$**

WHERE TO EAT AND DRINK The two eateries described below possess plenty of character as well as free Wi-Fi. Most of the hotels listed above have decent restaurants, but none warrants a special mention.

✷ **Grassroots Café & Deli** [192 C5] Elgin Rd; m 0702 988467; f; ⊕ 09.30–20.00 Mon–Sat. This 1st-floor café with terrace seating is a great place to stop for a quick & inexpensive lunch en route between Kampala & the southwest. Fresh sandwiches, pizzas, salads, wraps & other mostly vegetarian dishes are supplemented by juices, smoothies, wine, cocktails, & homemade produce. *Mains cost around US$5.*

✷ **Plot 99** [192 B3] Hill Rd; m 0700 151649; ⌚ 10.30–23.00 Wed–Mon. Popular with the younger volunteer crowd, this chilled restaurant, bar & coffee shop is housed in a bungalow & green gardens overlooking the former golf course. The menu includes burgers, pizzas, grills, curries & salads, as well as a good selection of coffees, smoothies, juices & cocktails. *Mains mostly in the US$5–8 range.*

ENTERTAINMENT AND NIGHTLIFE

Club Ambiance [192 D2] Broadway Rd; m 0701 415748; f clubambiancemsk; ⌚ 18.00–late Tue–Sun. One of Uganda's best-known nightclubs, the original Ambiance – now also represented by branches in Kampala & Mityana – is a monumental glass-fronted building that uses 6 different DJs. Popular with locally based volunteers, the club peaks in popularity on Fri & Sat nights, when the dancefloor action really only kicks in after midnight. Tue is ladies' night, Wed old school, Fri campus night, Sat variety night & Sun oldies' night.

Nyama Choma Bar [192 C6] Victoria St. A ramshackle wooden exterior hides a popular central bar that is most vibey at w/ends, when it often hosts DJ sets. There's a pool table, TVs for live Premier League football, grilled pork & other inexpensive local meals.

SHOPPING Several good supermarkets are dotted around the town centre, especially at the northern end of Elgin Road. **Smart Shoppers** on Broadway Road [192 C4] is the best stocked when it comes to imported goods.

SPORTS AND ACTIVITIES The Hotel Brovad [192 C3] charges day visitors US$4 to use its swimming pool. The Masaka Sports Club [192 B4] near Plot 99 has tennis and squash courts, table tennis, a pool table and a decent local-style restaurant.

TOUR OPERATOR Allied to Elite Backpackers (page 193), and situated in the same premises, **EBS Tours** (m 0701 352736; e info@ebstoursandsafaris.com; w ebstoursandsafaris.com) offers a variety of local day excursions, including farm tours, a community walk, and bike and boda tours of Masaka, as well as two-day safaris to nearby Lake Mburo National Park and longer itineraries to most other points of interest in the southwest.

WHAT TO SEE AND DO

Nabajjuzi Wetland [190 B2] Listed as a Ramsar Wetland and Important Bird Area, the 17.5km² Nabajjuzi Wetland, which follows a tributary of the Katonga River as it flows west past Masaka, is also the town's sole source of drinking water. Though it incorporates some open water, the wetland is dominated by papyrus and reed swamps, which support large numbers of lungfish and mudfish. Otters and sitatunga antelope are still reputedly common in Nabajjuzi, as are a host of alluring birds, including shoebill, rufous-bellied heron, papyrus yellow warbler, papyrus gonolek and blue swallow. The prime viewpoint is located beside the Masaka Water Treatment Plant (⊕ -0.33695, 31.71873), just beyond the roundabout at the western end of the bypass. The site is further identified by a wooden viewing platform from a long-defunct ecotourism project now seemingly converted into a home.

Camp Ndegeya [190 B2] (⊕ -0.29306, 31.72941; m 0777 006726; f campndegeyauganda; entry US$2) Situated on a eucalyptus-covered hilltop near the village of Ndegeya (literally 'Place of Weaverbirds') 5km north of Masaka, this open-air sculpture garden displays the work of six Ugandan contemporary artists. The grounds also offer great views over the Nabajjuzi Wetland 1.5km to the west, while amenities include a campsite (US$7 per tent) using common showers.

Camp Ndegeya is most easily reached from Ssaza junction (⊕ -0.31916, 31.73998), on the Kampala–Mbarara Bypass about 3km from the junction with the eastern feeder road into Masaka and 3.3km from the junction with the western feeder. From Ssaza junction, head north for 3km to the village of Ndegeya, whose main traffic circle is adorned with a prominent sculpture. A boda from Nyendo or Masaka shouldn't cost more than US$1.50. When arranging transport to Ndegeya, be warned that a better-known village of the same name straddles the Mbarara Road, 25km west of Masaka.

Villa Maria Church [190 B1] One of Uganda's most historic buildings, Villa Maria was established in 1892 in the wake of a religious civil war that resulted in the temporary exile from Kampala of Kabaka Mwanga and his fellow Catholics. The exiles briefly settled in Buddu, the most westerly country of Buganda, where Chief Alex Ssebbowa, a supporter of Mwanga, donated a tract of land north of present-day Masaka to Henri Streicher, a French missionary of the White Father order, so that he could establish a church there. In 1897, when Streicher was appointed Bishop of Northern Victoria Nyanza, he made Villa Maria the headquarters of a vicariate that included 30,000 baptised Catholics. Uganda's first indigenous Catholic priests – Fathers Basil Lumu and Victor Mukasa – were ordained at Villa Maria in 1913, and it was also the diocese that produced Africa's first indigenous Catholic bishop, Doctor Joseph Kiwanuka, who was ordained into Kitovu Diocese in 1940. Henri Streicher, who died in 1952 aged 89, was interred in the church, along with several of the young African priests he trained.

The main point of interest at Villa Maria is the original cruciform church (⊕ -0.22875, 31.74559) built by Streicher in the 1890s. It is one of the country's largest churches, with a floor area of 1,800m^2, and its 60cm-thick walls are composed entirely of unbaked clay bricks and mud mortar. The roof was thatched up until the early 1930s, and the original wooden struts have been retained to support the modern topping of red-painted iron sheets. Still in active use, the church has recently undergone extensive restoration work, and part of the building is earmarked to become a museum documenting the mission's history. Also of historic interest, about 1km south of Villa Maria, Bwamba Convent (⊕ -0.23722, 31.74941) is home to the Banna-Biikira ('Daughters of Mary'), Africa's oldest indigenous society of Catholic nuns, founded in 1910 at the urging of Bishop Streicher by Mother Mechtilde, a Dutch White Sister. The Banna-Biikira are now responsible for administering the 125-bed Villa Maria Hospital, which was established by Streicher in 1902, primarily to assist victims of sleeping sickness.

To get to Villa Maria Church from central Masaka, follow the Kampala Road out of town for about 2km past Club Ambiance to Nyendo, then turn left on to Villa Road, crossing the Kampala–Mbarara Bypass after about 1km, and keep going straight for another 12km. Coming directly from Kampala, follow the bypass downhill past the first roundabout for about 1km (⊕ -0.30866, 31.75636), then turn right on to Villa Road.

Kiyanja Wetlands [190 A2] This readily accessible 3km^2 reed marsh, part of the drainage system that feeds Lake Kacheera on the eastern border of Lake Mburo National Park, lies immediately south of the Mbarara Road some 42km west of Masaka. Kiyanja is an important breeding and foraging site for the spectacular grey crowned crane (Uganda's national bird), with some 20 breeding pairs resident and much larger temporary aggregations often recorded. Other aquatic birds

BARKCLOTH

A stiff, neat barkcloth cloak or *mbugu* was the conventional form of attire throughout Baganda for at least 100 years prior to the 1856 coronation of King Mutesa of Baganda. One of the earliest descriptions of it is by Speke, who prepared for his first audience with Mutesa in 1862 by putting on his finest clothes, but admitted that he 'cut a poor figure in comparison with the dressy Baganda [who] wore neat bark cloaks resembling the best yellow corduroy cloth, crimp and well set, as if stiffened with starch'. Exactly how and when the craft arose is unknown. One legend has it that Kintu, the founder of Baganda, brought the craft with him from the heavens, which would imply that it was introduced to the kingdom, possibly from Bunyoro. Another story is that the Bachwezi leader Wamala discovered barkcloth by accident on a hunting expedition, when he hammered a piece of bark to break it up, and instead found that it expanded laterally to form a durable material.

Whatever its origin, barkcloth has been worn in Baganda for several centuries, though oral tradition maintains that the cloth was originally worn only by the king and members of his court, while commoners draped themselves more skimpily in animal skins. In the late 18th century, however, King Semakokiro decreed that all his subjects should grow and wear barkcloth – men draped it over their shoulders, women tied it around their waist – or they would be fined or sentenced to death. At around the same time, barkcloth exported from Baganda grew in popularity in most neighbouring kingdoms, where it was generally reserved for the use of royalty and nobles.

Ironically, the historical association between barkcloth cloaks and social prestige was reversed in Baganda towards the end of the 19th century, when barkcloth remained the customary attire of the peasantry, but the king permitted his more favoured subjects to wear cotton fabrics imported by Arab traders. During the early decades of colonial rule, the trend away from barkcloth spread through all social strata. W E Hoyle, who arrived in Kampala in 1903, noted that barkcloth clothing was then 'so very common'. By 1930, when Hoyle departed from Uganda, it had been 'discarded in favour of "amerikani" (cotton sheeting); and later *kanzus* (of finer cotton material known as "bafta"), with a jacket of the cheaper imported cloth and a white round cap, the ideal "Sunday best"'. Hoyle also noted that while 'women kept to barkcloth much longer than men…by the 1920s many were attired in the finest cotton materials and silks'. In the early 1930s, Lucy Mair recorded that 'European [cloths] are popular and barkcloth is made for sale by not more than three or four men in each village'. By the time of independence, barkcloth had practically disappeared from everyday use.

Barkcloth – *olubugo* in Luganda – can be made from the inner bark lining of at least 20 tree species. The best-quality cloth derives from certain species in the genus *Ficus*, which were extensively cultivated in pre-colonial Baganda and regarded as the most valuable of trees after the plantain. Different species of tree yielded

are exceptionally well represented: at least 30 species were noted during a recent 15-minute stop, among them saddle-billed and open-billed storks, African jacana, spur-winged goose, pink-backed pelican and long-toed lapwing. A 12km footpath used by local farmers encircles the wetland, and you'd doubtless see a great many more species if you followed it in part or full.

Coming from Masaka, the 600m feeder road to the edge of the wetland runs south from the Mbarara Road at an inconspicuous junction (⊕ -0.4043, 31.37248)

different textures and colours, from yellow to sandy brown to dark red-brown. The finest-quality rusty brown cloth, called *kimote*, is generally worn on special occasions only. A specific type of tree that yielded a white cloth was reserved for the use of the king, who generally wore it only at his coronation ceremony.

The common barkcloth tree can be propagated simply by cutting a branch from a grown one and planting it in the ground – after about five years the new tree will be large enough to be used for making barkcloth. The bark will be stripped from any one given tree only once a year, when it is in full leaf. After the bark has been removed, the trunk is wrapped in green banana leaves for several days, and then plastered with wet cow dung and dry banana leaves, to help it heal. If a tree is looked after this way, it might survive 30 years of annual use.

The bark is removed from the tree in one long strip. A circular incision is made near the ground, another one below the lowest branches, and then a long line is cut from base to top, before finally a knife is worked underneath the bark to ease it carefully away from the trunk. The peeled bark is left out overnight before the hard outer layer is scraped off, and then it is soaked. It is then folded into two halves and laid out on a log to be beaten with a wooden mallet on alternating sides to become thinner. When it has spread sufficiently, the cloth is folded in four and the beating continues. The cloth is then unfolded before being left to dry in the sun.

There are several local variations in the preparation process, but the finest cloth reputedly results when the freshly stripped bark, instead of being soaked, is steamed for about an hour above a pot of boiling water, then beaten for an hour or so daily over the course of a week. The steaming and extended process of beating is said to improve the texture of the cloth and to enrich the natural red-brown or yellow colour of the bark.

Although it is used mostly for clothing, barkcloth can also serve as a blanket or a shroud, and is rare but valued as bookbinding. At one time, barkcloth strips patterned with the natural black Muzukizi dye became a popular house decoration in Kampala. Sadly, however, barkcloth production appears to be a dying craft, and today it would be remarkable to see anybody wandering around Kampala wrapped in a bark cloak. It is still customary to wear it in the presence of the king, and at funerals, when barkcloth is also often wrapped around the body of the deceased.

One place where you can be certain of seeing some impressive strips of red barkcloth is at the Kasubi Tombs in Kampala (page 153). If you're interested in looking for barkcloth at source, the forests around Sango Bay in Buddu County, south of Masaka, are traditionally regarded as producing the highest-quality material in Baganda. The Ugandan artist Mugalula Mukiibi is dedicated to reviving the dying craft through his work, and a number of his abstracts painted on traditional barkcloth can be viewed online (w mugalulaarts.com).

about 1km past the small trading centre of Kyawagonya, which is passed through by all public transport along this trunk road.

LAKE NABUGABO

Lake Nabugabo [190 C2], 20km east of Masaka, is a shallow 33km^2 freshwater body set within the 225km^2 Lwamunda Swamp on the western shore of Lake

Victoria. Nabugabo was isolated from its larger neighbour around 4,000 years ago, when a narrow sand bar drifted across what was formerly a large shallow bay. Silt accumulation has subsequently reduced the extent of open water fourfold, and all but the western shore of Nabugabo is now lined by more-or-less impenetrable papyrus and reed swamps. Despite its relatively recent formation, Nabugabo has a substantially different mineral composition from the main lake: its calcium content, for instance, is insufficient for molluscs to form shells, hence the alleged absence of the freshwater snails that transmit bilharzia. Impressively, a full five of nine cichlid fish species indigenous to Nabugabo are endemics that evolved since it was separated from Lake Victoria, one of the most recent incidents of speciation known from anywhere in the world. Unfortunately, however, the introduction of the predatory Nile perch and red-belly tilapia in the 1950s has had a negative effect on indigenous fish populations, which are now most common in a few small satellite lakes. The lake and surrounding swamp are listed as an Important Bird Area and Ramsar Wetland.

More popular with Kampala weekenders than it is with foreign visitors, Nabugabo is nonetheless an excellent place to rest up for a day or two. Its largely marsh-free western shore is serviced by a handful of tranquil and reasonably priced resorts, though be warned that these tend to transform into local party spots over the weekends. The forest patches that line the lakeshore, interspersed with grassy clearings and cultivated smallholdings, are rustling with small animals such as tree squirrels, vervet monkeys and monitor lizards, and can easily be explored along several roads and footpaths. Birdlife is prolific, too – look out for broad-billed roller, Ross's turaco, black-and-white casqued hornbill, African fish eagle and a variety of sunbirds and weavers. Lwamunda Swamp is an important stronghold for papyrus endemics such as shoebill, white-winged swamp warbler and papyrus canary, but these are unlikely to be seen from Nabugabo's western shore.

GETTING THERE AND AWAY In a **private vehicle**, there are two routes to Nabugabo. The simplest and smoothest leaves the roundabout at the eastern end of the Masaka bypass and passes through Nyendo town for 2km before turning left on to a recently surfaced road to the Ssese Island ferry landing at Bukakata. After 14km, a 5km dirt side road (⊕ -0.31393, 31.85918) leading to the lake resorts is signposted to the right. Alternatively, if coming from Kampala, you can take a potentially rough short cut across country from Kadugala (⊕ -0.27903, 31.79795) to join Bukakata Road (⊕ -0.30983, 31.83881) 2.5km before the turning to the lake.

Using **public transport**, you have two broad options. The first is to catch a matatu (or any other transport) along the Bukakata Road, hop off at the junction for Nabugabo, then walk the last (very flat) 5km to the resort of your choice. Alternatively, take a bus or matatu to Kadugala, from where a boda to Nabugabo should cost around US$4, and a special hire in the ballpark of US$15.

WHERE TO STAY AND EAT

Budget

Nabugabo Holiday Centre [190 A2] (10 rooms spread across 5 cottages) ⊕ -0.35246, 31.8771; **m** 0752 539300, 0772 433332; **e** info@nabugabo.com; **w** nabugabo.com. This long-serving Church of Uganda resort has a friendly atmosphere & lovely setting in a shady glade sloping down to a good swimming beach. All but 1 of the 5 cottages have 2 dbl or twin rooms, shared bathroom & common lounge with DSTV, while the other has 2 en-suite dbl rooms. You can also pitch a tent by the lake. Simple meals cost US$4 (b/fast) or up to US$10 (lunch or dinner). Soft drinks, tea & coffee are sold but you'll need to bring your own alcohol with you. *US$13/21 sgl/dbl using common shower; US$26 en-suite dbl; US$8 pp camping.* **$$**

✵ **Nabugabo Sand Beach** [190 A1] (12 units) ⊕ -0.34723, 31.87948; m 0702 416047, 0772 453030; e sandbeachnabugabo@yahoo.com. Boasting 200m of lake frontage, this is a lovely, peaceful spot during the week, but at w/ends it transforms into Uganda's version of the good old British migration to the seaside – as reflected by a holiday camp-style row of glass-fronted chalets, boat & donkey rides, canoe hire, cheap beer & a fish 'n' chips menu with mains for around US$7. Despite the regimental layout, the tiled cottages are well maintained with fitted nets, en-suite hot shower & DSTV & are great value. *US$18/21 dbl/twin cottage exc b/fast.* **$$**

Terrace View Lodge [190 A1] (6 rooms) ⊕ -0.34961, 31.87953; m 0758 280400. Whether the 'terrace' refers to the pleasant veranda of the thatched main building or the low clifftop on which the resort stands is an open question, but the elevation does mean that this isn't the best resort for swimming. Accommodation is in a row of spacious & airy en-suite brick-face rooms with nets & hot shower. Facilities include a bar, pool table & restaurant. *US$21 dbl B&B.* **$$**

THE SSESE ISLANDS

Situated in the northwest of Lake Victoria, the Ssese Archipelago comprises 84 separate islands, some large and densely inhabited, others small and deserted, but all lushly forested thanks to an annual average rainfall in excess of 2,000mm. By far the largest island in the Ssese group is Buggala, which accounts for more than half the archipelago's land area, and lies around 40km southwest of Entebbe as the crow flies. Buggala's principal settlement is Kalangala, which lends its name to, and serves as the administrative centre of, a thinly populated district comprising a 468km^2 terrestrial component and 8,635km^2 of open water. Kalangala, or more accurately the tiny lakeshore village of Lutoboka 1km to its north, is also the archipelago's main tourist focus, supporting as it does around half-a-dozen low-key beach resorts, as well as being the landing point for a daily vehicle ferry from Entebbe.

The Ssese Islands have a chequered history as a tourist destination. In the mid 1990s, when tourism to Uganda was dominated by backpackers, Buggala emerged as the country's most popular word-of-mouth chill-out destination. That changed later on in the decade, when the discontinuation of the Port Bell Ferry limited safe access to Buggala to a more roundabout approach via Masaka and Bukakata, and opened the way for the more accessible Lake Bunyonyi to capture the hearts of independent travellers. In recent years, the introduction of a daily passenger ferry from Entebbe has initiated a renaissance in tourism activity on Buggala, though facilities are geared towards Kampala weekenders rather than backpackers. That said, Buggala, with its scenic lake vistas and practically limitless opportunities for casual rambling along lush forest-fringed roads and footpaths, remains a beguiling retreat, particularly on weekdays (when it tends to be very tranquil) and for those seeking a more off-the-beaten-track and uncontrived alternative to the ever-busy Bunyonyi.

Although Buggala remains the main tourist focus on the Ssese Archipelago, a significant number of travellers also head to tiny Banda Island. Other islands that can be visited with varying degrees of ease are Bubeke, Bukasa and Bufumira.

GEOLOGY AND WILDLIFE The Ssese Islands came into being about 12,000 years ago when the then reduced Lake Victoria refilled at the end of the last Ice Age, forming the lake as we know it today. The archipelago supports a cover of mid-altitude rainforest, similar in composition to the forest that once swathed the facing mainland, but far less affected by agriculture and other forms of encroachment. The most common large terrestrial mammal is the vervet monkey, which is often seen in the vicinity of Lutoboka and Kalangala. Bushbuck and black-and-white

A DYING LAKE

Known to the Baganda as Nalubaale – Home of the Spirit – Lake Victoria is the world's second-largest freshwater body, set in a shallow basin with a diameter of roughly 250km on an elevated plateau separating the eastern and western forks of the Great Rift Valley, and shared between Tanzania, Uganda and Kenya. The environmental degradation of the lake began in the early colonial era, when the indigenous lakeshore vegetation was cleared and swamps were drained to make way for plantations of tea, coffee and sugar. This increased the amount of topsoil washed into the lake, with the result that its water became progressively muddier and murkier. A more serious effect was the wash-off of toxic pesticides and other agricultural chemicals whose nutrients promote algae growth, and as a result a decrease in oxygenation. The foundation of several lakeshore cities and plantations also attracted migrant labourers from around the region, leading to a rapid increase in population and – exacerbated by more sophisticated trapping tools introduced by the colonials – heavy overfishing.

By the early 1950s, the above factors had conspired to create a noticeable drop in yields of popular indigenous fish, in particular the Lake Victoria tilapia (*ngege*), which had been fished close to extinction. The colonial authorities introduced the similar Nile tilapia, which restored the diminishing yield without seriously affecting the ecological balance of the lake. More disastrous, however, was the gradual infiltration of the Nile perch, a voracious predator that feeds almost exclusively on smaller fish, and frequently reaches a length of 2m and a weight exceeding 100kg. How the perch initially ended up in Lake Victoria is a matter of conjecture, but they regularly turned up in fishermen's nets from the late 1950s onwards. The authorities, who favoured large eating fish over the smaller tilapia and cichlids, decided to ensure the survival of the alien predators with an active programme of introductions in the early 1960s.

It would be 20 years before the full impact of this misguided policy hit home. In a UN survey undertaken in 1971, indigenous cichlids belonging to the genus *Haplochromis* still constituted their traditional 80% of the lake's fish biomass, while the introduced fish had effectively displaced the indigenous tilapia without otherwise altering the ecology of the lake. A similar survey undertaken ten years later revealed that the perch population had exploded to constitute 80% of the lake's fish biomass, while *Haplochromis* cichlids – the favoured prey of the perch – now accounted for a mere 1%. Lake Victoria's estimated 150–300 endemic cichlid species, all of which have evolved from a mere five ancestral species since the lake dried out 10,000–15,000 years ago, are regarded to represent the most recent comparable explosion of vertebrate-adaptive radiation in the world. In simple terms, this is when a large number of species evolve from a limited ancestral stock in a short space of time, in this instance owing to the lake having formed rapidly to create all sorts of new niches. Ironically, at least 65% of these species are now thought to be extinct, and several others are headed that way, an ecological disaster described as 'the greatest vertebrate mass extinction in recorded history' by Les Kauffman of Boston University.

For all this, the introduction of perch could be considered a superficial success within its own terms. The perch now form the basis of the lake's thriving fishing industry, with up to 500 metric tonnes of fish meat being exported from the lake annually, at a value of more than US$300 million, by commercial fishing concerns in the three lakeshore countries. The tanned perch hide is used as a substitute for leather to make shoes, belts and purses, and the dried swim bladders, used to filter beer and make fish stock, are exported at a high profit too. The flip side of this is that as fish exports increase, local fishing communities are forced to compete against large commercial companies with better equipment and more economic clout. Furthermore, since the perch is too large to roast on a fire and too fatty to dry in the sun, it does not really meet local needs.

The introduction of perch is not the only damaging factor to have affected Lake Victoria's ecology. It is estimated that the amount of agricultural chemicals being washed into the lake has more than doubled since the 1950s. Tanzania alone is currently pumping 2 million litres of untreated sewage and industrial waste into the lake daily, and while legal controls on industrial dumping are tighter in Kenya and Uganda, they are not effectively enforced. The agricultural wash-off and industrial dumping has led to a further increase in the volume of chemical nutrients in the lake, promoting the growth of plankton and algae. At the same time, the cichlids that once fed on these microscopic organisms have been severely depleted in number by the predatorial perch.

The lake's algae levels have increased fivefold in the last four decades, with a corresponding decrease in oxygen levels. The lower level of the lake now consists of dead water – lacking any oxygenation or fish activity below about 30m – and the quality of the water closer to the surface has deteriorated markedly since the 1960s. Long-term residents of the Mwanza area say that the water was once so clear that you could see the lake floor from the surface to depths of 6m or more. Today visibility near the surface is more like 1m.

A clear indicator of this deterioration has been the rapid spread of water hyacinth, which thrives in polluted conditions leading to high phosphate and nitrogen levels, and then tends to further deplete oxygen levels by forming an impenetrable mat over the water's surface. An exotic South American species, unknown on the lake prior to 1989, the water hyacinth has subsequently colonised vast tracts of the lake surface, and clogged up several harbours. To complete this grim vicious circle, Nile perch, arguably the main cause of the problem, are known to be vulnerable to the conditions created by hyacinth matting, high algae levels and decreased oxygenation in the water. On a positive note, hyacinth infestation on the Ugandan waters of Lake Victoria has decreased markedly since 2001, though a resurgence caused several fishing vessels to be trapped in the middle of the lake in 2017, forcing a major rescue operation. It was estimated to cover at least 40km^2 of the surface in late 2018, most of it in Kenya, and in shallow water close to ports.

As is so often the case with ecological issues, what might at first be dismissed by some as an esoteric concern for 'bunny-huggers' in fact has wider implications for the tens of millions of people resident in the Lake Victoria basin. The infestation of hyacinth and rapid decrease in indigenous snail-eating fish has led to a growth in the number of bilharzia-carrying snails. The deterioration in water quality, exacerbated by the pumping of sewage, has increased the risk of sanitary-related diseases such as cholera spreading around the lake. The change in the fish biomass has encouraged commercial fishing for export outside the region, in the process depressing the local semi-subsistence fishing economy, leading to an increase in unemployment and protein deficiency. And the risk remains that Africa's largest lake will eventually be reduced to a vast expanse of dead water, with no fish in it at all – and ecological, economic and humanitarian ramifications that scarcely bear thinking about.

colobus are also present, but seldom observed. Since Buggala was separated from the mainland, one endemic creek rat and three endemic butterfly species have evolved on the island. Water and forest birds are prolific. Expect to see a variety of hornbills, barbets, turacos, robin-chats, flycatchers and weavers from the roads around Kalangala. Particularly common are the jewel-like pygmy kingfisher, the brown-throated wattle-eye and a stunning morph of the paradise flycatcher intermediate to the orange and white phases illustrated in most East African field guides. African fish eagles and palm-nut vultures are often seen near the lake, while immense breeding colonies of little egret and great cormorant occur on Lutoboka and other bays.

HISTORY Little is known about the earliest inhabitants of Ssese, but some oral traditions associated with the creation of Buganda claim that its founder Kintu hailed from the islands, or at least arrived in Buganda via them. The Baganda traditionally revere Ssese as the Islands of the Gods. In pre-colonial times it was customary for the Kings of Buganda to visit the islands and pay tribute to the several balubaale whose main shrines are situated there. These include shrines to Musisi (spirit of earthquakes) and Wanema (physical handicaps) on Bukasa Island, as well as the shrine to Mukasa, spirit of the lake, on Bubembe. Some Baganda historical sources romanticise this relationship, claiming that in pre-colonial times Ssese, because of its exalted status, was never attacked by Buganda, nor was it formally incorporated into the mainland kingdom. In reality, while Ssese probably did enjoy a degree of autonomy, it was clearly a vassal of Buganda for at least a century prior to the colonial era. Furthermore, while the Baganda revered the islands' spirits, Stanley recorded that they looked down on their human inhabitants for their 'coal-black colour, timidity, superstition, and generally uncleanly life'.

The most popular legend associated with a deity from the Ssese Islands dates from the mid 16th-century war, when Buganda, led by King Nakibinge, was being overwhelmed in a war against Bunyoro. Nakibinge visited the islands in search of support, and was offered the assistance of the local king's youngest son, Kibuuka, who leaped to the mainland in one mighty bound to join the war against Bunyoro. Tall and powerful though he was, Kibuuka – which means the flier – was also possessed of a somewhat more singular fighting skill. A deity in human form, he was able to fly high above the clouds and shower down spears on the enemy, who had no idea from where the deadly missiles emanated. Led by Kibuuka's aerial attacks, rout followed rout, and the tide of war reversed swiftly in Nakibinge's favour as the Baganda army proceeded deeper into Banyoro territory.

Although Buganda went on to win the war, Kibuuka didn't survive to enjoy the spoils of victory. After yet another successful battle, the Baganda soldiers captured several Banyoro maidens and gave one to Kibuuka as his mistress. Kibuuka told the Munyoro girl his secret, only to find that she had vanished overnight. The next day, Kibuuka sailed up into the sky as normal, and was greeted by a barrage of Banyoro spears and arrows projected up towards the clouds. Kibuuka fell wounded into a tall tree, where he was spotted the next morning by an elder, who attempted to rescue the wounded fighter, but instead accidentally let him drop to the ground, where he died on impact. The scrotum, testes, penis and certain other body parts of the great Ssese warrior – now regarded as the greatest lubaale of war – were preserved in a shrine, where his spirit could be called upon before important battles. The shrine, which lies close to the Mpanga Forest, can still be visited today, as can a nearby shrine to Nakibinge, also revered as a deity on account of his successful campaign against Bunyoro. The shrine to Kibuuka was desecrated by the British during the colonial era, and the contents, including his jawbone, are on display in a museum in Cambridge.

The Bassese people of the islands, who speak a distinct Bantu language closely related to Luganda, and were described by Stanley as 'the principal canoe builders and the greater number of the sailors' of Buganda, played a more verifiable – albeit less overtly aggressive – role in Baganda expansionism during the second half of the 19th century. At this time, Kabaka Suuna and his successor Mutesa dispatched regular military fleets of 300-plus fighting canoes across Lake Victoria to present-day northwestern Tanzania. These fleets consisted almost entirely of canoes built on Ssese, which – in comparison with the simple dugouts used on the mainland – were highly sophisticated in design, constructed with several pieces of interlocking timber, and boasted an extended prow that could be used to batter other boats. Speke described one such fleet as follows: 'some fifty large [boats]... all painted with red clay, and averaged from ten to thirty paddles, with long prows standing out like the neck of a siphon or swan, decorated on the head with the horns of the Nsunnu [kob] antelope, between which was stuck upright a tuft of feathers exactly like a grenadier's plume.' The islanders were also more skilled as oarsmen and navigators than their landlubber Baganda neighbours, and although they played no role in the fighting, it was they who generally powered and directed the war fleets.

In the late 19th century, the demands of the Buganda military became a heavy drain on the Ssese economy. So much so that in 1898 the islanders petitioned the British governor, complaining that they were 'regarded in Uganda as being inferior and subordinate to that country' and that the 'severe strain upon the island labour resources [was] so serious as to endanger the canoe service, now so essential with the increasing demands on the Victoria Nyanza lake transport'. In 1900, an agreement between Buganda and Britain placed Ssese and nine other formerly autonomous counties under the full jurisdiction of Buganda. Over the next ten years, Ssese was hit by a sleeping sickness epidemic that claimed thousands of lives annually, forcing the government to relocate 25,000 islanders to the mainland.

Resettlement of Ssese was gradual, and it is largely due to the sleeping sickness epidemic that the islands' total population was estimated at fewer than 20,000 as recently as the mid 1990s. Since then, however, the population has risen rapidly, doubling from around 35,000 in 2002 to an estimated 70,000 in 2015. Although much of the land remains uncultivated and supports a cover of natural forest, Buggala also supports a major palm oil industry, which until recently consisted mainly of local farmers who grew a few oil palm trees on their smallholding and sold the produce on to the Jinja-based processor Bidco Uganda. That changed in 2011 when Oil Palm Uganda Limited (OPUL), a subsidiary of Bidco Uganda, controversially razed 61km^2 of natural forest and smallholdings west of Kalangala to make way for new oil palm plantations. Displaced local community members, some of whom were effectively squatters but nevertheless lost their homes or livelihood in the land grab, have since taken OPUL to court, demanding compensation.

GETTING THERE AND AWAY There are two reliable options for Buggala Island, either using a direct daily ferry or boat from Entebbe, or a more roundabout route via Masaka and Bukakata. When the Entebbe ferry is non-operational (as happens from time to time), you could also use a motorised lake-taxi from nearby Kasenyi, which comprises the only public transport to the other smaller islands. However, it is possible to charter a lake-taxi from Lutoboka (Buggala Island) to Banda Island for around US$50.

By ferry from Entebbe The MV *Kalangala* is a daily passenger/vehicle ferry service that connects Lutoboka Port [190 E2] on Buggala Island to Nakiwogo Port (⊕ 0.08054, 32.44919), which lies only 3km (and less than 10 minutes by boda) west of central Entebbe. The ferry leaves Nakiwogo at 14.00 daily and starts the return trip from Lutoboka at 08.00 the next morning (3½hrs one-way; US$3 for 2nd-class passage and US$4 for 1st class, the latter with padded seating and tables). Bottled drinks and snacks are available on board. Vehicles pay US$13 and SUVs US$18 for a one-way crossing. Phone m 0705 116773 to reserve a vehicle spot; payment is in advance using Mobile Money. Alternatively, you can travel as a foot passenger after parking your car in a compound just west of the ferry landing (a small fee applies); approach this using Kiwafu Road from Kitoro rather than Nakiwogo Road to avoid a snarl-up in the trading centre by the ferry. If this all sounds a bit organised, be reassured that, when the gates are opened, it can be a proper scramble to get on board (prospective passengers frequently exceeding the number painted on the Plimsoll Line) and even if you've paid for a first-class seat, you'll need to be both quick and agile to get one. The return trip to Entebbe can be busy at the end of holiday weekends, and drivers should park on the jetty the night before and have a quiet word with the captain.

Fortunately, there is another option and passengers can travel faster and in greater style on the 50-seat launch *MV Natalie* (m 0752 371829, 0786 275187). This travels from Nakiwogo to Lutoboka on Monday (dep 08.00; US$9). Then it shuttles to Nakiwogo and back to Lutoboka on Tuesday, Thursday (dep 08.00, rtn 13.00; US$9 each way) and Friday (dep 09.00, rtn 14.00; US$12). On Sunday it makes a one-way trip back to Nakiwogo to return weekenders to the mainland (dep 14.00; US$12).

By ferry via Bukakata A free vehicle ferry service connects the mainland port of Bukakata [190 D2] (40km east of Masaka) to Luko [190 D1] (30km west of Kalangala) several times daily. Two different ferries cross back and forth regularly, leaving in either direction at 07.00, 08.00, 10.00, noon, 14.00, 15.00, 16.00 and 18.00 Monday to Saturday, and at 08.00, 10.00, 14.00 and 18.00 on Sunday, and taking 30 minutes in either direction. Self-drivers who want to catch the first ferry in either direction should be at the port at least 30 minutes before the scheduled departure time, or they risk being too far back in the vehicle queue.

To get to Bukakata in a private vehicle, you can head towards Lake Nabugabo detailed on page 198, but continue straight on at the final junction, for 22km to Bukakata (⊕ -0.27205, 32.02629). Using public transport, a daily bus service (7–8hrs; US$7) to Kalangala via Bukakata leaves Kampala's New Taxi Park at 08.00, and starts the return trip from Kalangala at around 06.30. Coming from Masaka, a few matatus run daily between Nyendo and Kalangala via Bukakata (3hrs; US$5). There are also matatus between Luko and Kalangala (45mins; US$2).

By lake-taxi from Kasenyi The main port for motorised lake-taxis to Ssese is Kasenyi, 7km out of Abaita Abibiri township (⊕ 0.09516, 32.50251), which is 4km north of Entebbe on the Kampala Road. Given the alternative craft described above, there is no reason to risk a 5-hour lake-taxi to Lutoboka given that they are uncomfortable, usually overloaded and frequently sink. Lake-taxis from Kasenyi to Banda or Bukasa are no safer but they remain the only direct option from the mainland. You may, however, prefer to take a ferry to Lutoboka and take a shorter boat voyage to these islands.

WHERE TO STAY Buggala Island offers a broad selection of accommodation, while options on Banda and Bukasa islands are more limited.

Buggala

Accommodation on Buggala is concentrated along sandy Lutoboka Bay (the landing point for ferries from Nakiwogo) & around Kalangala.

Upmarket

Brovad Sands Lodge [190 A4] (39 rooms) ⊕ -0.31893, 32.28068; ☎ 041 4237477; m 0774 334655; e info@brovadsandslodge.com, brovadsandslodge@gmail.com; w brovadsandslodge.com. The smartest lodge on the island lies at the southwest end of Lutoboka Bay, 2km from the ferry jetty. The large stone-&-thatch cottages, which wouldn't look out of place in a game lodge, are spaced around well-wooded gardens with a restaurant, bar, spa, swimming pool, sandy beach & long activities list. Very reasonably priced for a place of this quality. *US$80/100 sgl/dbl B&B; US$115/155 sgl/dbl FB.* **$$$**

Moderate

Ssese Islands Beach Hotel [190 B3] (38 rooms) ⊕ -0.31431, 32.28735; ☎ 041 4220065; m 0772 408244; e sibh@sseseislandsbeachhotel.com; w sseseislandsbeachhotel.com. Perhaps we aren't the only ones to report that this pleasant resort was looking a touch down-at-heel because it's now closed for renovations, reopening 2025. Anyway, the grounds run down to a sandy swimming beach overlooked by a terrace restaurant & by the time you read this, the 'semi-operational' 9-hole golf course might be fully operational. *Expect the current rates of US$35/55 sgl/dbl B&B to increase.* **$$$**

Victoria Forest Resort [190 B3] (50 rooms) ⊕ -0.30223, 32.28933; ☎ 031 3239205; m 0776 663389; e info@victoriaforestresort.co.ug; w victoriaforestresort.co.ug. This collection of 2-storey blocks & thatched circular cottages has an isolated beachfront location 1.2km northwest of the ferry, & a backdrop of dense forest alive with birdsong. The terracotta-tiled rooms are modern & spacious while amenities include a swimming pool, sauna/massage centre & restaurant. A bit characterless but easily the pick in this range. *From US$38/70 sgl/dbl B&B.* **$$$**

Budget

Panorama Cottages [190 B3] (16 rooms) ⊕ -0.3129, 32.29383; m 0782 310629. Stronger on the cottages than the panorama, this friendly owner-managed lodge lacks a beachfront location, but has an attractive garden setting in a forest clearing 500m inland from the ferry landing. A selection of spacious but rather tired-looking chalets all come with nets, TV & en-suite hot shower. *US$26–40 dbl, depending on size & furnishing.* **$$**

Shoestring and camping

Philo Leisure Gardens [190 C4] (11 rooms) ⊕ -0.31821, 32.30098; m 0772 165431/0705 317205; e reserve@philoleisuregardens.ug; w philoleisuregardens.ug. Set in tranquil fruiting gardens off the main road between Kalangala & Lutoboka, this chilled lodge is centred on a slate-terraced restaurant serving a good selection of grills, curries & other dishes in the US$4–6 range. It can rent out mountain bikes at US$9/day. *From US$20 dbl using common shower; US$7 pp camping.* **$$**

Upland Guesthouse [190 B4] (25 rooms) ⊕ -0.31988, 32.2951; m 0773 310006. Tucked away behind the main road through Kalangala opposite the prominent Cruise Safari, this clean & friendly place is the pick of a few basic guesthouses dotted around the small town. All rooms are en suite & have nets. *US$8/10/12 sgl/dbl/twin.* **$**

Banda Island

✷ **Banda Island Resort** [190 F1] (2 beach cabins, 1 cottage, 1 dorm, 1 safari tent) ⊕ -0.25543, 32.39765; m 0772 222777; e banda.island@gmail.com; w bandaisland.biz. This marvellously idiosyncratic & laid-back island camp has survived the untimely death of its hedonist creator Dominic Symes, with family & friends making sure that his legend lives on. It remains on a different planet from the beachfront resorts on Buggala Island & a significant number of budget travellers forsake Lutoboka in search of the more authentic experience on Banda. A wide range of activities & services includes sailing, swimming, paddle boats, fishing, birding, nature & village walks, darts, pétanque & massage, facial & pedicure/manicure. Nile perch trawling is available & kayaks for hire. Food is fantastic. *US$54 pp 2-room en-suite cottage; US$54 pp en-suite beach cottage or safari tent; US$48 dorm bed or lazy camping; US$37 pp camping in own tent. All rates FB.* **$$**

Bukasa Island

Bukasa Guesthouse [190 G3] (4 rooms) m 0764 956668. Still the only place to stay in

Bukasa (long-standing plans for a resort yet to come to fruition), this simple guesthouse with twin rooms opens on demand; call at least 2 days ahead to make arrangements. Rates include b/fast, dinner & 2hrs of generator-powered electricity. *US$12 pp.* **$$**

WHERE TO EAT AND DRINK All of the resorts on Buggala Island serve adequate to good meals, with the standouts being Brovad Sands, Victoria Forest Resort and Philo Leisure Gardens.

Cruise Safari Restaurant [190 B4] ⊕ -0.32064, 32.29517; m 0771 913987, 0758 706108; ⊕ 07.00–midnight daily. This stilted wooden restaurant stands upstairs of Kalangala's only quad-biking setup & serves a varied & unexpectedly cosmopolitan menu of b/fasts, fajitas, grills & other dishes. It also has a good vegetarian & juice selection, & sells freshly baked bread over the counter. *Mains in the US$5–8 range.*

OTHER PRACTICALITIES The Ssese Islands feel very undeveloped by comparison with the rest of Uganda, but even so Kalangala now has a Stanbic Bank with an ATM [190 B4]. Internet facilities are almost non-existent, though the smarter resorts have Wi-Fi.

WHAT TO SEE AND DO

Buggala Island The narrow and irregularly shaped Buggala Island, which is nowhere much more than 10km wide, extends for more than 25km to the west and the south from the town of Kalangala on its northeastern pivot. If you don't fancy exploring on foot, note that Cruise Safari Restaurant in Kalangala (see above) rents out quad bikes at US$17 per person per hour inclusive of a guide. Mountain bikes can be rented from Philo Leisure Gardens (page 205) and local guides arranged through the **Ssese Island Tourism Centre** [190 B4] (m 0772 686772, 0772 537222) next to the police station in Kalangala.

Lutoboka There's more to this beautiful bay than a ferry jetty. Situated 1km downhill from Kalangala, the sandy forest-fringed bay offers a variety of beach activities, including swimming, though bilharzia is certainly a risk (see page 70 for more information). Canoeing is available at some resorts. The forest encircling the bay hosts a wealth of birdlife, best seen from the dirt road running northwest of the jetty towards Victoria Forest Resort.

Further afield Strike out in any direction from Kalangala town for pleasing views over forests and grassy clearings to the lakeshore and more distant islands, as well as the opportunity to see a variety of forest birds and vervet monkeys. One potentially interesting goal further afield is the marshy southwestern shore, which harbours small numbers of hippo as well as a population of sitatunga antelope with larger horns than the mainland equivalent, regarded by some authorities to represent an endemic island race. Another popular cycling excursion is to Mutumbula swimming beach [190 D2], which lies off the road towards Luko, and is reputedly but unverifiably free of bilharzia.

Other islands The second-largest island in Ssese is **Bukasa** [190 G2], which lies on the eastern end of the archipelago and is widely regarded to be even more attractive than Buggala. Extensively forested, it supports a profusion of birds and monkeys, and can be explored on foot along a network of fair roads. Individual points of interest include an attractive beach at Misenyi Bay [190 G2], and a plunge-pool ringed by forest and a waterfall, about an hour's walk from the ferry jetty. Several other small, mostly uninhabited islands can be reached by fishing boat as day trips from Buggala.

8

Ankole and Lake Mburo

The modern administrative subregion of Ankole, which lies to the west of Buganda and east of Kigezi, has its roots in an eponymous kingdom established more than 500 years ago. The subregion is administered from Mbarara, a bustling and rapidly growing town that holds little of interest to tourists, but now ranks as the country's most populous urban area outside the immediate vicinity of Kampala. The main tourist attraction in Ankole is Lake Mburo National Park, a fine savannah reserve whose acacia woodland supports substantial herds of zebra and various antelope, along with an increasingly visible population of leopard and recently introduced giraffe. Lake Mburo makes for a great overnight stop between the far southwest and Kampala, and it's also the only place in Uganda to offer horseback safaris. The most worthwhile cultural site in Ankole, the fine museum at the Igongo Cultural Centre, 15km east of Mbarara, is a popular place to stop for lunch and a leg stretch en route to or from Kampala.

HISTORY

The ancient kingdom of Ankole (also known as Nkore) was founded c1500 in the power vacuum created by the demise of the Bachwezi. Although Ankole was a centralised polity like Buganda or Bunyoro, its social structure differed from the other pre-colonial kingdoms of present-day Uganda insofar as it recognised two rigidly stratified but interdependent castes: the pastoralist Bahima nobility and the agriculturist Bairu peasantry. Ankole was ruled by a hereditary king, called the *omugabe*, a role reserved for prominent members of the Bahinda clan of the Bahima. The omugabe was served by an appointed *enganzi* (prime minister) and a number of local chiefs.

Ankole rose to regional prominence in roughly 1700, after Omugabe Ntare IV Kiitabanyoro, the 11th in the dynasty, defeated the Banyoro army (Kiitabanyoro means 'Killer of the Banyoro'). By the mid 19th century, the kingdom, bounded by the Katonga River in the north and the Kagera River in the south, extended from east of Lake Mburo to the shores of Lake Albert. After 1875, however, Ankole went into decline, attributable partly to a combination of disease and drought, but primarily to the rejuvenation of Bunyoro under Kabalega, who might well have co-opted Ankole into his realm were it not for outside intervention.

In 1898, the 21-year-old Omugabe Kahaya II, then just three years into a troubled five-decade reign, decided that the only way to safeguard his kingdom against Bunyoro was to enter into an alliance with the British administration in Buganda. Three years later, the kingdom was incorporated into the British Protectorate of Uganda on 25 October 1901 with the signing of the Ankole Agreement. The Ankole royalty became increasingly irrelevant and powerless during the course of the colonial era, and it was abolished by President Obote in 1967. Unlike the other traditional monarchies of Uganda, it has never been restored (page 224).

LAKE MBURO NATIONAL PARK

Extending over 260km² of undulating territory in southern Ankole, Lake Mburo National Park (LMNP) is an underrated gem dominated scenically by the eponymous lake, whose forest-fringed shores hemmed in by rolling green hills recall Kenya's more celebrated Lake Naivasha. Until recently, LMNP, despite its relative accessibility, was bypassed by the majority of safaris and independent travellers due to its low Big Five count, in particular the lack of elephants and lions. These days, however, the park is an increasingly common overnight stop en route between Bwindi or QENP and Kampala, as well as being a popular weekend break from the capital. In part, this is because it offers some excellent game viewing, despite the absence of the aforementioned heavyweights. Indeed, visitors are now likely to see as many different large mammal species over the course of a day as they would in any Ugandan national park. LMNP is also of great interest to birders for its wealth of acacia-associated and aquatic species,

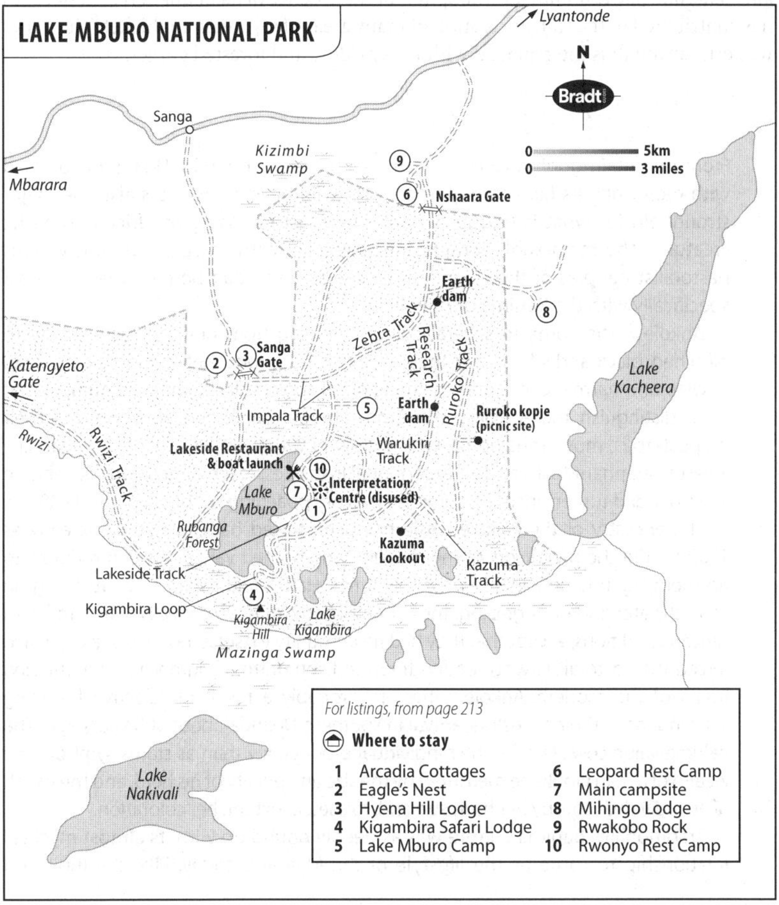

while more active travellers have the opportunity to view wildlife on horseback, on foot, or from a mountain bike.

FEES Entrance to Lake Mburo National Park costs US$30/40/25 FR/FNR/ROA per 24 hours. The standard vehicle entrance fees are also charged (page 9), but only once per entry. Entrance fees can be paid by card or Mobile Money at any gate, while activity fees are paid at Rwonyo (page 216).

GEOGRAPHY AND VEGETATION Spanning altitudes of 1,220m to 1,828m, LMNP is a hilly park underlaid by pre-Cambrian granitic rocks and sandy soils. Although the park has a relatively low average annual rainfall of around 800mm, some 20% of its surface area consists of wetland habitats. The most important of these is Lake Mburo, which extends over some 13km^2 and is fringed by lush riparian woodland and significant areas of papyrus swamp. Mburo is the largest of five lakes that lie within the park boundaries, and the second-most westerly component in a chain of 16 lakes and connecting swamps fed by the Rwizi River on its course from Mbarara to Lake Victoria. The remainder of LMNP supports a cover of open savannah and woodland dominated by thorny acacia trees such as *Vachellia hockii*, *V. gerrardii*, *V. sieberiana* and *Senegalia polyacantha*. It is thought that the absence of elephant in recent decades has contributed to the transformation of many areas of savannah to thicket. The park's western savannah is interspersed with rocky ridges and forested gorges.

ANKOLE CATTLE

From mountain gorillas to lions, from elephants to shoebills, Uganda is blessed with more than its fair share of impressive wild beasties. But it is also the major stronghold for what is unquestionably the most imposing of Africa's domestic creatures: the remarkable long-horned breed of cattle associated with various pastoralist peoples of the Ugandan–Tanzanian–Rwandan border area, but most specifically with the Bahima of Ankole.

Ankole cattle come in several colours, ranging from uniform rusty-yellow to blotched black-and-white, but they always have a long head, short neck, deep dewlap and narrow chest, and the male often sports a large thoracic hump. What most distinguish the Ankole cattle from any familiar breed, however, are their preposterous, monstrous horns, which grow out from either side of the head like inverted elephant tusks and, in exceptional instances, reach dimensions unseen on any Ugandan tusker since the commercial ivory poaching outbreak of the 1980s.

The ancestry of the Ankole cattle has been traced back to Eurasia as early as 15000BC, but the precursors of the modern long-horned variety were introduced to northern Uganda only in late medieval times. Hardy, and capable of subsisting on limited water and poor grazing, these introduced cattle were ideally suited to harsh African conditions, except that they had no immunity to tsetse-borne diseases, which forced the pastoralists who tended them to keep drifting southward. The outsized horns of the modern Ankole cattle are probably a result of selective breeding subsequent to their ancestors' arrival in southern Uganda about 500 years ago. The Bahima value cows less for their individual productivity than as status symbols: the wealth of a man would be measured by the size and quality of his herd, and the worth of an individual cow by her horn size and, to a lesser extent, her coloration.

Traditionally, Bahima culture was as deeply bound up with its almost mystical relationship to cattle as the lifestyle of the Maasai is today. Like the Inuit and

WILDLIFE LMNP harbours several **mammal** species not easily observed elsewhere in the country. It supports Uganda's only substantial remaining population of impala, the handsome antelope after which Kampala is named, and is one of only two national parks where zebras occur. Other antelope species likely to be seen by casual visitors are topi, common duiker, oribi, waterbuck, Bohor reedbuck and bushbuck – the last, rather unusually, often seen standing sentinel on top of thicketed termite mounds. The sitatunga antelope is confined to swamp interiors, while the rock-loving klipspringer is occasionally observed on hills, notably in the grounds of Mihingo Lodge. The roan antelope, once common, is now locally extinct, but 50-strong herds of the majestic eland still move seasonally through parts of the park.

The lake and its lush fringing vegetation also support healthy populations of buffalo, warthog, bushpig and hippopotamus. Some 15 giraffe from Murchison Falls were introduced to LMNP in 2015, since when the population has increased to about 50, and herds are reliably seen on game drives in the savannah northeast of Lake Mburo.

Only two diurnal primate species are present, namely vervet monkey and olive baboon, but Lake Mburo is one of the very few places in Uganda where the greater galago has been recorded. Up to eight of these cat-sized nocturnal primates make a nightly appearance at a feeding table at Mihingo Lodge, and the jet-black coloration of most individuals suggests they belong to a little-known and taxonomically

their physical landscape, the abiding mental preoccupation of the Bahima is reflected in the 30 variations in hide coloration that are recognised linguistically – the most valued being the uniform dark-brown *bihogo* – along with at least a dozen peculiarities of horn shape and size. The Bahima day is traditionally divided up into 20 periods, of which all but one of the daylight phases is named after an associated cattle-related activity. And, like the Maasai, the Bahima traditionally regarded any activity other than cattle herding as beneath contempt. They also declined to hunt game for meat, with the exception of buffalo and eland, which were sufficiently bovine in appearance for acceptable eating.

In times past, the Bahima diet did not, as might be expected, centre on meat, but rather on blood tapped from a vein of a living cow, combined with the relatively meagre yield of milk from the small udders that characterise the Ankole breed. The Bahima viewed their cattle as something close to family, so that slaughtering a fertile cow for meat was regarded as akin to cannibalism. It was customary, however, for infertile cows and surplus bullocks to be killed for meat on special occasions, while the flesh of any cow that died of natural causes would be eaten or bartered with the agriculturist Bairu for millet beer and fresh produce. No part of the cow would go to waste: the hide would be used to make clothing, mats and drums, the dung used to plaster huts and dried to light fires, while the horns could be customised as musical instruments.

The Ankole region is not as defiantly traditionalist as, say, Ethiopia's Omo Valley or Maasailand, and most rural Bahima today supplement their herds of livestock by practising mixed agriculture of subsistence and cash crops. But the Ankole cattle and their extraordinary horns, common in several parts of Uganda but most prevalent in the vicinity of Mbarara and Lake Mburo, pay living tribute to the bovine preoccupations of Ankole past.

controversial population of silvery greater galago restricted to woodland habitats in the Lake Victoria basin, and designated as *Otolemur monteiri argentatus* by some authorities.

As for predators, leopards are abundant and quite commonly seen, especially on night drives out of Mihingo Lodge, which has identified a dozen different individuals over the past few years based on photographs taken in the northeast of the park. The eerie, rising, nocturnal call of the spotted hyena is often heard from the camps, and individuals are also observed crossing the road at night or shortly after dawn with increasing frequency. Side-striped jackal and various smaller predators are also present, most visibly white-tailed mongoose (at dusk and dawn) and three otter species resident in the lakes. The lions for which LMNP was once famed are now extinct. For some years, the odd individual or pride still found its way there, most recently a solitary male that showed up in 2008 and was seen with some regularity for at least ten years after that, but he has since died.

Some 315 species of **bird** have been recorded in Lake Mburo National Park, and it is probably the best place in Uganda to see acacia-associated birds. Rwonyo Rest Camp is as good a place as any to look for the likes of mosque swallow, black-bellied bustard, bare-faced go-away bird and Rüppell's starling. A handful of birds recorded at Lake Mburo are essentially southern species at the very northern limit of their range, for instance the southern ground hornbill, black-collared and black-throated barbets, and green-capped eremomela. Of special interest to birders are the swamps, in which six papyrus endemics are resident, including the brilliantly coloured papyrus gonolek, the striking blue-headed coucal, and the highly localised white-winged warbler and papyrus yellow warbler, the last recorded nowhere else in Uganda. Lake Mburo itself is known as a reliable site for the elusive African finfoot.

FURTHER INFORMATION The informative *Lake Mburo National Park Information Guide*, written by Mark Jordhal and published by UWA in 2014, is well worth a look. Sheet 5 in the 'Uganda Maps' series covers Lake Mburo National Park and includes lists of wildlife and birding highlights.

GETTING THERE AND AWAY Four dirt access roads run south from the surfaced Masaka–Mbarara Road to Lake Mburo National Park. All require 4x4 vehicles.

Coming from Kampala, the first approach road leads to Mihingo Lodge and Kyanyanshara Gate. Follow the Mbarara Road past Lyantonde for 15km to Akagati trading centre and turn left on to an excellent graded road. This passes through Akashenshero village after 17km before, 1.4km further on, a right turn follows an indistinct and seasonally boggy tangle of tracks to Kyanyanshara Gate. Another 800m brings you to a signposted right turn that leads to Mihingo Lodge.

The more popular approach from the east is the signposted 8km road to Nshaara Gate that branches south at a junction (⊕ -0.46966, 31.02603) about 1.5km west of the village of Akagati.

Coming from the west, the most popular route is the 10km road to Sanga Gate that branches south at Sanga (⊕ -0.49823, 30.90681), 35km east of Mbarara.

The most westerly, longest, roughest and least-used route leads south from Biharwe (⊕ -0.52188, 30.74215), which straddles the Mbarara Road 21km past Sanga and only 200m east of Igongo Cultural Centre, then passes through Katengyeto Gate before emerging at Rwonyo after about 50km.

There is no public transport along any of the approach roads. Backpackers heading to Rwonyo Rest Camp (page 216) should catch a bus or matatu travelling from Masaka or Mbarara to Sanga, then pick up a special hire (around US$30 one-way) or boda (around US$8–10). For Leopard Rest Camp (page 216), ask any bus or matatu travelling between Masaka and Mbarara to drop you at Akagati, from where a boda should cost around US$2.

WHERE TO STAY *Map, page 209*

A good selection of small, mid-range and upmarket camps and lodges serves LMNP. The only budget option within the park is Rwonyo Rest Camp, but there are plenty of affordable hotels in Lyantonde, a small town beside the Masaka Road about 16km east of the junction for Nshaara Gate.

Upmarket

Kigambira Safari Lodge (12 cottages) ⊕ -0.61805, 30.98085; m 0775 162835, 0777 571597; e info@kigambirasafarilodge.com; w kigambirasafarilodge.com. The most isolated of all of Lake Mburo's lodges stands on a remote headland overlooking Lake Kigambira & the broad, swamp-filled Rwizi Valley. Though the thatched & canvas-sided architecture melds nicely with the natural setting, a certain smoothness of style makes it tempting to categorise it as a hotel in the bush. As such, it's a perfect retreat from the cares of the world, while as a base for serious wildlife viewing it's less ideal, the park's game-rich grasslands lying beyond several kilometres of dense bush. **$$$$$**

Lake Mburo Camp (9 tents) ⊕ -0.61805, 30.98085; m 0772 401391; e info@kimbla-mantanauganda.com; w lakemburocamp.com. Also sometimes referred to as Kimbla-Mantana after the company that runs it, this classic luxury tented camp offers a genuine bush experience in secluded & fully furnished en-suite tents, all with solar lighting, eco-friendly toilets & private verandas. The camp runs along a lightly wooded ridge, which is rattling with birds, lizards & other small animals. If the views towards Lake Mburo are impressive from the thatched dining/lounge shelter, they are even more memorable from the sundowner fireplace on the summit just above the camp. The tented camp lies off Impala Track & is clearly signposted about 7km from Sanga Gate. **$$$$$**

✷ **Mihingo Lodge** (12 tents) ⊕ -0.60298, 31.0484; m 0752 410509; e reservations@mihingolodge.com; w mihingo-lodge.com. One of the best lodges associated with any Ugandan national park, Mihingo is superbly positioned atop an extensive kopje (rock outcrop) within a private 97ha wilderness area abutting the eastern boundary of LMNP & offering views eastward to Lake Kacheera. The privately positioned luxury tents all enjoy outward views from a veranda & spacious bathroom, with 6 units dramatically placed on the summit of the kopje & others along less giddy contours around the flanks. Attention to detail is evident throughout, from the loo handles to the organic thatched lounge/dining shelter supported by gnarled olive-wood branches. The setting for excellent 3-course dinners is perfectly positioned (as is an adjacent rock-sided swimming pool) to enjoy the breeze, sunsets & the wildlife visiting a salt lick in the valley below. Visitors with walking difficulties or small children should note that some tents are accessed by varying numbers of rough stone steps. Mihingo is the only base for horseback safaris in & around the national park (page 217). It also offers mountain-biking excursions outside the park, guided walks, night drives & cultural visits to a nearby village, as well as the opportunity to hire out the lodge's open-sided 4x4 vehicle. It is a good place to see klipspringer by day & greater galago by night. Mihingo Lodge reinvests a portion of its income in community & ecological projects, notably by supporting the local school & by compensating locals for livestock killed by leopard & hyena, which has enabled the populations of these predators to recover. *Substantial discounts available seasonally & for East African residents.* **$$$$$**

Moderate

Arcadia Cottages (8 cottages) ⊕ -0.64151, 30.95343; m 0785 623366; e arcadialodgesuganda@gmail.com; w arcadialodges.com. Down in Kigezi, this lodge's luxurious & eponymous sister establishment enjoys a Lake Bunyonyi panorama that defies superlatives. The Lake Mburo version is altogether more basic &, though the lake is just a couple of hundred metres distant, it is hidden behind a screen of bush. Hence this lodge's best feature is

LAKE MBURO: SOME HISTORY

Many centuries ago, according to oral tradition, the valley in which Lake Mburo stands today was dry agricultural land, worked by a pair of brothers named Kigarama and Mburo. One night, Kigarama dreamed that he and his brother would be in danger unless they moved to higher land. The next morning, as Kigarama prepared to relocate to the surrounding hills, he shared the warning with Mburo, who shrugged it off and decided to stay put. Within days, the valley was submerged, and Kigarama watched on helplessly from the hills as his younger brother drowned. The lake was named for the unfortunate Mburo and the surrounding hills after Kigarama.

In pre-colonial times, the area around Lake Mburo, known as Nshara and referred to by Bahima pastoralists as Karo Karungyi (literally 'good grazing land'), was probably rather thinly populated. Pastoralist settlement would have been inhibited by the periodic prevalence of *Glossina morsitans*, a species of tsetse fly that transmits a strain of trypanosome harmless to wild animals and humans, but fatal to domestic cattle. Furthermore, the Omugabe of Ankole favoured Nshara as a royal hunting ground, and forbade the Bahima from grazing and watering their cattle there except during times of drought.

In the early 1890s, Mburo – like the rest of Ankole – was hit severely by the rinderpest epidemic that swept through East Africa, and the resultant depletion of livestock precipitated a famine that claimed thousands of human lives. The decreased grazing pressure also led to widespread bush regeneration, paving the way for a devastating tsetse fly outbreak c1910. Those pastoralists who had resettled the Mburo area were forced to relocate their herds to the more arid savannah of Nyabushozi, north of the present-day Kampala–Mbarara Road.

In 1935, the colonial government set aside the vast tract of largely depopulated land centred on Mburo as a Controlled Hunting Area in which both regulated hunting and traditional human activities were permitted. Ten years later, another tsetse outbreak – this time not only *G. morsitans*, but also *G. palpalis*, which spreads sleeping sickness to humans – forced the pastoralists out of the Mburo area. As a result, the colonial authorities instituted a radical programme to eradicate the tsetse from Ankole in the 1950s – its premise being that if every last wild animal in the area were killed, then the bloodsucking tsetse would surely be starved to extinction.

Brian Herne includes a scathing account of this first phase of the anti-tsetse campaign in his book *African Safaris*:

> They employed vast teams of African hunters with shot-bolt rifles...with orders to shoot every single animal, irrespective of age or sex. Everything was to be exterminated. We watched in horror and anger. They did slaughter everything they could...anything and everything that crossed their gunsights. The wildlife was decimated almost out of existence...after the grass fires in July, the plains were richly scattered with bleached skeletons and gaunt sun-dried carcasses.

According to Herne, the 'wondrous final solution had proved a disastrous and expensive bloodbath...It is of course almost possible to kill off entire populations but some stock always survives, especially of more elusive animals like duiker and bushbuck. Of course, some did survive – enough to ensure the survival of the tsetse fly!'

The authorities reasoned that if it was not possible to starve the tsetse to death, then the only solution was to eradicate the shady bushes and trees around which it lived. Hundreds of square kilometres of bush around Mburo were stripped, cut and/or burned, until barely any trees were left. After the first rains fell, however, a dense cover of secondary undergrowth quickly established itself, offering adequate cover for tsetse flies to survive, Herne wrote, 'voracious and hungry and as indiscriminate in their hunger as ever'. Over the next season, the authorities implemented a new campaign, aimed directly at the tsetse, employing teams of locals to spray every inch of Ankole with insecticide. This final phase did result in the virtual elimination of the tsetse, but at considerable ecological cost, since it also took its toll on almost every other insect species, as well as insectivorous birds and small mammals.

In the early 1960s, with tsetse-borne diseases all but eradicated, Bahima pastoralists flocked back to the controlled hunting area. It soon became clear that, were any wildlife to survive, the resettlement of Mburo would need to be regulated. In 1964, the first Obote government de-gazetted a large portion of the controlled hunting area to make way for subsistence farmers and herders, while the remainder was upgraded to become the Lake Mburo Game Reserve. Pastoralists were granted transit and dry-season watering rights to the newly gazetted reserve, but were forbidden from residing within it.

This stasis was undermined in the 1970s, after some 650km^2 of gazetted land were excised to become a state cattle ranch. Conservation activities in what remained of the game reserve practically ceased, allowing for considerable human encroachment along the borders. The volume of wildlife, largely recovered from the anti-tsetse slaughter 20 years earlier, was again severely depleted, this time as a result of subsistence poaching. The park's lions – unpopular with local herders not only because they occasionally hunted cattle, but also for their long-standing reputation as man-eaters (one particularly voracious male reputedly accounted for more than 80 human lives in the 1960s) – were hunted to local extinction.

In 1983, the second Obote government gazetted Lake Mburo as a national park, following the boundaries of the original game reserve and forcibly evicting some 4,500 families without compensation. As a result, local communities tended to view the park somewhat negatively – a waste of an important traditional resource from which they had been wrongly excluded. As the civil war reached its peak in 1986, Lake Mburo was almost wholly resettled, its facilities and infrastructure were destroyed, and subsistence poaching once again reached critical levels. In 1987, the Museveni government agreed to reduce the area of the national park by 60%, and it allowed a limited number of people to live within the park and fish on the lake, but still tensions between the park and surrounding communities remained high.

The turning point in Mburo's fractious history came in 1991, with the creation of a pioneering Mburo Community Conservation Unit, established with the assistance of the Africa Wildlife Foundation. A community representative was appointed for each of the neighbouring parishes, to be consulted with regard to decisions affecting the future of the park, and to air any local grievances directly with the park management. Between 1991 and 1997, the remaining inhabitants of the park were relocated outside its borders and awarded a negotiated sum as compensation. Since 1995, 20% of the revenue raised by park entrance fees has been used to fund the construction of local clinics and schools, and for other community projects.

not the cement cabins rendered to look like logs but a storyed wooden restaurant that manages to salvage a view. *US$120/180 sgl/dbl FB.* **$$$$**

Eagle's Nest (12 tents) ⊕ -0.6014, 30.91981; ☎ 031 2294894; **m** 0777 820071; **e** reservations@gorillatours.com; **w** gorillatours.com. Perched on a cliff just outside Sanga Gate, this sensibly priced bush camp offers accommodation in large standing twin tents with en-suite eco-toilet & bush shower, solar lights, & private balcony offering a splendid view over the plains below. *US$90/140/140 sgl/dbl/twin FB.* **$$$**

Hyena Hill Lodge (8 cottages) ⊕ - 0.58879, 30.92722; **m** 0751 898 014; **e** info@hyenahilllodge.com; **w** hyenahilllodge.com. Since opening on a lofty hill overlooking the park in 2019, this eco-friendly lodge has quickly established itself as a favourite with visitors and expatriates. Nearby Sanga Gate is your starting point for a game drive while mountain-biking and community walks are other options. *US$110/165/260 sgl/dbl/family cottages.* **$$$**

✷ **Rwakobo Rock** (12 cottages, 5 rooms) ⊕ -0.52825, 31.00011; **m** 0755 211771; **e** info@rwakoborock.com; **w** rwakoborock.com. This lodge, 1.5km outside Nshaara Gate, is spread across a rock outcrop looking into the national park. The simple but comfortable & meticulously constructed en-suite cottages are individually positioned in secluded sites across the kopje. Though each has a view, don't miss the 360° regional panorama from the top of the kopje. En-suite rooms are also available within Hornbill Hse. Can arrange mountain-bike tours. *Cottages US$150/250 sgl/dbl; rooms US$100/160 sgl/dbl; all rates FB; discounts for residents.* **$$$–$$$$$**

Budget

✷ **Leopard Rest Camp** (24 units) ⊕ -0.53087, 31.01089; **m** 0789 787856, 0753 666984; **e** info@leopardrestcamp.com; **w** leopardrestcamp.com. Situated in an attractive patch of bush a short distance outside Nshaara Gate, this well-organised budget camp is a popular base for travellers without transport. Options range from simple 'lazy camping' tents using common showers to luxury en-suite standing tents with private balcony, all with proper wooden beds & mattresses. The gardens are dotted with hammocks & sitting areas, there's plenty of birdlife, & larger wildlife occasionally passes through. Activities on offer include nature walks (US$15 pp), community walks (US$10 pp) & guided bike safaris outside/inside the park (US$30 pp exc park entry). *US$55–75 pp en-suite safari tents; US$30 pp lazy camping; US$10 pp own tent. B/fast costs US$5 pp & other meals US$10 pp.* **$$$**

Shoestring and camping

Main campsite ⊕ -0.63754, 30.95308. This lakeshore campsite 1.5km from Rwonyo is serviced by a clean ablution block & the Lakeside Restaurant. Birdlife is plentiful & hippos come ashore at night to keep the lawns cropped short. If you have your own transport & provisions, & aren't too fussed by tsetse flies, lakeshore camping is also possible at a 2nd campsite 5km further south. *US$11 pp.* **$**

✷ **Rwonyo Rest Camp** (7 tents, 4 bandas) ⊕ -0.63388, 30.96506; **m** 0751 046904, 0784 752874; **e** info@ugandawildlife.org; **w** ugandawildlife.org. Perched on a hillside 1km from the lakeshore, this stalwart UWA camp offers the choice of a new and rather institutional accommodation block and a more discreetly placed group of standing tents, most of which use communal showers & toilets. You can self-cater or eat at the nearby Lakeside Restaurant (travellers without transport will need to be walked there by a ranger). Waterbuck, warthog & the occasional bushpig wander through at night. Aspects of the camp are a bit rundown, but it offers a genuine bush experience at a bargain price. *Guesthouses US$35 dbl room B&B; tents US$9/16 sgl/dbl; dorm bed US$7.* **$**

WHAT TO SEE AND DO

Game drives The part of the national park to the east of Lake Mburo is traversed by a network of game tracks. The quality of game viewing in particular locations is influenced by the season as well as long-term vegetative changes. Overall, though, the best game viewing is in the park-like savannah north and east of Rwonyo along the Research Track (where two earth dams were recently excavated) and the Zebra, Impala and Warukiri tracks. This area usually hosts substantial concentrations of impala, zebra, waterbuck, topi and buffalo. The relatively open savannah along the Kazuma and Ruroko tracks is also good for game viewing, passing through a landscape interspersed with rocky hills where pairs of klipspringer are frequently observed. Giraffe are most commonly seen in the vicinity of the Kazuma and Research tracks. You should also park up and walk to the Kazuma Lookout atop the eponymous hill for the southern panorama over four of the park's lakes.

Historically, during the dry season, when animals congregate around the swamps and lakes, the best game viewing was often along the stretch of Lakeside Track south of the junction with Kazuma Track, together with the more southerly Kigambira Loop. These days, however, the increasingly dense bush cover near the lake has complicated game viewing (unless you're searching specifically for bush-dwelling birds, or hoping to spot a leopard), and it is also often infested with tsetse flies. The 360° panorama from the once-grassy summit of Kigambira Hill has been all but obscured by scrub.

To the west of Rwonyo, starting near Sanga Gate, the Rwizi Track leads through an area of light acacia savannah where impala, eland and zebra are common. After 12km, the track approaches the Rwizi River and fringing swamps, before veering west to follow the wooded watercourse for 33km to Bisheshe Gate. This road is particularly rewarding for birds but tsetse flies can be a problem.

The standard US$10 for a self-guided game drive fee applies. If you prefer to take a UWA guide, this costs US$15/20 FR/FNR per vehicle per drive. For those without their own transport, most lodges can arrange game drives.

Horseback safaris Mihingo Lodge (page 213) has introduced horseback safaris in the east of the park, a first in a Ugandan protected area, and a great opportunity to get close to animals such as zebra and buffalo, which are far more relaxed around horses than around cars. Rides are tailored to individual experience and requirements. Kids can be led on good-natured ponies while (at the other extreme) experienced riders can help a couple of retired racehorses burn off some calories. Day rates vary from US$35/70 per person for a 30-/60-minute taster in the grassy valley floor below the lodge (an area habitually filled with game) to US$240 for a half-day excursion to various hilltop viewpoints with a bush breakfast. Guests staying at Mihingo get substantial discounts on these rates. Further details and rates are posted at w mihingo-lodge.com.

Cycling Because the number of seriously stroppy wildlife species in Lake Mburo is limited, cycling is allowed within the park, though at an additional cost (US$25/30 FR/FNR plus park entry) since you'll need a ranger escort on his own bike. The porous nature of the park boundary means that you can have a similar but significantly cheaper experience cycling past eland, zebra and impala in the surrounding rangelands, though you won't find giraffe outside the park.

Guided night drives The success of Mihingo Lodge's compensation scheme for locals whose livestock is killed by leopards or hyenas means that numbers of these once-elusive nocturnal predators have increased greatly in recent years, particularly in the northeast of the park. Night drives out of Mihingo now come with a 30–40% chance of seeing leopards, which are often quite relaxed around vehicles, while packs of up to 20 hyena are regularly observed. The cost is US$30 per person in your own vehicle, or for those without a vehicle, Mihingo Lodge can provide one for US$60 per group.

Boat trips (US$25/30 pp FR/FNR) Motorboat trips on Lake Mburo leave from the jetty at the main campsite 1km from Rwonyo Camp. In addition to the attractive scenery and simple pleasure attached to being out on the water, the boat trip reliably produces good sightings of hippo, crocodile, buffalo, waterbuck and bushbuck, and it's also worth looking out for the three species of resident otter. Among the more conspicuous waterbirds are African fish eagle, marabou stork, pied kingfisher and various egrets and herons, while Ross's turaco and Narina trogon are frequently seen in lakeside thickets. Lake Mburo is possibly the easiest place in Uganda to see the African finfoot, which is generally associated with still water below overhanging branches. The excursions last 90 minutes and, subject to demand, leave every 2 hours between 08.00 and 16.00 as well as at 17.30.

Guided walks (US$20/25 pp FR/FNR) Visitors are permitted to walk anywhere in LMNP in the company of an armed ranger. Near to the rest camp, a derelict hilltop Interpretation Centre occupies a good viewpoint, while the road to the jetty is also a good place to walk, being rich in birds and regularly visited by hippos. An even better target is a viewing platform that overlooks a salt lick about 2km from the camp – an excellent place to see a wide variety of animals. Of particular interest to walkers and birders is the **Rubanga Forest**, which lies off the Rwizi Track and can only be visited with the permission of the warden, who will provide you with an armed ranger.

Cultural tours Under the banner 'Beyond the Park', this new community initiative presents a variety of participatory activities in the Rurambira Community Conservancy on the eastern edge of LMNP. These demonstrate the work of a volunteer Community Wildlife Scout, showcase local cattle culture, present traditional dance and drama, get visitors involved in craft making and send them trundling through local villages on bicycles. To organise an activity call Wycliffe on m 0753 321009 or ask your lodge to take charge.

MBARARA

Situated 260km southwest of Kampala at the junction of the main roads running south to Kabale and Bwindi and north to QENP and Kasese, Mbarara is a rapidly growing town that now ranks as Uganda's largest urban centre outside the environs of Greater Kampala. It hasn't always been this way, though – in 1955, when Alan Forward arrived here to serve as the new district officer, he found himself 'choking in the dust' of what 'seemed to have the atmosphere of a one-horse town'. Even as recently as 1992, when the first edition of this guidebook was researched, Mbarara was a sleepy and nondescript kind of place, its moribund infrastructure still visibly scarred by the Tanzanian invasion during the Amin era.

By contrast, post-millennial Mbarara has evolved into what is surely the most modern and vibrant urban centre in western Uganda, though surprisingly its population of 281,000 lags slightly behind that of Masaka. Yet, paradoxically, while its urban hotels and shops are as good as any west of Kampala, the former are aimed mostly at the conference market, and the town

MBARARA

For listings, see from page 221

Where to stay

Where to eat and drink

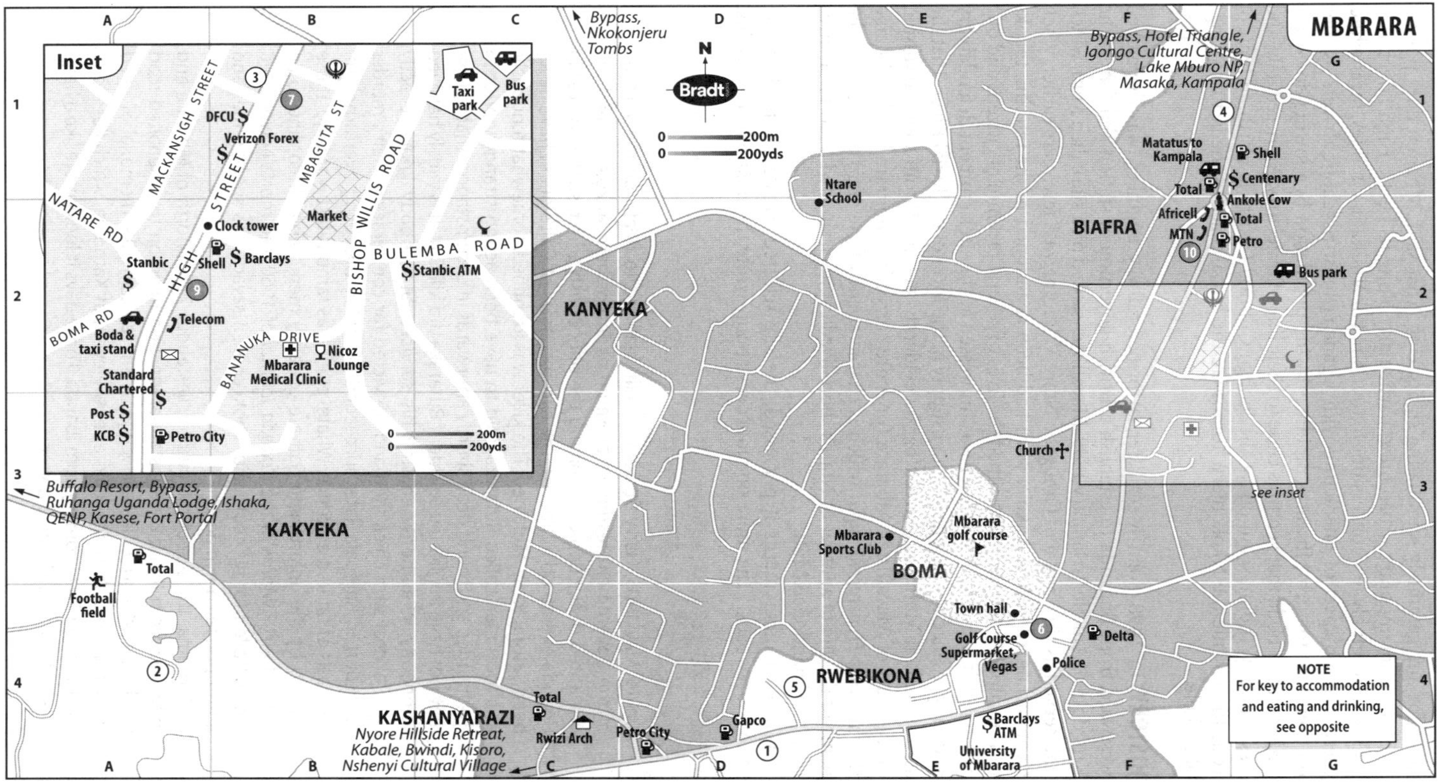
MBARARA
Inset
Bypass, Nkokonjeru Tombs
Bypass, Hotel Triangle, Igongo Cultural Centre, Lake Mburo NP, Masaka, Kampala
Buffalo Resort, Bypass, Ruhanga Uganda Lodge, Ishaka, QENP, Kasese, Fort Portal
Nyore Hillside Retreat, Kabale, Bwindi, Kisoro, Nshenyi Cultural Village
N
Bradt
0 200m
0 200yds
MACKANSIGH STREET
HIGH STREET
MBAGUTA ST
BISHOP WILLIS ROAD
BULEMBA ROAD
NATARE RD
BOMA RD
BANANUKA DRIVE
DFCU
Verizon Forex
Market
Clock tower
Stanbic
Shell
Barclays
Stanbic ATM
Telecom
Boda & taxi stand
Standard Chartered
Post
KCB
Petro City
Mbarara Medical Clinic
Nicoz Lounge
Taxi park
Bus park
KANYEKA
KAKYEKA
BIAFRA
BOMA
RWEBIKONA
KASHANYARAZI
Ntare School
Matatus to Kampala
Shell
Centenary
Total
Ankole Cow
Africell
Total
MTN
Petro
Bus park
Church
see inset
Mbarara Sports Club
Mbarara golf course
Town hall
Golf Course Supermarket, Vegas
Delta
Police
Barclays ATM
University of Mbarara
Gapco
Petro City
Rwizi Arch
Total
Total
Football field
NOTE
For key to accommodation and eating and drinking, see opposite

lacks for any genuinely scintillating sightseeing. That said, Mbarara does possess a certain contemporary urban buzz, particularly along its hectic High Street, that makes refreshingly few concessions to tourism. For adrenaline junkies, meanwhile, there's the prospect of interacting with Uganda's most psychotic drivers as they do their best to curb Mbarara's rapidly growing population by mowing down any pedestrian or boda that ventures close to their line of trajectory. More sedately, and less centrally, the museum out at the Igongo Cultural Centre is worth an hour of your time, while the Nkokonjeru Tombs are the burial place of the last two kings of Ankole.

HISTORY In 1898, John Macallister, a former railway engineer, was dispatched westward from Buganda to establish a British government station and fort in the Kingdom of Ankole. In January 1899, Macallister settled on a site called Muti, which had served as the capital of Omugabe Ntare V Rugingiza a few years earlier, when Captain Lugard visited Ankole. Muti had been abandoned in the interim, thanks to a smallpox epidemic that claimed the lives of several prominent citizens and one of Ntare V's sons, but Macallister was impressed at the site's eminent defendability and the presence of a perennial water supply in the form of the Rwizi River. That the station built at Muti was called Mbarara evidently stemmed from some confusion on the part of Macallister. Mbarara (or more correctly Emburara, the local name for the grass *Hyperemia ruffa*, which is characteristic of the area) was actually the name of the site of another of Ntare's short-lived capitals, situated a few kilometres from the abandoned Muti.

Whatever other merits it possessed, the site selected by Macallister had one serious drawback. 'The more one journeys about', wrote the missionary J J Willis,

MURDER IN ANKOLE

On 19 May 1905, Harry St George Galt, stabbed to death on the veranda of the government resthouse at Katooma in northern Ankole, earned the unwanted distinction of becoming the only British administrative officer in Uganda ever to be murdered. The circumstances of Galt's death have never been satisfactorily explained. The killer was identified, somewhat tenuously, as a local man called Rutaraka, said to have been acting strangely prior to the murder, and found dead shortly afterwards in circumstances that may or may not have implicated suicide. If Rutaraka did kill Galt, it is widely believed somebody in authority enlisted his services, but nobody knows exactly who: a local Saza chief, tried and convicted for conspiracy in Galt's murder at a court in Kampala, later succeeded in having the ruling overturned on the basis of tainted evidence. Whatever else, as famous last words go, those uttered by the unfortunate Galt are certainly memorable. According to an article by H F Morris in the *Uganda Journal* of 1960, the mortally wounded officer 'called for his cook, said "Look, cook, a savage has speared me", and thereupon fell down dead'.

Katooma, the site of the murder, lies about 75km north of Mbarara and only 3km from Ibanda, a substantial junction town on the asphalted road north to Fort Portal via Kamwenge. A 3m-tall cairn-like memorial of piled stones was erected a few days after the event at Katooma, which lies along the Kagongo Road coming from Ibanda. These days it looks more like a heap of rubble, but you'll know better.

'the more one is impressed with the fact that [Mbarara] is the one spot in all Ankole where you have to march a whole day or two days before you come on any cultivation worth the name.' The scarcity of food around Mbarara was rooted less in the area's geography than in local cultural attitudes – the Bahima, like so many other African pastoralists, had no tradition of cultivation. The British administration, supported by Enganzi Mbaguta, did much to encourage the growth of agriculture in Ankole during the early years of the 20th century. In 1905, Mbaguta remarked that, following the establishment of Mbarara, the annual famines were 'becoming yearly less severe'. Within a few years, the new capital of Ankole, accorded township status in 1906, would be practically self-sufficient in food, and its future role as the main centre of trade in Ankole secure.

Mbarara grew slowly during the colonial era. Indeed, following a census undertaken in the late 1950s, it was too small to be ranked among 12 towns countrywide whose population exceeded 4,000. It remained something of a one-horse town in the 1990s, but by the turn of the millennium it had grown to become one of the ten largest towns in Uganda, with a population of almost 70,000 in 2002. Mbarara has developed rapidly since then, partly due to its strategic importance as a regional transport hub at the junction of roads connecting Kampala to Rwanda, Burundi, Tanzania and the DRC, but also as a result of increased industrialisation and government investment. Surprisingly, Mbarara, which was afforded city status in 2020, now ranks as Uganda's second-largest urb, slightly ahead of Gulu and a country mile behind the conurbation created by Kampala and its contiguous municipalities.

GETTING THERE AND AWAY Mbarara is a major route focus, situated at the junction of the surfaced roads northeast to Kampala via Masaka, southwest to Kabale and Kisoro, and north to Fort Portal via either QENP and Kasese or Ibanda and Kibale National Park. Distances and approximate driving times in a **private vehicle** are 50km/1 hour to Lake Mburo National Park (Sanga Gate), 140km/2 hours to Masaka, 270km/4–5 hours to Kampala, 115km/1½–2 hours to Katunguru (QENP), 145km/2–3 hours to Kasese, 235km/4 hours to Fort Portal, 140km/2½ hours to Kabale, and 180km/3–4 hours to Buhoma (Bwindi).

Until such time that the daily Post Bus (page 130) is revived, your best bets from Kampala are the Global and Link buses that leave the Kasenyi bus terminal throughout the day. Mbarara's central taxi park [219 C1] is also the place to pick up matatus to Ishaka (US$2), Ibanda (US$3), Kasese via Katunguru (US$4–5), Kabale (US$4–5) and Kisoro (US$8–9).

WHERE TO STAY Mbarara boasts an extraordinary number of hotels, most of them falling at the superior end of the budget range and catering mainly to the conference market, but which are also perfectly adequate for unfussy tourists. The listings on below are highly selective.

Moderate

Acacia Hotel [219 D4] (38 rooms) 7 High St; t 039 2916391; m 0772 487559; e acaciahotelmbarara@gmail.com. The centrepiece of this smart & reasonably central hotel is a small but wonderfully fussy garden that brings to mind the worst excesses of English suburbia. There's ample secure parking & an attractive, open-sided restaurant in the aforementioned garden serving grills, pasta, Indian & local dishes for around US$8. *From US$37/48 sgl/dbl B&B.* **$$**

Lake View Resort Hotel [219 A4] (80 rooms) t 048 5422112; m 0764 000356, 0753 374528; e info@lakeviewresorthotelmbarara.com; w lakeviewresorthotelmbarara.com. Mbarara's largest hotel lies in expansive green grounds set around a papyrus-lined manmade lake off the Fort Portal Rd, some 2km west of the town centre. It's a definite notch down from the Igongo Country Hotel (the only comparable option in the immediate vicinity of Mbarara; page 225) in terms of quality, but it's also substantially cheaper & more central, & facilities include spacious well-equipped rooms, swimming pool, gym & sauna. *From US$61/77/120 sgl/dbl/suite B&B*. **$$$**

✷ **Nyore Hillside Retreat** [map, page 98] (4 cottages) ⊕ -0.6805, 30.44176; m 0783 356142; e info@nyoreretreat.com; w nyoreretreat.com. Aimed more at people heading on to Kigezi than as a base for exploring Mbarara, this wonderful owner-managed lodge is set in a flowering hillside garden near the village of Nyakaguruka, 25km along the Kabale Rd. The bright stone-&-thatch en-suite cottages are individually decorated, & there is also a campsite with the option of hiring a tent. The restaurant, earthily decorated with stone, wood & cane, serves tasty grills, stews & salads in the US$6–7 range, & gives a commanding view of the surrounding steep terraced slopes, which offer plenty of walking possibilities & are teeming with birds & butterflies. The retreat lies 2km south of Nyakaguruka along a dirt road, & the junction (⊕ -0.66735, 30.44556) is clearly signposted. *US$56/96/153 sgl/dbl/family cottage B&B; camping US$10 per tent; US$10/14 to rent a sgl/dbl tent*. **$$$**

Budget

New Classic Hotel [219 B1] (22 rooms) High St; m 0772 666107; e newclassic@gmail.com. Centrally located & close to the main taxi park, this place has clean rooms with fans, nets, DSTV, Wi-Fi & en-suite hot tub/shower. *US$22/24 sgl/dbl B&B*. **$$**

Ruhanga Uganda Lodge [219 A3] (20 bandas) m 0701 536197, 0774 768090; e info@ugandalodge.com; w ugandalodge.com. Situated in Ruhanga, on the Kabale Rd 50km past Mbarara, this guesthouse operates as a social enterprise whose profits go towards helping the local community. It accommodates both passing visitors & long- or short-term volunteers in 1–4-bed bandas, all with bedding, nets, hot shower & electric power points. Meals are freshly cooked on a help-yourself basis. Set near the eastern limit of the Kigezi Highlands, the lodge offers plenty of scope to explore the surrounding hills & visit markets, lakes & hot springs. Volunteer accommodation & projects are available. *US$24 pp FB*. **$$**

University Inn [219 D4] (20 rooms) High St; ☎ 020 0917946. Built in 1933, this fabulously outmoded hotel is set in magnificent wooded grounds beyond the golf course & university. Recently reopened, the crumbly old rooms have been done up; there are tiled floors in the dbls & reasonable carpets in the sgls, & we can describe the rooms as 'en suite' without feeling slightly guilty. A simple garden restaurant stands in a leafy glade just downhill from the main building. Mains US$4. *US$17/26 sgl/dbl B&B*. **$–$$**

Shoestring

Tobiz Guesthouse [219 F1] (20 rooms) Masaka Rd; m 0782 872418. The spacious & well-equipped rooms at this well-priced multi-storey lodge all come with fans, DSTV & en-suite hot shower. *US$9/12 sgl/dbl*. **$**

WHERE TO EAT AND DRINK Several of the hotels recommended on page 221 have good restaurants, with the Acacia Hotel and Lake View Resort being the picks of the more central options. For those passing through Mbarara en route to Kabale, the out-of-town Nyore Hillside Retreat (see above) makes for a scenic lunch stop, but best call ahead with your order.

Numerous bars and *muchomo* (meat) joints come to life at night in the Rwebikona market area just up the Fort Portal Road. They serve cheap drinks and barbecue tilapia, pork, chicken and goat with matoke, cabbage and the like.

Ark Café [219 F4] Lower Circular Rd; ☎ 048 5443046; ⏲ 07.30–midnight daily. This excellent 1st-floor restaurant above the Golf Course Supermarket has a long & varied menu embracing salads, soups, burgers, pasta, grills, Indian dishes & several vegetarian selections. There's also free Wi-Fi, comfortable leather seating indoors, a terrace, excellent fresh coffee & ice cream, & a disco from 21.00 over w/ends. *Most mains in the US$6–8 range.*

Buffalo Resort [map, page 98] ⊕ -0.60241, 30.61855; ☎ 039 2829250; m 0777 188418; ⏱ 08.00–23.00 daily. Situated about 4km out of town on the main circle where the Kampala, Kasese & Kabale roads meet, this thatched restaurant set in pleasant gardens serves an excellent buffet lunch complete with soup & fruits. *US$5 pp.*

Café Havana [219 B1] High St; m 0779 494447; ⏱ 07.00–23.00 daily. Burgers, pizzas, salads, ice cream & Cuban coffee are the specialities at this efficient 1st-floor restaurant with terrace seating. *Mains in the US$6–9 range.*

Curry in a Hurry [219 A2] High St; ☎ 048 5420555; ⏱ 09.00–22.00 daily. Excellent Indian restaurant with plenty of choice for meat-eaters & vegetarians alike. *Mains in the US$5–7 range.*

Moonlight Restaurant [219 F2] High St; m 0701 891617; ⏱ 24/7. Popular & perennially busy local eatery with a central location, terrace seating, fresh juice & a good range of meals. *Mains in the US$3–4 range.*

ENTERTAINMENT AND NIGHTLIFE

Nicoz Lounge [219 B2] Bananuka Dr; m 0779 199022; f NicozLoungeMbarara. Smarter than it looks from the outside, this sports bar has large screens showing live football at w/ends & a nice terrace. The biggest attraction is live music starting at 20.00 on Wed & Sat night, when a US$3 entrance fee is charged & it's worth phoning ahead to reserve a table.

Vegas [219 E4] Lower Circular Rd; ⏱ 15.00–late. Set on the 2nd floor of the same building & under the same management as Ark Café (see above), this rooftop cocktail bar is an attractive sundowner spot that transforms into a pumping music venue late at night.

SHOPPING A lack of parking opportunities makes shopping in the busy town centre a frustrating experience. Less of a headache is the **Golf Course Supermarket** [219 E4] (Lower Circular Rd; m 0702 974729; ⏱ 24hrs daily). In the same building as Ark Café (see opposite), this place is very well stocked, especially when it comes to imported packaged goods, wines and spirits.

SPORTS AND ACTIVITIES Day visitors can use the swimming pool at the Lake View Resort Hotel (page 221) for a small fee.

WHAT TO SEE AND DO The main tourist attractions in the vicinity of Mbarara are the Igongo Cultural Centre and Lake Mburo National Park, both covered under separate headings within this chapter.

Nkokonjeru Tombs

[219 C1] The last two kings of Ankole, Omugabe Edward Solomon Kahaya II, who died in 1944, and Omugabe Sir Charles Godfrey Rutahaba Gasyonga II, who ruled from 1944 until 1967 and died in 1982, were buried at Nkokonjeru, 3km northwest of central Mbarara. Unfortunately, by comparison with the impressive and lovingly tended royal tombs at Kasubi and Mparo, Nkokonjeru is utterly anticlimactic: two bland concrete slabs protected within a rundown colonial-style tiled house. To get there, follow Ntare Road out of town for 1.5km, then just after it curves sharply to the left, take a right turn and continue for another 800m to a three-way junction whose central fork leads to the tomb after 500m.

Nshenyi Cultural Village

[219 C4] (m 0777 972915; w nshenyi.com; US$120/200 sgl/dbl FB, plus an additional US$50 per group for all activities) Situated on a traditional Ankole cattle farm about 60km south of Mbarara, this secluded cultural retreat lies in the Mirama Hills, close to the village of Kitwe, only

THE ANKOLE MONARCHY TODAY

The untended state of the Nkokonjeru Tombs is symptomatic of a popular ambivalence to the Ankole royalty that stretches back to the early years of independence. In 1967, the constitutional abolition of the monarchies under Obote was hotly protested in Buganda, Bunyoro and Toro. In Ankole, by contrast, the reaction was closer to muted indifference. In 1971, Idi Amin opened a short-lived debate with regard to reinstating all the ancient monarchies, a notion that garnered strong support in Buganda and elsewhere. Not so in Ankole, where a committee of elders signed a memorandum stating that the matter 'should not be raised or even discussed', since it would 'revive political divisions and factionalism' and stand in the way of the 'march forward to our stated goal of freedom and progress'.

The widespread anti-royalist sentiment in Ankole is so fundamentally at odds with popular attitudes in the other kingdoms of Uganda that it requires explanation. Two main factors can be cited. The first is that the traditional social structure of Ankole, like that of pre-colonial Rwanda but not of Buganda or Bunyoro, was informed by a rigid caste system. For the majority of Banyankole – who are of Bairu descent – reinstating the Bahima monarchy would smack of retrogression to that obsolete caste system. Secondly, Ankole, as it was delineated from the early colonial era until post-independence, was an artificial entity, one that encompassed several formerly independent kingdoms – Igara, Sheema, Bweju and parts of Mpororo – that had no prior historical affiliation or loyalty to the omugabe.

Ankole is the only one of the ancient Ugandan kingdoms that was not officially restored by Museveni in 1993. And although the recognised heir to the throne John Patrick Barigye was clandestinely crowned as Omugabe Ntare VI in November of that year, Museveni annulled the ceremony immediately afterwards. Following Barigye's death in October 2011, his 21-year-old son Charles Aryaija Rwebishengye was installed as Crown Prince of Ankole, and vowed to continue lobbying for the restoration of the kingdom, but it seems unlikely anything of the sort will happen in the foreseeable future.

10km from the borders with Rwanda and Tanzania. Accommodation ranges from a basic grass-thatched or clay-and-brick hut to a room in a modern farmhouse, and it also offers traditional meals. A wide range of activities encourage direct interaction with the local community; these include milking the long-horned Ankole cattle, joining the pastoralists as they graze the cattle, a market-day experience, nature walks and birdwatching in the undulating hills that overlook the Kagera River (the border with Tanzania), tribal encounters, visits to rock art and historical sites, traditional cooking and cultural singing and dancing.

IGONGO CULTURAL CENTRE

Set in neat gardens abutting the Masaka Road 15km northeast of Mbarara, this smart multi-faceted development has quickly become a popular lunch stop en route between sites further west and Kampala. The centre incorporates a modern and well-organised museum that achieves its goal of preserving and promoting the history and culture of the dormant Ankole kingdom with far greater success than any similar installation associated with Uganda's officially recognised kingdoms. Other facilities include the most upmarket hotel in the vicinity of Mbarara, as well as a good restaurant that serves a top-notch buffet lunch, a well-stocked craft and book shop, and clean toilets. Something of an annex to the centre is the Biharwe Eclipse Monument, which stands conspicuously on the opposite hill since being unveiled by President Museveni in August 2014.

GETTING THERE AND AWAY Prominently signposted, Igongo (⊕ -0.52183, 30.73998) stands on the north side of the Masaka Road in a village called Biharwe. For those without private transport, any matatu running east from Mbarara can drop you at the entrance, or you could take a boda.

WHERE TO STAY

Igongo Country Hotel (52 rooms) Igongo Cultural Centre; ☎ 039 2722828/9; e reservations@igongo.co.ug; w igongo.co.ug. Situated in Biharwe, 15km out of town along the Kampala Rd, this hotel in the Igongo Cultural Centre is as swanky as it comes in the vicinity of Mbarara. The ostentatious lobby, complete with instrumental muzak & AC, leads through to an attractively decorated restaurant, while the stylish rooms are split between the main building & a cluster of garden cottages. *From US$120/140 sgl/dbl B&B.* **$$$$**

WHERE TO EAT AND DRINK

Kaahwa Kanuzire Restaurant Igongo Cultural Centre; m 0705 867027, 0782 553564; w igongo.co.ug; ⌚ 10.00–23.00 daily. This smart garden restaurant is well known for its daily lunchtime buffet (⌚ noon–15.30), which is popular with tour groups. An à la carte menu of Ankole & continental dishes is available at other times. *Buffet US$11; main-menu dishes in the US$6–8 range.*

WHAT TO SEE AND DO

Igongo Museum (m 0704 629921; e museum@igongo.co.ug; w igongo.co.ug; ⌚ 07.00–20.00 daily; entry US$7/3 foreigners/East African residents) Arguably the finest museum anywhere in Uganda, Igongo houses a number of detailed and well-annotated displays covering everything from the development of currency in Uganda to traditional Ankole and Bakiga dress, drums and other musical instruments, agricultural practices and herbal medicine. There are also plenty of informative displays relating to the foundation and history of the Ankole and Bakiga kingdom and its rulers, and to the 18th-century warrior queen Kitami kya Nyawera, whose murder by a rival king presaged a series of local disasters and led to the establishment of the Nyabingi cult at her shrine in the vicinity of Lake Bunyonyi. All in all, it is a veritable treasure trove for those with the time and interest.

Biharwe Eclipse Monument (Make arrangements with the museum or the hotel at Igongo; US$4/3 foreigners/East African residents) This striking hilltop monument – comprising a golden orb supported by a trio of pillars representing the three kings of Bunyoro, Ankole and Buganda – commemorates a historic solar eclipse associated with the emergence of the Ankole kingdom. Oral history holds that the collapse of Bachwezi in the 15th century led to the formation of several smaller polities of which Bunyoro initially emerged as the most powerful. In the early 16th century, Omukama Olimi I of Bunyoro took advantage of his prowess by orchestrating a series of cattle raids that depopulated what are now Buganda and

Ankole of livestock, and led to a devastating famine. The tide of events turned when one day the sky fell ominously dark during daylight hours, prompting the terrified omukama to flee back to Bunyoro, leaving behind a large number of stolen cattle, from which the Ankole people were able to start breeding new herds. This incident is now regarded to be the only accurately datable event in the region's early history, since the ominous darkening of the sky witnessed by the omukama was almost certainly the solar eclipse of AD1520.

Part Three

EASTERN UGANDA

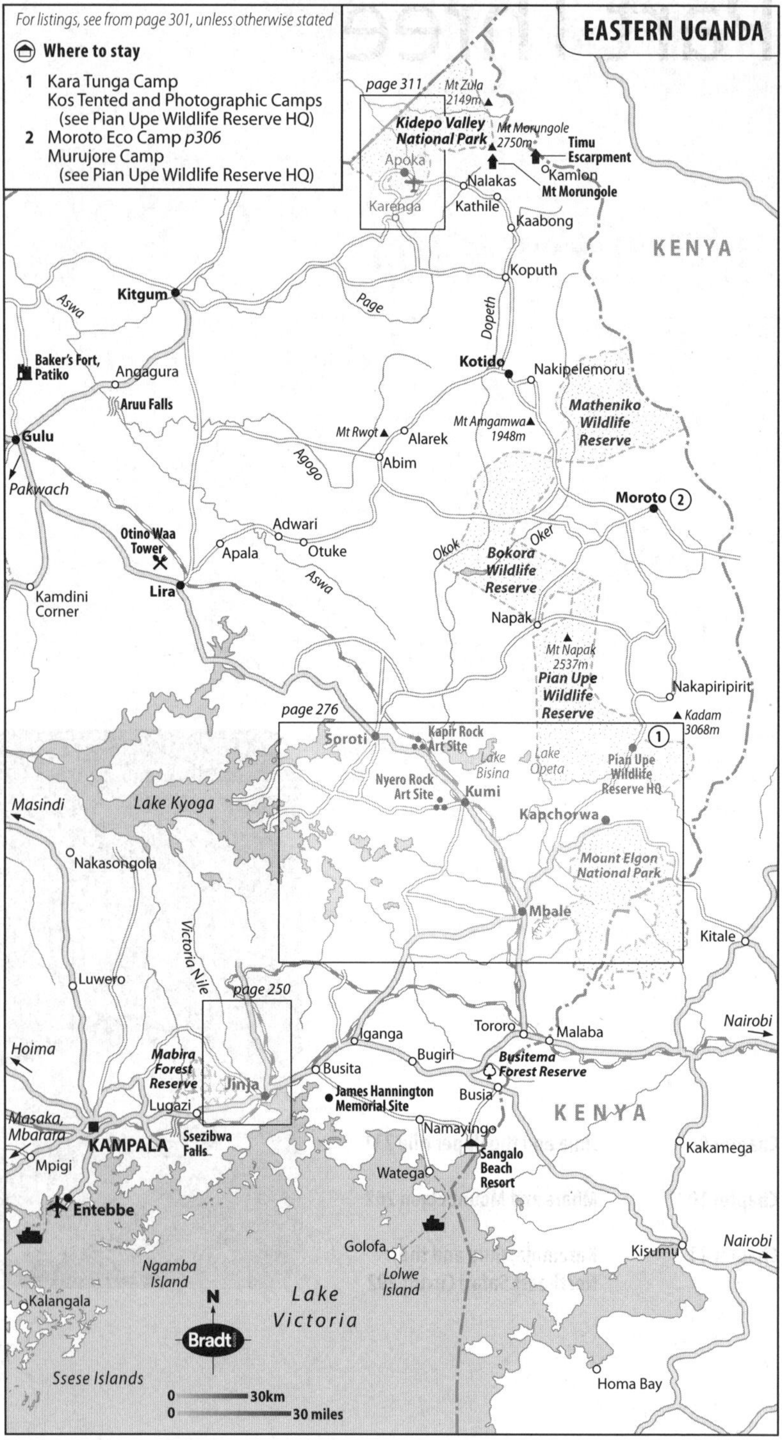
EASTERN UGANDA
For listings, see from page 301, unless otherwise stated
Where to stay
1 Kara Tunga Camp
Kos Tented and Photographic Camps
(see Pian Upe Wildlife Reserve HQ)
2 Moroto Eco Camp p306
Murujore Camp
(see Pian Upe Wildlife Reserve HQ)
page 311
Mt Zula 2149m
Kidepo Valley National Park
Mt Morungole 2750m
Timu Escarpment
Apoka
Kamion
Nalakas
Mt Morungole
Karenga
Kathile
Kaabong
KENYA
Koputh
Kitgum
Aswa
Page
Dopeth
Baker's Fort, Patiko
Angagura
Kotido
Nakipelemoru
Aruu Falls
Matheniko Wildlife Reserve
Mt Rwot
Alarek
Mt Amgamwa 1948m
Gulu
Agogo
Abim
Pakwach
Moroto
Adwari
Otino Waa Tower
Apala
Otuke
Okok
Oker
Bokora Wildlife Reserve
Aswa
Kamdini Corner
Lira
Napak
Mt Napak 2537m
Pian Upe Wildlife Reserve
Nakapiripirit
page 276
Kadam 3068m
Soroti
Kapir Rock Art Site
Lake Bisina
Lake Opeta
Pian Upe Wildlife Reserve HQ
Masindi
Lake Kyoga
Nyero Rock Art Site
Kumi
Kapchorwa
Nakasongola
Mount Elgon National Park
Mbale
Victoria Nile
Kitale
Luwero
page 250
Nairobi
Iganga
Tororo
Malaba
Hoima
Mabira Forest Reserve
Bugiri
Busitema Forest Reserve
Busita
Jinja
James Hannington Memorial Site
Busia
Lugazi
KENYA
Masaka, Mbarara
KAMPALA
Ssezibwa Falls
Namayingo
Sangalo Beach Resort
Mpigi
Kakamega
Watega
Entebbe
Nairobi
Golofa
Kisumu
Ngamba Island
Lolwe Island
Kalangala
Lake Victoria
Bradt
Ssese Islands
Homa Bay
0 30km
0 30 miles

OVERVIEW

Uganda's emerging eastern safari circuit may be under-publicised by comparison with its western counterparts, and lacks for opportunities to track gorillas or chimpanzees, but it offers plenty of chances for off-the-beaten-track exploration. Traditionally, the region's main draw is the white-water rafting and other adventure activities that can be undertaken along the White Nile a few kilometres north of Jinja, where the world's longest river starts its extensive journey from the island-studded expanse of Lake Victoria to the Mediterranean. Further east, immense Mount Elgon is an extinct volcano whose slopes are streaked with pretty waterfalls and offer plenty of hiking opportunities, while the drier, flatter expanses of Karamoja are home to the charismatic Karamojong people and the superb Kidepo Valley National Park, which is fast emerging as perhaps the country's top safari destination. This section of the book is divided into three chapters that respectively cover Jinja and the upper waters of the White Nile to its immediate north, the more remote and relatively little-visited Kenyan border region centred on Mbale, Mount Elgon and Lake Kyoga, and the vast untrammelled swathes of Karamoja and the far northeast.

HIGHLIGHTS

BUJAGALI AND KALAGALA Situated on the west and east banks of the Upper Nile, Bujagali and Kalagala exist to cater for devotees of Uganda's white-water rafting scene. Page 249.

KIDEPO VALLEY NATIONAL PARK Uganda's third-largest and most remote national park combines a spectacular submontane setting with plentiful wildlife, including elephant, lion and thousand-strong buffalo herds. Page 310.

SIPI FALLS Overlooked by a scattering of attractive lodges and backpackers, this 99m-high waterfall is the last in a series of three formed by the Sipi River as it cascades downhill from Mount Elgon into the Kyoga Basin. Page 284.

MOROTO The largest town in Uganda's remote 'Wild Northeast' is the best place to arrange day or overnight visits to a traditional Karamojong *manyatta* or *kraal*, as well as being the base for hikes up scenic Mount Moroto. Page 303.

MOUNT ELGON NATIONAL PARK Towering to a lofty 4,321m, this massive extinct volcano, topped by an immense collapsed caldera, is a hiker's paradise and far more budget-friendly than East Africa's other major mountains. Page 273.

NYERO ROCK PAINTINGS Uganda's finest prehistoric rock-art site was painted by unknown hunter-gatherers many hundreds – possibly thousands – of years ago. Page 295.

JINJA Though it's no longer the second-largest town in Uganda, sleepy but well-equipped Jinja retains a historic architectural flavour befitting its geographically poignant location overlooking the White Nile as it exits Lake Victoria. Page 231.

NAKIPELEMORU This sprawling Karamojong *manyatta* near Kotido is reputedly the largest traditional settlement in East Africa, supporting a population of around 10,000. Page 308.

GULU A bustling hub of economic activity, northern Uganda's largest town is also notable for its friendly vibe and surprisingly cosmopolitan amenities. Page 321.

PIAN UPE WILDLIFE RESERVE One to watch, this 2,788km^2 tract of semi-arid country is Uganda's second-largest protected area, and while its potential as a safari destination is largely unrealised, it is earmarked for an upgrade to national park status and associated tourist development. Page 300.

9

Jinja and the Upper Nile

Set on the northern shore of Lake Victoria 80km east of Kampala, Jinja is a large and historic town whose main claim to fame is as the source of the Nile: the place where the world's longest river exits Africa's largest lake to commence an epic 6,500km journey to the Mediterranean via the deserts of Sudan and Egypt. It was here, back in 1862, that the explorer John Speke recognised Ripon Falls to be the geographic holy grail that had lured the obsessed, and hopelessly misdirected, David Livingstone to a feverish death near Lake Bangweulu (in present-day Zambia) less than a decade earlier. These days, however, the Upper Nile's main touristic draw is not so much Jinja's poignant location as its status as East Africa's main adventure tourism capital. For some years now, white-water rafting on the rapids upriver of Jinja has vied with gorilla tracking as Uganda's most popular tourist activity. Although the construction of a series of hydro-power dams since 2010 has submerged several of the best rapids, this stretch of the Nile remains a great rafting centre, with several exciting Grade V rapids on offer. Other activities along the Upper Nile include kayaking, motorboat trips, bungee-jumping, horseback safaris and quad-biking.

JINJA

Uganda's second-largest settlement for most of the 20th century, Jinja (sometimes referred to in Lusoga as 'Idindha') occupies a lush wide peninsula flanked by Lake Victoria to the south and east, and the Nile and now-submerged Ripon Falls to the west. In colonial times and the early years of independence, Jinja was the industrial heart of Uganda, but its economy collapsed during the Amin years, and has never quite recovered. The town's years of economic torpor are reflected in what must surely be the tardiest population growth rate of any major town in East Africa. In 1991, Jinja was still Uganda's second-largest town, according to a census that recorded its population as 65,000. By the time of the 2014 census, however, it had dropped to 14th – a place behind the once-insignificant village of Njeru directly across the river – with a population of 73,000.

Partly as a result of this slow growth, Jinja retains the spacious and attractive layout of its colonial-era incarnation, and its roads are lined with some fine Asian architecture, giving it a sense of place that is further enhanced by the spread of thickly vegetated residential suburbs carved from the jungle between the town centre and the lake and river. Tourism is big business, though the main focal point of rafting and other adventure activities is further upriver at Bujagali, and most of Jinja's hotels cater primarily to the conference market. A significant contributor to the local economy is the plethora of NGO workers, volunteers and missionaries who can be seen lunching in the unexpected glut of deli- and bistro-style eateries that dot the old town centre.

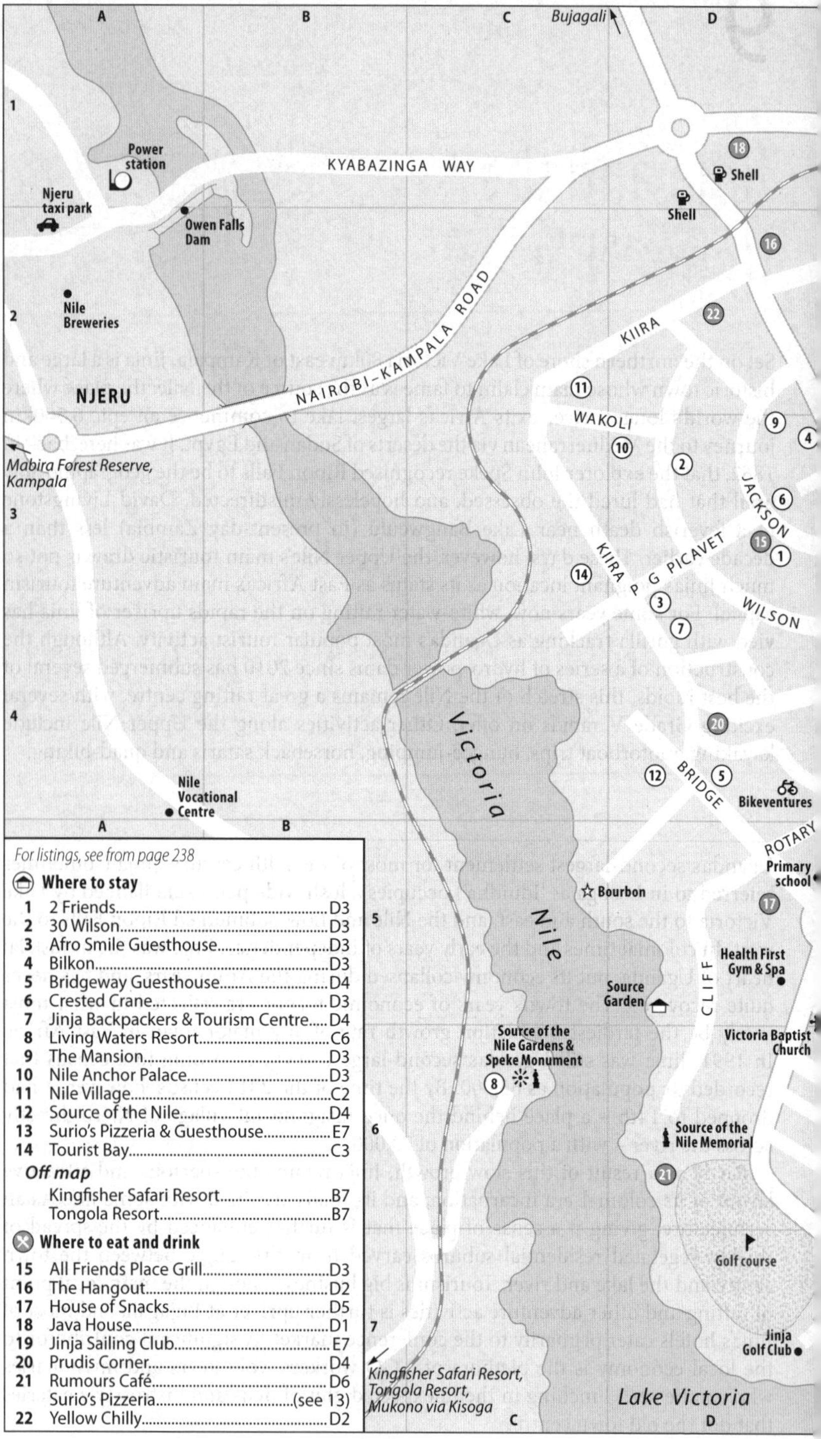
A
B
C
D
1
2
3
4
5
6
7
Bujagali
Power station
Njeru taxi park
Owen Falls Dam
KYABAZINGA WAY
Shell
Shell
Nile Breweries
NAIROBI–KAMPALA ROAD
KIIRA
WAKOLI
JACKSON
KIIRA
P G PICAVET
WILSON
NJERU
Mabira Forest Reserve, Kampala
Victoria
Nile
BRIDGE
Bikeventures
ROTARY
Primary school
Nile Vocational Centre
Bourbon
Health First Gym & Spa
CLIFF
Source Garden
Victoria Baptist Church
Source of the Nile Gardens & Speke Monument
Source of the Nile Memorial
Golf course
Jinja Golf Club
Kingfisher Safari Resort, Tongola Resort, Mukono via Kisoga
Lake Victoria
For listings, see from page 238
Where to stay
1 2 Friends D3
2 30 Wilson D3
3 Afro Smile Guesthouse D3
4 Bilkon D3
5 Bridgeway Guesthouse D4
6 Crested Crane D3
7 Jinja Backpackers & Tourism Centre D4
8 Living Waters Resort C6
9 The Mansion D3
10 Nile Anchor Palace D3
11 Nile Village C2
12 Source of the Nile D4
13 Surio's Pizzeria & Guesthouse E7
14 Tourist Bay C3
Off map
Kingfisher Safari Resort B7
Tongola Resort B7
Where to eat and drink
15 All Friends Place Grill D3
16 The Hangout D2
17 House of Snacks D5
18 Java House D1
19 Jinja Sailing Club E7
20 Prudis Corner D4
21 Rumours Café D6
Surio's Pizzeria (see 13)
22 Yellow Chilly D2

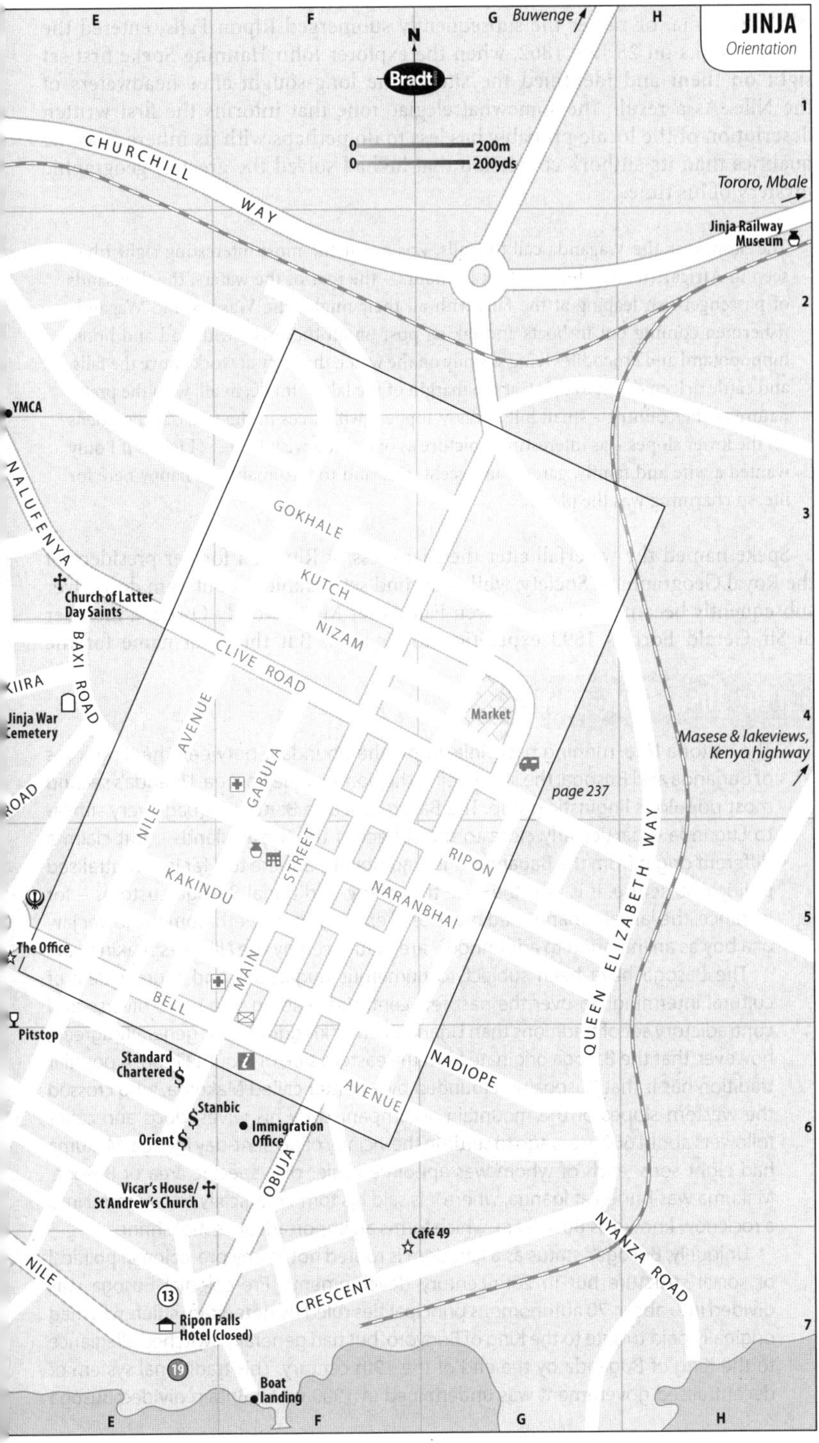
JINJA
Orientation
N
Bradt
0 200m
0 200yds
Buwenge
Tororo, Mbale
Jinja Railway Museum
CHURCHILL WAY
YMCA
NALUFENYA
Church of Latter Day Saints
BAXI ROAD
KIIRA
Jinja War Cemetery
ROAD
GOKHALE
KUTCH
NIZAM
CLIVE ROAD
Market
Masese & lakeviews, Kenya highway
page 237
AVENUE
GABULA
NILE
STREET
RIPON
KAKINDU
NARANBHAI
QUEEN ELIZABETH WAY
The Office
MAIN
BELL
Pitstop
Standard Chartered
NADIOPE
AVENUE
Stanbic
Immigration Office
Orient
OBUJA
Vicar's House/ St Andrew's Church
NYANZA ROAD
Café 49
NILE
CRESCENT
13
Ripon Falls Hotel (closed)
19
Boat landing
E F G H
1 2 3 4 5 6 7

HISTORY Jinja, or rather the subsequently submerged Ripon Falls, entered the history books on 28 July 1862, when the explorer John Hanning Speke first set sight on them and identified the site as the long-sought-after headwaters of the Nile. As a result, the somewhat elegiac tone that informs the first written description of the locale probably has less to do perhaps with its inherent scenic qualities than its author's conviction that he had solved the greatest geographic mystery of his time:

> The 'stones', as the Waganda call the falls, was by far the most interesting sight I had seen in Africa…It attracted one to it for hours – the roar of the waters, the thousands of passenger-fish leaping at the falls with all their might; the Wasoga and Waganda fishermen coming out in boats and taking post on all the rocks with rod and hook, hippopotami and crocodiles lying sleepily on the water, the ferry at work above the falls, and cattle driven down to drink at the margin of the lake – made, in all, with the pretty nature of the country – small hills, grassy-topped, with trees in the folds, and gardens on the lower slopes – as interesting a picture as one could wish to see…I felt as if I only wanted a wife and family, garden and yacht, rifle and rod, to make me happy here for life, so charming was the place.

Speke named the waterfall after the Marquess of Ripon, a former president of the Royal Geographical Society, while a second set of rapids about 1km downriver subsequently became known as Owen Falls, after Major Roddy Owen, a member of Sir Gerald Portal's 1893 expedition to Uganda. But the local name for the

THE BUSOGA KINGDOM

The Victoria Nile, running past Jinja, forms the boundary between the Kingdoms of Buganda and Busoga, the latter being the home of the Basoga, Uganda's second most populous linguistic group. The Basoga speak a Bantu language very similar to Luganda – particularly close to the dialect of the Ssese Islands – but claim a different origin from the Baganda, and traditionally adhere to a far less centralised political structure. It is also the case that many traditional Basoga customs – for instance, the largely abandoned practice of extracting six teeth from the lower jaw of a boy as an initiation to adulthood – are influenced by the Nilotic-speaking Luo.

The Basoga have been subject to numerous migrations and a great deal of cultural intermingling over the past few centuries, leading to a more diverse and contradictory set of traditions than Uganda's other kingdoms. It is generally agreed, however, that the Basoga originate from the eastern side of Mount Elgon. A popular tradition has it that Busoga was founded by a hunter called Makuma, who crossed the western slopes of the mountain accompanied by his wives, dogs and other followers about 600 years ago to settle in the vicinity of present-day Iganga. Makuma had eight sons, each of whom was appointed ruler of a specific area of Busoga. Makuma was buried at Iganga, where it is said his tomb magically transformed into a rock now known as Buswikara, which forms an important ancestral shrine.

Uniquely, Busoga's status as a kingdom is rooted not in any pre-colonial political or social structure but in 20th-century developments. Pre-colonial Busoga was divided into about 70 autonomous principalities ruled by hereditary chiefs who had originally paid tribute to the King of Bunyoro, but had generally switched allegiance to the King of Buganda by the end of the 19th century. This traditional system of decentralised government was undermined in 1900 when Britain divided Busoga

site has survived, too, since Jinja is a corruption of Ejjinja (Stones), the original Luganda name for the Ripon Falls, as well as for a nearby village and associated sacrificial stone.

An informal European settlement was founded at Jinja in 1900, when the rocky waterfall was selected as the most suitable place for the telegraph line to Kampala to cross the Nile. At this time, the administrative centre for Busoga was at Iganga, regarded by Governor Sir Harry Johnston to be 'not a very healthy place, and, so to speak, "nowhere"'. In 1901, however, Johnston relocated the headquarters to Jinja, with its 'aggregation of European settlers' at the head of a potentially important riverine transport route north along the Nile and Lake Kyoga.

Jinja's rapid emergence as a pivotal commercial centre and international transport hub was further cemented by the completion of the railway line from Mombasa to the lake port of Kisumu, and the introduction of a connecting ferry service. The local economy was further boosted by the successful introduction of cotton as a cash crop for export, and by the construction of a railway line north to Namasagali in 1912. Even so, Sir Frederick Treves, writing in 1913, dismissed Jinja as 'a little tin town…a rough settlement of some size [but] purely utilitarian and without the least ambition to be beautiful'. Jinja's importance as a port undoubtedly diminished after the late 1920s, when the railway line was extended to Kampala, but by this time the town was firmly established as an administrative and retail centre servicing the local cotton industry.

Instrumental in Jinja's post-World War II emergence as Uganda's major industrial and manufacturing centre was the construction of a dam and an associated

into 14 larger principalities for administrative and tax purposes. It was shattered entirely six years later, when Busoga was amalgamated into one cohesive political entity, modelled on Buganda, and administered by a Muganda 'president', Semei Kakungulu. The office occupied by Kakungulu was abandoned after his retirement in 1913, but the traditional leaders of Basoga put pressure on the British authorities for it to be reinstated – and awarded to a prominent Musoga.

In 1919, Britain created the title of *kyabazinga*, transforming Busoga into a centralised monarchy that enjoyed a similar status within the Uganda Protectorate to the ancient kingdoms of Bunyoro or Buganda. Ezekieri Wako Zibondo was crowned as the first kyabazinga, to be succeeded by Sir Wilberforce Nadiope II, whose active rule was terminated when Obote abolished the traditional kingdoms of Uganda in 1967. In 1996, when the kingdoms were reinstated, Henry Wako Muloki – the son of the first kyabazinga – was installed on the throne. Today, the kyabazinga is regarded as the overall leader of Basoga, but he is supported by a parliament of 11 semi-autonomous hereditary Saza chiefs. Five of these chiefs claim accession from Makuma, the founder of Busoga, and the kyabazinga is picked from one of these elite families using a system of rotating accession, to be succeeded only upon death, abdication or serious illness. Muloki ruled until his death in 2008. Perhaps not surprisingly, given the vague process set out for succession, the clans of Busoga took several years to identify an heir acceptable to all. The six-year deadlock was broken only in September 2014 when 26-year-old William Gabula Nadiope IV – the grandson of Sir Wilberforce Nadiope II – was instated as the fourth Kyabazinga of Busoga at a ceremony attended by President Museveni.

hydro-electric plant at Owen Falls. As early as 1904, the Uganda Company had mooted erecting 'an electric generating station to be worked by waterpower from the Ripon Falls'. Winston Churchill, who visited the falls three years later, supported this notion enthusiastically: 'So much power running to waste, such a coign of vantage unoccupied, such a lever to control the natural forces of Africa ungripped, cannot but vex and stimulate imagination. And what fun to make the immemorial Nile begin its journey by driving through a turbine!'

Only in 1946, however, did the colonial administration look seriously at damming the lower Nile, initially as part of a proposed Equatorial Nile Project that involved Egypt, Sudan, Uganda and other indirectly affected nations. The broad idea behind this scheme was that Egypt would fund the construction of a large dam at the outlet of each of the two largest lakes along the Nile's course: Victoria and Albert. The advantage to Uganda was that the dams could be harnessed as a reliable source of hydro-electric power, not only for domestic use, but also to sell to neighbouring Kenya. At the same time, the dams would transform the lakes into vast semi-artificial reservoirs from where the flow of the Nile downriver to Sudan and Egypt could be regulated to prevent the sporadic flooding and droughts that had long been associated with annual fluctuations in the river's water level.

Protracted and often acrimonious negotiations between the various governments over the next two years eventually broke down as both Uganda and to a lesser extent Kenya objected to the significant loss of land that would result from the construction of the proposed dams. In 1949, Egypt reluctantly signed a treaty allowing Uganda to build a hydro-electric plant at Owen Falls, provided that it did not significantly disrupt the natural flow of the river and that an Egyptian engineer would regulate the water flow through the dam. The Owen Falls Dam cost £7 million to construct, and was officially opened by Queen Elizabeth II on her 1954 visit to Uganda and Kenya.

Jinja's proximity to this reliable source of cheap electricity proved attractive to industry, and several textile and other manufacturing plants, including the country's major cigarette factory and brewery, were established. For two decades, the local economy boomed. The modern town centre – one of the few in East Africa to display much indication of considered urban planning – essentially dates to the early 1950s, when the population increased from 8,500 to more than 20,000 in the space of three years. This included a settler community of 800 Europeans and 5,000 Asians, reflected today in the ornate Indian façades of the town centre, as well as the sprawling double-storey mansions that languish in the suburbs. Other relics of this period are the impressive town hall and administrative buildings at the southern end of the town centre.

Jinja's fortunes slumped again following the expulsion of Asians from Uganda in 1972. Most of the town's leading industries had been under Asian management, and the cohorts of Amin who were installed in their place generally lacked any appropriate business experience or managerial skill, resulting in a total breakdown in the local economy. In the early 1990s, the town centre's boarded-up shops and deeply pot-holed roads epitomised a more general aura of lethargy and economic torpor. Today, however, while Jinja remains somewhat sleepy in comparison with Kampala, the freshly painted shopfronts that line the town centre's sporadically tarred roads seem emblematic of its urban rejuvenation, as do the once-rundown suburban mansions that have been restored as private houses or hotels. In terms of population, Jinja has seen a remarkable resurgence. Though its 65,000 residents earned it second place in the 1991 census, a modest increase to 73,000 in 2014 saw it drop to 14th in the rankings. It was something of a surprise therefore in 2024 when

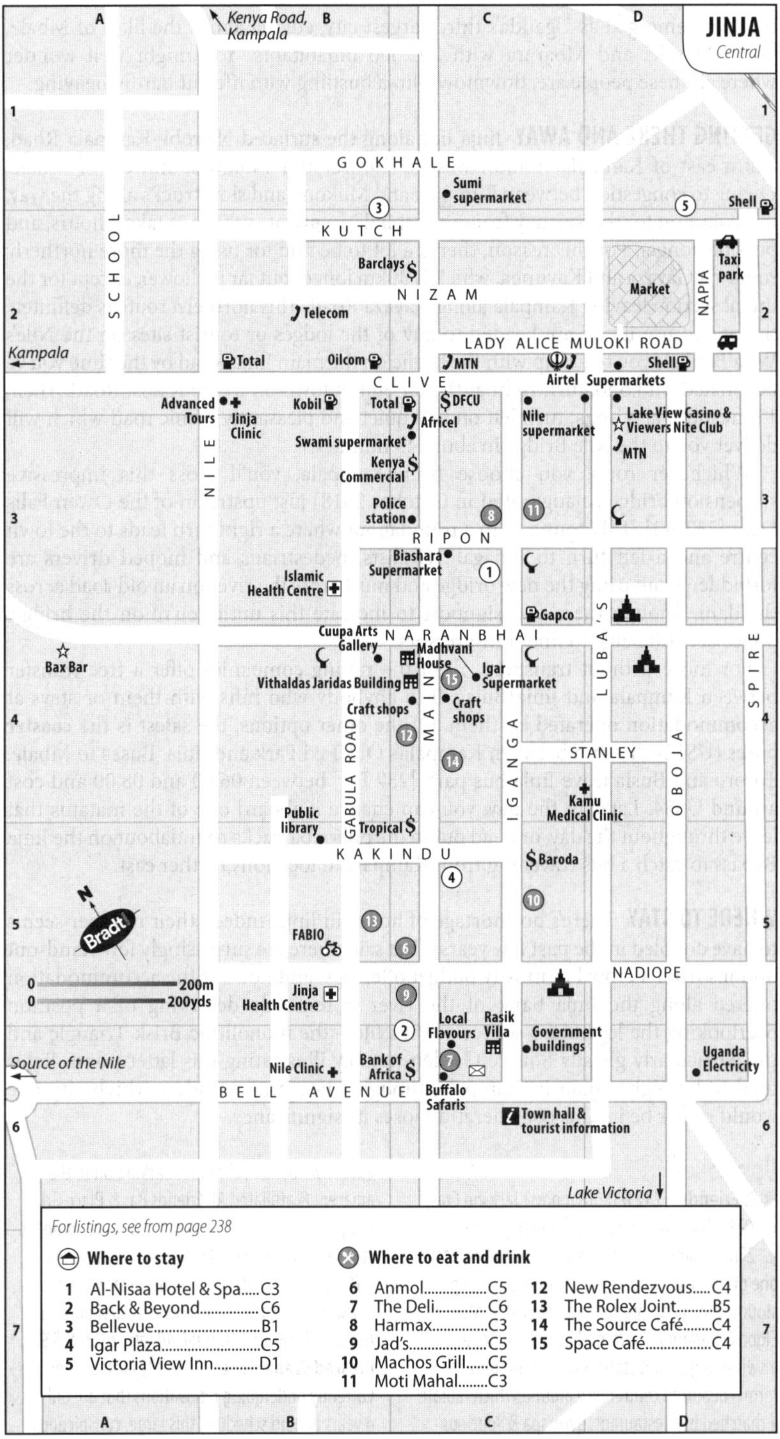
JINJA
Central
Kenya Road, Kampala
Kampala
Source of the Nile
Lake Victoria
GOKHALE
KUTCH
NIZAM
LADY ALICE MULOKI ROAD
CLIVE
RIPON
NARANBHAI
STANLEY
KAKINDU
NADIOPE
BELL AVENUE
SCHOOL
NILE
GABULA ROAD
MAIN
IGANGA
LUBA'S
OBOJA
SPIRE
NAPIA
Sumi supermarket
Shell
Taxi park
Market
Barclays
Telecom
Total
Oilcom
MTN
Airtel
Supermarkets
Advanced Tours
Jinja Clinic
Kobil
Africel
DFCU
Nile supermarket
Lake View Casino & Viewers Nite Club
Swami supermarket
Kenya Commercial
Police station
Biashara Supermarket
Islamic Health Centre
Gapco
Cuupa Arts Gallery
Madhvani House
Igar Supermarket
Bax Bar
Vithaldas Jaridas Building
Craft shops
Kamu Medical Clinic
Public library
Tropical
Baroda
FABIO
Jinja Health Centre
Local Flavours
Rasik Villa
Government buildings
Uganda Electricity
Nile Clinic
Bank of Africa
Buffalo Safaris
Town hall & tourist information
200m
200yds
Bradt
For listings, see from page 238
Where to stay
1 Al-Nisaa Hotel & Spa.....C3
2 Back & Beyond................C6
3 Bellevue.............................B1
4 Igar Plaza..........................C5
5 Victoria View Inn............D1
Where to eat and drink
6 Anmol.................C5
7 The Deli.............C6
8 Harmax...............C3
9 Jad's....................C5
10 Machos Grill......C5
11 Moti Mahal........C3
12 New Rendezvous.....C4
13 The Rolex Joint..........B5
14 The Source Café........C4
15 Space Café.................C4

the town emerged as Uganda's third-largest city, edging above the likes of Mbale, Gulu, Masaka and Mbarara with 292,000 inhabitants. You might well wonder where all these people are, downtown Jinja bustling with life but hardly heaving.

GETTING THERE AND AWAY Jinja lies along the surfaced Nairobi–Kampala Road, 82km east of Kampala, 130km west of Tororo, and 145km southwest of Mbale. Owing to congestion between Kampala and Mukono and slow trucks along the way, it is common for the journey from the capital in a **private vehicle** to take 3 hours, and possibly longer. For this reason, there's a lot to be said for using the more northerly route via Gayaza and Kayunga, which is 30km longer but far mellower, except for the initial section leaving Kampala along Gayaza Road. This northern route is definitely the one to use if you are headed to any of the lodges or tourist sites on the Nile's West Bank. If you're fed up with the traffic on the main Jinja Road by the time you've negotiated Mukono, turn right at the far end of town on to the Katosi Road. Then, 15km south at Kisoga, turn left on to a quiet and pleasantly scenic road which will deliver you to the Nile Bridge in about 45 minutes.

Whichever route you choose from Kampala, you'll cross this impressive suspension bridge (inaugurated in October 2018) just upstream of the Owen Falls Dam [232 A2]. This connects to a roundabout where a right turn leads to the town centre and a left turn to Bujagali. Cyclists, pedestrians and moped drivers are forbidden from using the new bridge and must cross the river on an old road across the dam. Though there's no signpost to indicate this until you're on the bridge, police are still liable to fine transgressors.

For those without transport, all of the rafting companies offer a free transfer between Kampala and Jinja/Bujagali to anybody who rafts with them or stays at accommodation operated by them. Of the other options, the safest is the **coaster buses** (US$2) that run between Kampala's Old Taxi Park and Jinja. Buses to Mbale, Tororo and Busia leave Jinja bus park [237 D2] between 06.00 and 08.00 and cost around US$4. Later in the day, you can chance it aboard one of the matatus that leave throughout the day, or head out to the police barracks roundabout on the Jinja Bypass to catch a bus travelling from Kampala to locations further east.

WHERE TO STAY There's no shortage of hotels in Jinja, indeed their number seems to have doubled in the past few years. That said, there are surprisingly few stand-out options from a crowd of mostly budget offerings, and none of the accommodation offered along the Jinja bank of the river is remotely deserving of a position overlooking the legendary source of the Nile – the monolithic Brisk Triangle and the particularly ghastly Source Garden notably illustrating this latter point. Rates tend to be higher than in Kampala, though when one considers which city one would rather be in, this consideration loses its significance.

Upmarket

✱ **2 Friends** [232 D3] (18 rooms) Jackson Cres; m 0783 160804; e post@2FriendsJinja.com; w 2FriendsJinja.com. Jinja's only boutique hotel & one of its most characterful, 2 Friends is a popular stopover for safari groups headed east to Mount Elgon & Karamoja. Softened by tropical foliage, a swimming pool & stone-flagged sun terrace form a beautiful centrepiece around which radiate a thatched bar-restaurant, gym/spa & spacious executive rooms. Off centre, backing on to the adjacent & affiliated All Friends Bar & Place Grill (page 242), is a block of cheaper & more compact standard rooms. *US$143/162 sgl/dbl poolside; US$112/130 sgl/dbl std. 2 rooms upstairs in main house with kitchen, small private pool & barbecue terrace US$180/210 sgl/dbl. All rates B&B.* **$$$**

Crested Crane Hotel [232 D3] Jackson Cres. Currently undergoing renovations that are only 4 years behind schedule, this large, conspicuous former government hotel will eventually reopen as a Tourism & Hotel Training Institute: a meticulously planned & architecturally innovative centre of excellence charged with moulding & showcasing the prodigious talents of an up & coming generation. Other than this sarcasm has to stop, more we cannot say at present.

The Mansion [232 D3] (21 rooms) Jackson Cres; m 0773 286445; e info@themansionjinja.com; w themansionjinja.com. A decades-overdue makeover at the former Timton Hotel has been at the expense of the period charm & the large green garden – now mostly car park or monoblock/lawn. Still, there's now a swimming pool, & rooms in a modern extension are a definite improvement on the previous crumbling colonial-era suites. *US$66/94 sgl/dbl B&B; suites from US$120.* **$$$**

Nile Village Hotel [232 C2] (42 rooms) Kiira Rd; ☎ 043 4120879; m 0773 826420; e reservations@nilevillagehotel.com; w nilevillagehotel.com. Though walled in & lacking any sort of view, this is still the most agreeable of Jinja's larger hotels by a country mile. A smart, service-oriented facility, it is notable for its fast maturing garden with a great swimming pool area & lovely terrace restaurant serving Thai, Indian & continental dishes for US$8–11. The reasonably priced rooms start at *US$100/120 sgl/dbl B&B.* **$$$**

✷ **Surjio's Pizzeria & Guesthouse** [233 E7] (23 rooms) Kisinja Rd; m 0772 500400; e bookings@surjios.com; w surjios.com. This renovated colonial house is set in lush gardens centred on a sparkling swimming pool. Despite being a block back from Nile Crescent, it's the closest thing in Jinja to an attractive waterfront hotel, though the Nile view – from the veranda or a communal balcony accessed through the bedrooms – is inevitably far from panoramic. An excellent pizzeria is attached. *US$85/130/160 sgl/dbl/trpl B&B.* **$$$**

Moderate

Afro Smile Guesthouse [232 D3] (11 rooms) Kiira Rd; m 0754 476666; e afrosmilehotel@gmail.com. This Indian-owned & -managed guesthouse in quiet Nalufenya suburb is set in serene leafy gardens with a swimming pool & terrace bar/restaurant. *US$55/65 sgl/dbl indoor room without terrace; US$75 poolside room; US$110 for family room sleeping 4. All rates B&B.* **$$**

Igar Plaza Hotel [237 C5] (38 rooms) Main St; ☎ 048 5660682; e info@igarplazahotel.com; w igarplazahotel.com. The smartest hotel in the city centre is a blue-glass 7-storey high-rise in which smart modern rooms, accessed by a lift, lack for character but are decent value. The excellent ground floor café (known for its w/end buffet: US$7) is a comfortable place to wonder how this garish structure, which includes a well-stocked supermarket & underground parking, was allowed to intrude into Jinja's architecturally historic Main St. The probable truth, of course, is that this is just the beginning. *US$61/66/71 sgl/dbl/twin B& – an exceptional buffet – B.* **$$**

Source of the Nile Hotel [232 D4] (44 rooms) Bridge St; ☎ 039 3249292; m 0709 711587; e sourceofthenilehotel@gmail.com; w sourceofthenilehotel.ug. Set in large grounds, this well-managed but unmemorable hotel is the best of the mid-range hotels perched on the east bank of the Nile in Jinja. Having named itself after a landmark that Sir Harry Johnston called 'the greatest geographical secret after the discovery of America', management has belatedly decided to enable guests to have a proper look at it. To this end, a large & fine-looking annex with pool, bar/restaurant & river view terrace is under construction, its pitched roof offering a jaunty contrast to the main hotel's sober, box-like outline. If only the whole complex had been similarly thought out. *From US$80/100 sgl/dbl B&B.* **$$$**

Budget

✷ **30 Wilson** [232 D3] (3 cottages, 4 dbl rooms, 2 dorms) Wilson Rd; m 0781 887082; e 30wilsonventures@gmail.com; w thirtywilson.com. The most appealing of Jinja's budget listings, 30 Wilson owes much of its charm to a shady garden setting with some mature trees, a large thatched bar/restaurant with an excellent menu & a stone-flagged swimming pool. Accommodation is carved out from original buildings on site with, hopefully, something for everyone. *3 bedroom cottage with lounge & kitchen US$130 (US$40–50 individual rooms); dbl rooms with small sitting room US$34–40 sgl/dbl; dorms US$15 pp. All rates B&B.* **$$**

Al-Nisaa Hotel & Spa [237 C3] (12 rooms) Iganga Rd; m 0780 897119; e info@alnisaahotelandspa.com; w alnisaahotelandspa.com. This smart, central hotel comprises a colonial-style building with a wide terrace (with an evening pavement barbecue) plus a good restaurant inside (no alcohol served) & a spa. Good value. *From US$37/43 sgl/dbl B&B.* **$$**

Bilkon Hotel [232 D3] (37 rooms) Nalufenya Rd; m 0702 504452, 0782 154236; e bilkonhotel@gmail.com. Marred only by the noise from the main road running past, this characterless but friendly multi-storey hotel offers reasonably priced en-suite rooms with fitted nets, DSTV, fans, private balcony & hot water. *US$21/24/32 sgl/dbl/twin; US$32/54 dbl/twin B&B.* **$$**

Bridgeway Guesthouse [232 D4] (11 rooms) Bridge Rd; m 0772 480142; e bridgewayguesthouse@yahoo.com. This friendly 2-storey house set in quiet suburban gardens has the feel of a B&B & the neat & variously priced rooms should have something to match your requirements. *US$16/37/43/43 small sgl/sgl/dbl/twin B&B.* **$$**

Jinja Backpackers & Tourism Centre [232 D4] (3 rooms, 6 eco tents, 5 dorms) Kira Rd; m 0763 287604; e info@jinjabackpackers.net; w jinjabackpackers.net. After many challenges to Jinja's mantle as Uganda's favourite backpacker haunt, this excellent setup on Kira Rd has emerged to keep the flag flying. The creation of Nash Karanja, a youthful employee of Nile River Explorers during its heyday (& whose greying beard testifies to the years that have passed since), the facility occupies a large garden site with a converted townhouse & bolt-on thatched bar/restaurant serving pizzas, grills etc (mains US$8). Accommodation is offered in an assortment of rooms, dorms & half a dozen yurt-like things at the back of the large garden. As the new, go-to place for backpackers in Jinja, this is as much a centre for things to do as a place to sleep. All the usual adrenalin activities (page 251) can be arranged here, as well as short & extended mountain-bike trips, overland truck safaris to the national parks & walking tours of Jinja. *US$60 dbl room en suite; US$45/60 dbl/twin shared bathroom; US$70/85 dbl/trpl en-suite eco tents; dorms US$15 pp. All B&B. Camping US$7 exc b/fast.* **$$**

Nile Anchor Palace [232 D3] (24 rooms) Wakoli Rd; m 0754 575005; e nileanchorpalace@yahoo.com; w nileanchorpalace.com. Set in secure palm-shaded suburban gardens, this renovated & expanded 3-storey hotel has comfortable & acceptably priced rooms behind a reception/dining area unaffected by recent improvements. *US$40/45 sgl/dbl B&B.* **$$**

Tourist Bay [232 C3] (39 rooms) Nile Cres; m 0784 858026. As a place to simply lay down your head & sleep, the small rooms in this no-frills hotel are far & away the best value in the exclusive Nalufenya suburb. If, however, your daily calisthenics app is pinging for attention, your room will allow space to swipe it open but little more. *From US$25/28 sgl/dbl B&B.* **$$**

Shoestring

Back & Beyond [237 C6] (30 rooms) Kutch Rd; m 0701 944806. This centrally located lodging house offers decent en-suite rooms at the southern end of Main St, temptingly close to the Anmol curry house, the Deli & Jad's shawarma parlour. On-street parking only. *US$13 sgl exc b/fast.* **$**

Bellevue Hotel [237 B1] (38 rooms) Kutch Rd; m 0708 578134; e info@bellevue.ug. This long-standing & well-priced favourite lies on the slightly smarter side of Main St, 5mins' walk from the bus & taxi parks. Rooms are clean & facilities include a restaurant, bar & lounge with DSTV & pool table. *US$8 sgl with common showers; US$13/20 en-suite sgl/dbl exc b/fast.* **$**

Victoria View Inn [237 D1] (30 rooms) Kutch Rd; m 0704 130947. Although the implied outlook is restricted to the rooftop laundry area, this venerable high-rise is the closest hotel to the taxi park & the en-suite tiled rooms with cold shower are decent value following renovations in 2018. *US$13/19 en-suite sgl/dbl; US$8 sgl shared bathrooms.* **$**

Dorms and camping

See Jinja Backpackers & 30 Wilson on page 239.

Njeru and the West Bank

The following facilities are located west of Jinja on the Njeru side of the Nile. All are accessible by vehicle or by chartering a boat from the landing beside the Jinja Sailing Club.

Kingfisher Safari Resort [232 B7] m 0772 632063, 0752 080987; e jinja@kingfisher-hotels.com; w kingfisher-hotels.com. Located beside the lake at the southern end of Njeru, this popular camp centres on 3 connected swimming pools of perennial appeal to missionaries & others blessed with large families. Those seeking quiet & more private communion will appreciate the verdant tropical gardens that extend down to the water, where a super lake view opens up. Boat trips can be arranged; day visitors can pay US$3 to use the pool. Accommodation is in pleasant thatched rondavels. *US$60/70–80 sgl/dbl B&B; camping US$15 exc b/fast.* **$$**

Living Waters Resort [232 C6] (10 units) m 0706 283822; e info@sourceofthenile.org; w sourceofthenile.org. Situated on the West Bank of the Nile, directly opposite Jinja, this attractive small lodge boasts the finest view in town, the outlook occupying the very spot where Speke saw the Nile exit Lake Victoria. The pick of the accommodation is 4 elevated en-suite standing tents, all of which enjoy the historic view. 6 additional rooms, all with river-view balconies, are in a storeyed & stilted timber block that looks adventurously ramshackle – & even more so when viewed from the Jinja side of the river. Facilities include a smart new restaurant, a 15min walking trail through the lightly wooded grounds circling the Speke Memorial & boat trips at US$7 pp. *US$53/67 sgl/dbl B&B; US$114/132 sgl/dbl FB; US$5 pp camping.* **$$$**

Tongola Resort [250 D6] m 0776 202555; e info@tongolaresort.com. This isolated resort across the bay from Jinja town boasts immaculate, lightly wooded grounds sloping down to the Lake Victoria shore. Banda accommodation is provided – pleasantly spacious but set back from the lake view. Even if you don't stay over, Tongola is a lovely excuse for a boat trip from Jinja to enjoy a plate of fresh tilapia & chips (US$9). Otherwise, follow the tarmac Kisoga Rd for 5km from the Nile Bridge, then follow the signposts south on murram from Kafunta trading centre (the signs for the neighbouring but inferior Fancy Resort are more conspicuous). *US$66 sgl/dbl B&B.* **$$**

WHERE TO EAT AND DRINK

In addition to the places listed below, numerous small bars and local eateries are scattered along the south end of Main Street and around the market area.

Town centre

Moderate to expensive

✱ **The Deli** [237 C6] Main St; m 0789 5888892; e thedeliug@gmail.com; f thedeliug; ⌚ 07.30–19.00 Mon–Sat, 08.00–17.00 Sun. Jinja's most happening lunch spot, this excellent Finnish-owned snack bar occupies a large, shady terrace at the side of the post office. Specialising in DIY wraps & sandwiches using a wide choice of fresh ingredients, it also serves salads, burgers, steak pies (Uganda's best), cakes, an all-day b/fast, fresh coffee & smoothies. For self-caterers, a butchers/deli section (closed Sun) stocks fresh & cured meats, cheeses, fresh veggies & other goodies. *Mains US$4–8.*

✱ **Moti Mahal** [237 C3] Iganga Rd; m 0718 357199, 0757 879048; ⌚ 09.30–22.30 daily. The spartan dining room inside this excellent Indian restaurant might not be much to look at but the thalis & curries are truly superb with plenty of choice for vegetarians. *Mains cost around US$7–9.*

The Source Café [237 C4] Main St; ☎ 043 4120911; ⌚ 07.30–18.00 Mon–Sat. A non-profit initiative supporting several local schools, this characterful café, set in a restored 1920s warehouse, looks & smells like an old-time European coffee house, though the busily whirring fans place it firmly in the tropics. Freshly brewed coffee, juices, cakes & light meals can be imbibed indoors or on the terrace, though the menu also includes more substantial dishes such as burgers, whole grilled tilapia & filled wraps. An internet café, small library & craft shop are attached. *Most mains in the US$6–9 range.*

Cheap to moderate

✱ **Anmol Restaurant** [237 C5] Main St; m 0755 703434; ⌚ until 22.00 daily. Popular with the local Asian community, which is always a good thing, this unpretentious corner restaurant serves an extensive selection of Manchurian, Nepali, Chinese & Indian meat & vegetarian dishes, with thalis & Chinese hotties being the main speciality. Drinks include lassis, juices & a full bar. *Mains US$9 exc rice/naan.*

Harmax [237 C3] Cnr Iganga & Ripon rds; m 0700 794347. Cocooned within a screen of hanging plants & with an astroturf floor, this chlorophyll-filled corner *nyama choma* (roast meat) joint is the greenest place in town. Chunks of beef & goat, chicken pieces & whole fish fried or grilled to order. *Mains from US$3.*

Jad's [237 C5] Main St; m 0701 944806. If you're not in the mood for an Anmol curry (page 241), try a Thai dish from Jad's on the opposite corner; or if time & funds are considerations, the tasty shawarmas, which are quicker & cheaper. *Thai mains US$5–8.*

Machos Grill [237 C5] Iganga Rd; m 0762 387960; ⌚ daily. This popular café, rather oddly designed to resemble a castle by the original owner, offers a tempting selection of burgers, sandwiches, pizzas & more. *Mains US$7–9.*

New Rendezvous [237 C4] Main St; ⌚ 08.00–late daily. This brick-fronted restaurant has been dishing out beer & tasty local food for more than 2 decades. *US$2.50 vegetarian dishes, US$3 with meat.*

The Rolex Joint [237 B5] Gabula Rd; m 0775 669178, 0758 639591; f; ⌚ 09.30–21.00 daily. Specialising in fast food Uganda-style, this cheap 'n' cheerful wooden shack serves a varied selection of filled rolexes to take away or eat on the small terrace. *Rolexes US$1.50–2.*

Space Café [237 C4] Main St; m 0794 004803; f spacecafejinja; ⌚ 07.00–22.00 daily. This small modern café with leather-&-wood furniture serves smoothies, coffee, juices, Mexican dishes, grills & burgers. *Mains US$4–6.*

Suburban

✱ **All Friends Place Grill** [232 D3] Jackson Cres; m 0772 984821; w allfriendsgrill.com; ⌚ 09.00–midnight daily. Affiliated to the neighbouring 2 Friends (page 238), this popular & chilled-out garden restaurant serves some fabulously filling steaks, chops & whole fish from an outside grill tempered by some less outstanding offerings from the house kitchen. *Mains in the US$7–11 range.*

The Hangout [232 D2] Nalufenya Rd; m 0773 451414; w thehangoutjinja.com; ⌚ until 20.30 Mon–Fri, until 22.00 w/ends. Occupying a row of converted containers, 500m off the Kampala–Kenya road (just beyond the railway underpass on the way into town), Jinja's first food court venture is an ideal stop even if you're just passing through. Wraps, noodles, rolexes, pizzas, shawarmas, grills, coffees, juices & more are on offer; the website contains all the menus. *Meals in the US$3–8 range.*

House of Snacks [232 D5] Off Bridge Rd; ⌚ 06.00–18.00 daily. This large open-air eatery in the Jinja Showground caters mainly to locals, serving perhaps the best buffet in town, starting at around 11.00, with plenty to keep vegetarians interested. Great value. *Buffet US$5 pp.*

✱ **Java House** [232 D1] Churchill Way; m 0703 042306; f Java-House-1187277841293713; ⌚ 06.00–22.00 daily. The fan-cooled Jinja branch of this popular franchise sits alongside a filling station on the main circle with the Kampala Rd – ideal for a break if driving to Mbale or Kenya; indeed the clean toilets are an attraction in their own right. It serves great coffee & smoothies as well as the usual long & varied menu of meals & snacks. *Meals in the US$5–10 range.*

✱ **Jinja Sailing Club** [233 E7] Nile Cres; ☎ 039 3193491; m 0750 035901; w jinjasailingclub.com; ⌚ 10.00–23.00 daily. Set in lovely lakeshore gardens complete with an incongruous dinosaur statue, Jinja's once-prestigious sailing club is now the town's priciest restaurant. The varied menu is longest on Indian dishes, but it also has a good selection of grills & a wide choice of desserts & cakes. *Mains mostly in the US$9–12 range.*

✱ **Prudis Corner** [232 D4] Main St; m 0759 338216; ⌚ daily. Occupying a shelter in a vacant corner plot, this friendly diner serves pizzas (US$7) plus a selection of affordable Ethiopian meat & vegan dishes with the traditional, pancake-like staple *injera. US$5–7 range.*

Rumours Café [232 D6] Cliff Rd; m 0772 401508; ⌚ daily until 20.00. Located in the Source of the Nile complex, Rumours' ramshackle timber platforms are as close as you can get to the Nile without actually being in it – & subject to the current water level, the latter might be an option. Not surprisingly, perhaps, whole-fish & chips are the house speciality, while curries are also served. Note that you'll have to pay the Source of the Nile entrance fee to reach the restaurant. *Mains US$8–11.*

Surjio's Pizzeria [233 E7] Kisinja Rd; ☎ 043 4122325; m 0772 500400; w surjios.com; ⌚ 11.00–21.30 daily. Quite simply the best pizzas in Jinja, supplemented by a few dishes of the day, served in a lovely old terraced colonial homestead with lush green gardens. *Mains US$8–10.*

Yellow Chilly [232 D2] Kiira Rd; m 0750 655683. This large, modern (& less than atmospheric) diner at the Nalugenya Rd end of the long, looping Kiira Rd offers a wide-ranging menu with its excellent Indian one being the most popular. *Meals in the US$5–10 range*.

ENTERTAINMENT AND NIGHTLIFE

Nightclubs

Bourbon [232 C5] Bridge Close; m 0750 745090; ⏲ 11.00–late daily. This popular bar slopes down through a pretty wooded glade to a pontoon beer platform on the Nile water via a series of terraces, steps, decks & bridges that link various vantage points. Towards the end of the day, these are perfect for a riverside sundowner or some boozy aquatic birdwatching before the changes in level start causing complications for an increasingly befuddled nocturnal clientele.

Café 49 [232 C5] Nile Cres. This popular, open-air nightspot is found at the less salubrious end of Nile Cres, where the mansions give way to industrial activity. At its core is a covered hub containing semi-private lounges in which the town's elite enjoys VIP service while the rest of us flap for a waiter's attention.

The Office [233 E5] Grant Rd; m 0752 925371; f; ⏲ noon–04.00 daily. This quirky 2-storey suburban venue is most popular on Fri & Sat nights, when there's usually a DJ & occasionally live music. On other nights it functions as a more relaxed bar with Tue being quiz night.

Viewers Nite Club [237 D3] Luba's Rd; m 0750 982734; f; ⏲ 08.00–late Wed–Sat. Another popular nightclub, set in the Nile View Casino, this caters to a more local clientele than other such clubs listed.

Bars

Jinja Golf Club [232 D7] Nile Cres; ⏲ 08.00–late daily. A pleasant location for a quiet drink in green surrounds, the members' clubhouse attached to the Jinja Golf Course is open to the public & serves the usual drinks as well as snacks for around US$5.

Pitstop [233 E5] Nile Cres; ⏲ 09.00–late daily. Facing the margins of the golf course, this is a relaxed place for a drink or *nyama choma* (grilled meat, US$5 per plate) in stylish surrounds.

SHOPPING Jinja is well supplied with supermarkets. The highest concentration lies along Clive Road, while **Biashara Supermarket** [237 C3] and **Igar Supermarket** [237 C4] on Main Street are closer to the main cluster of craft shops and cafés frequented by tourists. If you're looking for fresh fruit and vegetables – or, for that matter, you are short of dried fish, door handles, traditional cloth, secondhand T-shirts, cow's stomachs, spanner sets or whatever – visit the **main market** [237 D2] near the taxi park, which is now a covered multi-storey building.

You'll find a couple of dozen craft shops at the western end of Main Street, most of them selling the usual stuff, largely from Kenya, that you buy for your friends. Having done that, head for **Local Flavours** [237 C6] (m 0781 150745, 0750 599683) two doors down from **The Deli** to find something for yourself. The **Cuupa Arts Gallery** [237 B4] (Naranbhai Rd; m 0706 265287; f; ⏲ 08.00–19.00 Mon–Sat) also sells quality handicrafts including jewellery and coffee mugs, as well as original paintings and other artworks.

OTHER PRACTICALITIES

Bicycle hire Jinja, being relatively flat, is ideal for exploration by bike; a single-speed machine will do at a pinch but a tour on the town's variable road surfaces will be far more enjoyable on a mountain bike with gears. The latter can be hired from Jinja Backpackers (page 240) at US$15/25 half/full day. Another option on nearby Victoria Close is an NGO called **Bikeventures** [232 D4] (m 0778 366007; e uganda@bikeventures.org; w bikeventures.org), which charges US$15–20 per day for mountain bike hire. Also linked to a social venture is the centrally located **First African Bicycle Information Organisation** [237 B5] (FABIO; m 0700 504966;

THE RIDDLE OF THE NILE

The first European to see Lake Victoria was John Hanning Speke, who marched from Tabora to the site of present-day Mwanza in 1858 following his joint 'discovery' of Lake Tanganyika with Richard Burton the previous year. Speke named the lake for Queen Victoria but, prior to that, Arab slave traders called it Ukerewe (still the name of its largest island). It is unclear what name was in local use, since the only one referred to by Speke was Nyanza, which simply means 'lake'.

A major goal of the Burton–Speke expedition had been to solve the great geographical enigma of the age, the source of the White Nile. Speke, based on his brief glimpse of the southeast corner of Lake Victoria, somewhat whimsically proclaimed his 'discovery' to be the answer to that riddle. Burton, with a comparable lack of compelling evidence, was convinced that the great river flowed out of Lake Tanganyika. The dispute between the former travelling companions erupted bitterly on their return to Britain, where Burton – the more persuasive writer and better respected traveller – gained the backing of the scientific establishment.

In 1862–63, Speke and Captain James Grant returned to Lake Victoria, hoping to prove Speke's theory correct. They looped inland around the western shore of the lake, arriving at the court of King Mutesa of Buganda, then continued east to the site of present-day Jinja, where a substantial river flowed out of the lake after tumbling over a cataract that Speke named Ripon Falls. From here, the two explorers headed north, sporadically crossing paths with the river until they reached Lake Albert, then continued following the Nile to Khartoum and Cairo.

Back home, Speke's declaration that 'The Nile is settled' met with mixed support. Burton and other sceptics pointed out that Speke had bypassed the entire western shore of his purported great lake, had visited only a couple of points on the northern shore, and had not attempted to explore the east. Nor, for that matter, had he followed the course of the Nile in its entirety. In other words, according to his detractors, Speke might have encountered several different lakes and rivers that were unconnected except in his deluded mind. But while the naysayers did have a point, it is equally true that the geographical evidence gathered by Speke lent a great deal of credibility to his theories, which were also supported by anecdotal information gathered from local sources along the way.

Matters were scheduled to reach a head on 16 September 1864, when an eagerly awaited debate between Burton and Speke – in the words of the former, 'what silly tongues called the "Nile Duel"' – was due to take place at the Royal Geographic Society (RGS). And reach a head they did, but in circumstances more tragic than anybody could have anticipated. On the afternoon of the debate, Speke went out shooting with a cousin, only to stumble while crossing a wall, in the process discharging a barrel of his shotgun into his heart. The subsequent inquest recorded a verdict of accidental death, but it has often been suggested – purely on the basis of the curious timing – that Speke deliberately took his life rather than face up to Burton in public. Burton, who had seen Speke less than 3 hours earlier, was by all accounts deeply troubled by Speke's death, and years later he was quoted as stating 'the uncharitable [say] that I shot him' – an accusation that seems to have been aired only in Burton's imagination.

Speke was dead, but the 'Nile debate' would keep kicking for several years. In 1864, Sir Samuel and Lady Baker became the first Europeans to reach Lake Albert and nearby Murchison Falls in present-day Uganda. The Bakers, much to the delight of the anti-Speke lobby, were convinced that this newly named lake was a source of the Nile, though they openly admitted it might not be the only one. Following the Bakers' announcement, Burton put forward a revised theory, namely that the most remote source of the Nile was the Rusizi River, which he believed flowed out of the northern head of Lake Tanganyika and emptied into Lake Albert.

In 1865, the RGS followed up on Burton's theory by sending Dr David Livingstone to Lake Tanganyika. Livingstone, however, was of the opinion that the Nile's source lay further south than Burton supposed, and so he struck out towards the lake along a previously unexplored route. Leaving from Mikindani in the far south of present-day Tanzania, Livingstone followed the Ruvuma River inland, continuing westward to the southern tip of Lake Tanganyika. From there, he ranged southward into present-day Zambia, where he came across a new candidate for the source of the Nile, the swampy Lake Bangweulu and its major outlet, the Lualaba River. It was only after his famous meeting with Henry Stanley at Ujiji, in November 1871, that Livingstone (in the company of Stanley) visited the north of Lake Tanganyika and Burton's cherished Rusizi River, which, it transpired, flowed into the lake. Burton, nevertheless, still regarded Lake Tanganyika as the most likely source of the Nile, while Livingstone was convinced that the answer lay with the Lualaba River. In August 1872, Livingstone headed back to the Lake Bangweulu region, where he fell ill and died six months later, the great question still unanswered.

In August 1874, ten years after Speke's death, Stanley embarked on a three-year expedition every bit as remarkable and arduous as those undertaken by his predecessors, yet one whose significance is often overlooked. Partly, this is because most histories have painted such an unsympathetic picture of Stanley: a grim caricature of the murderous, pre-colonial White Man blasting and blustering his way through territories where Burton, Speke and Livingstone had relied largely on diplomacy. It is also the case, however, that Stanley set out with no intention of seeking headline-making fresh discoveries. Instead, he determined to test methodically the theories advocated by Speke, Burton and Livingstone about the Nile's source. First, Stanley sailed around the circumference of Lake Victoria, establishing that it was indeed as vast as Speke had claimed. Stanley's next step was to circumnavigate Lake Tanganyika, which, contrary to Burton's long-held theories, clearly boasted no outlet sufficiently large to be the source of the Nile. Finally, and most remarkably, Stanley took a boat along Livingstone's Lualaba River to its confluence with an even larger river, which he followed for months with no idea as to where he might end up.

When, exactly 999 days after he left Zanzibar, Stanley emerged at the Congo mouth, the shortlist of plausible theories relating to the source of the Nile had been reduced to one. Clearly, the Nile did flow out of Lake Victoria at Ripon Falls, before entering and exiting Lake Albert at its northern tip to start its long course through the sands of the Sahara. Stanley's achievement in putting to rest decades of speculation about how the main rivers and lakes of East Africa linked together is estimable indeed. He was nevertheless generous enough to concede that: 'Speke now has the full glory of having discovered the largest inland sea on the continent of Africa, also its principal affluent as well as its outlet. I must also give him credit for having understood the geography of the countries we travelled through far better than any of us who so persistently opposed his hypothesis.'

e info@fabio.or.ug; w fabio.or.ug; ⏰ 09.00–17.00 Mon–Fri) on Gabula Road. This rents out basic bikes with gears for US$5 per day or US$8 with a guide who can show you various sights of interest around town.

Immigration If your three-month tourist visa is stamped for only one month on arrival in Uganda, you can get it extended for free at the Immigration Office [233 F6] behind the town hall (opposite Stanbic Bank).

Maps A free map of Jinja, accurate but curiously short on landmarks, can be picked up at the tourist office [237 C6]. Far more detailed, the *Jinja and the Nile* title in the 'Uganda Maps' series (on sale at The Deli and Local Flavours) includes a map of the Upper Nile on its reverse. An app and downloadable map of historical buildings in Jinja, supported by the European Union, was published by the Cross-Cultural Foundation of Uganda in 2019 and is available at w crossculturalfoundation.or.ug/historical-sites-more-resources.

Spa The spa in the central Al-Nisaa Hotel and Spa (Iganga Rd; 043 4122660; w alnisaahotelandspa.com) has been recommended.

Swimming The Jinja Golf Club, Nile Village Hotel and Jinja Nile Resort all charge around US$3.

TOUR OPERATORS

Buffalo Safaris [237 C6] m 0758 098428; e info@buffalosafaricamps.com; w buffalosafaricamps.com. Organised & self-drive safaris.

Tubale Safaris [250 D2] Bujugali Rd; m 0785 907173; e info@tubalesafaris.com; w tubalesafaris.com

WHAT TO SEE AND DO

Note that the many activities listed on page 251 can be (and frequently are) undertaken as day excursions from Jinja. Any hotel, backpackers' or local tour operator can book such excursions, or put you in touch with the right organisation.

Historic Jinja The roads of central Jinja are lined with several colonial-era British and Asian architectural gems, some now restored to their former glory, others in varying states of disrepair. To help you locate these, an app and downloadable map of historical buildings in Jinja (page 586), supported by the European Union, was published by the Cross-Cultural Foundation of Uganda in 2019. The *Jinja and the Nile* map also locates many interesting buildings.

The most presentable of Jinja's historic buildings on Main Street are the handsome **Madhvani House** [237 C4], which dates to 1919, and **The Source Café** [237 C4], which occupies a warehouse built in 1924 by the Kampala Oriental Company. In poorer shape are **Rasik Villa** [237 C6] (built 1935) on nearby Iganga Road, the **police station** [237 C3] (1928) on Main Street, and **Vithaldas Jaridas Building** [237 C4] (1919) on Naranbhai Road.

Southwest of the town centre, **Nile Crescent**, an erratically surfaced avenue lined by palm trees laden with fruit bats, leads past the attractive golf course and some fine old colonial homesteads. Probably the oldest building in this part of town is the 1914 **Vicar's House** [233 E6] behind St Andrew's Church on Busoga Road. Many other old houses between the town centre and Nile Crescent have been beautifully renovated as hotels or private residences. Sadly, however, no attempt has been made to restore and reopen the historic **Ripon Falls Hotel**, which stands semi-derelict opposite the Jinja Sailing Club [233 E7].

Jinja Railway Museum [233 H2] (Churchill Way; ⌚ 11.00–18.00 Tue–Sun; entry US$5 FR) Housed in Jinja's long-dormant station, this excellent initiative driven by the Cross-Cultural Foundation of Uganda opened in 2022 to tell the century-long story of railways in Uganda, starting with the construction of track inland from Mombasa at the end of the 19th century and ending with the inglorious collapse of the domestic network during the 1990s. In addition to some clear and informative panels with excellent period photos, there's a model railway (based on the state of Uganda Railways in the late '80s, I'd say; erratic but still functioning) while outside, visitors get to clamber over a locomotive and watch a short film in a railway carriage. It's a sobering thought that of the thousands of schoolkids brought to the museum, this must be the first train that 99.9% of them have ever been on. It's an exciting thought, however, that if all goes to plan (page 127), people might soon be taking a train from Kampala to visit the museum.

Jinja War Cemetery [233 E4] (Baxi Rd; w cwgc.org; ⌚ 06.00–18.00 Mon–Fri) Tended by the Commonwealth War Graves Commission, this well-maintained cemetery comprises 178 graves of Ugandan and British soldiers killed in World War II, when Jinja was the Ugandan centre for the King's African Rifles. It also contains one World War I grave, and four of servicemen who died after 1945. Within the cemetery, the Jinja Memorial is a screen wall inscribed with the names of 127 East African servicemen who died during World War II but whose graves were too remotely located to be maintained properly. Every year, on the second Sunday of November, the British High Commissioner to Uganda and various other representatives of Commonwealth states visit the cemetery to pay their respects.

Jinja Golf Club [232 D7] (1 Nile Cres; m 0750 472287, 0774 787289) Established in 1912, Jinja's lovely nine-hole golf course overlooks the Nile and was at one time famous for games being interrupted by stray hippos. Day membership costs US$8, clubs can be hired at US$15 per day, and the caddie fee is US$3 per round. A fee of US$3 is charged to non-members who want to use the 25m swimming pool or squash or tennis courts.

Source of the Nile (East Bank) [232 D6] (Cliff Rd; entry US$10 pp; parking fee US$3 per vehicle) About 1km west of the town centre, Jinja Municipality maintains a landscaped park on the east bank of the now-submerged Ripon Falls, the natural landmark associated with the source of the Nile prior to the construction of the Owen Falls Dam a short distance upriver in the 1950s. It's a pleasant spot and deserving of a once-in-a-lifetime visit, and while its significance has been diminished by the disappearance of Ripon Falls, a prominent plaque is there to remind you it 'marks the place where the Nile starts its long journey to the Mediterranean'. An additional plaque with a sculpted bust commemorates Mahatma Gandhi, some of whose ashes were scattered into the river here following his death in 1948. Drinks and basic refreshments are served by a couple of bars on a concrete terrace at what passes as the main tourism hotspot. Alternatively, for greater choice, drop in at Rumours, a waterfront bar/restaurant set in a patch of riverine woodland 100m distant. A Tourism Masterplan has recently been prepared to jazz up the Source of the Nile experience and, though pigs will fly before you see the proposed glass observation tower and cable car, you may well find a revamped entrance corridor descending to a new pier.

Source of the Nile Gardens (West Bank) [232 C6] (⊕ 0.420531, 33.193013; entry US$3 pp) Now operated privately by Living Waters (page 241), the Source of the Nile Gardens incorporates the spot from where Speke viewed Ripon Falls in 1862, and is altogether prettier and more enjoyable than its eastern counterpart. surthermore, unlike the outlook from the Jinja side, the magnificent view from

A SOURCE OF CONTROVERSY

The first plaque erected in the Source of the Nile Gardens read 'Speke discovered this source of the Nile on the 28th July 1862'. This was removed some years back on the basis that local people knew of the place long before any European arrived there. Of course, it is true enough that Speke didn't really 'discover' Lake Victoria or the Ripon Falls: people had been living there for millennia before he arrived. But Speke *was* the first person to make a connection between this 13m-high waterfall and the life-bearing river that flows through the deserts of Egypt before emptying into the Mediterranean 6,500km further north.

Being nit-picky, the newer plaque that replaced the original is also somewhat contentious. For while Ripon Falls is unambiguously *a* source of the Nile, its semi-official status as *the* source of the Nile could be said to be arbitrary and sentimental – posthumous recognition of Speke's momentous but contemporarily controversial discovery – rather than being based on geographical logic.

Strictly speaking, the truest source of the Nile is the most remote headwater of the Kagera, which is the longest river to feed Lake Victoria. And the location of this landmark is also open to debate. In 1892, the German explorer Oscar Baumann traced the Kagera to a source in Burundi's Kabera Forest, while 11 years later his countryman Richard Kandt located a possibly more remote spring in Rwanda's Nyungwe Forest. In 1937, however, the German explorer Burkhart Waldecker located what has since been recognised as the most remote of the Nile's headwaters, the source of the Kagera River, a hillside spring known as Kasumo (Gusher) and situated some 4° south of the equator in Burundi. But the mantle was handed back to Rwanda in 2006, when a modern-day GPS-guided expedition following the Nile all the way from Alexandria hit on a 'new' source in Nyungwe Forest, 15km from the location identified by Kandt. One implication of this most recent discovery is that the Nile, if traced to its most remote source, is actually 6,718km long – a full 107km more than previously accepted.

There are other sources to consider. Before crossing into Sudan, the Victoria Nile flows through Lake Kyoga and into the northern tip of Lake Albert, from where it emerges as the Albert Nile. And Lake Albert is also fed by the Semliki River, several of whose tributaries rise on the Rwenzori Mountains, which count as the highest and most fabulous source of the Nile. In truth, depending on how you look at these things, Nyungwe Forest, the Rwenzori Mountains or even the point where the river exits Lake Albert all vie with Ripon Falls as the point where the Nile can be considered to start its long journey to the Mediterranean.

the West Bank puts the whole thing into context. As you behold the sight seen by Speke – of the river being funnelled towards you out of a broad bay of Lake Victoria – you'll appreciate his conviction that he had solved the age-old mystery. Speke's visit is remembered by an inscribed pillar-like **Speke Monument**, which, erected in 1954, has thus far survived any attempt to replace it with something more politically correct. Other facilities include accommodation, a restaurant and wooded grounds that offer much to birders. The gardens can be reached by canoe from the East Bank or by crossing the Nile Bridge and turning left on to the Kisoga Road. The dirt road to the gardens is signposted on the left after 2km. The entrance fee will likely be waived if you are eating at the restaurant.

Boat trips A variety of locations along the Jinja waterfront offer motorboat trips on the Nile. These usually visit a few islands dotted around the Nile's emergence from the lake as well as a supposed spring on a small island (currently greatly reduced by a rise in lake level), locally considered to be the true source of the Nile. Of the available operators, the most professional is the Jinja Sailing Club [233 E7] (m 0750 035901), where an hour costs US$16 per person for four (minimum) to ten people. Cheaper excursions in the Source of the Nile Gardens [232 C6] cost US$32/50 for 30 minutes/1 hour for up to 15 people. An altogether faster and superior craft, which plies as far out as Samuka Island in Napoleon Gulf, launches from the adjacent Rumours restaurant [232 D6] and costs US$130/210/370 for 30 minutes/1 hour/2 hours for up to 20 people. A speedboat from Bourbon bar [232 C5] (m 0750 745090) costs US$80/hour while a wooden canoe costs US$66. Cheapest of all, though dependent on your haggling skills, are the local boat operators at the fish landing adjacent to (but accessed separately from) the Jinja Sailing Club. If a lifejacket is not offered, ask to be given one.

BUJAGALI, KALAGALA AND THE UPPER NILE

The stretch of the Victoria Nile immediately downriver of its source at Jinja blossomed as one of the world's top white-water rafting venues in the late 1990s, and subsequently became the most important centre of adventure and adrenalin activities in East Africa. Until recently, the focal point for all this activity was the village of Bujagali, which stands on the East Bank some 7km north of Jinja. Overlooking Bujagali Falls, the first in a series of Grade V rapids, this became the established launch point for rafting excursions. Since then, however, Bujagali's star has steadily waned. The first blows were the submergence of Bujagali Falls and other major rapids behind two hydro-electric dams. Fortunately – both for tourists, and for the great many locals whose income is dependent on them – there's a great deal more to the Upper Nile than white-water rafting. Tourism has been bolstered by supplementary options such as bungee-jumping, horseriding and quad-biking, as well as more laid-back activities on the becalmed Lake Bujagali such as birdwatching, sit-on-top kayaking, stand-up paddleboarding and down-yer-neck booze cruises.

An additional complication for Bujagali is the mushrooming of tourism facilities on the opposite bank of the Nile, most notably a rival activity centre at Kalagala Falls. Located on the West Bank, closer to what remains of the action on the river and closer to Kampala too, smart, modern facilities at Kalagala Falls are in direct competition with setups at Bujagali that have changed little in 20 years. The winner is not entirely a forgone conclusion, however, for this state-of-the-art infrastructure comes at a price. Given the choice between paying US$30 for

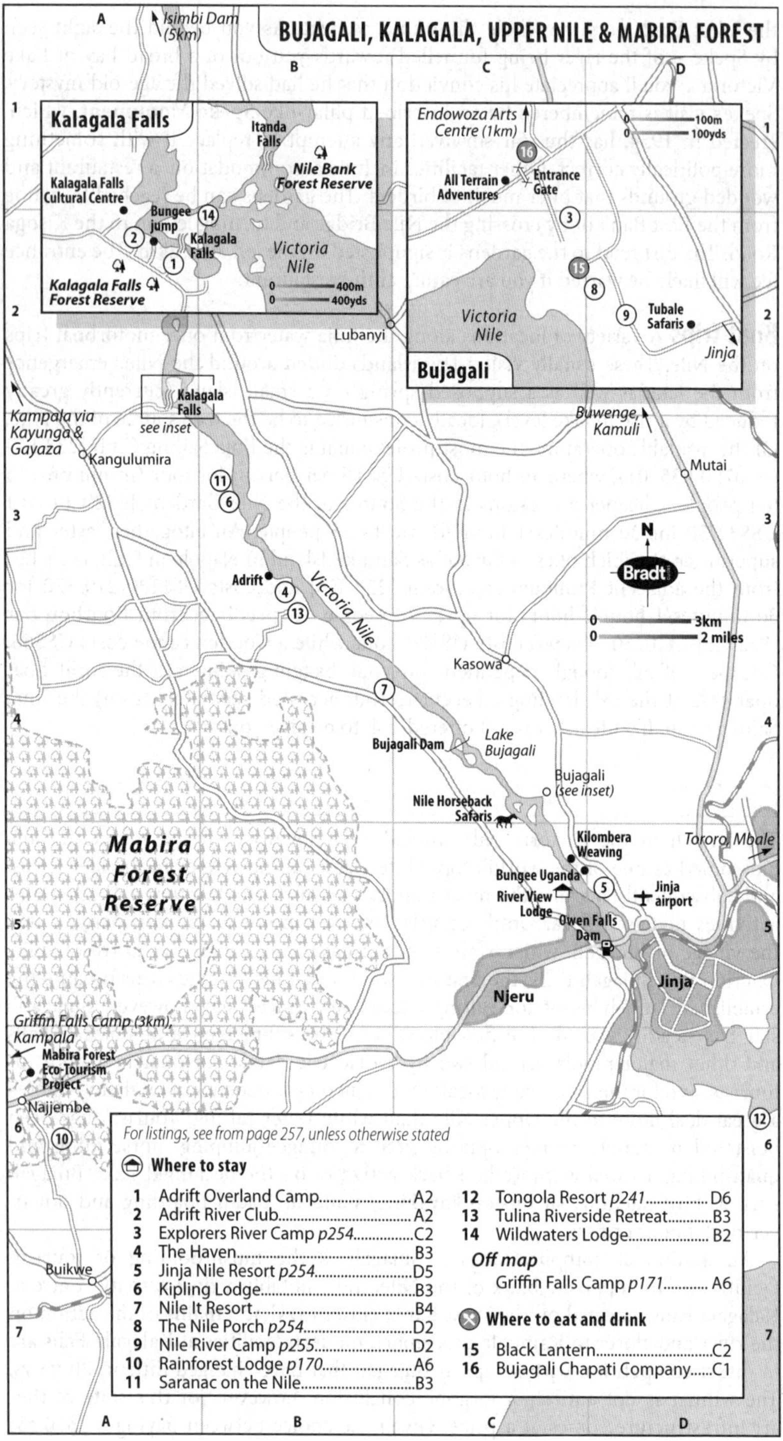
BUJAGALI, KALAGALA, UPPER NILE & MABIRA FOREST
Isimbi Dam (5km)
Kalagala Falls
Itanda Falls
Nile Bank Forest Reserve
Kalagala Falls Cultural Centre
Bungee jump
Kalagala Falls
Victoria Nile
Kalagala Falls Forest Reserve
Endowoza Arts Centre (1km)
All Terrain Adventures
Entrance Gate
Tubale Safaris
Jinja
Bujagali
Lubanyi
Kampala via Kayunga & Gayaza
see inset
Kangulumira
Buwenge, Kamuli
Mutai
Adrift
Victoria Nile
Bradt
Kasowa
Bujagali Dam
Lake Bujagali
Bujagali (see inset)
Nile Horseback Safaris
Kilombera Weaving
Tororo, Mbale
Bungee Uganda
River View Lodge
Jinja airport
Owen Falls Dam
Mabira Forest Reserve
Njeru
Jinja
Griffin Falls Camp (3km), Kampala
Mabira Forest Eco-Tourism Project
Najjembe
Buikwe
For listings, see from page 257, unless otherwise stated
Where to stay
1 Adrift Overland Camp........A2
2 Adrift River Club........A2
3 Explorers River Camp p254........C2
4 The Haven........B3
5 Jinja Nile Resort p254........D5
6 Kipling Lodge........B3
7 Nile It Resort........B4
8 The Nile Porch p254........D2
9 Nile River Camp p255........D2
10 Rainforest Lodge p170........A6
11 Saranac on the Nile........B3
12 Tongola Resort p241........D6
13 Tulina Riverside Retreat........B3
14 Wildwaters Lodge........B2
Off map
Griffin Falls Camp p171........A6
Where to eat and drink
15 Black Lantern........C2
16 Bujagali Chapati Company........C1

a dorm bed at Kalagala Falls and US$15 at Buj', there will inevitably be plenty of takers for the latter. There is, however, no avoiding the reality that Bujagali is no longer the automatic go-to destination on the Upper Nile. Consequently, after an overview of rafting options below, we have split this section into two, separating accommodation and activities at Bujagali and the East Bank from those around Kalagala Falls and the West Bank.

HISTORY AND BACKGROUND When the first edition of this book was researched in 1992, tourism activity on the Upper Nile immediately downstream of Jinja amounted to one peaceful and little-visited picnic site overlooking the Bujagali Falls. The region has undergone three major transformations since then. The first was initiated in 1996, when Adrift established a commercial white-water rafting operation on the East Bank overlooking Bujagali, thereby kickstarting an adventure tourism industry that soon grew to embrace a dozen riverside lodges and camps, along with numerous small operators offering a plethora of aquatic and terrestrial adventure activities. By the early 2000s, Bujagali had become entrenched as the undisputed adventure tourism capital of East Africa, attracting up to 50,000 rafters annually, and for several years outstripping the gorillas of Bwindi as Uganda's most important tourist draw.

The second transformation took place in 2011, when the construction of a 250MW hydro-electric dam at Dumbbell Island caused several sets of white water, including the Grade V rapids Total Gunga and Silverback/Big Brother, and the emblematic Bujagali Falls itself, to be submerged below the reservoir now known as Lake Bujagali. This forced the rafting companies to relocate their embarkation point from the East Bank below Bujagali to the West Bank at Overtime, 8km downriver.

Rafting options were further contracted in 2018, following the completion of the 180MW Isimbi Hydro-electric Dam which flooded several more rapids below Kalagala and Itanda falls, including Nile Special, an internationally renowned kayaking wave. As a result, rafting trips now conclude just below Itanda Falls and though this is still offered as a full day trip, it is a slower and more relaxed journey down the river than before.

WHAT TO SEE AND DO ON THE UPPER NILE

White-water rafting Though white-water rafting remains the flagship activity on the Upper Nile, a host of other activities are available and can be booked directly with the rafting operators listed on page 252, or indirectly through any tour company in Jinja or backpacker hostel in Kampala. In case you're thinking of doing more than one activity, the rafting companies usually offer discounted packages combining rafting with other pursuits such as paddleboarding, tandem kayaking and bungee-jumping.

The companies listed on page 252 offer similar itineraries starting below Bujagali Dam and finishing near Kalagala Falls. Though several rapids were lost to the flooding associated with Isimbi Dam in 2019, the trip still includes ten white-water events including the Grade V Overtime. It also offers an opportunity to see a variety of birds, and to swim in calm stretches of water. All companies charge US$145 for a half-day excursion inclusive of return transportation from Kampala or Jinja, buffet lunch, and a couple of beers and/or sodas.

The rafting outfits are the oldest and most established, boasting high safety standards and an excellent track record. A host of other rafting companies come and go and their prices may be significantly cheaper than the operators listed. Before you sign up, however, ask yourself whether or where corners are being cut.

Adrift [250 B3] **m** 0755 225587, 0752 225587; **e** info@adrift.ug; **w** adrift.ug
Nalubale Rafting [232 D3] **m** 0782 638938; **e** bookings@nalubalerafting.com; **w** nalubalerafting.com
Nile River Explorers (NRE) [232 D3] **m** 0772 422373; **e** rafting@raftafrica.com; **w** raftafrica.com

Lake Bujagali and the East Bank Bujagali's iconic waterfall might have been sacrificed to the march of progress, but scenically, the qualities of the narrow, serpentine lake that has replaced it make for a very acceptable Plan B. With the water visible through a fringe of riparian forest rattling with birds and

THE NILE RIVER

Based partially on text kindly supplied by Laura Sserunjogi

The Nile is the world's longest river, flowing for 6,718km (4,174 miles) from its most remote headwater in Rwanda to the delta formed as it enters the Mediterranean in Egypt. Its vast drainage basin occupies more than 10% of the African mainland and includes portions of ten countries: Tanzania, Burundi, Rwanda, the DRC, Kenya, Uganda, Ethiopia, South Sudan, Sudan and Egypt. While passing through South Sudan, the Nile also feeds the 5.5-million-hectare Sudd or Bar-el-Jebel, the world's most expansive wetland system.

A feature of the Nile Basin is a marked decrease in precipitation as it runs further northward. In the East African lakes region and Ethiopian Highlands, mean annual rainfall figures are typically in excess of 1,000mm. Rainfall in south and central Sudan varies from 250mm to 500mm annually, except in the Sudd (900mm), while in the deserts north of Khartoum the annual rainfall is little more than 100mm, dropping to 25mm in the south of Egypt, then increasing to around 200mm closer to the Mediterranean.

The Nile has served as the lifeblood of Egyptian agriculture for millennia, carrying not only water, but also silt, from the fertile tropics into the sandy expanses of the Sahara. Indeed, it is widely believed that the very first agricultural societies arose on the floodplain of the Egyptian Nile, and so, certainly, did one of the earliest and most enduring of all human civilisations. The antiquity of the name 'Nile', which simply means 'river valley', is reflected in the Ancient Greek (Nelios), Semetic (Nahal) and Latin (Nilus).

Over the past 50 years, several hydro-electric dams have been built along the Nile, notably the Aswan Dam in Egypt and the Owen Falls Dam in Uganda. The Aswan Dam doesn't merely provide hydro-electric power; it also supplies water for various irrigation schemes, and protects crops downriver from destruction by heavy flooding. Built in 1963, the dam wall rises 110m above the river and is almost 4km long, producing up to 2,100MW and forming the 450km-long Lake Nasser. The construction of the Aswan Dam enforced the resettlement of 90,000 Nubians, while the Temple of Abu Simbel, built 3,200 years ago for the Pharaoh Ramesses II, had to be relocated 65m higher.

The waterway plays a major role in transportation, especially in parts of Sudan between May and November, when transportation of goods and people is not possible by road owing to the floods. Like other rivers and lakes, the Nile provides a variety of fish as food. And its importance for conservation is difficult

monkeys, the lofty plateau above Lake Bujagali is, given a half-decent sunset, a quite delightful spot with a suitable sundowner. Though there is always an element of chance concerning the former, three very good camps are perched atop the river cliff to guarantee the second. If relaxing isn't your thing, activities on offer in and near Bujagali include bungee-jumping, quad-biking, kayaking and tubing.

Note that there have been reports of nocturnal muggings in Bujagali village, so it's advisable not to walk around unaccompanied after dark.

Getting there and away Bujagali lies 7km from Jinja along a clearly signposted road – murram with sections of poor tarmac – running north from the main roundabout (⊕ 0.44523, 33.19784) on the Kampala Road. The junction to Jinja Nile Resort is about 2.5km along this road. From Jinja, a boda to Bujagali will cost less

to overstate. The Sudd alone supports more than half the global populations of Nile lechwe and shoebill (more than 6,000), together with astonishing numbers of other water-associated birds – aerial surveys undertaken between 1979 and 1982 counted an estimated 1.7 million glossy ibis, 370,000 marabou stork, 350,000 open-billed stork, 175,000 cattle egret and 150,000 spur-winged goose.

The Nile has two major sources, often referred to as the White and Blue Nile, which flow respectively from Lake Victoria near Jinja and from Lake Tana in Ethiopia. The stretch of the White Nile that flows through southern Uganda is today known as the Victoria Nile (it was formerly called Kiira locally). From Jinja, it runs northward through the swampy Lake Kyoga, before veering west to descend into the Rift Valley over Murchison Falls and empty into Lake Albert. The Albert Nile flows from the northern tip of Lake Albert to enter Sudan at Nimule, passing through the Sudd before it merges with the Blue Nile at the Sudanese capital of Khartoum, more than 3,000km from Lake Victoria.

The discovery of the source of the Blue Nile on Lake Tana is often accredited to the 18th-century Scots explorer James Bruce. In fact, its approximate (if not exact) location was almost certainly known to the ancients. The Old Testament mentions that the Ghion (Nile) 'compasseth the whole land of Ethiopia', evidently in reference to the arcing course followed by the river along the approximate southern boundary of Ethiopia's ancient Axumite Empire. There are, too, strong similarities in the design of the papyrus *tankwa* used on Lake Tana to this day and the papyrus boats depicted in ancient Egyptian paintings. Furthermore, the main river feeding Lake Tana rises at a spring known locally as Abay Minch (literally 'Nile Fountain'), a site held sacred by Ethiopian Christians, whose links with the Egyptian Coptic Church date to the 4th century AD. Bruce's claim is further undermined by the Portuguese stone bridge, built c1620, which crosses the Nile a few hundred metres downstream of the Blue Nile Falls and only 30km from the Lake Tana outlet.

By contrast, the source of the White Nile was for centuries one of the world's great, unsolved mysteries. The Roman emperor Nero once sent an expedition south from Khartoum to search for it, but it was forced to turn back at the edge of the Sudd. In 1862, Speke correctly identified Ripon Falls as the source of the Nile, a theory that would be confirmed by Stanley in 1875. Since then, the river has been traced to various headwaters of the Kagera – the largest river flowing into Lake Victoria – in Rwanda and Burundi (page 248).

THE SPIRIT OF BUJAGALI

Bujagali is named after a set of fast-flowing rapids long held sacred by the local community as the home of an eponymous river spirit that manifested in more than 30 human incarnations over several centuries. Traditionally, anybody who claimed to be the spirit's newest reincarnation was required to prove it by sitting on a magical piece of barkcloth and drifting across the rapids. Only if he succeeded in this risky venture would the local villagers accept him as their new spiritual leader.

The last uncontested Bujagali died without nominating an heir in the 1970s, and the identity of his successor became the subject of a heated dispute. Most villagers believed the spirit resided in a local called Ja-Ja, who reputedly crossed the rapids on the magical barkcloth while evading military arrest under Idi Amin. Ja-Ja's rival for the title was an outsider called Jackson, who dreamed that he was the reincarnation of Bujagali, travelled to the village with a companion to stake his claim, then ran off with the magic barkcloth in order to float over the rapids. Before Jackson could attempt the crossing, however, he was caught by the villagers, who killed his companion. Jackson was banished to live out his days on a nearby island. In 2011, both the rapids and the island were submerged below what is now known as Lake Bujagali, making it unlikely there will ever be another reincarnation of the spirit for which it is named.

than US$2.50 and a private hire will charge around US$7. Alternatively, you can get a matatu from the main roundabout to Bujagali for less than US$1.

Where to stay

Moderate

Jinja Nile Resort [250 D5] (140 rooms) ⊕ 0.45757, 33.17981; ☎ 043 4122190; m 0774 676832; e reservations.ug@madahotels.com; w madahotels.com. Once one of the country's most sumptuous hotels but now starting to look a little ragged at the edges, this Ugandan component of the Kenyan Mada chain overlooks a stretch of the Nile studded with forested islands, about 2km downriver of the Owen Falls Dam. Facilities include a fabulous swimming pool & outdoor bar area, gym, massage parlour, business centre, & squash & tennis courts. Unfortunately, some refurbishment is required to justify the price tag. *From US$190/235 sgl/dbl B&B.* **$$$$**

✷ **The Nile Porch** [250 D2] (8 tents, 2 family cottages) ⊕ 0.48361, 33.16386; m 0782 321541; e relax@nileporch.com; w nileporch.com. Superbly located on an elevated plateau fringed by acacia trees inhabited by red-tailed & vervet monkey, Nile Porch overlooks Lake Bujagali, a lovely sight in the misty dawn or at sunset. The luxury tents are spacious yet marvellously cosy, with 1 sgl & 1 dbl bed, walk-in mosquito nets, solar-powered hot water & river-facing verandas. 2-bedroom cottages for families are also available. Facilities include a swimming pool & the superb Black Lantern restaurant (see opposite). *US$100/120 sgl/dbl; US$220 cottage (sleeps 5). All rates B&B.* **$$$**

Budget and camping

Explorers River Camp [250 C2] (30 rooms & tents, 10 4- to 28-bed dorms) ⊕ 0.48432, 33.16346; m 0772 422373; e rafting@raftafrica.com; w raftafrica.com. Located on a high bluff above Lake Bujagali, this popular & sociable base for rafting & other activities has a lively bar serving good meals in the US$4–8 range. It's operated by Nile River Explorers (NRE), & facilities include a day spa, book-swap service, mountain bike hire, a slide into the lake & a zip-line. *US$50 en-suite dbl room; US$30 tents with lake view using shared shower; US$10 pp dorm bed; US$5 pp camping.* **$$**

Nile River Camp [250 D2] (10 standing tents, 8 dorms) ⊕ 0.48243, 33.16457; m 0776 900450; e bookings@camponthenile.com; w camponthenile.com. This popular, budget-friendly camp next to the Nile Porch (see opposite) enjoys the same great lake view. Facilities include a swimming pool & a sociable bar serving mains in the US$3–5 range. Standing tents facing the lake are being replaced by some lovely, if closely spaced, en-suite cottages. *US$45 dbl tent; US$12 dorm bed; US$6 pp camping.* **$$**

Where to eat and drink

Though most travellers will end up eating at the same place they stay, there are two stand-out, bespoke eateries – at opposite ends of the quality and price spectrum – at Bujagali.

✷ **Black Lantern** [250 C2] ⊕ 0.48361, 33.16386; m 0782 321541; e relax@nileporch.com; w nileporch.com; ⊙ 07.00–21.30 daily. Attached to Nile Porch (see opposite) & under the same management, this stylish restaurant, with indoor & terrace seating facing Lake Bujagali, serves good salads & a cosmopolitan selection of mains including excellent steak, Mexican & Indian dishes, & various other grills. The house speciality is a full rack of spare ribs (US$18) but vegetarians are also well catered for. *Most dishes are in the US$8–10 range.*

Bujagali Chapati Company [250 C1] ⊕ 0.48494, 33.16316; m 0774 158346; ⊙ 05.00–23.00 daily. This cheap 'n' cheerful stall opposite the entrance to Explorers River Camp (see opposite) serves a great selection of filled chapatis – meat, vegetarian or sweet (eg: banana & Nutella). *Dishes around US$1.*

What to see and do

Kayaking In addition to white-water rafting (page 251), the Upper Nile is a top spot for adventure kayaking, attracting experienced enthusiasts from across the world. Kayaking is a more testing activity than rafting, since it offers, in the words of an appreciative reader, 'the opportunity to develop your own skills, rather than just bouncing along in a raft controlled by the professionals'. Courses and expeditions are offered by **Kayak the Nile** (m 0772 880322; e info@kayakthenile.com; w kayakthenile.com), a specialist kayaking operation based at Bujagali's Explorers River Camp (see opposite), whose instructors are trained to the UK's BCU standard. Options start with a half-/full-day introductory course (US$95/125) and progress to longer and more testing two-, three- or five-day courses. Full-on Grade V tandem kayaking (US$160) is also offered.

Placid Lake Bujagali is ideal for short beginner or family kayaking trips, which are also offered by Kayak the Nile (US$40/2hrs).

Lake cruises NRE (page 252) offers lunch and sunset cruises on Lake Bujagali in comfortable two-storey aluminium crafts (minimum group size is five). The lunch cruise costs US$30 inclusive of a buffet meal, while the sunset cruise is US$45 inclusive of snacks, all the lager you can drink in 2 hours and, if you're paying attention, a sunset.

Quad-biking Based in Bujagali but likely to relocate to Kalagala at some point, **All Terrain Adventures** [250 C1] (m 0772 377185; e info@atadventuresjinja.com; w atadventuresjinja.com; ⊙ 08.00–17.00 daily) runs quad-biking trips following local footpaths and tracks that connect some stunning Nile viewpoints. Rates range from US$55 per person for an hour-long ride to US$95 per person for a twilight tour starting at 17.00 and including dinner in a local village. A two-day trip along the Nile Valley, including overnight accommodation and meals, is also offered.

Mountain biking Mountain bikes can be hired from several hotels and lodges on the Upper Nile. A recommended specialist, based at Nile River Camp (page 255), is **Alex Dot Com** (m 0782 063780, 0776 900450; e alexdotcombiked260@gmail.com), which charges US$30/45 per person for a 2-/4-hour guided trip. Rates for unguided bike usage are negotiable.

Bungee-jumping A 38m bungee jump next to the Jinja Nile Resort (operated by Adrift before their relocation to Kalagala Falls), is now being run by Bungee Uganda (m 0778 317100; e info@bungeeuganda.com; w bungeeuganda.com).

Kilombera Weaving [250 D5] (⊕ 0.46951, 33.16979; m 0793 439619; f; ⊕ 09.00–17.00 Mon–Fri, 09.00–13.00 Sat) Named after a species of weaver bird that spends hours weaving its intricate nest in order to attract a mate, Kilombera Weaving specialises in colourful and lightweight handwoven cotton kikois, hammocks, bedspreads and other items made using traditional looms. Its new workshop and retail outlet, overlooking the Nile midway between Jinja Nile Resort and Bujagali, can provide a demonstration of the weaving process by arrangement.

Kalagala Falls and the West Bank

It is perfectly possible for a traveller to whizz down the last 25km of the Kampala–Gayaza–Njeru road towards Jinja in complete ignorance of the fabulous river scenery that lies just a couple of kilometres to the east. The only indication is a series of roadside signs that distinguish a select few of the dirt tracks that lead off into the roadside jungle. These are well worth following (assuming you have booked in advance) for each leads to a lodge with a delightful view of the Nile; maybe of a rapid, perhaps an island-strewn panorama. There's a variety to choose from; upmarket, mid-range, budget and glamping are all on offer but what most have in common is an emphasis on relaxation. You may be motivated to sit on a horse or take a boat trip or farm tour, but (with the exception of Kalagala Falls) there is nothing to compare to the sort of activities you will be expected to undertake at Bujagali.

All of the West Bank tourism sites overlook something pretty special, but the undoubted jewel in the crown is a kilometre section of river flanked by the Kalagala Falls Forest Reserve on the West Bank and the Nile Bank Forest Reserve on the far side. Though themselves unremarkable – the former reserve is recovering from years of degradation and the latter is a plantation – they lie either side of a cluster of magnificent forested islands separated by three of the most violent rapids on the Jinja Nile. Starting on the eastern side, the Nile Bank Forest Reserve overlooks Itanda Falls – a watery hellhole known to rafters, and with good reason, as 'The Bad Place'. The central channel, a heaving 500m-long serpent of water, thrashes wildly between the two largest mid-river islands and is known, reasonably enough, as Hypoxia. It is on the hypnotic views of this maelstrom that the reputation of the superb Wildwaters Lodge (⊕ 0.5818535, 33.0265732) on the western island is largely founded. The main obstacle on the westernmost channel, between Wildwaters Island and Kalagala Falls Forest Reserve, is an abrupt 4m plunge over Kalagala Falls. None of these three channels is raftable. Indeed, while Kalagala Falls Forest Reserve lies just 5km from the tarmac at Kangulumira town, the Nile Bank Forest Reserve, though considerably more remote, was better known for many years as the place where rafters landed and carried their boats safely around the Bad Place.

The profile of Kalagala Falls Forest Reserve is rising fast, however, for it is now the site of a new, multi-faceted tourism development in direct competition to Bujagali.

Leased to the South African lodge chain Lemala, which owns the rafting company Adrift, the reserve now has a range of quality lodgings that cater for all budgets, namely the upmarket Wildwaters Lodge, the Adrift Overland Camp, a state-of-the-art backpacker/overlander facility complete with bungee tower, and the mid-range Adrift River Club.

Getting there and away The West Bank lodges all lie 2–3km east of a surfaced road that loops around the top of Mabira Forest from Kampala to Jinja via Gayaza. Though all are signposted in some form, it is easy to miss the turnings so we have included grid references to help you locate them.

If driving from Kampala, the quiet Gayaza route (page 238) will leave you better disposed towards your lodge experience than the truck-clogged crawl along the main Jinja Road. If coming from Jinja (or from the directions of Mukono or Kisoga; page 162) head north from the roundabout on the west side of the Nile Bridge roundabout and then continue north from the next intersection on the Kampala–Jinja road at Njeru (⊕ 0.44033, 33.1783) opposite Nile Breweries [232 A2].

Where to stay

Exclusive/luxury

✷ **Wildwaters Lodge** [250 B2] (10 cottages) ⊕ 0.59432, 33.05497 (parking); t 039 2776669; m 0754 237500; e info@wild-uganda.com; w wildwaterslodge.com. This magnificent lodge extends across a forested island at Kalagala Falls, 28km upriver of Jinja. It's a truly exclusive experience, walk-in visitors being discouraged by a US$85 day entrance fee. Not that walking in is an option, given the island is reached by a boat ride from the mainland; it's only a minute long, but the sound of roaring rapids just downstream ensures the voyage has your full attention. The huge thatch-&-canvas cottages are individually shaped to the terrain & the forest setting with beautifully appointed interiors & a private river-view balcony with outdoor bathtub. 6 cottages stand broadside on to the Nile, looking down into the thunderous Hypoxia rapid; settings that come with 24/7 sound effects. The remainder face upstream & enjoy a more placid view of the oncoming river. The smart lodge building & swimming pool manage to combine both prospects; the perfect place to while away an afternoon monitoring fluctuating water levels (these are controlled by the dam upriver) & supervising the sinking sun as it imbues the swirling waters with crepuscular hues. Shortly after, when you retreat to the dining area, leaving the river to roar through the darkness, you'll find your selections from the à la carte menu to be quite superb. For safety reasons, children under 12 are not allowed on to the island. High/low season & week/weekend rates apply with substantial discounts for residents. **$$$$$$**

Upmarket

✷ **Adrift River Club** [250 A2] (16 rooms) Contacts as for Wildwaters Lodge (see left). Intended to fill the niche between the upmarket Wildwaters & the budget Adrift Overland Camp (page 258), the River Club stands on a high river cliff overlooking the Nile. More specifically, the superbly placed bar-restaurant enjoys a picture-postcard view of Wildwaters Island & the confluence of the channels containing Kalagala Falls & Hypoxia, while the chalets offer full frontal views of Kalagala Falls. Walk-in guests are welcomed; 3-course meals cost US$25. *US$242/342 sgl/dbl B&B. Discounts for residents.* **$$$$**

The Haven [250 B3] (10 units) ⊕ 0.54195, 33.08996; m 0702 905959, 0782 905959; e thehavenuganda@yahoo.com; w thehaven-uganda.com. This riverside lodge, 17km along the road from Njeru (⊕ 0.521586, 33.080036), boasts a great location overlooking the Grade V Overtime Rapid. The spacious en-suite bungalows & bandas, constructed using natural materials & decorated in earthy tones, have hammock, river-facing balcony & UV-filtered spring water hot shower. There's also a Honeymoon Cottage with a floor-level bathtub in front of a picture window overlooking the rapids. Pitch-your-own & lazy camping are also available. Facilities include a swimming pool, children's play area, silent solar-powered boat (popular with birders) & restaurant serving European cuisine. Shoreline wildlife includes fish eagle, red-tailed monkey, otter & monitor lizard. *US$320 dbl honeymoon cottage; US$320 dbl family suite, plus US$45 per child; bandas from US$165/275 sgl/dbl; US$85/150 sgl/dbl lazy camping; US$55 pp camping. All rates FB.* **$$$$**

✷ **Kipling Lodge** [250 B3] (5 cottages) ⊕ 0.56583, 33.07305; m 0782 390243; e bookings@thekiplinglodge.com; w thekiplinglodge.com. A day or 2 at owner-managed Kipling Lodge, which enjoys a super view of the oncoming Nile from a bend in the river, is a genuine pleasure. Start off by taking your morning cuppa from your cottage to the top of the boulder-topped river bluff to watch the swirling currents below & plan your programme. Many guests will find lounging beside the pool sufficiently time consuming but some make time for a cruise up to Overtime Rapid, a tour of the vanilla gardens or even a session with a local potter; exertions fuelled by thrice-daily offerings from the dedicated Belgian-Ugandan kitchen. *From US$165/220 sgl/dbl FB.* **$$$$**

✷ **Saranac on the Nile** [250 B3] (5 cottages) ⊕ 0.56583, 33.07305; m 0787 117999; e bookings@saranaconthenile.com; w saranaconthenile.com. Right next door to Kipling Lodge, this delightful self-catering setup stands in extensive grounds that flow around chunky, water-smoothed boulders to the water's edge. An attractive pool with an attached, open-sided lounge & kitchen is provided, along with kayaks if you prefer the river. Bring your own food; a cook can be arranged on request. Accommodation is in modern units beneath thatched roofs. *Main house (sleeps 6) US$290; 1-bedroom bedsit/kitchen US$145; 2-bedroom bedsit/kitchen with private room; US$175.* **$$$**

Budget and camping

Adrift Overland Camp [250 A2] Contacts as for Wildwaters Lodge (page 257). This superb new 'budget' facility at Kalagala Falls has set a completely new benchmark for backpacker/overland accommodation in Uganda. Accommodation is in state-of-the-art dorms (1 2-tier bunk in each partitioned pod; pristine shared bathrooms) & spacious standing tents (shared facilities). An open-sided bar-restaurant beside the river offers pizzas, burgers (US$8–10) & salads (US$6). There's even a bungee jump on site (see opposite). Though popular with overland groups welcoming a bit of relative luxury, the rates may not appeal to penny-pinching backpackers. *Dorm bed US$31; standing tents US$45 pp; camping US$15. Rates exc b/fast (full English costs US$7).* **$$–$$$**

Nile It Resort [250 B4] ⊕ 0.5041152, 33.1232947; m 0772 222777; e nileitresort@gmail.com; w nileitresort.com. Owned & managed by the same people as Ssese's legendary Banda Island Resort (page 205), this rather luxurious riverside campsite offers the choice between pitching your own tent or lazy camping in a cosy standing tent with mattress & bedding. A restaurant serves favourites from around the world & a variety of activities includes birding, with 120 species recorded so far. Nile It is 10km north of Njeru & within walking distance of the main road. *US$44/72 sgl/dbl lazy camping; US$25 pp in own tent. All rates B&B.* **$$$**

✷ **Tulina Riverside Retreat** [250 B3] (8 rooms) ⊕ 0.54076, 33.09108; m 0776 460354; e tulina@tulinariverside.com. This budget lodge next to The Haven has a fabulous riverside setting in large pretty gardens, & functional but comfortable & well-priced en-suite rooms. An adequate restaurant has terrace seating. *US$60/70 sgl/dbl; US$20 pp camping. B&B.* **$$**

What to see and do

White-water rafting The new Kalagala Falls tourism hub is a staging point for Adrift's white-water rafting (page 252) excursions, while Nile River Explorers also launch and conclude their trips on the west side of the river.

Horseriding All horseback excursions offered by various operators in and around Jinja are run by **Nile Horseback Safaris** [250 C4] (⊕ 0.47585, 33.15479; m 0774 101196; e info@nilehorsebacksafaris.com; w nilehorsebacksafaris.com), whose stables, housing around 20 calm and well-cared-for horses, stand on the West Bank about 4.5km north of Njeru. Short (1–2 hour) safaris leave daily at 10.00 and 14.00, and sunset safaris leave on demand at 16.30 on Fridays and Saturdays. For more experienced riders, overnight and multi-day safaris using upmarket lodges on the West Bank of the Nile and in Mabira Forest are also available, as are kids' pony rides. Day rates range from US$45 per person for 1 hour to US$65 per person for 2 hours.

Bungee-jumping Adrift Overland Camp (see opposite) has constructed a 52m bungee jump above the Nile at Kalagala Falls (US$115; US$100 for residents). A second jump is half price; a third is free.

Other activities Many lodges offer walks and tours to experience the local way of life, learn more about coffee or vanilla, etc. Adrift Overland Camp and the adjacent Nile Club run community walks that include visits to Kalagala Falls (alternatively just pay US$1.50 at the gate) and the nearby Kalagala Cultural Centre. The latter site includes a massive tree beneath which visiting kabakas sat, while an ancient shrine, still of considerable importance to traditionalists, is found within a jumble of massive riverside boulders. If you're keen to show a new route on your Strava, a jogging trail with a local runner is also an option (Ush10,000)

EXCURSIONS FURTHER AFIELD

Jinja is a feasible base for two sites of historical interest in the lake hinterland east of the town.

JAMES HANNINGTON MEMORIAL SITE (⊕ 0.43389, 33.42887; m 0757 992485, 0701 500452) Situated in the village of Kyando (pronounced Chando) about 25km east of Jinja as the crow flies, this memorial site forms part of a church and health centre named after the Anglican missionary Bishop James Hannington, who was killed in 1885, together with 50 of his porters, by an emissary of Kabaka Mwanga (page 260). It is an important pilgrimage site that attracts thousands of Anglicans from all over East Africa on 29 October, the anniversary of the bishop's death. The stone where Hannington was speared to death is now a covered shrine, and the caretaker will also show you other sites associated with the bishop. These include a concreted-up spring of holy water once drunk from by the bishop, as well as a pair of rocky shelters on a nearby hill, one of which is reputedly where he slept, and the other where he stored the books he was carrying. There is no entrance fee but a tip will be expected.

The signposted and newly surfaced road to Kyando runs south from a junction in the small town of Busita (⊕ 0.5281, 33.38455) on the Tororo Road about 21km east of Jinja. Follow this road south for 8km to Bufululubi (⊕ 0.49543, 33.43143), then turn right at the signpost for the memorial, passing through Nkombe after 7km, then continuing for another 2.5km to the prominent church and shrine. There is no public transport past Bufululubi, but bodas are available at Busita.

LOLWE ISLAND Also known as Lolui or Dolwe, this remote island, some 30km by boat from the mainland landing at Bwondha, is strewn with giant granite outcrops that harbour some of the most intriguing archaeological sites anywhere in Uganda. Several prehistoric rock-art sites exist on the island, the best known being the Sanctuary, a chamber supported by four extensively painted granite boulders near the lakeside village of Golofa. Reminiscent of Nyero near Kumi, the artwork at Lolwe

THE DEATH OF BISHOP HANNINGTON

The Rev James Hannington first set foot in East Africa in June 1882 as the leader of a reinforcement party for the Victoria Nyanza Mission in Kampala, but he was forced to return to England before reaching Uganda owing to a debilitating case of dysentery. In June 1884, he was consecrated in London as the first bishop of Eastern Equatorial Africa. In November of the same year, he left England to assume his post, inspired by Joseph Thomson, who months earlier had become the first European to travel to Lake Victoria through Maasailand, rather than the longer but less perilous route pioneered by Speke around the south of the lake.

Thomson advised future travellers against attempting to reach Buganda through the territory occupied by the militant Maasai, but Bishop Hannington – attracted by its directness and better climatic conditions – paid him no heed. And, as it transpired, Hannington and his party of 200 porters negotiated the route without encountering any significant resistance from the Kikuyu or Maasai, to arrive at Mumias (in present-day western Kenya) on 8 October 1885. A few days later, accompanied by a reduced party of 50 porters, Hannington continued the march westward, obtaining his first view of Lake Victoria on 14 October.

Hannington had been fully aware of the risks involved in crossing Maasailand, but he had no way of knowing about the momentous change in mood that had marked Buganda since the death of King Mutesa a year earlier. Mutesa was succeeded by his son Mwanga, who became increasingly hostile towards outsiders in general and the Anglican Church in particular during the first year of his reign. Worse still, Mwanga was deeply affected by a vision that foretold the destruction of Buganda at the hands of strangers who entered the kingdom through the 'back door' – the east – as opposed to the more normal approach from the southwest.

mostly comprises geometric patterns – sets of concentric circles, or sausage and dumbbell shapes – painted with ochre pigments. The island is also liberally scattered with ancient rock gongs, ceramics and cairns dating back more than 500 years, several rock shrines to important Luo deities, and literally thousands of artificial stone hollows whose purpose is unknown.

Getting to Lolwe used to involve a long and potentially dangerous boat trip but matters have been simplified by the 2022 launch of the *MV Sigulu*, a modern ferry capable of carrying 300 passengers. This departs daily except Sunday from Watega landing (⊕ 0.1456324, 33.8077785), roughly 35km south of Namayingo (⊕ 0.3422932, 33.8763372) on the surfaced Busita–Mayuge–Busia Road. Once on the island, accommodation can be found at the La Fang Eco Resort (m 0702 728335, 0752 220780). Alternatively, Maleng Safaris (m 0778 278853) is developing a small campsite/lodge.

On 21 October 1885, Hannington and his party entered the fort of Luba, an important Basoga chief with strong loyalties to the King of Buganda. Hours later, the bishop was attacked and imprisoned, and Luba sent a party of messengers to Mwanga to seek instructions. The messengers returned on 28 October accompanied by three Baganda soldiers. The next morning, Hannington wrote in his diary: 'I can hear no news. A hyena howled near me last night, smelling a sick man, but I hope it is not to have me yet.' On the afternoon of 29 October, Hannington was informed that he would be escorted to Buganda immediately. Instead, he was led to a nearby execution rock, stripped of his clothes and possessions, and speared to death. That night, Luba's soldiers massacred the bishop's entire party of 50 porters, with the exception of three men who managed to escape and one boy who was spared on account of his youth.

It is said locally that the murder of Bishop Hannington displeased the spirits and resulted in a long famine in Busoga. King Mwanga, not entirely plausibly, would subsequently claim that he had never ordered Hannington's death; instead, his instructions to release the bishop had been misinterpreted or disregarded by overzealous underlings. In 1890, the bishop's skull – identifiable by his gold fillings – and some of his clothes were brought to Sir Frederick Jackson in Mumias by the one member of Hannington's party who had been spared by Luba's soldiers. The mortal remains of Bishop Hannington were interred at Namirembe Cathedral on 31 December 1892 in a lavish ceremony attended by Mwanga. On 29 October 1939, the 54th anniversary of his death, a bronze memorial dedicated to James Hannington was erected on a boulder near the small port of Buluba (Place of Luba), some 20km east of Jinja as the crow flies. In 2013, a more lavish memorial was unveiled at the Bishop Hannington Church and Health Centre in Nkombe, the site of his death, some 7km south of Buluba (page 259).

10

Mbale and Mount Elgon

Straddling the Kenyan border east of Kampala and Jinja, freestanding Mount Elgon is the centrepiece of the eponymous national park on both sides of the border. At 4,321m, it is the second-highest massif in Uganda, and it boasts the largest base of any extinct volcano in the world. Although it is a worthwhile and relatively affordable hiking destination, the national park sees little tourist traffic compared with the Rwenzori, though Sipi Falls, on its western footslopes, has long been popular with resident weekenders and backpackers seeking a relaxed rambling destination to settle into for a few days. The main town in the region, set at the base of the mountain, is Mbale, an agreeable but unremarkable place associated with the unusual Abayudaya, a Jewish community founded by a Ugandan in the early 20th century. Also of interest is Tororo, a small but rather pretty town set below a large and eminently climbable volcanic plug known as Tororo Rock.

BUSIA

The busiest border crossing between Kenya and Uganda is Busia (⊕ 0.46521, 34.09958), which lies on the main highway between Nairobi and Kampala. Busia is also the name of the similarly sized twin towns that flank the border post, both of which are significant trade and market centres with a population of around 55,000 apiece. Arriving from Kenya by bus, most travellers continue straight on through to Jinja or Kampala, but if you need to stop over, there are several banks with ATMs, including an Absa only 100m from the border post.

GETTING THERE AND AWAY Busia lies about 450km west of Nairobi, 120km northwest of Kisumu, 120km east of Jinja and 200km east of Kampala. All coaches running between the two countries stop there to complete border formalities. There are also plenty of matatus from the taxi park to the likes of Tororo, Jinja, Mbale and Kampala..

WHERE TO STAY AND EAT The pick of the lodgings is the quiet, friendly and comfortable **Jireh Guesthouse** (m 0782 330595; f jirehguest; **$**) which stands on the main road to Kampala 3km from the border post. On the Kenyan side, about 1.5km from the border post, is the superior **Farmview Hotel** (⊕ 0.45769, 34.10547; +254 (020) 2315443; e info@farmviewhotel.co.ke; **$$**).

WHAT TO SEE AND DO

Majanji The closest thing to an established tourist attraction in the Busia District, Majanji stands on an attractive bay on the Lake Victoria shore about 30km south of town. Here, the **Sangalo Beach Resort** (⊕ 0.24081, 33.99119; m 0774 282506; f sangalosandbeach) is a pleasant and low-key setup with a stunning location on a palm-lined peninsula facing the small Kenyan port of Sio. Motor and rowing boats are available for birding and hippo spotting on the lake. The 40 rooms are decent value for the location (US$21 sgl/dbl; US$40 sgl/dbl for a thatched banda; all rates B&B; **$$**), and the restaurant serves decent enough meals. Beaten-up matatus run to Majanji from the Busia police station, but you may need to transfer to a boda for the last few kilometres to the resort. Alternatively, a special hire from Busia will cost around US$5.

Busitema Forest Reserve Bisected by the Kampala–Tororo Road as it runs northeast from the junction to Busia, this reserve protects 28km^2 of semi-deciduous woodland comprising more than 200 tree species depleted by recent encroachment and a voracious bush fire in 2015. Baboons and other monkeys are frequently seen from the roadside, and the reserve supports a variety of birdlife, though claims that it supports a population of Fox's weaver, a swamp-associated Ugandan endemic, seem improbable. No entrance fee is charged.

TORORO

Situated 10km west of the Malaba border post with Kenya, this backwater of around 45,000 people is best known as the site of the iconic Tororo Rock, an isolated volcanic plug that rises about 300m above the town centre to an altitude of 1,485m, where it is capped by a copse of radio and satellite masts. For much of the 20th century, Tororo was one of Uganda's important rail, road and trade hubs, but it has fallen off the travel map in recent years – partly because of the railway's closure, partly because Busia is now the more popular border crossing with Kenya, and partly because there is now a more direct and westerly surfaced road connecting Mbale to Kampala/Jinja. Still, Tororo's exaggeratedly wide pavements, lined with a straggle of flowering trees and colonial-era façades, pay testament to its former prosperity, as does a trio of impressive Hindu temples.

HISTORY Although little information is available about the early history of Tororo, the Catholic Apostolic Vicariate of Upper Nile was established immediately north of the present-day town centre in 1894. The original Uganda Railway terminated at Tororo when it started operation in 1926, and it remained an important rail hub after 1931 when it became the junction of new lines running west to Kampala and north to Soroti. Well located for cross-border trade and the site of Uganda's main cement factory from 1952 onwards, Tororo supported roughly 1,000 Asian and European settlers by the time of independence, when it ranked among Uganda's ten most populous and prosperous towns. Its economic significance has since diminished, partly because of the closure of the railway in the 1990s and associated ascent of more southerly Busia as the more important border crossing with Kenya.

Looking ahead, Malaba, 10km to the east of Tororo, is one of two alternative designated sites (the other being Kisumu) for a US$120 million dry port where containers railed up from the Kenyan coast will be stored for clearance prior to being transported into Uganda or on to other neighbouring countries. More certainly, the cement industry in Tororo is currently enjoying a boom: the Tororo Cement Company (privatised back in the 1990s) recently invested US$50 million to expand its annual production from 1.8 to 3.0 million metric tonnes, while the Kenyan company Simba Cement and western Uganda's Hima Cement opened new plants at Tororo in 2017 and 2018 respectively.

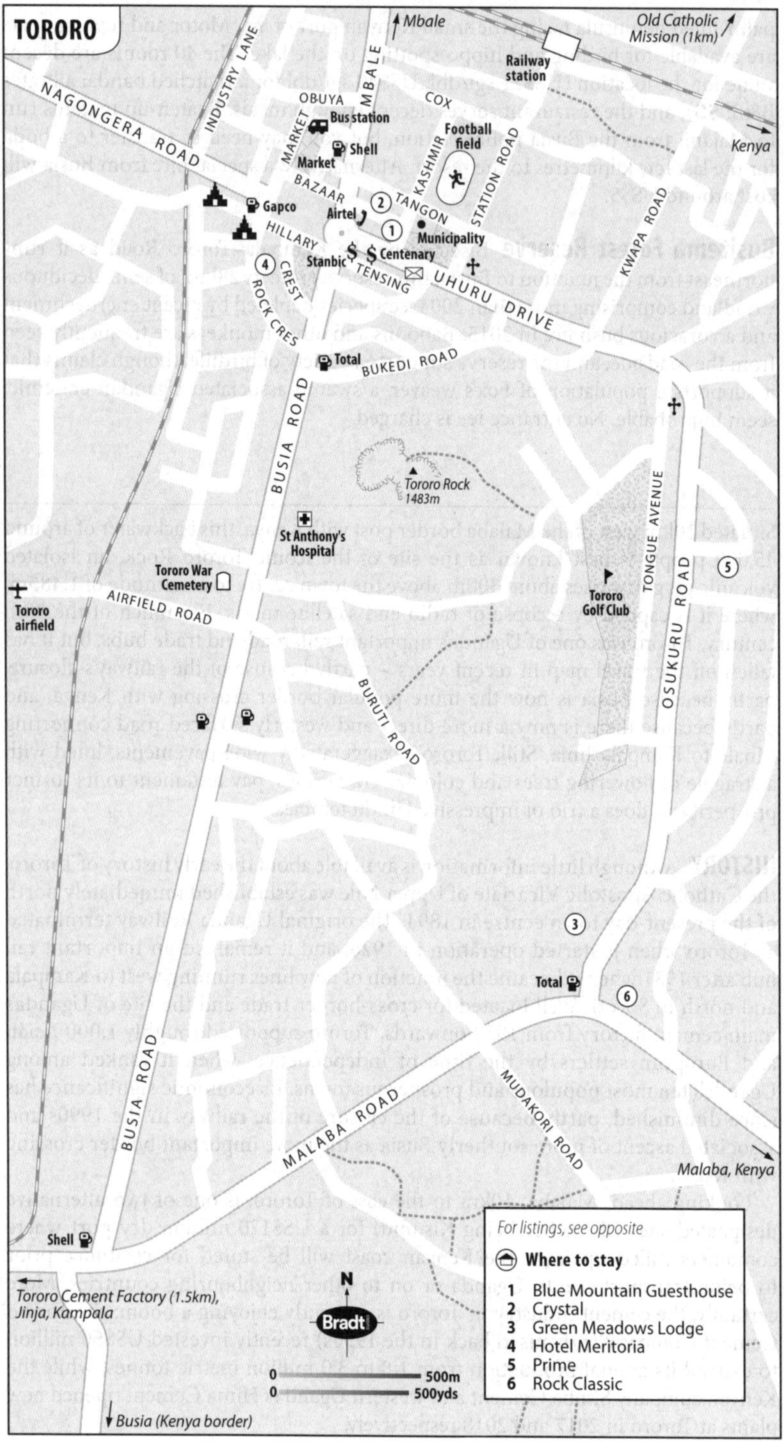

TORORO
Mbale
Old Catholic Mission (1km)
Railway station
Kenya
NAGONGERA ROAD
INDUSTRY LANE
MBALE
OBUYA
COX
Bus station
MARKET
Shell
Market
Football field
KASHMIR
STATION ROAD
BAZAAR
Gapco
Airtel
TANGON
Municipality
KWAPA ROAD
HILLARY
Stanbic
Centenary
TENSING
UHURU DRIVE
CREST
ROCK CRES
Total
BUKEDI ROAD
BUSIA ROAD
Tororo Rock
1483m
St Anthony's Hospital
Tororo War Cemetery
Tororo airfield
AIRFIELD ROAD
TONGUE AVENUE
OSUKURU ROAD
Tororo Golf Club
BURUTI ROAD
Total
MUDAKORI ROAD
MALABA ROAD
Malaba, Kenya
Shell
Tororo Cement Factory (1.5km), Jinja, Kampala
Busia (Kenya border)
N
Bradt
0 500m
0 500yds
For listings, see opposite
Where to stay
1 Blue Mountain Guesthouse
2 Crystal
3 Green Meadows Lodge
4 Hotel Meritoria
5 Prime
6 Rock Classic

GETTING THERE AND AWAY Tororo lies on the old surfaced road between Jinja (130km to the west) and Mbale (40km to the north), at the junction with the road running 10km east to the Malaba border post. A daily Gateway Bus (m 0778 092178) leaves Tororo for Kampala at 06.30 and starts the return trip at 13.30. In addition, regular matatus run to/from Kampala (US$5.50), Jinja (US$3), Mbale (US$1.50) and Malaba (less than US$1).

WHERE TO STAY AND EAT *Map, opposite*

Moderate

✱ Green Meadows Lodge (12 rooms) Buwesa Cl, off Osukuru Rd; m 0776 435063, 0743 564699; e greenmeadowstororo@gmail.com. Easily the nicest place to stay in Tororo, this quiet out-of-town lodge stands in well-tended gardens on the slopes below the main cement quarry. The neat, spacious & modern-looking rooms come with 1 queen-size or 2 ¾ beds with fitted nets, garden view, flatscreen DSTV & en-suite hot shower. A restaurant serves a selection of fried & grilled meat & vegetarian dishes in the US$6–8 range. *US$43/52 sgl/dbl B&B.* **$$**

Rock Classic Hotel (100 rooms) Malaba Rd; ☎ 045 4448102; m 0775 024945; e rockclassichotel@yahoo.com; f rockclassicht. The imposing stone-clad frontage of Tororo's best-known hotel flatters to deceive, as does the attractive garden complete with swimming pool. Tired en-suite rooms with AC, DSTV, balcony & fitted nets are poor value compared with Green Meadows though renovations are promised. That said, the poolside bar is a nice spot for a drink & possibly a meal. *From US$35/52 dbl/twin.* **$$**

Budget

Crystal Hotel (14 rooms) Bazaar Rd; m 0702 555174; e crystalhoteltororo@gmail.com. This central multi-storey building has been the budget standout in Tororo since the early 1990s. Clean, tiled en-suite rooms come with nets, fans, DSTV, & private balcony facing Tororo Rock. The inexpensive ground-floor restaurant remains the best central option, too. *US$11/13 sgl/dbl B&B.* **$**

Hotel Meritoria (16 rooms) Rock Cres West; ☎ 048 4437693; m 0752 736679; e info@hotelmeritoria.com; w hotelmeritoria.com. Another good central hotel, despite the preposterous name, this has acceptable but rather small tiled rooms with DSTV, Wi-Fi, balcony & en-suite hot shower. A decent restaurant is attached. *US$11/14 sgl/dbl exc b/fast.* **$**

Prime Hotel (24 rooms) Off Osukuru Rd; m 0772 591862. Set in a green garden compound in leafy Malakasi suburb, this efficiently run & justifiably popular hotel has spacious tiled rooms with nets, fans & DSTV. The restaurant serves good continental & Indian food. Well priced. *US$23/28 sgl/dbl B&B.* **$$**

Shoestring

Blue Mountain Guesthouse (6 rooms) Bazaar Rd; ☎ 045 4448253. The pick of Tororo's cheapies, this small guesthouse opposite Crystal Hotel has well-priced tiled en-suite rooms. *US$8 dbl.* **$**

OTHER PRACTICALITIES Forex services are provided at the **Stanbic Bank** in the town centre. Some good **supermarkets** are located at the western end of Bazaar Road, and there are a few internet cafés.

WHAT TO SEE AND DO

Tororo Rock This steep and partly forested volcanic plug, which protrudes about 300m above the town centre's southern skyline, is reputedly visible from everywhere in Tororo District. It takes about an hour to climb, a short but very steep hike using steps and ladders on the trickier bits, and up to an hour to descend again. The peak offers panoramic views towards Mount Elgon, 35km to the northeast, as well as across the border into Kenya. The trailhead (⊕ 0.68375, 34.18743) is on High Road (off Tongue Avenue) behind the northern end of the golf course. There's no entrance fee. Guides are optional but recommended, and can be arranged through Green Meadows Lodge (see above) and most other hotels in town, and usually ask around US$5 per party. The best time to hike is in the relative cool of the early morning.

Tororo Golf Club (Tongue Av; m 0700 355870) Visitors are welcome at this venerable club, whose nine-hole golf course, set at the southeast base of Tororo Rock, was constructed during the town's 1950s heyday and is still very well tended but rather undersubscribed to. Other facilities include a badminton court, snooker table, tennis court, the best swimming pool in town and a good restaurant/bar. A nominal fee is charged to outsiders for use of the pool or to play a round of golf.

MBALE

Perched at a temperate altitude of 1,200m on the western footslopes of Mount Elgon, Mbale is an agreeable and substantial town whose compact and rather hectic centre is surrounded by leafy suburbs, sprawling eastward to the foot of the dramatic Wanale Cliffs, the westernmost extent of Mount Elgon. The town was established at the start of the 20th century (page 270) and soon grew to become Uganda's third most populous settlement, a status it retained until the mid 1990s, since when it has slipped to seventh place, with a population of 289,000. Relatively few travellers visit Mbale, and those who do generally pass through briefly in transit to Mount Elgon or the Sipi Falls. Despite this, Mbale has a greater sense of place than most Ugandan towns east of the Nile, thanks largely to its striking cliff-base location below Mount Elgon, whose volcanic peaks are sometimes visible in clear weather. Also in its favour, Mbale was left relatively unscarred by the events of 1971–86, and its streets are lined with many well-preserved examples of colonial-era Asian and European architecture.

GETTING THERE AND AWAY Mbale lies about 230km from Kampala along an excellent surfaced road through Jinja and Iganga (turn left about 3km east of Iganga to avoid Tororo and follow the lightly trafficked tarmac road to its west). Traffic congestion on the outskirts of Kampala, plus slow trailers and tankers on the Jinja Road, mean that the trip often takes up to 6 hours. Other distances and estimated driving times are 144km/2½ hours from Jinja, 55km/45 minutes from Tororo, 100km/90 minutes from Soroti, and 45km/45 minutes from Sipi.

There is plenty of public transport from Kampala to Mbale. The most reliable option from Kampala is the **YY Coach**, which leaves from the Namayiba Bus Terminal (f yycoaches) and arrives at Mbale's main bus station. Regular **matatus** out of the Old Taxi Park are quicker but driven with less care. An alternative, recommended at Casa del Turista (page 269), is the 11-seater **O-Express** (m Kampala: 0775 364540, Mbale: 0775 757853). This leaves Kampala's Colville Street (near Theatre La Bonita) for Mbale daily at 04.30, 08.00, 10.00 and noon and departs Bishop Wasike Road in Mbale at 03.00, 09.00 and 13.00 (US$8). Matatus also run from Jinja, Tororo or Soroti. Most local places of interest can be reached by matatu and details are given under the individual sites later in this chapter.

TOURIST INFORMATION All aspects relating to hikes on Mount Elgon, including equipment hire, can be arranged at the national park's helpful tourist information office in the **MENP HQ** [267 E3] (t 039 2176475; m 0774 288053; e menp@ugandawildlife.org) on Masaba Road, 1km southeast of the town centre. A good source of information online is w exploreelgon.com.

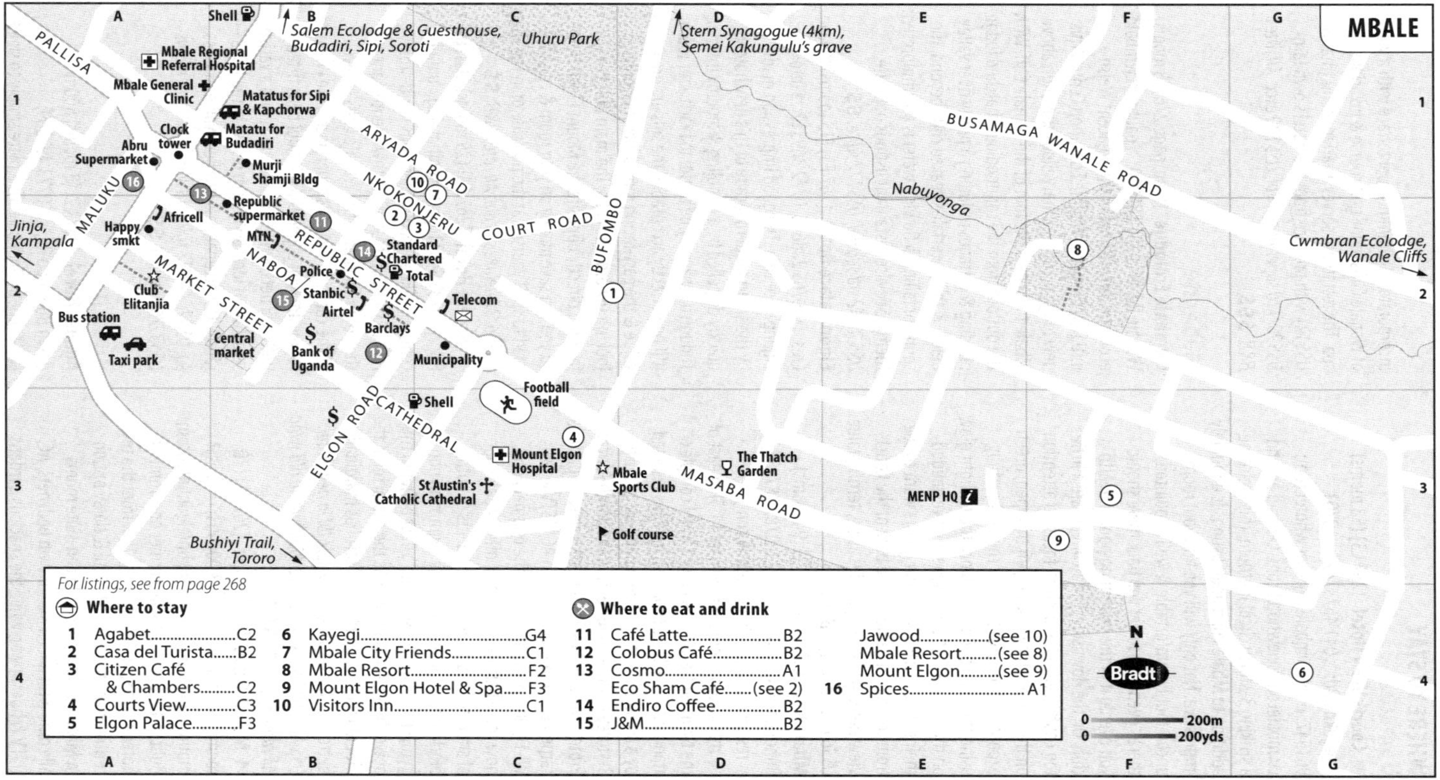
MBALE
A
B
C
D
E
F
G
1
2
3
4
Salem Ecolodge & Guesthouse, Budadiri, Sipi, Soroti
Uhuru Park
Stern Synagogue (4km), Semei Kakungulu's grave
Cwmbran Ecolodge, Wanale Cliffs
Jinja, Kampala
Bushiyi Trail, Tororo
PALLISA
MALUKU
MARKET STREET
NABOA
REPUBLIC STREET
ARYADA ROAD
NKOKONJERU
COURT ROAD
BUFOMBO
BUSAMAGA WANALE ROAD
Nabuyonga
ELGON ROAD
CATHEDRAL
MASABA ROAD
Shell
Mbale Regional Referral Hospital
Mbale General Clinic
Matatus for Sipi & Kapchorwa
Matatu for Budadiri
Clock tower
Abru Supermarket
Murji Shamji Bldg
Republic supermarket
Africell
Happy smkt
MTN
Police
Stanbic
Airtel
Standard Chartered
Total
Telecom
Barclays
Bank of Uganda
Municipality
Club Elitanjia
Bus station
Taxi park
Central market
Shell
Football field
Mount Elgon Hospital
St Austin's Catholic Cathedral
Mbale Sports Club
The Thatch Garden
Golf course
MENP HQ
N
Bradt
0 200m
0 200yds
For listings, see from page 268
Where to stay
1 Agabet....C2
2 Casa del Turista....B2
3 Citizen Café & Chambers....C2
4 Courts View....C3
5 Elgon Palace....F3
6 Kayegi....G4
7 Mbale City Friends....C1
8 Mbale Resort....F2
9 Mount Elgon Hotel & Spa....F3
10 Visitors Inn....C1
Where to eat and drink
11 Café Latte....B2
12 Colobus Café....B2
13 Cosmo....A1
Eco Sham Café....(see 2)
14 Endiro Coffee....B2
15 J&M....B2
Jawood....(see 10)
Mbale Resort....(see 8)
Mount Elgon....(see 9)
16 Spices....A1

WHERE TO STAY

Upmarket

✷ **Courts View Hotel** [267 C3] (58 rooms) Bungukho Rd; ☎ 041 4673742; m 0701 961547; e info@mbalecourtsviewhotel.com; w mbalecourtsviewhotel.com. Centred around a striking 3-storey circular atrium, this welcome addition to Mbale's upmarket listings is genuinely impressive. Not only will you find your room uncommonly comfortable & well appointed, there's even a lift to get you back there should you overdo it in the swimming pool or health club. On the downside, the architects are a little too chuffed with themselves, focusing attention on their creation by blocking off the open, green expanses of the adjacent golf course & artfully using the main building to block the twilight glow on the Wanale Cliffs. Or maybe they've gauged their market perfectly & what guests want to see from the pool & garden is the back of the Courts View Hotel. Aesthetic quibbles aside, terrific value. *US$65/72 sgl/dbl B&B*. **$$**

Mbale Resort Hotel [267 F2] (94 rooms) Bungukho Rd; m 0758 210121, 0782 787333; e reservation@mbaleresorthotel.com; w mbaleresorthotel.com. Situated 1.5km east of the town centre, Mbale's largest hotel complex stands in large, leafy suburban gardens bisected by a stream. On the northern bank sits a plush 3-storey block – briefly part of the South African Protea hotel chain – that boasts smart & spacious carpeted rooms provided with AC, DSTV & fast Wi-Fi. On the southern side, the original hotel, now the Mbale Resort Annex, offers a selection of smaller, cheaper rooms. Residents of both blocks enjoy the use of a large swimming pool, gym, spa, 2 bars & a splendid b/fast buffet in the newer hotel. Although it lacks the character of the Mount Elgon Hotel, Mbale Resort has marginally better facilities. *US$100/112 sgl/dbl in new hotel; US$40/53/67/67 small sgl/sgl/dbl/twin in old wing. All rates B&B*. **$$–$$$**

✷ **Mount Elgon Hotel & Spa** [267 F3] (30 rooms) Masaba Rd; m 0773 008903; e sales@mountelgonhotel.com; w mountelgonhotel.com. Built in 1958, this stalwart former government hotel, set in spacious grounds, 1km from the town centre, is the most characterful & classy option in Mbale. Stylishly decorated en-suite rooms all come with queen-size or twin bed, nets, AC, DSTV & hot shower, while the spacious gardens incorporate a swimming pool terrace with a view of Wanale Cliffs, mini-golf course & luxurious spa. The restaurant serves a varied menu (mains US$12) with produce from the hotel's own farm. *US$90/110 superior sgl/dbl; US$180 exec. All rates B&B*. **$$$**

Moderate

Cwmbale Ecolodge [map, page 276] (8 rooms) Wanale Rd; m 0781 785030; e paulm@cwmbale.ecolodge. An offshoot of the adjacent Welsh-initiated Cwmbale Wildlife Education Centre, this new lodge occupies a marvellous site, high above Mbale town near the foot of the Wanale Cliff. With the outlook from the commodious thatched lodge building & cottages including a pretty river valley below & the waterfall-streaked cliffs beyond, the sound of falling & flowing water is an omnipresent theme. See also restaurant listings opposite. *US$50/62 std sgl/dbl; US$177 suite*. **$$**

Elgon Palace Hotel [267 F3] (15 rooms) Bwayo Cres; m 0765 208646, 0772 369512; e info@elgonpalace.com. The good impression made by the smart modern façade of this new hotel is quickly dispelled by a rambling & gloomy interior. Though a torch may be useful to reach your room, it'll be perfectly acceptable; the sgls are great value & the east-facing rooms have balconies looking towards the cliffs. The main plus is a location directly opposite the Mount Elgon Hotel, so you can save money on your room & cross the road to spoil yourself at the poolside or in the spa. *US$16/32 deluxe sgl/dbl. All rates B&B*. **$$**

✷ **Kayegi Hotel** [267 G4] (25 rooms) Masaba Rd; m 0789 543316; e kayegihotelug@gmail.com; f. Like so many others, this multi-storey hotel 2km southeast of the town centre ignores the potential view of the Wanale Cliffs in favour of the car park, but ticks other boxes; the en-suite rooms are well appointed with dbl beds fitted with box nets, while a restaurant serves a varied selection of local & Western dishes in the US$3–4 range. Dbl occupancy is excellent value; sgl less so. *US$26/30/32 sgl/dbl/twin; larger exec rooms US$32/66 sgl/dbl*. **$$**

Budget

Agabet Hotel [267 C2] (8 rooms) 800m down Bufombo Rd; m 0773 497209; f AgabetHotelMbale. As a place simply to sleep, the Agabet does the job with spotless, recently renovated cottages at a bargain price. However, the restaurant & grounds are more ordinary & its location is slightly out on a limb, so ideally you'll have a vehicle for wining & dining elsewhere. *US$17/22 sgl/dbl en-suite cottage B&B.* **$$**

✷ **Casa del Turista** [267 B2] (12 rooms) Nkokonjeru Tce; m 0772 328085, 0702 328085; e hello@casaugandasafaris.com; w exploreelgon.com. Mbale's hottest backpacker & volunteer hangout has a relaxed & friendly vibe. Comfortable rooms with stylish wood & iron furniture are supplemented by the rooftop Eco Sham Café, which offers a view of Wanale Cliffs & a tempting & affordable menu. Salads, stir-fries, wraps, sandwiches & pasta fall into the US$4–8 range, while a variety of generously laden pizzas cost US$6–8. Street parking only. *US$19/30 sgl/dbl; 2-room apartment with kitchen US$22/room; basic dorms with shared facilities US$10 pp.* **$$**

Citizen Café & Chambers [267 C2] (4 rooms) m 0772 210414, 0759 764952. Behind an unloved road frontage lie some small but comfortable & reasonably priced apartments (lounge/bedroom). There's also a rooftop café attached – an affordable but less atmospheric version of the nearby Eco Sham Caféat Casa del Turista (see above). A percentage of profits support young surgeons, that deserving yet often overlooked sector of medical society. Compound parking available. *US$16/26 sgl/dbl B&B.* **$$**

Salem Ecolodge & Guesthouse [map, page 276] (16 cottages) ⊕ 1.14213, 34.1493; m 0772 505595; e salem-uganda@salem-mail.net. Situated in a wooded 10ha stand about 10km north of Mbale, this praiseworthy guesthouse is run by the Salem Brotherhood to help fund health-care projects & orphan support. The large clean bandas have 1–3 beds & en-suite hot shower. A great vegetarian restaurant using locally sourced ingredients serves tasty pizzas, & various stews & salads (lunch/dinner US$5.50), as well as a selection of alcoholic & soft drinks. A variety of improving walks in the vicinity explore village, agricultural, natural & educational themes. To get there, follow the Kumi Rd out of town (or catch a Kumi-bound matatu) to Nakaloke, then take a left turn on to the Kolonyi Rd (a phone mast behind the junction is a useful pointer) & follow it for another 2km to the guesthouse. *US$13/18/26 sgl/dbl/trpl B&B.* **$$**

Shoestring

Mbale City Friends [267 C1] (32 rooms) Nkokonjeru Tce; m 0789 751321. Only 100m from the Visitors Inn, this recently completed hotel is also good value & scores over its rival with secure compound parking. *US$9/12/14 sgl/dbl/twin exc b/fast.* **$**

✷ **Visitors Inn** [267 C1] (46 rooms) Nkokonjeru Tce; m 0700 470344; e info@visitorsinn.co.ug; w visitorsinn.co.ug. This high-rise above the Jawood Restaurant (page 272) has clean en-suite tiled rooms with nets, DSTV & hot shower. Exceptional value but street parking only. *US$7/10/17 sgl/dbl/twin exc b/fast.* **$**

WHERE TO EAT AND DRINK Of the hotels listed, the suburban **Mount Elgon Hotel** and **Mbale Resort Hotel** both serve good Western food in agreeable settings. The **Eco Sham Café** in Casa del Turista is a popular and affordable central option.

Moderate to expensive

Café Latte [267 B2] Republic St; m 0757 072729; ⏲ 08.00–22.00 Mon–Sat, 09.00–20.30 Sun. This unassuming café serves a varied selection of sandwiches, salads, grills, curries & pizzas. It has a good internet café & free Wi-Fi, while the extensive drinks menu includes a tempting choice of coffees, liqueurs & cocktails. *Main with naan US$9.*

Colobus Café [267 B2] Court Rd; m 0781 332796. Stylishly decorated with large monochrome artworks depicting local themes, this light, airy & clearly popular new café offers salads, grills & burgers & a variety of juices, smoothies & milkshakes. Colobus Café is affiliated to a local NGO that attempts to persuade local families to adopt fashionable & environmentally responsible alternatives to killing a colobus & putting its skin on their sons' heads during the circumcision season. *Mains US$8.*

Cwmbale Ecolodge [map, page 276] See opposite for contact details. Though 6km out of town up a poor tarmac road, the Ecolodge is worth the trip for the view & the wide-ranging & superbly presented menu. A truly international array of signature dishes from around the world – Jamaica, Hungary,

EARLY DAYS IN MBALE

In 1900, the narrow belt of no-man's-land that divided the cultivated footslopes of Nkokonjeru and its Bagisu inhabitants from the pastoralist people of the Kyoga Basin made a less than favourable impression on visitors. C J Phillips described the area as 'a long wilderness of scrub', William Grant deemed it 'a dreary waste', while one early Muganda visitor called it 'a small and fearsome place, swarming with wild animals'. Back then, certainly, it would have taken a bold soul to suggest this area would become the site of the third-largest town in Uganda! But then Mbale is possibly unique among comparably sized East African towns in that it isn't rooted in a pre-colonial settlement, nor is it truly a colonial creation, but was instead founded by the controversial Muganda administrator and soldier Semei Kakungulu.

Between 1889 and 1901, Kakungulu had single-handedly – or rather with the assistance of a private army of 5,000 Baganda soldiers – subjugated and administered the region of eastern Uganda known as Bukedi (a disparaging Luganda term meaning 'Land of Naked People') as an agent of the British Crown. By 1901, however, Kakungulu was perceived by his colonial paymasters to have developed into a tyrannical force – the self-appointed 'King of Bukedi' – that they could neither stem nor control. In the words of A L Hitching, Kakungulu had indeed 'first reduced [Bukedi] to order, cut the roads, and began to direct the local chiefs', but it was 'rather after the method of making desolation and calling it peace'. And bad enough, that Kakungulu and his army evidently regarded Bukedi 'as a sort of El Dorado', raiding the local cattle and crops at whim. Worse still, the authorities at Entebbe had every reason to believe that their employee was less than scrupulous when it came to declaring and returning the tax he had collected in his official capacity for the Crown.

The Entebbe administration decided that this untenable situation could be resolved only by retiring the self-styled King of Bukedi from the colonial service. But how to achieve this when any hint of force might prompt Kakungulu's army to stage a rebellion the authorities would find difficult to contain? A series of tense communications resulted in a mutually agreeable compromise: Kakungulu would resign his post and hand over his fort at Budoka (30km west of present-day Mbale). In exchange, he would be given 20 square miles (52km^2) of land at a site of his own choosing. Kakungulu selected the plains below Nkokonjeru, which, although practically unoccupied, were run through by several perennial streams and lay close to a reliable supply of the favoured Baganda diet of *matoke*.

Kakungulu and his Baganda followers relocated to Mbale in March 1902, and immediately set about building a new township, one that by several accounts bore strong similarities to the Buganda royal enclosure on Kampala's Mengo Hill. The first European visitors to trickle through Mbale in early 1903 were astonished at the transformation wrought by Kakungulu in one brief year. Bishop Tucker reported that 'on what was little better than a wilderness...we found ourselves surrounded by gardens, well cultivated and well kept; houses, too, had sprung up on every hand, most of them well built'. An equally gushing William Grant described Mbale as 'flourishing with gardens, teeming with life' and added that 'good wide roads have been cut, rivers have been bridged and embankments made through marshy ground, all at [Kakungulu's] expense and for public use'. A map of Mbale dating to 1904 indicates that the central market was situated roughly where the clock tower stands today. Running southwest from the market, a wide road lined with shops and houses approximated the equivalent stretch of present-day Kumi Road. This road continued southwest for about 300m to Kakungulu's fortified compound, which consisted of a large rectangular stone building and seven smaller huts protected within a tall reed fence.

This rapid growth of Mbale was not solely due to its founder's estimable ambition and drive. One contemporary visitor, the missionary J J Willis, described the town's location as 'a natural centre' for trade, elaborating that: 'An excellent road connects Mbale with Jinja to the southwest. A caravan route, very far from excellent, connects it with Mumias to the south. Caravans [from Karamoja] pass through Mbale laden with ivory. And to the northwest a caravan route passes through Serere and Bululu to the Nile Province.' Mbale usurped nearby Mumias as the most important regional trading centre; indeed its market soon became the largest anywhere in the protectorate after Kampala and Entebbe. The permanent population of the nascent metropolis – estimated by Willis to stand at around 3,000 – comprised not only Kakungulu's Buganda followers, but also a substantial number of Greek, Arab, Indian and Swahili traders.

In hindsight, it might be said that when Kakungulu handed over Budoka Fort to Britain, he did not so much abandon his 'El Dorado' as relocate it (and expand it) at his personal estate of Mbale. That much was recognised by the new commissioner, James Sadler, when he made a tour of Bukedi in January 1904. Sadler characterised the established administrative centre at Budoka as consisting of 'two wattle and daub houses and some dilapidated police lines' on a 'bad' site that was 'neither liked by Europeans nor natives'. Mbale, by contrast, impressed him as 'the natural trade centre of the district [and] centre of a Baganda civilisation [of] flourishing plantations [and] substantially built grass-roofed houses'. Sadler decided that Mbale should forthwith replace Budoka as the administrative centre of Bukedi, and attempted to rein in Kakungulu by reappointing him to the regional administration. In 1906, the authorities realised that they would gain full control over Bukedi only in the physical absence of Kakungulu, which they achieved not by retiring him, but by tantalising him away to Jinja to serve as the official head of state of Busoga, a position he held until 1913.

Mbale's rise to prominence had its setbacks. In 1909, Cook described it as a 'thriving little place entered along a broad well-kept road, nearly a mile in length, bordered by thousands of *emsambya* trees and numerous native houses… crowded with the once-turbulent Bagisu engaged in the peaceful activity of bartering their native produce'. A year later, the colonial administration – for a variety of opaque reasons – banned the ivory trade from Karamoja, causing foreign traders to desert Mbale and the district commissioner to bemoan that 'a legacy of debts is about all that remains of what used to be a profitable and flourishing business'. A few years later, tentative plans to relocate the regional administration to Bugondo, a newly developed ferry port on Lake Kyoga and the site of two large ginneries, were shelved following the outbreak of World War I. As it transpired, Bugondo's brief heyday would be curtailed by a post-war drought that left it high and dry, while the strategic location chosen by Kakungulu took on fresh significance with the rise of the motor vehicle as the natural hub of the road network east of Lake Kyoga.

Mongolia, Indonesia & Italy to name but a few influences – is on offer, together with some telling pen portraits. 'British food is usually quite plain & simple.' A fair point & yes, a plate of fish 'n' chips is apparently as good as it gets in the UK. *Mains US$10.*

✷ **Endiro Coffee** [267 B2] Republic St; ☎ 045 4437783; w endirocoffee.com; ⏲ 07.00–22.00 daily. Set in a converted warehouse tucked away below street level opposite the Stanbic Bank, this rustically funky restaurant serves an imaginative selection of gourmet burgers, wraps, salads & sandwiches, with several vegetarian & healthy options, as well as cheaper tapas & cakes. There's also coffee & an ambitious selection of fruit & vegetable juices, herbal teas & smoothies, but no alcohol. Proceeds support various projects assisting vulnerable children. Free Wi-Fi. *Meals mostly in the US$6–7 range.*

✷ **Spices** [267 A1] Off Tororo Rd, opposite Abru Shopping Centre; m 0759 830000; ⏲ 08.30–22.30 daily. The red décor is a little overdone, but since this is now the only Indian restaurant in Mbale, you'll be in a forgiving mood. *Mains with naan around US$9.*

Cheap to moderate

✷ **Cosmo Restaurant** [267 A1] Republic St (clock tower end); m 0790 916393; f cosmo.mbale; ⏲ 08.00–21.30 daily. This simply but brightly decorated 1st-floor restaurant serves local dishes supplemented by a globetrotting selection of pricier mains – risottos, burritos, curries, goulash, pizza, etc. The vegetarian selection is unusually diverse, too. *Mains in the US$3–5 range, local dishes US$2.*

J&M [267 B2] Mumias Rd. Conveniently located just off Republic St. J&M has a forgettable 1st-floor restaurant & a great rooftop space with pallet furniture & thatch shades, & yes, the cliffs are visible. Local dishes, barbecue chicken, juices, smoothies & milkshakes are on offer, plus beer too, making it a potential sundowner venue. *Local dishes US$3.*

Jawood Restaurant [267 C1] Nkokonjeru Rd; ⏲ 06.30–22.00 daily. This popular local eatery on the ground floor of the Visitors Inn (page 269) serves filling portions of pilau & meat or beans with matoke. *Mains around US$3–4.*

ENTERTAINMENT AND NIGHTLIFE

Club Elitanjia [267 A2] Cathedral Rd; m 0772 552150. Mbale's top nightclub hosts a disco most nights & live music on occasion.

Mbale Sports Club [267 C3] Off Masaba Rd; m 0787 462100. Built in 1952 & attached to a recently revived golf course, the old sports club in the eastern suburbs is now a popular dance venue with DJs most nights.

The Thatch Garden [267 D3] Masaba Rd; ☎ 039 2943405; m 0701 119299. This suburban garden complex a short walk east of the town centre, dominated by a large thatched building, is a pleasant spot for music, drinks & grilled snacks.

SHOPPING Good, centrally located **supermarkets** are found on the road to Tororo and on Republic Street. By far the largest of these, **Abru Supermarket** [267 A1], is hidden inside the Abru Shopping Centre adjacent to the clock tower and includes a bakery. The **central market** [267 B2] on Market Street is usually overflowing with fresh produce from the surrounding agricultural lands.

WHAT TO SEE AND DO The main tourist attractions in the Mbale area are Mount Elgon National Park and Sipi Falls, both covered deeper into this chapter. The following sites also make for interesting excursions out of Mbale.

Wanale Cliffs The waterfall-streaked cliffs of Wanale Ridge dominate Mbale's eastern skyline, marking the end of the 2,348m Nkokonjeru 'Arm', a ridge of lava extruded through a parasitic vent on the western flank of Mount Elgon. A 20km road from Mbale climbs up on to the ridge through a cleft in the cliffs, meandering through superb mountain scenery before terminating at a cluster of radio masts that provide a map-like view of Mbale and vast panoramas towards distant horizons.

The ridge is also accessible from Mbale using a steep footpath (find a guide from Casa Turista or at the UWA office) or on one of the few daily matatus. Mount Elgon National Park extends along Nkokonjeru to Wanale, and the UWA offers two guided walking trails of 3km and 6km in length through regenerating forest. An interesting geological feature along the trail is **Khauka Cave**, which contains logs of petrified wood. However, the cost (US$30/40/25 FR/FNR/ROA plus US$25/35 FR/FNR park entrance fee) is rather off-putting, since walking along the road or public lands is equally attractive.

Stern Synagogue and Semei Kakungulu's grave [267 D1] Situated 4km northeast of central Mbale as the crow flies, Nabugoye Hill is the spiritual home to the Abayudaya, an isolated Jewish community established in 1920 under the Musoga politician Semei Kakungulu (page 270). The community's centrepiece is the Stern Synagogue. The most interesting time to visit Nabugoye, especially if you're prepared to stay overnight, is for the weekly Shabbat, which starts on Friday night and runs into Saturday morning, climaxing with a reading from the Torah by Rabbi Gershom Sizomu (the first indigenous black African rabbi, having been ordained in the USA in 2008). The synagogue has evidently become something of a pilgrimage site for curious Israeli and other Jewish visitors to Uganda, but it is open to people of all religious backgrounds, and the rabbi speaks good English. No fee is charged but donations are gratefully accepted, and do be aware that all forms of photography are forbidden between Friday sunset and Saturday sunset. Of minor interest, 10–15 minutes' walk east of the synagogue, is the covered grave of Semei Kakungulu (entrance US$1.50), marked with a Star of David and three spears, which lies alongside those of his brother and daughter.

Getting there and away Nabugoye Synagogue (⊕ 1.09886, 34.20375) lies 5.5km from Mbale by road, close to the village of Makadui. To get there from the town centre, follow Masaba Road east from the post office for 200m, then turn left on to Bufombo Road and continue for 1.7km until you reach a fork where you need to branch right along the Namwanyi Road. Makadui lies about 3km along this road, and a sharp left turn there will take you to the parking area outside the synagogue compound after about 600m. Matatus from Mbale to Makadui cost less than US$1, a boda shouldn't cost a great deal more one-way, or you can phone the guesthouse and arrange to be collected for around US$7. A rough but motorable 1.5km track winds east from the car park to Semei Kakungulu's grave (⊕ 1.09654, 34.19443).

Where to stay and eat *Map, page 276*

Abayudaya Guesthouse (4 rooms & 4 dorms) ⊕ 1.099, 34.20268; m 0782 654611. Situated 100m downhill from the synagogue, this quiet & comfortable guesthouse offers the choice of en-suite twin rooms or a bed in a 4-berth dorm. All beds have nets. Simple meals cost around US$3. *US$30 pp dorm bed FB; US$75 twin FB.* **$$**

MOUNT ELGON

An extinct shield volcano straddling the Kenyan border east of Mbale, Mount Elgon is Africa's eighth-highest massif, rising to 4,321m at Wagagai Peak, and it has the broadest base of any free-standing mountain anywhere in the world. Two contiguous national parks share a 10km border on the massif's upper slopes. Kenya's 169km^2 Mount Elgon National Park was created in 1968, while its larger Uganda namesake, gazetted in 1993, extends over 1,145km^2 above the 2,000m contour. The highland

THE ABAYUDAYA OF MBALE

Situated on the outskirts of Mbale, Nabugoye Hill is the site of the Moses Synagogue, spiritual home to a small, isolated community of Ugandan Jews known as Abayudaya. The Abayudaya are not formally accepted as Jews, nor will they be until they undergo an official conversion recognised by a court of rabbis, but this seems likely to change in the coming years. Either way, the Abayudaya are devout in their observance of Jewish customs and rituals, recognising the same holidays as other Jews, holding their Sabbath services on Friday evening and Saturday morning, and keeping kosher according to Talmudic law. They do not participate in local Basigu circumcision rituals, but instead circumcise males eight days after birth. And those who marry outside the community are no longer considered Abayudaya unless their spouses agree to convert.

Abayudaya is the Luganda word for Jews, coined in the late 19th century when missionaries attempted to dissociate their outside religion from British colonialism by explaining to locals that the Bible was written not by Europeans but by Jews – the People of Judea or Ba-Judea. This ploy backfired somewhat when the first Luganda translation of the Bible appeared and literate Muganda started to question why their local tradition of polygamy was condemned by the missionaries when many of the Abayudaya in the Old Testament unashamedly possessed more than one wife.

The most prominent of these religious dissidents was Malaki Musajakawa, whose Africanist Christian sect called the Malakites managed to attract up to 100,000 Ugandans away from more conventional denominations during its short-lived heyday. The Malakite doctrine was based on a fairly random selection of Old Testament verses: it was vehemently against the consumption of pork and the use of any medicine whatsoever, and – of course – it came out in strong support of polygamy. Not surprisingly, the British colonists were less than enamoured with this development and tensions between the authorities and the sect came to a head in 1926, when the plague swept through Uganda and the Malakites launched a violent protest against the use of inoculations to combat the disease. In the aftermath, Malaki Musajakawa was imprisoned and exiled to northern Uganda, where he died after a protracted hunger strike, and the sect gradually disbanded.

The main proponent of the spread of Malakitism in eastern Uganda was Semei Kakungulu, who – embittered with the colonial authorities after his retirement from the 'presidency' of Busoga in 1913 – heartily embraced the anti-establishmentarianism of the breakaway faith. Kakungulu withdrew from politics to focus his attention on spiritual matters, dedicating his life to reading the Bible and other Christian tracts. And, somewhat inevitably, he soon started to develop his own variations on the established Malakite doctrines, leading to a dispute that would eventually split the Mbale Malakites into two opposing factions. The key issue was male circumcision, which Kakungulu and his followers believed to be in line with Old Testament teachings, but which most other Malakites regarded as sacrilege. The true reason behind the widespread Malakite objection to circumcision was rooted in Kiganda tradition, which forbade bodily mutilation of any sort. But this was rationalised away by claiming that circumcision was the way of the Abayudaya, people who don't believe in Jesus Christ.

The present-day Abayudaya community was founded in 1920, when Kakungulu, fed up with the quarrelling, announced to the Malakites that 'because of your insults…I have separated completely from you and stay with those who want to be circumcised: and we will be known as the Jews.' Kakungulu – at the age of 50 –

was circumcised along with his first-born son. He circumcised all his subsequently born sons eight days after their birth, and gave them all Old Testament names. In 1922, he published an idiosyncratic Luganda religious text steeped in the Jewish religion, demanding complete faith in the Old Testament and its commandments from himself and his followers.

In reality, Kakungulu's version of Judaism was a confused hotchpotch of Jewish and Christian customs. Neither he nor any of his followers had actually ever met a genuine Jew, and they knew little of real Jewish customs. As a result, the Abayudaya referred to their temple not as a synagogue but as a 'Jewish Church', and they placed as much emphasis on the Christian baptism of children as on the severing of their foreskins! That would change after 1926, however, when Kakungulu spent six months under the instruction of one Yusufu, the Jewish settler who effected the community's final conversion to Judaism. Under Yusufu's guidance, Kakungulu deleted all the Christian prayers from his book, and he instructed his followers to cease baptising their children, to observe the Saturday Sabbath, and to eat meat only if it had been slaughtered within the community according to Jewish custom. Ever the iconoclast, however, Kakungulu did remain vehement when it came to at least one pivotal Malakite doctrine that has no place in modern Judaism: the rejection of medicine. On 24 November 1928, Semei Kakungulu died of pneumonia, refusing to the last to touch the medication that might have saved his life.

By this time, a community of 2,000 Jewish converts lived on Kakungulu's estate at Nabugoye Hill, also known as Galiraya, a Luganda rendition of Galilee. After their founder's death, the Abayudaya had little contact with their neighbours and eschewed materialistic values: it is said that they could be recognised in a crowd by their 'backward' attire of animal hides and barkcloth. The Abayudaya suffered mild persecution during these early years, especially from neighbouring Christian communities who regarded Jews to be Christ killers. But essentially the community thrived until 1971, when Idi Amin banned Judaism, closed 32 synagogues and ordered the Abayudaya to convert to Christianity or Islam. During the Amin years, some 3,000 Abayudaya abandoned their faith rather than risk being beaten or tortured by the military, and some of the more stubborn among them – one group, for instance, who were beaten to death by Amin's thugs for collecting remnants of a synagogue roof that had blown away in a storm – did not survive. By the end of the Amin era, the total number of practising Abayudaya numbered a few hundred. Since then, the Abayudaya have been able to follow their faith without persecution, and the national community has grown to roughly 2,000 individuals, most of whom live around Nabugoye Hill, the site of Kakungulu's original 'Jewish Church'. A smaller community and synagogue exist at nearby Namanyoyi, and two others lie further afield in the town of Pallisa and in a village called Namatumba. There is still some debate within Jewish circles as to whether the Abayudaya should be fully accepted as members of the faith, but great strides towards integration have been made under the recent leadership of Gershom Sizomu, the Chief Rabbi of Uganda.

Under Kakungulu, the Abayudaya developed a distinct style of spiritual music, setting the text of recognised Jewish prayers to African melodies and rhythms. Several of these songs, sung in Hebrew or Luganda over a simple guitar backing, are collected on two CDs *Shalom Everybody Everywhere* and *Lecha Dodi*, available online. The Stern Synagogue at Nabugoye Hill welcomes visitors with a genuine interest in its faith (page 273). For more information, see w kulanu.org.

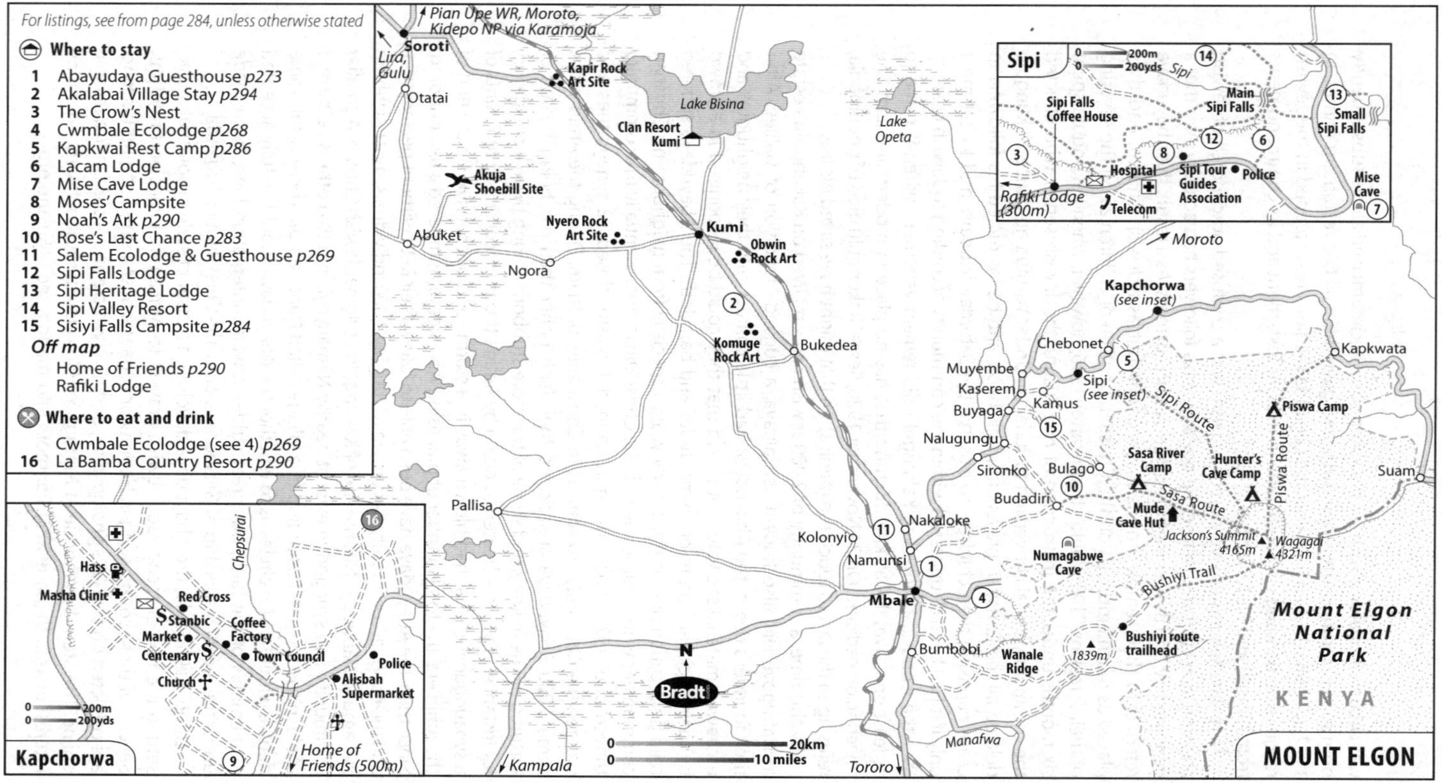

MOUNT ELGON
For listings, see from page 284, unless otherwise stated
Where to stay
1 Abayudaya Guesthouse p273
2 Akalabai Village Stay p294
3 The Crow's Nest
4 Cwmbale Ecolodge p268
5 Kapkwai Rest Camp p286
6 Lacam Lodge
7 Mise Cave Lodge
8 Moses' Campsite
9 Noah's Ark p290
10 Rose's Last Chance p283
11 Salem Ecolodge & Guesthouse p269
12 Sipi Falls Lodge
13 Sipi Heritage Lodge
14 Sipi Valley Resort
15 Sisiyi Falls Campsite p284
Off map
Home of Friends p290
Rafiki Lodge
Where to eat and drink
Cwmbale Ecolodge (see 4) p269
16 La Bamba Country Resort p290
Pian Upe WR, Moroto, Kidepo NP via Karamoja
Soroti
Lira, Gulu
Otatai
Kapir Rock Art Site
Lake Bisina
Clan Resort Kumi
Lake Opeta
Akuja Shoebill Site
Abuket
Nyero Rock Art Site
Kumi
Obwin Rock Art
Ngora
Komuge Rock Art
Bukedea
Pallisa
Kolonyi
Namunsi
Nakaloke
Mbale
Bumbobi
Tororo
Kampala
Manafwa
Muyembe
Kaserem
Buyaga
Kamus
Nalugungu
Sironko
Bulago
Budadiri
Chebonet
Sipi (see inset)
Kapchorwa (see inset)
Moroto
Kapkwata
Piswa Camp
Piswa Route
Sipi Route
Sasa River Camp
Hunter's Cave Camp
Sasa Route
Mude Cave Hut
Jackson's Summit 4165m
Wagagai 4321m
Suam
Numagabwe Cave
Bushiyi Trail
Bushiyi route trailhead
1839m
Wanale Ridge
Mount Elgon National Park
KENYA
0 20km
0 10 miles
N
Bradt
Sipi
0 200m
0 200yds
Sipi
Main Sipi Falls
Small Sipi Falls
Sipi Falls Coffee House
Hospital
Sipi Tour Guides Association
Police
Mise Cave
Rafiki Lodge (300m)
Telecom
Kapchorwa
0 200m
0 200yds
Hass
Masha Clinic
Red Cross
Stanbic
Market
Centenary
Coffee Factory
Town Council
Church
Police
Alisbah Supermarket
Chepsurai
Home of Friends (500m)

moors and forests protected within these national parks harbour an impressively varied flora and fauna, while the lower slopes outside the national park are the site of Sipi Falls, the most popular tourist attraction in the Elgon region.

Elgon has enormous potential as a hiking destination, but it lacks the iconic status of Kilimanjaro, Mount Kenya or the Rwenzori, and sees far fewer visitors. Nevertheless, for budget travellers seeking a relatively affordable off-the-beaten-track opportunity to explore East Africa's weird and wonderful Afro-alpine vegetation, Elgon is a far less financially draining prospect than any other comparably lofty massif. The mountain can be climbed from either side of the border, but the Uganda trailheads are more accessible on public transport, and Wagagai, the tallest peak, falls on that side of the border. It is possible to do a cross-border traverse, ascending on the Ugandan side and descending in Kenya (ask at the national park office in Mbale for further details). For less serious walkers, the Mount Elgon foothills outside the national park offer plenty of alluring prospects, with Sipi Falls and to a lesser extent Kapchorwa being particularly popular bases in a coffee-growing area endowed with many scenic vistas.

PARK FEES As a Category B protected area, the US$25/35 FR/FNR entrance fee applies to Mount Elgon National Park. In practice, however, this is levied only for the little-used trail to Khauka Cave on Wanale Ridge since day fees have been waived for trails around the Kapkwai Exploration Centre and separate fees apply to overnight trails to the peaks (see page 282 for more on costs for extended hikes).

No UWA fee is charged for visiting Sipi Falls or any other sites that are associated with the mountain but lie outside the national park boundaries.

GEOLOGICAL AND HISTORICAL BACKGROUND Like most other major East African massifs, Elgon is an extinct volcano whose formation was associated with the tectonic activity that created the Rift Valley several million years ago. It is the region's oldest extinct volcano, having first erupted 20–25 million years ago, and would have remained active for at least 14 million years, standing far higher than Kilimanjaro does today in its explosive prime. Today, Elgon's tallest peaks form a jagged circle around the more-or-less-intact caldera, which has a diameter of about 8km (making it one of the largest in the world) and is dotted with small crater lakes and hot springs created by Pleistocene glacial activity. The tallest peak, set on the Uganda side of the border, is Wagagai (4,321m), which lies on the southwestern rim. Of the next four tallest peaks, three fall within Uganda: Sudek (also known as Kiongo, 4,302m) in the south; Mubiyi (4,210m) in the north; and Jackson's Summit (also known as Masaba, 4,165m) in the east. Elgon is one of the region's most important watersheds, feeding rivers that empty into both Lake Victoria and Lake Turkana, and forming the main source of fresh water for more than 2 million people in Uganda alone.

The local Bagisu know the mountain as Masaba, the name of their founding ancestor, who legendarily emerged from a cave on its slopes several centuries ago. Masaba's spirit is personified by Jackson's Summit, which appears to be the mountain's tallest peak from most vantage points, while Wagagai is named after and associated with Masaba's wife. It seems that Elgon was well known to the Arab slave traders who passed through the area throughout the 19th century, but the first person to document its existence was the explorer Henry Morton Stanley, who obtained a distant view of its peaks in 1875. The first European to reach the lower slopes was Joseph Thomson, who approached it from the direction of Maasailand in 1883, and named it Elgon, an anglicisation either of the Maasai name Ol Doinyo Ilgoon (literally 'Breast Mountain') or else of El Kony, the name of the tribe that

BAGISU CIRCUMCISION CEREMONIES

The western slopes of Mount Elgon are home to the Bagisu, a Bantu-speaking people with few cultural or historical links to the linguistically affiliated kingdoms of western Uganda. The origin of the Bagisu is uncertain; their oral traditions assert simply that the founding ancestor Masaba emerged from a cave in the eponymous mountain perhaps 500 years ago. Masaba – also the local name for the mountain – is said to still inhabit Elgon's upper slopes, where he holds meetings with lesser deities at a place where stones have been laid out to form chairs and tables. Bagisu society recognises no central leadership and each autonomous clan is presided over by its own non-hereditary chief, appointed by a committee of elders.

The Bagisu, together with their Sebei neighbours, are the only Ugandans to practise male circumcision (unlike the Sebei, however, the Bagisu do not circumcise females; page 288). The origin of this custom is obscure, and several contradictory traditions have been recorded. One somewhat improbable legend has it that the first Bagisu man to be circumcised had a reputation for seducing the wives of his neighbours, and was taken before the committee of elders, who decreed that he should be semi-castrated as both punishment and deterrent. This plan backfired when, having recovered, the offender went back to his seductive ways, and – it was whispered – had become an even more proficient lover following the operation. After that, his rivals decided that they too would have to be circumcised in order to compete for sexual favours! Nice story, but all things considered it's more likely that the custom arose through contact with a neighbouring people who had an existing tradition of circumcision, for instance the Kalenjin of western Kenya.

Whatever its origin, the circumcision ceremony or *imbalu*, held on even-numbered years, is the pivotal occasion in Bagisu society, an individual rite of passage to manhood that involves the entire local community. Unusually among those African societies that practise circumcision, the year in which an individual will undergo the ritual is dictated not by strict convention nor by the council of elders, but by his own personal choice – any age between 16 and 26 is considered acceptable. Those who elect to be circumcised in any given year announce their intention in May or June, and spend the next few months preparing for the main ceremony. The most visible facet of the preparations involves the initiate, adorned in plantain fronds or animal skins and ash-plastered face, and accompanied by a band of cheering friends, parading and dancing through the streets to visit all his close relatives and seek their approval.

The climactic ceremony, according to certain historical sources, is traditionally held in August by the Bagisu and in December by the Sebei, but these days it appears that both groups hold ceremonies during both of these months, though mainly in December. It normally takes place in the morning, well before 10.00, and involves all the initiates from a given clan – anything from one to several dozen young men – being marched by a whistling, cheering crowd to the circumcision ground. The initiates have their faces plastered in ash, and they are stripped below the waist on the way to the circumcision ground, where they must line up in front of a crowd of family and friends of both sexes and all ages before the initiates and their 'surgeon' withdraw to a long-established cutting ground, often a discreet grove or patch of bush, to get down to business.

The operation lasts for about a minute. The initiate holds both his arms rigid in front of him, clasping a stick in his hands, and staring forward expressionlessly. The circumcisor then makes three bold cuts around the foreskin to remove it from the penis. When the operation is complete, a whistle is blown and the initiate emerges from the cutting ground, his hands triumphantly in the air, then starts dancing, proudly displaying his bloodied member to an ululating crowd. Any initiate who cries out during the painful procedure is branded a coward (as is any Bagisu man who is circumcised by a doctor under local anaesthetic). Once the crowd is satisfied of his bravery, the initiate is led away to a quiet place by a few friends, and seated on a stool and wrapped in cloth while he waits for the bleeding to cease. He is then taken to his father's house, where he will be hand fed by his relatives for three days. Finally, the initiate's hands are ritually washed, after which he is permitted to eat with his own hands, and his rite to manhood is completed.

While it is wholly acceptable for a Bagisu man to delay circumcision into his late 20s, he will not be considered a 'true' man until he has undergone the rite, and will be forbidden from marrying or attending important clan meetings. A man who refuses to be circumcised past the accepted age parameters may be hunted down by his peers, and cut by force. These days, however, an increasing number of people are circumcised privately and unceremoniously at home or in a hospital, a surgical approach that carries a far lower risk of infection or other complications. Furthermore, while the traditional ceremony is still condoned by the government, President Museveni personally denounced it as retrogressive when he presided over the launch of the 2014 circumcision season, and used the occasion to call on the Bagisu elite to encourage their communities to discontinue the practice.

Official attitudes have changed since and government is actively trying to promote the imbalu to a wider audience, and in August 2024 Mbale's hotels were packed for the weekend of the opening ceremony at the Bumototo Ceremonial Grounds. Unfortunately, the itinerary was poorly publicised and most visitors missed a spectacular dance-off between local clans on the Friday before enduring an interminable act of cultural appropriation at Bumutoto on Saturday afternoon. Centre stage at this event was a host of dignitaries including the visiting king of Ghana, Kenyan and Ugandan politicians and the king of the Bagisu and local leaders, who addressed the 1,200 seated occupants of a huge tent on the importance of tradition and culture for fully 3 hours. During this eternity, those participants actually at (or rather waiting for) the cutting edge of Bagisu culture stood patiently outside in the sun, the effects of the magic root that when chewed, makes a chap visibly excited about the prospect of having his foreskin hacked off, steadily wearing off. Meanwhile, their entourages and a distinctly grassroots audience numbering several thousand, waited with growing impatience outside an enclosing metal barricade. Eventually, their ire reached boiling point and, breaking down the barricade, they stormed the enclosure to reclaim their culture and rescue their champions. The riot swiftly shifted into 10 minutes of frenzied dancing – this bit *was* fun – after which they marched off to their sacred grove and that was that. It may be better organised in future, but you'd still do well to avoid Bumutoto. If boredom is not sufficient disincentive, the prospect of being flattened in a stampede ought to be. Pending improvements to the programme, the best visitors can hope for is to encounter some of the hundreds of colourful processions in which the candidates and their entourages tour their home areas. By all means join in the dancing and clapping as they pass – you'll make their day – and be sure to contribute a few thousand shillings to the fund that will be presented to the young man when he emerges, bloodied and sore, into adulthood.

inhabited the eastern footslopes. The first recorded summit took place in February 1890, when Frederick (later Sir Frederick) Jackson and Ernest Gedge ascended to the caldera from a base camp at modern-day Kapchorwa, and climbed one of the subsidiary peaks (long assumed to have been Jackson's Summit, but now more widely thought to have been Sudek).

FLORA AND FAUNA Elgon's vegetation zones are similar to those of other large East African mountains. Below the 3,000m contour, the mountain supports a contiguous belt of evergreen forest extending over roughly 750km^2 within Uganda. This forest belt can be divided into two broad strata: tall Afro-montane forest below 2,500m; and low canopy montane forest and bamboo between 2,500m and 3,000m. The slopes below the 2,000m contour, which lie outside the national park, also supported significant forest cover a century ago, but much of this has since been cleared for cultivation. Above 3,000m lies the heather belt, giving way at around 3,500m to other-worldly Afro-alpine vegetation studded with stands of giant lobelia and groundsel, including the endemic *Senecio barbatipes* and *S. elgonensis*.

The mammalian fauna of Mount Elgon is poorly known. The most common species, or at least the most visible to hikers, are blue monkey and black-and-white colobus. A small number of elephant are resident in the forests, as is the striking De Brazza's monkey, along with leopard, bushpig, buffalo, sitatunga and common duiker. The bird checklist stands at more than 300 species and includes a rich variety of forest birds, as well as several Afro-montane moorland endemics. Twelve of the species listed for Elgon occur in no other Ugandan national park, in many instances because Elgon lies at the most westerly extent of its range. Of particular interest are Jackson's francolin (recorded only once), moorland francolin (elsewhere common only in Ethiopia's Bale Mountains), moustached green tinker-bird, red-throated wryneck, black-collared apalis, Hunter's cisticola, alpine chat, marsh widow-bird and Weyn's weaver. The endangered bearded vulture or lammergeyer is regularly observed soaring at higher altitudes.

ACCESS AND ORIENTATION Mount Elgon National Park can be explored only on foot, but the trailheads are all accessible by road. The most established of these trailheads is Budadiri, which lies on the western slopes 38km by road from Mbale via Sironko, and forms the starting point of the perennially popular Sasa Trail. Two less frequently traversed trails can be accessed from the tarmac road running around the northern footslopes to the Kenyan border town of Suam. These are the Sipi Trail, whose trailhead is at Kapkwai, 60km from Mbale, and the Piswa Trail, which starts at Kapkwata, 100km from Mbale. Kapkwai is also the site of the national park's Forest Exploration Centre, an excellent goal for anyone who wants to do a day hike in the forest zone. Other important landmarks along the road to Suam include Sipi Falls, 45km from Mbale, and the town of Kapchorwa another 20km past that. A fourth and recently established trailhead is found 30km to the southeast of Mbale at Bushiyi, which is reached from a newly tarmacked road that leads to the Kenyan border at Lwakahku.

TOURIST INFORMATION It's well worth dropping into the national park tourist office in Mbale (page 266) before heading to the mountain or trailheads. The best map is 'Uganda Maps' Sheet No 10 *Mount Elgon*, which also includes good coverage of Mbale town and the Sipi area. Up on the mountain itself, the go-to people for all things Elgon are Daan and Eliza at Home of Friends guesthouse in Kapchorwa (m 0780 548202; e info@homeoffriends.com; w homeoffriends.com). Whether you want to run a half marathon, take in a coffee tour, cook with local ladies, sing and dance local songs or lose yourself in an evening of traditional stories, they will be happy to oblige. In addition to visiting their excellent website, which details these activities, prospective mountain climbers should view their informative park guide (w homeoffriends.com/blog/mount-elgon-national-park).

WHERE TO STAY Accommodation of some sort exists at or near all four trailheads, as well as at Sipi and Kapchorwa, as listed under the header for the individual site. Once on the trail, there's only one hut for hikers, so you'll need a tent and sleeping bag. Porters will cut grass to make you a 'mattress' for comfort and warmth at higher altitudes. Tents (US$3), as well as sleeping bags and roll mats (US$1.50 each), can be hired from Rose's Last Chance in Budadiri (page 283).

OVERNIGHT HIKES ON MOUNT ELGON Elgon is not a difficult mountain to climb. Aspirant hikers need to be reasonably fit, but no specialised equipment or skill are required to reach the peaks. Elgon can be climbed at any time of year, though the dry seasons (June to August and November to March) are best, in particular November and December when the highland flowers are in bloom. As you'll see on page 282, another noteworthy attraction of Elgon is the relatively low cost compared with other large East African mountains.

There are two types of route to the top of Mount Elgon: those managed by UWA and another, the Sasa Trail, which has recently been taken over by a concessionaire, Elgon Trekking Services (ETS). The former should be arranged through the Mount Elgon National Park tourist office in Mbale, which lies about 100m from the Mount Elgon Hotel & Spa. In theory, hikes on these routes can be planned at the equivalent offices at the trailheads of Budadiri, Kapkwata or Kapkwai Forest Exploration Centre, but it's best to pass by the Mbale office for an overview first. An ascent of the Sasa Trail can be arranged through ETS's offices on Kampala's Bukoto Street, near Acacia Mall (m 0774 114499; w rwenzoritrekking.com) or in Budadiri (m 0743 564780) next to the UWA office.

A few **warnings**: altitude sickness (page 458) can occur on Mount Elgon with symptoms starting as low as 2,700m. That said, acute cases have historically been rare since the Sasa, Piswa and Sipi routes ascend the mountain slowly and most people feel nothing worse than a headache near the peaks. The new Bushiyi Trail, which ascends 2,480m from the trailhead to reach Wagagai peak on Day Two, is a different matter altogether. If considering this route, be sure to prepare yourself beforehand by visiting the US Centre for Disease Control's webpage w wwwnc.cdc.gov/travel/yellowbook/2024/environmental-hazards-risks/high-elevation-travel-and-altitude-illness. There, *Box 4-08: Acclimatisation Tips: A checklist for travellers* and *Table 4-04: Risk categories for developing acute mountain sickness* in particular spell things out for you.

Water on the mountain should be purified or boiled before drinking. Be aware that it is mandatory for trekkers visiting the hot springs area between Mude and Hunters caves to be escorted by an armed ranger.

In addition to the mandatory fees, guides, porters and cooks will expect to be tipped at the end of a successful hike. Rough guidelines are upwards of US$15 per party for the guide and US$10 per party for each cook or porter.

Sasa Trail (22km each way; 3 nights/4 days) The hike up and down the Sasa Trail between Budadiri and Wagagai has long been the most popular route on Mount

Elgon. It was previously a there-and-back affair, but ETS have created a loop trail through the forest and moorland above Mudangi Cliffs as follows:

- Day One: On the first day out of Budadiri (1,250m), you can drive or boda a rough 8km to the Bugiboni Trailhead. A stiff ascent of the Mudangi Cliffs leads to a new hut on Mukoola Ridge (2,830m).
- Day Two: A newly opened trail leads to Masaba Camp (3,800m), close to Masaba peak.
- Day Three: Trekkers summit Wagagai (4,321m) before following the old Sasa Trail down to a new mountain hut at Mude Cave (3,500m).
- Day Four: Climbers can descend to Budadiri or spend a fourth night on the mountain at Sasa River Camp (2,900m).

Rather than rushing off the mountain from Wagagai, it is possible to descend into the caldera to visit the hot springs and ETS is planning an additional camp in this area. You could also descend via the Piswa or Sipi route, though this would mean moving from the ETS trail to a UWA-managed route with whatever costs and bureaucracy this involves.

The standard three-night/four-day ascent costs US$350 plus a US$35/day concession fee. Costs for alternative itineraries are available on request.

Sipi Trail (41km each way; 3 nights/4 days or 4 nights/5 days) This trail starts at Kapkwai Exploration Centre (2,050m) near Sipi Falls and uses two campsites, Tutum Cave (Night 1) and Kajere (Night 2), to reach the summit. After returning to Kajere for a second night (Night 3), climbers can descend to Kapkwai (a 23km slog) or spend a second night at Tutum Cave (Night 4) before concluding. This route starts at a significantly higher altitude than Budadiri, making for a more gradual and far less strenuous ascent. The experienced national park staff can give more detailed advice on the various options.

Expect to pay US$40/50/15 FNR/FR/Ugandan per day for trekking this route (a guide is included) and US5.50/day for camping. However, unless you plan to carry all your gear and cook your own meals, you'll also need to hire a porter or two (US$12 each/day) and a cook (US$9/day). If you don't have your own food, the cook will be happy to cater for you (approx US$12/day). There are no huts on this route so a tent is essential. Two-person tents can be hired, as can mats and sleeping bags. You should budget about US$95/87/58 per day FNR/FR/Ugandan.

Piswa Trail (30km each way; 4 nights/5 days) This route ascends from a new trailhead at Kapkwai (2,190m), 23km beyond Kapchorwa town. Again, the higher starting point makes for a more gradual and far less strenuous ascent than the Budadiri trail. The route involves two overnight camps, Piswa (Night 1) and Hunter's Cave (Night 2) before reaching the summit. You can then return to Kapkwata on the same route (Nights 3 & 4) or descend to Kapkwai. There are no huts so you'll need a tent. Costs are the same as for the Sipi Trail (page 282).

Bushiyi Trail (20km; 2 nights/3 days) The shortest, steepest and most direct route of all, this new trail climbs some 2,480m up the southern side of the mountain to reach the summit on the second day. The first day ascends 1,004m to Sayum Cave (2,438m) before climbing 1,478m on Day Two to reach the peak. Though altitude sickness (page 281) is a risk, the prospect of a cheaper and quicker ascent is enticing and UWA charges a flat rate of US$150 per person plus US$5.50 camping/

day for this route to encourage climbers – it's not mandatory – to spend two nights acclimatising at Sayum Cave. As an additional bonus, this fee also allows unlimited time on the mountain. Thus trekkers can take extra days to explore the caldera and potentially descend using the Sipi or Piswa route. The Bushiyi trailhead is reached by turning east from the Mbale–Tororo Road at Bumbobi, 8km south of Mbale. The first 15km of this road is surfaced as far as Bulobo, where you'll turn left and ask for directions. There are no huts on this route so you'll need a tent.

AROUND THE MOUNTAIN The main sites and trailheads in the Elgon foothills are described clockwise from Mbale, starting at Budadiri and ending at the remote Kenyan border town of Suam. Traditionally, the most popular destination in the area is **Sipi Falls**, which is readily accessible on public transport and has accommodation to suit all budgets, as well as offering several day-walking possibilities outside the national park. The **Kapkwai Forest Exploration Centre** on the northern slopes is a more worthwhile goal for those with a strong interest in natural history.

Budadiri This small trading centre 10km west of the park boundary is the trailhead for the Sasa route and best-established starting point for hikes on Mount Elgon. Although non-hikers seldom visit Budadiri, one interesting local attraction is the **Numagabwe Cave**, which lies about 7km to the southwest and is decorated with ancient rock paintings. Either of the hotels in Budadiri can organise a day trip to the caves, as well as longer caving expeditions for those with the necessary equipment.

Getting there and away Budadiri (⊕ 1.17051, 34.33575) lies about 38km from Mbale by road. The best route entails following the surfaced Kapchorwa Road out of town for 27km through Sironko to the village of Nalugungu (⊕ 1.24814, 34.27223), then turning right into a signposted 11km dirt road. Matatus from Mbale to Budadiri cost around US$1.25, take 45–60 minutes, and leave from the Kumi Road about 100m north of the clock tower.

Where to stay and eat *Map, page 276*

Rose's Last Chance (7 rooms & 1 dorm) ⊕ 1.168999, 34.339357; m 0772 623206; e mananarose@gmail.com. This long-serving & friendly setup occupies basic premises in a pretty garden next to the UWA office, 200m east of the town centre. Inexpensive meals & day tours are offered, & it also rents out tents, sleeping bags, roll mats & hiking boots. *Rooms (presumably negotiable) cost US$40/50 en-suite sgl/dbl or US$30/40 with shared facilities; US$20 dorm bed. All rates HB.* **$**

Bulago An attractive detour on the way up to Sipi leads to the scenic village of Bulago (also known as Buluganya). Approaching from Mbale along the surfaced Sipi Road, turn right on to the old Sipi Road at Kaserem (⊕ 1.32139, 34.33612), 6.5km past the junction with the Moroto Road. After 3km you reach Kamus, where you need to turn left up the mountain. From here, a 15km road winds beneath some superb cliffs and passes through a small but pretty rock gorge before reaching Bulago, which stands on a clifftop above a lovely waterfall dropping into a pretty, grassy meadow. A rocky plateau beyond the village overlooks the Simu Valley to Butandiga Ridge, and a path climbs to the cliffs bordering the national park, over which a couple of streams fall. There is no formal accommodation in Bulago, and the steep road there deteriorates quickly after rain, so be ready to retreat if necessary.

Sisiyi Falls This pretty waterfall is visible for miles around as it plunges over a lofty cliff from the direction of Bulago village. The base of the falls is occupied by the basic but beautifully located **Sisiyi Falls Campsite** [map, page 276] (⊕ 1.278333, 34.318056; m 0750 618869; f sisiyi.falls; basic en-suite bandas US$12/24 sg/dbl; US$8 pp camping with own tent B&B; **$$**). Dotted with house-sized basalt boulders softened by lichen and surrounded by lush, tropical vegetation, the result is a delightful 'Lost World' feel. The falls are a couple of minutes' walk uphill but their constant sound permeates the gardens. A camping ground set among the boulders is one of the loveliest in the whole country. A variety of guided nature walks, hikes and other activities can be arranged. Sisiyi Falls lies 5km off the main tarmac road at Buyaga, about 7km north of Sironko town; the turning is identified by a phone mast. A boda from Buyaga should cost around US$1.50. Day visitors pay US$3 entrance.

Sipi Falls Elgon's main tourist focus is the small trading centre of Sipi, which lies at an altitude of 1,775m on the mountain's northeastern footslopes, only 45km from Mbale along a good surfaced road. The village overlooks the 99m-high Sipi Falls, the last in a series of three pretty waterfalls formed by the Sipi River as it cascades downhill from the upper slopes of Mount Elgon into the Kyoga Basin. Serviced by half-a-dozen resorts and lodges that collectively cater to most tastes and budgets, Sipi is a very peaceful and pretty spot, and it makes a most agreeable base for gentle day walks in the surrounding hills, which offer spectacular views to the lowlands further west and – weather permitting – occasional glimpses of the Elgon peaks.

Getting there and away Sipi trading centre lies about 45km from Mbale along the surfaced road to Kapchorwa. Self-drivers must follow the Kumi Road out of town for 5km to Namunsi (⊕ 1.12395, 34.16863), where they need to turn right on to the Moroto Road and follow it for another 28km before turning right on to the Kapchorwa Road at a junction (⊕ 1.3357, 34.29741) 1km past Muyembe. Sipi lies about 12km along this road. Matatus from Mbale to Sipi cost US$3, take 60 minutes, and leave from the Kumi Road about 100m north of the clock tower.

Where to stay and eat *Map, page 276*

Upmarket

Sipi Heritage Lodge (9 cottages & bandas) ⊕ 1.33805, 34.38308; m 0751 796109. Set in wooded grounds at the foot of the middle waterfall, this terrific little lodge was, for many years, comfortably the best in the Mount Elgon region. One wonders about the future, however, following the local owner's eviction of the English leaseholder from his greatly improved property. Though an eventual drop in standards is anticipated, it's business as usual at the moment – the rates, menu & indeed the cook remaining the same. *US$175/260 sgl/dbl cottage; US$80/128 sgl/dbl banda with common shower. All rates HB.* **$$$$**

Moderate

Lacam Lodge (7 rooms) ⊕ 1.33598, 34.37989; m 0752 292554; e info@lacamlodge.co.uk; w lacamlodge.co.uk. Lacam occupies a steep hillside provided with plenty of steps immediately beside the main Sipi Falls – so close that the waterfall is mostly heard rather than seen. Though the steep cliff below the site will give parents with young kids the willies, it will be easy enough to keep them safely in the restaurant; the Endiro coffee shop chain now handles the catering & has brought its popular burger & wrap-oriented menu to Sipi (mains US$7–9). Accommodation is in rustic cottages fashioned from log offcuts & topped with roofs thatched in the local style. *US$60–80/100–120 sgl/dbl B&B; US$35/60 sgl/dbl using common showers B&B.* **$$$**

Mise Cave Lodge (9 rooms) m 0740 515550; e info@misecave.com. Named after an on-site cave of local cultural significance (day visitors US$1), this pleasant little lodge is found close to the main road between the 1st & 2nd waterfalls.

Though there is no view to speak of, the pleasantly wooded hillside site has its own appeal. It also has its own small waterfall which, if you choose a chalet close by, goes some way to diminishing the noise from the road. *US$69/75 sgl/dbl B&B.* **$$$**

Rafiki Lodge (10 units) ⊕ 1.33661, 34.36729; m 0757 449360, 0783 817748; e info@rafikilodgesipi.com; w rafikilodgesipi.com. This acceptable lodge is tucked away on a hillside above The Crow's Nest & affords a similarly memorable view over the main waterfall & Kyoga Basin. 2-bedroom family cottages & 1-bedroom bandas are comfortable & pleasantly furnished but rather lacking in character. There is also a row of dbl rooms & dorms using shared facilities. A good restaurant with a view is attached (3-course meals US$15). *US$75/100 sgl/twin B&B; US$200 B&B family cottage sleeping 4; US$25 pp B&B room or dorm using common shower.* **$$$**

Sipi Falls Lodge (9 cottages) ⊕ 1.33596, 34.3773; m 0702 328085; e casaugandasafaris@gmail.com; w gotouruganda.com. Sipi's oldest resort started life in the 1950s as a quaint retreat for Sir Andrew Cohen, Governor of the Uganda Protectorate, who with the prerogative afforded his office, chose & developed the site with the best possible view of the main waterfall. Post-independence, thousands of guests have had cause to appreciate this colonial-era imposition, the outlook beating those offered by other local lodges by a country mile (only the ramshackle Moses Campsite comes close). Though Sir Andrew's compact 2-bedroom cottage still stands, options have been expanded & improved by the addition of simple but attractive rustic cottages made of wood & bamboo thatch. *US$60/90 sgl/dbl B&B.* **$$$**

Sipi Valley Resort (14 rooms) ⊕ 1.3423288, 34.3771011; m 0700 292008; e sipivalleyresort@gmail.com; w sipivalleyresort.com. Sipi's newest resort occupies a large open site, perched on the northern rim of the Sipi valley & facing the main cluster of lodges on the opposite side. A row of box-like chalets diminishes the valley panorama from the latter, while doing little to facilitate the enjoyment of the resort either. Laid out perpendicular to the dramatic valley & turning their backs on the plains beyond, these glass-fronted cubes – though comfortable & enhanced by use of local stone within – face nothing more exciting than a couple of acres of lawn. *US$62/70 sgl/dbl B&B.* **$$$**

Shoestring and camping

✷ **The Crow's Nest** (7 cabins & 10 dorms) ⊕ 1.33519, 34.3693; m 0772 687924, 0772 093930; e crowsnest1998@gmail.com. This well-established shoestring resort, set on a small hill to the left as you enter Sipi trading centre, offers a grandstand view of all the waterfalls along the Sipi River as well as the peaks of Mount Elgon. Accommodation is in simple log cabins or dorms with 4–12 beds, & a simple restaurant/bar serves a selection of stir-fries, spaghetti & local dishes for around US$4. A short nature trail encircles the hill above the camp. *US$17 twin cabin; US$10 pp dorm; US$8 pp camping.* **$–$$**

Moses Campsite (4 rooms) ⊕ 1.33554, 34.37555; m 0752 208302, 0787 756283; e mosescampsitesipi@yahoo.com. By far the simplest of Sipi's offerings, this friendly & long-serving family-run setup has a wooded clifftop location with a terrific waterfall view (again, not one for parents with young kids). Accommodation is either in basic bandas using common showers or (preferably) in your own tent. *Both cost US$8 pp exc b/fast.* **$**

What to see and do

Guided walks The most popular walking trail, only 20 minutes each way, leads from behind the post office in Sipi trading centre to the base of the main waterfall. If you choose, you can continue for another 20 minutes to reach a cluster of caves on the cliff above the river. The largest cave extends for about 125m into the rock face, and contains rich mineral salt deposits that have clearly been worked extensively at some time in the past, as well as traces of petrified wood. Walking back to the trading centre along the main road, you'll pass the top of the main waterfall, as well as Mise Cave, an important local shrine set within a small forest-fringed cavern and now within the grounds of an eponymous lodge.

More ambitiously, it is possible to undertake a day hike from the main waterfall to the three smaller falls that lie upstream, one of which has a tempting swimming pool at its base. Another interesting option is a coffee tour to local subsistence farms where you can learn about the coffee farming process from harvesting and drying the beans to roasting and grinding them for consumption.

It is more-or-less mandatory to take a guide on walks to the waterfalls, other local hikes and coffee tours. This not only helps you locate some of the sites, but also the guiding fees include a contribution to local landowners for access to the falls. A guide can be arranged through any of the lodges listed on page 284, or through the **Sipi Tour Guides Association** (⊕ 1.33527, 34.37639; m 0785 504314, 0752 994294; w sipifallstouristguidesassociation.wordpress.com) at the entrance to the Sipi Falls Lodge (page 285). The going rate is US$5 per person for each waterfall visited.

Abseiling Two local operators can arrange abseiling and rock climbing on the cliffs around the waterfall for US$50. Try the long-standing **Rob's Rolling Rock** (m 0776 963078, 0775 1963078; e robsrollingrocks@yahoo.com; w rollingrocksipifalls.wordpress.com) or get in touch with **Mulima Mountain Adventures** (m 0753 340235; e info@mulimaadventures.com).

Kapkwai Forest Exploration Centre

Only 3km east of Sipi as the crow flies and easily accessed by foot or by road, the Kapkwai Forest Exploration Centre is an attractive destination for hikers and wildlife enthusiasts who don't want to overnight on the upper slopes of Mount Elgon. Set at an altitude of 2,050m immediately inside the national park boundary, the centre was originally designed as an educational facility but now doubles as a base for tourism. Its main attraction is a network of day trails that provide access to the surrounding Afro-montane forest and offer a good opportunity to see associated monkeys and birds. Kapkwai is also the starting point for the overnight Sipi Route, which leads to the Elgon peaks, and the site of a comfortable rest camp consisting of four log cottages offering affordable banda and dormitory accommodation as well as a good canteen.

Fees Forest walks cost US$15/30 FR/FNR inclusive of a mandatory guide. As of 2024, this activity is exempted from the park entrance fee. Note that trekkers bound for the peaks pay the hiking/camping fee described on page 282.

Getting there and away Kapkwai entrance gate (⊕ 1.33518, 34.41142) lies 12km from Sipi by road. To drive there, follow the surfaced Kapchorwa Road out of Sipi for 6km, then turn right at a prominently signposted junction (⊕ 1.36778, 34.39141) on to the 6km dirt feeder road, which may require a 4x4 after heavy rain. For those without private transport, any vehicle running between Mbale or Sipi and Kapchorwa can drop you at the junction, from where the walk to Kapkwai shouldn't take longer than 90 minutes. Alternatively, the guides in Sipi can lead you along a more direct 90-minute walking trail for about US$7 per person. Another option is a boda out of Sipi or even Mbale.

Where to stay and eat *Map, page 276*

Kapkwai Rest Camp (3 bandas, 1 dorm) ⊕ 1.33479, 34.41462; 039 2176475. Sprawling across forested slopes near the source of the Sipi River 500m east of the entrance gate, this attractive rest camp offers the choice of en-suite timber cabins, a dorm bed or camping. The Bamboo Grove Canteen serves basic but decent meals for around US$4, as well as air-cooled beers & sodas. As of 2024, the national park entrance fee no longer applies to overnight visitors, making this very good value indeed. *US$8.50/15 sgl/dbl.* **$$**

What to see and do

Hiking Three connecting, circular day trails run through the exploration centre. The **Mountain Bamboo Loop** (7km; 4hrs) leads past a cave before climbing to the main viewpoint (from where, on a clear day, the peaks of Mount Elgon can be seen), and then runs north along a ridge, through montane forest, to a large bamboo forest. The popular **Chebonet Falls Loop** (5km; 3hrs) passes the eponymous waterfalls, and also involves a climb up a rock chimney and passing through areas of montane and bamboo forest leading to the main viewpoint. The **Ridge View Loop** (3km; 2hrs) involves a relatively easy ascent of the ridge, where it connects with the other trails at the main viewpoint.

In addition to passing through areas of regenerating forest, fields of colourful wild flowers and extensive stands of bamboo, the day trails offer a good chance of sighting black-and-white colobus and blue monkeys.

Birding Kapkwai is highly rewarding to birders, since a high proportion of the 305 species recorded in the national park are present in the vicinity. The lovely cinnamon-chested bee-eater, Doherty's bush-shrike and golden-winged sunbird head a long list of highland species resident in the riverine scrub close to the rest camp. The Mountain Bamboo Loop is probably the most productive trail for true forest birds, including black-and-white casqued hornbill, Hartlaub's turaco, bar-tailed trogon, grey-throated barbet, montane oriole, mountain greenbul and black-collared apalis.

Kapchorwa Administrative headquarters of the eponymous district, Kapchorwa lies at the heart of Uganda's main Arabica coffee-production area, and its major development is a vast and rehabilitated coffee-processing plant. Kapchorwa is an odd little place: a vast but unfocused semi-urban sprawl of fewer than 15,000 inhabitants that somehow manages to straddle the Suam Road for more than 2km. An attractive and breezy montane setting goes some way to compensating for the town's rather scruffy appearance, but you could argue that the best thing about Kapchorwa is the scintillating ascent road from Sipi, which offers some wonderful views to Lake Kyoga and the isolated Mount Kadam. If you're up for some

TOWN OF CHAMPIONS

The Sebei people of Kapchorwa District are a subgroup of the Kalenjin, the so-called 'running tribe' renowned for having produced a high proportion of Kenya's Olympic medallists. Like the neighbouring part of Kenya, Kapchorwa and its immediate environs are the birthplace of and training ground for several world-class runners. Most lauded among these is Stephen Kiprotich, who took gold in the marathon at London 2012, earning Uganda its second ever Olympic gold medal, and then repeated the feat at the World Championships in Moscow a year later. Other established athletes hailing from the vicinity of Kapchorwa include Moses Kipsiro, winner of six gold medals at the All Africa and Commonwealth Games between 2006 and 2014. Mount Elgon's women are also doing their country proud. Stella Chesang caused great excitement in her remote home district of Kween when she won the 10,000m gold medal at the 2018 Commonwealth Games in Australia. More recently, at the Tokyo Olympics in 2021, Peruth Chemutail triggered similar rejoicing in nearby Bukwo when she won the 3,000m steeplechase to become the first Ugandan woman to earn an Olympic gold.

GENITAL MUTILATION IN KAPCHORWA

The Sebei (or Sabiny) people of Kapchorwa District are the only ethnic group in Uganda to practise female genital mutilation (FGM) – often and somewhat euphemistically referred to as female circumcision. Traditionally, Sebei girls are expected to succumb to the knife shortly after reaching puberty but before marriage, in the belief that having the clitoris removed reduces the temptation to indulge in promiscuity. Traditionally, should a female Sebei refuse to be cut, she will forever be accorded the social status of a girl – forbidden from marrying, or from speaking publicly to circumcised women, or from undertaking women's tasks such as milking cows, collecting dung to plaster walls and drawing grain from the communal granary.

FGM is traditionally performed during the December of every even-numbered year. Several girls will participate in one communal ceremony, and the festivities last for several days before and after the actual operation, which takes only a few minutes to perform. One by one, the girls are instructed to lie down with their arms held aloft and their legs spread open. Cold water is poured on the vulva, and the clitoris is pulled and extended to its fullest possible length before it is sliced off, together with part of the labia minora. Should a girl cry out during the procedure, she will be branded a coward and bring shame and misfortune to her family. When all the participants have endured the operation, they are herded to a collective enclosure. Here, according to J P Barber, who witnessed a ceremony in the 1950s: 'they bend and kneel, they moan and whistle, in an attempt to lessen their extreme agony. Their faces…are drawn and contracted. They are too conscious of pain to notice or care about anything or anybody.'

No anaesthetic or disinfectant is used, and the operation is often performed on several girls in short succession using a non-sterilised knife or razor, or even a scrap of sharp metal or glass. Short-term complications that frequently follow on from the procedure include haemorrhaging, urinary retention and temporary lameness. In the years that follow, mutilated women often experience extreme pain during sexual intercourse, and bear an increased risk of complications related to childbirth. For some, circumcision will prove fatal. A small proportion of girls will die immediately or shortly after the operation from uncontrolled bleeding, shock or infection. Others face a lingering death sentence: the HIV virus is occasionally transmitted during mass operations, and mutilated women are often prone to vaginal tearing during intercourse, which makes them especially vulnerable to sexually transmitted diseases.

Public debate around the subject of FGM is traditionally taboo. The first local woman to come out strongly against the custom was Jane Frances Kuka, who served as head of a local teacher-training college in the 1970s. Herself defiantly uncircumcised, Kuka educated her students about the dangers of FGM, hoping they would act as ambassadors to the wider community. In 1986, encouraged by Museveni's strong commitment to women's rights, and assisted by the local representative of the WHO, Kuka launched a more open campaign, one that met strong opposition from community leaders who felt that outsiders were criticising and interfering with their culture. In response to this provocation, a district by-law was passed in 1988 requiring all Sebei women to undergo FGM – any woman who did not submit to the knife voluntarily would do so by force. Kuka visited the cabinet minister for women in Kampala, and together they flew a helicopter to Kapchorwa to rescue as many victims as they could. At the minister's insistence, the by-law was revoked shortly after it came into being, but still too late for the hundreds of women that had been seized, bound and forcibly circumcised by the district authorities.

Kuka's major breakthrough came in 1992, with the formation of the Sebei Elders Association, which aimed to protect the Sebei culture by preserving songs, dances and other positive customs, but also wanted to eliminate more harmful traditions, notably FGM. At the same time, Kuka consolidated her network of local women's groups to launch the UN-funded REACH programme, which adopted a culturally sensitive strategy, endorsing most Sebei traditional values but highlighting the health risks associated with FGM. In 1996, coinciding with the start of the initiation season, the two organisations staged the first Sebei Culture Day, which highlighted the positive aspects of local traditions while doubling as a substitute for the traditional female initiation ceremony. In place of a rusty knife, female initiates were given a symbolic gift, and counselled on subjects such as HIV prevention, family planning and economic empowerment. The number of girls who underwent FGM in 1996 was 36% lower than it had been in 1994. In 1996, Kuka swept to a landslide victory in local elections for a parliamentary representative, to be appointed Minister of State for Gender and Cultural Affairs, giving her a more prominent forum for her campaign. Her new appointment also ensured that she had the ear of President Museveni, who made a personal appearance at the 1998 Culture Day to deliver a speech about the dangers of FGM.

Many Sebei traditionalists regard female circumcision as integral to their cultural identity: the rite of passage that transforms a girl into a woman. In more remote parts of the district, uncircumcised women still experience social discrimination, and their families stand to gain materially from the substantial gifts they customarily receive from friends and relatives on the day of initiation. One strongly reactionary element is the female elders who are paid to perform the operations – finance aside, these women are not eager to relinquish their elevated status as community advisors and custodians of tradition and magic.

In recent years, Museveni and his government have made great strides towards the total abolition of FGM in Uganda. In 2010, it was made illegal to carry out FGM, or to participate in any event leading to its practice, or to discriminate against a woman who hasn't undergone it. Clandestine ceremonies are still held in remote areas, but illegal practitioners of the operation now risk being arrested – indeed, five such individuals each received a four-year jail sentence in 2014 – and the number of women who undergo FGM today is a fraction of what it would have been in the 1990s. In the 2013 Tumaini Awards Programme, Jane Frances Kuka was named a Lifetime Achiever for her role as a heroine in the fight against FGM.

The remarkable progress made towards eradicating FGM locally within the space of one generation can be attributed partially to the Sebei being culturally anomalous in Uganda – the rest of the population has never subscribed to the practice. It is sobering to realise that, according to WHO estimates, up to 140 million women across 28 countries elsewhere in Africa have suffered some form of genital mutilation, and every year another 3 million girls in Africa are at risk of being subjected to FGM.

exploration, Kapchorwa now has a decent selection of budget accommodation, and the surrounding slopes offer plenty of good walking, with one possible goal being a little-known series of caves on a cliff outside town.

Getting there and away Kapchorwa lies about 60km from Mbale along a good surfaced road that can be covered in under an hour. Directions are as for Sipi (page 284), which the road passes through 15km before it reaches Kapchorwa. Regular matatus to Kapchorwa (US$3) leave Mbale from a taxi park on the Kumi Road 100m north of the clock tower, stopping at Sipi on request.

Where to stay *Map, page 276*

Moderate

✷ **Home of Friends** (11 rooms) ⊕ 1.38836, 34.44569; m 0780 548202; e info@homeoffriends.com; w homeoffriends.com. Perched on a hilltop on the southern outskirts of Kapchorwa, this excellent guesthouse is affiliated to From Coach to Coach, a small Dutch-founded social enterprise committed to helping young Sebei athletes achieve self-reliance. The guesthouse caters to casual visitors, offering a wide variety of activities ranging from hiking to Sipi Falls & mountain biking around Kapchorwa to coffee tours & cultural programmes, but (inspired by the likes of Joshua Cheptegei) it also doubles as a top-notch high-altitude training base for dedicated runners (page 287). The tiled en-suite rooms have fitted nets & private balcony while the restaurant serves a healthy selection of chicken & vegetarian dishes in the US$5–8 range, plus fresh juices & great coffee. *US$52/60 en-suite sgl/dbl; US$20/25 sgl/dbl using common showers; US$14 pp dorm bed; US$8 pp camping. All rates B&B.* **$$**

Budget

Noah's Ark Hotel (20 rooms) ⊕ 1.395709, 34.447432; m 0774 27401; e info@noahsarkhotel.co.ug; w noahsarkhotel.co.ug. 2 sister establishments are signposted from the main road to the northern side of town, the supposedly superior Noah's Ark Resort – billed 'For VIP use only' – and the nearby Noah's Ark Hotel. As is common with Ugandan hotels, both are strangely rambling setups, with limited funds imposing processes of gradual evolution rather than sudden Creationism. You should head for the hotel, where the rooms are half the price & every bit as good as those in the resort. *US$11–13/21–26 sgl/dbl B&B.* **$$**

Where to eat and drink *Map, page 276*

La Bamba Country Resort ⊕ 1.40368, 34.45239; m 0782 112801. Located on a clifftop on the northern edge of town, La Bamba is both ordinary & more than usually disjointed in conception. It is, however, a great place to pop in to enjoy a drink & some wonderful views towards the wide-open plains of Pian Upe. There's even a waterfall on the edge of the site. A restaurant serves simple meals for around US$4.

Kapkwata Kapkwata trading centre, some 35km from Kapchorwa along the dirt road to Suam, is of interest mainly as the trailhead for the little-used **Piswa Trail** up Mount Elgon. Any transport heading between Kapchorwa and Suam can drop you there.

Suam Set at an altitude of 2,070m on the Kenyan border, Suam is likely to see increasing (though far from heavy) tourist traffic when tarmacking works are completed on the road from Kapchorwa. First up, it will facilitate a cross-border excursion to Kitale and points beyond in Kenya's lovely Western Highlands. If this is not an option, the drive to Suam and back might be considered sufficient reward, the new tarmac penetrating a scenic and hitherto extremely isolated region with, as an additional bonus, some tremendous views towards Karamoja. Though the roadworks should be completed during the lifespan of this book, we said that for the last edition too, so, pending a conclusion, be prepared for some muddy sections during the rainy months. When you reach Suam, you find a few basic lodgings as well as a **UWA Suam Guesthouse** (9 rooms; 039 2176475; US$6/10 dbl with en-suite/common showers; **$**). The ongoing road improvements mean that matatus now run to Suam – a potentially white-knuckle ride on this winding mountain route – while, if crossing into Kenya, Suam is connected to Kitale by a reasonable surfaced road and regular matatus.

11

Karamoja, Gulu and the Northeast Safari Circuit

Culturally, linguistically and economically, northern Uganda has always been a land apart. This sense of dislocation is partly attributable to Lake Kyoga, the amorphous centrepiece of a vast shallow sump whose spidery, swamp-lined fingers form a significant geographical barrier between the predominantly Bantu-speaking south and Nilotic-speaking north. Politically, this isolation intensified after 1986, when the Lord's Resistance Army (LRA) subjected much of northern Uganda to a brutal civil war that rendered it unsafe for travel. Fortunately, however, the expulsion of the LRA in 2005 (coupled with the successful disarming of the cattle-rustling Karamojong in 2011) has ushered in a new era of peace in northern Uganda, and once war-ravaged towns such as Lira and Gulu now positively bustle with commercial activity.

Northern Uganda lies off the beaten tourist track, and is arguably worth visiting for that reason alone, but it would be disingenuous to pretend towns such as Gulu, Lira and Kitgum are brimming with potential attractions. Far more alluring is Kidepo Valley National Park, a spectacularly scenic safari destination abutting the remote border with South Sudan. No less compelling is the opportunity to interact with the iconic Karamojong pastoralists who inhabit the semi-arid Karamoja plains and slopes running south from Kidepo to the town of Moroto. Further south, Soroti is a useful base for visiting the fascinating Nyero Rock Art Site and searching for shoebill and the endemic Fox's weaver in the Kyoga Basin.

Coverage in this chapter is structured to follow a *very* rough anti-clockwise circuit from Mbale via the Kyoga Basin and/or Pian Upe and/or Karamoja to Kidepo, then returning south via a more westerly route through Kitgum to Gulu, which is the largest town in the north and a springboard to travel on westwards to West Nile District and Murchison Falls National Park, or south back to Kampala and Entebbe.

HISTORY

Northern Uganda has a very different ethnic and historical identity from the south. Historically, the region is inhabited by a mosaic of politically decentralised Nilotic-speaking tribes whose cultural and linguistic affiliations point north towards South Sudan rather than south towards the centralised Bantu-speaking areas of the south and west of Uganda. The most populous of these northern tribes are the Acholi (a relatively recent confederation of chiefdoms created by the British and centred on Gulu), the Langi (centred on Lira) and the semi-nomadic Karamojong pastoralists of Karamoja. The Nilotic languages spoken by these people are quite distinct from the Bantu dialects spoken in the south, having as much in common as English has with, say, Chinese.

During the colonial era, it was northern cotton and tobacco rather than any southern produce that enabled the fledgling Uganda Protectorate to turn a profit. Northerners earned a reputation as tough and hard-working that still persists today. By 1959, Gulu had become Uganda's second-largest town with 30,000 residents, and Lira was placed third with 14,000 – a combined population not far short of the 46,000 that then lived in Kampala. Northerners formed the backbone of the protectorate army, and many, used to hard graft on plantations in their homeland, migrated south to work on sugar estates in Buganda. But if the north provided the raw materials and the manpower for Uganda's development, it was the south that tended to enjoy the rewards.

In the immediate post-independence era, this long-standing economic divide festered into tribal persecution and bloodshed. During Obote's two terms as president, the Acholi- and Langi-dominated army terrorised southerners. In between, Amin and his West Nile cronies (known as 'Sudanese') terrorised everyone; though curiously it was their fellow northerners, the Acholi and Langi, who were most heavily targeted on ethnicity grounds. Come 1986, when Museveni seized power, the north had good cause to fear, their menfolk having brutalised the Ugandan population over the best part of 20 years. They were right to be worried, for Museveni's southern-dominated army mounted a decidedly heavy-handed campaign to stamp their authority on northern Uganda. Amid an atmosphere of fear, resentment and hatred of the National Resistance Movement (NRM) regime, the stage was set for Alice Lakwena's short-lived rebellion, and the subsequent 20-year campaign waged by Joseph Kony and his LRA – see pages 318 and 322.

The LRA ceased to be active in Uganda in 2005, and the north has been peaceful ever since. Nevertheless, the legacy of those long years is still apparent in the likes of Gulu, Lira and Kitgum. While the rest of the country enjoyed a 20-year head start when it comes to the stability and economic growth that characterise the Museveni era, the majority of the north's rural populace was forced to live under military guard in squalid and insanitary camps for Internally Displaced People (IDP), or to migrate into large towns. For up to 20 years, these IDPs were stuck in protected camps where they were fed by aid agencies and were unable to do any useful work. Then finally when they did return home, their houses had crumbled, termites had reduced their furniture to dust, once-fertile fields had been reclaimed by the bush, and boundary lines with neighbouring properties had been lost. Indeed, with no other source of support, many disadvantaged northerners are still dependent on charity today.

TESO, LANGI AND THE KYOGA BASIN

Northwest of Mbale, the subregions of Teso and Langi are dominated by a sprawl of marshy wetlands formed by the Nile as it flows northwest from Jinja towards Lake Albert and a number of lesser tributaries that rise on Mount Elgon and other massifs on the Kenyan border. The region's amorphous centrepiece is Lake Kyoga, a marshy, lily-covered, multiple-armed body of shallow water (nowhere more than 6m deep) that extends across some 1,720km^2 of central Uganda, hosting large numbers of hippo and water-associated birds (including a sizeable population of shoebill) but largely ignored by the tourist industry. Best explored from the moderately sized town of Soroti, Teso is also home to a scattering of spectacular volcanic outcrops, several of which – most notably Nyero – are adorned with mysterious prehistoric rock art.

Further east, lakes Bisina and Opeta are eastern extensions of the Kyoga Basin and of special interest to dedicated birders as the core territory of the endemic Fox's weaver. The other main settlement in the Kyoga Basin is Lira, which is the largest town in the Langi subregion and attracts plenty of NGO activity, but is of limited interest to tourists, though you will need to pass through it if you travel directly between the Mount Elgon region and Murchison Falls.

SOROTI With a population estimated at around 65,000, Soroti is the largest town in the Teso subregion and headquarters of an eponymous district mainly populated by Iteso people. It lies along the main route connecting Mbale to Murchison Falls, and is also a potential springboard for the northeastern route to Kidepo via Karamoja (page 302). The town itself would be unremarkable were it not set below the striking, 90m-high granite landmark known as Soroti Rock. Soroti also serves as a possible base for exploring rock-art sites such as Nyero and for birding on Lake Bisina and looking for shoebills at Akuja.

Getting there and away Soroti lies 100km northwest of Mbale along a good surfaced road passing through Kumi and the marshy western fringes of Lake Bisina. Allow 90 minutes in a private vehicle to make the journey. The surfaced road continues from Soroti to Lira, 125km (2–3hrs) to the northwest. The 170km road running northeast from Soroti to Moroto has recently been surfaced and the onward journey can be completed in under 3 hours.

Plenty of bus and matatu traffic connects Soroti to Kampala (US$7), Mbale (US$2) and Lira (US$3.50). The pick of the private bus companies is YY Coaches (m 0759 932500; f yycoaches), which runs several times daily in either direction between Kampala and Lira via Mbale and Soroti. Kakise Bus Services covers the same route but continues from Lira on to Gulu. Transport into Karamoja is more limited but Teso Coaches (m 0758 999881) operates a service from Kampala to Kotido via Mbale, Soroti and Moroto, while Gateway Buses (☎ 041 4250930; m 0778 092178) operates a service from Kampala to Kaabong via Soroti.

Where to stay

Akalabai Village Stay [map, page 276] (4 rooms) m 0772 515776; e akalabaivillagestay@gmail.com. Situated in the village of the same name about 60km south of Soroti & 10km south of Kumi, this low-key cluster of en-suite thatched cottages aims to provide visitors with an immersive experience in local Iteso culture. It incorporates an interesting ethnological museum & offers various interactive activities ranging from cattle market visits & walking safaris to dining & storytelling with village elders. *US$45 dbl.* **$$**

Hursey Resort (15 rooms) ☎ 039 2001682; m 0779 557903; e admin@hursey.co.ug; w hursey.co.ug. This modern hotel stands in large, peaceful manicured grounds some 4km out of town off the Moroto Rd. Local sources say the rooms are the best in town, but they prefer the food at Timisha Hotel. *US$35/43 sgl/dbl B&B; suites from US$57.* **$$**

Paxland Hotel (23 rooms) m 0777 721222. Situated in neat gardens about 1km from the town centre along the Lira Rd, this comfortable hotel offers a range of attractively priced rooms. Excellent value. *US$8 sgl exc b/fast; US$11/30 dbl/large dbl B&B.* **$**

Soroti Hotel (63 rooms) m 0772 301154; e hotelsoroti2001@gmail.com; w sorotihotel.inn.fan. Situated 800m southwest of the town centre beyond the defunct golf course, Soroti's inheritance from the long-gone Uganda Hotels chain provides the standard combination of characterful but slightly rundown original infrastructure & modern 'bolt-on' additions. As usual, the rooms are larger & smarter in the new block; an unexpectedly modern-looking restaurant serves a varied selection of mains for around US$7. *US$30/33/36 sgl/dbl/twin B&B.* **$$**

Timisha Hotel (17 rooms) ⊕ 1.7129588, 33.6076408; ☎ 0774 557719; e timishahotel@gmail.com; w hursey.co.ug. This pleasant modern hotel is found in a quiet suburb, a few mins' walk from the (seasonally) green expanse of the defunct cricket ground & golf course, with the town centre just beyond. *US$25/35 sgl/dbl B&B; suites from US$57.* **$$**

Where to eat and drink

Arch Restaurant Edyegu Rd; ☎ 039 2963502; ⏲ 07.00–21.00 daily. Set at the base of Soroti Rock, the town's busiest eatery has indoor & terrace seating, & serves a variety of local dishes (eg: goat, chicken or beef stew with rice or matoke), supplemented by a Western-style menu of salads, grills & curries. *Local dishes in the US$1–2 range; Western-style dishes around US$4.*

Café Canunu Main Rd; m 0702 733070; ⏲ 24hrs daily. Situated above Stanbic Bank, this 1st-floor café (access from the alley at the back) has terrace seating offering views across the town centre to Soroti Rock & a long, varied menu of b/fasts, pasta, wraps, burgers, pizzas & curries. *Meals in the US$3–4 range.*

Tour operator Soroti is a potential staging point for the range of rather low-key attractions described below. It's possible to locate most of them by yourself, but a variety of local day trips and longer packages are also offered by **Homestead Tours** (m 0702 475378, 0773 521380; e info@homesteadtoursandsafaris.com; w homesteadtoursandsafaris.com). Activities include guided walks, cycle rides and boat trips, fishing, visits to the rock paintings on Kapir Hill, processing and eating traditional foods including peanut butter, ox ploughing, birdwatching (including wetland rarities), singing, dancing and storytelling, and visiting local markets.

What to see and do The town centre doesn't offer much in the way of scintillating sightseeing. Its most prominent feature is **Soroti Rock**, a striking, domed granite formation whose climbable pinnacle stands 90m above the town centre and offers good views across to Mount Elgon and Lake Kyoga. However, as the summit is the site of a government communication installation, permission for an ascent must be obtained from the City Council Office first. Since the authorisation form must be signed by the town clerk, mayor and district commissioner, this is a slow process which, inevitably, requires a small payment at each stage. This works out cheaply enough for a group – around US$5 pp – if you send a local guide to handle matters, but will be more costly and time consuming if you take on the challenge yourself. Either way, plan a day in advance.

Otherwise, Soroti retains a large central green space as well as some pleasantly leafy lanes which reward an early morning walk from Timisha or Soroti Hotel towards the rock. Your route will take you past the small **Soroti Museum** (⊕ 1.7076045, 33.6128342), a perennially incomplete initiative which should open to the public during the lifespan of this edition (we said that in the last book, too). Call Peter, the museum curator, for an update on m 0773 771823. Some 10 minutes' walk beyond the museum, a spectacularly pot-holed road lined with warehouses and maize mills encircles Soroti Rock. If you find your way behind this, a short northwards walk along the base of the looming outcrop will decant you in the town centre near the market. The path is lined with small quarries in which local people are slowly but steadily reducing Soroti Rock towards ground zero by bashing it into building aggregate with hammers (it is, you will appreciate, a long-term project).

Nyero Rock Art Site (⊕ 1.47114, 33.84699; entrance US$5 pp) Far and away the finest of the 20-odd prehistoric rock-art sites identified on the granite outcrops that scatter the plains between Mount Elgon and Lake Kyoga, Nyero is also one of the most accessible, situated only 10km west of the main road between Mbale and Soroti. The site is managed by the Ministry of Tourism, Wildlife and Antiquities, which has built a small visitor centre bearing plasterwork depictions of the Nyero artwork but has yet to provide any additional information or context; indeed, the site curator was pleased to photograph these pages for his personal edification. Meanwhile, a tree-planting project is attempting to recreate the forest environment in which, presumably, Nyero's unknown artists would have worked – though the initiative does assume that eastern Uganda was a monoculture of teak. The site comprises six discrete painted panels set within a few hundred metres of each other on a prominent granite outcrop called Moru Ikara. Most impressive is **Panel Two**, a 6m-high rock face reached via a narrow cleft between two immense boulders. At least 40 sets of red concentric circles are partially or wholly visible on the face, as is one 'acacia pod' figure. At the top right is a (very faded) painting of three zebras. The most striking naturalistic figures on the panel are two large canoes, of which one is about 1.5m long and evidently carrying people. **Panel One** is far less elaborate, consisting of six sets of white concentric circles and a few 'acacia pod' figures. **Panel Three** is painted on the underside of a low rock shelter. Though limited in area and subject, it is the most distinctive and (in an admittedly limited circle) iconic of all of Uganda's rock art, consisting of a single, sun-like motif in which a dozen spokes/rays, each of distinct and abstract design, radiate from a core of concentric circles. Unless you're intent on full value for your US$5 fee, this is where you call it a day, for the remaining three panels are either very faded or damaged.

ROCK ART OF EASTERN UGANDA

Almost 50 discrete panels of prehistoric rock art have been identified at 29 different localities in southeast Uganda, the best-known being Nyero, Kakoro, Komuge, Obwin Rock, Ngora and Lolwe Island (Lake Victoria). Collectively added to the tentative list of UNESCO World Heritage sites in 1997, these 'hunter-gatherer geometric rock-art sites of eastern Uganda' are in most cases monochromatic – typically either red or white – and the predominant figures are sets of four or five concentric circles, and strange compartmentalised sausage-shaped figures reminiscent of acacia pods. It would be misleading to compare the impact of these geometric rock paintings, many of which are very faded, with their more naturalistic and better-preserved counterparts in central Tanzania or southern Africa. Nevertheless, a visit to one of the more accessible sites, in particular Nyero, is recommended to anybody with a passing interest in archaeology or human prehistory.

The limited palate drawn on by the artists of eastern Uganda was sourced from whatever natural materials were available to them. Red pigments were created by scraping the surface of a ferruginous rock, while white paint was derived from a combination of clay, dung and sap, and black from oxidised organic matter such as charcoal and burned fat. The raw ingredients would be ground finely then mixed into a thick liquid such as albumin to form an adhesive paste that was applied to the rock surface using a rudimentary brush of animal hair. Unless you assume that the artists had one eye focused on posterity, it is reasonable to think that the surviving paintings constitute a minute proportion of their work, much of which would have been painted on to exposed rocks or more ephemeral surfaces such as animal hide.

The age of the rock art is a matter for conjecture, as is the identity of the artists. The Iteso people who have inhabited the region for the last 300 years

The springboard for visits to Nyero is Kumi town, halfway along the surfaced road between Mbale and Soroti. Founded in 1904 by Semei Kakungulu as an administrative substation of Mbale, it is named after the jackal-berry or African ebony (*Diospyros mespiliformis*), known locally as *ekum*, that proliferates in the vicinity. From the crossroads in Kumi (⊕ 1.48913, 33.93674), head west along the Ngora Road for 8km, passing through the tiny trading centre of Nyero (somewhat incongruously, the site of a large private university), then 2km later you'll see the 100m side road to the rock-art site signposted clearly to the right.

For dedicated rock-art enthusiasts, several other low-key sites in the vicinity of Soroti are worth a look. Perhaps the most accessible is the Kapir Rock Art Site (⊕ 1.6585, 33.78199; entrance US$3 pp), which comprises one worn and graffiti-scarred panel of mostly geometric patterns on a prominent granite outcrop on the northeast side of the Mbale Road some 20km from Soroti. Other sites, for hardcore rock-art fans only, include Obwin Rock, which lies about 7km south of Soroti along the dirt road to Akuja, and Komuge (⊕ 1.2147582, 34.0904162), which lies about 3km west of the Mbale Road along a signposted junction 85km southeast of Soroti, just before Kachumbale. For more information and a map showing the rough location of all identified sites in Uganda, download Catherine Namono's fascinating 2010 thesis *Resolving the Authorship of the Geometric Rock Art of Uganda* from w researchgate.net.

Where to stay If you plan careful scrutiny of the rock art at Nyero and perhaps other sites in the vicinity, a variety of accommodation in the area is available – indeed, a

reckon that the art has always been there. Iteso tradition does relate that the region's rock shelters were formerly occupied by a short, light-skinned race of people, and excavations at Nyero have unearthed several microlithic tools of a type not used by the Iteso. For this reason, it was long thought that the artists might have ethnic and cultural affiliations to the San peoples responsible for much of the rock art in southern Africa, but Catherine Namono's paper *Resolving the Authorship of the Geometric Rock Art of Uganda*, published in the *Journal of African Archaeology* in 2010, makes a convincing case that they are more likely to have been Pygmy hunter-gatherers with no ethnic affinities to their southern counterparts. Either way, the paintings must be at least 300 years old, and are possibly much more ancient.

As for the intent of the artists, the field is wide open. The circle is a universal theme in prehistoric art and its use could be mythological, symbolic (for instance, a representation of the cycle of the seasons) or more literal (the sun or moon). A possible clue to interpreting the rock art of eastern Uganda comes from a style of house painting practised in northeast DRC in association with rainmaking ceremonies. Here, concentric circles represent the sun, while wavy lines symbolise the moon's feet, which – it is said – follow the rain (a reference to the link between the new moon and stormy weather). Could a similar purpose reasonably be attributed to the rock art of eastern Uganda? Quite possibly, since Nyero is known to have been the site of Iteso rainmaking ceremonies in historic times. But it is a considerable part of these ancient paintings' mystique that they pose more questions than there are answers forthcoming – the simple truth is that we'll never know.

cluster of small cottages is under construction right at the entrance to the Nyero site. A few kilometres further down the road at Ngora, you'll find the expansive and unexpectedly grand **Galaxy Hotel** (m 0772 401039; e info@galaxycountryclub.com; US$20–28 std/exec sgl;, US$28–35 std/exec dbl, B&B; **$$**). Back on the main highway in Kumi, **Kumi Hotel** (m 0772 490659; US$21/26 sgl/dbl B&B; **$$**), signposted to the right as you arrive from Mbale, is the first choice for many visiting NGO workers.

Akuja Shoebill Site Situated on an arm of Lake Kyoga known locally as Agu or Achola, the tiny village of Akuja, some 25km south of Soroti as the crow flies, is home to Teso Community Action For Nature (TESCAN; m 0782 308292, 0778 209048, 0777 074813), which offers visitors dugout canoe trips on a papyrus-lined stretch of water whose wealth of aquatic birds includes a resident population of shoebill. It is a scenic location, with the open water scattered with blue and white water lilies and surrounded by several barre granite outcrops. Odds of seeing shoebill are better than even, especially if you arrive early in the day (ideally leaving Soroti before 06.00 to arrive at Akuja before 07.00) and phone through to arrange a boat in advance. The other birdlife is also impressive, and includes fulvous and white-faced whistling duck, purple and squacco heron, long-toed lapwing and African jacana. The boat excursion costs around US$28 per person, including the canoe and a local guide.

Transport from Soroti can be arranged with Homestead Tours (page 295). Alternatively, self-drivers should head out of Soroti south along the Serere Road for about 5km, fork to the left at Otatai, then continue south for another 21km until they reach a T-junction at Kyere. Turn left here, then after another 4km, left again at Abuket, and you will reach Akuja after another 2km, and a tree-shaded parking spot close to the lake after another 1km. After the boat trip, a left turn at Abuket would bring you to the Nyero Rock Art Site after 25km and Kumi (on the main Soroti–Mbale Road) after another 10km.

Lake Bisina Shaped like a wobbly smiley, this narrow and shallow freshwater body extends over roughly 190km^2 along an eastern arm of the Kyoga Basin, some 12km northeast of Kumi as the crow flies. Bisina is an attractive lake, fringed by extensive swamps and towered over by the (normally obscured) peaks of Elgon to the south and the jagged outline of Mount Kadam to the east. More significantly, it is the largest component in the Lake Opeta–Bisina Wetland System, a vast mosaic of open lakes, permanent swamps and seasonal floodplains that submerge the eastern Kyoga Basin. In 2006, Lake Bisina and the smaller Lake Opeta, together with their soggy catchments, were recognised as a 550km^2 Ramsar Wetland Site due to their scientific importance. Both lakes harbour endemic cichlid fish species considered extinct in the more accessible lakes of Kyoga and Victoria. Lake Bisina and its enclosing swamps also support a number of localised bird species, including the legendary shoebill and localised papyrus gonolek, white-winged warbler, pygmy goose and lesser jacana. Bisina is also one of a handful of localities known to harbour Fox's weaver, a swamp fringe-associated bird endemic to this one small part of eastern Uganda.

Tourist development on Lake Bisina is all but non-existent. The shortest route to its southern shore is from the village of Kapir, 25km north of Kumi, where a 4km side road runs to the western tip of Bisina. Once at the lakeshore, you'll need to negotiate for a local dugout to ferry you towards the reedy northwestern shore, where up to 50 pairs of Fox's weaver have been recorded breeding. Homestead Tours (page 295) have experience arranging birding trips to Bisina. Alternatively, head north from Kumi crossroads for 15km to the lake at Agule, where a vehicle ferry crosses to Okolorro on the northern shore to connect to Katakwi. Motorboats at Agule can be hired for lake excursions while the new Clan Resort Kumi (m 0772 479176; US$110 dbl B&B; **$$$**) should be open for business by the end of 2024.

Lake Opeta Part of the same Ramsar Wetland Site as the larger and more accessible Bisina, Lake Opeta comprises about 12km² of shallow open water enclosed by a much larger area of papyrus swamp. The lake and its swampy environs support one of Africa's most prolific shoebill populations, as well as the marsh-dwelling sitatunga antelope, breeding colonies of the endemic Fox's weaver, and other localised bird species including rufous-bellied heron and papyrus gonolek.

Lake Opeta cannot be reached on any conventional form of public transport. To get there in a private vehicle, follow the Moroto Road out of Soroti for 55km, turning right a few hundred metres past the village of Katakwi. From here, it's another 50km or so to the lakeshore village of Peta, passing en route through the villages of Toroma and Magoro. A trip to Lake Opeta could be combined with a diversion to the northern shore of Lake Bisina at Okolorro (see opposite), which lies about 10km south of Toroma.

LIRA The term 'backwater' might have been coined specially to describe the principal town of the Langi subregion. Lake Kyoga provides the water, with all main roads between south and north diverting around its shores, and Lira lies behind it, on the road to nowhere of specific interest to tourists. Despite its isolation, Lira is a pleasant and bustling place, with unusually narrow streets for Uganda, and a rather crowded feel befitting its status as the country's seventh-largest town (population 246,437).

As with Gulu, Lira suffered greatly at the hands of the LRA. The conflict's most notoriously heart-rending episode, the abduction of 139 schoolgirls in 1996, took place at St Mary's School in Aboke, 28km to the northwest of Lira. By 2004, 39% of Lira District's total population had been displaced to the town, whose population increased from 27,568 to 89,781 between 1991 and 2002. Though many of these displaced people have returned to their rural homes, others have opted to remain in town.

Getting there and away Coming from the southeast, the surfaced 125km road from Soroti to Lira can be covered in 2–3 hours and is traversed by several buses daily, including the well-regarded YY Coaches from Kampala via Mbale and Soroti (page 133). Fares are US$10 from Kampala, US$4 from Mbale and US$3 from Soroti.

For self-drivers coming from Kampala, the most direct approach is the 340km (5–6hrs) route that entails following the Gulu Road north across the Nile, then turning right on to a 70km road running east to Lira from Kamdini Corner (⊕ 2.24648, 32.33084). A good surfaced road and regular buses also connect Lira to Gulu (100km/2hrs) via Kamdini Corner. By contrast, the unpaved 125km road north to Kitgum is very rough in parts and not recommended unless you genuinely need to travel that way.

Where to stay

Moderate

Lillian Towers Hotel (18 rooms) Inomo Rd; m 0774 192310; e lilliantowershotellira@gmail.com. This 2-storey hotel is the smartest central option, offering spacious tiled rooms with understated décor, nets, DSTV & (uniquely for Lira) AC. *US$50/56/59 sgl/dbl/twin B&B*. **$$**

St Lira Hotel (20 rooms) Erute Rd; m 0772 594184; e stlirahotel@gmail.com. This long-serving, slightly rundown & self-canonised former government hotel is set in large quiet grounds near the former golf course. A restaurant serves decent meals in the US$5–6 range & opens on to a central courtyard. Strong on character & good value. *US$26 sgl or dbl in old block; US$32/40 sgl/dbl in old block B&B.* **$$**

Budget

Hotel Komar (47 rooms) Soroti Rd; ☎ 0788 507527, 0766 095409. This large & conspicuous blue glass building on the southern edge of town offers a welcome & easily locatable stopover if you're late coming in from Mbale or Soroti. *US$21/26/32 sgl/dbl/twin B&B.* **$$**

Kanberra Hotel (14 rooms) Oyam Rd; ☎ 039 2176379; m 0775 714808; e reception@kanberrahotel.com. Far & away the best option in this category, this small 2-storey hotel lies in compact green grounds where a garden restaurant serves international cuisine in the US$6 range. *US$20/26/32 sgl/dbl/twin B&B.* **$$**

Shoestring

Garden Inn Hotel (25 rooms) m 0775 493550. A notch up from the row of cheapies lining Oyam Rd, this hotel offers adequate en-suite rooms with nets & cold shower, set in large untended gardens around the corner from the bus station. *Rooms from US$9.* **$**

Where to eat and drink While eateries serving local fare still abound in the middle of Lira, a once-tempting array of international menus was drastically reduced by the Covid-19 pandemic. If you prefer to self-cater (not a bad idea under current circumstances), the town's best supermarkets are **Pari** on Obote Road, opposite KCB, and **New Lira** on Olwol Road.

Path Centre Café Ireda Rd; ☎ 039 2619385; m 0789 445763; e info@otinowaa.org; w otinowaa.org; ⌚ 08.00–20.00 Mon–Sat. The central branch of the out-of-town Otino Waa Tower has terrace & garden seating & doubles as a craft shop selling quality local produce. It serves all-day b/fasts, burritos, burgers, pizzas & typical local fare, as well as juices, smoothies & good coffee. Proceeds support an orphanage housing 300 children. Travellers with their own transport might prefer to head to the original **Otino Waa Tower** [map, page 228] (⊕ 2.29163, 32.78937), set in a small landscaped garden 7km along the Kampala Rd. *Meals in the US$3–5 range.*

PIAN UPE WILDLIFE RESERVE

Little-known Pian Upe extends over 2,788km^2 of semi-arid country to the north of Mount Elgon, making it Uganda's second-largest protected area after Murchison Falls. It hosts a diverse but scattered dry-country fauna, ranging from patas monkey and cheetah to Burchell's zebra and roan antelope, but populations are very thin and scattered. The reserve is also home to two pastoralist tribes: the Pian being a subgroup of the Karamojong, while the Upe are a Kalenjin-speaking people also known as the Pokot. The two have a history of armed conflict related to cattle rustling, having at times teamed up together to take on neighbouring tribes in Kenya or Uganda, and at other times directed their violence towards each other. This insecurity is the main reason why Pian Upe remains so obscure, but following the recent disarmament of the two tribes, it is earmarked for further development, including the introduction of giraffes from Kidepo. There is also serious talk of upgrading the reserve – currently administered as an annex of the Mount Elgon Conservation Area – to a standalone national park.

FEES An entrance fee of US$35/25 per FR/FNR per 24 hours is levied, and a ranger costs US$20 (FR & FNR) per vehicle. No fee is charged for using the public road through the reserve.

FLORA AND FAUNA Pian Upe protects a tract of semi-arid country that usually receives some rain in April and more substantial showers from June to early September, but is also subject to regular rainfall failure. The predominant cover of mixed *Acacia-Commiphora* savannah is essentially the Ugandan extension of an eastern savannah belt encompassing much of northern Kenya and the Amboseli–Tsavo–Mkomazi complex of reserves on the border between Kenya and Tanzania.

No reliable wildlife population estimates exist for Pian Upe, and poaching has taken a heavy toll since the 1970s, but the park still harbours a wide variety of large mammals and populations have stabilised or even increased since 2011. Leopard, spotted hyena and cheetah (the reserve hosts Uganda's largest population of the last) are all seen quite regularly by ranger patrols, and a small number of lion are present. Ungulates include Burchell's zebra, buffalo, eland, hartebeest, greater kudu, topi, oribi, dik-dik and Uganda's last population of roan antelope. In addition to the widespread vervet monkey and olive baboon, the far more localised patas monkey is quite common on the savannah.

Wildlife concentrations are highest in the vicinity of the Loporokocho Swamps, which lie near the eastern border and are inhabited by Upe pastoralists who (unlike the Pian) have no tradition of killing wild animals for food. Pian Upe is of some ornithological interest, with 250 species recorded, notably several dry-country species with a restricted distribution in Uganda, for instance ostrich, yellow-necked spurfowl, Hartlaub's bustard, Jackson's hornbill and white-headed buffalo weaver.

GETTING THERE AND AWAY The headquarters at Murujore is situated right alongside the direct Mbale–Moroto Road, roughly 90km north of Mbale (11km north of the reserve's southern boundary) and 50km south of Nakapiripirit. Coming from the south, for the first 30km, as far as the junction for Sipi, the road is surfaced and in a good state of repair. However, the condition of the subsequent dirt road is erratic and can be pretty dire after rainfall. You'll know you've entered the reserve when, shortly after passing through the trading centre of Chepsikunya, the road crosses a bridge over the forest-fringed Kerim River. In theory, a couple of daily **buses** run right past the reserve headquarters on their way between Mbale and Moroto but in practice, because of the condition of the road between Pian Upe and Muyembe, public transport has ceased on this route.

WHERE TO STAY AND EAT *Map, page 228*

Kara-Tunga Camp ☎ 039 3225630; m 0776 833901; e info@kara-tunga.com; w kara-tunga.com. Karamoja-specialist Kara-Tunga is in the process of extending its network of eco-camps to include a camp close to Pian Upe.

Kos Tented & Photographic Camps (6 tents) ⊕ 1.69032, 34.58253; m 0777 294754, 0757 294754; e jammeski@gmail.com. This simple private camp next to the reserve headquarters has en-suite standing tents with hot shower. *US$80/120 pp self-catering/FB.* **$$$**

Murujore Camp (6-room guesthouse; 2 dbl bandas; 1 sgl banda) ⊕ 1.69032, 34.58253; UWA Reservations: ☎ 03123 55000. This small camp is situated at the reserve headquarters alongside a canteen that serves a limited selection of drinks. Expect to bring anything else you need with you, unless advised to the contrary. *Guesthouse US$21/room; sgl banda US$15; dbl banda US$21; US$10 pp camping.* **$**

WHAT TO SEE AND DO The main obstacle to exploring Pian Upe is the restricted internal road network. Other than the main road between Mbale and Moroto, this is limited to a track leading towards the Loporokocho Swamps. Guided game walks can be arranged, accompanied by an armed ranger, as can informal visits to one of the Pian/Karamojong villages within the reserve. Another point of interest is the Napeded Rock Art Site, which stands in a cave about 30 minutes' drive from the main road and can only be visited with a ranger. The UWA now runs the reserve in partnership with a private operator (Karamojong Overland Safaris), and improved facilities and an expanded game track network are planned. Though self-guided game drives are an option (the US$10 per vehicle fee applies), we'd suggest you take a guide (US$20).

KARAMOJA

Uganda's most overtly absorbing cultural destination, the thinly populated administrative subregion of Karamoja extends over 27,900km^2 of semi-arid country along the northeastern border with Kenya. Karamoja is named after the Karamojong people, Nilotic-speaking, semi-nomadic pastoralists whose traditionalist lifestyle still revolves around their precious cows. For many years, it ranked among the most unsafe parts of East Africa due to the prevalence of cattle raids and large number of guns in circulation, but it has been stable since the disarming campaign of 2011 (page 305). Despite this, it remains one of the least-touristed parts of the country, thanks partly to its remoteness from the gorilla-tracking hub in the southwest, but also due to a limited network of rough roads and relatively poor amenities. This is gradually changing, however, not least due to the efforts of the Moroto-based operator Kara-Tunga, and the realisation among adventurous travellers and operators that the main road through Karamoja forms an excellent off-the-beaten-track alternative to the tamer Gulu–Kitgum route to Kidepo Valley National Park.

GETTING THERE AND AROUND Two main routes (with several minor variations) run to Kidepo Valley via Karamoja, both arriving at the park's Nataba Gate, 13km southeast of Apoka Rest Camp (page 314). Coming from Kampala, the more interesting but longer route entails skirting east of Lake Kyoga along the surfaced road to Mbale, then following a rougher 420km road north to Nataba Gate via Pian Upe Wildlife Reserve (page 300), Nakapiripirit, Moroto, Kotido and Kaabong (or, as a less bumpy variation, with better public transport opportunities, travelling via Soroti to Moroto and picking up the route there). The other option involves taking the surfaced Gulu Road as far as Kamdini Corner and branching right to Lira, from where a very rough 300km road runs to Nataba Gate via Abim, Kotido and Kaabong. In a private vehicle, assuming a very early start, you could drive from Mbale or Lira to Apoka Rest Camp in a long dusty day, but it will be a push, and you'll get more from the experience by allowing for an overnight stop. You can also get through using public transport, possibly supplemented by the occasional boda, but assign two to three days for the trip, and be prepared for some bumpy travel.

The roads through Karamoja pass through wild country with some challenging conditions, so check with recent visitors about the road surface. If driving yourself, you'll need a 4x4 with good clearance, recently serviced and checked over by a mechanic. Pack something for digging yourself out and take a tow rope if you can. Keep plenty of drinking water and snacks in the car as a matter of routine. Fill your fuel tank whenever you can and don't bank on finding further supplies past Kitgum or Moroto.

SECURITY Karamoja experienced regular instability associated with armed domestic and cross-border cattle raids prior to the disarming campaign of 2011.

Things have improved greatly since then and it is now widely regarded as safe for travel by locally based officials and expatriates. It would still be prudent to ask local advice before heading east of Soroti or north of Mount Elgon. Driving after dark should definitely be avoided, as should off-road exploration in the direction of the Kenyan border.

NAKAPIRIPIRIT Situated about 130km north of Mbale along a road through Pian Upe Wildlife Reserve, Nakapiripirit is a rambling Karamojong village (population 2,800) set at the northern base of Mount Kadam, an isolated range of spectacularly tortured turrets and bleak volcanic plugs whose forest-clad slopes rise to an altitude of 3,063m. If you have provisions and tents, it's possible to climb this 40km-long range. Plan for at least one night on the mountain, two if you want to reach the summit. Guides can be obtained in the village.

The road from Mbale to Nakapiripirit is surfaced for the first 40km until Muyembe (also known as Sironko), at the junction for Sipi. Though surfacing works are underway beyond Mutembe, they never seem to get finished and self-drivers should still allow at least 3 hours. Matatus between Mbale and Nakapiripirit (3–5hrs; US$8.50) tend to fill up slowly, and breakdowns are commonplace, especially during the rains. Gateway Buses (☎ 041 4250930) operate a service from Kampala to Moroto via Mbale and Nakapiripirit. The pick of Nakapiripirit's modest lodges are the **Panaora Hotel** (m 0778 014151; US$11/12/18 en-suite sgl/dbl/trpl B&B; **$**) and the **Hill View Resort** (m 0776 589937, 0751 589937; from US$12/15 sgl/dbl B&B; **$**), which is set in large gardens facing Mount Kadam, and has en-suite cottages and rooms, as well as a fair restaurant and TV lounge.

MOROTO Nestled at the western base of an eponymous 3,084m volcanic massif, Moroto is Karamoja's largest urban centre (with a population of 15,000), and the obvious place for an overnight break driving between Mbale and Kidepo. Mount Moroto, which dominates the landscape for miles, is far more impressive than the small town, whose central business district consists of a 100m length of tarmac lined by shabby single-storey trading premises and interspersed with a few freshly painted and whitewashed bank façades. Moroto has recently emerged as a fledgling tourist centre, being the best base not only for hikes up Mount Moroto but also for day or overnight visits to a traditional Karamoja manyatta, and for exploring the area's little-known rock art. Other attractions in town include a small museum, and a fantastic livestock market held on Mondays.

Getting there and away Moroto lies 105km north of Nakapiripirit along a good surfaced dirt road. It can also be reached directly from Soroti on a smart new 170km road via Katakwi. Using public transport, Gateway Buses (m 0778 092178) operates several services daily from Kampala to Moroto via Mbale, some routing through Soroti, others through Nakapiripirit, and some continuing on to Kotido and Kaabong. Night buses are more comfortable and much quicker. Teso Coaches (m 0758 999881) operates a coach service from Kampala to Kotido via Mbale, Soroti and Moroto and YY Coaches will most likely extend its Soroti service to Moroto once the surfaced road to Nakapiripirit is complete.

Where to stay and eat

Africana Hotel (40 rooms) m 0752 644686; e hotelafricanamoroto@gmail.com; w hotelafricanamoroto.com. The latest attempt to beef up Moroto's unremarkable hotel listings is this smart new hotel on the western edge of town towards the main north–south highway. Rooms

THE KARAMOJONG *Adapted from* Uganda Safari *by Andrew Roberts*

The northeast is home to Uganda's most distinctive ethnic group, the Karamojong; nomadic agro-pastoralists known primarily for their love of cattle and cattle rustling and their resistance to the trappings of the modern world. The idea of 'the Karamojong people' is in fact an administrative invention, a convenient lumping together of several tribes. These do admittedly have plenty in common. The various Karamojong factions are all 16th- or 17th-century migrants from Ethiopia, all speak dialects of a common language, Akarimojong, and, most significantly, most are obsessively keen cattle keepers. This last point is a dividing rather than a uniting factor, thanks to the fact that 'keeping thy neighbours' cattle', ideally after obtaining them by force, is equally central to Karamojong ideology. Without a patchwork of distinct tribes and clans to enable feuds, grudges, reprisals, alliances and understandings, cattle rustling would lose much of its appeal.

The so-called Karamojong people arose from a southerly migration by the Jie, an Abyssinian pastoralist tribe, 300–400 years ago. On reaching the Kenyan–Ugandan–Sudanese border region, the Jie split to create the Toposa of Southern Sudan, the Turkana of Kenya and the Dodoth of northern Karamoja. Some of the Turkana Jie then crossed the mountains that line the present-day Kenyan border on to the plains of northeastern Uganda. Some groups remained around Kotido as the Uganda Jie. Others continued further until they were, quite literally, fed up with walking; the gist of the word 'Karamojong' means 'the old men sat down'. Some Jie groups reached southern Karamoja where they gave rise to the Matheniko (around Mount Moroto), the Bokora (on the plain to the west) and the Pian (on the plains below Mount Kadam), while others continued southwest to become the Iteso people around Soroti. The 'old men…' line is in fact attributed to a hardcore group of walkers who continued even further west before finally 'sitting down' as the Langi of Lira District.

The language of the Karamojong people is an interesting and apparently ancient curiosity. Scotsman John Wilson, who lived in and around Karamoja for 30 years, has identified numerous words and phrases of similar meaning in Akarimojong and Gaelic. Subsequent investigation has identified further similarities with other widely spaced languages including Hebrew, Spanish, Sumerian, Akkadian and Tibetan among others. To give just a few examples, we have *bot* (a house in Gaelic) and *eboot* (a temporary dwelling in Akarimojong); *cainnean* (live embers in Gaelic) and *ekeno* (a fireplace in Akarimojong); *oibirich* (ferment in Gaelic) and *aki-pirichiar* (to overflow as beer foam in Akarimojong); *cuidh* (an enclosure in Gaelic) and *aki-ud* (to drive cattle into an enclosure in Akarimojong).

Elsewhere, the Spanish word *corral*, for a circular stock enclosure, is uncannily close to the Akarimojong synonym *ekorr*, and the Spanish *ajorar* for 'theft of cattle' is not dissimilar to the Akarimojong *ajore* meaning 'cattle raid'. The thinking is that these various, far-flung modern languages are legacies of a common tongue spoken by an ancient human population, presumably before the Tower of Babel incident and perhaps as far back as the late Pleistocene. If corroborated, this would be of more than just a passing interest, for such linguistic evidence helps us to identify practices that fail to show up on the archaeological radar. From the commonalities

are provided with AC & balcony. Acceptable meals are available. *US$70/100/150 deluxe room/junior suite/exec suite B&B.* **$$$**

✷ **Karamoja Safari Camp** (7 standing tents & 4 rooms) ⊕ 2.527332, 34.665212; ☎ 039 3225630; m 0784 414528, 0776 833901; e info@kara-

identified we might infer that, before they went their separate ways, the speakers of this mother tongue were (for example) cultivating land, harvesting ears of grain, creating simple reservoirs, getting drunk, plastering houses and pinching each other's cows (source: w treasuresofafricamuseum.blogspot.com).

More recently, the Karamojong have been something of an embarrassment to more Westernised Ugandans. The common view was that they were a backward lot who ran around naked and, half a century ago, the latter point was certainly true. Male attire consisted solely of an elaborately styled hairdo, a feathered headdress, a small, T-shaped stool and a spear, while female dress was represented by a heavy roll of neck beads and a bit of a skirt. These minimalist styles were driven underground in the 1970s when Idi Amin sent soldiers to force Western dress on the Karamojong at gunpoint. Men took to wearing, at the very least, a light blanket/cloak, usually of a striped or – interestingly given the suggestion of a Gaelic connection – tartan pattern. During the 1990s, this was frequently worn as a sole item of clothing but these days, some additional layers now seem mandatory, most obviously in the undercarriage department. Nudists – at least along the routes you're likely to explore – are now rare in Karamoja.

Despite expanding wardrobes and pressure from Kampala to join the modern world, most rural Karamojong remain true to their traditional way of life. Communities still commonly inhabit *manyattas*: traditional homesteads in which concentric, defensive rings of thorny brushwood surround a central compound containing huts, granaries and cattle pens. Unlike the rest of Uganda, some semblance of cultural dress remains part of everyday attire. For men this is epitomised by the cloak and some form of Western hat with ostrich feathers added to indicate status. Though the great beaded ruffs of yesteryear are less common, neck beads remain very much in vogue with women.

The recent history of the region owes much to another, more sinister addition to the well-dressed warrior's kit. In 1979, when Amin's army fled north, leaving a well-stocked arsenal in Soroti barracks unattended, the Karamojong, who had suffered terribly at the hands of the dictator's soldiers, took the opportunity to arm themselves against future depredations. Thereafter, a warrior's personal effects consisted of an AK47 as well as a spear. This development transformed the nature of regional cattle raiding. Outgunned, the Pokot and Turkana sourced their own armaments from the perennial conflict in southern Sudan. Traditional cattle rustling escalated from a violent form of football hooliganism (with perhaps more spear wounds than usually recorded on the terraces) to intentionally murderous assaults. The possibility of being caught up in such events meant that few risked visiting the region and Karamoja's isolation deepened. Between 2006 and 2011, however, the Ugandan army managed to effectively disarm the Karamojong warriors, a process sometimes nastier than the violence it sought to suppress, but which has restored security to the region. That being said, the immediate border region remains subject to armed cattle raids since the Kenyan government has not disarmed its own pastoralists; now reduced to their traditional spears, the Karamojong in this area are at a distinct disadvantage.

tunga.com; w kara-tunga.com. Home to the tour operator Kara-Tunga, this guesthouse stands in compact wooded grounds about 1km east of the town centre. Accommodation is in standing tents with balcony (comfortable but can be hot during daylight hours), apartments with kitchens &

verandas, & small but clean rooms. A terrace café/bar sells 2 or 3 dishes of the day for around US$10, & there's a new & well-equipped campsite with self-catering facilities & power points opposite. *US$70/80 sgl/dbl standing tent; US$30/40/70 sgl/dbl/trpl room; US$60/65/70 sgl/dbl/trpl studio room; US$10 pp camping. All rates B&B. 25% discount for East African residents.* **$–$$**

Lavender Inn (20 rooms) ⊕ 2.53425, 34.65852; m 0781 636987, 0772 710333. This popular hotel is centred around a neat hedged courtyard bar & restaurant. En-suite rooms have fitted nets & TV. *US$14/22 dbl with fan/AC.* **$**

Moroto Eco Camp [map, page 228] (7 standing tents) ☎ 039 3225630; m 0784 414528, 0776 833901; e info@kara-tunga.com; w kara-tunga.com. Another offshoot of the ubiquitous Kara Tunga (see below), this small camp occupies a delightful location on the side of Mount Moroto about 4km southeast of the town. *US$70/80 sgl/dbl standing tent, with 25% discount for East African residents.* **$$$**

Mount Moroto Hotel (38 rooms) ⊕ 2.523696, 34.670535; ☎ 039 2897300; m 0751 493000; e info@morotohotel.com. This agreeably time-warped former government hotel has a superb setting in a grassy bowl in the Mount Moroto foothills, 1.5km southeast of the town centre. Rooms in the main building have seen better days but the tiled en-suite cottages are very nice, & all have fitted nets, flatscreen TV & hot shower. Acceptable meals are available. *US$22 sgl room; US$43/48 sgl/dbl cottage. All rates B&B.* **$$**

Shalosa Hotel (12 rooms) ⊕ 2.53132, 34.66479; m 0782 430198. Well-priced family-run guesthouse whose spacious, cool, clean & brightly decorated rooms come with fitted nets & TV. *From US$17 dbl/twin.* **$**

Tour operator

Kara-Tunga Tours m 0776 833901; e info@kara-tunga.com; w kara-tunga.com. This dynamic Dutch-Karamojong operator offers a couple of dozen different tours & activities, all detailed fully on their website, organised in collaboration with local communities & led by Karamojong guides. These range from an afternoon visit to a Karamojong *manyatta* (homestead) or an overnight stay in a Karamojong kraal (cattle pen) to day & overnight hikes on the region's highest 4 mountains (Kadam, Moroto, Napak & Morungole).

What to see and do

Karamoja Museum and Cultural Centre (⊕ 2.52105, 34.68452; m 0783 330644; ⌚ 09.00–15.00 Mon–Fri; entrance US$4 pp) Inaugurated in 2012, this French-funded one-room museum stands isolated on the slopes of Mount Moroto about 3km southeast of the town centre. Displays relating to Karamojong culture and history include giraffe-skin shoes handed down from father to son over eight generations, ostrich-shell and bead jewellery, traditional leather clothes and a replica of a traditional manyatta. It also contains some interesting 20-million-year-old fossils unearthed in the 1960s on the volcanic slopes of Mount Napak, which lies about 50km southwest of Moroto. These include a semi-bipedal proto-hominid *Ugandapithecus major*, the earliest known cercopithecoid monkey *Victoriapithecus macinnesi*, the smallest known ape *Micropithecus clarki* and a bizarre leaf-eating odd-toed ungulate of the extinct group Chalicotheres.

Naitakwai Cattle Market This fascinating market takes place every Monday on the south side of the Soroti Road about 3km west of the town centre. Cattle and other livestock are the market's main focal point, with going rates being around US$200 for a calf or cow and US$500 for a bull. But plenty of other rural produce and other merchandise is on sale, from maize and sorghum to rope and clothes – not to mention a type of local hat made from human hair! And although Karamojong people predominate, you might also encounter traditional Turkana women with their trademark Mohican hairstyle. Activity peaks mid-morning but it's worth a look any time from around 08.00 until mid-afternoon.

Mount Moroto A popular Sunday afternoon activity for local expats is a ramble up grass- and scrub-covered Mount Moroto, an ancient extinct volcano that rises to 3,084m immediately east of town. The mountain is home to around 40,000 Tepeth people, mixed farmers who speak a different language from the Karamojong and are believed to be the region's earliest extant inhabitants of Karamoja, and whose dwellings are concealed among jumbles of rocks. Options range from a 2-hour round hike to a Tepeth homestead set on a bald rock offering splendid views back towards Moroto, to a three-day round hike to the highest peak. There's a waterfall up there, as well as cave paintings, while the 480km^2 Mount Moroto Forest Reserve harbours some 220 bird species, including Karamoja apalis, Boran cisticola and blue-capped cordon bleu, the last otherwise unrecorded in Uganda. Guided hikes are best arranged through Kara-Tunga Tours (see opposite).

Karamojong cultural visits Kara-Tunga Tours (see opposite) offers a wide range of Karamojong cultural experiences, ranging from beekeeping and gold-panning tours to bicycle outings, woodcarving workshops and a visit to a traditional healer. Most popular is a trip to a labyrinthine traditional manyatta, which usually incorporates a performance of traditional dances, starting with a tag-like courting game and tug-of-war, and culminating in pogo-like jumping reminiscent of the Maasai and Samburu of neighbouring Kenya. More interesting still is an overnight camping stay at a traditional kraal (cattle and goat pen) in the company of a dozen or so local shepherds drinking local beer around the campfire, sharing stories (through the medium of a translator) and, if you're lucky, singing strange polyphonic chants that recall Gregorian or Buddhist monks, except that the subject of these eerie paeans of appreciation is usually their favourite bulls. Day outings cost US$65 for one person, reducing to US$20 per person for a group of four, while the overnight experience is US$125 per person.

KOTIDO Dusty Kotido, Karamoja's second-largest town (population 25,000), is an important local route hub, situated at the junction of the roads running southwest to Abim and Lira, south to Moroto and Mbale, and north to Kaabong and Kidepo. It's an undistinguished but reasonably well-equipped town, hosting a few modest hotels, a Stanbic Bank with ATM, a large market, a Shell filling station and, alongside it, the best supermarket in Karamoja (though you'd probably need to have spent quite some time in the area to fully appreciate this accolade). Points of interest include the immense traditional manyatta at Nakipelemoru, the weekly cattle market, and the so-called 'sliding rock' at nearby Kalikruk.

Getting there and away Kotido lies about 110km northwest of Moroto, a slow 3-hour drive on a dirt road with some bad sections. It lies 190km northeast of Lira along a somewhat better road through Abim that takes up to 4 hours. Coming from the direction of Moroto, the best public transport options are the daily Gateway Bus and Teso Coach from Kampala via Soroti and Moroto (US$12). Coming from Lira, there's one daily bus via Abim (US$8). There are also two buses daily connecting Soroti to Kotido via Abim, one of which continues to Kaabong. If headed for Kidepo or Moroto, you could pop into the UWA office (just off the central roundabout) in case one of their pick-ups is going your way.

Where to stay and eat

Karamoja Arts Community Resthouse (3 bandas) ⊕ 3.00397, 34.10494; m 0753 246873, 0788 335442; e karamoja.arts@yahoo.com; w karamojaarts.com. This Christian NGO operates a simple but pleasant guesthouse & campsite, as well as a nursery & primary school, in a large sandy compound about 1km west of the town centre. Traditional-style thatched huts come with fitted nets, while a kitchen serves a limited menu of vegetarian & meat dishes in the US$4–5 range. *US$30 dbl using common shower; US$35 en-suite dbl; dorm bed US$15. All rates B&B.* **$$**

Kotido Discovery Hotel (12 rooms) ⊕ 3.00344, 34.11169; m 0771 469470, 0772 688357. This simple budget hotel on the west side of the town centre has tiled en-suite rooms with nets & cold shower. *US$8/10 en-suite sgl/dbl.* **$**

St Peters Community Centre (12 rooms) ⊕ 3.00139, 34.10818; m 0784 036178. Run by the Church of Uganda, this slightly down-at-heel lodge offers rooms & banda accommodation with nets & cold shower in large leafy gardens about 1km west of the town centre. *US$10/14 en-suite sgl/dbl.* **$**

What to see and do The main attraction close to Kotido is the vast Karamojong village of Nakipelemoru, as described below. But the cattle market that takes place every Wednesday and Thursday is also well worth a visit, and Karamoja Arts arranges day outings to the so-called 'sliding rock' of Kalikruk, a large boulder so smooth you can slide from the top to the base (US$5 pp).

Nakipelemoru This sprawling complex of wood-and-thatch Karamojong manyattas is reputedly East Africa's largest traditional settlement, supporting a population estimated at 10,000, and one of its oldest. The name 'Nakipelemoru' means ('The Rock is Seen') and refers to a sacred rock where the Jie people first settled after arriving from Ethiopia many hundreds of years ago. It was reputedly also the birthplace of Nayeche, the legendary female founder of the Turkana people of northwest Kenya.

There's nothing stopping independent travellers with wheels from visiting the Nakipelemoru independently, but it is one of those situations where you'll get more from it – and experience less hassle – if you go with a local guide. This is best arranged through Karamoja Arts (m 0788 335442) at a cost of US$70 per carload, a fee that takes care of community expectations for you. The best time to visit is Sunday afternoon, when the Karamojong of Nakipelemoru perform a traditional dance. Otherwise, the standard procedure is to visit a low hill from which the full extent of the settlement can be appreciated and then have a look around one of the individual manyattas. It's a fascinating experience but it can be a bit of a procession dogged by hordes of overexcited children. You may well get a more intimate – and cheaper – experience by visiting a smaller village with Karamoja Arts (US$40/vehicle) or with Kara-Tunga Tours in Moroto.

Nakipelemoru lies about 12km east of Kotido. To get there, head north from the main roundabout, with the Stanbic Bank to your right, turn right after 300m at the first main junction on that side of the road, then left after 800m, right again after 600m, and keep going until you see the District Headquarters to your right. Coming from Moroto, a quicker route entails turning right about 18km before Kotido at a major intersection for the army barracks (⊕ 2.97161, 34.2224), then left after another 5km and continuing through the village for 3km to the District Headquarters.

ABIM Situated 70km from Kotido on the little-used road running southwest to Lira, Abim is a junction town of 15,000 inhabitants set in a region characterised by wildly spectacular mountains and rock formations. The most impressive of these is Mount Rwot (⊕ 2.79088, 33.69215), a massive volcanic outcrop whose name is the Acholi word for 'Chief', which towers several hundred metres above the west side of the Kotido Road some 10km north of Abim near the village of

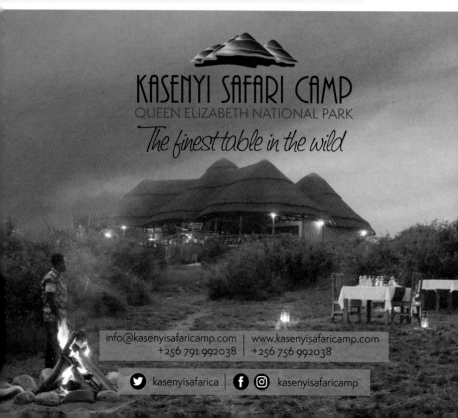

Isunga Lodge
Isunga Lodge at Kibale National Park
contact@isungalodge.com
+256 704 578783
www.isungalodge.com
Via Via
taste the world
BAR
RESTAURANT
GUESTHOUSE
Entebbe@viavia.world
+256 781 524 991
entebbe.viavia.world
Follow us on: &
FIND US IN ENTEBBE
PLACE TO
CONNECT
A PLACE TO
ENJOY
A PLACE TO
RELAX
A PLACE TO
EXPLORE

Alarek. If you feel like exploring, the **Green Star Hotel** (8 rooms; 039 2889420; m 0772 641666; e greenstarhotel2010@gmail.com; w greenstarhotelabim.com; US$10/15 sgl/dbl; **$**) on the main junction has clean and comfortable en-suite rooms with nets. All public transport between Lira or Soroti and Kotido stops at Abim.

KAABONG Possibly the most remote town in Uganda, Kaabong (population 23,000) runs southward from the banks of the seasonal Dopeth River in a spectacular and somewhat surreal landscape of scattered volcanic plugs and giant standing boulders that look like an unintentional parody of the Easter Island statues. Its bustling daily market attracts plenty of rural Karamojong in traditional attire, while modern amenities include a Stanbic Bank complete with Karamoja's most northerly ATM. The Saturday cattle market is similar to its Monday counterpart in Moroto and well worth a visit.

Getting there and away Kaabong lies 69km north of Kotido along a fair dirt road that can usually be covered in under 90 minutes. Though some maps suggest that the main road to Kaabong runs north directly out of central Kotido, you actually need to follow the Soroti Road west out of town for about 5km to an obvious junction (⊕ 3.01017, 34.07817) then turn right towards the north. Several matatus cover this road daily (2hrs). Masochists could also travel directly from Kampala with the dreaded Gateway Bus, whose daily run from the Kasenyi Bus Terminal in Kampala takes about 14 hours.

Heading on to Kidepo from Kaabong in a private vehicle, the 53km drive to Nataba Gate takes about 1 hour. No public transport runs to Nataba, but one or two matatus daily trundle along the 70km road from Kaabong to Karenga (US$5).

Where to stay and eat

Kaabong Resort (20 rooms) ⊕ 3.53529, 34.12483; m 0778 908449; e info@kaabongresorthotel.com; w kaabongresorthotel.com. Situated below a prominent rock outcrop about 2km north of town, this place has a lovely location, en-suite rooms with nets, a decent restaurant/bar, & pretty manicured gardens centred around a large fig tree that attracts plenty of birds. *US$14/28 dbl/twin; US$32 cottage.* **$$**

Rock Motel (17 rooms) m 0775 977873. Acceptable & reasonably priced town hotel. *US$14/16 dbl/twin; US$31 exec dbl. B&B.* **$$**

Sachavian Hotel (16 rooms) ⊕ 3.51544, 34.1286; m 0786 602221. Overlooking the river on the edge of town along a 400m road leading west through the market, this place has rather rundown en-suite rooms with nets. No restaurant. *US$8.50 dbl.* **$**

Tourist Guesthouse (11 rooms) ⊕ 3.51261, 34.1342; m 0782 795264. Located towards the southern end of town, this has en-suite rooms with fitted nets & Asian-style toilets. *US$8.50 dbl.* **$**

KARENGA Situated just 8km south of Lokumoit Gate, and most easily approached from Kitgum, Karenga is the main urban gateway to Kidepo Valley National Park. In a private vehicle, in good conditions, it's a 2-hour/115km drive from Kitgum. Happily, if you lack your own wheels, the days of perching in an open-backed truck from Kitgum are gone – or at least there are other options. A daily Roblyn bus leaves Kitgum for Karenga around 10.00 and costs US$7. Alternatively, you can take it all the way from Kampala's Namayiba bus terminal (US$20) departing at 22.00 and arriving around 14.00 the next day. Karenga can also be reached from the direction of Moroto or Kotido using the Gateway bus or some equally ramshackle matatu from Kaabong. For onwards travel into Kidepo Valley National Park, see page 312.

Where to stay and eat *Map, opposite*

Buffalo Base (5 rooms & 1 6-bed dorm) ⊕ 3.57525, 33.69697; m 0772 334506; e halfvocationalinstitute@gmail.com. This roadside lodge on the northern end of the village has basic rooms & serves decent meals in the US$2–8 range. *US$13/22 sgl/dbl; US$8 pp dorm bed B&B.* **$$**

KIDEPO VALLEY NATIONAL PARK

Lynchpin of the nascent northeastern safari circuit, Kidepo Valley National Park (KVNP) is Uganda's third-largest national park after Murchison Falls and Queen Elizabeth, and it vies with these two as Uganda's most alluring safari destination. It has a remote location in the extreme northeast of Karamoja subregion, more than 500km from Kampala, bordering South Sudan to the northwest, and only 5km from the easterly border with Kenya. Notable for its rugged mountain scenery and compelling wilderness atmosphere, KVNP also offers some exceptionally good game viewing, particularly in the Narus Valley with its dense populations of lion, buffalo, elephant and many smaller ungulates. Prior to 2011, the expense and difficulty of reaching the park meant it attracted a low volume of tourists, but this has changed in recent years as a result of increased stability in northern Uganda, greatly improved approach roads, and the opening of several lodges. Even so, KVNP retains a genuinely off-the-beaten-track character by comparison with most other comparably wildlife-rich savannah reserves in East Africa.

FEES Entrance to KVNP costs US$30/40/25 per FR/FNR/ROA per 24 hours. The standard vehicle entrance fees are also charged (page 9), but only once per visit. Fees are payable by card or MoMo.

HISTORY AND GEOGRAPHY KVNP was gazetted as a game reserve in 1958, with the dual purpose of clearing the bush in the name of tsetse-fly control, and protecting its larger wild inhabitants from hunters. Prior to this, the area had been inhabited by two ethnic groups: the Dodoth Karamojong pastoralists who herded their cattle in the valleys, and the semi-nomadic Ik who eked out a hunter-gatherer existence on higher land. Tragically, the Ik, who speak a relict Nilo-Saharan language of uncertain affiliations, were evicted from the game reserve when it was gazetted in 1958, and forced to turn their hand to agriculture, resulting in the drought-related famine in the early 1960s, and the deaths of hundreds of elderly people and children.

The original 1,259km² reserve was upgraded to national park status following independence in 1962, and extended to its present size of 1,442km² seven years later. Altitudes range from 914m above sea level to the 2,750m peak of Mount Morungole, the highest point on an extinct volcanic range running along the park's southeastern border. The slightly taller Mount Lutoke (2,797m), which lies on the opposite side of a 50km border shared with South Sudan, is also visible from several points in the park. This ruggedly mountainous terrain is broken by the Narus Valley in the southwest and the Kidepo Valley in the northeast.

KVNP has a moister climate than other parts of Karamoja, but almost all the average annual rainfall of 800mm falls between April and October, so the plains become very hot and parched towards the end of the dry season. The park is named after the river Kidepo, a derivative of the Karamojong '*akidep*' which means 'to pick', and refers to the fruits of the borassus palms that line this seasonal waterway and formed an important source of nourishment in past times of drought. The only perennial river is the Narus, which flows through the eponymous valley, and attracts a profusion of game in the dry season.

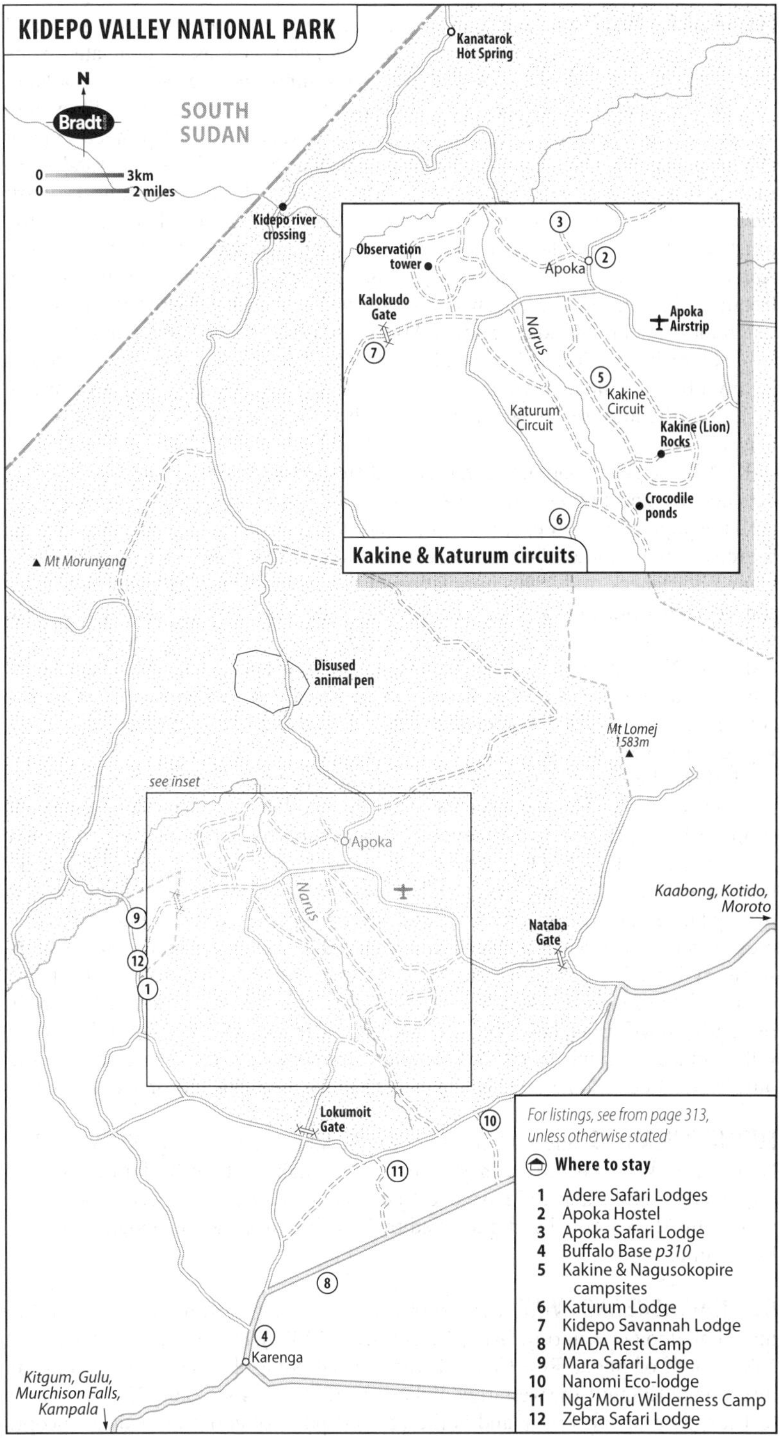

For listings, see from page 313, unless otherwise stated

Where to stay

1 Adere Safari Lodges
2 Apoka Hostel
3 Apoka Safari Lodge
4 Buffalo Base *p310*
5 Kakine & Nagusokopire campsites
6 Katurum Lodge
7 Kidepo Savannah Lodge
8 MADA Rest Camp
9 Mara Safari Lodge
10 Nanomi Eco-lodge
11 Nga'Moru Wilderness Camp
12 Zebra Safari Lodge

FLORA AND FAUNA The dominant habitat in the Narus Valley is open grassland studded with tall sausage trees (*Kigelia africana*) and the massive elongated fruits for which they are named. The Kidepo Valley supports drier acacia woodland, though some significant stands of borassus palms line the watercourses. Elsewhere are patches of montane forest and riparian woodland. KVNP protects one of the most exciting faunas of any Ugandan national park, although its total of 86 **mammal** species has been reduced to 77 after a rash of local extinctions in recent years. Predators are particularly well represented. Of 20 resident species, the most conspicuous predator is lion, but side-striped jackal are common around Apoka Safari Lodge and Narus Valley is also gaining a reputation for increasingly frequent sightings of cheetah, which might possibly cross between the park and neighbouring parts of South Sudan. Also present are leopard and spotted hyena, while black-backed jackal, bat-eared fox, aardwolf and caracal are not to be found in any other Ugandan national park. Five primate species have been recorded, including the localised patas monkey, which is often seen in and around Apoka Safari Lodge.

KVNP's elephant population has surged from around 200 in the mid 1990s to between 650 and 1,000 today. The African buffalo is the most numerous ungulate, with the population now estimated at 10,000–15,000. KVNP is an important refuge for the localised Rothschild's giraffe, which has bred up to more than 50 individuals from a bottleneck mid 1990s population of three, supplemented by another three translocated from Kenya. Other conspicuous ungulates include Burchell's zebra, warthog, Jackson's hartebeest, Bohor reedbuck, oribi and, to a lesser extent, eland. KVNP is the only park in Uganda to harbour populations of greater kudu, lesser kudu, Guenther's dik-dik and mountain reedbuck, none of which is all that common. The localised white-eared kob and Mongalla gazelle are occasional vagrants from South Sudan.

The **bird** checklist of 470 species is second only to Queen Elizabeth National Park, and includes more than 60 birds recorded in no other Ugandan national park. It supports East Africa's only population of Clapperton's francolin and the spectacular rose-ringed parakeet. Raptors are particularly well represented: there are 56 species in total, of which the most commonly observed include dark chanting goshawk, pygmy falcon, tawny eagle, bateleur and several types of vulture. Other birds that must be regarded as Kidepo specials in a Ugandan context include common ostrich, secretary-bird, fox kestrel, greater kestrel, white-bellied go-away bird, northern carmine bee-eater, little green bee-eater, Abyssinian roller, Abyssinian scimitarbill, red-and-yellow barbet, black-breasted barbet, northern red-billed hornbill, eastern yellow-billed hornbill, Jackson's hornbill, Karamoja apalis, rufous chatterer and purple grenadier – to name only a few of the more colourful and/or visible species.

FURTHER READING Sheet 11 in the 'Uganda Maps' series covers Kidepo Valley National Park (w east-africa-maps.com) and contains lists of bird and mammal highlights. An informative 72-page *Kidepo Valley National Park Information Guide*, written by Mark Jordhal and published by UWA in 2014, can be bought at Apoka Rest Camp.

GETTING THERE AND AWAY Three entrance gates are regularly used by tourists. The main Lokumoit or Katarum Gate (⊕ 3.64032, 33.71571), 8km north of Karenga and 16km south of Apoka Rest Camp, is the normal point of entry coming from the direction of Kitgum. The westerly Kalokudo Gate (⊕ 3.71486, 33.67322) stands next to Kidepo Savannah Lodge and is the obvious point of entry and exit for people staying there. The more easterly Nataba Gate (⊕ 3.69709, 33.80248), 12km from Apoka, is more useful coming from the direction of Kaabong.

By air Flights from Entebbe to KVNP's Apoka Airstrip (⊕ 3.71763, 33.74991), 3km southeast of the eponymous safari lodge and rest camp, take 2 hours. Aerolink (031 7333000; e info@aerolinkuganda.com; w aerolinkuganda.com) operates a return flight on Wednesday, Friday and Sunday. The fare is a stiff US$504/1,008 single/return and a minimum of seven passengers is required.

By road Driving to KVNP is increasingly straightforward, though it remains a push to try to get through from Kampala in a day. The most direct route, through Gulu and Kitgum to Lokumoit Gate, is covered from north to south on page 320. It is a total drive of around 565km (the last 130km all on dirt tracks) and takes about 10 hours, excluding stops. The trip can be broken up with an overnight stop at Ziwa Rhino and Wildlife Ranch, Chobe Safari Lodge (in the far east of Murchison Falls National Park), Gulu or Kitgum.

Two longer routes pass through Karamoja subregion, arriving at Nataba Gate. These are the 740km drive via Mbale and Moroto or 650km road through Lira/Abim, as outlined in the Karamoja section (page 302). Coming from Murchison Falls National Park, the 380km drive from Paraa via Pakwach, Gulu and Kitgum is doable in a day, ideally with a very early start.

Try to arrive at KVNP with as much fuel as you require for your safari (the last opportunity to fill up at a reliable brand station, depending on which route you are using, will be in Kitgum or Kotido). If need be, you might be able to top up at the UWA workshop at Apoka, assuming the pump is working, and you can also usually get fuel by the litre in Karenga. You'll find a mechanic at Apoka if your vehicle is making strange noises.

By public transport It is possible to reach KVNP from Kampala or Kitgum without your own vehicle. The most straightforward option is the Roblyn bus to Karenga (page 309). Once there, the management at Buffalo Base (page 310) will help you find a special hire to get you to Apoka Hostel or call the UWA game drive vehicle to come and pick you up (min charge US$90/day). Alternatively, take a boda or special hire up to Kalukudo to find a bed and hire a vehicle at Savannah Lodge (US$45/70 pp half/full day) or Zebra Lodge (US$160/game drive). It is also possible to get to Karenga via Karamoja, as covered stage by stage in the Karamoja section, but allow at least three days coming from Kampala.

WHERE TO STAY AND EAT *Map, page 311*

Kidepo is served by an ever-expanding selection of lodges which cater for all budgets. For budget travellers, Buffalo Base (page 310) at Karenga also makes a good overnight springboard for safaris into the park.

Exclusive/luxury

✷ **Apoka Safari Lodge** (10 units) ⊕ 3.73962, 33.72406; 041 4251182; m 0772 489497; e info@wildplacesafrica.com; w wildplacesafrica.com. This stunning lodge stands on a rocky hillside in the heart of the park & overlooks the rolling plains of the Narus Valley & its mountainous backdrop. A nearby waterhole attracts steady ungulate traffic, as well as troops of patas monkey & regular side-striped jackal. The thatched main building, set into the side of a kopje, comprises a large timber deck where all meals are served & leads out to a magnificent swimming pool with a natural rock floor. The spacious & stylish canvas-walled en-suite cottages have walk-in nets & a private balcony facing the plains. *Significant resident* *discounts offered. Rates inc drinks, game drives & walking safari but exc park entrance.* **$$$$$$**

Moderate

Adere Safari Lodges (20 cottages) m 0706 269726; e book@aderesafarilodges.com; w aderesafarilodges.com. This large & conspicuous resort-like facility near Kalokudo Gate offers guests a magnificent panorama across the park. Residents of other lodges, however, are less appreciative when, after dark, it introduces the hitherto unknown concept of light pollution to KVNP, lighting up the wilderness like the proverbial Christmas tree. A pool is provided. **$$$$$**

Katurum Lodge (18 rooms) ☎ 039 2474487; w katurumlodge.com. Nestled into the cliffs of Katurum Kopje, this magnificent creation of Danish architect Hans Munk Hanssen was never quite completed. Abandoned & trashed when the Asian contractor was deported in 1972, it stood as a ruin for half a century & only now – 60 years on – has it finally opened its doors to visitors. Though it's doubtful that the renovations would have met with the approval of its original creator, the view across the park remains as fabulous as ever. *US$120/180 sgl/dbl FB.* **$$$**

✷ **Kidepo Savannah Lodge** (17 units) ⊕ 3.71277, 33.66963; ☎ 031 2294894; m 0773 447343; e booking@naturelodges.biz; w naturelodges.biz. Situated just outside the park next to Kalokudo Gate, this well-priced & well-run old-school safari camp has a thatched hilltop lounge & restaurant offering superb views over the Narus Valley. En-suite tents are simply furnished & have private hot shower & balcony. There are also budget tents using common shower. It's well placed for game drives in the Narus Valley & b/fast opens at 05.30 to accommodate dawn starts. Hard to fault at the price. *US$135/205 std sgl/dbl; US$65/120 budget sgl/dbl; all rates FB.* **$$$**

Mara Safari Lodge (12 rooms) ⊕ 3.71277, 33.66963; m 0772 334994; e info@marasafarilodgekidepo.com; w marasafarilodgekidepo.com. This new lodge just outside the park's Kalokudo Gate has no Kenyan connections; *'Mara'* is a greeting among the Ik people up on Mount Morungole, just about visible in the distance. Closer to hand, the nearby Amukwas Rock is a favourite perch for lions while the game-rich Narus plains lie just beyond. *US$120/200 sgl/dbl FB.* **$$$**

Nga'Moru Wilderness Camp (5 cottages) ⊕ 3.62903, 33.7425; m 0785 551911; e lyn@ngamorukidepo.com. Set on private land bordering the park 2km east of Lokumoit Gate, this owner-managed lodge overlooks the Narus Valley & is well positioned for game drives there. *US$95/165 sgl/dbl FB.* **$$$**

Zebra Safari Lodge (10 rooms) m 0783 837346; w kenturegyelodges.com. This lovely little lodge near Kalokudo Gate enjoys the great easterly panorama across the park towards the Morungole Mountains. It's outside the park but a waterhole on site means that buffaloes etc are regular visitors. While the cottages are already a good mid-range deal, driver/guides' rooms (shared facilities) are available to all-comers, making it a fabulous budget option too. *US$115/192 sgl/dbl FB; budget rooms US$15 pp; meals US$10 each.* **$–$$$**

Budget

Apoka Hostel (aka Apoka Rest Camp) (21 bandas) ⊕ 3.73516, 33.72839; m 0775 299765; e info@ugandawildlife.org. Comprising renovated rondavels formerly occupied by park rangers, this rest camp doesn't offer many luxuries, but it has most things a budget traveller could ask for, & the price is right. The location close to the Narus Valley game tracks is also very convenient, & an observation tower with telescope allows you to scan the surrounding plains for wildlife. All bandas have fitted nets, & towels are supplied. A restaurant/bar serves surprisingly good meals for around US$4, as well as cheap beers & sodas. You can call ahead to make food reservations. Electricity is supplied by an erratic generator which shuts off at 22.00 so bring a headlamp & solar-powered charger or power bank for your phone. Overall, an excellent no-frills setup. *US$26/45 old bandas sgl/dbl; US$34/50 new bandas; US$54/66 deluxe. US$10 pp camping.* **$$**

Kakine & Nagusokopire campsites ⊕ 3.69877, 33.73335 (Kakine) & 3.72926, 33.68935 (Nagusokopire). UWA plans to open bandas similar to those at Apoka at these 2 splendid hilltop campsites, both of which overlook the Narus Valley, & have observation towers with telescopes as well as ablution blocks with showers & flush toilets for campers. You may need to fill water jerry cans at Apoka before heading out to pitch a tent. *US$5 pp camping.* **$**

Nanomi Eco-lodge (6 bandas) 039 3225630; m 0776 833901; e info@kara-tunga.com; w kara-tunga.com. Yet another venture from the ever-active Kara Tunga, this basic camp is located close to the southern boundary of the national park. Convenient for either Lokumoit or Nataba Gate, it has a great view across the Narus Valley towards Apoka & beyond. *US$90/95 sgl/dbl FB*. **$$**

Shoestring

MADA Rest Camp (21 bandas) ⊕ 3.25296, 33.42377; 039 2899500; e info@ugandawildlife.org. We learn that a Karenga-based NGO called MADA has built a small camp of brick & thatch huts with sgl beds. En suite with cold showers. B/fast is not included & meals need to be ordered in advance but the price is nice! *US$9 pp*. **$**

WHAT TO SEE AND DO

Self-drive game drives If you have your own 4x4 vehicle, you'll have no problem exploring the park, though it would be wise to enquire about road conditions. The standard US$10 per vehicle for a self-guided game drive fee applies. If you prefer to take a UWA guide, this costs US$20/25 FR/FNR per vehicle per drive.

Narus Valley Apoka Safari Lodge and Apoka Rest Camp both lie in the prime game-viewing territory of the Narus Valley, as does Kidepo Savannah Lodge. Wildlife here is prolific throughout the year, but doubly so in the later dry season (January to March) when the Narus River is the only reliable water source for miles around. The valley can be explored along two excellent road loops, both around 15–20km long, that run south from Apoka. These are the Kakine Circuit, whose centrepiece Kakine Rocks (⊕ 3.68412, 33.75041), also known as Lion Rock, is often frequented by lions, and Katurum Circuit, named after a (currently disused) cliffside lodge built in the Amin era. A landmark along the road connecting these two circuits is a pair of lily-covered crocodile ponds (⊕ 3.66874, 33.74029) which often attract large herds of buffalo and reliably host a profusion of waterbirds, including African jacana, yellow-billed stork, white-faced whistling duck and various herons and egrets.

On either circuit, you should look out for the herds of 20 or 30 elephant that come to drink from the river in the mid-morning, before marching back to more remote grazing grounds mid-afternoon. They are usually quite relaxed around vehicles, but be warned that recent returnees from South Sudan, where poaching is still rife, can sometimes be wary or aggressive when approached too closely. A feature of the Narus Valley is the spectacular thousand-strong herds of buffalo that are frequently encountered around Apoka, generally preferring wooded savannah to completely open grassland. These buffalo are the main prey of the park's 100-odd lion population, which currently includes two large prides of more than 20 individuals each. KVNP's lions are often seen on top of the park's trademark granite outcrops, which they use as lookout points. Other large mammals likely to be seen along these circuits are Rothschild's giraffe, Burchell's zebra, warthog, eland, Jackson's hartebeest, Bohor reedbuck and oribi.

For birders, Clapperton's francolin and rose-ringed parakeet are quite common around Apoka – the latter usually seen in small squawking flocks – while other conspicuous 'specials' include Abyssinian ground hornbill, bateleur, Meyer's parrot, black coucal (rainy season only) and superb starling.

Kidepo Valley Game is scarce in the Kidepo Valley, partly because it is drier than the Narus Valley, and partly as a result of poaching by South Sudanese visitors. Worth a visit is the Kidepo River itself, which is beautiful in its unorthodox fashion. Lined by lovely borassus palm forest, it is completely dry for 95% of the year and its 50m-wide course is a swathe of white sand. The Kanatarok Hot Spring near the

South Sudanese border is a low-key event that doesn't compare with its counterpart in Semuliki National Park. The thicker bush here looks promising for greater and lesser kudu, and it's the place to look for Uganda's only population of common ostrich, as well as secretary-bird, Jackson's hornbill, speckle-fronted weaver (look out for its conspicuous nests) and Karamoja apalis (often associated with the whistling-thorn acacia *Vachellia drepanolobium*).

Guided drives UWA also offers very reasonably priced guided game drives in an open-sided 4x4 car at a cost of US$25/30 FR/FNR per day subject to a minimum of three passengers or payment of equivalent fee. Game drives led by highly knowledgeable driver/guides are part of the all-inclusive package offered by Apoka Safari Lodge, while other lodges offer their own services. Zebra Lodge charges US$160 and Savannah Lodge charges US$45/70 per person half/full day (min 2 people).

Guided hikes It is possible to arrange guided walks around the Apoka area in the hope of seeing more common species such as elephant, buffalo, zebra, waterbuck and hartebeest. UWA also now offers an exciting 15km hike across the ridges of the Narus Valley, which costs US$30 per person, with no minimum group size.

Mount Morungole Rising to 2,750m on the eastern border of KVNP, Morungole is a rugged, remote, forest-swathed range best known as the main stronghold of Uganda's last 10,000 or so Ik people, who hold the mountain sacred. Immortalised in Colin Turnbull's 1972 publication *The Mountain People*, the Ik are traditional hunter-gatherers who probably originate from present-day Ethiopia and speak a unique Nilotic language quite distinct from the Karamojong tongue. Today the Ik rank among the most marginalised and isolated of Uganda's people, having been forced to turn to subsistence farming and beekeeping in response to outside factors such as their eviction from KVNP and victimisation by Karamoja cattle raiders. But they also retain a strong sense of tradition, with ritual hunts for small game being held several times a year, usually over the period between January and February.

Day visits to an Ik community on Morungole can be arranged through the UWA office at Apoka Rest Camp (page 314) or Kara-Tunga Tours (page 306). No park entrance fees apply since the people live outside the boundary, but there are other considerations: you'll need a guide, a security escort is a good idea and the Ik need to get something out of your visit. If you sign up with Kara Tunga, you'll pay US$35/30/25/20 each for 1/2/3/4 people. An additional US$50 pp gets you an interactive cultural experience with the Ik. As a day trip, it's a long outing involving a 1–4-hour drive depending on the season, then an 8–9-hour return hike. For a less rushed and more insightful experience, Kara-Tunga Tours offers a two- to three-day tour using two ecocamps on Mount Morungole and Timu Escarpment, the latter offering spectacular views into the Kenyan rift valley. These cost US$60/110 single/double full board, while day hikes from these locations cost US$60/50/40/30 for 1/2/3/4 people.

Cultural tours Under the banner Kidepo Connections, this new community initiative presents a variety of activities in the lands neighbouring the national park. Among other things, these demonstrate the work of a volunteer Community Wildlife Scout, showcase local cuisine and dance, and visit a traditional manyatta. To organise an activity, call Maraika on m 0771 454362 or ask your lodge to take charge.

ACHOLI

Named after its eponymous Nilotic-speaking inhabitants, the administrative subregion of Acholi lies in the far north of the country, bordered by Karamoja to the east and West Nile to the west. Its largest town, Gulu, lay at the epicentre of the civil war that tore the north apart between 1986 and 2005, and was for many years after that the main focal point of NGO activity outside Kampala. Few travellers ventured into the region in those dark days, and even now that things are superficially normalised and few visible scars of the war remain, Acholi is of interest to travellers primarily for logistical reasons, bisected as it is by the more direct (but less interesting) of the two main routes between Kidepo and Kampala. With an early start, and a private 4x4, this 560km route could, at a push, be covered in one long day (allow 10 hours without stops). It's more realistic, however, to break it up over two or more days, with possible stops at Ziwa Rhino and Wildlife Ranch (page 172) or, within Acholi, at Kitgum, Aruu Falls or Gulu. Acholi is also bisected by the most direct route between Kidepo and Pakwach (for Murchison Falls National Park), a 350km drive that is easily covered in a day, assuming you have private transport.

KITGUM Situated 435km from Kampala, Uganda's most northerly major town, set in a landscape only a sweet potato farmer could love, has some strategic significance to tourists as a staging or stocking-up post for Kidepo Valley National Park. Kitgum suffered much deprivation and housed several IDP camps during the LRA's reign of terror, as documented in the National Memory and Peace Documentation Centre

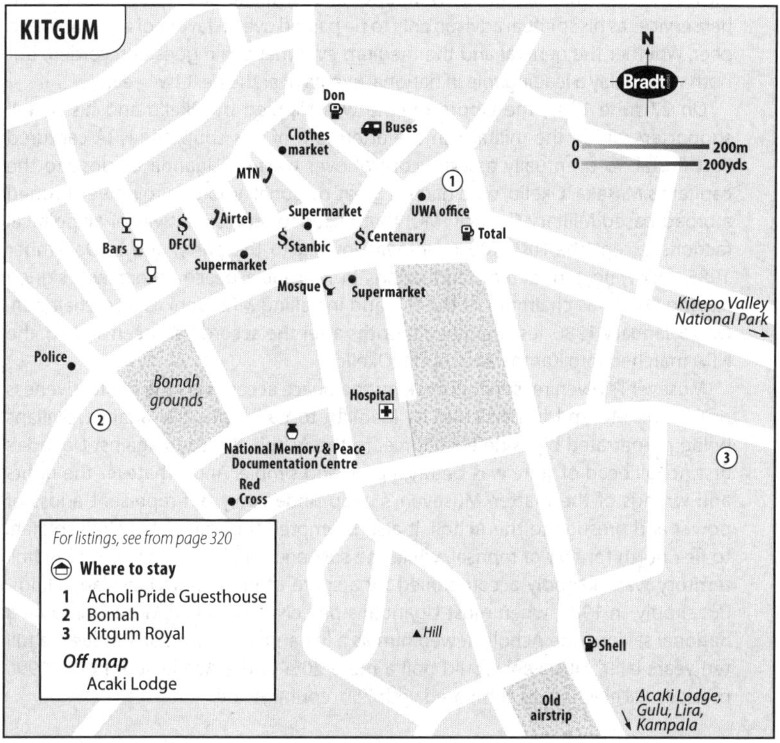

THE RISE AND FALL OF ALICE LAKWENA

The civil war that consumed the Acholi districts of Kitgum and Gulu until 2005 has deep roots. They stretch to the beginning of the colonial era, when the culturally divergent northern territories were arbitrarily annexed to the Uganda Protectorate and effectively placed under joint British–Baganda rule. And they reach back through 60 years of colonial underdevelopment: education in the northwest, and associated prospects of employment were deliberately stifled by the British, in order that the region might remain a ready source of military recruits and manual labourers. The roots of the present-day conflict are also embedded in the complex Jok system of spiritual belief, possession and sorcery that informs Acholi culture past and present. And they cannot easily be disentangled from the teachings of the early Christian missionaries who appropriated traditional Acholi spiritual concepts and icons into their biblical translations, in order that they might better hawk their foreign religious product to the locals.

As good a place to start as any, however, is June 1985 when Alice Auma, or Alice Lakwena as she had recently started calling herself, was introduced to General Tito Okello at Gulu's Acholi Inn. Auma was then a 29-year-old Acholi woman whose largely undistinguished life – divorced, childless and eking out a living as a fish-seller in Pakwach – had been transformed three months earlier when she was possessed by the spirit of an Italian soldier called Lakwena. Okello, by contrast, was the chief of the defence force (UPDF), slowly coming to the realisation that his troops would be unable to hold out indefinitely against the rebel National Resistance Army (NRA) and frustrated at President Obote's refusal to negotiate with NRA leader Yoweri Museveni. Lakwena was made aware of Okello's plans to oust Obote, and offered her services as his spiritual advisor, only to be passed over in favour of an established peer. Whether the general and the medium ever met again goes unrecorded, but both would play a leading role in national events over the next two years.

On 27 June 1985, the Obote regime was toppled by Okello and his Acholi supporters within the military. In the aftermath of this coup, the NRA captured Fort Portal, to eventually assume control over western Uganda as close to the capital as Masaka. Okello, who had no great personal ambition to power, formed a broad-based Military Council (MC) that included representatives of all political factions except the NRA. Museveni was invited to the party, and in December 1985, following protracted negotiations in Nairobi, a peace accord was signed leaving Okello as chairman of the MC and installing Museveni as vice-chairman. On 25 January 1986, less than two months after the accord had been signed, the NRA marched into Kampala to topple Okello.

Museveni's given reason for breaking the peace accord was the ineffectiveness of Okello's MC and in particular its inability to curb atrocities against civilians being perpetrated by its defence force. To the Acholi, the coup against Uganda's first Acholi head of state was betrayal pure and simple. And, whatever the rights and wrongs of the matter, Museveni's coup undeniably did represent a loss of power and prestige to the Acholi. It also prompted thousands of Acholi soldiers to flee north for fear of reprisal, while the subsequent NRA occupation of Acholi territory was allegedly accompanied by a spate of unprovoked civilian killings. Put simply, in 1986, when most Ugandans perceived or willed Museveni to be a national saviour, the Acholi viewed him as a liar and an oppressor – indeed, a full ten years later, Museveni would poll a mere 20% of the Acholi vote in the 1996 presidential election, as compared with 75% countrywide.

After being rebuffed by Okello, Alice Lakwena continued using her powers as a medium and healer to tend wounded Acholi soldiers. On 6 August 1986, however, the spirit Lakwena ordered his medium to abandon her healing to form the Holy Spirit Mobile Forces (HSMF) and lead a war against the forces of evil in Uganda. Alice assembled an initial force of 150 Acholi men, all of whom had served in the UPDF prior to the NRA coup, and made them undertake an elaborate purification ritual, laced with elements of both Christian and traditional Acholi ritual, as laid out to her by the spirit Lakwena. The newly inducted soldiers were also issued with a list of 20 commandments – the Holy Spirit Safety Precautions – ranging from the predictable 'Thou shalt not commit adultery' to the decidedly left-field 'Thou shalt have two testicles, neither more nor less'.

A compelling book could be – and indeed has been – written about the outwardly contradictory aims and beliefs of the HSMF. One central aim of the movement was the elimination of witchcraft (allegations of which were rife in the early days of the HIV pandemic) in favour of Christian values. Yet it could be argued that the movement's obsession with sorcery itself stood in contravention of biblical teachings, as certainly did some of its more obtuse beliefs, for instance that smearing a soldier's body with shea butter would make him immune to bullets. And even if Alice herself was sincere in her beliefs, it is difficult to say whether her mostly ex-UPDF followers – at least 3,000 at the movement's peak – were motivated primarily by spiritual considerations or simply by the prospect of exacting revenge on the hated NRA.

Whatever their motives, this improbable army came closer to ousting Museveni than anybody has before or since. Led by the spirit Lakwena and his earthly vessel Alice, the HSMF marched through Kitgum, Lira, Soroti, Kumi, Mbale and Tororo, inflicting significant defeats on the NRA and replacing the dead and wounded with new recruits along the way. Defeat came finally in November 1987, on the outskirts of Jinja, where the HSMF enjoyed little public support and its movements were relayed to the government forces by local villagers. After the defeat, the spirit of Lakwena abandoned Alice in favour of her father Severino Lukoya, who resuscitated the HSMF with some success, at least until March 1988, when 450 of his followers were killed in an attack on Kitgum. Six months later, Severino was captured and beaten up by the Uganda People's Democratic Army (UPDA – a rival anti-NRA army) and informed by a leading officer – an HSMF deserter – that there would be no more talk of spirits.

Following the defeat at Jinja, Alice fled into exile in Kenya, and spent the rest of her days in a refugee camp at Dabaab near Garissa, despite having been pardoned in January 2003 under an act granting amnesty to combatants who surrender voluntarily. She died of an unknown illness, possibly HIV/AIDS-related, in January 2007. Her father Severino escaped from the UPDA in May 1989, and was arrested by the NRA six months later, only to be released in 1992. Severino was later abandoned by the spirit of Lakwena, but – having renounced violence in favour of prayer and fasting – he remains active as a self-proclaimed prophet in Kitgum at the age of 94. The UPDA officer who so violently exhorted Severino against spiritual talk back in 1988 has subsequently stated that he is possessed by Lakwena, a claim publicly refuted by Severino, who describes his former tormentor as a 'devil'. And that former UPDA officer, whether spirit medium or devil, would go on to exert a murderously destabilising influence over the whole of northern Uganda for almost two decades. His name is Joseph Kony, and the chilling story of his subsequent career continues in the box on page 322.

(m 0770 553464; f NMPDC; ⌚ 09.00–17.00), an exhibition that features photos and artefacts relating to the conflict between 1986 and 2006. Today, Kitgum is a pleasant little town whose 50,000 inhabitants enjoy the services of a Stanbic Bank with ATM, reliable fuel stations, and an internet signal to keep them in touch with global trends in the sweet potato market.

Getting there and away It takes about 8 hours to drive from Kampala to Kitgum via Gulu, following a road that is now surfaced in its entirety. Using public transport, the bus fare from Kampala is US$10 and from Gulu is US$3. The best private services are Homeland Northern Express, which operates five coaches daily in either direction between Kampala and Kitgum via Gulu, HMK Coaches and Makome Buses. The 105km road between Gulu and Kitgum is also serviced by regular matatus.

Heading between Kitgum and Karenga (for Kidepo Valley National Park) it's a 2-hour drive in a private vehicle on a good unsurfaced 115km road, but it might take twice that time in the occasional open-backed trucks that serve as the closest thing to public transport along this route.

Tourist information The UWA office in the town centre is a useful source of information, especially if looking for transport to Kidepo Valley National Park.

Where to stay and eat *Map, page 317*

As far as bed and board goes, there is little to commend Kitgum. If you want a decent hotel or meal on the way to Kidepo, you're better off stopping over in Gulu. On the other hand, its budget options are cheaper and you'll get to Kidepo that much earlier in the morning. Also in its favour, there are a couple of very well-stocked little supermarkets near the Stanbic Bank for those last-minute provisions.

Acaki Lodge (22 rooms) Off Acholibur-Kitgum Rd; ⊕ 3.2674541, 32.8987159; ☎ 039 3242288; m 0783 377001, 0707 377000; e info@acakilodge.co.ug; w acakilodge.co.ug. Another popular stopover for Kidepo-bound travellers, this cottage-style hotel is located south of town & just off the approach road from Gulu. An apex of deluxe hospitality in Kitgum, it offers 'international comfort & standards combined with local charm'. I'm quoting from the website here, a remarkably honest text – for, as anyone who has travelled any distance in Uganda knows, 'local charm' is a euphemism for all manner of things, & indeed this is borne out by travellers' feedback. Order your food well in advance, for a start, & make sure the hotel isn't planning an all-night party during your visit. *US$41/50 B&B.* **$$**

Acholi Pride Guesthouse (13 rooms) m 0777 758069. This basic lodge next to the UWA office is conveniently close to the bus station & has a popular local restaurant. *US$8 en-suite dbl; US$4 sgl with shared facilities.* **$**

Bomah Hotel (22 rooms) Uhuru Dr; ⊕ 3.293786, 32.876475; m 0775 593123; e bomahhotelktgm@yahoo.com. Set in pleasant grounds bordering the town centre, this rather institutional hotel isn't anything like as smart as its posh namesake in Gulu, though recent renovations have narrowed the gap from a gulf to more of a fair-sized chasm. There's a pleasant enough compound offering secure parking & a swimming pool (in which baptismal immersions provide additional entertainment at w/ends). Though there's a tempting array of continental dishes & curries on the menu, availability depends whether anyone's bothered to go to the market. If not, you may as well go eat at the market. *US$25/30–40 poky sgl/ dbls B&B.* **$$**

✱ **Kitgum Royal Hotel** (11 rooms) m 0770 656887. Behind the smart stone-clad façade, the courtyard is softened by pot plants & a fountain (which sometimes works), while the en-suite rooms are tiled, with nets & fans. There's an indoor restaurant & a barbecue guy roasts pork outside in the evenings. Cheap, cheerful & ticks all the right boxes. Street parking only. *US$15/18/24 sgl/dbl/twin.* **$$**

ARUU FALLS (Entrance US$3) This impressive 250m-wide waterfall comprises five different streams that cascade westwards down a series of moss-covered rocks on a tributary of the Aswa River called the Agogo or Aruu. Situated about 8km south of the surfaced road between Kitgum and Gulu, it is easily visited as a day trip from either of these towns, or en route between them travelling to or from Kidepo Valley National Park, provided that you have private transport (ideally a 4x4). To reach the falls, first head for Angagura trading centre (⊕ 2.9661, 32.6399), which straddles the surfaced road about 47km northeast of Gulu and 57km southwest of Kitgum. As you enter the trading centre, turn right on to an unsignposted dirt road and follow it for 8km, passing Aruu Falls Primary School on the way, until the Agogo River effectively blocks the road (⊕ 2.89664, 32.64884). Follow the fast-flowing river downstream for about 300m, and you'll reach the top of the waterfall. Plans exist to develop the site further as a private wildlife conservancy and centre of adventure activities.

Where to stay and eat

Aruu Falls Campsite (5 tents) m 0774 591229; e atisilvie@yahoo.com, nokrobinson@gmail.com. This small tented camp stands alongside the falls & makes a great place for budget travellers to break up the drive between Kidepo & Kampala. 5 sgl, dbl & family standing tents use a common shower & pit toilet. A simple restaurant serves meals for around US$7 per plate, as well as beers & sodas. You can also bring your own food & the chef will prepare it for a small fee. Booking at least a week in advance is advised if possible. *US$7 pp standing tent; US$3 pp camping in own tent; rates inc entrance fee*. **$**

GULU Gulu will be a name familiar to anyone who takes the slightest interest in Uganda's recent history, as for many years it was at the heart of the territory terrorised by the LRA. By 2002, the sanctuary provided by the town had caused its population to grow to 113,000, making it Uganda's third largest town. Though it has since doubled in size to 232,000, its expansion has slowed during the subsequent peace and, overtaken in the rankings by other cities, it has slipped to eighth place.

As its reputation as a remote and besieged outpost fades into the past, it comes as less of a surprise to find that Gulu is a perfectly normal-looking town. Like many others in Uganda, it is formed by two distinct halves, in this case, separated by a gentle marshy valley alluded to in its Acholi name (literally meaning 'pot'). To the north of the valley, a network of quiet curving avenues is lined with government offices, smartish hotels and green gardens. To the south, the compact town centre is both busy and prosperous-looking; roads are choked with bicycle traffic, shops are filled with goods, the central market overflows with fresh produce, and a rash of banks and other corporate concerns occupy freshly painted premises with smartly tiled verandas – the same buildings that once served as sleeping quarters for the 15,000-odd children who filed into town every evening to escape the clutches of the LRA.

Getting there and away

By air Scheduled flights to Arua via Gulu with Eagle Air were put on hold during the Covid-19 pandemic and have yet to resume. Check w eagleair-ug.com for updates.

By road The 335km drive north from Kampala to Gulu takes around 6 hours along a good surfaced road that crosses the Nile at Karuma Falls, then 13km further on passes through Kamdini Corner, a nondescript junction town that enjoys almost legendary status as *the* place to stop for roasted roadside chicken. If driving yourself,

JOSEPH KONY AND THE LORD'S RESISTANCE ARMY

For most of the 20 years after Museveni assumed power in January 1986, the districts of Gulu and Kitgum in northern Uganda were seldom at peace. After the demise of the HSMF (page 318) in November 1987, the government sought to defuse the surviving UPDA, an army of ex-soldiers who'd served under Obote and Okello, and in 1988 a peace deal was signed. But although some 20,000 rebels accepted the offered amnesty, others remained dubious – Museveni had, after all, reneged on a similar accord with Okello in 1985 – and were persuaded to throw their lot in with a newly formed Ugandan People's Democratic Christian Army (now known as the Lord's Resistance Army, or LRA) and their charismatic leader, Joseph Kony.

Kony's sketchy biography varies with the teller. Born in a village outside Gulu in 1961, he claimed to be related to Alice Lakwena, and to be possessed by her spirit (and by others), and he almost certainly served briefly with the HSMF. Sometime in 1987, when Kony first became possessed, he was instructed to start a new movement to 'liberate humans from disease and suffering'. Initially, Kony's doctrines were based primarily on the Christian HSMF's 20 'safety precautions', but many Muslim rituals were added in the 1990s. Kony's ferment of possessive spirits often guided him along paths less ascetic than those cut by Lakwena – the edict 'Thou shalt not fornicate', for instance, was evidently discarded in favour of something along the lines of 'Thou shalt abduct, rape and sexually enslave schoolgirls at whim'.

The actual political objectives of the LRA eluded most observers. It never seriously attempted to topple the government, and after 1989, when Kony attacked several villages he perceived as disloyal to his cause, its main target was the people it was ostensibly trying to liberate: the rural Acholi. In 1991, a government campaign called Operation North significantly reduced rebel activity, but violence flared up again in 1993. An attempt at peace talks failed and the next three years saw suffering like never before in the form of mass abduction of children and the callous massacre of villagers.

Perhaps the single most important reason why the LRA survived all attempts by the Ugandan government to defeat it was the support it received from the National Islamic Front (NIF) government of Sudan. In a tit-for-tat scenario, the NIF aided Kony in retaliation for Ugandan support for the rebel Sudanese People's Liberation Army (SPLA) in southern Sudan. Between 1993 and early 2002, Kony and the LRA were based in Sudan, able to flee across the border whenever things heated up in Uganda.

This changed in March 2002, when Sudan signed a protocol allowing the Uganda People's Defence Force (UPDF) to follow LRA rebels into southern Sudan. Despite some victories, the ensuing Operation Iron Fist failed to destroy the rebels, and sparked off the LRA's most vicious civilian attacks yet. On 24 July, Kony's rebels killed 48 people in a village near Kitgum – the adults hacked apart with machetes and knives, the young children beaten against a tree until their skulls smashed open – before abducting an estimated 100 teenagers. On 24 October, *New Vision* printed a chilling picture of a singularly callous attack: the LRA executed 28 villagers, chopped off their heads and limbs, boiled them in a pot, and had been about to force the surviving villagers to eat the human stew when the government army arrived.

Following the signature of a peace accord between the Sudanese government and SPLA in January 2005, the LRA moved outside Uganda and Sudan into the forests of Garamba in northeastern DRC. Over the course of the next 18 months, the International Criminal Court (ICC) in The Hague issued warrants against Kony and four of his deputies for crimes against humanity, and Interpol issued wanted persons' notices to 184 countries. In July 2006, negotiations began in the South Sudanese town of Juba. An estimated 3,000 rebels amassed there to be demobbed before returning to the Acholi society from which most of them had been abducted. But Kony failed to turn up. And although many rebels did return home, others melted back into the bush. This period of uncertainty saw new divisions in the LRA's ranks. Kony's deputy, Vincent Otti, reputedly in favour of a peace deal, was executed in November 2007, casting doubt on Kony's own commitment to the negotiation process. And while the Acholi people seemed content for returning rebels to be reabsorbed into society through traditional ceremonies of cleansing and forgiveness, and the Ugandan government was prepared to give amnesty, the ICC's insistence that their warrants against Kony and his deputies could not be revoked remained a stumbling block.

By the end of 2008, the peace process was going nowhere. On 14 December, the forces of Uganda, the DRC and southern Sudan reacted to reports from the DRC that the LRA was rearming and abducting fresh recruits by attacking the rebel stronghold in Garamba. Operation Lightning Thunder was aptly named, with plenty of flashes and bangs, but no Kony, dead or alive. The rebels fled towards the Central African Republic (CAR), murdering hundreds of Congolese people living in their path.

The legacy of Kony's war is a brutal one. The civilian death toll in Gulu and Kitgum districts exceeded 10,000 while a similar number of schoolchildren were abducted and thousands more people maimed or disabled. However, some 2 million people – 90% of the rural population in the affected areas – were forced to take refuge in towns or protected IDP camps offering limited food and facilities, and appalling sanitation for up to 18 years. Dozens of schools were destroyed, while lamentable medical facilities were highlighted by a 30% mortality rate among children under the age of five. Average annual per-capita household income (US$30) was just 10% of the national average, while the number of cattle in the region fell to only 2% of 1986 figures (compared with an increase of 100% countrywide).

The LRA has not operated in Uganda since 2005. But the question remains: why did the war drag on for so long? The standard answer cites a lack of motivation in Kampala to end it. A more telling reason was a general feeling in northern Uganda that although Kony might be bad, Museveni was worse. Since 2005, however, the social and economic climate in the north has improved beyond recognition. And were Kony to return now, he would find that antipathy towards the government, and any associated support for the LRA, has been largely overtaken by the desire for, and fruits of, peace.

Despite this, Kony himself remains at large, probably in the CAR, possibly elsewhere. In January 2015, Dominic Ongwen, an LRA commander charged with seven counts of crimes against humanity and war crimes by the ICC, surrendered himself to US forces in the CAR. Two years later, the US and Uganda both officially abandoned the search for Kony, the latter stating that neither he nor the LRA – reputedly now reduced to fewer than 100 members – posed any ongoing security risk.

Joseph Kony's story is well told in Matthew Greens's Wizard of the Nile *(page 582) and the 30-minute film* Kony 2012.

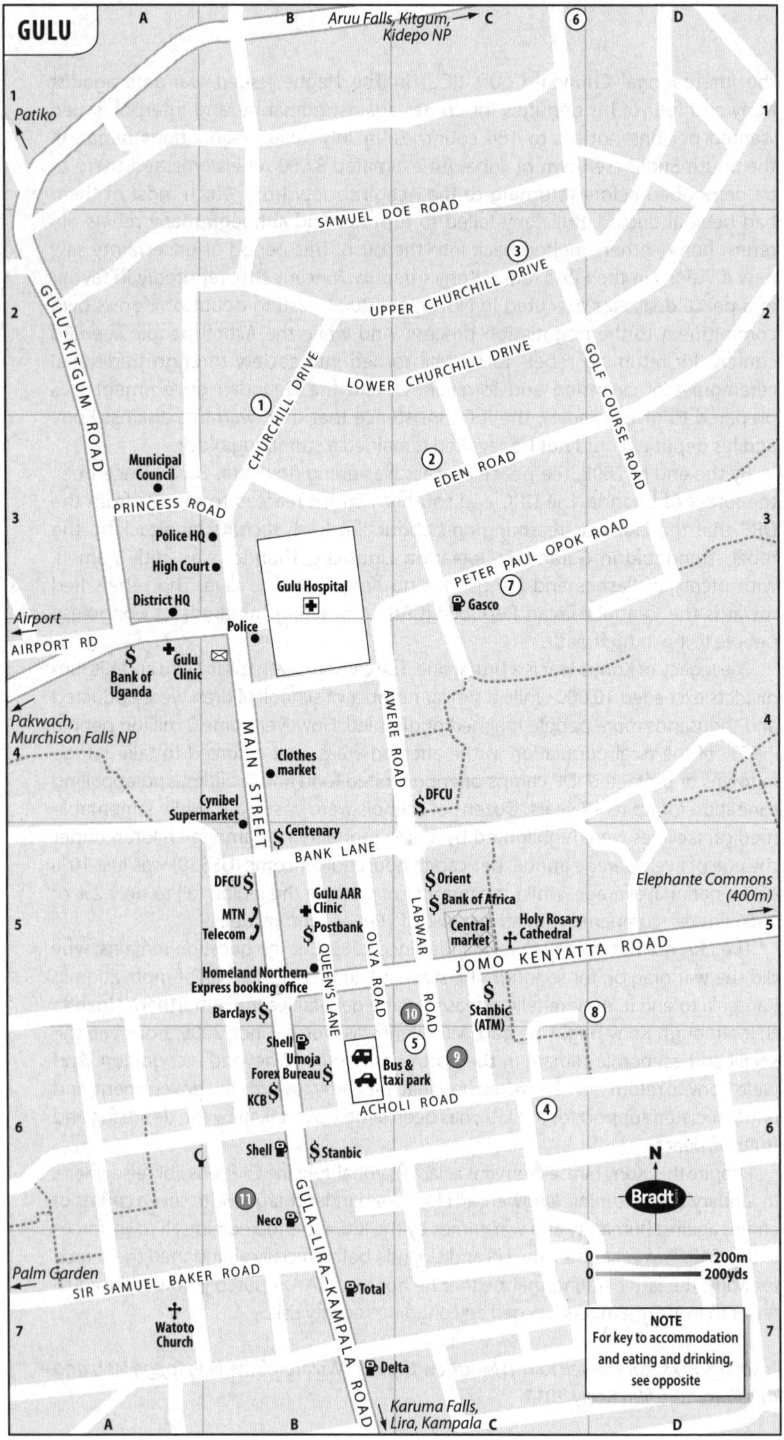
GULU
A
B
C
D
1
2
3
4
5
6
7
Aruu Falls, Kitgum, Kidepo NP
Patiko
SAMUEL DOE ROAD
UPPER CHURCHILL DRIVE
LOWER CHURCHILL DRIVE
CHURCHILL DRIVE
GOLF COURSE ROAD
GULU–KITGUM ROAD
EDEN ROAD
Municipal Council
PRINCESS ROAD
Police HQ
High Court
Gulu Hospital
PETER PAUL OPOK ROAD
Gasco
District HQ
Airport
AIRPORT RD
Police
Bank of Uganda
Gulu Clinic
Pakwach, Murchison Falls NP
MAIN STREET
AWERE ROAD
Clothes market
DFCU
Cynibel Supermarket
Centenary
BANK LANE
DFCU
Orient
Bank of Africa
Elephante Commons (400m)
Gulu AAR Clinic
MTN
Telecom
Postbank
LABWAR ROAD
Central market
Holy Rosary Cathedral
OLYA ROAD
QUEEN'S LANE
JOMO KENYATTA ROAD
Homeland Northern Express booking office
Barclays
Stanbic (ATM)
Shell
Umoja Forex Bureau
Bus & taxi park
KCB
ACHOLI ROAD
Shell
Stanbic
N
Bradt
Neco
GULA–LIRA–KAMPALA ROAD
0 200m
0 200yds
Palm Garden
SIR SAMUEL BAKER ROAD
Total
Watoto Church
Delta
NOTE
For key to accommodation and eating and drinking, see opposite
Karuma Falls, Lira, Kampala

GULU

For listings, see below

Where to stay

1	Acholi Inn	B2
2	Bomah	C3
3	Churchill Courts	C2
4	Gulu Crystal	C6
5	Lexus Guesthouse	C6
6	Northern Pearl	C1
7	Paula Guesthouse	C3
8	Pearl Afrique	D5
Off map		
	Palm Garden	A7

Where to eat and drink

9	Abyssinia Ethiopian	C6
10	New Florida	C5
	Northern Pearl	(see 6)
11	The Rolling Donkey	B6
Off map		
	Elephante Commons	D5
	Palm Garden	A7

reliable (ie: Shell or Total) opportunities to refuel along the way are few and far between beyond Luwero, especially on the 60km sections north and south of Karuma. Many buses run between Kampala and Gulu daily (US$7). Other options leave from Kampala's Kasenyi Bus Terminal and include Homeland Northern Express, Gulu Coach and Friendship and HMK Coaches.

Gulu lies 100km southwest of Kitgum and the road between them is surfaced in its entirety and easily covered in less than 2 hours. A worthwhile stop along the way is Aruu Falls (page 321). Using public transport, HMK is your best option for Kitgum, but matatus also cover this route. In the event that you're trying to get to Gulu from Masindi, you'll need to take a taxi to Kigumba on the Kampala–Gulu Road to board an onward bus or taxi. If you want to travel between Gulu and southeastern Uganda your best bet is the Kakise Bus Service, which travels to/from Kampala via Lira, Soroti and Mbale.

If you've left it a bit late to reach Gulu from Kampala, you'll find an overnight refuge at the homely **Karuma Travellers Lodge** (⊕ 2.20214, 32.23434; m 0756 840651, 0776 830651; US$48/66 sgl/dbl B&B; **$$**) 4km before the Nile crossing at Karuma. Should you reach this decision when crossing the bridge, look out for the imposing façade of the comfortable but bland **Northern Gateway Hotel** [map, page 370] (m 0772 440560; US$50/70 std sgl/dbl B&B; **$$**) on your left, 1km before Kamdini.

To continue south from Gulu to Murchison Falls, follow the Nimule road southwest from the town centre for 2km to a roundabout. You should go straight on (the route to South Sudan branches right) and after 60km of smooth tarmac, you'll join the Pakwach Road at Olwiyo. Turn right to enter the park through the Tangi or Wankwar Gate (page 376). Alternatively, if you are specifically headed for the easterly Chobe sector, take the Karuma/Kampala Road south from Gulu.

Where to stay

Moderate

Acholi Inn [324 B2] (100 rooms) Churchill Dr; 0780 468107; e info@acholinn.com; w acholinn.com. Could the *Extreme Makeover* TV people have passed through Gulu's oldest hotel since our last visit? Gone are the dismal compound & shabby public areas (including the lino-floored bar in which MPs, army officers & retired rebels mingled in the book *Wizard of the Nile*), replaced by an appealing meld of light & airy spaces, inside & out. Spacious en-suite rooms come with nets, AC & free use of the swimming pool & health club. Good value but book ahead, as it's a popular venue for government conferences. *US$54/66/75 sgl/dbl/twin B&B.* **$$**

Bomah Hotel [324 C3] (130 rooms) Eden Rd; m 0393 238127; e reservations@bomahhotel.com. While the main hotel occupies a forgettable 5-storey block, a pleasant swimming pool & lovely storeyed thatch restaurant-bar make the Bomah an attractive stopover on the way to Kidepo. En-suite rooms come with nets, DSTV, AC & hot water, while the restaurant serves grills & curries in the US$7–12 range. Facilities include a health club with steam/sauna. *US$54/60 sgl/dbl B&B. Tiny sgls US$37.* **$$**

Churchill Courts Hotel [324 C2] (38 rooms) Upper Churchill Dr; m 0777 764409, 0741 432245; e gcchotel@gmail.com. This friendly, secluded & comfortable hotel has generously sized rooms with nets, AC, DSTV & en-suite hot shower. Bland but decent value. *US$45/54/65 sgl/dbl/twin B&B.* **$$**

Northern Pearl [324 C1] (12 rooms) ⊕ 2.78080, 32.30126; Lasto Oketch Rd; m 0709 080808. With comfortable & affordable cottage accommodation attached to Gulu's best & smartest Indian restaurant (see below) & a convenient suburban location on the road in from Kidepo & Kitgum, this is an appealing option. *US$28/36 std rooms; US$42/50 deluxe B&B.* **$$**

Budget

Gulu Crystal Hotel [324 C6] (25 rooms) Acholi Rd; m 0790 912182. This central 4-storey hotel has clean tiled rooms with fitted nets, fans, TV, Wi-Fi & plenty of cupboard space. Very good value. *US$13/17/20 sgl/dbl/twin.* **$$**

The Iron Donkey This popular backpacker/volunteer haven is currently homeless, living on as the Rolling Donkey restaurant listed on page 328. We're hopeful that a resurrection is imminent, so phone Rita, the manager, for updates on m 0777 581303. **$$**

✱ **Palm Garden** [324 A7] (6 rooms) ⊕ 2.75983, 32.29008; m 0782 207118; e palmgardengulu@gmail.com. Perhaps the best-value place to stay in Gulu, this Italian-managed guesthouse is affiliated to an NGO that sponsors the education of local schoolchildren. Plain but clean bandas come with fans, fitted nets & hot shower. The large green compound supports an affordable restaurant/bar. To get there follow the Kampala Rd south from the Stanbic Bank for 350m, then turn right on to Lakana Odong Kara Rd. Follow this for 1km (straight over the wiggle at the 5-way junction) until the road curves to the right. Take the tarmac road on the left &, immediately after crossing the disused railway, turn right to find Palm Gardens. Most boda drivers know it. *US$13/18 small/large sgl; US$32 dbl; dorm bed US$8. All rates B&B.* **$–$$**

Paula Guesthouse [324 C3] (10 rooms) Peter Paul Opok Rd; ☎ 039 2419607; m 0772 613998; e paulagh@gmail.com. This family-run guesthouse stands in a large suburban garden within easy walking distance of the town centre. The spacious en-suite rooms in the main house are superior to the smaller rooms at the back. *US$20/24 sgl/dbl B&B.* **$**

Pearl Afrique Hotel [324 D5] (36 rooms) Off Acholi Rd; m 0781 569049. Once the first choice for NGO workers, this storeyed hotel is no better than 'acceptable' these days. Still, there's secure parking & though the on-site restaurant is currently closed, the New Florida Restaurant is 5mins' walk away. Though the standard rooms are small, larger ones are available. *US$20/24 std sgl/dbl; US$35 exec dbl. B&B.* **$$**

Shoestring

Lexus Guesthouse [324 C5] (13 rooms) Labwar Rd; m 0779 885467. The pick of several central cheapies clustered south of the market, this has clean tiled rooms with fitted nets, fans & en-suite cold shower. There's a terrace restaurant on the road frontage & a courtyard bar at the side. *US$11/13 sgl/dbl.* **$**

Where to eat and drink

Abyssinia Ethiopian Restaurant [324 C6] Labwar Rd; m 0777 111666. Down-to-earth vegan-friendly eatery serving typical Ethiopian dishes such as *tibs* (fried meat), *shiro* (spicy chickpea stew), *kitfo* (minced beef) & *atkilt* (mixed vegetables) with rice or an injera 'pancake'. Tasty food & good value. *Mains US$4–7.*

Elephante Commons [324 D5] Jomo Kenyatta Rd; m 0794 073820, 0783 115811; e hello@elephantecommons.org; w elephantecommons.org; ⏲ 09.00–21.00 daily. Situated 600m east of the central market, this hip Portlander-run venue serves burritos, pizzas, salads & other mains, as well as cocktails, smoothies, coffee & wine by the glass. Profits support an attached skill training centre. *Mains in the US$5–8 range.*

New Florida [324 C5] Olya Rd; m 0777 004338, 0779 825683; ⏲ 08.00–22.00 daily. On a good day, this no-frills central restaurant serves tasty & affordable Ethiopian & Indian dishes in a ground-floor dining room or on an airy 1st-floor balcony. During our last visit a series of delays & disasters ended with the confession that the chef was away burying his mother & that the guy who peels the potatoes was filling in. *Mains US$5 exc carbs.*

✱ **Northern Pearl** [324 C1] ⊕ 2.78080, 32.30126; Lasto Oketch Rd; m 0782 207118. Coming into town from the wilds of Karamoja, a feast in this excellent Indian restaurant could be just what you need! I haven't eaten there – yet – but I've seen the trays of delicious curries going out on those little copper warming pots & I'm

THE BAKERS AT PATIKO

Samuel and Florence Baker made repeated visits to Patiko (which they recorded as Fatiko). On the first two occasions, both in 1864, they were just passing through, firstly as explorers en route from Gondokoro (Sudan) to Lake Albert and Murchison Falls, then again on the return journey to Gondokoro. Patiko then was the southernmost outpost of a vast territory from which Egypt's Turkish rulers and their mercenaries plundered slaves, cattle and ivory.

The Bakers returned to Patiko in 1872 on a crusade to stamp out slavery. On this occasion they marched under a different flag; ironically, that of Egypt. The wind had changed in Cairo with the opening of the Suez Canal in 1869. Egypt's ruler, the Khedive Ismail, was aware that while this ultra-modern development had gained him recognition from the great powers, Egypt's international standing remained tempered by the ongoing medieval barbarism in Sudan and northern Uganda. Slavery, banned a full half-century earlier by Britain and France, needed to be stopped or at any rate, a high-profile attempt to do so needed to be seen to be made. Samuel Baker, whose 1865 travelogue *The Albert N'yanza* had exposed the practice to the world, was the ideal candidate and in due course (after accepting the fabulous salary of £10,000 per year) Baker returned to central Africa with his wife and nephew to formalise Egypt's presence in southern Sudan and northern Uganda by officially annexing it as a province, to be named Equatoria. Specifically, he was to establish a chain of forts to pacify the region and end the slave trade. He found the territory around Patiko so ravaged by the Egyptian Turks that they struggled to capture sufficient people or cattle to transport their vast hauls of ivory north to Khartoum. Baker headed south to Masindi in his vain attempt to include Bunyoro into the Egyptian Empire (page 363), before returning to Patiko where he established his headquarters around the kopje, from which he was able to banish the enslavers and pacify local tribes made belligerent by their activities, at least in Gulu region. A long-running wrangle with a notorious enslaver, Abu Saood, culminated in the enslavers being routed in a battle at Patiko. When Baker finally returned to Britain, he felt able to write: 'The White Nile, for a distance of 1,600 miles from Khartoum to Central Africa was cleansed of an abomination of a traffic which had hitherto sullied its waters.' In truth, Baker had merely inconvenienced the enslavers of Equatoria; he had lopped off their tentacles around Gulu – an area too despoiled to be of further interest – but more soon grew elsewhere. It was, for the time being, a hopeless cause anyway, for little real success could be achieved without the support of the Egyptian administration in Khartoum. By way of example, the defeated Abu Saood fled north to Gondokoro where, to Baker's outrage, Egyptian officials did not detain him but allowed him to return to Khartoum to regroup.

Baker's legacy in Uganda is interesting. Speke and Stanley are remembered simply as explorers who passed through and their achievements are cited as historical fact. Baker, however, was the first to spend any significant time in the region, in the process making both friends and enemies. Around Masindi, he is remembered with little warmth as the colonial aggressor who sought to conquer Bunyoro (and kick-started a history of poor relations between Britain and Bunyoro). It's a different story in Gulu though, where Baker is still remembered to this day with genuine warmth as the man who drove the Arabs from Patiko.

giving it a star in expectation. *Mains inc naan in the US$8–10 range.*

Palm Garden [324 A7] ⊕ 2.75983, 32.29008; m 0782 207118. This out-of-town guesthouse serves acceptable burgers & meat/chips dishes plus (given a few hours' notice) pizza, homemade ice cream & Italian coffee. *Mains in the US$4–10 range.*

✷ **The Rolling Donkey** [324 C5] Jivan Abji Rd; m 0777 581303; ⏲ 08.00–20.00 Tue–Sat. This excellent café just beyond the western edge of the town centre serves a great selection of wraps, toasted sandwiches, filled pancakes, quiches, burritos, smoothies, fresh juices, iced & hot coffee & cupcakes. Expect the café to move to new premises in 2025. *Meals in the US$4–8 range.*

Shopping The exceptional **Cynibel Supermarket** [324 B5] (⏲ 07.00–22.30 daily) is the place to stock up on packaged goods and wines and spirits before heading on to Kidepo or other more remote areas. The **central market** [324 C5] sells all the things you'd expect a market to sell.

Sports and activities The Bomah Hotel (page 325) has an excellent pool (US$3 for day visitors), as does the nearby Acholi Inn (US$3), though the latter is still let down by the dilapidated changing rooms (refurbishment is planned).

What to see and do

Baker's Fort, Patiko Remnants of the fort established in 1872 by Sir Samuel Baker (page 327) can be found at Patiko, 25km north of Gulu. The fort centres on a large kopje consisting of several rock outcrops and a number of massive boulders. Three mortared stone structures still stand on the central plateau, but rather disappointingly they were grain stores rather than part of the Bakers' residence. The mud houses that stood below the kopje are long gone, but an encircling defensive ditch, 100m in diameter, still curves into opposite ends of the kopje like the ring through a bull's nose. This ditch was reinforced with a wooden palisade with access through a small surviving gatehouse with a narrow doorway and rifle ports. Your guide, if you find one, will show you fissures between the rocks which acted as holding cells in which men and women captured by Arab slavers were separately confined prior to 'sorting' on an adjacent rock plateau. You'll also see the passage between two boulders through which rejected wretches were led to be speared to death and tossed off the kopje for the hyenas. On a lighter note, the tour includes two massive boulders – separated by a gap and a drop slightly too wide for carefree leaping – between which Baker is said to have regularly jumped 'for exercise'; a feat which you'll be invited to emulate, but probably shouldn't!

The road to Patiko leads out of Gulu opposite the Bank of Uganda, just beyond the government offices. Bear right after 800m or you'll end up in Kitgum. The drive takes about 45 minutes. A special hire will cost around US$40–50 return, while boda riders quote US$5–8. Upon reaching Patiko, pass through the small trading centre and turn left immediately in front of a row of metal police huts. A visitors' book is kept in a caretaker's hut on the right of the access track but it's usually locked. Guides are available for US$3 and the site is more interesting with local interpretation, however skewed.

Part Four

NORTHWEST UGANDA

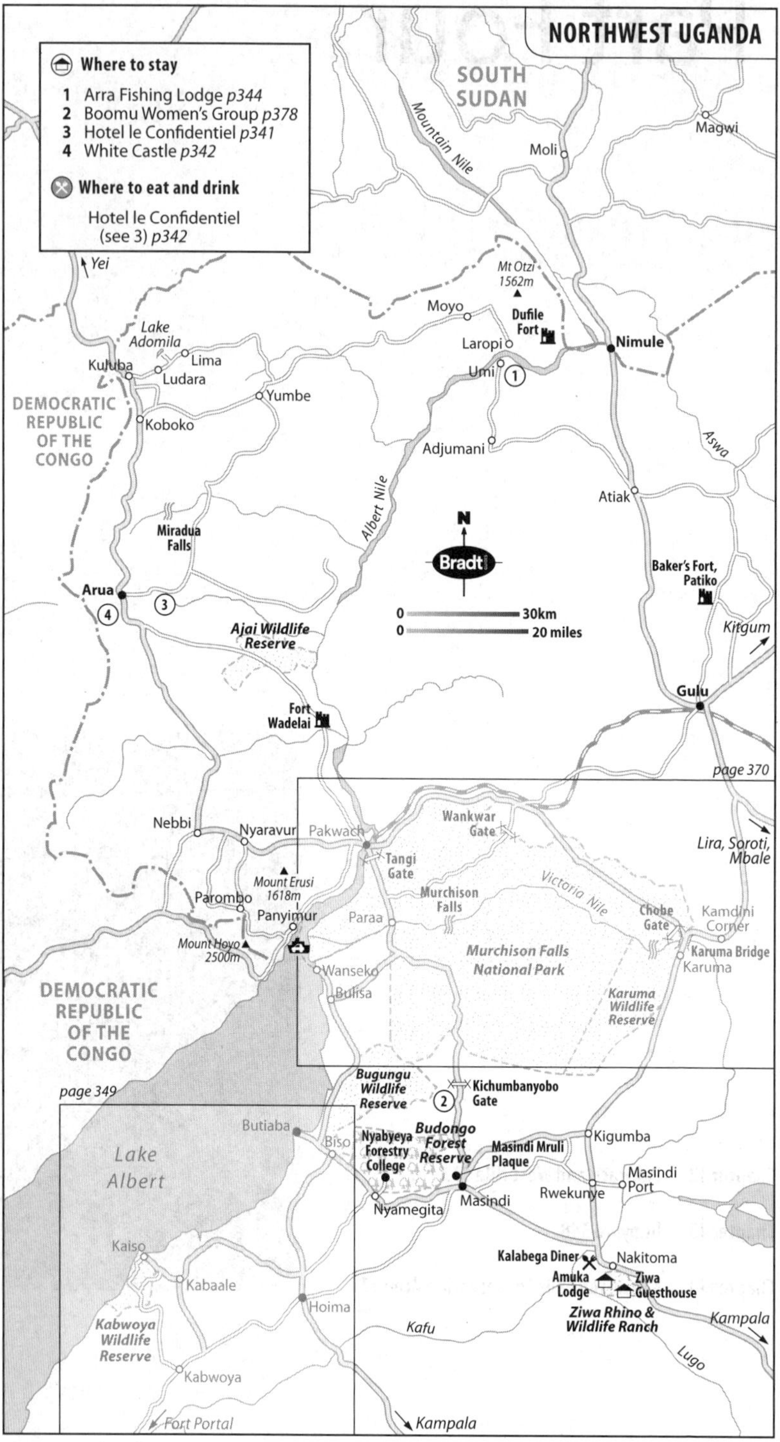

NORTHWEST UGANDA
Where to stay
1 Arra Fishing Lodge p344
2 Boomu Women's Group p378
3 Hotel le Confidentiel p341
4 White Castle p342
Where to eat and drink
Hotel le Confidentiel (see 3) p342
SOUTH SUDAN
Mountain Nile
Magwi
Moli
Yei
Mt Otzi 1562m
Moyo
Dufile Fort
Laropi
Nimule
Umi
Lake Adomila
Lima
Kuluba
Ludara
Yumbe
DEMOCRATIC REPUBLIC OF THE CONGO
Koboko
Adjumani
Aswa
Atiak
Albert Nile
Miradua Falls
Bradt
0 30km
0 20 miles
Baker's Fort, Patiko
Arua
Kitgum
Ajai Wildlife Reserve
Gulu
Fort Wadelai
page 370
Wankwar Gate
Nebbi
Nyaravur
Pakwach
Lira, Soroti, Mbale
Tangi Gate
Victoria Nile
Mount Erusi 1618m
Murchison Falls
Parombo
Chobe Gate
Kamdini Corner
Panyimur
Paraa
Mount Hoyo 2500m
Murchison Falls National Park
Karuma Bridge
Karuma
Wanseko
Bulisa
Karuma Wildlife Reserve
DEMOCRATIC REPUBLIC OF THE CONGO
Bugungu Wildlife Reserve
Kichumbanyobo Gate
page 349
Butiaba
Biso
Nyabyeya Forestry College
Budongo Forest Reserve
Masindi Mruli Plaque
Kigumba
Lake Albert
Masindi Port
Rwekunye
Nyamegita
Masindi
Kaiso
Kalabega Diner
Nakitoma
Amuka Lodge
Ziwa Guesthouse
Kabaale
Ziwa Rhino & Wildlife Ranch
Hoima
Kampala
Kafu
Kabwoya Wildlife Reserve
Lugo
Kabwoya
Fort Portal
Kampala

OVERVIEW

The northwest of Uganda, defined for the purposes of this book as pretty much everywhere north of the river Kafu and west of the town of Gulu, is dominated in touristic terms by Murchison Falls Conservation Area, which forms the focal point of almost all organised tours passing through the region. Other less-developed natural attractions include the bird-rich Budongo Forest Reserve, scenic Lake Albert, and the untrammelled Albert Nile as it courses north from Pakwach to the South Sudanese border. The northwest is bisected by the Victoria Nile as it flows through Murchison Falls National Park; the area to the north of the river suffered terribly during the decades-long civil war that embroiled northern Uganda until as recently as 2005, and it remains quite undeveloped for tourism and offers little in the way of prescribed sightseeing.

This section on northern Uganda is divided into three chapters. The first covers the town of Pakwach, an increasingly important gateway to Murchison Falls, whether coming from Kidepo Valley National Park or Kampala, along with the remote and little-visited administrative subregion of West Nile. The second covers Bunyoro, an ancient kingdom whose major towns, Hoima and Masindi, are frequently passed through by tourists crossing between Murchison Falls and the southwest or Kampala. And the final chapter focuses tightly on Murchison Falls Conservation Area, which incorporates the eponymous national park as well as Kaniyo Pabidi Forest, a popular site for chimp tracking and forest birding.

HIGHLIGHTS

MURCHISON FALLS Boat trips from Paraa upstream to the base of Murchison Falls follow a mesmerising stretch of the tropical Nile, alive with hippo, crocodile and waterbirds, to a rocky peninsula from where you have the option to hike to the stunning viewpoint at the top of the falls. Page 385.

BULIGI AND THE DELTA CIRCUIT The most rewarding game-viewing in Murchison Falls National Park traverses palm-studded hills inhabited by large herds of giraffe to emerge at a wildlife-rich delta where elephant, lion and shoebill are often encountered. Page 389.

KANIYO PABIDI FOREST Set within Murchison Falls Conservation Area but outside the national park, this forest offers the opportunity to track Uganda's densest chimpanzee population. Page 384.

KABWOYA WILDLIFE RESERVE This small and scenic reserve fringing Lake Albert offers a great range of activities including horseback safaris, mountain biking and day hikes. Page 359.

MPARO TOMBS The former capital of Bunyoro's King Kabalega, situated on the outskirts of Hoima, now houses a fantastic domed thatch construction where he and his successor are buried. Page 353.

PAKWACH AND SURROUNDS The gateway to little-visited West Nile, Pakwach is the only town to front the Nile on its meandering journey from Jinja to the South Sudanese border, and is a useful budget base for day visits to Murchison Falls. Page 334.

BUDONGO FOREST RESERVE Superseded as a chimp-tracking destination by Kaniyo Pabidi, this vast forest west of Masindi remains a birding hotspot of note. Page 355.

KIBIRO SALT GARDENS The goal of a truly off-the-beaten-track day hike down the Rift Escarpment to the shore of Lake Albert, Kibiro has been Bunyoro's most important source of salt since the 13th century. Page 354.

LAROPI At the foot of the dramatic Mount Otzi, the Laropi vehicle ferry shuttles across the Nile to enable an appealing (if low-key) loop through northwestern Uganda. Birders may be tempted to dally to explore the papyrus-fringed river and the forested mountain slopes above. Page 343.

ARUA A focal point for NGO activity but seldom visited by tourists, Arua might be the most remote of Uganda's main towns, but it possesses an engaging vitality epitomised by its lively market. Page 339.

12

Pakwach and West Nile

The subregion of West Nile is a remote northwestern protrusion hemmed in on three sides by international borders, and bordered to the east by the Nile as it meanders northward from Lake Albert towards South Sudan. Integrated into the Uganda Protectorate as late as 1910, West Nile still feels somewhat isolated from the rest of the country, and its main ethnic groups (the Alur of Nebbi, Lugbara of Arua, Kaka of Koboko and Madi of Moyo) maintain strong cultural and trade links with their Congolese and South Sudanese neighbours. This isolation is emphasised by the fact that the only road between West Nile and the rest of Uganda is over a solitary bridge that spans the Albert Nile at Pakwach, though this is supplemented by ferry services linking Wanseko to Panyimur and Umi to Laropi.

West Nile holds one under-recognised touristic trump card in the form of Pakwach, a tropical river port and the only substantial town set alongside the Nile on its long journey from Jinja to the South Sudanese border. Since the Lord's Resistance Army (LRA) left Uganda in 2005, Pakwach has also emerged as an increasingly popular base for exploring Murchison Falls National Park, whose northerly Tangi Gate lies just 3km out of town. Some 40km north of Pakwach, Fort Wadelai is a remote and little-visited historical site associated with Emin Pasha.

Elsewhere, West Nile ranks among the least-visited parts of Uganda, but it is known for the friendliness of its people, while its traditionalist character is reflected by the widespread use of thatch as opposed to iron sheet roofing. Adventurous travellers coming from Bunyoro might be tempted to make use of the ferry service linking Wanseko, on the Lake Albert shore immediately south of the Victoria Nile Delta, to Panyimur, on the west bank of the Albert Nile close to where it leaves the lake. Arua, the subregion's largest town, is a pleasant enough place and an important NGO base, but situated as it is 130km northwest of Pakwach, it feels rather out of the way unless you have specific business there, or you plan to follow the thoroughly off-the-beaten-track northern road loop that connects it to Gulu via the Laropi ferry.

HISTORY

Remote though it is today, the far northwest was the first part of Uganda to attract the interest of the outside world. In 1839, Khedive Muhammad Ali Pasha, of Ottoman Egypt, instructed Captain Salim Kapudan to lead an expedition up the White Nile in search of its source. In 1842, following two failed attempts to cross the swampy Sudd, Salim made it past Gondokoro into what is now West Nile. This expedition led to a spate of mercantile activity, and by the late 1850s up to 80 Egyptian boats were docking at Gondokoro annually to buy ivory and other goods. By the early 1860s, West Nile's once-plentiful elephant population had been depleted, and enslaved people had replaced ivory as the main item of export.

In 1862, West Nile was traversed by Samuel and Florence Baker, who became the first Europeans to see Lake Albert. An ardent abolitionist, Baker returned to the region in 1869 to establish and serve as the first Governor-General of Egypt's Equatoria Province. Baker succeeded not only in suppressing the slave trade but also in opening up the area to legitimate trade. West Nile and the rest of Equatoria became part of the British Empire following the occupation of Egypt in 1862. However, a treaty signed with King Leopold only two years later led to the region – then known as the Lado Enclave – being administered by the Belgian Congo until 1910.

In the post-independence era, West Nile became known for spawning Uganda's most famous son: Idi Amin Dada. Oddly, it is not certain that Amin was actually born in West Nile, but with a mother from Arua and a father from Koboko, he strongly identified with the area. Under Amin, West Nile and its people enjoyed preferential treatment, and after his downfall in 1979, the region's isolation was exacerbated by memories of his brutal excesses elsewhere in the country. Over the next 25 years, while West Nile was not directly involved in the civil war with the LRA, the only road routes to the region passed through a conflict zone characterised by regular rebel ambushes. Agricultural production slumped, since nobody dared come to buy any produce, with revenue from cotton, for instance, dropping by 50% between the late 1970s and mid 1990s. Access has improved dramatically since the evacuation of the LRA, and the surfacing of the 500km road between Kampala and Arua means the journey can now be made in a single (though long) day. There is also talk of rehabilitating the railway line that, until 1993, connected Pakwach to Tororo, where it meets the line between Kampala and the Kenyan port of Mombasa, and possibly extending it from Pakwach to the South Sudanese capital, Juba.

PAKWACH

It may not rank among the country's 50 largest settlements, nor is it designated a district headquarters, but modest Pakwach (population 23,000) can boast the most interesting location of any town in northern Uganda. Perched on the west bank of the Albert Nile as it flows out of Murchison Falls National Park, Pakwach is also the only road gateway to West Nile, linked to the east bank by a large modern bridge, as well as the northern railhead of a defunct line running via Tororo to Nairobi and Mombasa.

Despite this, Pakwach, on first glance, comes across as little more than a broad main street lined with the usual motley collection of local shops, restaurants and guesthouses. Explore further, however, and you'll find that away from that main street, this is one of the most overtly traditional towns in Uganda, its side roads lined with a mix of circular and rectangular adobe huts distinguished by neatly layered thatch roofs. The town's Alur inhabitants, who speak a sub-dialect called Jonam (literally, 'People of the River'), also come across as unusually friendly, though the woodcarving sellers who tend to lurk opposite the Sunrise Guesthouse can be rather persistent.

For self-drivers and those on organised safaris, Pakwach – or, more accurately, an expanding cluster of lodges along the opposite, eastern bank of the Nile – is rapidly emerging as a popular base from which to explore Murchison Falls National Park, whose Tangi Gate lies only 3km out of town. Pakwach is also the closest town to the historic Fort Wadelai.

For backpackers, this readily accessible small town has two main attractions. Remarkably, it is the only substantial riverside settlement anywhere along the Nile's lengthy northwesterly course from Jinja to the South Sudanese border, and several footpaths and tracks run down from the main road to the lushly vegetated

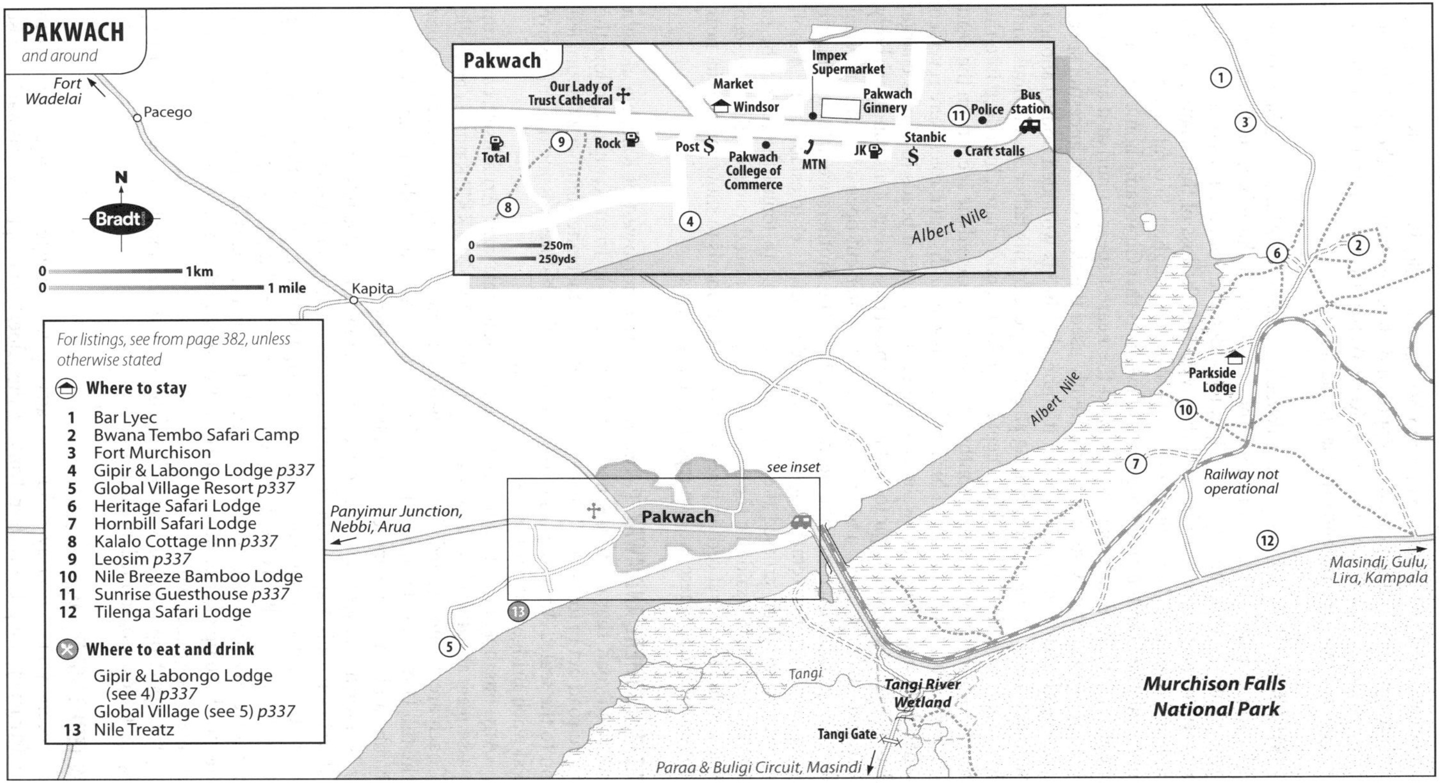
PAKWACH
and around
Fort Wadelai
Pacego
Kapita
N
Bradt
0 1km
0 1 mile
Pakwach
Our Lady of Trust Cathedral
Market
Windsor
Impex Supermarket
Pakwach Ginnery
Police
Bus station
Total
Rock
Post
Pakwach College of Commerce
MTN
JK
Stanbic
Craft stalls
Albert Nile
0 250m
0 250yds
For listings, see from page 382, unless otherwise stated
Where to stay
1 Bar Lyec
2 Bwana Tembo Safari Camp
3 Fort Murchison
4 Gipir & Labongo Lodge p337
5 Global Village Resort p337
6 Heritage Safari Lodge
7 Hornbill Safari Lodge
8 Kalalo Cottage Inn p337
9 Leosim p337
10 Nile Breeze Bamboo Lodge
11 Sunrise Guesthouse p337
12 Tilenga Safari Lodge
Where to eat and drink
Gipir & Labongo Lodge (see 4) p337
Global Village (see 5) p337
13 Nile Treatz
Panyimur Junction, Nebbi, Arua
see inset
Pakwach
Parkside Lodge
Railway not operational
Masindi, Gulu, Lira, Kampala
Tangi
Tangi River Wetland
Tangi Gate
Paraa & Buligi Circuit, Masindi
Murchison Falls National Park

riverbank. Thanks to its proximity to Murchison Falls, Pakwach also has plenty of birding and wildlife potential: hippos and shoebills frequent the shallows and swamps close to town, while the Tangi River Wetland, only 1km from town, is often frequented by elephants and other large mammals.

HISTORY Local legend has it that Pakwach is where the Alur and Acholi peoples split into separate tribes c AD1450. The rift is said to have been initiated by an argument between Labongo and Gipir, the elder and younger sons of a Luo ruler who then lived on the east bank of the river, over the loss of their clan's ancestral hunting spear and the resultant death of Labongo's daughter. Several variations are in circulation, but the broad sequence of events is that Gipir came home to find an elephant raiding their crops and grabbed the nearest spear to hurl at it and chase it away. Unfortunately, he had inadvertently used the clan's sacred ancestral spear, and the elephant walked away with it embedded in his wounded body. Labongo, who had been charged with looking after the spear by his father, was furious with his younger brother, refused to accept his apologies, and chased him deep into the forest. Gipir returned several months later having retrieved the spear from the dead elephant, but still furious with his brother. A few months later, roles were reversed when Labongo's daughter swallowed one of the ancestral beads in Gipir's charge. Labongo pleaded with Gipir to wait until the bead passed out of his daughter's body naturally. Gipir refused, and had Labongo's daughter cut open with the ancestral spear in order to retrieve the bead. After that, the brothers went their separate ways, with Labongo remaining on the east side of the river to establish the Acholi people, while Gipir crossed the river with his people to found the Alur tribe of Nebbi District. It is said that the troublesome spear, or bead, can sometimes be seen floating in the river at certain places. You could ask locals to show you the site near Pakwach Bridge where the two reputedly parted ways.

GETTING THERE AND AWAY Pakwach lies 370km northwest of Kampala along a surfaced road that continues north to Arua. Coming from Kampala, follow the Gulu road out of town for 260m to Karuma Bridge, then after another 2km turn left on to the sealed Arua Road and follow it for 108km before crossing the impressive Pakwach Bridge at the eastern entrance to town.

Any bus headed between Arua Stage in Kampala and Arua itself can drop passengers at Pakwach; Gaagaa Coaches (m 0785 202322), KKT Kampala and Nile Coach are recommended. These take 6–8 hours and you may be expected to pay the full US$10 fare to Arua. Plenty of matatus run between Pakwach and Arua via Nebbi, and between Pakwach and Gulu via Purongo.

Pakwach can also be reached via either Hoima or Masindi, passing through Murchison Falls National Park (individual park entry and vehicle fees apply) to cross the new Victoria Nile bridge at Paraa, and exiting the park through Tangi Gate. Finally, an alternative (in more than one sense of the word) route to Pakwach utilises a free (daily except Sunday) vehicle ferry which plies often choppy waters at the northern tip of Lake Albert between Wanseko on the eastern shore to Panyimur on the west (page 339).

Transport options for visiting Murchison Falls National Park via the nearby Tangi Gate are described on page 377.

WHERE TO STAY *Map, page 335*

In recent years, an array of lodges catering for a range of budgets have been constructed along the eastern bank of the Albert Nile opposite Pakwach. These lodges all lie within 10km of town by road, but since they exist to service nearby Murchison Falls National Park rather than Pakwach, they are covered separately in that chapter, under the heading *The Albert Nile and Northwest* (page 382).

Moderate

Gipir & Labongo Lodge (30 rooms) m 0770 757909. Pakwach's smartest & most attractively placed offering enjoys a terrific riverside site facing the wilderness of Murchison Falls National Park on the opposite bank. In a starker setting, the grey, concrete-block cottages might be merely utilitarian but, softened by lush tropical shrubs & with comfortable, uncluttered en-suite interiors, they contrive to be fashionably modern. The dirt track to the lodge leaves the main road at the western end of the town centre where it is signposted & further identified by a mobile phone mast, just beyond the junction for Wadelei. *Std rooms cost US$53/80 while identical units on the river front cost US$67/93. All rates B&B.* **$$**

Global Village Resort (20 rooms) ☎ 039 2848729; m 0771 170629; e marketing@globalvillageaccommodation.com. Located at the western end of town, Global Village occupies a large but unremarkable site beside the Nile. A substantial tract of no-man's-land separates the generously sized & comfortably furnished rondavel cottages from a less attractive 2-storey glass-sided restaurant-bar near the river. Indeed, the former are thoughtfully provided with everything you might need – fridge, microwave & kettle, TV & AC – to avoid the hike down to the latter. *US$40/55 sgl/dbl B&B.* **$$**

Kalalo Cottage Inn (11 rooms) m 0789 014861, 0750 678013. Set alongside a dirt backroad 1km southwest of the town centre, this quiet & pleasant lodge has modern clean rooms with fitted nets, fans & en-suite cold shower. *US$16/26/32 sgl/dbl/twin.* **$$**

Leosim Hotel (31 rooms) m 0777 838721; e pakwach@leosimhotel.co.ug; w leosimhotelltd.com. This 3-storey building on the western edge of town offers clean, modern en-suite rooms with fitted nets, fans, writing desk, hot shower & balcony. It has a restaurant, bar & a welcome swimming pool. *US$18/26/35 sgl/dbl/twin.* **$$**

Shoestring

Sunrise Guesthouse (11 rooms) m 0777 260750. Located on the main road at the eastern end of town, this place has very clean & spacious en-suite rooms with fans & nets. Meals can be prepared by advance order. Fair value. *From US$8/11/16 sgl/dbl/lge dbl.* **$**

WHERE TO EAT AND DRINK For a meal or a drink in Pakwach, the river is the place to head to, ideally at sundowner time when the vegetation on the opposite (Murchison) bank glows in the orange light. The following are all accessed from Jobi Road which runs between and parallel to the river and the main road. First choice by a country mile is the **Gipir & Labongo Lodge** (see above), where grills, stews and pizzas served in an attractive, open-fronted dining area cost US$7–12. Upstream, **Nile Treatz** and **Global Village Resort** (see above) both serve variations on the ubiquitous meat 'n' chips theme. Main courses at the former, which has a pleasant garden and an airy, stone-floored restaurant, cost US$10. Meals at Global Village are cheap (US$5) and tasty but the open setting is bland and the glass-sided restaurant hot during the day.

OTHER PRACTICALITIES The **Impex Supermarket** is the best place to stock up on packaged goods for a day safari to Murchison Falls. If you need funds for shopping, there's a Stanbic Bank with ATM on the south side of Main Street.

WHAT TO SEE AND DO The main attraction in the area is Murchison Falls National Park (page 371), which lies directly across the Nile from Pakwach with the Tangi Gate just 3km distant. This, of course, is where this nondescript town comes into its own, as a springboard for backpacker visits into this superb park. Having reached Pakwach by public means, you will of course now need a vehicle to enter the park for a game drive, to visit the top of the falls and to get to Paraa for the perennially popular boat ride. If you want to do things in style – or if you are travelling in a group – Global Village Resort (page 337) has a superb open-sided ten-seater safari truck. The US$150/170 half/full day fee includes a driver, fuel and car entrance fee. Extras include a UWA guide fee (US$20 per group) and individual park entrance fees, as well as any meals or additional activities such as the Paraa boat trip.

Wildlife and birding Any track or road leading south from the main road through Pakwach will bring you to the banks of the Nile, opposite the papyrus-lined confluence with the Tangi River on the northwest border of Murchison Falls National Park. Hippos are frequently seen here – indeed they sometimes wander into the town at night – and the birding can be very good. Better still, follow the Kampala Road east out of town across the Pakwach Bridge, which offers a great vantage point over the east bank and an extensive papyrus swamp where shoebill are seen with some regularity. About 750m beyond the bridge, at the junction for the national park's Tangi Gate (⊕ 2.45236, 31.51123), the surfaced main road runs for about 1km along the northern flank of the Tangi River Wetland. This semi-seasonal mosaic of open pools, mudflats and vegetated marshland is home to Uganda kob, Defassa waterbuck and warthog, with elephant passing through on a regular basis, and a profusion of waterbirds (you might easily see 30 species in 15 minutes) includes various herons, egrets and smaller waders and sometimes shoebills.

Fort Wadelai (Entry US$7) Named after a 7ha fort constructed by Emin Pasha in 1885, the fishing village of Fort Wadelai, set on the west bank of the Nile 40km north of Pakwach, is locally infamous for having served as an Arab trade outpost and slave-holding pen earlier in the 19th century. By 1876, when the former slave trading post was visited by General Gordon's lieutenant Romolo Gessi, it had been adopted as the capital of one Chief Wadelai, the local vassal of Omukama Kabalega of Bunyoro. Three years later, the site by then known as Wadelai became headquarters of the Egyptian province of Equatoria under Emin Pasha. The fort was abandoned by him in December 1888, only to be captured by the Mahdists and held by them for several years. Wadelai resumed service as a British government post in 1894, but when Winston Churchill visited it in 1907, it was recently abandoned and already going to ruin.

No trace of Emin Pasha's fort remains, and for many decades the only evidence of Wadelai's past significance was a plaque affixed to a concrete obelisk. This has been supplemented by a small information centre constructed as part of the Emin Pasha Historical Fort Preservation and Development Project. Long-talked-about future plans include the opening of a campsite and boat trips upriver from Murchison Falls National Park. For the time being, Wadelai is most easily visited along a 40km road leading north from Pakwach at a signposted junction (⊕ 2.4609, 31.49486) 100m west of the Windsor Hotel.

Nebbi The capital of Nebbi District is a substantial but unremarkable town straddling the main surfaced road through West Nile, 50km west of Pakwach and 80km south of Arua. The only site of potential interest, some 2km west of the town centre along the road to Paidha, is the palace where Phillip Olarker Rauni III, the 34th Rwot (King) of Alur, was crowned on 30 October 2010. Logistically, Nebbi is where travellers using matatus between Pakwach and Arua might need to change, and the only reason you'd be likely to stay overnight is if you missed that connection. A few lodgings are strung along the main road, the pick being the **Leosim Hotel** (45 rooms; ⊕ 2.48051, 31.09471; ☎ 039 3241371; e nebbi@leosimhotel.co.ug; w leosimhotelltd.com; US$15/18 en-suite dbl/twin; **$**), a very pleasant sibling of its Pakwach namesake.

PANYIMUR

This small fishing village, 35km southwest of Pakwach, has a fabulous location on the west bank of the Albert Nile close to where it exits Lake Albert below the 1,618m Mount Erusi on the Rift Valley Escarpment. Though there are some hot springs in the vicinity, Panyimur is of interest mainly as the western terminus of a free vehicle ferry connecting West Nile to Wanseko on the eastern shore of Lake Albert. Should you need to spend the night in Panyimur, a few basic guesthouses do exist.

GETTING THERE AND AWAY

By boat According to the (not entirely reliable) official timetable, the free vehicle ferry to Panyimur (2hrs) departs from Wanseko at noon on Monday, Wednesday and Friday, and at 07.00 and 16.00 on Tuesday, Thursday and Saturday. In the opposite direction, the boat leaves Panyimur at 07.00 and 16.00 on Monday, Wednesday and Friday, and at noon on Tuesday, Thursday and Saturday. There are no boats on Sundays. If you're not constrained by a vehicle, fishing boats travel between Wanseko and Panyimur throughout the day (1hr; US$3), but they tend to be overloaded and regularly capsize with fatal results during the tempests for which Lake Albert is renowned, so stay put if there's any hint of an oncoming storm.

By road A 35km murram road runs southwest to Panyimur from the surfaced Arua Road; the junction (⊕ 2.45991, 31.46844) is only 2.5km west of Pakwach. A few matatus trundle back and forth between Pakwach and Panyimur daily.

For self-drivers arriving at Panyimur by ferry, a more adventurous onward option would be to follow the murram road that leads west out of the village to the northernmost stretch of the Rift Valley Escarpment. This steep climb provides good views of the higher Rift Valley wall as it follows Lake Albert's Congo shore south towards the 2,500m Mount Hoyo. The road then passes through a pretty, hilly and distinctly rural hinterland, reaching the small town of Parombo about an hour from Panyimur. From Parombo, the most direct route to Arua runs north to meet the main road at Nyaravur, 18km before Nebbi. Attractive pottery is sold by the roadside. Alternatively, a longer but considerably more scenic route passes around Mount Erusi before heading north to arrive at the main road a short distance east of Nebbi. Aside from being achievable in a private vehicle, this is potentially a great trip on a motorcycle, hot work on a bicycle, and a real adventure (or chore) using public transport, which consists mostly of pick-up trucks.

ARUA

Set in undistinguished scrubland 10km east of the Congolese border, Arua was long notable (and that only to the few that took an interest) as the largest settlement in the isolated northwesterly province of West Nile. Over the years, however, Arua has steadily crept up the rankings to become Uganda's second-largest city with a population of 380,000. Despite its remote location, Arua – whose name reputedly derives from the Lugbara word 'Aru', meaning 'prison' – has much in common with other Ugandan towns, with its tight central street grid, bustling open market and smarter 'senior quarters' centred on the golf course. Arua is also a significant centre

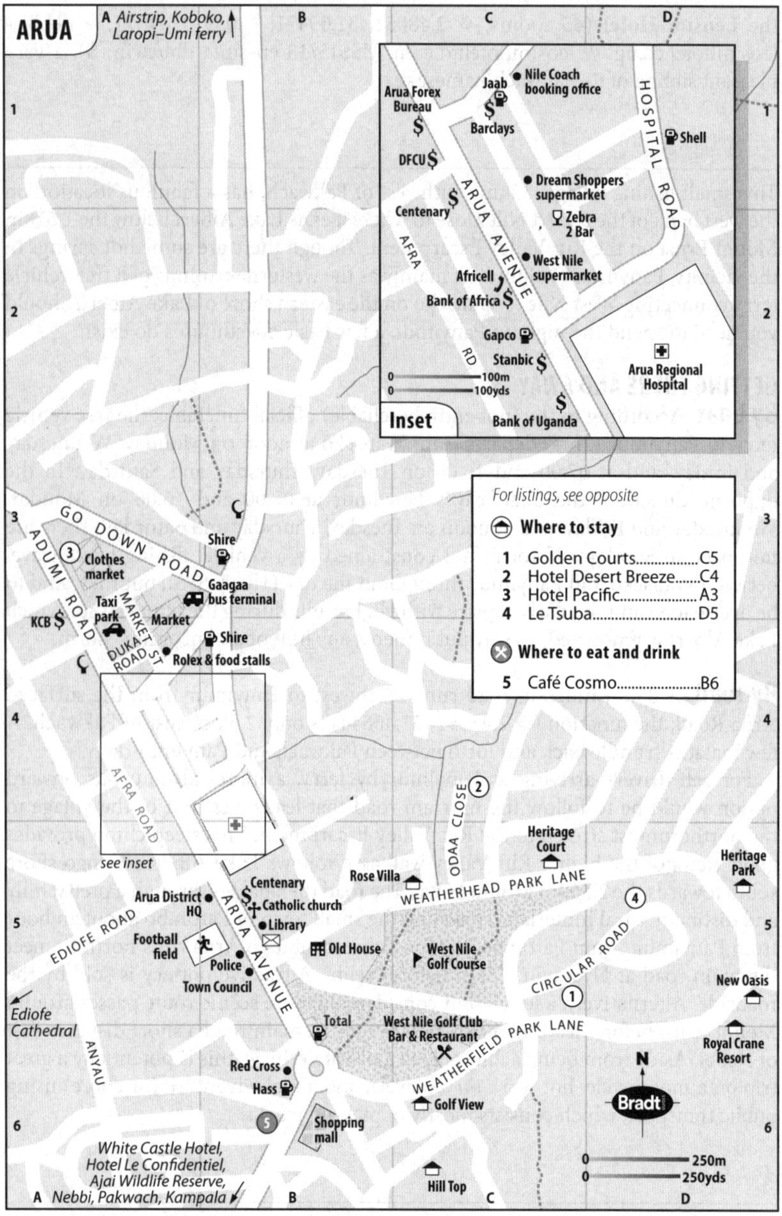

of NGO activity and an important transport hub along the supply corridor to the South Sudanese towns of Yei and Juba.

While Arua lacks for essential tourist attractions, it makes up for this with its friendly aura, economic vitality, and dense weave of bicycle traffic. There's no better way to explore this busy little town than to engage a boda to pedal you about Arua's excellent tarmac streets and point out such major landmarks as the hospital and police station, several mosques, and a market rated to be one of the biggest in Uganda, with a wide selection of Congolese *vitenge* (sarongs) on sale. Ediofe Cathedral, which was built by Catholic missionaries in 1917, lies 2km west of the town centre along Ediofe Road. Elsewhere, the hill above the main roundabout is worth climbing for views east towards the Nile and west into DRC, while the West Nile Golf Course is a pleasant setting for a stroll, a doze in the shade, or indeed a round of golf.

GETTING THERE AND AWAY

By air Eagle Air makes return flights from Entebbe to Arua on Mondays and Fridays (US$190/340 sgl/rtn), each leg taking 1 hour 20 minutes. Their Arua office (Arua Av; m 0772 777331/400341; w eagleair-ug.com) is close to the Hotel Pacific [340 A3]. The airstrip is about 2km north of the town centre on the Kiboko Road.

By road Arua is a 500km drive on a surfaced road from Kampala via Karuma, Pakwach and Nebbi. In theory, the journey should be doable in 7–8 hours but deteriorating sections on the approaches to Pakwach and Arua mean that you should anticipate a longer day or plan for an overnight stop. The best bus service between Kampala and Arua is Gaagaa Coaches (m 0785 202322; 3 buses daily; 8–10hrs; US$10). Buses leave Kampala from Arua Stage on Johnstone Street. Plenty of matatus run between Pakwach and Arua, though you might have to change vehicles at Nebbi.

WHERE TO STAY

Upmarket

Hotel le Confidentiel [map, page 330] (52 rooms) Off Pakwach Rd, 200m beyond Vurra junction; m 0708 808182, 0761 688181; e reception@hotelleconfidentiel.com; w hotelleconfidentiel.com. What goes in le Confidentiel might as well stay in le Confidentiel for, once there, there is little reason to go anywhere else. Though plonked incongruously into an expanse of barren scrub, 7km south of Arua (you may find yourself swerving gratefully through its gates, exhausted by the interminable pot-holes beyond Nebbi) this new hotel ticks all boxes & the staff are clearly & justifiably proud of their swish dining room & other offerings, including a pool, sauna & stylish en-suite rooms with AC. Should life in the hotel compound become a little insular, excursions can be arranged to local attractions (page 342). *Very reasonably priced at US$60/90 sgl/dbl B&B*. **$$$**

Moderate

Golden Courts Hotel [340 C5] (20 rooms) Circular Rd; m 0786 391876, 0754 075415; e info@goldencourtshotel.com. This attractive hotel has a prime location next to the golf course & smart modern rooms with walk-in nets, flatscreen DSTV, telephone, AC, Wi-Fi & en-suite hot shower. A stylish restaurant is attached. *US$43/52 sgl/dbl B&B*. **$$**

Hotel Desert Breeze [340 C4] (50 rooms) Odaa Clse (off Weatherhead Park Ln); m 0781 620905, 0754 900343; e desertbreezehotel@gmail.com; w desertbreezehotel.com. This characterless but efficiently run 3-storey hotel, complete with shiny fittings from Dubai, has spacious rooms with fans or AC, flatscreen DSTV, nets & free Wi-Fi. A restaurant serves decent food. Good value. *From US$50/60 sgl/dbl B&B*. **$$**

Le Tsuba [340 D5] (58 rooms) Off Circular Rd; 039 2246190; w letsubahotel.com. This smart new hotel occasioned great excitement locally when it opened in 2022, thanks to the glass-fronted elevator that glides up the storeyed façade to provide giddy views of a receding car park. The ascent terminates at a 4th-floor bar-restaurant which, open on 2 sides, enjoys a cooling breeze while the northerly aspect looks beyond the town towards what we'll generously call scenery. The immediate environs are actually more appealing, with the pretty Weatherhead Lane & the golf course close by. The en-suite rooms, enlivened with local artwork & fabrics plus AC & DSTV, are good value. *US$55/85 dbl/deluxe dbl*. **$$$**

Budget

White Castle Hotel [map, page 330] (28 rooms) 4km along Pakwach Rd; ⊕ 2.97555, 30.91885; m 0772 880830; e info@whitecastlehotel.com; w whitecastlehotel.com. Distinguished by a pleasantly green setting, this popular hotel has become a veritable oasis within the messy suburban sprawl that now follows the Pakwach Rd out of town for several kilometres. You'll find decent en-suite rooms with TV, nets & fans in 4-unit cottage blocks in a garden of sorts, while other attractions include one of Arua's most reliable restaurants, serving continental, Indian & Italian dishes in the US$7–10 range, & a clean pear-shaped swimming pool. *From US$45/56 sgl/dbl B&B.* **$$**

Shoestring

Hotel Pacific [340 A3] (28 rooms) Adumi Rd; m 0702 057599, 0776 057599. This long-serving & suitably timeworn 3-storey hotel has a central location, clean rooms with nets, tiled floors & en-suite shower, & a characterful ground-floor bar & restaurant serving meals in the US$3–4 range. *US$10/12 sgl/dbl.* **$**

WHERE TO EAT AND DRINK

✷ **Café Cosmo** [340 B6] Off Pakwach Rd; m 0756 335577; f; ⊕ 11.00–23.00 daily. This superb Indian-owned restaurant at the south end of the town centre has a cosmopolitan menu dominated by Indian tandooris & curries, but also including salads, pizzas, wraps, burgers, Chinese sizzlers & plenty of vegetarian options. Coffee & a varied selection of alcoholic & non-alcoholic beverages are served indoors or in the large garden. Free Wi-Fi. *Mains mostly in the US$5–10 range.*

Hotel le Confidentiel [map, page 330] (52 rooms) Off Pakwach Rd. Even if only half of the impressive array of salads, sandwiches, grills, burgers & local dishes on offer at this smart new hotel are actually available, the classy setting more than justifies the 7km drive out of town. The menu includes some sumptuous descriptions, the soups alone promising 'silky-smooth', 'refreshing & soothing' & 'deliciously creamy' experiences, further enlivened 'with tender bites'. Sounds irresistible! *US$5–12.*

SHOPPING Expect shopping options to expand dramatically with the completion of a large mall currently under construction on the Pakwach Road roundabout on the southern edge of town. Meanwhile, **West Nile Supermarket** [340 C2]and **Dream Shoppers** [340 C1] are among the best of a few supermarkets to line Arua Avenue and the **central market** [340 B4] is one of the largest and busiest in Uganda, with stalls selling everything from rolexes and fresh produce to colourful Congolese cloth and car spares.

SPORTS AND ACTIVITIES

Golf Founded in the 1950s, the West Nile Golf Course [340 C5] (Circular Rd; m 0772 620680/874384) still boasts a playable nine holes – a commendable achievement up on the northwestern frontier. The green fees are around US$3. Willing caddies and ball spotters can be recruited for around US$1. Club hire is also available. The clubhouse is a pleasant spot for a beer in green surrounds.

Swimming The White Castle Hotel on the Nebbi Road (see above) has a swimming pool (US$2 Mon–Fri, US$3 w/ends), as does the smarter Hotel le Confidentiel (US$5).

WHAT TO SEE AND DO Though sightseeing opportunities in and around Arua are in short supply, you might visit Miriadua Falls, a pretty stepped cascade off the Kiboko Road, 20km north, or climb the nearby 1,250m-high Mount Wati.

Ajai Wildlife Reserve This 158km² reserve, which flanks the west bank of the Nile east of Arua, was set aside in the 1960s to protect what was then the world's largest population of northern white rhino, estimated at 60 individuals. By 1975, only six survivors remained in Ajai, and today the northern race of white rhino is listed as extinct. In an exciting new development, it appears probable that, during the lifetime of this book, UWA will relocate a number of rhinos from Ziwa Rhino and Wildlife Ranch to Ajai. Contact UWA for updates.

Otherwise, despite considerable human encroachment, Ajai supports around 35km² of papyrus swamp, along with grassy floodplains and savannah woodland. Large mammals present include leopard, Uganda kob, sitatunga, hippo, black-and-white colobus and warthog. A limited ornithological survey undertaken in 1993 recorded 115 species. To get there from Arua, follow the surfaced Pakwach Road south for 15km to Olevu (⊕ 2.94641, 30.96312), then branch left on to a 40km dirt road running east to the reserve. Category B UWA tariffs apply (page 8).

ARUA TO GULU VIA THE LAROPI FERRY

A contender for the most remote road in Uganda, the 320km northern loop from Arua to Gulu via Koboko, Laropi and Adjumani passes through a region whose main allure is its genuinely off-the-beaten-track feel rather than any must-see travel highlights. The only real scenic drama lies in the Moyo–Laropi Hills, which also provide opportunities to visit the site of Emin Pasha's fort at Dufile, go sport fishing or search for shoebills on the Nile, or climb Mount Otzi and watch birds in the Otzi Forest Reserve.

KOBOKO For many Ugandans, this small town in their country's northwestern corner close to the borders with Sudan and the DRC is the epitome of remoteness. It's little more than a disproportionately wide main street with a roundabout at the northern end. The left branch leads to Yei in South Sudan, and the border crossing at Oraba, and the right to Moyo. Amenities include a Stanbic Bank with an ATM and perhaps the most expensive fuel stations in Uganda.

The only potential tourist attraction in the vicinity of Koboko is the 250m-long Lake Adomila, which despite its serpentine shape is claimed locally to sit in a volcanic crater. To get there, follow the Yei Road out of town for 12km, then turn right on to a dirt road that leads to Ludara after another 8km. The lake lies about 5km north of Ludara and you can drive to within a few hundred metres of it in a 4x4.

A 55km tarmac road runs north from Arua to Koboko, from which a 100km dirt road of variable condition runs west to Moyo. A right fork at a roundabout on the Koboko Road, 4km out of Arua, offers a dirt road short cut to Yumbe, roughly midway between Kiboko and Moyo.

Buses and taxis pass through Koboko on their way between Arua and the South Sudanese border. The fare works out at US$13 from Kampala and US$3 from Arua. Traffic headed east to Moyo is lighter but you should find a bus before resorting to a perch in the back of a truck. The pick of a handful of basic lodgings is the **Hotel de L'Ambiance** (7 en-suite rooms; **$**).

MOYO AND THE LAROPI FERRY Once a prosperous hub of cross-border trade, Moyo is an unassuming and rather pretty backwater of 25,000 people, perched on an elevated plateau 10km north of the Nile and 7km south of the South Sudanese border. Though not much in itself, Moyo lies about 25km from the small and sleepy but strategically important villages of Laropi and Umi, which respectively form the west bank and east bank landings for the only vehicle ferry to cross the Albert Nile downriver of Pakwach. Though most through traffic is simply intent on crossing the river, this area has plenty to offer an interested visitor and, if you've taken the trouble to travel all the way up there, it's well worth taking a few days to explore. The Nile itself is an obvious attraction, flanked as it is by a 5km floodplain of papyrus swamps and open lakes that support a fantastic variety of birdlife. The superb riverine scenery is complemented by the cliff-topped Mount Otzi, which towers to an altitude of 1,562m above the west bank. For all that, the area is only intermittently troubled by tourists, most of whom are guests of the Arra Fishing Lodge near Umi.

Getting there and away The free ferry between Laropi (⊕ 3.55175, 31.81256) and Umi (⊕ 3.54462, 31.81078) lies about 175km from Arua (via Kiboko), 25km from Moyo, 20km from Adjumani and 140km from Gulu. While the descent to the river from Moyo is rough and often rocky, on the eastern side, the road is surfaced all the way to Gulu. See notes on page 86 about using ferries. At Laropi, the lunchtime break is between noon and 14.00 so bear in mind that Laropi is one of the lowest spots in Uganda and at midday is also one of the hottest. Diversions on the Laropi side are limited to the nearby village of that name while Umi, on the opposite bank, offers only a shelter for passengers and a few stalls peddling refreshments. If you care to brave the heat, there are some impressive rock outcrops close by but you may prefer to delay in the relative cool of either Moyo or Adjumani.

Arra Fishing Lodge near Umi (see below) offers free boat transfers to the lodge for guests arriving at Laropi by public transport or taxi, or for safari groups with a driver to cross later with the vehicle.

Regular buses run throughout the day to connect Moyo with Arua (US$4) and Adjumani (US$3). Zawadi Buses run to Moyo (US$12) via Adjumani from its Kampala office on William Street. A special hire between Moyo and Laropi costs around US$40.

Where to stay and eat

Moyo

Penthouse Inn (24 rooms) m 0776 988266, 0775 454931; e sales@penthouseinns.com; w penthouseinns.com. Located 2km out of town past Moyo Hospital, the friendly Penthouse Inn offers a hotchpotch of indoor & outdoor spaces within a lush garden setting. The remote location is no disadvantage since the hotel compound contains the best of everything that Moyo has to offer. Accommodation options include some genuinely smart deluxe rooms, en suite with walk-in nets & AC, & a cluster of 6 more attractively priced 'cottage' rooms; the latter share an equipped kitchen that enables travellers to take catering matters into their own hands & avoid the limitations of the house menu. *Deluxe rooms US$60/70 sgl/dbl; cottage rooms US$26 sgl/dbl. All rates B&B.* **$$**

Laropi

Arra Fishing Lodge [map, page 330] (20 rooms) Umi; ⊕ 3.53387, 31.80884; m 0770 686076; e sales@penthouseinns.com; w penthouseinns.com. Situated on the eastern bank of the Nile, across from Laropi & 2km south of Umi landing, Arra Fishing Lodge (AFL) has enjoyed almost legendary status as Uganda's most remote tourism hotspot since its inception in 1999. In its original incarnation, AFL was a low-key tented camp built by the late Horst Pirker as a retreat for German tourists seeking genuine solitude. With vehicle access from the east blocked by the LRA insurgency, & complicated to the west by a roundabout approach on appalling roads, one can only assume they got what they were looking for. After years teetering on the edge of collapse, Arra has been revived & transformed by a Moyo tycoon. Spacious, en-suite thatched cottages now look past colourful gardens & acacia-shaded lawns towards the river, while on the terrace outside the main lodge building a substantially sized swimming pool offers essential respite from the heat. It's early days for Arra's renaissance, however, & even allowing for the relaxed standards of northern

Uganda, current standards of food & service will add a new layer to the Zen-like shell you will have cultivated since crossing the Nile at Pakwach. These minor details will, I am sure, soon be resolved, & AFL should be considered an essential stop, indeed the highlight, of the loop through the northwest. For activities, see below. *US$200/300 sgl/dbl B&B; US$15 pp camping.* **$$$**

What to see and do The activities described below are operated by Arra Fishing Lodge at the prices quoted. It is possible to find local guides and boatmen to assist you at a reduced cost, though you are unlikely to enjoy the same level of safety or expertise.

Boat cruises (Hourly rates are US$30 for 1 passenger; US$20 pp for up to 5 passengers; or US$80 for up to 25) Arra Fishing Lodge boasts three boats, the 25-seater *White Angel*, the ten-seater *White Rhino* and the diminutive *White Cock*, the latter being the emblem of Moyo. A variety of waterbirds can be sighted along the banks of the Nile. The prize is undoubtedly the shoebill, but other species often seen include open-billed and yellow-billed storks, African spoonbill, knob-billed duck, pygmy goose, giant kingfisher, and various herons. For those lacking ornithological intent, an early evening cruise to enjoy a cool beer and the terrific scenery is highly recommended.

Fishing The Nile at Arra provides a good chance of catching sizeable Nile perch (the local record with rod and line is 75kg), catfish, and to battle with the aggressive tiger fish. Boat hire with gear and a guide costs US$30/hour for one or US$20/hour for two to five people.

Mount Otzi Northwest Uganda's most distinctive peak, the 1,562m Mount Otzi rises a full 960m above the Nile's banks on the South Sudanese border 18km northeast of Moyo. Its slopes support the 188km^2 Otzi Forest Reserve, whose dominant cover of *Butyrospermum-Hyparrhenia* and *Combretum* savannah is interspersed with semi-deciduous thicket and riverine forest. More than 260 tree species are known from the reserve, which is identified as an Important Bird Area, with 168 bird species recorded. This checklist includes 14 of Uganda's 22 Sudan–Guinea savannah biome species: fox kestrel, white-crested turaco, red-throated bee-eater, Uganda spotted woodpecker, Emin's shrike, red-pate and foxy cisticolas, chestnut-crowned sparrow weaver, black-bellied firefinch, brown-rumped bunting, black-rumped waxbill, bronze-tailed glossy starling, purple glossy starling and piapiac. A chimpanzee population estimated at 20–40 individuals was documented in the early 1990s, but surveys undertaken in 2009 and 2015 suggest it is either extinct or seasonal (crossing into South Sudan for part of the year). Other primates include Anubis baboon, patas and vervet monkey, and what might turn out to be East Africa's only population of the western black-and-white colobus (*C. g. occidentalis*).

Arra Fishing Lodge offers full day excursions to Otzi at US$100 for four to five people including transport to the trailhead. If you're driving yourself, a track into the mountains – mostly good but with some extremely steep and rocky 4x4 sections – leaves the main road midway between Moyo and Laropi.

Dufile Fort Perched on the northern bank of the Albert Nile 20km downstream of Laropi, Dufile was established by Emin Pasha in 1879 as a station of Equatoria, and housed some 4,000 people at its busiest. By 1885, however, most of its inhabitants had been relocated south to Wadelai, increasing their distance from the Mahdist insurgents in Sudan, though a reduced garrison remained to guard the northern limit of Emin's shrinking domain. In 1888, when Henry Stanley arrived to assist Emin's withdrawal from Equatoria, the soldiers ensconced at Dufile turned mutinous and refused to follow their leader. Instead, Emin and another British officer were briefly imprisoned in the fort before the mutineers allowed them to return to Stanley's camp on Lake Albert. Shortly after this, Dufile was attacked by the Mahdist army, and while Emin's men won the battle, they recognised they were bound to lose the war, so they hotfooted it south to Lake Albert in January 1889, only to find that Emin and Stanley had already left for the coast. The mutineers remained near Lake Albert until 1890, when they were sought out and headhunted by Frederick Lugard to add some backbone to his understaffed fort in Old Kampala.

The future restoration of Dufile Fort is earmarked as part of the same Emin Pasha Historical Fort Preservation and Development Project as Fort Wadelai (page 338). For the time being, however, the only obvious evidence of the former fortification is part of the perimeter ditch. Archaeological excavations over 2006–07 were able to ascertain the positions of a few buildings whose age and significance is uncertain, since the original fort was overlaid by Belgian structures during 1902–07, when West Nile was part of the Congo's Lado Enclave. Nevertheless, the site can be reached by 4x4 or boat, the latter being preferable as the river journey is far more rewarding than the actual destination. The return boat trip from Arra Fishing Lodge costs US$100 plus US$50 for guide and entrance fees.

ADJUMANI Adjumani is a substantial town (population 45,000) with very little going for it in terms of tourism other than a location only 20km south of the Laropi ferry. Adjumani District has long been the site of Uganda's largest refugee camp, and while many of its Sudanese inhabitants returned home following the peace agreement that led to South Sudan's independence, subsequent events north of the border have led to a fresh influx and the total number of refugees had risen to around 250,000 in 2018. Pekelle, 6km out of town along the Atiak Road, is the site of the region's oldest Catholic church, founded by missionaries who baptised their first 22 converts in November 1911.

Getting there and away Adjumani lies 117km north of Gulu on the murram road that branches off the main South Sudanese route at Atiak, 72km from Gulu. The town is well served by public transport. Zawadi's Moyo-bound buses run through Adjumani (US$10) from Kampala's William Street. Other services run to Gulu and Arua.

Where to stay and eat

Zawadi Hotel (27 rooms) Magni Rd; m 0780 585699. This vaguely Mediterranean-style hotel has a clay-tiled roof & white walls softened with climbing plants surrounding a courtyard. Clean rooms come with nets, fans & TV. A pleasant restaurant serves main courses for around US$6. *US$12 sgl using common shower; US$25/32 en-suite sgl/dbl.* **$–$$**

ATIAK Situated 45km southeast of Adjumani, this small junction town is remembered as the site of one of the LRA's most notorious atrocities: the Atiak Massacre of 20 April 1995. After repulsing an enthusiastic but ill-advised attack by a newly trained home guard, the rebels drove the vigilantes back into the town, handpicked a number of young boys and girls to conscript into their ranks as child soldiers or sex slaves, then slaughtered the remaining 200 to 300 in a

burst of gunfire. A memorial erected by the surviving townsfolk still stands in the town.

Our loop through the less travelled byways of the northwest is close to completion at Atiak, assuming you have no interest in turning north towards the uncertainties of South Sudan beyond Nimule. For here, a right turn leads south towards the bright lights (and so they will now seem) of Gulu, just 90 minutes away. There is, however, an additional option to prolong your explorations: a dirt road that cuts east across very remote country to Kitgum, with the prospects of Kidepo Valley National Park and Karamoja beyond. Should your resolve quickly falter along the way, a right turn after some 20km leads south to Gulu past Patiko, where Baker's Fort (page 327) offers a worthwhile diversion.

13

Bunyoro

Extending over 18,580km^2 of Rift Valley floor and escarpment immediately east of Lake Albert, the administrative subregion of Bunyoro is bounded by the Victoria Nile in the north and another of the lake's effluents, the Muzizi, to the south. The modern subregion approximates the late 19th-century shape of the Bunyoro kingdom, which was founded in the 16th century, unwillingly incorporated into the Buganda Protectorate in 1894, disbanded under Milton Obote in 1967, then revived in 1994 with the coronation of the still incumbent Omukama (King) Gafabusa Iguru I. For much of the 20th century, Bunyoro's largest town was Masindi, an important trade centre set at the crossroads of three transport routes. In recent years, however, Hoima has superseded Masindi both in size and in terms of economic vibrancy.

TWINS

Traditionally, within what is today Uganda, the birth of twins was seen as an event of great significance, though some cultures regarded it as a great blessing while others perceived it to be an omen of ill. Speke, while stuck in Bunyoro in 1862, compared some of the customs he had come across on his travels:

> A Munyoro woman, who bore twins that died, now keeps two small pots in her house, as effigies of the children, into which she milks herself every evening, and will continue to do so for five months, fulfilling the time appointed by nature for suckling children, lest the spirits of the dead should persecute her. The twins were not buried, as ordinary people are buried, under ground, but placed in an earthenware pot, such as the Banyoro use for holding pombe [beer]. They were taken to the jungle and placed by a tree, with the pot turned mouth downwards. Manua, one of my men, who is a twin, said, in Nguru, one of the sister provinces to Unyanyembe, twins are ordered to be killed and thrown into water the moment they are born, lest droughts and famines or floods should oppress the land. Should any one attempt to conceal twins, the whole family would be murdered by the chief; but, though a great traveller, this is the only instance of such brutality Manua had ever witnessed in any country.
>
> In the province of Unyanyembe, if a twin or twins die, they are thrown into water for the same reason as in Nguru; but as their numbers increase the size of the family, their birth is hailed with delight. Still there is a source of fear there in connection with twins, as I have seen myself; for when one dies, the mother ties a little gourd to her neck as a proxy, and puts into it a trifle of everything which she gives the living child, lest the jealousy of the dead spirit should torment her. Further, on the death of the child, she smears herself with butter and ashes, and runs frantically about, tearing her hair and bewailing piteously; while the men of the place use towards her the foulest language, apparently as if in abuse of her person, but in reality to frighten away the demons who have robbed her nest.

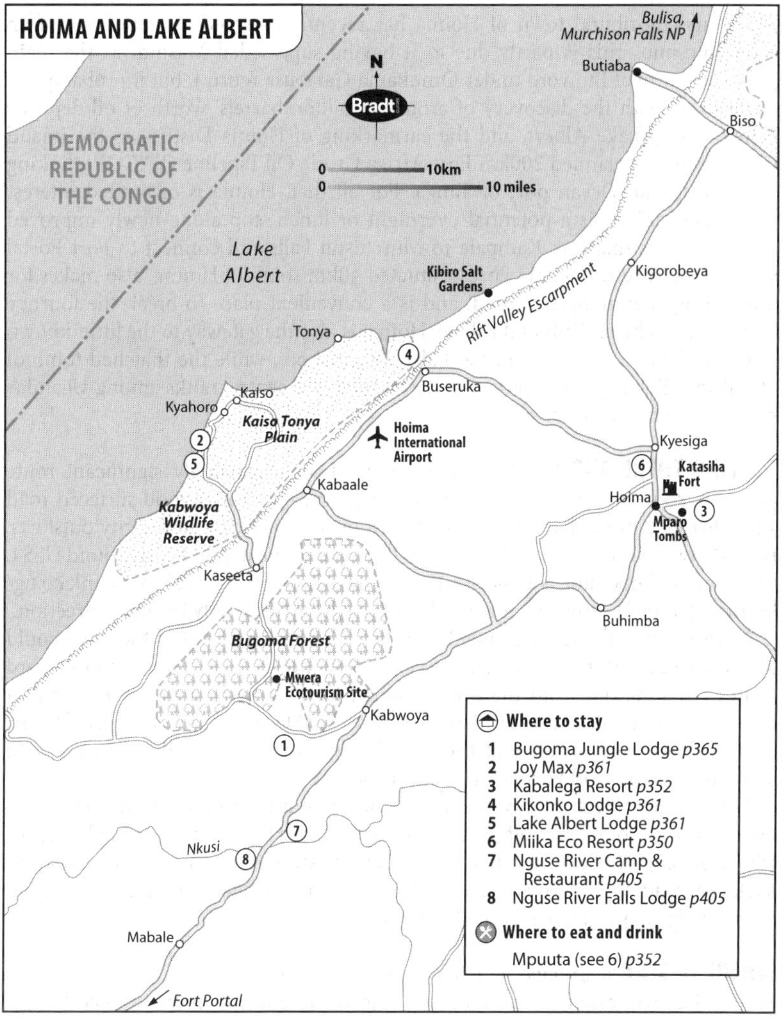

For tourists, Bunyoro is of interest primarily as the southern gateway to Murchison Falls National Park (page 371), whose main Kichambanyobo Gate lies only 22km north of Masindi, though the park can also be accessed from Masindi along a longer, rougher route via Wanseko on the Lake Albert shore. Those travelling between Murchison Falls and Fort Portal, or elsewhere in the southwest, will need to pass through both Hoima and Masindi. Bunyoro hosts a few other worthwhile but under-publicised attractions, notably the Mparo Tombs outside Hoima, the bird-rich Budongo Forest Reserve west of Masindi, and the Kabwoya Wildlife Reserve and Kibiro Salt Gardens on the shores of Lake Albert.

HOIMA

With a population that has more than doubled from a modest 60,000 at the turn of the millennium to tip over the 140,000 mark in the 2024 census, the once rather pokey and moribund town of Hoima has recently emerged as something of an economic hub. This is partly due to it having superseded Masindi as the main political centre of Bunyoro under Omukama Gafabusa Iguru I, but it probably has more to do with the discovery of around 3 billion barrels' worth of oil deposits below nearby Lake Albert, and the earmarking of Hoima District as the inland terminus of the planned 200km East Africa Crude Oil Pipeline (EACOP), linking it to the Indian Ocean port of Tanga. For all that, Hoima is of limited interest to tourists, except as a potential overnight or lunch stop along newly improved surfaced roads that link Kampala to Murchison Falls and connect to Fort Portal and the southwest. Bugoma Forest, situated 40km south of Hoima, also makes for a diverting stop along this road, and is a convenient place to break the journey between Murchison Falls and Kibale. Hoima is also the gateway to the little-known Kabwoya Wildlife Reserve on the Lake Albert shore, while the thatched tomb of Omukama Kabalega at Mparo, 4km from the town centre, ranks among Uganda's more interesting cultural sites.

GETTING THERE AND AWAY Hoima stands at an increasingly significant route junction, some 200km northwest of Kampala; the drive on a good surfaced road shouldn't take more than 2½ hours, at least once you've cleared the city outskirts. Buses between Kampala and Hoima run throughout the day and cost around US$4. The preferred operator is Link Bus (📞 041 4255426; m 0757 222743; w link.co.ug/hoima_terminal), which operates at least four departures daily in either direction.

Until recently the tarmac ended at Hoima and driving beyond the town could be quite an adventure during rainy seasons. Now, however, all of the major onward routes radiating out from the town – north to the emergent oil town of Bulisa and Murchison Falls National Park, northeast to Masindi (and Murchison Falls), southwest to Lake Albert and the little-known Kabwoya Wildlife Reserve, and south to Kyenjojo and Fort Portal – are surfaced.

Given time, travel improvements will not be limited to terrestrial access. The eventuality is some way off, but the out-of-town Hoima International Airport (⊕ 1.556403, 31.088247), currently under construction some 40km along the surfaced road to Kabwoya, may well be a game changer for safari circuits in western Uganda when it eventually opens.

WHERE TO STAY *Map, opposite, unless otherwise stated*

Hoima has witnessed a recent burgeoning of decent but unremarkable budget hotels catering primarily to the conference market and other NGO and business travellers. The options listed here are highly selective.

Upmarket

Miika Eco Resort Hotel [map, page 349] (63 rooms) Butiaba Rd; m 0700 235008; e reservations@mereho.com; w mereho.com. Though the 'Eco Resort' tag is a bit of a stretch, this smart new hotel, 2km north of the town centre, does have a lovely location in terraced 13ha grounds that incorporate a small & quite delightful river valley complete with waterfall & ancient trees inhabited by black-&-white colobus & red-tailed monkey. It is also home to the excellent Mpuuta Restaurant (page 352) & the site of what remains of Katasiha Fort (page 354). Coming from Hoima, take the 1st signposted turning for the restaurant & the 2nd for the hotel. *From US$66/86 sgl/dbl B&B.* **$$$**

Moderate

✱ **Hotel KonTiki** (45 rooms) ⊕ 1.41021, 31.37278; 📞 046 5442890; m 0772 775005; e info@hoimakontiki.com; f hotelkontikihoima. This family-run lodge, located off the Kampala Rd, 3km out of town & just after the Masindi turning, is set in large landscaped gardens that

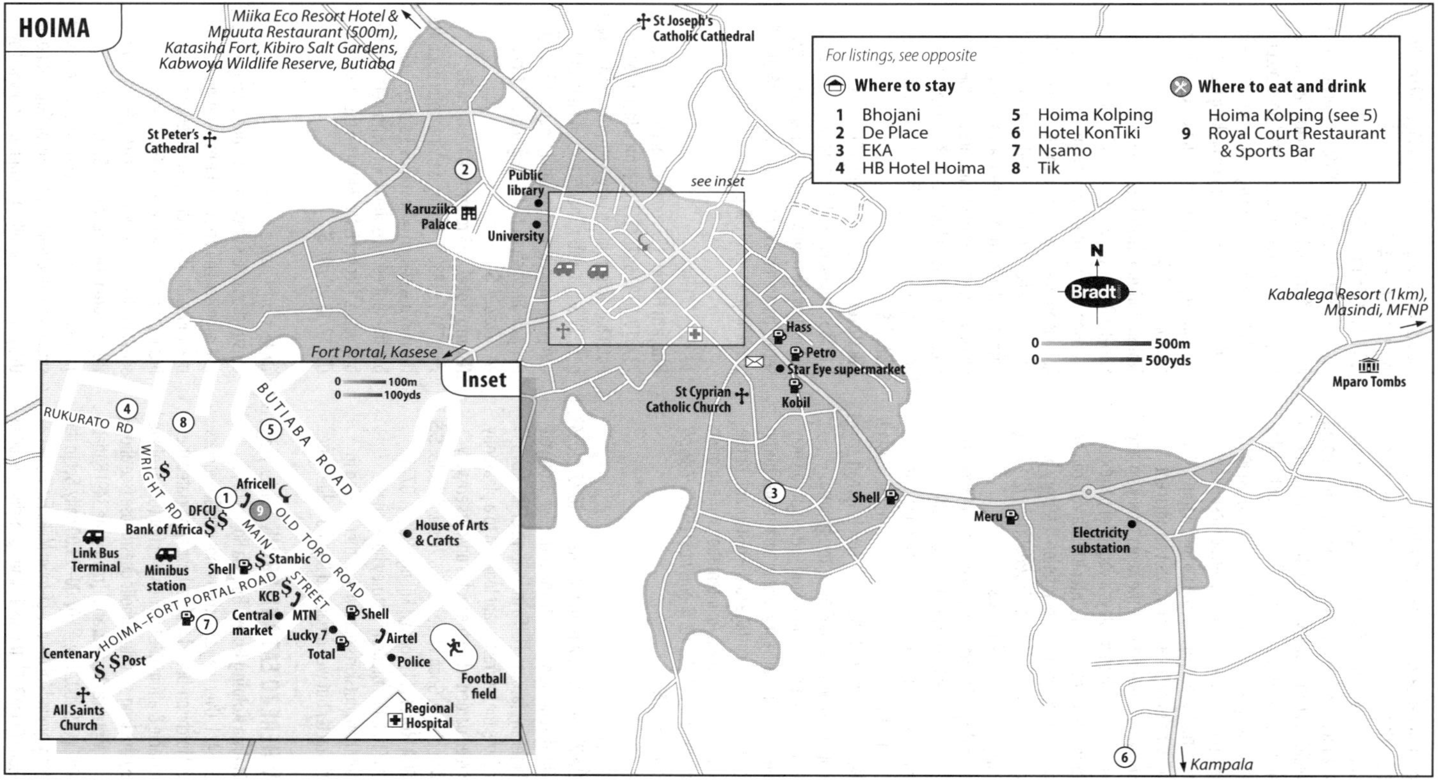
HOIMA
Miika Eco Resort Hotel & Mpuuta Restaurant (500m), Katasiha Fort, Kibiro Salt Gardens, Kabwoya Wildlife Reserve, Butiaba
St Joseph's Catholic Cathedral
For listings, see opposite
Where to stay
1 Bhojani
2 De Place
3 EKA
4 HB Hotel Hoima
5 Hoima Kolping
6 Hotel KonTiki
7 Nsamo
8 Tik
Where to eat and drink
Hoima Kolping (see 5)
9 Royal Court Restaurant & Sports Bar
St Peter's Cathedral
Public library
Karuziika Palace
University
see inset
N
Bradt
0 500m
0 500yds
Kabalega Resort (1km), Masindi, MFNP
Mparo Tombs
Fort Portal, Kasese
Hass
Petro
Star Eye supermarket
Kobil
St Cyprian Catholic Church
Shell
Meru
Electricity substation
Kampala
Inset
0 100m
0 100yds
RUKURATO RD
BUTIABA ROAD
WRIGHT RD
Africell
DFCU
Bank of Africa
OLD TORO ROAD
MAIN STREET
House of Arts & Crafts
Link Bus Terminal
Minibus station
Shell
Stanbic
HOIMA–FORT PORTAL ROAD
KCB
Central market
MTN
Shell
Lucky 7
Total
Airtel
Police
Football field
Centenary
Post
All Saints Church
Regional Hospital

get lovelier each time we update this book. As regards the accommodation, opt for one of the standalone thatched stone cottages rather than the more ordinary rooms in a nondescript modern building. Either way, you'll probably spend most of your waking hours scanning the trees for birdlife (including the superb Rwenzori turaco), lying by the pool or in the charming terrace restaurant (international dishes in the US$6–7 range). You might also be interested to visit an adjacent showroom – another of the Kooja family's many ventures – which displays a variety of bamboo products. If you're really interested, a visit can be arranged to a bamboo plantation & factory just out of town. *US$50/60/65 sgl/dbl/twin; US$10 pp camping. All rates B&B.* **$$**

Kabalega Resort [map, page 349] (49 rooms) ☎ 046 5442890; m 0393 193860; e info@kabalegaresort.com; w kabalegaresort.com. Situated in a quiet location 3km down the Masindi Rd beyond Mparo, Kabalega Resort is spread across impressively spacious & attractive grounds – estate might be a better word – though you may be less appreciative if you're in a particular hurry to get from your cottage to the restaurant, or the car park to the pool. An international menu offers mains from US$8–10. *Rooms from US$54/68/sgl/dbl B&B.* **$$**

Budget

De Place (30 rooms) Butiaba Rd; m 0772 220243. The daft name doesn't do this attractive, storeyed hotel any favours. Half a mile north of the town centre, the bar/restaurant looks on to a pleasantly green garden while the rooms upstairs are very acceptable. Good value. *US$21/26 sgl/dbl B&B.* **$$**

EKA Hotel (45 rooms) Kijungu Rd; m 0771 937104. This modern 3-storey hotel on the southern outskirts of town is rather lacking in character but well organised & good value. Rates include use of a gym & sauna. *US$32/40 small/large room B&B.* **$$**

HB Hotel Hoima (60 rooms) Circular Rd; m 0789 099949, 0701 570836; e reservations@hoimabuffalohotel.com; w hoimabuffalohotel.com. This smart & centrally located hotel occupies a modern storeyed building on the northern edge of the town centre with ample parking plus a swimming pool in an adjacent annex. *US$26/32 sgl/dbl B&B.* **$$**

Hoima Kolping Hotel (22 rooms) Butiaba Rd; m 0772 516421, 0705 898501; e hoimakolpinghotel@gmail.com; w hoima.kolpinghotelsug.com. This clean & central Catholic guesthouse has recently trebled its room capacity with the addition of a modern accommodation block. Rooms in the new wing are far superior to those in the original hotel. *US$32/43 sgl/dbl in new wing; US$21/26 sgl/dbl in old wing. All rates B&B.* **$$**

Tik Hotel (35 rooms) Kijungu Rd; m 0761 219135. This older establishment in the shadow of the new HB Hoima remains a good deal with secure parking & a central location. *US$18/26/30 small/large/exec dbl B&B.* **$$**

Shoestring

Bhojani Hotel (27 rooms) Main St; m 0712 737319, 0782 542642. This central Indian-owned hotel has acceptable & very well-priced rooms with nets, TV & hot water. There's also an affordable, curry-dominated residents-only menu. *US$5 sgl using common shower; US$6/8 ground/1st-floor en-suite dbl.* **$**

Nsamo Hotel (25 rooms) Off Kyenjojo Rd; m 0781 763880. This long-serving hotel opposite the minibus station now stands 3 storeys tall, but the spotless en-suite rooms with nets remain fine value. Alcohol is forbidden on the premises. *US$12/13 sgl/dbl.* **$**

WHERE TO EAT AND DRINK *Map, page 351, unless otherwise stated*

Hoima Kolping Hotel Butiaba Rd; m 0772 516421. Over the years, thousands of NGO workers & Murchison-bound tourists have appreciated the reliable & affordable lunchtime buffet (US$5) offered by this long-serving Catholic guesthouse (see above).

✵ **Mpuuta Restaurant** [map, page 349] Butiaba Rd; ☎ 039 2002486; ⌚ 07.00–23.00 daily. Set in the leafy grounds of the out-of-town Miika Eco Resort Hotel (page 350), this sprawling open-sided wooden construction offers views into the tree canopy as well as a large-screen TV next to the bar. A cosmopolitan menu includes Thai, Indian & continental dishes including pasta, salads & grills. Good dessert selection, too. *Mains mostly in the US$8–10 range.*

Royal Court Restaurant & Sports Bar Old Toro Rd; m 0758 113371. Long experience would suggest yet another spurious 'royal' tag, but not in this case – this excellent restaurant is owned by a real life Banyoro princess. The veranda restaurant fronting on to Old Toro Rd is the most attractive place to sit out in the town centre & as an added bonus, to enjoy a curry fit for a . . . well . . . for Princess Bagaya's uncle, King Solomon Gafabusa Iguru I of Bunyoro. You can then retreat to the courtyard bar behind to watch a Premier League match or 2 on DSTV before a sound system fires up to give your ears a good drubbing. That's your Saturday in Hoima sorted! *Curries & grills US$7–9.*

SHOPPING The best stocked of several small supermarkets are the **People's Supermarket** and **Lucky 7** on Main Street.

SPORTS AND ACTIVITIES KonTiki charges day visitors US$3 to use its swimming pool; the Miika Eco Resort charges a dollar more, though you get to enjoy loud poolside music at weekends.

WHAT TO SEE AND DO

Mparo Tombs (Masindi Rd; ⊕ 1.42753, 31.3831; m 0782 802651 (Bwogo Fred); ⊕ no fixed opening hours; entry US$5) Now situated on the eastern outskirts of Hoima, the village of Mparo was chosen as the capital of Omukama Kabalega of Bunyoro in 1872, after Sir Samuel Baker forced his retreat out of Masindi. It was from Mparo that Kabalega led his raids into the neighbouring kingdoms of Toro and Buganda before the British drove him into hiding in 1891. After Kabalega's death at Jinja in 1923, his body was returned to Hoima and interred at Mparo. The burial ceremony was traditional in most respects, but certain customs were deemed obsolete. The grisliest of these discarded practices involved digging a 10m-deep hole, the floor of which would be covered in barkcloth on the morning of the burial. One of the late king's wives – usually the eldest or the favourite – would be seated in the hole, holding in her lap a parcel containing the dead man's jawbone. Onlookers were then seized randomly from the crowd, their limbs were amputated, and then they were thrown into the hole one by one until it was filled.

Today, the main tomb at Mparo is protected within a large domed construction made mostly from natural materials, and not dissimilar in appearance to the more famous Kasubi Tombs in Kampala, though considerably smaller. Kabalega's grave is covered with a type of white spotted brown cowhide called *entimba*, held in place by nine traditional hoes, and surrounded by many of his personal effects, including some spears and crowns said to be handed down from the Bachwezi dynasty. Kabalega's son and successor Omukama Tito Winyi is also buried at Mparo, while a plaque and monument outside the main enclosure marks the spot where Kabalega granted an audience to Emin Pasha in 1877 (page 363).

Coming from Hoima, Kabalega's grass-roofed tomb and the whitewashed Emin Pasha monument are visible about 100m south of the Masindi Road, 1.6km past the junction with the Kampala Road. If you don't have a vehicle, a return boda from Hoima shouldn't set you back more than a few US dollars. In theory, Bwogo Fred, the curator, will be there to provide you with a tour and some fiercely partisan insights into Banyoro-Baganda history. In practice, he may be busy elsewhere so it would be safer to ring ahead.

Karuziika Palace (⊕ 1.43397, 31.34543) The palace of the Omukama of Bunyoro lies 500m northwest of Hoima town centre, just past the main university campus and library. Though the building itself is modern, a fierce sense of tradition is still evident in the Throne Room, which contains a wealth of ancient royal regalia, some said to date from the Bachwezi era. These include a stool-like nine-legged throne swathed in leopard skins and barkcloth, as well as an array of spears, royal headdresses and musical instruments. To arrange a visit, you should phone Princess Kasagama on m 0772 656085.

Katasiha Fort Constructed in 1893, Katasiha was the largest of the forts built by General Colville in the wake of Kabalega's abandonment of Mparo two years earlier. All that remains of the fort is the 8m dry moat (now filled in) that surrounded it, and a small cave used as a hiding place by Kabalega and later as an arsenal by the British. It now stands in the grounds of the Miika Eco Resort Hotel (page 350).

LAKE ALBERT AND THE ESCARPMENT FORESTS

Until very recently, the shores of the 160km-long Lake Albert were all but inaccessible, Butiaba Port being the only place that could be reliably reached by vehicle between the extremities of Ntoroko town on the southern tip and Wanseko at the northern end. Indeed, Lake Albert was the only part of Africa to defeat Ewart Grogan on his famous Cape to Cairo walk; he gave up trying to follow its steep, gullied and often precipitous shore and hired a boat. Road improvements related to the imminent extraction of oil from the Albertine Rift Valley have changed all this, making a number of destinations easily accessible from Hoima town and thus also potential weekend excursions from Kampala.

The big game changer in this respect is a trio of newly surfaced roads running out of Hoima. These are the 145km road southeast to Kyenjojo (linking to Kibale National Park and Fort Portal), the 120km road north to Murchison Falls via Bulisa, and the surreal and almost traffic-free 80km road west to the Lake Albert port of Kaiso and Kabwoya Wildlife Reserve.

Another attraction of this region is the steep and scenic Rift Valley Escarpment that rises from the eastern shore of Lake Albert. Two of Uganda's most important protected forests are associated with this escarpment. These are Budongo and Bugoma forest reserves, which respectively lie to the north and south of Hoima. Budongo Forest Reserve is home to Uganda's longest-running chimp research project, and is one of the country's most rewarding destinations for forest birding, but the tourist development is currently quite limited (though chimp tracking is available in the Kaniyo Pabidi extension protected within Murchison Falls Conservation Area; page 371). By contrast, the once-neglected Bugoma Forest Reserve opened as Uganda's newest chimp tracking destination in 2024.

The following attractions are listed as they occur driving out from Hoima, firstly in a northwesterly direction towards Murchison, and then to the south.

NORTHWEST OF HOIMA

Kibiro Salt Gardens and hot spring The Lake Albert fishing village of Kibiro, 25km north of Hoima as the crow flies, is an appealing goal for travellers who enjoy a short but steep off-the-beaten-track hike. Kibiro stands on the narrow plain that divides the lake from the Rift Valley Escarpment, where it is distinguished from other similarly inaccessible lakeside settlements by its proximity to a saline hot spring that has supplied Bunyoro with salt for centuries. In 1885, Emin Pasha, probably the first foreign visitor to Kibiro, described the gardens and salt-making process, observing helpfully that 'when taken in large quantities, [the spring water] acts as a moderate purgative'. But the salt industry at Kibiro is much, much older than this: indeed, glass beads found by archaeologists indicate that salt was bartered for here in the 13th century, and most probably earlier.

The salt-gardeners of Kibiro employ a clever technique to obtain an unusually pure product. Their so-called gardens are patches of salty ground from which all grass and topsoil has been removed. These mineral-rich depressions are saturated with water diverted in earthen channels from a searingly hot stream fed by a spring hidden deep within a cleft in the Rift Valley Escarpment. This already slightly salty water dissolves additional salts from the soil. Loose dry soil is then scattered across the 'garden' into which, over a week or so, the salty water is drawn up by capillary action. When the enriched earth changes colour, it is scraped into jars to be repeatedly leached by a further quantity of spring water. The result is a concentrated solution of 14% salt which is boiled off to produce crystals of 97.6% pure sodium chloride. In contrast, the product at Lake Katwe, the region's other major salt supplier, is only 85% pure.

Salt gardens aside, the short but steep hike to Kibiro provides a rare opportunity to appreciate a dramatic out-of-the-way stretch of the Rift Valley on foot. And as you follow the footpath to Kibiro, you'll notice it becomes steeper as you approach the base. This is because the escarpment actually comprises three distinct planes, each corresponding to a different phase of uplift. The highest section is 4.5 million years old and has eroded into a relatively gentle slope, while the lowest section was heaved above the lake within the last 1.5 million years and remains much steeper.

To get to Kibiro from Hoima, follow the Butiaba Road north for 24km to Kigorobeya (⊕ 1.61602, 31.30792), where a left turn on to a decent 8km track leads to the top of the Rift Valley Escarpment. If you have a strong 4x4 vehicle, it's just about possible to drive down to the lake, otherwise it's a 45-minute descent on foot which can be hot going, so take plenty of water. Once there, a guide should appear to take you around; expect to pay about US$5.

Budongo Forest (West) One of East Africa's most extensive and ecologically diverse blocks of contiguous rainforest, the Budongo Forest Reserve extends over an area of 435km² in the Rift Valley hinterland between Biso and Masindi, where it borders and partially overlaps with the Murchison Falls Conservation Area (MFCA). In pre-colonial times, Budongo, a Runyoro name meaning 'fertile soil', was accorded protection by the Omukama of Bunyoro, who used it as a royal hunting ground and forbade his subjects from hunting there without permission. In 1926, the colonial authorities opened a sawmill in the forest, which was producing 600 tonnes of hardwood timber per month by the 1960s. The sawmill closed in the 1980s, by which time an estimated 35m³ of timber per hectare had been removed from Budongo, at least 65% of which comprised mahogany. The forest has recovered well since then, with *Ficus* and other fruiting trees having taken the place of many of the felled mahoganies and ironwoods, though some illegal logging still takes place.

Today, Budongo is renowned both for harbouring Uganda's largest population of chimpanzees and as one of its key ornithological destinations. Indeed, such is its avian wealth that the track nicknamed the 'Royal Mile' (because it was once a favourite haunt of Omukama Kabalega) is widely regarded to be the country's single most rewarding birding hotspot. In 1993, an internationally funded ecotourism project was established in Budongo with the objective of helping to conserve the forest through the implementation of tourist projects that benefited local communities. Two ecotourism sites were created: Busingiro at the western edge of Budongo near Biso, and Kaniyo Pabidi in a northeasterly extremity that overlaps what is now the UWA-managed Murchison Falls Conservation Area (MFCA). Though chimp tracking is still operational at Kaniyo Pabidi (this is covered in the Murchison Falls chapter on page 384), the Busingiro site is currently inactive and tourism in the western part of Budongo is limited to birdwatching in the Royal Mile (see below). However, plans for a USAID-funded renaissance at Busingiro are afoot and, assuming that Uganda does nothing further to offend donor sensibilities, may be implemented during the course of this edition.

Flora and fauna Classified as a moist semi-deciduous medium-altitude forest, Budongo supports at least 450 species of tree, the most impressive being those large buttressed giant mahoganies that have been left unfelled and now stand up to 60m tall. More than 250 butterfly and 360 bird species have been recorded in Budongo and/or Kaniyo Pabidi. The bird checklist includes 60 West or central African bird species known from fewer than five locations in East Africa. Yellow-footed flycatcher, often associated with ironwood trees, has not been recorded elsewhere in Uganda, while Ituri batis, lemon-bellied crombec, white-thighed hornbill, black-eared ground thrush and chestnut-capped flycatcher are known from only one other East African forest.

Together with Kaniyo Pabidi, Budongo supports an 800-strong chimpanzee population, the largest anywhere in Uganda. Budongo's chimpanzees were first studied in 1962 by Professor Vernon Reynolds, who went on to publish the book *Budongo: An African Forest and its Chimpanzees* in 1965. In 1990, Reynolds established the Budongo Forest Project, subsequently renamed the Budongo Conservation Field Station (w budongo.org), an ongoing research project dedicated to a habituated chimp community located near Busingiro. Other primates resident in Budongo include red-tailed monkey, blue monkey, black-and-white colobus, potto and various forest galago species. The forest is also occasionally visited by elephants and other large mammals associated with the adjacent MFCA.

Getting there and away Budongo Forest is flanked by the Butiaba Road some 30km west of Masindi. To get to Nyabyeya Forestry College, the springboard for the Royal Mile, from Hoima, leave the tarmac road to Bulisa and Murchison Falls at Biso at the top of the Rift Valley Escarpment and head east towards Masindi for 25km to Nyamegita, where you turn north on to a signposted 2km feeder road. Alternatively, if coming from Masindi, turn off the surfaced Masindi–Hoima Road 2km south of town and head west for about 30km to Nyamegita. In the event that the inactive Busingiro Tourist Site is revived, you'll find it on the same road, 5km east of Biso and 10km past Nyabyeya.

Using public transport, any matatu heading from Masindi to Butiaba or Wanseko can drop you at Nyamegita or Busingiro, though you'll probably have to pay the full fare for Biso or Butiaba. A 4x4 with driver can be hired in Masindi through Yebo Tours (page 369).

What to see and do

The Royal Mile The best place to do a guided bird walk in Budongo Forest is along the Royal Mile, a 2.5km stretch of dirt road that runs north from Nyabyeya Forestry College to the Budongo Conservation Field Station. Unfortunately, the Royal Mile lies about 14km from Busingiro, so it's not really a viable option for a day trip unless you have private transport. Generally regarded as being one of Uganda's best forest-birding sites, the Royal Mile supports a wide variety of localised species, with the sought-after African dwarf, blue-breasted and chocolate-backed kingfishers all very common. A long list of other local specials includes Cassin's hawk eagle, Nahan's francolin, white-thighed hornbill, yellow-billed barbet, lemon-billed crombec, black-capped apalis, forest flycatcher, yellow-footed flycatcher and Jameson's wattle-eye. Various monkeys are also likely to be seen, along with giant forest squirrels and the bizarre chequered elephant-shrew. Equally bizarre in this remote patch of forest is Our Lady Queen of Poland Catholic Church, which was built during World War II by Polish refugees who were settled in the area and in some cases were buried in the adjacent cemetery.

Around Busingiro An alternative to visiting the Royal Mile is simply to park up and walk along the main road through the forest between Nyamegita and Busingiro. Though not on a par with the Royal Mile, the birding here is still excellent and it is generally easier to locate birds than it is in the forest proper. Among the species to look for on the road and around the campsite are rufous-crowned eremomela, Ituri batis, chestnut-capped flycatcher, Cassin's and Sabine's spinetails, and grey and yellow longbills. The chocolate-backed kingfisher, common in the area, is most easily located by call. A small pool by the side of the road about 1km back towards Masindi is a reliable place to see the shining blue kingfisher and black-necked weaver. In addition to birds, you should also see at least three types of primate on this stretch of road. There's nothing to prevent you from walking along the road alone, but it's worth taking a guide from the tourism site – they are very knowledgeable, particularly with regard to bird calls, and they all carry binoculars and a field guide. With a vehicle and spotlight, the road could be worth exploring at night – a colony of gigantic hammerhead bats roosts along the road between Busingiro and the aforementioned pool, and the nocturnal potto and tree pangolin are also resident.

Bugungu Wildlife Reserve This small reserve protects an area of savannah and seasonal swamp lying on and along the base of the Rift Valley Escarpment. It's not a tourist destination as such – there are no tourism facilities at present – but awareness of its existence helps to explain the uninhabited wilderness that lies to of the tarmac road between Biso and Bulisa, starting during the winding descent towards the Rift Valley floor. Bugungu supports many of the same species as the contiguous Murchison Falls National Park to the east, with an estimated 1,200 oribi and 600 Ugandan kob. Leopard, buffalo, warthog, hippo, reedbuck, sitatunga, waterbuck, bushbuck, dik-dik, black-and-white colobus and baboon are also found. Roughly 240 bird species have been recorded, including Abyssinian ground hornbill, shoebill and saddle-billed stork.

Butiaba You'd scarcely credit it today, but the port of Butiaba, set on the lakeshore 8km west of the Hoima–Bulisa Road, was a commercial centre of some significance back in the colonial era. In the 1920s, the colonial government earmarked the existing administrative station – contemporaneously described by Etta Close as 'a few native huts, an Indian store, and three little European houses by the edge of the water' – for a major harbour development. A regular steamer service was established out of Butiaba, effectively extending the existing import–export route between Masindi and Mombasa further west, to the Congolese port of Mahagi and to Nimule on the Sudanese border.

Butiaba's stock rose further in 1931, when it was selected as a landing site for the first seaplane flights between Cairo and East Africa. Over the subsequent decade, it also became something of a tourist focus, after a freshly dredged channel through the Victoria Nile Estuary allowed boats from Butiaba to divert to a landing point a short distance downstream of Murchison Falls. During the production of the classic Bogart/Hepburn movie *The African Queen*, a boat called the *Murchison* was chartered by director John Huston to carry supplies and run errands between

HEMINGWAY AND BUTIABA

The American writer Ernest Hemingway and his fourth wife Mary Welsh arrived at Butiaba on 23 January 1954, somewhat the worse for wear after a bruising 24-hour trip to Murchison Falls. The day before, their chartered Cessna had dipped to avoid hitting a flock of birds, in the process clipping a wing on an abandoned telegraph wire and forcing a crash landing in which Hemingway dislocated his right shoulder and Mary cracked several ribs. The injured passengers and their pilot spent the night huddled on the riverbank below Murchison Falls, to be rescued the next morning by a boat headed to Butiaba.

At Butiaba, Hemingway chartered a De Havilland to fly him and his wife back to Entebbe the next morning. On take-off, however, the plane lifted, bumped back down, crashed, and burst into flames. Mary and the pilot escaped through a window. Hemingway, too bulky to fit through the window and unable to use his dislocated arm, battered open the buckled door with his head, to emerge with bleeding skull and a rash of blistering burns. The battered couple were driven to Masindi to receive medical attention and spent a few days recuperating at the Masindi Hotel. On 25 January 1954, New York's *Daily News* broke the news of the accident under the headline 'Hemingway Feared Dead in Nile Air Crash'. A spate of premature obituaries followed before it was discovered that the writer had survived, if only just.

Hemingway had, in addition to the dislocated arm and several first-degree burns, limped out of the burning plane with a collapsed intestine, a ruptured liver and kidney, two crushed vertebrae, temporary loss of vision in one eye, impaired hearing, and a fractured skull. In October of that year, he was awarded the Nobel Prize in Literature, but was too battered to attend the ceremony. Nor did he have the energy to work the 200,000 words he wrote on safari into publishable shape – an edited version finally appeared in 1999 under the name *True at First Light*. It is widely asserted, too, that the injuries Hemingway sustained at Butiaba sparked the gradual decline in his mental well-being that led ultimately to his suicide in 1961.

Butiaba and the nearby filming location. Butiaba's celebrity connections don't end with Bogart and Hepburn – see above.

In 1962, coincidentally the same year that Uganda gained independence, unusually heavy rains caused Lake Albert to rise several metres overnight, sinking all of the ships in Butiaba harbour and leaving much of the town submerged. The port was officially abandoned in 1963, never to be redeveloped. Today it is little more than an overgrown fishing village. The airstrip where Hemingway so nearly died in 1954 (see above) reputedly still flies a windsock, but it sees little aerial traffic other than ducks and herons flapping overhead. There is now little other evidence of Butiaba's former significance. Even the once-imposing wreck of the SS *Robert Coryndon*, a historic passenger boat built in 1930 named after Sir Robert Coryndon (Governor of Uganda 1918–22), and described by Hemingway as 'magnificence on water' and Sir Winston Churchill as 'the best library afloat', which foundered at Butiaba during the floods of 1962, is gone – dismantled in 2012 and removed for scrap metal. If you feel like making the diversion to Butiaba, the junction lies about 10km past Biso, shortly after the Wanseko Road reaches the Rift Valley floor.

Bulisa and Wanseko At the northern tip of Lake Albert, the small, nondescript towns of Bulisa and, 7km further on, end-of-the-road Wanseko are changing out of all recognition as the area gears up for the exploitation of oil deposits hidden far beneath them. Visible on the surface of each are networks of new tarmac roads that have replaced and extended the rough, sandy tracks that previously permeated the area. The pace of construction is as confusing as it is astonishing and a good rule of thumb is, if a sign for a turning doesn't make sense – Crocodile VI Revision, for example – then it doesn't concern you; it leads to a fenced and highly secured compound in which the attention of its serious-minded occupants is concentrated, in various unfathomable ways, on an ancient rock strata 1,750m beneath them.

The highway from Hoima – the widest oil road of all – terminates at a massive jetty in Wanseko which, being far larger than necessary for the modest vehicle ferry that shuttles across to Panyimur in West Nile, hints at a similar scaling-up of activities out on the lake. What is unchanged is the Rift Valley scenery, Wanseko offering impressive views west across the lake towards the Blue Mountains and north to the Victoria Nile's papyrus-choked Nile Estuary, home to the odd hippo or crocodile, as well as a profusion of birds, notably crowned crane and, with a bit of luck, shoebill. As regards accommodation, Bulisa seems to offer a superior choice of lodgings (page 381).

SOUTH OF HOIMA

Kabwoya Wildlife Reserve and Kaiso-Tonya Some 50km long and up to 15km in width, Kaiso-Tonya is a flat, alluvial plain sandwiched between the Albertine Rift Valley Escarpment and Lake Albert. Once one of the remotest and least accessible parts of Uganda, the area has been shunted into the limelight by the discovery that it lies above a significant oil field. As a result, an excellent surfaced road now links Hoima to the lakeside village of Kaiso, and getting to Kaiso-Tonya and its varied (though admittedly low-key) attractions could not be simpler.

Kaiso-Tonya's main tourist focus is the 87km^2 Kabwoya Wildlife Reserve, a relatively new protected area with an isolated location on the central part of the plain. Kabwoya cannot be mentioned in the same breath as the likes of Murchison Falls or Queen Elizabeth national parks when it comes to viewing big game, and it is seldom visited on rushed tour itineraries. That said, it's a very scenic reserve, and the attractive Lake Albert Lodge offers a variety of outdoor activities, including guided walks, night safaris, birdwatching and fossil hunting, while, logistically, the new road from Hoima makes Kabwoya a viable prospect to break the drive from Murchison Falls to Fort Portal. Entrance costs US$5/10/5 FR/FNR/ROA per 24 hours.

History Kabwoya was originally set aside for conservation in 1963 as part of the 227km^2 Kaiso-Tonya Controlled Hunting Area (KTCHA), which then represented an important component in a migration route along the east shore of Lake Albert between Murchison Falls National Park and the Toro-Semliki Wildlife Reserve. Sadly, however, the large herds of buffalo, waterbuck, Ugandan kob and Jackson's hartebeest once associated with the KTCHA had all but vanished when a survey was undertaken there in 1982. Most of these animals were wiped out by poachers during the long years of civil war, while others dispersed elsewhere as a result of competition with cattle herders. At the turn of the millennium, a belated effort to protect the remnant wildlife led to an 87km^2 portion of KTCHA southwest of the Hohwa River being upgraded in status to form the Kabwoya Wildlife Reserve, while the northeast was rebranded as the Kaiso-Tonya Community Wildlife Area (KTCWA), the country's lowest and most meaningless category of protected area.

In 2002, Kabwoya and the KTCWA was leased to Lake Albert Safaris, a private concessionaire that works in partnership with the UWA and the Hoima District administration to manage the reserve and develop it for tourism. It has been an uphill task for the new management team which, after winching its Land Rovers over the escarpment, took charge of a reserve empty of large mammals other than cattle. The opening of a lodge overlooking Lake Albert coincided with the discovery of oil reserves beneath Kabwoya and the arrival of prominent and ecologically unfriendly exploratory rigs. Despite this, impressive progress has been made in Kabwoya. With the backing of local politicians and Bunyoro royalty, most of the cattle have been relocated from the wildlife reserve to KTCWA, resulting in an increase in wildlife. And while oil rigs are soon expected to open offshore, the significance of Kaiso (a fishing village 5km northeast of the lodge) to the imminent East Africa Crude Oil Pipeline is not without a silver lining since the new surfaced road from Hoima has made Kabwoya highly accessible to tourists.

Flora and fauna Wildlife populations in Kabwoya, though still recovering from years of poaching and encroachment, are steadily on the increase. Of the so-called Big Five, lion and elephant have not been seen regularly in decades, but buffalo and presumably leopard are still present in small numbers. The most common large mammals are Ugandan kob, oribi, Anubis baboon and warthog, but Jackson's hartebeest, waterbuck, bushbuck and common duiker are also present in significant numbers. More localised species include hippo, which have recolonised the lake close to the lodge, and the small numbers of giant forest hog, chimpanzee, black-and-white colobus and vervet monkey that dwell in the riparian forest along the rivers Hohwa and Wambabya. A full bird list has yet to be compiled, but a mix of habitats including grassland, wooded savannah, riverine forest and lakeshore suggests birders are unlikely to be disappointed – indeed, while a survey undertaken in 2009 recorded just 176 species, the lodge claims an unofficial checklist of 460 species for Kabwoya and KTCWA.

Getting there and away Getting to the Kaiso-Tonya plain and Kabwoya Wildlife Reserve from Hoima could not be easier. Simply follow the Butiaba road north out of town for 6km then turn left at the Kyesiga roundabout (⊕ 1.4795, 31.3439) to follow what is quite possibly the best (and least trafficked) road anywhere in Uganda for 76km all the way to the end.

If, on the other hand, you're feeling adventurous, after just 28km you'll reach a more challenging Rift Valley access point at the village of Buseruka (⊕ 1.5481426, 31.1358510), where a right turn signposted for Kikonko Lodge (see opposite) follows an increasingly steep and windy route down the Rift Valley Escarpment. After 2km, you'll pass the lodge, which you may well, and possibly wisely, consider sufficient diversion, before a rough road decorated by rockfalls and hairpin bends leads down on to the Rift Valley plain. There, you can continue to the shores of Lake Albert at Tonya fishing village or turn left to follow a scenic but very poor 4x4 track along the base of the waterfall-streaked escarpment. After 25km – if you make it all the way – you'll rejoin the tarmac road near Kaiso. The safer option to reach Kaiso is to backtrack up the hill to the main highway at Busuruka and continue south. After another 15km, you'll see signs for Hoima International Airport which, currently under construction, is expected to increase traffic levels in the vicinity on completion. Shortly after, you'll pass two tarmac turnings to your left heading into the Rift Valley hinterland, first at the small town of Kabaale and shortly after that, at Kaseke. By the time you read this, both should be surfaced as far as the Hoima–Fort Portal road.

This will be of huge significance for tourism sites in Kaiso-Tonya, making them part of a Murchison–Fort Portal circuit rather than a detour down a lengthy cul de sac.

Just beyond Kaseke, the road descends through a large cutting to the Rift Valley floor, where a UWA gate (⊕ 1.41688, 30.96524) marks the entrance to Kabwoya Wildlife Reserve. The road then runs for 12km to a T-junction (⊕ 1.52473, 30.96238) where you'll see the Joy Max Hotel to your immediate left and Kaiso village to your right. A left turn, still on tarmac, passes the 1.5km signposted track turning to Lake Albert Safari Lodge (⊕ 1.493, 30.94296) after 5.5km, as it loops back towards the UWA gate. Although the last 5km of this section reverts to dirt, it offers a shorter route to/from the lodge with kob and warthogs along the way.

Thanks to the new road and employment opportunities generated by the oil programme, matatus run regularly during weekdays from Hoima to Kaiso village with a reduced service at weekends.

Where to stay and eat *Map, page 349*

Upmarket

Kikonko Lodge (10 rooms) ⊕ 1.5621619, 31.119312; m 0787 999447; e info@kikonko.com; w kikonko.com. An attractive stop between Murchison & Kibale, Kikonko enjoys a giddy view across Lake Albert & the Kaiso-Tonya plain from the top of the steepest & most recently uplifted plane of the Rift Valley Escarpment. If you're looking for more than an overnight stopover, the lodge site may feel quite limited once you've exhausted the appeal of the pool & an unexpected art gallery. It's time to get out & about, either on foot or mountain bike to explore some Rift Valley routes & drive out to visit Kibiro Salt Gardens or a local tea factory. The dining is excellent & your appreciation will be heightened immeasurably if you time dinner to marvel at the apparent appearance of a city below you, as fishermen on the lake attach thousands of floating lights to their nets to attract the diminutive mukene fish. *US$175/260 sgl/dbl*. **$$$$**

Lake Albert Lodge (10 cottages) ⊕ 1.49543, 30.93253; m 0776 729609, 0781 851018; e safarilodgelakealbert@gmail.com; w lodgelakealbert.com. Built by the reserve concessionaire at a stunning location atop 60m-high cliffs rising from the lakeshore, this excellent little lodge with its immaculately thatched cottages is the perfect place to watch the sun set over the Congolese Blue Mountains across 40km of water. A variety of activities can be arranged, including day & night game drives, bush b/fasts, fossil hunting, guided walks & waterfall hikes, while a small swimming pool is a welcome feature in the hot trough of the Albertine Rift Valley. *US$110/175 sgl/dbl HB*. **$$$**

Budget

Joy Max Hotel (11 rooms) ⊕ 1.52405, 30.96241; m 0773 439437. Situated on the left side of the T-junction where the roads for Kaiso & Kabwoya split, this adequate guesthouse has small but clean en-suite rooms with fitted nets & cold shower, as well as a restaurant/bar with terrace seating & pool table. *US$12/18 sgl/dbl*. **$$**

What to see and do In addition to the activities listed for the lodges above, the KTCWA could be explored independently on foot or in a private vehicle by day visitors or those using Joy Max Hotel as a base. Kaiso itself is a rather surreal lakeshore fishing village dominated by traditional reed-and-thatch huts encircled by a pristine loop of asphalt road associated with the soon-to-come oil-drilling industry. Its busy fishing beach is lined with several dozen boats, and there's a large market where you can see fish being dried using traditional methods. A 20-minute walk along a sandy spit northwest of the main fishing beach leads to the tip of the marshy delta through which the Hohwa River enters the lake. In the opposite direction, where the road towards Lake Albert Lodge crosses the Hohwa floodplain about 1km southwest of the Joy Max, is a series of small swamps and pools where you are likely to see kob, baboon and a good variety of water-associated birds.

BUNYORO 1862–77

On 9 September 1862, Speke and Grant became the first Europeans to set foot in the Bunyoro capital of Mruli, near present-day Masindi Port. Grant described the site as 'bare and dreary'. Speke dismissed the royal palace as 'a dumpy, large hut, surrounded by a host of smaller ones…nothing could be more filthy', adding that 'it was well, perhaps, that we were never expected to go there, for without stilts and respirators it would have been impracticable'. Nor were Speke and Grant much taken with the reigning Omukama Kamurasi Kyebambe IV, who – understandably troubled by 'absurd stories which he had heard from the Baganda' about the cannibalistic, mountain-eating, river-drying powers of the white man – left his European visitors waiting for nine days before finally granting them an audience. When finally they met, Speke wrote:

> Kamurasi was enshrouded in his *mbugu* dress, for all the world like a pope in state – calm and actionless. One bracelet of fine-twisted brass wire adorned his left wrist, and his hair, half an inch long, was worked up into small peppercorn-like knobs by rubbing the hand circularly over the crown of the head…Kamurasi asked [Speke's translator] Bombay, 'Who governs England?' 'A woman.' 'Has she any children?' 'Yes', said Bombay, with ready impudence; 'these are two of them' (pointing to Grant and myself). That settled, Kamurasi wished to know if we had any speckled cows, or cows of any peculiar colour, and would we like to change four large cows for four small ones, as he coveted some of ours.

Speke was clearly frustrated by the mixed reception accorded to him by Kamurasi, not to mention the king's endless demands for gifts, but he also regarded him to be more benevolent than the despotic Kabaka Mutesa of Buganda. 'Kamurasi conducts all business himself', Speke wrote: 'awarding punishments and seeing them carried out. The most severe instrument of chastisement is a knob-stick, sharpened at the back…for breaking a man's neck before he is thrown into the lake. But this severity is seldom resorted to, Kamurasi being of a mild disposition compared with Mutesa, whom he invariably alludes to when ordering men to be flogged, telling them that were they in Buganda, their heads would suffer instead of their backs.' The king's attitude towards his family, Speke explained, was somewhat dictatorial:

> Kamurasi's sisters are not allowed to wed; they live and die virgins in his palace. Their only occupation in life consisted of drinking milk, of which each one consumes the produce daily of from ten to twenty cows, and hence they become so inordinately fat that they cannot walk. Should they wish to see a relative, or go outside the hut for any purpose, it requires eight men to lift any of them on a litter. The brothers, too, are not allowed to go out of his reach. This confinement of the palace family is considered a state necessity, as a preventive to civil wars, in the same way as the destruction of the Baganda princes, after a certain season, is thought necessary for the preservation of peace there.

The only other Europeans to visit Bunyoro during Kamurasi's rule were the Bakers (page 387), who arrived at Mruli on 10 February 1864, remarking that it was a 'delightful change to find ourselves in comparative civilisation'. Baker waxed lyrical about 'the decency of the clothing' in the 'thickly populated and much cultivated' kingdom. 'The blacksmiths,' he noted 'were exceedingly clever and used iron hammers instead of stones…they made a fine quality of jet black earthenware, producing excellent tobacco pipes, extremely pretty bowls and also bottles. The huts are very large...made entirely of reeds and straw, and very lofty...like huge inverted baskets, beehive shaped.'

Kamurasi, once again, made a poor impression, badgering his guests with interminable demands for gifts, culminating in the suggestion that Baker leave his wife behind at Mruli as a royal consort. But after the Bakers left Mruli for Lake Albert, they received a message from Kamurasi requesting another meeting, at which it transpired that the 'king' they had met at Mruli was an impostor, installed by Kamurasi for reasons that remain unclear. The real Kamurasi impressed Baker as 'a remarkably fine man, tall and well-proportioned...beautifully clean', but still perturbed by the earlier deceit in Mruli, he also observed in Kamurasi a 'peculiarly sinister expression'. When the king started with the customarily outrageous requests for gifts, Baker 'rose to depart, telling him I had heard that Kamurasi was a great king, but that he was a mere beggar, and was doubtless [another] impostor'.

In April 1872, the recently knighted Sir Samuel Baker returned to Bunyoro as governor of Egypt's Equatoria Province, accompanied by a detachment of Egyptian troops, and charged with stopping the Arab slave trade out of the region. Kamurasi had died three years earlier, to be succeeded by his son Chwa II Kabalega. Baker was impressed by the physical attributes of the new king, describing him as 'excessively neat [and] very well clad, in a beautifully made bark-cloth striped with black... about twenty years of age...five feet ten inches in height, and of extremely light complexion'. Kabalega welcomed Baker's attempt to suppress the slave trade, but he also resented his kingdom being placed under Egyptian sovereignty, and relations between the two men swiftly deteriorated. On 8 June 1872, Kabalega led a surprise attack on Baker's Fort, expecting that resistance would be minimal, since he had craftily arranged for poisoned beer to be supplied to the Egyptian troops on the previous day. But Baker repulsed the attack, and having done so burned Kabalega's capital to the ground. Kabalega retreated southward to Mparo (close to modern-day Hoima), where he established a new capital. A decade earlier, Baker had written of Bunyoro that 'the deceit of this country was incredible'. The apparently unprovoked attack on Masindi only confirmed his earlier judgement.

Sir Samuel Baker, who left Equatoria in 1873, repeatedly expressed a strong antipathy towards Bunyoro's 'cowardly, treacherous, beggarly drunkard' of a ruler, one that went on to mould Britain's colonial policy towards the kingdom. Yet a very different impression is given in the writings of the first European to build a lasting relationship with Kabalega: Emin Pasha, who visited Mparo in 1877 to negotiate the peace between Equatoria and Bunyoro, and then served as Governor of Equatoria between 1878 and 1889. 'I have often visited Kabalega,' he wrote, 'and cannot say that I have ever heard him utter an improper word or make an indecent gesture, or that he was ever rude...Kabalega is cheerful, laughs readily and much, talks a great deal, and does not appear to be bound by ceremony, the exact opposite to Mutesa, the conceited ruler of Buganda. I certainly cannot charge Kabalega with begging; on the contrary he sent me daily, in the most hospitable manner, stores...which although they were intended to last one day, could easily have been made to last us a fortnight. I received a detailed account of all the events that happened during Baker's visit, a curiously different account from that given [by Baker]. I had to listen to a long account of the doings of the Danaglas [Egyptian soldiers]...the sum and substance of all being that [Kabalega] had been continually provoked and attacked by them, although he, as occupant on the throne, was entitled to rule over them.'

Bugoma Forest Reserve Gazetted in 1932, the 411km^2 Bugoma Forest Reserve (w bugomaconservation.org) stands on top of the Albertine Rift Escarpment about 25km southwest of Hoima as the crow flies. Although it ranks among the largest and most biodiverse of Uganda's forests, it was until recently relatively unknown in scientific terms and totally undeveloped for tourism. Bugoma is one of Uganda's most important chimpanzee strongholds, supporting an estimated 550–600 individuals (around 10% of the national population), including one community that has been habituated for tourist visits. The forest also harbours an important population of the endemic Ugandan mangabey, as well as substantial numbers of black-and-white colobus, olive baboon, red-tailed monkey and blue monkey. A small and possibly transient elephant population reflects Bugoma's location on an otherwise rather encroached-upon wildlife migratory corridor connecting Murchison Falls Conservation Area to the Semliki Valley. Other seldom-seen large mammals include buffalo, bushpig, golden cat and side-striped jackal. Highlights of a (probably incomplete) checklist of 260 bird species include Nahan's francolin, white-thighed hornbill, yellow-billed barbet, rufous-sided broadbill, great blue turaco, green-breasted pitta, green-tailed bristlebill, black-eared ground thrush, green hylia and buff-throated apalis.

Although it has been neglected as a tourist destination in the past, Bugoma Forest Reserve is potentially a worthwhile stop travelling between the Fort Portal area and Murchison Falls. A pleasant mid-range lodge was established in the forest several years ago, and it is also quite easily visited as a day trip from any of the lodges associated with Kabwoya Wildlife Reserve. General forest walks to see Uganda mangabey and other forest wildlife have been available for some time, but the long overdue introduction of chimp tracking in 2024 is likely to be a real game-changer, especially for those who don't want to track in the far busier Kibale National Park.

In recent years, Bugoma has made the headlines for all the wrong reasons. Following several years of legal wrangling, the Hoima Sugar Company cleared around 24km^2 of forest in 2020 to make way for a sugarcane plantation. Permission to do this was controversially granted by the so-called National Environment Management Authority, and while a strong legal challenge was mounted by a group of local campaigners called Save Bugoma Forest, it was eventually thrown out by the Uganda High Court. Our understanding is that another, even larger, section of Bugoma is earmarked for the same fate, which makes recent moves to develop the forest reserve as a chimp tracking and ecotourism site, together with a proposal to upgrade it to national park status, doubly welcome.

Getting there and away The focal point for chimp tracking and other guided activities is Mwera Ecotourism Site (⊕ 1.29409, 30.99776). This lies in the heart of the forest about 17km from Kabwoya, a small trading centre that straddles the surfaced road between Kyenjojo and Hoima about 100km north of the former and 45km southwest of the latter. The dirt access road is clearly signposted from Kabwoya, and you need to follow it straight for about 13km, passing Bugoma Jungle Lodge to your left, then cutting through Kisaru Tea Estate, before turning right at a small junction (⊕ 1.2607, 30.97775) that leads to Mwera Ecotourism Site after 4km.

An alternative route to Mwera, coming from the west, branches southeast from the small trading centre of Kaseeta (⊕ 1.39151, 30.99535), which lies about 55km from Hoima on the surfaced road to Kaiso. From Kaseeta, it is about 12km on a fair dirt road south to the ecotourism centre. This makes Mwera less than an hour's drive from either Lake Albert Lodge (30km) or Kikonko Lodge (40km).

Note that the direct road between Kabwoya and Mwera can become very muddy and practically impossible after heavy rain. In that case, your best option coming from Kabwoya is to continue for 18km along the Hoima Road to Kiziranfumbi, then turn left on to an excellent new surfaced 25km link road that connects with the main road to Kaiso about 8km north of Kaseeta.

Where to stay *Map, page 349*

In addition to the lodge listed below, Bugoma Forest can be visited as a day excursion from Lake Albert Lodge or Kikonko Lodge (page 361), as well as from any hotel in Hoima (page 350).

Bugoma Jungle Lodge (5 standing tents) ⊕ 1.23029, 31.03826; m 0787 220107; e info@ugandajunglelodges.com; w ugandajunglelodges.com. This agreeable small ecolodge is located in a large patch of private forest close to the southeastern border of Bugoma Forest Reserve. The 5 comfortable standing tents have an agreeable organic feel & come with thatched roof, private terrace, walk-in netting & en-suite hot shower. A wonderful feature of this lodge is the nocturnal sounds: shrieking tree hyrax in the depth of night & the loud guttural purr of back-&-white colobus at sunrise. The well-wooded grounds feel like an extension of the forest proper & offer good birding, & the staff can arrange guided activities including chimp tracking & forest walks. The lodge lies 6km from the main Kyenjojo–Hoima road along a signposted dirt road that runs west from the small town of Kabwoya. *US$206/312 sgl/dbl FB.* **$$$$**

What to see and do Chimp tracking opened in Bugoma in 2024 and currently costs a modest US$80 FNR/FR while a full-day habituation experience is also attractively priced at US$130. The FNR rates being significantly cheaper than similar activities elsewhere, don't be surprised if they increase as the site becomes busier. Though we are told that the community visited by tourists is fully habituated, as yet we have no feedback about the ease of locating and seeing them from people who have tracked there. Other activities include general forest walks (US$40 pp), birding walks (US$40 pp), mangabey tracking (US$50 pp) and community tours arranged by Bugoma Jungle Lodge (US$15 pp).

MASINDI

The second-largest town in Bunyoro, with a population of around 100,000, Masindi comes across as rather sleepy and economically subdued in comparison with Hoima. Located in the hinterland of the Albertine Rift Valley, 215km northwest of Kampala and 95km south of Paraa, the town has become best known, in tourism circles at least, as the gateway to Murchison Falls National Park. Travellers refuel there, stock up on last-minute essentials (and treats) and may spend the night in Uganda's oldest hotel before heading into the wilderness. However, even this modest status is now under threat with growing numbers of tourists accessing the park via Hoima and Pakwach.

The modern town centre isn't much to look at: a tight grid of erratically surfaced roads emanates from a central market, lined with the faded colonial-era shopfronts that characterise so many small Ugandan towns. Rather more appealing is the green, leafy stretch of suburbia that runs north from the town centre past the defunct golf course. In 1924, Etta Close was charmed by this part of Masindi and its 'European officials [who] live in trim little bungalows with little gardens full of European flowers placed in a circle around a golf course and two lawn tennis courts, the one and only hotel being not far off'. The European officials are long

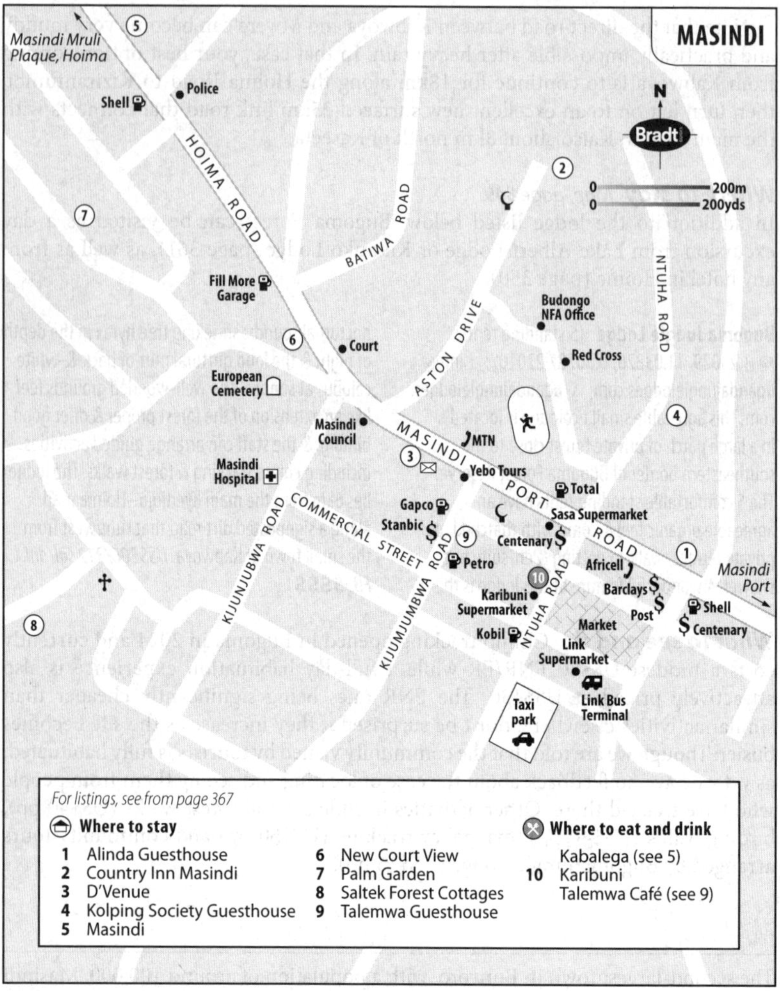

gone, but this description otherwise feels surprisingly apposite today, right down to the renovated Masindi Hotel, built in 1923 and still going strong. Indeed, this is Uganda's oldest surviving hotel – Kampala's Speke Hotel (1925) coming in a close second – and its significance was recognised when it was listed as a National Heritage Site in 2024.

HISTORY Masindi served as the capital of Bunyoro and a major centre of ivory trade prior to 1872, when Omukama Kabalega relocated his court to Mparo to distance himself from the military attentions of Sir Samuel Baker. In the early colonial era, Masindi re-emerged as a thriving hub of trade, thanks to its location at the pivot of three key international transport routes: from Butiaba across Lake Albert to what was then the Belgian Congo, north along the Nile to what is now South Sudan, and southeast across Lake Kyoga to the Busoga Railway (which connected the main line to the Kenyan port of Mombasa). Commerce declined after 1962, when the rising level of Lake Albert enforced the closure of Butiaba Port, and it was further undermined by the havoc wrought on the national economy and transport infrastructure under Idi Amin. Masindi's post-1986 recovery has been restricted by several factors, among them the effective closure of the Congolese and (until recently) South Sudanese borders, the long years of unrest in Uganda north of the Nile, and the collapse of the road–rail–steamer transport network that once linked lakes Albert, Kyoga and Victoria. In recent years, Masindi has been superseded by Hoima, the fast-growing seat of the omukama situated some 50km to its southwest, in terms of both population size and economic vibrancy.

GETTING THERE AND AWAY

To/from Kampala Masindi lies 215km north of Kampala on a surfaced road. The drive can take up to 4 hours, with heavy traffic slowing the first 40km to Luwero. To reach Masindi, follow the Kampala–Gulu Road north for 170km before turning left at a conspicuous junction (⊕ 1.54471, 32.04156) about 200m north of Kafu Bridge. A popular overnight or afternoon stop between Kampala and Masindi, the Ziwa Rhino and Wildlife Ranch (page 172) lies immediately west of the main road about 8km before Kafu Bridge.

Also worth a stop is the excellent Kabalega Diner (page 174), 2km past the turning to Ziwa Rhino and Wildlife Ranch, which, in addition to a wide-ranging menu, boasts clean flushing toilets. This can get busy so large groups might want to phone ahead (m 0774 582296). Prices (and the standard of food) are geared to the tourist market, so if you're on a budget you might check out a supermarket/diner complex and a Shell filling station with a café between Ziwa junction and the Kabalega Diner.

Regular buses run between Kampala and Masindi (3hrs; US$4). The most reliable service is Link Bus (041 4255426; m 0702 855482; w link.co.ug), which operates several departures daily in either direction.

To/from Hoima and Fort Portal Southwest of Masindi, the 260km road to Fort Portal via Hoima is now smooth tarmac all the way. Allow 4 hours in a private vehicle. Though plenty of matatus cover this road, the route is now served by the reliable Link Bus (page 133).

To/from Murchison Falls and Budongo Forest Heading for Paraa (Murchison Falls) on the direct 85km route via the Kaniyo Pabidi sector of Budongo Forest, you need to follow the Hoima Road for 500m beyond the town centre, then turn right opposite the Shell petrol station (the last opportunity to fill up at reasonable fuel prices), then turn left after another 6km. This route is surfaced all the way to Paraa; take note of the strict speed limit when entering the national park. A longer and more scenic 135km route runs through the western part of Budongo Forest and Bulisa; follow the Hoima Road as it loops back south, then turn right on to a dirt road which connects to the tarmac Hoima–Bulisa Road at Biso after 55km. There is no public transport to Paraa along either of the routes described. If coming from Kampala, you're better taking a daily Link Bus to Bulisa/Wanseko via Hoima to find onward transport.

WHERE TO STAY *Map, opposite*

Upmarket

Masindi Hotel (30 rooms) Hoima Rd; m 0772 420130, 0709 752881; e reservations@masindihotel.com; w masindihotel.com. Located almost 1km northwest of the town centre, Masindi's oldest hotel was built in 1923 by the East Africa Railways & Harbours Company as a transit point between ferries on lakes Kyoga & Albert.

Following an effective facelift, the long verandas, airy, tiled en-suite rooms & revamped public areas once again exude the charm of its salad days, when the hotel register read like a Who's Who of celebrity safari-goers (Hemingway, Bogart, Bacall, Hepburn...). The Kabalega Restaurant is attached (see below). *US$45/90 sgl/dbl; Hemingway's Room US$120 dbl B&B.* **$$$**

Moderate

Country Inn Masindi (51 rooms) Aston Dr; m 0772 463203; f. This modern hotel has a pleasant setting in large manicured gardens opposite the old golf course, 5mins' walk from the town centre. It's a bit characterless but has a large swimming pool (which can get rowdy with day visitors at w/ends) & very spacious en-suite rooms with fan & TV. *From US20/34 sgl/dbl B&B.* **$$**

Kolping Society Guesthouse (30 units) Ntuha Rd; m 0782 394992; e masindikhotel@kolpingug.org; w ugandakolpinghotels.com. This well-run Catholic guesthouse stands in large green gardens 200m north of the town centre. Older rooms in the main building are nothing special but come with king-size bed, fitted nets, DSTV & en-suite hot shower. Spacious & contemporarily decorated garden cottages have similar facilities, plus fans, fridge & private balcony, & seem like exceptional value at the price. A fair restaurant & bar is attached. *US$33/40 sgl/dbl room; US$26/32 sgl/dbl cottage. All rates B&B.* **$$**

✷ **Saltek Forest Cottages** (8 units) Off Kijunjubwa Rd; m 0772 589301, 0773 097368; e saltekhotels@grp.com; w saltekhotels.com. Set in a quiet & shady pine plantation 1km west of the town centre, this new complex comprises a main building with small but brightly decorated en-suite dbls & self-catering cottages with well-equipped kitchens. Meals available by arrangement. Exceptional value. *US$32/42 dbl room/cottage B&B.* **$$**

Budget

D'Venue Hotel (14 rooms) Masindi Port Rd; t 046 5420160; m 0751 684370; w dvenuehotel.com. Set in large gardens, this very well-priced hotel has large spotless tiled rooms with fitted nets, TV & en-suite hot shower, set back far enough from the main road that traffic noise shouldn't be an issue. *US$19/22/24 sgl/dbl/twin B&B.* **$**

New Court View Hotel (21 rooms) Hoima Rd; m 0752 446463; e info@newcourtviewhotel@gmail.com; w newcourtviewhotel.com. Best known for its excellent garden restaurant (mains US$8-12), this hotel also has a cluster of en-suite bandas with nets & fans. Though a bit cramped & closely spaced, these have recently been spruced up & the NCVH deservedly remains a popular & affordable stopover on the way to Murchison Falls. *US$23/31 sgl/dbl B&B.* **$$**

Palm Garden Hotel (11 rooms) Off Hoima Rd; m 0774 721532, 0779 791378. This low-key family-run hotel, in a quiet location around the corner from the Masindi Hotel, is very literal about its singular palm, the most impressive feature of the small grassy garden. Clean tiled rooms have fans, nets &, in some cases, DSTV. *US$14 en-suite dbl; US$13 dbl using common showers.* **$$**

Talemwa Guesthouse (20 rooms) Market St; m 0772 406074. This likeable central guesthouse has small but brightly decorated rooms with nets, DSTV, fans & en-suite hot shower. An equally attractive coffee shop is attached (page 368). *US$13 sgl sharing bathroom with 1 other room; US$15/18 en-suite sgl/dbl.* **$$**

Shoestring

Alinda Guesthouse (40 rooms) Masindi Port Rd; m 0782 640100. This long-serving 2-storey guesthouse has clean & otherwise adequate rooms with fans & nets. *US$5 sgl using common shower; US$12 en-suite dbl with TV.* **$**

WHERE TO EAT AND DRINK *Map, page 366*

Kabalega Restaurant Hoima Rd; t 046 5420023; ⌚ 07.00–23.00 daily. Set in the grounds of the venerable Masindi Hotel (page 367), this relatively stylish restaurant has indoor & courtyard seating & a long menu of Indian, Chinese & continental dishes. *Mains around US$9.*

Karibuni Restaurant Ntuha Rd; ⌚ 07.30–22.00 daily. This busy local eatery opposite the market has indoor & outdoor seating. *Mains in the US$2–3 range.*

Talemwa Café Cnr Commercial & Kijumjumbwa rds; m 0772 406074; ⌚ 07.30–22.00 daily. The funky little coffee shop which is attached to the Talemwa Guesthouse (see opposite) serves the best coffee & fruit juice in town, as well as a selection of local dishes. *Mains around US$3.*

SHOPPING Several supermarkets are scattered around the market area. The **Karibuni Supermarket** opposite the market is a good place to stock up before heading to Murchison Falls, as are the **Link Supermarket** next to the Link Bus Terminal and **Sasa Supermarket** on Masindi Port Road.

TOUR OPERATORS

Yebo Tours Cnr of Kijumjumbwa Rd & Masindi Port Rd; 046 5420029; m 0778 345545; e yebotours2002@yahoo.com; masinditravel. Reliable Masindi-based operator which can provide 4x4/minibus hire to Murchison Falls at around US$100/day, inclusive of driver & unlimited kilometres, but exclusive of fuel. It also arranges all-inclusive camping tours to Murchison Falls.

WHAT TO SEE AND DO

Masindi Town Walking Trail If you have a spare afternoon, pick up this informative brochure (compiled by a group of Masindi-based VSO volunteers) from the Masindi or New Court View hotels (page 367), and follow the route described past several historical sites. Central landmarks include an overgrown European Cemetery established in 1894, Masindi or New Court View hotels, which started life in the 1920s as a sick bay for railway workers, and the bustling central market. Probably the most interesting of a few scattered out-of-town sites is the Masindi Mruli (or M'rooli) Plaque, a conical brick monument of unknown progeny that commemorates the site where Omukama Kamurasi met Sir Samuel and Lady Baker in 1864 (page 362). To get there, follow the Hoima Road northwest out of town for 600m past the Masindi Hotel, then turn right into the hectic market suburb of Kijuura, right after another 150m, then left on to a dirt road after 400m just after you pass the Terrace Hotel. The monument stands on the raised grassy ground on the left side of the road less than 200m along this dirt road.

Masindi Port Situated almost 50km east of Masindi town, the eponymous port fringes the 500m-wide Victoria Nile a short distance downriver of the marshy area where it exits Lake Kyoga. The port peaked in importance during the colonial era, when it formed part of a trade network linking Lake Albert to the Kenyan coast, but no commercial boats sail from it today. The surrounding marshes are of potential interest to birdwatchers, and there are quite a few hippos around. You'd be unlikely to have any problems organising a dugout to explore Lake Kyoga, and the Nile River is navigable to the top of Karuma Falls, 70km downstream.

Masindi Port lies just 7km east of the main Kampala–Gulu Road along a dirt road signposted at Rwekunye junction (⊕ 1.70989, 32.02877). Little formal public transport runs there, but you could wait at Rwekunye junction for a lift or a boda, or even walk out from the main road. A free ferry service crosses the Nile between Masindi Port and Kungu on the opposite bank. When it's not running, you can hire a dugout to take you across for a small consideration. From Kungu, a dirt road of variable condition meanders across Lake Kyoga's boggy hinterland in a northeasterly direction, eventually reaching Lira.

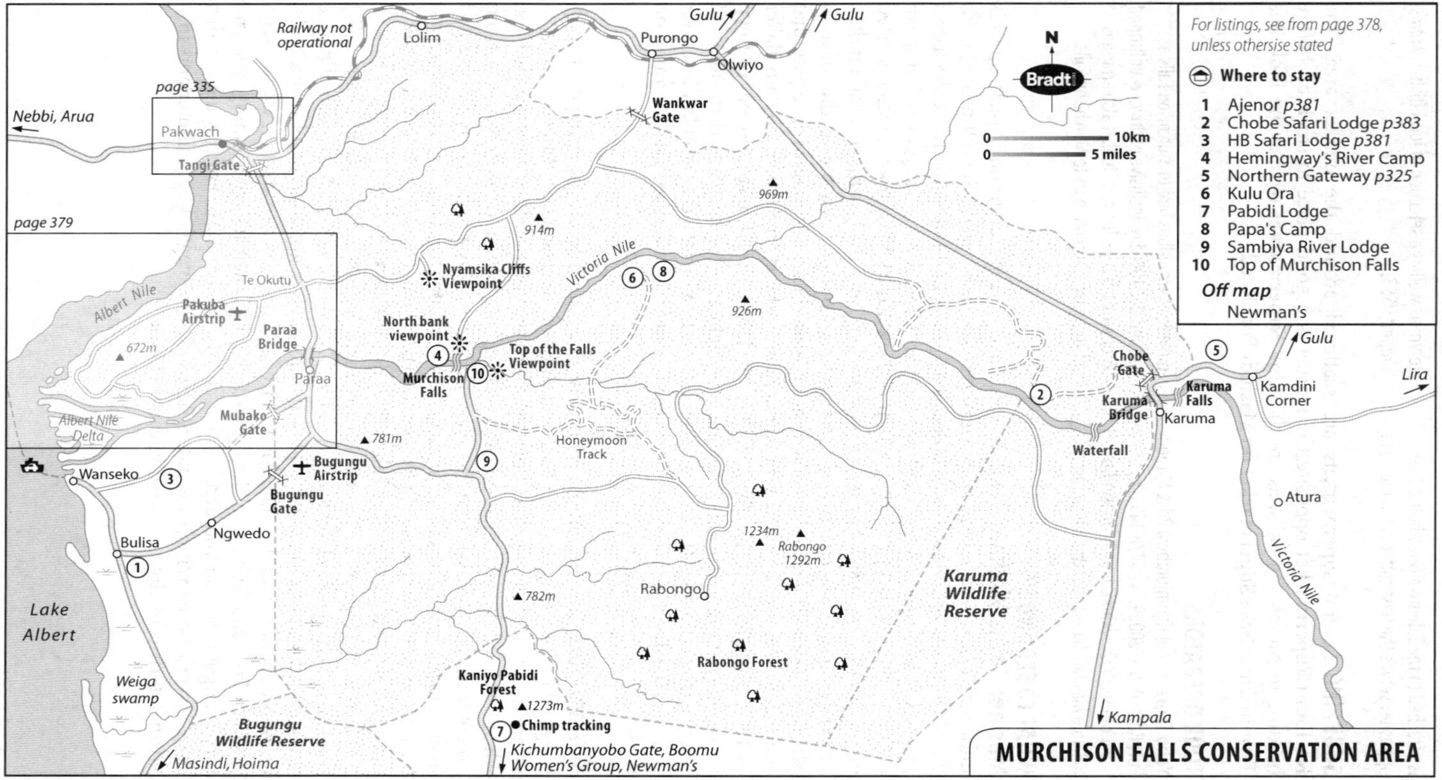
MURCHISON FALLS CONSERVATION AREA
For listings, see from page 378, unless otherwise stated
Where to stay
1 Ajenor p381
2 Chobe Safari Lodge p383
3 HB Safari Lodge p381
4 Hemingway's River Camp
5 Northern Gateway p325
6 Kulu Ora
7 Pabidi Lodge
8 Papa's Camp
9 Sambiya River Lodge
10 Top of Murchison Falls
Off map
Newman's
N
Bradt
0 10km
0 5 miles
Nebbi, Arua
page 335
page 379
Pakwach
Tangi Gate
Railway not operational
Lolim
Purongo
Olwiyo
Gulu
Gulu
Wankwar Gate
969m
914m
926m
Victoria Nile
Nyamsika Cliffs Viewpoint
North bank viewpoint
Top of the Falls Viewpoint
Murchison Falls
Albert Nile
Te Okutu
Pakuba Airstrip
Paraa Bridge
Paraa
672m
Mubako Gate
Albert Nile Delta
781m
Bugungu Airstrip
Bugungu Gate
Honeymoon Track
Wanseko
Ngwedo
Bulisa
Lake Albert
Weiga swamp
Bugungu Wildlife Reserve
Masindi, Hoima
782m
Rabongo
1234m
Rabongo 1292m
Rabongo Forest
Kaniyo Pabidi Forest
1273m
Chimp tracking
Kichumbanyobo Gate, Boomu Women's Group, Newman's
Karuma Wildlife Reserve
Chobe Gate
Karuma Bridge
Karuma Falls
Karuma
Waterfall
Kamdini Corner
Gulu
Lira
Atura
Victoria Nile
Kampala

14

Murchison Falls Conservation Area

Flanking the 100km stretch of the Victoria Nile that arcs west from Karuma Bridge towards Lake Albert, the 3,840km^2 Murchison Falls National Park (MFNP) is the largest protected area in Uganda, and one of the most exciting. Its centrepiece Murchison Falls is the most electrifying sight of its type in East Africa, with the fast-flowing but wide Nile being transformed into an explosive froth of thunderous white water as it funnels through a narrow cleft in the Rift Valley Escarpment. MFNP offers some superb terrestrial and boat-based game viewing, with lion, elephant, hippo, buffalo and giraffe being particularly common along the north bank of the Nile. The park is the largest component in the greater Murchison Falls Conservation Area (MFCA), which also incorporates the collectively managed 750km^2 Bugungu and 720km^2 Karuma wildlife reserves to its south. From a visitor's perspective, the most important feature of Bugungu and Karuma is the Kaniyo Pabidi Forest, which harbours a chimpanzee community that's been habituated for tourists, as well as a number of localised forest birds. For most birders, however, the star attraction among the 550-plus species recorded in the MFCA is the shoebill, an elusive and bizarre waterbird frequently seen in the delta where the Nile empties into Lake Albert.

GENERAL INFORMATION

HISTORY Gazetted in 1952, Murchison Falls National Park formerly fell within the Bunyoro Game Reserve, which was set aside in 1910 following a sleeping-sickness epidemic that forced the local human population to be evacuated. In its early days, Murchison Falls was universally regarded as one of East Africa's most compelling national parks, thanks to its spectacular waterfall, prolific game, and a clutch of outstanding lodges built in the 1950s and 1960s. A census undertaken in 1969 confirms the park then supported some quite incredible large mammal populations, including 14,500 elephant, 26,500 buffalo, 14,000 hippo, 16,000 Jackson's hartebeest, 30,000 Ugandan kob and 11,000 warthog, as well as substantial populations of giraffe, black rhinoceros, and northern white rhinoceros (introduced from the West Nile in the early 1960s). Ironically, the main conservation issue associated with Murchison Falls back then was environmental destruction caused by the overpopulation of elephant, some 3,500 of which were eventually culled, along with 4,000 hippo.

Murchison Falls remained a popular tourist draw in the early days of the Amin regime, but the gates closed in September 1972 when foreign visitors were banned from Uganda. It was at around this time that Amin rechristened both the waterfall and the national park as Kabalega Falls after the former king of Bunyoro (this name still appears on some maps of Uganda, though it fell into disuse in the 1980s).

Following the ban on foreigners, conservation activities within the national park also dwindled, and the wildlife became easy prey for commercial and subsistence poachers. An aerial survey undertaken in 1980, the year after Amin was ousted, indicated that the number of elephant and hippo had been reduced to around 10% of their 1969 levels, while populations of buffalo and most other large mammals had halved. The slaughter continued unabated during the turbulent early to mid 1980s, as a succession of military factions occupied the park and treated it as a moving larder. By 1990, the future of MFNP looked bleak in the extreme: rhino and African hunting dog had been hunted to local extinction and dwindling giraffe and lion populations seemed to be headed the same way, while elephant numbers stood at around 250, buffalo at 1,000, and the total head count of Jackson's hartebeest and Ugandan kob had plummeted to around 3,000 and 6,000 respectively. Furthermore, declining tourist arrivals coupled with ongoing guerrilla activity had rendered all three of the park's lodges inoperative.

The downward trend was reversed in the early 1990s, and although wildlife numbers have yet to reapproach their pre-Amin highs, most large mammal populations have experienced a steady and significant growth since the late 1980s. The early 1990s saw a revival of low-key tourism following the opening of a very basic rest camp (where Red Chilli Rest Camp now stands) on the south bank, and the subsequent construction of the more upmarket Nile Safari Lodge and reopening of Paraa Safari Lodge. Despite this, MFNP's proximity to Acholi enabled the Lord's Resistance Army (LRA) to launch sporadic attacks in the vicinity of Paraa and elsewhere north of the Nile until 2005, when it ceased operations within Uganda. Following the withdrawal of the LRA, Murchison Falls has been regarded to be as safe as anywhere in the country, and several new lodges have opened in the vicinity of Pakwach, Pakuba and Karuma Bridge – areas that were previously practically off-limits to tourists. Currently, the main threats to the park's future are ecological: an increase in poaching and snare setting on the banks of the Albert Nile outside the park, and the consequences of oil extraction within Murchison's prime tourism and wildlife areas (page 392).

GEOGRAPHY AND VEGETATION Although it spans altitudes of 619m to 1,292m, MFNP is mostly quite low-lying by Ugandan standards, and it often experiences stiflingly hot weather, with average daily highs peaking at 32–33°C through December to March. The average annual rainfall of 1,085mm, though significantly lower than in the forests of the southwest, compares favourably with most other East African savannah ecosystems. A long, steady rainy season runs from March to November, when average rainfall hovers at around 100mm per month, most of it falling in the form of short drenching storms. December to February is somewhat drier.

The park's most important geographical feature is the Victoria Nile, which bisects it for around 100km as it flows in a northwesterly then southwesterly direction between lakes Kyoga and Albert. The Nile drops 420m in altitude along this relatively short stretch, which incorporates many rapids and two major cataracts: Karuma Falls immediately east of the Kampala–Gulu Road where it skirts MFNP's eastern gate; and the more explosive Murchison Falls about 30km upriver of Lake Albert. The Nile divides MFNP into two parts of comparable area. North of the river, the vegetation broadly consists of tall, green grassland interspersed with isolated stands of borassus palms, acacia trees and riverine woodland. South of it, denser woodland gives way to closed canopy forest around Rabongo Hill (the park's highest peak) in the southwest, and Kaniyo Pabidi on the Masindi Road. In total, 755 plant species have been identified in the park.

WILDLIFE MFCA's varied habitats support an impressive array of wildlife with at least 144 mammal, 556 bird, 51 reptile and 51 amphibian species. As noted elsewhere, large mammal populations have yet to climb back to their pre-Amin highs, but they are impressive all the same. MFCA is one of the few areas where African elephants are increasing in number: aerial surveys counted 900 individuals in 2010 and 1,330 in 2013, and anecdotal evidence suggests the number has subsequently increased. It also supports the world's largest population of the endangered Rothschild's giraffe (now considered by some authorities to be genetically identical to Nubian giraffe; page 50). This population was recently estimated at around 1,250 individuals but is now probably closer to 1,500. Historically, the giraffes exclusively inhabit the sector north of the Nile, but some 20 individuals were translocated to the southern sector in 2016, with the dual goal of creating a second, viable free-ranging giraffe population in MFCA, and boosting tourism in the south. The buffalo population has increased from fewer than 4,000 in 1999 to more than 10,000 today, while Ugandan kob numbers have leaped from around 7,500 to more than 35,000 over the same period. The lion population is credibly estimated at a healthy 150–200 individuals split across 15–20 prides, and other large predators such as leopard and spotted hyena are present in significant numbers. Also common in varying degrees are Jackson's hartebeest, oribi, bushbuck, waterbuck, Bohor reedbuck and warthog. In the savannah and woodland areas, vervet monkey, Anubis baboon and the localised patas monkey are also present. The Rabongo and Kaniyo Pabidi forests harbour chimpanzees, black-and-white colobus and other forest primates.

The bird checklist is headed in desirability by the shoebill, which is most common along the stretch of river approaching the Lake Albert Delta. Many other water-associated birds are prolific along the river, while raptors make a strong showing on the checklist with 53 species recorded. MFNP is perhaps the best place in East Africa for sightings of the localised white-crested turaco, red-headed lovebird and red-winged grey warbler, all of which are associated with the riparian woodland in the vicinity of the south bank camps running west from Baker's Lodge. Key birds of the northern plains include Abyssinian ground hornbill, Denham's bustard, black-headed lapwing and black-billed barbet, while Kaniyo Pabidi supports a wealth of localised forest birds including chocolate-backed kingfisher, green-breasted pitta and East Africa's only known population of the localised Puvel's illadopsis.

ORIENTATION The focal point of tourist activities is Paraa, which flanks the Nile about 15km downstream of Murchison Falls. This has long been a strategic location as the only river crossing between Karuma and Pakwach and so almost all roads into the park converge there. Now crossed in moments by a bridge, the river was formerly negotiated by a ferry crossing which put lodges on the southern bank at a distinct disadvantage to those on the north side near the prime game viewing areas. The park headquarters lie on the south bank of the Nile at Paraa, as does the park reception/ticket office, the main launch site for boat trips operated by UWA and Wild Frontiers (page 386), and Red Chilli Rest Camp (page 381). Paraa Safari Lodge lies on the north bank at Paraa, as does the launch site for its own boat trips, while the stretch of south bank a few kilometres further downriver, immediately outside the park's Mubako Gate, is lined with a dozen tourist accommodations, starting with Anyadwe House in the east and terminating with Nile Safari Lodge in the west. Other important sites within or bordering MFCA are Kaniyo Pabidi Forest (alongside the road from Masindi about 2 hours' drive south of Paraa), the Top of the Falls Viewpoint (45 minutes' drive east of Paraa), the Buligi and Delta game-viewing circuit (on the north bank west of Paraa) and the small town of Pakwach (overlooking the Albert Nile a

HEALTH

Murchison (and Paraa in particular) has long had a reputation as a malarial hotspot – curiously, one would think, given the low human population in the area. As a result, many expats who wouldn't think of taking prophylactics in heaving Kampala take precautionary pills when visiting Murchison.

few kilometres outside the park's main northern entrance gate). Note that whereas all the aforementioned sites are to some extent visitable from each other, this is not really true of Chobe Safari Lodge, which lies out on a limb in the far east of the park close to Karuma Bridge. Though Chobe is a popular upmarket weekend retreat from Kampala, and a useful potential overnight staging point en route between the capital and Gulu/Kidepo, it cannot really be classed as a safari destination in its own right or as a base for exploring the rest of MFNP.

FEES Entrance to Murchison Falls National Park costs US$35/45/30 FR/FNR/ROA per 24 hours. The standard vehicle entrance fees are also charged (page 9), but only once per entry. Note that although Kaniyo Pabidi Forest, which is split between Bugungu and Karuma wildlife reserves, technically falls outside MFNP, it does fall within the MFCA and full park fees are levied, even if you never actually cross into the national park. Entrance fees can be paid by card or MoMo at any of the gates or at the UWA reservations office in Kampala where cash is also accepted.

FURTHER READING The informative *Murchison Falls National Park Information Guide*, written by Mark Jordhal and published by UWA in 2014, is well worth a look. Sheet 8 in the 'Uganda Maps' series contains maps of the national park and Buligi game tracks plus a wildlife checklist and general information.

GETTING THERE AND AWAY

For many years, the LRA presence in Acholi enforced a southern approach to MFNP via Masindi. Most safaris still do arrive from the south, but since the LRA withdrew, three new routes to the park have opened to the north of the Nile, all accessible from Kampala via Karuma Bridge on the Kampala–Gulu Road. With the exception of the Hoima approach, all direct overland routes between Kampala and Murchison Falls follow the Kampala–Gulu Road at least as far as Kafu Bridge (the junction for Masindi) and can thus be broken up with a day or overnight visit to Ziwa Rhino and Wildlife Ranch (page 172), or a pit stop at the nearby Kabalega Diner.

TOURS Organised fly-in or overland tours to Murchison Falls can be arranged through any operator in Kampala (page 136). For budget travellers, a popular option is the three-day, two-night trips offered by Kampala-based **Red Chilli Hideaway**, using its Red Chilli Rest Camp at Paraa; these start at US$350 per person inclusive of all transport, entrance fees and meals, and incorporate a game drive, a launch trip on the Nile, and a visit to the Top of the Falls Viewpoint.

BY AIR **Aerolink** (☎031 7333000; e info@aerolinkuganda.com; w aerolinkuganda.com) flies daily from Entebbe to Pakuba Airstrip, 15km north of Paraa (US$264/441 sgl/rtn plus taxes). From Pakuba, the plane returns to Entebbe via Kasese and

Kihihi, enabling stops to visit Queen Elizabeth National Park and/or Bwindi while following a dramatic route along the edge of the Albertine Rift Valley.

SELF-DRIVE

Southern approaches Masindi town has long been the main staging point for a visit to Murchison Falls, a status boosted by three trump cards. The first of these is the Ziwa Rhino and Wildlife Ranch, which lies on the approach to Masindi from Kampala, the second is the chimpanzee tracking site at Kaniyo Pabidi on the Masindi–Paraa road and third is the more or less mandatory Top of the Falls Viewpoint, which is accessed further along the same road. That said, Masindi is no longer the automatic choice it once was, following extensive tarmacking along the eastern margins of the Albertine Rift Valley. There are certainly good reasons to consider an approach via Hoima (303km), a route made feasible by a brand-new ribbon of tarmac that drops dramatically down into the Rift Valley to enter the park at Mubako Gate. Though the routes to Paraa via Masindi and Hoima are equidistant from Kampala, the latter is both more scenic and more lightly trafficked, the crawl out of Kampala on the Hoima Road hardly comparing with the congestion on the Masindi/Gulu road. An additional consideration is that the Hoima route enters the park just 8km from Paraa Bridge and most of the approach to the Nile is therefore subject to the national 100km/h speed limit, while once inside Kichumbanyobo Gate near Masindi, you'll be crawling along at a maximum of 60km/h for 65km to Paraa. Secondly, UWA entry fees do not apply to the Hoima route until Mubako Gate is reached, so this is the obvious route if you plan to overnight in one of the lodges just outside this gate before visiting the park. Note that it is also possible to reach Mubako from Masindi (page 376), though this involves a 55km drive on variable murram to join the surfaced Hoima–Mubako Road at Biso.

An additional route to/from Murchison Falls connects to Fort Portal, a drive that is now surfaced all the way. Routes leaving the park from Mubako and Kichumbanyobo gates converge at Hoima then continue south. From the former, it's a total of 320km to Fort Portal, the drive taking about 5 hours. The latter route is slightly longer at 340km and is further slowed by the park speed limit.

If driving yourself to Murchison through Masindi, be sure to fill up with fuel; the last opportunity is the Shell station opposite the turning to the national park. Your next chance for brand-name fuel will be a Shell pump at Paraa Safari Lodge (expensive and subject to a slow, prior-payment system at the lodge) or the Total at Pakwach outside the northern boundary of the park. Hoima should be another mandatory topping up point, though a Total station at Bulisa provides further reassurance.

Visitors entering the park through Kichumbanyobo, Mubako and Tangi gates will find brand new tarmac roads constructed to facilitate oil operations within the national park. The speeds thus enabled obviously pose a risk to wildlife so a speed limit of 40km/h has been established. UWA, appreciating that this is painfully slow on a surfaced road in an empty wilderness, informs us – strictly off the record, you understand – that speeds up to 60km/h are tolerated. Go any faster and a ranger with a speed gun will stop and fine you. This situation may change so make your own enquiries. Our view is that trundling for 25km across the open, game-rich plains between Tangi and Paraa Bridge at 60km/h is both surreal and enjoyable, while the onward, 85km/h drive south through bushier landscapes to Kichumbanyobo Gate is simply tiresome. The oil companies, incidentally, enforce the lower limit for their vehicles, both in the park and as far as Bulisa, so when you see their minibuses and pickups crawling along, feel free to slowly overtake.

Important note: An additional complication regarding access to Murchison Falls concerns the deteriorating bridge spanning the Nile at Karuma Falls. As we go to print, this is closed for major repairs and all traffic to northern Uganda has been rerouted through the national park via Bugungu and Tangi gates. Pending the construction of a new bridge, it is probable that the old bridge will be reopened to light vehicles, though whether trucks and buses will continue to pass through the park is unclear.

Kichumbanyobo Gate (⊕ 1.85323, 31.70965) The 85km tarmac road from Masindi to Paraa, passing through Kichumbanyobo Gate after 22km, takes about 90 minutes if you observe the park speed limit. This is the best choice for those heading to Budongo Eco Lodge and Sambiya River Lodge (respectively 7km and 40km inside the park).

Mubako Gate (⊕ 2.25855, 31.53536) This gate on the western edge of the national park serves a string of riverbank lodges just outside the park. Mubako Gate can be reached via either Hoima or Masindi using routes that converge at Biso at the top of the Rift Valley Escarpment. The Hoima route is surfaced in its entirety while the road between Masindi and Biso is still murram. Both approaches mean that if you are staying at a Mubako lodge, you won't need to pay UWA entry fees to reach your accommodation. At Bulisa, follow a wide tarmac road east out of town, passing through the village of Ngwedo after 8km. After another 2.5km turn left on to another surfaced road and after 6km, you'll find a cluster of lodge signs indicating the 9km dirt road to Mubako Gate.

Bugungu Gate If headed directly to Paraa from Bulisa, ignore the left turn after Ngwedo to follow tarmac all the way to Paraa via Bungungu Gate.

Northern and eastern approaches Murchison Falls can be approached from three gates north of the Nile. These are Chobe Gate on the Kampala–Gulu Road, Wankwar Gate about 10km south of Purongo, and Tangi Gate 3km from Pakwach.

Chobe Gate (⊕ 2.25505, 32.24194) The most easterly entrance to MFNP, Chobe Gate, 2km north of Karuma Bridge on the surfaced Kampala–Gulu Road, is also the quickest gate to reach from Kampala, a 260km drive that takes around 3 hours. It is aimed mainly at people overnighting at Chobe Safari Lodge, which lies 15km further into the park along a relatively well-maintained dirt road. From Chobe Safari Lodge it is possible to continue west all the way to Paraa following the 95km Chobe Track. Be warned, however, that the first 40km of this follows a poor road through dense, tsetse-infested woodland that tends to be poor for game viewing. It may also be closed entirely after heavy rain.

Wankwar Gate (⊕ 2.47214, 31.81893) Situated about 10km south of Purongo, Wankwar Gate is particularly well suited to those travelling between Paraa and Gulu or Kidepo Valley National Park following the recent surfacing of the direct 65km Gulu–Olwiyo Road, which connects to the Karuma–Pakwach Road 4km east of Purongo. It is also a useful access point coming from Kampala: just follow the Kampala–Gulu Road for 200m past Chobe Gate, then turn left on to the sealed Arua Road and follow it for 58km to Purongo. Once there, Wankwar Gate is only 45km northeast of Paraa along a reasonably well-maintained road that usually offers excellent game viewing, even though the first few kilometres pass through a wooded area that sporadically hosts large numbers of tsetse flies. Allow at least 5 hours to the gate driving directly from Kampala, and another hour to reach Paraa.

Tangi Gate (⊕ 2.44579, 31.51188) This once little-used gate is situated only 3km from Pakwach (page 334), a small town set on the west bank of the Albert Nile immediately after it exits MFNP. Tangi Gate has become rather busy in recent years thanks to the opening of a variety of lodges on the east bank of the Albert Nile opposite Pakwach. Although these lie outside the park, they are well situated for exploring it, since Tangi Gate is just half an hour's drive from Paraa and the Buligi game-viewing circuit. Coming from Kampala or Gulu, follow directions for Wankwar Gate as far as Purongo, where instead of branching south on to a dirt road, you need to continue for another 50km west towards Pakwach. Tarmac along this section is currently very poor so if headed for Paraa, a lengthy game drive via Wankwar may be preferable. Tangi Gate lies almost 1km south of the main road along a turn-off signposted 700m before the Pakwach Bridge crosses the Albert Nile. Allow 6 hours to the gate driving directly from Kampala.

PUBLIC TRANSPORT No public transport actually runs into MFNP, and all things considered, wheel-less travellers who can afford it are probably best off joining a budget tour with Red Chilli. If you prefer to go it alone, the closest public transport access point is technically Chobe Gate, on the west side of the Kampala–Gulu Road, 2km north of Karuma Bridge. While any passing bus or matatu could drop you here, your only onwards option is the upmarket Chobe Lodge; and if you can afford a night there, you won't be hitch-hiking to reach it. A far better option is to continue to Pakwach to hire a vehicle to explore the more interesting northwest sector of the park. Alternatively, a daily Link Bus will get you as far as Bulisa via Hoima where you'll need to arrange transportation to enter the park's Mubako Gate.

From Masindi via Kichumbanyobo Gate No public transport runs along the 85km newly surfaced road from Masindi to Paraa via Kichumbanyobo Gate. It is possible, however, to arrange a special hire (expect to pay upwards of US$50 one-way) or to rent a vehicle from Yebo Tours (page 369) from around US$100 per day. You could think about trying to hitch from the junction opposite the Shell petrol station in Masindi, though make sure that the vehicle will be going as far as Paraa to drop you at Red Chilli Rest Camp. Boda bodas are not allowed in the national park, reasonably enough, given the risk of encountering buffalo and other potentially dangerous animals, so you'll need to find four wheels in Masindi to get from Paraa and the chimp-tracking site at Kaniyo Pabidi.

From Bulisa via Mubako Gate A daily Link Bus from Kampala will get you as far as Bulisa or Wanseko via Hoima (US$10). From Bulisa, you could try to hitch a ride with other tourists through to Mubako Gate (25km) or Red Chilli. Alternatively, continue to Wanseko for a shorter (20km) boda ride to the gate. However, the preferred and failsafe option seems to be a special hire to either Red Chilli in the park or Yebo at Mubako (page 381). A vehicle for a game drive can be hired at both of these camps.

From Pakwach via Tangi Gate A choice of buses from Kampala will get you to Pakwach (page 334), the only substantial town to front the Nile along its course from Jinja to the South Sudanese border. Pakwach lies only 3km beyond the Tangi Gate and an hour's drive from Paraa. Global Village Resort (page 337) rents out an open-sided game-viewing vehicle that seats up to nine people. Alternatively, find a special hire to take you into the park, if only to see what is out and about beside the new tarmac road on the way to and from a Nile launch trip at Paraa.

WHERE TO STAY AND EAT

KANIYO PABIDI AND THE MASINDI ROAD *Map, page 370, unless otherwise stated*

The accommodation options listed here all lie alongside the newly surfaced 85km main road between Masindi & Paraa. The lodges are all well situated for activities in Kaniyo Pabidi Forest, make a viable base for the launch trip from Paraa and for exploring the so-called Honeymoon games tracks east of Sambiya. Even with the new bridge at Paraa, speed limits on the tarmac road through the park mean that they are still too distant for early morning game drives north of the river. Backpackers trying to hitch to Paraa or Kaniyo Pabidi will find a couple of reassuring backups just outside Kichumbanyobo Gate.

Upmarket

Pabidi Lodge ☏ 039 3267153; m 0701 426368; e info@ugandalodges.com; w ugandalodges.com. Opening in 2025, this brand new tented camp will offer 10 suites on a sunny hilltop rising out of the forest, 4km south of the Kaniyo Pabidi chimp-tracking trailhead. **$$$$$**

Sambiya River Lodge (26 cottages & 12 bandas) ⊕ 2.1816, 31.69871; m 0764 001797/0703 589370; e reservations@sambiyariverlodge.com; w sambiyariverlodge.com. This reasonably priced lodge sprawls across large wooded grounds off the main road to Paraa, 35km north of Kaniyo Pabidi. Though it lacks a Nile frontage, it is only 15mins' drive from the Top of the Falls Viewpoint, a great place to be at sunset. It is also conveniently located for those who want to use a single base to track chimps at Kaniyo Pabidi & do a launch trip out of Paraa. The stone-&-thatch en-suite bandas are colourfully decorated & come with fans, nets & screen doors. A canopy walkway has recently been completed (free to guests, otherwise US$8) & a zipline too (US$16). *From US$235/318 FB; low-season discounts apply.* **$$$$**

Shoestring

Boomu Women's Group [map, page 330] (10 rooms) ⊕ 1.8499, 31.70888; m 0772 448950; e boomuwomensgroup@yahoo.com. Traditional accommodation & experiences don't come any more authentic than at this community tourism project located immediately outside Kichumbanyobo Gate. A traditional mango-shaded homestead brightened by flowers & shrubs, it provides accommodation in small, simple & spotless thatched bandas, as well as an interesting variety of activities & demonstrations offering insights into rural Ugandan life. *US$20 pp B&B*. **$**

Newman's [map, page 370] m 0772 618603. If learning to weave a basket isn't your thing, you should find basic self-catering rooms on the other side of the road by the time you read this. Call for prices.

Camping

Top of Murchison Falls ⊕ 2.27618, 31.68962. Visitors with a private 4x4 vehicle can pitch a tent at this secluded & little-used campsite set a couple of hundred metres upstream from the waterfall. It is a beautiful location above a natural pool & there's great birding – look out for the localised bat hawk towards dusk. *US$10 pp*. **$**

KISANGANI *Map, page 370*

Newly opened to tourism in 2023, Kisangani is a remote low-usage zone situated to the east of the main road from Masindi to Paraa. It is accessed from the Honeymoon Track by an unbridged crossing of the Murchison (also known as Mopina) River, whose confluence with the Nile lies just upriver of Murchison Falls. Kisangani is the site of a private 8ha riverside concession that has been leased to Wildplaces. One camp is already operational & another will be opened by the time you read this. Although the rest of Kisangani is theoretically open to all, an additional entrance fee is charged to enter a surrounding low usage zone, so it effectively functions as a 400km^2 private reserve used almost exclusively by the 2 Wildplaces camps. Scenically, it protects an attractive area of rolling grassland & woodland running south from the forested bank of the Nile. Plentiful wildlife includes buffalo, giraffe, hippo, warthog, Ugandan kob, hartebeest, waterbuck, oribi, olive baboon & black-&-white colobus. Elephants also pass through regularly, & the resident lion prides (which sometimes climb trees) are already overcoming their initial shyness & becoming very relaxed around vehicles.

Kulu Ora ⊕ 2.35669, 31.84967; ☎ 041 4251182; m 0772 489497; e info@wildplacesafrica.com; w wildplacesafrica.com. Scheduled to open in late 2024, this 10-unit camp lies about 1km downstream of Papa's Camp. It is likely to have a similar bush feel to its neighbour, & to offer identical activities, but will be more luxurious, with better amenities which include a swimming pool. **$$$$$$**

✷ **Papa's Camp** ⊕ 2.36235, 31.84177; ☎ 041 4251182; m 0772 489497; e info@wildplacesafrica.com; w wildplacesafrica.com. Highly recommended to those seeking an untrammelled wilderness experience, this wonderfully isolated bush camp is named after the writer Ernest 'Papa' Hemingway (page 358). Exclusive as opposed to luxurious, it consists of 5 standing tents perched alongside a raging stretch of the Nile 26km upriver of Murchison Falls. The jungle-lined riverbank is alive with birds & monkeys, while hippos grunt in the shallows between the roaring rapids. The old-school tents

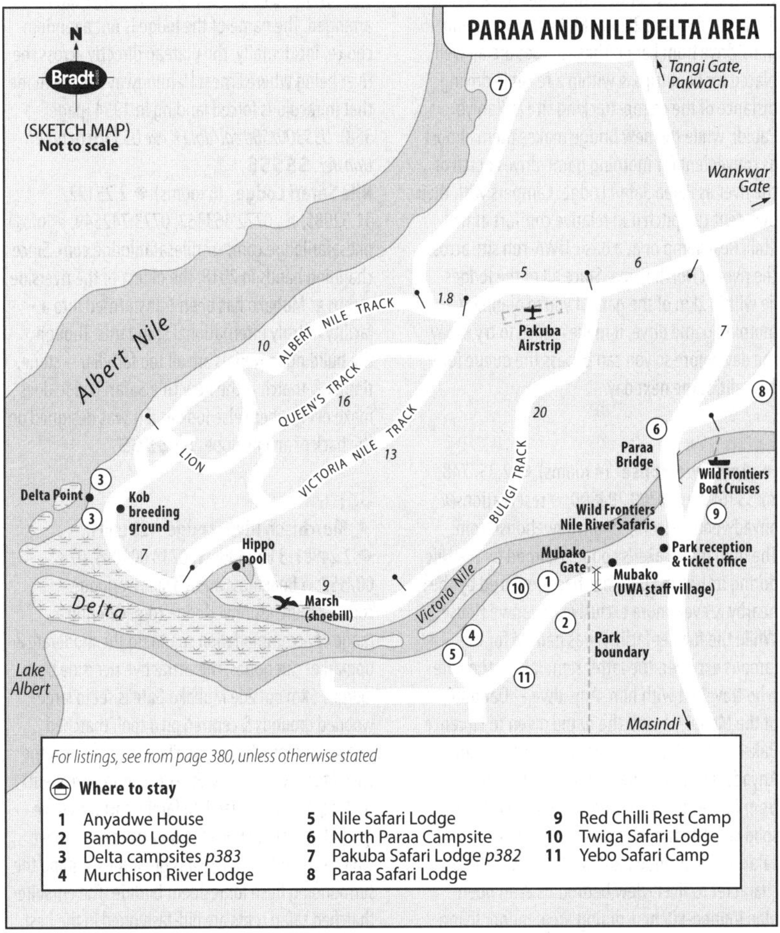

here are simply but comfortably furnished, & come with bucket showers, solar lighting & a small private riverside veranda. Activities include guided game drives & walks in the Kisangani sector, & day excursions to Paraa & the Top of the Falls. There are also plans to install a boat to punt visitors across to the north bank for game drives there. All activities, meals & drinks are included in the room rates. **$$$$$$**

PARAA AND THE VICTORIA NILE *Map, page 379, unless otherwise stated*

Of the accommodation listed here, only 3 facilities lie within the park. Paraa Safari Lodge lies just north of the Paraa Bridge, Red Chilli Rest Camp just south, while Hemingway's Camp lies upriver near the Falls. All other options lie just outside the park, close to the south bank of the Victoria Nile & clustered within 2km of Mubako Gate, about 15 mins' drive from Paraa. These lodges are all well placed for boat trips & within a feasible driving distance of the chimp-tracking site at Kaniyo Pabidi, while the new bridge makes them almost as convenient for morning game drives north of the river as Paraa Safari Lodge. Campers with their own tent can pitch it in relative comfort at Red Chilli Rest Camp or at a basic UWA-run site across the river at North Paraa. Since all of the lodges lie within 2km of the gate, if you're planning a morning game drive, it makes sense to try & pay the day before so you can bypass the queue for formalities the next day.

Exclusive

✷ **Anyadwe House** (4 rooms) ⊕ 2.257748, 31.531659; m 0709 294800; e reservations@anyadwehouse.com; w anyadwehouse.com. The upmarket Baker's Lodge, claimed by the Nile during its rise in 2020, has been replaced by the nearby & even more exclusive Anyadwe House. While the former facility was named for the famous explorer, the latter remembers the wife who travelled with him, Anyadwe – 'Daughter of the Moon' – being the name given to Florence Baker by the Acholi people. With just 4 rooms, Anyadwe House is the luxurious Nile-side home from home you always dreamed of. While the solid construction eschews the usual African safari style, antique hardwood furniture lends character to river-view bedrooms & an open-plan lounge-kitchen-dining area. Indoor living is just 1 option; alternative settings include the river-facing veranda, a lounge-balcony upstairs & the swimming pool terrace. Self-catering is an option; alternatively on-site staff will take charge. Anyadwe is 1min from Mubako Gate, with Paraa Bridge & the launch jetties just 10mins beyond. **$$$$$**

✷ **Hemingway's River Camp** [map, page 370] (9 rooms) ⊕ 2.25122, 31.52085; m 0781 851018, 0773 742549; e info@murchisonrivercamps.com; w murchisonrivercamps.com. With an elevated site overlooking the Nile at the head of Fajao Gorge & accessible only by river launch, this new facility enjoys the most exciting location of any camp in Uganda. The west-facing cottages overlook the Nile crocodile banks & face the sunset, while to the east, a 30min nature trail leads to a full-frontal view of Uhuru Falls. Fishing in the gorge can be arranged. The name of the lodge is not a random choice, incidentally, the plateau directly across the river being where Ernest Hemingway's plane made that miraculous forced landing in 1954 (page 358). *US$300/500 sgl/dbl FB exc US$50 rtn boat transfer*. **$$$$$**

Nile Safari Lodge (8 rooms) ⊕ 2.25122, 31.52085; m 0772 363362, 0773 742549; e info@nilesafarilodge.com; w nilesafarilodge.com. Since changing hands in 2018, the oldest of the riverside camps at Mubako has been transformed into a facility of truly international standards. Though the building materials are all too familiar – stone, timber & thatch – the new Nile Safari Lodge does make everywhere else look as if it was designed on the back of an envelope. **$$$$$$**

Upmarket

✷ **Murchison River Lodge** (20 units) ⊕ 2.24981, 31.52496; m 0714 000085, 0782 007552; e bookings@murchisonriverlodge.com; w murchisonriverlodge.com. Offering a range of accommodation spanning the moderate & upmarket categories, this attractive riverside bush lodge 1.5km outside Mubako Gate is set in large wooded grounds & centred on a cool, thatched restaurant/bar which is ideally placed to enjoy the view of the River Nile & the consistently excellent cooking. Spacious thatched family cottages have ground-floor twin beds & a mezzanine dbl above, while a veranda at the rear is great for scanning the surrounding bush for resident birdlife. The en-suite thatched safari tents are old-fashioned in the best possible way, while simpler furnished tents at the back of the site use shared facilities in a palatial bathroom block. Facilities include a swimming pool & viewing platform. *US$200/330/430/530 cottage for 1/2/3/4 people FB; US$155/260/350 sgl/twin/trpl thatched safari tents FB; US$90/150 tent sgl/twin using shared facilities FB. Special family packages available for families with children up to 16 yrs.* **$$$$**

Paraa Safari Lodge (57 rooms) ⊕ 2.29013, 31.57286; ☎ 0312 260261; e reservations2@marasa.net; w paraalodge.com. Overlooking the north bank of the Nile at Paraa, this dbl-storey monolith was reconstructed in 1997 using the shell of a derelict lodge built in 1959. Indeed, the feel of solidity makes it a reassuring choice for nervous first-time visitors to Africa, while children will enjoy the large swimming pool with its view over the Nile. Logistically – though the new bridge makes this less of a selling point – Paraa Lodge is the most convenient accommodation to combine game drives in the north with boat trips on the river. *From US$300/440 sgl/dbl FB. Safari tents US$340/510 FB.* **$$$$$**

Twiga Safari Lodge (10 rooms) ⊕ 2.25432, 31.53188; m 0755 098635, 0779 492404; e info@twigasafarilodge.com; w twigasafarilodge.com. This pleasant lodge is found just outside the park at Mubako, in lightly wooded grounds that run down to a papyrus-fringed river shore. Large standing tents are set on wooden platforms & come with walk-in nets & private balcony. A pool has recently been added. *US$210/340 sgl/dbl FB.* **$$$$**

Moderate

Bamboo Lodge (14 units) m 0788 829730; e bamboovillagemubako@gmail.com. Conveniently located near Mubako Gate but some distance from the river, this new facility occupies a large site in which hippo-grazed lawns are interspersed with stands of bamboo. Thatched cottages of earthy, adobe-rendered construction are smallish but adequate, while an accommodation block contains generously proportioned rooms with high, airy ceilings that open on to private verandas through a mesh frontage. A swimming pool is a welcome feature while a lofty, elevated deck reveals the views lacking at ground level. *US$125/180 sgl/dbl cottage; US$160/260 sgl/dbl room. All rates FB.* **$$$–$$$$**

Budget

Ajenor Hotel [map, page 370] m 0774 442285. Located in fast-changing Bulisa town, just 16km from Bugungu Gate, this small hotel (& several like it) show that you don't have to sleep under a thatched roof to enjoy a trip to Murchison Falls National Park. *US$25 sgl shared facilities; US$32/40 en-suite sgl/dbl B&B.* **$$**

HB Safari Lodge [map, page 370] ⊕ 2.199890, 31.463911; ☎ 031 2202903; m 0765 266186. Located on a new tarmac road midway between Wanseko & Mubako, this new setup isn't a safari lodge at all but accommodates oil-related workers. It is, nonetheless, conveniently located for the national park's western gates & is very reasonably priced. The compact, prefab 'pods' won't be to everyone's taste, but it's hard to fault the more spacious 'banda' rooms. The large bar/dining room/DSTV lounge gets lively on Sun afternoons when local expats are released from their (mostly teetotal) oil camps. *US$25 sgl pod B&B, US$32/45 sgl/dbl banda room B&B.* **$$**

✱ **Red Chilli Rest Camp** ⊕ 2.27702, 31.56434; ☎ 031 2202903; m 0772 509150; e reservations@redchillihideaway.com; w redchillihideaway.com. This scion of Kampala's Red Chilli Hideaway (page 142) provides pocket-friendly bandas & tents in the heart of the park. Chilled drinks & meals are served in the welcome shade of a thatch restaurant & while river views are rather distant, it's only 10mins' walk to the launch jetty. The camp itself is frequented by warthog, hippos & a wide variety of birds. It's frequently fully booked so make an advance reservation. If you've arrived without your own wheels & can get a group together, Red Chilli has an open-top, 6-seater game-viewing vehicle for hire (US$130 for 4hrs). *US$55/65/90/100 en-suite banda sleeping 2/3/4/5 people; US$35/40 twin tent/banda with shared facilities; US$8 pp camping. All rates bed only.* **$$**

Shoestring

Yebo Safari Camp (12 rooms) ⊕ 2.24798, 31.52133; ☎ 046 5420029; m 0778 345545; e yebotours2002@yahoo.com; f masinditravel. Run by Masindi-based Yebo Tours (page 369), this distinctly rustic lodge is set 500m back from the river, 2km west of Mubako Gate, where a dining shelter provides meals & much-needed shade; book in advance so they can turn on the fridge to cool the drinks. With the traditional en-suite mud-&-thatch bandas looking a bit tired, the main attraction is the money saved by nipping in & out of Mubako Gate to do Murchison in a single day. *US$50 pp FB.* **$$**

Camping

North Paraa Campsite This public campsite stands close to the bridge on the north bank, making it well placed for morning drives to the delta. Book in advance to ensure the water tank is filled. *US$10 pp.* **$**

THE ALBERT NILE AND NORTHWEST

Map, page 335, unless otherwise stated

Of the places listed here, only Pakuba Safari Lodge, set on the east bank of the Albert Nile between the Buligi Circuit & Tangi Gate, actually lies within MFNP. The other lodges are all clustered on the east side of the Albert Nile opposite Pakwach, between 5km & 10km north of Tangi Gate. Any of the lodges listed would make a good base for a day trip combining a game drive on the Buligi Circuit with a boat trip from Paraa. For budget-conscious travellers, the lodges outside Tangi Gate are mostly moderately priced & their location would allow you to get a good look at the park while paying only 1 day's entrance fee. If they're too pricey, then the selection of inexpensive town lodges listed under Pakwach (page 336) are equally well positioned for day trips into MFNP.

Moderate

Bwana Tembo Safari Camp (10 units) ⊕ 2.4799, 31.54309; m 0772 957850; e info@bwanatembo.com; w bwanatembo.com. Owned & managed by a hands-on Italian family, this relaxed hilltop camp 7km north of Tangi Gate is named after the elephants that regularly pass through at night, & it also offers fabulous views towards the papyrus-lined river 1km to its west. The circular en-suite cottages are clean & comfortable, while en-suite standing tents offer a more canvas-soaked safari ambience. Set menus have a strong Italian flavour. *US$85/125 sgl/dbl cottages & safari tents FB.* **$$$**

✷ **Fort Murchison** (12 rooms, 12 standing tents) ⊕ 2.4891, 31.53613; ☎ 031 2294894; m 0773 447343; e booking@naturelodges.biz; w naturelodges.biz. Situated on a rise overlooking the Nile about 10km north of Tangi Gate, this architecturally innovative lodge is inspired by the chain of riverside forts established by imperialists & traders along the Nile corridor, & looking out from the 1st-floor rooftop lounge, it doesn't take much imagination to picture General Gordon's exploratory flotillas of canoes & steamships coming into sight. A bold break from the usual safari style, the imposing storeyed gatehouse is a good take on a period etching of Dufile Fort (page 345), & it serves excellent 3-course meals in generous quantities. The brightly decorated en-suite rooms come with fitted nets, fans & private river-facing balcony, while the simple standing tents with twin bed, nets & thatched roof are hard to fault at the price. A swimming pool was recently added. *US$150/175 sgl/dbl room; US$60/85 sgl/dbl tent with shared facilities; US$40 pp camping. All rates FB.* **$$$–$**

Nile Breeze Bamboo Lodge (17 cottages) m 0776 920729; w nilebreezelodge.com. With cottages scattered across a large grassy site broken up by stands of bamboo (planted to convert the breeze from the river into a peaceful rustle), & monoblock paved roads & the odd golfcart to get around, this smart new development has a country club feel. The wildlife themes of individual cottages are brought to life by original artwork, daubings limited by neither conventional talent nor parochial checklists; it's definitely the first time we've mentioned a Tiger Cottage in this book. Trips are offered on the lodge speedboat which looks tremendous fun. *US$130/200 sgl/dbl B&B.* **$$$$**

✷ **Pakuba Safari Lodge** [map, page 379] (41 rooms) ⊕ 2.38969, 31.48535; ☎ 041 4253597; m 0706 725822; e info@pakubasafarilodge.com; w pakubasafarilodge.com. Set in magnificent isolation on the east bank of the Albert Nile 20km downstream of where it exits Lake Albert, the current incarnation of Pakuba Lodge opened in 2013 near the ruins of a long-abandoned 1960s government hotel. AC is a welcome bonus in the spacious, stone-flagged rooms, while a tempting swimming pool provides further scope for keeping cool. The park-like woodland around the lodge is teeming with kob & giraffe, & has a good reputation for leopard sightings. It's also the closest lodge to the Buligi Circuit & the new tarmac means that it's only 30mins' drive from the boat launch at Paraa. There are slicker & more stylish options in Murchison, but nothing else offers such good value in the thick of the wildlife action. *US$200/270 sgl/dbl FB.* **$$$$**

Tilenga Safari Lodge (15 cottages) m 0789 390350; e bookings@kikorongosafarilodge.com; w tilengasafarilodge.com. This attractive new lodge is located on the main Karuma–Pakwach road, 1km east of the Tangi junction. Well thought out public areas include a spacious thatched lodge building & pool, while the interiors of the comfortable, clay-tiled cottages are enhanced by the use of traditional materials & fabrics, king-sized beds & AC. Though the adjacent highway allows excellent access to the park, some traffic noise is audible; the rooms, however, which are at the back of the site, seem to be exempted. *From US$210/285 sgl/dbl FB*. **$$$$**

Budget

Bar Lyec (10 rooms) m 0778 159479; e barlyecsafarilodge@gmail.com. At the northern end of the string of lodges on the 'East Bank' opposite Pakwach, the sweeping river panorama from Bar Lyec's hillside site is the best of the lot. Thatched roofs keep temperatures down inside the en-suite cottages, while a swimming pool offers further opportunities to keep cool. *US$100 sgl/dbl cottage FB*. **$$$**

Heritage Safari Lodge (21 rooms) ⊕ 2.47969, 31.53773; ☎ 041 4200026; m 0752 890009; e info@heritagesafarilodge.com; w heritagesafarilodge.com. Perched above the Albert Nile 6km from the Tangi Gate, this agreeable lodge is the pick of a growing number of (unlisted) budget lodges along the east bank of the Nile. With accommodation in mud-&-thatch bandas on patches of bare, carefully swept ground, it's also as close as you're likely to get to sleeping in a traditional Jonam homestead. Happily, the quest for authenticity does not extend inside the comfortable en-suite cottages. Although the lodge lies outside the park, the river corridor is frequented by elephant & hippo, & boat trips (US$120 for up to 6 people; US$20 per additional passenger) come with a fair chance of spotting both these large mammals as well as shoebill. Good value. *US$70/100 sgl/dbl FB*. **$$$**

Hornbill Bush Lodge (5 bandas) ⊕ 2.46234, 31.52657; m 0702 747758, 0772 482462; e info@woodlandlodgesug.com; w woodlandlodgesug.com. One of 3 low-key lodges found down a side track off the Fort Murchison road. A safari vehicle is available for hire (morning game drive US$150). *US$90/120 sgl/dbl FB*. **$$$**

Camping

Delta campsites [map, page 379] ⊕ 2.27413, 31.37866. Not for the faint of heart, these amenity-free campsites are located to the north & south of Delta Point, with the northern one being only 1min's drive from the toilet block used by day visitors. The sites lie in prime game-viewing territory; plenty of noisy nocturnal wildlife activity is guaranteed & dawn/dusk game drives can be undertaken before/after the 1st/last vehicles from Paraa. You need your own vehicle & camping gear. An armed ranger for protection must be arranged at Paraa. *US$40 pp*. **$**

CHOBE SECTOR *Map, page 370*

Upmarket

Chobe Safari Lodge (63 rooms) ⊕ 2.24243, 32.13573; ☎ 041 4259390/4/5; m 0772 788880; e reservations2@marasa.net; w chobelodgeuganda.com. Situated in the far east of the park, 15km from Chobe Gate & Karuma Bridge, Chobe Safari Lodge, built on the site of an older 1960s lodge, has a magnificent setting on a jungle-lined stretch of the Nile that rushes by audibly between dozens of islands & minor rapids. The stylish décor, well-managed spa, classy restaurant, sumptuous accommodation (in rooms or luxury standing tents) & a quartet of tiered swimming pools make it a popular upmarket venue for w/end breaks & conferences from Kampala. Plenty of wildlife frequents the well-wooded grounds, notably giraffe, buffalo, hippo, warthog & black-&-white colobus. Unfortunately, the location is otherwise unpromising for wildlife viewing: this stretch of the Nile is too rough for boat trips & the limited road network passes through thick woodland where tsetse flies are rife, while Paraa & the Buligi Circuit are about 3hrs distant. *From US$199/345 sgl/dbl B&B; add US$24 pp for FB*. **$$$$$**

WHAT TO SEE AND DO

MFCA offers a diverse selection of activities to visitors. Most popular, and best undertaken in the afternoon with the sun in the west, is the atmospheric and all-but-obligatory return boat trip that follows the Nile from Paraa to the base of Murchison Falls. This is closely followed in the must-do stakes by a morning game drive on the Buligi Circuit, a network of game-viewing tracks traversing the 10km-wide peninsula that separates the Victoria and Albert Niles as they course in and out of Lake Albert. For those with more time, other highlights include chimpanzee tracking or forest birding at Kaniyo Pabidi, the spectacular Top of the Falls Viewpoint and associated Honeymoon Track on the south side of the river, the boat trip downriver from Paraa to the bird-rich Lake Albert Delta, and the oft-neglected game-viewing road running northeast of Paraa towards Wankwar Gate.

Those with their own vehicle are permitted to undertake game drives without an armed ranger, though safari novices might feel it is worth the investment of US$20 to have some assistance navigating the often poorly marked game-viewing tracks, and to help locate well-camouflaged animals such as lion and leopard. For those without their own transport, organised game drives are offered by Red Chilli Rest Camp (page 381) or (more expensively) Paraa Safari Lodge (page 381).

KANIYO PABIDI (EASTERN BUDONGO) FOREST The 28km^2 Kaniyo Pabidi Forest, which lies in the south of MFCA, split between the Bugungu and Karuma wildlife reserves, is essentially a northeastern extension of the larger Budongo Forest Reserve. It harbours similar (though not identical) fauna and flora to Budongo, and because it has never been logged it contains a far higher proportion of large buttressed mahogany and ironwood trees. Forest primates include black-and-white colobus, red-tailed monkey and blue monkey, while large troops of olive baboon are a regular sight along the main road through the forest. It also supports Uganda's densest chimp population, recently estimated at around 6.5 individuals per square kilometre, along with an alluring selection of forest birds. The focal point for tourist activities in Kaniyo Pabidi is located on the east side of the surfaced road to Paraa, 29km north of Masindi (via Kichumbanyobo Gate), and can easily be visited driving between the two, or as a day trip from either. Chimp-tracking permits and other activities at Kaniyo Pabidi can be booked and paid for online (w ugandalodges.com/book-online) or arranged on the spot, assuming they are not sold out in advance.

Chimp tracking Kaniyo Pabidi supports two chimpanzee communities, each estimated to number around 90 individuals, and the one centred closest to Budongo Eco Lodge has been habituated for tourist visits since the late 1990s. Up to 36 permits are issued by the lodge daily, with trackers setting off in up to six guided groups, each comprising up to six people, at 08.00 then again at 14.00, though they can be quite flexible about departure times when not fully booked. Tracking at Kaniyo Pabidi is not quite as reliable as it is at Kibale Forest, but the terrain is flatter and easier, and the success rate currently stands at around 80%, with most groups locating chimps within an hour of setting off, in which case the full activity should take around 3 hours. It may take longer if the chimps are more difficult to locate. Permits cost US$130; a full-day habituation experience (6–12hrs, starting at 07.00; max 6 participants) is US$230 per person.

Bird walks One of the top forest birding sites in Uganda, Kaniyo Pabidi protects a similar range of species to Budongo Forest. The best place to look for birds is around the lodge, especially the gallery forest along the main road, which offers good views into the canopy and can be explored freely and without a guide if you so choose. Among the more interesting species we've observed here are African shrike-flycatcher, chestnut wattle-eye, Narina trogon, little greenbul, chestnut-winged starling, grey apalis, dwarf and pygmy kingfishers, and a great many forest sunbirds and hornbills. A local speciality is Puvel's illadopsis, which is quite common in Kaniyo Pabidi, but known from no other locality in East Africa. This bird is quite easily located by call, so ask your guides to listen out for it if you are hoping to see it. The extremely localised and magnificently garish green-breasted pitta has also been recorded. To stand a realistic chance of seeing these and other more elusive denizens of the forest interior, you're best off organising a formal bird walk with a specialised guide through the lodge. This costs US$60/110 for a half/full day.

SOUTH OF THE NILE The main attraction on the southern side of the Nile is the spectacular Top of the Falls Viewpoint. The turning lies about 30 minutes' drive from Paraa on the newly surfaced road to Masindi, with the falls 15 minutes beyond, also on tarmac. A visit to this viewpoint can also be tagged on to the boat trip to the base of the falls by prior arrangement. Game drives south of the river are possible but, other than the Honeymoon Track described on page 386, are complicated by dense bush and a local prevalence of tsetse flies.

Top of the Falls Viewpoint Murchison Falls is an impressive sight from the boat, but for sheer sensory overload, be sure to visit this spectacular south bank viewpoint, which is reached along a newly surfaced 15km road that branches north from the main Paraa Road at a signposted junction (⊕ 2.18259, 31.69194) about 500m past Sambiya River Lodge. From the car park (⊕ 2.27718, 31.6872), a short footpath leads downhill to the waterfall's head and a fenced viewpoint from where one can truly appreciate the staggering power with which the Nile crashes through the narrow gap in the escarpment, not to mention the deafening roar and voluminous spray it generates. Although you've already paid park entrance, you'll be charged an additional US$10 to view the Top of the Falls.

From this main viewpoint, a longer footpath, perhaps 20 minutes' walking time, leads to Baker's View on a ridge looking directly towards Murchison Falls, as well as the broader Uhuru Falls a hundred metres or so to the north. Historical records suggest that this latter falls was an impermanent (possibly seasonal) feature until the great floods of 1962, since when it has been more-or-less constant, though it is still subject to dramatic variations in volume. The face-on view of the two cataracts – separated by a lushly forested hillock – is truly inspiring, but surpassed perhaps by following another footpath down to the base of the short gorge below the two waterfalls. If you want to check out all the viewpoints, allow at least 2 hours – ideally in the afternoon, when the sun is better positioned for photography.

There is not much wildlife in the vicinity of the falls and it is considered safe to walk unaccompanied between the viewpoints, though you may encounter troops of baboons and black-and-white colobus. The so-called 'bat cliff' immediately south of the main waterfall (visible from Baker's View) is worth scanning with binoculars for raptors and swallows. Wait around until dusk and you should see some impressive flocks of bats emerging from the caves in this cliff, as well as a few bat hawks soaring around in search of a quick dinner. After dusk, the drive from the Top of the Falls back to the main road is particularly good for nocturnal birds, including spotted eagle owl and (seasonally) Africa's three most spectacular and distinctive nightjar species: long-tailed (Mar–Aug); pennant-winged (Mar–Sep); and standard-winged (Sep–Apr).

Although the Top of the Falls is easily visited by road, the most satisfying way to get there is to tag it on to a launch trip from Paraa. This entails disembarking from the boat at a landing point a few hundred metres below the falls, then ascending a tree-shaded footpath through the gorge to the viewpoints at its rim, where you will need to arrange for a vehicle to collect you. Be aware that while it is only 1km or so in length, the footpath is rather steep and involves at least 100 steps, so it can be challenging in the equatorial heat. Alternatively, you could be driven to the viewpoint and then walk down in time to be collected by the launch, with the considerable disadvantage that the boat's captain tends to stop less often to look at wildlife on the return leg to Paraa. In both cases, a hiking fee of US$10/15 FR/FNR must be paid in advance at the ticket office at Paraa, and a ranger will be allocated to escort you on foot between the landing point and Baker's View. This fee, you'll be glad to know, includes the US$10 levy to view the Top of the Falls.

Honeymoon Track A combination of dense vegetation, low wildlife concentrations and rampant tsetse flies means that game viewing south of the river is generally poor. An exception is the recently opened Honeymoon Track, and associated Kob and Hartebeest loops, which run to the east of the main Masindi–Paraa Road, making it particularly useful to people staying at Sambiya River Lodge, or as an extension to a visit to the Top of the Falls. The loop starts at a junction (⊕ 2.24098, 31.69228) about 8km along the feeder road to the Top of the Falls, then runs east through thick woodland for about 15km before arriving at the three-way junction (⊕ 2.22563, 31.80182) that marks the start of the Kob Track. Turn left here and you can follow a series of winding roads through open green hilly country where Uganda kob, Jackson's hartebeest, waterbuck, baboon and oribi are plentiful, and you might also find lion, elephant, buffalo and some of the giraffes that were relocated from the north bank in 2016 and are now thriving in the area. After about 15km of this, you reach the junction of the Hartebeest Loop and Honeymoon Track (⊕ 2.2198, 31.82822), where a right turn takes you back towards the Top of the Falls and a left turn leads you to the junction for Rabongo Forest, where you need to keep to the right before reconnecting with the Masindi–Paraa Road after about 25km. It should be noted that wildlife here is less prolific and more skittish than it is on the Buligi and Delta Circuit, so you are still best conducting your game drives north of the river if ticking off the Big Five is your first priority, but the compensation is that very few tourists head out this way, so it has a real wilderness feel.

Rabongo Forest Situated in the far southeast of the park, little-visited Rabongo Forest is smaller and less ecologically interesting than Kaniyo Pabidi, and the 40km access road there – branching from the main Paraa Road a few kilometres south of Sambiya River Lodge – is both rough and tsetse-infested. General forest walks are available on the spot, but are of interest mostly to birdwatchers, though black-and-white colobus and red-tailed monkeys are also likely to be seen, and the number and variety of butterflies is impressive.

BOAT TRIPS FROM PARAA A highlight of any visit to MFNP is one of the boat trips that follow the Victoria Nile east or west from Paraa. For many years, these were operated on a monopolistic basis by UWA, which still runs twice-daily trips from Paraa to the base of Murchison Falls, bookable through the reception and ticket office a few hundred metres south of the jetty (US$25/30 FR/FNR). Two private operators now also run daily boat trips from Paraa to the base of the falls, charging similar prices for what is generally regarded to be a better service. Paraa Safari Lodge (page 381) operates from the north bank and charges US$28/32 FR/FNR while the more specialised **Wild Frontiers Nile River Safaris** (⊕ 2.28301,

THE BAKERS AT MURCHISON FALLS

Murchison Falls is first alluded to in the writings of Speke, who upon visiting Karuma Falls to the east in 1862 was told that a few other waterfalls lay downriver, mostly 'of minor importance' but 'one within ear-sound...said to be very grand'. Speke does not record the name by which this waterfall was known locally, but his guide did inform him that a few years earlier 'at the Grand Falls...the king had the heads of one hundred men, prisoners taken in war against Rionga, cut off and thrown into the river'. Two years later, partially to fulfil a promise they had made to Speke, Samuel and Florence Baker became the first Europeans to explore the stretch of river between Lake Albert and Karuma Falls. As they were paddling about 30km east of the estuary, Samuel Baker wrote:

> We could distinctly hear the roar of water [and] upon rounding the corner a magnificent site burst upon us. On either side of the river were beautifully wooded cliffs rising abruptly to a height of about 300 feet [100m]; rocks were jutting out from the intensely green foliage; and rushing through a gap that cleft exactly before us, the river, contracted from a grand stream, was pent up in a passage of scarcely 50 yards [46m] in width; roaring furiously through the rock-bound pass, it plunged in one leap of about 120 feet [36m] perpendicular into a large abyss below. The fall of water was snow white, which had a superb effect as it contrasted with the dark cliffs that walled the water, while the graceful palms of the tropics and wild plantains perfected the beauty of the view. This was the greatest waterfall of the Nile, and in honour of the distinguished president of the Royal Geographic Society, I named it the Murchison Falls, the most important object through the entire course of the river.

31.5648; m 0773 897275, 0702 152928; e reservations@wildfrontiers-uganda.com; w wildfrontiers.co.ug) is on the south bank immediately east of the Paraa Bridge and charges US$35 per person. Where UWA and Paraa Safari Lodge focus mainly on trips to the base of the falls, Wild Frontiers also operates additional excursions to the Lake Albert delta and bespoke fishing and birding cruises.

Base of the falls The 3-hour return launch trip to the base of Murchison Falls has been MFNP's most popular attraction since Queen Elizabeth, the Queen Mother made the inaugural voyage in a spanking-new boat back in 1959. Starting at Paraa, the boat cruises slowly eastward along an archetypically African stretch of the Nile, fringed by borassus palms, acacia woodland and mahogany stands, before finally docking in a small bay a few hundred metres away from the crashing waterfall.

Game viewing along the way is excellent. Expect to see hippos in their hundreds, along with some of Africa's largest surviving crocodiles, and small herds of buffalo, waterbuck and kob. Giraffe, bushbuck and black-and-white colobus are also regularly seen, while elephants are frequently observed playing in the water, often within a few metres of the launch. A bit more luck is required to see lion or leopard.

The birdlife is reliably stunning, though the exact species composition varies depending on season and sandbank exposure. Look out for African fish eagle, Goliath heron, saddle-billed stork, African jacana, pied and malachite kingfishers, African skimmer, piapiac, rock pratincole, black-headed gonolek, black-winged red bishop, yellow-mantled widow-bird, yellow-backed weaver and, at the right time of year, a variety of migrant waders. The dazzlingly colourful red-throated bee-eater nests in sandbanks between Paraa and the falls, and is more likely to be seen here than anywhere in East Africa. The top avian prize is of course the shoebill, which is spotted here less frequently than it is around the delta, but remains a fair possibility in the dry season.

There's not a great deal to choose between the three operators offering daily trips to the base of the falls. All use double-decker boats, follow the same route, take 2–3 hours there and back, and charge a similar price (page 386). All operators can collect passengers from either side of the river, but it is advantageous to be on the boat early in order to take one of the better seats (the left side of the boat gives you the better view towards the wildlife-rich north bank on the slower outbound leg), which means passengers embarking on the north bank are best off booking with Paraa Safari Lodge, while those on the south bank should go with Wild Frontiers or UWA. It is also worth noting that the newer craft used by Wild Frontiers are more comfortable and take the return trip from the falls to Paraa at a faster pace (a useful consideration if travelling with kids). All three operators usually offer morning and afternoon trips (Wild Frontiers, for example, departs 08.30, 11.00 and 14.30), with the former offering better birdwatching but the latter being better for photography, since the sun is behind you on the outbound leg and when you reach the falls. An advantage of being on the first morning or first afternoon boat is that it is quite likely to scare off shyer animals coming down to drink before the other boats come past. Keen photographers, however, would certainly want to take the last afternoon departure in order to capture the best light. On that note, Wild Frontiers also offers a couple of additional options, one being a daily Falls Sundowner Cruise leaving at 15.30 for US$45 per adult. Also, since the scheduled cruises can be a bit crowded and day-trippy, they offer private trips on a smaller, five-person boat for US$216. All boats are provided with lifejackets and river guides.

Delta cruise The 20km voyage downriver from Paraa to the Lake Albert Delta is reckoned by birdwatchers to be one of the best opportunities in Africa to see the rare shoebill, particularly during the rainy season. More often than not, those who take the boat trip are rewarded with multiple shoebill sightings, but nothing is guaranteed and occasionally they dip totally. Without the shoebill as a motivating factor, the delta trip is not as worthwhile as the one to the falls, since there's less wildlife to be seen, and the general birding is more-or-less duplicated, though other papyrus endemics are sometimes observed. Wild Frontiers runs a daily delta cruise in a shaded 15-seater boat that leaves Paraa at 07.00 (5hrs return; US$56 pp; min 2 passengers).

Fishing excursions There is good fishing along the Murchison Nile, with large Nile perch and tiger fish offering the main challenge. The record for rod and line in Murchison was established by Kevin Nicholson in 2013. His mammoth catch weighed 114kg, just eclipsing Tim Smith's 113kg catch in 2009, but far heavier than the previous official record of 73kg, set by C D Mardach in 1959. Local fishermen claim to have netted specimens weighing up to 160kg. Wild Frontiers offers fishing cruises starting at US$180/223 FR/FNR per person for three people. A sport-fishing permit must be bought from UWA at a cost of US$50/day.

NORTH OF THE NILE The northern half of MFNP is far more rewarding than the bushier south when it comes to game drives. The most popular and best game-viewing circuit is Buligi, which stretches west from the tarmac road between Paraa and Tangi Gate to the Lake Albert Delta. However, the area to the east of the Paraa–Tangi Road, off-limits until 2005 or so due to security concerns, can also be very worthwhile, and it attracts far less safari traffic.

Buligi and the Delta Circuit The bulk of Murchison Falls' wildlife is concentrated to the north of the Nile, and the established area for game drives is a circuit of tracks within the Buligi area, an extensive promontory of grassland running west from the Paraa–Tangi Road to the promontory flanked by the Victoria Nile and Albert Nile as they enter and exit Lake Albert. Although the area is known as Buligi today, older sources refer to it as Bugili, in reference to the far-carrying 'bugle' reveille that routinely awoke General Gordon's troops at nearby Fort Magungo in the 1870s. To reach the Buligi area from Paraa, follow the surfaced road towards Tangi Gate north of Paraa Bridge, then after 7km turn left on to a dirt road at Te Okutu junction (⊕ 2.34323, 31.56463).

About 3km from here, the road passes through a patch of whistling thorns, a type of acacia whose marble-sized round pods – aerated by insects – whistle softly when a wind comes up. About 3km further (⊕ 2.33035, 31.51938), you have the option of branching left along the **Buligi Track**. This relatively little-used route runs southwest for 20km, passing through an area characterised by dense tsetse-friendly thickets, before reaching the eastern extreme of the delta. It then veers southeast through a swampy area – good for elephant and waterbirds including shoebill – that connects with the other tracks after another 9km or so.

Carrying on straight past the junction for the Buligi Track, the road runs through a scenic area of rolling grassland studded with tall borassus palms, where game concentrations are unpredictable, but generally highest in the rainy season. About 3km further on, it passes the fenced Pakuba Airstrip (⊕ 2.32931, 31.49921) to the left.

About 2km past the airstrip, the road forks twice in the space of a kilometre, giving you the option of following three different tracks, all of which lead west towards the delta. For those with limited time, the central 10km **Queen's Track** is not only the shortest route, but also the smoothest, and generally the most productive for game viewing. The northerly 12km **Albert Nile Track**, branching right at the first junction (⊕ 2.32316, 31.48511), passes through patches of dense acacia woodland that will be as attractive to birdwatchers as they are, unfortunately, to tsetse flies. The more southerly 13km **Victoria Nile Track**, which branches left at the second junction (⊕ 2.31765, 31.48123), also tends to support low game concentrations except as it approaches the delta.

These three tracks converge with each other and the Buligi Track on a grassy peninsula flanked by the delta to the south and the Albert Nile to the north. The delta is crossed by a network of interconnecting tracks that run through several kob breeding grounds. A good place to stop here, unsignposted but now adorned with a conspicuous public toilet (the only such amenity in this part of the park), is the lookout known as Delta Point (⊕ 2.28352, 31.38682), though it might as well be called Hippo Point, given the numbers of these animals that languish in the surrounding water. The convention at Delta Point is to hop out of the vehicle and wander down to the shore to gawp at the profusion of hippos and birds in the reedy shallows. Large concentrations of Ugandan kob are a certainty in this area, as are family parties of waterbuck and the doleful-looking Jackson's hartebeest, as well as small groups of the dainty oribi. A striking feature of the area is its giraffe herds, which often number 50 or more, something you seldom see elsewhere in Africa on a regular basis. Substantial buffalo herds are also common around the delta, usually

IN SEARCH OF KING WHALE-HEAD

Perhaps the most eagerly sought of all African birds, the shoebill is also one of the few that is likely to make an impression on those travellers who regard pursuing rare birds to be about as diverting as hanging about in windswept railway stations scribbling down train numbers. Three factors combine to give the shoebill its bizarre and somewhat prehistoric appearance. The first is its enormous proportions: an adult might stand more than 150cm (5ft) tall and typically weighs around 6kg. The second is its unique uniform slate-grey coloration. Last but emphatically not least is its clog-shaped, hook-tipped bill – at 20cm long, and almost as wide, the largest among all living bird species. The bill is fixed in a permanent Cheshire-cat smirk that contrives to look at once sinister and somewhat inane, and when agitated the bird loudly claps together its upper and lower bill, rather like outsized castanets.

The first known allusions to the shoebill came from early European explorers to Sudan, who wrote of a camel-sized flying creature known by the local Arabs as Abu Markub – Father of the Shoe. These reports were dismissed as pure fancy by Western biologists until 1851, when Gould came across a bizarre specimen among an avian collection shot on the Upper White Nile. Describing it as 'the most extraordinary bird I have seen', Gould placed his discovery in a monotypic family and named it *Balaeniceps Rex* – King Whale-Head! Gould believed the strange bird to be most closely allied to pelicans, but it also shares some anatomic and behavioural characteristics with herons, and until recently it was widely held to be an evolutionary offshoot of the stork family. DNA studies support Gould's original theory, however, and the shoebill is now placed in a monotypic subfamily of Pelecanidae.

The life cycle of the shoebill is no less remarkable than its appearance. One of the few birds with an age span of up to 50 years, it is generally monogamous, with pairs coming together during the breeding season (April to June) to construct a grassy nest up to 3m wide on a mound of floating vegetation or a small island. Two eggs are laid, and the parents rotate incubation duties, in hot weather filling their bills with water to spray over the eggs to keep them cool. The chicks hatch after about a month, and will need to be fed by the parents for at least another two months until their beaks are fully developed. Usually only one nestling survives, probably as a result of sibling rivalry.

The shoebill is a true swamp specialist, but it avoids dense stands of papyrus and tall grass, which obstruct its take-off, preferring instead to forage from patches of low floating vegetation or along the edge of channels. It consumes up to half its weight in food daily, preying on whatever moderately sized aquatic creature might come its way, ranging from toads to baby crocodiles, though lungfish are especially favoured. Its method of hunting is exceptionally sedentary: the bird might stand semi-frozen for several hours before it lunges down with remarkable

containing a few individuals whose coloration indicates some genetic input from the smaller, redder forest buffalo of West Africa. This area is also a good place to look for the endearingly puppyish side-striped jackal, and troops of the localised and rather skittish patas monkey.

The limitless supply of kob has attracted several prides of lion to the delta area. The best place to look for these languid predators is along the series of short anonymous tracks that connect the Albert Nile and Queen's tracks. At least one pride maintains an almost permanent presence in this area, often lying out in the

speed and power, heavy wings stretched backward, to grab an item of prey in its large, inescapable bill. Although it is generally a solitary hunter, the shoebill has occasionally been observed hunting co-operatively in small flocks, which splash about flapping their wings to drive a school of fish into a confined area.

Although the shoebill is an elusive bird, this – as with the sitatunga antelope – is less a function of its inherent scarcity than of the inaccessibility of its swampy haunts. Nevertheless, BirdLife International has classified it as Vulnerable, and it is classed as CITES Appendix 2, which means that trade in shoebills, or their capture for any harmful activity, is forbidden by international law. Estimates of the global population vary wildly. In the 1970s, only 1,500 shoebills were thought to exist in the wild, but this estimate has subsequently been revised to 5,000–10,000 individuals concentrated in five countries – Sudan, Uganda, Tanzania, DRC and Zambia. Small breeding populations also survive in Rwanda and Ethiopia, and vagrants have been recorded in Malawi and Kenya.

The most important shoebill stronghold is the Sudd floodplain on the Sudanese Nile, where 6,400 individuals were counted during an aerial survey in 1979–82, a figure that dropped to 3,830 when a similar survey was undertaken in 2005. Another likely stronghold is western Tanzania's rather inaccessible Moyowosi-Kigosi Swamp, whose population was thought to amount to a few hundred prior to a 1990 survey that estimated it to be greater than 2,000, though recent reports suggest a maximum of 500. Ironically, although Uganda is the easiest place to see the shoebill in the wild, the national population probably amounts to no more than 250 adult birds, half of which are concentrated in the Kyoga–Bisina–Opeta complex of wetlands. For tourists, however, the most reliable locations for shoebill sightings are Murchison Falls National Park, Toro-Semliki Wildlife Reserve, Mabamba Swamp near Entebbe, and to a lesser extent Akuja near Soroti – none of which is thought to hold more than a dozen pairs. Visitors to Uganda who fail to locate a shoebill in the wild might take consolation from the Wildlife Orphanage in Entebbe, where a few orphaned individuals are kept in a large aviary.

The major threat to the survival of the shoebill is habitat destruction. The construction of several dams along the lower Nile means that the water levels of the Sudd are open to artificial manipulation. Elsewhere, swamp clearance and rice farming pose a localised threat to suitable wetland habitats. A lesser concern is that shoebills are hunted for food or illegal trade in parts of Uganda. In the Lake Kyoga region, local fishermen often kill shoebill for cultural reasons – they believe that seeing a shoebill before a fishing expedition is a bad omen. As is so often the case, tourism can play a major role in preserving the shoebill and its habitat, particularly in areas such as the Mabamba Swamp, where the local community has already seen financial benefits from ornithological visits.

open in the early morning and late afternoon, but generally retreating deep into the thicket during the heat of the day. The most reliable way to locate the lions is by observing the behaviour of the male kobs that always stand sentry on the edge of a herd. If one or two kobs persistently emit their characteristic high wheezing alarm whistle, they are almost certainly conscious that lions are around, so follow their gaze towards the nearest thicket. Conversely, should you hang around a kob herd for a few minutes and not hear any alarm calls, you can be reasonably sure that no lions are to be found in the immediate vicinity. The lions of MFNP aren't

OIL IN MURCHISON FALLS

Adapted from Andrew Roberts' Uganda Safari. *Thanks to Justine Namara of the UWA Planning Unit and Kizza Fred, Chief Park Warden, MFCA.*

The presence of oil beneath the Albertine Rift has long been suspected. The first report on the subject, *Petroleum in Uganda*, was completed by E J Wayland in 1927. Some 80-odd years later, it became official when, in 2006, test drilling programmes found significant reserves of oil in the Lake Albert–Edward basins along the Ugandan–Congolese border. The area is now known to contain at least 6 billion barrels of oil, some 25% of which is viable for commercial exploitation. The catch? Unfortunately, most of these oil deposits are clustered beneath the Albertine Rift Valley, home of western Uganda's primary tourism destinations, most notably Murchison Falls. So, while fistfuls of oil dollars could theoretically do much to boost Uganda's economy and substandard infrastructure, it could be at the expense of tourist revenue, which is currently the country's single highest source of foreign exchange.

Initial suggestions that oil-rich sectors should be excised from national parks created an outcry from the tourism industry and environmentalists. Doubly so once it became clear that Murchison's most prolific oilfields are found directly below the Buligi area, where most of the park's wildlife and tourist activity is concentrated, and under the public lands directly south of the Nile, where much of the area's tourism accommodation is located.

Inevitably, with such riches at stake, conservation interests were not allowed to curtail progress and preparations for oil extraction from the Tilenga Oil Field are now well underway. This comprises the Pakuba–Buligi sector of MFNP west of the Tanga–Paraa Road, together with the Bulisa–Bugungu area outside the park on the southern side of the Nile. To provide an overview of what will happen, oil pumped from ten well pads within this sector of the park will be sent through a pipeline to a Central Processing Facility (CPF) near Bulisa for initial treatment. This 20km conduit will be entirely underground, including the necessary Nile crossing. Operations within the park are a relatively small part of the Tilenga Oil Field, with a further 24 wells being planned around the CPF. Apparently, up to 6,000 barrels/day will be piped from the CPF to a refinery near Hoima for local distribution, with the remainder sent down a 1,440km-long East Africa Crude Oil Pipeline (EACOP) to the Tanzanian coast. This US$5 billion investment will be heated, to reduce the gluey oil to a moveable consistency, and buried to reduce visual impact, complications to transport routes, and theft.

With preparations well underway, production is set to commence in 2026; though 2027 is probably a more realistic and indeed appropriate goal, neatly marking a full century since E J Wayland's pioneering report. In fairness, it must be said that so far, everything seems to have been done properly, including extensive roadworks to facilitate movement of equipment. These have included the surfacing of the dirt road through the park linking Masindi to Pakwach, and the replacement of the Paraa ferry with a concrete bridge. Though devotees of Murchison's wildernesses are predictably outraged by these latter developments, even the most fervent of these admits to the convenience of the bridge.

The extraction of oil has been mandated to the French multi-national Total Energies. Given that the alternative might have been the Chinese National Offshore Oil Company (CNOOC), which is operating beside Lake Albert in Kabwoya Wildlife

Reserve, this is perhaps a reassuring choice. As France's top-grossing company in 2023, Total can be expected, or if necessary, pressured, to follow internationally acceptable standards of operation, safety, environmental compliance, etc. At present, significant visual impact is limited to the current whereabouts of the single drilling rig being used sequentially to open ten well pads; the construction of a pipeline to the CPF; and an increase in traffic associated with these activities. Though detrimental to both tourism and wildlife, these are short-term impacts and mitigation measures are in place. Strict speed limits apply on the tarmac roads and Total is using coaster buses instead of numerous small vehicles to transport workers.

When the production phase commences, human activity will be reduced to routine maintenance of the ten operational well pads while visual impacts will be limited to whatever can be seen of these compounds. Though one would have wished them located in some remoter corner of the protected area, it is a 30km drive across extensive and undulating savanna from the Paraa–Tangi tarmac to the peninsula's extremity at Delta Point and the reality is that – at the time of writing – the fence surrounding Pakuba Airfield remains the most prominent intrusion in this area. This is in part a consequence of 9m-high earth banks screening the pad compounds, and the pumping technology is expected to use an alternative to the prominent 'nodding donkey' mechanism. There will be some light pollution at night, but nothing to compare with the existing illuminations from Adere Safari Lodge outside Kidepo Valley National Park.

With each well pad measuring 4ha in size, the equivalent of ten football pitches, one might flag the habitat loss involved, until considering their combined area of $0.4km^2$ in the context of the $5,310km^2$ Murchison Falls Conservation Area. By the same token, the loss of $0.4km^2$ of grazing and browsing land is unlikely to be much of a loss to wildlife. That said, UWA reports that wildlife is noticeably stressed by the increased level of activity in the park – reduced breeding activity is one concern – and that animals are migrating to quieter areas beyond the tarmac road to the east. Hopes that the security associated with Total's presence would lead to a reduction in poaching have also proved unfounded. According to UWA sources, the oil company's patrol vehicles ignore poachers sighted in the vicinity of their operations while the number of snares found in the vicinity of the oil pads has actually increased. This, you will appreciate, raises some serious questions.

It is also inevitable that wildlife will be affected by developments *outside* the park. Since the end of the LRA war, the return of displaced park boundary communities has already led to an increase in poaching and pressure on firewood and other natural resources within MFNP. This situation is now being exacerbated by migration in response to oil-related employment opportunities. While the oil and gas sector is expected to generate 160,000 jobs nationwide, 4,400 workers, mostly migrants, have been employed in the Tilenga Oil Field. To these can be added a host of unsuccessful applicants, still in the area and ready to turn their hand to any activity including poaching. In this endeavour, plenty of tips can be provided by workers with an intimate knowledge of the park, including UWA's shortcomings and the indifference of their company's own patrols. They will, moreover, find a ready market for bushmeat in the shanties already emerging on the edges of Bulisa and Wanseko, as well as for 160,000 newly monied workers across a wider area.

continued overleaf

OIL IN MURCHISON FALLS (continued)

So much for the national park, which is only part of the greater Tilenga project area. If the Buligi grasslands are not going to be turned into a tundra littered with nodding donkeys, who is to say what will happen in the supposedly less sensitive Bulisa area immediately adjacent across the river. I certainly can't, since Total don't respond to my emails. There are also wider environmental issues to consider, the Nile being a river subject to international treaties and one which South Sudan, Sudan and Egypt would not wish diluted with oil. These things happen, of course, as evidenced by BP's disastrous spill into the Gulf of Mexico in the 2010 Deepwater Horizon incident. Total, however, insists that the comparison is an irrelevant one, that BP's failure was caused by stretching the limits of available technology in a far harsher environment, while the extraction and piping of oil to Bulisa, Hoima and Tanzania are routine operations. Perhaps of greater concern is that the Chinese company CNOOC has been contracted to extract oil from beneath the Kaiso-Tonya plain and on a narrow strip of Lake Albert shoreline further south, an area known as the Kingfisher Field. Only time will tell whether their environmental and technological standards will be tested to – or beyond – the limit or will prove to be equally routine.

traditionally known to climb trees, but we heard reports of this behaviour in the vicinity of Pakuba Airstrip in 2018.

The delta area offers some great birdwatching. Noteworthy ground birds include the preposterous eye-fluttering Abyssinian ground hornbill, the majestic grey crowned crane and saddle-billed stork, the localised Denham's bustard, the handsome black-headed and spur-winged lapwings, and the Senegal thick-knee. The tall acacia stands that line the Albert Nile Track, immediately north of the junction with the Queen's Track, harbour a host of good woodland birds, including the rare black-billed barbet and delightfully colourful swallow-tailed, northern Carmine, blue-breasted and red-throated bee-eaters. Herds of grazers – in particular buffalo – are often attended by flocks of insectivorous cattle egret, piapiac and red-billed and yellow-billed oxpeckers. An abundance of aquatic habitats – not only the rivers and lake, but also numerous small pools – attracts a wide variety of waterfowl, waders, herons and egrets, while the mighty African fish eagle and both species of marsh harrier are often seen soaring above the water. All birders should take a slow drive along the extension of the Victoria Nile Track that branches southwest at an easily missed junction (⊕ 2.27576, 31.38234) about 1.5km south of Hippo Point, then runs adjacent to the papyrus-lined Victoria Nile for 3km to a seasonal hippo pool only 200m from the riverbank. Shoebills are frequently observed in this area, flying over the delta or standing stock still in the papyrus beds, while a solitary osprey is often observed at the hippo pool itself.

The Buligi Circuit is also readily accessed from Pakwach and the Tangi Gate. To get there, turn right on to the Pakuba Track at a signposted junction (⊕ 2.40878, 31.51421) 5km south of Tangi Gate, and follow it for 15km (passing Pakuba Safari Lodge to your right) until you come to a T-junction with the Albert Nile Track (⊕ 2.32503, 31.46849), where a right turn leads towards the delta. Driving in the vicinity of Pakuba, keep an eye on the canopy for a large and reasonably habituated male leopard that is frequently seen close to the lodge or along the road that connects it to the Albert Nile Track.

Northeast of Paraa Although it doesn't quite compare with the Buligi Circuit for general game viewing or aquatic birds, the road running east from Te Okutu junction (7km north of Paraa) towards Wankwar Gate can still be very rewarding and tends to carry far less tourist traffic. A recommended 2km diversion, albeit a very rough one, branches south at a junction (⊕ 2.34386, 31.64009) some 10km east of Te Okutu crossroads and leads to the **Nyamsika Cliffs Viewpoint** (⊕ 2.33133, 31.64951). Named for the sandy waterway it overlooks, this craggy cliff hosts seasonal colonies of several types of bee-eater, while lion and buffalo sometimes come to drink at the river below. It is also one of the few places in East Africa where the dashing Egyptian plover is frequently recorded. Another 2km past Nyamsika junction, a series of roadside waterholes often attracts giraffe, elephant, buffalo, hartebeest, waterbuck, Ugandan kob, oribi, duiker and warthog. Another 4km past this, game viewing tends to dry up at about the same time as the road reaches a wooded area where tsetse flies are numerous and visitors on a short game drive would be well advised to turn back to Paraa.

Alternatively, continue for another 12km towards Wankwar to the signposted junction (⊕ 2.41308, 31.75815) for the **north bank viewpoint** over Murchison Falls. Be warned, however, that the reality of this northern viewpoint falls way short of expectations, with the main waterfall being identifiable only by a distant plume of spray. The theoretical prospect of eyeballing the comparably voluminous Uhuru Falls is also thwarted, since the flight of concrete steps that descends from the parking area terminates at a nondescript riverside spot in sight of neither waterfall. All that might change should vague plans to open a trail to Uhuru Falls and rebuild the bridge across the gorge ever come to fruition. Until that time, however, it's a poor incentive for a 3-hour, 110km round trip from Paraa.

Shortly before reaching Wankwar Gate, a turning (⊕ 2.43465, 31.78508) to the right eventually reaches Chobe Lodge, 53km away. It's worth driving a kilometre or so down this track to enjoy some super southerly panoramas of the Murchison wilderness. If you intend to continue to Chobe (enquire about road conditions first) note that the route passes through long tracts of woodland where little wildlife is seen and tsetse flies are numerous, so best wind up your windows.

Walking safaris Bush Wonderers (m 0783 291399; w bushwonderers.com) offers a variety of tailor-made walking safaris in lovely country lying to the north of the river between Paraa and Murchison Falls. It's an exciting prospect, boating upriver to disembark at the Nyamsika River's delta and then heading off into the wilderness to follow the valley upstream to an overnight camp close to the lovely Nyamsika Cliffs viewpoint. It's not all walking, of course, with additional activities including afternoon game drives, boat trips and a visit to the Top of the Falls. Three nights/ four days costs US$1,500 pp and covers everything except park entry.

KARUMA FALLS Crossed by the Kampala–Gulu Road 2km south of MFNP's Chobe Gate, Karuma Bridge is the spot where, a couple of decades ago during the LRA insurgency, a fearful tension gripped northbound travellers, while the mood on vehicles headed south lightened immeasurably. Today, it's a beautiful location: beneath the bridge, the river races down rapids between high, forested banks. On the north side these lie within Murchison Falls National Park, and on the southern, downstream side, in the Karuma Wildlife Reserve.

Though the bridge crosses a lovely section of rapids, the main Karuma Falls lies 1.5km upriver below. The first major plunge in an 80km-long stretch of rapids ending at Murchison Falls, Karuma represents the point where an older and much larger incarnation of Lake Kyoga burst its banks, causing the present-day Nile to scour its present-day course towards the Rift Valley. It's quite a sight, despite the curious fact that Speke, who visited in 1864, was sufficiently underwhelmed to record it by its local name rather than allocating it to a contemporary royal or sponsor. It's also easily accessible, an elevated north-bank viewpoint lying only a 600m walk from the junction to Pakwach-Gulu junction. Unfortunately, the path runs through the national park and you'll need to report to the adjacent Chobe Gate to pay park entrance fees and hire a ranger guide. Visiting the south bank is cheaper, but complicated by the need to obtain permission at the office of the Karuma Falls power station.

CULTURAL TOURS Under the banner Beyond the Park, this new community initiative presents a variety of activities in the lands neighbouring MFNP. Among other things, these demonstrate the work of a volunteer Community Wildlife Scout, showcase local folklore and dance, and take visitors fishing in a dugout canoe. To organise an activity, call Okello on m 0783 468031 or 0709 007664, or ask your lodge to take charge.

Part Five

AROUND THE RWENZORI

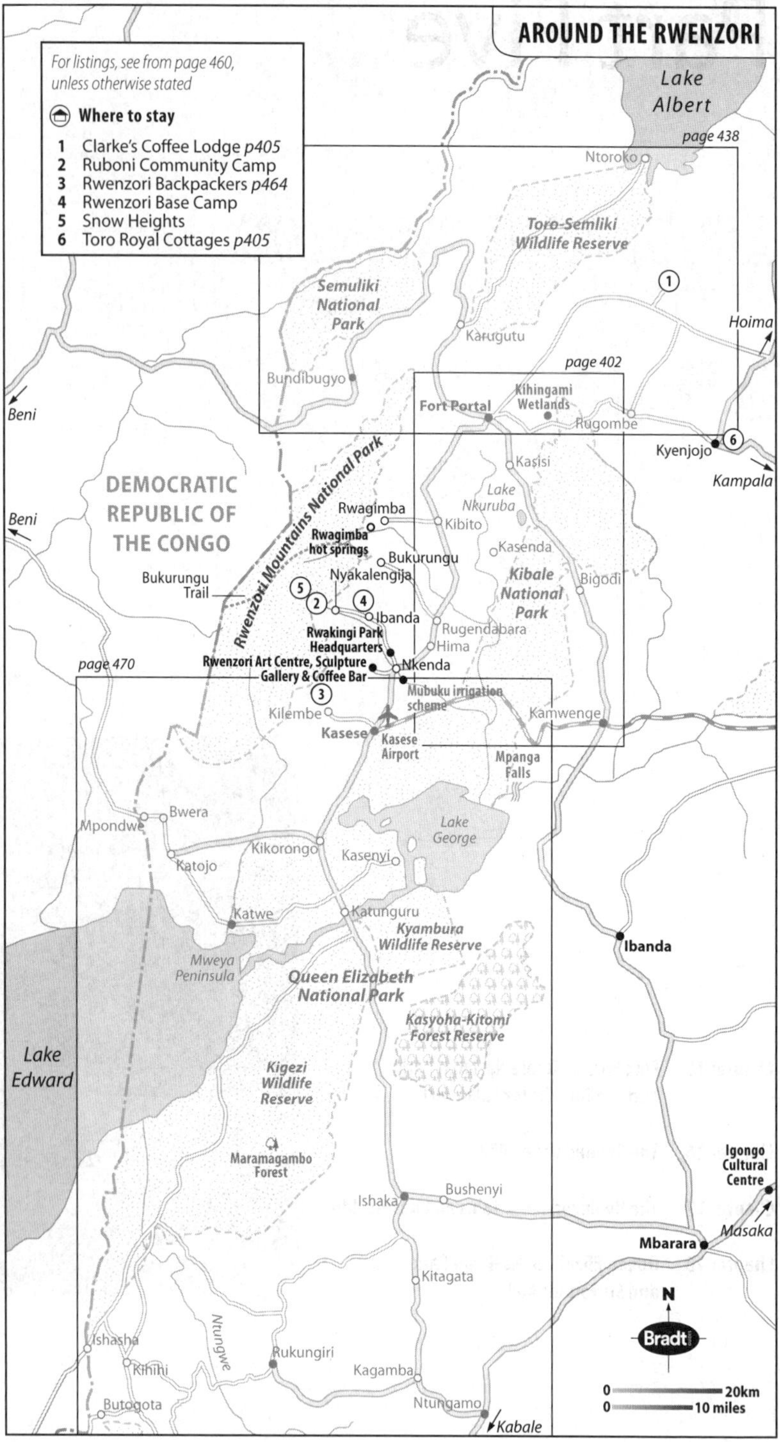

AROUND THE RWENZORI
For listings, see from page 460, unless otherwise stated
Where to stay
1 Clarke's Coffee Lodge p405
2 Ruboni Community Camp
3 Rwenzori Backpackers p464
4 Rwenzori Base Camp
5 Snow Heights
6 Toro Royal Cottages p405
Lake Albert
page 438
Ntoroko
Toro-Semliki Wildlife Reserve
Semuliki National Park
Karugutu
Hoima
page 402
Bundibugyo
Beni
Fort Portal
Kihingami Wetlands
Rugombe
Kyenjojo
Kampala
Kasisi
DEMOCRATIC REPUBLIC OF THE CONGO
Rwenzori Mountains National Park
Lake Nkuruba
Rwagimba
Kibito
Rwagimba hot springs
Kasenda
Bukurungu
Bukurungu Trail
Nyakalengija
Kibale National Park
Bigodi
Ibanda
Rugendabara
Rwakingi Park Headquarters
Hima
page 470
Rwenzori Art Centre, Sculpture Gallery & Coffee Bar
Nkenda
Mubuku irrigation scheme
Kilembe
Kamwenge
Kasese
Kasese Airport
Mpanga Falls
Bwera
Mpondwe
Lake George
Kikorongo
Kasenyi
Katojo
Katwe
Katunguru
Kyambura Wildlife Reserve
Ibanda
Mweya Peninsula
Queen Elizabeth National Park
Kasyoha-Kitomi Forest Reserve
Lake Edward
Kigezi Wildlife Reserve
Maramagambo Forest
Igongo Cultural Centre
Bushenyi
Ishaka
Masaka
Mbarara
Kitagata
N
Bradt
Ntungwe
Ishasha
Rukungiri
Kihihi
Kagamba
Butogota
Ntungamo
Kabale
0 20km
0 10 miles

OVERVIEW

One of the most ecologically varied regions anywhere in Africa stands in the shadow of the legendary and routinely cloud-shrouded range known as the Mountains of the Moon or the Rwenzori. Here, a quintet of national parks and wildlife reserves shields a range of habitats that embraces everything from snow-capped glacial peaks and frosty Afro-alpine moorland to marsh-fringed Rift Valley lakes and tangled montane and lowland rainforest – not forgetting some vast tracts of archetypal African savannah.

Although it covers quite a small area in geographic terms, this section breaks up into four chapters. Starting in the north, the first chapter covers the town of Fort Portal along with the nearby Toro Crater Lakes and Kibale National Park. The next three respectively cover the remote Semliki Valley, the hiker-oriented Rwenzori National Park, and the all-round safari charms of the biodiverse Queen Elizabeth National Park.

HIGHLIGHTS

QUEEN ELIZABETH NATIONAL PARK Arguably the most biodiverse conservation area in East Africa with a bird checklist topping the 600 mark, QENP's variety embraces the elephant, hippo and giant forest hogs that haunt the Kazinga Channel – serviced by several boat trips daily – as well as the chimps of Kyambura Gorge and celebrated tree-climbing lions of Ishasha. Page 469.

KIBALE NATIONAL PARK Uganda's top chimpanzee-tracking venue also protects the country's densest and most varied monkey population and a fabulous variety of forest birds. Page 425.

RWENZORI MOUNTAINS NATIONAL PARK The montane forest, Afro-alpine moorland and craggy glacial peaks of the 5,109m-high Mountains of the Moon provide some of the most challenging and rewarding high-altitude hiking anywhere in Africa. Page 453.

TORO CRATER LAKES Studding the volcanically formed Rwenzori footslopes like a ribbon of green and blue gemstones, the 30-plus crater lakes of Toro provide the setting for some of Uganda's most attractive upmarket lodges and budget camps. Page 415.

BIGODI SWAMP WALK This respected community project bordering Kibale National Park offers the opportunity to see a fabulous variety of forest birds along with localised primates such as red colobus and Uganda mangabey. Page 433.

KALINZU ECOTOURISM SITE This under-publicised forest reserve bordering QENP is second only to Kibale National Park when it comes to reliable chimp tracking, but at prices far better suited to budget-conscious backpackers. Page 500.

SEMULIKI NATIONAL PARK Set in Albertine Rift below the northern Rwenzori footslopes, this remote national park is famed for its ecological affinities to the Ituri Forest in the neighbouring Congo Basin and the presence of several dozen bird species recorded nowhere else in Uganda. Page 442.

TORO-SEMLIKI WILDLIFE RESERVE The game viewing at this scenic national park is a bit hit-and-miss, but it has a wonderfully untrammelled atmosphere, provides the best chance in Uganda of spotting forest elephant, and supports a varied avifauna including shoebills, which are easily seen on boat trips on Lake Albert. Page 437.

FORT PORTAL Arguably the most pleasant town in Uganda, Fort Portal has an appealing highland climate and makes a great urban base for day trips to Kibale Forest, the Toro Crater Lakes and Semliki Valley. See opposite.

MPANGA FALLS One for aficionados of off-the-beaten-track exploration, this impressive 50m waterfall is enclosed by a steep gorge whose lush cover of spray forest is dominated by the Uganda giant cycad, a critically endangered and primitive-looking endemic tree. Page 435.

15

Fort Portal, Kibale National Park and the Toro Crater Lakes

The principal town of Toro subregion, likeable Fort Portal forms the urban gateway to a circuit of magnificent natural attractions that includes one of the country's most biodiverse rainforests, several dozen lushly vegetated crater lakes, and the spectacular northern Rwenzori foothills. The top attraction, situated to the southeast of Fort Portal, is Kibale National Park, which forms Uganda's premier chimp-tracking destination, as well as supporting its greatest primate diversity and a thrilling variety of forest birds. Running Kibale a close second, the Toro Crater Lakes are nestled within a longitudinal band of volcanic calderas that run west of the national park border from Fort Portal south to Kasenda. The region's other main attraction, stretching west from Fort Portal to the Congolese border, is the more remote Semliki Valley, covered in *Chapter 16*.

Approximating the borders of the 19th-century Kingdom of Toro, the area covered in this chapter is endowed with plenty of appealing accommodation. At the top end, you have the choice of intimate jungle-fringed bush camps or boutique-style lodges perched above aquamarine crater lakes, while budget travellers are catered for by an above-par selection of inexpensive hotels and simple banda/camping sites. The area also supports several budget-friendly community projects, notably the Bigodi Wetland Sanctuary bordering Kibale National Park and Lake Nkuruba Nature Reserve near Rwaihamba. It is worth emphasising that, where accommodation is concerned, the division between Fort Portal, the Toro Crater Lakes and Kibale National Park can be quite arbitrary. In reality, most places covered in this chapter lie within an easy hour's drive of each other, which means, for instance, that many tourists use a lodge in Fort Portal or at one of the crater lakes as a base for chimp tracking and other activities in Kibale National Park.

FORT PORTAL

The administrative centre of Kabarole District and seat of the Toro kingdom, Fort Portal is perhaps the most attractive town in Uganda, situated amid lush rolling hillsides swathed in neat tea plantations and – clouds permitting – offering excellent views across to the glacial peaks of the Rwenzori Mountains to the west. Some 300km from Kampala along a good surfaced road, this well-equipped town is also a useful springboard for exploring Kibale National Park and the Toro Crater Lakes, though most organised tours literally just pass through en route to one of the many upmarket lodges around the forest and lakes. The town centre has seen a great deal of renovation since the early 1990s, making it barely recognisable from the

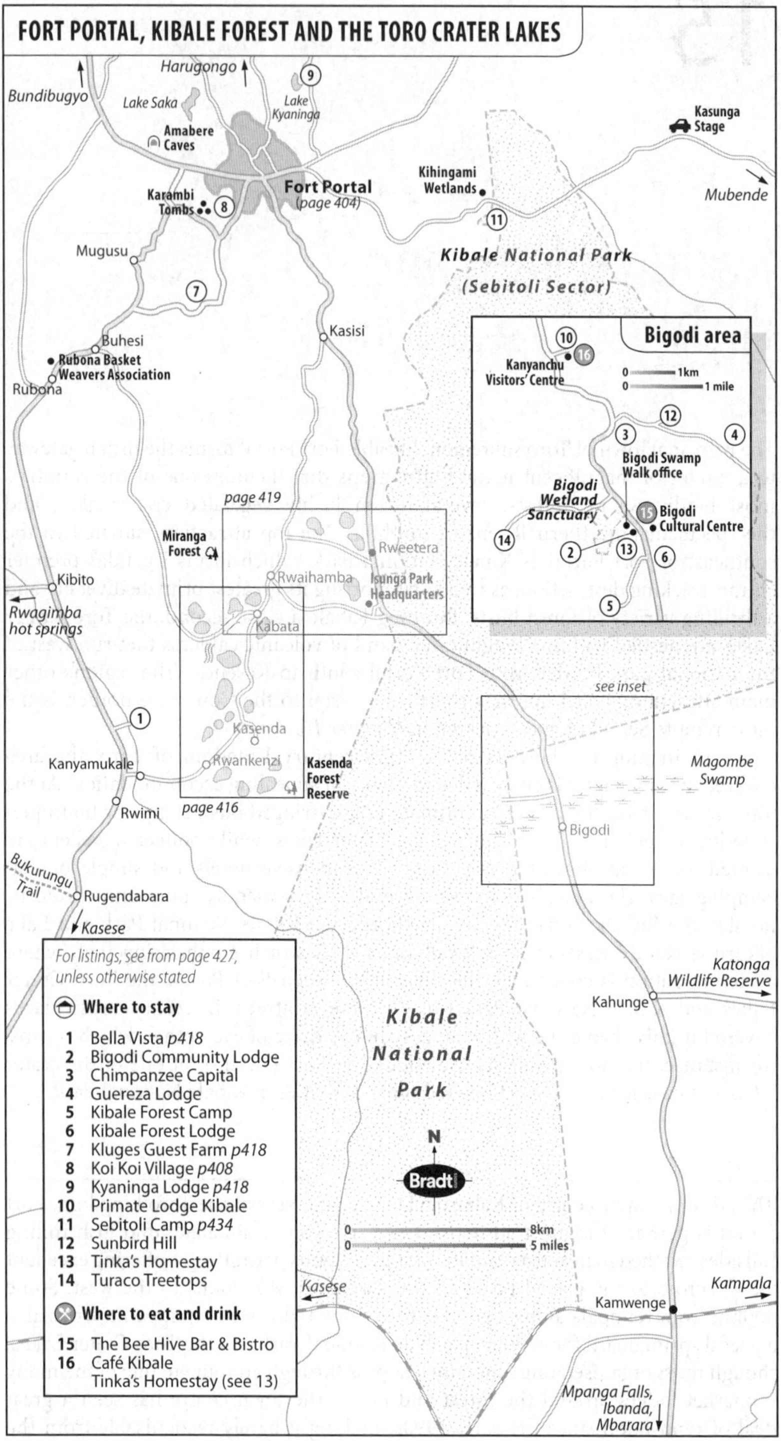
FORT PORTAL, KIBALE FOREST AND THE TORO CRATER LAKES
Harugongo
Bundibugyo
Lake Saka
Lake Kyaninga
Amabere Caves
Kasunga Stage
Fort Portal (page 404)
Kihingami Wetlands
Mubende
Karambi Tombs
Mugusu
Kibale National Park (Sebitoli Sector)
Kasisi
Buhesi
Rubona Basket Weavers Association
Rubona
Bigodi area
Kanyanchu Visitors' Centre
1km
1 mile
Bigodi Swamp Walk office
Bigodi Wetland Sanctuary
Bigodi Cultural Centre
page 419
Miranga Forest
Rweetera
Rwaihamba
Isunga Park Headquarters
Kibito
Rwagimba hot springs
Kabata
see inset
Kasenda
Magombe Swamp
Kanyamukale
Rwankenzi
Kasenda Forest Reserve
page 416
Rwimi
Bigodi
Bukurungu Trail
Rugendabara
Kasese
Katonga Wildlife Reserve
Kahunge
Kibale National Park
N
Bradt
8km
5 miles
Kasese
Kampala
Kamwenge
Mpanga Falls, Ibanda, Mbarara
For listings, see from page 427, unless otherwise stated
Where to stay
1 Bella Vista p418
2 Bigodi Community Lodge
3 Chimpanzee Capital
4 Guereza Lodge
5 Kibale Forest Camp
6 Kibale Forest Lodge
7 Kluges Guest Farm p418
8 Koi Koi Village p408
9 Kyaninga Lodge p418
10 Primate Lodge Kibale
11 Sebitoli Camp p434
12 Sunbird Hill
13 Tinka's Homestay
14 Turaco Treetops
Where to eat and drink
15 The Bee Hive Bar & Bistro
16 Café Kibale
Tinka's Homestay (see 13)

rundown 'Fort Pot-hole' of a few years back. It is also rather short on noteworthy landmarks, unless perhaps you count the hilltop Toro Palace built in the 1960s and restored more recently with Libyan funds, but it does offer a very good selection of hotels, restaurants and nightspots, making it an agreeable place to settle into for a few days.

HISTORY The area around Fort Portal has strong associations with the legendary Bachwezi Empire. It is said the Ndahura, the first Bachwezi king, retired from his capital in Mubende after he abdicated in favour of his son Wamala, and that the many crater lakes in the vicinity were his creation. It seems probable that the site of the modern-day town served as the capital of Toro prior to 1891, when a British fort was constructed there to protect it from guerrilla raids by Omukama Kabalega of Bunyoro. Situated where the golf club is today, Fort Gerry, as it was originally known, was named posthumously after the British Consul General of Zanzibar Sir Gerald Portal, who arrived in Buganda in late 1892 to formalise its protectorateship and died of typhoid in London just over a year later. Norma Lorimer, who travelled to Fort Portal in 1913, referred to the settlement as 'Toro', adding that it then consisted of 'about six bungalows, the bank, the Boma, the huts for a few KARs (King's African Rifles), the Indian bazaar and the native settlement'. By 1980, it had grown to become the largest town in western Uganda, and fifth countrywide, with a population of 28,800. It has grown at a relatively modest rate since then, but a population of 135,000 still places it just inside the country's ten largest settlements.

GETTING THERE AND AWAY Coming directly from Kampala, the 300km road to Fort Portal via Mubende is surfaced almost in its entirety, though the Mityana–Mubende section is currently in rotten condition, stretching the drive in a private vehicle to around 6 hours.

Fort Portal also lies on an established north–south safari circuit between Murchison Falls and Queen Elizabeth National Park, usually with a short diversion to Kibale National Park. The fastest drive from Murchison Falls via Bulisa and Hoima is 320km, follows good tarmac and takes about 5 hours. The alternative via Masindi town is 340km (page 367). Heading south from Fort Portal, still on tarmac, Kasese is 60km distant, with Queen Elizabeth National Park's Kasenyi Gate 33km further on. If headed to Lake Mburo National Park or Mbarara, follow a surfaced road south through Kibale Forest to Ibanda. Head through the town for Mbarara or turn left to join the Kampala–Mbarara Road between Lyantonde and Lake Mburo, a drive of 210km.

The Link Bus [410 E4] (m 0701 966181; w link.co.ug/fort_portal_terminal) operates on all of the above routes arriving and departing from a private terminal on Kahinju Road. The journey from Kampala costs around US$8, buses leaving hourly between 06.00 and 19.00 from Kasenyi Bus Station.

Matatus to Kasese (60–90mins), Bundibugyo (2–3hrs), Mbarara (4–5hrs), Kampala (4–6hrs) and Hoima (5–7hrs) leave from Nyakaseke Taxi Park [410 E3] off Bwamba Road. Transport for Kibale National Park, Bigodi and the nearby crater lakes leaves from a separate park close to the Mpanga Bridge.

WHERE TO STAY

Between Murchison Falls and Fort Portal

The once-notoriously bad road from Murchison Falls to Fort Portal might have been transformed by tarmac but it's still quite a drive, especially if you detour along the way to (for example) the top of Murchison Falls or Kibero Salt Gardens. In this case, an overnight stop might be in order, so, in addition

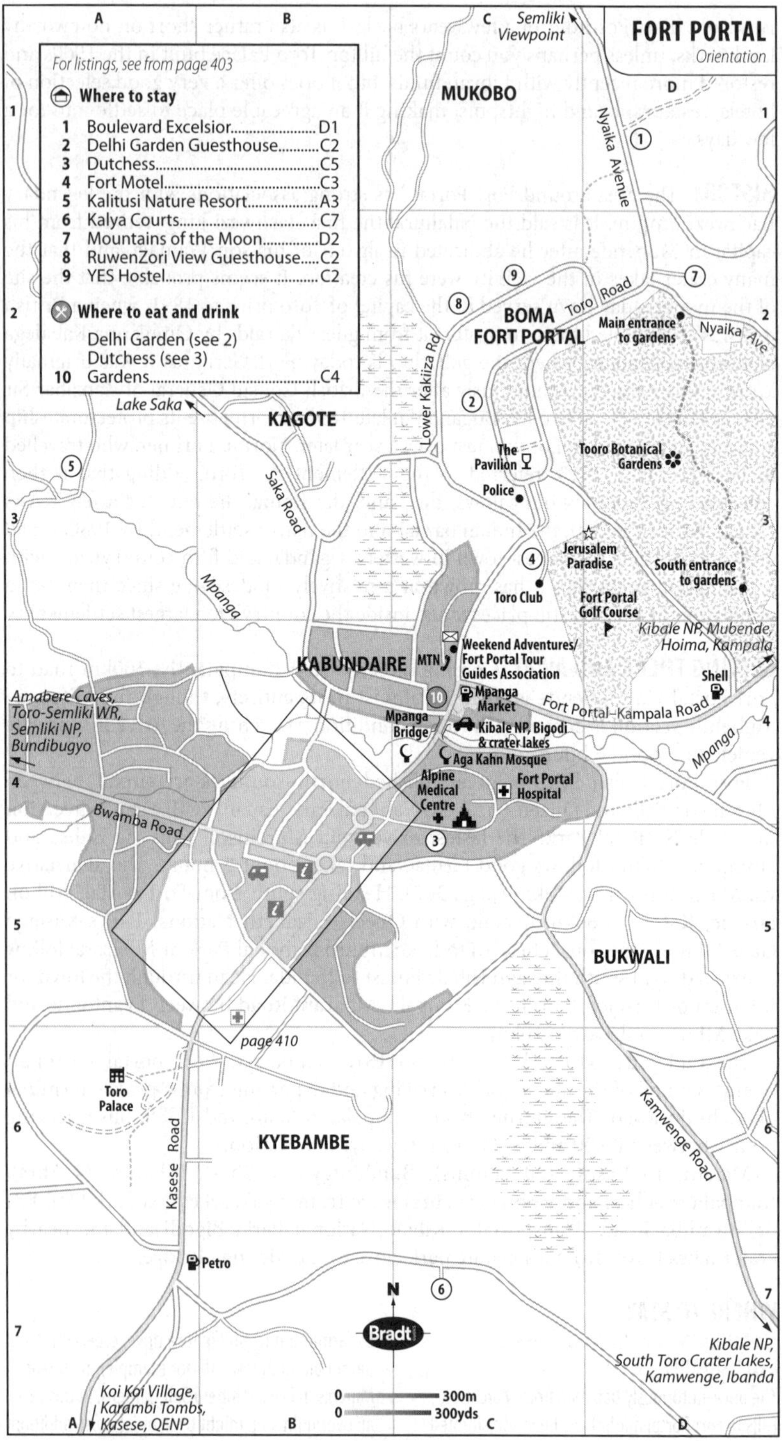
FORT PORTAL
Orientation
For listings, see from page 403
Where to stay
1 Boulevard Excelsior.....D1
2 Delhi Garden Guesthouse.....C2
3 Dutchess.....C5
4 Fort Motel.....C3
5 Kalitusi Nature Resort.....A3
6 Kalya Courts.....C7
7 Mountains of the Moon.....D2
8 RuwenZori View Guesthouse.....C2
9 YES Hostel.....C2
Where to eat and drink
Delhi Garden (see 2)
Dutchess (see 3)
10 Gardens.....C4
Semliki Viewpoint
MUKOBO
Nyaika Avenue
Toro Road
BOMA
FORT PORTAL
Main entrance to gardens
Nyaika Ave
Lower Kakiiza Rd
Lake Saka
KAGOTE
The Pavilion
Police
Tooro Botanical Gardens
Saka Road
Jerusalem Paradise
South entrance to gardens
Toro Club
Fort Portal Golf Course
Mpanga
Kibale NP, Mubende, Hoima, Kampala
Weekend Adventures/ Fort Portal Tour Guides Association
MTN
KABUNDAIRE
Shell
Mpanga Market
Fort Portal–Kampala Road
Amabere Caves, Toro-Semliki WR, Semliki NP, Bundibugyo
Mpanga Bridge
Kibale NP, Bigodi & crater lakes
Aga Kahn Mosque
Alpine Medical Centre
Fort Portal Hospital
Bwamba Road
BUKWALI
page 410
Toro Palace
KYEBAMBE
Kasese Road
Kamwenge Road
Petro
N
Bradt
Kibale NP, South Toro Crater Lakes, Kamwenge, Ibanda
Koi Koi Village, Karambi Tombs, Kasese, QENP
0 300m
0 300yds

to the Rift Valley lodges listed on page 361, we've included some further options here.

Before the recent tarmacking of the Hoima–Kyenjojo highway, the crossing of the swampy Nguse (or Nkusi) River Valley was a regular complication during rainy seasons. Back in the day, heatstroke nearly claimed the life of Florence Baker when she and husband Samuel struggled through the swamp on foot in 1864. Today, though a surfaced causeway now enables vehicles to whizz across the river & away, a new budget lodge on either side of the crossing offers opportunities to stop for a meal or the night. Otherwise, there are plenty of budget hotels, albeit in less agreeable settings, in fast-growing Kagadi town 22km to the south.

Upmarket

Clarke's Coffee Lodge [map, page 398] (33 rooms) ⊕ 0.8789539, 30.5887065; ☎ 039 2201400; e patricia@clarke_group.org; w clarke-farm.com. This delightful lodge occupies a dramatic, eyrie-like hilltop in the heart of a 1,500-acre coffee estate. Though located – more or less – on the route between Murchison Falls & Fort Portal, it would be stretching it to plug it as a convenient stopover since it's 40km off the Hoima–Kyenjojo tarmac & another 40km down to the Kampala–Kyenjojo–Fort Portal road. If, however, you can factor in the time – & it deserves at least 2 nights – the Coffee Lodge is a worthwhile diversion. It's very relaxing & with a fabulous view, but there are also options to bestir yourself to explore the estate, tick off a few birds & better your knowledge of Robusta coffee farming. *US$140/200/200 sgl/dbl/twin FB.* **$$$**

Budget

Nguse River Camp & Restaurant [map, page 349] (4 units) m 0776 862153; e rivercampsuganda@gmail.com. Sited on the north edge of the Nguse Valley, this low-key lodge is set in acacia woodland that sustains a variety of birdlife including Ross's & white-crested turaco, grey-headed oliveback & olive-bellied sunbird. Accommodation is provided in simple & reasonably priced en-suite chalets, while the restaurant is becoming an established lunch stop on the Murchison–Kibale leg of the safari route (mains, ideally ordered in advance, cost US$8). *US$70/80 sgl/dbl B&B.* **$$**

Nguse River Falls Lodge [map, page 349] (6 units) ⊕ 1.1298633, 30.9929054; m 0773 910932; e riverfallslodge@yahoo.com; f riverfallslodgenguse. This pretty lodge stands on the southern edge of the Nguse Valley where the river tumbles noisily out of the swamp. Though the lodge building & boulder-strewn gardens are delightful, the wooden cottages are optimistically priced when compared to the nearby River Camp. It still looks like a lovely stop for lunch, though (meat 'n' chips dishes, best ordered in advance, cost US$6–8). *US$110/150 sgl/dbl B&B.* **$$$**

Toro Royal Cottages [map, page 398] (30 rooms) m 0776 277775. Should darkness overtake you at Kyenjojo town at Hoima Rd's merger with the Kampala–Fort Portal Rd, turn into this welcoming hotel, 100m before the junction. Come daylight, you'll appreciate that this storeyed, drum-shaped building is a modern take on the Royal Palace of Toro in Fort Portal, a theme reinforced by some dreadful statues of Omukama Oyo I & loyal attendants in the gardens. *US$24/32/40 sgl/dbl/twin.* **$$**

Fort Portal

Although good accommodation suited to most tastes & budgets can be found within Fort Portal, the most exclusive option in the immediate vicinity is the out-of-town Kyaninga Lodge (page 418), set on the rim of the eponymous crater lake. At the other end of the price scale, Kibale National Park's Sebitoli Camp (page 434) is an under-utilised budget forest retreat situated only 16km out of town along the Fort Portal–Kampala Rd. In addition to the hotels listed here, plenty of decent cheapies can be found on Malibo Rd uphill of Nyakaseke Taxi Park, as well as on Balya Rd, which runs parallel to the Kasese Rd.

Upmarket

Fort Motel [404 C3] (16 rooms) Off Toro Rd; m 0776 970677; e reservations@fortmotel.com; w fortmotel.com. Centred on a restored 2-storey colonial house, this excellent hotel stands on the hilltop close to the site of Fort Gerry. Though the grounds are compact compared to the expansive Mountains of the Moon Hotel on page 408, the verandas, balconies, lawns & pool enjoy outward views towards the mountains beyond the town. *US$80/110 sgl/dbl B&B.* **$$$**

THE TORO KINGDOM

Fort Portal lies at the physical and political heart of Toro, the youngest of Uganda's traditional kingdoms, ruled – aptly – by the world's most youthful monarch, not quite four years old when he took the throne in 1995. Toro started life as a southern principality within the Bunyoro kingdom, from which it broke away to become an independent kingdom in the late 1820s under Prince Kaboyo, the son of the Bunyoro king, Nyakamaturu. The original kingdom corresponded roughly with the present-day administrative districts of Kabarole (which includes Fort Portal), Kyenjojo, Kamwenge, Bundibugyo and Kasese, but the last two are not considered to be part of Toro today.

In the mid 1820s, Nyakamaturu, reaching the end of his 50-year reign, was evidently regarded as a weak and unpopular ruler. As a result, Kaboyo, the king's favourite son and chosen heir to the throne, had become impatient to claim his inheritance. In part, Kaboyo's haste might have been linked to a perceived threat to his future status: Nyakamaturu had already survived at least one attempted overthrow by a less-favoured son, while the elders of Bunyoro openly supported his younger brother Mugenyi as the next candidate for the throne. While on a tour of Toro c1825, Kaboyo came to realise the full extent of his father's unpopularity in this southern part of Bunyoro, and he was persuaded by local chiefs to lead a rebellion that left Toro a sovereign state.

Nyakamaturu's army had the better of the rebels in the one full-scale battle that occurred between them, but the ageing king was not prepared for his favourite son to be killed, and he eventually decided to tolerate the breakaway state. It has even been suggested that Kaboyo was invited to succeed the Banyoro throne after Nyakamaturu's death in the early 1830s, but declined, leaving the way clear for Mugenyi to be crowned King of Bunyoro. By all accounts, Kaboyo's 30-year reign over Toro was marked by a high level of internal stability, as well as a reasonably amicable relationship with Bunyoro.

The death of Kaboyo c1860 sparked a long period of instability in Toro. Kaboyo's son and nominated successor Dahiga proved to be an unpopular leader, and was soon persuaded to abdicate in favour of his brother Nyaika, who was in turn overthrown, with the assistance of the Baganda army, by another brother called Kato Rukidi. Nyaika was exiled to the present-day DRC, where he rebuilt his army to eventually recapture Toro, killing Kato Rukidi and reclaiming the throne as his own. Toro enjoyed a brief period of stability after this, but Nyaika was not a popular ruler, and the long years of civil strife had left his state considerably weakened and open to attack.

The start of Nyaika's second term on the Toro throne roughly coincided with the rise of Bunyoro's King Kabalega, who avowed to expand his diminished sphere of influence by reintegrating Toro into the ancient kingdom, along with various other smaller breakaway states. In 1876, Kabalega led an attack on Toro that left its king dead. The Banyoro troops withdrew, and a new Toro king was crowned, but he too was captured by Kabalega and tortured to death, as was his immediate and short-lived successor. The remaining Toro princes fled to Ankole, where they were granted exile, and for the next decade Banyoro rule was effectively restored to Toro.

And that might have been that, had it not been for a fortuitous meeting between the prominent Toro prince Kasagama (also known as Kyebambe) and Captain Lugard in May 1891, at the small principality of Buddu in Buganda. Kasagama was eager for any assistance that might help him to restore the Toro throne, while Lugard quickly realised that the young prince might prove a useful ally in his plans to colonise

Bunyoro – 'Inshallah, this may yet prove a trump card', he wrote of the meeting in his diary. Kasagama and his entourage joined Lugard on the march to Ankole, where they gathered together a small army of exiled Toro royalists. They then proceeded to march towards Toro, recapturing one of its southern outposts and most important commercial centres, the salt mine at Lake Katwe, then continuing north to the vicinity of Fort Portal, where a treaty was signed in which Kasagama signed away Toro sovereignty in exchange for British protection.

When Lugard left for Kampala in late 1891, leaving behind a young British officer named De Winton, the Kingdom of Toro had to all intents and purposes been restored, albeit under a puppet leader. De Winton oversaw the construction of a string of small forts along the northwestern boundaries of Toro, designed to protect it from any further attacks by Kabalega, and manned by 6,000 Sudanese troops who had been abandoned by Emin Pasha on his withdrawal from Equatoria a few years earlier. In early 1892, however, De Winton succumbed to one or other tropical disease, leaving Toro at the mercy of the Sudanese troops, who plundered from communities living close to the forts, and rapidly established themselves as a more powerful force than Kasagama and his supporters. The withdrawal of the Sudanese troops to Buganda in mid 1893 proved to be a mixed blessing: in the absence of any direct colonial presence in Toro, Kasagama briefly enjoyed his first real taste of royal autonomy, but this ended abruptly when Kabalega attacked his capital in November of the same year. Kasagama retreated to the upper Rwenzori, where several of his loyal followers died of exposure, but was able to return to his capital in early 1894 following a successful British attack on Kabalega's capital at Mparo.

Toro functioned as a semi-autonomous kingdom throughout the British colonial era. Kasagama died in 1929, to be succeeded by King George Rukidi II, a well-educated former serviceman who is regarded as having done much to advance the infrastructure of his kingdom prior to his death in 1965. In February 1966, King Patrick Kaboyo Rukidi III ascended to the Toro throne, only eight months before the traditional monarchies of Uganda were abolished by Obote. The king lived in exile until the National Resistance Movement took power in 1986, after which he enjoyed a distinguished diplomatic career serving in Tanzania and Cuba.

In July 1993, the traditional monarchies were restored by Museveni, and two years later Patrick Rukidi returned to Fort Portal for a second coronation. He died a few days before this was scheduled to take place, to be succeeded by his son Prince Oyo Nyimba Kabamba Iguru Rukidi IV who was only three years old when he came to power. The first years of the restored monarchy were marked by controversy. The sudden death of the former king just before he would have been restored to power attracted allegations of foul play from certain quarters. The plot thickened when Toro prime minister John Kataramu (one of three regents appointed to assist the young Oyo) was convicted for ordering the murder of another prince in 1999.

Following his official coronation in 2010, King Oyo is doing what he can to develop Toro through various charitable organisations. Thus far, however, he has yet to match the fundraising prowess of his mother Best Kemigisha, a close associate of Muammar Gaddafi, whose munificence funded the restoration of the derelict Toro Palace on a hill outside Fort Portal as well as the expensive educations enjoyed by Oyo and his sister Komuntale. As a result, King Oyo named Gaddafi the 'defender' of his kingdom, and the Libyan dictator's miserable end in 2011 was deeply mourned in Toro, at least by those who had benefited from his philanthropy.

Mountains of the Moon Hotel [404 D2] (33 rooms) Nyaika Av; 048 3422201; m 0775 557840, 0752 557840; e info@motmh.com; w motmh.com. Set in manicured 7ha gardens, this colonial-era landmark has comfortable rooms with terracotta floors & veranda, flatscreen TV, tea-/coffee-maker, private balcony & en-suite hot shower. The delightful veranda is the most attractive place in Fort Portal to relax with a drink. More active residents can enjoy a gym, sauna & stone-lined swimming pool. A comprehensive menu includes stir-fries, fajitas, grills, stews, salads & pizzas, with most mains falling in the US$7–12 range. Service is variable. *From US$100/125–45 sgl/dbl B&B; discounts for East African residents.* **$$$**

Moderate

Dutchess Hotel [404 C5] (5 rooms) Mugurusi Rd; m 0704 879474; e info@dutchessuganda.com; w dutchessuganda.com. Boasting a quiet but central location on the 1st floor above the Dutchess Restaurant (& the town's most varied & appetising menu; see opposite), this small owner-managed hotel offers stylish & brightly coloured rooms with twin or dbl beds, fitted nets, ceiling fans, screened windows, built-in safe, flatscreen DSTV, Wi-Fi & en-suite hot shower. *US$51/64/81 sgl/dbl/twn exc b/fast (US$8).* **$$**

Kalya Courts Hotel [404 C7] (33 rooms) Maguru Itaara Rd; 039 2080215; e info@kalyacourtshotel.com; w kalyacourtshotel.com. This modern hotel stands in extensive suburban grounds of hedge & lawn that look towards the Toro Palace south of the town centre. The spacious & airy white-tiled rooms have a modern look, with fitted nets, flatscreen DSTV, Wi-Fi & en-suite hot shower. A restaurant with terrace seating is attached. Excellent value. *US$46/66/80 sgl/dbl/twin B&B.* **$$**

Koi Koi Village [map, page 402] (16 rooms) ⊕ 0.63434, 30.26489; m 0751 569569; e koikoivillage@gmail.com; w koikoi.co.ug. Situated 2km out of town along the Kasese Rd, this attractive cultural centre has stylish & spacious rooms with slate tile floors, DSTV, twin ¾ beds & private balcony offering views towards the Rwenzori. A restaurant is attached (page 413) & the location is quite idyllic, though it could be noisy on Sun when the cultural show is in full swing (page 413). Excellent value, & all proceeds go to the NGO Ensi Women. *US$58/69/69 sgl/dbl/twin.* **$$**

✱ **RuwenZori View Guesthouse** [404 C2] (12 rooms) Lower Kakiiza Rd; 048 3422102; m 0772 722102; e ruwview@gmail.com; w ruwenzoriview.com. A perennial favourite since it opened its doors back in 1997, this suburban guesthouse is top pick for independent-minded travellers on a middling budget. Comfortable rooms with nets & hot water are mostly en suite & rates include an exceptional b/fast. Most guests also stick around for the wonderful home-cooked 4-course dinners, which are served communally to create a sociable ambience in keeping with its homestay feel. More than 60 bird species have been recorded in the pretty flowering gardens, which face the glacial peaks of the Rwenzori. A selection of baskets & other local crafts are on sale. Highly recommended at the price. *US$24/37 sgl/dbl using common showers; US$46/69 sgl/dbl. All rates B&B.* **$$**

Budget

Boulevard Excelsior [404 D1] (20 rooms) Rukurato Rd; m 0788 606345. This adequate but rather dated establishment enjoys a quiet location in a pleasant part of town, within easy walking distance of the swimming pools & gym at the Mountains of the Moon (turn left out of the gate) & Nyaika hotels (turn right). The Botanical Garden provides further scope for active enjoyment. *US$26/32–48 sgl/dbl B&B.* **$$**

Delhi Garden Guesthouse [404 C2] (17 rooms) Government Rd; m 0752 857074. Beneficiary, one suspects, of a bulk sell-off of purple paint, this guesthouse's quirky feel is furthered by its courtyard being shaded by a rickety stilted wooden platform bearing the eponymous Indian restaurant above. Pleasant clean rooms come with fitted nets, fans, flatscreen DSTV & en-suite hot shower. Good value, assuming you can live with the colour scheme. *From US$11/19 sgl/dbl B&B.* **$**

Jade Hotel [410 D4] (22 rooms) Kahinju Rd; m 0758 873777. Right next door to the New Fort View, this modern, 3-storey block is slightly smarter, slightly more expensive & slightly closer to the Link Bus terminal. *US$22/26 sgl/dbl B&B.* **$$**

New Fort View Hotel [410 D4] (22 rooms) Kahinju Rd; m 0774 924785. There's no fort in sight but, since the view does include the Link Bus terminal across the road, this hotel is perfect for an early morning departure or late arrival. *US$20/22 sgl/dbl B&B.* **$$**

Rwenzori Travellers Inn [410 C3] (22 rooms) Kasese Rd; t 048 3422075; m 0712 400570, 0774 504020; e reservations@rwenzoritravellersinn.com. This sensibly priced 3-storey block has comfortable en-suite rooms, a covered terrace restaurant serving simple but tasty mains (US$5–7) & a suspended orchid garden in the atrium. You'll sleep most soundly in rooms as far as possible from the road & 1st-floor bar. *US$13/20/21 std sgl/twin/dbl; US$32 superior dbl. All rates B&B.* **$$**

Sam's Place [410 G4] (8 rooms) Cnr Mugurusi Rd; m 0702 724261. Set in a pretty, colonial-era bungalow, this small & super-central hotel is located just behind Stanbic Bank. The clean, tiled en-suite rooms are unbeatable value & (while everything on offer in central Fort Portal is conveniently close by) a small bar/restaurant is included. *US$16/19 sgl/dbl. B&B.* **$$**

Shoestring and camping

Kalitusi Nature Resort [404 A3] (5 rooms, 3 dorms) ⊕ 0.66381, 30.26757; m 0772 957573; e info@kalitusi.com; w natureresort.kalitusi.com. This attractive, nature-oriented facility occupies a large, well-wooded compound on the edge of town beside the Mpanga River. There are wooden 6-bed dorms, equally simple private rooms with nets, & a massive camping area, all using common showers. B/fast costs US$8 & a 3-course dinner is US$15. Fun when busy but less so when quiet. To get there, follow the Bundibugyo Rd for 700m then turn right to follow a newly tarmacked road across Mpanga Bridge to find Kalitusi on the left. *US$30/60 sgl/dbl; US$15 dorm bed; US$10 pp camping.* **$–$$**

Tabes Resthouse [410 B3] (18 rooms) Malibo Rd; m 0789 189086. This above-par cheapie offers clean, tiled 1st-floor rooms with nets above a spartan courtyard. An external balcony even provides Rwenzori views. *US$4 sgl with common facilities; US$5/8 en-suite sgl/dbl.* **$**

Visitours Guesthouse [410 E3] (39 rooms) Lugard Rd; m 0772 634159. Adequate cheapie conveniently located on the corner of Bwamba Rd. *US$5 sgl with shared facilities; US$8/11 en-suite sgl/dbl.* **$**

YES Hostel [404 C2] (1 room, 10 dorms) Lower Kakiiza Rd; m 0772 780350; e yesuganda@gmail.com; w yesuganda.org. This popular hostel, run by Youth Encouragement Services (an NGO that supports orphans), stands in a suburban plot north of the town centre facing a delightful pastoral setting with mountain views beyond. *US$13 dbl; US$8 pp dorm bed; US$4 pp camping all with shared facilities inc hot showers. Rates exc b/fast (US$4).* **$**

WHERE TO EAT AND DRINK

In addition to the restaurants listed here, the covered terrace facing the manicured gardens at the Mountains of the Moon Hotel (see opposite) is a fabulous spot for a relaxed outdoor meal, though the food is a touch pricey and the service variable. Another very pleasant spot for a meal or drink is the Koi Koi Village out along the Kasese Road (page 413). See also the entry for Lake Kyaninga on page 418.

Moderate to expensive

✷ **Dutchess Restaurant** [404 C5] Mugurusi St; m 0704 879474; w dutchessuganda.com; ⌚ 07.00–23.00 daily. This brightly decorated Dutch-owned & -managed deli & restaurant is rated to be the best in Fort Portal. It offers the choice of indoor, terrace or garden seating, with views to the Rwenzori peaks on a clear day. An innovative & varied menu, with light meals & mains, includes pizzas, salads & sandwiches, & specialities include crocodile burgers, porterhouse steak, homemade pasta & chicken cordon bleu. The best coffee in town is complemented by a good wine list. Self-caterers will appreciate the range of cheeses, breads & salamis on offer. *Mains in the US$4–10 range.*

Gardens Restaurant [404 C4] Junction of Lugard & Kabundaire rds; m 0774 648235; ⌚ 07.00–22.30 daily. Occupying a wide shady terrace 400m downhill from the town centre, opposite the Mpanga Bridge & main market, Fort Portal's favourite rendezvous serves good pizzas, burgers & grills & has a well-stocked bar & great coffee, juices & smoothies. It's also a near-mandatory safari stop, the clean toilets & lunchtime buffet being firm favourites with tour groups on the go. *Buffet US$8, mains in the US$5–10 range.*

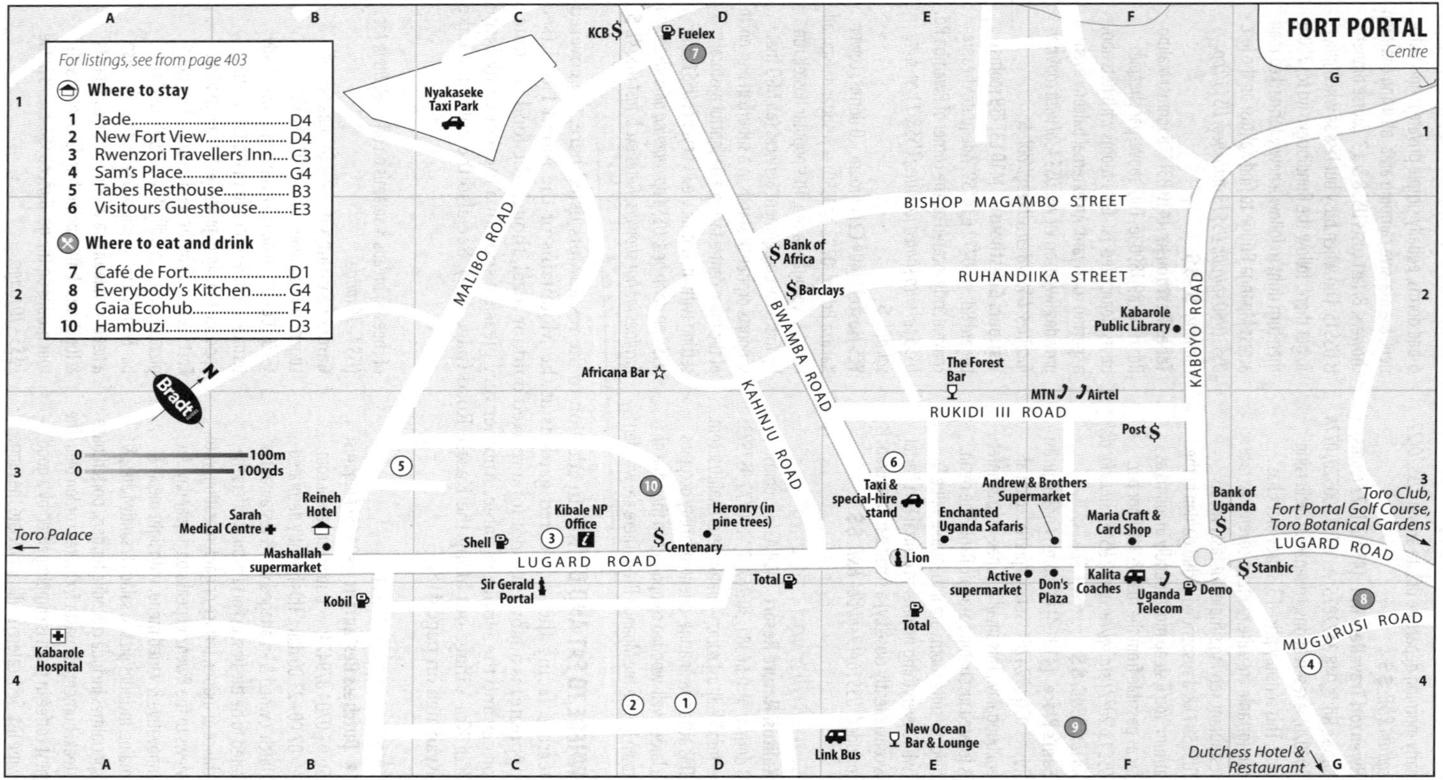
FORT PORTAL
Centre
For listings, see from page 403
Where to stay
1 Jade.....D4
2 New Fort View.....D4
3 Rwenzori Travellers Inn.....C3
4 Sam's Place.....G4
5 Tabes Resthouse.....B3
6 Visitours Guesthouse.....E3
Where to eat and drink
7 Café de Fort.....D1
8 Everybody's Kitchen.....G4
9 Gaia Ecohub.....F4
10 Hambuzi.....D3
Nyakaseke Taxi Park
KCB
Fuelex
MALIBO ROAD
BISHOP MAGAMBO STREET
RUHANDIIKA STREET
Bank of Africa
Barclays
BWAMBA ROAD
KAHINJU ROAD
Kabarole Public Library
KABOYO ROAD
Africana Bar
The Forest Bar
MTN
Airtel
RUKIDI III ROAD
Post
0 100m
0 100yds
Taxi & special-hire stand
Andrew & Brothers Supermarket
Enchanted Uganda Safaris
Maria Craft & Card Shop
Bank of Uganda
Toro Club, Fort Portal Golf Course, Toro Botanical Gardens
Reineh Hotel
Sarah Medical Centre
Toro Palace
Mashallah supermarket
Kibale NP Office
Shell
Heronry (in pine trees)
Centenary
LUGARD ROAD
Lion
Stanbic
Sir Gerald Portal
Total
Active supermarket
Don's Plaza
Kalita Coaches
Uganda Telecom
Demo
Kobil
Total
MUGURUSI ROAD
Kabarole Hospital
Link Bus
New Ocean Bar & Lounge
Dutchess Hotel & Restaurant

Cheap to moderate

Café de Fort [410 D1] Bwamba Rd. A polar opposite to the quirky Delhi Gardens, this rival Indian restaurant occupies brightly lit but characterless restaurant premises in the Fuelex Petrol Station (so plenty of parking). Though local opinions vary as to which is the better curry house, Café de Fort, despite being more expensive, probably edges it: if nothing else, you can see what you're eating. *Mains US$7 plus naan.*

Delhi Garden Restaurant [404 C2] Government Rd; m 0712 857074; ⌚ 08.00–23.00 daily. Bizarrely set on a sparsely furnished & oddly lopsided wooden platform – a walk to the loo gives the impression of being on a rolling ocean steamer – this Indian-owned restaurant serves very good & affordable Indian food, as well as a few Ugandan selections for those who prefer their meals low on spice. *Meat dishes around US$6, vegetarian selections US$3–4; naan or rice will add another US$1.*

Everybody's Kitchen (EBK) [410 G4] Mugurusi Rd; m 0744 346036; ⌚ closed Mon. Created to cater for a constant community of Spanish volunteers in Fort Portal, this sail-shaded diner occupies a leafy patio overlooking Lugard Rd as it ascends from the market. The menu offers an enterprising array of Iberian favourites including tortillas, crepes, 'real' Spanish omelettes, *patatas* & coffees. Fair weather dining only until they get a roof. *Mains US$3–5.*

Gaia Ecohub [410 F4] Kibonja Rd; m 0788 681554. Set in an open-sided shelter in a green garden on the edge of the town centre, this eco-conscious & family-friendly German/Ethiopian setup has a relaxed & friendly vibe. In addition to an Ethiopian menu, Gaia sells a range of recycled products & hosts a monthly farmers' market & regular art exhibitions. *Genau! Meat/veg mains US$5–6 inc injera.*

Hambuzi Restaurant [410 D3] Off Lugard Rd; m 0757 483481. Superior & reliably busy local eatery set in a converted old house just off the main road. It serves a varied selection of meat & vegetarian dishes. *Mains in the US$1–2 range.*

ENTERTAINMENT AND NIGHTLIFE

Africana Bar [410 D2] Off Bwamba Rd. This down-to-earth bar & club behind the Old Bus Park has terrace seating where you can cool off between dances.

The Forest Bar [410 E3] Rukidi III St; m 0772 912349. The place to be before the Pavilion opened its mesh gates, this courtyard bar remains a good place for an evening drink, to watch football & other sporting action on large screens, or to play a game of pool.

Jerusalem Paradise [404 D3] Toro Rd; m 0775 619557, 0704 161421. This curious setup, sandwiched between the golf course & Toro Botanical Gardens, is convenient for those staying in the northern suburbs. A garish indoor bar is complemented by a large garden, while a bewildering variety of fruit & vegetable cocktails (complete with New-Age hype about their benefits) share menu space with a more conventional selection of alcoholic drinks & bar snacks.

New Ocean Bar & Lounge [410 E4] Off Kibonja Rd. The newest entry to Fort Portal 's nightlife scene is found just downhill from the Link Bus terminal. Though billed as a quieter & more sophisticated venue than the rest, it apparently gives in to market forces as the night goes on.

The Pavilion [404 C3] The Boma Grounds; ⌚ lunchtime–late. Fort Portal's hottest bar occupies the old pavilion facing what was, long ago, the town's cricket ground, & the sporting theme continues with multiple screens showing Premier League football at the w/end. That said, local expats need no excuse to put in regular shifts during w/days as well, & (while conceding that the Wed quiz night might be a valid reason) one wonders when they find time to run their lodges or put on a safari. An array of freshly roasted snacks is available to buffer local rates of consumption.

SHOPPING The best general store is **Andrew & Brothers Supermarket** [410 F3] (Lugard Rd; m 0772 554602), which stocks a good range of local and imported food and drinks. Across the road, **Active Supermarket** [410 F3] is also pretty good. In third place, up at the top of the town beyond the Shell station, **Mashallah supermarket** [410 B3] beneath the storeyed Reinah Hotel offers the convenience of off-street parking. For fresh bread, your best bet is the **Dutchess Restaurant**

[404 C5] (page 409), which also sells cheese and other goodies. The large **Mpanga Market** [404 C4] opposite Gardens Restaurant is the place to buy fresh produce and much else besides. The **Maria Craft and Card Shop** [410 F3] on Lugard Road sells cards, clothes and other handicrafts made by a Church-affiliated vocational training centre near Fort Portal.

SPORTS AND ACTIVITIES The Mountains of the Moon Hotel (page 408) charges US$5 for non-residents to use its swimming pool.

Kyaninga Lodge (page 418) organises an series of annual events throughout the year, including a triathlon, marathon/half-marathon and a 100km or 200km cycling event in December to raise money for children living with disabilities (page 34). Golfers can also enjoy a round at the nine-hole golf course in the Toro Club (see below).

TOURIST INFORMATION

Kibale National Park Office [410 C4] Lugard Rd ☎ 039 2175976; e knp@ugandawildlife.org; ⌚ 08.00–17.00 Mon–Fri, 08.00–14.00 Sat. Now that chimp-tracking permits have to be arranged through UWA HQ in Kampala, this main purpose of this office appears to be to inform visitors of the fact.

TOUR OPERATORS

Enchanted Uganda Safaris [410 E3] Lugard Rd; m 0781 965467/0704 297469; e info@enchantedugandasafaris.com; w enchantedugandasafaris.com. This centrally located operator has been recommended by readers.

Weekend Adventurers/Fort Portal Tour Guides Association [404 C4] m 0779 775790, 0783 493177; e kenneththugume729@gmail.com; f forttourguides2017association2. Based in the old Post Office uphill of the market, these affiliated organisations can arrange a wide selection of day & longer tours in & around Fort Portal, as well as offering mountain-bike hire at US$10/day.

WHAT TO SEE AND DO This section covers most sites of interest within or close to Fort Portal, but it excludes several popular day trips detailed elsewhere in this chapter under the headings *Toro Crater Lakes* (page 415) and *Kibale National Park* (page 425). Fort Portal is the sole road gateway to the Semliki Valley, the subject of *Chapter 16*, and the usual starting point for the Northern Rwenzori mini-hike between Kazingo and Bundibugyo detailed in *Chapter 17* (page 467).

For those who enjoy unguided rambling, details of a trio of great day walks – a 9.3km city tour, a 12.6km circular hike on the city outskirts, and an 8.6km one-way hike to Lake Kyaninga – designed by former Fort Portal resident Jozef Serneels are posted as three separate downloadable PDFs with maps at w bradtugandaupdate.wordpress.com/2019/01/09/day-hikes-in-and-around-fort-portal. Hard copies of each hike are available at RuwenZori View Guesthouse (page 408).

Northern suburbs Both the sites listed here lie a short walk north of the town centre, amid the green administrative suburbs that also house the Mountains of the Moon Hotel, RuwenZori View Guesthouse and YES Hostel.

Fort Gerry and the Toro Club The short-lived 1891 construction after which Fort Portal is named once stood on a hill about 1km north of the modern town centre. All that survives of it today is a defensive trench that now partially encloses the **Toro Club** [404 C3], where a bronze plaque commemorating Fort Gerry is still displayed. The focal point of the Toro Club is the lovely nine-hole

Fort Portal Golf Course [404 D4], which was laid out across 3ha of well-wooded land back in 1914. Non-members pay US$10 to play a round, and caddies are available along with clubs for hire. The sociable clubhouse bar is reliably busy on weekend evenings.

Tooro Botanical Gardens [404 D3] (Nyaika Av; e tooboga@yahoo.com; f TooroBotanicalGardens; ⌚ 08.00–17.00 Mon–Sat, 09.00–16.00 Sun; entry US$3) Founded in 2001 with the objective of conserving and promoting awareness of the Albertine Rift flora, this commendable garden occupies around 50ha of forested valley between the Mountains of the Moon Hotel and the golf course. It contains demonstration gardens of medicinal plants, herbs and spices, fruits, flowers and trees, and the entrance fee includes an optional guided tour. It is also a good place to look for typical woodland and forest birds, including great blue turaco, Ross's turaco and black-and-white flycatcher, and birding guides are available for US$7. The main entrance on Nyaika Avenue is almost opposite the Mountains of the Moon Hotel, but if you're coming from the town centre, it's quicker to walk out to the second entrance 1km along the Fort Portal–Kampala Road. Organised birding tours can be booked through the RuwenZori View Guesthouse (page 408).

Kasese Road The attractions listed here lie alongside the Kasese Road as it runs southwest from Fort Portal, and can easily be reached by boda or matatu.

Toro Palace [404 A6] (⊕ 0.64716, 30.26848) Perched on Kabarole Hill immediately south of the town centre, Toro Palace is an imposing but rather charmless two-storey circular monolith constructed in 1963 for Omukama Rukidi III. Looted in the wake of the abolition of the old kingdoms under Obote, the palace had been reduced to little more than a concrete shell by the time Omukama Oyo was crowned in 1995, but it was fully restored in 2001, at considerable expense to royal benefactor President Gaddafi of Libya. It's worth walking or driving up Kabarole Hill for the panoramic view over the town and surrounding countryside, and there's some talk of eventually opening a proper museum within its crowning palace. For the time being, however, the palace remains unoccupied, casual visitors are forbidden from entering it, and those who approach too closely might be asked to pay the caretaker an 'entrance fee' equivalent to US$5 for being informed of this fact.

Koi Koi Village Cultural Centre [map, page 402] (⊕ 0.63383, 30.2652; m 0751 569569; e koikoivillage@gmail.com; w koikoi.co.ug; ⌚ 09.00–23.00 daily) The brainchild of the NGO Ensi Women (w ensiwomen.org), this stylish tourist 'one-stop shop' is set in lush gardens looking towards the Rwenzori, 2km along the Kasese Road. In addition to good accommodation (page 408), it incorporates a quality handicraft shop, a gallery showcasing contemporary local art, a museum displaying traditional items from Toro and elsewhere in Uganda, and a modern restaurant with indoor and terrace seating and a varied menu that includes whole tilapia, pepper steak, grilled half chicken, burgers and pasta (US$5–7). The biggest draw is the charismatic music and dance performance of the cultural troupe Angabu Za Toro (Tradition of Toro; w engabuzatooro.blogspot.com) held every Sunday from 13.00 to 21.00, when a nominal entrance fee is levied.

Karambi Tombs [map, page 402] (⊕ 0.6342, 30.24553; m 0779 357646; ⌚ 08.00–18.00 daily; entry US$3) Situated 3km southwest of Toro Palace as the crow flies, the Karambi Tombs comprise a thatched construction housing the graves of three former Toro kings – Kasagama (died 1928), Rukidi II (died 1965) and Rukidi III (died 1995) – along with an open-air cemetery where several lesser members of the royal family are buried. The friendly and soft-spoken caretaker – grandson of the original guardian appointed after the death of Omukama Kasagama – will happily show visitors inside the tombs, which are decorated with various royal paraphernalia. To reach the unsignposted site, follow the Kasese Road out of town for 5.5km to Karambi, then turn right 50m before a large whitewashed mosque on the left, and continue for another 150m.

Rubona Basket Weavers Association [map, page 402] (RUBOWA; m 0782 562640; f rubonabasketsuganda) Situated on the west side of the Kasese Road in the village of Rubona, 22km from Fort Portal, the Rubona Basket Weavers Association is a co-operative of more than 200 women that produce *ekibo*-style baskets – colourful, flattish and circular – using raffia palm fibre and organic pigments made from *Rubia* roots and other indigenous plants. The intricately patterned baskets make wonderful wall hangings, and while most are sold to international markets or through outlets in Kampala, a good selection is available to be bought directly from RUBOWA for up to US$10 apiece.

Mugusu and Rwimi markets The colourful weekly markets at Mugusu (⊕ 0.61229, 30.21278) and Rwimi (⊕ 0.37734, 30.2171), which lie along the Kasese Road below the Rwenzori peaks, are important social events, and well worth visiting if you're in town on the right day. The Wednesday market at Mugusu, 10km south of Fort Portal, is mostly concerned with secondhand clothing, attracting buyers from as far afield as Kampala. The more conventional Friday vegetable and food market at Rwimi, about 45km south of Fort Portal, is very large and colourful, with a spectacular setting.

Rwagimba hot springs [map, page 398] This little-visited site is set in the deep Rwimi River Valley in the shadow of the Rwenzori, 12.5km west of the Kasese Road. Don't expect too much from the actual springs – this is not Iceland or Yellowstone – but rather go for the walk there, which provides a great opportunity to stretch your legs in superb mountain scenery with no national park entry fees. The actual springs comprise a pair of excavated pools beside the Rwimi River, one for women, the other for men. Despite the calm and contented expressions of the folk sitting in the pool, the water is hot! And the possibility of a temperature-related incident is not limited to the pools. Paddle in the adjacent river and shuffle your feet down into its sandy bed, and you'll experience confusingly contrasting sensations as your ankles numb in the glacial meltwaters while the soles of your feet heat up to the point of pain. To get there, first head to Kibito, roughly 30km south of Fort Portal on the Kasese Road, then drive or catch a boda west for 6km to the village of Rwagimba. From here, the up-and-down 6km hike to the springs takes around 2–3 hours, culminating in a particularly steep descent to the narrow rocky floodplain of the Rwimi River.

Semliki Viewpoint [map, page 438] The rift escarpment near Harugongo, about 10km north of Fort Portal, offers some spectacular views over the Semliki Valley to Lake Albert almost 1,000m below. To get there, follow Toro Road north out past the Mountains of the Moon Hotel for about 8km until you reach Harugongo trading centre, then continue north for 500m to a T-junction (⊕ 0.73846, 30.27895), where you need to turn right. After 1.2km, you'll pass Harugongo Sub-County

Headquarters, then after another 1km, you'll see St Raphael Catholic Church signposted to the left (⊕ 0.74583, 30.2965). Take this left turn and continue for about 2.5km to the main viewpoint (⊕ 0.76472, 30.29277). Using public transport, you could catch a matatu to Harugongo, then walk the last 5km, or take a boda all the way from Fort Portal. Kyaninga Lodge (page 418) organises guided day hikes to the viewpoint for its guests.

TORO CRATER LAKES

A scenic highlight of Toro subregion is the concentration of jewel-like crater lakes that runs between Fort Portal and Kibale National Park, providing the setting for some wonderfully sited upmarket and budget lodges from which to explore the fertile countryside or track Kibale's chimps. A total of more than three-dozen permanent crater lakes can be found in Toro, scattered across a 10km-wide longitudinal band that runs parallel to the western boundary of Kibale National Park from Fort Portal south to Kasenda. Geographically, there are two main groups of lakes: an isolated quintet set in the hilly countryside immediately north of Fort Portal, and a much larger and more sprawling cluster that starts about 15km south from Fort Portal as the crow flies. For logistical reasons, however, we have divided the southern lakes into three further subgroups: the Rweetera cluster of three lakes on the west side of the main road between Fort Portal and Kibale Forest; the Rwaihamba cluster of about ten lakes focused around Nkuruba, Rwaihamba and Kabata; and the Kasenda cluster of about 20 lakes sprawling in all directions from Kasenda trading centre. Set below a majestic Rwenzori backdrop and offering easy access to Kibale National Park, this fertile lakes region is dominated by lush cultivation, but it also supports many relict pockets of indigenous forest and swamp, together with a profusion of birds, monkeys and butterflies, providing almost limitless opportunities for casual exploration.

GEOLOGY, FLORA AND FAUNA The Toro Crater Lakes are the most northerly component in a vast field of volcanic calderas that runs south from Fort Portal via Queen Elizabeth National Park to the Rift Valley Escarpment around Bunyaruguru. Legend has it that these fertile craters, overshadowed by the glacial peaks of the Rwenzori, and numbering more than 100 in total, are the bountiful handiwork of Ndahura, the first Bachwezi king. Geologically, the craters – many of which formed within the last 10,000 years and host small freshwater or saline lakes – provide a graphic reminder of the immense volcanic forces that have moulded the landscapes of western Uganda.

The fertile volcanic soils and high annual rainfall of the lakes region ensures it supports a lush mosaic of verdant tropical cultivation, forest, grassland and swamp. While the region lacks the biodiversity of neighbouring Kibale National Park, the relict forest patches associated with the steep-sided calderas wherein the lakes are nestled are often conspicuously inhabited by monkeys and forest-associated turacos, hornbills, barbets and sunbirds. For wildlife enthusiasts, the highlight of the region is probably the community-managed Lake Nkuruba Nature Reserve, but the grounds of upmarket lodges such as Ndali and Kyaninga are also very rewarding.

GETTING THERE AND AWAY All lodges and places of interest associated with the Rweetera, Rwaihamba and Kasenda clusters can be approached from Fort Portal along the route described here. Exceptions are Kluges Guest Farm and Bella Vista, which are most easily accessed from the Kasese Road, and Kyaninga Lodge to the north of Fort Portal (see individual entries for more details).

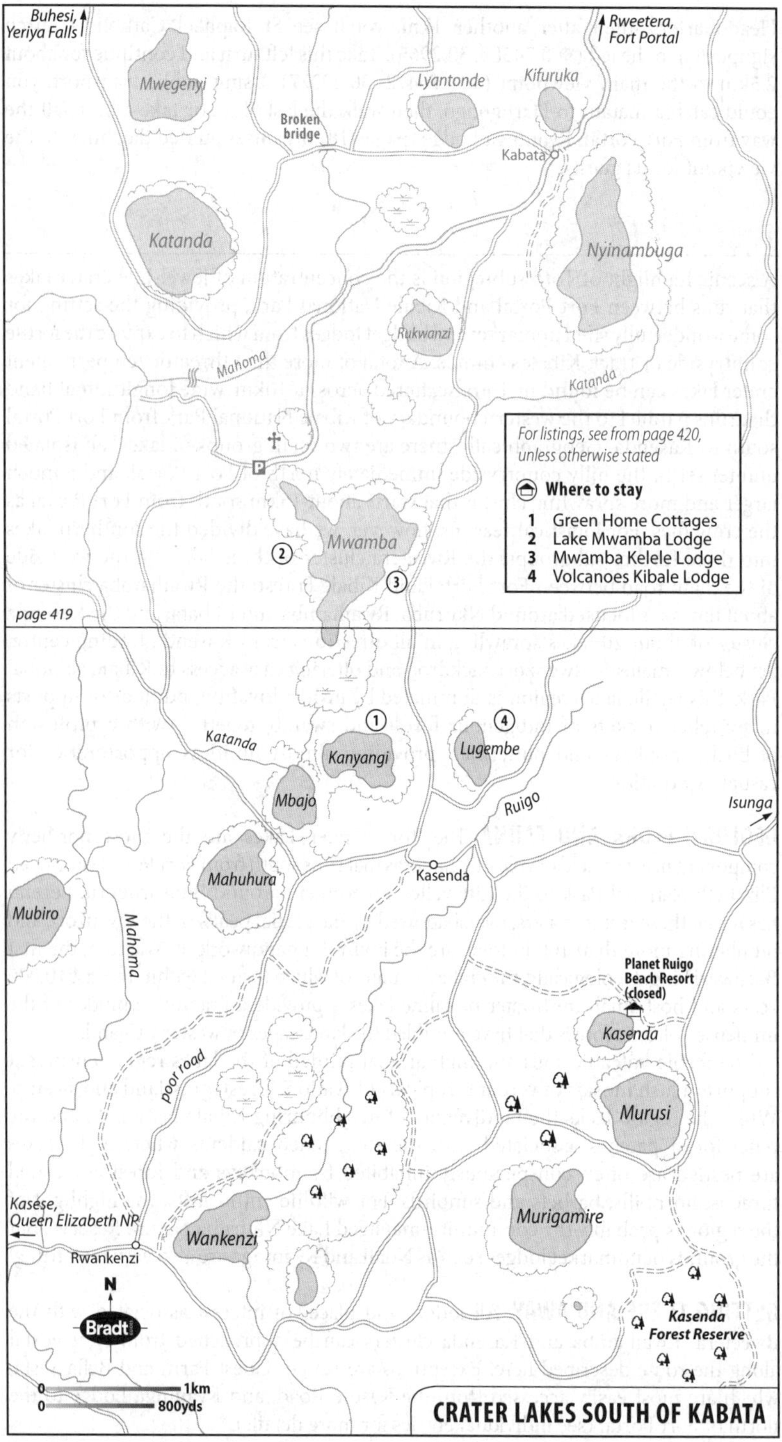
Buhesi, Yeriya Falls
Rweetera, Fort Portal
Mwegenyi
Lyantonde
Kifuruka
Broken bridge
Kabata
Katanda
Nyinambuga
Rukwanzi
Mahoma
Katanda
For listings, see from page 420, unless otherwise stated
Where to stay
1 Green Home Cottages
2 Lake Mwamba Lodge
3 Mwamba Kelele Lodge
4 Volcanoes Kibale Lodge
Mwamba
page 419
Katanda
Kanyangi
Lugembe
Mbajo
Ruigo
Isunga
Mahuhura
Kasenda
Mubiro
Mahoma
Planet Ruigo Beach Resort (closed)
Kasenda
poor road
Murusi
Kasese, Queen Elizabeth NP
Murigamire
Wankenzi
Rwankenzi
N
Bradt
Kasenda Forest Reserve
0 1km
0 800yds
CRATER LAKES SOUTH OF KABATA

Self-drive Heading from central Fort Portal to any of the crater lakes further south, follow Lugard Road north for a few hundred metres, then turn right on to the newly surfaced road to Ibanda immediately before the Mpanga River bridge. Just beyond Kasisi, after 12km, a right fork decorated with lodge signposts (⊕ 0.57552, 30.31015) marks the start of a dirt road leading to the Rwaihamba and Kasenda clusters, taking in Lake Nkuruba, Rwaihamba village, Kabata/Ndali Lodge and Kasenda after 8km, 10km, 13km and 18km respectively. To reach the Rweetera cluster, continue straight on the asphalt Ibanda Road (as if heading to Kibale National Park) and you'll reach the lodges associated with lakes Nyinabulitwa and Nyabikere after another 8–11km.

Coming from Queen Elizabeth National Park or elsewhere in the south, an unsurfaced short cut to Kasenda and Rwaihamba branches east from the Kasese Road about 1.5km north of Rwimi.

Public transport A few matatus run daily from Fort Portal to both Rwaihamba and Kasenda, along a road that tends to be busiest on Rwaihamba's market days (Mon & Thu). They leave Fort Portal from a stand close to Mpanga Bridge, and can drop you anywhere en route. If you are heading to a lodge in the Rweetera cluster, you need a matatu for Bigodi (page 426). It is also possible to charter a boda from Fort Portal to any of the lakes.

WHERE TO STAY AND EAT In addition to the lodges and camps listed here, any hotel in Fort Portal can be used as a base for exploring the Toro Crater Lakes. Equally,

KYANINGA: A LODGE WITH A HEART... *By Chris Gibbons*

Thankfully, many lodges in Uganda choose to support their local communities. And at Kyaninga Lodge, community involvement really is at the heart of the enterprise. By staying there, you will support the valuable work it does in supporting local children with disabilities. Steve Williams, the lodge's owner, has a son with disabilities, and the realisation of the total lack of support for children in this position in rural Uganda motivated him to set up the Kyaninga Child Development Centre (w kyaningacdc.org) in 2014. The organisation has since grown and now consists of a Therapy and Rehabilitation Centre, an Inclusive Model School, an Education Hub offering training in inclusive education to local Ugandan schools and an Assistive Technology workshop, producing bamboo wheelchairs for local children. Today, it employs 85 people and has so far helped over 7,000 children.

It is important to note that the charity work done by Kyaninga is not forced upon you during your stay; if you choose, you can simply enjoy a relaxing visit to the lodge and think no further about it, knowing that merely by staying there you have made a contribution. However, for those travellers who wish to have a deeper insight into local people's lives and the positive impact that tourism can have, you can choose to find out more by taking a walk through the lovely lodge grounds down to the mobility workshop or the showcase, which sensitively tells of the story of the organisation. For those travellers who would like to venture further afield, a visit to the Inclusive School and Therapy and Rehabilitation Centre are the making of an inspirational short excursion into Fort Portal town.

most lodges associated with the crater lakes are well placed for chimp tracking in Kibale National Park, assuming you have private transport.

The Fort Portal cluster and Kasese Road

Map, page 402

Of the 3 lodges listed here, Kyaninga Lodge lies on the rim of the eponymous crater lake a few kilometres north of Fort Portal, while the other 2 lie alongside or a short distance east of the main Kasese Rd. Kyaninga Lodge & Kluges Guest Farm rank among the most popular bases from which to track Kibale's chimps, while Bella Vista is uniquely well positioned as a base from which to explore both Kibale & Queen Elizabeth national parks.

Exclusive

✷ **Kyaninga Lodge** (9 cottages) m 0772 999750; e info@kyaningalodge.com; w kyaningalodge.com. This masterpiece of imaginative engineering, built using massive eucalyptus logs, comprises a central dining/reception area connected by a tall timber catwalk to the spacious luxury cottages with king-size bed, walk-in nets, en-suite hot shower & private balcony. Perched on the rim of the 220m-deep Kyaninga Crater Lake, lodge & cottages look across startlingly blue waters hemmed in by forested cliffs towards rolling green hills backed (weather permitting) by the snow-speckled Rwenzori peaks. The 60ha grounds incorporate a 2.4m-deep swimming pool, lawn tennis, badminton & croquet courts, & a vegetable garden/orchard providing organic produce to the kitchen. Activities include a 3hr forest walk (good for colobus monkeys & birds) & a 90min walk around the crater rim. A footpath leads down to the shore of the bilharzia-free lake, where you can swim or explore by canoe. To get here, head 2km out of town along the Kampala Rd, then turn left up the Kijura Rd, then left again after 2km at a signposted turning & carry on for 4.5km. *Discounts for East African residents.* **$$$$$$**

Moderate and budget

Bella Vista (12 rooms, 10-bed dorm) m 0773 204364; e booking@lodgebellavista.com; w lodgebellavista.com. This attractively priced & Italian-owned lodge is perched on the rim of Nyamiteza Crater Lake, 2km east of the main Kasese Rd. Bright en-suite rooms have balconies on both sides, 1 facing the swimming pool & the other the lake. In addition to a fabulous lake view, the 1st-floor Italian-themed restaurant displays eye-catching monochrome images of Uganda, captured in 1906 by photographer-mountaineer Vittorio Sella, & serves a pasta & pizza-based menu, with most mains in the US$7–12 range. There's a pool on site while activities further afield include mountain bike hire & swimming or boating down at the lake. *US$80/100 sgl/dbl B&B; US$15 pp dorm bed B&B; US$5 pp camping.* **$$–$$$**

Kluges Guest Farm (10 rooms, 7 standing tents) m 0775 440099; e klugesguestfarm@gmx.de; w klugesguestfarm.com. In a break from local lodge-siting convention, this owner-managed guest farm occupies a pretty pastoral site above the Mahoma River Valley rather than a volcanic crater rim. The entrance is a delight: a 1km avenue of gorgeous flowering plants beneath twin lines of trees. The comfortable en-suite rooms are set in a formal terrace softened by a pastoral setting. A swimming pool is provided & forest walks are offered to look for some of the 175 bird species so far recorded. Popular with expats seeking an affordable & family-friendly getaway, Kluges is located a few kilometres east of the main Kasese Rd, with turnings signposted at Kasusu & Buhesi, 3km & 15km south of Fort Portal respectively. *US$175/205 sgl/dbl HB; discounts for East African residents. US$15 pp camping.* **$$$$**

Rweetera cluster

Map, page 419

Set among tea estates close to the Isunga Park Headquarters, the lodges listed here stand on the west side of the main road from Fort Portal, a few kilometres south of Rweetera & 12km north of Kanyanchu, meaning that they are very convenient for chimp tracking in the national park.

Moderate

Chimpanzee Forest Lodge (9 garden cottages, 2 rooms) m 0772 486415; e reservations@chimpanzeeforestguesthouse.com; w chimpanzeeforestlodge.com. This lovely hillside guesthouse centres on the 1950s house of one C W Switzer, a British tea planter, & is run by his Ugandan descendants who have added 9 cottages in the lovely garden. The old man chose a super site for his home, the site enjoying a distant view

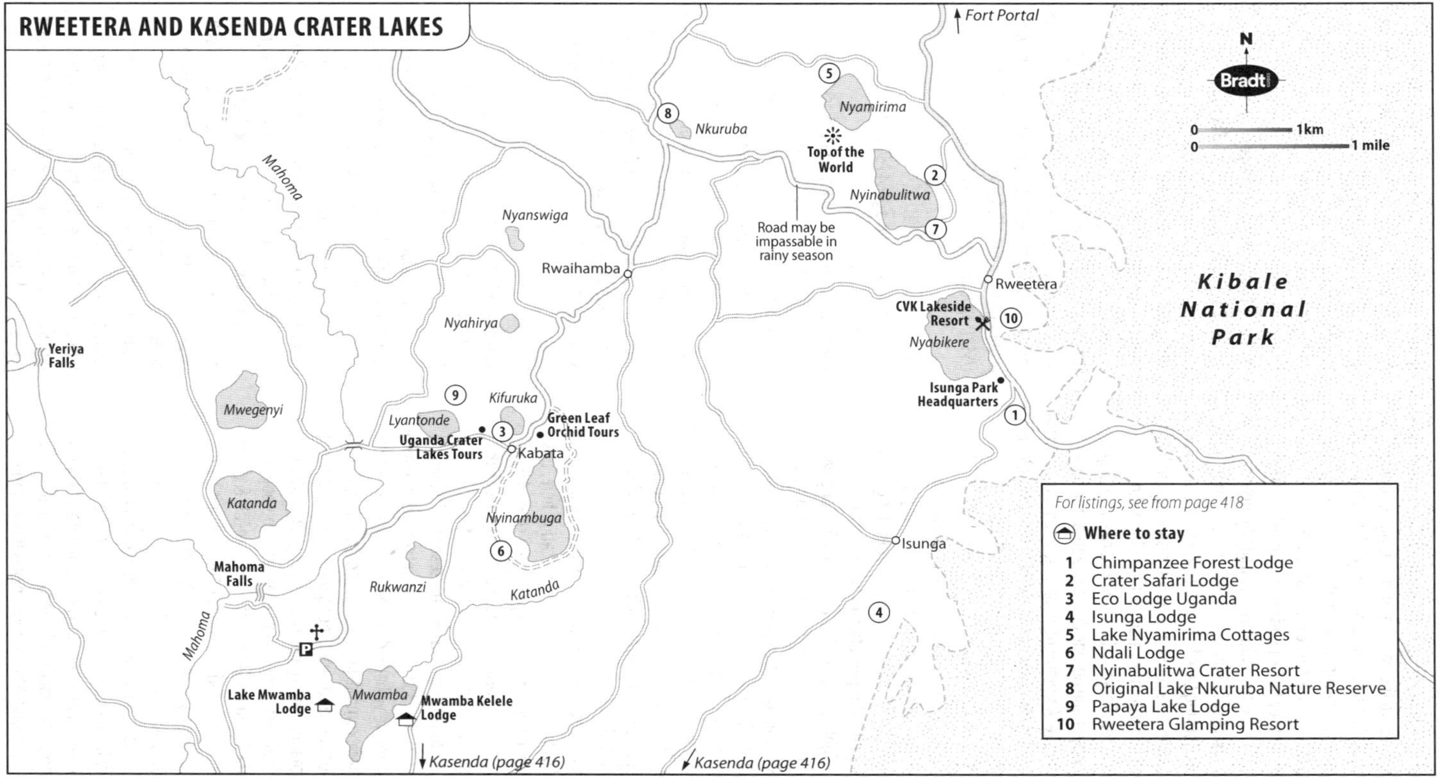

RWEETERA AND KASENDA CRATER LAKES
Fort Portal
N
Bradt
0
1km
0
1 mile
Kibale National Park
Nkuruba
Nyamirima
Top of the World
Nyinabulitwa
Road may be impassable in rainy season
Rweetera
CVK Lakeside Resort
Nyabikere
Isunga Park Headquarters
Mahoma
Nyanswiga
Rwaihamba
Nyahirya
Yeriya Falls
Mwegenyi
Kifuruka
Lyantonde
Uganda Crater Lakes Tours
Green Leaf Orchid Tours
Kabata
Katanda
Nyinambuga
Isunga
Mahoma Falls
Rukwanzi
Katanda
Mahoma
Lake Mwamba Lodge
Mwamba
Mwamba Kelele Lodge
Kasenda (page 416)
Kasenda (page 416)
For listings, see from page 418
Where to stay
1 Chimpanzee Forest Lodge
2 Crater Safari Lodge
3 Eco Lodge Uganda
4 Isunga Lodge
5 Lake Nyamirima Cottages
6 Ndali Lodge
7 Nyinabulitwa Crater Resort
8 Original Lake Nkuruba Nature Reserve
9 Papaya Lake Lodge
10 Rweetera Glamping Resort

of Lake Nyabikere to the north with tea plantations & forest to the east & south. A range of guided walks is offered. *US$95/140 sgl/dbl cottage B&B; rooms in the main house US$85/110 sgl/dbl B&B; US$10 pp camping exc b/fast.* **$$$**

✷ **Crater Safari Lodge** (24 units) m 0765 207119; e reservations@crystallodgeuganda.com; w cratersafarilodge.com. Occupying a large site overlooking Lake Nyinabulitwa, this extensive setup centres on a commodious & stylish lodge building, while accommodation is offered in spacious wooden-floored lake-view cottages, plus slightly cheaper one up-one down chalets at the back of the site. A swimming pool is included & residents & low season discounts are offered. *US$160/320 std chalet; US$185/370 cottage. FB.* **$$$$**

✷ **Isunga Lodge** (8 cottages) m 0704 578783, 0774 181966; e contact@isungalodge.com; w isungalodge.com. Owned & managed by a hands-on Scottish couple, this new lodge has a superb hilltop location overlooking the forest of neighbouring Kibale National Park, along with more distant views to Lake George, Lake Edward, Kichwamba Escarpment & the Rwenzori peaks. A useful base for chimp tracking, only 3km on dirt from the Isunga Park Headquarters & surfaced road to Kanyanchu, it also has a small swimming pool & offers bikes for exploring the surrounding crater lake landscape. Great value. *US$105/135 sgl/dbl B&B.* **$$$**

Nyinabulitwa Crater Resort (6 rooms) m 0782 061462. No giddy crater rim location here, this small lodge occupies a pretty site shaded by remnant forest trees close to the shore of Lake Nyinabulitwa. *US$80/100 B&B.* **$$$**

✷ **Rweteera Glamping Resort** (12 units) m 0751 735727; e info@rweteeraglampingsite.com. We've backed ourselves into a bit of a corner here, committing ourselves to awarding stars for lodges which are, among other things, 'unusually characterful' (page 87). A strong contender for the strangest lodge you've ever seen, this adjunct to the Rweteera Tea Factory serves meals & drinks in a converted warehouse. Unusual, but hardly bonkers, you might say – but bear with us. An adjacent semi-circle of 2-storeyed accommodation comprises individually themed & cement-rendered units that include, among other things, a shoe, teapot, pineapple, log cabin, tomato & what is possibly a maize cob. Unconventional to say the least, while the location makes it even more surreal. Sensibly, the attached swimming pool is normal enough. *US$180 family banda sleeping up to 6 FB; US$80 dbl cabin B&B; US$35 pp standing tent B&B.* **$$$**

Budget

✷ **Lake Nyamirima Cottages** (5 rooms) m 0772 447120. Located on a lofty ridge, 1.5km from the Kibale tarmac, this lovely & very affordable little lodge looks over a fringe of forest trees into the still jungle-fringed Nyamirima crater. Set in a neat garden, the round thatched cottages are very reasonably priced & though a lodge building is currently lacking, you should find this deficiency remedied by the adjacent & newly acquired viewpoint. *US$50/60 sgl/dbl B&B. Add US$10 pp for additional meals.* **$$**

Rwaihamba and Kasenda clusters *Map, page 419, unless otherwise stated*

The main cluster of accommodation associated with the Toro Crater Lakes lies along the 5km stretch of road running south from Lake Nkuruba to the junction village of Kabata. With private transport, these lodges are conveniently based for chimp tracking, whether you follow the main road back through Kasisi, or take 1 of 2 4x4-only short cuts – an 8.5km dirt track between Rwaihamba & Isunga, or a 5km dirt track between Lake Nkuruba & Rweetera – that may be impassable after rain.

Exclusive

Volcanoes Kibale Lodge [map, page 416] (8 cottages) ☎ 041 4346464; m 0772 741718; e salesug@volcanoessafaris.com; w volcanoessafaris.com. Situated some 45mins' drive from Kibale's Kanyanchu trailhead, the latest offering from the upmarket Volcanoes safari company enjoys an unsurpassed, broadside-on view of the Rwenzori from an elevated site above Lake Lugembe. The luxurious cottage accommodation is spacious, with open fires; the food is both imaginative & excellent; while a superb library will have Africa-philes heading immediately online to order their own copies.

Outdoors, the regional panorama is magnificent while an indigenous landscaping revegetating former farmland already rattles with abundant birdlife. Diversions include a walk around the crater lake & a pool-spa. **$$$$$$**

Upmarket

Ndali Lodge (8 cottages) m 0772 221309; e info@ndalilodge.co.ug; w ndalilodge.co.ug. Situated 1km south of Kabata along a narrow private road, Ndali has long been ranked among Uganda's best regarded lodges. Set on a lofty crater rim, verandas face east above lovely Lake Nyinambuga while the westerly outlook from the pool & cottages looks across rolling hills & crater lakes towards the Rwenzori peaks. An English country-house ambience is generated by an airy lounge decorated with period etchings of flora & fauna, an excellent library & candlelit 5-course dinners served with silver cutlery. **$$$$$**

Papaya Lake Lodge (9 cottages) m 0793 388277; e info@papayalakelodge.com; w papayalakelodge.com. This modern Polish-owned & -managed lodge sprawls across the forested inner slope of the crater that encloses beautiful Lake Lyantonde. The secluded cottages, with wooden floors & tall thatched ceilings, are complemented by a magnificent lodge building adorned with ethnic artefacts & lovely elevated swimming pool area behind the main lodge. Birds & monkeys are plentiful. **$$$$$**

Budget and camping

Eco Lodge Uganda (4 rooms) m 0772 562513; e emmanueltugume@gmail.com. This basic facility overlooks Kifuruka Crater Lake only 100m from Kabata junction. The site is rather bare & exposed, but the accommodation is tucked below the crater rim & enjoys a good view over the lake. The lodge also arranges excursions to Mahoma & Nsongya waterfalls plus a 6hr circuit taking in 9 crater lakes. *US$6 pp banda using shared bathrooms; US$14/27 sgl/dbl en-suite cottages; camping US$5 pp. Rates exc meals.* **$$**

Green Home Cottages [map, page 416] (4 cottages) m 0772 333203. This serene retreat lies about 1km north of Kasenda village on the west side of the road back to Kabata. The wood-&-concrete cottages lie in the rim of Lake Kanyangi, which is nestled in a steep crater surrounded by lushly vegetated cliffs. Several other crater lakes lie within 1km of the lodge. *US$27/40 sgl/dbl B&B.* **$$$**

Lake Mwamba Lodge (4 rooms) ⊕ 0.46258469, 30.267992; m 0754 770628, 0779 669842; e lakemwambalodge@gmail.com; w lakemwambalodge.com. A fabulously elevated location provides panoramic views in all directions from this simple lodge, 5km south of Kabata trading centre. Rustic en-suite cottages face towards the Rwenzori snow peaks (view weather permitting) while the restaurant looks across Lake Mwamba & the rolling hills of Toro (views guaranteed between 07.00 & 19.30). *US$39/75 sgl/dbl B&B.* **$$**

Mwamba Kelele Lodge (6 rooms) m 0701 428216. Situated on the eastern rim of Lake Mwamba close to the main Kasisi–Rwimi road, this worthy, Spanish-founded setup includes basic accommodation & a school which supports orphaned and disadvantaged children. US$40-60/60 sgl/dbl B&B. **$$**

✷ **Original Lake Nkuruba Nature Reserve** (10 rooms) m 0773 266067; e enquiries@nkuruba.com; w nkuruba.com. Protecting a jungle-fringed crater lake 2km north of Rwaihamba, this laid-back community-run reserve & rest camp (proceeds fund a local primary school) is an ideal base from which to explore the crater lakes, though price hikes following recent improvements (all cottages are now en suite) may have alienated their traditional backpacker market. Amenities include mountain-bike hire & a short hiking trail from where you're likely to see red colobus, black-&-white colobus & red-tailed monkey along with a good variety of forest birds. Be aware that boda & matatu drivers have, in the past, been incentivised to drop travellers asking to stay at Nkuruba at the inferior Enfuzi Community Campsite overlooking the same lake. *US$100/140 B&B/FB en-suite lake view cottage; US$50/100 B&B/FB Hilltop & Rwenzori view cottages; US$8 pp camping.* **$$**

WHAT TO SEE AND DO As with accommodation, the activities described on the following pages are grouped together under the four main crater lake clusters: Fort Portal, Rweetera, Rwaihamba and Kasenda. The lodges serving the crater lakes are also regularly used as bases for chimp tracking in Kibale National Park and the swamp walk in Bigodi.

Fort Portal cluster The sites listed here are associated with the small group of crater lakes that lies immediately north of Fort Portal. They all make straightforward targets for a day trip out of the town.

Lake Kyaninga The most spectacular of the crater lakes north of Fort Portal is also the site of Kyaninga Lodge (page 418), which offers a superb view across the blue waters and forested cliffs of the twin calderas to the Rwenzori peaks. When the lodge isn't too busy, day visitors are usually welcome to enjoy a two-/three-course lunch/dinner – a thoroughly enjoyable outing, but booking is essential and availability depends on overnight occupancy. Lunch and dinner guests are also welcome to swim in the lake and explore the trails on the lodge property. More ambitiously, RuwenZori View Guesthouse (page 408) can organise a guided 8km hike from Fort Portal to Lake Kyaninga, culminating in lunch or dinner, though once again this depends on how busy the lodge is.

Lake Saka The largest water body in the immediate vicinity of Fort Portal, Saka is not strictly speaking a crater lake, but rather a flooded valley dammed by a crater. It is one of the few lakes in the area to support fish large enough for commercial harvesting, and it is reputedly safe to swim in. Birding is also fantastic; the Kibale Bird Population Monitoring Team recorded 82 species in 90 minutes on a recent early morning transect. It's possible to walk there directly from Fort Portal in 1½–2 hours. From the landmark Gardens Restaurant beside the Mpanga Bridge, head straight through the adjacent industrial area to follow the Saka Road for about 5km until you see the Mountains of the Moon University signposted to the left (this is a pretty boring route, mostly through ribbon development, so you might hop on a boda at some stage). Follow this track, passing the campus on your right, for 1km and you'll see Lake Saka on the right. A left turn here along the base of a high, pyramidal hill leads between Lake Kigere on your left and a larger, swamp-lined lake on the right. At a T-junction beyond, you can either turn right and right again, or left and then keep left (the last bit is a footpath) to loop back to the University–Lake Saka track. The left turn passes a homestead on the western rim of Lake Kigere (which means 'foot') where, for a small fee, you can see the Giant's Footstep, an impression made in a lava flow by the legendary Bachwezi king Ndahura, while he was scooping out the crater lake. From here, you can also find a way on local paths to the Amabere Caves (see below).

Amabere Caves Situated 5km west of Fort Portal as the crow flies, the small cave known as Amabere (⊕ 0.67602, 30.22594; ⊙ 07.00–18.00 daily; entry US$10) is notable less perhaps for its visual impact than for its cultural significance as the reputed birthplace of the founding Bachwezi king Ndahura (page 10). The main cave is very small, really more of an exaggerated overhang, though it is supported by several pillar-like formations of connected stalactites and stalagmites. Alongside it, you can stand on the moss-covered rocks behind a powerful small waterfall and watch the ice-cold water plunge down right in front of you, kicking spray back into your face. It's said to be safe to swim in the pool below the falls, though the water is very chilly. The riparian forest around the waterfall is rattling with birds, and it supports a few black-and-white colobus monkeys.

Amabere used to be a popular goal for a day hike out of Fort Portal, but following a threefold increase in the entrance fee a few years back, it gets mixed reviews, since many people feel the attraction is too low-key to justify the cost. To get there by car

NYINAMWIRU'S BREASTS

The Amabere Caves are named after the live stalactite formation Amabere ga Nyinamwiru (literally, Breasts of Nyinamwiru), which supposedly resembles the twin breasts of a woman. The woman in question is Nyinamwiru, a legendary princess who would most likely have lived in the 14th century and is said to have been so beautiful that no man could leave her alone. When Nyinamwiru's father King Bukuku became weary of receiving marital requests from unsuitable suitors, he took the extreme measure of cutting off his daughter's breasts in order to make her less attractive. But even this proved to be insufficient to deter Nyinamwiru's many admirers, so the king hid her away in the cave now known as Amabere. Here, she was discovered by the Batembuzi king Isaza, who impregnated her with a son. Since Nyinamwiru lacked breasts herself, she stayed on in the cave with her infant, feeding him on the cloudy limestone 'milk' that drips from its stalactites. The child nurtured by the stalactite formation would grow up to become King Ndahura, founder of the Bachwezi dynasty, which was based out of Mubende, 150km east of Fort Portal. However, after he abdicated in favour of his son (and Nyinamwiru's grandson) Wamala, Ndahura retired back to his birthplace, where his footprints can still reputedly be seen in the vicinity of Amabere.

or boda, follow the Bundibugyo Road out of Fort Portal for 6km to a signposted junction to the right (⊕ 0.66331, 30.22881), from where it's another 2km to the caves, turning right halfway, immediately before the entrance to Nyakasura School (founded by an eccentric Scotsman in 1926 and whose male students still wear kilts). You can also follow paths across country to reach the caves from Lake Kigere (see opposite).

Rweetera cluster The most popular activity here is a circular walking trail along the rim of Lake Nyabikere from CVK Lakeside Resort (a safe place to park for a modest fee and a pleasant spot to enjoy a drink after your exercise). There is no charge for walking this trail, nor is any guide required. Black-and-white colobus and other monkeys are often encountered, while a varied selection of resident birds includes Ross's turaco, great blue turaco, pygmy goose, little bittern and black-crowned night heron. Unfortunately, it is possible that a full circuit will be prevented by the construction of the Tabebuia Spa & Safari Resort on the western crater edge. Alternatively, you could hike up to Nyinabulitwa and Nyamirima, both of which lie on the west side of the Fort Portal Road, respectively 1.5km and 2.5km north of CVK. Another attractive walk follows the driveable track from Rweetera to emerge on the Kasenda Road a few hundred metres south of Lake Nkuruba. There are great views over the three crater lakes from Mpurumu Hill to the south of this track.

Rwaihamba cluster The activities listed here can all be undertaken independently, but they can also be organised as guided outings. The three outfits listed below all offer guided nature walks, crater-lake exploration, village tours, birding and swamp walks of varying duration for around US$8–15 per person.

Green Leaf Orchid Tours Roadside office overlooks Lake Nyinambuga between Rwaihamba & Ndai; m 0778 125903; e greenleaforchid@gmail.com

Nkuruba Community Tours m 0782 972756; e mukubwa2008@gmail.com; w nkurubatours.com. An affiliate of Lake Nkuruba Nature Reserve (see below).

Uganda Crater Lakes Tours Near Lake Kifuruka; m 0777 293248; e ataryebwanoah@gmail.com; w ugandacraterlakestours.weebly.com

Lake Nkuruba Nature Reserve Known mainly for the budget camp on its rim (page 421), Lake Nkuruba, though small, is also very beautiful, and well worth a visit even if you are staying elsewhere. The lake is enclosed by a steep forest-lined crater in which red-tailed monkey, red colobus and black-and-white colobus are resident, while at least 100 species of bird might be seen on the limited network of walking trails near the lake (a regularly updated checklist is pinned up in the office). The water is considered to be free of bilharzia, which if true means there's no obstacle to swimming. An entrance fee of US$2.50 is charged to day visitors but not to overnight guests.

Lake Nyahirya From Lake Nkuruba, the tiny forest-fringed Lake Nyahirya can be reached by walking south along the road to Kabata, passing through Rwaihamba trading centre after 2km, then continuing 1km further to a sharp westward kink in the road. The lake lies 500m west of this kink – if you're uncertain, ask in Rwaihamba for directions. A second crater lake, Nyanswiga, lies 1km directly to the north of Nyahirya. Rwaihamba hosts a large, colourful market on Mondays and Thursdays.

Around Kabata This small junction village, 5km south of Lake Nkuruba by road, is the site of Ndali Lodge (page 421) and Eco Lodge Uganda (page 421). On the left side of the road as you approach Kabata, you'll see the rustic office of Green Leaf Orchid Tours overlooking Lake Nyinambuga, named for its mildly saline water. You'll also find this view, incidentally, on the Ush20,000 banknote. On the other side of the road, the smaller, murkier, forest-fringed Lake Kifuruka is a good place to look for black-and-white colobus as well as Ross's turaco, great blue turaco, African grey parrot, yellow-billed duck and pygmy goose.

After another 100m, a right turn leads to still more craters. Lake Lyantonde is set in a thickly vegetated crater that contains Papaya Lake Lodge (page 421), while beyond the Mahoma River Valley, the road skirts a considerably deeper crater holding the impressive Lake Katanda with the shallower Lake Mwegenyi beyond. The appeal of the nearby Mahoma Falls, an attraction for many years, has unfortunately been reduced by a hydropower plant, though it still impresses during the rainy months. The local Green Leaf Orchid Tours (page 423) has responded by taking visitors to the more distant but also more dramatic Yeriya Falls, where a significant difference in level between the Nsonge River and its arriving tributary, the Yeriya, is resolved by a sudden and dramatic cascade.

Kasenda cluster Three further crater lakes can easily be seen from the 6km road running south from Kabata to Kasenda trading centre. About 1.5km past the main junction in Kabata, Lake Rukwanzi lies only 100m to the right of the road, but is invisible from it. Another 1.5km further, also on the right, the much larger Lake Mwamba has an irregular outline suggesting that it fills several different collapsed calderas. Finally, another 1.5km towards Kasenda, and again on the right, the stunning Lake Kanyangi, overlooked by Green Home Cottages (page 421), lies within 200m of the road, also hidden by a cliff. Directly opposite Kanyangi, Lake Lugembe, overlooked by the new and very plush Volcanoes Kibale Lodge, lies at the base of a very deep and sheer-sided steep crater, no more than 25m left of the road, but invisible from it. To the south of Kasenda, lushly forested Lake Kasenda is the site of the defunct Planet Ruigo Beach Resort.

KIBALE NATIONAL PARK

Uganda's premier chimpanzee-tracking destination, Kibale National Park protects 766km^2 of predominantly forested habitat that extends more than 50km south from the main Fort Portal–Kampala Road to the northeast border of Queen Elizabeth National Park. Originally gazetted as a forest reserve in 1932, Kibale was upgraded to national park status, and extended southward to form a contiguous block with the Queen Elizabeth National Park, in 1993. The trailhead for chimp tracking and main centre of tourist activity within the park is the Kanyanchu Visitors' Centre, which lies 35km south of Fort Portal along a newly surfaced road that continues south to Kamwenge and Ibanda. Chimps aside, Kanyanchu offers some superb forest birding and monkey viewing, with the community-run Bigodi Wetland Sanctuary, only 5km away immediately outside the park boundary, being a particular highlight in this respect. While Kibale National Park and Kanyanchu are practically synonymous so far as most visitors are concerned, a lesser-known secondary point of entry – no chimp tracking offered, but good for forest walks – can be found at the northerly Sebitoli Sector, 15km east of Fort Portal along the Fort Portal–Kampala Road.

FLORA AND FAUNA Kibale National Park is dominated by rainforest, but this is interspersed with tracts of grassland and swamp. Spanning altitudes of 1,100–1,590m, Kibale boasts a floral composition transitional to typical eastern Afro-montane and western lowland forest with more than 200 tree species recorded in total. Unlike Budongo Forest to its north, Kibale wasn't logged commercially until the 1950s, when it became an important source of timber for the Kilembe Copper Mine near Kasese, and logging was discontinued during the civil war. As a result, areas of mature forest are still liberally endowed with large-buttressed mahoganies, tall fruiting figs, and other hardwood trees whose canopy is up to 60m above the ground. It also supports a dense tangle of lianas and epiphytes, while the thick undergrowth includes wild Robusta coffee.

At least 60 mammal species are present in Kibale National Park. It is particularly rich in **primates**, with 13 species recorded, the highest for any Ugandan national park. Kibale Forest is the most important stronghold of Ugandan red colobus, but it supports eight other diurnal primate species: vervet, red-tailed, L'Hoest's and blue monkeys; Uganda mangabey; black-and-white colobus; olive baboon; and chimpanzee. It also supports four species of nocturnal prosimian including the sloth-like potto.

Most prominent among Kibale's primates is a chimpanzee population of up to 1,500 individuals, divided into at least a dozen different communities, four of which are habituated to humans. Two of these are tracked by tourists. The Kanyantale community has been visited by tourists since 1993, while the neighbouring Buraiga community was upgraded from a habituation group for tracking in 2023. The other two are reserved for researchers and include Ngogo, which is the world's largest chimp community, numbering more than 200 individuals. You might already be familiar with this group, as it contains the stars of the hugely popular Netflix docuseries *Chimp Empire*. Though why their homeland was presented as the 'Ngogo Forest' rather than promoting Kibale to millions of viewers is known only to the filmmakers and researchers from Yale University; it's certainly a mystery to the UWA's marketing department.

While Kibale Forest offers superlative primate viewing, it is not an easy place to see other large **mammals** – this is despite an impressive checklist that includes lion, leopard, elephant, buffalo, hippo, warthog, giant forest hog, bushpig, bushbuck, sitatunga, and Peter's, red and blue duikers. The elephants found in Kibale Forest belong to the forest race, which is smaller and hairier than the more familiar savannah elephant. Elephants frequently move into the Kanyanchu area during the wet season, but they are not often seen by tourists.

Roughly 370 **bird** species have been recorded in Kibale, including four species not recorded in any other national park: Nahan's francolin, Cassin's spinetail, blue-headed bee-eater and lowland masked apalis. Otherwise, the checklist for Kibale includes a similar range of forest birds to Semuliki National Park, with the exclusion of the 40-odd Semliki 'specials' and the inclusion of a greater variety of water and grassland species. The discovery of a resident population of the gorgeous green-breasted pitta by ranger Harriet Kemigisha in 2005 caused some excitement in Ugandan ornithological circles, and Kibale is now entrenched as the best place to look for this elusive central African endemic. For the truly optimistic, there's also the taxonomically ambiguous Kibale ground-thrush (*Geokichla (camaronensis) kibalensis*), which was described based on two specimens collected by Alexandre Prigogine at Kibale in 1978, and is thought to be endemic to Uganda, though the jury's out on whether it's a full species or a race of the more widespread black-eared ground-thrush. The most productive birding spots are generally Bigodi Wetland Sanctuary and the stretch of main road running either side of Kanyanchu Visitors' Centre.

FURTHER INFORMATION A very useful and inexpensive 60-page UWA-produced booklet on Kibale National Park can be bought at Kanyanchu. Uganda Maps Sheet 7 *Fort Portal & Kibale Forest* shows the national park and crater lake area in great detail.

ENTRANCE FEE The park entrance fee is US$30/40/25 FR/FNR/ROA per 24 hours. It applies only to those undertaking activities within the park, not to those merely staying at accommodation set within it (eg: Primate Lodge Kibale and Sebitoli Camp) or driving along the public road that bisects it. The entrance fee is included in the price of a chimp-tracking or habituation-experience permit. Since this permit is valid for 24 hours, no additional entrance fee will be charged for any other activity undertaken within that timeframe. This means that the only circumstance in which a standalone entrance fee is charged is when somebody does a guided day or night walk or birding excursion outside of the 24-hour timeframe in which they also tracked chimps. Though chimp permits must be booked and paid for at the UWA reservations office in Kampala, fees for other activities can be paid at Kanyanchu, Sebotoli or Isunga Park Headquarters (⊕ 0.49331, 30.33223) on the Kibale Road, about 23km out of Fort Portal. Payment is by card or MoMo, though a poor MTN signal at Kanyanchu complicates the latter.

KANYANCHU AND BIGODI The Kanyanchu Visitors' Centre and the village of Bigodi, situated only 5km apart on the main road to Kamwenge, form the focal point of most tourist visits to the Fort Portal area. A common itinerary for rushed tour parties is to track chimps from Kanyanchu in the morning, then – assuming they still have the energy – to do the Bigodi Swamp Walk (outside the national park) in the afternoon. There is a good case, however, for bucking the trend and doing it the other way around, as the Bigodi Swamp Walk tends to be far more productive for birding and monkey viewing in the relative cool of the early morning. More importantly perhaps, the 50 chimp-tracking permits available in the morning are now almost invariably fully booked, leading to a situation where you may well find yourself jostling with a couple of dozen other tourists for the best angle on a single sighting, a situation that can be stressful for all trackers and chimps alike. By contrast, relatively few people track in the afternoon, which means you've a much better chance of an intimate and unstressed encounter. Also, because the national park entrance fee of US$40 is included in the chimp-tracking fee, you could do another activity in the park the following morning (ie: within the same 24-hour period) without having to pay an additional entrance fee.

Getting there and away Kanyanchu Visitors' Centre and Bigodi respectively lie 35km and 40km south of Fort Portal on a surfaced road that runs to Mbarara via Kamwenge and Ibanda. Three alternative approaches to Kanyanchu are possible. The first, coming from Ankole, follows the surfaced road from Mbarara while the second, also surfaced, runs north from Lyantonde to join the Mbarara route at Ibanda; ideal if coming from Lake Mburo National Park. The last option, from Queen Elizabeth National Park and Kasese, is an unsurfaced short cut that branches east from the Kasese Road about 1.5km north of Rwimi and cuts across country to join the Fort Portal–Kibale Road at Isunga.

Matatus from Fort Portal to Bigodi leave from close to Mpanga Bridge. Some matatus also run from Bigodi on to Kamwenge, Ibanda and Mbarara. Traffic is generally busiest early in the morning, so long waits for the vehicle to fill up become more likely as the day progresses.

Where to stay *Map, page 402*

The accommodation described here is found on or close to the 5km stretch of road between Kanyanchu Visitors' Centre and Bigodi, a small village next to the Bigodi Swamp Walk. Though these are well placed for chimp tracking, a wider choice of accommodation can be found just 40 minutes away in the vicinity of Fort Portal (page 403).

Upmarket

✷ **Primate Lodge Kibale** (16 rooms) ⊕ 0.43735, 30.39498; t 039 3267153; m 0701 426368, 0772 426368; e info@ugandalodges.com; w ugandalodges.com. Perfectly located just a couple of mins' walk from the Kanyanchu trailhead, allowing aspiring chimp trackers rather longer to lie abed & enjoy the build-up of sound from the awakening forest. Not that the nights are entirely silent either, being washed over by a white noise of cicadas & other insects punctuated by occasional shrieks from the diminutive hyrax. The food is top notch & the service excellent, & the accommodation leaves nothing to be desired. *FB inc laundry & drinks.* **$$$$$**

✷ **Turaco Treetops** (16 units) m 0757 152323; e info@turacotreetops.com; w turacotreetops.com. This excellent lodge is set in a 5ha tract of regenerating forest on the eastern side of the Dura River Valley. Kibale National Park lies directly beyond the river & the luxury cottages are all oriented towards a wall of luxuriant rainforest strata. The 1st-floor lounge in the airy thatched lodge enjoys an even better view, looking across the full width of the park towards the Rwenzori Mountains. It is ideal for families; kids can exhaust themselves in the swimming pool & enclosed play/TV room before sleeping soundly on the 2 sgl sofa beds provided in each cottage. Guided walks (US$5) explore the forest margin, which contains plenty of birds & monkeys, plus evidence of visiting chimps & elephants. The lodge, which is just 15mins' drive from Kanyanchu trailhead, is reached via a 3km dirt road signposted west from Nkingo village (between Kanyanchu & Bigodi). Unbeatable value in this category. *US$240/310 luxury sgl/dbl; US$160/210 sgl/dbl std room. All rates B&B; add US$25 pp for FB. Discounts for residents.* **$$$–$$$$**

Moderate

Guereza Lodge (11 rooms) ⊕ 0.40225, 30.41156; m 0772 339494; e office@guerezalodge.com; w guerezalodge.com. Situated 4km off the main tarmac road, this new lodge enjoys a quiet location with cottage accommodation within sight & sound of Kibale Forest. *US$150/230 sgl/dbl FB.* **$$$$**

✷ **Kibale Forest Camp** (17 tents) ⊕ 0.3903, 30.40486; ☎ 031 2294894; m 0773 447343; e booking@naturelodges.biz; w naturelodges.biz. This long-serving tented camp, set in a pretty forest patch 2km south of Bigodi, is now managed by Nature Lodges, who spruced up the rooms & slashed the prices to make it a contender for the best-value facility in the vicinity of Kibale Forest. Classic en-suite safari tents have slate floors & bright ethnic décor, & there are also some cheaper & more basic tents using common showers on a slope leading down to a lily-covered river. Monkeys & birds are plentiful around the camp, which is centred on a 2-storey wood-&-thatch restaurant/bar. *US$125/185 en-suite sgl/dbl; US$65/120 sgl/dbl with common shower. FB.* **$$$**

Budget

Chimpanzee Capital (11 rooms) m 0772 455301. This small lodge is the closest accommodation to Kanyanchu (if you exclude the on-site Primate Lodge Kibale; page 427). Though this prime location is complemented by a bushy, valley-side garden alive with birdlife, the rooms are a bit ordinary. Discounts available. *US$90/140 sgl/dbl FB.* **$$$**

Kibale Forest Lodge (11 rooms) ⊕ 0.40225, 30.41156; m 0778 566148. At the southern end of Bigodi village, this small guesthouse is anything but forested, though a small but leafy compound does its best. Owned by guide Harriet Kemigisha, the spotless rooms are popular with budget birding tours. *US$100/160 sgl/dbl FB.* **$$$**

✷ **Sunbird Hill** (5 units) ⊕ 0.42466, 30.41453; m 0701 577784; e hello@sunbirdhill.com; w sunbirdhill.com. Run by a British-Ugandan family to support the NGO In the Shadow of Chimpanzees (page 432), this private 17ha site is aimed at wildlife enthusiasts seeking an immersive nature experience rather than the creature comforts of a conventional lodge. Overnight guests can do guided nocturnal activities & have exclusive access to the Birders Lounge, an open-sided thatched construction that is designed for armchair birding & photography, & houses an excellent library of natural history tomes. The lounge is also the start point for Wednesday Bird Club, a relaxed 3–5hr outing on foot that attracts an enthusiastic gang of local guides & morphs into a Butterfly Club mid-morning. The cosy Butterfly Cottage comes with a solar-powered drinks fridge, en-suite warm shower & wide wooden veranda. For the adventurous, there's a trio of elevated en-suite cottages with wide balconies offering views into the forest canopy, as well as an atmospheric treehouse. The focus here is on smaller creatures – birds, reptiles, nocturnal mammals, butterflies, moths & other insects – but elephants often pass by at night, while the resounding dawn chorus is frequently capped by pant-hooting chimps. There's an equipped self-catering kitchen, simple local meals (US$8–10) can be booked in advance, & take-aways can be delivered from The Bee Hive (see opposite). Preference is given to natural history experts who can share their knowledge with the Sunbird Hill team, which then trains children in the local community. *US$145 dbl inc activities but exc meals.* **$$$**

Shoestring and camping

Bigodi Community Lodge (11 rooms) ⊕ 0.40616, 30.40846; m 0772 997289. Conveniently located close to the Bigodi Swamp Walk, this is a private lodge with no community links. Still, the simple rooms with ¾ bed & nets & use of common cold showers are affordable. *US$9 per room.* **$**

✷ **Tinka's Homestay** (4 rooms) ⊕ 0.40505, 30.40879; m 0772 468113; e comm-tour@infocom.co.ug. Owned by an articulate & engaging local conservationist who helped set up the nearby Bigodi Swamp Walk, this homestay offers visitors the chance to share local meals with the family, assist with food preparation, & plant or harvest crops in the garden. The tiled twin rooms are en suite & clean. *US$26 pp FB.* **$$**

Where to eat and drink *Map, page 402*

Most people will eat at their lodge or camp, but two standalone eateries aimed at tourists can be found in Kanyanchu and Bigodi, close to the office for the swamp walk, with a third in Kanyanchu.

The Bee Hive Bar & Bistro ⊕ 0.40676, 30.40855; m 0742 569140, 0765 321982; f beehivebigodi; ⏲ 08.00–20.00. Set in a conspicuous yellow-&-brown 2-storey building almost opposite the reception for Bigodi Wetland Sanctuary, this pub-like venue has a pool table, a TV for watching Premier League & other major football matches & a 1st-floor veranda offering views to the Rwenzori in clear weather. A tempting menu of stews, curries & grills is supplemented by cheaper burritos, b/fast (inc rolexes), fresh coffee & desserts. *Mains in the US$8–10 range.*

Café Kibale m 0759 697895 – use WhatsApp due to poor phone signal; e cafekibale@ugandalodges.com. Operated by the adjacent Primate Lodge Kibale, this café is right next to the Kanyanchu trailhead – perfectly placed to refresh or revive returning chimp trackers with a coffee, juice or beer. A limited menu of rolexes, burgers & chicken is offered. Commendably, the café is also a community-oriented initiative that gives young people a grounding for a career in hospitality. *US$7.*

Tinka's Homestay m 0772 468113. Perhaps 200m from the Bigodi Swamp Walk office, this place offers filling buffets, eaten barefoot on floor mats, of various traditional meat & vegetarian dishes. It's a popular diversion for safari groups, but needs to be arranged in advance. *US$6 pp.*

What to see and do

Chimp tracking and habituation A highlight of any visit to Kibale National Park will be the chimp-tracking excursions that leave twice daily from Kanyanchu, at 08.00 and 14.00. Chimp sightings are not guaranteed on these walks, but the odds of an encounter now stand at greater than 95%. Trackers visit one of two groups. The large Kanyantale community, which comprises around 90 individuals, is very well habituated, with the result that individuals feeding or grooming on the ground can often be approached to within 8–10m. A second group, Buraiga, having been under habituation for several years, opened for tracking in 2023. Tracking usually takes up to 3 hours, including the maximum period of an hour with the chimps.

Chimp tracking costs US$200/250 FR/FNR. Up to 50 tracking permits are available every morning, another 50 every afternoon, and these should be booked as far in advance as possible. The procedures for booking chimp permits for various tourist categories (FR, FNR, etc) are the same as those described on page 560 for gorilla permits.

Trackers leave in six parties of up to six individuals; in theory each party goes its own way, but in practice several often end up converging on the same sighting, particularly in the morning, when permits are more often than not fully booked throughout the year. Fortunately, there are plans to tackle the congestion. The new Buraiga community will help in the short term, and additional groups are undergoing habituation at Mainaro, south of Bigodi, and at Sebitoli, near Fort Portal. The former seems the most likely option; researchers from the Jane Goodall Institute are studying the latter and seem to think there is scope for several more years of learning.

Another option for a less crowded experience is to track in the afternoon, when permits tend to be less heavily subscribed. This strategy is also advisable for those hoping for last-minute availability. Details and availability can be checked at the national park office in Fort Portal or at Kanyanchu, but permits can only be issued and paid for at the UWA office in Kampala. The easiest months to get permits at short notice (though nothing can be guaranteed) are April, May and November.

For those who want to spend longer with the chimps, or to avoid potential crowding, a good alternative to the standard tracking permit is the full-day chimp-habituation experience, which costs US$250/300 FR/FNR and focuses on the Kisonge community.

As for preparing for chimp tracking, long trousers are essential, as are socks of sufficient length that you can turn your trousers into them – a safeguard against

CHIMPANZEES

Most likely you'll hear them before you see them. An excited hoot from somewhere deep in the forest; just one voice at first, then several, rising in volume and tempo and pitch to a frenzied unified crescendo, before it stops abruptly or fades away. Jane Goodall called it the 'pant-hoot' call, a kind of bonding ritual that enables any chimpanzees within earshot of each other to identify exactly who is around at any given moment, through the individual's unique vocal stylisation. To the human listener, this eruptive crescendo is one of the most spine-chilling and exciting sounds of the rainforest, and a strong indicator that visual contact with man's closest genetic relative is imminent.

It is, in large part, our close evolutionary kinship with chimpanzees that makes these sociable black-coated apes of the forest so enduringly fascinating. Though different DNA studies have yielded different percentages, it is universally agreed that humans, chimpanzees and bonobos (also known as pygmy chimpanzees) are more closely related to each other than to any other living creature, gorillas included. A few superficial differences notwithstanding, the similarities between humans and chimps are consistently striking, not only with regard to the skeletal and skull structure, but also the nervous system, the immune system, and many behaviours – bonobos, for instance, are the only animals other than humans to copulate in the missionary position.

Unlike most other primates, chimpanzees don't live in troops, but instead form extended communities of up to 100 individuals, which roam the forest in small, socially mobile subgroups that often revolve around a few close family members such as brothers or a mother and daughter. Male chimps normally spend their entire life within the community into which they were born, whereas females often migrate into a neighbouring community after reaching adolescence. A high-ranking male will occasionally attempt to monopolise a female in oestrus, but the more normal state of sexual affairs is non-hierarchical promiscuity. A young female in oestrus will generally mate with any male chimp that takes her fancy, while older females tend to form close bonds with a few specific males, sometimes allowing themselves to be monopolised by a favoured suitor for a period, but never pairing off exclusively in the long term.

Within each community, one alpha male is normally recognised – though coalitions between two males, often a dominant and a submissive sibling, have often been recorded. The role of the alpha male, not fully understood, is evidently quite benevolent – chairman of the board rather than crusty tyrant. This is probably influenced by the alpha male's relatively limited reproductive advantages over his potential rivals, most of whom he will have known for his entire life. Other males in the community are generally supportive rather than competitive towards the alpha male, except for when a rival consciously contests the alpha position, which is far from being an everyday occurrence. One male in Tanzania's Mahale Mountains maintained an alpha status within his community for more than 15 years between 1979 and 1995!

Little was known about chimpanzee behaviour until the early 1960s, when three separate pioneering studies – all still active today – were established in East Africa. Best known is the behavioural study established by Jane Goodall in Tanzania's Gombe Stream National Park in 1960, but other projects were founded in 1962 in Uganda's Budongo Forest by Prof Vernon Reynolds and in 1965 in Tanzania's Mahale Mountains National Park by Prof Toshisada Nishida.

The longstanding assumption that chimps are strictly vegetarian was rocked when Jane Goodall witnessed her subjects hunting down a red colobus monkey in Gombe Stream. Such behaviour has since been discovered to be common and widespread, particularly during the dry season when other food sources are depleted. An average of 20 kills is recorded in Gombe annually, with monkeys being the prey on more than half of these occasions, though young bushbuck, young bushpig and even infant chimps have also been victimised and eaten. Closer to home, researchers in Uganda's Kalinzu Forest have observed blue monkeys and red-tailed monkeys being eaten by chimps, as well as unsuccessful attempts to hunt black-and-white colobus. The normal *modus operandi* is for four or five adult chimps to slowly encircle a monkey troop, then for another chimp to act as a decoy, creating deliberate confusion in the hope that it will drive the monkeys into the trap, or cause a mother to drop her baby.

Chimp communities are by-and-large stable and peaceful entities, but intensive warfare has been known to erupt within the several habituated communities. In Mahale, one of the two communities originally habituated by researchers in 1967 had exterminated the other by 1982. A similar thing happened in Gombe Stream in the 1970s, when the Kasekela community, originally habituated by Goodall, divided into two discrete communities. The Kasekela and breakaway Kahama community coexisted alongside each other for some years. Then in 1974, Goodall returned to Gombe Stream after a break to discover that the Kasekela males were methodically persecuting their former community mates, isolating the Kahama males one by one, and tearing into them until they were dead or terminally wounded. By 1977, the Kahama community had vanished entirely.

Chimpanzees are essentially inhabitants of the western rainforest, but their range does extend into the extreme west of Tanzania, Rwanda and Uganda, which have a combined population of perhaps 7,000 individuals. These are concentrated in Tanzania's Mahale and Gombe national parks, Rwanda's Nyungwe Forest, and about 20 Ugandan national parks and other reserves, most notably Budongo, Kibale, Semuliki, Maramagambo and Bwindi. Although East Africa's chimps represent less than 3% of the global population, much of what is known about wild chimpanzee society and behaviour stems from the region's many ongoing research projects.

An interesting pattern that emerged from the parallel research projects in Gombe Stream and Mahale Mountains, which lie little more than 100km apart on the shore of Lake Tanganyika, is a wide variety of social and behavioural differences between the two populations. Of the plant species common to both national parks, for instance, as many as 40% of those utilised as a food source by chimps in the one reserve are not eaten by chimps in the other.

In Gombe Stream, chimps appear to regard the palm-nut as something of a delicacy, but, while the same plants grow profusely in Mahale, the chimps there have yet to be recorded eating them. Likewise, the 'termite-fishing' behaviour first recorded by Jane Goodall at Gombe Stream in the 1960s has a parallel in Mahale, where the chimps are often seen 'fishing' for carpenter ants in the trees. But the Mahale chimps have never been recorded fishing for termites, while the Gombe chimps are not known to fish for carpenter ants. Mahale's chimps routinely groom each other with one hand while holding their other hands together above their heads – once again, behaviour that has never been noted at Gombe. More than any structural similarity, more even than any single quirk of chimpanzee behaviour, it's such striking cultural differences – the influence of nurture over nature if you like – that bring home our close genetic kinship with chimpanzees.

biting safari ants. Otherwise, a lightweight raincoat is an excellent precaution. Note that the on-site Café Kibale doesn't sell mineral water in single-use plastic bottles and nor, for that matter, do they sell multiple-use bottles to fill, so bring drinking water with you. You will also need to bring a surgical face mask with you to put on when approaching close to the chimps.

Other forest walks Unguided walking is no longer permitted in Kibale National Park, except within the immediate vicinity of Kanyanchu Visitors' Centre, where dedicated birders should look out for the localised red-chested paradise flycatcher (a stunning bird that's easy to locate by call), as well as various robin-chats, weavers and greenbuls. Daytime guided walks into the forest are available out of Kanyanchu, and offer a good chance of spotting several types of monkey, including the endemic Uganda mangabey, but at a cost of US$30/40 FNR/FR excluding park entrance, they seem like poor value compared with the guided trail at Bigodi. Rather more alluring are spotlighted night walks (US$30/50 FNR/FR exc park entrance), which run from 19.30 to 22.00 daily, and offer a good chance of sighting nocturnal creatures such as galagos, various small predators, and the peculiar potto. This is worth considering if staying on site at Kibale Primate Lodge after chimp tracking, since your permit covers park entry for the rest of the day. Serious birdwatchers might also consider a birding walk (US$30/40 exc park entrance), since the forest proper has a very different species composition from Bigodi. However, the most rewarding option for first-time birders in Kibale is the forest-flanked section of the Fort Portal Road that runs for several kilometres north of Kanyanchu. This area often throws up the likes of Sabine's spinetail, blue-breasted kingfisher and Afep pigeon, as well as butterflies in their hundreds and a decent selection of monkeys.

Sunbird Hill/In the Shadow of Chimpanzees (m 0701 577784; e info@sunbirdhill.com; w sunbirdhill.com) Brainchild of primatologist Julia Lloyd, Sunbird Hill is a private birding site that co-ordinates the NatureUganda Bird Population Monitoring Programme in Uganda's western region and is affiliated to registered community/conservation charity In the Shadow of Chimpanzees. It comprises 17ha of regenerating farmland bordering the national park, and is regularly visited by chimps, monkeys and (nocturnally) elephants, but the emphasis is on smaller stuff such as birds, butterflies, reptiles and frogs. Almost 300 bird species have been recorded, including 14 of 38 sunbird species listed for Uganda, and the keenly sought green-breasted pitta. For serious birders, the species composition at Sunbird Hill is quite different from Bigodi Swamp Walk or the national park proper, with a higher proportion of birds associated with forest fringe and cultivation. It is also a bird-ringing site and training centre for local wildlife enthusiasts. Accommodation is available (page 428). Birding and tailor-made nature walks cost from US$40 per person, with prebooking a must. Also on offer for those seeking deeper insight into chimpanzee behaviour is a question-and-answer session with Julia, whose experience as a researcher at Kibale stretches back to 1998. All proceeds from Sunbird Hill go to In the Shadow of Chimpanzees, which is developing a quality community-tourism programme for day visitors at neighbouring Kyabakwerere village. Here, a dedicated community area includes a medicinal plant garden, butterfly garden, bird trails, beehives, elephant trench and a much-loved football pitch (visitors are welcome to join in for a kick-around during practices). Activities on offer include a guided walk with an ex-poacher, but more are planned – check the website for details.

The site lies about 1km east of the main road and the junction (⊕ 0.42393, 30.4051) is 2.25km past Kanyanchu in the direction of Bigodi.

CHRIS ROBERTS FOREST FOUNDATION

An alarming rate of deforestation in Uganda means that tracts of natural tree cover are increasingly restricted to parks and reserves. Study, for example, the outline of the forested northern section of Kibale National Park on the map; now look for it on Google Earth. You'll see an identical shape leap off the screen, a dark green block of foliage hemmed in by a sea of banana gardens, pasture and tea plantations.

The Chris Roberts Forest Foundation (CRFF) is working to reverse this trend and push forest cover back out into the farmlands around Kibale National Park, contributing to the protection of vital habitat of chimpanzees, forest elephants, golden cats and many other species. CRFF was named after the late Chris Roberts, conservation champion and founder of the Turaco Treetops lodge. On a 40-acre demonstration site adjoining the lodge, the foundation spearheads rainforest conservation, boundary zone restoration and agroforestry development. A program for nearby farmers encourages the extension of these efforts into the surrounding area. Turaco Treetops (page 427) offers explanatory walks in the protected CRFF area; in the meantime, you can learn more at w crff.earth.

Bigodi Wetland Sanctuary Offering some of the finest birding and monkey viewing in Uganda, Bigodi Wetland Sanctuary is also an admirable example of conservation and tourism having a direct mutual benefit at grassroots level. The award-winning programme is run by the Kibale Association for Rural and Environmental Development (KAFRED), and all profits are used to support education-related and other such projects in Bigodi trading centre. The reasonable fee of US$20 (or an even more favourable 'equivalent' of Ush50,000) is inclusive of a knowledgeable guide, making Bigodi a far more affordable prospect than a guided walk in the national park, particularly as the guides know the terrain intimately and can usually identify even the most troublesome species by sight or call.

The sanctuary's main ornithological virtue is quality rather than quantity. You'd be lucky to identify more than 40 species in one walk, but most will be forest-fringe and swamp specials, and a good number will be West African species at the eastern limit of their range. A spectacular bird strongly associated with the swamp is the great blue turaco, which will be seen by most visitors. A more elusive speciality is the papyrus gonolek, which is occasionally seen from the wooden walkway about halfway along the trail. Other regularly observed birds include: grey-throated, yellow-billed, yellow-spotted and double-toothed barbets; speckled, yellow-rumped and yellow-throated tinkerbirds; blue malkoha (a recent split from green malkoha); brown-eared woodpecker; blue-throated roller; African grey parrot; bronze sunbird; black-crowned waxbill; grey-headed nigrita; swamp flycatcher; red-capped and snowy-headed robin-chats; thick-billed and northern brown-throated weavers; and black-and-white casqued hornbill. The most common monkey is red colobus, but red-tailed monkey, L'Hoest's monkey, black-and-white colobus and Uganda mangabey are also regularly sighted. If you are extremely fortunate, you might see chimpanzees, which occasionally visit the swamp to forage for fruit, or the shy sitatunga antelope.

The 4.5km circular trail starts in Bigodi trading centre at the Bigodi Swamp Walk office (⊕ 0.406843, 30.40729; m 0772 468113; e tinkabigodi@gmail.com; w bigoditourism.com; ⌚ 07.30–17.00 daily), where serious birdwatchers should mention their special interest, since some guides are better at identification than others. Walks technically start at 07.30 and 15.00, and generally take around 3 hours, but dedicated birders will require longer. For general monkey viewing, it doesn't matter greatly whether you go in the morning or afternoon, but birders should definitely aim to do the morning walk. For morning walks, it is worth getting to the office as early as you can, or possibly even arranging a dawn start a day in advance. For afternoon walks, it's advisable to get going an hour earlier than the scheduled departure. The trail is very muddy in parts, so it's worth taking advantage of the free gumboots offered at the KAFRED office.

KAFRED also now offers guided 3–4-hour community tours, also at US$20/ Ush50,000 per person. These include visits to a traditional healer and clan elders, as well as to a school, church and the local trading centre.

Finally, be aware that several rival organisations now offer prominently signposted 'Bigodi Swamp Walks' that could be mistaken for the real thing. These are often cheaper than Bigodi Wetland Sanctuary, but they also tend to be less productive, and usually have no formal community involvement. Guides and safari drivers from out of town are quite often incentivised to take clients to these other swamp walks, claiming them to be Bigodi Wetland. So before paying anything to anyone, do make sure you actually are at KAFRED – coming from the direction of Fort Portal, the office is on the right-hand side of the road, 200m from The Bee Hive (page 429) on the opposite side of the road.

Bigodi Cultural Centre (m 0782 541164; entrance US$10) Situated just uphill from The Bee Hive, this small museum displaying traditional clothes, grinding stones, musical instruments and other such artefacts offers a sedate alternative for those who don't feel like doing the swamp walk. A private venture, it is the brainchild of an experienced and articulate national park guide whose lengthy explanation of the various exhibits is arguably more interesting than the artefacts themselves.

SEBITOLI SECTOR This northerly sector of Kibale National Park opened in 2002 to help ease tourist pressure on Kanyanchu. However, it has never really caught on with travellers, despite its convenient location a few hundred metres off the main Fort Portal–Kampala Road. This is partly because no chimp tracking is offered, but it doesn't help that Sebitoli has received little publicity, nor that activities are relatively costly since they attract full national park fees. Outside the national park, by contrast, guided walks in the Kihingami Wetlands, only 1km from Sebitoli, are very good value, and make for a thoroughly worthwhile budget outing from Fort Portal.

Getting there and away Coming from Fort Portal, Sebitoli Camp is signposted to the right 16km along the Fort Portal–Kampala Road, some 1.5km before a bridge across the Mpanga River. Using public transport, any matatu between Fort Portal and Kyenjojo can drop you at the junction, from where it's a 5-minute walk to the camp, though you may need to pay full fare (US$1.50).

Where to stay and eat *Map, page 402*

✷ **Sebitoli Camp** (5 rooms) ⊕ 0.64381, 30.38491; 039 2175976; m 0788 843931; e knp@ugandawildlife.org. Set in a forest clearing only 600m south of the main road to Kampala, this very reasonably priced UWA facility lies at the northern tip of Kibale National Forest. Plenty of monkeys & birds can be seen in the camp. En-suite rooms have electricity & a canteen serves simple meals. No entrance fee is charged unless you do activities within the national park. *US$12 sgl/dbl; 2-room cottage US$22; US$5 pp camping. Payment by MoMo only*. **$**

What to see and do

Sebitoli Forest hikes A general Nature Walk and a more focused Birding Walk are both offered. The latter should be booked in advance so that a specialist guide can be arranged. Walks offer a good chance of seeing red colobus, black-and-white colobus, Uganda mangabey, red-tailed monkey and blue monkey, as well as a wide range of bird species. Chimpanzees are often heard but seldom seen, while elephants are occasionally encountered close to the Mpanga River. All hikes cost US$30 per person, plus US$40 park entrance per 24 hours. At night, Sebitoli is reportedly a superb site for spotlighting for nocturnal creatures such as galagos and potto.

Kihingami Wetlands (⊕ 0.64378, 30.37751; m 0779 775790; e kihingamiwetland2002@gmail.com) Protected as part of a community project, the 13km² Kihingami Wetlands border Kibale National Park on the north side of the Fort Portal–Kampala Road about 15km out of Fort Portal and 1km from Sebitoli. Home to more than 230 bird species, it is best known as a refuge for the localised white-spotted flufftail, an elusive and largely nocturnal swamp-dweller that is very difficult to see despite its often persistent calling. Other alluring species associated with the forest fringes and swamp are great blue turaco, papyrus gonolek, masked apalis, white-winged warbler, black-faced rufous warbler, Jameson's wattle-eye, Holub's golden weaver, grey-winged robin-chat and blue-shouldered robin-chat. Guided birdwatching tours leave at 07.30 and 15.00 daily (3–4hrs) with morning generally being most productive. Guided forest walks leave at 08.00 and 15.00 daily and come with a good chance of spotting red colobus, black-and-white colobus and red-tailed monkeys. All walks cost US$11 per person – considerably cheaper than a walk at Sebitoli and with no park entrance fees either. The wetlands office is clearly signposted at Sebitoli village, and easily reached from Fort Portal by matatu.

Mpanga Falls This impressive waterfall is formed by the Mpanga River as it tumbles over the rim of the 1,200m Mount Karubaguma some 15km before emptying into Lake George. Estimated to be about 50m high, the waterfall, which marks the northeastern extremity of Queen Elizabeth National Park, is enclosed by a steep gorge and supports a lush cover of spray forest. A remarkable feature of the gorge's vegetation is one of Africa's largest cycad colonies, consisting entirely of the so-called Uganda giant cycad (*Encephalartos whitelockii*), a critically endangered species endemic to this single location. Perhaps the closest thing among trees to living fossils, the cycads are relicts of an ancient order of coniferous plants that flourished some 300 to 200 million years ago, with the aptly prehistoric appearance of an overgrown tree fern perched on top of a palm stem up to 10m tall. Like *E. whitelockii*, many modern cycad species are classified as 'Endangered', due to their extremely localised distribution and very slow life cycle.

The outside world caught up with *E. whitelockii* in 2008, when a controversial hydro-power scheme for the gorge was pushed through. Dozens of cycads were bulldozed before a public outcry led to mitigation measures, including the establishment of local nurseries to grow cycads. Though the colony survived this adventure substantially intact, most of it lies outside the national park and is now threatened by cattle grazing and watering.

Mpanga Gorge can be reached with reasonable ease as a day trip from Kibale Forest or as a diversion from the surfaced main road between Kamwenge and Ibanda. Kamwenge is well served by public transport from both directions. From there, the gorge is 22km from town on the northern side and more like 30km on the south. You could, as we did, make your own way there – we found plenty of cycads in the valley but failed to locate the falls. Alternatively (as we subsequently learned) you could ensure success by booking the services of Mackay, a local cycad enthusiast and emergent tourism entrepreneur (m 0794 887799).

FEEL THE FOREST
TURACO TREETOPS
Kibale Forest
+256 757 152 323 | www.turacotreetops.com | turacotreetops

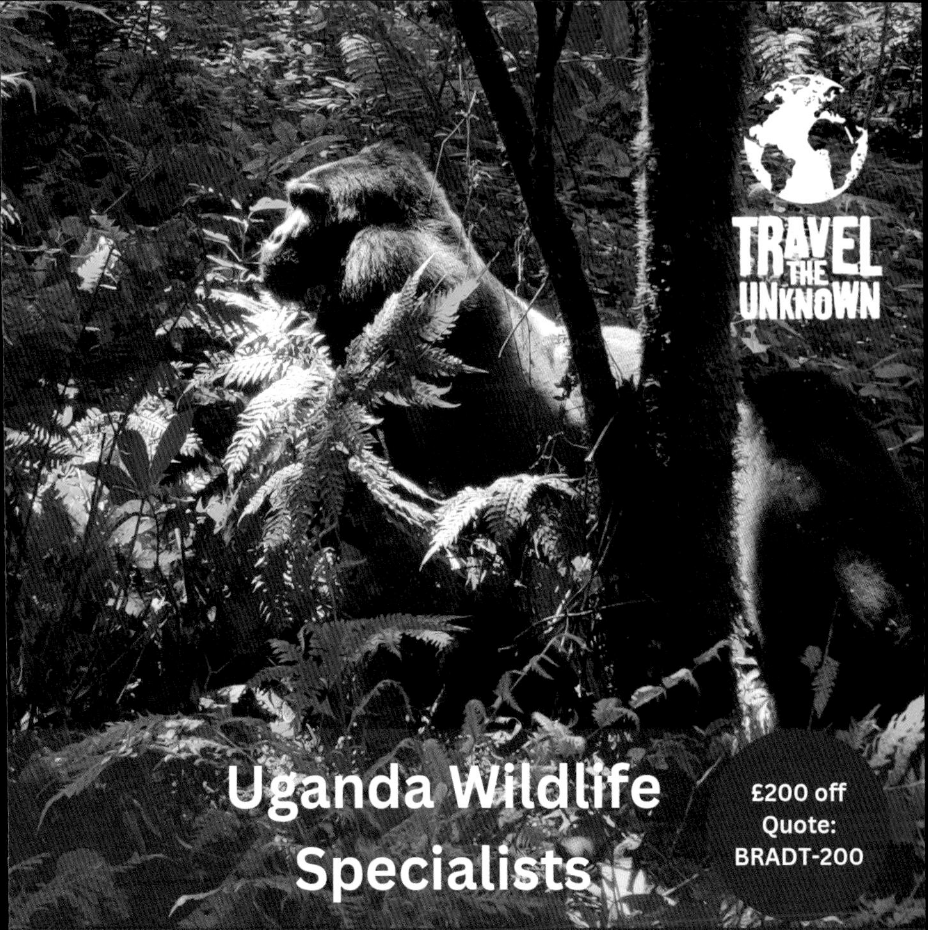
TRAVEL THE UNKNOWN
Uganda Wildlife Specialists
£200 off
Quote:
BRADT-200

ALSO POSSIBLE
WITH DRIVER-GUIDE
Drive your own adventure
Self-drive tours. 4x4 rental. Camp gear
roadtripafrica.com
Roadtrip
Africa

16

The Semliki Valley

Set at the base of the Albertine Rift west of Fort Portal, the spectacular but little-visited Semliki Valley is hemmed in by Lake Albert to the north and by the Semliki River along the Congolese border, while the Rwenzori foothills protrude into it from the south to create two geographically discrete and ecologically divergent sectors. Northeast of the Rwenzori, the Toro-Semliki Wildlife Reserve protects a tract of moist woodland running towards the marshy southern shores of Lake Albert. By contrast, the northwest Rwenzori footslopes give way to the steamy lowland jungle of Semuliki National Park, whose affinities with the contiguous Congolese rainforest are reflected by the presence of dozens of birds and other creatures found nowhere else in Uganda.

Foreigners who make it to the Semliki Valley generally fall into one of three categories: upmarket tourists headed to the wildlife reserve's excellent lodge for an off-the-beaten-track safari; dedicated birders in search of the national park's many avian rarities; or backpackers doing the Northern Rwenzori mini-hike (page 467). But, even if you're none of the above, the new surfaced 85km road that rounds the Rwenzori foothills between Fort Portal and Bundibugyo (the region's largest town) is one of the most breathtaking in Uganda.

The Semliki Valley area is covered by Sheet 7 in the 'Uganda Maps' series, *Fort Portal & Kibale Forest.*

TORO-SEMLIKI WILDLIFE RESERVE

Uganda's oldest wildlife reserve was originally gazetted in 1932 as the Toro Game Reserve. Extending over 543km^2, it runs northeast of the Bundibugyo Road to

SEMLIKI VS SEMULIKI

Both these spelling variations are widely used in Uganda, even by the Uganda Wildlife Authority, which officially refers to the national park as Semuliki (with a 'u') and the wildlife reserve as Toro-Semliki (without one). Arbitrary as this seems, there is, according to locals, some logic behind it: the Bamba people who live around Bundibugyo and the national park pronounce the name 'Semuliki', whereas the Batoro and Batuku living around Ntoroko say 'Semliki'.

Paradoxically, the Semliki River, which runs through the national park and lends its name to the entire region, is generally spelt without a 'u'. This inconsistency may be associated with the probability that Semliki was not originally a local name. The story is that the first European explorer to see the river asked a local Mukonjo woman carrying an empty basket on her head what it was called. She thought he was asking what was in the basket and replied '*sem lik*', which means 'nothing', and the river has been known as Semliki ever since.

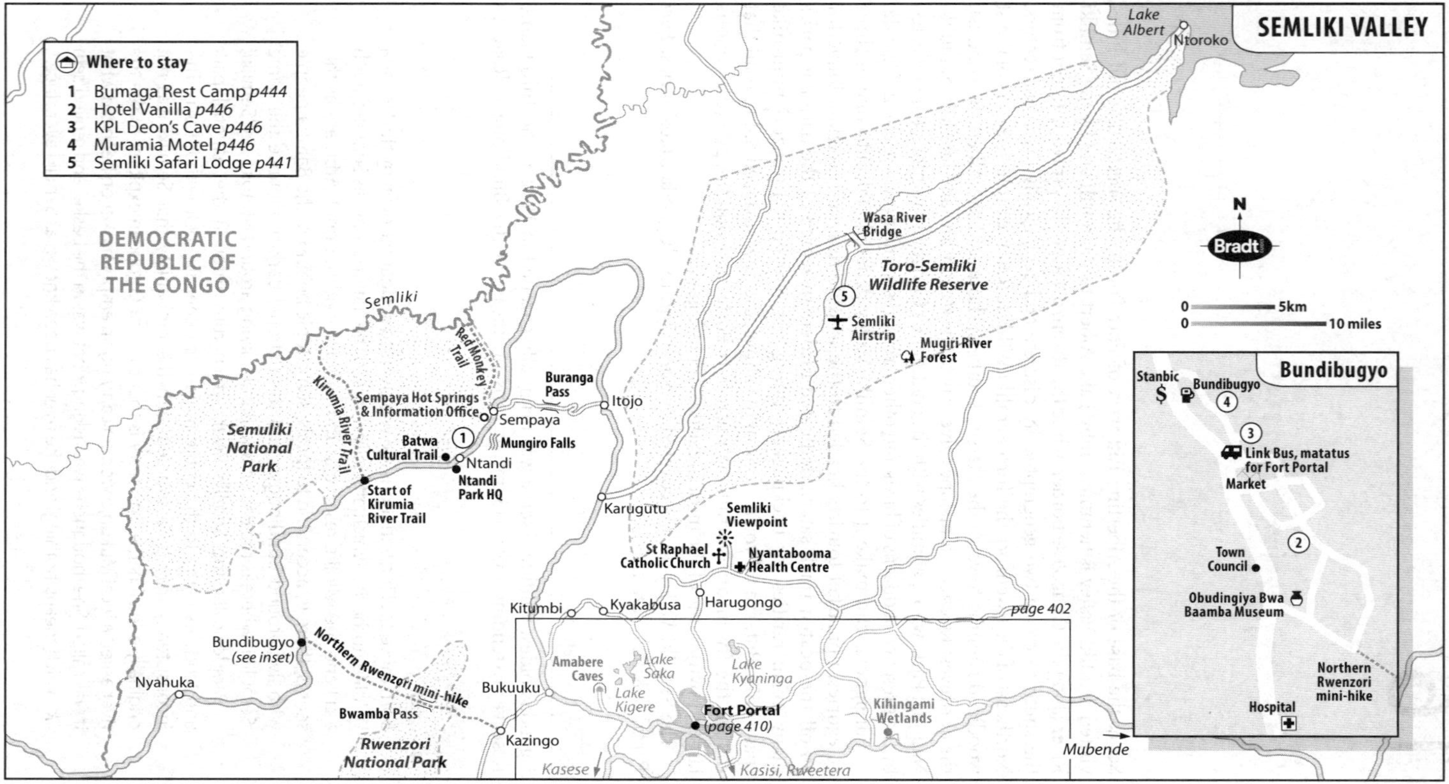
SEMLIKI VALLEY
Where to stay
1 Bumaga Rest Camp p444
2 Hotel Vanilla p446
3 KPL Deon's Cave p446
4 Muramia Motel p446
5 Semliki Safari Lodge p441
DEMOCRATIC REPUBLIC OF THE CONGO
Lake Albert
Ntoroko
Wasa River Bridge
Toro-Semliki Wildlife Reserve
Semliki Airstrip
Mugiri River Forest
Semliki
Red Monkey Trail
Kirumia River Trail
Sempaya Hot Springs & Information Office
Sempaya
Buranga Pass
Itojo
Semuliki National Park
Batwa Cultural Trail
Mungiro Falls
Ntandi
Ntandi Park HQ
Start of Kirumia River Trail
Karugutu
Semliki Viewpoint
St Raphael Catholic Church
Nyantabooma Health Centre
Kitumbi
Kyakabusa
Harugongo
page 402
Bundibugyo (see inset)
Nyahuka
Northern Rwenzori mini-hike
Bwamba Pass
Rwenzori National Park
Bukuuku
Kazingo
Amabere Caves
Lake Saka
Lake Kigere
Lake Kyaninga
Fort Portal (page 410)
Kihingami Wetlands
Kasese
Kasisi, Rweetera
Mubende
0 5km
0 10 miles
Bundibugyo
Stanbic
Bundibugyo
Link Bus, matatus for Fort Portal
Market
Town Council
Obudingiya Bwa Baamba Museum
Northern Rwenzori mini-hike
Hospital

SEMLIKI IN 1898

One of the first Europeans to enter the Semliki Valley was Dr Albert Cook, who visited it on foot in 1898, an experience he would later describe vividly in his memoir *Ugandan Memories*:

> The ground descended abruptly at our feet, and we looked out over a vast plain. Beneath us the Semliki River twisted in and out across the plain like a large snake. Beyond to the west was the commencement of Stanley's Great Forest. It looked like a dark green carpet, stretching away until it was lost in the haze...After a short rest, we began to descend from the summit of the pass into the Semliki Valley. Down, down, down for seven thousand feet, we had to leap like goats from rock to rock, and it was with bleeding fingers that we reached the bottom, for there were plenty of thorns.
>
> At the bottom...was a village of the Bwamba, hill tribes who inhabit the western slopes of the Rwenzori. The village was composed of little beehive shaped huts, each with its own porch. The people were splendid specimens...stalking about with spears in their hands...They file their front teeth to a point, and dress their hair very carefully, frizzing it into long curls like a poodle dog. They wear brass rings on their arms and legs [and] nothing but a wisp of cloth passed between the legs and secured by a girdle.
>
> In the afternoon we went to the celebrated hot springs...Emerging from the long grass we suddenly came on a belt of rich tropical foliage...paved with slabs of rock. From these, great sheets of steam were rising...all along the upper edge were springs of boiling water, bubbling furiously...in front were clouds of steam. In some of the holes, we boiled plantains, in other potatoes, and in a third we stuck our kettle.

Ntoroko, a sprawling fishing village and district administrative centre set on the southern shore of Lake Albert. The reserve itself is topographically unremarkable, set at a relatively low altitude of around 600–700m above sea level, but on a clear day the setting is truly awesome, with the sheer Rift Valley Escarpment rising sharply from the eastern shore of Lake Albert, the 2,500m-high Congolese Blue Mountains on the western horizon, and the glacial peaks of the Rwenzori visible to the southwest. The reserve's touristic centrepiece is the isolated and rather wonderful Semliki Safari Lodge, which offers all-inclusive packages to tourists seeking a holistic wilderness experience rather than wall-to-wall game viewing. Ntoroko is now the centre of more low-key tourist developments including a mid-range lakeshore lodge and affordable UWA camping and banda site.

FLORA AND FAUNA The dominant vegetation of Toro-Semliki is open Acacia-Combretum woodland and grassy savannah, interspersed with patches of borassus palm forest, significant belts of riparian woodland along the main watercourses, and extensive swamps towards Lake Albert. In its pre-Amin heyday, the vast geographic scale of Toro-Semliki Wildlife Reserve was complemented by some of East Africa's most prolific plains game. More than 10,000 Ugandan kob were resident, together with large herds of Jackson's hartebeest, waterbuck, elephant and buffalo. As for predators, the hunter Brian Herne wrote: 'The area is famous for the number of massive maned lions that live there. I have never seen so many big lions in other parts of Africa...Leopard were numerous throughout...None of the cats in Semliki had to work very hard for their dinner; they could simply lie in the grass and throw out a paw, for some animal or another was always about.' Isolated from similar habitats by various mountain ranges, Toro-Semliki was also at one point mooted as the site of a bizarre scheme to introduce commercial tiger hunting to Uganda – indeed, six pairs of tiger made it as far as Entebbe before the scheme was abandoned as potentially detrimental to indigenous predators.

Wildlife has partially recovered from the poaching that took a heavy toll during the civil war. The Ugandan kob population, which plummeted below 1,000 in the early 1990s, today totals several thousand. More than 1,000 buffalo are resident, up from about 50 in the early 1990s, and waterbuck numbers are growing, too. Leopards are still common, while lions were present in small numbers until as recently as 2010, but are now thought to be locally extinct. Toro-Semliki is one of the few places where both African elephant species live alongside each other. The two are easily told apart by the much smaller size of the African forest elephant, which also has far straighter tusks than the more widespread African bush elephant.

Primates are well represented. Large troops of olive baboon are often seen along the main road, while smaller groups of black-and-white colobus are common in riverine forests and red-tailed monkeys are often seen in the grounds of Semliki Safari Lodge. Vervet and reputedly DeBrazza's monkeys are also present, while a chimpanzee community inhabits the Mugiri River Forest.

The reserve is highly alluring to birdwatchers: more than 460 species have been recorded and it is one of the best places in Uganda to see shoebill.

FEES The entrance fee is US$25/35/20 FR/FNR/ROA per 24 hours. No fee applies to using the public road from Karagutu to Ntoroko, nor to using accommodation at Ntoroko. The fee is levied to guests staying at Semliki Safari Lodge, and for any guided walks, boat trips or other activities undertaken out of Ntoroko. Note that the fee does not cover Semuliki National Park, so if you were to visit the national park as a day trip from Semliki Safari Lodge, you'll end up paying two sets of entrance fees.

GETTING THERE AND AWAY

By air Flights to Semliki airstrip near Semliki Safari Lodge can be chartered from Entebbe with Aerolink. The alternative is a scheduled flight with the same company to Kasese (page 449) which is about 3 hours' drive to Semliki.

By road The drive from Fort Portal to Toro-Semliki takes around 90 minutes in a private vehicle. Follow the surfaced Bundibugyo Road for 30km to Karagutu (⊕ 0.78903, 30.22645), where a signposted turn-off to the right leads on to a recently upgraded 40km murram road that terminates at Ntoroko. If you are headed to Semliki Safari Lodge, look out for the signposted junction (⊕ 0.92979, 30.36787) to the right after about 25km, shortly after crossing the Wasa River bridge. It's 3km from this junction to the lodge.

Using public transport, a few matatus (2–3hrs) run directly between Fort Portal and Ntoroko, usually leaving in the early morning. Alternatively, any vehicle heading to Bundibugyo can drop you at Karagutu, from where matatus run to Ntoroko throughout the day.

By boat Overloaded passenger boats travel erratically along the lakeshore between Ntoroko, Butiaba and Wanseko, but fatal accidents are commonplace, especially in squally weather.

WHERE TO STAY AND EAT *Map, page 438*

Tourist accommodation is limited in the reserve following a rise in the level of Lake Albert that claimed a waterfront safari lodge and a UWA campground. What remains is the upmarket option Semliki Safari Lodge, halfway between Karagutu and Ntoroko, and a newly opened UWA camp at the reserve's Karagutu. If you're not too fussy, you'll find plenty of basic hotels in Ntoroko catering for business travellers crossing the lake to/from the Congo.

Exclusive

✷ **Semliki Safari Lodge** (2 suites, 6 standing tents) ⊕ 0.9091, 30.35583; ☎ 041 4251182; m 0772 489497; e info@wildplacesafrica.com; w wildplacesafrica.com. Uganda's oldest upmarket tented camp still ranks as one of its best & most remote. Overlooking a stretch of riverine forest inhabited by black-&-white colobus, red-tailed monkey & plentiful birds, the main stone, wood & thatch lodge exudes an earthy open-air feel & there's a large swimming pool area. Accommodation is in large thatched tents with wooden floors, walk-in nets & stylish ethnic décor, or massive canvas-sided, thatched-roofed stilted suites decorated in contemporary colonial style, with indoor showers & tubs on the massive deck. Guided game drives & birdwatching walks are included in the rates & emphasise a holistic wilderness experience rather than ticking off wildlife. Rates are FB & inc drinks & 2 game activities per day, but chimp tracking, Lake Albert boat trips & excursions to Semuliki National Park are charged extra. **$$$$$$**

Budget, shoestring and camping

Karagutu Campsite Recently established following the flooding of the lovely lakeshore UWA camp at Ntoroko, the setting of this replacement facility at the reserve's HQ on the edge of Karagutu hardly compares. *Camping US$10.* **$**

WHAT TO SEE AND DO Two activities daily are included in the rate for Semliki Safari Lodge, though chimp tracking and boat trips on Lake Albert are billed as extras.

Game drives For self-drivers, game-drive options are more-or-less limited to the main road between Karagutu and Ntoroko, which runs through the reserve for most of its length, though a couple of short 4x4-only loops now run either side of this. Game viewing along this road is rather hit-and-miss, but taken slowly it can be quite rewarding, especially if you've an interest in birds. Guests at Semliki Safari Lodge are offered guided day and night drives in open 4x4s, which can explore tracks and off-road areas closed to less robust vehicles. Either way, look out for black-and-white colobus monkey in areas of gallery forest, and olive baboon and vervet monkey in lighter woodland. Small herds of Ugandan kob and waterbuck inhabit the grassy plains, along with shyer pairs of common reedbuck and family parties of warthog.

Elephant and giant forest hog are also around, but are not seen on an everyday basis and they tend to be rather skittish when approached by a vehicle. Leopards are very occasionally seen, most usually on night drives. Both species of elephant are quite often seen crossing the main road from east to west in the morning and in the opposite direction in the evening.

Birding is excellent. The open grassland hosts Abyssinian ground hornbill, while areas of rank vegetation are good for marsh tchagra and African crake. Wooded areas are home to a wide variety of raptors, with grey kestrel, long-crested eagle and palm-nut vulture being especially common. The Mugiri River Forest is regarded to be the best site in Uganda for the elusive leaf-love, and it also hosts a variety of other localised forest species. Night drives are good for owls, as well as the improbable pennant-winged and standard-winged nightjars.

Boat trips Boat trips on scenic Lake Albert are a highlight of any visit. For birdwatchers, this is one of the best places in Uganda to see shoebill at close quarters. The local shoebill population is estimated at around 30–35 individuals and the success rate on boat trips is better than 80%. Other common waterbirds are also present, and breeding colonies of the dazzling red-throated bee-eater can be seen on a sandbank near Ntoroko. Less ornithologically minded visitors are usually boated to the base of the impressive Nkusi Falls. A smaller and much older version of Murchison Falls, this explodes through a cleft in the Rift Valley Escarpment before tumbling into the lake. Boat rides can be arranged at the Ntoroko waterfront (insist on a lifejacket: a shade/roof is also a good idea) while guests at Semliki Safari Lodge (page 441) can arrange trips directly through the lodge.

Walks Guided primate walks run through the Mugiri River Forest, near Semliki Safari Lodge, which supports a partially habituated community of 70 chimpanzees. The chimps of Mugiri do most of their diurnal foraging in the surrounding savannah and tend to travel much longer daily distances than their counterparts in Kibale or Budongo, so sightings are far from guaranteed, and most individuals are quite shy. Odds of locating chimps stand at around 40% in July, when trees are fruiting, but are lower at other times. Either way, you should also see a variety of smaller forest primates. If you make it down to the lakeshore at Ntoroko, you can walk freely in the immediate vicinity of the town where the lake shallows are teeming with birdlife.

SEMULIKI NATIONAL PARK

Gazetted in 1993, Semuliki National Park – previously known as Bwamba Forest, a name that often crops up in old ornithological literature – protects a practically unspoilt 220km^2 tract of rainforest bounded to the northwest by the Semliki River as it runs along the Congolese border into Lake Albert, and to the southeast by the surfaced main road connecting Fort Portal to Bundibugyo. The tropical lowland forest of Semuliki, set at an average altitude of 700m, forms an ecological continuum with the Ituri Forest, which extends eastward for more than 500km to the Congo River, and it supports a wealth of wildlife unknown elsewhere in East Africa, including more than 35 bird species. Despite this, the relative remoteness of the park means it is seldom visited, even by ornithological tours.

Back in the late 1990s, Semuliki National Park and indeed the whole of Bundibugyo District was off-limits to travel during a brutal insurgency by the DRC-based Allied Democratic Forces (ADF). It was assumed that this situation was long resolved, but a series of attacks in western Uganda by an apparently resurgent ADF in 2023 suggest that it would be prudent to check the situation before heading this way.

FEES The entrance fee is US$25/35/20 for FR/FNR/ROA per 24 hours. No fee is charged for driving or walking along the main road to Bundibugyo, which follows the park's southeastern boundary, or for staying overnight at Bumaga Rest Camp. There is no additional charge for the short walk to Sempaya Hot Springs. Other activities such as birding walks attract a guide fee of US$30/40 per FR/FNR over and above the entrance fee. Because Semuliki National Park and Toro-Semliki Wildlife Reserve are separate entities, you need to pay two sets of entrance fees if you visit both, even if it falls within the same 24-hour period.

FLORA AND FAUNA Seated at the juncture of several ecological zones, Semuliki National Park has an exceptionally diverse flora. The dominant tree is the Uganda ironwood (*Cynometra alexandri*), but the forest also contains several Congolese species at the easternmost extent of their range. A checklist of 60 **mammal** species includes at least a dozen that occur nowhere else in Uganda, among them two types of flying squirrel and six types of bat. Semuliki National Park is also the only East African stronghold of the oddball water chevrotain (or fanged deer), a superficially duiker-like relic of an ancient ungulate family that shares several structural features with pigs and is regarded to be ancestral to all modern-day antelopes, deer, cows and giraffes. In 2018, motion-sensor camera traps set by scientists from the UK's Chester Zoo snapped the first East African record of the lowland bongo (*Tragelaphus eurycerus*), a hefty (up to 1.3m tall and 180kg) and handsome nocturnal spiral-horned antelope associated with forests in western and central Africa. Eight diurnal primates have been recorded: red-tailed monkey; vervet monkey; blue and De Brazza's monkeys; grey-cheeked mangabey; olive baboon; black-and-white colobus; and chimpanzee. Other large mammals include elephant, bushpig, buffalo, sitatunga and white-bellied duiker. Hippos are common along the Semliki River, as are crocodiles. More than 300 species of butterfly have been identified, including 46 species of forest swallowtail, together with 235 moth species.

Over 435 **bird** species have been recorded in Semuliki National Park. The checklist includes a full 36 Guinea–Congo forest biome bird species unknown elsewhere in East Africa. These are spot-breasted ibis, Hartlaub's duck, Congo serpent eagle, chestnut-flanked sparrowhawk, red-thighed sparrowhawk, long-tailed hawk, Nkulengu rail, black-throated coucal, chestnut owlet, Bates's nightjar, black-casqued hornbill, white-crested hornbill, black dwarf hornbill, red-billed dwarf hornbill, red-rumped tinkerbird, spotted honeyguide, lyre-tailed honeyguide, Zenker's honeyguide, African piculet, Gabon woodpecker, white-throated blue swallow, palm swamp greenbul, simple greenbul, eastern bearded greenbul, Sassi's olive greenbul, yellow-throated nicator, forest scrub-robin, lowland akalat, grey ground thrush, rufous flycatcher-thrush, fiery-breasted bush-shrike, red-eyed puffback, black-winged oriole, Maxwell's black weaver, blue-billed malimbe and Grant's bluebill. Furthermore, another 11 species with an extremely limited distribution in East Africa are reasonably likely to be seen by visitors spending a few days in Semuliki National Park. These are western bronze-naped pigeon, yellow-throated cuckoo, piping hornbill, rufous-sided broadbill, Xavier's greenbul, Capuchin babbler, yellow longbill, blue-headed flycatcher, red-billed helmet-shrike, crested malimbe and chestnut-breasted nigrita.

For amateur ornithologists, Semuliki is not only certain to throw up a clutch of 'lifers' – it also offers a faint but real possibility of a brand-new East African record. Indeed, three of the seven 'recent records' depicted in Stevenson and Fanshawe's 2002 *Field Guide to the Birds of East Africa* – namely Congo serpent-eagle, grey-throated rail and black-throated coucal – were discovered in Semuliki during the 1990s.

GETTING THERE AND AWAY The gateway to the park is Sempaya Information Office (⊕ 0.8359, 30.16721), which is signposted along the right side of the surfaced Bundibugyo Road, 60km from Fort Portal, only 300m past the intersection with the old road. The drive from Fort Portal shouldn't take longer than 1 hour. Any public transport heading between Fort Portal and Bundibugyo can drop you there.

If possible, try to avoid visiting on a Thursday, as this is when locals are allowed in the park to remove 'dead timber' – a process that involves a prevalence of chopping noises.

WHERE TO STAY AND EAT *Map, page 438*

If the facility on page 444 doesn't appeal, Semuliki can be visited as a day trip from Fort Portal, 90 minutes away, or Bundibuygo.

Bumaga Rest Camp ⊕ 0.82203, 30.15294; m 0786 741890. This no-frills UWA-run facility is located just off the main road, 2km beyond Sempaya, where it offers a selection of basic en-suite bandas. Though birding possibilities are excellent, the midges that plague the forest margins at dawn & dusk are less attractive – take a good insect repellent. Meals & drinks can be arranged to order. *US$13/21/32 sgl/dbl/family cottage.* **$$**

WHAT TO SEE AND DO Note that all the guided walks described here cost US$30 per person, excluding the park entrance fee of US$30/40 FR/FNR.

Buranga Pass Even if you opt not to enter Semuliki National Park, it's worth taking a day trip to Sempaya or Bundibugyo just for the drive. You used to be able to combine the new and old road to form a scenic loop around the northern Rwenzori, but fallen trees along the route mean that nothing larger than a boda gets through these days. You can still drive 4km up the old road as far as the watershed, however, turning off the new road at Itojo, about 10km beyond Karagutu (⊕ 0.84051, 30.2273). If you have a vehicle with a driver, you can be dropped off to enjoy a gentle 10km walk down to Sempaya to be collected by your vehicle (⊕ 0.8388, 30.16788). This lovely route passes through the rocky and forested Buranga Pass before a long and tightly winding descent which offers fantastic views across the Rift Valley towards the DRC. If more exercise is required, the forest-fringed tarmac immediately west of the junction at Sempaya borders but lies outside the national park, so no park fee or guide is required to walk (or drive) along it to look for monkeys and birds. You might also seek out the 100m path to the pretty Mungiro Falls on the Rwenzori side of the road, which slides down a precipitous fault face. Further along, the patch of fig and palm forest about halfway between Sempaya and Ntandi is worth scanning

THE BAMBUTI OF BUNDIMASOLI

A community of roughly 40 Bambuti Pygmies live at Bundimasoli (⊕ 0.80596, 30.13866; look out for the sign reading 'Batwa Cultural Trail') on the Bundibugyo Road about 5km past Sempaya and 500m from the park headquarters at Ntandi. They are close cultural kin of the Basua Pygmies of the Congolese Basin, but suffer from much the same sort of discrimination and prejudice as is experienced by the Batwa Pygmies of Kigezi and Rwanda (page 540). Among their neighbours, the Bambuti are regarded to be dirty ne'er-do-wells, stigmatised by such unacceptable customs as eating snakes and monkeys, growing and smoking marijuana, and the women walking around topless. Until recently, tourist fees supposedly paid to the Ntandi community were regularly confiscated by non-Bambuti guides and the Bambuti, like the Batwa of Kigezi, were forbidden to use their traditional hunting grounds after Semuliki National Park was gazetted in 1993.

Today, the Bambuti live outside the forest in a cluster of basic shacks on the edge of Bundimasoli village, 10 minutes' walk from the Semuliki National Park headquarters at Ntandi. Several Bambuti have learned enough English to deal directly with tourists rather than through the medium of crooked guides. The Bambuti's relationship with the national park has also improved greatly following a concession allowing them limited rights to fish and hunt within its boundaries (the main restriction being against hunting larger mammals such as elephant, buffalo and chimps) and to barter the forest produce with other local communities. They also claim to be the only people in Uganda who are legally permitted to grow and smoke marijuana. The latter they do constantly and with

carefully for the likes of swamp greenbul and various forest hornbills. You can then return to Sempaya and use the new tarmac road back to Fort Portal.

Sempaya and surrounds The most popular attraction in Semuliki National Park is the cluster of hot springs at Sempaya, which can be reached via a short guided walking trail (no more than 500m) from the Sempaya Information Office. Ringed by forest and palm trees, and veiled in a cloud of steam, these springs are a primeval, evocative sight: the largest geyser spouts up to 2m into the air from an opening in a low salt sculpture. Take care, though: the emerging water has a temperature of more than 100°C and the surrounding pools are hot! The trail to the springs leads through a patch of forest where red-tailed monkey, grey-cheeked mangabey and black-and-white colobus are common. Among the more interesting birds regularly seen here are various forest hornbills, blue-breasted kingfisher, red-rumped and yellow-throated tinkerbird, rufous flycatcher-thrush and honeyguide greenbul. Another spring, more of a broad steaming pool than a geyser, lies on the far side of the swampy clearing reached by a boardwalk. Rather than retracing your steps to Sempaya, you might ask whether the UWA has finally reopened an old trail that creates an attractive loop, passing through forest and a lovely tract of swamp/grassland.

Red Monkey Trail Following the eastern margin of the national park to the Semliki River, this wilderness trail takes at least 3 hours in either direction, but offers exposure to a far greater variety of localised birds than the trail to the springs. It can be undertaken as a day trip, or, if you carry your own tent and food, as an overnight trip camping on the bank of the river. In addition to birds, you can expect

great enthusiasm, through bubble pipes, especially – and somewhat incredibly – before they go hunting.

It's not all roses for the Bambuti by any means. Their women are regularly impregnated by outsiders, partially due to the belief that sleeping with one cures certain diseases, and the men have little hope of finding a partner outside their own community on account of their unacceptable customs. Interbreeding means that the genetic stock of Uganda's most ancient inhabitants is rapidly being diluted – the average height of its teenagers far exceeds that of the adults. Historically, their main sources of income are digging on local farms and entertaining tourists. One is hardly a key to advancement, while opportunities for the other are increasingly rare. Few visitors find their way to Bundimasoli these days, and many who do must feel that the experience veers uncomfortably close to a freak-show exhibit – look at the short people, shake their hand, snap a photograph, and off we go. It would, I think, be more edifying for all parties were the community to be facilitated to offer guided walks into the national park and to show off their consummate knowledge and mastery of the forest setting. As it stands, after paying the community fee of US$10 per person, you'll get some semblance of a traditional dance and the opportunity to buy a selection of crafts, mostly dope pipes. It might not be the most edifying of encounters, but it's also true that the Bambuti of Bundimasoli, caught in limbo between their hunter-gathering heritage and an uncertain future in the modern world, need the money more than most.

to see a variety of monkeys, hippos and crocodiles on the river, and possibly even buffalo and elephant.

Kirumia River Trail Highly recommended to birdwatchers, this 15km trail runs north from Kirumia (⊕ 0.79606, 30.09608) on the main Bundibugyo Road to the banks of the Semliki River, crossing the Kirumia River twice, as well as passing a succession of forest-fringed oxbow lakes. The first 4km, as far as the first crossing of the Kirumia River, can be undertaken as a guided day hike, and passes through secondary and riparian forest where African piculet, long-tailed hawk, rufous-sided broadbill, black-faced rufous warbler and lemon-bellied crombec are resident. The full round hike offers birders the best opportunity to see a good selection of Semuliki 'specials', but realistically it can only be undertaken as a two- to four-night self-sufficient camping expedition. Among the 20–30 bird species associated with the oxbow lakes and their environs, but unlikely to be seen in the vicinity of the main road or elsewhere in Uganda, are spot-breasted ibis, Nkulengu rail, black-throated coucal, yellow-throated cuckoo, lyre-tailed honeyguide, grey ground thrush, blue-billed malimbe, Maxwell's black weaver and Grant's bluebill, while Hartlaub's duck and white-throated blue swallow are resident on the Semliki River.

BUNDIBUGYO

This pretty, rather remote little town, situated only 10km from the Congolese border, lies some 25km west of Fort Portal as the crow flies, but more than three times that distance by road, thanks to the intervention of the northern Rwenzori. It is the largest town in the Semliki Valley, supporting a population of around 20,000, as well as being the western terminus of the Northern Rwenzori mini-hike (page 467) and a relatively comfortable base from which motorised travellers can explore Semuliki National Park. The town itself is short on tourist attractions other than a small and modest museum. Amenities are limited but include a decent hospital and one bank with an ATM.

GETTING THERE AND AWAY The scenic drive from Fort Portal to Bundibugyo via Semuliki National Park once followed one of the roughest roads anywhere in Uganda, but it is now surfaced in its entirety and the 85km drive should take no longer than 90 minutes. Using public transport, Link Bus (t 041 4255426; m 0703 236441; w link.co.ug/Bundibudgyo) operates two buses daily in either direction between Kampala and Bundibugyo via Fort Portal. These leave Kampala at 09.00 and 11.00 and Bundibugyo at 07.00 and 09.00 (5–6hrs; US$10). Regular matatus between Fort Portal and Bundibugyo take up to 2 hours.

WHERE TO STAY AND EAT *Map, page 438*

Hotel Vanilla (27 rooms) m 0772 912110; e hotelvanilla@gmail.com. This long-serving 2-storey hotel has clean tiled en-suite rooms with nets & fans. The courtyard restaurant is about as good as it gets in Bundibugyo, serving basic local meals for around US$4. A 1st-floor balcony at the front enjoys mountain views. **$**

KPL Deon's Cave (8 rooms) m 0772 903212; f kplhotel. This has clean en-suite rooms with nets set around a neat green courtyard. Good value. **$**

Muramia Motel (12 rooms) m 0782 623276. This new central hotel is marginally the smartest in Bundibugyo. It has solar power & rooms come with AC, DSTV & balcony. **$$**

WHAT TO SEE AND DO

Obudingiya Bwa Baamba Museum (m 0772 966094; ⌚ 08.00–16.30 Mon–Fri; entry US$3) This small museum displays basketwork, household and farm utensils, fish traps and other traditional artefacts associated with the region's three main cultural groups, the Bamba, Babwisi and Bavanuma. Though rather underwhelming, it is just about worth a look.

Nyahuka This little-visited but easily accessible trading centre 20 minutes' drive from Bundibugyo offers marvellous views of the Rwenzori peaks, a bustling Saturday market, and access to the 100m-high Ngite Falls and smaller Nyahuka Falls in the Rwenzori foothills. Once there, it would be a shame not to enjoy the pretty 10km drive to the border, where a large concrete bridge over the Lamia River leads to the Congolese bank. Do note, however, that the bridge represents the end of the road in Ugandan terms, since it is not advisable to cross into the DRC here for security reasons.

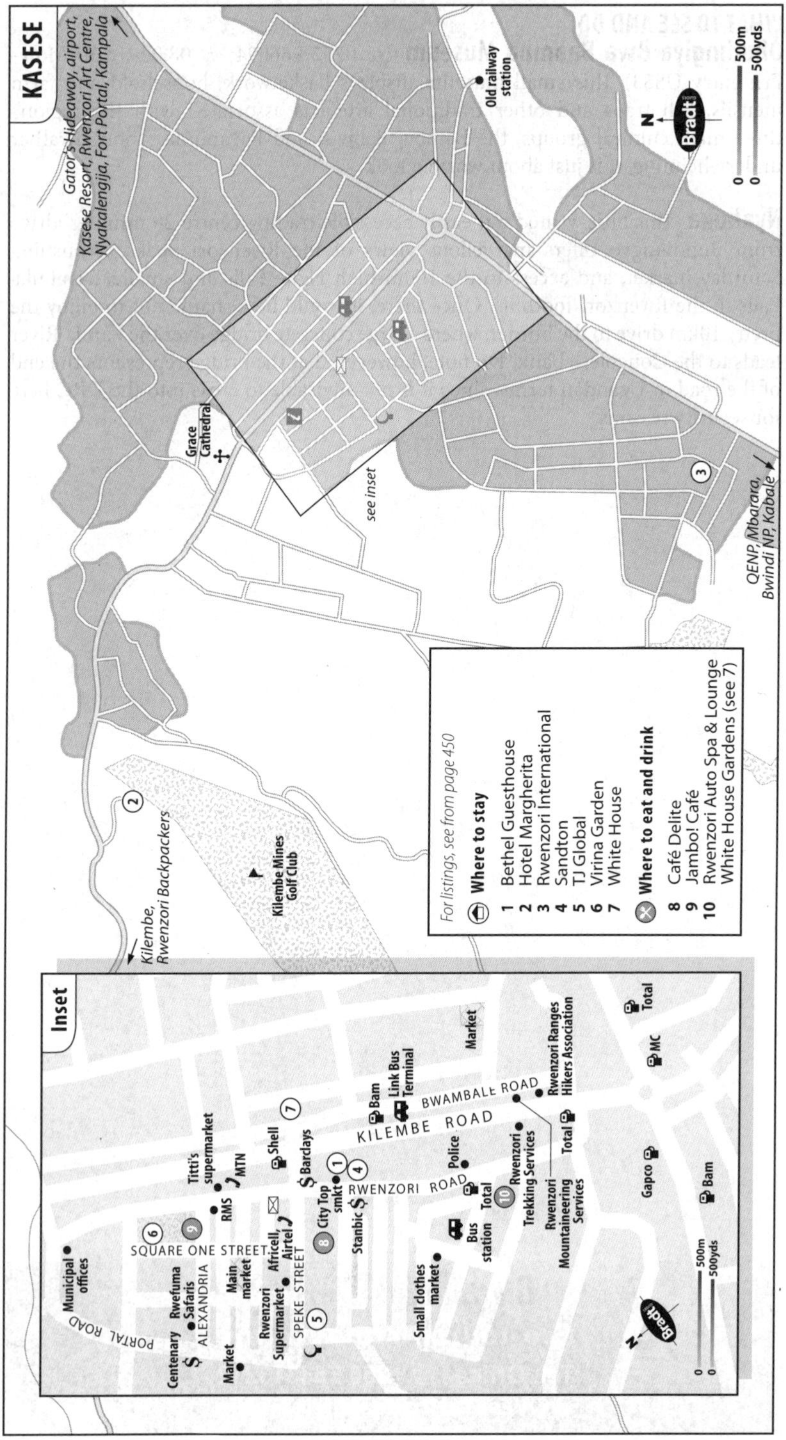
KASESE
Gator's Hideaway, airport, Kasese Resort, Rwenzori Art Centre, Nyakalengija, Fort Portal, Kampala
Old railway station
Grace Cathedral
see inset
QENP, Mbarara, Bwindi NP, Kabale
Kilembe, Rwenzori Backpackers
Kilembe Mines Golf Club
500m
500yds
For listings, see from page 450
Where to stay
1 Bethel Guesthouse
2 Hotel Margherita
3 Rwenzori International
4 Sandton
5 TJ Global
6 Virina Garden
7 White House
Where to eat and drink
8 Café Delite
9 Jambo! Café
10 Rwenzori Auto Spa & Lounge
White House Gardens (see 7)
Inset
PORTAL ROAD
Municipal offices
Centenary
Market
Rwefuma Safaris
ALEXANDRIA
SQUARE ONE STREET
Main market
Rwenzori Supermarket
SPEKE STREET
Africell
Airtel
RMS
Titti's supermarket
MTN
Shell
Barclays
City Top smkt
Stanbic
RWENZORI ROAD
KILEMBE ROAD
BWAMBALE ROAD
Bam
Link Bus Terminal
Police
Total
Bus station
Small clothes market
Rwenzori Trekking Services
Rwenzori Mountaineering Services
Rwenzori Ranges Hikers Association
Market
Gapco
MC
Total
Bam
500m
500yds

17

The Rwenzori Mountains and Kasese

Often associated with Ptolemy's legendary Mountains of the Moon, the majestic Rwenzori Mountains – a UNESCO World Heritage Site since 1994 – are protected in a 996km^2 national park that runs along the Congolese border between Semliki Valley and Queen Elizabeth National Park. The range's upper slopes constitute an aptly lunar landscape of bare black rocks and tussocked moorland studded with surreal giant lobelias and groundsels, while the lower contours are swathed in a tangled jungle inhabited by shy forest elephants and chimpanzees, as well as a wealth of forest monkeys and birds including several Albertine Rift Endemics. Above all this, towering to a maximum altitude of 5,109m, a series of craggy black peaks is coated in permanent equatorial snow and ice. Now served by two different hiking circuits, both of which offer more experienced climbers access to the glacial peaks, Rwenzori Mountains National Park is the most popular hiking destination in Uganda, less iconic perhaps than Kilimanjaro in neighbouring Tanzania, but offering far more of a wilderness experience, as well as being significantly more affordable.

KASESE

The gateway town to the Rwenzori, Kasese lies at an altitude of 950m on the open plains that separate this ice-capped massif from Lake George and Queen Elizabeth National Park. Hot and humid, Kasese isn't the most prepossessing of towns (through a recent and extensive roadworks programme certainly makes it easier to get around) and its rather pokey and parochial feel is at variance with its dramatic setting at the base of the legendary Mountains of the Moon, the snowy source of the Nile first postulated by geographers 2,000 years ago. For many years, Kasese's economic wellspring was the nearby Kilembe Copper Mine, a Canadian venture that started up in 1950 and led to the town becoming the railhead of a line connecting western Uganda to the Kenyan coast via Kampala in 1956. The mine was sold to the Ugandan government in 1975 and ceased operations seven years later. It is theoretically set to reopen in the near future under an agreement granting extraction rights of its 4 million tonnes of copper (and untold cobalt reserves) to the Chinese-owned Tibet Hima Mining Company, but this is currently on hold (page 452). Even after the mine collapsed, Kasese's railhead status ensured it remained a popular springboard for independent travel in western Uganda, but it fell off the travel map somewhat after 1995, when passenger services from Kampala were suspended. Now the ninth-largest town in Uganda with a population of 108,000, Kasese is a convenient place to stay overnight and shop for provisions prior to a Rwenzori hike, and it could also be used as a cheap base for visits to Queen Elizabeth National Park, but in most respects it has far less going for it than Fort Portal, only 75km to the north.

GETTING THERE AND AWAY

By air Aerolink (w aerolinkuganda.com) operates a daily flight (US$286/475 sgl/rtn exc taxes) connecting Kasese to Entebbe via Kisoro and Kihihi. The airport is on the northeastern outskirts of town about 2km from the centre along the Fort Portal Road.

By road Coming directly from Kampala, the best route is the 370km road through Fort Portal. This is well maintained and surfaced in its entirety except for the 50km or so between Kyenjojo and Fort Portal, and can be covered in 6–7 hours. There's also a more southerly route via Mbarara, but it's 50km longer and more heavily trafficked, at least as far as Mbarara. Distances to other key locations in the southwest are: 35km/30 minutes to Katunguru (for Queen Elizabeth National Park); 75km/90 minutes to Fort Portal; 155km/2–3 hours to Mbarara; 170km/4 hours to Buhoma (Bwindi National Park) via the Ishasha Road; and 220km/4–5 hours to Kabale on a direct road between Ishaka and Ntungamo.

Plenty of matatus connect Kasese to Katunguru, Mbarara, Kabale and Fort Portal. The pick of the private operators is the Link Bus (m 0701 548686; w link.co.ug; 6hrs; US$12), which runs ten times daily in either direction via Fort Portal.

WHERE TO STAY *Map, page 448*

Kasese has a decent selection of accommodation at the lower end of the price scale, but if you are looking for something more upmarket, you're better off in Queen Elizabeth National Park or Fort Portal.

Moderate

Hotel Margherita (36 rooms) ⊕ 0.18627, 30.06115; m 0772 695808; e info@hotel-margherita.com; w hotel-margherita.com. Situated 3km from the town centre just off the Kilembe Rd, this former government hotel offers a commanding view of the Rwenzori & there's plenty of birdlife in the flowering garden. The spacious & comfortable rooms come with nets, DSTV, optional AC & en-suite tub/shower. The restaurant serves an unexciting menu of grills & stews in the US$7–8 range. The most inherently tranquil & appealing option in Kasese, with plenty of potential to be a tourist oasis, it suffers from institutional architecture, bland décor, & an overall aura of neglect, & it feels quite overpriced. *US$70/95 sgl/dbl without AC; US$95/107 with AC. All rates B&B.* **$$$**

Sandton Hotel (42 rooms) Rwenzori Rd; m 0761 999699; e sandtonhotel@ymail.com; w sandtonhotel-kasese.com. Easily the smartest option in the town centre, this business hotel has small but modern rooms with AC, net, fan, DSTV & en-suite tub or shower, & a good AC restaurant with mains in the US$5–7 range. *US$48/62 sgl/dbl B&B.* **$$**

Budget

Bethel Guesthouse (15 rooms) m 0774 007051, 0701 443750; e guesthousebethel@gmail.com. Set around a neatly hedged courtyard next to the landmark Sandton Hotel, this Church-affiliated guesthouse has clean en-suite tiled rooms with flatscreen TV & hot shower. *US$11/16/22 sgl/dbl/twin.* **$$**

Rwenzori International Hotel (36 rooms) Mbogo Rd; ⊕ 0.16051, 30.07573; m 0782 282008, 0702 212754; e info@rwenzoriinternationalhotel.com; w rwenzoriinternationalhotel.com. Set in a quiet suburban garden off the Mbarara Rd, 2km south of the main roundabout, this pleasant hotel has a restaurant/bar with garden seating (mains US$3–5) & sauna. Very good value. *US$24/27/32 sgl/dbl/twin B&B.* **$$**

TJ Global Hotel (29 rooms) Speke St; 039 2175965; e info@tjglobalhotel.com; w tjglobalhotel.com. This 3-storey hotel has very spacious rooms, & the option of AC is a definite bonus in Kasese. Attempts to market itself as a honeymoon destination seem a touch delusional, but it's a great choice for passing travellers looking for smart & affordable central accommodation. *US$35/43 dbl without/with AC.* **$$**

Virina Garden Hotel (50 units) Square One St; m 0751 805838, 0772 588161; e virinagarden@yahoo.com; f. This well-established central hotel offers the option of conventional rooms in the main building or thatched mock-traditional cottages in the garden. *US$13/21 sgl/dbl.* **$$**

Shoestring

White House Hotel (23 rooms) Bwambale Rd; m 0703 467660, 0782 536263; e whitehse_hotel@yahoo.co.uk. A long-serving backpackers' favourite well placed for the Link Bus terminal, this hotel has small but clean rooms in an old block & superior ones in a new extension. A popular garden restaurant is adjacent (see below). Good value. *US$6/11 sgl/twin with common showers; US$8/14 en-suite sgl/dbl with hot water. New rooms US$12/26. All rates B&B.* **$–$$**

WHERE TO EAT AND DRINK *Map, page 448*

The standout in terms of location is the restaurant at the out-of-town Hotel Margherita (see opposite), though the food is best appreciated after a week or so of privations on the Rwenzori. The Sandton Hotel (see opposite) has the best continental menu in the town centre, while cheap drinks and snacks can be found at any number of unpretentious bars and roadside barbecues on Stanley Road.

Café Delite Stanley St. This pleasant café with terrace seating serves fresh coffee & a cosmopolitan menu embracing everything from rolexes, omelettes & burgers to pizzas, curries & stir-fries. *Most mains US$4–6.*

Jambo! Café Alexandria St; Mon–Sat. Run by 3 local women, this chilled-out Church-affiliated co-operative serves good locally sourced coffee, smoothies & juices, light meals (fajitas, filled pancakes, pizza, salads) & cakes geared towards the palates of volunteers & travellers. It also sells a range of local handicrafts. *Most drinks & meals in the US$2–3 range.*

✱ **Rwenzori Auto Spa & Lounge** Junction of Kilembe Rd & Rwenzori Rd. Easily the smartest place to hang out in Kasese, this popular open-air complex offers a tempting array of burgers, grills & curries. Ideal sustenance to keep you going while you have your car washed or before you get stuck in to an evening in the bar. Regular theme nights – movies, live music, quizzes, etc – add to the fun. *US$7.*

White House Gardens Bwambale Rd. This open-air restaurant opposite the eponymous guesthouse (see above) has a long, varied & well-priced menu embracing Indian & Ugandan dishes, pasta & excellent whole grilled tilapia. It's also the greenest spot in town for a drink. *Mains in the US$1.50–3.50 range.*

SHOPPING For groceries, try the well-stocked **Rwenzori Supermarket** on Margherita Street, or the **Titti's** and **City Top** supermarkets on Rwenzori Road. For handicrafts, your best bet is the **Jambo! Café**, which also has a few secondhand novels for sale.

SPORTS AND ACTIVITIES Kasese can get hot, so you'll be glad to know that there are a couple of swimming pools, both a little out of town on the Fort Portal Road. Kasese Resort is opposite the airstrip, while further along beyond the District Offices, Gator's Hideaway has a novel, guitar-shaped pool. Swimming costs US$4.

Kilembe Mines Golf Club (m 0706 593059; e kilembeminesgolfclub@gmail.com) Revived after years of disuse, this 18-hole golf course is one of the most beautiful and reputedly the most challenging in Uganda. It was founded in 1960 at the foot of the Rwenzori Mountains, and stands 3km out of town close to the Hotel Margherita. A round costs around US$15 and caddies and clubs are available to hire.

TOURIST INFORMATION AND TOUR OPERATORS

Rwefuma Safaris 13 Alexander St; m 0772 573399, 0756 573399; e rwefuma@gmail.com; w rwefumasafaris.com. Kasese-based operator offering day & longer trips to QENP, the Rwenzori & further afield. A half-/full-day trip to QENP in a Landcruiser costs US$150/200 including driver & fuel but excluding tourist entrance fees.

Rwenzori Mountaineering Services (RMS) Kilembe Rd; m 0785 257635; e trek@rwenzorimountaineeringservices.com; w rwenzorimountaineeringservices.com. The primary operator on Rwenzori's Central Circuit maintains an information & booking office on Kilembe Rd opposite the Total fuel station.

Rwenzori Ranges Hikers Association Kilembe Rd; m 0753 523208, 0750 767973, 0771 224021; e rwenzorihikers@gmail.com; w rwenzorihikers.com. The main operator on the Rwenzori's Bukurungu Trail has an office next to RMS.

Rwenzori Trekking Services Kilembe Rd; m 0774 114499, 0709 747700; e traveluganda@rwenzoritrekking.com; w rwenzoritrekking.com. The organisation responsible for the Rwenzori's Kilembe Trail has an office across the road from RMS.

WHAT TO SEE AND DO Kasese is a potential springboard for day and overnight hikes in Rwenzori National Park, though in truth there is no need to stop in town if you'll be exploring the Central Circuit out of Nyakalengija, while those doing the Kilembe Trail could continue directly to the trailhead at Kilembe. Budget-conscious self-drivers might settle on Kasese as a base for visits to Queen Elizabeth National Park.

Kilembe Situated on the Rwenzori footslopes about 8km west of Kasese, the small town of Kilembe was established in 1950 to service the adjoining copper mine of the same name. It remains a strangely time-warped place, dotted with 1950s-style buildings, most of which survived being damaged by boulders washed down in 2013 by the flooded Nyamwamba River. How long Kilembe will retain its late-colonial-era aura is an open question, given that the mine is theoretically set to reopen under new Chinese management soon (a project that appears to be on hold in the wake of a recent government ban on all exports of raw and unprocessed ores, in order to allow Uganda the opportunity to build its own metal-processing industry) but as things stand it's an intriguing, albeit inessential, diversion from Kasese.

Mubuku irrigation scheme One of Uganda's largest irrigation schemes, Mubuku takes water from the eponymous river, which rises in the Rwenzori, and disperses it across almost 500ha of plains. Established in the 1960s, the original scheme ran into difficulties and collapsed, but it has been recently rehabilitated under the management of the Abasaija Kweyamba Mubuku Farming Co-operative Society, whose 150 members each own 2.23ha of land to produce rice, maize and vegetable seeds for processing companies such as Fica and Naseco, as well as mangoes, guavas and other fruits. The co-operative is signposted to the right about 8.5km north of Kasese along the main Fort Portal Road and visitors are welcome. Guided tours cost around US$4; for details contact the Agrotourism office in advance (m 0784 010221). If going by car, or you can convince your guide to walk along the scheme's eastern roads, there are amazing views of the upper Rwenzori.

Rwenzori Art Centre, Sculpture Gallery and Coffee Bar (⊕ 0.25728, 30.10788; m 0782 238036; e rfkasese@yahoo.com; w rwenzorifounders.com;

⌚ 10.00–16.00 daily) Set on a 60ha tract of bush owned by Rwenzori Founders, this gallery displays the bronze work of 15 Ugandan sculptors, several of whom were trained in the lengthy lost-wax casting process in the UK in 2008. Permanent exhibits include a series of more than 30 magnificent bronzes representing the different clan totems of Uganda, as well as soapstone and marble carvings made by local artists. The land on which the gallery stands has been rehabilitated as a private nature sanctuary through the extensive replanting of indigenous trees, and the checklist now includes 150-plus bird species, as well as various small mammals and reptiles. A guided tour of the foundry costs US$10, and there is also a gallery with items for sale (at very reasonable prices by international standards), and a coffee shop serving hot drinks, biscuits and snacks. Proper loos, too. To get there from Kasese, follow the Fort Portal Road out of town for 10km to Kyemihoko trading centre (⊕ 0.24941, 30.11631), then turn left on to the signposted feeder road and follow it for 1.5km. You should call in advance, particularly if you want a tour.

RWENZORI MOUNTAINS NATIONAL PARK

Gazetted in 1991, the 996km² Rwenzori Mountains National Park protects the upper slopes and glacial peaks of the immense 5,109m-high mountain range that runs along the Congolese border for a full 120km south of Lake Albert and north of Lake Edward. Rwenzori is Uganda's most alluring hiking destination, traversed by three six- to nine-day trail circuits. The southernmost trailhead at Kilembe lies a few kilometres behind Kasese while Nyakalengija and Rugendabara lie 20km and 40km respectively to the north, off the Fort Portal road. All of these trails pass through a fascinating succession of altitudinally defined vegetation zones, ranging from montane rainforest to Afro-alpine moorland, and the scenery can be breathtaking. Be warned, however, that the upper Rwenzori is widely regarded to present tougher hiking conditions than the ascents of mounts Kilimanjaro or Kenya, largely due to the mud, which can be knee-deep in places after rain, and as such it requires above-average fitness and stamina. Unlike on Kilimanjaro, normal Rwenzori hikes stick below the snowline (around 4,500m), which reduces the risk of altitude-related illness, but the glacial peaks are accessible to experienced technical climbers. At the other end of the commitment scale, those with limited time, money or stamina can choose from a number of day or short overnight hikes through the forested slopes above Kilembe or Nyakalengija, or head up to Fort Portal and follow the Northern Rwenzori mini-hike between nearby Kazingo and Bundibugyo.

GEOLOGY AND HISTORY Rising from the western base of the Albertine Rift, the ancient gneissic, quartzite and other crystalline rocks of the Rwenzori peaks were uplifted to their present altitude about 3 million years ago, during the same tectonic upheaval responsible for the creation of lakes Albert, Edward and George more than 4,000m below. Roughly 120km long and 65km wide, the range incorporates six main massifs, the tallest being Mount Stanley, whose loftiest peaks are Margherita (5,109m) and Alexandra (5,083m). Margherita is exceeded in altitude elsewhere in Africa only by the free-standing volcanic cones of Kilimanjaro and Kenya, meaning that the Rwenzori is the highest proper mountain range anywhere on the continent. There are four other glacial peaks – Speke (4,890m), Emin (4,791m), Gessi (4,715m) and Luigi di Savoia (4,627m) – but global climate change has caused the combined extent of glacial coverage to retreat from 7.5km² in 1906 to a mere 1.5km² today.

Habitually obscured by clouds, the Rwenzori, though obviously well known to the local Bakonjo people (page 456), eluded European geographers until as recently

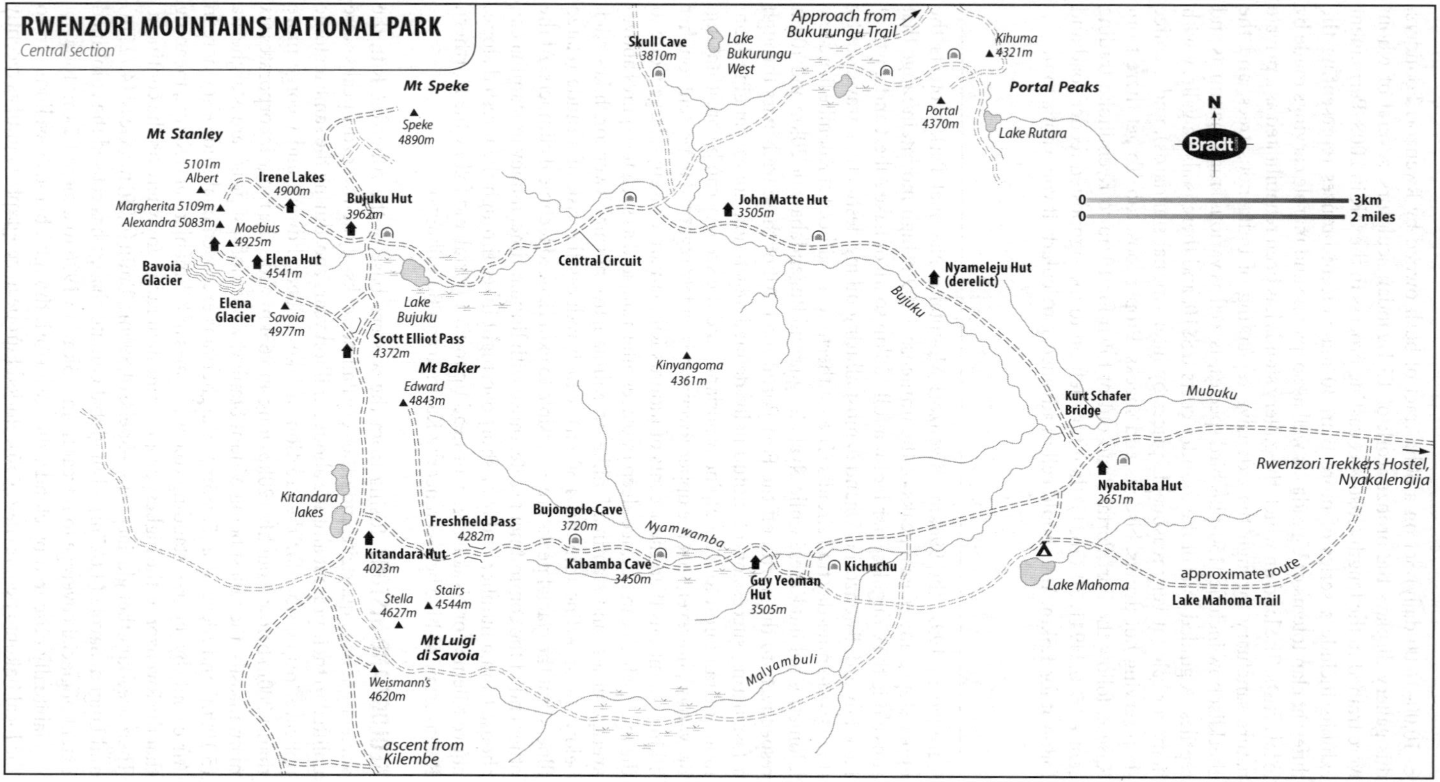
RWENZORI MOUNTAINS NATIONAL PARK
Central section
Mt Speke
Speke 4890m
Mt Stanley
5101m Albert
Margherita 5109m
Alexandra 5083m
Moebius 4925m
Irene Lakes 4900m
Bujuku Hut 3962m
Elena Hut 4541m
Bavoia Glacier
Elena Glacier
Savoia 4977m
Lake Bujuku
Scott Elliot Pass 4372m
Mt Baker
Edward 4843m
Central Circuit
Skull Cave 3810m
Lake Bukurungu West
Approach from Bukurungu Trail
Kihuma 4321m
Portal 4370m
Portal Peaks
Lake Rutara
N
Bradt
0 3km
0 2 miles
John Matte Hut 3505m
Nyameleju Hut (derelict)
Bujuku
Kinyangoma 4361m
Kurt Schafer Bridge
Mubuku
Nyabitaba Hut 2651m
Rwenzori Trekkers Hostel, Nyakalengija
Kitandara lakes
Kitandara Hut 4023m
Freshfield Pass 4282m
Bujongolo Cave 3720m
Kabamba Cave 3450m
Nyamwamba
Guy Yeoman Hut 3505m
Kichuchu
Lake Mahoma
approximate route
Lake Mahoma Trail
Stella 4627m
Stairs 4544m
Mt Luigi di Savoia
Weismann's 4620m
Malyambuli
ascent from Kilembe

as 1889, when the peaks were observed by Arthur Jephson and Thomas Parke, members of Henry Morton Stanley's cross-continental expedition to rescue Emin Pasha. Stanley's second in command, William Stairs, ascended the slopes as high as the 3,250m contour, followed in 1895 by the geologist George Scott Elliot and in 1900 by the biologist J E S Moore, both of whom managed to reach the 4,500m snowline. Margherita was summited for the first time in 1906, when Duke Luigi di Savoia's expedition – comprising more than 150 porters, a miscellany of scientists and the photographer Vittorio Sella – undertook a pioneering cartographic and biological survey of the Rwenzori, conquering all the major peaks in the process.

Ever since the Stanley expedition observed its distant glacial peaks in 1889, Rwenzori has been popularly identified as the snow-capped 'Montes Lunae' (Mountains of the Moon), which Ptolemy's *Geography*, written circa AD150, cited as the primary source of the Nile. According to Ptolemy, the existence of the Mountains of the Moon was based on a report by a Greek merchant named Diogenes, who followed a waterway inland from a port called Rhapta for 25 days to reach their base. Some modern geographers speculate that Diogenes's story is pure fabrication, and that the existence of several snow-capped ranges in equatorial Africa is mere coincidence. But even if Diogenes's account is true, it seems most likely that the mountain he saw was either Kilimanjaro or Kenya – both of which lie far closer to the coast, are reachable from it along rivers, and have more frequently visible snow caps – and that its supposed connection with the Nile was based on hearsay or extrapolation.

FLORA AND FAUNA As is the case with other comparably lofty East African mountains, the vegetation of the Rwenzori can be divided into several altitude zones, each with its own distinct microclimate, flora and fauna. The Afro-montane forest zone, which starts at 1,800m, has the most varied fauna. Above 2,500m, closed canopy forest starts to give way to dense bamboo stands. Higher still, spanning altitudes of 3,000m to 4,500m, the open vegetation of the heather and alpine zones has an otherworldly quality, with forests of giant heather trees throughout, and the striking 10m-high *Lobelia wollastonii* and giant groundsel (*Senecio admiralis*) most common above 3,800m.

The diverse fauna of the Rwenzori includes 70 mammal and 177 bird species, several of the latter being Albertine Rift Endemics. It is the only national park in Uganda where the Angola colobus has been recorded, though identification of this localised monkey will require careful examination as the similar and more widespread black-and-white colobus also occurs on the mountain. The only other mammal you're likely to see in the forest is the blue monkey, but elephant, buffalo, golden cat, servaline genet, chimpanzee, yellow-backed duiker and giant forest hog are all present. At night, the forest resounds with the distinctive and eerie call of the southern tree hyrax. Mammals are scarce above the forest zone.

Birds of the forest zone include Rwenzori turaco, barred long-tailed cuckoo, handsome francolin, cinnamon-chested bee-eater, Archer's ground robin, white-starred forest robin, Rwenzori batis, mountain sooty boubou, Lagden's bush-shrike, slender-billed starling, blue-headed sunbird, golden-winged sunbird, strange weaver, and several varieties of barbet, greenbul, apalis, illadopsis, flycatcher and crimsonwing. At higher altitudes, look out for lammergeyer (bearded vulture) and Verreaux's eagle soaring overhead, as well as alpine and scarce swifts, and the stunning scarlet-tufted malachite sunbird.

CLOTHING AND EQUIPMENT Wet conditions and sub-zero temperatures are normal, so it is essential you are properly prepared. Bring plenty of layered warm clothing for the nights. Rain is to be expected at all times of year (even the relatively dry months from late December to early March and late June to early September), so pack a decent waterproof jacket and trousers which you've tried on before the climb, and take plenty of plastic bags to keep clean clothes dry and to quarantine wet or dirty garments. Some paths are incredibly muddy after rain (knee-deep in parts), so while you'll need hiking boots if scaling any peaks, you'll be happier wearing locally bought gumboots elsewhere above the forest and bamboo zone.

THE BAKONJO

The guides and porters on the Rwenzori are almost exclusively Bakonjo, a group of Bantu-speaking agriculturists who inhabit the Rwenzori footslopes and are known for their stocky build and hardy nature. Some 500,000 Bakonjo (also sometimes called Bakonzo) live in Uganda, compared with more than 4 million in the DRC. Unlike most other Bantu-speaking peoples in Uganda, the Bakonjo have no clear traditional origin. Some say that they migrated westward from Mount Elgon, not settling anywhere until they found a similar montane environment to cultivate. Other traditions claim that the Bakonjo are descended from an ancient ancestor who emerged from one of the caves in the Rwenzori – oddly echoing the prevalent creation legend among the Bagisu of Elgon. They also have no paramount leader, but are divided into a number of small clans, each of which is associated with a particular spur on the Rwenzori foothills.

Traditionally, the Bakonjo seldom ventured on to the higher slopes of the Rwenzori, which is inhabited by a number of powerful deities and spirits that place a curse on any human who glimpses them, and will sometimes strike the observer dead. Paramount among these is Kitasamba – The God Who Never Climbs – said to live on the apex of the jagged peaks, in a snowy environment associated by the Bakonjo with semen and potency. Tradition has it that Kitasamba will only remain the source of Bakonjo procreative powers so long as he is untainted by the act itself – for which reason his spirit manifests itself only in male virgins, and adult men will abstain from intercourse for a period before ascending to the Rwenzori snowline.

Kitasamba has one wife, called Mbulanene (Heavy Rain), but a more important female spirit is his sister Nyabibuya, who safeguards female fertility and protects children. The third most important spirit of the mountains is Endioka, a dark serpentine inhabitant of rivers, capable of rendering men or women infertile, as well as indulging in other acts of black sorcery. The centrality of fertility and potency in their spiritual affairs notwithstanding, sex before marriage is frowned upon in traditional Bakonjo society, monogamy is customary, divorce rare, and pregnancy outside wedlock was formerly punishable by execution.

Agriculture has always been the main food-producing activity of the Bakonjo, but hunting also plays an important role in their traditional society, partly as sport, but also for food. The spirit of hunting, and shepherd of all wild animals, is a one-eyed, one-legged, one-armed being called Kalisa, known for his addiction to pipe smoking, as well as his partiality to fresh meat. Before setting off on any hunting expedition, Bakonjo men traditionally leave an offering of *matoke* or chicken to Kalisa in a shrine consisting of a pair of small hut-like shelters (the largest about 1m high) made of bamboo and/or thatch, then place a small fence of bamboo stakes across their path to prevent evil spirits following. After a successful hunt, a further offering of meat offcuts is left for Kalisa at the site of the slaughter.

Rwenzori Trekking Services includes all meals in its package rates, but Rwenzori Mountaineering Services (RMS) gives you the option of feeding yourself. If you decide to self-cater, you'll need to plan meals and quantities for a week or more. Vegetables and dried foods – noodles, rice, packet soups, posho, groundnut flour, etc – are available in Kasese and Fort Portal. You'll also need to bring or hire a camping stove (US$50 from RMS) and utensils. At altitude, eating can be a bit of a chore so do what you can to generate an appetite by varying meals. Whichever you

The advent of colonial rule robbed the Bakonjo of Uganda of much of their former independence, since their territory was placed under the indirect rule of the Toro monarchy, to which they were forced to pay hut taxes and other tributes. Widespread dissatisfaction with this state of affairs led to the Bakonjo Uprising of 1919, which endured for two years before its leader, Chief Tibamwenda, and his two leading spiritual advisers, were captured by the authorities and executed. But the strong resentment against Toro that still existed among the Bakonjo and their Bwamba neighbours resurfaced 40 years later, during the build-up to independence.

In 1961, the Bakonjo and Bwamba, frustrated by Toro's unwillingness to grant them equal status within the kingdom, demanded that they be given their own federal district of Ruwenzururu (Land of the Snow), to be governed independently of Toro. This request was refused. In August 1962, two months before Uganda was to gain independence, the Bakonjo took up arms in the Ruwenzururu Rebellion, attacking several Toro officials and resulting in a number of riots and fatalities. In February 1963, the central government declared a local State of Emergency in affected parts of Toro, and the Bakonjo were invited to elect their own government agents to replace the local representatives of Toro. Instead, the Bakonjo and Bwamba unofficially but effectively ceded from Uganda, by establishing their own Ruwenzururu kingdom, ruled by King Mukirania, and placing border posts and immigration officers at all entry points.

In 1967, the researcher Kirstin Alnaes, who had made several previous study trips to the region, noted that:

> The difference…from 1960 was marked…Earlier…spirit possession rituals were performed surreptitiously. Now people sported houses and shrines for the spirits, and were more than willing to talk about it. It was as if the establishment of their own territory in the mountains had released a belief in themselves and their cultural identity [formerly] suppressed not only by government regulations and missionary influence, but also by their own fear of seeming 'backward', 'uncivilised', 'monkeys' and the many other epithets the Batoro had showered upon them.

The situation in Ruwenzururu deteriorated after 1967, as government troops made repeated forays into the breakaway montane kingdom to capture or kill the rebel ringleaders. Ironically, it was only under Amin, who came to power in 1971, that the right to self-determination among the Bakonjo and Bwamba was finally accorded official recognition, with the creation of the Rwenzori and Semliki districts, which correspond to the modern districts of Kasese and Bundibugyo. Even so, clan elders must still today obtain a permit from the authorities before they may visit centuries-old sacrificial shrines to the various mountain spirits situated within the national park.

choose, take a few snacks – chocolate and the like – and include some for the poor soul who's carrying your luggage!

If you intend to climb one of the glacial peaks, bring climbing boots and equipment such as ropes, ice-axes, harnesses, crampons and walking sticks, or hire gear from your mountain operator. Make sure they are aware of your requirements and allow plenty of time so that shoes, etc, can be sized, fitted and paid for, ideally the day before departure to avoid misunderstandings and other delays. Snow goggles, a compass and an altimeter will also be useful.

MOUNTAIN HEALTH Do not attempt to climb the Rwenzori unless you are reasonably fit, or if you have heart or lung problems (asthma sufferers should be all right). Once above 3,000m, hikers may not feel hungry, but they should try to eat. Carbohydrates and fruit are recommended, while rich or fatty foods are harder to digest. Dehydration is one of the most common reasons for failing to complete the climb. Drink at least 3 litres of liquid daily, and bring enough water bottles to carry this. If you dress in layers, you can take off clothes before you sweat too much, thereby reducing water loss.

Altitude-related illness is not a major concern below the snowline. That said, few people climb above 3,500m without feeling minor symptoms such as headaches, nausea, fatigue, breathlessness, sleeplessness and swelling of the hands and feet. You can reduce these by allowing yourself time to acclimatise by taking an extra day over the ascent, eating and drinking properly, and trying not to push yourself. If you walk slowly and steadily, you will tire less quickly than if you try to rush each day's walk. Acetazolamide (Diamox) also helps speed acclimatisation. Take 250mg twice a day for five days, starting two or three days before reaching 3,500m. Be warned that the side-effects of Acetazolamide may resemble altitude sickness, so best try the medication for a couple of days about two weeks before the trip to check it suits you.

The risk of developing full-blown altitude sickness is greatest if you ascend the peaks. But at any altitude, should symptoms become severe or suddenly get worse, you may be developing pulmonary or cerebral oedema, both of which can be fatal. Symptoms of pulmonary oedema include shortness of breath even when at rest and coughing up frothy spit or blood. Symptoms of cerebral oedema are headaches, poor co-ordination, staggering, disorientation, poor judgement and even hallucinations. Sleeping at high altitudes with significant symptoms of altitude sickness is dangerous, and the only treatment is to descend as quickly as possible; even going down 500m is enough to start recovery. Sufferers often don't realise how sick they are, and may argue against descending. Fortunately, guides are trained to recognise altitude-related symptoms, and will force their clients to turn back immediately if they feel it is unsafe to continue.

Hypothermia is a lowering of body temperature usually caused by a combination of the cold and the wet. Mild cases typically manifest themselves as uncontrollable shivering. Put on dry, warm clothes and get into a sleeping bag; this will normally raise your body temperature sufficiently. Severe hypothermia is potentially fatal: symptoms include disorientation, lethargy, mental confusion (including an inappropriate feeling of well-being and warmth) and coma. In severe cases the rescue team should be summoned.

BOOKS AND MAPS The definitive written guide is the revised 2006 edition of the late Henry Osmaston's self-published *Guide to the Rwenzori*, which is now out of print but can be tracked down at a price through the usual online outlets. As regards maps, the most detailed is Andrew Wielochowski's excellent *Rwenzori Map and Guide* which shows contours and routes with plenty of practical and background information on the reverse side. Unfortunately, this is increasingly scarce and you will have to search for it online. Also useful for the peak area is the Department of Lands and Surveys' 1:25,000 Central Rwenzori Contour Map. Though hardly portable for the climb, Andrew Roberts' *Uganda Safari* contains chapters on the centuries-long search for this rumoured snowy source of the Nile, the eventual discovery of the Rwenzori and its subsequent ascent.

OVERNIGHT HIKING ROUTES Two main hiking circuits traverse Rwenzori Mountains National Park. The longer **Kilembe Trail**, which starts near Kilembe just northwest of Kasese, then ascends to the upper moorland via the Nyamwamba River Valley, is operated exclusively by the Australian-managed **Rwenzori Trekking Services** (RTS; m 0774 114499, 0709 747700; e traveluganda@rwenzoritrekking.com; w rwenzoritrekking.com). The more established option is the **Central Circuit**, which ascends to the peak area from Nyakalengija via the Mubuku and Bujuku valleys, and is in theory operated exclusively by **Rwenzori Mountaineering Services** (RMS; m 0784 308425, 0756 678224; e trek@rwenzorimountaineeringservices.com; w rwenzorimountaineeringservices.com), a community tourism group established in the 1990s to provide local Bakonjo people with the opportunity to benefit from tourism on the mountain.

Comparing the two routes, the main advantages of the Central Circuit are that it is shorter and slightly cheaper. The ascendant Southern Circuit is gaining greater popularity, however, for the simple reason that RMS, for all its ostensible worthiness, has a poor record by comparison with RTS when it comes to quality of guides, safety and rescue procedures, transparency with clients, environmental practices, and pretty much every other organisational facet of a successful trek.

There is now a third route to the high Rwenzori from Omukorukumi trailhead which, accessed from Rugendabara village on the Fort Portal–Kasese Road, ascends the eastern flank of the mountain. There is, as yet, no exclusive operator for the **Bukurungu Trail** and climbers are free to pay their park fees and cut out the middle men by arranging their own food, tents, porters, etc. The simpler option, however, would be to engage the locally based **Rwenzori Ranges Hikers Association** (RRHA; m 0753 523208, 0750 767973, 0771 224021; e rwenzorihikers@gmail.com; w rwenzorihikers.com) to handle all matters for you. A breakaway from RMS, this outfit aims to offer a more professional service on the mountain and feedback certainly appears to be good. Like RTS and RMS, the RRHA offers various summiting options in the high Rwenzori.

A fourth and much shorter option, suited to time- or budget-conscious travellers who just want to spend a day on the mountain, is an ascent from Kazingo, 13km from Fort Portal. The **Northern Rwenzori mini-hike** clambers over the medial ridge to Bundibugyo, while an alternative route detours to the additional 3,014m Karangora Peak. Park fees are paid to UWA but guides (and porters if required) can be arranged through **Abanya-Rwenzori Mountaineering Association** (AMA; m 0772 621397; e azolibahati@gmail.com; w abanyarwenzori.wixsite.com/rwenzorihiking) or **Karangura Trekking Services** (m 0779 775790, 0753 323699; e info@karanguratrekking.com; w karanguratrekking.com).

Nyakalengija and the Central Circuit For many years the only trail network in Rwenzori Mountains National Park, the Central Circuit ascends from Nyakalengija trailhead, which lies off the Fort Portal Road about 25km northwest of Kasese. Although hikes on this circuit can be booked through any tour operator in Uganda, on-the-ground arrangements are officially the exclusive domain of RMS, which maintains offices in Kampala and Kasese, as well as at Nyakalengija. The standard circuit is six days and five nights, but extra nights are required to ascend Margherita or any other peaks, while other options include day hikes into the forest around Nyakalengija.

Costs The advertised six-day guided hike along the Central Circuit loop works out at US$200 per person per day, inclusive of one porter per client (carrying a maximum of 25kg), meals, hut accommodation, guide and park entrance fees. A seven-day package including the ascent of Margherita or Mount Stanley costs an additional US$140 per person. Rates exclude mountaineering equipment such as climbing boots, sleeping bags, ropes, crampons and the like, which can be rented from RMS at US$25 per item.

Getting there and away The Nyakalengija trailhead (⊕ 0.35538, 30.02741) lies about 25km northwest of Kasese and takes approximately 40 minutes to reach in a private vehicle. To get there, follow the Fort Portal Road north out of town for 10km to the junction village of Nkenda (⊕ 0.25423, 30.11683), where the junction for Rwenzori Mountains National Park is signposted to the left. The various accommodation options listed below lie alongside the road between Nkenda and Nyakalengija. Matatus between Kasese and Fort Portal can drop passengers at Nkenda, and there are also matatus to Ibanda, about 6km before Nyakalengija, but no further. Most travellers charter a boda from Kasese (US$6–8) or arrange a special hire (US$20–30). Transport from Kasese (or indeed Kampala, or anywhere else in Uganda) can be arranged with RMS.

Where to stay and eat *Map, page 398*

Many people overnight in Kasese immediately before and after their ascent, but there are also several prettier and pricier accommodation options in the Mubuku Valley alongside the main road between Nkenda and Nyakalengija.

Upmarket

Snow Heights (8 cottages) ⊕ 0.35456, 30.02814; m 0784 404454; e snowheightslt@gmail.com. Situated less than 1km from Nyakalengija trailhead, this smart lodge is set at a chilly altitude of 1,600m in a lovely forest patch bisected by the babbling Mubuku River & inhabited by Rwenzori duiker, giant forest hog, various monkeys & at least 110 species of forest bird. The spacious stone cottages all have a sitting area with fireplace & balcony with a view through the forest to the river. A lovely forest retreat even if you've no intention of hiking higher. *US$150/260 sgl/dbl FB*. **$$$$**

Budget

Ruboni Community Camp (6 rooms) ⊕ 0.35023, 30.03007; m 0773 650049, 0752 503445; e visitruboni@gmail.com; w rubonicamp.com. This worthy community project has a lovely hillside location on the western slopes of the Mubuku River Valley in the village of Mihunga, 1km from Nyakalengija trailhead. It offers guided cultural & nature walks through local Bakonjo communities at US$20 pp, as well as overnight hill treks to view Margherita Peak at US$100 pp. Meals cost US$6–8. Coming from Nkenda, make sure you aren't deposited at its administrative office (also signposted for Ruboni Community Camp), in Ruboni village 2–3km before the camp itself. Again, a little expensive compared with similar accommodation in Kasese, but what price fresh air & mountain views? *US$20/25 pp room with common/en-suite showers B&B; US$5 pp camping*. **$$**

Rwenzori Base Camp (23 rooms) ⊕ 0.3325, 30.07163; m 0772 482248, 0774 723617. Situated in Ibanda, 10km from Nkenda along the

Nyakalengija Rd, this agreeable hotel is set in a pretty green garden on the edge of the village. The rooms are spacious & clean while a restaurant with garden seating serves meals in the US$5–7 range. On the high side compared with similar accommodation in Kasese. *US$45/50/55 sgl/dbl/twin B&B.* **$$$**

Hiking and walking routes In addition to the Central Circuit, Nyakalengija is also the starting point for the three-day Lake Mahoma Trail, and a number of day trails.

Central Circuit For many years, this six- or seven-day circuit out of Nyakalengija provided the only available access to the upper Rwenzori. Issues with RMS notwithstanding, it remains an exciting and superbly scenic experience. Note that the ascents of Margherita or Mount Stanley each require an additional day, slotting in between days three and four of the circuit described below. Mount Speke is reached from Bujuku Hut, where you will need to spend one extra night to allow you a full day to summit and return. To ascend the 5,109m Margherita Peak, the Rwenzori's highest point, you need to spend a night at Elena Hut (4,541m), 2km off the Central Circuit trail, and 3–4 hours on foot from either Bujuku or Kitandara huts.

Day one: Nyakalengija (1,615m) to Nyabitaba Hut (2,651m) (5hrs; altitude gain: 1,036m) From the trailhead at Nyakalengija, it's a 10km ascent to Nyabitaba Hut, passing first through cultivation then through forest. There's a piped water supply at the hut.

Day two: Nyabitaba Hut (2,651m) to John Matte Hut (3,505m) (7hrs; altitude gain: 854m) This is the longest and most strenuous day's walk. From Nyabitaba Hut, the path descends through forest for a short time before it crosses the Bujuku River at the Kurt Schafer Bridge (built in 1989). Between the bridge and Nyamileju Hut, the path is good for the first couple of hours, but it becomes steeper and very rocky as you enter the moorland zone, where heather plants are prolific. After about 5 hours you will emerge at Nyamileju, where the little-used hut is supplemented by a rock shelter, making for a good lunch stop. From Nyamileju, the path passes a giant heather forest and follows the Bujuku River for 2 hours to John Matte Hut, which is in good condition and stands about 200m from the Bujuku River, where water can be collected.

Day three: John Matte Hut (3,505m) to Bujuku Hut (3,962m) (5hrs; altitude gain: 457m) This stage takes up to 5 hours, depending on the condition of the two Bigo Bogs, which are often knee-deep in mud, though a boardwalk has now been constructed across part of it. On the way, Lake Bujuku has a magnificent setting between mounts Stanley, Speke and Baker.

Day four: Bujuku Hut (3,962m) to Kitandara Hut (4,023m) (3–4hrs; altitude gain: 61m) From Bujuku Hut you will ascend to Scott Elliot Pass (4,372m), which is the highest point on the Central Circuit trail, before descending to the two Kitandara lakes. The hut is next to the second lake.

Day five: Kitandara Hut (4,023m) to Guy Yeoman Hut (3,505m) (5hrs; descent: 518m) This stage starts with a steep ascent to Freshfield Pass (4,282m) then a descent to Bujongolo Cave (3,720m), which formed the base of Duke Luigi di Savoia's 1906 expedition. Further along the trail, there is an attractive waterfall and rock shelter at Kabamba Cave (3,450m), where you can overnight as an alternative to Guy Yeoman Hut.

Day six: Guy Yeoman Hut (3,505m) to Nyakalengija (1,615m) (8hrs; descent: 1,890m) It's a 5-hour trek down from Guy Yeoman Hut to Nyabitaba Hut (a descent of 854m), followed by a stiff descent to the trailhead at Nyakalengija, which takes a further 3 hours. If money is no object, the sensible thing is to rest overnight at Nyabitaba and descend slowly the following morning. Most people, however, push straight on downwards, motivated by the thought of a hot bath and saving themselves fees for an extra night on the mountain.

Lake Mahoma Trail This relatively new one- to three-day route forms a shorter and more wildlife-oriented alternative to the Central Circuit. The shortest variation, a day hike out of Nyakalengija (up to 6hrs; US$70 pp), involves a reasonably gentle climb to an altitude of 2,088m, and offers a good opportunity to see forest monkeys and birds, and occasionally even elephants. The full three-day route climbs from Nyakalengija trailhead into the bamboo forest zone, where the glacial Lake Mahoma offers fine views towards the high peaks, weather permitting. Nights are spent at Omu'ka Kizza Camp (2,977m) and Lake Mahoma Camp (3,515m), neither of which offers hutted accommodation, but are geared to wilderness camping only. It's debatable, however, whether the rewards associated with the three-day hike justify the exertion of what is probably the stiffest bit of legwork on the whole Central Circuit – having willed yourself that far, it would be a shame not to see some Afro-montane vegetation. A far better three-day option is the first two days (then one day to return) of the Kilembe Trail, which is equally tough on the first day, but gets you up with the giant heathers, lobelias and groundsels on the second.

Kilembe Trail Based out of Kilembe (or more accurately the village of Kyanjuki), 14km west of Kasese, the southerly Kilembe Trail follows a combination of trails along (and between) the Nyamugasani, Kamusoni and Nyamwamba river valleys to reach the peaks area. This route was first used by Professor Scott Elliot in 1895, 11 years before Luigi di Savoia pioneered the more direct route from Nyakalengija via the Bujuku River Valley. Coming from the Kilembe trailhead, the hiking distance to the peaks is significantly longer than on the established Central Circuit, and the ascent of Margherita will push the full duration of the excursion to nine days unless you are very fit. On the plus side, the trails run through some pristine and astonishingly beautiful landscapes, most of which had been unvisited by hikers for decades prior to the trail opening. All hikes on this route are operated by RTS, which has a top reputation when it comes to guiding and safety standards.

Costs The cost of the five-day hike to Mount Luigi di Savoia is US$1,080 for one person, or US$990 per person for two or more. The nine-day trek to Margherita plus other peaks costs US$1,870 for one person, or US$1,780 per person for two or more. Day hikes are priced at US$50 per person (or US$45 for more than two people), while two-/three-day hikes work out at US$290/520 for one person or US$250/475 per person for two or more.

In all cases, these prices include guides, porters, meals and accommodation while on the mountain, but they exclude the national park entrance fee of US$25/35 FR/FNR per day.

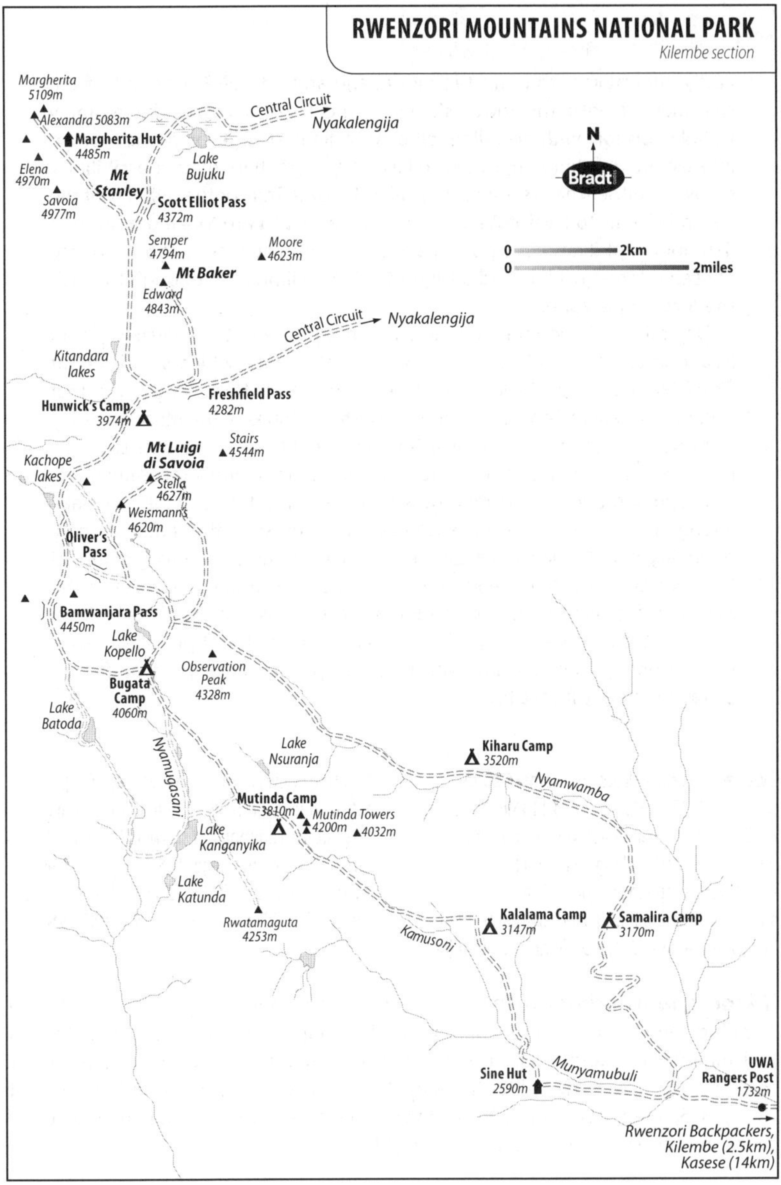

Getting there and away The base camp for the Kilembe Trail is Rwenzori Backpackers in Kyanjuki, a tiny village situated in the Nyamwamba River Valley, 3.5km past Kilembe's small town centre coming from Kasese. A boda from Kasese costs US$1.50–3 and a special hire around US$10.

Where to stay and eat *Map, page 398*

If the only accommodation in Kyanjuki is too basic for your tastes, it is perfectly possible to stay overnight in Kasese and head up to the trailhead on the day of departure.

DAY HIKES FROM NYAKALENGIJA

Easily undertaken from most lodges in and around QENP, a day hike from Nyakalengija into the lower slopes of the Rwenzori is an increasingly popular option with travellers who have limited time or money, or no interest in gruelling multi-day hikes. There are two main possibilities, following either the first day of the Lake Mahoma Trail, or the first day of the Central Circuit to Nyabitaba Hut. In both cases you are looking at around 5–6 hours uphill and 2–3 hours back down, and you stand a good chance of seeing forest wildlife and birds, but will not climb high enough to reach the Afro-alpine zone.

Day hikes can be arranged directly through UWA at the Rwakingi Park Headquarters (⊕ 0.26783, 30.10923; ☎ 039 2855758), which stands about 2km from Nkenda on the left side of the feeder road to Nyakalengija. Another option is a walk to Sebwe Falls on the southern slopes of the Mubuku Valley from Bugoye trading centre near Rwakingi. In all cases, the cost is US$70 per person including park entrance. An early start is highly recommended, as is phoning ahead or visiting Rwakingi the day before you hike to make arrangements. More inexpensive day hikes outside the national park boundary near Nyakalengija can be arranged on the spot through Ruboni Community Camp (page 460). You might also ask about a day out in the Rwenzori foothills outside the park (Rwenzori Snow Peaks Coffee; m 0760 950352). On a coffee tour you'll be picking, roasting and grinding beans, while a honey tour will have you dressed up in a beekeeper's outfit and extracting honey from a hive.

Rwenzori Backpackers (6 rooms, 4 dorms) ⊕ 0.21748, 30.00049; m 0774 114499, 0709 747700; e traveluganda@rwenzoritrekking.com; w rwenzoritrekking.com. Run by RTS, this hostel is set at an altitude of 1,450m in an old mine-associated building overlooking the deep Nyamwamba River Valley & offering enticing (or daunting) views of the high Rwenzori. Simple but clean rooms & 5-/6-/7-bed dorms all have nets but use common hot showers & flush toilets. Services include massages (US$25 pp) & meals in the US$4–6 range. *US$15/25 sgl/dbl rooms; US$12 dorm bed; US$8 pp camping. All rates B&B.* **$$**

Hiking and walking routes The most popular option, requiring no technical climbing ability or equipment, is a six-day loop trail summiting the 4,620m Weismann's Peak and 4,627m Stella Peak on Mount Luigi di Savoia. A longer variation on this is the nine-day loop trail incorporating a summit of Mount Stanley's 5,109m Margherita Peak. Even longer variations taking in both these peaks, and possibly others, can be arranged, too.

Six-day hike to Mount Luigi di Savoia

Day one: Kyambogho trailhead (1,450m) to Sine Hut (2,590m) (altitude gain: 1,140m) Starting at the main trailhead 2km past Rwenzori Backpackers, the route runs along the side of the Nyamwamba River Valley for 3km before entering the park for a long, steady climb through montane forest, followed by a stiff ascent through bamboo to reach the Sine Hut in the heather zone. Strong climbers can push on to Kalalama Camp, which lies at 3,147m, and allows longer to acclimatise before continuing to Mutinda the next day. Though this latter stage is a chore at the end of the day, you'll enjoy the morrow all the more for having it behind you.

Day two: Sine Hut (2,590m) to Mutinda Camp (3,810m) (altitude gain: 1,220m) After a stiff climb through bamboo to Kalalama Camp, the route follows the Kamusoni River Valley up to Mutinda. The overnight camp enjoys a particularly pretty setting among giant groundsels and moss-draped Erica at the foot of the 4,200m multi-pronged Mutinda Towers.

Day three: Mutinda Camp (3,810m) to Bugata Camp (4,060m) (altitude gain: 250m) From Mutinda, the landscape becomes bleaker and more dramatic as the trail traverses open moorland between the Kamusoni and Nyamugasani river valleys. The third night's campsite, set on a high rocky bluff above the Nyamugasani, enjoys a terrific, map-like view of Lake Kopello (one of eight glacial lakes in this valley) far below and north towards Mount Luigi di Savoia.

Day four: Climb Mount Luigi di Savoia (4,627m) and return to Bugata Camp (4,060m) (altitude gain and loss: 567m) Spend another night at Bugata Camp in order to climb to the two main peaks of Mount Luigi di Savoia. This day hike through superb Afro-montane vegetation provides the possibility (weather permitting, of course) of viewing the high peaks to the north and encountering patches of equatorial snow. The climb is not normally technical, but ropes may be required when the rock is snowy or icy.

Day five: Bugata Camp (4,060m) to Kiharu Camp (3,520m) (altitude loss: 542m) This lovely hike back towards Kilembe follows a different route through a valley to an area of evergreen forest where tree hyrax can be heard at night, and monkeys and Rwenzori turacos call by day. It is possible to continue further downhill to Samalira Camp (3,170m), which makes for a shorter and less knee-crunching day six.

Day six: Kiharu Camp (3,520m) to Kyambogho trailhead (1,450m) (altitude loss: 2,070m) The trail descends along a long ridge through bamboo and montane forest to the hostel at Kilembe.

Nine-day hike to Mount Stanley (Margherita Peak)

Days one to three As for the six-day hike to Mount Luigi di Savoia (see opposite).

Day four: Bugata Camp (4,060m) to Hunwick's Camp (3,974m) (altitude loss: 86m) Though this day ends with a net descent of 86m, it involves several ups and downs through magnificent scenery. The trail starts with a short but stiff climb to Bamwanjara Pass (4,450m), before a long descent through groundsel forest to the Kachope lakes. The route flanks Mount Luigi di Savoia before climbing on to a moraine ridge to find the camp. This faces Mount Baker and overlooks the Butawu Valley which drains on to the Rift Valley floor – visible in clear conditions – in the DRC.

Day five: Hunwick's Camp (3,974m) to Margherita Hut (4,485m) (altitude gain: 511m) A great day, this one. The route passes the two lovely Kitandara lakes before ascending the great glacier-carved chasm between mounts Stanley and Baker to Scott Elliot Pass. Hopefully you'll be able to see Lake Bujuku, far below in the classic U-shaped vast Bujuku Valley on the eastern side of the pass, before turning up on to Mount Stanley where you'll find Margherita Hut just below RMS's Elena Hut.

Day six: Climb Margherita Peak (5,109m) and return to Hunwick's Camp (3,974m) (altitude gain: 624m; altitude loss: 1,135m) An early start is required to ascend Mount Stanley before cloud obscures the views. The route then descends to Hunwick's Camp.

Days seven to nine Return to Bugata Camp, then continue as for days five and six of the six-day hike to Mount Luigi di Savoia (page 465).

Shorter variations from Kilembe A good option for birders and wildlife lovers, the **Munyamubuli River Trail** is a 6–7-hour day hike passing through pristine Afro-montane forest rich in plants, primates and birds. A two-night variation of this follows the same valley further, before climbing a steep ridge to sleep in Omusitha Camp (2,792m). Better for scenery but less wildlife-oriented, the two-night **Samalira Trail** leads over 5–6 hours to the eponymous camp, set at an altitude of 3,170m, and offers the option of climbing a bit higher for better views over Lake George and Queen Elizabeth National Park. The three-day **Kalevala Loop Trail** passes through the Munyamubuli Valley before climbing a heavily forested ridge where black-and-white colobus, blue monkey and L'Hoest's monkey are often seen. Overnight stops are at Samalira Camp, then at Kalalama Camp, which stands at an altitude of 3,147m in an area characterised by giant heather forest.

Bukurungu Trail This new trail starts at Omukorukumi trailhead on the western flank of the mountain, above Rugendabara trading centre on the main Fort Portal–Kasese Road. The standard ascent takes five nights and six days on the mountain. After ascending the mountain from a trailhead 20km north of Nyakalenjia, the route joins and follows the Central Circuit up the Upper Bujuku Valley, where it follows an alternative route to Margherita Peak up the northeastern side of Mount Stanley. First climbed in 1954 (and notable for 'the first ascent of Margherita by a lady'), this is described on page 104 of Henry Osmaston's Rwenzori guidebook as '7(i) East ridge of Margerita from Irene Lakes'. Prospective climbers would do well to read this beforehand. After summiting, climbers follow the Central Circuit in reverse (descending RMS's ascending route) down to Nyakalengija. Though, as previously stated, UWA will allow climbers to make their own arrangements for an expedition and will provide a ranger escort, an experienced guide and porters will need to be hired separately from the Rwenzori Ranges Hikers Association (page 452). The logistics and complications of a six-day trek being what they are, it would be simpler to engage the RRHA to take care of everything.

Costs The cost of the standard five-night hike to Mount Stanley with the RRHA is US$1,350 for 1–2 climbers with small discounts for larger numbers. This includes food, tents and bedding, porters, guides, return transport from Kasese to the Omukorukumi trailhead, and the park entrance fee. Expect to pay an additional US$125 if you don't have the specialist equipment necessary to summit.

Hiking and walking route

Six-day hike to Mount Stanley (Margherita Peak) Detours as additions or alternatives to this standard itinerary are possible. Mounts Emin (4,798m) and Gessi (4,715m) can be climbed from Bigo Camp, while Mount Speke (4,890m) can be summited from the Irene Lakes.

Day one: Omukorukumi trailhead (1,560m) to Kambeho Camp (3,288m) (altitude gain: 1,728m) A long day climbing through forest ends at Kambeho Camp.

Day two: Kambeho Camp (3,288m) to Lamia Camp (3,577m) (altitude gain: 289m) The second day ascends through bamboo and heather to the mountain's medial watershed at the head of the Lamia River, which drains west down to the Semliki Valley.

Day three: Lamia Camp (3,577m) to Bigo Camp (3,463m) (altitude loss: 114m) Groundels and lobelias abound as the route passes the Portal Peaks (4,391m) and descends to cross the infamous Bigo Bog and join the Central Circuit.

Day four: Bigo Camp (3,463m) to Irene Lakes Camp (4,495m) (altitude gain: 1,032m) The route follows the Central Circuit up the moraine-stepped Bujuku Valley as far as Lake Bujuku before continuing on to camp by the Irene Lakes.

Day five: Irene Lakes Camp (4,495m) to Bigo Camp (3,463m) (altitude gain: 614m; altitude loss: 1,646m) This day follows a route up the northeastern side of Mount Stanley to summit Margherita Peak (5,109m).

Day six: Bigo Camp (3,463m) to Nyakalengija (1,615m) (altitude loss: 1,848m) A long final day follows the Central Circuit all the way down to Nyakalengija trailhead.

Kazingo and the Northern Rwenzori mini-hike This long day hike crosses from the trading centre of Kazingo (13km from Fort Portal) to Bundibugyo via the northern tip of the Rwenzori Mountains National Park using the Bwamba Pass, which once served as the only access route between Fort Portal and the Semliki Valley. Despite being relatively strenuous, and taking 6–8 hours from the trailhead at Kazingo, the mini-hike has become popular with travellers reluctant to pay the high fees asked for longer Rwenzori hikes based out of Kasese. From the 1,650m trailhead at Kazingo, a choice of routes traverses the range, ascending through farmland/grassland, Afro-montane forest and bamboo forest to the medial ridge before descending to Bundibugyo. It's hard going, especially if your trail takes in the 3,012m Mount Karangora. Consolation for the leg strain is provided by excellent regional views (weather permitting) and the chance to spot four monkey species, including Angola colobus.

Guided hikes out of Fort Portal can be arranged through the RuwenZori View Guesthouse (page 408). Day hikes with a UWA guide cost US$65/85 FR/FNR including park entrance. Alternatively, you can make arrangements with one of the Kazingo specialists listed on page 459, who will provide lunch, water, porter and return transport if required.

To get to Kazingo in a private vehicle, follow the Bundibugyo Road out of Fort Portal for 9.5km as far as Bukuuku, then turn left at a junction (⊕ 0.67437, 30.19814) signposted for Rwenzori Mountains National Park, and continue for another 3.5km. Using public transport, occasional matatus run from Fort Portal to Kazingo or you just take a boda all the way. Inexpensive bandas, camping facilities and basic meals are available at the Rwenzori Unique Campsite, 2km from the Kazingo trailhead.

4x4 safari car hire
Tailored safari packages
Inland transport
Guiding · Hotel booking
Birding · Rafting on the Nile
Rwenzori mountain hike
Plot 13 Speke Street
Rwefuma House
Kasese Town
Kampala Office:
Plot 4982 Kitende
Entebbe Road
Email: rwefuma@gmail.com
www.rwefumasafaris.com
rwefuma safaris and Car rental
Rwefuma
SAFARIS & CAR HIRE
CONTACT US
+256 772 573 399
+256 756 573 399
+256 776 573 399
Your Preferred Local Travel Agency

RWENZORI EXPEDITIONS
Rwenzori Expeditions
Take me to the mountains
+256 392 159 498
Namasuba- Kikajjo, Semakula Road
info@rwenzoriexpeditions.com
www.rwenzoriexpeditions.com

Queen Elizabeth National Park and Surrounds

Uganda's second-largest, joint-oldest and most biodiverse national park is set in the low-lying Rift Valley where it crosses the equator south of the lofty Rwenzori Mountains and north of the Kigezi Highlands. Protected as a wildlife reserve since the late 1920s, it was gazetted under the name Kazinga National Park in 1952, but renamed two years later to commemorate the first visit to Uganda by Queen Elizabeth II and Prince Philip. Extending over 1,978km^2, Queen Elizabeth National Park (QENP) protects a fabulously diverse landscape of tropical habitats: rolling grassland, moist acacia woodland, tropical rainforest, sheer-sided volcanic calderas, and a variety of wetland habitats including the open waters and swampy shores of lakes Edward and George, the 40km-long Kazinga Channel that connects them, and several freshwater and saline crater lakes.

Uganda's busiest safari destination, QENP makes for a convenient stopover en route between Kibale and Bwindi Impenetrable national parks. The park's most popular attraction is a scenic boat trip that runs out of the Mweya Peninsula along the Kazinga Channel past large herds of elephant, buffalo and hippo. But there are plenty of other potential highlights: game drives on the Kasenyi Plains; chimp tracking at Kyambura Gorge (inside the park) or Kalinzu Ecotourism Project (outside it); birding and monkey viewing in Maramagambo Forest; exploring the Katwe or Bunyaruguru crater lakes; and – last but emphatically not least – heading off in search of the legendary tree-climbing lions that inhabit the remote Ishasha Plains.

GENERAL INFORMATION

GEOLOGY Set on the floor of the Albertine Rift, Queen Elizabeth National Park broadly took its present geological shape around 3 million years ago, when the uplifting of the Rwenzori Mountains split the paleo-lake Obweruka – then similar in extent to present-day Lake Tanganyika – into what are now lakes Albert, Edward and George. Today, most of the Ugandan shore of Lake Edward lies within QENP, as does the northern and western shore of Lake George, and the connecting Kazinga Channel. Despite their common origin and identical surface altitude of 913m, lakes Edward and George could scarcely be more different in character. Elongated Lake Edward, extending over almost 2,000km^2 and up to 120m deep, is the smallest of a quartet of major freshwater bodies that arc through the base of the Albertine Rift floor, a broadly north–south orientation, to form the Congolese border with Uganda, Rwanda, Burundi and Tanzania. The 250km^2 Lake George, by contrast, is essentially an extension of Lake Edward fed by the Kazinga Channel: roughly

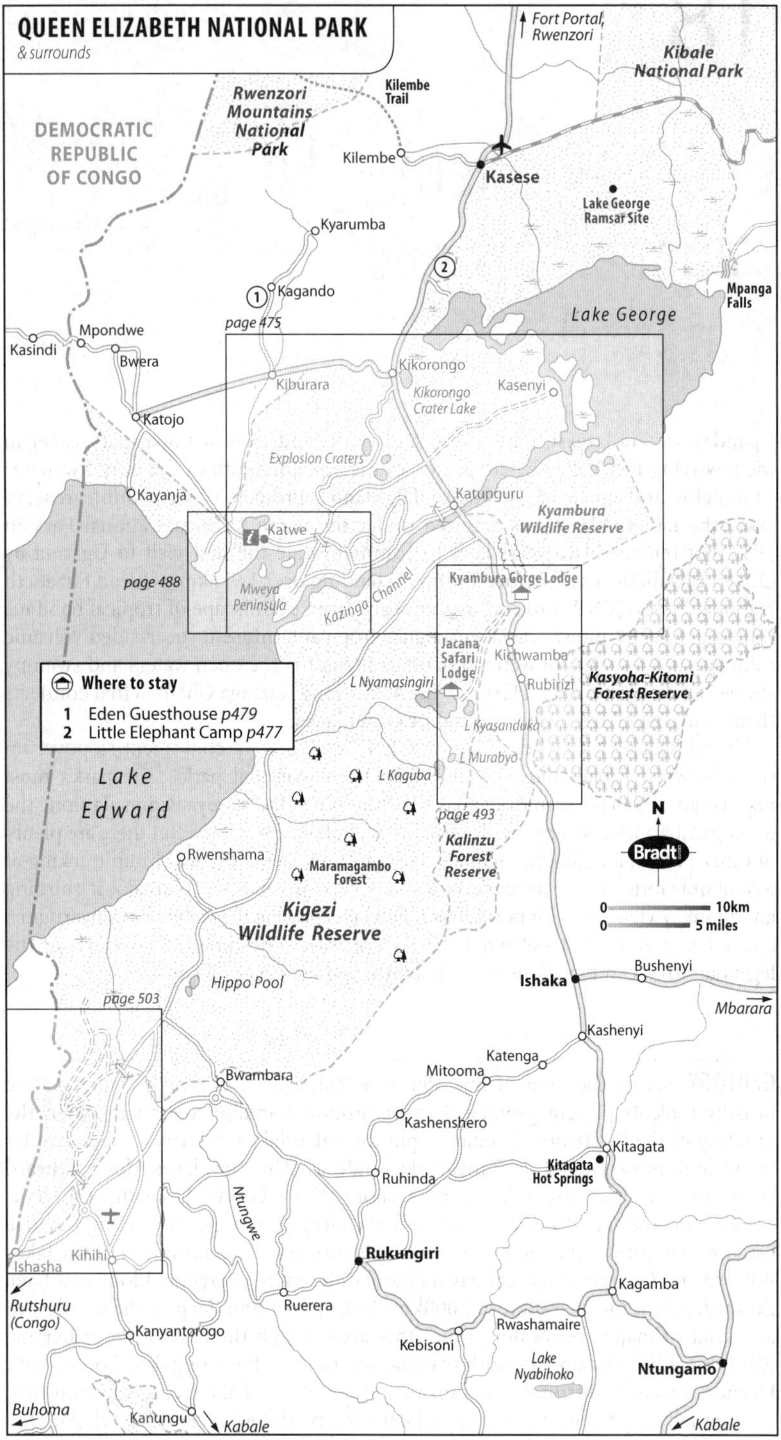

QUEEN ELIZABETH NATIONAL PARK
& surrounds
Fort Portal, Rwenzori
Kibale National Park
Rwenzori Mountains National Park
Kilembe Trail
DEMOCRATIC REPUBLIC OF CONGO
Kilembe
Kasese
Lake George Ramsar Site
Kyarumba
Kagando
Mpanga Falls
Lake George
page 475
Mpondwe
Kasindi
Bwera
Kikorongo
Kiburara
Kikorongo Crater Lake
Kasenyi
Katojo
Explosion Craters
Kayanja
Katunguru
Kyambura Wildlife Reserve
Katwe
page 488
Mweya Peninsula
Kazinga Channel
Kyambura Gorge Lodge
Jacana Safari Lodge
Kichwamba
Rubirizi
Kasyoha-Kitomi Forest Reserve
L Nyamasingiri
Where to stay
1 Eden Guesthouse p479
2 Little Elephant Camp p477
L Kyasanduka
L Murabyo
Lake Edward
L Kaguba
page 493
Kalinzu Forest Reserve
Bradt
Rwenshama
Maramagambo Forest
Kigezi Wildlife Reserve
0 10km
0 5 miles
Ishaka
Bushenyi
Mbarara
Hippo Pool
page 503
Kashenyi
Katenga
Mitooma
Bwambara
Kashenshero
Kitagata
Kitagata Hot Springs
Ruhinda
Ntungwe
Rukungiri
Ishasha
Kihihi
Kagamba
Rutshuru (Congo)
Ruerera
Rwashamaire
Kanyantorogo
Kebisoni
Lake Nyabihoko
Ntungamo
Buhoma
Kanungu
Kabale
Kabale

circular in shape, nowhere more than 3.5m deep, and bordered by extensive marshes. Although geologically calm in recent millennia, the area around lakes Edward and George has been subject to massive tectonic upheaval over the past 500,000 years, as evidenced by a total of at least 35 crater lakes and numerous dry volcanic calderas within 20km of the Kazinga Channel. Fecund as QENP is today, the geological and archaeological records indicate that only 7,000 years ago, the area was temporarily denuded of practically all its fauna and flora as a result of a particularly violent bout of volcanic activity.

FLORA AND FAUNA Most of QENP comprises open grassland and savannah, which tends to be moister and woodier in the west than in the east. A variety of thorny acacias predominate in savannah habitats, though a striking feature of the park is its high concentrations of the candelabra shrub *Euphorbia candelabrum*, a cactus-like succulent that grows to tree-like dimensions along the Kazinga Channel and on the Kasenyi Plains. The park also incorporates substantial areas of papyrus swamp around Lake George, which is listed as a Ramsar Wetland, as well as the extensive rainforest of Maramagambo Forest and riparian woodland in the Kyambura Gorge (bordering Kyambura Wildlife Reserve) and the Ishasha and various tributary rivers in the southwest. The park's terrestrial biodiversity is increasingly threatened by the spread of exotic invasive plants such as *Lantana camara* and *Parthenium hysterophorus*, neither of which provides suitable forage to antelope, buffalo and other grazers.

QENP supports at least 95 **mammal** species, the highest for any Ugandan national park. Ten primate species are present, including chimpanzee, vervet, blue, red-tailed and L'Hoest's monkeys, black-and-white colobus and olive baboon. A checklist of around 20 carnivores is headed by lion and leopard, but spotted hyena and side-striped jackal are also quite common, and a habituated banded mongoose troop is conspicuous on the Mweya Peninsula. The most common antelope is Ugandan kob, some 20,000 of which are resident in the park, but bushbuck, topi and waterbuck are also locally common, while the elusive semi-aquatic sitatunga occurs in papyrus swamps around Lake George, and four duiker species are primarily confined to the Maramagambo Forest. Buffalo are common and often reddish in colour due to interbreeding with the redder forest buffalo of the Congolese rainforest. The park's elephants are also sometimes said to display affinities with the smaller and slightly hairier forest-dwelling race of elephant found in the DRC. Among other ungulates, notable absentees include rhino, giraffe and zebra, but more than 5,000 hippos inhabit the park's waterways, warthogs are very common, and the Kazinga Channel is one of the few non-forested places in Africa where giant forest hog are regularly seen.

Although it now ranks as Uganda's most popular safari destination, QENP suffered an alarming loss of wildlife during the years of instability that followed Amin's 1971 coup. The elephant population, for instance, dropped from a high of 4,000 in the 1960s to perhaps 150 in 1980, and buffalo numbers were reduced from 18,000 to 8,000. Since the late 1980s, however, the situation has improved greatly. An aerial survey undertaken in May 2015 estimated that almost 3,000 elephants – about 60% of the national population – inhabit QENP, while the buffalo population now stands at around 16,000. Lions became very uncommon and elusive in the 1980s but numbers have since increased, probably peaking at around 200 circa 2010, since when they have once again declined slightly, primarily due to conflict with and persecution by people living in and around the park. All the same, QENP remains a very important stronghold for lions, which are concentrated on the Kasenyi Plains and around Ishasha and Mweya.

RETURN OF THE CROCODILES

An enduring casualty of the most recent volcanic cataclysms in what is now QENP was the Nile crocodile, which occurs naturally in almost all suitable aquatic habitats south of the Sahara, but vanished from the local archaeological record some 7,000 years ago, and was absent from Lake Edward, Lake George and the Kazinga Channel until recent historical times. This anomaly was a subject of considerable debate during the colonial era. Some biologists attributed the absence to a physical or chemical factor in the water, a theory that had little grounding in fact, since crocodiles elsewhere are tolerant of more extreme water temperatures, higher levels of alkalinity and more toxic chemical dilutes than are presented by either of the lakes in question. As a Cambridge scientific expedition to Uganda in 1931 noted, 'Lake Edward seems to be an ideal habitat for crocodiles; there are plenty of quiet beaches and swamps and an abundance of fish and other food.'

The other prevalent notion was that the crocodiles, having been wiped out by volcanic activity 7,000 years ago, were unable to recolonise QENP due to their inability to navigate the rapids and gorges along the Semliki River, the only major associated waterway they still inhabited. Implausible as this may sound, subsequent events suggest it was at least halfway correct. However, it was probably not the rapids or gorges per se that inhibited the crocodiles' movement, but the obstacle they presented in tandem with the surrounding rainforest. As a result, deforestation along the Semliki Gorge in the 1980s led to crocodiles making an unexpected reappearance on Lake Edward towards the end of that decade. Since then numbers have proliferated. Large crocodiles are frequently observed on Kazinga launch trips, while local fishermen now regard them as a hazard in the reedy shallows of Lake George.

Some 610 **bird** species have been recorded in QENP, a remarkable figure for what is a relatively small national park by continental standards (to place this in some perspective, that's more birds than have ever been seen in the Serengeti or Kruger national parks, fine birding destinations that are seven- and ten-times larger than QENP respectively). In addition to 54 raptors, the checklist includes virtually every aquatic species resident in Uganda, and a variety of woodland and forest birds, the latter largely confined to the Maramagambo Forest. Birding anywhere in the park is good, but the Mweya Peninsula stands out for the myriad waterbirds on the Kazinga Channel, while the riparian forest at Ishasha is a good place to see certain more unusual species.

ORIENTATION QENP is a park of many parts – and, it might be said, one adorned with an above average quota of appendages in the form of tourist sites that technically lie outside its boundaries but are most often visited in conjunction with it, for instance the Kalinzu Forest, Lake Katwe, Kyambura Wildlife Reserve and Kasenyi fishing village.

The park might simplistically be broken up into five main sectors, starting in the north as follows:

Lake George Ramsar Site The most northerly part of QENP comprises an all-but-inaccessible expanse of papyrus swamp that divides Lake George from Kasese and Kibale National Park.

Northern Plains and Kazinga Channel Historically, the Kazinga Channel and plains running for about 10km to its north form QENP's main focus of tourist development. The area incorporates the Mweya Peninsula, Kasenyi Plains, the western shore of Lake George, the northeast shore of Lake Edward, and the Katwe crater lakes.

Between Kazinga and Maramagambo Bounded by Maramagambo Forest in the south, the part of QENP immediately south of the Kazinga Channel is largely undeveloped for tourism, one notable exception being the chimp-tracking site at Kyambura Gorge. It is, however, integrated with several of the aforementioned appendages, including the Bunyaruguru Crater Lakes, Kyambura Wildlife Reserve, a chimp-tracking site at Kalinzu Ecotourism Project, and a cluster of lodges perched on the Kichwamba Escarpment above the QENP's eastern boundary.

Maramagambo Forest This vast tract of medium-altitude rainforest is largely inaccessible, bar a limited number of tourist developments in the vicinity of Lake Nyamasingiri in the far northeast.

Ishasha Sector This small but wildlife-rich area of savannah running along the Congolese border south of Lake Edward is now well developed for tourism and a popular overnight stop en route to or from Bwindi Impenetrable National Park.

The circuits In practice, QENP and environs can be split up into two distinct but very unequal tourist circuits. The larger of these, and the more loosely defined, is North-Central QENP, which comprises the first four aforementioned sectors, and is serviced by more than 30 lodges and guesthouses centred on half-a-dozen nuclei, eg: Kikorongo, Kasenyi, Katunguru, Katwe, Mweya and the Kichwamba Escarpment. The smaller circuit, flanking the murram road to Bwindi Impenetrable National Park some 2 hours' drive southwest of North-Central QENP, consists of the isolated Ishasha Sector, which is serviced by around five lodges and offers just one game-viewing circuit.

Logistically, the common thread linking the lodges and sites associated with North-Central QENP is a 50km stretch of the surfaced Kasese–Ishaka Road that runs between Kikorongo in the north and the Kalinzu Ecotourism Project in the south, crossing the Kazinga Channel en route at Katunguru Bridge. Almost all lodges and sites of interest in North-Central QENP lie alongside this road, or are connected to it by a short (up to 20km) feeder road, which means that (with a few extreme exceptions) you can drive between almost any of the circuit's lodges and main attractions in under an hour.

FEES The entrance fee for QENP is US$30/40/25 FR/FNR/ROA per 24 hours. The standard vehicle entrance fees are also charged (page 9), but only once per entry. No fee is charged for driving along the surfaced Mbarara–Kasese Road, the main dirt roads to Katwe and Kasenyi villages, the dirt road between Katunguru and the Ishasha border post, or any other public roads that run through the park. Entrance fees should be paid by debit card or MoMo at the UWA reservations office in Kampala, at any of the entrance gates, or at the Katunguru Park Headquarters 3km south of Katunguru Bridge (⊕ -0.14916, 30.06394). All charges relating to accommodation, camping and activities at Mweya must be paid for at the visitors' centre there. Other activities can usually be paid for at the relevant gate or ranger post, but chimp tracking in Kyambura is best booked ahead at the UWA reservations office in Kampala or at Katunguru Park Headquarters.

Although it is not mandatory to take a ranger/guide on private game drives, it is strongly recommended, at least until you get to know your way around the park, and it will greatly improve your odds of seeing lion and leopard. The fee for a guide is US$20 per vehicle or US$10 for a self-guided drive.

Fees for individual activities are given under the relevant section later in the chapter.

FURTHER READING Andrew Roberts's *Uganda Safari* book contains a chapter on QENP, and the park is also covered by Sheet 6 in the 'Uganda Maps' series. The latter is available at the park entrance gates for around US$7/Ush25,000.

SECURITY IN QENP Queen Elizabeth National Park adjoins the troubled east of the Democratic Republic of Congo, which has for many years been overrun by rebel groups. Occasionally, their activities spill over into Uganda, as in October 2023 when two tourists and their driver were killed on the Katwe Road. Though security was beefed up, the authorities considered this an isolated incident and (while visits from British and American tourists reduced for a while) European tourists clearly agreed with them. Indeed, during our fieldwork for this book in February 2024, the park was as busy as ever.

NORTH-CENTRAL QENP AND THE KASESE–ISHAKA ROAD

This main developed part of QENP incorporates a remarkable diversity and number of tourist attractions and amenities in a relatively compact area. Prime activities are the boat trip out of the Mweya Peninsula and game drives on the Kasenyi Plains, but North-Central QENP and its immediate environs also include two chimpanzee-tracking sites, a couple of dozen crater lakes, scenic lakes George and Edward, and a variety of worthwhile community projects – not to mention around three-dozen lodges and other accommodation facilities. Despite this diversity, almost everything covered in this section lies within 10km of the Kazinga Channel as the crow flies, and with private transport, most sites of interest can be visited as a day trip from any of the lodges.

QUEEN ELIZABETH NATIONAL PARK
Northern Circuit
For listings, see from page 482, unless otherwise stated

Where to stay

1 Aardvark Safari Lodge
2 Buffalo Safari Lodge
3 The Elephant Home *p477*
4 Elephant Plains Lodge *p476*
5 Engiri Game Lodge
6 Enshama
7 Euphorbia Lodge *p480*
8 Honey Bear Bush Camp *p492*
9 Kasenyi Lake Retreat *p480*
10 Kasenyi Safari Camp *p480*
11 Kazinga Wilderness Safari Camp
12 Kikorongo Safari Lodge *p476*
13 Marafiki Safari Lodge *p477*
14 Queen Elizabeth Bush Lodge
15 The River Station *p494*
16 Simba Safari Camp *p477*
17 Tabingi Safari Lodge
18 Tembo Safari Lodge

Where to eat and drink

19 Nyamihanda & Sons
20 Tibs

GETTING THERE AND AWAY

By air Aerolink (031 7333000; e info@aerolinkuganda.com; w aerolinkuganda.com) flies daily from Entebbe Airport to Kasese (page 449). Flights cost US$286/474 single/return excluding taxes. There is also a small airstrip on Mweya Peninsula and, subject to a minimum of four passengers, Aerolink will also land there.

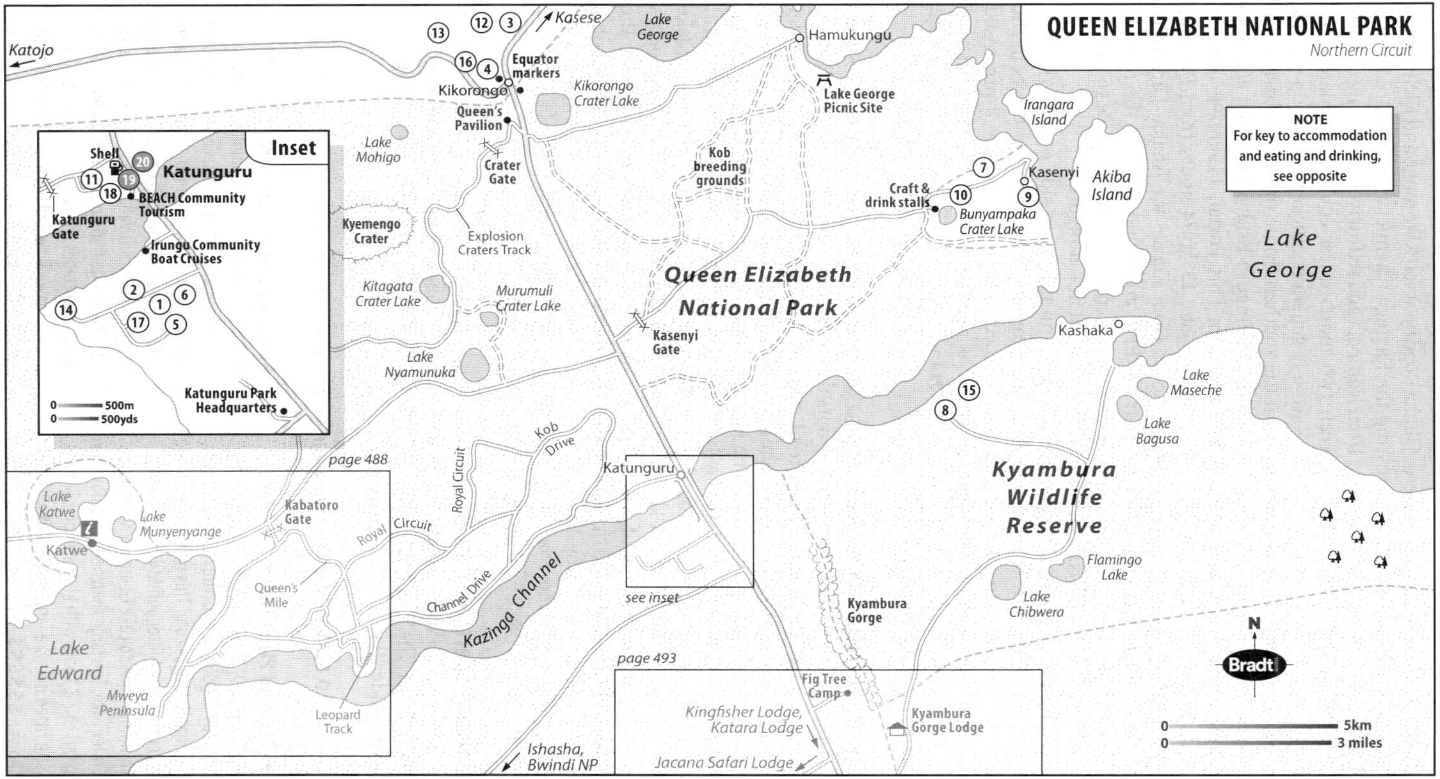
QUEEN ELIZABETH NATIONAL PARK
Northern Circuit
NOTE
For key to accommodation and eating and drinking, see opposite
Katojo
Kasese
Lake George
Hamukungu
Equator markers
Kikorongo
Kikorongo Crater Lake
Queen's Pavilion
Lake George Picnic Site
Irangara Island
Akiba Island
Kasenyi
Lake George
Crater Gate
Lake Mohigo
Kob breeding grounds
Craft & drink stalls
Bunyampaka Crater Lake
Kyemengo Crater
Explosion Craters Track
Queen Elizabeth National Park
Kitagata Crater Lake
Murumuli Crater Lake
Kasenyi Gate
Kashaka
Lake Nyamunuka
Lake Maseche
Lake Bagusa
Kob Drive
Royal Circuit
Katunguru
Kyambura Wildlife Reserve
page 488
Lake Katwe
Lake Munyenyange
Katwe
Kabatoro Gate
Royal Circuit
Queen's Mile
Channel Drive
Kazinga Channel
see inset
Kyambura Gorge
Flamingo Lake
Lake Chibwera
Lake Edward
Mweya Peninsula
Leopard Track
page 493
Fig Tree Camp
Kingfisher Lodge, Katara Lodge
Kyambura Gorge Lodge
Ishasha, Bwindi NP
Jacana Safari Lodge
N
Bradt
0 5km
0 3 miles
Inset
Shell
Katunguru
BEACH Community Tourism
Katunguru Gate
Irungu Community Boat Cruises
Katunguru Park Headquarters
0 500m
0 500yds

By road The stretch of the Kasese–Ishaka Road between Kikorongo and Kichwamba bisects North-Central QENP, crossing the Kazinga Channel at Katunguru Bridge. The park lies about 400km by road from Kampala and self-drivers travelling directly between the two can choose between two more-or-less equidistant routes. The northern route via Fort Portal and Kasese is generally quicker – bank on around 6 hours – as there is less traffic than on the southern route through Mbarara and Ishaka. Driving from elsewhere in Uganda, Katunguru Bridge lies about 40km/45 minutes from Kasese, 115km/90 minutes from Fort Portal, 115km/90 minutes from Mbarara, 73km/2 hours from Ishasha Gate, 135km/4 hours from Buhoma (Bwindi National Park) and 182km/4 hours from Kabale via Ishaka. Directions for individual sites within North-Central QENP are included under the relevant heading later in the chapter. For self-drivers, the most convenient place to fuel up in North-Central QENP is the Shell filling station in Katunguru.

Using public transport, Katunguru village (on the north side of the bridge) is the most useful goal for travellers wanting to organise budget game drives in the Kasenyi Sector, or to take a special hire to Mweya. Katwe, with its well-organised and affordable community tourism project, is another good option for shoestring travellers. Both are accessible on public transport as detailed under the relevant heading later in the chapter.

KIKORONGO AND SURROUNDS Only 22km south of Kasese, the village of Kikorongo lies on the Ishaka Road immediately outside the northern boundary of QENP, at the junction of a little-used surfaced road running west towards the Congolese border town of Mpondwe. Kikorongo is a blink-and-you'll-miss-it kind of place, distinguished mainly by its hemisphere-straddling location (although the equator officially crosses the Ishaka Road at a signposted lay-by 400m further south, a gradual northward drift means it now more-or-less runs through the village) and proximity to the crater lake for which it is named (about 1km to the southeast). A number of relatively new lodges scattered in the vicinity of Kikorongo are well positioned for game drives on the Kasenyi Plains and boat trips out of Mweya. Other possible activities include birding in the vicinity of nearby Lake George, drives into the Rwenzori foothills around Kyarumba, and a more far-flung excursion to the backpacker-friendly Pan-Afrique Hippo Resort (page 479) on the shores of Lake Edward.

Getting there and away The drive from Kasese to Kikorongo takes 20–30 minutes on a tarmac road. Any matatu heading south from Kasese can drop you there, or at The Elephant Home 1km to the north. Directions to other lodges are given under the individual listing.

Where to stay and eat *Map, page 475, unless otherwise stated*

Exclusive

✱ **Elephant Plains Lodge** (10 rooms) ⊕ 0.0036, 29.99032; ☎ 039 3267153; m 0701 426368; e info@ugandalodges.com; w ugandalodges.com. This new top-end lodge is centred on a hilltop infinity pool offering stunning views to Lake George & Kikorongo Crater Lake. The large thatched bungalows exude safari chic & come with king-size or 2 ¾ beds with fitted nets & a large bathroom with tub & shower. **$$$$$$**

Upmarket

Kikorongo Safari Lodge (9 rooms) m 0775 692334; e info@kikorongosafarilodge.com; w kikorongosafarilodge.com. Conveniently located close to the main tarmac road, & within easy reach of Kasenyi for the morning game drive, this lodge enjoys a terrific Rift Valley view, albeit beyond the tatty Kikorongo trading centre in the foreground. Spacious cottages are spread across the bushy hillside above & behind the main lodge building; guests with mobility issues or small children might want to avoid the higher units. Sensibly, since it gets hot on the Rift Valley floor, a pool is included with an attractive dining terrace attached. The lodge is signposted off the Kasese Rd on the edge of Kikorongo village. *US$120/226 sgl/dbl FB.* **$$$$**

Marafiki Safari Lodge (14 rooms) ⊕ 0.00586, 29.99253; m 0775 941189, 0784 056831; e info@marafikisafaris.com; w marafikisafaris.com. This hillside lodge offers a choice of spacious & stylish cottages & tents set on wooden platforms or smaller 4-bed budget cottages. A small but beautifully positioned infinity pool overlooks Lake George & the Rift Valley plains. From Kikorongo, follow the Mpondwe Rd west for 2km, then turn right on to a signposted dirt road that leads to the lodge after another 1km. *Luxury tents & cottages US$200/300/420 sgl/dbl/trpl FB; std cottages US$165/260/390 pp FB.* **$$–$$$$**

Moderate

✷ **Little Elephant Camp** [map, page 470] (5 tents) ⊕ 0.04385, 30.02681; m 0787 722355, 0706 596452; e info@littleelephantcamp.com; w littleelephantcamp.com. Owned & managed by a hands-on Canadian couple living in nearby Kasese, this unique self-catering tented camp has a tranquil location on the edge of the park at Muhokya, just off the main road between Kasese & the Crater Gate at Kikorongo. Passing wildlife includes waterbuck, Ugandan kob & more occasionally elephant, & it is well placed for game drives into the Kasenyi Plains. The glamping tents have lovely outdoor showers & come with a private dining/kitchen tent with hotplates, barbecue, fridge & utensils. These can be converted to family units by adding dome tents for children. A varied & well-priced selection of delicious self-catering food (from pre-marinaded steak or chicken curry to b/fast & fruit/vegetables) can be ordered in advance online & delivered to you upon arrival. Inexpensive beer & wine is sold on site. Half-/full-day guided safaris into QENP cost US$125/140 for up to 5 people, exclusive of park entrance fees. *U$140/220 sgl/dbl or twin; US$50 extra for dome tent. Discounts for residents.* **$$$$**

Simba Safari Camp (19 rooms, 1 dorm) ⊕ 0.00135, 29.98901; ☎ 039 3267153; m 0701 426368; e info@ugandalodges.com; w ugandalodges.com. This unpretentious lodge 1.5km along the Mpondwe Rd offers a row of budget rooms & an altogether nicer block of new rooms facing a lovely swimming pool. At the other end of the scale, there's a dorm using common showers. Simba is both well priced & well placed for early morning game drives to the Kasenyi Plains, the only downer being noise from truck traffic on the main road. *US$70/100 sgl/dbl (old rooms); US$115/140 sgl/dbl (new rooms).* **$$$**

Budget and camping

The Elephant Home (3 rooms) ⊕ 0.01041, 29.99996; m 0706 581477, 0787 822299; e info@theelephanthome.com; w theelephanthome.com. Situated in farmland on the west side of the Kasese Rd 1km north of Kikorongo, this community project offers the choice of spacious rooms or camping sites. The restaurant has views of the countryside, serving local delicious meals in the US$4–7 range, & a gift shop sells locally made handicrafts, paintings & cards. It further engages local community members by arranging boda safaris (US$15 pp) & other guided tours. *US$25 pp en-suite room B&B; US$10 pp camping.* **$$**

What to see and do The lodges are all less than 30 minutes' drive from the Kasenyi Plains and no more than an hour away from the Mweya Peninsula, making them very useful bases for general exploration of northern QENP.

Queen's Pavilion This bandstand lookalike, perched on a low ridge above the west side of the Kasese–Ishaka Road, 1km south of the official equator lay-by, affords a great view to the 1.5km² Kikorongo Crater Lake. The pavilion was built in 1958 to receive the British Queen Mother and Omukama Rukidi III of Toro, on a site previously visited by Queen Elizabeth II and the Duke of Edinburgh in 1954, and restored for the latter's return in 2007. The adjacent Queen's Pavilion Coffee Shop (⊕ -0.01033, 30.00199; m 0772 330139; e supporter@ctph.org; w ctph.org), a community project operated by the NGO Conservation Through Public Health, serves coffee, snacks and light meals. The pavilion stands just outside QENP's

Crater Gate, so no fees are payable unless you enter the park to follow the Explosion Craters Track (see below) or do a guided walk around Kikorongo Crater Lake.

Explosion Craters Track This scenic 15km drive runs south from the Queen's Pavilion through a magnificent landscape of volcanic calderas, each with its own microhabitat – some are lushly forested from rim to rim, while others host circular lakes or support a practically treeless savannah. The drive is particularly beautiful in the early morning, when the low eastern sun illuminates forested crater walls overhung with mist, and the clouds sometimes lift to reveal the glacial peaks of the Rwenzori. Wildlife volumes are low, but the craters frequently attract large elephant and buffalo herds in the dry season, and the thick woodland is the best place in QENP for acacia-associated birds.

The Explosion Craters Track is a rough, rocky and occasionally vertiginous road, so it is best tackled in a 4x4 or other high-clearance vehicle. Starting from the Queen's Pavilion, you must enter the park through Crater Gate, then after about 5.5km you'll reach a wooden viewing platform that offers views across to Lake George and the Rwenzori. You then pass the massive forest-swathed Kyemengo Crater to the right, followed by the pretty Kitagata Crater Lake, a good place to look for wildlife. The road then forks, with the better option being to head left along a short road that passes the small Murumuli Crater Lake to the right, before emerging on the main Katwe Road at a junction (⊕ -0.09399, 29.99631) about 500m east of Lake Nyamunyuka (literally, 'rotting meat'), an impressive near-circular crater lake whose green and malodorous waters are often attended by herds of buffalo. Alternatively, if you stick to the right fork after passing Kitagata Crater Lake, a longer road (about 9km extra) leads past several dry craters to connect with the Katwe Road more-or-less opposite Kabatoro Gate (⊕ -0.13509, 29.92819). If you are starting the track in the south, both these junctions are quite easy to find, and you can't really go wrong once you locate them.

Lake George Ramsar Site Extending across 150km^2 of swampland to the northwest of Lake George, Uganda's oldest Ramsar Wetland, listed in 1988, falls almost entirely within the expansive but inaccessible northern sector of QENP. It has the highest avian diversity of any Ugandan wetland, with 491 bird species recorded, including 167 wetland specialists and nine listed as globally threatened. The papyrus swamps of the Lake George Ramsar Site also support one of Uganda's most substantial breeding populations of the elusive shoebill. Other residents include papyrus endemics such as white-winged warbler, papyrus gonolek, papyrus canary and papyrus yellow warbler, while large concentrations of migrant waders and waterfowl aggregate in the area during the northern hemisphere winter. The localised sitatunga antelope is also resident. You can approach the southern tip of the wetland along a 10km dirt road that runs east from the Kasese–Ishaka Road, leaving it at a junction (⊕ -0.01337, 30.0032) 200m south of the Queen's Pavilion, to the fishing village of Hamukungu on the western shore of Lake George. To reach the swamp proper, however, you'll need to enquire about a ranger/guide at Mweya Visitor Centre or the Katunguru Park Headquarters.

Southern Rwenzori foothills If you've had your fill of lakes and savannah, and have some time at your disposal, the little-visited southern Rwenzori foothills to the west of Kikorongo are worth exploring. Some 40km west of Kikorongo and linked to it by regular matatus, the twin towns of Mpondwe and Bwera support a population of around 52,000 and – situated less than 5km east of the Congolese border – are also regarded to be the busiest centres of trade between the two countries. The most worthwhile time to visit is on Tuesday or Friday, when the daily market in Mpondwe, 2km beyond Bwera, is at its busiest and most colourful. If you want to spend the night, the Islander Guest House has en-suite rooms with DSTV, and a garden bar and restaurant.

On other days, travellers with access to a vehicle could follow a lovely road loop to the village of Kyarumba, by striking north from the Mpondwe Road at the small town of Kiburara (⊕ 0.00936, 29.89679), 12.5km west of Kikorongo. If you fancy overnighting in the area, try the cosy **Eden Guesthouse** at the Kagando Mission Hospital [map, page 470] (⊕ 0.06313, 29.89816; m 0705 389652; US$22 pp FB; **$$**) about 7km north of Kiburara.

Pan-Afrique Hippo Resort (⊕ -0.0931, 29.76291; m 0779 592561, 0788 115628; e afriquehitours@gmail.com) Set in Kayanja fishing village on the northern shore of Lake Edward, this quirky setup feels like a throwback to what passed for a beach resort elsewhere in Uganda in the 1980s. The massive grassy compound, cropped by hippos at night, leads to a rickety but breezy and well-shaded wooden lakeside platform ideally placed to enjoy a chilled beer while the sun sets over the Congolese shore, before partaking from a deceptively lengthy menu that usually boils down to the choice of goat or fish and accompanying starch for US$5–8. Boat trips cost around US$30 per party and come with a near certainty of seeing hippos and waterbirds, and an outside chance of spotting elephants. Basic en-suite rooms with nets and cold water cost US$10 per person, or you can brave the hippos and pitch a tent for a negotiable fee.

To get there, follow the Mpondwe Road out of Kikorongo for 27.5km to Katojo (⊕ -0.0177, 29.76856), where you need to turn left on to a conspicuously signposted dirt road, then right after another 900m at a junction (⊕ -0.02441, 29.77383) signposted for Kayanja but not for the resort. From here, it's 8km along a rough dirt road to Kayanja and the Pan-Afrique Hippo Resort. Using public transport, any Mpondwe-bound matatus can drop you at Katojo, but you'll need to charter a boda from there. Note that the Pan-Afrique Hippo Resort can also be reached from Katwe (page 485) by following a good dirt road that runs northeast to Katojo, passing the same junction for Kayanja mentioned above after about 19km.

KASENYI AND SURROUNDS QENP's most popular game-drive circuit traverses a plain that extends east from the Kasese–Ishaka Road to the rundown fishing village of Kasenyi on the western shore of Lake George. Being far more open than the North Kazinga plains on the opposite side of the main road, and if lions are your sole measure of quality, Kasenyi probably ranks as Uganda's best game-viewing spot anywhere. That said, plenty of others are of the same opinion and in the busier months you may find yourself part of a trail of safari vehicles crawling behind or clustered around a solitary lion. For a more enjoyable experience, get to Kasenyi for sunrise, accompanied by a guide who knows the areas currently favoured by the plains' resident prides. Locate your lions and, when the masses turn up, withdraw to enjoy the solitude of the surrounding plains.

One worthwhile destination is a lakeside viewpoint in the northeast of the sector which is a good place to watch hippos, as indeed is the shoreline at Kasenyi village. Another interesting feature, 2km before the village, is the scenic Bunyampaka Crater Lake. Overlooked by a cluster of kiosks selling handicrafts and chilled drinks, this is still active as a traditional salt extraction site. Logistically, the Kasenyi Plains are easily accessed from most lodges covered in this chapter, the main exception being those listed under Ishasha, but there's no better base for locating lions in the early morning – when they tend to be most active, and before the traffic from further afield starts trickling in – than the upmarket lodge overlooking Bunyampaka Crater Lake or their budget counterparts in Kasenyi village.

Getting there and away Access to the Kasenyi Plains is from a public dirt road that runs east from the Kasese–Ishaka Road to terminate on the Lake George shore at Kasenyi village after 16km. The signposted junction, sometimes referred to as Kasenyi Crossroads (⊕ -0.08187, 30.03027), is 10km south of Kikorongo, 5km north of Katunguru, and stands almost directly opposite the public road west to Katwe and Mweya.

Coming from Kasenyi Crossroads, the southern and northern game-viewing circuits both depart from the public road after 1.2km, where Kasenyi Gate (⊕ -0.07403, 30.03821) stands on the left side of the road. Those making a beeline for prime lion territory would be better off following the public road for another 7km, where they have the choice of turning south at the junction signposted 'Janet Track' (⊕ -0.03851, 30.08118), or north at an unsignposted junction (⊕ -0.03933, 30.08239) 150m past this. Bunyampaka Crater Lake and the two associated lodges both lie 5km past the junction for Janet Track.

Park entrance fees need not be paid to use the public road to Kasenyi, nor to visit Bunyampaka Crater Lake or any of the lodges listed below (all fall within an enclave of community land surrounded by the national park on three sides). It is mandatory, however, to pay park entrance fees in advance, most conveniently at Kasenyi Gate on Kasenyi Road, 1km off the tarmac, if you plan to leave the public road on a game drive.

Where to stay and eat *Map, page 475*

Upmarket

✷ **Kasenyi Safari Camp** (10 tented rooms) ⊕ -0.03346, 30.12609; **m** 0756 992038, 0791 992038; **e** info@kasenyisafaricamp.com; **w** kasenyisafaricamp.com. This excellent tented camp occupies a 20ha plot on the rim of Bunyampaka Crater Lake. Technically located outside the national park (being within an enclave containing the salty lake & Kasenyi fishing village), it is in the thick of the wildlife action. Lion & elephants roam the crater as they do the park that surrounds it, while the Kasenyi kob leks are just 10mins' drive away. Night drives within the crater (US$50 pp but no park fees) offer the chance to see lion, hippo, genet, leopard, spotted hyena & occasionally aardvark. The large standing tents have king-size beds with walk-in nets, spacious bathrooms with quality fittings & a large private deck facing the lake. **$$$$$**

Budget and camping

Euphorbia Lodge (8 rooms) **m** 0782 877127; **e** info@euphorbiasafarilodge.co.uk; **w** euphorbiasafarilodge.co.uk. This pleasant lodge within the Kasenyi enclave has an engaging history. Several years ago, Pascal, the Congolese owner, was guiding a European tourist through Kasenyi when they noticed an abundance of small kids running wild with no adults in sight. Turned out they were out fishing or working in the salt lake. Funds were obtained & a nursery school built to occupy the children; a health centre & a clean drinking water initiative followed &, eventually, this small lodge. Though a commercial venture, the latter trains local youngsters hoping to work in tourism/hospitality. There's no view but plenty of wildlife passes through the site & the kob leks are just 15mins away by car. The lodge comprises an attractive open-fronted bar-restaurant with plain cottage accommodation, en suite with cold showers. Good value. *US$55/90 sgl/dbl FB*. **$$$**

Kasenyi Lake Retreat (4 rooms) ⊕ -0.04158, 30.15202; **m** 0701 536197, 0774 297164. Located beside Lake George within the Kasenyi enclave, 1km south of the fishing village, this basic lodge is regularly visited by hippo, buffalo & various antelope, & more occasionally by elephant, lion & leopard. Birding is exceptional & the staff can arrange local boats to go out & look for shoebills in nearby swamps. A proportion of proceeds goes towards community projects in Kasenyi, & funding orphan education. Simple en-suite bandas are offered (hot water comes in jerrycans on request) & small tents with mattresses are available for campers. Check that the planned lodge building has appeared; shade during the heat of the day is currently limited to a small thatched shelter. *US$50 pp banda; US$10 pp camping in your/their tent exc meals.* **$$$**

What to see and do

Kasenyi Plains Criss-crossed by a labyrinthine network of (confusingly) signposted game-viewing roads, the plains running east from the Kasese–Ishaka Road to Kasenyi cover a moist short-grass savannah interspersed with solitary euphorbia trees and low clumps of bushy thicket. The area is an important breeding ground for Ugandan kob – thousands congregate here at times – and it is also frequented by numerous buffalo and fewer and more skittish pairs of bushbuck. The main attraction for most visitors, however, is the trio of lion prides that lurk around the 'new' kob breeding grounds, picking off the occasional unwary antelope or buffalo for dinner. The open habitat of Kasenyi means that its super-habituated lions are unusually easy to locate, particularly in the first hour or two after sunrise, when they are usually still active (and the cubs are often very playful) and the heat and/or attention of safari vehicles has yet to drive them into the shade of thicker bush. If you can't locate the lions directly by sight or sound, pay attention to the male kobs, whose high whistling alarm call may warn of a predator lurking in a nearby thicket. Vultures – most commonly white-backed and white-headed – either circling or perched purposefully in a tree may indicate a kill, with lions possibly still in attendance. Such bush craft may actually be necessary in prime lion-viewing hours, from sunrise to around 07.00, at which point the main morning influx of 4x4s starts rolling up. At other times of day, it may be more effective to watch where safari vehicles are congregating and tag along. Hiring a UWA guide – they generally have a good idea where to look – could also help provide you with a more exclusive sighting. Lion, kob and buffalo aside, you're unlikely to see too many other large mammals on the Kasenyi Plains, but an interesting selection of grassland birds includes grey crowned crane, red-throated spurfowl and yellow-throated longclaw. It is also emphatically worth diverting along an unsignposted track that branches northeast from the old breeding ground track at two points (⊕ -0.02417, 30.08823 and ⊕ -0.00341, 30.09231), then crosses the equator en route to a waterside viewpoint, aka the Lake George Picnic Site (⊕ 0.00754, 30.10254) facing a papyrus-lined island in Lake George. Home to a couple of dozen hippos, the viewpoint is also a good place for a short leg stretch and to look for other waterbirds, including pied kingfisher (which breeds in holes in the mudbanks) and African fish eagle.

Bunyampaka Crater Lake An interesting spot to take a break after the morning's first intense burst of lion seeking, circular Lake Bunyampaka lies at the base of a steep but small crater whose rim is covered in thick natural bush. It is one of only two crater lakes in this part of Uganda that supports a salt-extraction industry, albeit on a far smaller scale than the better-known Lake Katwe. A mosaic of small individual plots worked by villagers from nearby Kasenyi encloses the lake's green open water on three sides, accounting for roughly half its total surface area of 40ha. Waterbirds are also prolific, with large flocks of flamingos and pelicans often congregating on the unmined southern shore, particularly in the early evening.

Although the lake water is way too saline for most animals to drink, the freshwater springs on its southern shore sometimes attract thirsty herds of elephant, buffalo and other wildlife. Most safari groups stop at the northwest crater rim viewpoint (⊕ -0.03818, 30.12311), where there's a cluster of kiosks selling chilled drinks and curios, but it is also possible to breakfast or lunch at Kasenyi Safari Camp (page 480) by prior arrangement. To see the salt workings or lakeshore birdlife up close, you can follow a rough motorable track below Kasenyi Safari Camp to a parking spot on the northern shore (⊕ -0.03638, 30.12891).

Kasenyi fishing village Having come this far, it's worth continuing the last couple of kilometres to Kasenyi, a small and scruffy but friendly fishing village where hippos can reliably be seen basking a few metres offshore while buffaloes rest on the edge of the settlement. There are lots of birds around too, most strikingly the marabou storks that scavenge around a fishing beach lined with small local boats and nets. If you are thinking of chartering a boat to look for shoebills, or whatever else, talk to the staff at Kasenyi Lake Retreat (page 480), 2km south of the village.

KATUNGURU AND THE EASTERN KAZINGA CHANNEL It may not be much to look at in itself, but the small town of (North) Katunguru could scarcely have a wilder or more strategic location. An enclave of public land surrounded by park, this straddles the Kasese–Ishaka Road immediately north of the only bridge across the Kazinga Channel. The springboard for backpackers looking to set up a budget foray into QENP, Katunguru is visited multiple times daily by the reliable Link Bus, has its own cluster of tourist boats and lies at the junction for Mweya Peninsula. Don't be fooled by the town's paper-thin urban veneer: hippos are plentiful in the nearby channel, while buffalo, elephant and the like regularly pass within a few hundred metres of town, and the birdlife in and around the channel is fantastic.

The wilderness theme – and likelihood of encountering visiting wildlife – is even stronger across the channel in the sister enclave of South Katunguru. Back in the day it was home to a thriving fish factory, but though still considerably larger than its namesake on the north bank, today it has nothing remotely like the same buzz. Aside from a few roadside homes, it is dominated by bush, out of which space has been carved for an ever-expanding number of mid-range lodges favoured by budget-conscious group safaris.

Getting there and away Flanking the Kasese–Ishaka Road 40km south of Kasese and 55km north of Ishaka, Katunguru is easy to reach and difficult to miss in a private vehicle. Coming directly from Kampala on public transport, Kalita Coaches and Link Bus operate buses to Kasese via Mbarara and Katunguru (7–8hrs) but do make sure you get on the right vehicle, as they also operate a service to Kasese via Fort Portal. More locally, any matatu heading between Fort Portal or Kasese and Ishaka or Mbarara can drop you at Katunguru, though you may be asked to pay full fare. It is also easy enough to pick up transport out of Katunguru in either direction along the main Kasese–Ishaka Road. The south bank lodges are reached along a 2km dirt road that runs west from the Kasese–Ishaka Road at a clearly signposted junction (⊕ -0.13206, 30.05485) 1km south of Katunguru Bridge.

Where to stay *Map, page 475*

All the lodges listed here lie within the two Katunguru enclaves, surrounded by QENP but technically outside it, meaning that no park fees are charged just for staying overnight. They are also centrally located for game drives on the Kasenyi

Plains (18km to the north), boat trips on the Mweya Peninsula (25km to the west) and chimp tracking in Kyambura Gorge (8km to the south).

South Katunguru

With the exception of the channel-side Queen Elizabeth Bush Lodge, the first to be built in the area, accommodation on the south bank is much of a muchness. None of the locations has any sense of place, an elevated deck to salvage some sort of view is standard & if I had US$10 for every time I could add 'thatched & timber lodge building' & 'thatched cottages with tented walls', I'd be taking the rest of the day off.

Upmarket

Buffalo Safari Lodge (9 cottages) ⊕ -0.13694, 30.04925; m 0772 378565; e bookings@savannahlodges.com; w savannahlodges.com. This smart lodge combines the usual safari architecture with a corporate, resort feel. The spacious & cool thatched cottages lack a direct channel view, but there is a tempting swimming pool – assuming that the path is not blocked, as it was during our visit, by a contentedly browsing bull elephant. Other regular obstacles include buffalo, kob & giant forest hog. *US$160/250–350 sgl/dbl FB.* **$$$$**

Moderate

Aardvark Safari Lodge (5 cottages) ⊕ -0.13694, 30.04925; m 0701 114256; e info@aardvarksafarilodge.co.ug; w aardvarksafarilodge.co.ug. The swankiest of the south bank lodges boasts a stylish, elevated lodge building which conjures up a Rwenzori backdrop from an otherwise unpromising site. This serves 5 widely spaced & massively proportioned thatched cottages, all with high canvas sides enclosing a generous 90m² of floorspace – yes 9 x 10m – in the bedroom, not counting a 1st-floor balcony & a bathroom with indoor & outdoor showers. *The right to roam this expanse costs US$180/300 sgl/dbl FB.* **$$$$**

Engiri Game Lodge (8 cottages) ⊕ -0.13935, 30.05171; m 0776 649426; e info@engirigamelodge.com; w engirigamelodge.com. Set in a nondescript patch of bush 800m south of the channel, this small lodge offers accommodation in compact cabins. Elephant, buffalo & other wildlife regularly pass through. A viewing deck is under construction. *US$80/100 sgl/dbl FB.* **$$$**

Enshama (8 cottages) m 0702 385658; e info@enshamagamelodge.com; w enshamagamelodge.com. Tucked into an acacia grove on the south bank of the Kazinga Channel, this attractively priced setup has no view at ground level but a 2nd-floor viewing deck attached to the main lodge provides a 360° panorama across Rift Valley plains extending north to the Rwenzori & south to the Kichwamba Escarpment. *US$80/140 sgl/dbl FB.* **$$$**

✱ **Queen Elizabeth Bush Lodge** (12 cottages, 13 tents) ⊕ -0.13726, 30.04141; ☎ 031 2294894; e booking@naturelodges.biz; w naturelodges.biz. This popular & reasonably priced camp is set in bush beside the Kazinga Channel, 2km west of the Kasese–Ishaka Rd. There's the choice of canvas-sided cottage or more basic standing tents, some en suite, others using a shared ablution block. The dining tent faces the channel, & the grounds are bristling with chattering birdlife & honking hippos. *US$135/205 sgl/dbl cottage; US$90/145 sgl/dbl en-suite tent; US$65/120 sgl/dbl tent using shared ablutions. All rates FB.* **$$$**

✱ **Tabingi Safari Lodge** (12 cottages, 13 tents) m 0778 672262, 0704 295232; e info@tabingisafarilodge.com; w tabingisafarilodge.com. This attractively constructed lodge might be a gold standard for mid-range accommodation in western Uganda. Anything comparable & cheaper might be considered very good value; any costlier & there should be a good reason. There's not much to be excited about at ground level but the lodge structure has an elevated deck to take in the Rift Valley geography, while 1st-floor balconies attached to the roomy cottages overlook an expanse of bush in which anything might be – & probably is – lurking. A pool is planned which will be a great addition. *US$100/200 sgl/dbl cottage FB.* **$$$**

North Katunguru

Moderate

Kazinga Wilderness Safari Camp (10 tented cottages) m 0772 873106; e info@kazingawildcamp.com; w kazingawildcamp.com. Though this new lodge is located right on the edge of Katunguru fishing village (on the north side of the channel), its northwards orientation actually manages a pretty decent wilderness outlook with the Rwenzori (weather permitting) as a backdrop. The canvas & mesh-sided cabins are cool & comfortable, if rather closely spaced. A raised deck is a perfect spot to enjoy a drink & look out for whatever animals are in the vicinity. The camp is located beside the track to Katunguru Gate, 400m off the tarmac. *US$100/170 sgl/dbl cottage FB.* **$$$**

Budget

Tembo Safari Lodge (5 rooms) ⊕ -0.12475, 30.04615; m 0772 628803, 0701 628803. Perched on the north bank of the Kazinga Channel above the fish landing, this recently upgraded facility gets full marks for its multi-faceted waterside setting. It really is one of those views that could occupy you all day, the foreground being a hive of activity – fishing boats being offloaded, kids jumping off the road bridge into the channel, tourists going off on boat cruises & hawkers peddling their wares – while the far shore of the channel is worth scanning for wildlife. Enjoy all this from the bar/restaurant, which serves meals for around US$7, or the balcony of your simple but adequate wooden cottage. It's ideally located for those using public transport; just walk behind the Shell petrol station & ask the way. Those with wheels will need to drive down the track leading to Katunguru Park Gate & turn left after 400m. Very good value. *US$50/70 sgl/dbl FB.* **$$**

Where to eat and drink

Nyamihanda & Sons m 0772 454656. Next to Katunguru Shell, this small restaurant offers sandwiches, pizzas & local meals. *Around US$6.*

Tibs m 0776 887398. Across the road from the Shell station in Katunguru trading centre, this new restaurant is quickly becoming a popular safari stop. In addition to a tasty menu of continental, local & veg dishes, a 1st-floor deck is well placed to escape the heat of the day & enjoy the afternoon breeze. As an additional bonus, there's a good view down the length of the Kazinga Channel, though an electricity pylon in the foreground is less than ideal. *Mains US$9.*

Tour operators

BEACH Community Tourism On the north bank of the channel adjacent to Katunguru village; m 0703 700500, 0776 573000; e bakingwe@gmail.com, muzamilu@gmail.com. Founded in 2016, BEACH (Bakingwe for Economic Advancement & Cultural Heritage) is a grassroots organisation whose profits go to educational & other community projects in Katunguru. In addition to channel boat trips (see below), it offers community walks around Katunguru (US$10 pp) & can arrange safaris into QENP (US$100/day per car exc park entrance fees; negotiable for half days) & chimp tracking in Kalinzu Forest Reserve (page 500).

Irungu Community Boat Cruises m 0774 392047. Set on the south bank of the channel opposite Katunguru, this offers a similar boat cruise along the channel.

What to see and do Katunguru is entrenched as the most common and accessible base for backpackers to arrange budget day safaris into QENP. The options generally boil down to around US$100–140 for a full-day safari, including a morning game drive in Kasenyi and a trip to Mweya for the afternoon boat trip, or around US$80 for a half-day safari including one or other of the above. Prices quoted locally will include car hire, fuel, driver/guide and vehicle entrance fees, but exclude individual entrance fees and any boat trip or other activity costs. The two community projects listed above are a good first port of call for arranging safaris, but it can also be done through private operators.

BEACH and Irungu Community Boat Cruises (see above) both offer boat trips on the adjacent stretch of the Kazinga Channel (US$50 for 2 people, US$25 per additional person; but negotiable for large groups). Wildlife here is less prolific than on the launch trip from the Mweya Peninsula, but you should see plenty of hippos and waterbirds, as well as buffaloes and crocodiles, and – with a bit of luck

– elephants. Note that park entrance must be paid in addition to the boat fee so if you will be entering the park anyway, you're better off doing a launch trip out of Mweya, as the scenery is more interesting and the more open channel shoreline better suited to bird and animal viewing.

KATWE Lined with rundown, partially boarded-up buildings that give it the aura of a recently resettled ghost town, the small but sprawling settlement of Katwe occupies an odd urban enclave within QENP, enclosed by park boundaries on three sides, and lapped by the waters of Lake Edward to the south. A potentially interesting goal for backpackers who cannot afford a full-scale safari into QENP, Katwe is named after and owes its existence to a bordering crater lake that has formed one of Uganda's most important sources of coarse salt for at least 500 years. Lake Munyenyange, also bordering Katwe, is seasonally good for flamingos, while the nearby Lake Edward shoreline is a reliable location for elephant, hippo, warthog, waterbuck and an abundance of waterbirds (though, for obvious reasons, it should be explored on foot only with considerable caution – indeed, a small area of shore has been fenced off to allow townsfolk to collect water without being taken by crocodiles).

History The first written report of Lake Katwe was penned by Speke, who heard secondhand about a legendarily wealthy source of salt close to the base of the Mountains of the Moon. By that time, the lake had been mined for at least 400 years, and with salt being regarded as more valuable than precious metal in pre-colonial Uganda, control of this prized possession regularly shifted between the region's different kingdoms. Indeed, when Speke visited Uganda in 1862, Lake Katwe had for some years been part of Toro, but in the late 1870s it was recaptured by Omukama Kabalega, a coup that led to the first military confrontation between Bunyoro and a combined British–Toro expedition led by Captain Frederick Lugard.

Lugard arrived at Katwe in 1890 and recorded that: 'Everywhere were piles of salt, in heaps covered with grass, some beautifully white and clean. On our right was the Salt Lake, about three-quarters of a mile [1.2km] in diameter, at the bottom of a deep crater-like depression with banks some 200ft [61m] high. The water was of a claret red, with a white fringe of crystallised salt about its margin. A narrow neck, only some 40 yards [36m] across at the top, and perhaps 300 yards [274m] at its base, divided the Salt Lake from [Lake] Edward.' Lugard and his Toro entourage had little difficulty claiming the site – the resident Banyoro were not soldiers but miners and businessmen, and evidently they subscribed to the view that discretion forms the better part of valour – and built there a small fort, of which little trace remains today, before continuing northwards to Fort Portal.

Today, you'd be fortunate to encounter Lake Katwe in the rich claret incarnation encountered by Lugard and other early European visitors. This seems to happen only when the level of salt in the water approaches a certain concentration. However, this phenomenon is frequently seen in individual salt pans when they are almost ready to be 'harvested'. Particularly in the harsh midday light, however, Lake Katwe still retains the vaguely foreboding atmosphere described by E J Wayland: 'stifling and malodorous…a fiend-made meeting place for the Devil and his friends'. Commercial salt extraction from the lake peaked in the early 1970s when the faded plant that dominates Katwe village briefly pumped out an annual 2,000 tonnes before breaking down owing to corrosion of the pipework. Extraction of the lake's characteristic pink-hued coarse salt remains the main source of local income – though judging by the state of the village, it's not quite so lucrative an activity as it was in Katwe's heyday. However, a relatively recent university study suggests that the lake holds more than 20 million tonnes of crystalline salts, enough to support commercial extraction of 40,000 tonnes per annum for longer than 30 years, and the Uganda Development Board is currently looking for an investor to build a new factory.

Getting there and away A well-maintained 18km dirt road runs west from a clearly signposted junction (⊕ -0.08187, 30.03027) on the Kasese–Ishaka Road, 5km north of Katunguru and 8km south of Kikorongo. The road passes Kabatoro Gate (only 6km from the Mweya Peninsula) to the south about 4km before it enters Katwe. Coming from the north, Katwe can also be reached via the Explosion Craters Track that leaves the main road at Queen's Pavilion (page 477). A few matatus run back and forth between Kasese and Katwe daily.

Where to stay and eat *Map, page 488*

All the lodges listed here lie within the Katwe enclave or along the main road, so no park fees are charged just for staying overnight. Katwe is also a useful base for game drives on the Kasenyi Plains (15–20km to the east) and boat trips on the Mweya Peninsula (6–10km to the south).

Moderate

Muyenyange Caves (22 rooms) ⊕ 0.13826, 29.89424; m 0772 418296. This new lodge on the eastern slopes above Lake Muyenyange has the best view of any accommodation in Katwe & a new restaurant is under construction to better appreciate it. Prices being based on those at the related but far superior Kikorongo Safari Lodge, one assumes that either the rates or standard of this facility will adjust to achieve parity. *US$170/210 sgl/dbl FB.* **$$$$**

Budget

Forest Hog Safari Lodge (4 rooms) ⊕ 0.13826, 29.89424; m 0772 418296. Straddling the hillside north of Katwe, this rustic place has attractive bandas & a massive dining area under a tall *makuti* roof. *US$60/100 sgl/dbl FB.* **$$$**

Njovu Park Lodge (11 rooms) ⊕ -0.13598, 29.89542; m 0776 023058, 0752 992551; e njovuparklodge@yahoo.com; f. Enclosed by a concrete-&-wire fence, this characterless lodge 500m north of Katwe has neat, clean & spacious rooms with nets. Hippo & elephant come past regularly, & it's only 300m from the rim of Lake Munyenyange. *US$70/90 sgl/dbl FB.* **$$$**

Shoestring

Excellent Lodge (12 rooms) m 0752 501905. 'Excellent' overstates the case, but this just-about-acceptable shoestring lodge – the finest in downtown Katwe – is better than the flaking frontage might suggest. *US$6–9 en-suite dbl.* **$**

✱ **Kabatoro Guesthouse** (6 rooms) ⊕ -0.13713, 29.9246; m 0775 766132, 0787 426478. This unique guesthouse 400m west of Kabatoro Gate occupies the only inhabited building in the otherwise-abandoned colonial-era village of Kabatoro. The time-warped façade & sleepy veranda, which could be transplanted from any medium-sized Ugandan town, feel rather surreal in this bush environment, thrillingly so on the regular occasions when elephants stroll past. The en-suite dbl rooms have fitted nets & hot water, while a restaurant serves a limited selection of meals for around US$4. A fabulous shoestring safari option. *US$20 dbl B&B.* **$**

Tour operators

Katwe Tourism Information Centre m 0752 397354; e katic.org@gmail.com; f Katic Katwe Tourism Centre; ⏲ 08.00–19.00 daily. Located just west of what passes for downtown Katwe, KATIC is a community-based organisation that charges US$10 pp for a variety of guided activities including salt lake tours, birding excursions & visits to the bustling Fri & Tue markets at Mpondwe.

What to see and do

Katwe Bay The 30km² bay separating Katwe from the Mweya Peninsula isn't technically part of QENP, but the surrounding shore is, and it hosts plenty of wildlife, including elephant, buffalo, kob and warthog. Hippos are resident in the offshore shallows, and the aquatic birdlife is prodigious. The Katwe Tourism Information Centre no longer offers boat trips but you could probably make a deal with a local fisherman; if you do, insist on a lifejacket.

Lake Katwe Separated from the northern shore of Lake Edward by its 400m-wide rim, the 2.5km² hyper-saline Lake Katwe occupies the base of a volcanic caldera that last erupted between 6,000 and 10,000 years ago. It is one of the oldest and most productive sources of coarse salt anywhere in Uganda (page 485), and the view from the rim – with a honeycomb of individually worked extraction plots running around the shore – is quite stunning. If you are interested in seeing the salt extraction process up close, there's nothing stopping you from driving or walking down the short road that leads out of town to the lakeshore. However, you'll get far more from the experience, as will the local salt miners toiling away in the sun, by arranging a tour via Katwe Tourism Information Centre (see opposite). This costs US$10 per person and enables you to see (and photograph) the various mining processes in the company of well-informed and articulate local guides.

Lake Munyenyange Even closer to town than Lake Katwe, but hidden from view by an enclosing caldera, the small and shallow Lake Munyenyange is known for the large numbers of lesser (and sometimes greater) flamingos that gather there when conditions are right, most usually from September to March. It also usually supports an interesting selection of resident (and, seasonally, migrant) waders. You can watch the birds from the road that skirts the lake's rim, but if you want to head closer to the water, you need to make arrangements with the Katwe Tourism Information Centre (see opposite), which charges US$10 per person whether you visit independently or are guided by its informative flamingo expert.

Pelican Point Immediately west of Katwe, the Pelican Point Sector of QENP was suggested as the location for the park's first lodge in the 1950s, but Mweya was selected owing to its more central location. Despite its proximity to Katwe, this sector has a remote, unspoiled flavour, and although wildlife volumes are relatively low, the likes of buffalo, kob, warthog, hippo and lion are all present. The main attractions are excellent views across Lake Edward and the opportunity to explore off-road. There are currently no facilities in the area, not even tracks, but the QENP management plan has proposed that a basic campsite be cleared in the future.

MWEYA PENINSULA Historically, the main tourist focus in QENP is the 10km² Mweya Peninsula, an elevated arrowhead of bushy land connected to the northern mainland by a natural isthmus little wider than the road that traverses it. Protruding between Lake Edward and the Kazinga Channel, immediately north of where the two waters merge, the peninsula has an inspirational setting, overlooking an archetypal equatorial African riverbank scene, with elephant and buffalo milling around the opposite shore, subverted by occasional glimpses of the snowy Rwenzori peaks (at least when they're not blanketed in cloud). Logistically, Mweya remains a popular base for exploring QENP, since it houses the park's oldest and arguably swankiest lodge, along with several budget-friendly UWA-managed

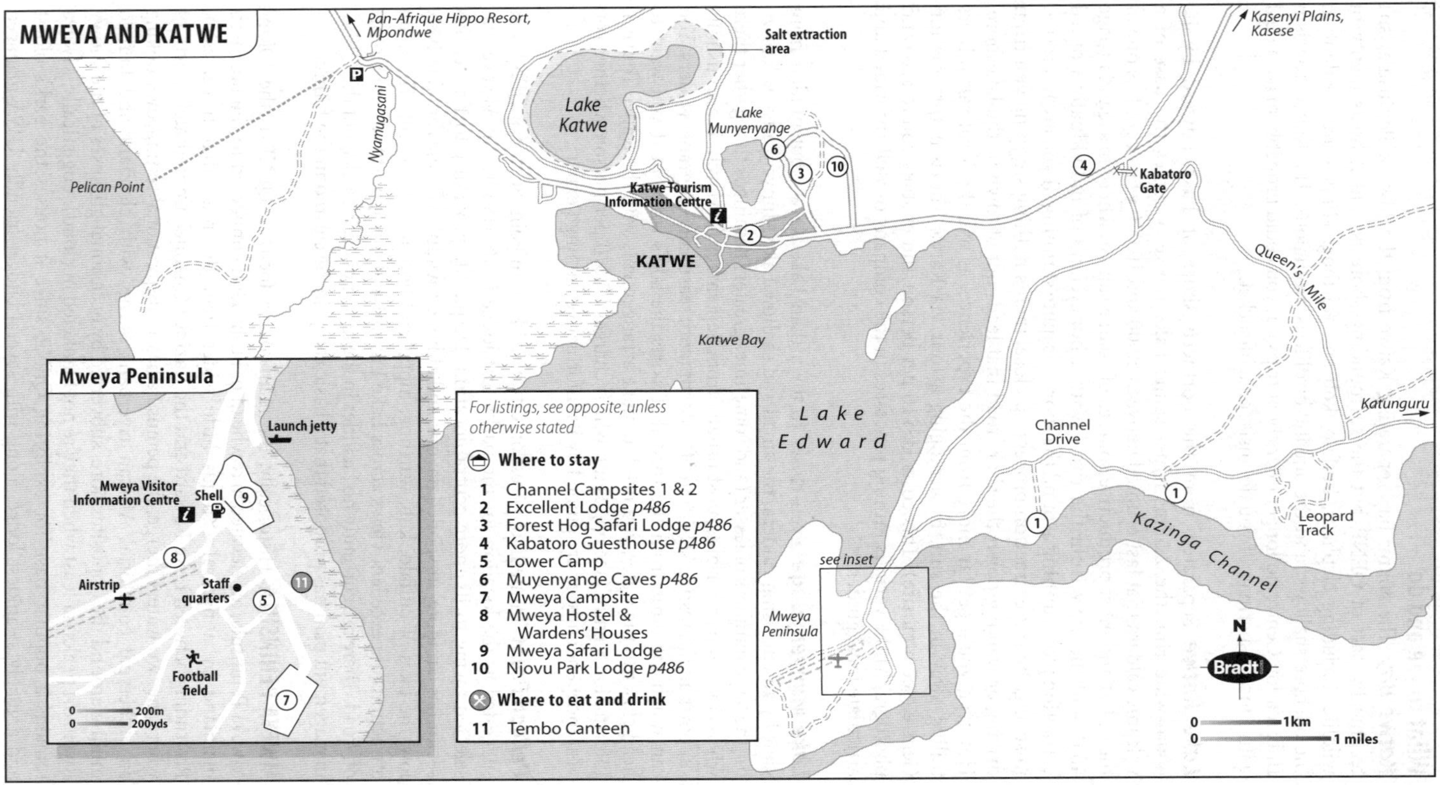
MWEYA AND KATWE
Pan-Afrique Hippo Resort, Mpondwe
Kasenyi Plains, Kasese
Salt extraction area
Lake Katwe
Lake Munyenyange
Nyamugasani
Pelican Point
Katwe Tourism Information Centre
KATWE
Katwe Bay
Kabatoro Gate
Queen's Mile
Katunguru
Channel Drive
Leopard Track
Kazinga Channel
Lake Edward
see inset
Mweya Peninsula
N
Bradt
0 1km
0 1 miles
Mweya Peninsula
Launch jetty
Mweya Visitor Information Centre
Shell
Airstrip
Staff quarters
Football field
0 200m
0 200yds
For listings, see opposite, unless otherwise stated
Where to stay
1 Channel Campsites 1 & 2
2 Excellent Lodge p486
3 Forest Hog Safari Lodge p486
4 Kabatoro Guesthouse p486
5 Lower Camp
6 Muyenyange Caves p486
7 Mweya Campsite
8 Mweya Hostel & Wardens' Houses
9 Mweya Safari Lodge
10 Njovu Park Lodge p486
Where to eat and drink
11 Tembo Canteen

guesthouses, and lies less than 45 minutes' drive from the game-viewing circuit on the Kasenyi Plains. While the peninsula may no longer be the be-all and end-all when it comes to tourist activity in QENP, it remains the launch point for the park's most iconic activity – boat excursions on the Kazinga Channel.

Getting there and away Mweya lies 20km west of the Kasese–Ishaka Road. Coming from the south, the most direct route runs from just north of Katunguru Bridge via Katunguru Gate (⊕ -0.12801, 30.03428) and Channel Drive. Coming from the north, follow the Katwe Road for 14km until you reach Kabatoro Gate (⊕ -0.13546, 29.92814), then turn left, and it's 8km to Mweya.

Using public transport, the easiest option is to bus or matatu to Katunguru, from where a special-hire taxi to Mweya should cost US$10–15 one-way. Bodas are not allowed into the park. Alternatively, catch a matatu from Kasese to Katwe, and ask to be dropped at Kabatoro Gate, where the rangers will usually help you find a lift (and you have the shoestring Kabatoro Guesthouse, 400m to the west, as a fall-back). When you're ready to leave Mweya, wait for a lift with outgoing lodge or park staff at the barrier guarding the entrance to the peninsula.

Where to stay *Map, opposite*

Upmarket

✷ **Mweya Safari Lodge** (54 units) ⊕ -0.18882, 29.90011; ☎ 031 2260260, 041 4255992; e reservations@marasa.net; w mweyalodge.com. Aptly described by both admirers & detractors as a 'Sheraton in the Bush', this plush lodge lacks the intimate wilderness feel associated with smaller tented camps, but this is compensated for by the fabulous location & proximity to QENP's main attractions. On a clear day, the Rwenzori Mountains provide an incomparable backdrop, while the dining veranda & pool terrace enjoy a grandstand view of buffalo & elephant drinking from the opposite bank of the Kazinga Channel. The gardens rustle with animal life, including warthog, banded mongoose & myriad birds. The standard rooms are more than adequate (ask for one facing the channel as opposed to the drive) but pale in comparison with the palatial safari tents. Additional activities offered include daily game drives & boat trips on the channel. *From US$203/354 sgl/dbl FB.* **$$$$–$$$$$**

Budget and shoestring

Lower Camp (17 rooms) m 0760 868545. A few hundred metres west of Mweya Safari Lodge, a line of former ranger accommodation has been renovated by a private operator to provide affordable en-suite accommodation. Food is not provided, nor is there any view, but both are available 200m away at the Tembo Canteen under the same management. Take a torch to spot the hippos if you'll be returning after dark. *US$21/30 sgl/dbl; 2-room cottage US$54. Exc meals.* **$$**

Mweya Hostel & Wardens' Houses Mweya Hostel: ☎ 039 3206439; m 0759 697976; Wardens' Houses: m 0772 415184. For years, the Mweya Hostel opposite the Visitor Information Centre offered affordable if run-down rooms while an adjacent row of one-time wardens' houses provided no-frills self-catering accommodation. At the time of writing both are out of service pending renovation & reopening by private operators whose contacts are given above.

Camping

Channel Campsites 1 & 2 ⊕ -0.17839, 29.91791 & -0.17492, 29.93383. If you have your own vehicle & are self-sufficient in food & water, you might prefer to camp at one of the secluded exclusive campsites that lie along Channel Dr about 5km from Mweya. Camping here is relatively expensive, but nocturnal encounters with large mammals are thrown in for free. Campsite No 2 has a good reputation for leopard sightings, but do seek advice about security in advance. *US$30 pp.* **$$**

Mweya Campsite ⊕ -0.19625, 29.90173. This fabulously located campsite on the southern end of the peninsula has few facilities & is passed through by hippo en masse nightly & lions with some regularity, making it potentially dangerous after dark if you don't have a vehicle. If you intend on cooking for yourself, bring your own food. Alternatively, you could brave the hippos & wander up to the Tembo Canteen for a meal, but again, be careful after dark, & carry a good torch. *US$5 pp*. **$**

Where to eat and drink *Map, page 488*

✷ Tembo Canteen ⊕ -0.19276, 29.90193; m 0760 868545; ⏲ 07.00–22.00 daily. Situated about 300m south of the entrance to Mweya Safari Lodge (page 489) & sharing its more illustrious neighbour's fabulous view over a stretch of channel frequented by buffalo, elephant & hippo, this unpretentious canteen with indoor, terrace & garden seating & a well-stocked bar serves a fair range of tasty meat & vegetable dishes. *Meals in the US$6–8 range*.

Tourist information

Mweya Visitor Information Centre ⊕ -0.19008, 29.89845; m 0782 387805; ⏲ 06.30–18.00 daily. This purpose-built facility 100m west of Mweya Safari Lodge contains clear & concise (though now somewhat weathered) interpretive exhibits including a topographic model illustrating QENP's setting within the dramatic Albertine Rift Valley. It handles bookings & payments for UWA-operated boat trips on the Kazinga Channel, the lion- or leopard-tracking experience with the Queen Elizabeth Predator Project, & ranger-guides for game drives out of Mweya.

What to see and do

Around the peninsula Plenty of wildlife can be seen on or from Mweya Peninsula, and there is no restriction on walking around the developed area between Mweya Safari Lodge, the airstrip and the campsite, though you should be cautious of any wildlife, and hippos in particular. Herds of buffalo and elephant routinely gather to drink on the channel shore facing Mweya Safari Lodge and Tembo Canteen, while waterbuck, hippo and warthog are often seen milling along the peninsula's road. Giant forest hogs sometimes emerge on to the airstrip towards dusk, a family of habituated banded mongooses lives in the lodge grounds, and lion and spotted hyena are heard – and seen – with a frequency that might unnerve solitary campers. Birdlife is prolific, too. Marabou storks regularly roost on a bare tree between the lodge and restaurant, while the exquisite red-chested sunbird, black-headed gonolek and a variety of weavers are among the more common residents of the lodge grounds. It's also well worth taking a bottle of beer down to the end of the peninsula airstrip to watch the sun set behind the DRC mountains – but ask which track to use, as driving down the airstrip itself is prohibited for obvious reasons.

Kazinga Channel boat trips The most popular activity at Mweya is the 2-hour boat trip from a jetty below the lodge to the mouth of the Kazinga Channel. Although not as spectacular as the equivalent boat trip in Murchison Falls, this is a great excursion, and wildlife viewing is excellent. Elephant, buffalo, waterbuck, Ugandan kob and large hippo pods are seen on a daily basis, while giant forest hog, leopard and lion are observed with unexpected frequency. Keep an eye open for the enormous water monitor lizard, which is common in the riverine scrub, as well as crocodiles, seen with increasing regularity since first colonising the area in the early 1990s. Waterbirds are plentiful, in particular water thick-knee, yellow-billed stork and various plovers, while pink-backed pelicans and white-bellied cormorants often flock on a sandbank near the channel mouth. One smaller bird to look out for is the black-headed gonolek, a type of bush-shrike with a dazzling red chest.

Boat trips are operated by UWA (US$25/30 FR/FNR) and by Mweya Safari Lodge (US$28/32 FR/FNR) which has more comfortable boats. UWA trips leave daily at 09.00, 11.00, 13.00, 15.00 and 17.00, while the lodge boats leave at 11.00, 14.00

and 16.15, as well as at 07.00 and 09.00 by special request for groups. The 14.00 and 15.00 departures are most likely to yield good elephant sightings, particularly on hot days, when these thirsty creatures generally gravitate towards water from midday onwards, sometimes bathing in the channel. The odds of seeing predators and other nocturnal creatures coming to drink are highest in the late afternoon. In theory, departures are subject to minimum numbers, which used to be a concern for single travellers and couples, but these days the tourist volume through Mweya is so high that you can be confident there will be several departures daily. The posh *MV Kazinga* launch (m 0772 426368; e info@ugandalodges.com) also runs out of the Mweya jetty at 08.30 and 14.00 (US$30 pp). Its enclosed 60-seat cabin is ideal if it rains, while a rooftop deck provides a less detached wildlife-viewing experience.

Lion and leopard tracking The Queen Elizabeth Predator Project, overseen by Dr Ludwig Siefert, monitors the activities of several lion prides and a few individual leopards living to the north of the Kazinga Channel. At least one member of each research pride has been fitted with a radio collar, as have all the leopards under study, which means it is easy to locate them at any time of day. A limited number of tourists is permitted to join the research team as part of an Experiential Predator Tourism activity offered twice-daily by the Mweya Visitor Information Centre (see opposite). Lion sightings are all but certain, and close-up leopard encounters are also very likely. The experience can, however, be a bit of a procession, with several vehicles following a tracking technician in a lead car, while the impact of off-track driving on ground-nesting birds has been flagged as a concern. The excursion leaves at 06.30 or 16.00, takes up to 3 hours, and costs US$150/200 FR/FNR plus a US$10 payment which goes directly to local communities.

Mongoose tracking Subject of an ongoing behavioural research project, the banded mongooses of Mweya – around 400 individuals split between a dozen groups – are possibly the most habituated anywhere in the world. Tracking these intelligent, social and playful small carnivores with a knowledgeable guide and field assistant from the mongoose project is a thoroughly delightful and engaging experience. The excursion must be booked in advance through the Mweya Visitor Information Centre. It leaves at 07.00, takes up to 3 hours, and costs US$30 per person.

Channel Drive circuit Running roughly parallel to the Kazinga Channel's northern shore, Channel Drive now serves mainly as a through route between Katunguru Bridge and the Mweya Peninsula. However, the compact network of tracks that emanates from the main road can provide some excellent game viewing, albeit a little more hit and miss than the Kasenyi Plains due to dense vegetation that grew unchecked when the numbers of grazing and browsing animals were reduced by poachers in the 1970s. This issue is being addressed by a bush clearance scheme which has already opened up several hundred hectares. It remains to be seen whether wildlife numbers are sufficient to maintain this as grassland or whether scrub will simply grow back again. The most common large mammals in the area are warthog, bushbuck and waterbuck, but elephants often cross through from midday onwards, heading to or from the water. Leopard Track and the side road to Channel Campsite No 2 (page 489) are the best places to look for the – unusually habituated – leopards that frequent the area, while lions are seen fairly regularly, and it is also a good place to spot the localised giant forest hog. Because it lies so close to Mweya and consists of several interconnecting tracks, the circuit can easily be explored from the lodge over 2 hours. Potentially rewarding night drives are also permitted provided you take a guide/ranger, which costs US$30 per person and can be arranged at Mweya Visitor Information Centre.

KYAMBURA, MARAMAGAMBO AND THE KICHWAMBA ESCARPMENT Relatively undeveloped for tourism compared with the plains north of the Kazinga Channel, southeastern QENP is dominated by the 750km² Maramagambo Forest, some 60% of which lies within the park boundaries, while the remainder is divided between the abutting Kalinzu Forest Reserve and Kigezi Wildlife Reserve. Maramagambo is regarded to be one of the most biodiverse forests anywhere in East Africa, with strong faunal affinities to the Congo Basin, and it can be explored on a network of guided trails emanating from a pair of jungle-bound crater lakes called Nyamasingiri and Kyasanduka. A popular tourist activity in this part of QENP is chimp tracking in the Kyambura Gorge, a forested ravine carved into the surrounding flat savannah along the border with Kyambura Wildlife Reserve, a little-visited tract of savannah notable for the waterbirds – in particular flamingos – attracted to its lovely crater lakes. Although Maramagambo Forest is serviced by a solitary upmarket lodge and a couple of low-key campsites, the stretch of the Rift Valley wall that overlooks it, known as the Kichwamba Escarpment, supports an ever-growing proliferation of lodges used by mid-range safaris primarily as a base for day trips to Mweya, Kasenyi and elsewhere north of the Kazinga Channel. A short distance further south, the affordable chimp-tracking experience offered by the Kalinzu Ecotourism Project (page 495) in the eponymous forest reserve is rapidly becoming a firm favourite with budget-minded travellers. Another attraction for birders, keen walkers and others on a budget is the Bunyaruguru Crater Lakes, many of which are within easy striking distance of the Ishaka Road.

Getting there and away

All the sites described under this heading are accessed from the Kasese–Ishaka Road as it runs south from Katunguru Bridge. Plenty of public transport runs along this main road, but most sites lying off it are accessible only in a private vehicle, on foot, or by special hire or boda from Kichwamba trading centre, 13km south of Katunguru Bridge. Directions to individual lodges and sites are included as required in the relevant listing descriptions.

Where to stay and eat *Map, opposite, unless otherwise stated*

Except where noted, the lodges listed here lie alongside or within 1.5km of the main Kasese–Ishaka Road. With the exception of Jacana Safari Lodge, Honey Bear Bush Camp and The River Station, they all sit outside park boundaries, so no park fees are charged simply for staying there. Many are strung along the Kichwamba Escarpment, where they enjoy a terrific view north across the plains of QENP to the Kazinga Channel as it zigzags between lakes George and Edward, stretching all the way to the Rwenzori peaks on a clear day. Conveniently located for visits to Maramagambo Forest, or for chimp tracking in Kyambura Gorge or Kalinzu Forest Reserve, these lodges also offer good access to the Kasenyi Plains (20km north of Kichwamba trading centre) and Mweya Peninsula (35km northwest).

Exclusive

✱ **Honey Bear Bush Camp** [map, page 475] (5 rooms) 041 4251182; m 0772 489497; e info@wildplacesafrica.com; w wildplacesafrica.com. Established in 2023, this superb 5-unit bush camp is named after a character played by Oscar-nominated Ava Gardner in the movie *Mogambo*, some of which was filmed on location in Uganda in 1952. It stands on the south bank of the Kazinga Channel as it flows along the northern border of the Kyambura Wildlife Reserve – a classic African riverside setting, alive with hippo

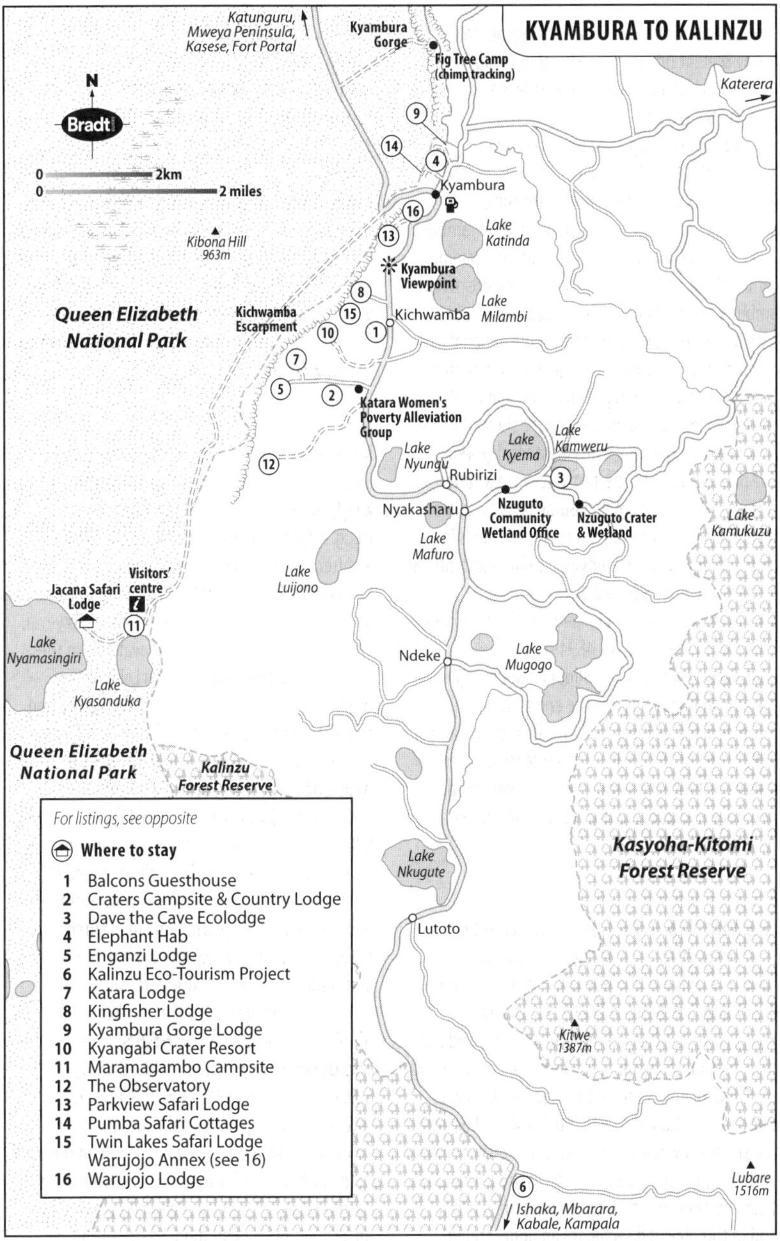

& waterbirds, & boosted by a stunning snow-capped Rwenzori backdrop in clear weather. Although the location is remote by road, the camp is accessible from Katunguru on a delightful boat trip through a stretch of the channel that is rich in wildlife but sees little boat traffic. Especially in the dry season, plenty of wildlife passes through, including elephant & buffalo by day & leopard at night. Accommodation is in classic standing tents with private balconies, solar lighting & hot bucket showers at the back. Activities include guided wildlife, bird & crater lake walks, boat trips to Lake

George, chimp tracking in nearby Kyambura Gorge, & day & night drives in the Kyambura Wildlife Reserve, which functions more-or-less as a private reserve. **$$$$$$**

☀ **Kyambura Gorge Lodge** (8 cottages) ⊕ -0.20698, 30.10333; ☎ 041 4346464; m 0772 741718; e salesug@volcanoessafaris.com; w volcanoessafaris.com. Overlooking the Kyambura River Valley about 1km north of Kyambura trading centre, this excellent lodge is the centrepiece of an ambitious project by Volcanoes Safaris to rewild a 5km buffer zone along the edge of the national park. Fronted by a neat garden that gives way to bush & forest, the main building has been imaginatively converted from an abandoned coffee shed while the 8 cottages are spacious & unashamedly luxurious. The pool terrace is the perfect place to relax after chimp tracking in Kyambura Gorge before a tour of the apiary & other community ventures. *Rates inc meals, drinks, laundry & massage & drop substantially in the low season*. **$$$$$$**

The River Station [map, page 475] (10 rooms) ☎ 041 4251182; m 0772 489497; e info@wildplacesafrica.com; w wildplacesafrica.com. Scheduled to open before the end of 2024, this more upmarket sibling to Honey Bear Bush Camp will consist of 10 classic standing tents situated a short distance upstream towards Lake George. Activities & attractions are identical to Honey Bear. **$$$$$$**

Upmarket

Elephant Hab (12 rooms) ☎ 039 3206439; m 0759 697976; e info@elephanthablodge.com; w elephanthablodge.com. Located at the dwindling, northern end of the Kichwamba Escarpment, & accessed through Kyambura Village, this pleasant lodge has an infinity pool overlooking the QENP plains. Some of the thatched & canvas-sided rooms share the view; others at the back of the site are, by way of compensation, rather larger with a generously sided veranda in the garden. Ticks the relevant boxes but even at the bottom end of this elevated sector, it's an undeserving entry. **$$$$$**

Enganzi Lodge (9 cottages) ⊕ -0.24375, 30.07701; m 0756 702583, 0702 386244; e info@enganzilodge.com; f. In its original incarnation, this escarpment setup was a blatant copy of the adjacent Katara Lodge, barely meriting separate inclusion, but it has, over time, evolved its own identity. As things stand, it is just as attractive & scenically located as its neighbour, with more pocket-friendly rack rates. **$$$$$**

Katara Lodge (8 cottages) ⊕ -0.24116, 30.07803; m 0773 011648, 0712 812560; e info@kataralodge.com; w kataralodge.com. Scenically perched on the escarpment edge overlooking the rolling plains of QENP, this highly rated lodge offers accommodation in thatched wood-&-canvas cottages which includes a private balcony where you can sleep under the stars if you so choose. There's a swimming pool, good wine list & cocktail menu. **$$$$$**

Moderate

Kingfisher Lodge (20 rooms) ⊕ -0.23026, 30.08988; m 0774 159579; e bookings@kingfisherlodge.co.ug; w kingfisherlodge.co.ug. Influenced by whitewashed Swahili-style architecture, the longest-serving lodge on the Kichwamba Escarpment has the best panorama of all & the pool terrace remains a delight. However, when you consider what else is available in the vicinity nowadays (notably Twin Lakes Lodge right next door), it's hard to avoid the conclusion that the rooms seem cramped & tired & the rates excessive. *US$140/260 sgl/dbl B&B*. **$$$$**

Kyangabi Crater Resort (32 rooms) ⊕ -0.23555, 30.07908; m 0706 439247, 0787 765222; e kyangabicrater@gmail.com; w kyangabicrater.com. This well-managed & relatively large lodge has a great view over the plains of QENP & stands in large manicured gardens centred on a swimming pool. It doubles as a conference venue & the sterile aesthetic is perhaps more geared to that market than to tourists. *US$120/213 pp FB*. **$$$$**

The Observatory (3 rooms) ⊕ -0.2577, 30.07333; m 0782 574271, 0701 563437; e reservations@geolodgesafrica.com; w geolodgesafrica.com. Perched high on the edge of the Kichwamba Escarpment, this attractively decorated wooden house sleeping up to 6 stands on a small coffee plantation 2.5km southwest of the main road. Views towards the Kazinga Channel & Rwenzori are peerless. Facilities include an equipped kitchen, sitting room with games & books, solar & generator power, jacuzzi & fabulous balcony aimed to catch the sunset. Guests must bring their own food. Ideal for self-catering family parties. *US$70/40 adult/child*. **$$$$**

Parkview Safari Lodge (20 cottages) ⊕ -0.21963, 30.09461; m 0707 002855, 0751 070855; e parkviewsafarilodge@gmail.com; w parkviewsafarilodge.com. This attractive lodge on the edge of the escarpment doesn't have the best of views but it does have an impressive 2-storey thatched bar/restaurant & spacious & beautifully constructed cottages in a shady pine plantation. *US$180/280 sgl/dbl FB.* **$$$$**

✷ **Twin Lakes Safari Lodge** (14 units) ⊕ -0.2314, 30.08911; m 0772 892866/348509; e info@twinlakesafarilodge.com; w twinlakesafarilodge.com. Perched high above the plains on the lip of the Kichwamba Escarpment, the centrepiece of this super lodge is the restored 1940s residence of the regional Fisheries Officer. It is tempting to assume he was anticipating a biblical-style flood within the Rift Valley trough (as occurred 3 million years ago) but the simple fact is that the breezy uplands are an altogether more pleasant place to live than the hot & dusty fishing villages down below. The lodge premises also include a timber bunkhouse built by the engineers who erected the bridge over the Kazinga Channel in 1954 & who, when locating their camp, followed exactly this line of reasoning. The subsequent 75 years have done nothing to diminish the splendour of the panorama, which is now shared with 14 stylish slate-roofed chalets with wooden balconies. An infinity pool only adds to the fun. Quite wonderful! *US$170/240 sgl/dbl FB.* **$$$$**

Warujojo Lodge (8 rooms, 4 cottages, 4 bandas) m 0780 761221, 0707 909034; e info@warujojosafarilodge.com; w warujojosafarilodge.com. Set on a bluff above the main road as it winds up the escarpment, the stylish, open-fronted lounge-restaurant at the heart of this attractive new lodge has a great Rift Valley view, notwithstanding a bit of noise from ascending vehicles. It is accessed from Kyambura village through a garden curiously pocked with large grassy mounds. The work of neither Bachwezi kings or Teletubbies, these are apparently simply 'for decoration'. Decent value for a dbl room. *US$150/210 sgl/dbl FB.* **$$$$**

Budget

Dave the Cave Ecolodge (5 rooms, 1 4-bed dorm) ⊕ -0.261, 30.12255; m 0706 825615, 0772 863399; e nyanzibiriecotour@gmail.com; w mirtheboerdijk.wix.com/dave-the-cave. Set in lush gardens on the southwest rim of Lake Kamweru, 2km east of Nyakasharu (on the main Kasese–Ishaka Rd), this rustic owner-managed lodge has no shortage of character, comprising wooden Tarzan-style huts with lake views, twin or dbl beds, nets, & en-suite semi-outdoor eco-toilets. Camping is also permitted. Room rates are a little steep by standards elsewhere in Uganda, but seem more reasonable when you consider its proximity to Kichwamba & QENP, & that they include meals & access to Izoguto Cave & the boardwalk around Kamweru. *US$38/77 sgl/dbl FB; US$10 camping exc food.* **$$$**

Pumba Safari Cottages (3 cottages, 1 standing tent) ⊕ -0.21013, 30.10055; m 0772 482462; e info@mamalandsafaris.com; w pumbasafaricottages.n.nu. This unpretentious cluster of basic en-suite cottages, situated a few hundred metres north of Kyambura trading centre, has a home-away-from-home mood, but feels overpriced for what it is. *US$100/130 sgl/dbl FB.* **$$$**

Shoestring and camping

Balcons Guesthouse (8 rooms) ⊕ -0.23338, 30.09416; m 0772 873542. Genuine old-fashioned Ugandan small-town guesthouse with simple but adequate en-suite rooms with cold shower & ¾ bed in Kichwamba town. *US$4 sgl.* **$**

Craters Campsite & Country Lodge (6 rooms, more under construction) ⊕ -0.24563, 30.08429; m 0782 504900, 0757 869503; f campsiteandlodge.craters. Set in large grassy gardens 1km west of the main road, this friendly setup lies 5mins' walk downhill from the rim of the forested Kyemengo Crater. Rooms are quite basic but have nets, balcony & en-suite shower. *US$26/40 sgl/dbl bed only; US$10 pp camping. Meals in the US$6–9 range.* **$$**

Kalinzu Eco-Tourism Project ⊕ -0.37565, 30.11526; t 041 4230365/6; m 0772 568168; w nfa.org.ug. The only overnight option at Kalinzu itself is a campsite with toilet & shower right next to the chimp-tracking office. There's no restaurant, so campers should ideally be self-sufficient, but basic supplies can be purchased at a nearby trading centre. *US$5 pp.* **$**

Maramagambo Campsite ⊕ -0.28491, 30.05089. Rustic campsite cut into a forest glade close to (but not in sight of) Lake Kyasanduka.

Facilities are limited to cold showers & firewood & you'll need to take all provisions; note that the nearby Jacana Safari Lodge is closed for renovations with no date set for reopening, so don't plan on treating yourself there. The birdlife around the campsite is superb, & monkeys are everywhere. *US$5 pp.* **$**

Warujojo Annex (6 rooms) m 0780 761221, 0707 909034; e info@warujojosafarilodge.com; w warujojosafarilodge.com. Essentially drivers' quarters attached to the eponymous safari lodge (page 495), this roadside block of en-suite sgl rooms is very reasonably priced. Eat at the lodge, 5mins' walk away, or get a simpler meal in the adjacent bar. *US$10 sgl; extra bed US$10. Exc meals.* **$**

What to see and do The sites listed here are described in the sequence you'd encounter them – or the primary junction for the associated access road – driving from north to south between Katunguru and Ishaka.

Kyambura Gorge chimp tracking The only habituated chimpanzee community in QENP inhabits an isolated strip of riparian forest in the 100m-deep Kyambura Gorge, which runs for 16km on the park's eastern boundary with Kyambura Wildlife Reserve. The confined nature of the forested gorge makes it quite easy to locate the chimps by sound, and once you've found them, they can usually be approached quite closely. Even if you don't see chimps, it is a quite lovely patch of forest, with an open understorey typical of riparian woodland, and the river that runs through it is very beautiful too. The topography can make for interesting sightings, as when trackers, ascending the side of the gorge, are level with or above chimps sitting in the top of an adjacent tree.

Chimps aside, black-and-white colobus, vervet monkey, red-tailed monkey and olive baboon are also regularly observed in the gorge, while less visible residents include bushbuck and giant forest hog. Buffalo, elephant and even lion pass through from time to time and are occasionally seen by chimp trackers. The river is home to several hippo pods, which – rather amusingly – tend to respond to the chimps' pant-hoot calls with some loud harrumphing of their own. For birdwatchers, great blue turaco and black-and-white casqued hornbill are also very vocal (Kyambura Gorge can get pretty noisy, actually) and the forested rim is one of the best places in Uganda to look for black bee-eater and blue-bellied kingfisher.

Guided chimp-tracking excursions depart twice-daily from Fig Tree Camp on the gorge's western rim. Permits cost US$80/100 FR/FNR, inclusive of the guide but excluding the park entrance fee, and can be booked and paid for in advance at the UWA headquarters in Kampala or at Katunguru Park Headquarters 8km to the north. Up to 16 permits are issued for any given day, with trackers leaving in two groups of up to four people each at 08.00 or 13.00. The excursion typically takes about 3 hours but this depends greatly on whether you locate the chimps,

RIVER OF THE BLIND

Local tradition maintains that the Kyambura River had no name until one day, without warning, it flooded, surprising the locals who lived along its banks or washed their clothing there. As the waters subsided, the locals one by one waded upriver to Lake George in search of the possessions that had been washed away in the flood. Invariably, they would return empty-handed and announce 'Kyambura' – a local phrase meaning 'I cannot see it'. This eventually became the river's name.

CHIMPS OF THE LOST GORGE

The long-term prognosis for the chimps of Kyambura is less than glowing. Deforestation and cultivation on the surrounding plains left this relict population of 28 individuals isolated from other forests c1990, and so far as can be ascertained it's had no subsequent interaction with other larger chimp communities – for instance, those at Maramagambo 10km to the southwest or Kasyoha-Kitomi 8km to the southeast. As a result, the Kyambura chimp population has become worryingly inbred, a situation exacerbated by the unfortunate circumstance that its members are predominantly male, which means the birth rate is unusually low.

Though the odd female does join the group, there is some talk of speeding things up by introducing a few more from other communities. Another option is to create a corridor of fig and other fruiting trees to encourage chimp movement between Kyambura and Maramagambo, but it remains to be seen whether it will be a case of too little, too late. For more information, check out the 2011 BBC documentary *Chimps of the Lost Gorge*.

and how quickly. A few years ago, Kyambura was one of the most reliable tracking sites in Uganda, with a success rate of 85%, and this is still the case when the chimps have easy access to fruiting trees, but it dips to around 50% at other times of year, when the Kalinzu Ecotourism Project (page 495), only 28km further south, is a better prospect.

The chimp-tracking trailhead at Fig Tree Camp (⊕ -0.1885, 30.10085) lies 2.5km east of the Ishaka Road. The junction (⊕ -0.19579, 30.08567) is 9km south of Katunguru Bridge.

Maramagambo Forest The immense Maramagambo Forest, which runs west from the Katunguru–Ishaka Road almost as far as the shore of Lake Edward, is largely inaccessible to tourists, the only exception being the northeastern tip around the crater lakes Nyamasingiri and Kyasanduka. The vastness of this forest is alluded to in its name, which derives from a local phrase meaning 'the end of words' and refers to a legend about a group of young people who got lost there many years ago, and took so long to find their way out they were unable to speak when they returned home. A medium-altitude rainforest with strong affiliations to its counterparts on the opposite side of the Congolese border, Maramagambo supports a rich selection of birds, along with forest mammals, including an unhabituated population of at least 300 chimpanzees, several types of monkey, and the likes of potto, giant forest hog, yellow-backed duiker, pygmy antelope and giant elephant shrew.

The main tourist development in northeast Maramagambo is Jacana Safari Lodge beside Lake Nyamasingiri. However, since this is currently closed for a major redevelopment, the only option at present is a campsite close to the shore of the smaller Lake Kyasanduka. The adjacent road passes through a tract of lush primary forest and can be walked unguided at no charge other than the standard entrance fees. Plenty of monkeys are likely to be seen – most commonly black-and-white colobus, red-tailed and vervet – and there's a slimmer chance of encountering the lovely L'Hoest's monkey, chimpanzees and even leopard. Birdwatchers could pace up and down several times without exhausting the opportunities to identify a confusing assembly of forest greenbuls, sunbirds, woodpeckers and other more elusive species.

Three different **guided walks** can be undertaken from the visitors' centre at a cost of US$20/25 FR/FNR per person per activity. The most straightforward trail loops around the forested shore of Lake Kyasanduka, and shouldn't take much longer than an hour, depending on how interested you are in the prolific birdlife. For dedicated birdwatchers, the most rewarding walk is likely to be the half day around the back of Lake Nyamasingiri, which comprises five interlocking craters and extends over 4km^2. The forest here hosts rarities such as scaly-breasted illadopsis, snowy-headed robin-chat and chestnut wattle-eye, while the lake itself is a good site for African finfoot.

More popular than either of the above is the 2–3km Nyamasingiri Trail, which leads from the eponymous lake to a bat cave and the so-called Blue Lake. The former is a rubble-strewn lava funnel whose interior hosts a massive colony of bats, as well as a few rock pythons that feed on them. The cave is viewed from a platform 15m away, a precaution imposed after a visitor died of Marburg fever contracted through contact with a bat inside the cave. About 300m past it, the Blue Lake sits at the bottom of a small deep volcanic crater and owes its coloration to high levels of copper in the water. It is also known as Lake Kamilanjojo (literally 'Swallowed Elephant'), in reference to a legend that an elephant running away from local hunters fell into the crater and couldn't escape.

The feeder road to Jacana Safari Lodge departs from the west side of the Ishaka Road (⊕ -0.21623, 30.09302), 2.5km south of the junction for Kyambura Gorge and 1km before Kyambura trading centre. The road reaches the visitors' centre and campsite after 14km, then terminates at Jacana Safari Lodge after another 1km.

Kyambura Wildlife Reserve Designated as a low usage zone within the greater Queen Elizabeth Conservation Area in 2023, the 157km^2 Kyambura Wildlife Reserve protects a magnificent tract of hilly savannah and tangled woodland bordering the national park. Kyambura Gorge, with its habituated chimps, forms the reserve's western boundary, while the wild eastern section of the Kazinga Channel, flowing out of Lake George, runs along the northern border. Geographically, the reserve's most striking feature is a cluster of seven scenic crater lakes enclosed by riparian forest. Wildlife includes large herds of elephant, buffalo and waterbuck, while prodigious hippo inhabit the Kazinga Channel, and lion, leopard and giant forest hog are seen with varying degrees of regularity. Historically, this beautiful wilderness area has largely been neglected by tourists, thanks to its remote location and a lack of suitable tracks. This is set to change, however, following the recent construction of two Wild Places concession camps, Honey Bear (page 492) and The River Station (page 494), on the south bank of the Kazinga Channel, opposite the Kasenyi Plains. These camps offer near-exclusive access to Kyambura Wildlife Reserve, as well as expertly guided walks, boat trips and game drives that provide a similar experience to some of the top private reserves and concessions in neighbouring countries such as Kenya and Tanzania. Those not staying at the Wild Places camps are technically free to explore Kyambura Wildlife Reserve in a 4x4, but the additional low usage zone entrance fees of US$40 (over and above the standard park entrance fee) is a deterrent to most.

Three of the crater lakes in Kyambura Wildlife Reserve are accessible from a bumpy 4x4-only public road that connects Kyambura trading centre to Kashaka, a fishing village sited where the Kazinga Channel exits Lake George. About 10km out of Kyambura village, the bumpy track to Kashaka runs along the northern rim of

Lake Chibwera offering the opportunity to alight from the car and scan the surface for waterbirds such as little grebe and various ducks. About 3km further on, the road offers distant views over Lake Nshenyi, which is also known as Flamingo Lake, after the concentrations of several thousand greater and lesser flamingos that gather there when conditions are conducive, and black-and-white colobus swing through the fringing forest. Some 6km further the Kashaka Road skirts Lake Bagusa, then passes a breached crater connected to Lake George immediately before it arrives at the fishing village. No fees are payable for driving along this pubic road, but step or drive off it, and you will be liable for full park and low usage zone fees. A steady trickle of shared taxis connects Kichwamba to Kashaka.

Kyambura Viewpoint and lakes Katinda and Milambi Set on the west side of the Ishaka Road about 1.5km south of Kichwamba trading centre, the Kyambura Viewpoint (⊕ -0.22515, 30.09418), situated on the escarpment overlooking QENP and the Kazinga Channel, is a scenic spot to stop for a cold drink. There's a well-stocked handicraft shop, and it also sells good locally produced honey. The viewpoint is the home of the Bunyaruguru Community-Based Tourism Association (BUCOBATA; m 0772 873542, 0754 206569), which offers guided hikes to the twin 'love lakes', Katinda (vaguely heart-shaped) and Milambi (vaguely egg-shaped), 1km to the east. The scenic walk takes about an hour, and also includes visits to a local coffee plantation and beer brewery, which seems like a fair return for the guide fee of US$7 per person. Incidentally, an official road authority sign in Kyambura trading centre indicating 'Katanda-Mirembe Twin Lakes' offers road access along the rim of Lake Katinda only, Mirembe being hidden in a crater beyond.

Kataara Women's Poverty Alleviation Group (KWPAG; ⊕ -0.24481, 30.08948; m 0774 373794; e katarawomens@gmail.com; w kwpag.wordpress.com) Operating out of a handicraft centre situated 300m west of the Ishaka Road towards Katara Lodge, this community-based NGO specialises in making paper from dried elephant dung collected in and around the borders of QENP. It's an innovative and laudable way to create local support for animals that are frequently destructive to subsistence farms bordering the park. Elephant dung is bought from locals who collect it at a rate of US$3 per basin, and the project also provides partial employment to 30 (mostly female) craftspeople, while profits are used to help support orphans or to finance a local savings and credit scheme. Visitors are welcome to watch the paper being manufactured at the back of the shop, or to shop for the reasonably priced products, which include elephant-dung cards, notebooks, beads and purses, as well as some basketwork and engraved calabashes.

Nzuguto Community Wetland The Nzuguto Environmental Conservation Association (NECA; ⊕ -0.26238, 30.1139; m 0703 630944; e ugandapal@gmail.com) was established in 2012 to save a 56ha wetland nestled within Nzuguto Crater, an important water source and wildlife refuge that had been degraded as a result of pollution. The main activity offered by NECA is a guided 1.6km walk (US$10 pp), incorporating a 600m boardwalk, through the papyrus swamp. The sitatunga antelope, once resident, is now extinct, but more than 130 bird species have been recorded, with grey crowned crane, Ross's turaco, marsh tchagra, dark-capped yellow warbler, white-collared oliveback and red-headed bluebill ranking among the more interesting regulars.

NECA also offers a 5km guided walk around the rim of Lake Kyema (US$10 pp), which is nestled in a deep, steep crater about 500m to the east of its office. On a clear day, the highest point on the Kyema rim offers views over QENP to the Rwenzori. A small group of hippos is reputedly resident in the lake.

The NECA office lies 1km east of the Ishaka Road. The junction is at Nyakasharu trading centre (⊕ -0.26593, 30.10685), just south of the larger settlement of Rubirizi. Any transport running along the main road can drop you at Nyakasharu, from where a boda to NECA (or on to Dave the Cave) shouldn't cost more than US$1.

Lake Kamweru Accessible through the grounds of Dave the Cave Ecolodge (page 495), this small crater lake is best known as the site of the large but low Izoguto Cave (entrance US$3 pp), which has been carved by a subterranean river that originates in the Nzuguto Wetland and empties into the lake. Dave the Cave also offers guided walks around the lake, which supports more than 100 bird species, incorporating a visit to the cave (US$15 pp), and canoe trips on the lake (US$15/hr).

Kasyoha-Kitomi Forest Reserve (m 0772 568168; w nfa.org.ug) Separated from QENP's Maramagambo Forest by a corridor of cultivation some 2km wide at its narrowest, Kasyoha-Kitomi is a 400km² tract of medium-altitude evergreen forest that harbours a varied fauna, including an estimated 300 elephants, 350 chimpanzees and an abundance of monkeys. The forest is of particular interest to birders, with more than 300 species recorded, including African grey parrot, red-chested owlet, black bee-eater, chocolate-backed kingfisher and equatorial akalat. Kasyoha-Kitomi is poorly developed for tourists at present, but NECA does offer guided day hikes to Lake Kamukuzu (US$10 pp), a pretty body of transparent water bordering the forest reserve. The lake is safe for swimming, and wildlife likely to be seen includes black-and-white colobus, red-tailed and L'Hoest's monkey, giant kingfisher and great blue turaco. To get to the forest reserve from the NECA office, you need to drive for 30 minutes to the trailhead, or catch a boda, then it's an hour's walk in either direction. Future plans include the construction of a community-run campsite next to the lake, and the introduction of canoeing. There is also talk of starting up chimpanzee tracking and constructing a canopy walk in the forest.

Kalinzu Chimp-Tracking and Ecotourism Project The highly accessible Kalinzu Ecotourism Project (⊕ -0.37565, 30.11526; ☎ 041 4230365; m 0783 000890;

THE FORMATION OF LAKE KAMWERU

Kamweru translates as 'fertile place', and legend has it that the crater in which the lake now nestles had a dry floor that was covered in agriculture until about 100 years ago. Back then, it was Nzuguto Crater that hosted a lake, one whose secretive spirit guardian served as an oracle to a local king called Heru. One day, when Heru was away on safari, his wife had sex with another man, and revealed the secret of the lake's spirit to her lover. This indiscretion so incensed the spirit that he lured the king's eldest son into the lake's waters, and pulled him under to drown. When Heru returned home, he in turn was angry at the spirit, and told it to leave the lake, threatening never to leave it another sacrifice. The next day, when Heru woke up, the spirit had indeed vanished. But so had the lake itself, as the spirit caused its water to flow through the subterranean river that passes through Izoguto Cave into Kamweru Crater, which has hosted a lake ever since.

w nfa.org.ug), set alongside the Kasese–Ishaka Road 35km south of Katunguru, now ranks as Uganda's most reliable chimpanzee-tracking site for those who want to avoid the high tourist volumes associated with doing this activity in Kibale National Park. The project is centred on the 137km² Kalinzu Forest Reserve, an eastern extension of QENP's Maramagambo Forest that comprises more than 400 tree species and supports a similar range of forest wildlife than its better-known neighbour. The main draw of this medium-altitude forest is chimpanzees, but five other diurnal primate species are present, namely olive baboon, black-and-white colobus and red-tailed, blue and L'Hoest's monkeys, along with the nocturnal potto and two varieties of galago. Kalinzu also provides refuge to the rare pygmy antelope. Other wildlife includes 378 bird, 262 butterfly and 97 moth species.

Kalinzu harbours around 320 chimpanzees, including a 50-strong community habituated for tourist visits, and a much larger one reserved for researchers. Chimp tracking (US$130/65 FNR/FR, inclusive of entrance fee) now comes with a success rate close to 95%, making the site almost as reliable as Kibale Forest, and the quality of sightings is usually very good. There is no fixed departure time; tracking can start from 07.30 until around 14.00, but an early start offers the best chance of a good sighting. The walk from the project to the habituated troop's territory is around 3–4km and it is steep in parts, so the round trip usually takes up to 4 hours.

Also on offer are 3–4-hour guided forest walks, which provide an opportunity to see all or most of the forest's monkey species, as well as alluring forest birds such as great blue turaco, black-billed turaco, black bee-eater, African pygmy kingfisher, white-tailed ant-thrush and red-tailed bristlebill. These nature walks cost US$40/20 FNR/FR, excluding an entrance fee of US$20 (FNR only). Travellers with a specialised interest in birds or butterflies should specify this before they set out.

Exciting future plans for Kalinzu include the construction of a new upmarket eco lodge and Uganda's first suspended canopy walkway. Both projects will be undertaken with World Bank funding and if all goes to plan they should be operational in 2026.

Any public transport heading along the main road between Kasese and Mbarara can drop you at Kalinzu's clearly signposted office, trailhead and campsite, which stand on the west side of the road 22km south of Rubirizi. Camping is permitted or you could overnight in Ishaka, only 20km to the south, and come through by boda, which shouldn't cost more than US$5 one-way.

ISHAKA AND BUSHENYI Arguably the most important route focus in southwest Uganda, Ishaka is where travellers coming from QENP or Kasese must choose between heading east via Mbarara towards Kampala, south via Ntungamo to Kabale, or southwest via Rukungiri to Buhoma (Bwindi Impenetrable National Park). Together with Bushenyi less than 5km further east, it forms the rapidly growing Bushenyi-Ishaka Metropolitan Area, which supports a combined population of 41,000. Ishaka is home to the Kampala International University's Western Campus, a medical college that attracts students from all around East Africa, and it forms a useful base for tracking chimps at nearby Kalinzu.

Getting there and away Ishaka lies at the three-way junction of the main road between Fort Portal and Mbarara, and a surfaced road running south to join the Ntungamo–Rukungiri tarmac at the small junction village of Kagamba. There, if you turn left you can reach Kabale and southern Bwindi, while a right turn will lead you to Rukungiri where a brand new 50km tarmac road connects to Kihihi for Buhoma (Bwindi) and Ishasha. Distances and approximate driving times are

55km/60 minutes to Katunguru (QENP), 95km/100 minutes to Kasese, 175km/3 hours to Fort Portal, 60km/45 minutes to Mbarara, 330km/4½–6 hours to Kampala, 100km/2 hours to Kabale, 140km/2½–3 hours to Ishasha and 160km/3½ hours to Buhoma.

Using public transport, those coming directly from Kampala are best off trying to catch a bus to Kasese via Mbarara (as opposed to via Fort Portal) and hopping off in Ishaka. Alternatively, take a bus to Mbarara and pick up an onward matatu there. More locally, regular matatus connect Ishaka to Kasese, Mbarara and Kabale. There is no taxi park as such; matatus out of Ishaka all leave from within 100m or so of the main central junction, on the left side of the appropriate road.

Where to stay and eat In addition to the two places listed here, a few indifferent shoestring guesthouses line the main road through Ishaka and Bushenyi.

Belline Hotel (11 rooms & more under construction) ⊕ -0.54145, 30.13108; m 0750 546366. Another 1km towards central Ishaka from the Cielo, this conspicuous blue-glass hotel block is difficult to miss. Urban in style, it lacks the leafy & intimate setting of its competitor, but the large 1st-floor lounge/bar/restaurant has views of green hills beyond the town. *US$38/50 sgl/dbl B&B.* **$$**

Cielo Country Inn (15 rooms) ⊕ -0.5321, 30.12378; m 0703 082597, 0772 934697; e reservations@cieloinn.com; w cieloinn.com. This welcoming hotel is set in a compact but pleasant garden compound alongside the Kasese Rd, 2km north of the town centre. En-suite rooms, accessed directly off the gardens, are clean & comfortable & there's a good restaurant though not much in the way of a bar/lounge area. Car hire to explore Kalinzu &/or QENP is available at US$100 per day inclusive of driver. *US$40/50 sgl/dbl B&B.* **$$**

What to see and do Ishaka is the closest town to the Kalinzu Ecotourism Project and, with private transport, its budget hotels would also make an affordable base for a day trip into QENP. The only other attraction in the area is the Kitagata Hot Springs, which lie along the recently surfaced and upgraded direct road to Kabale via Ntungamo.

Kitagata Hot Springs (⊕ -0.6782, 30.1603; no entrance fee) Situated 16km south of Ishaka and 1.5km south of Kitagata trading centre, these sulphuric hot springs hold few mysteries for linguists – Kitagata translates somewhat prosaically as 'boiling water' – and it could be argued that they are also of limited visual interest, bubbling as they do into a clear, shallow, steaming pool about 200m west of the Kabale Road. Kitagata has long been believed to possess therapeutic qualities (and so probably does, should you be suffering from creaky joints or aching muscles, though it's doubtful it would do much to cure malaria or several other ailments as it claims) and the surrounding rocks are generally draped in a couple of dozen half-naked bathers who, needless to say, will be less than enamoured of any passing tourist who pulls out a camera. Facilities are limited to the communal hot bath created naturally by the springs. South of Kitagata, the road to Ntungamo passes through some impressively scenic hills, and follows a papyrus-fringed river for several kilometres, offering excellent views over patches of swamp that might potentially prove to be excellent for papyrus endemics.

ISHASHA AND KIHIHI

Renowned for the unusual tree-climbing behaviour of its lions, the remote Ishasha Sector of QENP supports plenty of other wildlife and is serviced by one of Uganda's most alluring wilderness lodges. Although it is somewhat removed from the rest of the park, Ishasha is bisected by the 150km road that connects Katunguru to Buhoma, and as such it is often visited as a day trip or overnight safari destination travelling between northern QENP and Bwindi. The largest town in the vicinity is Kihihi, which is also traversed by the main road to Buhoma. Kihihi hosts an airport that is serviced by regular flights from Entebbe and Kampala, and in addition to being a potential base for safaris to Ishasha, it is also the main springboard for fly-in gorilla-tracking expeditions in Bwindi.

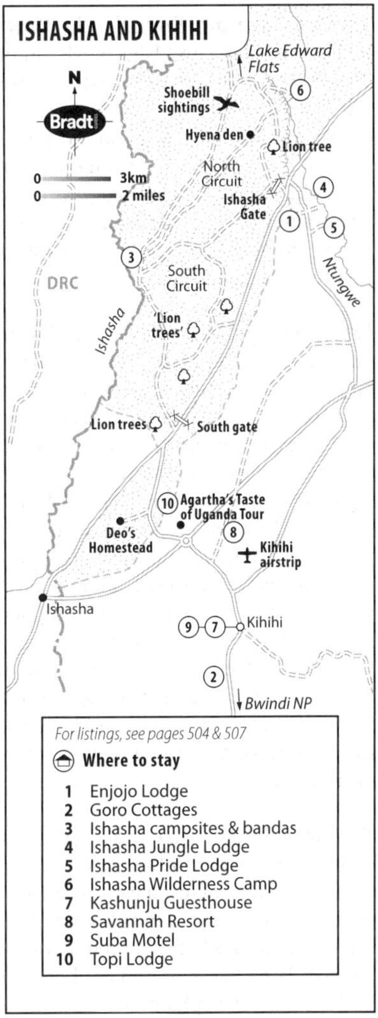

GETTING THERE AND AWAY

By air Aerolink (031 7333000; e info@aerolinkuganda.com; w aerolinkuganda.com) flies daily from Entebbe Airport to Kihihi (page 507), 30 minutes' drive from Ishasha. Flights cost US$286/474 single/return excluding taxes. Aerolink flights also connect Ishasha to other airports in western Uganda, including Kasese for northern QENP and Kibale Forest, and Pakuba in Murchison Falls National Park.

By road Ishasha is most normally approached from one of three directions: from the north, via Katunguru on the main Kasese–Ishaka Road; from the east (Kampala and Lake Mburo) via Mbarara and Rukungiri; or from Kabale and Bwindi National Park in the south via Kihihi. It is thus easily visited en route between central QENP and Bwindi, though road conditions are such that the game-viewing tracks can be explored thoroughly only on an overnight stay.

To/from Katunguru Ishasha Gate (⊕ -0.58543, 29.71733) lies 70km southwest of the Kasese–Ishaka Road along a fair dirt road that starts 4km south of Katunguru Bridge and continues to the Congolese border at Ishasha town. The gate is clearly signposted 1km beyond the Ntungwe River bridge, and 17km before the border post. The drive between Katunguru and Ishasha Gate shouldn't take more than 2 hours, but the road tends to deteriorate during the wet season, so ask local advice before using it. A 4x4 is recommended, though any robust saloon car should get through with ease in normal conditions. If you don't have private transport, hitching along the main road is a possibility, but getting into the park will be problematic.

To/from Kabale/Bwindi via Kihihi In a private vehicle, the 60km drive between Buhoma and Ishasha via Butogota, Kanyantorogo and Kihihi takes about 90 minutes on decent dirt roads. From Kabale, the best route is through Hamurwa, Kanungu and Kihihi, connecting with the road from Buhoma at Kanyantorogo, a distance of around 120km on mostly dirt that should take at least 4 hours (but best to allow longer). Coming from elsewhere in Bwindi, it's an 85km/4-hour drive from the Ruhija area, connecting with the road from Buhoma at Butogota, while the best route from the Rushaga or Ntungamo areas entails returning to the surfaced Kisoro–Kabale Road, driving northwest to Hamurwa, then using the same route (via Kanungu and Kihihi) as you would from Kabale.

From Kampala and the east Coming from Kampala or Lake Mburo, the best route to Ishasha follows the surfaced Kabale Road for 60km past Mbarara to Ntungamo, then turns right on to a surfaced 45km road to Rukungiri. From there, an impressive new tarmac road arcs west through the highlands of northeast Kigezi for 48km to a conspicuous roundabout. While a left turn on tarmac leads to Kihihi, a right turn on to a poor dirt road runs to the Katunguru-Ishasha road near the Ishasha sector's Southern Gate. Alternatively, you could follow the tarmac straight on to the Ishasha border post with a right turn on to the aforementioned road to head north to whichever gate or lodge you are looking for.

Using public transport, a daily Starlink bus runs between Kampala and Kihihi, which is also connected to Butogota, Kanungu and Rukungiri by buses and matatus. From Kihihi, you'd need to charter a special hire to enter Ishasha, where the only budget accommodation is the UWA bandas (bodas are only allowed as far as the gate and won't get you all the way). Alternatively, you could base yourself cheaply in Kihihi and have your special hire take you on a full-day game drive to Ishasha – expect to pay around US$80 inclusive of fuel and the driver's entrance fee.

ISHASHA Bounded by Lake Edward to the north, the Ishasha River (also the Congolese border) to the west, and the Ntungwe River to the east, Ishasha ranks among the most alluring game-viewing areas anywhere in the country. It supports a population of tree-climbing lions that comprised around 40 individuals a while back, but is said to have halved in number in recent years. The grassy plains of Ishasha also support large herds of buffalo, kob and topi, smaller family groups of waterbuck, and the likes of elephant, warthog and various monkeys. Ishasha retains a relatively untrammelled wilderness character, one best appreciated by spending a night or two within the sector, or failing that at one of the flurry of lodges constructed a short distance outside it. However, those intent on seeing lions up trees, which most often happens in the heat of the day, could think about visiting as a (long) day trip from one of the lodges listed elsewhere in this chapter, or (better) as a diversion en route between other sectors of QENP and Bwindi Impenetrable National Park.

Where to stay and eat *Map, page 503*

In addition to the listings below, you could also stay in nearby Kihihi, particularly if your focus is the tree-climbing lions, which tend not to clamber up on to their perches before the day is well underway.

Exclusive

✷ **Ishasha Wilderness Camp** (10 tents) ⊕ 0.54908, 29.72112; ☎ 041 4321479; m 0772 721155; e reservations@ugandaexclusivecamps.com; w ugandaexclusivecamps.com. Arguably the only true wilderness facility in Uganda, & the only lodge actually set within the park's Ishasha Sector, this excellent camp is carved into the riparian forest along the Ntungwe River & located in the thick of the wildlife action. Elephant regularly cross the river within view of the camp & lion & leopard are often found close by, while colobus monkeys emit their guttural croak in the trees overhead. The place is alive with birds, including African finfoot & Pel's fishing owl on the river & the gorgeous Narina trogon in & around the car park. The en-suite canvas-sided cottages with fitted nets & river-facing balconies are comfortable & beautifully appointed, with large mesh windows to bring the river views indoors. Tasty, ample & beautifully presented 4-course dinners demonstrate that isolation is no excuse for mediocre catering. Excellent in every respect. **$$$$$**

Upmarket

✷ **Enjojo Lodge** (8 cottages, 3 huts, 4 standing tents) ⊕ -0.59403, 29.72267; t 041 4669487; m 0758 880521, 0782 803518; e info@enjojolodge.com; w enjojolodge.com. This characterful lodge stands on the national park border only 3km from Ishasha Gate, in a steamy jungle-like stand of fever trees & palms overlooking a waterhole that regularly attracts elephant, buffalo & other wildlife. Upmarket thatched & stilted cottages, reached via delightfully atmospheric wooden walkways through the swamp, are decorated with colourful local fabrics & geometric Rwandan paintings. A separate campsite with common showers offers the choice between a standing tent on a raised wooden platform or pitching your own tent. *Thatched cottage US$190/320 sgl/dbl; forest cottage US$150/260 sgl/dbl; tents US$130/220 sgl/dbl; US$50 pp camping. All rates FB.* **$$$$**

Ishasha Jungle Lodge (1 treehouse, 6 cottages, 6 standing tents) ⊕ -0.59101, 29.73002; t 041 4232754; e info@ugandajunglelodges.com; w ugandajunglelodges.com. Situated about 3km from Ishasha Gate in densely wooded gardens some 200m from the Ntungwe River, this agreeable lodge offers accommodation in neat thatched cottages with 1 dbl & 1 sgl bed, walk-in nets, & private wooden balcony. *US$200/330/435 sgl/dbl/trpl FB.* **$$$$**

Moderate

Ishasha Pride Lodge (7 cottages) m 0784 454991, 0772 409510; e reservations@mbzgroup.africa; w mbzgroup.africa/ishashapridelodge. 'Suburban safari chic' seems to sums up this new lodge plonked on the floodplain of the Ntungwe River. The storeyed lodge structure does just enough to keep wildlife tourists happy, but in a more accessible location, the accommodation blocks would appeal more to urban weekenders. Located close to the river, these are sensibly raised on concrete pillars against seasonal flooding but one wonders, given the experiences of neighbouring lodges, how long they will withstand the erosive power of the meandering Ntungwe. While the standing tents appear a fair budget option, the characterless rooms don't cut it at the price. *Tents US$65/120 sgl/dbl; rooms US$130/200 sgl/dbl. Rates FB.* **$$$**

✷ **Topi Lodge** (7 cottages) m 0702 747758; e info@woodlandlodgesug.com; w topilodgeishasha.com. Reached from the Kihihi–Ishasha Road, this agreeable new lodge appears to be located in the middle of the QENP wilderness, albeit an unremarkable tract. It's a canny trick, the access track passing right through a 500m-wide strip of the contiguous Kigezi Wildlife Reserve to find the lodge in regenerating farmland on other side. The rustic lodge building & cottage accommodation manage a homely feel, while the bushy site is mitigated by elevated timber viewing decks. Reasonably priced & just 10mins' drive from Ishasha's southern gate. *US$110/180 sgl/dbl FB.* **$$$**

Budget and camping

Aside from the options listed here, budget tents are available at Enjojo Lodge (see left).

✷ **Ishasha campsites & bandas** ⊕ -0.6161, 29.65791 & -0.61388, 29.65711. These 2 lovely UWA-run campsites are flanked by the Ishasha River a few hundred metres north of the UWA offices. Set in riverine forest, they provide guaranteed views of (& sometimes encounters with) hippos. There are showers & flush toilets, & bottled drinks & simple meals are available in a canteen at the park offices. A couple of simple bandas (⊕ -0.61877, 29.65987) are also available close to the park offices. *US$12 dbl banda; US$5 pp camping.* **$**

What to see and do

Game drives Two main game circuits run out of Ishasha: the northern and southern loops, both roughly 20km in length. The southern circuit is the more productive for lion sightings, since it passes through the main kob breeding grounds – as in Kasenyi, the predators frequently stick close to their prey, and their presence is often revealed by the antelope's alarm calls. This area is also better provided with the trees favoured by lions. Navigating the **South Circuit** is a tricky task, being confused by side tracks leading to lion trees and diversions to bypass boggy sections. Though the 'Uganda Maps' QENP sheet has a good stab at making sense of all this, it's a good idea to take a guide. The simpler **North Circuit** is better for general game viewing, and the open landscape and boundless horizons on the northwestern part of the loop represent some of the finest wilderness in southwestern Uganda, even though it's actually only 4km from the main road to Katunguru. This section of the North Circuit also overlooks the Ntungwe River floodplain, a long low trough punctuated by pools and wallows enjoyed by buffalo; look out here for redder animals related to the forest buffalo of the DRC.

At the northern part of the loop, these boggy wallows develop into a full-blown wetland where birdwatchers might look out for black coucal, compact weaver, fan-tailed widow and other water-associated birds. A cairn in this area marks an 8km track extending north towards the marshy Lake Edward Flats. This papyrus-fringed site is good for waterbirds, including various herons, storks and plovers, and shoebills are quite often seen too, though that is far from definite. They also often harbour decent concentrations of elephant, buffalo, kob, topi and waterbuck. Road conditions are erratic, however, so seek advice from the rangers before striking out alone, particularly after rain, when getting stuck is a very real risk.

The Ishasha River, which can be explored on foot from the campsites along its bank, supports a healthy hippo population, most easily observed from Campsite 2. The fringing riparian forest harbours good numbers of bushbuck and black-and-white colobus monkey, and an interesting variety of birds including black bee-eater, broad-billed roller and the localised Cassin's grey flycatcher. Away from the river, light acacia woodland and savannah support large herds of Ugandan kob, topi and buffalo, while elephants are seasonally common.

ISHASHA'S TREE-CLIMBING LIONS

As a rule, lions are strictly terrestrial. Indeed, Ishasha is one of a handful of places anywhere in Africa where these regal predators regularly take to the trees (the others being Lake Manyara National Park and parts of the Serengeti, both in Tanzania), and it is probably the most reliable site of the lot. The explanation for this localised behaviour is open to conjecture. Limited studies undertaken in Lake Manyara indicate that the custom of ascending trees is culturally ingrained rather than a response to any immediate external stimuli, though it may well have been initiated to escape the attention of biting flies during an epidemic of these irksome creatures. In Ishasha, sycamore fig and to a lesser extent Albezias are favoured over other trees, with around 20 specific individual trees being favoured – which makes it quite easy to locate the lions when they are up in the canopy. The behaviour might be observed throughout the year but it is most frequent during the rainy seasons. Ishasha's lions are most likely to be seen in arboreal action in the heat of the day, between 11.00 and 15.00, and they invariably descend back to the ground well before dusk.

Following the kidnapping of a US tourist and local driver in Ishasha in April 2019, it might be advisable to take an armed ranger on any game drives in the sector.

KIHIHI Kihihi is a smallish (population around 25,000) but well-equipped town notable not only as the road funnel for southerly and easterly approaches to QENP's Ishasha Sector, but also for an out-of-town airport that forms the main fly-in springboard for gorilla tracking at Bwindi's Buhoma and Ruhija trailheads. Few travellers linger long in Kihihi, but it does boast some useful amenities, including a Stanbic Bank with an ATM, a few filling stations and small supermarkets, and several guesthouses. The airport is clustered together with the upmarket Savannah Resort Hotel and Garuga Golf Course about 4km along the Ishasha Road.

Where to stay and eat *Map, page 503*

✷ **Goro Cottages** (20 rooms) ⊕ 0.7516242, 29.6954983; m 0777 031654; e bookings@gorocottages.com; w gorocottages.com. Set in large & well-tended gardens & provided with a swimming pool (day visitors US$4) & sauna, plus adjacent dining area with bar & campfire in a *Grevillia* shaded glade, first appearances make the Goro Cottages look very promising indeed. Though some of the cottage-style rooms are a bit poky, it's easily the best value in the vicinity & perfectly do-able as a base for Ishasha. Clearly signposted as you leave town down the Bwindi Rd, Goro is 200m off to the right. *US$52/61 sgl/dbl B&B.* **$$**

Kashunju Guesthouse (9 rooms) 039 2949199. This place is much of a muchness with the Suba next door. *US$13/26 sgl/dbl B&B.* **$$**

Savannah Resort Hotel (44 rooms) ⊕ -0.71726, 29.69381; m 0751 382916; e reservations@savannahresorthotel.com; w savannahresorthotel.com. Set in large, park-like grounds, this 'country club'-style hotel stands adjacent to Kihihi Airstrip & the Garuga Golf Course, some 4km north of Kihihi town. A rare oasis of comfort between Bwindi (Buhoma, 1hr) & Ishasha Gate (30mins), its facilities include a swimming pool, steam/sauna & good restaurant. A justifiably popular stop for safari groups in transit or using the airstrip, & the grid of cottage accommodation is also fair value for the location. *US$120/160 sgl/dbl B&B; US$150/220 sgl/dbl FB.* **$$$$**

Suba Motel (9 rooms) 039 2905978; m 0776 905978; e info@subamotel.com; w subamotel.com. This old-style courtyard guesthouse – restaurant at the front, a U-shaped block of rooms at the back – is still as good as it gets in the town centre. The tiled en-suite rooms are superior to some examples of the genre but for the price, you'd expect a hotel rather than the classic shoestring layout. *US$17/26 sgl/dbl B&B.* **$$**

What to see and do

Agartha's Taste of Uganda Tour (⊕ -0.71424, 29.6756; m 0775 646665, 0776 453121) Well signposted on the east side of the Ishasha Road about 5km out of Kihihi, Agartha's is the flagship for the Ishasha Community Uplift Group. Her informative and enjoyable 30-minute tour provides an introduction to the daily life of a Bakiga woman, as well as typical regional millet- and sorghum-based foods such as *hakab* (a soft bread), *amagwa* (millet beer) and *omalamba* (sorghum beer). Proceeds are split three ways between Agartha, the community and a savings scheme for local women. A recommended stop en route between Ishasha and Bwindi.

Deo's Homestead (⊕ -0.70979, 29.66631; m 0781 201368) Deo's fascinating tour used to be affiliated to the Ishasha Community Uplift Group but he has now gone his own way. A typical local farmer, Deo shows how he and his kind cope in their daily battle to defend their crops from wildlife resident in the nearby Ishasha Sector of QENP. Life on this front line is aided by a 20km-long trench dug with support from the Uganda Conservation Foundation, one of several strategies employed by park-edge communities to keep hungry elephants out of the crops.

Deo's homestead is in the village of Bukorwe, which lies 1.5km off the road from Kihihi to Ishasha, along a track signposted to the west 1km past Agartha's.

Sana Gorilla Rafting (Rukungiri town; ⊕0.791412, 29.925668; m 0754 944695; e gorillarafting@gmail.com; w gorillaraftinguganda.com) When the latest dam on the Jinja Nile inundated the famous Nile Special rapid (and others), kayaker and rafting guide Sadat Kawawa set out to find himself another river. What he found was the Birira, the turbulent and still jungle-fringed headwater of Ishasha's Ntungwe River and he's now in a position to share it with you. A day out with Sana Gorilla Rafting covers 26km, includes several Grade IV rapids and takes 4–5 hours with all the gear and safety considerations you would expect from a major rafting outfit at Bujagali. The cost of US$145/125 FNR/FR includes lunch and return transport to Rukungiri (50km east of Kihihi on tarmac). Prices for two- to three-day camping excursions are available on request.

Part Six

THE GORILLA HIGHLANDS

OVERVIEW

Nudged up against the Rwandan and Congolese borders, the self-styled Gorilla Highlands, comprising the southwesterly districts of Kabale and Kisoro, are named after the small towns that serve as their administrative capitals and are best known to travellers for the opportunity to track some of the world's last few remaining mountain gorillas. Coming face-to-face with these gentle giants in one of the region's two national parks – Bwindi Impenetrable and Mgahinga Gorilla – is undoubtedly one of the world's most thrilling wildlife encounters. But the fertile and scenic highlands around Kabale and Kisoro rank as arguably the most picturesque part of Uganda, a kind of equatorial counterpart to Switzerland, where steep slopes covered in terraced cultivation frame expansive blue lakes that sparkle tantalisingly below the magnificent Virunga Mountains, a cross-border range of eight dormant and active volcanoes whose highest peak tops 4,500m.

This section comprises three chapters. The first covers the small town of Kabale and the popular resorts lining the shore and islands of nearby Lake Bunyonyi, while the second is dedicated to Mgahinga Gorilla National Park, which protects the upper slopes of the Virungas, as well as the town of Kisoro and various lakes that scatter its footslopes. The third is dedicated entirely to Bwindi Impenetrable National Park and the four gorilla-tracking trailheads that service it: Buhoma, Ruhija, Nkuringo and Rushaga.

For further information, a comprehensive interactive e-book, *Gorilla Highlands: Travel Guide to Southwestern Uganda,* compiled by the management of Edirisa (page 523), is available from the Apple iTunes Store for US$14.99. You can also download a smaller pocket guide from its informative website w gorillahighlands.com. More conventionally, Sheet 5 in the 'Uganda Maps' series, *Bwindi & the Gorilla Highlands*, illustrates the regional topography, main tourist routes and hotspots, viewpoints and home ranges of all Bwindi's habituated gorilla groups.

HIGHLIGHTS

GORILLA TRACKING IN BWINDI IMPENETRABLE NATIONAL PARK Home to 25 habituated groups, Bwindi is the ultimate mountain gorilla-tracking destination, with 200 tracking permits available daily. Page 546.

GORILLA TRACKING IN MGAHINGA GORILLA NATIONAL PARK This small but scenic national park is home to a single habituated mountain group notable for including four fraternal silverbacks that seem significantly heftier than their counterparts in Bwindi. Page 535.

GOLDEN MONKEY TRACKING The opportunity to track a habituated troop of these gorgeous bamboo-guzzling Albertine Rift Endemics in Mgahinga is an excellent add-on to gorilla tracking. Page 539.

LAKE BUNYONYI A flooded riverine valley set between the steep terraced slopes of Kigezi, lovely Lake Bunyonyi is entrenched as the place to chill out for a few days before or after gorilla tracking. Page 517.

VOLCANO HIKES All three of the volcanic Virunga peaks protected within Mgahinga can be tackled on guided day hikes. Most challenging is the slog up and

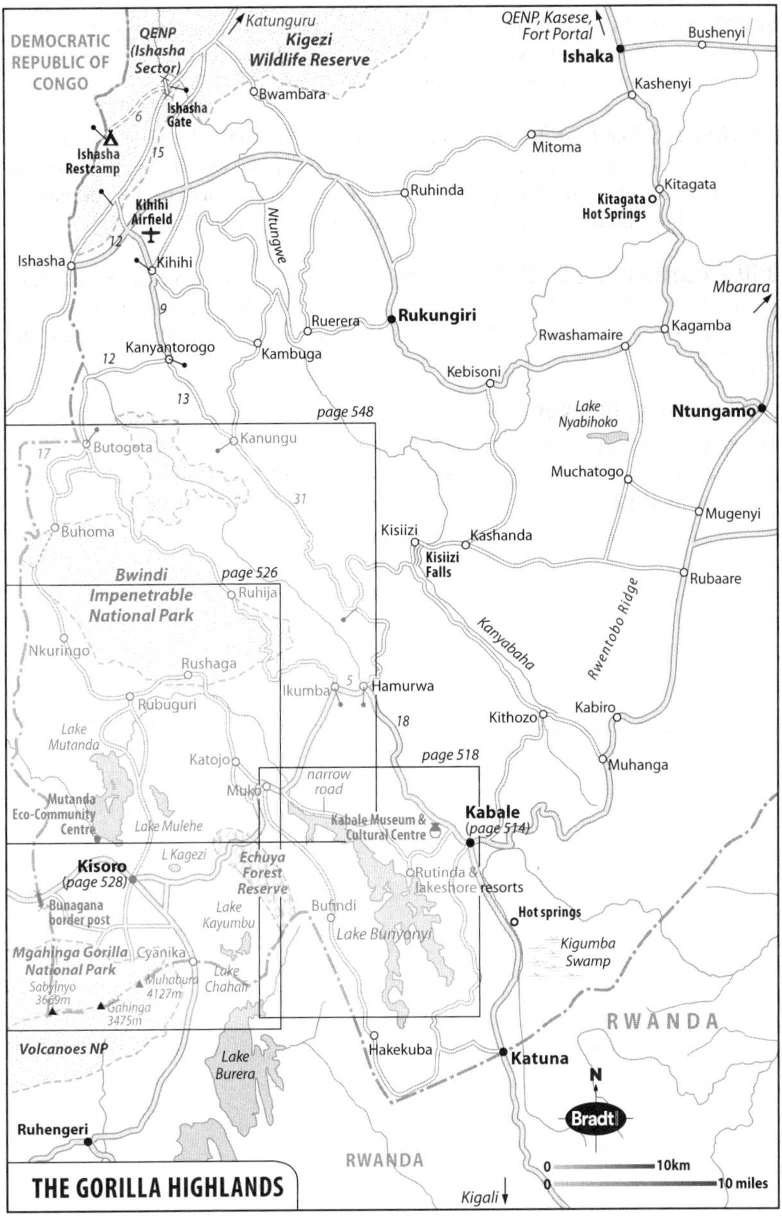

THE GORILLA HIGHLANDS

down the 4,127m-high Muhabura; more popular is the vertiginous scramble to the 3,669m-high peak of Sabyinyo, which marks the three-way border with Rwanda and the DRC. Page 537.

LAKE MUTANDA Visually reminiscent of the larger and better-known Lake Bunyonyi, Mutanda is if anything even more scenic, thanks to the backdrop provided by the volcanic cones of the Virunga Mountains. Page 542.

BATWA TRAIL This excellent initiative at Mgahinga provides a genuine opportunity to experience traditional Batwa 'Pygmy' culture, culminating with a memorable music performance in the council chamber of Garama Cave. Page 542.

MUBWINDI SWAMP TRAIL This scenic day hike through the densely forested slopes near Bwindi's Ruhija trailhead offers great monkey viewing, occasional elephant encounters, and the opportunity to tick off several bird species endemic to the Albertine Rift, most notably the rare African green broadbill. Page 568.

BUNIGA COMMUNITY FOREST A 2–3-hour guided trail through this tiny patch of regenerating forest bordering Nkuringo allows you to see it through the eyes of the local Batwa, who demonstrate various aspects of their traditional forest life. Page 575.

ECHUYA FOREST RESERVE Bisected by the main road between Kabale and Kisoro, the little-visited highland forest of Echuya protects at least a dozen bird species endemic to the Albertine Rift, and is the best place to seek them outside the national park system. Page 534.

19

Kabale and Lake Bunyonyi

Nestled amid the green slopes of Kigezi some 400km southwest of Kampala, Kabale stands at a refreshing altitude of 1,900m, making it one of the country's highest and most climatically agreeable larger towns. For many years, it was an important springboard for budget travellers tracking gorillas in Bwindi or Mgahinga (or indeed Rwanda or the DRC), but the town has faded in significance in recent years, thanks partly to the surfacing of the once-appalling road to Kisoro, but also to the closure of its UWA gorilla-permit booking office and to the opening of other, better access routes into Bwindi.

Though few tourists stay in Kabale overnight, the town remains the main gateway to Lake Bunyonyi, which lies only 8km away by road. In recent years, Bunyonyi has superseded Lake Victoria's Ssese Islands as Uganda's most popular waterfront chill-out venue. In part this is because Bunyonyi is easily visited in tandem with the gorilla-tracking trailheads of Bwindi and the Virungas. Further in Bunyonyi's favour, its greater elevation ensures a more temperate climate and lower prevalence of malaria, while swimming is more-or-less hazard-free due to the absence of hippos and crocodiles.

KABALE

The breezy highland town of Kabale is one of the largest in western Uganda, with a population of around 50,000. It was founded in 1913, when the British government station at Ikumba was relocated to Makanga Hill, then known as Kabaare after a trough-like depression at its summit. Today, the original hilltop site houses an expansive green golf course, a few old government buildings, and a handful of relatively smart hotels, all shaded by eucalyptus trees planted in the 1920s as part of a swamp-clearance and malaria-control programme. Immediately southwest and downhill of Makanga Hill, the modern town centre is dotted with budget hotels and restaurants, but its rather scruffy appearance is seemingly designed to discourage new arrivals from lingering any longer than is required to arrange transport on to Bunyonyi or Kisoro.

GETTING THERE AND AWAY Kabale is connected to Kampala by a 400km surfaced road through Mbarara; allow at least 7 hours in a private vehicle. Coming from Kasese (or Fort Portal or North-Central QENP), the best option is the 220km 4-hour route taking in the surfaced road between Ishaka and Ntungamo. Directions for Kisoro, the various gorilla-tracking trailheads at Bwindi and other relatively local sites are included in the relevant sections.

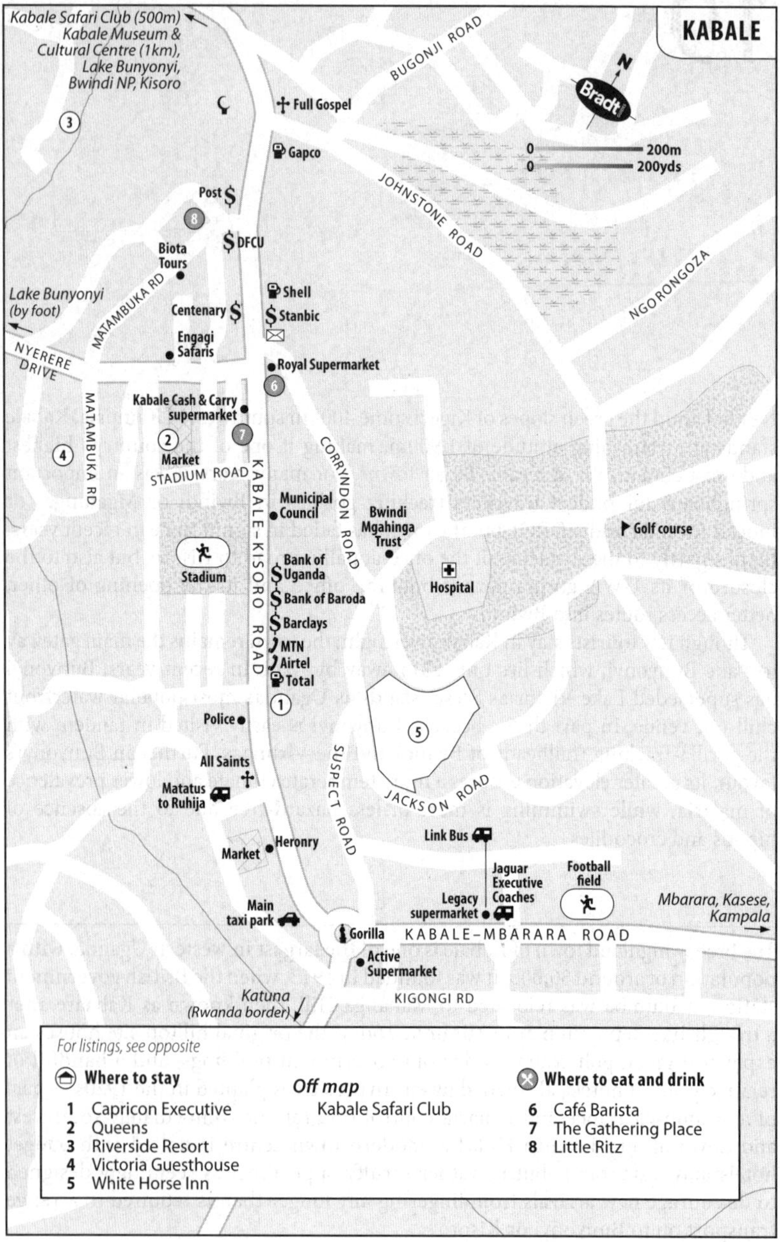

Buses from Kampala take 7–9 hours. The superior Rwandan company Trinity Coaches (US$17 one-way) runs a couple of services daily to Kigali via Kabale which can be booked online at w ugabus.com. The fare for most other buses is US$10. The most popular pick is Jaguar Executive Coaches (m 0782 811128, 0758 178951 (Kampala)) which operates at least five executive buses to Kisoro or Kigali (Rwanda) daily, all passing through Kabale, from its terminal on Namirembe Road.

Modern Coach (m 0705 700888) is a reputable Kenyan company that operates a couple of very comfortable coaches daily from Nairobi to Kigali via Kampala and Kabale. Other buses to Kabale leave Kampala throughout the morning, mostly from Namirembe Road, and generally stopping at Mbarara en route. Surprisingly, Link Bus's comprehensive routes through southern Uganda do not reach Kabale from Kampala, but there is a daily service (in both directions) between Hoima and Kabale, taking in Fort Portal, Kasese and Ishaka along the way – very useful if trying to get from Murchison Falls, Kibale or Queen Elizabeth National Park to southern Bwindi and Lake Bunyonyi.

Regular matatus connect Kabale's main taxi park to Kampala and Kisoro (90mins). A few matatus also run to Ruhija in Bwindi National Park (2–3hrs), on weekdays (but usually not Saturday, Sunday or public holidays), leaving from the junction behind the All Saints Church between 13.00 and 16.00. Transport to Muko and Rutinda (Lake Bunyonyi) leaves from a small taxi park at the north end of town near the Highland Hotel.

WHERE TO STAY *Map, opposite*

A generally low standard of hotels in Kabale reflects a downturn in overnight tourist traffic. Far better out-of-town accommodation is available at Lake Bunyonyi, though prices tend to be higher.

Moderate

Kabale Safari Club (9 rooms) ☎ 020 0910812, 041 4660379; e reservations@kabalesafariclub.com; w kabalesafariclub.com. Out on the western side of the town towards the Lake Bunyonyi junction, the smartest (and most ambitiously priced) place in Kabale offers modern rooms in a cluster of semi-detached chalets set in a pleasant garden. A restaurant/bar is attached: mains US$10. *US$80/120/130 sgl/dbl/twin B&B.* **$$$**

✷ **White Horse Inn** (40 rooms) m 0705 809994, 0779 414 342; e info@whitehorseinnkabale.ug; w whitehorseinnkabale.ug. Kabale's oldest & best-known hotel was established on Makanga Hill in 1927 in large green grounds that lie adjacent to the golf course & overlook the town centre. A perennial appeal lies in the attractive shingle-roofed buildings, lovely grounds that overlook the town & a cosy bar in which a fire is lit on cooler nights; the carpeted older rooms, on the other hand, though adequate, are small & feel a bit institutional. A restaurant with a choice of indoor or terrace seating serves decent international mains for around US$9. *US$39/52 sgl/dbl old rooms; US$80 dbl new wing. All rates B&B.* **$$–$$$**

Budget

Capricon Executive Hotel (28 rooms) m 0774 464908, 0705 872727; e capriconexecutivehotel@gmail.com. A distinct cut above anything else in the town centre, this smart 3-storey hotel serves good international meals & an uncommonly varied selection of wines & spirits. *US$30/45 sgl/dbl B&B.* **$$**

Riverside Resort Hotel (7 rooms) ⊕ 1.2505312, 29.9822062; m 0788 571411. Popular with self-drive tourists, the large, stream-side garden attached to this pleasant guesthouse is perfect for stretching your legs after a long day on the road. The rooms are acceptable & the food, given plenty of notice, excellent. Beer is not stocked & (if you don't have your own supply) must be ordered from outside at an eyebrow-raising US$3 (if nothing else, it'll prepare you for Bwindi prices). *US$30/45 sgl/dbl B&B.* **$$**

Shoestring

Queens Hotel (7 rooms) m 0752 390105. On a quieter road behind the market & main street, this agreeable cheapie has its own restaurant & veranda; alternatively, the Gathering Place is just 5mins' walk away. *US$13/16 sgl/dbl.* **$**

Victoria Guesthouse (20 rooms) m 0753 577776. This friendly & long-serving budget hotel has a quiet backroad location a couple of mins' walk from the town centre. The en-suite rooms are small & a little dated but remain pretty good value. *US$20 dbl B&B.* **$**

WHERE TO EAT AND DRINK *Map, page 514*

Aside from the limited selection of standalone restaurants listed here, the White Horse Inn on Makanga Hill is the place to head for an alfresco lunch or dinner with a view.

Café Barista m 0780 828668; ⏲ 07.00–midnight daily. This smart little high-street eatery with wrought-iron furniture & a pleasant terrace serves coffees & smoothies (US$3–4), as well as a varied selection of burgers, pizzas, grills, curries & pasta dishes. *Mains in the US$5–6 range.*

The Gathering Place m 0754 834355; ⏲ 07.00–midnight daily. The latest place to meet & eat in the town centre occupies 1st-floor premises on the main street. Coffees, teas & juices are served while the menu, though broadly similar to nearby Café Barista, is enlivened by some Mexican dishes. Profits go to Lot 2545, an NGO dedicated to helping street kids get back on track. *Mains in the US$5–6 range.*

Little Ritz Central Kabale's longest-serving bar/restaurant occupies 1st-floor premises with balcony seating & serves a limited selection of mains including good chicken masala. There's DSTV in the bar & a warming log fire in chilly weather. *Mains US$4–6.*

SHOPPING There are a couple of good supermarkets in Kabale, notably the **Royal Supermarket** next to Café Barista and **Active Supermarket** in a new mall on the Cyanika roundabout. The latter has its own bakery and off-street parking.

TOUR OPERATORS Any of the operators listed here can arrange transport to the gorilla-tracking trailheads, as well as other local excursions.

Biota Tours m 0777 408098, 0750 745970; e info@kigezibiotasafaris.com; w kigezibiotatours-ug.com

Engagi Safaris m 0782 421519; e engagisafaris@gmail.com; w africagorillasafaris.net

Safari 2 Gorilla Tours m 0774 608916, 0754 608916; w safarigorillatrips.com

Safari for All m 0772 703846; w safariforall.net

WHAT TO SEE AND DO The most popular tourist attraction in the immediate vicinity of Kabale is Lake Bunyonyi, covered later in this chapter, and the town also makes a possible base for gorilla tracking at Ruhija, 55km to the north.

Kabale Museum and Cultural Centre

(⊕ -1.24522, 29.97276; m 0752 500435; ⏲ 10.00–17.30 Mon–Fri & w/end by arrangement; entrance for foreign tourists is US$6) This small out-of-town museum has some interesting displays relating to Kigezi's four main ethnic groups: the Bakiga of Kabale; the Mpororo of Rukungiri; the Bafumbira of Kisoro; and the Kinkizi of Kanungu. Traditional artefacts on display, some evidently very old, include musical instruments, jewellery, weapons, pots and iron-smelting equipment. It is situated off the Kisoro Road along the junction to Lake Bunyonyi about 1.5km northwest of Kabale town centre.

Kisiizi Falls

(⊕ -0.99824, 29.94392; ☎ 039 2700806; e kisiizifalls@gmail.com; w kisiizifalls.com; entrance US$1.50) This 30m-high waterfall lies on the Rushoma River above its confluence with the Kyanabaha a few hundred metres from Kisiizi Hospital, which was founded by the Church of Uganda in 1958, some 65km north of Kabale by road. The waterfall is a very pretty and peaceful spot, with plenty of birdlife around including Ross's turaco and double-toothed barbet, and the surrounding forests and quiet roads offer some pleasant rambling possibilities.

The waterfall is used to provide hydro-electric power to the hospital – in Uganda's darker days, Kisiizi was one of the few places countrywide that had a reliable 24-hour electricity supply and functional street lamps.

The tranquil atmosphere around the waterfall belies its macabre historical association with the local custom described somewhat euphemistically by one Ugandan source as 'damping'. In traditional Bakiga society, virginity was a highly prized asset and an unmarried girl who fell pregnant could, at best, hope to be a social outcast for the rest of her days. More often, however, the offender would be mortally punished: tied to a tree and left at the mercy of wild animals, thrown from a cliff, or abandoned to starve on an island. Many disgraced girls were 'damped' at Kisiizi: tossed over the waterfall, arms and legs tightly bound, to drown in the pool below. On a hillside above the river, a graphic sculpture depicts an unmarried pregnant girl being killed in this manner. Though it takes two to tango, history glosses over the consequences, if any, for the man involved.

Kisiizi formally opened as a tourist site in 2017 and the gorge below it is now spanned by a suspended footbridge offering fine views to the main attraction, as well as a three-stage zip-line for over-16s only (US$11.50) and a mini zip-line for children (US$1.50). Canoes and mountain bikes are available for hire at US$1.50 per 30 minutes. Comfortable accommodation is available at the recently renovated **Kisiizi Falls Guest House** (10 rooms; m 0759 512764; other contact details as for the tourism site above; US$8 pp in room using common showers; US$30/35 en-suite cottage sleeping 3/4; **$$**) and it can also provide meals in the US$3–4 range. All amenities are operated by Kisiizi Hospital and proceeds support a fund to help poor and mentally ill patients, diabetics and premature babies.

Several roads connect Kabale to Kisiizi, but the best option is to follow the surfaced Kampala Road for 32km as far as Muhanga, from where a 33km dirt road leads north to the hospital and waterfall. The drive should take less than 2 hours in a private vehicle. Using public transport, regular matatus run between Kabale and Muhanga.

LAKE BUNYONYI

Serpentine Lake Bunyonyi, as its shape suggests, comprises a flooded river valley that extends northwards for 25km, following the steep contours of the hills separating Kabale from Kisoro, but is nowhere more than 5km wide. The lake formed about 8,000 years ago, when a lava flow blocked off the Ndego River at present-day Muko to create a natural dam. The 60km^2 lake stands at the core of a larger wetland incorporating the Ruhuma Swamp and several other permanent marshes. Set at an altitude of 1,950m, it is encircled by steep terraced hills that rise to above 2,500m, and although estimates of its depth vary wildly, it is probably nowhere more than 45m deep.

Bunyonyi translates as 'place of little birds', presumably in reference to the weaver colonies that proliferate on the shore, but larger birds are also represented by the likes of grey crowned crane and a variety of herons and egrets. The spotted-necked otter is unusually common and visible at Bunyonyi, presumably due to the lack of competition from larger aquatic carnivores.

A popular venue for chilling out before or after gorilla tracking in Bwindi or Mgahinga, Bunyonyi is regarded to be safe for swimming due to the absence of hippos, crocodiles and – by most accounts – bilharzia (although occasional localised outbreaks of the last cannot be ruled out entirely). It also offers some great opportunities for rambling, hiking and canoeing. Tourist development is

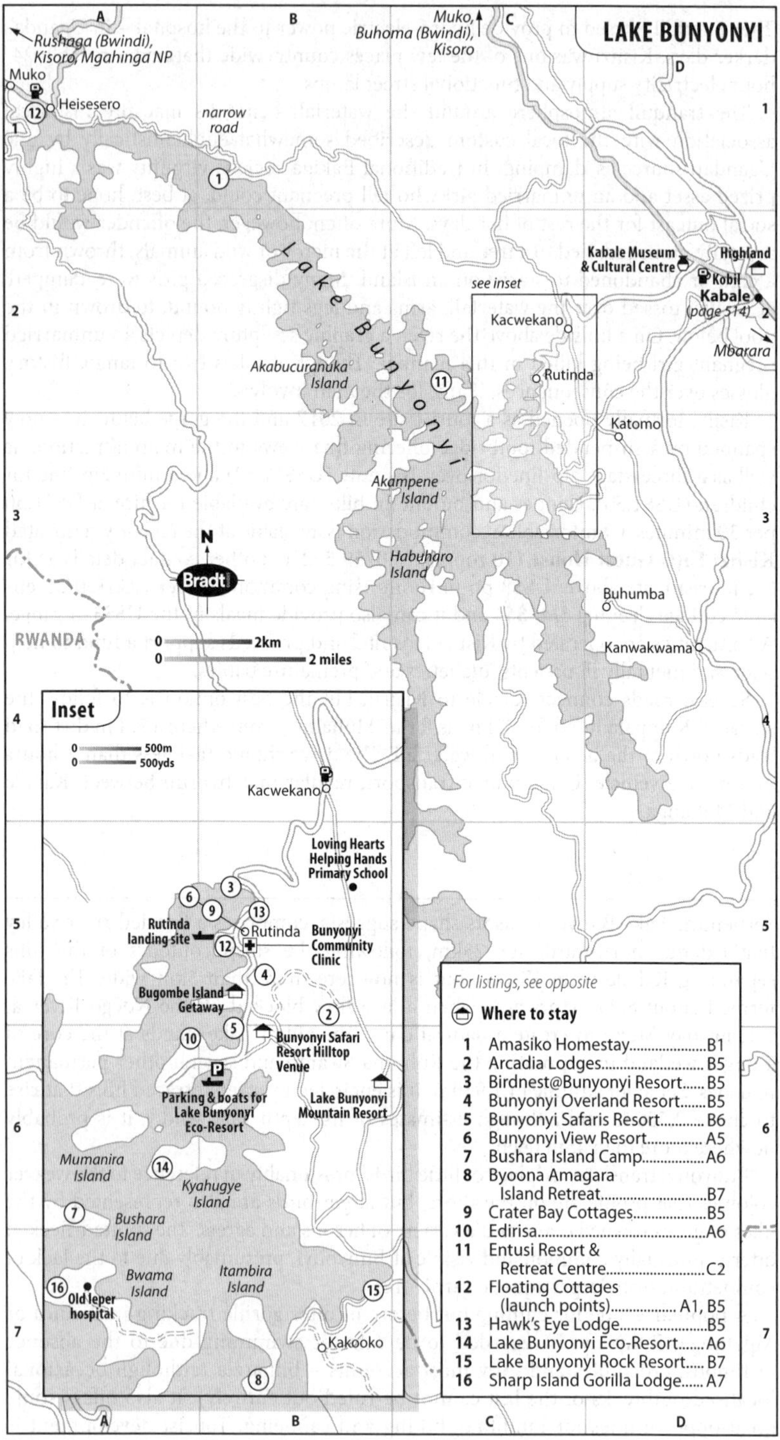

LAKE BUNYONYI
Rushaga (Bwindi), Kisoro, Mgahinga NP
Muko, Buhoma (Bwindi), Kisoro
Muko
Heisesero
narrow road
Lake Bunyonyi
Akabucuranuka Island
Akampene Island
Habuharo Island
see inset
Kacwekano
Rutinda
Katomo
Buhumba
Kanwakwama
Kabale Museum & Cultural Centre
Highland
Kobil
Kabale
(page 514)
Mbarara
RWANDA
Bradt
N
0 2km
0 2 miles
Inset
0 500m
0 500yds
Kacwekano
Loving Hearts Helping Hands Primary School
Rutinda landing site
Rutinda
Bunyonyi Community Clinic
Bugombe Island Getaway
Bunyonyi Safari Resort Hilltop Venue
Parking & boats for Lake Bunyonyi Eco-Resort
Lake Bunyonyi Mountain Resort
Mumanira Island
Kyahugye Island
Bushara Island
Bwama Island
Itambira Island
Old leper hospital
Kakooko
For listings, see opposite
Where to stay
1 Amasiko Homestay.....B1
2 Arcadia Lodges.....B5
3 Birdnest@Bunyonyi Resort.....B5
4 Bunyonyi Overland Resort.....B5
5 Bunyonyi Safaris Resort.....B6
6 Bunyonyi View Resort.....A5
7 Bushara Island Camp.....A6
8 Byoona Amagara Island Retreat.....B7
9 Crater Bay Cottages.....B5
10 Edirisa.....A6
11 Entusi Resort & Retreat Centre.....C2
12 Floating Cottages (launch points).....A1, B5
13 Hawk's Eye Lodge.....B5
14 Lake Bunyonyi Eco-Resort.....A6
15 Lake Bunyonyi Rock Resort.....B7
16 Sharp Island Gorilla Lodge.....A7

focused on Rutinda, a fishing village that stands on a pretty bay halfway along the eastern shore, only 8km from Kabale by road. Close to a dozen different resorts and hotels are clustered in and around Rutinda, whose jetty is also the best place to pick up a boat to the lake's 29 small islands, several of which also support rustic retreats.

GETTING THERE AND AWAY An 8km all-weather dirt road connects Kabale to Rutinda. Self-drivers should follow the Kisoro Road out of town for 1.5km, then turn left at a junction (⊕ -1.24479, 29.97408) signposted for the lakeshore resorts. After 5km, you reach a four-way junction at Kacwekano (⊕ -1.25861, 29.94471) on a summit overlooking Lake Bunyonyi. The track to the left leads to Arcadia Lodge, while the road on the right follows a lovely (but narrow) 20km route along the lakeshore to Muko on the main Kabale–Kisoro Road. Otherwise, keep going straight ahead for the 2km descent to Rutinda.

Regular matatus run between Kabale and Rutinda (30mins), with market days (Monday and Friday) being busiest; otherwise hire a boda or special hire. Alternatively, it's possible to walk from Kabale in around 2 hours. Either follow the road described above, with a slight chance of hitching a lift, or take the quieter and more scenic direct route, which involves following Butambuka Road west out of town then using local footpaths (there are plenty of villagers around to point the way). Either way, the walk out is a delight, passing by traditional homesteads and patches of forest rustling with birdlife, though it does involve a very steep ascent as you approach the summit above the lake. One thing you don't want to do, unless you're supremely fit, is hire a bicycle – you'll spend more time pushing it up steep hills than you will actually cycling.

If you'll be staying on one of the islands, head to Rutinda landing site [518 B5] (⊕ -1.26916, 29.93648), where those without pre-arranged transfers can expect to pay a negotiable fare of US$6–8 per party for a short one-way motorboat transfer, or US$2 per person for a 30 to 45-minute transfer in a dugout canoe. Motorists should find safe overland parking in a compound provided by their intended destination, but failing that they can leave their vehicle at Bunyonyi Overland Resort (page 521) for a small charge.

WHERE TO STAY AND EAT

Rutinda and surrounds

Upmarket

✱ **Arcadia Lodges** [518 B5] (25 cottages) m 0785 623366; e arcadialodgesuganda@gmail.com; w arcadialodges.com. The sensational map-like panorama of Lake Bunyonyi & its myriad islands from this ridge-top lodge must surely appear in some top 50 list of views to see before you die. A stylish new lodge building with external decks complements the view, while the octagonal cottages, complete with domed reed ceiling & thatch roof are very pleasant indeed. Coming from Kabale, turn left at Kacwekano, then continue south for 2km. If a walk along the scenic ridge seems over energetic, quad-bikes can be hired. *US$150/220 sgl/dbl B&B; add US$35 pp FB.* **$$$$**

✱ **Birdnest@Bunyonyi Resort** [518 B5] (25 rooms) m 0754 252560; e reservations@birdnestresort.com; w birdnestatbunyonyi.com. This plush 4-storey hotel, set on a quiet bay 500m north of Rutinda, originally opened in 1965 but stood derelict for decades after its original owner, the Kigezi-born politician Frank Kalimuzo, was abducted & killed by Amin's soldiers in 1972. Still owned by the Kalimuzo family but restored & extended by Belgian investors, it is now the chicest lodge on the shore of Bunyonyi, with a dining room leading out on to a deck offering splendid views over the lake, & spacious rooms whose modernist lines & contemporary country décor – rough wood floor, slate-tiled lake-facing balcony, cheerful fabrics – is complemented by a fabulous cave-like bathroom at the back. There's a swimming pool,

FISHY TALES

According to the late Paul Ngologoza, an eminent Kigezi politician and historian, Lake Bunyonyi harboured 'no fish at all, just *encere*, which are edible frogs' prior to 1919. While this claim seems rather unlikely, several other sources do imply that Bunyonyi naturally harbours very low fish densities. Presumably, this is because the lake slopes underwater too sharply and deeply from the shoreline to provide suitable habitat for shallow-water species such as tilapia and Nile perch, which would have lived in the river before Bunyonyi became a lake.

Whatever the situation before 1919, great efforts were made to stock Lake Bunyonyi during the colonial era. The most valiant of these was initiated in 1927 by District Commissioner Trewin, who arranged for a volume of fish to be relayed manually from Lake Edward to Lake Bunyonyi. 'This was a very involved task,' writes Ngologoza, 'because of the difficulty created by fish dying in transit. Many people [were] divided into groups...The first group brought fish from a place called Katwe...This group raced at great speed to hand over the fish to the second group, who raced to hand over to the third group, and so on, putting in fresh water, pouring out the old water, and finally bringing them to Lake Bunyonyi. It took a day and a night to cover the distance of about 80 miles [120km].'

Initially, the introduced fish flourished, as did commercial fishing, and the rapidly multiplying schools were used to restock several other lakes in the region. Then, in the early 1950s, for reasons that remain unclear, they died out en masse, so that 'one might see the whole lake full of floating bodies of dead fish'. Following this disaster, Ngologoza himself experimented with digging a shallow pool next to the lake and stocking it with 50 fish, which rapidly reproduced, allowing him to distribute 4,500 fish to local fishermen, to be bred in the same way.

The only fish to thrive in the lake today is *Claria mozambicus*, known locally as *evale*, which forms an important component of the local subsistence diet. Bunyonyi is also well known for its small freshwater crayfish, a delicacy served in curries at most of the tourist resorts along the shore.

Quotes extracted from the late Paul Ngologoza's excellent and often amusing introduction to the history and culture of Kigezi entitled Kigezi and its People, *first published in 1967, reprinted by Fountain Publishers in 1998 and still widely available.*

free canoe usage & a cosmopolitan menu of meat-based & vegetarian dishes (mains US$12–15; 3-course set menus US$20). *US$160/190/210 sgl/dbl/trpl B&B.* **$$$**

Moderate

Bunyonyi Safaris Resort [518 B6] (46 units) 041 4547460; m 0772 119852, 0706 485538; e hotel@bunyonyisafaris.com; w bunyonyisafarisresort.com. Set on an isolated stretch of lakeshore about 750m south of Rutinda, this 3-storey hotel has large open-plan public areas with a contemporary African feel, but limited lake views & no outdoor seating. The spacious parquet-floored en-suite rooms in the main building are attractively furnished, but the garden cottages make more of the setting by having private balconies. A restaurant is attached. A touch institutional, & more like a city hotel than a beach resort, but decent value at the asking price. *US$21/40/50/65 pp dorm/room/cottage/suite B&B. Additional meals US$10 each.* **$$**

✷ **Lake Bunyonyi Rock Resort** [518 B7] (14 rooms) m 0702 421519; e engagisafaris@gmail.com. Boasting a wonderfully isolated location on a tranquil papyrus-fringed bay about 6km south of Rutinda, this exceptional new lodge offers the choice of en-suite wood-&-bamboo-roof cottages with king-size bed, fitted net, solar power & glass front leading out to a wide balcony with lake view, or simpler budget rooms using common showers. A good restaurant built around a lakeside rock serves mains in the US$8–10 range. A boda from Rutinda will cost around US$4, while a boat transfer costs US$1.50. *US$100/120 sgl/dbl B&B; US$15/25 sgl/dbl bed-only in budget rooms.* **$$$**

Budget

Bunyonyi Overland Resort [518 B5] (66 rooms, 2 dorms) m 0772 409510, 0784 454991; e info@mbzgroup.africa; w mbzgroup.africa. This vast, long-serving & justifiably popular resort sprawls down a terraced green slope to a lovely papyrus-fringed bay immediately south of Rutinda. Facilities include a sociable open-sided restaurant/bar with pool table, DSTV, well-priced & tasty meals, & private swimming beach. Away from the main camping area are several rows of comfortable en-suite chalets, smaller twin rooms using common showers, & furnished tents. The latest addition is a 2-storey block of superior rooms with private lake-facing balconies. Even though several overland trucks might congregate there on a busy night, it is spacious enough that this won't disturb people staying in rooms. *US$90/100 sgl/dbl superior room; US$60/70 sgl/dbl cottage; US$40/50 sgl/dbl rooms using common showers; US$35/45 sgl/dbl furnished tent; US$20 pp dorm bed; US$12 pp camping. All rates bed only; add US$5 pp b/fast.* **$$**

Bunyonyi View Resort [518 A5] (8 rooms, 1 dorm) m 0772 666331; e bunyonyiviewresort@gmail.com. Situated at the south end of Rutinda on the opposite side of the road to the lake, this has cool, comfortable en-suite rooms with hot shower & balcony with lake views. Fair value. *US$35/40 sgl/dbl; US$80/100 deluxe dbl/family; US$15 pp dorm bed. All rates B&B.* **$–$$**

Crater Bay Cottages [518 B5] (22 units) m 0782 558088, 0772 643996; e craterbaybookings@gmail.com; w craterbaycottageslakebunyonyi.com. Situated within Rutinda, this owner-managed lodge comprises a row of clean & comfortably furnished round cottages with nets & en-suite hot showers, as well as smaller rooms & furnished standing tents using common showers, & space for pitching a tent, all set in compact flowering grounds that drop down to the lake. Friendly, quiet, uncrowded & decent value. *US$55/70/75/120 sgl/twin/dbl/trpl cottage B&B; US$45/60/75 sgl/dbl/trpl room; US$40/55 sgl/dbl tent; US$10 pp camping.* **$$**

Hawk's Eye Lodge [518 B5] (10 rooms) m 0789 573926, 0771 272933; e reservations@hawkseyelodge.co.ug. Reached by a steep road that ascends the hillside immediately above Rutinda village, this attractive lodge enjoys great lake views. Accommodation is in en-suite standing tents set on stilted wooden platforms while an open-sided wooden restaurant serves meals in the US$5–7 range. *US$43/48 sgl/dbl en-suite tent; US$40/43 sgl/dbl in a tent using common showers. All rates B&B.* **$$**

Shoestring

Edirisa [518 A6] (3 rooms, 1 dorm) m 0761 365593; e edirisa@gorillahighlands.com; w edirisa.org. A multi-faceted organisation that works towards peace & prosperity in the region shared between Uganda, Rwanda & the DRC, Edirisa offers an isolated Robinson Crusoe-style camp that sprawls across a wooded peninsula 2km south of Rutinda. Accommodation options comprise a 2-bed family house, a dbl hut & a 4-bed dorm (shared ablutions) and a self-contained family bedsit sleeping 4–5. Edirisa is also a site for volunteering at the adjacent primary school & in award-winning multimedia productions. Activities include free canoeing & swimming in a submerged pool in the lake while a range of excursions further afield are offered. Meals cost US$5–10 with specialities from the firewood oven, as well as crayfish & giant samosas. *Family bedsit US$40; US$20/40 1/both rooms in family hut; US$25 dbl hut; US$10 pp dorm bed; US$7 pp camping in your own tent.* **$–$$**

Island retreats

The accommodation listed here is – with one exception - set on one or other of the lake's 29 islands &, except where otherwise stated, is usually accessed by motorboat or canoe transfer from Rutinda landing site.

Upmarket

✷ **Lake Bunyonyi Eco-Resort** [518 A6] (8 rooms) t 041 4372067; m 0776 280344;

w lakebunyonyiecoresort.com. Set on the elevated west side of wooded Kyahugye Island, this excellent & well-managed retreat offers accommodation in rustically stylish wooden cabins with nets & en-suite bathrooms. In addition to birding & canoe trips, the island is stocked with zebra, waterbuck, kob, & impala translocated from Lake Mburo National Park. It lies 500m south of the same peninsula that houses Edirisa, 2km south of Rutinda, & is usually accessed from a landing & parking site (⊕ -1.27857, 29.93654) on the left side of the road to Edirisa. *US$110/140 sgl/dbl FB.* **$$$**

Sharp Island Gorilla Lodge [518 A7] (4 rooms) m 0783 864900, 0718 864900. This small lodge on Bwama Island accommodates guests in thatched en-suite cabins built on stilted wooden platforms whose decks offer a fine view over the lake. Meals should be ordered well in advance. *US$100/200 sgl/dbl.* **$$$**

Budget

Bushara Island Camp [518 A6] (10 units) m 0772 464585, 0774 499613; e busharaislandcamp@gmail.com; w busharaislandcamp.com. The community resort on the medium-sized island of Bushara, 2.5km southwest of Rutinda by motorboat, comprises a selection of en-suite furnished tents, cottages & elevated wooden 'treehouses'. Accommodation set in secondary vegetation along the island's southern side is preferable to that located within the dark eucalyptus forest in the north. Amenities include a checklist of the 100-plus bird species recorded on the island & free transfers from Rutinda. *From US$35/40 sgl/dbl bed-only or US$60 pp FB; US$10 pp dorm bed; US$6 pp camping.* **$$**

Byoona Amagara Island Retreat [518 B7] (9 units & 2 dorms) m 0752 652788; e bookings@lakebunyonyi.net; w lakebunyonyi.net. This popular & very chilled backpackers' haunt stands on the south side of Itambira Island, 3km south of Rutinda. A range of accommodation is available, the most popular option being the fresh-air 'geodomes' consisting of a round thatched roof & a rear wall over twin or dbl beds (nets provided). *US$70 family cottage (sleeps 5); US$17 pp en-suite wood cabin (sleeps 5); US$14/20 pp basic/luxury geodome; US$11/17/21 sgl/dbl/trpl room; US$4 dorm bed; US$4 camping.* **$$**

✷ **Entusi Resort & Retreat Centre** [518 C2] (15 units) m 0777 660098, 0779 252150; e raymond@globallivingston.org; w entusi.org. This superb budget lodge, affiliated to the Global Livingston Institute, doesn't actually stand on an island, but it feels like it does, & it's most easily reached from Rutinda by a 10min boat ride. The lovely setting at the end of a remote peninsula is complemented by the likeable staff & a varied selection of activities including swimming, birding & boat trips. There's a terraced block of simple but stylish en-suite rooms with private balconies, as well as standing tents & a dorm. *US$20/35/50 pp dorm bed/tent/room B&B. Other meals US$10 apiece.* **$$**

✷ **Floating Cottages** [518 B5] (3 boats) m 0793 930006, 0772 409510; e bcbunyonyi@gmail.com. If an island retreat sounds a little static, give your wanderlust free rein with a houseboat on Lake Bunyonyi. Propelled by a silent, solar-powered engine, you can sleep out on the water where you – & not geography – decide. It'll be a self-catering voyage, enabled by a fully equipped galley on board; alternatively, food can be boated out from Bunyonyi Overland Resort or Birdnest@Bunyonyi by arrangement. Your houseboat can be brought to you at Rutinda or Muko at the northern end of the lake. *US$100.* **$$**

Northern lakeshore

Budget

✷ **Amasiko Homestay** [518 B1] (5 bandas) m 0782 583815, 0704 224184; e info@amasiko.org; w amasiko.org. The only lakeshore facility not accessed via Rutinda, this small Dutch-run enterprise – whose name means 'hope' – is committed to permaculture & other sustainable agricultural practices. Accommodation is in rustic, solar-lit earth-bag or wooden constructions set in a quiet lakeshore compound with communal showers & compost toilets, & rates include simple but tasty local meals eaten communally with other guests & management. Visitors can get involved in the farming project or stick to recreational activities: swimming, boating, a 2½hr hike to the Echuya Forest or a village visit to Hamukaka. Amasiko lies on the back road along the northeast Bunyonyi shore, a 5km drive southeast of Muko & 15km northwest of Kacwekano. Alternatively, a 30min boat transfer along the lake from Rutinda is a fabulous way to get there. An enjoyable, unique & worthy setup, & good value too. *US$20 pp B&B; US$38 pp FB.* **$$**

TOUR OPERATOR

Edirisa m 0761 365593, +250 784 112355 (Rwanda); e tours@gorillahighlands.com; w gorillahighlands.com. Edirisa is the Ugandan arm of Gorilla Highlands, recipients of a global responsible tourism award, specialising in adventure, culture & cuisine in Uganda & Rwanda. Specifically, it runs canoeing, trekking & culinary excursions from a lakeside base 2km from Rutinda [518 A6]. Day trips include the 2hr Bunyonyi Dugout Dining (US$25), which culminates with a crayfish meal in a treehouse; the 5hr Culture on the Crest Tour (US$55) taking in Kyabahinga viewpoint, a craftmaker & a herbalist; & the full-day Islands of Miracles (US$110), which extends the previous visits to 3 islands. Trips include all meals. Multi-day expeditions towards Mgahinga & Bwindi national parks (US$360–490) include tented accommodation at pretty lakeshore & island campsites (upgrades available) & visits to Batwa Pygmy partners.

WHAT TO SEE AND DO Lake Bunyonyi is a great place to chill out, but it also caters well to more active travellers, with canoes, kayaks and mountain bikes available for hire, and enough potential excursions to keep you busy for days. Visits to most of the places of interest described on the following pages can be arranged through any of the lakeshore resorts and hotels, and it's also possible to reach some sites using public transport and/or dugout canoes chartered at a negotiable rate from the landing site at Rutinda.

The lakeshore near Rutinda Rutinda itself [518 B5], though rather small, is considerably enlivened on Mondays and Fridays, when dozens of canoes arrive in the early morning from all around the lake, carrying local farmers and their produce to a colourful market on the main jetty. A pleasant **short stroll** out of town, roughly 1.5km in either direction, leads south past Bunyonyi Safari Resort then to the left and uphill to the same resort's Hilltop Venue [518 B6] (⊕ -1.27625, 29.93988), which is open to the public and offers fabulous views over the lake.

A **longer circuit** entails following the Kabale Road north out of Rutinda, past the smart Birdnest@Bunyonyi Resort, before it begins the steep ascent to the summit above the lake. Just before the climb, the road skirts a patch of papyrus swamp where various colourful bishop- and widow-birds breed, and a few pairs of the peculiar thick-billed weaver construct their distinctive neat nests. From here, more energetic travellers could ascend via a series of switchbacks to the small ridge-top village of Kacwekano. Turn right here, and after about 2km you'll reach Arcadia Lodge, with its stunning view over the lake and islands. Using local footpaths, it's possible to descend directly from Arcadia to the lakeshore about 1km south of Rutinda, but the paths are very steep and probably best avoided after rain.

For those with private transport, a lovely **drive** out of Rutinda runs north from the five-way junction at Kacwekano along a 20km back road that offers some fantastic views over the northern part of the lake before connecting with the surfaced main road between Kabale and Kisoro at Muko.

The islands Several of the 20-plus islands on Bunyonyi are worth a visit, with the most accessible being the half-dozen or so situated in the central part of the lake close to Rutinda. Aside from Bushara Island, which uses its own motorboat for transfers, the best way to reach most of the islands is by dugout canoe. This is easily arranged through any lakeshore lodge or with local fishermen at Rutinda landing site. Rates are negotiable but expect to pay around US$25–30 per person for a trip taking in up to three islands.

Bwama Island [518 A7] The largest island on Lake Bunyonyi is the site of a well-known mission, school and handicraft centre for people with disabilities. Most of the buildings on Bwama date to 1929, when Leonard Sharp, a British doctor with several years' medical experience in southwest Uganda, established a leper colony on the island. Leprosy was a serious problem in Kigezi at that time, and for longer than three decades the island provided refuge for up to 100 victims of the disease. Leprosy was eradicated from Kigezi in the 1960s and the colony ceased operating in 1969. Also known as Njuyera or Sharp's Island, it remains of interest for its scenery, architecture and handicraft shop.

Bushara Island [518 A6] Immediately north of Bwama, Bushara is well developed for tourism, and although the accommodation is highly recommended, day trips are also encouraged. The ideal would be to go to the island for a lingering lunch, then either arrange to take a dugout canoe around its circumference or else to walk the self-guided trail along the shore – both options cost day visitors US$2–3.

Akampene Island [518 C3] Shaded by a solitary tree, the tiny 'Island of Punishment' is visible both from the north shore of Bwama and the east shore of Bushara. Like Kisiizi Falls, this island is traditionally associated with the Bakiga taboo against pre-marital sex. In times gone by, unmarried girls who became pregnant would be exiled to Akampene, where they faced one of two possible fates. Any man who did not own sufficient cows to pay for an untainted bride was permitted to fetch the disgraced girl from the island and make her his wife. Failing that, the girl would usually starve to death.

Akabucuranuka Island A rather fanciful legend is attached to this island, whose name literally means 'upside down'. Many years ago, it is said, a group of male revellers on Akabucuranuka refused to share their abundant stock of beer with an old lady who had disembarked from her canoe to join them. Unfortunately for the drinking party, the woman was a sorceress. She returned to her canoe, paddled a safe distance away, and then used her magical powers to overturn the island – drowning everybody in the party – and then flip it back the right way up as if nothing had happened.

Kyahugye Island [518 A6] This medium-sized island only 500m from the mainland is the site of Lake Bunyonyi Eco-Resort (page 521), and day visitors are charged an entrance fee of US$3 to wander around in the company of its introduced populations of zebra, impala, waterbuck and kob antelope. A solitary De Brazza's monkey of unknown provenance also inhabits the island.

Muko and the Ruhuma Swamp The small trading centre of Muko [518 A1], situated 45km from Kabale along the main road to Kisoro, is where the Ndego River flows out of Bunyonyi's northern tip to form the vast Ruhuma (or Kigeyu) Swamp, which meanders river-like north and then west to skirt Bwindi Impenetrable National Park before entering Lake Mutanda, and forms one of the best places in Uganda to see the likes of papyrus gonolek and papyrus yellow warbler. A good access point to the swamp is a rough motorable track that leads north from the tar road to Kabale about 10km northeast of Muko. Fred Hodgson, who visited the area in 2015, recorded 'white-winged warbler, fan-tailed widowbird and papyrus canary as well as two mysterious weaver species that are currently before the East African Rarities Committee'.

Any vehicle heading along the main road between Kabale and Kisoro can drop you at Muko, and one elevated stretch of this road also affords good views over the swamps. Self-drivers could also follow the 20km back road between Rutinda and Muko via Kacwekano and Hamukaka. Bushara Island Camp (page 522) charges US$25 for a motorboat to Muko, or you could charter a dugout canoe from Rutinda for a few dollars less.

Batwa Pygmy cultural visits Kigezi once supported a large population of Batwa, ancient Pygmoid hunter-gatherers (page 539) who have been evacuated from traditional forest haunts such as Mgahinga Gorilla and Bwindi Impenetrable national parks in modern times. Batwa visits on the shores of Bunyonyi tend to be a sad affair supporting community degradation through alcohol. A respectable alternative in the vicinity of the lake is the community experience by Edirisa (page 523) which involves a Batwa group on the outskirts of Echuya Forest Reserve (w gorillahighlands.com/batwa-today). It costs US$80 per person and ensures that the community benefits appropriately.

MGAHINGA AND THE VIRUNGA FOOTHILLS

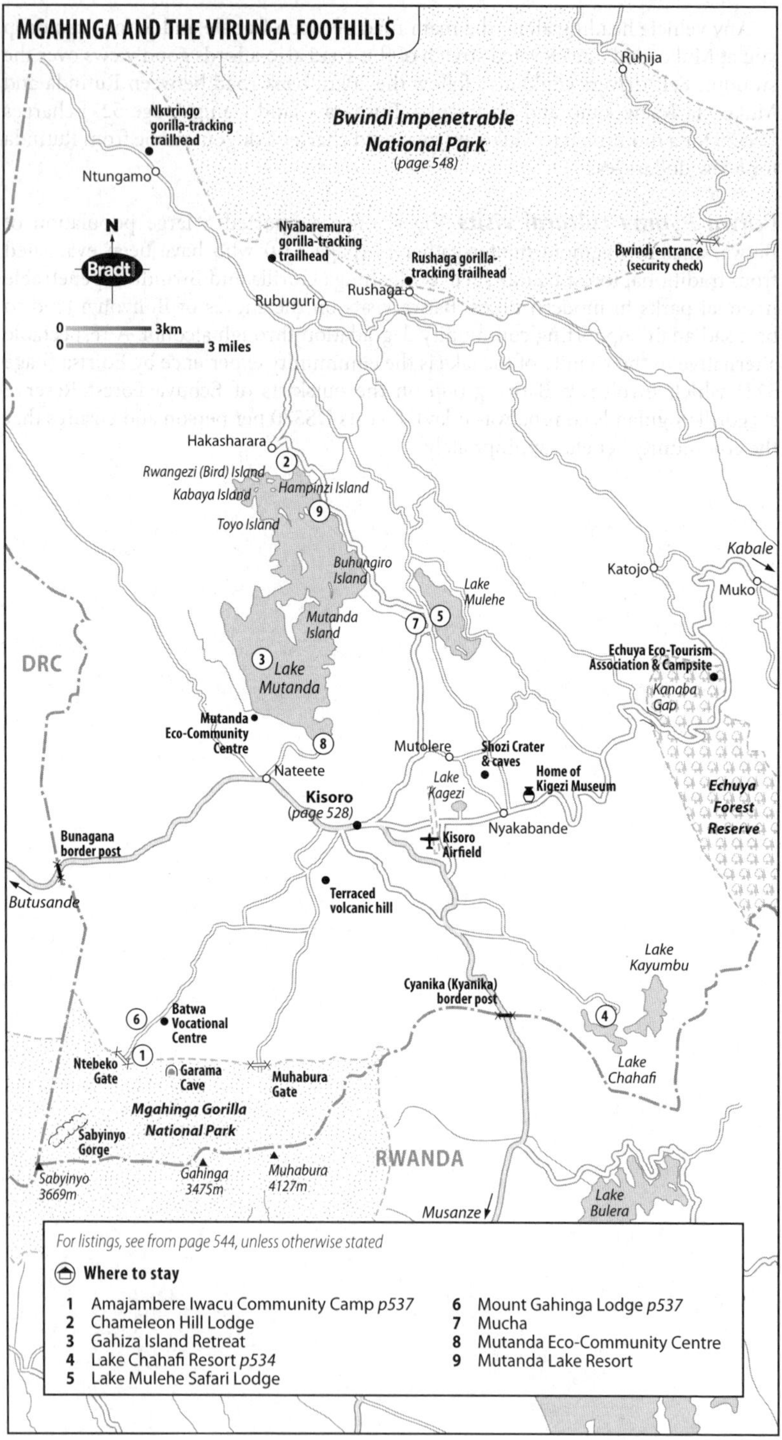

For listings, see from page 544, unless otherwise stated

Where to stay

1 Amajambere Iwacu Community Camp *p537*
2 Chameleon Hill Lodge
3 Gahiza Island Retreat
4 Lake Chahafi Resort *p534*
5 Lake Mulehe Safari Lodge
6 Mount Gahinga Lodge *p537*
7 Mucha
8 Mutanda Eco-Community Centre
9 Mutanda Lake Resort

20

Mgahinga and the Virunga Foothills

The most southwesterly corner of Uganda is also one of the most scenic, a landscape of rolling green hills whose preposterously fertile soils are a product of their location at the base of the majestic chain of forest-swathed volcanoes known as the Virungas. Home to more than half the world's remaining mountain gorillas, the Virungas run along the border of Uganda, Rwanda and the DRC, all of which have set aside their portion of the volcanic range as a national park. The Ugandan component in this cross-border protected area is Mgahinga Gorilla National Park, which tends to be overlooked as a gorilla-tracking venue (understandably, given that it hosts just one habituated group by comparison with Bwindi's tally of 25), but it also offers a range of other worthwhile activities, notably golden monkey tracking in the bamboo zone, and the challenging hikes to its trio of volcanic peaks. Other important regional tourist focal points are Kisoro, the district capital and main road gateway to Mgahinga, and scenic Lake Mutanda, which forms a popular and increasingly well-developed base for gorilla tracking in southern Bwindi and Mgahinga. Minor attractions include Lake Chahafi and the Echuya Forest Reserve.

KISORO

Set at an altitude of 1,900m within 10km of the Rwandan and Congolese borders, Kisoro is an inherently unremarkable small town with an utterly stupendous setting in an area of rolling green hills at the base of the Virunga volcanoes. A few years back, Kisoro came across as a scruffy and amorphous backwater, set on something of a limb in terms of Kigezi's main tourist circuit, and even today it is only one-third the size of Kabale, with a population estimated at 18,000. But Kisoro of late has acquired an altogether more modern and economically vibrant feel, as reflected in its relatively new sealed main road and freshly painted shopfronts, and an overdue upgrade to municipal status in 2015. It has also taken over from Kabale as Kigezi's busiest urban tourist hub, partly as a result of improved access following the surfacing of the main road to Kampala, but also thanks to the opening of gorilla-tracking trailheads at Nkuringo and Rushaga in southern Bwindi, and of several lodges on nearby Lake Mutanda. Kisoro's most striking feature, at least in clear weather, is its stupendous Virunga backdrop, in particular the 4,127m peak of Muhabura, which stands only 10km to the south. The town is a potential base for gorilla tracking not only in southern Bwindi, but also in Mgahinga Gorilla National Park or across the border in Rwanda's Volcanoes National Park and the Congolese Virunga National Park, both of which are accorded full chapters in the companion Bradt guide to Rwanda.

GETTING THERE AND AWAY Kisoro and Kabale are connected by a very scenic 75km surfaced road through Hamurwa, Muko and the Echuya Forest Reserve.

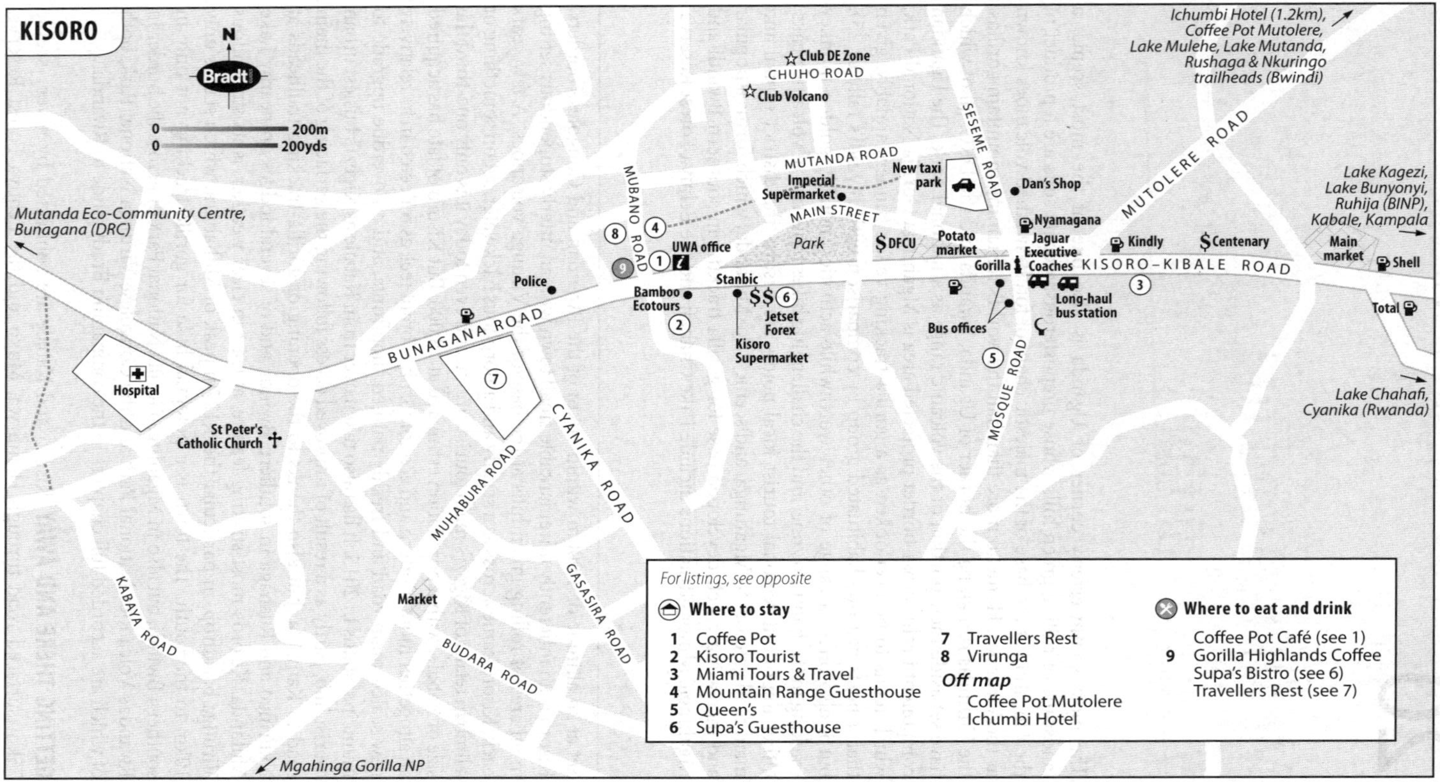
KISORO
N
Bradt
0 200m
0 200yds
Club DE Zone
CHUHO ROAD
Club Volcano
MUTANDA ROAD
New taxi park
Imperial Supermarket
SESEME ROAD
Dan's Shop
MUTOLERE ROAD
Ichumbi Hotel (1.2km), Coffee Pot Mutolere, Lake Mulehe, Lake Mutanda, Rushaga & Nkuringo trailheads (Bwindi)
Lake Kagezi, Lake Bunyonyi, Ruhija (BINP), Kabale, Kampala
Mutanda Eco-Community Centre, Bunagana (DRC)
MUBANO ROAD
MAIN STREET
Park
DFCU
Potato market
Nyamagana
Jaguar Executive Coaches
Kindly
Centenary
Main market
Shell
UWA office
Gorilla
KISORO–KIBALE ROAD
Police
Stanbic
Bamboo Ecotours
Jetset Forex
Kisoro Supermarket
Bus offices
Long-haul bus station
Total
BUNAGANA ROAD
Hospital
St Peter's Catholic Church
CYANIKA ROAD
MOSQUE ROAD
Lake Chahafi, Cyanika (Rwanda)
MUHABURA ROAD
GASASIRA ROAD
KABAYA ROAD
Market
BUDARA ROAD
Mgahinga Gorilla NP
For listings, see opposite
Where to stay
1 Coffee Pot
2 Kisoro Tourist
3 Miami Tours & Travel
4 Mountain Range Guesthouse
5 Queen's
6 Supa's Guesthouse
7 Travellers Rest
8 Virunga
Off map
Coffee Pot Mutolere
Ichumbi Hotel
Where to eat and drink
Coffee Pot Café (see 1)
9 Gorilla Highlands Coffee
Supa's Bistro (see 6)
Travellers Rest (see 7)

Crossing through Echuya, do stop at the lofty Kanaba Gap, where on a clear day you'll see all the Virunga volcanoes laid out in front of you, from Muhabura in the east to the tempestuous Congolese twins Nyiragongo and Nyamuragira in the west. The drive takes up to 90 minutes, or 2 hours allowing for a few scenic stops. About 10km shorter, but no quicker unless you are coming from Rutinda as opposed to Kabale, is the back road between Kabale and Muko via Kacwekano and the northeast shore of Lake Bunyonyi. Coming from Kampala, the main road, which previously crossed the airfield, now curves south around it to join the Kisoro–Cyanika (Rwanda) Road. Turn right for Kisoro. If headed out of Kisoro for Kabale, turn right on to the Cyanika Road at the Shell/Total junction; otherwise you'll fetch up at a dead end at the airfield.

Several **buses** run daily between Kampala and Kisoro (10hrs). The priciest and most upmarket service is the overnight Trinity Coaches service (m 0772 422451), which charges US$20 for a wide and comfortable reclining seat. Best of the rest is the significantly cheaper Jaguar Executive Coaches (m 0782 811128 (Kampala), 0777 763491 (Kisoro); around US$13), which operates two buses in either direction daily, leaving Kampala from its terminal on Namirembe Road. A more conservative choice is the Post Bus, should it revive, though with numerous stops along the way, it is far from being the fastest. More locally, **matatus** between Kabale and Kisoro (90mins) run back and forth throughout the day. Bodas are available for those continuing to the Rwandan border at Cyanika (aka Kyanika) or Congolese border at Bunagana.

By air The nearby border crossing at Cyanika is only 3 hours by road from the Rwandan capital Kigali, meaning that catching an international flight to Kigali to visit Kisoro (unlikely as a standalone activity) or track gorillas in nearby Bwindi or Mgahinga Gorilla national parks is perfectly feasible. Alternatively, Aerolink flies daily to/from Kisoro Airfield from Entebbe Airport (031 7333000; e info@aerolinkuganda.com; w aerolinkuganda.com). Return flights cost US$475 plus U$20 taxes. Kisoro is an interesting airfield – during the course of the day, winds blowing down from the nearby volcanoes increase in strength, making afternoon landings and departures lively propositions. This has two consequences for air travellers: firstly, that all flights must leave Kisoro before noon, and secondly, a US$70 per person surcharge is levied to cover costs in case the weather builds up early and flights must divert to Kihihi on the far side of Bwindi.

WHERE TO STAY *Map, opposite*

Kisoro is well supplied with budget hotels, though they tend to be costlier than in other similarly sized Ugandan towns. Upmarket options listed are upmarket in the context of Kisoro. Superior options are available at Mgahinga Gorilla National Park's Ntebeko Gate and around Lake Mutanda. Use water sparingly as Kisoro suffers from a chronic shortage due to the porous nature of the underlying volcanic rock.

Upmarket

Coffee Pot Hotel (8 rooms) m 0772 625493, 0772 704131; e info@coffee-pot-cafe.com; w coffee-pot-cafe.com. With a central location right next to the eponymous café, this brand new hotel includes a wellness centre with sauna (free to guests); just what you'll need after climbing Mt Muhuvura! Guests enjoy a free transfer to the hotel from the Rwanda border or the airstrip. *US$45–60/95 sgl/dbl B&B.* **$$**

✱ **Ichumbi Hotel** (8 rooms & more under construction) ⊕ 1.2326395, 29.7200842; m 0709 000028, 0788 118233; e reservations@ichumbigorillalodge.com; w ichumbigorillalodge.com. Kisoro's newest & smartest offering lies 1.2km out of town on the Rushaga/Nkuringo Rd.

THE VIRUNGAS

Straddling the borders of Uganda, Rwanda and the DRC, the Virungas are not a mountain range as such, but a chain of isolated free-standing volcanic cones strung along a fault line associated with the same geological process that formed the Rift Valley. Sometimes also referred to as the Birunga or Bufumbira Mountains, the chain comprises six inactive and two active volcanoes, all of which exceed 3,000m in altitude – the tallest being Karisimbi (4,507m), Mikeno (4,437m) and Muhabura (also known as Muhavura, 4,127m). Three of the eight mountains lie partially within Uganda: Muhabura and Gahinga (3,475m) straddle the Rwandan border, while Sabyinyo (3,669m) stands at the junction of the three national borders.

The names of the individual mountains in the Virunga chain reflect local perceptions. Sabyinyo translates as 'old man's teeth' in reference to the jagged rim of what is probably the most ancient and weathered of the eight volcanoes. The lofty Muhabura is 'the guide', and anecdotes collected by the first Europeans to visit the area suggest that its perfect cone, topped today by a small crater lake, still glowed at night as recently as the early 19th century. The stumpier Gahinga translates as 'small pile of stones', a name that becomes clear when you see local people tidying the rocks that clutter their fields into heaps named *gahingas*. Of the volcanoes that lie outside Uganda, Karisimbi – which occasionally sports a small cap of snow – is named for the colour of a cowrie shell, while Bisoke simply means 'watering hole', in reference to the crater lake near its peak.

The vegetation zones of the Virungas correspond closely with those of other large East African mountains, albeit that much of the Afro-montane forest below the 2,500m contour has been sacrificed to cultivation. Between 2,500m and 3,500m, where an average annual rainfall of 2,000mm is typical, bamboo forest is interspersed with stands of tall *hagenia* woodland. At higher altitudes, the cover of Afro-alpine moorland, grassland and marsh is studded with giant lobelia and other outsized plants similar to those found on Kilimanjaro and the Rwenzori.

The most famous denizen of the Virungas is the mountain gorilla, which inhabits the forested slopes of all six of the inactive volcanoes, but not – for obvious reasons – the denuded slopes of their more temperamental kin. The Virungas also form the main stronghold for the endangered golden monkey and support relic populations of elephant and buffalo along with typical highland forest species such as yellow-backed duiker and giant forest hog. The mountains' avifauna is comparatively poorly known, but some 150 species are recorded, including about 20 Albertine Rift Endemics.

Still in their geological infancy, none of the present Virunga Mountains is more than 2 million years old, and two of the cones remain highly active. However, eruptions of earlier Virunga volcanoes 10 to 12 million years ago marked the start of the tectonic processes that have formed the western Rift Valley. The most dramatic volcanic explosion in recorded history was the 1977 eruption of

The smart, modern rooms are easily the best in town, & to cap it all there's a swimming pool too – Kisoro's first! A tempting money saver for your gorilla safari if you're prepared to drive up to your trailhead on the morning of tracking. *US$90/130 sgl/dbl. Add US$20 pp FB.* **$$$**

✷ **Travellers Rest Hotel** (11 rooms) m 0777 820071, 0701 453031; e reservations@gorillatours.com. Built by pioneering gorilla enthusiast Walter Baumgärtel back in the 1950s, Kisoro's oldest – & favourite – hotel hosted such eminent personages as George Schaller & Dian

the 3,470m Mount Nyiragongo in the DRC, about 20km north of the Lake Kivu port of Goma. During this eruption, a lava lake that had formed in the volcano's main crater back in 1894 drained in less than an hour, emitting streams of molten lava that flowed at a rate of up to 60km/h, killing an estimated 2,000 people and terminating only 500m from Goma Airport.

In 1994, a new lake of lava started to accumulate within the main crater of Nyiragongo, leading to another highly destructive eruption on 17 January 2002. Lava flowed down the southern and eastern flanks of the volcano into Goma itself, killing at least 50 people. Goma was evacuated, and an estimated 450,000 people crossed into the nearby Rwandan towns of Rubavu (Gisenyi) and Musanze (Ruhengeri) for temporary refuge. Three days later, when the first evacuees returned, it transpired that about a quarter of the town – including large parts of the commercial and residential centre – had been engulfed by the lava, leaving 12,000 families homeless. The 50m-diamater lava lake in the crater of Nyiragongo remains active, and although there has been no major eruption since 2002, a minor one did occur in 2011.

Only 15km northwest of Nyiragongo stands the 3,058m Mount Nyamuragira, which also erupted in January 2002. Nyamuragira is probably the most active volcano on the African mainland, with 34 eruptions recorded since 1882, though only the 1912–13 incident resulted in any fatalities. Nyamuragira most recently blew its top on 7 November 2011, emitting a 400m-high column of lava – its largest eruption in 100 years – that destroyed large tracts of cultivated land and forest. In mid 2014, a new lava lake appeared in Nyamuragira for the first time since the last one was emptied in a 1938 eruption. Thought to be 500m deep and still growing, the lake has caused locally based volcanologists to study the possibility of evacuating Goma once again.

It is perhaps worth noting that these temperamental Congolese volcanoes pose no threat to visitors to Uganda. The three cones shared by Uganda are all long inactive – indeed, while plumes from the Congolese volcanoes might well be seen around Kisoro at night, no active lava flow has touched Ugandan soil in recorded history. That might change one day: there is a tradition among the Bafumbira people of the Ugandan Virungas that the fiery spirits inhabiting the crater of Nyamuragira will eventually relocate to Muhabura, reducing both the mountain and its surrounds to ash.

Another Bafumbira custom has it that the crater lake atop Mount Muhabura is inhabited by a powerful snake spirit called Indyoka, which only needs to raise its head to bring rain to the surrounding countryside. It is said that Indyoka lives on a bed of gold and protects various other artefacts made of precious metal, and that it can extend itself as far as Lake Mutanda to a lakeshore sacrificial shrine at Mushungero. An indication of its presence at the lake and associated shrine is the inundation of the seasonal Gitundwe Swamp near Lake Mutanda.

Fossey before being nationalised by Idi Amin in the 1970s & falling apart in the '80s. Restored in the '90s, & once again under private management, it is still rich in period character, the hotel & L-shaped accommodation block surrounding a well-tended garden which, shaded by indigenous trees, offers great in-house birding. The rooms are on the small side, but lounge chairs are provided outside under a communal veranda facing the lovely garden – though with rooms & windows opening directly on to this throughfare, the rooms are slightly lacking in privacy. The hotel is located at the turn-off to Mgahinga Gorilla National Park. Meals, taken indoors or on the courtyard terrace, cost around US$8. Good value. *US$90/115 sgl/dbl B&B.* **$$$**

Budget

Coffee Pot Mutolere (8 rooms) ⊕ 1.2634664, 29.7187575; m 0777 010997; w coffee-pot-cafe.com. Out of town next to Mutolere Hospital, this attractive guesthouse is set in a delightful flowering garden, while the attached café is an extension of the excellent & eponymous Kisoro diner. Head up the Bwindi Rd for 5km then turn right, then follow the signs from the hospital roundabout. *US$30 pp B&B.* **$$**

Kisoro Tourist Hotel (16 rooms) m 0772 483136; e kisorotouristhotel@gmail.com. Once the automatic mid-range choice if funds didn't stretch to Travellers Rest, this centrally located 2-storey block has now seen better days. Having drastically reduced its rates, it is fair value in its new category. *US$18/26 sgl/dbl B&B.* **$$$**

Mountain Range Guesthouse (7 rooms) m 0786 751921. This previously overlooked hotel is a convenient Plan B if next-door Golden Monkey, a long-time backpacker favourite, insists on US$26/52 sgl/dbl B&B for identical rooms. There's no restaurant but the Coffee Pot diner is just around the corner. *US$16/18 sgl/dbl exc b/fast.* **$$**

Queen's Hotel (28 rooms) m 0756 565665; e bamkisoro@gmail.com. Conveniently located for early morning buses, services at this 3-storey hotel include a wake-up call, courtesy of the mosque across the road. Secure compound parking. *US$16 sgl/dbl exc b/fast.* **$$**

Supa's Guesthouse (9 rooms) m 0784 478605; e supasbistro@gmail.com. Located in a courtyard behind the popular Supa's Bistro, the neat rooms at this owner-managed high-street guesthouse come with nets & en-suite hot shower. *US$15/20 sgl/dbl plus US$3 pp b/fast.* **$$**

Virunga Hotel (30 rooms) m 0778 360820. The current favourite with the NGO crowd, this long-established budget hotel offers smart rooms in a new, storeyed block & cheaper & more basic rooms with ¾ bed in the original hotel. *US$50 dbl B&B in new block; US$20/25 dbl/twin B&B in old block; US$5 dorm bed; US$7 pp camping.* **$$**

Shoestring

Miami Tours & Travel (8 rooms) m 0786 823208. A minute's walk from the bus park, this above par shoestring lodge offers en-suite rooms with nets. The restaurant at the front is notable for a popular US$5 lunchtime buffet. *US$8 sgl/dbl exc b/fast.* **$**

WHERE TO EAT AND DRINK *Map, page 528*

For a break from urban settings, the pick in terms of aesthetics is undoubtedly the garden terrace at the **Travellers Rest Hotel**, whose continental-style mains are very reasonably priced at around US$8. In pure culinary terms, however, the more central restaurants listed here are more interesting. If you're looking to stay up late, **Club Volcano** and **Club DE Zone** can both get lively at night.

Coffee Pot Café m 0772 625493; w coffee-pot-cafe.com; ⌚ 08.30–22.00 Mon–Sat. Conspicuously located on a corner plot at the western end of the town centre – the junction is marked by an impressive tree that surely predates the town – Kisoro's most perennially popular country-style eatery serves everything from vegetable curry or chilli con carne to pizzas or fish & chips. There's also delicious coffee & juice, wonderful cakes, packed lunches for hikers at US$5 & a well-stocked craft shop. The menu is duplicated at the out-of-town Coffee Pot Mutolere (see above). *B/fast US$4, mains around US$5–8.*

Gorilla Highlands Coffee m 0786 224527. A little beyond the Coffee Pot, this attractive-looking café stands out from adjacent businesses of more 'local' character. A range of burgers & sandwiches is offered & locally produced coffee is also available. *US$4–7.*

Supa's Bistro m 0784 478605. Attached to the eponymous guesthouse, this high-street bistro opposite the central park has indoor & pavement seating & a tempting menu of light meals, burgers & sandwiches. Freshly brewed coffee & juices are available, too. *Meals in the US$4–7 range.*

KYANINGALODGE
info@kyaningalodge.com || +256 772 999750 || www.kyaningalodge.com

MUTANDA
LAKE RESORT
www.mutandalakeresort.com - info@mutandalakeresort.com

Manya Africa
Experiencing Is Better Than Being Told
Your sustainable Tour operator in Uganda and Rwanda.
Gorilla tracking, Tailor made and small group safaris.
Highly trained guides in your language.
Modern fleet of Landcruisers.
info@manyaafricatours.com
www.manyaafricatours.com
: +256 775 554 791

SHOPPING Despite its new-found commercial vigour, Kisoro remains short on supermarkets. Try **Kisoro Supermarket** on the main road facing the park, **Imperial Supermarket** on the road behind it, and **Dan's Shop** on nearby Seseme Road. The main market – busiest on Mondays and Thursdays – is a short distance along the Kabale Road, roughly opposite the junction for the Cyanika border post. For crafts, a good selection is on sale at the Coffee Pot Café (see opposite), while a wide selection of 'antique' Congolese carvings and masks decorate the foyer of the Travellers Rest Hotel.

TOURIST INFORMATION, OPERATORS AND GUIDES If you need a guide, ask for a recommendation at your hotel or the Coffee Pot Café rather than engaging a self-styled tourist guide off the street (and be warned that the UWA office will often suggest the same chaps who accost travellers in the street).

Bamboo Ecotours m 0779 499670, 0789 862680; e info@bambooecotours.com; w bambooecotours.com. Gorilla tracking, golden-monkey tracking & volcano hikes in Mgahinga & neighbouring parts of Rwanda & the DRC.

Experience Kigezi m 0783 782082, 0701 126050; w experiencekigezi.wordpress.com. This social enterprise shares premises with Gorilla Highlands Coffee (near the Coffee Pot Café) & offers a variety of guided 2–4hr tours out of Kisoro (around US$8–20 pp), as well as mountain-bike trips for US$35 & kayaking at US$15/hr.

Nkuringo Walking Safaris 039 2176327; m 0774 805580; e info@nkuringowalkingsafaris.com; w nkuringowalkingsafaris.com. With bases in Kampala & Nkuringo (Bwindi), this excellent operator specialises in hikes in the Kisoro area, ranging from a couple of hours to 5 days in duration. It offers volcano climbs in Mgahinga Gorilla National Park & a 2-day overnight hike from Kisoro to Nkuringo via Lake Mutanda, with a possible day extension through Bwindi to Buhoma.

Uganda Wildlife Authority Office 08.00–18.00 daily. Situated at the west end of the town centre, 100m before the turning to Mgahinga Gorilla National Park, the helpful UWA office provides information about Mgahinga & southern Bwindi, as well as other tourist attractions in the region. Fees for golden monkey tracking & mountain climbing can also be paid here, & staff will assist with booking gorilla permits subject to the various complications described on page 560. Even if you've pre-bought gorilla-tracking permits for Mgahinga, you should pop in here the day before to check which of the 2 trailheads will be used.

WHAT TO SEE AND DO Kisoro is the main springboard for gorilla tracking and other hikes in Mgahinga Gorilla National Park, while the surrounding hills host several pretty lakes, of which the largest and best-developed for tourism is Mutanda, whose southernmost shore is only 5km from the town centre. Kisoro also lies within striking distance of the two southern gorilla-tracking trailheads detailed in the chapter on Bwindi Impenetrable National Park.

Around town There's not much to see in the town centre. The small central park serves as a roost for large numbers of black-headed and other herons, while the central 'Irish potato' market, where the region's main crop is sold to traders from Kampala and elsewhere, can be a hive of economic activity in season. Also of interest is the enormous Monday and Thursday market out along the Kabale Road. For a more rigorous leg stretch, try hiking up the insular and distinctively terraced volcanic hill that lies about 1.5km south of Kisoro overlooking the right side of the road to Mgahinga Gorilla National Park. A small but perfectly formed dry crater lies within the rim, which also offers terrific views of the surrounding region.

Lake Kagezi Kigezi subregion is named after Uganda's most southwesterly colonial-era district, whose name is in turn bastardised from that of the region's first

British government station, established by Captain Coote in 1910. The site chosen by Coote stood next to a lake called Kagezi, and though the station was abandoned two years later in favour of Ikumba (on the Kabale Road near the junction to Ruhija), the name endured. The site of Coote's short-lived station is easily reached along a rough 800m track that leads north from the Kabale Road alongside a conspicuous church 1km east of Kisoro Airstrip. The lake itself, rather disappointingly, is little more than a grassy seasonal swamp set in what appears to be an old volcanic caldera. No trace of any former government building remains.

Lake Chahafi This small lake, 12km southeast of Kisoro, lies in a wedge of Ugandan land surrounded by Rwandan territory to the southeast and southwest. Fringed with papyrus and covered in water lilies, it's a pretty spot, particularly on clear days with Muhabura towering above the western horizon, and it supports plenty of otters and birds. The setting wasn't always so tranquil. On 1 January 1915, German forces attacked an Anglo-Belgian outpost positioned on nearby Murora Hill, where some remnants of trenches remain. Then a few days later, according to an account in the *Uganda Journal*, '1,500 natives attacked the base in a fighting that took 6 hours, claiming that they had come to pay taxes but armed with spears.' A 10-minute walk east from Chahafi leads to the slightly larger Lake Kayumbu.

Getting there and away To get to Lake Chahafi from Kisoro, follow the surfaced Kabale Road east out of town for 500m, then turn right on to the signposted Cyanika Road and follow it for 4km to a signposted junction to the left (⊕ -1.305, 29.72468). From here it is about 8km along a maze of dirt roads to the lakeside resort.

Where to stay and eat *Map, page 526*

Lake Chahafi Resort (8 cottages) m 0772 131533, 0782 754496; e reservations@lakechahafiresort.com; w lakechahafiresort.com. This pretty lakeshore resort has recently upgraded from simple standing tents to 'tented cabins with rock finish,' a move accompanied by a remarkable hike in rates. Facilities include a swimming pier, a boat for birding trips & a restaurant/bar. After 4 years of stocking, fishing for mirror carp is set to be introduced in mid 2025. **$$$$$**

Shozi Crater and caves Shozi Crater, reaching an altitude of 2,000m, is a relic of the volcanic activity that shaped this mountainous corner of Uganda. Close by is a 400m-long cave, formed by a petrified lava flow, which houses a colony of thousands upon thousands of bats. The crater and cave are located near the trading centre of Mutolere (⊕ -1.26312, 29.72249), off the road to Mutanda about 5km northeast of Kisoro.

Home of Kigezi Museum (⊕ 1.2756756, 29.7481445; m 0702 874427; e home.kigezi@gmail.com) Advertised by a prominent signboard at the western end of Kisoro's central park, this facility is a couple of kilometres beyond the airstrip on the Kabale Road. Inside you'll find a quirky but insightful array of cultural and historical artefacts plus a permaculture garden showcasing a range of traditionally useful plants. A tour costs US$15 per person, including a local meal. Gerald, the owner-curator, can arrange a number of interesting tours in the vicinity. Advance booking is essential.

Echuya Forest Reserve Extending over 34km^2 of hilly terrain between Lake Bunyonyi and Kisoro, Echuya Forest Reserve is one of Uganda's least-visited and most under-researched protected areas, yet it still ranks among the top six sites in the country in terms of forest biodiversity. With an altitude span of 2,200m to 2,600m, the reserve protects a range of montane habitats including evergreen forest dominated by *Macaranga kilimandscharica* and *Hagenia abyssinica* trees, and dense bamboo forest. The forested slopes of Echuya also enclose the 7km-long Muchuya Swamp, which is one of the most extensive perennial high-altitude wetlands in East Africa, and harbours the largest-known population of the globally endangered Grauer's swamp warbler. Little information is available about the reserve's non-avian fauna, but it is likely to be similar to the forest belt of nearby Mgahinga Gorilla National Park and includes at least four small mammal species endemic to the Albertine Rift. Until recent times, Echuya was permanently inhabited by Batwa Pygmies (page 540). Several Pygmy communities living on the verge of the forest still derive their livelihood from bamboo and other resources extracted from within the reserve.

Echuya's bird checklist of 150-plus species includes 18 Albertine Rift Endemics (for a full list, see page 52), and it is the only locality outside the national park system where a comparable selection of these sought-after specialities is resident. The easiest and cheapest way to explore the reserve under your own steam is along the 5km of the main Kisoro–Kabale Road that passes through it. This was easier, or at least a lot more peaceful, before the road was surfaced, but the wide verge means it is not unsafe, and the birding is excellent. Among the commoner birds noted by Fred Hodgson, who explored the area extensively in 2015, were the following: regal sunbird, strange weaver, white-starred robin, mountain masked apalis, long-tailed barred cuckoo, Shelley's greenbul, chestnut-throated apalis, Rwenzori batis and red-throated alethe. Fred also notes that African black duck and cinnamon bracken-warbler were seen at the swampy area where a stream crosses under the road in the summit area at Kanaba Gap.

Formed c2010 with the support of Nature Uganda, the **Echuya Eco-Tourism Association** (☎ 039 2584982; m 0750 084211; e echuyaforest@gmail.com; w echuya.wordpress.com) is a community initiative based at a prominently signposted reception area and campsite on the northwest side of the main Kabale Road some 25km out of Kisoro. The association theoretically offers guided hikes into the forest (US$8.50 pp for up to 3 hours; US$17 pp for a full day), but the initiative hasn't really taken off, so best call a few days ahead to make arrangements. Two trails are available, one of which crosses the forest, while the other descends to Muchuya Swamp (water levels permitting) via hardwood forest and bamboo forest. Self-sufficient camping (US$2 pp) is permitted at the reception area, which stands in a lovely wooded glade on the east side of the forest and would make a superb base for exploring the reserve from the main Kabale–Kisoro Road.

MGAHINGA GORILLA NATIONAL PARK

Comprising the Ugandan portion of the Virungas, the 34km^2 Mgahinga Gorilla National Park (MGNP) is the smallest component in a 430km^2 cross-border system of protected areas that incorporates the Rwandan and Congolese sectors of the same volcanic mountain range. Established in 1930 as the Gorilla Game Sanctuary, MGNP was gazetted in 1991, when more than 2,000 people were relocated from within its boundaries in order to allow the cultivated land below the bamboo zone to regenerate as forest. Small MGNP might be, but it is arguably the most scenic park in Uganda, offering panoramic views that stretch northward to Bwindi, and a southern skyline dominated by the steep volcanic cones of the Virungas, surely one of the most memorable and stirring sights in East Africa. MGNP's main attraction, as its name suggests, is tracking mountain gorillas, though it harbours only one habituated group as opposed to Bwindi's 25. Other activities, aimed mainly at keen hikers and walkers, include a challenging day hike to the peaks of Muhabura, Gahinga and Sabyinyo volcanoes, as well as golden monkey tracking, birdwatching in the spectacular Sabyinyo Gorge, a Batwa cultural trail, caving, and forest walks.

WILDLIFE The best-known residents of MGNP are the iconic mountain gorilla (around 30 individuals split between one habituated and two unhabituated groups) and the charismatic golden monkey (an Albertine Rift Endemic whose range is now restricted to the Virungas and one other forest in Rwanda). The checklist of 76 mammal species also includes black-and-white colobus, leopard, elephant, giant forest hog, bushpig, buffalo, bushbuck, black-fronted duiker, and several varieties of rodents, bats and small predators. A bird checklist of 180 species includes 14 Albertine Rift Endemics, notably Kivu ground thrush and Rwenzori turaco, and many other localised forest specialists.

FEES The entrance fee of US$30/40/25 FR/FNR/ROA per 24 hours is incorporated into the per person activity fees for gorilla tracking (US$700/800/500 FR/FNR/ROA), volcano climbs (US$80/100 FR/FNR), the Batwa Experience (US$70/80 FR/FNR), golden monkey tracking (US$50/60 FR/FNR) and the golden monkey habituation experience (US$80/100 FR/FNR), but not the Sabyinyo Gorge hike (US$15/30 FR/FNR) or the short Platform Walk (US$10) to a viewing deck above Ntebeko. All activities, with the exception of gorilla tracking, can be booked and paid for at the UWA headquarters in Kampala or the UWA office in Kisoro. No entrance fee is applied for simply staying overnight at the community campsite or lodge immediately outside Ntebeko Gate.

GETTING THERE AND AWAY There are two points of entry: the westerly Ntebeko Gate (⊕ -1.3541, 29.61905) 14km from Kisoro; and the easterly Muhabura Gate (⊕ -1.35496, 29.66157) 9km from Kisoro. Ntebeko Gate is the site of the lodge, community campsite and visitors' centre, as well as being the trailhead for golden monkey tracking and hikes to Gahinga Peak, Sabyinyo Peak, Sabyinyo Gorge and the short version of the Batwa Trail. Muhabura Gate is the trailhead for hikes to Muhabura Peak and the long version of the Batwa Trail. The habituated gorillas move between the two gates so it is advisable to check which will be used as a trailhead the day before you track (this can be done at the office in Kisoro or the visitors' centre at Ntebeko).

Both gates are reached along a rough and seasonally slippery dirt road that runs south from Kisoro next to the Travellers Rest Hotel. Allow an hour for the journey, and be warned that a 4x4 may be necessary after heavy rain. If you are driving yourself, 2km out of Kisoro you'll reach a junction (⊕ -1.29672, 29.67824) where you need to fork to the left, then after another 2km a second junction (⊕ -1.3147, 29.67848) where you need to fork right for Ntebeko and left for Muhabura Gate.

If you don't have a vehicle, the UWA office in Kisoro will know whether any official vehicles are heading out to the appropriate entrance gate. Failing that, a boda costs US$8–10 one-way and is best arranged through the UWA office in Kisoro.

WHERE TO STAY AND EAT *Map, page 526*

It's perfectly possible to visit Mgahinga on a day trip from Kisoro or Lake Mutanda, but the accommodation at Ntebeko Gate is difficult to beat scenically, and puts you right on the spot for those early starting hikes.

Amajambere Iwacu Community Camp (6 rooms) m 0705 474409, 0785 947571; e info@amajambere.com; w amajambere.com. This community campsite just outside Ntebeko Gate has a truly spectacular setting, with Muhabura, Gahinga & Sabyinyo peaks forming an arc to the south, & a grandstand view over Lake Mutanda & the rolling hills of Bwindi to the north. Simple meals cost about US$6 & there is a bar, too, with a fireplace for cold nights. Simple but reasonably priced accommodation is provided & camping is permitted (though chilly). *US$55/100 sgl/dbl en-suite banda; US$45/70 sgl/dbl banda with shared facilities; US$30 dorm bed; US$25 pp camping. All rates FB.* **$$**

✷ **Mount Gahinga Lodge** (7 cottages) 041 4346464; e salesug@volcanoessafaris.com; w volcanoessafaris.com. This wonderful lodge, 500m outside Ntebeko Gate, offers accommodation in very spacious stone cottages with wooden floor, papyrus roof, a massive dressing room, en-suite solar hot shower & private terrace. Plenty of birdlife passes through the grounds, rock hyraxes are resident, & amenities include free Wi-Fi & laundry. **$$$$$$**

WHAT TO SEE AND DO All activities described here can be arranged at the visitors' centre at Ntebeko Gate or the UWA office in Kisoro. Most activities start at Ntebeko Gate, though the hike to Muhabura Peak starts at Muhabura Gate, and gorilla tracks might start from either gate, depending on the expected location of the habituated group.

Gorilla tracking Eight permits are issued daily to track the Nyakagezi Group, which currently consists of three silverbacks, one blackback, one subadult male, three females and one youngster. Nyakagezi's trio of hefty silverbacks are all half-brothers, whose mutual father Bugingo died of natural causes in 2016, aged around 55, and they appear to co-exist peacefully under the leadership of the current dominant male. For the time being, the high proportion of silverbacks makes tracking in MGNP particularly impressive, especially as the gorillas usually stick to the relatively open vegetation of the bamboo and regenerating forest zones. The group does, however, have something of a reputation for unreliability, after having spent most of its time in Rwanda's Volcanoes National Park between 2004 and 2012. Many tour operators shun Mgahinga in favour of Bwindi as a gorilla-tracking destination for this historical reason, but the Nyakagezi Group has actually maintained a permanent presence in MGNP since its last return from Rwanda in November 2012, and local opinion is that it would be unlikely to stray back across the border since the regeneration of a large tract of former cultivation below the bamboo zone means it has far more food available to it than was the case a few years back.

As with Bwindi, gorilla-tracking permits cost US$700/800/500 FR/FNR/ROA, inclusive of all park entrance and guiding fees. Permits must be prebooked through the UWA headquarters in Kampala, but if any are still available when you pass through Kisoro, they can, in theory, be bought there and payment sent to HQ during business hours (page 560). Odds of getting one at short notice are pretty slim in the peak seasons, but fair over March to May and September to November. In the unlikely event that the Nyakagezi Group were to cross the border into Rwanda between the time of booking and the time of tracking, UWA will transfer the permit to Bwindi, or refund the cost. The Nyakagezi Group's territory lies between the Ntebeko and Muhabura entrance gates, so check a day in advance which trailhead will be used the next morning.

Mountain hikes Guided day hikes to each of the three volcanic peaks in MGNP leave on demand daily at 07.30 at a cost of US$100 per person, inclusive of park entrance and guiding fees. A reasonable level of fitness is required for these hikes,

CLIMBING SABYINYO *By Ariadne Van Zandbergen*

The climb from Ntebeko to the 3,669m summit of Sabyinyo, a demanding round trip that takes at least 8 hours, involves an elevation gain of around 1,300m, and the thin air will more than likely make you very out of breath. Leaving from the visitors' centre, you first hike through regenerating forest, home to bushbuck and buffalo, before entering a beautiful bamboo forest where you might be lucky and see the rare golden monkey. The bamboo soon gives way to a fairytale Afro-montane forest dominated by *hagenia* trees whose boughs are laden with wispy old-man's beard. The forest is home to a wide variety of birds, most strikingly the Rwenzori turaco, a beautiful Albertine Rift Endemic that is often spotted in flight as the red from the underwings flashes in the forest greenery.

As you ascend further, the upper slopes support a cover of alpine moorland vegetation studded with eerie giant lobelias and groundsels. The path is very steep and there are little wooden ladders along the way to prevent erosion and help you on more difficult parts of the ascent. The final part of the hike entails summiting a trio of peaks linked by high-altitude saddles. The ascent from the second to the third and highest peak – located at the tripartite border of Uganda, Rwanda and the DRC – is particularly spectacular and not for the faint-hearted, since it involves a very long vertical climb on a wooden ladder. Expect some white-necked ravens to follow you around the peaks as they hope to pick up some scraps from your lunch.

As is the case on all mountains, the weather can change in a flash at any time. The upper slopes of the mountains are often shrouded in mist, and even when the temperature is pleasant at the base it can be very cold at higher altitudes. Make sure to bring warm clothing and a rain jacket as well as plenty of water and something to eat. Depending on your fitness and how many stops you make along the way, the hike can take anything from 7 to 10 hours. If it proves to be very strenuous for you or if you battle with the altitude, you can always opt to turn back after summiting the first peak. That way, you'll still get to experience all the different vegetation zones and, on a clear day, you'll be rewarded with an amazing view from the top.

all of which take between 7 and 9 hours, and good boots, rain gear and warm clothes are recommended. Most popular is the strenuous ascent from Ntebeko Gate to Sabyinyo (see above), a hike that culminates in three challenging ladder climbs up rock faces that will sorely test anyone with a poor head for heights, before summiting at the three-way border with Rwanda and the DRC.

Less vertiginously challenging but far more of a slog, the hike to the park's highest point, the 4,127m Muhabura Peak, involves a 1,793m climb from the trailhead at Muhabura Gate, which means that hikers may well feel mild altitude-related symptoms near the peak. The open moorland on Muhabura's higher slopes offers great views in all directions, though unless you're lucky this will be reduced by haze by the time you reach the top. Look out for Afro-alpine endemics such as the beautiful scarlet-tufted malachite sunbird and the small crater lake at the top of Muhabura, encircled by giant lobelias. This hike can now also be done as an overnight trip, staying at one of two newly built cabins that can accommodate eight people sharing. Note that this option needs prior booking so that arrangements can be made.

Less demanding than either of the above is the 1,100m climb from Ntebeko to Mount Gahinga, which offers a good chance of seeing various forest birds in the bamboo zone, while duikers and bushbuck inhabit the marshy crater at the peak.

Golden monkey tracking The next-best thing to seeing the mountain gorilla is the chance to track the golden monkey (*Cercopithecus kandti*), a little-known bamboo-associated primate listed as 'Endangered' by the IUCN. Endemic to the Albertine Rift, the golden monkey is characterised by a bright orange-gold body, cheeks and tail, contrasting with its black limbs, crown and tail end. Once quite widespread in the forests of southwest Uganda and northwest Rwanda, it is now near-endemic to the Virunga volcanoes, though a small number still inhabit the relict forests protected within Rwanda's recently gazetted Gishwati-Mukura National Park. Within this restricted range, however, it is the numerically dominant primate – indeed a 2003 survey estimated a population of 3,000 to 4,000 in MGNP alone. Visitors to Mgahinga might luck a glimpse of this charismatic monkey on any hike that passes through the park's bamboo zone, but to be sure of seeing them close up, it is best to do the golden monkey tracking excursion that leaves from Ntebeko at 08.30 to 09.00 daily. This operates in much the same fashion as gorilla tracking. The park's experienced trackers go ahead to locate the habituated Kasinje troop of about 80–100 golden monkeys, and a group of tourists (no limit on numbers) is guided up the mountain to join them. The hike to the habituated troop's territory entails a gradual 60- to 90-minute ascent through regenerating secondary forest to the edge of the primary forest, which is also the beginning of the bamboo zone. The golden monkey's main diet comprises bamboo leaves and shoots, the latter being a particular delicacy that is only available in the wet season. Tracking is particularly rewarding during April, May, October and November, when you can count on finding the monkeys foraging in the bamboo zone, and they often come down to the ground to pull out fresh shoots. In the dry season, food tends to be scarcer and the monkeys are sometimes more difficult to find as they roam further afield to feed on the fruit of different trees. Either way, the monkeys are very habituated, and once located, you can expect to get within a few metres of them. Tracking costs US$50/60 FR/FNR (including park entrance), and you are allocated a maximum of 1 hour with the monkeys. Alternatively, you can opt for the golden monkey habituation experience (US$80/100 FR/FNR) where you get a chance to join a researcher and stay with the semi-habituated Kabakyondo troop for up to 4 hours.

Sabyinyo Gorge Trail (US$15/30 FR/FNR plus entrance fee) Of particular interest to birders in search of Albertine Rift Endemics and other localised forest species, this half-day nature trail ascends from Ntebeko Gate through an area of regenerating forest where you might see bushbuck or buffalo, along with mountain buzzard, mountain greenbul, Chubb's cisticola and various waxbills and finches. It continues into a spectacular stand of atmospheric bamboo forest inhabited by golden monkey (unhabituated, so you are far less likely to see them than if you are on a dedicated tracking excursion), as well as handsome francolin and Kivu ground thrush. It then follows a small stream through the lushly forested Sabyinyo Gorge to a maximum altitude of around 2,900m, crossing several rickety ladders and bridges en route. The evergreen forest in the gorge is very reliable for the sensational Rwenzori turaco, and it also harbours such localised birds as western green tinkerbird, olive woodpecker, African hill babbler, yellow mountain warbler, Archer's and white-starred robin-chat, Rwenzori batis, stripe-breasted tit,

BATWA PYGMIES

We have always lived in the forest. Like my father and grandfathers, I lived from hunting and collecting in this mountain. Then the Bahutu came. They cut the forest to cultivate the land. They carried on cutting and planting until they had encircled our forest with their fields. Today, they come right up to our huts. Instead of forest, now we are surrounded by Irish potatoes!

Gahut Gahuliro, a Mutwa born 100 years earlier on the slopes of the Virungas, talking in 1999

The most ancient inhabitants of inter-lacustrine Africa, the Batwa (singular Mutwa) are a Pygmoid people easily distinguished by their short stature – an adult male seldom exceeds 1.5m in height – and paler, more bronzed complexion. Semi-nomadic by inclination, small egalitarian communities of Batwa kin traditionally live in impermanent encampments of flimsy leaf huts, set in a forest clearing, which they abandon when food becomes scarce locally, upon the death of a community member, or on a whim. Traditionally, the Batwa lifestyle is based around hunting, which is undertaken as a team effort by the male community members, usually using nets or poisoned arrows. Batwa men also gather wild honey, while the women gather edible plants to supplement the meat. In times past, the Batwa wore only a drape of animal hide or barkcloth, and had little desire to accumulate possessions – a few cooking pots and some hunting gear was about it.

According to the most recent survey, around 6,500 Batwa live in Uganda, mostly concentrated in Kigezi. Only 2,000 years ago, however, East and southern Africa were populated almost solely by Batwa and related hunter-gatherers, whose lifestyle differed little from that of our earliest common human ancestors. Since then, agriculturist and pastoralist settlers, through persecution or assimilation, have marginalised the number to a few small and mostly degraded communities living in habitats unsuitable to agriculture or pasture, such as rainforest interiors and deserts.

The initial incursions into Batwa territory were made when the Bantu-speaking farmers settled in Kigezi, sometime before the 16th century, and set about clearing small tracts of forest for subsistence agriculture and pasture. This process of deforestation was greatly accelerated in the early 20th century: by 1930 the last three substantial tracts of forest remaining in Kigezi were gazetted as the Impenetrable and Echuya forest reserves and Gorilla Game Sanctuary by the colonial authorities. In one sense, this move to protect the forests was of direct benefit to the Batwa, since it ensured that what little remained of them would not be lost to agriculture. But the legal status of the Batwa was altered to their detriment – true, they were still permitted to hunt and forage within the reserves, but where formerly these forests had been recognised as Batwa communal land, they were now government property.

Only some three generations later would the Batwa be faced with the full ramifications of having lost all legal entitlement to their ancestral lands. In 1991, the Gorilla Game Sanctuary and Impenetrable Forest Reserve were regazetted to become Mgahinga and Bwindi national parks, a move backed by international donors who stipulated that all persons resident within the national parks were to be evicted, and that hunting and other forest harvesting should cease. Good news for gorillas, perhaps, but what about those Batwa communities that had dwelt within the forest reserves for centuries? Overnight, they were reduced in status to illegal squatters whose traditional subsistence lifestyle had been criminalised. Adding insult to injury, while some compensation was awarded to non-Batwa farmers who had settled within the forest since the 1930s and illegally cleared it for cultivation, the evicted Batwa received compensation only if they had destroyed part of the forest reserve in a similar manner.

Today, more than 80% of Uganda's Batwa are officially landless, and none has legal access to the forest on which their traditional livelihood depends. Locally, the Batwa are viewed not with sympathy, but rather as objects of ridicule, subject to regular unprovoked attacks that occasionally lead to fatalities. The extent of local prejudice against the Batwa can be garnered from a set of interviews posted on the website w edirisa.org. The Batwa, report some of their Bakiga neighbours, 'smoke marijuana…like alcohol…drink too much…make noise all night long… eat too much food…cannot grow their own food and crops…depend on hunting and begging…don't care about their children…the man makes love to his wife while the children sleep on their side' – a collection of circumstantially induced half-truths and outright fallacies that make the Batwa come across as the debauched survivors of a dysfunctional hippie commune.

Prejudice against the Batwa is not confined to their immediate neighbours. Richard Nzita's otherwise commendable *Peoples and Cultures of Uganda*, for instance, contrives, in the space of two pages, to characterise the Pygmoid peoples of Uganda as beggars, crop raiders and pottery thieves – even cannibals! Conservationists and the Western media, meanwhile, persistently stigmatise the Batwa as gorilla hunters and poachers – this despite the strong taboo against killing or eating apes that informs every known Batwa community. Almost certainly, any gorilla hunting that might be undertaken by the Batwa today will have been instigated by outsiders.

This much is incontestable: the Batwa and their hunter-gatherer ancestors have in all probability inhabited the forests of Kigezi for some half-a-million years. Their traditional lifestyle, which places no rigorous demands on the forest, could be cited as a model of that professed holy grail of modern conservationists: the sustainable use of natural resources. The Batwa were not major participants in the deforestation of Kigezi, but they have certainly been the main human victims of this loss. And Batwa and gorillas co-habited in the same forests for many millennia prior to their futures both being imperilled by identical external causes in the 20th century. As Jerome Lewis writes: 'They and their way of life are entitled to as much consideration and respect as other ways of life. There was and is nothing to be condemned in forest nomadism…The Batwa…used the environment without destroying or seriously damaging it. It is only through their long-term custody of the area that later comers have good land to use.'

Travellers to Kigezi might well be approached by self-styled guides offering to take them to a local Batwa community. The answer to this query should be no. Unofficial encounters set up by street guides are almost invariably dodgy or exploitative. If you want to meet Batwa in a culturally sensitive environment, the best places to do so are at Mgahinga Gorilla National Park, at a few sites listed in the Bwindi chapter, or through Edirisa, which arranges visits to Echuya Forest from Lake Bunyonyi. Should you witness any incident where Batwa are exploited or victimised, contact the Forest Peoples Project (w forestpeoples.org), a UK-based charity that works with the Batwa of Uganda to help them determine their own future, control the use of their lands, and carry out sustainable use of the forest resources.

For further information, Karsten Tadie's fascinating self-published book *The Batwa of Uganda: A Forgotten People* (2010) can be bought at Crater Bay Cottages (page 521) for around US$13. Also check out the website: w minorityrights.org.

montane sooty boubou, Lagden's bush-shrike, strange weaver, dusky and Shelley's crimsonwing, and regal, blue-headed and Rwenzori double-collard sunbird.

The Batwa Trail (Book through UWA; ☎ 041 4355000; e info@thebatwatrail.com; w ugandawildlife.org) A welcome alternative to the usual tawdry visits to impoverished Batwa Pygmy communities, this initiative provides a genuine opportunity to experience something of traditional Batwa forest culture. The event follows a trail along the lower slopes of the Virungas to Garama Cave, and involves Batwa guides demonstrating a range of practical traditional skills such as lighting a fire by rubbing together sticks, bivouac building, target practice with a bow and arrow (meat must have been a rare dish indeed) and food gathering. The trail culminates with a memorable performance of Batwa song and music in the council chamber of Garama Cave, a dramatic setting with powerful acoustics. Importantly, the Batwa Trail is no 'pretty Pygmy' celebration; the day should include a discussion of the current plight of the Batwa, who have been reduced to squatting in bivouacs on Bakiga-owned farmland along the forest margins. The activity costs US$80 per person (including park entrance), and the fee is split approximately 50–50 between UWA and the Batwa. Two variations are possible, both leaving at 08.30 to 09.00 and culminating in a visit to Garama Cave. The short trail leaves from Ntebeko Gate and takes around 3 hours while the longer trail leaves from Muhabura Gate and takes up to 7 hours.

LAKES MUTANDA AND MULEHE

A compelling attraction in its own right as well as being a useful base for gorilla tracking and other activities in Mgahinga Gorilla and Bwindi Impenetrable national parks, pretty 22km² Lake Mutanda follows the 1,800m contour of the steep-sided hills immediately north of Kisoro. Like the larger and better-known Lake Bunyonyi, Mutanda is a narrow flooded valley system that formed several thousand years ago when the Rutshuru River, its main effluent, was dammed by a lava flow from the Virungas, whose immense volcanic outlines still dominate the lake's southern skyline. About 3km east of Mutanda, and linked to it by the babbling waters of the short Mucha River, Mulehe is a relatively shallow but equally pretty lake with a surface area of 9km². Recent years have seen the emergence of several tourist developments around the two lakes, which are conveniently located en route from Kisoro to the gorilla-tracking trailheads at Rushaga and Nkuringo. This includes a sextet of moderate and upmarket lodges situated between 8km and 20km north or northeast of Kisoro by road, and aimed mainly at gorilla trackers, as well as the more low-key Mutanda Eco-Community Centre, which is primarily of interest to budget travellers and day trippers out of Kisoro, and stands at the southern end of the lake, off the road running west to Bunagana near the border with the DRC.

GETTING THERE AND AWAY Coming directly from Kisoro to any of the five upmarket lodges in the vicinity of the lakes, follow the unsurfaced road towards Nkuringo that leads northeast from the Kindly petrol station (⊕ -1.2823, 29.69693). After 8km, the road passes the Mucha Hotel to the left, then after another 100m it arrives at a three-way junction (⊕ -1.2235, 29.71628). Turn right here, and you'll reach Bwindi Jungle Lodge after about 500m. Bear left, and you'll reach the Mutanda Lake Resort after another 8km, and Chameleon Hill 3km past that. Coming from Kabale or points further east, you can take a short cut that leads north from the

MUTANDA'S ISLANDS

Despite its relatively small size, Lake Mutanda is studded with a dozen islands, of which the following are the most interesting:

RWANGEZI (BIRD) ISLAND This smallish island in the far north of the lake supports an avian breeding colony dominated by African spoonbill, black-headed heron, sacred ibis, white-breasted cormorant and black kite.

HAMPINZI ISLAND Legend has it that this tiny islet close to Rwangezi was once much larger, but when its inhabitants refused to give sorghum beer to a visiting sorceress, she cast a spell to make it sink, and everybody living on it died.

KABAYA ISLAND A small cave on this island was once a burial place for dead people whose spirits were so powerful it was feared they would cause havoc on the mainland were they interred there. It is still an important local pilgrimage site associated with ancestor worship, especially in August, the height of the sorghum-harvesting season.

TOYO ISLAND One of the few places in the immediate vicinity of Mutanda to support a cover of predominantly indigenous vegetation, Toyo is good for woodland birds such as Ross's turaco and various bee-eaters, and a large *Ficus* tree visible from the western shore supports a colony of pink-backed pelican and black-headed night heron.

MUTANDA ISLAND Sharing its name with the lake that laps its shores, this is the largest island on Mutanda, with an area of almost 1km^2. It supports a population of around 200 fishermen and farmers, and the short but steep hike to its summit offers great views towards the Virunga volcanoes.

GAHIZA ISLAND This tiny island, now home to a lovely lake retreat, has a grim history as a place where unmarried girls who became pregnant were marooned to die of thirst and starvation. Skeletons of the victims are still sometimes unearthed there.

BUHUNGIRO (FREEDOM) ISLAND Still covered in indigenous forest, this small island reputedly acquired its name when a group of local fishermen took refuge there to escape an attack by spear-wielding Batwa.

main road to Kisoro at Nyakabande (⊕ -1.27832, 29.74225) and connects with the Nkuringo road about 1.5km before the Mucha Hotel (⊕ -1.23357, 29.71201).

Mutanda Eco-Community Centre lies on the marshy southern lakeshore, about 2.5km southeast of where the Rutshuru River flows out of the western shore, and a similar distance north of Kisoro as the crow flies. In a car, the best way to get there from Kisoro is to follow the Bunagana Road for 3km west out of town to Nateete, then turn right at the signposted junction (⊕ -1.26856, 29.6647) and continue for another 3.5km to the lakeshore. You could also walk out along the road in about 90 minutes, or try to make your way via a maze of footpaths running north out of town. A boda will cost around US$1.50.

WHERE TO STAY AND EAT *Map, page 526*

Exclusive

✷ **Chameleon Hill Lodge** (12 cottages) m 0772 721818; e welcome@chameleonhill.com; w chameleonhill.com. Set on a high hill offering a panoramic view across the island-studded northeast corner of the lake to the Virungas, this refreshingly different lodge is distinguished by its boldly painted turreted exteriors, whose use of primary colours makes it look like a fairytale castle from a children's colouring-in book, & spacious stylish interiors decorated with mosaic & contemporary African art. The cottages all have dbl or twin beds with walk-in net, en-suite hot shower with imported fittings & a private lake-facing balcony & garden. Mainly used as a base for gorilla tracking in southern Bwindi, the lodge also arranges village walks, coffee-farm visits, boat trips on the lake & canoeing. There's also charmingly quirky budget accommodation available in an original 1970s VW combi that's been converted into a room with a view. *Rates are FB.* **$$$$**

Upmarket

Lake Mulehe Safari Lodge (4 cottages) m 0772 787733; e reservations@lakemulehesafarilodge.com; w lakemulehesafarilodge.com. Overlooking the western shore of lovely Lake Mulehe, this small lodge offers spacious & cosy cottages 8km north of Kisoro along the road to the gorilla-tracking trailheads at Rushaga & Nkuringo. *US$220/270/370 sgl/dbl/trpl FB.* **$$$$**

✷ **Mutanda Lake Resort** (17 rooms & cottages) m 0789 951943, 0787 971220; e info@mutandalakeresort.com; w mutandalakeresort.com. Set on a peninsula 45mins' drive from Kisoro, this lodge enjoys a stupendous southerly outlook across peaceful island-studded waters towards the Virunga volcanoes. The location, right on the lakeshore, is ideal for taking a dip from the wooden sundeck, for birdwatching, or for exploring the lake on a stand-up paddleboard, local canoe or motorboat cruise. The cosy standard rooms are stilted constructions with wooden floors & walls, while a row of 5 much larger & very attractively decorated luxury cottages stands on an isolated stretch of lakeshore behind the main cluster. Set menus are eaten in a lovely wooden restaurant/bar, also with lake views. It's a justifiably popular base for gorilla tracking in southern Bwindi or Mgahinga & very reasonably priced. *US$130/185 std sgl/dbl B&B.* **$$$$**

Moderate

Gahiza Island Retreat (5 rooms) m 0775 235579; e reservationsgahizaisland@gmail.com; w gahizaisland.com. Though Lake Mutanda is famous for its island-studded scenery, Gahiza Island Retreat is currently the only offshore lodge. Just 2ha in size, it really is a retreat with just 5 rooms, though more are planned. Despite the compact size, there is plenty of birdlife, including fish eagles, turacos & kingfishers. The volcanic backdrop to the south is superb, while the northern prospect looks the length of the lake towards the Bwindi hills. If you tire of the views from the island, take a dugout canoe on the water to find one that takes your fancy. Swimming is also possible, the lake being considered bilharzia free & with no hippos or crocs either. Gahiza Island is accessed by boat from the southern end of Lake Mutanda off the Bunagana Rd; head west from Kisoro, & after 4km turn north at Natete trading centre then follow the signs to the boat landing. *US$100/150 sgl/dbl FB.* **$$$**

Mucha Hotel (10 rooms) m 0776 556674. Nestled on the south bank of the Mucha River about 8km north of Kisoro, this small lodge has spacious, uncluttered & stylishly furnished rooms with fitted nets & en-suite hot showers. A highly rated restaurant serves à la carte meals for around US$7. It's a slightly odd location, nestled between the road, rural shambas & a swamp, & the view is limited to the fast-moving stream (which in a less scenic area might be considered attraction enough), but it's well priced & conveniently located for gorilla tracking in southern Bwindi. *US$40/80 sgl/dbl B&B; add US$21 pp FB.* **$$$**

Budget

Mutanda Eco-Community Centre (5 rooms) m 0784 850959, 0773 107795; e info@lakemutandacamp.com; w lakemutandacamp.com. Set on the papyrus-fringed southern lakeshore, this community-oriented development enjoys a fantastic location & offers accommodation in stilted wooden cabins. A restaurant serves a fair selection of meals for US$5–6. *US$40/50 sgl/dbl; US$10 pp dorm bed.* **$$**

WHAT TO SEE AND DO Lake Mutanda is a great place to chill out before or after gorilla tracking or other hikes in Bwindi Impenetrable and Mgahinga Gorilla national parks. It is regarded to be safe for swimming, since there are no hippos (hunted out in the 1990s) and no crocodiles (too cold), and it is reputedly free of bilharzia. The surrounding countryside offers some great rambling and birdwatching opportunities, with a good chance of seeing spotted necked otters swimming close to shore, especially in the vicinity of Mutanda Lake Resort. Motorboat trips to explore the lake and its dozen islands (page 543) can be arranged through Mutanda Eco-Community Centre (US$50 per boat for 2–3hrs) or Mutanda Lake Resort (see w view.publitas.com/mutandalakeresort for a full rates list).

21

Bwindi Impenetrable National Park

Uganda's single most important tourist hotspot is the 331km² Bwindi Impenetrable National Park (BINP), which protects a rugged landscape of steep hills and valleys abutting the Congolese border south of Ishasha and north of Kisoro. Rolling eastward from the Albertine Rift Escarpment, the tangled forested slopes of Bwindi provide shelter to one of Africa's most diverse mammalian faunas, including 45% of the global mountain gorilla population. Unsurprisingly, the main tourist activity in BINP is gorilla tracking, which was first established at the Buhoma park headquarters in 1993, but now operates out of four trailheads – the others being Ruhija, Nkuringo and Rushaga – all of which are serviced by a selection of tourist lodges. Today, 25 habituated gorilla groups can be tracked in Bwindi, a thrilling venture regarded by most who have undertaken it to be a true once-in-a-lifetime experience. BINP is also one of the finest birding destinations in Uganda, thanks in part to the presence of 23 Albertine Rift Endemics, while other attractions include forest walks in search of smaller primates such as black-and-white colobus and L'Hoest's monkey. There are also a few reputable cultural programmes that offer the opportunity to interact with the Batwa Pygmies who were evicted from the forest interior following the gazetting of the national park.

GENERAL INFORMATION

FLORA AND FAUNA Bwindi is one of Africa's most biodiverse forests, due to its altitudinal span of 1,160m to 2,607m and an antiquity of more than 25,000 years, and its **flora** includes 160 tree and more than 100 fern species. It formed part of a much larger forest belt that stretched south to the slopes of the Virunga Mountains until about 500 years ago, when agriculturists started planting crops in the Kisoro area. The area was first accorded protection in 1932 with the creation of the Kayonza and Kasatora Crown Forest, which had a combined area of 207km². In 1964, the protected area was extended to its present-day size, renamed the Impenetrable Central Forest Reserve, and designated as a gorilla and wildlife sanctuary. Gazetted as a national park in 1991, it protects a true rainforest that receives an average annual rainfall of almost 1,500mm, and a vital catchment area at the source of five major rivers that flow into Lake Edward. The park was listed as a UNESCO World Heritage Site in 1994 on account of its biodiversity and wealth of International Union for Conservation of Nature (IUCN) red-listed wildlife.

BINP harbours at least 120 **mammal** species, more than any national park except Queen Elizabeth. Its most famous residents are the mountain gorillas, which number around 460 individuals split across 30 or so troops according to the most recent survey, undertaken in 2018. Another ten primate species are present, a list that includes a healthy population of (unhabituated) chimpanzees, and substantial numbers of olive baboon, black-and-white colobus, L'Hoest's monkey, red-tailed monkey and blue monkey. Of the so-called Big Five, only elephants are present, though the herd of 30 animals in the southeast of the park – assigned to the forest race – is very seldom seen by tourists. Buffaloes and leopards were present until recent times, but they are thought to have been hunted to extinction. Six antelope species occur in the park: bushbuck and five types of forest duiker. Small mammals such as rodents and bats are well represented, too.

A total of 350 **bird** species has been recorded in Bwindi, a remarkably high figure when you consider that it includes very few water-associated birds. Of particular interest to birders are 23 species endemic to the Albertine Rift, and at least 14 species recorded nowhere else in Uganda, among them the African green broadbill, white-tailed blue flycatcher, brown-necked parrot, white-bellied robin chat and Frazer's eagle owl. In addition to its extensive bird checklist, Bwindi is also home to at least 200 **butterfly** species, including eight Albertine Rift Endemics, and dedicated butterfly watchers might hope to identify more than 50 varieties in one day. Bwindi is also home to many **reptiles and amphibians**, notably the Rwenzori three-horned chameleon (*Trioceros johnstoni*), a spectacularly colourful foot-long Albertine Rift Endemic.

ORIENTATION Tourism in BINP focuses on four separate locations: Buhoma in the northwest; Ruhija in the east; Nkuringo in the southwest; and Rushaga in the south. Each of these four bases functions as a self-standing gorilla-tracking destination, insofar as it has its own habituated gorilla groups, is serviced by its own set of accommodation options, and is reached by a different approach road from the other locations. For this reason, coverage of the park is divided up into four sections corresponding to the four above-mentioned locations, which are dealt with in a clockwise direction, starting with Buhoma, which is the oldest trailhead,

BWINDI IMPENETRABLE NATIONAL PARK

For listings, see from page 554, unless otherwise stated

Where to stay

1 Agandi Uganda Ecolodge *p565* ... H6
2 Albertine Gorilla Campsite *p575* ... G3
3 Bakiga Lodge *p565* ... H6
4 Bigambo Cottages ... B1
5 Broadbill Forest Camp *p565* ... E4
6 Buhoma Community Rest Camp ... A6
7 Buhoma Gorilla Camp ... A4
8 Buhoma Lodge ... A7
9 Bwindi Lodge ... A6
10 Bwindi Safari Lodge *p574* ... B5
11 Clouds Mountain Gorilla Lodge *p574* ... G3
12 Crested Crane Hotel Bwindi ... B1
13 Engagi Lodge ... B5
14 Gorilla Bluff ... A5
15 Gorilla CloseUp Lodge *p574* ... B5
16 Gorilla Conservation Lodge ... A6
17 Gorilla Friends Lodge ... A4
18 Gorilla Heights *p574* ... H4
19 Gorilla Leisure Lodge *p570* ... H1
20 Gorilla Mist Camp *p565* ... H6
21 Gorilla Safari Lodge *p570* ... G1
22 Gorilla Valley Lodge *p570* ... H1
23 Haven Lodge ... A6
24 Ichumbi Gorilla Lodge *p571* ... G1
25 Karungi Camp *p571* ... E1
26 Kiho Gorilla Safari Lodge *p564* ... E4
27 Mahogany Springs ... B5
28 Mist Lodge ... A6
29 Nkuringo Bwindi Gorilla Lodge *p574* ... H4
30 Nkuringo Guesthouse *p575* ... H4
31 Nshongi Camp *p571* ... G1
32 Ride 4 A Woman ... A4
33 Ruhija Community Rest Camp *p565* ... H6
34 Ruhija Gorilla Friends Resort *p565* ... H6
35 Ruhija Gorilla Safari Lodge *p565* ... H6
36 Ruhija Gorilla Tours Hotel *p567* ... H6
37 Ruhondeza Lodge & Campsite ... B5
38 Rushaga Gorilla Haven *p571* ... H2
39 Rushaga Gorilla Lodge *p571* ... G1
40 Sanctuary Gorilla Forest Camp ... A7
41 Trackers Safari Lodge ... A5
42 Trekkers Tavern *p566* ... H6
43 Wagtail Eco Camp *p571* ... E1

Where to eat and drink

44 Bwindi Bar ... A6
45 Bwindi Gorilla Coffee Cup ... A6
46 Mapera Lounge ... A4
47 Terrace Junction *p571* ... F2

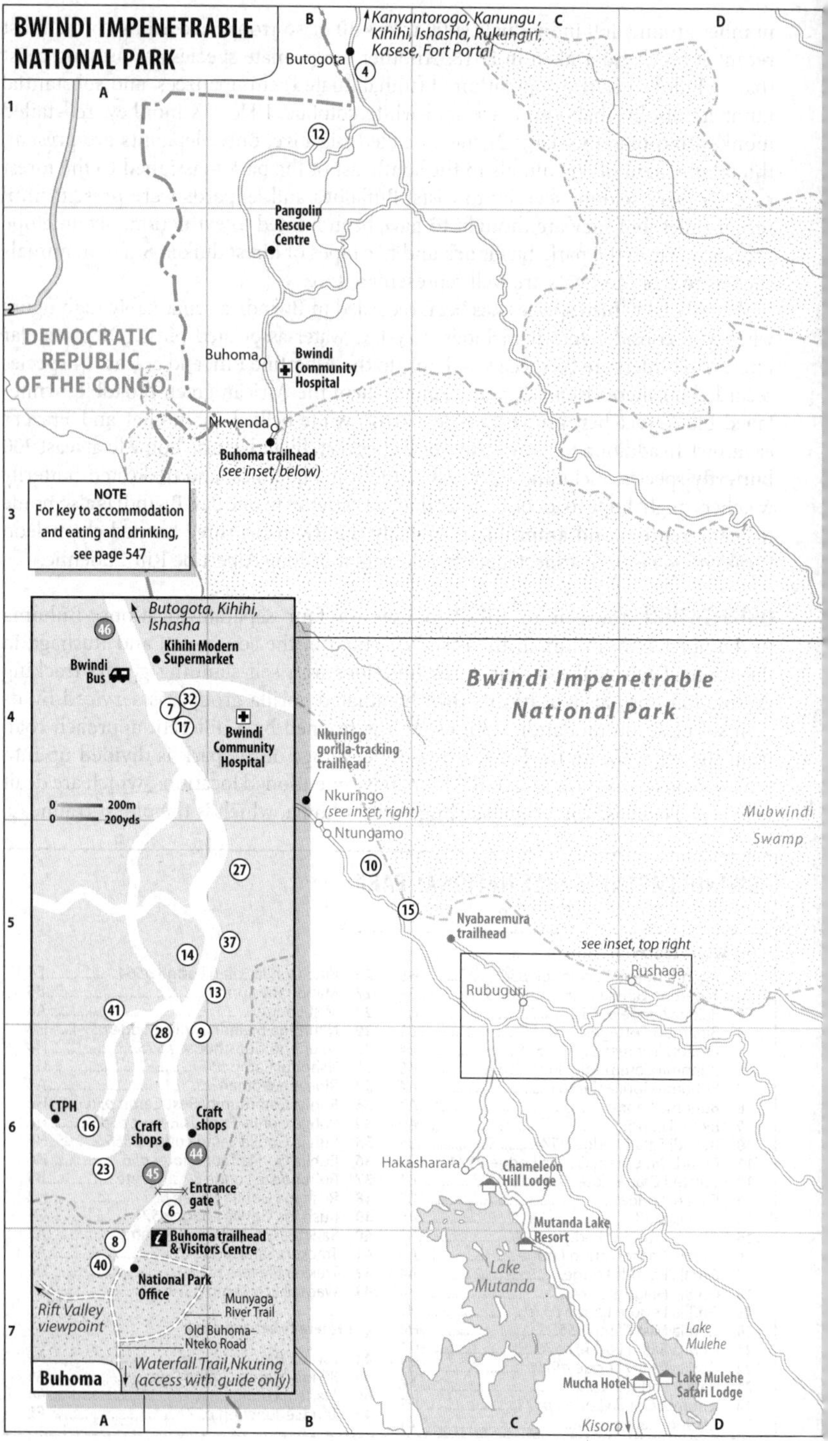
BWINDI IMPENETRABLE NATIONAL PARK
A
B
C
D
1
2
3
4
5
6
7
Kanyantorogo, Kanungu, Kihihi, Ishasha, Rukungiri, Kasese, Fort Portal
Butogota
4
12
Pangolin Rescue Centre
DEMOCRATIC REPUBLIC OF THE CONGO
Buhoma
Bwindi Community Hospital
Nkwenda
Buhoma trailhead
(see inset, below)
NOTE
For key to accommodation and eating and drinking, see page 547
Butogota, Kihihi, Ishasha
46
Kihihi Modern Supermarket
Bwindi Bus
32
7
17
Bwindi Community Hospital
0 200m
0 200yds
27
37
14
13
41
28
9
CTPH
16
Craft shops
Craft shops
44
23
45
Entrance gate
6
8
Buhoma trailhead & Visitors Centre
40
National Park Office
Rift Valley viewpoint
Munyaga River Trail
Old Buhoma–Nteko Road
Waterfall Trail, Nkuring (access with guide only)
Buhoma
Bwindi Impenetrable National Park
Nkuringo gorilla-tracking trailhead
Nkuringo
(see inset, right)
Ntungamo
10
15
Nyabaremura trailhead
Mubwindi Swamp
see inset, top right
Rushaga
Rubuguri
Hakasharara
Chameleon Hill Lodge
Mutanda Lake Resort
Lake Mutanda
Lake Mulehe
Mucha Hotel
Lake Mulehe Safari Lodge
Kisoro

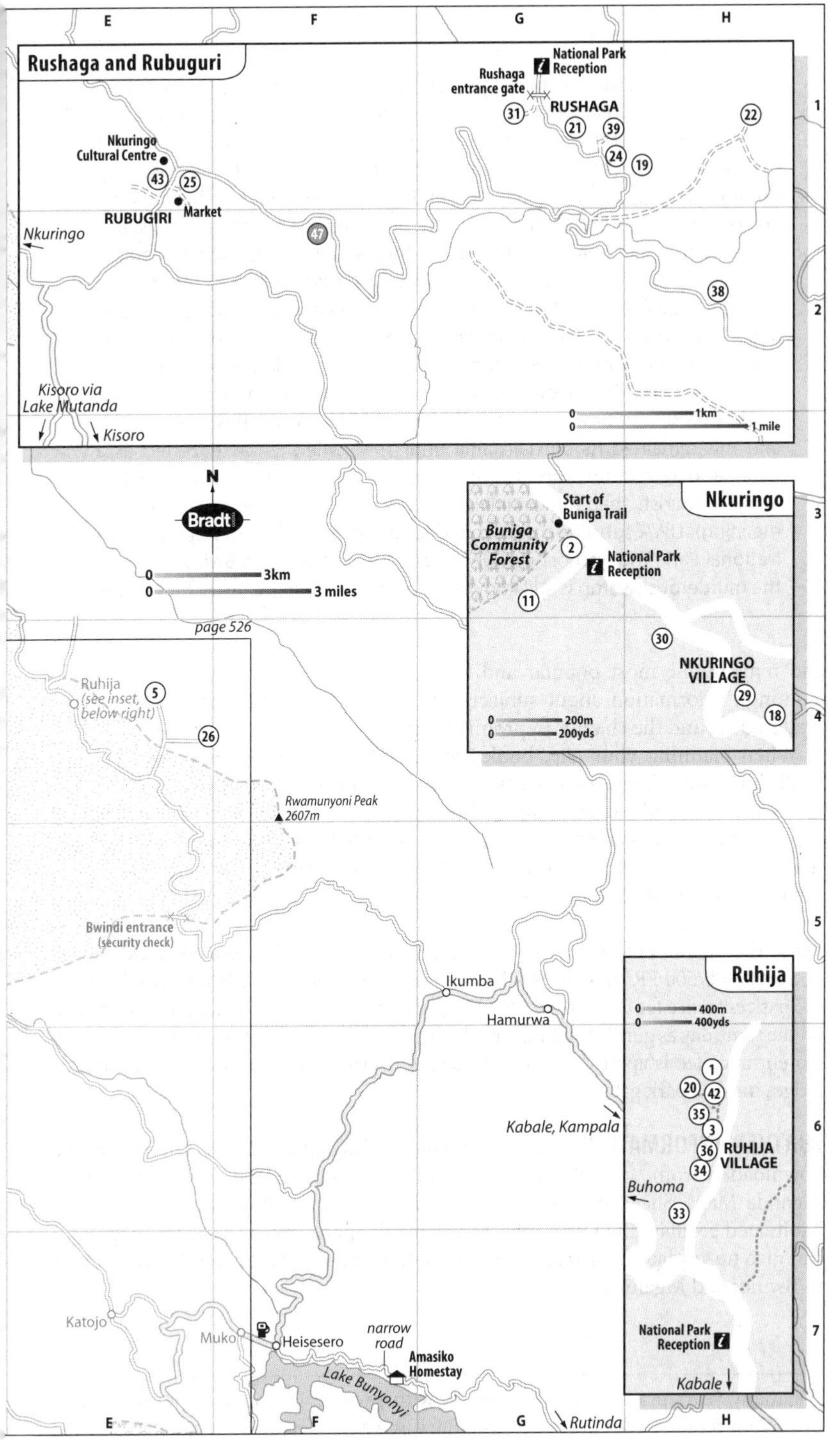

E
F
G
H
Rushaga and Rubuguri
National Park Reception
Rushaga entrance gate
RUSHAGA
31
21
39
24
19
22
Nkuringo Cultural Centre
43
25
RUBUGIRI
Market
Nkuringo
47
38
Kisoro via Lake Mutanda
Kisoro
0 1km
0 1 mile
1
2
3
4
5
6
7
N
Bradt
0 3km
0 3 miles
Nkuringo
Start of Buniga Trail
Buniga Community Forest
2
National Park Reception
11
30
NKURINGO VILLAGE
29
18
0 200m
0 200yds
page 526
Ruhija (see inset, below right)
5
26
Rwamunyoni Peak 2607m
Bwindi entrance (security check)
Ikumba
Hamurwa
Kabale, Kampala
Ruhija
0 400m
0 400yds
1
20
42
35
3
36
RUHIJA VILLAGE
34
Buhoma
33
National Park Reception
Kabale
Katojo
Muko
Heisesero
narrow road
Amasiko Homestay
Lake Bunyonyi
Rutinda

BWINDI IMPENETRABLE

The name 'Bwindi' derives from the local phrase 'Mubwindi bwa Nyinamukari', which most probably originally referred to the Mubwindi Swamp, near Ruhija in the southeast of the park, rather than to the forest itself. The story behind this name goes back to about a century ago, when, it is said, a family migrating northwards from the Kisoro area found themselves standing at the southern end of a seemingly impenetrable swamp. The parents asked the swamp spirits for guidance, and were told that only if they sacrificed their most beautiful daughter, Nyinamukari, would the rest of the family cross without mishap. After two days of deliberation, the family decided that they could not turn back south, and so they threw the girl into the water to drown, and went on their way safely to the other side. When news of the sacrifice spread, people began to avoid the swamp, calling it 'Mubwindi bwa Nyinamukari' – 'Dark Place of Nyinamukari'.

The forest was proclaimed as the Impenetrable Forest Reserve in 1932, and this remained its official name until 1991 when it was gazetted as a national park and renamed Bwindi. Realising that this local name has less allure to tourists than the colonial name (though the two words are close in meaning), UWA subsequently expanded the name to Bwindi Impenetrable National Park. Today, most people refer to the park as plain Bwindi, though the murderous swamp is still known by the more correct name of Mubwindi.

and remains the most popular and the most directly accessible from Kampala. Common information about subjects such as gorilla tracking and behaviour is scattered around the chapter in prominent grey boxes.

When planning your trip, book accommodation as close as possible to the trailhead from which you'll track gorillas. If you don't, you'll be looking at a very early start and a drive of up to 2 hours before you even start on the tracking expedition. Permit availability at all the trailheads tends to be more problematic than finding a room, so we'd advise you to book your permit first, then choose your accommodation once you know from where you'll be tracking.

FEES The park entrance fee is incorporated into the gorilla-tracking fee (US$700/800/500 FR/FNR/ROA). Nature walks cost US$30/40 FR/FNR, exclusive of the park entrance fee (US$30/40 FR/FNR per 24 hours), unless the walk is undertaken on the same day as gorilla tracking, in which case no additional entrance fee is charged. No entrance fee is applied for simply staying overnight at community campsites or lodges inside a park gate.

FURTHER INFORMATION The useful *Gorilla Highlands Pocket Guide* can be downloaded from w gorillahighlands.com. The excellent and regularly updated 'Uganda Maps' Sheet 5 *Bwindi & the Gorilla Highlands* shows the ranges of the habituated gorillas. The UWA offices in Kampala (page 149) and Kisoro (page 533) can give up-to-date information on gorilla tracking and other travel practicalities in Bwindi and Mgahinga.

BUHOMA

For many years practically synonymous with Bwindi, Buhoma, set at an altitude of 1,500m on the park's northern boundary, is where Uganda first launched gorilla tracking back in 1993, and for 11 years after that, it remained the only trailhead for an activity that accounts for 99% of tourist visits to the national park. Despite the opening of three other gorilla-tracking trailheads since 2004, Buhoma remains the park's busiest tourist focus, partly perhaps as a matter of convention, but also due to its excellent selection of upmarket lodges, the relative ease of access from Kampala (being 45 minutes from tarmac connecting to the capital) and proximity to the main western safari circuit (Ishasha in Queen Elizabeth National Park is little more than an hour distant). Given the additional ease of reaching Buhoma by public transport and the availability of some excellent and affordable budget accommodation, it is clear that Buhoma caters for all markets. On the downside, the daily rigmarole of processing 48 gorilla trackers takes place in a Visitor Centre complex of such egregious proportions and construction that it might have been designed primarily to offend.

Buhoma's popularity means that it is usually the first of the trailheads to be booked solid. Indeed, such is the demand for permits in the high season that many upmarket tours base themselves at Buhoma but do their tracking at Ruhija, about 45km to the southeast. Gorilla tracking aside, Buhoma is also the site of Bwindi's park headquarters, and a rewarding base for birdwatchers, with 190 species, most associated with relatively low-altitude forest, having been recorded in the vicinity, among them ten listed in the *Red Data Book* and/or endemic to the Albertine Rift.

GETTING THERE AND AWAY

By air Aerolink (☎ 0317 333000; e info@aerolinkuganda.com; w aerolinkuganda.com) flies daily to/from Kihihi Airfield from Entebbe Airport. Return flights cost US$475 plus taxes. Savannah Resort Hotel (page 507), right next to Kihihi Airfield, is a possible base for exploring Bwindi Impenetrable National Park in tandem with the Ishasha Sector of QENP. Otherwise, you'll need to arrange a transfer from Kihihi with your lodge.

By road Buhoma can be approached along several different routes that converge near the town of Butogota, 17km north of the park entrance. All approach routes involve some driving along dirt roads that may become slippery after rain, so an early start is advised. Your last brand name fuel stations on the three routes described below will be in Katunguru (coming from QENP), Rukungiri (from Kampala) and Kabale. After that, you'll find local brands in Kihihi, Butogota and Buhoma.

From Kampala and the east Buhoma is about 475km west of Kampala and 205km west of Mbarara by road. The best route follows the surfaced Kabale Road for 60km past Mbarara to Ntungamo, then turns right on to a surfaced 45km road to Rukungiri. At the central roundabout turn right and shortly outside the town you'll join an impressive new tarmac road. After some 50km, by which time you'll have descended from the Kigezi highlands on to the plains beyond, you'll reach a new roundabout in the middle of nowhere. Turn left to follow the tarmac through the town of Kihihi (3km) to Kanyantorogo (another 9km). A right turn here on to murram passes through the town of Butogota (11km). At a cluster of lodge signposts, 1km beyond the town, turn right for Buhoma (12km). The drive can take up to 10 hours so aim for an early start.

From Kasese and the north Two main routes connect Kasese, Fort Portal and North-Central QENP to Buhoma. The more direct and interesting route branches

MOUNTAIN GORILLAS: ECOLOGY AND TAXONOMY

The largest living primates, gorillas are widespread residents of the equatorial African rainforest, with a global population of 250,000–300,000 concentrated mainly in the Congo Basin. Until 2001, all gorillas were assigned to the species *Gorilla gorilla*, split into three races: the western lowland gorilla (*G. g. gorilla*) of the western Congo Basin; the eastern lowland gorilla (*G. g. graueri*) in the eastern DRC; and the mountain gorilla (*G. g. beringei*), which lives in highland forest on the eastern side of the Albertine Rift. The western race was formally described in 1847, but the mountain gorilla remained unknown to zoologists until 1903, when the German army officer Captain Friedrich Robert von Beringe shot the first two documented individuals on the Rwandan slopes of Mount Sabyinyo, and the eastern lowland gorilla remained undescribed until 1914.

Post-millennial advances in DNA testing and fresh morphological studies have forced the revision of this conventional taxonomic classification. It seems that the western and eastern populations, whose ranges lie more than 1,000km apart, diverged at least 250,000 years ago and should be treated as two species, usually referred to as the western gorilla (*G. gorilla*) and eastern gorilla (*G. beringei*).

The western race (*G. g. gorilla*) has a total population estimated at 150,000 which, though centred on the DRC, spans half-a-dozen countries. It is classified by the IUCN Red List as Critically Endangered, a status attributed to a number of threats, notably hunting for bush meat, the lethal Ebola virus and rapid habitat loss throughout its range. Also listed as Critically Endangered is the Cross River race *G. g. dielhi* which lives in five fragmented populations in the Cameroon–Nigeria border region. With a combined total of fewer than 250 individuals, this is one of the world's most threatened primate taxa.

The fate of the eastern gorilla – still split into a lowland and mountain race – is more precarious still. As recently as the mid 1990s, an estimated 17,000 eastern lowland gorillas remained in the wild, but by 2016 it was thought that the population had dropped to below 4,000, largely as a result of ongoing civil war in the DRC. Rarer still, but more numerically stable, is the mountain gorilla, with a global population of slightly more than 1,000 individuals split between the border-straddling Virunga volcanoes and Uganda's Bwindi Impenetrable National Park.

The first study of mountain gorilla behaviour was undertaken in the 1950s by George Schaller, whose pioneering work formed the starting point for the better-publicised research initiated by Dian Fossey in the 1960s. The brutal – and still unsolved – murder of Fossey at her Rwandan research centre in December 1985 is generally thought to have been the work of one of the many poachers with whom she crossed swords in the Virungas. Fossey's acclaimed book *Gorillas in the Mist* remains perhaps the accessible starting point for anybody who wants to know more about mountain gorilla behaviour, while the eponymous movie, a posthumous account of Fossey's life, drew global attention to the plight of the mountain gorilla.

The mountain gorilla is distinguished from its lowland counterparts by several adaptations to its high-altitude home, most visibly a longer and more luxuriant

west from the Mbarara Road near Katunguru, then runs past the Ishasha Sector of QENP and south through Kihihi and Butogota. From Kasese, this 170km route takes around 5 hours driving non stop, but most people divert to Ishasha to look for its tree-climbing lions (page 506). The alternative route via Ishaka, Kagamba

coat. It is on average bulkier than other races, with the heaviest individual gorilla on record being Guhondo, the 220kg dominant silverback in Rwanda's Sabyinyo Group. The mountain gorilla is a highly sociable creature, living in defined groups of anything from five to 50 animals. A group typically consists of one dominant silverback male (the male's back turns silver when he reaches sexual maturity at about 13 years old) and sometimes one or more subordinate silverbacks, as well as a harem of three or four mature females, and several young animals. Unusually for mammals, it is the male who forms the focal point of gorilla society; when a silverback dies, his troop normally disintegrates. A silverback will start to acquire his harem at about 15 years of age, most normally by attracting a young sexually mature female from another troop. He may continue to lead a troop well into his 40s.

A female gorilla reaches sexual maturity at the age of eight, after which she will often move between different troops several times. Once a female has successfully given birth, however, she normally stays loyal to the same silverback until he dies, and she will even help defend him against other males. (When a male takes over a troop, he generally kills all nursing infants to bring the mothers into oestrus more quickly, a strong motive for a female to help preserve the status quo.) A female gorilla has a gestation period similar to that of a human, and if she reaches old age she will typically have raised up to six offspring to sexual maturity. A female's status within a troop is based on the length of time she has been with a silverback: the alpha female is normally the longest-serving member of the harem.

The mountain gorilla is primarily vegetarian. Its dietary mainstay is bamboo shoots, but it has been recorded eating the leaves, shoots, stems or other parts of more than 140 different plant species. About 2% of its diet is made up of insects and other invertebrates, with ants being the most favoured protein supplement. A gorilla troop will spend most of its waking hours on the ground, but climbs into the trees at night, when each group member builds its own temporary nest. Gorillas are surprisingly sedentary creatures, typically moving less than 1km in a day, which makes tracking them on a day-to-day basis relatively easy for experienced guides. A group will generally only move a long distance after a stressful incident, for instance an aggressive encounter with other gorillas. But this is quite rare, as gorillas are fundamentally peaceable animals. They have few natural enemies and often live for up to 50 years in the wild, but their long-term survival is critically threatened by poaching, deforestation and exposure to human-borne diseases.

The Virunga and Bwindi populations do display some quite distinct behavioural differences. Gorillas in Bwindi, for instance, tend to eat more fruit than their Virunga counterparts, to travel further on the average day to forage, and to climb and build overnight nests in trees with greater regularity. This is most likely due to environmental rather than genetic factors, and it is widely held that the two populations are racially identical, a not unreasonable assumption given that a corridor of mid-altitude forest linked the Virungas to Bwindi until about 500 years ago.

and Rukungiri is worth considering if you hear the Ishasha Road is in poor shape, and is as good as equidistant and probably slightly faster coming from the vicinity of Kichwamba Escarpment. Alternatively, a shorter option via Mitooma bypasses Rukungori but includes 20km of rough murram.

From Kabale and the south The 108km drive from Kabale to Buhoma follows dirt roads most of the way, and takes at least 3 hours. Follow the surfaced Kisoro Road out of Kabale for 18km to Hamurwa, then turn right at the turn-off signposted for Buhoma and continue for 60km via Kanungu to Kanyantorogo, where you turn left to Butogota. A far more scenic but slightly slower alternative, often offering excellent monkey viewing, is to travel through Ruhija (page 563), taking the signposted short cut left turn 5km before Butogota.

By public transport These days, reaching Buhoma on public transport couldn't be simpler, though you might wish it quicker. The reliable Bwindi Bus (m 0782 608325, 0782 570898) leaves Kampala's Kasenyi Bus Terminal for Buhoma at 09.00 and 20.00 and starts the return journey at 03.00 and 15.00. The trip costs US$12 and takes 10–12 hours. Other options are the Highway and Starlink buses. With an US$800 gorilla-tracking permit at stake, be sure to book your ticket at least one day ahead, and to allow a spare day in case of breakdowns.

Coming from elsewhere, you'll be dependent on matatus. From the north or east, your first goal will most likely be Rukungiri, a substantial but unremarkable town now connected by good surfaced roads and plenty of matatus to Ishaka (on the Kasese–Mbarara Road) and Ntungamo (on the Mbarara–Kabale Road). Coming from the south, your first goal will be Kanungu, which is connected to Kabale by regular matatus. You won't have any problem finding transport from Rukungiri or Kanungu to Butogota, a small town with several hotels only 17km from Buhoma. From Butogota, you could either wait for one of the buses coming from Kampala, or – more convenient – engage a special-hire taxi (US$20–25) or a boda (US$6).

On foot The most unusual and perhaps exciting way to get to or from Buhoma is the day hiking trail that follows an abandoned logging road through the national park to the southwestern trailhead of Nkuringo. The hike is not particularly steep and takes up to 5 hours, with a good chance of spotting black-and-white colobus, L'Hoest's monkey and red-tailed monkey, as well as forest birds. Like other nature walks, it costs US$50/60 FNR/FR, plus the national park entrance fee. If you are on an organised safari, you can arrange for your driver to drop you at one trailhead and meet you at the other, though bear in mind that they might actually take longer to drive between Nkuringo and Buhoma, since the two are 130km apart by road, mostly on dirt. The hike can be arranged at either trailhead a day in advance.

WHERE TO STAY The camps and lodges servicing Buhoma are spread along the steeply sloping, well-wooded and rather damp Munyaga River Valley. Most enjoy a memorable view of the wall of verdant forest covering the opposite side of the valley, but getting around them tends to involve negotiating an inordinate number of steps. Accommodation often costs considerably more than comparable facilities elsewhere, partly due to the isolated location, and partly because it includes several of the country's swankiest lodges. If we're going to be correct, the emergent village (the main purpose of which is seemingly to satisfy an insatiable demand for Congolese masks and carved gorillas) immediately outside the park gate, which the tourist industry knows as Buhoma, is really called Nkwenda. Buhoma proper is 1.5km back down the road. Most of the accommodation listed on the following pages is in Nkwenda, and in the few instances that a lodge is located in Buhoma proper, we'll emphasise the distinction by calling it Old Buhoma.

Exclusive

✷ **Buhoma Lodge** [548 A7] (10 cottages) m 0772 721155; e reservations@ugandaexclusivecamps.com; w ugandaexclusivecamps.com. Located 300m inside the park gate & 2mins' walk from the gorilla trailhead, this terrific lodge faces a wall of forest on the far side of the Munyaga River. With a comfortable 1st-floor lounge taking in the view, an excellent array of books provided, & superb 3-course meals, there is no better place in Buhoma to stay put after tracking gorillas & resisting blandishments to meet the Batwa, see a pangolin & support women's empowerment at Ride 4 A Woman, etc. Perched upslope behind the lodge, the cottages enjoy even giddier views, &, being constructed using mesh windows & gumpole-&-plaster walls (a lightweight version of a half-timbered medieval building), they avoid the clinging dampness common to tropical forest accommodation. **$$$$$**

✷ **Bwindi Lodge** [548 A6] (10 cottages) ☎ 041 4346464/5; m 0772 741720; e enquiries@volcanoessafaris.com; w volcanoessafaris.com. Set in regenerating forest between Nkwenda village & the Munyaga River, Buhoma's standout lodge manages an atmosphere of effortless seclusion, exclusivity & understated luxury, just metres below the budget hordes & mid-range masses moving along the main road. With an eclectic range of fabrics, furnishings, colours & framed botanical prints within & the usual forest view without, the spacious cottages are, without doubt, Buhoma's finest. A 20min trail within the property descends into beautiful forest beside the river & offers a good chance of seeing red-tailed monkey, black-&-white colobus & a range of forest birds. The rates are, of course, unapologetically immodest. **$$$$$$**

Mahogany Springs [548 B5] (8 cottages) ☎ (UK) +44 208 736 0713; e barrie@mahoganysprings.com; w mahoganysprings.com. This popular lodge is set in a tract of wooded farmland on the northern edge of Nwenda village, about 1.5km outside the park entrance gate. The lodge & cottages present a modernistic take on the usual safari style & if this results in some austere interiors, the scales are tipped the other way by the warmth of the service & the excellence of the food. **$$$$$**

Sanctuary Gorilla Forest Camp [548 A7] (8 tents) m 0772 753619 (camp), 0776 340290 (reservations); e reservations.kenya@sanctuaryretreats.com; w sanctuaryretreats.com. Situated inside the park entrance, 100m beyond Buhoma Lodge (see left) this meticulously managed tented camp boasts a superb location in a forest glade at the top of a 91-step staircase. Though vegetation prevents much of an outward panorama, the forest takes on a particularly tangible presence, with plenty of monkeys passing through & great blue turacos, emerald cuckoos & tinker barbets calling from high in the canopy. **$$$$$$**

Upmarket

Engagi Lodge [548 B5] (8 cottages) m 0772 401391; e info@kimbla-mantanauganda.com; w engagilodge.com. A good-value alternative to the exclusive lodges listed above, this lovely camp on the edge of Nkwenda has an open-fronted, wooden-floored dining & sitting area with lounge chairs & fireplace, fascinating historical prints, a library, bar, veranda & the usual great forest view. These priorities within a structure of local stone, timber & thatch bring to mind the home of a (wealthy) colonial-era settler. **$$$$$**

Haven Lodge [548 A6] (8 rooms) m 0788 047194, 0772 384965; e havenlodgebwindi21@gmail.com; w buhomacommunityug.com. In a location in which fabulous forest views are ten a penny, this upmarket venture by the Buhoma Community Rest Camp people (page 556) enjoys one of the very best. Set high above Nkwenda village, the lodge & slate-roofed cottages look directly down the forested Munyaga River Valley towards Bwindi's southerly Nkuringo trailhead, 8km as the crow flies but about 6hrs by car. *US$216/338 sgl/dbl FB*. **$$$$**

Trackers Safari Lodge [548 A5] (13 cottages) m 0772 411715, 0706 662537; e trackerssafarilodge@gmail.com; w trackerssafarilodge.com. Reached by a steep road ascending above Nkwenda, this upmarket establishment offers large & luxurious log cabins connected by an elevated walkway that leads through manicured gardens towards a nice swimming pool area. There is, of course, the usual verdant forest backdrop, but though the rates are similar, it isn't in quite the same league as the exclusive lodges listed above. **$$$$$$**

Moderate

Crested Crane Hotel Bwindi [548 B1] (10 rooms) ⊕ -0.90975, 29.62711; ☎ 039 2176063; **m** 0792 200380; **e** reservations@thecrestedcranebwindi.com; **w** thecrestedcranebwindi.com. Set on a grassy green hill overlooking rolling farmland 10km north of Buhoma alongside the road to Butogota, this rather institutional-looking complex of round bandas lacks the character of the upmarket options close to the national park, but it is more competitively priced. Rooms have nets, DTSV, Wi-Fi, balcony & en-suite hot shower. The restaurant has a fine view towards the forest. Flocks of several dozen crowned crane are semi-resident. Despite (or perhaps because of) its relative remoteness, a good-value base for gorilla tracking. *US$160/200 sgl/dbl FB.* **$$$**

Budget

Buhoma Community Rest Camp [548 A6] (11 rooms, 1 dorm) **m** 0772 384965; **e** buhomacommunity@yahoo.com; **w** buhomacommunityug.com. Located just inside the park gate, this popular camp has a great jungle setting. Once the go-to place for travellers on a budget, this worthy establishment has abandoned its humble roots by upgrading its cheaper rooms with shared facilities to costlier en-suite accommodation. While allowing for the contribution the BCRC makes to local community development, you'll now find better for less elsewhere. *US$115/166 en-suite sgl/dbl FB; US$12 pp camping.* **$$$**

Buhoma Gorilla Camp [548 A4] (8 rooms) **m** 0784 728516. This new lodge counters a location in Old Buhoma village with a pleasantly forested location beside a babbling brook. One suspects the rates may moderate in time. *US$180/280 sgl/dbl cottages.* **$$$$**

✷ **Gorilla Bluff** [548 A5] (9 rooms) **m** 0772 439756; **e** info@gorillablufflodge.com; **w** gorillablufflodge.com. Just beyond the northern end of Nkwenda village, this smart new hillside lodge offers refreshingly sensible prices for rooms in the lodge building & cottages with a view. Good value. *Rooms US$100/120, cottages US$80/120 sgl/dbl FB.* **$$$**

Gorilla Conservation Lodge [548 A6] (5 rooms) **m** 0780 484259, 0778 331025; **e** supporter@ctph.org; **w** ctph.org/gorilla-conservation-camp. The highest lodge in – or rather above – Nkwenda, this sensibly priced facility enjoys the broadest panorama, looking south towards Nkuringo. It's an appendage to Conservation Through Public Health, an NGO that works to further conservation by improving local health care, & guests are welcome to visit the adjacent research centre to learn about ongoing work. Non-residents pay US$250/group. Accommodation is provided in a block of 5 simple rooms facing the view; more luxurious cottages are planned. *US$80/120 sgl/dbl FB.* **$$$**

✷ **Ride 4 A Woman** [548 A4] (11 rooms) Old Buhoma; **m** 0785 999112, 0772 607317; **e** info@ride4awoman.org; **w** ride4awoman.org. Part of a women's co-operative that originally rented out bicycles to tourists (but no longer does), this lovely guesthouse lies in the NGO's large green gardens in Buhoma village. Brightly decorated twin or dbl en-suite rooms have fitted nets, hot shower & private balcony & there's a cheerful restaurant on the property, as well as the Ride 4 A Woman gift shop. *US$100/150 sgl/dbl FB.* **$$$**

Ruhondeza Lodge & Campsite [548 B5] (4 rooms) Nkwenda; **m** 0773 465938; **e** info@ruhondezalodge.com; **w** ruhondezalodge.com. Owned & managed by a former guide, this pleasant low-key lodge stands in riverside undergrowth between the tea estates 200m downhill from the main road. The rustic en-suite wood-&-thatch bandas have stone floor, hot shower & private balcony. There is also a secluded grassy campsite with a hot shower. *US$75/130 sgl/dbl FB; US$10 pp camping.* **$$$**

Shoestring

Bigambo Cottages [548 B1] (11 rooms) **m** 0782 822043; **e** bwindiforestsafariresort@yahoo.co.za. Situated 18km from Buhoma on the northern edge of the distinctly ordinary Butogota town, this extremely affordable facility offers basic but perfectly acceptable en-suite accommodation in round, 4-unit bandas. Excellent value if you don't mind being based in town & have wheels to get to the gorilla-tracking trailhead in time. *US$8/13 sgl/dbl bed-only.* **$**

✷ **Gorilla Friend's Lodge aka Magezi's** [548 A4] (8 rooms) **m** 0782 822043; **e** mistlodgebuhoma@gmail.com. This basic & eminently affordable lodge in Old Buhoma has long been a favourite with safari driver/guides & backpackers. *US$8 sgl. Bed only.* **$**

✷ **Mist Lodge** [548 A6] (8 rooms) m 0764 416476; e mistlodgebuhoma@gmail.com. Friendly, clean & unpretentious, this standard shoestring Ugandan guesthouse in the heart of Nkwenda village is a refreshingly affordable alternative to anything else within 5mins' walking distance of the entrance gate. *US$5/11 en-suite sgl/dbl; US$4 with shared facilities.* **$**

WHERE TO EAT AND DRINK Most visitors eat at their lodge or camp, but there are a few eateries in Nkwenda and Buhoma villages.

Bwindi Bar [548 A6] m 0772 595155; ⏲ 07.00–22.00. In addition to providing hospitality training to disadvantaged local youngsters, this Nkwenda restaurant & bar serves a variety of local dishes, along with beer, wine, coffee & other beverages. You can sit indoors or in a back garden offering a great view to the forested slopes opposite. Rolex-making classes at 16.00 on Wed, Sat & Sun. *Most mains in the US$3–6 range.*

Bwindi Gorilla Coffee Cup [548 A6] m 0772 399224. Set right outside the park entrance, this neat café with outdoor seating serves fresh coffee & chilled beers throughout the day, but meals must be ordered in advance. *Meals US$3–5.*

Mapera Lounge [548 A4] Old Buhoma; m 0764 146159. Locals flock to this bar complex at w/ends to watch Premier League football on a large screen TV, while on w/days tourists come to see Batwa & Bakiga dances in the large, wooded compound. There's no charge for the latter but donations are obviously welcomed.

SHOPPING While most lodges contain some sort of sales area, take the time to browse through the **roadside craft shops** in Nkenda village. In particular, check out the Batwa Crafts outside the national park gate [548 B6], which, affiliated to the highly regarded Batwa Development Programme, sells a variety of handicrafts made by local Batwa communities. You should also be sure to have a look at the colourful Ride 4 A Woman shop, 1.5km away in Old Buhoma [548 B2] (page 562).

OTHER PRACTICALITIES There are no banks or foreign exchange facilities in Buhoma; the closest banks and ATMs are in Kihihi, 40km along the Ishasha Road.

TOURIST INFORMATION AND TOUR OPERATORS

Buhoma Mukono Community Development Association [548 B6] m 0772 384965; e buhomacommunity@yahoo.com. Based out of the community rest camp just inside the park gate (see opposite), this association can organise a variety of community-based activities outside the park.

Buhoma Visitors Centre [548 B7] A new visitors' centre 300m inside the park entrance gate doubles as the gorilla-tracking reception & briefing point, & a booking & information office where you can enquire about & pay for all activities out of Buhoma with the exception of gorilla-tracking permits. Be warned, however, that this concrete structure is so astonishingly at odds with its World Heritage Site location that aesthetic types might want to select an alternative trailhead for their gorilla adventure.

WHAT TO SEE AND DO

Gorilla tracking Buhoma is the trailhead for tracking seven habituated gorilla groups, all of which currently have one silverback. These are the Mubare Group (nine individuals), Habinyanja Group (11), Rushegura Group (16), Katwe Group (6), Binyindo (6), Kanywali (6) and Muyambi (6). The Mubare Group, named after the hills where it was first observed, was the first to be habituated for tourism in Uganda, a process that started in October 1991 and culminated with the first tourist visit exactly two years later. It numbered 15 individuals prior to 2017

THE GORILLA-TRACKING EXPERIENCE

Tracking mountain gorillas in the Virungas or Bwindi ranks among the absolute highlights of African travel. The exhilaration attached to first setting eyes on a wild mountain gorilla is difficult to describe. These are enormous animals: up to three times as bulky as the average man, their size exaggerated by a shaggily luxuriant coat. Yet despite their fearsome appearance, gorillas are remarkably peaceable creatures – tracking them would be a considerably more dangerous pursuit were they possessed of the aggressive temperament of, say, vervet monkeys or baboons, or for that matter human beings.

More impressive even than the gorillas' size and bearing is their unfathomable attitude to people, which differs greatly from that of any other wild animal I've encountered. Anthropomorphic as it might sound, almost everybody who visits the gorillas experiences an almost mystical sense of recognition. Often, one of the gentle giants will break off from the business of chomping on bamboo to study a human visitor, soft brown eyes staring deeply into theirs as if seeking a connection – a spine-tingling wildlife experience without peer.

Gorilla tracking should not present a serious physical challenge to any reasonably fit adult whatever their age, but the hike can be tough going. Exactly how tough varies greatly, and the main determining factor is basically down to luck, specifically how close the gorillas are to the trailhead on the day you trek (1–2 hours is typical, anything from 15 minutes to 6 hours possible). Another variable is how recently it has rained, which affects conditions underfoot – June to August are the driest months and March to May are the wettest.

The effects of altitude should not be underestimated. Tracking in Bwindi usually takes place at around 1,400–2,000m above sea level, but in the Virungas the gorillas are often encountered closer to 3,000m – sufficient to knock the breath out of anybody who just flew in from low altitude. For this reason, travellers might want to leave gorilla tracking until they've been in the region for a week and are reasonably acclimatised – most of Uganda lies above 1,000m.

Trackers must meet (with passport or photocopy thereof to hand) at the relevant trailhead at 08.00 to receive a short briefing about what to expect before they depart into the forest. Though permits don't specify which gorilla group you will track, the rangers try to match older or relatively unfit-looking trackers to whichever group they expect to be easiest to reach on the day. If you need special consideration in this regard, best get there a bit early. Take advantage when the guides offer you a walking staff before the walk; this will be invaluable to help you keep your balance on steep hillsides. Once on the trail, don't be afraid to ask to stop for a few minutes whenever you feel tired, or to ask the guides to create a makeshift walking stick from a branch. Drink plenty of water, and do carry some

when a young silverback from the Habinyanja Group staged a violent takeover by killing the existing silverback and all youngsters. Subsequent splits from this latter group have produced the Rushegura and Binyindo families, both of which are tracked. From this history it will be apparent that the size and number of gorilla groups can change significantly and the figures on page 557 for 2024 will probably have changed by the time you visit. In most cases, though overall numbers of gorillas within each sector will merely reflect a few births and deaths, these totals may well be redistributed as groups, usually the larger ones, split up to form two smaller ones.

quick calories such as biscuits or chocolate. The good news is that in 99% of cases, whatever exhaustion you might feel on the way up will vanish with the adrenalin charge that follows the first sighting of a silverback gorilla!

Put on your sturdiest walking shoes for the trek, and wear thick trousers and long sleeves as protection against vicious nettles. It's often cold at the outset, so bring a sweatshirt or jersey. The gorillas are used to people, and it makes no difference whether you wear bright or muted colours. Whatever clothes you wear are likely to get very dirty, so if you have pre-muddied clothes, use them! During the rainy season, a poncho or raincoat might be a worthy addition to your daypack, while sunscreen, sunglasses and a hat are a good idea at any time of year, as are gloves to protect against nettles.

In all reserves, ordinary trackers are permitted to spend no longer than 1 hour with the gorillas (people who sign on for the habituation experience can stay for up to 4 hours). It is forbidden to eat, smoke, urinate or defecate in the vicinity of a gorilla group. Gorillas are susceptible to many human diseases, and it has long been feared by researchers that one ill tourist might infect a gorilla, resulting in the possible death of the whole troop should no immunity exist. For this reason, people who know they are harbouring a potentially airborne infection such as a flu or cold should not track gorillas (the permit fee will be refunded). Once in the forest, trackers should not approach the gorillas more closely than 7m (a rule that is often contravened by curious youngsters and sometimes adults approaching their human visitors) and should turn their head away if they need to sneeze.

As for photography, our advice, unless you're a professional or serious amateur, is to run off a few quick snapshots, then put the camera away, enjoy the moment, and buy a postcard or coffee-table book later. Gorillas are tricky photographic subjects, on account of their sunken eyes, the gloomy habitat in which they are often found, and a jet-black skin that tends to distort light readings. Flash photography is forbidden, so carrying a tripod or monopod will help you to get sharper results. It is also worth pre-programming your camera to a relatively high ISO (around 800), and pushing it even higher if conditions demand it. Make sure, too, that your camera gear is well protected – if your bag isn't waterproof, seal your camera in a plastic bag.

Above all, do bear in mind that gorillas are still wild animals, despite the 'gentle giant' reputation that has superseded the old King Kong image. An adult gorilla is much stronger than a person and will act in accordance with its own social codes when provoked or surprised. Accidents are rare, but still it is important to listen to your guide at all times regarding the correct protocol in the presence of gorillas.

Eight permits are available for each of Buhoma's groups, bringing the daily total to 56. These are often booked up months in advance, especially during the high season. Assuming you have obtained your permit, you'll need to present it at the Visitor Centre by 08.00 and be ready to set off after a short briefing. The round trip might take anything from 3 to 10 hours, depending on the proximity of the gorillas and how easily they are located. The success rate is as good as 100%, though it may sometimes depend on the age, fitness and determination of individual permit-holders, who will occasionally turn back before reaching the gorillas because they are too tired to continue. If you are concerned about your age or fitness, let the rangers

GORILLA-TRACKING PERMITS AND LOGISTICS

When gorilla tracking was introduced to Uganda in 1993, it was limited to a single habituated group at Buhoma. Today, by contrast, 25 fully habituated groups can be tracked from four different sites in Bwindi (seven from Buhoma, five from Ruhija, nine from Rushaga and four from Nkuringo), while another habituated group can be tracked in Mgahinga Gorilla National Park (page 535). This means that 208 gorilla-tracking permits are available daily, 200 for Bwindi and eight for Mgahinga.

Two types of permit are available. The vast majority of visitors buy a standard permit, which costs US$700/800/500/80 FR/FNR/ROA/EAC. The alternative, applicable only to the group currently under habituation at Rushaga, is a habituation permit which allows you 4 hours with the gorillas. This costs US$1,000/1,500/800/300 per FR/FNR/ROA/EAC and is reserved for one group of up to six people daily. In all cases, the permit includes park entrance fees, guides and trackers, but not a porter if one is required.

In addition to this initial outlay, other financial considerations must be taken into account. One is the cost of transport. Public transport is tricky, Buhoma being the only trailhead accessible by bus. For the remainder you'll need to get to a regional town before resorting to some rough and ready form of public transport or chartering a boda or special hire. When you finally reach the trailhead, you'll find the cost of accommodation to be on the high side – plenty of opportunities to splash out US$500-plus per night on an upmarket lodge or tented camp – but each of the tracking trailheads also has at least one more affordable (though in most cases, still relatively overpriced) budget option in the vicinity.

If you're tracking gorillas as part of an organised tour, you can safely assume that your operator will have booked permits in advance and will get you down to Bwindi (or Mgahinga) by car or plane and find you a comfortable bed. Independent travellers will obviously need to make other arrangements to obtain a permit. Since UWA is yet to implement an online system, someone will need to contact the Kampala Reservations Office to establish availability, make payment in cash, by card, bank transfer or MoMo, and collect your permit. If

know, and they will probably allocate you to the group they expect to be easiest to locate, based on its location the day before. Mubare and Katwe are probably the most reliably physically undemanding groups to track, since they generally stick close to the park's northern boundary, and often stray outside it. Rushegura, whose territory incorporates Buhoma, occasionally passes through lodge and camp grounds within the park boundary, and is often very quickly located close to the trailhead, but it also sometimes moves deeper into the forest. The Binyindo and Habinyanja groups are usually the most remote from Buhoma and trackers will need a vehicle to reach an isolated trailhead along the Ruhija to start the hike.

Nature walks from Buhoma Several guided nature walks, ranging from 30 minutes to 8 hours in duration, lead from Buhoma, offering the opportunity to enjoy the tranquillity and broader biodiversity of the forest, and to see a variety of monkeys and birds. For monkeys and general scenery, the best of the guided walks is probably the 3-hour **Waterfall Trail**, which leads for 2km along the Old Buhoma Road, a disused logging track, to Nkuringo before ascending through a beautiful area of forest to a 33m-high waterfall on the Munyaga River. The **Mazubijiro Loop**

you're a Foreign Resident or Ugandan citizen, that person could be you, and good luck; you could spend several hours waiting with tour operators on the same errand. A better option is to go to the much quieter UWA Booking Office at the Sheraton Hotel. Alternatively, you could pay remotely and have the permit scanned and sent to your phone. You can do this by MoMo or bank transfer (the latter must be done online; filling in forms at a bank creates a complicated paper chase).

If, on the other hand, you're a Foreign Non Resident or a visitor from the Rest of Africa, you'll need to contract a registered tour company to buy your permit for you. This service obviously comes at a cost – money well spent, perhaps, if it spares you a trip to UWA – and a few phone calls brought in quotes averaging out at US$50. Initiate the process well in advance so your agent doesn't need to make a special trip to UWA on your behalf and charge you accordingly. To find an agent, visit the Uganda Tourism Board website (w utb.go.ug/licenced-tour-companies), which lists safari companies licenced to handle the transaction. To help decide which of the 600-plus registered companies to select, you might want to do a bit of online research for testimonials from happy clients.

Whatever you do, don't go to a gorilla tracking trailhead hoping to snap up a vacant permit at the last minute. That's not going to happen. Though this is not to say that you have to physically be in the capital to secure a permit within a day or two (if, of course, one is available). It would be perfectly possible for a Foreign Non Resident taking time out at Lake Bunyonyi, for example, to spontaneously contact a tour operator on Monday morning and find themselves tracking gorillas in Rushaga or Ruhija on Wednesday. A Foreign Resident could also buy a permit remotely, though good luck with finding a local agent to load US$800 worth of shillings on to your Mobile Money account. The main complication is likely to be permit availability and the likelihood of getting one for a given date during the high season (Jul–Sep & Dec–Feb) is low. It is, however, often possible to obtain permits for trailheads other than Buhoma in the shoulder season (Mar, Jun, Oct) and often quite easy in the low season (Apr, May, Nov).

Trail and **Rushara Hill Trail**, each of which takes about 3 hours, offer good views across to the Virunga Mountains. The 8-hour **Ivo River Walk**, which leads to the Ivo River on the southern boundary of the park, offers a good opportunity for seeing monkeys, duikers and a variety of birds. Guided nature walks cost US$30/40 FR/FNR, exclusive of the US$30/40 park entrance fee, which is waived on walks undertaken on the same day as gorilla tracking. Tipping the guide is not mandatory but it is customary, bearing in mind that the rangers are poorly paid.

Birdwatching There are a couple of options for birders with a limited amount of time in Buhoma. One is a guided forest walk along the Old Buhoma Road with an option to divert on to the Waterfall Trail (see opposite). The open road provides better birding opportunities than a narrow forest path and on a good morning you could hope to see around 40–50 species, a high proportion of which are more easily seen here than in any similarly accessible part of Uganda. Among the great many remarkable birds commonly seen along this road, some of the more readily identifiable include the great blue turaco, black-billed turaco, barred long-tailed cuckoo, bar-tailed trogon, black bee-eater, grey-throated barbet, Petit's cuckoo-shrike, Elliot's woodpecker, red-tailed greenbul, mountain greenbul, icterine greenbul, yellow-whiskered greenbul, white-bellied robin-chat, white-tailed ant-thrush, rusty-faced woodland warbler, white-browed crombec, yellow-eyed black flycatcher, white-tailed blue flycatcher, white-tailed crested flycatcher, narrow-tailed starling, McKinnon's shrike, Doherty's bush-shrike and black-headed waxbill. In addition to the outstanding birding, this road supports a dazzling array of colourful butterflies, and the lovely L'Hoest's monkey is often encountered. Birders who specify their area of interest when they book a walk could ask for one of several UWA guides with above average birding skills.

If time (or money) is really tight, the answer is the self-guided Munyaga River Trail. This short (600m) route diverts left from the Old Buhoma Road at the entrance to the forest proper and loops back along the Munyaga Valley, following the river along the forest edge before climbing to the Visitor Centre. Entrance or guide fees do not apply to this trail, the reason being that the area between the gate and the forest is land held in trust for conservation rather than officially gazetted as part of the national park.

Ride 4 A Woman (m 0772 607317; e info@ride4awoman.org; w ride4awoman.org) This worthy initiative in Old Buhoma operates a workshop and gift shop on the side road to the Bwindi Community Hospital as well as offering accommodation (page 556). While a couple of dozen seamstresses work on site, the shop displays the work of some 300 craftswomen whose products range from beaded jewellery and basketwork to clothes, shopping bags and handbags. Made-to-measure items can be ordered and shipped to your home. A variety of participatory activities are also offered, including collecting and cooking ingredients for a local meal, basket weaving and guided walks/cycle trips.

Village walk This 3-hour stroll through Buhoma and its margins immerses visitors in the customs and practices of the Bakiga and Batwa people. The tour takes in varied activities such as farming, brewing local beer and dispensing traditional medicines, and concludes with dancing displays by members of the Batwa community. The walk is organised through the BMCDA (w bmcda.org) and costs US$15 per person.

Batwa visits The most authentic and best regulated Batwa visit is provided by the Batwa Experience [548 B6] (m 0772 901628; e info@batwaexperience.com; w batwaexperience.org), a half-day encounter that takes place in a patch of private forest contiguous with the national park and provides a fascinating insight into the traditional forest life and lore of this hunter-gatherer culture. The experience is organised by the well-regarded Batwa Development Programme and can be arranged through their sales outlet at Batwa Crafts (page 557). The outing runs from around 09.00 to 14.00 and costs US$60–85 per person depending on group size. A shorter (1-hour) Batwa walk costs US$30 per person.

Dance performances Based at the Watoto School past the Bwindi Community Hospital in Old Buhoma [548 B2], the Bwindi Orphan's Group, affiliated to the NGO Educate Bwindi (w educatebwindi.org), is dedicated to helping educate orphaned and disadvantaged children living in and around Buhoma. Traditional dances, supplemented by rather contrived but enjoyable 'gorilla dances', can be arranged on site or at any of the nearby lodges. There is no fixed charge but a significant donation will be welcomed. The Bwindi Cultural Heritage Programme also stages Batwa dances, held on weekdays at Mapera Lounge in Old Buhoma (page 557).

Pangolin Rescue Centre (⊕ 0.9245100, 29.6126900; m 0782 386972) Initiated by local conservationist Arineitwe Moses, this exciting new initiative receives forest pangolins found in farmland or rescued from poachers. After keeping them for a few days to recover from stress or injuries, they are then released in Bwindi Forest. Tourists are welcome to visit the project's rustic premises (signposted 6km north of Buhoma, 1km beyond the Ruhija short cut) to view these rarely seen nocturnal creatures, either in the morning (before 09.30) or afternoon (after 16.00), ie: when they are not fast asleep. It is also possible to schedule a visit to assist with a pangolin release into the forest. Prior booking is essential to make sure pangolins are currently in residence. There is no fixed charge (yet) but a donation of US$20 per person would seem reasonable to help cover project costs.

RUHIJA

Bwindi's highest and arguably most beautiful gorilla-tracking trailhead, sited at an altitude of 2,340m in the hills abutting the park's eastern boundary, affords fabulous southerly views over forested ridge after forested ridge to the distant Virunga volcanoes. Equally panoramic views towards the western Rift Valley are offered from sections of the road leading beyond Ruhija towards Buhoma, as well as from the hill a short distance beyond the main cluster of lodges (page 564). Prior to the opening of the Bitukura gorilla group for tracking in 2008, Ruhija was accessible only by very rough roads, and tourist activity was limited to the odd visiting birdwatcher in search of the super-localised green broadbill and various other high-altitude Albertine Rift Endemics associated with the area. Recently, however, this backwater status has changed. Five gorilla groups can now be tracked out of Ruhija, which handles a lot of overspill from the upmarket lodges at Buhoma during the peak tourist season. In addition, several mid-range and budget lodges are scattered in and around Ruhija, while the road there from Buhoma or Kabale – though hardly pristine – is sufficiently improved that it is usually negotiable by saloon cars.

GETTING THERE AND AWAY Coming directly from Kampala, the best option is through Kabale, where you'll probably need to spend a night before continuing to Ruhija.

From Kabale and the southwest Driving from anywhere in southern Kigezi, first head to the village of Ikumba, on the surfaced Kisoro Road 26km out of Kabale, then turn right at the clearly signposted junction (⊕ -1.12301, 29.87668) for Ruhija and Buhoma. After 12km, you'll pass through a park entrance gate (security check but no fees payable), from where the road continues through lush forest to reach the Ruhija tracking trailhead and park information office (⊕ -1.05161, 29.77815) after another 13km. About 800m past this, a multi-signposted junction to the right (⊕ -1.04695, 29.77535) leads outside the park and straight into Ruhija village – site of most of the accommodation servicing the area – after another 500m or so. The road between Ikumba and Ruhija is currently well maintained, but allow 2 hours coming from Kabale, and be aware there are some rocky sections that might deteriorate during the rainy season, so if you are setting off in a saloon car, ask for an update first.

Matatus run between Kabale and Ruhija most days (2–3hrs), but this cannot be depended on. Most of these matatus all overnight in Ruhija, then set off for Kabale in the early morning (typically around 05.00) arriving in time for breakfast. They then spend the morning in Kabale before starting the return trip in the early afternoon, between 13.00 and 16.00. There are no matatus on Saturday, Sunday or public holidays. Alternatively, a special hire is likely to cost up to US$100, depending on whether it has 4x4, while a boda costs around US$25. Some travellers opt to overnight in Kabale before they go gorilla tracking at Ruhija, but this enforces a very early start and leaves no margin for error in the event of a breakdown or delay.

From Buhoma and the north It's a straightforward 50km, 2-hour drive from Buhoma to Ruhija, passing through the park and some lovely scenery for much of the way, and ideally using the short cut that avoids Butogota and cuts about 6km from the route passing through that town. Quite a lot of organised tours now use Buhoma as a base for gorilla tracking in Ruhija, in which case a 05.00 start is advisable. Coming from QENP, Kasese, Fort Portal or other sites to the northwest, directions are as for Buhoma, except that when you reach the forest of signposts indicating the right turn to Buhoma (⊕ -0.90618, 29.64535) 1.5km past Butogota, you need to continue straight on instead. No public transport runs to Ruhija from the north, but you could presumably arrange a special hire or boda from Butogota.

By air Aerolink (☎ 031 7333000; e info@aerolinkuganda.com; w aerolinkuganda.com) flies daily to both Kisoro and Kihihi airstrips (US$475 return plus US$20 airport tax) with the latter being the better option. Not only is the vehicle transfer from Kihihi slightly shorter, a US$70 per person surcharge is levied on Kisoro in case weather conditions force the plane to redirect to Kihihi (page 507). So best just book a flight there in the first place.

WHERE TO STAY AND EAT With one upmarket exception, Ruhija's lodges are more down-to-earth than Buhoma's finest while offering little in the way of decent budget options. The result is an overblown mid-range sector in which value for money should not be taken for granted. Except where noted, the places listed here lie adjacent to Ruhija village, which lies on a ridge extending north from the main road. Easily identified by a cluster of signposts, the junction lies 800m northwest of the Ruhija tracking trailhead. Most of Ruhija's camps and lodges enjoy terrific views over the forest and adjacent terraced hills towards (weather permitting) the Virungas, but it does get chilly at night so come prepared. Ruhija also has a serious water shortage: when it doesn't fall from the sky, it has to be fetched from a valley stream spring located a parachute-worthy distance below the ridge. Consequently, in place of the usual grass thatch, you'll find roofs covered by tiles or corrugated sheets to maximise the potential for rainwater harvesting. To note an additional potential concern, Ruhija has recently been connected to mains electricity, so evening noise from bars may become an issue for lodges closest to the village unless they have sufficient clout in the community to tackle the matter.

Upmarket

✷ **Kiho Gorilla Safari Lodge** [549 E4] (9 rooms) m 0758 736454, 0700 682266; e reservations@kihogorillalodge.com; w kihogorillalodge.com. Hitherto, upmarket visitors to Ruhija were limited to those who booked too late in the season to get a permit in Buhoma – & endured a 3hr round trip to Ruhija as a result. Now, in the form of this welcome new development, which borders the forest 7km southeast of Ruhija trailhead, they finally have the accommodation they deserve. Though the modernistic architecture is a brutal break with the usual safari style, purists need not worry. From the outside, each cottage, nestled into stands of bamboo, grasses & exotic-looking species of giant lobelia, is merely a door at the end of a brick paved corridor through the jungle. Nor are the luxurious & well-thought-out interiors anything to worry about, with a 'mud room'/lobby (to divest yourself of forest-sodden garments) connecting to a generously sized bedsit with warming firewood stove & minibar, & a bathroom with indoor & outdoor showers plus jacuzzi tub. If the Chinese landscape represented in the AI-generated artwork isn't to your taste, a sliding glass door connects to a pergola-topped veranda & the bamboo-lobelia world beyond. A heated swimming pool is provided, plus spa facilities. **$$$$$**

Moderate

Agandi Uganda Ecolodge [549 H6] (9 rooms) m 0393 241250; e info@agandiuganda.com; w agandiuganda.com. Ruhija village's most stylish lodge offers accommodation in 3 distinct types of room, all of which have an organic feel offset by bright ethnic fabrics. The main lodge enjoys a grandstand view across steep farmed & forested hills towards the Virungas; unfortunately, a similar outlook from the cottages below is threatened by the growth of tree plantations downslope. *US$150/250 sgl/dbl FB.* **$$$$**

✷ **Bakiga Lodge** [549 H6] (12 rooms) m 0774 518421; e info@bakigalodge.org; w bakigalodge.org. This friendly & well-priced lodge in Ruhija village comprises a row of attractively furnished en-suite twin, dbl & family cabins. Both lodge & cottages enjoy an uninterrupted view of forest & farmland, the latter from a private balcony or through large glass windows. All profits go towards the Bakiga Community Project, which is mainly concerned with creating clean water sources in villages in the vicinity of Bwindi. *US$150/220/350 sgl/dbl/trpl FB.* **$$$$**

Gorilla Mist Camp [549 H6] (12 rooms) m 0772 563577, 0754 315151; e info@gorillamistcamp.com; w gorillamistcamp.com. This agreeable lodge set in manicured gardens at the north end of Ruhija village is distinguished by its on-the-ball staff & sensible rates. Again, it is the lodge that provides the forest/Virunga view while the pine trees of an unco-operative neighbour rise ever upwards in front of the stilted half-timbered cottages. Fair value. *US$170/220 sgl/dbl FB.* **$$$$**

Ruhija Community Rest Camp [549 H6] (10 rooms) m 0771 846635, 0754 166306; e ruhijac@gmail.com; w ruhijacommunityrestcamp.com. Revenue from this community-run camp helps fund local development & they are doing their best to maximise their impact by upgrading the rooms & doubling their rates. Though the new selection of en-suite tented cottages faces a stunning wall of forest on a facing mountainside, visitors may well feel short-changed by the standard of the accommodation. *US$100 pp FB en-suite; US$45 rooms using common shower.* **$$$**

Ruhija Gorilla Safari Lodge [549 H6] (14 rooms) \ 041 4503065; e reservation@gorillasafari.travel; w bwindigorillasafari.com. The most expensive place in Ruhija village enjoys a fine view across the forest towards the Virungas. *US$185/307 standard sgl/dbl. Just US$5 extra pp gets a larger 'superior' cabin with a fireplace. All rates FB.* **$$$$**

Budget and camping

Broadbill Forest Camp [549 E4] (5 tents) ⊕ -1.05781, 29.79623; m 0754 134875; e enquiries@broadbillforest.com; w broadbillforestcamp.com. This likeable tented camp has an isolated location on private land 7km from Ruhija trailhead, close to the upmarket Kiho Lodge. Simple but comfortable en-suite furnished tents have balconies offering great views into a glade sometimes visited by Bwindi's elusive elephants. The hands-on owner-manager is a superb naturalist & adept at locating Rwenzori 3-horned chameleons, as well as some of the rarer birds associated with the Ruhija area. Good value. *US$75/145 sgl/dbl B&B.* **$$$**

✷ **Ruhija Gorilla Friends Resort** [549 H6] (13 units) m 0786 613313, 0751 198193; e ruhijagorillafriends@gmail.com; w ruhijagorillafriends.com. This recently upgraded facility offers a splendid view over cultivated hills (as opposed to forest) behind Ruhija village. A selection of options with & without attached bathroom is offered in standing tents (plenty of warm bedding provided) & rooms. *US$80/160*

MOUNTAIN GORILLAS: TOURISM AND CONSERVATION

Over the two decades following the European discovery of mountain gorillas, at least 50 individuals were captured or killed in the Virungas, prompting the Belgian government to create Albert National Park in 1925. This protected what are now the Congolese and Rwandan portions of the Virunga Mountains, and was managed as a cohesive conservation unit.

The gorilla population of the Virungas is thought to have been reasonably stable in 1960, when a census undertaken by George Schaller indicated that some 450 individuals lived in the range. By 1971–73, however, the population had plummeted to an estimated 250. This decline was attributed to several factors, including the post-colonial division of Albert National Park into its Rwandan and Congolese components, the ongoing fighting between the Hutu and Tutsi of Rwanda, and a grisly tourist trade in poached gorilla heads and hands – the latter used by some sad individuals as ashtrays! Most devastating of all perhaps was the irreversible loss of almost half of the gorillas' habitat between 1957 and 1968 to local farmers and a European-funded agricultural scheme.

In 1979, Amy Vedder and Bill Webber initiated the first gorilla tourism project in Rwanda's Volcanoes National Park, integrating tourism, local education and anti-poaching measures with remarkable success. Initially, the project was aimed mainly at overland trucks, who paid US$20 per person – paltry by today's standards – to track gorillas. Even so, gorilla tourism was raising up to US$10 million annually by the mid 1980s, making it Rwanda's third-highest earner of foreign revenue. The mountain gorilla had practically become the national emblem, and was officially regarded to be the country's most important renewable natural resource. To ordinary Rwandans, gorillas became a source of great national pride: living gorillas ultimately created far more work and money than poaching them had ever done. As a result, a census undertaken in 1989 indicated that the local mountain gorilla population had increased by almost 30% to 320 animals.

Despite the success of ecotourism, there are still several threats to the ongoing survival of mountain gorillas in the wild. For the Virunga population, the major threat is undoubtedly political. In 1991, the long-standing ethnic tension between Rwanda's Hutu and Tutsi populations erupted into a civil war that culminated in the genocide of 1994. In context, the fate of a few gorillas does seem a rather trivial concern, even if you take into account the important role that gorilla tourism has played in rebuilding Rwanda's post-war economy, and the fact that the integrated conservation of their habitat will also protect a watershed that supplies 10% of the country with water.

Nevertheless, the Rwandan conflict had several repercussions in the Virungas. Researchers and park rangers were twice forced to evacuate the Volcanoes National Park, leaving the gorillas unguarded. Tourism to Rwanda practically ceased in 1991, but gorilla tracking resumed in 1999, and tourist arrivals now far exceed the level of the 1980s. Remarkably, however, when researchers were finally able to return to the Volcanoes National Park in the late 1990s, only four gorillas were unaccounted

en-suite tent/room; US$60/120 tent/room with shared facilities. **$$$**

Trekkers Tavern [549 H6] (5 cottages) 0774 112511, 0772 455423; e mutebihassan@yahoo.com. Set in a patch of woodland at the top end of Ruhija village, this basic lodge offers inferior but correspondingly cheaper copies of the upmarket cottages at Ndali Lodge (page 421). Fair value. *US$120/140 sgl/dbl FB.* **$$$**

for. Two were old females who most probably died of natural causes. The other two might have been shot, but could just as easily have succumbed to disease.

But in this most unstable part of Africa, little can be taken for granted. Just as Rwanda started to stabilise politically, the DRC descended into anarchy. For years, eastern Congolese officials, who lived far from the capital, received no formal salary and were forced to devise their own ways of securing a living, leading to a level of corruption second to none in the region. At least 20 gorillas were killed in the DRC between 1995 and 2007, during most of which time the Congolese Virunga National Park was effectively closed to tourists and researchers alike. Under the circumstances, it is remarkable to learn that the latest Virunga-wide gorilla count, undertaken in 2018, showed a further increase to at least 604 individuals – almost double the number recorded in the early 1970s, and a 25% increase since the 2010–11 census, which recorded 480 gorillas. The Bwindi population has also increased by more than 20% since 1997, with a 2019 census suggesting 460 individuals. Controversially, perhaps, these figures prompted the IUCN to downgrade the status of the mountain gorilla from 'Critically Endangered' to 'Endangered' in November 2018. They also seem to confirm that longstanding fears about the vulnerability of habituated gorillas to poachers are far outweighed by the positive effects of the revenue inflow generated by tourism, and the support it has generated among local communities, who receive 10% of tracking permit fees, and also operate community campsites and other grassroots projects outside the national parks.

A more tangible risk associated with tourism is that humans and gorillas are genetically close enough for there to be a real risk of passing a viral or bacterial infection on to a gorilla. To reduce this risk, there is a restriction on the number of people allowed to visit a troop on any given day, and visitors are now obliged to wear surgical masks and asked to keep a few metres' distance between themselves and the animals. It is up to individual tourists to forgo their gorilla-tracking permit if they are unwell – easier said than done when you've already spent a small fortune to get all the way to Uganda, but perhaps not if you imagine the consequences if even one individual were to be infected by a contagious disease to which gorillas have no acquired resistance.

Nevertheless, so long as gorilla tourism generates local revenue and employment opportunities, neighbouring communities are more likely to perceive the survival of the gorillas as being in their long-term interest. Without tourism, why would they give a damn? The benefits also extend much further afield: gorilla tracking is the cornerstone of Uganda's (and also Rwanda's) national tourist industry, and the majority of people who come for the gorillas will end up spending money elsewhere in the country, consequently generating foreign revenue and creating employment beyond the immediate vicinities of the mountain gorilla reserves. The end result is a symbiotic situation whereby a far greater number of people, both nationally and internationally, are motivated to take an active interest in the protection of the gorillas than would otherwise be the case.

Shoestring

Ruhija Gorilla Tours Hotel [549 H6] (10 rooms) m 0776 257118. This hotel in the middle of Ruhija village caters primarily for safari drivers & it's hard to see the basic rooms & communal bathrooms making their Top 100. The rates are as quoted but it's possible that the guy was taking the mickey. *US$30/40 exc b/fast.* **$$**

OTHER PRACTICALITIES There are no banks in Ruhija, but several craft shops line the main road through the village.

TOURIST INFORMATION

National Park Reception [549 H7] Situated on the west side of the main road to Kabale 1.3km south of Ruhija village, the Ruhija tracking trailhead & park information office is the best place to enquire about & pay for all activities out of Ruhija (except gorilla tracking). Check out the fabulous forest & volcano views from the old, protectorate-era Forest Station nearby – what a place that must have been to wake up of a morning!

WHAT TO SEE AND DO

Gorilla tracking Ruhija opened up as a gorilla-tracking destination in October 2008. Today, five groups can be tracked on the steep slopes that descend from the road passing along the Ruhija Ridge and the Mubwindi Swamp several hundred metres below. Bitakura, the first habituated group, has 13 animals while Mukisa, the largest group in Bwindi has 20. Kyaguliro, Oruzogo and Happy have eight, ten and seven respectively.

Eight daily tracking permits are available for each of these five groups. These are usually booked solid over June–August and December, but the odds of last-minute availability are good at other times of year. Permits can be booked at the national park offices in Kampala or Kisoro, but are also sold on the spot subject to availability. Trackers must be at the trailhead by 08.00. As with Buhoma, the success rate is practically 100%, but tracking conditions are generally slightly tougher due to the higher altitude and steeper slopes. Compared to Buhoma, the daily preparation for gorilla tracking is rather more low-key than Buhoma, what with tourist numbers being rather lower, and briefing takes place in a tented shelter rather than a purpose-built visitor centre. The Oruzogo and Happy groups roam the mountainside several kilometres west of Ruhija and trackers usually drive to a convenient roadside starting point.

Forest walks and drives It is permitted to walk or drive unguided along the public road through Ruhija Sector, which offers good wildlife viewing, with black-and-white colobus and L'Hoest's monkey being particularly common. It's also the part of the park where Bwindi's elephants – occasionally known to rock vehicles – are resident, so caution is required. Because it lies at a higher altitude than Buhoma, the tree composition is more characteristic of Afro-montane than lowland forest, and it supports a significantly different avifauna, making it an essential destination for enthusiasts. It is one of the few places where you stand a chance of seeing all four crimsonwings recorded in Uganda, and other specialities include a variety of apalis species, Lagden's bush-shrike and handsome francolin. The only Ugandan record for yellow-crested helmet-shrike is an unconfirmed sighting at Ruhija.

Guided nature walks out of Ruhija cost US$30/40 FR/FNR. Unlike at Buhoma, it is not really feasible to do any of these hikes on the same day as you track gorillas, so you will also need to pay an additional US$30/40 park entrance fee. For peak-baggers, the 6-hour **Bamboo Trail** leads to the 2,607m Rwamunyoni Peak, which is the highest point in the park, and notable for good birding.

Ruhija's top birding walk has to be the **Mubwindi Swamp Trail**, which descends several hundred metres from the trailhead to a swampy area that harbours 20 bird species listed in the IUCN *Red Data Book* and/or endemic to the Albertine Rift. The first part of the trail passes through highlands where there are several clearings offering good views into the canopy, and common birds include great blue turaco, black-billed turaco, Rwenzori batis, Chubb's cisticola, blue-headed sunbird and stripe-breasted tit. There are great views across to Mount Muhabura and other volcanoes in the Virunga Range. The trail descends into an area of thick-leafed scrubby marsh rated the most reliable site anywhere for the extremely localised African green broadbill. Odds of sighting this alluring Albertine Rift Endemic might be as good as 95% from May to July, when the guides usually know the location of a few breeding pairs, but you are very unlikely to see them at other times. As consolation, other good birds often seen here include cinnamon-chested bee-eater, Rwenzori apalis, banded prinia, Grauer's warbler, pink-footed puffback, yellow-eyed black flycatcher, Lagden's bush-shrike and dusky crimsonwing. Eventually you emerge on the edge of Mubwindi Swamp, where the main avian draws are the quite easily seen Grauer's rush warbler and Carruthers's cisticola, and the vocal but visually elusive red-chested flufftail. For non-birders, other wildlife includes black-and-white colobus, red-tailed and L'Hoest's monkey, and there is a chance of seeing elephant and sitatunga in the vicinity of the swamp. Technically, it is a 3-hour walk, but that would be quite a frog-march – 4 hours is more relaxed, and dedicated twitchers might be out for twice as long as they stop to look for rarities. An early start is recommended, and carry plenty of water.

RUSHAGA

Situated at an altitude of 1,900m near the southern tip of BINP, Rushaga became Uganda's newest gorilla-tracking site in October 2009, following an unusually high-profile launch whereby a brat pack of American film stars was flown in to make positive statements about the experience. Although Rushaga is less well known and less developed than Buhoma, accommodation facilities are steadily improving, and there are now nine habituated gorilla groups in the area, meaning that 72 tracking permits are available daily, while up to six permits are currently available daily for the 'habituation experience' with a tenth group. Scenically, unlike some parts of Bwindi, where you can't see the forest for the proverbial trees, Rushaga offers terrific views across deep jungle-clad valleys as well as glimpses of the Virunga volcanoes, and there's plenty to attract birders including the localised Rwenzori turaco and Shelley's crimsonwing. All of which means Rushaga is set to grow in popularity, not only with tour operators as a peak-season alternative to gorilla tracking at Buhoma and Ruhija, but also with independent travellers, overland truck groups and regional expatriates seeking a last-minute permit. Rushaga is also the most accessible of the four trailheads for visitors who opt to track gorillas as a day trip out of Kisoro or Lake Mutanda.

GETTING THERE AND AWAY

By air The options described for reaching Kisoro by air on page 529 also apply to Rushaga.

By road Road access to Rushaga is from the south only, via two murram roads linking to the main surfaced strip between Kabale and Kisoro. Coming **from Kabale** (or, indeed, from anywhere else to the north or east), you need to follow the Kisoro Road for 43km to a signposted junction to the right (⊕ -1.20511, 29.80237) some 4.5km past the northern tip of Lake Bunyonyi and 3km past Muko. From the junction, it's 24km on dirt to the gorilla-tracking trailhead and office at Rushaga (⊕ -1.11643, 29.71009), culminating in a long and winding descent into the Ruhezanyenda Valley via Rushaga village.

Approaching **from Kisoro**, it's only 35km to Rushaga via the small town of Rubuguri, following a poor murram road that might one day be surfaced. Follow the road running northeast towards lakes Mutanda and Mulehe from next to the Kindly filling station (⊕ -1.2823, 29.69693). After 8km, you'll arrive at a three-way junction (⊕ -1.2235, 29.71628) where you need to turn right if you want to use the direct route via Rubuguri and stick to the left if you want to follow the more scenic but rougher and slightly (2km) longer route via Lake Mutanda and Hakasharara.

The main focal point of **public transport**, such as it exists, is the small town of Rubuguri, which lies 10km from Rushaga along the road to Kisoro. A few pick-up trucks run between Kisoro and Rubuguri on Monday and Thursday (90mins) and between Kabale and Rubuguri on Tuesday and Saturday (3hrs). Transport from Kabale passes within 2km of Rushaga trailhead, so if you want to stay there, ask to be dropped at the junction for Rushaga. Coming from Kisoro, you'll need to catch a boda to Rushaga. Alternatively, with a prebooked permit, you could stay in Rubuguri, and catch a boda through for the day, which costs US$10–15 return.

If pick-ups and bodas don't appeal, then Nshongi Camp can arrange a transfer from Kisoro/Kabale for around US$60 for a party of up to five. If you prefer to travel from Kisoro on the day of tracking, a special hire should cost around US$50 and a boda around US$15; it's advisable to make these arrangements through the national park booking office there. Do be aware that a landslide or stuck truck might scupper your plans on these narrow mountain roads, in which event all is not lost, but you might have to find a boda to complete your journey.

If this sounds like hard work, Kampala's Red Chilli Hideaway (page 142) runs economy trips to Rushaga. One person pays US$1,860 for a whistlestop three-day/two-night excursion, reducing to US$1,280 per person if you can get six people together. This includes return transport, accommodation, meals and the all-important gorilla permit. A more relaxed option stops in Lake Mburo National Park on the way back and costs US$3,105/1,506/1,415 per person for 1/3/6 people.

WHERE TO STAY The main accommodation clusters serving Rushaga are in the village of the same name, which lies immediately outside the entrance gate no more than 15 minutes' walk from the tracking trailhead, and Rubuguri town 10km back along the road to Kisoro. If you're prepared to make an early start, it's also possible to stay in Kisoro or at Lake Mutanda – indeed, the two lodges at the northern end of this lake now function primarily as bases for gorilla tracking at Rushaga. While there is plenty of mid-range accommodation close to Rushaga, you might consider basing yourself in one of the exclusive lodges at Nkuringo, 50 minutes' drive to the west.

Upmarket

Gorilla Leisure Lodge [549 H1] (12 rooms) m 0772 082165; e info@gorillaleisurelodge.com; w gorillaleisurelodge.com. You might find better views in the vicinity of Rushaga, but there is no doubt that the level of comfort at this stylish new lodge is unrivalled for many miles around. From the lovely flowering gardens at the entrance to the large & luxurious accommodation, this is a notch above everything else – assuming you can turn a blind eye to the tacky gorilla statues. **$$$$$**

Gorilla Safari Lodge [549 G1] (11 rooms) ☎ 039 3255214; m 0773 388059; e reservations@crystallodgesuganda.com; w gorillasafarilodge.com. This gem of a lodge stands on a hillside facing the forest only 1km from the Rushaga trailhead. The en-suite cottages are attractively & colourfully decorated in ethnic style, & spread across a pretty garden site surrounded by scattered local homesteads. A touch overpriced though low season rates apply. *US$375 pp FB.* **$$$$**

Moderate

Gorilla Valley Lodge [549 H1] (12 cottages) ☎ 031 2294894; m 0773 447343; e booking@naturelodges.biz; w naturelodges.biz. This offering from Nature Lodges has an isolated position on the park boundary 1.5km east of the tracking trailhead as the crow flies, but more like 5km by road. Sprawling across a hillside, the comfortable en-suite cottages all offer views towards the nearby forest canopy. Decent value. *US$130/175 sgl/dbl FB.* **$$$**

Ichumbi Gorilla Lodge [549 G1] (13 units) ⊕ 1.2326395, 29.7200842; m 0782 118233; e reservations@ichumbigorillalodge.com; w ichumbigorillalodge.com. 1km from the tracking trailhead, this very agreeable & reasonably priced lodge offers standalone luxury cottages on sloping grounds with a forest view. *US$180/280 sgl/dbl cottage FB.* **$$$$**

Rushaga Gorilla Lodge [549 G1] (25 rooms) m 0774 633331, 0752 409510; e info@rushaga.com; w rushaga.com. This well-run camp 1km from the tracking trailhead is under the same management as the ever-popular Bunyonyi Overland Resort (page 521). It offers the choice of luxury rooms with forest views, or a row of smaller & cheaper rooms overlooking a eucalyptus plantation. The view aside, there's not that much to choose between them, making the latter excellent value. *US$200/300 sgl/dbl luxury; US$130/200 sgl/dbl budget; US$50 pp camping. All rates FB.* **$$$$**

Budget

Karungi Camp [549 E1] (3 rooms) m 0772 682718, 0779 806583; e bookings@karungicamp.com; w karungicamp.com. This cosy owner-managed lodge has bright, airy en-suite bandas with a private balcony secluded by a hedge. There is also a restaurant serving meals for around US$14 & a grassy campsite. It lies below the Rushaga Rd, just outside Rubuguri by the town road sign. *US$70/100 sgl/dbl FB.* **$$$**

✷ **Nshongi Camp** [549 G1] (4 cottages) m 0774 231913; e nshongicamp@gmail.com; w nshongicamp.altervista.org. This wonderful budget lodge is set in lush grounds next to a stream bordering the forest & national park, just behind Rushaga village & only 15mins' walk from the gorilla-tracking trailhead. Originally an unashamed shoestring option, it's now gone a bit upmarket & offers a range of accommodation including, happily, the original cheapie options. There's great on-site birding & monkey viewing, & even gorillas pass through from time to time. *US$115/190 sgl/dbl luxury; US$95/150 sgl/dbl std room; US$65/100 sgl/dbl economy; US$50 dorm bed; US$45 camping. All rates FB.* **$$–$$$**

✷ **Rushaga Gorilla Haven** [549 G1] (8 units) ⊕ 1.1322624, 29.7406990; m 0788 871046; e booking@rushagagorillahaven.com; w rushagagorillahaven.com. With a giddy hillside location high above the Ruhezanyindo River (audible far, far below), this lovely lodge enjoys a stupendous view into a wall of forest on the far side of the valley. The perfect spot to enjoy a drink the night before tracking & wonder where, exactly, in this vast expanse of greenery, your allocated gorilla group might currently be hanging out. Come the morning, it's a winding 4km drive down the mountainside to the river with the Rushaga trailhead 1.5km beyond. Excellent value. *US$70/130 sgl/dbl cottage FB.* **$$$**

✷ **Wagtail Eco Camp** [549 E1] (5 rooms) m 0787 719136; e info@wagtailforestlodge.com. This unpretentious facility in a lush jungle garden offers en-suite cottages in a shady compound alongside the main road through Rubuguri. *US$80/100 sgl/dbl FB.* **$$$**

WHERE TO EAT AND DRINK Though most people will carry a packed meal when gorilla tracking or lunch at their lodges afterwards, the restaurant listed below represents an unexpected treat to visitors on a half-board deal returning to accommodation in Rubugeri, Kisoro or beside Lake Mutanda.

Terrace Junction [549 F2] 039 3193264. Conspicuously signposted 2km out of Rubugeri on the way to/from Rushaga, this smart new roadside restaurant is strategically located to tempt returning gorilla trackers with a range of teas, coffees, juices, burgers, sandwiches & curries. It'll be a miracle if everything listed on the menu is available, but the clean toilets alone are bound to make this a popular stop. The glass-&-timber-framed structure overlooks the Bilala River Valley & guests with energy to spare after gorilla tracking can explore some caves below the site & follow a birding trail. Accommodation is under construction. *Mains US$8.*

TOURIST INFORMATION

National Park Reception [549 G1] ⊕ -1.11649, 29.71012; m 0782 35420. Situated just inside the eponymous park entrance about 500m from Rushaga village, the Rushaga tracking trailhead & park information office is the best place to enquire about & pay for all activities out of Rushaga, including gorilla tracking.

WHAT TO SEE AND DO

Gorilla tracking When gorilla tracking started up at Rushaga, the habituated Nshongi Group was the largest in Bwindi, comprising 34 individuals including three silverbacks, six blackbacks and eight infants. Between then and April 2019, the Nshongi and more recently habituated Busingye Group experienced several splits between rival silverbacks, meaning there are now nine habituated groups at Rushaga, and a total of 72 daily permits. The groups are: Nshongi (11), Busingye (16), Kahungye (15), Mucunguzi (14), Kutu (10), Bweza (8), Mishaya (10), Tindatine (6) and Bwindi's second-largest group, Rwigye (18). In addition, the Bikingi group (9) is currently being habituated and up to six people daily can join it for the all-day habituation experience, which costs US$1,000/US$1,500/800/300 FR/FNR/ROA/EAC.

The 72 tracking permits available each day at Rushaga are more often than not booked up on any given day over June to August, but even in peak season the odds of securing a permit from Kampala HQ at short notice are better than anywhere else in Bwindi (page 560).

Trackers must register at Rushaga by 08.00, and will leave after a short briefing. Note, however, that while formalities are carried out at Rushaga, there are actually two different tracking trailheads situated about 11km apart by road. The Rushaga trailhead stands next to the park reception, but to reach Nyabaremura trailhead [548 C5] (⊕ -1.10871, 29.6699) after your briefing, you need to drive 8km to Rubuguri, then turn right at a signposted junction (⊕ -1.12454, 29.6822) and continue northwest for 3km to a well-marked car park. The Kahungye, Busingye and Rwigye groups are usually tracked from Nyabaremura, while the Bweza and Mishaya groups are occasionally, depending on their movements.

Backtracking to Nyabaremura is obviously a pain for those who have already passed through Rubuguri to get to Rushaga (either from accommodation in the town or further afield) and plans to establish an additional reception either in Rubuguri or Nyabaremura are to be welcomed (this would have the additional benefit of reducing the processing and briefing of 72 gorilla trackers, plus the allocation of a similar number of porters, ranger escorts and guides, into two relatively small operations). As of now, however, the plan is nothing more than a plan.

The success rate for all groups at Rushaga is better than 99%, but trackers who are concerned about their age or fitness should let the rangers know, and they will allocate you to the group they expect to be easiest to reach. Usually this will be the ones tracked from Rushaga trailhead, as these are typically less than 2 hours' walk away on relatively easy terrain. Tracking from Nyabaremura generally entails a longer walk of up to 3 hours on steeper terrain.

Nature walks Nature walks are offered at the same fees as elsewhere in Bwindi. Birdlife is broadly similar to Buhoma, and L'Hoest's, blue and red-tailed monkey are often seen, along with black-and-white colobus, while chimpanzees have a large vocal presence but are seldom observed. The 3–4-hour **Waterfall Trail** descends into a steep valley dripping with giant tree ferns, then climbs upwards through a narrow, stream-filled fissure in the cliff face to reach a towering, rock-walled atrium containing a cascade of more than 30m. Outside the park, a candidate for further exploration would seem to be the dramatic and deeply incised Ruhezanyenda River Valley.

Community walks The 3–4-hour **Reformed Poacher walk**, guided by and offering the opportunity to chat to former poachers, takes in two waterfalls close to Rubuguri, as well as visits to local smallholdings and a coffee roastery. The **Rubuguri Origins Trail** connects a number of sites feted in local oral history, ranging from a place where the ancestors reputedly left their footprints to gold panning sites. Aimed mainly at birders, the **Kanyajondo Trail** runs through community land bordering the national park and offers a good chance of seeing the likes of Ross's turaco as well as Albertine Rift Endemics such as yellow-eyed black flycatcher, dusky crimsonwing and purple-breasted sunbird. In addition, the **Nyabaremura Batwa Experience** is run out of the Nkuringo Cultural Centre [549 E1], which stands alongside the road to the Nyabaremura trailhead a few hundred metres out of Rubuguri. Most of these activities cost around US$15–25 per person and can be arranged through any hotel or directly through Justus, the head of the Bwindi South Bird Guides Club (m 0773 780165; e ngabsjustus@gmail.com).

NKURINGO

Chronologically Bwindi's second gorilla-tracking trailhead, Nkuringo, which opened in 2004, lies at an altitude of 2,100m on the park's southwestern border north of Kisoro. The surrounding hills are densely settled by farming communities, but have a remote and undeveloped feel, on account of the location on a dead-end road ending at the nearby Congolese border. It is a very scenic area, set along the Nteko Ridge, which provides grandstand views across the Kashasha River Valley into BINP and the forest which cloaks the valley's northern slopes. 'Nkuringo' means 'round stone' and refers to a knoll-like forested hill that's set beside the river, but is dwarfed by loftier ridges above it. To the south and west, superb panoramas include the entire length of the Virunga volcanic range. The International Gorilla Conservation Programme has purchased a 10km-long by 400m-wide strip of public land along the river as a buffer zone for the growth of crops that are not appealing to gorillas and will encourage them to remain in the park.

GETTING THERE AND AWAY

By air The options described for reaching Kisoro by air on page 529 apply to Nkuringo.

By road Nkuringo trailhead is situated in the small village of Ntungamo, which lies 40km/90 minutes north of Kisoro by road, and 90km/3 hours from Kabale via Rubuguri. Coming **from Kisoro**, directions are the same as for Rushaga (page 569), except that you need to turn left at a junction 1km before Rubuguri (⊕ -1.13183, 29.67314), then continue driving northeast for about 8km to Ntungamo. Coming **from Kabale**, directions are also the same as for Rushaga, except that you need to continue past the last junction for Rushaga for about 10km and turn right 1km past Rubuguri. The dirt sections of these routes are generally in reasonable condition, but a 4x4 vehicle driven at a sensible speed is recommended in wet conditions.

Public transport, such as it exists, amounts to a few pick-up trucks that run between Kisoro and Rubuguri on Monday and Thursday (90mins). It would also be possible to pick up public transport to Rubuguri and take a boda from there.

Otherwise, the only reliable way to reach Ntungamo from Kisoro is by special hire or a long, bumpy boda ride.

WHERE TO STAY AND EAT Though accommodation in the vicinity of Nkuringo is limited, you'll find additional lodgings in Rubuguri (30–45 minutes distant), Lake Mutanda (45–60 minutes) or Kisoro (60–90 minutes). It's feasible to spend the night in any of these locations and then travel up to Ntungamo in the early morning. Like Ruhija, Ntungamo is located on a lofty ridge and water must be collected as rain or transported from streams in distant valleys. Do bear this in mind when you open a tap or flush a loo.

Exclusive

✷ **Clouds Mountain Gorilla Lodge** [549 G3] (8 cottages) 041 4251182; m 0772 489497; e info@wildplacesafrica.com; w wildplacesafrica.com. This stunning lodge stands on Nteko Ridge, a few mins' walk from the Nkuringo trailhead. It enjoys unparalleled views of the Virunga chain & the western Rift Valley by day & the glowing cone of the active Nyiragongo Volcano by night. The spacious (80m²) cottages, with lounge & bedroom with interconnected fireplace, are each decorated with work by an individual Ugandan artist. The comfort of guests in the main lodge building, a large & airy stone structure with massive timber roof beams, is also assured, not least through a generous ratio of 1:8 armchair/sofa spaces per guest. **$$$$$$**

Gorilla Heights [549 H4] (8 cottages) 039 4825265; m 0782 726526; e reservations@gorillaheightslodge; w gorillaheightslodge.com. This is, without a doubt, the most luxurious out-of-town hotel we have found yet. Architecturally modern & dramatic in both scale & vision, no expense has been spared to create the large, stylish & airy central building (a Virunga Terrace on one side & Bwindi Terrace on the other provide the usual views), swimming pool & spa, & the massive & widely spaced cottage-suites facing the forest. What this lavish development is doing at the end of one of the rockiest roads in the country, however – rather than on the edge of Kampala or Mbarara with a lake & golf course attached – is another matter entirely. One also wonders as to the target market. Gorilla trackers are unlikely to be impressed by the absence of safari style, while Uganda's monied elite – a more obvious clientele – may find the rigours involved in reaching Gorilla Heights off-putting. **$$$$$$**

✷ **Nkuringo Bwindi Gorilla Lodge** [549 H4] (18 units) 039 2176327; e bwindi@nkuringolodges.com; w mountaingorillalodge.com. Recent refurbishments have transformed this solid, mid-range setup into one of Bwindi's top lodges. Antique European & traditional African themes combine to good effect within a spacious lodge building constructed on a fabulous dual viewpoint. To the south, the Virunga volcanoes stretch across the horizon, while the northerly prospect looks across Bwindi towards Buhoma with (weather permitting) Lake Edward & the Rwenzori beyond. The luxurious cottages are warmed with a welcome charcoal hearth & are oriented towards one or other of the views; a clutter of cottages on the higher contours means that the best prospects are from the lowest suites on the Bwindi side. A state-of-the-art spa is on site to take care of any little twinges picked up during the trek into the Kashasha Valley to locate the gorillas. **$$$$$**

Budget

Bwindi Safari Lodge [548 B5] (12 rooms) m 0774 592925. It's extraordinary, given the myriad combinations derived from combining 'Bwindi', 'Gorilla', 'Safari' & 'Lodge' with various trailhead names, that no-one snapped up this simplest of names before. What it attaches to is a freshly painted but undistinguished storeyed road frontage with volcano-viewing balcony & 2 tiers of basic & overpriced rooms behind. *US$80/110 sgl/dbl shared bathrooms; US$100 sgl en suite. All rates FB.* **$$$**

Gorilla CloseUp Lodge (aka Bwindi Backpackers Lodge) [548 B5] m 0772 661854; e info@bwindibackpackerslodge.com. Located on the roadside with forest views behind, 5km before Nkuringo trailhead, the budget Bwindi Backpackers has expanded to offer additional, mid-range accommodation as Gorilla CloseUp Lodge. A communal lodge-restaurant caters for both categories. *CloseUp rooms US$120/230 sgl/dbl; Backpacker rooms US$85/140 sgl/dbl.* **$$$–$$$$**

Shoestring

Albertine Gorilla Campsite [549 G3] (5 rooms) m 0788 270164, 0779 241765. Simple rooms in a pretty compound sandwiched between Clouds & the Buniga Community Forest. Good value for the location. *US$15/25 in room with common/en-suite shower.* **$$**

Nkuringo Guesthouse [549 H4] (12 rooms) m 0782 193135. Situated in Ntungamo trading centre & just 500m from the Nkuringo tracking trailhead, this optimistically priced shoestring lodge is nothing special but it's cheap by Bwindi standards. Meals are available. *US$50 pp room only.* **$$**

TOURIST INFORMATION

National Park Reception [549 G3] m 0773 570094, 0772 590018. This purpose-built office, on the west side of the main road between Nkuringo village & Clouds, is the best place to enquire about & pay for all activities out of Nkuringo, including gorilla tracking.

WHAT TO SEE AND DO

Gorilla tracking Four habituated groups of gorillas can be tracked at Nkuringo, meaning that 32 permits are available daily. First to be habituated was the Nkuringo Group, which currently has 12 animals. Subsequent splits and habituation processes mean that three additional groups can be tracked: Bushaho (8 animals), Christmas (8) and Bwindi's third-largest group, Posho (17). The latter was previously tracked from Rushaga's Nyabaremura trailhead but is now visited from Nkuringo. You need to check in at 08.00. Permit availability at short notice used to be rare at Nkuringo, but now that there are four habituated groups, it is quite common, at least outside peak seasons.

Nkuringo is the most physically challenging of all gorilla-tracking locations. Unlike existing tracking sites at Buhoma and Mgahinga, there is no vehicle access from the Nteko Ridge to the park boundary which follows the Kashasha River. The closest road is the Rubuguri–Nkuringo–Nteko Road on the ridge 600m above the river. Trackers face a steep 1-hour descent simply in order to cross the river and enter the forest. After the arduous but rewarding business of gorilla tracking, you'll face the return climb back up to the ridge. This is not a problem for the fit, but Nkuringo is definitely not for the less-able or faint-hearted, though a number of routes have been improved by the addition of steps and gentler switchback turns.

Buniga Community Forest [549 G3] (⊕ -1.08016, 29.6268; w bunigaforestwalk.org) With the tagline, 'Meet the Batwa, then and now', this 3km^2 patch of regenerating forest on the outskirts of Nkuringo village is owned by the local Batwa and run as a community project. More than 100 bird species have been identified in the forest, and it also provides refuge to black-and-white colobus, red-tailed, blue, and L'Hoest's monkeys and black-backed duiker, while chimpanzees pass through occasionally. A 2–3-hour guided trail through the forest gives you the chance to see it through Batwa eyes, and is usually followed by a visit to the contemporary settlement of Sanuriio, where 150 of the former hunter-gatherers have been resettled about 4km from Nkuringo. Batwa guides demonstrate aspects of their traditional forest life – creating shelter, firing bows and arrows, making fire, identifying medicinal herbs, etc. You can choose between an enjoyable and informative guided walk (US$25 pp) or a cheaper self-guided walk (US$10 pp). No park fees or UWA guide fees are involved. Walks can be arranged through Clouds Mountain Gorilla Lodge or Nkuringo Bwindi Gorilla Lodge (see opposite), ideally a day in advance.

Hiking Nature walks into the national park can be arranged at the usual UWA rates, but the steep nature of the descent (and ascent) makes it a less appealing prospect than at the other trailheads. That said, Nkuringo is a superbly scenic area with great potential for hiking outside the forest, though the possibilities for haphazard exploration are pretty limited. The steepness of Nteko Ridge means that the main alternatives for a pleasant stroll are either west along the ridge-top road towards DRC or east towards Rubuguri. Bear in mind that Ntungamo lies about 8km from the Congolese border and it is a sensitive area. Tourism development has been subject to all manner of evaluations to ensure visitor safety and it's most unlikely that you'd wander off into the DRC, or indeed be allowed to.

Nkuringo community walk This community-run activity provides insights into Bakiga life and culture, with visits to a traditional healer, blacksmith, brewer and homestead in the vicinity of Nkuringo village. The walk costs US$30 per person and can be arranged through Clouds Mountain Gorilla Lodge (page 574) or Nkuringo Bwindi Gorilla Lodge (page 574).

Appendix 1

LANGUAGE

Although 33 local languages are spoken in Uganda, the official language is English, spoken widely by most urban Ugandans, and certainly by anybody with more than a moderate education level and/or who works in the tourist industry. It is not uncommon to come across Ugandans from different parts of the country using English to communicate, and most English-speaking visitors to the country will have no problem getting around. Of several indigenous languages, the most widely spoken is Luganda, which to some extent serves as a lingua franca for the uneducated. So, too, does Swahili, a coastal Bantu language that is no more indigenous to Uganda than is English.

LUGANDA Luganda is the first language of Buganda and most widely spoken of the languages indigenous to Uganda. Pronunciation is very similar to Swahili. Some words and phrases follow. A detailed phrasebook and dictionary can be viewed online at w buganda.com.

Greetings

Hello (informal)	*Ki kati*
How are you?	*Oli otya?*
I am OK	*Gyendi*
Have a nice day	*Siba bulungi*
Goodnight	*Sula bulungi*
Farewell	*Weraba*
See you later	*Tunalabagana*
Please	*Mwattu*
Thank you (very much)	*Webale (Nyo)*
Excuse me	*Owange*
Sorry	*Nsonyiwa*
Sir	*Ssebo*
Come here	*Jangu wano*
Madam	*Nnyabo*
Mr	*Mwami*
Mrs	*Mukyala*

Useful phrases

Where are you from?	*Ova mukitundu ki?*
I am from England	*Nva mu England*
Where have you come from?	*Ovude wa?*
I have come from Kampala	*Nvude Kampala*
Where are you going?	*Ogenda wa?*
I am going to Mbale	*Ngenda Mbale*
How can I get to Mbale?	*Ngenda ntya okutuka e Mbale?*
Does this bus go to Kampala?	*Eno baasi egenda e Kampala?*
Which bus goes to Kampala?	*Baasi ki egenda e Kampala?*
What time does the bus leave?	*Baasi egenda sawa meka?*
Where can I buy a bus ticket?	*Tikiti ya baasi nyinza kugigula wa?*
What time does the bus arrive?	*Baasi etuka ku sawa meka?*

Where is the road to Kampala?	*Olugudo lwe Kampala luliwa?*
Where is this taxi going?	*Eno taxi eraga wa?*
Where is it?	*Kiriwa?*
How far is it?	*Kiri wala wa?*
Is it far?	*Kiri wala?*
Is it near?	*Kiri kumpi?*
How much does it cost?	*Sente meka?*
Do you speak English?	*Oyogera oluzungu?*
Do you have any…?	*Olinayo ko…?*
I would like…	*Njagalayo…*
I want a room	*Njagala kisenge*
There is	*Waliwo*
There is not	*Tewali*
What is this called?	*Kino kiyitibwa kitya?*
What is your name?	*Amanya go gw'ani?*
My name is Philip	*Nze Philip*

Words

big	*kinene*	OK	*ye*
come (here)	*jangu (wano)*	please	*bambi*
good	*kirungi*	possible	*kisoboka*
here	*wano*	slow down	*genda mpola*
hurry up	*yanguwa*	small	*katono*
later	*edda*	today	*lero*
many	*bingi*	toilet	*toileti*
me	*nze*	tomorrow	*enkya*
morning	*kumakya*	water	*mazi*
no	*neda*	yes	*ye*
not possible	*tekisoboka*	yesterday	*jjo*
now	*kati*	you	*gwe*

Foodstuffs

avocado	*kedo*	melon	*wuju*
banana (green)	*matooke*	onion	*katungulu*
banana (sweet)	*menvu*	orange	*mucungwa*
beans	*bijanjalo*	pawpaw	*paapaali*
beef	*nte*	peanuts	*binyebwa*
cabbage	*mboga*	pepper	*kaamulali*
carrot	*kalati*	pineapple	*naanansi*
cassava	*muwogo*	pork	*mbizi*
chicken	*nkoko*	potato	*lumonde*
corn	*kasooli*	rice	*muceere*
fish	*kyenyanja*	salt	*munnyo*
goat meat	*mbuzi*	sugar	*sukali*
lamb/mutton	*ndiga*	sugarcane	*kikajo*
mango	*muyembe*	sweet potato	*lumonde*
meat	*nyama*	tomato	*nyanya*

Appendix 2

GLOSSARY

acacia woodland	any woodland dominated by thorn trees of the acacia family
Albertine Rift	western Rift Valley between Lake Albert and northern Lake Tanganyika
Amin, Idi	dictatorial President of Uganda 1971–79
Ankole	extant medieval kingdom centred on modern-day Mbarara
askari	security guard
Bachwezi	legendary medieval kingdom, centred on present-day Mubende
Baker, Lady Florence	wife and travel companion to Sir Samuel
Baker, Sir Samuel	first European to Lake Albert, Murchison Falls 1864, Governor of Equatoria 1872–73
balance	change (for a payment)
banda	any detached accommodation such as a hut or chalet
barkcloth	traditional material made from the bark of the fig tree
Batembuzi	legendary medieval kingdom, possibly centred on present-day Ntusi
Bell, Sir Henry Hesketh	Commissioner to Uganda 1905–09 after whom Port Bell (and thus Bell Beer) is named
Besigye, Kizza	Leader of the Forum for Democratic Change (FDC) who unsuccessfully contested the four presidential elections between 2001 and 2016
boda	short for boda-boda; motorbike, scooter or occasionally bicycle taxi
boma	colonial administrative office
Buganda	extant kingdom for which Uganda is named, centred on modern-day Kampala
Bunyoro	extant kingdom centred on modern-day Hoima
Bwana	Mister (polite Swahili term of address, sometimes used in Uganda)
chai	tea
Colville, Colonel	led the attack on Mparo that drove Kabalega into hiding, 1894
cowrie	small white shell used as currency in pre-colonial times
Daudi Chwa, Kabaka	crowned King of Buganda at age one in 1897, ruled until death in 1939
DSTV	South African multi-channel satellite television service
duka	stall or kiosk
endemic	unique to a specific area
exotic	not indigenous, for instance pine plantations
forest	wooded area with closed canopy
forex bureau	bureau de change
fundi	expert (especially mechanic)

Grant, Captain James	accompanied Speke on journey to source of the Nile, 1862
guesthouse	cheap local hotel
Hannington, Bishop James	missionary killed on Mwanga's instructions en route to Buganda in 1885
hoteli	local restaurant
indigenous	occurring in a place naturally
Interlacustrine Region	area between Lake Victoria and Albertine Rift Lakes: Rwanda, Burundi, south Uganda, northwest Tanzania
Isuza	legendary Batembuzi ruler
Kabaka	King of Buganda
Kabalega, Omukama	King of Bunyoro from 1870, exiled to Seychelles by the British 1897, died there 1923
Kaggwa, Sir Apollo	Katikiro of Buganda 1889–1926, and copious chronicler of Kiganda folklore and history
Kakunguru, Semei	Muganda leader who conquered east Uganda for the British in the 1890s and founded Kumi and Mbale
Kamurasi, Omukama	powerful Bunyoro king, ruled c1852–69, met by Speke and Baker
Katikiro	'Prime Minister' of Buganda
Kiganda	relating to the culture or religions of Buganda
Kiira	Luganda name for the Victoria Nile
Kintu	legendary founder of Buganda
Kony, Joseph	leader of the LRA
kopje	small, often rocky hill (from Afrikaans meaning 'little head')
Kyebambe III, Omukama	King of Bunyoro c1786–1835
LRA	Lord's Resistance Army
Lubaale (plural Balubaale)	important Kiganda spirit
Luganda	language of Buganda
Lugard, Captain Frederick	Representative of the Imperial British East Africa Company who signed a provisional treaty with Mwanga in 1890
mandazi	fried doughnut-like pastry
matatu	minibus used as a shared taxi carrying ten to 13 passengers
matoke	staple made from cooking plantains (bananas)
mazungu	white person
mbugo	barkcloth (traditional dress of Buganda)
minibus-taxi	see *matutu*
mishkaki	meat (usually beef) kebab
mobile	mobile satellite phone
MTN	main satellite-phone provider in Uganda
Muganda	citizen of Buganda kingdom (plural: Baganda)
murram	dirt road built with laterite soil
Museveni, Yoweri	President of Uganda 1986–present
Mutesa I, Kabaka	King of Buganda 1857–84, hosted Speke 1862
Mutesa II, Kabaka Edward	King of Buganda 1939–66, President of Uganda 1962–66, died in exile 1969
Mwanga, Kabaka	King of Buganda 1884–93, exiled to Seychelles 1897, died there 1903
Namasole	'Queen mother' or more accurately mother of the Kabaka of Buganda
Ndahura	legendary founder of Bachwezi dynasty, son of Isuza

netting	mosquito net
NRM	National Resistance Movement (governing part of Uganda)
Nyerere, Julius	President of Tanzania who initiated the war that ousted Amin in 1979
Obote, Milton	dictatorial President of Uganda, 1962–71 and 1981–85
Okello, Tito	military President of Uganda, July 1985–January 1986
Omugabe	King of Ankole
Omukama	King of Bunyoro/Toro
Owen, Roderick	companion of Portal in 1893 for whom Owen Falls at the source of the Nile is named
panga	local equivalent of a machete
Pasha, Emin	Governor of Equatoria 1878 until 'rescued' by Stanley 1889
pesa	money
pombe	local beer
Portal, Sir Gerald	Governor of Zanzibar, visited Uganda 1893, Fort Portal named in his honour
QENP	Queen Elizabeth National Park (often called QE or QENP)
riparian/riverine	strip of forest or lush woodland following a watercourse, often woodland rich in fig trees
Ruhanga	legendary king of the underworld and founder of the Batembuzi dynasty
Runyoro	language of Bunyoro
safari	Swahili word for journey, now widely used to refer to game-viewing trip
savannah	grassland with some trees
Saza chief	ruler of a County (Saza) of Buganda, answerable to the kabaka
shamba	small subsistence farm
short call	urinate
soda	fizzy drink such as Fanta or Coca-Cola
special hire	taxi
Speke, John Hanning	first European to visit Buganda, Bunyoro and the source of the Nile, 1862
Ssemogorere, Paul	one-time prime minister under Museveni, stood in the 1996 presidential election
Stanley, Henry Morton	explorer to Uganda in 1875–76 and 1889, discovering Rwenzoris on latter trip
surfaced (road)	road sealed with asphalt or similar
tented camp	rustic but generally upmarket small camp offering canvassed accommodation
Thomson, Joseph	in 1883, became the first European to enter present-day Uganda from the east
Toro	extant 19th-century kingdom centred on modern-day Fort Portal
tot packet	sachet of whisky or Waragi
track	motorable minor road or path
trading centre	small town or village where local villagers would go to shop
ugali	staple porridge made from maize (corn) meal
UPDF	Uganda People's Defence Force
UWA	Uganda Wildlife Authority
Wamala	legendary Bachwezi ruler, son of Ndahura
Waragi	local brand of gin
wazungu	plural of Mazungu
woodland	wooded area lacking closed canopy

Appendix 3

FURTHER INFORMATION

BOOKS

General interest

Roberts, Andrew *Uganda Safari* Mahiri Books, 2021. According to the blurb on the back cover, this is a wide-ranging and informative tour of the country Winston Churchill famously described as the 'Pearl of Africa'. Widely considered to be quite a good read.

History and background In addition to the books listed below, an excellent overview of literature about the Amin years, put together by reader Gavin Parnaby, is posted on w bradtugandaupdate.wordpress.com (click on the category 'Books').

Apuuli, K *A Thousand Years of Bunyoro-Kitara* Fountain, 1994. Inexpensive and compact locally published book that ranks close to being essential reading on pre-colonial events, despite being riddled with internal contradictions.

Behrend, Heike *Alice Lakwena & The Holy Spirits* James Currey, 1999. The bizarre and disturbing story of the emergence of the spirit medium in northern Uganda in 1986, which laid the foundation for the present-day Lord's Resistance Army and its brutal leader Joseph Kony.

Bussman, Jane *The Worst Date Ever* Macmillan, 2009. Readable investigation into the LRA war by a British comedienne/journalist and first-time visitor to Africa. Against a subplot of a supposed romantic agenda, Bussman combines a sharp wit and purported naivety while stumbling through murkier issues to raise some reasonable questions concerning the failure of government and the international community to end the conflict.

Carruthers, John *Mrs Carruthers is Black* Book Guild Publishing, 2005. Entertaining autobiographical account by a Scottish insurance chairman of his marriage to a Ugandan during the days when mixed-race marriages were something of an eyebrow raiser.

Chrétien, Jean-Pierre *The Great Lakes of Africa: Two Thousand Years of History* Zone Books, 2006. Scholarly one-volume history of a region centred on Rwanda and Uganda, with details of Bachwezi legends as well as more modern events.

Epstein, Helen *Another Fine Mess: America, Uganda, and the War on Terror* Columbia Global Reports, 2017. A damning indictment of the alleged US role and Museveni's complicity in regional conflicts in neighbouring countries.

Green, Matthew *The Wizard of the Nile* Portobello, 2008. This investigative travelogue tackles the war in northern Uganda and does much to explain the complex, internecine baggage behind this apparently futile conflict. Highly recommended.

Haden, John and Ondoma, John *Oh Uganda, May God Uphold Thee*. Barny Books, 2012. Readers with a particular interest in Arua and West Nile will enjoy this memoir by two erstwhile teachers. As Uganda starts to unravel after Idi Amin took power, you appreciate how the book's title, borrowed from the first line of the national anthem, must have

assumed equal significance as a prayer. (The book costs £12.99 + P&P from w barnybooks.biz; while the Kindle e-book costs £6.55 from Amazon.)
Jagielski, Wojciech *The Night Wanderers: Uganda's Children and the Lord's Resistance Army* Old Street Publishing, 2012. A harrowing award-nominated exploration of the lives led by children captured by the LRA during and after their reign of terror in northern Uganda.
Jeal, Tim *Stanley: The Impossible Life of Africa's Greatest Explorer* Faber and Faber, 2007. A readable biography that delves beneath the standard image of Stanley as an imperialist bully to paint a more nuanced portrait of Africa's most successful explorer.
Karugire, S *A Political History of Uganda* Heinemann, 1980. Concise and readable introduction to Ugandan history on the market, with a useful chapter covering pre-colonial events and razor-sharp commentary on the colonial period.
Miller, Charles *The Lunatic Express* 1971, reprinted Head of Zeus, 2016. Eminently readable account of the building of the Uganda Railway with an excellent history of the events in Uganda that brought about the project.
Moorehead, Alan *The White Nile* Hamilton, 1960. Classic example of the history-as-adventure-yarn genre, detailing the race to discover the source of the Nile and its leading characters.
Museveni, Yoweri *Sowing the Mustard Seed* Macmillan, 1997. Autobiography of Uganda's long-standing president, mostly devoted to his wilderness years fighting the Amin and Obote regimes.
Nzita, Richard *Peoples and Cultures of Uganda* Fountain, 1993, 3rd edition 1997. Useful introduction to the ethnic groupings of Uganda, with interesting monochrome photos.
O'Connor, Kevin *Uganda Society Observed* Fountain, 2006. A collection of light-hearted (sometimes exploring serious themes) articles written for *The Monitor* newspaper by an expat columnist.
Packenham, Thomas *The Scramble for Africa* Weidenfeld & Nicolson, 1991. Gripping and erudite 600-page account of the decade that turned Africa on its head – a 'must read', aptly described by one reviewer as 'Heart of Darkness with the lights switched on'.
Reid, Richard *History of Modern Uganda* Cambridge University Press, 2017. Encompassing the pre-colonial and post-millennial eras, this thematic and non-chronological book provides the best existing introduction to Uganda's history.
Reid, Richard *Political Power in Pre-colonial Buganda* James Currey, 2002. Accessible and clearly written introduction to the kingdom that lies at the heart of Uganda.
Rice, Andrew *The Teeth May Smile But The Heart Does Not Forget* Picador, 2010. Compelling journalistic account of Duncan Laki's four-year investigation into the murder of his father at the hands of Amin's henchmen, and attempt to bring the killers to justice.
Speke, John *Journal of the Discovery of the Source of the Nile* 1863, reprinted Dover Press, 1996. In this classic account of Victorian exploration, John Hanning Speke displays a wonderful ability to capture the flavour of local cultures, nowhere more so than in a series of chapters about the Buganda court under Mutesa. An enjoyable, instructive and occasionally mind-boggling read!
Turnball, Colin *The Mountain People* 1972, reprinted Touchstone, 1987. Fascinating, challenging and often disturbing anthropological study of the Ik people of the northeast.
Twaddle, Michael *Kakungulu and the Creation of Uganda* James Currey, 1993. Excellent and readable biography of the enigmatic and controversial Semei Kakungulu, a Muganda who started his career as a British expansionist and ended it as the founder of a Judaic sect that still thrives in the Mbale area to this day. Essential stuff!

Nature and wildlife

General

Briggs, Philip and Van Zandbergen, Ariadne *East African Wildlife* Bradt Travel Guides, 2024. A handy and lavishly illustrated one-stop handbook to the fauna of East Africa, with detailed sections on the region's main habitats, varied mammals, birds, reptiles and insects. It's the ideal companion for first-time visitors whose interest in wildlife extends beyond the Big Five but who don't want to carry a library of reference books.

Mammals

Erickson Wilson, Sandra *Bird and Mammal Checklists for Ten National Parks in Uganda* European Commission, 1995. Increasingly difficult-to-locate 88-page booklet containing a complete checklist of all mammals and birds known in Uganda, and in which national parks, if any, each species has been recorded.

Estes, Richard *The Safari Companion* Green Books UK, Chelsea Green USA, Russell Friedman Books South Africa, 1992. Not a field guide in the conventional sense so much as a guide to mammalian behaviour, this superb book is very well organised and highly informative, but rather bulky perhaps for casual safari-goers.

Fossey, Dian *Gorillas in the Mist* Hodder and Stoughton, 1983. Forty-plus years after its original publication, this seminal work remains the best introduction to gorilla behaviour in print.

Goodall, Jane *In the Shadow of Man* Collins, 1971. Classic on chimp behaviour based on Goodall's acclaimed research in Tanzania's Gombe Stream National Park.

Hanson, Thor *The Impenetrable Forest* Curtis Brown, 2014. First and foremost an account of the author's involvement in establishing gorilla tracking in Bwindi, this book also provides fascinating insights into day-to-day life in rural Uganda.

Kingdon, Jonathan *Field Guide to African Mammals* Academic Press, 1997. The definitive field guide of its type, with immense detail on all large mammals, a gold mine of information about the evolutionary relationships of modern species and good coverage of bats, rodents and other small mammals. Excellent illustrations. Arguably too pricey and heavy for casual safari-goers, but an essential reference for anybody with a strong interest in Africa's mammals. A useful pocket version is also available.

Schaller, George *The Year of the Gorilla* Chicago University Press, 1963. Subsequently overshadowed, at least in popular perception, by *Gorillas in the Mist*, thiş formative behavioural study of gorillas in the Virungas did much to dispel their violent image on publication. It remains a genuine classic, with the somewhat parochial advantage over later gorilla books in that most of the action takes place in Uganda rather than Rwanda.

Stuart, Chris and Tilde *Mammals of Southern and East Africa* Struik Publishers, 2002. Compact and well-organised field guide to all the larger mammals likely to be seen in Uganda.

Birds

Meunier, Quentin and McKelvie, Sherry *Birds of Uganda* Self-published, 2015. Attractive coffee-table-type book containing more than 900 photographs depicting about a quarter of Uganda's bird species in a variety of plumages. A Kindle version is available from Amazon.

Russouw, Jonathan and Sacchi, Marco *Where to Watch Birds in Uganda* Uganda Tourism Board, 1998. This excellent little book is out of print and hard to find these days so if you see a copy snap it up! The detailed descriptions and advice for all key birding sites in Uganda, with special reference to local rarities and specials, make for an ideal companion to a field guide.

Stevenson, Terry and Fanshawe, John *Field Guide to the Birds of East Africa* T & A D Poyser, 2002. The best bird field guide, with useful field descriptions and accurate plates and distribution maps covering every species recorded in Uganda as well as Kenya, Tanzania, Rwanda and Burundi. No other book will suffice for serious birdwatchers, but it is much bulkier and pricier than Van Perlo's competing title.

Butterflies

Carter, Nanny and Tindimubona, Laura *Butterflies of Uganda* Uganda Society, 2002. Very useful albeit non-comprehensive field guide illustrating and describing roughly 200 of the more common butterfly species in Uganda.

Health Self-prescribing has its hazards so if you are going anywhere very remote consider taking a health book. For adults there is *Bugs, Bites & Bowels* by Dr Jane Wilson-Howarth, published by Cadogan (2009); if travelling with the family look at *Your Child Abroad: A Travel Health Guide* by Dr Jane Wilson-Howarth and Dr Matthew Ellis, an eBook published by Bradt Travel Guides (2014).

Coffee-table books

Cross-Cultural Foundation of Uganda *Beyond the Reeds and Bricks – Historical Sites and Buildings in Kampala, Jinja and Entebbe* Cross-Cultural Foundation of Uganda, 2019. This plush coffee-table book, supported by the EU, contains over 150 pages of glossy photos and narrative of the history and development of this trio of Ugandan cities.

Gonget, Barbara, et al *Imagine Uganda*. Excellent and reasonably priced pocket-sized compilation of images by four Ugandan and expatriate photographers: an eclectic representation of landscapes, activities, people, wildlife, etc. Available locally.

Guadalupi, Gianni *Discovery of the Source of the Nile* Stewart, Tabori and Chang, 1997. This hefty and expensive-looking volume contains superb and lavish illustrated spreads of maps and coloured engravings from the age of exploration. The text (translated from the Italian) includes explorers usually omitted from the standard Anglophonic accounts of the search for the Nile's origins. The original hefty price tag notwithstanding, copies can be found for a few pounds on Amazon.

Kampala Attractively produced photo book with a difference. Instead of notable buildings and standard panoramas, *Kampala* depicts the reality of Uganda's hectic capital. Ugandans have complained that that reality does not present their city in a very complimentary light!

Michel, Kiguli, Pluth and Didek *Eye of the Storm: A Photographer's Journey across Uganda* Camerapix, 2002. Sumptuous book, which boldly contrasts evocative wildlife photography with more gritty urban and rural images reflecting the realities of daily life in Uganda.

Fiction

Baingana, Doreen *Tropical Fish: Tales from Entebbe* Crown, 2006. Shuttling between Entebbe, Kampala and Los Angeles, this is the story of how the lives of three sisters diverge towards separate fates in the years after Idi Amin.

Foden, Giles *The Freight Dogs* Wiedenfield & Nicholson, 2022. The tale of a Congolese refugee rescued by shady gun-runners operating out of Entebbe in the 1990s and pitched back into the turmoil whence he came.

Foden, Giles *The Last King of Scotland* Faber & Faber, 1998. The Whitbread Prize-winning fictional account of a young Scots doctor working in the service of Idi Amin.

Kingsolver, Barbara *The Poisonwood Bible* HarperCollins, 2000. Set in the Belgian Congo rather than Uganda, this is still a highly insightful novel, particularly about religion in Africa.

Isegawa, Moses *The Abyssinian Chronicles* Vintage, 2001. Uganda's best-known work of modern fiction (set in Uganda in the 1970s and 80s, not as the title suggests Ethiopia) has drawn comparisons to Salman Rushdie's *Midnight's Children* and Gabriel Garcia Marquez's *One Hundred Years of Solitude*.

Okorot, Mary Karooro *The Invisible Weevil* FemRite, 1993. Written by a Ugandan MP, this readable novel provides an insight into the many problems (notably men) that Ugandan women must endure.

MAPS A decent countrywide map can be a great asset. The 1:800,000 map of Uganda published by International Travel Maps and Books (ITMB) of Vancouver is the smallest-scale map available for the whole country, and more accurate than most (one major error in some editions being a displacement of latitudinal lines, causing the equator, for instance, to be marked as 1°N, etc). Other options are Nelles's 1:700,000 map and the excellent German-produced 1:600,000 Uganda sheet (w reise-know-how.de).

Superb illustrative maps are available in the popular and regularly updated 'Uganda Maps' series at around US$5 apiece (m 0772 462646; e ugandamaps@gmail.com).

TRAVEL MAGAZINES For readers with a broad interest in Africa, an excellent magazine dedicated to tourism throughout Africa is *Travel Africa* (w travelafricamag.com).

UGANDA ONLINE The internet is an increasingly valuable tool when it comes to researching most aspects of a trip to Uganda or elsewhere in Africa, though it is advisable to be somewhat circumspect when it comes to heeding advice on personal websites. Do also be aware that the internet is clogged up with sites constructed but never maintained and thus prone to be rather out of date. Websites for individual hotels, lodges, tour operators and other institutions are included alongside the relevant entries elsewhere in this guide. What follows is a list of more generic websites that might prove useful to travellers planning a trip in Uganda.

Uganda-specific sites

w **birdinguganda.blogspot.com** Run by Derek Kaverno, this is a superb free resource for independent travellers with the birding bug.
w **buganda.com** Detailed historical and cultural essays about the Buganda kingdom past and present.
w **crossculturalfoundation.or.ug** Apps and downloadable maps, supported by the European Union, of historical buildings in Kampala, Jinja and Entebbe.
w **diaryofamuzungu.com** Award-winning travel blog by Ugandan resident Charlotte Beauvoisin, covering 'adventure travel, birdwatching, conservation and cultural (mis)observations'.
w **exploreuganda.com** The official website of Tourism Uganda (aka Uganda Tourism Board) has some stunning photographs as section headers and a few useful links.
w **gorillahighlands.com** Comprehensive coverage of southwest Uganda.
w **monitor.co.ug** News, generally with a more independent stance than the government-backed *New Vision*.
w **my.viewranger.com/route/curations/921** Hiking route descriptions inside national parks.
w **my.viewranger.com/route/curations/922** Hiking route descriptions outside national parks.
w **newvision.co.ug** News, travel features, etc, posted by the country's most established English-language newspaper.
w **thecrag.com/climbing/uganda/guide** Database of rock climbs compiled by Matt Battani.
w **traveluganda.co.ug** The most useful site for independent travellers also has numerous links for tour companies and community-based tourism sites.
w **ugandawildlife.org** The website of the Uganda Wildlife Authority has the latest on gorilla-tracking permits and other fees and facilities in the national parks and wildlife reserves.

General sites

w **bradtugandaupdate.wordpress.com** Travel update service for Bradt readers sourced from and aimed at travellers, volunteers and service providers in Uganda.
w **fco.gov.uk/travel** British Foreign & Commonwealth Office site, containing up-to-date, generally rather conservative information on trouble spots and places to avoid.

w openstreetmap.org Free online maps of countries and major towns.
w travelafricamag.com Site for the quarterly magazine *Travel Africa* – good news section, travel archives and subscriptions.
w travel.state.gov/content/passports/en/country/uganda.html US State Department equivalent to FCO.

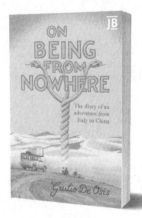

Index

Page numbers in *italics* indicate maps.

INDEX OF ADVERTISERS

THE BRADT STORY

In the beginning

It all began in 1974 on an Amazon river barge. During an 18-month trip through South America, two adventurous young backpackers – Hilary Bradt and her then husband, George – decided to write about the hiking trails they had discovered through the Andes. *Backpacking Along Ancient Ways in Peru and Bolivia* included the very first descriptions of the Inca Trail. It was the start of a colourful journey to becoming one of the best-loved travel publishers in the world; you can read the full story on our website (**bradtguides.com/ourstory**).

Getting there first

Hilary quickly gained a reputation for being a true travel pioneer, and in the 1980s she started to focus on guides to places overlooked by other publishers. The Bradt Guides list became a roll call of guidebook 'firsts'. We published the first guide to Madagascar, followed by Mauritius, Czechoslovakia and Vietnam. The 1990s saw the beginning of our extensive coverage of Africa: Tanzania, Uganda, South Africa, and Eritrea. Later, post-conflict guides became a feature: Rwanda, Mozambique, Angola, and Sierra Leone, as well as the first standalone guides to the Baltic States following the fall of the Iron Curtain, and the first post-war guides to Bosnia, Kosovo and Albania.

Comprehensive – and with a conscience

Today, we are the world's largest independently owned travel publisher, with more than 200 titles. However, our ethos remains unchanged. Hilary is still keenly involved, and **we still get there first**: two-thirds of Bradt guides have no direct competition.

But we don't just get there first. Our guides are also known for being **more comprehensive** than any other series. We avoid templates and tick-lists. Each guide is a one-of-a-kind expression of an expert author's interests, knowledge and enthusiasm for telling it how it really is.

And a commitment to wildlife, conservation and respect for local communities has always been at the heart of our books. Bradt Guides was **championing sustainable travel** before any other guidebook publisher. We even have a series dedicated to Slow Travel in the UK, award-winning books that explore the country with a passion and depth you'll find nowhere else.

Thank you!

We can only do what we do because of the support of readers like you – people who value less-obvious experiences, less-visited places and a more thoughtful approach to travel. Those who, like us, take travel seriously.